Global Crime

Global Crime

An Encyclopedia of Cyber Theft, Weapons Sales, and Other Illegal Activities

VOLUME I: A–L

Philip L. Reichel, Editor

ABC-CLIO™

An Imprint of ABC-CLIO, LLC
Santa Barbara, California • Denver, Colorado

Library of Congress Cataloging-in-Publication Data

Names: Reichel, Philip L., editor.
Title: Global crime : an encyclopedia of cyber theft, weapons sales, and other illegal activities / Philip L. Reichel, editor.
Description: Santa Barbara, CA : ABC-CLIO, [2019] | Includes bibliographical references and index.
Identifiers: LCCN 2018054480 (print) | LCCN 2019011370 (ebook) | ISBN 9781440860157 (eBook) | ISBN 9781440860140 (set : alk. paper) | ISBN 9781440860164 (volume 1) | ISBN 9781440860171 (volume 2)
Subjects: LCSH: Transnational crime—Encyclopedias. | International crimes—Encyclopedias.
Classification: LCC HV6252 (ebook) | LCC HV6252 .G5553 2019 (print) | DDC 364.1/3503—dc23
LC record available at https://lccn.loc.gov/2018054480

ISBN: 978-1-4408-6014-0 (set)
978-1-4408-6016-4 (vol. 1)
978-1-4408-6017-1 (vol. 2)
978-1-4408-6015-7 (ebook)

23 22 21 20 19 1 2 3 4 5

This book is also available as an eBook.

ABC-CLIO
An Imprint of ABC-CLIO, LLC

ABC-CLIO, LLC
147 Castilian Drive
Santa Barbara, California 93117
www.abc-clio.com

This book is printed on acid-free paper ∞

Manufactured in the United States of America

Dedicated to my friends and colleagues who graciously volunteered or agreed to provide one or more entries for this encyclopedia. And to Eva Jewell and Jay Albanese, who provide counsel and advice that I should more often follow.

Contents

VOLUME 2

Introduction

Crime is everywhere. That sentiment used to be expressed with thoughts about one's own locale. Citizens voiced concern about how crime seemed to be spreading throughout neighborhoods in their city or throughout their state. Actually, at least since the early 1990s, crime in the United States has declined. Statistics on reports of crime from the Federal Bureau of Investigation and on victimization from the Bureau of Justice Statistics show significant reduction in property and violent crime in the United States since 1993. Violent crime fell 48 percent from 1993 to 2016, and property crime fell 74 percent during the same period. Interestingly, public perception of crime does not match the data. Opinion surveys consistently find that Americans believe crime is up, even when the data show it is down (Gramlich 2018).

A similar phenomenon is found in most other Western countries. Violent and property crime rates rose in wealthy Western countries between the 1960s and 1990s, then began falling. Explanations for this global crime drop have included the security hypothesis, which argues that improvements in the quality and quantity of security measures have resulted in lower crime rates for many crimes (Reichel 2018, 33).

Although crime might be everywhere, it seems that there may also be less of it today than in the past. Domestic crime, consisting of such traditional crime types as burglary, auto theft, robbery, and assault, have indeed been in decline since the 1990s in most Western countries. However, there are new crimes and new iterations of old crimes that have effects beyond national borders. The global nature of these crimes must be understood from more than a domestic perspective. The entries in this encyclopedia provide that worldwide perspective on global crime.

GLOBAL CRIME

The concept of global crime is often used in two ways. In one sense, it refers to how crime is distributed around the world. That reference could be to the spread of traditional domestic crimes (for example, auto theft is found in virtually all countries today), or it could refer to the need to understand how a domestic crime like auto theft is linked to the activities of an organized crime network that steals cars in one country, transports them through another country, and then sells them in a third country. In this sense, the global nature of a crime requires it to be studied and responded to from a global, rather than only a domestic, perspective.

The second way that global crime as a concept can be used is through its link with globalization. In this manner, global crime is understood to be a consequence of the increased opportunities for trade in goods and services that has resulted from free market globalization. There certainly are positive aspects of globalization, not the least of which is how international trade and communication has been facilitated. Companies are using supply chain technology that has revolutionized the movement of products, created jobs for workers in developing countries, and brought less expensive goods to the global middle class. In addition, the Internet facilitates worldwide distribution of information and enhances freedom to speak and to listen (Gilman, Goldhammer, and Weber 2013).

But there are also negative aspects of globalization. Just as legitimate international trade and communication has been facilitated, so too has the illegitimate. Counterfeit goods now move as smoothly around the world as do the legitimate products. And for all the communication advancements brought by the Internet, there are as many examples of the Internet being used for illegitimate transactions and exploitative technology because they are of perfectly legal dealings and beneficial interactions. Today, from almost anywhere in the world, it is possible to purchase and receive anything from stolen art to trafficked people and wildlife.

TRANSNATIONAL CRIME

One of the most malevolent aspects of globalization's negative side—called deviant globalization by some—is transnational crime (Gilman, Goldhammer, and Weber 2013). Incidents of transnational crime are those that occur across national borders, that violate the criminal law of at least one country, and whose resolution requires the cooperation of two or more countries. Much of transnational crime occurs as a result of criminal organizations and networks rather than by the activities of just a few individuals. This makes sense because it would be difficult, if not impossible, for one or two people to have responsibility for all steps involved in carrying out a transnational crime. Using drug trafficking as an example, imagine one person harvesting the milky fluid from poppy seed pods in Afghanistan, packaging the dried resin for transportation, moving the packages over land and water through several countries, preparing the product for sale, and then actually selling the drug on the streets thousands of miles from where the poppy seeds were grown. Realistically, a network or organization of criminals is needed for this and most other crimes that involve the crossing of national borders.

Conceptualizing Transnational Crime

Beginning in the 1980s and early 1990s, the United Nations expressed concern about what was initially called transboundary crime—offenses involving more than one country. Five clusters of these crimes were identified: (1) internationally organized crime, (2) terrorist activities, (3) economic offenses involving more than one country, (4) crimes against cultural heritage, and (5) crimes against the environment (United Nations 1990). By the mid-1990s, the term *transnational crime* was replacing *transboundary crime*. and discussion was more likely to refer to specific crime categories such as money laundering, sea piracy, and human trafficking.

In 2000, with the adoption of the United Nations Convention against Transnational Organized Crime, attention remained on specific crime categories, but now the focus was on how organized crime groups were involved in those criminal activities. In 2010, the United Nations Office on Drugs and Crime (UNODC) identified eight crime categories in which organized crime was a key factor: (1) human trafficking, (2) migrant smuggling, (3) drug trafficking, (4) trafficking in small arms, (5) wildlife and forest crime, (6) counterfeit goods, (7) sea (maritime) piracy, and (8) cybercrime (UNODC 2010).

Today, transnational crime is often conceptualized in two ways. This first is reminiscent of the earlier "cluster" approach and is best explained by reference to the work of Jay Albanese, who groups transnational crimes into nine types that fall into three categories or clusters (Albanese 2011, 3). The "provision of illicit goods" category includes the crime types of drug trafficking, stolen property, and counterfeiting, whereas the "provision of illicit services" category includes human trafficking, cybercrime and fraud, and commercial vices such as sex and pornography. The category of "infiltration of business or government" includes the crime types of extortion and racketeering, money laundering, and corruption.

With these nine crime types placed in three categories, Albanese can find a place for all individual examples of currently recognized transnational crimes. For example, sea piracy is an example of extortion and racketeering, so it is understood as infiltration of business or government. Theft of cultural property is an example of stolen property (as is wildlife trafficking), so can be understood as an instance of providing illicit goods. Gambling, as a commercial vice, is an illicit service that organized crime has been providing for decades. By identifying all versions of transnational crime as falling into one of nine types within three categories, Albanese provides organization to what is a confusing array of criminal activities.

The second contemporary conceptualization of transnational crime is explained by the UNODC Studies and Threat Analysis Section as it argues for the need to focus less on the criminal groups that are engaged in transnational organized crime, and more on the illicit markets (UNODC 2010, v). Understanding and responding to transnational crime in terms of the market dynamics rather than the groups involved, UNDOC reasons, can be more effective since interrupting the market flow can have a bigger impact than does removing a few of the actors—who are quickly and easily replaced.

Characteristics of Transnational Crime

Organized crime has existed for decades, but traditionally it involved territorial-based groups operating in specific neighborhoods, cities, or regions.

The Mafia families in New York City and the Yakuza in Japan are examples. Those traditional crime groups have expanded or been partially replaced by flexible networks with branches across several jurisdictions in countries of supply, transit, or demand as transnational crime activities have evolved (UNODC n.d.).

United Nations data on an international sample of organized crime groups found that most of the groups that operate across national borders engage in multiple criminal activities, cooperate with other criminal groups, make extensive use of violence, and are likely to invest their illegally gained profits into legitimate business activities (van Dijk 2008, 146–147). These characteristics make it difficult for any single country or law enforcement entity to take effective action against the criminals involved. Modern organized crime presents a challenge to the world community and requires a global response—especially if, as UNODC argues for, strategies must be directed at the market dynamics and not only toward the individuals and groups involved (UNODC 2010). So what are some of the ways that countries are collaborating to respond to transitional crime, and especially transnationally organized crime?

NATIONS RESPOND

Countries have been cooperating in fighting crime for a very long time. But much of that cooperation was for domestic purposes in the sense of asking assistance from another country in tracking down suspects and/or extraditing suspects to stand trial in the requesting country. INTERPOL, for example, has been facilitating global communication among police agencies around the world since the 1940s. INTERPOL's mission statement identifies preventing and combating transnational crime as a current strategic goal—with specific emphasis on counterterrorism, cybercrime, and organized crime (INTERPOL n.d.). EUROPOL has been providing a similar information exchange service for European Union countries since 1992, and in 2009 it began focusing especially on organized crime. The Police Community of the Americas (Ameripol) provides a mechanism for police cooperation in the Americas, as does Afripol for member states of the African Union.

INTERPOL, Europol, Ameripol, Afripol, and other regional organizations that encourage and enable cooperative efforts among national police agencies are important tools in the fight against transnational crime. But the United Nations believes efforts that are more clearly international, rather than national and regional, are needed. In the first ever threat assessment of transnational organized crime, the UNODC explained that the threat posed by organized crime persists despite national responses that have seen armies mobilized to fight drug cartels and navies sent to thwart and capture pirates. National responses, and even regional efforts, directed at these transnational crimes are insufficient. The result, UNDOC argues, has had the effect of displacing the problem from one country to another rather than having an effective response to the problem (UNODC 2010).

When the United Nations Convention against Transnational Organized Crime (UNTOC) was adopted in 2000, the importance of international cooperation was made clear in Article 1, which identifies the convention's purpose as being "to promote cooperation to prevent and combat transnational organized crime more effectively" (United Nations 2000). The countries ratifying the convention committed to taking specific actions against transnational organized crime. Those actions include making certain activities criminal under domestic law (for example, participation in an organized criminal group, money laundering, corruption, and obstruction of justice) and making extradition, mutual legal assistance, and law enforcement cooperation more effective.

Interestingly, UNTOC provides no precise definition of transnational organized crime; neither is there even a list of the types of crimes that might be included. However, it is clear that criminal groups and more than one country are key aspects of what constitutes transnational organized crime. In addition, there are three protocols attached to UNTOC that provide clear examples of such crimes. The Protocol to Prevent, Suppress and Punish Trafficking in Persons, Especially Women and Children provides a model definition for trafficking in persons and has influenced the development of trafficking victims' rights. The Protocol against the Smuggling of Migrants by Land, Sea and Air created an agreed-upon definition for smuggling of migrants and seeks to prevent their exploitation. Finally, the Protocol against the Illicit Manufacturing of and Trafficking in Firearms, their Parts and Components and Ammunition promotes and facilitates the cooperative efforts among ratifying countries to prevent, combat, and eradicate the illicit manufacturing of and trafficking in small arms. Through UNTOC and its protocols, the United Nations is trying to provide a framework for the needed international cooperation to prevent and combat all forms of transnational organized crime.

WHY IS THIS IMPORTANT?

Global crime, and transnational organized crime especially, has far-reaching implications that affect everyone. The UNODC reminds us that the negative effect of some transnational crimes may not always be apparent or might not be considered something we should worry about personally. Persons who use drugs or who participate in migrant smuggling seem to be willing participants. When bad things happen to them because of their decisions, it is possible to simply take a "let the buyer beware" approach and dismiss any suggestion that there are social consequences in addition to those personal costs. Similarly, when the crime seems to be occurring in remote and foreign locations, it is difficult to understand how the resulting problems for those countries and their citizens can negatively influence our country and its citizens.

UNODC encourages everyone to take a less parochial and more global perspective to these events. Today, the negative and harmful consequences of crime, and transnational organized crime especially, extends well beyond the neighborhood where a criminal activity first occurs. When conflict and poverty in a remote country means local farmers must resort to providing opium to drug traffickers, or that young boys and girls are susceptible to recruitment techniques of human traffickers, those crimes will have an impact well beyond their local origin. When people believe that product counterfeiting simply means a loss of revenue to the legitimate company, they are ignoring the potential health and safety risks that are associated with products that avoid inspection and regulation. This is especially worrisome in instances of fraudulent medicine, which can not only harm the individual taking the medicine but can potentially pose a broader public safety threat (UNODC 2010).

In addition to those rather direct impacts of transnational crime, there are also some indirect consequences. Chief among those is the erosion of state control when organized crime groups undermine the authority and health of the official government (UNODC 2010). This happens primarily though corruption when the criminal networks are able to co-opt government (including elected) officials. The result is state organizations and institutions that operate to the advantage of crime groups rather than for the advancement of society.

CONCLUSION

Globalization, especially in terms of global production, global markets, and global communication, has clearly had a positive influence on developed and developing countries. Unfortunately, it is just as clear that globalization has also had a negative impact in terms of damage to the environment, increased economic inequality, and a growth in crime spreading across borders and throughout the world. The concept of transnational crime is generally used in reference to crime's global occurrence, and the international community is increasingly looking for ways to cooperate in preventing and combatting the groups and networks engaged in these criminal activities. The entries in the two volumes of this encyclopedia are designed to inform the reader about the events, people, organizations, and key terms that are relevant to global crime and its transnational aspects.

Philip L. Reichel

Further Reading

Albanese, Jay S. 2011. *Transnational Crime and the 21st Century: Criminal Enterprise, Corruption, and Opportunity.* New York: Oxford University Press.

Gilman, Nils, Jesse Goldhammer, and Steven Weber. 2013. "Deviant Globalization." In *Convergence: Illicit Networks and National Security in the Age of Globalization*, edited by Michael Miklaucic and Jacqueline Brewer, 3–13. Washington, D.C.: National Defense University Press.

Gramlich, John. 2018. "5 Facts about Crime in the U.S." Pew Research Center. Last modified January 30, 2018. Accessed January 15, 2019. http://www.pewresearch.org/fact-tank/2018/01/30/5-facts-about-crime-in-the-u-s.

INTERPOL. n.d. "Priorities: Strategic Framework 2017–2020." Accessed October 31, 2018. https://www.interpol.int/About-INTERPOL/Priorities.

Reichel, Philip L. 2018. *Comparative Criminal Justice Systems: A Topical Approach.* 7th ed. New York: Pearson.

United Nations. 1990. *Proposals for Concerted International Action against Forms of Crime Identified in the Milan Plan of Action, A/CONF.144/7.* Vienna: UN Crime Prevention and Criminal Justice Branch.

United Nations. 2000. "United Nations Convention against Transnational Organized Crime and the Protocols Thereto." Accessed July 16, 2018. https://www.unodc.org/unodc/en/organized-crime/intro/UNTOC.html.

United Nations Office on Drugs and Crime (UNODC). 2010. "The Globalization of Crime: A Transnational Organized Crime Threat Assessment." Vienna: UNODC. Accessed January 15, 2019. https://www.unodc.org/unodc/en/data-and-analysis/tocta-2010.html.

United Nations Office on Drugs and Crime (UNODC). n.d. "Organized Crime." Accessed October 29, 2018. https://www.unodc.org/unodc/en/organized-crime/intro.html.

van Dijk, Jan. 2008. *The World of Crime: Breaking the Silence on Problems of Security, Justice, and Development across the World.* Los Angeles: Sage Publications.

Chronology

1899
U.S. Congress passes the Refuse Act, which was the first environmental law to include criminal sanctions.

1930
The Forced Labour Convention is adopted by the General Conference of the International Labour Organisation and enters into force in 1932. The convention, which serves as one of the first legal documents on labor trafficking and exploitation, declares that forced labor is any work or service that is exacted from any person under the threat of any penalty and for which the person has not volunteered.

1945
The International Court of Justice (ICJ) is established by the UN Charter to be the main judicial organ of the United Nations. It has responsibility for settling legal disputes between UN member states. It is based in The Hague in the Netherlands.

1945
The International Military Tribunal (known as the Nuremberg Tribunal) is established by the four Allied powers (France, the Soviet Union, the United Kingdom, and the United States) following the end of World War II.

1948
The Convention on the Prevention and Punishment of the Crime of Genocide (known as the Genocide Convention) is adopted by the United Nations. It is an international agreement between countries to adopt laws to prevent and punish genocide, which the convention defines as the act of killing, mentally or physically harming, or creating conditions with the intent to destroy (in whole or in part) a national, ethnic, racial, or religious group.

1949
The Geneva Conventions are adopted. The third convention (Geneva Convention III) protects prisoners of war, and the fourth (Geneva Convention IV) protects civilians in times of war. As a result, these "protected persons" cannot be assaulted, tortured, murdered, raped, or mishandled.

1970

U.S. Congress passes the Racketeer Influenced and Corrupt Organizations Act (RICO) as part of the Organized Crime Control Act, which is designed to punish organized criminal activity. Racketeering includes such offenses as gambling, extortion, bribery, mail or securities fraud, prostitution, and narcotics trafficking.

1971

The Convention on Psychotropic Substances is adopted by the UN General Assembly to control the dissemination of narcotics and psychotropic drugs internationally with a goal of limiting the use of psychotropic substances and their precursors to medical and scientific purposes. The convention becomes effective in 1976.

1972

The Convention on the Prevention of Marine Pollution by Dumping of Wastes and Other Matter (the London Convention) is adopted and goes into force in 1975. It is the first global convention to protect the marine environment from human activities.

1977

U.S. Congress passes the Foreign Corrupt Practices Act prohibiting individuals and corporations in the United States from bribing or paying foreign officials with the intention of obtaining business contracts.

1982

The UN Convention on the Law of the Sea is adopted by the General Assembly and enters into force in 1994. The convention regulates the use of the oceans, the rights to natural resources therein, and maritime piracy. It has been called by some the constitution for the oceans.

1983

Transparency International (TI) is created in Berlin, Germany, with the mission of stopping corruption and promoting transparency across all sectors of society.

1988

The UN Convention against Illicit Traffic in Narcotic Drugs and Psychotropic Substances is adopted and becomes effective 1990. The convention provides comprehensive measures against drug trafficking, including provisions against money laundering for international cooperation through, for example, extradition of drug traffickers, controlled deliveries, and transfer of proceedings.

1989

Following the mysterious death of Shaykh Azzam in November, Osama bin Laden takes over the leadership of Al Qaeda, which bin Laden transforms into a multinational enterprise that becomes globally recognized via terrorist attacks in countries around the world.

1989

Robert Tappan Morris Jr. becomes the first person indicted under the Computer Fraud and Abuse Act of 1986 for unleashing the Morris worm—the first Internet virus.

1990

European Union (EU) member states adopt the Schengen Convention, which facilitates the ease with which borders can be crossed among EU countries and some contiguous countries that are not EU members. The convention not only eliminates internal border controls and provides a common visa policy, but it also includes provisions for police cooperation.

1992

The European Union Agency for Law Enforcement Cooperation (Europol) is established as the primary organization for cooperation among the various law enforcement agencies of the EU countries. Its main purpose is to assist the member states in combatting serious transnational crimes, such as organized crime, terrorism, and cybercrime.

1993

The International Criminal Tribunal for the former Yugoslavia (ICTY) is established in The Hague (the Netherlands) to deal with war crimes that took place during the conflicts in the Balkans during the 1990s. The ICTY was dissolved in 2017 after having indicted 161 individuals and sentencing more than 90. Individuals faced a variety of charges, but four specific war crimes were prosecuted: genocide, crimes against humanity, violations of the laws or customs of war, and grave breaches of the Geneva Conventions.

1993

Pablo Escobar, one of the world's most ruthless and successful cocaine traffickers and head of the Medellín Cartel in Colombia, is killed by an elite commando force in Medellín.

1994

Under its new name, the Organization for Security and Co-operation in Europe (OSCE) began playing a significant role in combating transnational crime. With 57 participating states from Europe, Asia, and North America, OSCE addresses such issues as radicalization and violent extremism, organized crime, cybercrime, trafficking in drugs and weapons, and human trafficking.

1995

April 19: At about 9:00 a.m., there is a massive explosion caused by the detonation of homemade explosives left in a parked truck in front of the Alfred P. Murrah Federal Building in Oklahoma City, Oklahoma. The final death toll counted 168 people killed in the blast, including 19 children who were being cared for at a daycare center.

1995

The first Corruption Perceptions Index (CPI) is published by Transparency International. The CPI is the leading global indicator of public-sector corruption, with each annual report providing a snapshot of the relative degree of corruption by ranking countries from around the globe.

1996

The Economic Espionage Act is signed into law by President Bill Clinton. The act criminalizes two types of trade secret misappropriations: economic espionage and theft of trade secrets. Individuals convicted of economic espionage can receive fines or a prison sentence. Organizations convicted under this statute can receive fines up to $10 million.

1998

The International Criminal Court (ICC) is established by the Rome Statute and enters into force in 2002. The ICC, an international organization, prosecutes violations of international criminal law.

1998

The Identity Theft and Assumption Deterrence Act is signed into law. The act defines identity theft and provides sentencing enhancements for defendants who are convicted for offenses based on the number of victims involved, whether the offense involves the stealing or destroying of a quantity of undelivered U.S. mail, and the potential loss that might result from such offense.

1998

The European Union adopts a regional Code of Conduct on Arms Exports that identifies common standards to be used when making arms export decisions and to increase transparency among EU countries on arms exports.

1998

Terry Nichols is sentenced in federal court to life in prison without parole for having conspired to use a weapon of mass destruction and on eight counts of involuntary manslaughter for his role in the Oklahoma City bombings in 1995. In 2004, he was sentenced in an Oklahoma state court to 161 consecutive life terms without the possibility of parole.

1999

The International Convention for the Suppression of the Financing of Terrorism (known as the Terrorist Financing Convention) is adopted by the UN General Assembly and enters into force in 2002. The convention's objective is to enhance international cooperation among states as they develop effective measures for the prevention of the financing of terrorism and for its suppression through the prosecution and punishment efforts.

1999

Kevin Mitnick, at one point the FBI's most wanted hacker, pleads guilty to wire fraud, computer fraud, and illegally intercepting a wire communication. He is sentenced to five years in prison but is released in 2000 to begin a three-year period of supervised release. He now serves as a consultant for a cybersecurity firm.

2000

The UN Convention against Transnational Organized Crime is opened for signatures in Palermo, Italy, and enters into force in 2003. The convention has three supplemental protocols that are aimed at specific acts of organized crime: trafficking in persons, especially women and children; smuggling of migrants; and illicit manufacturing and trafficking in firearms. The convention becomes an important in fighting transnational organized crime.

2000
The Trafficking Victims Protection Act (TVPA) is signed by President Bill Clinton and becomes the foundation for national and domestic legislation to combat human trafficking. The TVPA was reauthorized in 2003, 2005, 2008, and 2013. Each reauthorization provided additional protections and services for victims, tools for prosecution, and expanded sanctions.

2001
June 11: Timothy McVeigh is executed for his role in the 1995 bombing of the Alfred P. Murrah Federal Building in Oklahoma City—the worst act of terrorism on American soil prior to the September 11, 2001, attacks in New York City and Washington, D.C.

2001
September 11 ("9/11"): Terrorists hijack four planes and crash one into each tower of the World Trade Center in New York City and one into the Pentagon in Washington, D.C. The fourth plane crashed into a field in western Pennsylvania after its passengers attempted to overtake the hijackers. The attacks, the worst act of terrorism in U.S. history, killed nearly 3,000 people at the World Trade Center and almost 200 at the Pentagon.

2001
UN member states agree by consensus to adopt the Programme of Action to Prevent, Combat and Eradicate the Illicit Trade in Small Arms and Light Weapons in All Its Aspects (PoA). The PoA becomes the first major act of multilateral cooperation on the issue of excessive and destabilizing accumulation and transfer of small arms and light weapons, particularly in the context of armed conflict.

2001
The Kimberley Process Certification Scheme is established by a UN General Assembly resolution as a way to require diamond producers to certify that all unpolished diamond exports were produced through responsible mining and distributed through legitimate sales, and that they were not used to undermine legitimate governments or to finance conflict.

2001
The Convention on Cybercrime is opened for signatures by the Council of Europe. It encourages international cooperation in criminal matters as well as adoption of appropriate legal solutions to combat criminal offences against confidentiality, integrity, and availability of computer systems, networks, and data.

2002
The European Union's Judicial Cooperation Unit (Eurojust) is established with the mission of supporting and strengthening coordination and cooperation between national investigating and prosecuting authorities in the European Union.

2002
The George W. Bush administration begins holding prisoners, classified as "enemy combatants" at the Guantánamo Bay prison camp, a military prison at the U.S. naval facility at Guantánamo Bay in Cuba.

2003
The UN General Assembly adopts the Convention against Corruption, and it enters into force in 2005. It is the only legally binding universal anticorruption instrument designed to protect against public and private corruption.

2004
March 11: Nearly simultaneous coordinated bombings in Madrid, Spain, are launched in the morning against the city's commuter train system, killing 191 people and injuring about 1,700 others. The victims included citizens of 17 countries. The bombings are the deadliest terrorist attack in Spain's history.

2006
Oleg Khintsagov and three other Georgian citizens were arrested by Georgian law enforcement officials while attempting to smuggle approximately 100 grams of weapons-grade uranium in what is one of the largest publicly known cases of nuclear trafficking. The arrests were the result of a sting operation by the Georgian Secret Service after learning that a Russian national was looking to sell highly enriched uranium.

2008
Criminologists without Borders, with consultative status with the United Nations, is founded with the goal of applying scientific findings and best practices to the policies and operations of crime prevention and criminal justice systems.

2009
April 8: Four Somali pirates, armed with AK-47s, attack and hijack the *Maersk Alabama*, a U.S.-flagged cargo ship off the Somalian coastline. The attack was remarkable because it was the first pirate attack on a U.S.-flagged ship in roughly 200 years. Aboard the ship were 21 American crew members, including the ship's captain, Richard Phillips. A movie about the hijacking, *Captain Phillips*, was later released in 2013.

2011
May 1: Osama bin Laden is killed in an attack mounted by U.S. Navy SEALs on his compound in Pakistan. President Barack Obama calls it the "most significant achievement to date" in the effort to defeat Al Qaeda.

2011
Ross Ulbricht, the founder of the darknet marketplace Silk Road, is arrested by the FBI in San Francisco. Ulbricht realized that by using the encrypted data and hidden IP addresses provided by The Onion Router (Tor) and by allowing Bitcoins as the only method of payment, he could provide anonymity to persons wishing to purchase illicit items. In 2015, Ulbricht is convicted on charges of narcotics trafficking, money laundering, and computer hacking and sentenced to life without parole.

2011
Viktor Bout is found guilty of conspiring to kill American citizens, officers, and employees; conspiring to acquire and export surface-to-air antiaircraft missiles; and conspiring to provide support or weapons to a foreign terrorist organization. Nicholas Cage's character in the 2005 film *Lord of War* is said to have been inspired by Bout's career.

2012
Griselda Blanco, a high-profile drug trafficker of the Medellín Cartel, is killed, execution-style, by a motorcyclist in her hometown of Medellín, Mexico. Blanco had been one of the most prominent women involved with transnational organized crime and the Colombian drug trade. She was also the initiation godmother to several drug traffickers, most notably Pablo Escobar.

2013
April 15: Brothers Tamerlan and Dzhokhar Tsarnaev detonate two bombs near the finish line of the Boston Marathon, killing three people and wounding more than 260. The brothers were allegedly motivated by radical Islamic views,

2013
Dream Market, a hidden online service allowing users to browse for and purchase a variety of content, including illegal items, is founded. Following the shutdown of AlphaBay by federal authorities in 2017, Dream Market is believed by some to now be the largest online marketplace for illegal goods.

2013
The UN General Assembly adopts the Arms Trade Treaty, which strives to establish the highest possible common international standards for the regulation of international trade in conventional arms. The treaty enters into force in 2014.

2014
AlphaBay, an online darknet marketplace that facilitates the acquiring of illicit products and services, launches. It dominates the marketplace until it is shut down in 2017 during Operation Bayonet.

2015
January 7: Two brothers, Chérif and Saïd Kouachi, armed with Kalashnikov type machine guns, open fire in the offices of the satirical French magazine *Charlie Hebdo* in Paris. After killing 11 people, the brothers fled the offices, killing a police officer in the process. Two days later, police announce that the Kouachi brothers have been killed in a police shootout.

2015
November 13: A group of terrorists carry a series of highly coordinated, near simultaneous attacks aimed at multiple civilian targets in and around Paris. The next day, the Islamic State of Iraq and Syria (ISIS) claimed responsibility for the attacks. The ringleader was identified by police as Abdelhamid Abaaoud, and on November 18, Abaaoud and two others were killed in a five-hour-long shootout with police. The attacks are the deadliest to take place on French soil since World War II and the deadliest in Europe since the 2004 train bombings in Madrid, Spain.

2015

An anonymous source leaks the Panama Papers, which contain personal financial information about wealthy individuals and public officials that had previously been kept private. The first news stories, along with some of the documents, were published in 2016. The documents are important for showing the numerous ways in which the rich can exploit secretive offshore tax regimes.

2016

Ardit Ferizi, a citizen of Kosovo, is the first person to ever be convicted of cyberterrorism. Ferizi is sentenced to 20 years in prison for hacking crimes and providing material support to a foreign terrorist organization, the Islamic State of Iraq and Syria (ISIS).

2016

Joaquín Guzman (El Chapo) is arrested in Los Mochis, Sinaloa, after a shootout with Mexican authorities. He was extradited to the United States in 2017 to stand trial in New York for drug trafficking as head of the Sinaloa Cartel—one of the most powerful drug cartels operating during the 1990s and 2000s.

2017

May 22: Twenty-two concertgoers were killed and hundreds injured in a terrorist attack at the Manchester Arena in Manchester, United Kingdom, while attending a concert of American singer Ariana Grande. The assailant, Salman Ramadan Abedi, detonated a bomb in the foyer of the concert hall when people gathered to leave the venue. The attack was claimed by the terror organization the Islamic State of Iraq and Syria (ISIS).

2017

August 17: A van driven at a high rate of speed plows into throngs of pedestrians on Barcelona's Las Ramblas Boulevard, killing 14 people and injuring more than 100 others.

2017

October 31: Sayfullo Habibullaevic Saipov drives down a bike path in New York City, killing 8 people and injuring at least 12 others in what is New York's deadliest terror attack since 9/11. Saipov tells officials that he was heavily influenced by the Islamic State of Iraq and Syria (ISIS) and that he was proud to commit such an attack in their name.

2017

Operation Bayonet, a multinational law enforcement operation spearheaded by U.S. authorities, targets and seizes a multitude of darknet market infrastructures, including AlphaBay.

2017

Paulino Ramirez-Granados becomes the most recent member of the Granados sex trafficking organization to be sentenced. Since at least 1998, members of the Granados organization trafficked young women from Mexico into the United States, and as of 2018, five have been convicted on international sex trafficking charges.

2018

January 3: Greek Special Forces intercept a cargo vessel in the Sea of Crete on suspicion of arms trading. The ship, which was destined for Libya, held cargo that included containers loaded with explosives and detonators.

2018

An international Thai sex trafficking organization responsible for forcing hundreds of Thai women to engage in commercial sex acts across the United States was disrupted as 31 defendants pled guilty and 5 others were convicted in a U.S. District Court in Minnesota for their roles in the operation.

2018

The CEO of Backpage, a classified advertising website, pleads guilty in two states and a federal court to charges of money laundering and conspiracy to facilitate prostitution. Backpage was considered the dominant marketplace for illicit commercial sex, including sex trafficking.

2019

February 1: Hong Kong customs officials interrupt an endangered species smuggling operation trying to move pangolin (also known as scaly anteaters) scales and ivory tusks from Nigeria to Vietnam. The items, equating to about 500 elephants and up to 13,000 pangolins, were valued at more than $7.9 million.

2019

February 13: Joaquín Guzmán Loera, the Mexican drug kingpin known as El Chapo, is convicted on drug conspiracy charges by a federal jury in New York. His conviction is described by prosecutors as a watershed moment in America's war on drugs. He is scheduled for sentencing in June and faces life imprisonment.

2019

In February, the territory claimed by the Islamic State of Iraq and Syria (ISIS) for their physical caliphate is on the verge of collapse. Military and political leaders warn that the end of a physical territory for the militant group does not mean the end of the group itself.

A

Access Device Fraud Act of 1984

Congress passed the first cybercrime law, the Access Device Fraud Act of 1984 (ADFA; 18 U.S.C. §1029), on October 12, 1984. Congress passed this statute to give federal prosecutors a broad jurisdictional base to effectively prosecute a variety of credit card fraud schemes. This statute criminalizes the (1) use of counterfeit access devices, (2) use of unauthorized access devices where during a one-year period anything of value aggregating $1,000 or more is obtained, (3) possession of 15 or more counterfeit or unauthorized access devices, and (4) possession or use of device-making equipment. The term *access device* means any card, plate, code, account number, electronic serial number, mobile identification number, personal identification number, or other telecommunications service, equipment, or instrument identifier, or other means of account access that can be used, alone or in conjunction with another access device, to obtain money, goods, services, or any other thing of value or that can be used to initiate a transfer of funds. Defendants convicted under the statutes of this act can be sentenced to up to 15 years in prison and receive fines of up to $250,000. Judges may order the forfeiture of any property used to commit or to facilitate the commission of the crime.

For an offender to be convicted under the ADFA, a prosecutor must prove their case beyond a reasonable doubt that the offender (1) committed a criminal act under ADFA; (2) acted knowingly, willfully, and with the intent to defraud; and (3) affected interstate or foreign commerce to obtain a conviction (Wallin 2015; Kruk 1998). To act knowingly, willfully, and with the intent to defraud, the person acted with a conscious mind and was aware of his or her actions and did not commit the crime act out of ignorance, a mistake, or accident. Since the passage of the ADFA, 2,412 cases have been filed in federal courts, with 58 percent of the cases appealing to the Courts of Appeals and many cases coming from the state of New York, followed by Pennsylvania, California, and Florida.

The enactment of the Computer Fraud and Abuse Act in 1986 (CFAA; 18 U.S.C. §1030) strengthened the ADFA and specifically placed emphasis on the prosecution of those who knowingly or intentionally accessed computer(s) that they were not authorized to access. The purpose of the CFAA directly focused on three forms of illegal computer activities: (1) improper accessing of government information protected for national defense or foreign relations, (2) improper accessing of certain financial information from financial institutions, and (3) improper accessing of information on a government computer (Li 2017, 196–207).

David A. Rembert and Donna Ossorio

See also: Cybercrime

Further Reading

Access Device Fraud Act, 18 U.S.C.A. § 1029 (1984).

Computer Fraud and Abuse Act, 18 U.S.C.A. § 1030 (1984).

Kruk, Theresa. 1998. "What Constitutes Violation of 18 U.S.C.A. § 1029, Prohibiting Fraud or Related Activity in Connection with Credit Card or Other Credit Access Device." 115 A.L.R. Fed. 213 (Westlaw) (last updated 2011).

Li, Johannes Xingan. 2017. "Cyber Crime and Legal Countermeasures: A Historical Analysis." *International Journal of Criminal Justice Sciences* 12 (2): 196–207.

Wallin, Paul. J. 2015. "Federal Credit Card Fraud and Related Activity in Connection with Access Devices (18 USC 1029)." *Wallin & Klarich*, May 3, 2018. Accessed November 21, 2018. https://www.wklaw.com/practice-areas/federal-crimes/federal-credit-card-fraud-18-usc-1029.

Adler, Freda (1934–)

Freda Adler is a sociologist who specializes in criminology. She is best known for her pioneering work on female criminality and the book *Sisters in Crime: The Rise of the New Female Criminal* (1975). Contradicting existing pathological explanations of female crime, she posited that expanding opportunities for women, emanating from the feminist social movement, would also increase their opportunities and involvement in crime.

The significance of *Sisters in Crime* is difficult to capture, but Adler gave 300 media interviews within eight months of the book's publication, showing the tremendous interest in her ideas. Adler discussed some of her motivations for writing the book in a later interview:

> I didn't think that it was fair on the part of some scholars and some practitioners to say that, if women deviate in certain ways, they're mentally ill, and perhaps should be placed in mental institutions. I didn't think it was fair that theories of criminality were based on male behavior, I didn't believe that men should remain the sole subject of criminological research. (Faith 1993)

Freda Adler will be remembered for generating research interest in gender as a previously understudied topic in criminology and also for changing the focus from deviance as a correlate of crime to the impact of key social changes in creating new and unanticipated opportunities for crime (Cullen et al. 2015).

It is not a coincidence that the first panel on the topic of women and crime was held at the meetings of American Society of Criminology in 1975, which Adler chaired (ASC-DWC 2017). The growth in interest on the subjects of gender, women, and crime continued to build after that, resulting in the establishment of the Division on Women in Crime within the American Society of Criminology in 1984.

The pioneering role Freda Adler took in the field of criminology is further evidenced by the fact that there were very few women studying criminology at that time and very few female PhDs; she was the only female faculty member at the Rutgers University School of Criminal Justice at its founding. Dr. Adler received her PhD in 1971 at the University of Pennsylvania, which is known for its focus on criminology. She studied under Thorsten Sellin and returned there late in her career to serve as a visiting professor.

Freda Adler is also a distinguished academic. She was one of the founding faculty of the School of Criminal Justice at Rutgers University in 1974, and she now holds emeritus status there. She served as president of the American Society of Criminology in 1994–1995, as only the third woman elected to that position in the history of the ASC to that point.

Freda Adler also made significant contributions to international criminal justice, writing widely on topics that included international crime rates and maritime piracy. She was a consultant to the United Nations on crime issues. Her best-known book in this area was *Nations Not Obsessed with Crime* (1983), in which she again shifted the emphasis of previous research on the topic of international crime rates. Rather than focusing on jurisdictions with high crime rates, where much of the world was concentrating, she examined 10 countries with low crime rates to examine possible underlying reasons for their very low levels of crime.

After evaluating a large number of social, economic, and technological factors, which did not explain much variation in crime rates, she developed a new explanation called *synnomie*. Most theory in criminology concentrates on the absence of effective social controls that enforce conventional norms of conduct. Adler coined the term *synnomie* to emphasize that togetherness, rather than separateness, of norms and values was the foundation for low crime societies. Therefore, a wide sharing of values within a society, combined with tolerance for divergent values, results in synnomie where "harmonious accommodation" is achieved (Adler 1983, 157–158).

Similar to her work on female criminality, Adler's work on comparative crime trends attempted to change the focus of inquiry in criminology from the deviant to the normal in both producing opportunities and sometimes lowering crime rates. In some ways, this work foreshadowed the development of positive psychology, which looks to the causes and development of healthy adjustment by individuals in a society, rather than focusing on pathology and maladjustment of those who do not (Lopez and Snyder 2012).

Freda Adler is a prolific author who has written and edited more than 20 books and 100 journal articles. She was the recipient of the Beccaria Medal in Gold of the Deutsche Kriminologische Gesellschaft (representing Germany, Luxembourg, and Switzerland), the Chi Omega Sociology Award, the American Society of Criminology International Division Award, and the Academy of Criminal Justice Sciences Founders Award. The American Society of Criminology named its annual award for an international scholar after Freda Adler.

Freda Adler is a fellow of the Max-Planck Institute of Foreign and International Law and Criminology, the American Society of Criminology, and the Academy of Criminal Justice Sciences. She received a DHL (honoris causa) from the University of Scranton in 2011. She has three children, Mark, Jill, and Nanci. Her husband, noted criminologist and lawyer Gerhard O. W. Mueller, died in 2006.

Jay S. Albanese

See also: Mueller, Gerhard O. W.; Transnational, Global, and International Crime

Further Reading

Adler, Freda. 1975. *Sisters in Crime: The Rise of the New Female Criminal.* New York: McGraw-Hill.

Adler, Freda. 1983. *Nations Not Obsessed with Crime.* Littleton, CO: Rothman.

Adler, Freda. 1995. "Synnomie to Anomie: A Macrosocial Formulation." In F. Adler and W. Laufer, eds. *The Legacy of Anomie Theory.* New Brunswick, NJ: Transaction Books.

Adler, Freda, and Rita James Simon, eds. 1979. *The Criminology of Deviant Women.* Boston: Houghton Mifflin.

American Society of Criminology Division of Women and Crime (ASC-DWC). 2017. "History." Accessed November 21, 2018. http://ascdwc.com/about/history.

Cullen, Francis T., Pamela Wilcox, Jennifer L. Lux, and Cheryl Lero Jonson, eds. 2015. *Sisters in Crime Revisited: Bringing Gender into Criminology.* New York, NY: Oxford University Press.

Faith, K. 1993. "An Interview with Freda Adler." *Critical Criminologist* 5 (Spring): 3–10.

Flynn, Edith E. 1998. "Freda Adler: A Portrait of a Pioneer." *Women & Criminal Justice* 10: 1–26.

Lopez, Shane J., and C. R. Snyder. 2012. *The Oxford Handbook of Positive Psychology.* New York, NY: Oxford University Press.

Al Qaeda

Al Qaeda is an international terrorist organization, the hallmark of which is the perpetration of terrorist attacks against various Western and Western-allied interests. In the late 1980s, Al Qaeda (meaning the "base" or "foundation" in Arabic) fought against the Soviet occupation of Afghanistan. The organization is, however, best known for the September 11, 2001, terrorist attacks in the United States, the worst such attacks in the history of that nation. The founding of Al Qaeda, which is composed chiefly of Sunni Muslims, is shrouded in controversy. Research from a number of Arabic scholars indicates that Al Qaeda was created sometime between 1987 or 1988 by Sheikh Abdullah Azzam, a mentor to Osama bin Laden. Azzam was a professor at Jeddah University in Saudi Arabia. Bin Laden attended Jeddah University, where he met and was strongly influenced by Azzam.

GENESIS AND EARLY YEARS

The group Al Qaeda grew out of the Afghan Service Bureau, also known as the Maktab al Khidmat lil-mujahidin al-Arab (MaK). Azzam was the founder of the MaK, and bin Laden funded the organization and was considered the deputy director. This organization recruited, trained, and transported Muslim soldiers from any Muslim nation into Afghanistan to fight the jihad (holy war) against the Soviet armies in the 1980s. Sayyid Qutb, a philosopher of the Muslim Brotherhood, developed the credo for Al Qaeda, which is to arm all Muslims in the world and to overthrow any government that does not support traditional Muslim practice and Islamic law.

Following the mysterious death of Shaykh Azzam in November 1989, bin Laden took over the leadership of Al Qaeda. He continued to work toward Azzam's goal of creating an international organization composed of mujahideen (soldiers) who would fight the oppression of Muslims throughout the world. Al Qaeda has actually had several goals: to destroy Israel, to rid the Islamic world of the influence of Western civilization, to reestablish a caliphate form of government throughout the world, to fight against any government viewed as contrary to the ideals of Islamic law and religion, and to aid any Islamic groups trying to establish an Islamic form of government in their countries.

The organization of Al Qaeda follows the Shur majlis, or consultative council, form of leadership. The emir general's post has been held by Osama bin Laden, who was succeeded by Ayman al-Zawahiri upon bin Laden's death in May 2011. Several other generals are under the emir general, and there are additional leaders of related groups. There are 24 related groups as part of the consultative council. The council consists of four committees: military, religious-legal, finance, and media. The emir general personally selects the leaders of these committees, and each committee head reports directly to the emir general. All levels of Al Qaeda are highly compartmentalized, and secrecy is the key to all operations.

IDEOLOGY AND ACTIVITIES

Al Qaeda's ideology has appealed to both Middle Eastern and non–Middle Eastern groups that adhere to Islam. There are also a number of Islamist extremist groups associated with Al Qaeda that have established a history of violence and terrorism in numerous countries in the world today. Most notably, these associated groups have included Al Qaeda in Iraq, which merged with the Islamic State of Iraq and Syria (ISIS), and the al-Nusra Front in Syria. ISIS has been waging a bloody insurgency in both Iraq and Syria since 2011 and became a key player in the Syrian civil war. The al-Nusra organization has also been involved in the civil war in Syria and, like ISIS, is waging war against President Bashar al-Assad's government. Nigerian-based Boko Haram, another organization of jihadist extremists, also has alleged ties to Al Qaeda.

Bin Laden was able to put most of the Islamist extremist groups under the umbrella of Al Qaeda. Indeed, its leadership spread throughout the world, and its influence penetrates many religious, social, and economic structures in most Muslim communities. The membership of Al Qaeda remains difficult to determine because of its decentralized organizational structure. By early 2005, U.S. officials claimed to have killed or taken prisoner two-thirds of the Al Qaeda leaders behind the September 11 attacks. However, some of these prisoners have been shown to have had no direct connection with the attacks. Al Qaeda has continued to periodically release audio recordings and videotapes, some featuring bin Laden and Zawahiri, to comment on current issues, to exhort followers to keep up the fight, and to prove to Western governments that it is still a force with which to be reckoned.

AL QAEDA AFTER 9/11

Despite the decimation of Al Qaeda's core leadership in Afghanistan and Pakistan after 9/11, it continues to be a major threat. According to experts, the organization moved from a centralized organization to a series of local-actor organizations forming a broad, loosely organized terrorist network. Al Qaeda in Iraq was substantially weakened by the end of the Iraq War in 2011, but it subsequently regained control of many of its former staging areas and the ability to launch weekly waves of multiple car bomb attacks. It also joined forces with ISIS, and in so doing, it has greatly amplified its ability to sow chaos and terror within Iraq. On May 1, 2011, bin Laden was killed in an attack mounted by U.S. Special Forces on his compound in Pakistan. President Barack Obama called it the "most significant achievement to date" in the effort to defeat Al Qaeda.

In July 2013, however, more than 1,000 people were killed in Iraq, the highest monthly death toll in five years. Most of the attacks were led by Al Qaeda and its affiliates, including ISIS. That same year, in Syria, Al Qaeda's affiliate, the al-Nusra Front, rose to prominence. Until recently, al-Nusra had directly reported to Al Qaeda's leadership hierarchy. Between 2009 and 2018, in Libya, Al Qaeda–affiliated terror groups were blamed for scores of attacks, many of them including civilians. Indeed, Al Qaeda has been blamed for the September 11, 2012, attack on the U.S. consulate in Benghazi, Libya, that left the U.S. ambassador and three other Americans dead. In Yemen, Al Qaeda leaders in strongholds in the country's south have not been vanquished by a Yemeni military backed by U.S. and Saudi forces and drone strikes. Al Qaeda affiliates in Iraq, Syria, Yemen, and West Africa have expanded their operating areas and capabilities and appear poised to continue their expansion.

By January 2014, a resurgent Al Qaeda, along with ISIS, had secured much of Iraq's Anbar Province, including Fallujah, and was making significant headway in Afghanistan, often colluding with a resurgent Taliban. Al Qaeda has also successfully established itself in parts of Lebanon, Egypt, Algeria, and Mali. By early 2014, the Obama administration had begun shipping Hellfire missiles and other weaponry to the Iraqi government to suppress the growing insurgency there, which is now dominated by ISIS. In a telling sign of ISIS's recent excesses, Al Qaeda formally disassociated itself from the group in February 2014, citing the organization's brutality and inability to submit to authority.

In June 2015, Al Qaeda's second in command, Nasir al-Wuhayshi, died in a U.S. airstrike in Yemen. The Obama administration trumpeted this as a major blow to the Al Qaeda leadership, but the organization appears not to have suffered unduly because of it. Meanwhile, President Obama reluctantly agreed to keep a force of more than 10,000 troops in Afghanistan through 2016, in part because of increased activity by Al Qaeda and its affiliates throughout 2015. Saudi Arabia mounted a major military intervention in the Yemeni civil war in 2015, which was designed in large measure to defeat Al Qaeda in the Arabian Peninsula. Perhaps Al Qaeda's greatest influence in recent years has been its ability to form spin-off organizations—like ISIS—and to encourage allied groups, such as Boko Haram.

In 2017, the Donald Trump administration sent additional troops to Afghanistan, where the Taliban, ISIS, and Al Qaeda insurgency has continued. In 2018, Al Qaeda remained a viable terrorist group with the potential to carry out attacks in many corners of the world. Although it lacks the extreme potency of the late 1990s and early 2000s, it still poses a serious threat to Western interests. In 2016, Al Qaeda and al-Nusra split, with the al-Nusra leadership claiming that its alliance with Al Qaeda was inviting Western military operations within Syria.

Harry Raymond Hueston

See also: Bin Laden, Osama; Islamic State of Iraq and Syria (ISIS); September 11 Terrorist Attacks (2001); Terrorism, International

Further Reading

Bergen, Peter L. 2002. *The Holy War, Inc.: Inside the Secret World of Osama bin Laden.* New York: Free Press.

Gunaratna, Rohan. 2003. *Inside Al Qaeda: Global Network of Terror.* New York: Berkley Publishing Group.

Hueston, Harry R., and B. Vizzin. 2004. *Terrorism 101.* 2nd ed. Ann Arbor, MI: XanEdu Press.

Zuhur, Sherifa. 2006. *A Hundred Osamas: Islamist Threats and the Future of Counterinsurgency.* Carlisle Barracks, PA: Strategic Studies Institute, U.S. Army War College.

Albanese, Jay S. (1955–)

Jay S. Albanese is a professor in the Wilder School of Government & Public Affairs at Virginia Commonwealth University (VCU) in the United States. From 2002 to 2006, he served as chief of the International Center of the National Institute of Justice in Washington, D.C. He is internationally recognized for his research and publications in the areas of ethics and organized crime and has served as a consultant to United Nations groups, the National White Collar Crime Center, the Scottish Government, the United Kingdom, and others.

Albanese began his teaching career at Niagara University before accepting his current position at VCU. He teaches courses on organized crime, professional ethics, white-collar crime, comparative criminal justice, and great ideas of the social sciences. His research endeavors include those topics, plus transnational crime, corruption, gambling and crime, criminal justice education, and the future of crime and justice.

INTERNATIONAL SECTION CHIEF

From 2002 to 2006 Professor Albanese took leave from VCU to accept the position of International Center chief for the National Institute of Justice, which is the research, development, and evaluation agency of the U.S. Department of Justice. He developed research ideas and projects in the topic areas of terrorism, human trafficking, transnational organized crime and corruption, emerging crimes, and international justice system issues.

The International Center aimed to stimulate and facilitate research and evaluation on transnational and comparative crime and justice issues. In addition, the center disseminated that knowledge throughout the national and international criminal justice communities. Under his guidance, the International Center continued to identify and support the needed research and evaluation and coordinated the dissemination of that knowledge. Albanese was, and continues to be, especially adept at working with the United Nations to coordinate its efforts to combat transnational crime.

CONTRIBUTIONS TO THE STUDY OF GLOBAL CRIME

In 2017, Albanese received the Distinguished Scholar Award from the International Association for the Study of Organized Crime for his record of sustained and significant accomplishments and contributions to the scholarly knowledge of organized crime. Examples of those contributions include his recognition of the "ethnicity trap," wherein he argues that relying on ethnicity as a categorization of organized crime is misleading and misdirected (Albanese, 2015). He also applies "risk assessment" methods that allow a more rational way of responding to organized crime, has shown how organized crime groups mirror "enterprise" or business in their formation and operations, and has argued for the need to focus on organized crime "product markets" versus groups (Albanese, 2011). He also has a unique way of classifying and clarifying organized crime as falling into three categories: provision of illicit goods (e.g., drug trafficking and counterfeiting), provision of illicit services (e.g., human trafficking and cybercrime), and infiltration of business of government (e.g., extortion, racketeering, corruption, and money laundering). In this manner, he is able to group all recognized organized crime types in just three categories. By providing simplicity and clarity to a complex issue, Albanese assists researchers studying organized crime and aids policy makers in their understanding of responses to it.

In recognition of both his teaching and research skills, the United Nations Office on Drugs and Crime (Vienna, Austria) invited Albanese to serve on the UN Expert Group on the Education for Justice Initiative (E4J). He served as the principal drafter for all modules of the proposed course on organized crime and worked as a reviewer for the course modules on ethics—a topic for which he also has international recognition (Albanese 2016).

The courses are part of the UN University Module Series and will be used as a basis for teaching in universities and academic institutions across the world. The organized crime module, which was one of the first made available (UNODC n.d.-b), seeks to enhance students' understanding of organized crime, its implications, and the tools that can be used in the fight against it. The modules, consistent with Albanese's pedagogical approach, connect theory to practice, encourage critical thinking, and use innovative interactive teaching approaches, such as experiential learning and group-based work.

PROFESSIONAL ACTIVITIES AND RECOGNITION

Albanese is a past president of the Academy of Criminal Justice Sciences (ACJS), the Northeastern Association of Criminal Justice Sciences, and the White

Collar Crime Research Consortium. He also served as executive director of the International Association for the Study of Organized Crime. Recognition of his contributions to criminology and criminal justice include the ACJS Academy Founder's Award for service to the profession, the ACJS Academy Fellow Award for scholarly achievement, and the ACJS International Section's Gerhard O. W. Mueller Award for outstanding contributions to comparative and international criminal justice.

Philip L. Reichel

See also: Corruption; Illegal Gambling; Transnational, Global, and International Crime

Further Reading

Albanese, Jay S. 2010. "Never Cut a Class, because It Might Change Your Life? My Story." *Virginia Social Science Journal* 45: 82–84.

Albanese, Jay S. 2011. *Transnational Crime and the 21st Century: Criminal Enterprise, Corruption, and Opportunity*. New York: Oxford University Press.

Albanese, Jay S. 2015. *Organized Crime: From the Mob to Transnational Organized Crime*. 7th ed. New York: Routledge

Albanese, Jay S. 2016. *Professional Ethics in Criminal Justice: Being Ethical When No One Is Looking*. 4th ed. Boston: Pearson.

United Nations Office on Drugs and Crime (UNODC). n.d.-a. "Education for Justice." Accessed July 17, 2018. https://www.unodc.org/dohadeclaration/en/topics/education-for-justice.html.

United Nations Office on Drugs and Crime (UNODC). n.d.-b. "University Module Series: Organized Crime." Accessed July 17, 2018. https://www.unodc.org/e4j/en/tertiary/organized-crime.html.

Alliance of NGOs on Crime Prevention and Criminal Justice

The Alliance of NGOs on Crime Prevention and Criminal Justice (the Alliance) is a global network of international nongovernmental organizations (NGOs) in consultative status with the United Nations Economic and Social Council and active in crime prevention and criminal justice operating through the United Nations Office of Drugs and Crime (UNODC). The Alliance is simultaneously a committee of the Conference of NGOs (CoNGO) and one of the three major civil society coalitions partnering with the UNODC.

The Alliance framework for action is very broad to match that of the extensive work of the UNODC-guided Commission on Crime Prevention and Criminal Justice (CCPCJ). This allows its NGO members to participate in the Alliance as experts in their particular fields. In this way, the Alliance acts as an information-sharing advocacy and collaboration platform supporting informed engagement by NGOs with the UNODC and member states.

The mission of the Alliance is to enable the innovative contributions to global policy arising through civil society innovation, expertise, and activism to be considered, debated, adapted, and adopted through the United Nations' main crime prevention and criminal justice policy-making mechanism. In this way, civil society assists with the normalization of higher standards and improved practices as they pertain to the rule of law and a culture of justice.

For NGOs to be effective contributors in this intergovernmental arena, their staff and volunteers need to be adept at navigating global policy-making arenas, program development, and treaty monitoring. Therefore, in addition to providing essential information flow between UNODC and members, the Alliance provides ways for NGO representatives to enrich their understanding of the United Nations and how it works, decides, and is evolving in the light of global political, economic, and social changes.

Most of the Alliance's high-performing members have consultative status with the UN Economic and Social Council (ECOSOC), and some are also associated with the UN Department of Public Information (DPI). However, with increasing globalization and the worldwide impact of today's exponential technologies, there is also significant growth in the transnational nature of emergent problems. This, when combined with the particular difficulty transnational issues pose for the United Nations and member states and shrinking UN funding, informed support and partnerships with competent civil society actors has never been more crucial. Therefore, bolstering civil society actors as effective partners is needed.

The main intergovernmental meetings in which Alliance members are active include the annual Commission on Crime Prevention and Criminal Justice, the annual Conference of States Parties to the Convention against Transnational Organized Crime (UNTOC), and the quinquennial Crime Congress. Members also work with the Civil Society Coalition against Corruption (UNCAC) in their focus on implementing the UN Convention against Corruption (UNCAC).

Alliance representatives also represent the larger civil society grouping during high-profile UNODC-related meetings, high-level meetings of ECOSOC, and special sessions of the General Assembly.

HISTORY

The Alliance first formed in 1972 in New York City prior to the formation of UNODC. It was organized at the instigation of William Clifford, the first chief of the then Social Defense Section (now the Crime Prevention and Criminal Justice Branch) of ECOSOC. G. O. W. Mueller, of New York University, chaired the Alliance during its early years.

The Alliance was a small but active coalition of major NGOs with consultative status to ECOSOC and dedicated to crime prevention and criminal justice improvements. With the formation of UNODC and its subsequent move to Vienna in 1997, NGOs with representatives in Austria became more active.

Since its inception, the Alliance has laid great emphasis on the elaboration and application of the United Nations' minimum rules for justice administration and has contributed toward monitoring the implementation of standards, developing the Restorative Justice Handbook, addressing issues of border control, weapons control, and changing and updating policies on victims of such crimes as femicide, human trafficking, migrant smuggling, most often by enhancing civil relations.

Many NGO representatives active in the Alliance have contributed to the global work of crime prevention and criminal justice, including special representatives to the secretary-general, consultants to the United Nations, and primary actors in international governmental organizations, and as leaders in their own nation's crime prevention and criminal justice arenas.

ORGANIZATION AND MEMBERSHIP

Originally, Alliance members were all representatives of organizations with ECOCSOC or DPI status. Today, the Alliance includes individuals and organizations without formal UN status as associate members when they have an interest in, expertise, and willingness to contribute to areas of concern. This evolution of the Alliance began early on and has continued throughout its lifetime. Marked changes occurred as the UNODC formalized and became headquartered in Vienna in 1997, taking over the tasks and responsibilities originally under the purview of ECOSOC's Social Defense Section in New York.

The New York Alliance continuously met on the first Friday of every second month in New York City (with its working parties meeting as needed) until the end of 2012. NGOs started meeting at the Vienna International Center in 1997 and continue to liaise through the UNODC's Civil Society Team.

Today, the New York and Vienna arms of the Alliance support the worldwide membership overseen by the cochairs. The Vienna chair sustains the Alliance presence and engagement, and the New York chair largely serves the international community and facilitates virtual meetings and the online resources and social media. Alliance leadership in the United States also ensures that the civil society voice is heard at UNHQ meetings of the UNODC, the ECOSOC, or the General Assembly.

WORKING PARTIES AND FOCAL POINTS

The work of the Alliance is largely accomplished through its working parties. These form and dissolve around specific objectives. They develop their own rules of engagement, meeting schedules, objectives, resources, and teams. Working parties report to the larger Alliance community and share their resources and achievements through meetings, articles, and events using the Alliance Web site as an information and communications hub.

Working parties have organized around restorative justice, transnational border crime and technology, victims, corruption, religion and violent extremism, and more. They have been initiators of and major contributors to UNODC handbooks, such as the *Handbook on Restorative Justice Programmes* and the series of six *Femicide Reports* that also contributed to passing General Assembly resolution 68/191 on "taking action against gender-related killing of women and girls."

Working parties also produce civil society statements for distribution and consideration during the congresses, commissions, and other international meetings. Statements at high-level meetings of the United Nations have included but are not limited to the Conference of States Parties to the UNCAC Marrakech, Morocco (2011); the UN General Assembly Thematic Debate on "Drugs and Crime as a Threat to Development," UNHQ (2012); the Doha Civil Society Declaration (2015) contribution to the 2015 Crime Congress; and the high-level debate on the Convention against Transnational Organized Crime at UNHQ (2017).

During the 2015 Crime Congress, the Alliance members identified focal points as another way to provide organizational support. Focal points include corrections and sentencing, corruption, crime prevention, femicide, gender, artificial intelligence (AI) and cybercrime, lawyers and prosecutors, prison chaplains, restorative justice, Sustainable Development Goal 16, terrorism prevention, and victims' rights.

ADAPTATIONS TO GLOBALIZATION AND DIGITIZATION

Today, the Alliance helps to maximize the impact of civil society organizations and experts by leveraging technology to facilitate new conversations, share information, and drive new activity. For example, the Femicide Platform on the Alliance Web site became the largest online collection of femicide reports, stories, and resources. This organizing mechanism supported the work on the *Femicide Reports* and the related UNGA resolution.

Aware of the growing challenges wrought by organized crime leveraging new technologies, the Alliance is making new synergies possible between the various crime prevention and criminal justice stakeholders in the margins of intergovernmental meetings. For example, during the 27th UN Commission on Crime Prevention and Criminal Justice, under the banner of SOLVE2018, the Alliance is facilitating a process akin to a strategy sprint. This innovative framework for professionals, civil society actors, diplomats, and global policy specialists introduces an agile methodology new to UNODC's global strategy discussions and development.

Helping solve pressing crime prevention and criminal justice issues both through substance and process is the legacy and mission of the Alliance. To these ends, the Alliance continues to leverage the diverse resources and contributions of civil society as essential partners in strengthening the rule of law and a culture of lawfulness.

Karen Judd Smith

See also: Mueller, Gerhard O. W.; Nongovernmental Organization; UN Commission on Crime Prevention and Criminal Justice; UN Office on Drugs and Crime

Further Reading

The Alliance. 2015. *Doha Civil Society Declaration.* Accessed November 21, 2018. https://www.cpcjalliance.org/wp-content/uploads/2015/05/Doha-Civil-Society-Forum-Declaration-13th_6pm.doc.

The Alliance. 2018a. "Femicide Platform." Accessed April 21, 2018. https://www.cpcjalliance.org/femicide.

The Alliance. 2018b. "*Femicide Reports.* Vols. I–VI. Accessed April 22, 2018. https://www.cpcjalliance.org/femicide/documents-publications.

Judd Smith, Karen. 2016. *United Nations Unlocked: The Missing Link the UN Needs to Tackle Global Terrorism and the Coming Tech Tsunami.* Valley Springs, CA: GDE Press.

SOLVE2018. 2018. https://cpcjalliance.org/events/solve2018/.

United Nations Office of Drugs and Crime (UNODC). 2006. "Handbook on Restorative Justice Programmes." *Criminal Justice Handbook Series.* Accessed April 22, 2018. https://www.unodc.org/pdf/criminal_justice/Handbook_on_Restorative_Justice_Programmes.pdf.

Worley, Christopher G., Thomas Williams, and Edward E. Lawler III. 2016. "Creating Management Processes Built for Change." *MIT Sloan Management Review*, September 13. Accessed November 21, 2018. https://sloanreview.mit.edu/article/creating-management-processes-built-for-change.

AlphaBay

AlphaBay was an online marketplace—an e-commerce site that facilitates the acquirement of products and services by consumers from various third-party entities—that operated on the darknet via an onion service of the Tor anonymity network. Launched in December 2014, AlphaBay quickly became one of the largest darknet marketplaces in the world, with numbers peaking at over 369,000 listings and 400,000 users, approximately 10 times larger than the infamous Silk Road (Cimpanu 2017). Revenue accrued through AlphaBay ranged from $600,000 to $800,000 a day, with annual sales eclipsing hundreds of millions of dollars (DOJ 2017b). In July 2017, during the peak of its marketplace dominance, a multinational law enforcement operation known as Operation Bayonet shut AlphaBay down. Spearheaded by the United States, Operation Bayonet targeted and seized a multitude of darknet market infrastructures, with AlphaBay being one of the primary targets. On July 5, 2017, in conjunction with Operation Bayonet, authorities arrested the alleged founder and administrator of AlphaBay, Alexandre Cazes, in Thailand.

ANONYMITY

AlphaBay operated as a darknet marketplace that facilitated and brokered the commerce of illicit and legal goods. Products included stolen or fraudulent identification documents, controlled substances, firearms, noxious chemicals, stolen financial information and credit cards, counterfeit goods, fraudulent services, and malware. AlphaBay operated via an onion service, which is an anonymous hidden service that directs computer data around a number of Internet intermediaries before reaching the intended final destination (Walsh 2016). This feature allowed the traceability of information, provided by both the consumer and the seller, to be extremely diminished within the AlphaBay network. This onion service worked in conjunction with The Onion Router (Tor) anonymity network, which is a special network that obscures the true IP addresses of the computers within the network. Further anonymity aspects included the use of cryptocurrencies—a form of digital currency that has no central issuing or regulating authority—such as

Bitcoin, Monero, and Ethereum (DOJ 2017b). The use of cryptocurrencies, in conjunction with the anonymity aspects of the Tor network and onion service, provided AlphaBay users with a high sense of security, which helped foster the reported high levels of usage (DOJ 2017a).

OPERATION BAYONET

Operation Bayonet was a multinational law enforcement operation headed by the United States. It cooperated with law enforcement specialists in Thailand, Canada, the United Kingdom, the Netherlands, Lithuania, and France, with additional involvement coming from the European law enforcement agency Europol. Known events surrounding Operation Bayonet began in May 2016, when law enforcement officials began purchasing controlled substances, fake identification documents, and ATM skimmers from various AlphaBay vendors (DOJ 2017b). Access to, and utilization of, the AlphaBay network led investigating officials to believe that Cazes was the suspected founder and administrator of AlphaBay.

In December 2016, investigators uncovered that Cazes's personal e-mail was being utilized in a welcome e-mail sent out to all new AlphaBay users as well during the password recovery process of the AlphaBay forum. After tracing this e-mail back to Cazes, law enforcement officials issued an arrest warrant for Cazes detailing 16 criminal counts leveled against him, including several counts of conspiracy to engage in a racketeer influenced corrupt organization (DOJ 2017b). Under the direction of the U.S. Federal Bureau of Investigation (FBI) and Drug Enforcement Administration (DEA), the Royal Thai Police executed an arrest warrant for Cazes on July 5, 2017. During this arrest, Thai police gained access to Cazes's laptop, which was logged into his administrator role within the AlphaBay network, and found files relating to all of AlphaBay's servers, passwords, and associated identities. On July 12, 2017, while awaiting extradition to the United States, Cazes was found dead in his prison cell, with suicide being the suspected cause of death.

Jessie L. Slepicka

See also: Cryptocurrency; Cryptomarkets; Dream Market; Tor (The Onion Router) Network

Further Reading

AlphaBay Market. n.d. "Empire Market: A Replica of the Famous AlphaBay Launched." Accessed May 14, 2018. https://alphabaymarket.com.

Burrows, Ian. 2017. "Alexandre Cazes: Who Was the AlphaBay Founder and How Did Authorities Catch Him?" Accessed May 14, 2018. http://www.abc.net.au/news/2017-07-21/who-was-alphabay-founder-alexandre-cazes/8730680.

Cimpanu, Catalin. 2017. "AlphaBay Dark Web Market Taken Down after Law Enforcement Raids." Accessed May 14, 2018. https://www.bleepingcomputer.com/news/security/alphabay-dark-web-market-taken-down-after-law-enforcement-raids.

Federal Bureau of investigation (FBI). 2017. "Darknet Takedown: Authorities Shutter Online Criminal Market AlphaBay" Accessed May 14, 2018. https://www.fbi.gov/news/stories/alphabay-takedown.

U.S. Department of Justice (DOJ). 2017a. "AlphaBay, the Largest Online 'Dark Market,' Shut Down." Accessed May 14, 2018. https://www.justice.gov/opa/pr/alphabay-largest-online-dark-market-shut-down.

U.S. Department of Justice (DOJ). 2017b. "United States of America v. Alexandre Cazes." Accessed May 14, 2018. https://www.justice.gov/opa/press-release/file/982821/download.

Walsh, Dean. 2016. "A Beginner's Guide to Exploring the Darknet." Accessed May 14, 2018. https://turbofuture.com/internet/A-Beginners-Guide-to-Exploring-the-Darknet.

Anticorruption Efforts

There is a global debate on existing and possible anticorruption strategies and how to assess their effectiveness across different contexts. At least two lessons have been learned on the topic so far by criminal justice agencies. First, stricter laws do not necessarily guarantee an effective anticorruption campaign. Instead, success depends on the actual implementation of those laws (Project "DIGIWHIST" 2015–2018). Second, one-size-fits-all approaches are not likely to be successful, as the effectiveness of anticorruption policies is strictly dependent on the context.

MEASURES INCREASING THE RISKS OF CORRUPTION

The role of whistle-blowing polices have been internationally acknowledged by different anticorruption treaties, for example, the United Nations Convention against Corruption (Articles 8, 13, and 33), the Inter-American Convention against Corruption (Article III(8)), and the African Union Convention on Preventing and Combating Corruption (Article 5(6)). In the past decade, different countries have adopted such legislation to guarantee that employees in the public or private sector report illegal misconduct occurring at work to the judicial authorities. The legislation was conceived to safeguard the whistle-blower, to avoid revealing their identity, and to protect them from being fired for reporting. Although there are countries that have not yet guaranteed a full protection of whistle-blowers, a growing awareness is emerging on the issue. Indeed, Transparency International has committed itself to provide guidance to countries for the adoption and refinement of whistle-blowing legislation (Terracol 2018).

In different countries, international organizations and civil society strove to enhance civil oversight and monitor public decisions and spending. To meet such needs, various policies have been adopted to reduce corruption by increasing government transparency in its different facets (e.g., enable the monitoring of politicians' actions, publish legislative records). In Uganda, for example, the World Bank assessed the effect of a government transparency policy (Reinikka and Svensson 2005). Accordingly, the 80 percent of funds devoted to schools were leaked by local bureaucrats. This discovery led the government to deter such misbehavior by massively publicizing it. This policy not only had a strong impact in substantially decreasing leakages, but it also extended its benefits far beyond the initial aim by, for example, giving rise to school enrollments. Despite particularly successful cases as the one mentioned above, researchers agree that transparency should generally be accompanied with accountability measures to be fully effective (Lindstedt and Naurin 2010).

Another set of anticorruption policies aim at enhancing monitoring and enforcement. In different contexts, these resulted in the establishment of anticorruption agencies whose officers, ideally, must be carefully selected and trained to a culture of integrity and independence. The successfulness of such bodies mainly depends on the political willingness and commitment against corruption and, partly, on the support of the civil society (Svensson 2005). For example, the Hong Kong administration established an Independent Commission against Corruption (ICAC) specifically oriented toward prevention and community education. Its success depended on the fact that this body was answerable to institutions external to domestic politics (i.e., the colony's governor, who in turn was accountable to the British Parliament and to the queen at last). On the contrary, the Kenyan Anti-Corruption Commission (KACC) failed in its commitment due to its close dependence on local governors (Fisman and Golden 2017).

In the last years, both public and private institutions have been introducing technological tools within their anticorruption tool kits. For example, the Indian government introduced a smart card system based on biometric data to guarantee reaching the beneficiaries of a government policy aimed at fostering employment. The system was particularly successful, as it drastically reduced the leakage of funds perpetrated by officials to enrich themselves and their relatives (Muralidharan, Niehaus, and Sukhtankar 2016). The success of such tools usually requires human oversight to constantly ensure their performance and to prevent any kind of sabotage by lobbies who would lose out from their introduction. Further, many countries are recently showing a growing interest toward devices preventing rather than deterring corruption. In this regard, in the last years, the European Union (EU) has allocated funds for the development of risk assessment and management tools. For instance, the DIGIWHIST project (2015–2018) has developed software to assess corruption risks in public procurement both at the tender and company levels.

MEASURES REDUCING INCENTIVES AND REWARDS OF CORRUPTION

Policies aimed at increasing wages of officers to reduce their incentives to take bribes are among the most debated. Indeed, there are conflicting results on whether higher wages deter corruption (Rose-Ackerman 1999; Svensson 2005). A study carried out in India demonstrated that the introduction of a pay reform in 1997 that increased customs officials' salaries by up to 100 percent did not lead to a reduction of tariff evasion (Mishra, Subramanian, and Topalova 2008). Interestingly, a study conducted in Buenos Aires, Argentina, public hospital procurement showed that officers were less inclined to accept bribes if they thought they could be fired for it, irrespective of an increase of salary (Di Tella and Schargrodsky 2003). According to the authors, this policy should be combined with increased monitoring and enforcement to effectively reduce corruption. Other policies aimed at reducing corrupt incentives in the public sector include the rotation of civil servants, which makes it difficult for them to foster ties with clients and rewards those who reject bribes. Singapore is an example of the successful application of this policy (Svensson 2005).

Finally, many anticorruption policies combat corruption through deregulation measures aimed at reducing public intervention on the economy and enhancing its competitiveness. An example of these policies is the reduction of barriers to international trade (e.g., tariffs) and to the entry of firms in the market (e.g., licensing requirements). Again, Singapore constitutes a successful example: the extension of duty-free imports reduced corruption in customs. However, the same deregulation measures did not work in other contexts, as, for example, in the supply of indispensable goods in poor countries (Bardhan 1997).

Carlotta Carbone

See also: Corruption; Corruption in China; Corruption in Sub-Saharan Africa; Corruption Measurements; UN Convention against Corruption

Further Reading

Bardhan, Pranab. 1997. "Corruption and Development: A Review of Issues." *Journal of Economic Literature* 35 (3): 1320–1346.

Di Tella, Rafael, and Ernesto Schargrodsky. 2003. "The Role of Wages and Auditing during a Crackdown on Corruption in the City of Buenos Aires." *Journal of Law and Economics* 46 (1): 269–292.

Fisman, Raymond, and Miriam A. Golden. 2017. *Corruption: What Everyone Needs to Know*. New York: Oxford University Press.

Lindstedt, Catharina, and Daniel Naurin. 2010. "Transparency Is Not Enough: Making Transparency Effective in Reducing Corruption." *International Political Science Review* 31 (3): 301–322.

Mishra, Prachi, Arvind Subramanian, and Petia Topalova. 2008. "Tariffs, Enforcement, and Customs Evasion: Evidence from India." *Journal of Public Economics* 92 (10–11): 1907–1925.

Muralidharan, Karthik, Paul Niehaus, and Sandip Sukhtankar. 2016. "Building State Capacity: Evidence from Biometric Smartcards in India." *American Economic Review* 106 (10): 2895–2929.

Project "DIGIWHIST." 2015–2018. "DIGIWHIST—The Digital Whistleblower. Fiscal Transparency, Risk Assessment and Impact of Good Governance Policies Assessed." Horizon 2020 Research and Innovation Framework Programme, funded by the European Commission (Grant Agreement No: 645852). Accessed February 19, 2019. http://digiwhist.eu/about-digiwhist/

Reinikka, Ritva, and Jakob Svensson. 2005. "Fighting Corruption to Improve Schooling: Evidence from a Newspaper Campaign in Uganda." *Journal of the European Economic Association* 3 (2–3): 259–267.

Rose-Ackerman, Susan. 1999. *Corruption and Government Causes, Consequences, and Reform*. Cambridge: Cambridge University Press.

Svensson, Jakob. 2005. "Eight Questions about Corruption." *Journal of Economic Perspectives* 19 (3): 19–42.

Terracol, Marie. 2018. *A Best Practice Guide for Whistleblowing Legislation*. Berlin, Germany: Transparency International. Accessed February 19, 2019. https://www.transparency.org/whatwedo/publication/best_practice_guide_for_whistleblowing_legislation

Antiquities and Cultural Objects, Theft of

Trafficking in antiquities and cultural objects is a crime in which cultural property is stolen or illicitly trafficked from one place and sold in another. Trafficking is illegal transport and trade. Antiquities are objects, buildings, or works of art from the ancient past. Cultural objects are objects made by humans that give information about the culture of the people who made or used it. These objects can have significance regarding archeology, prehistory, history, literature, art, or science and all fall into the category of cultural objects.

Trafficked cultural property falls into one of two categories: looted antiquities or stolen art. Looted antiquities are pieces that are not known as individual objects, and stolen art is objects that are known as individual pieces. Despite overlap between these two categories, this section will focus on looted antiquities and cultural objects rather than art theft.

TRAFFICKING IN ANTIQUITIES

Cultural objects and antiquities from all over the world have been trafficked. Many examples of this trafficking involve objects from the Global South that end up being purchased in the Global North. Some common source regions include the Middle East (with some source countries being Egypt, Iraq, Jordan, and Syria); Latin America (Peru, Colombia, Ecuador, and Belize); West Africa (Mali, Niger, Ghana, and Burkina Faso); and Southeast Asia (India, Pakistan, Thailand, and Cambodia). The most common destination countries are the United States, Canada, and countries in Western Europe.

While the common paradigm has objects moving to the north, cultural objects can also be trafficked in other patterns. One pattern is objects moving from the Global North to other countries. Examples of this include objects from ancient Rome and Greece being trafficked to the United States and objects from indigenous communities in the United States or Canada being trafficked to Europe. Another pattern is objects from a source region being trafficked to another country within that region. An example of this is Khmer objects from Cambodia being trafficked to China or India.

The trafficking of antiquities and cultural objects is big business, with "the illegal trade in stolen art and antiquities [being] worth up to an estimated $6 billion annually" (Chonaill, Reding, and Valeri 2011, vii). It is difficult to find detailed information on the scope of trafficking in cultural objects because of the unknown nature of looted objects and the clandestine nature of many sales.

Much of this illegal trade is used to finance other crimes by organized criminal groups. Trafficking in cultural objects and antiquities has been linked to drug trafficking, arms trading, and terrorist organizations. One way this trade is linked to other criminal activities is through laundering money, and "dealing in art and antiquities is considered by some to be the most effective way of laundering criminal proceeds stemming from narcotics, gambling, extortion rackets, smuggling, merchandise pirating, and counterfeiting" (Chonaill, Reding, and Valeri 2011, 4).

UNDERSTANDING HOW ANTIQUITIES ARE TRAFFICKED

To better understand how antiquities are trafficked, a theory and a model can be applied to this crime. A criminological theory called the routine activity theory states that a crime event needs three conditions to take place. The three conditions are a likely offender, a suitable target, and the absence of a capable guardian. When all three of these conditions are met at one time and in one place, it is ripe for a crime to take place.

Building on this theory, a four-state progression model helps to understand how the crime takes place. The four stages, in order of occurrence, are theft, transit, facilitation, and sale or purchase. Because this process involves all of these different stages, several different crimes can be involved within trafficking in antiquities and cultural objects. Different key actors are typically involved at each stage. At the theft stage, the primary actors are extractors who are usually amateur thieves who loot antiquities or steal cultural objects to earn an income. In the transit stage, the actors are middlemen who are professional criminals that act as a bridge between the theft of an object in its source country and its sale in its destination country. With the facilitation stage, the actors are dealers of cultural objects who are professional dealers with connections to final markets. Finally, in the sale/purchase stage, the actors are the buyers, who may or may not know that the objects they are purchasing were obtained or transported illegally.

One special thing about the process of trafficking in antiquities and cultural objects is that it is a "gray market." The idea of a gray market is that it is neither all black nor all white, neither all illegal nor all legal. Both legal and illegal elements are present in most cases of trafficking in cultural objects, and objects can move back and forth between the legal and illegal sides during the four-stage process. An example of this gray market with both legal and illegal parts can be seen in the following case study.

FIGHTING THE TRAFFICKING OF ANTIQUITIES

Due to the broad scope of these criminal activities, a variety of different tools are needed to effectively address this problem. The three categories of activities to fight the trafficking of antiquities and cultural objects are legal instruments, operational instruments, and awareness-raising instruments. Legal instruments include international conventions, regional and national legislations, and bilateral agreements. Operational instruments include export and provenance certificates for cultural objects, databases of known cultural objects, criminal justice policies, and other practical tools. Awareness-raising instruments include codes of ethics, educational posters, news stories, and other public outreach methods.

Several international conventions have been very influential in the fight against trafficking in cultural objects. In chronological order, the four major international instruments are the following:

- The Convention for the Protection of Cultural Property in the Event of Armed Conflict—Commonly known as The Hague Convention of 1954, this instrument was adopted after World War II to protect cultural heritage during war and armed conflict.

- The Convention on the Means of Prohibiting and Preventing the Illicit Import, Export and Transfer of Ownership of Cultural Property—This convention, written in 1970 and orchestrated by the United Nations Educational, Scientific and Cultural Organization (UNESCO), sets standards for state signatories to enact preventative measures and to participate in international cooperative efforts to stop the illicit trafficking of cultural property.
- The Model Treaty for the Prevention of Crimes That Infringe on the Cultural Heritage of Peoples in the Form of Movable Property—This model treaty, adopted by the United Nations Economic and Social Council (ECOSOC) in 1990, sets an example for states who wish to enter bilateral agreements regarding prohibiting and punishing the illicit trafficking in cultural property that might occur between them.
- The UNIDROIT Convention on Stolen of Illegally Exported Cultural Objects—This convention, written by the International Institute for the Unification of Private Law (UNIDROIT) in 1995, complements the UNESCO Convention of 1970 by strengthening provisions regarding the repatriation of trafficked cultural objects to their state of origin.

THE IMPORTANCE OF CULTURAL PROPERTY

Addressing the crime of trafficking in antiquities and cultural objects is vitally important because these objects help people know their history and understand their heritage. When trafficked, cultural objects lose their context and sense of place, many are damaged, and nations lose parts of their identity. Four ways in which trafficking cultural objects is detrimental are that is removed from the public space where it can be seen and appreciated, the objects are more likely to be damaged or broken, cultural identity is lost when objects are stolen, and when property is removed from its original location its social or political function may be compromised. "When objects are looted and trafficked as collectible commodities, this results in not only the loss of physical objects from the human past but also the information and knowledge to be garnered from them" (Bowman 2018, 62).

Paula K. Priebe

See also: Cambodian Statue Theft; Convention on the Means of Prohibiting and Preventing the Illicit Import, Export, and Transport of Ownership of Cultural Property; Transnational, Global, and International Crime

Further Reading

Bowman, B. A. 2018. "Trafficking in Antiquities." In *Transnational Crime and Global Security*, edited by Phil Reichel and Ryan Randa, 61–72. Santa Barbara, CA: Praeger.

Campbell, P. B. 2013. "The Illicit Antiquities Trade as a Transnational Criminal Network: Characterizing and Anticipating Trafficking of Cultural Heritage." *International Journal of Cultural Property* 20: 113–153.

Chonaill, S. N., A. Reding, and L. Valeri. 2011. *Assessing the Illegal Trade in Cultural Property from a Public Policy Perspective.* Cambridge, UK: RAND Europe.

Deitzler, J. 2013. "On 'Organized Crime' in the Illicit Antiquities Trade: Moving beyond the Definitional Debate." *Trends in Organized Crime* 16: 329–342.

United Nations Educational, Scientific and Cultural Organization (UNESCO). n.d. "Illicit Trafficking of Cultural Property." Accessed January 13, 2019. www.unesco.org/new/en/culture/themes/illicit-trafficking-of-cultural-property.

United Nations Office on Drugs and Crime (UNODC). 2016. *Practical Assistance Tool to Assist in the Implementation of the International Guidelines for Crime Prevention and Criminal Justice Responses with Respect to Trafficking in Cultural Property and Other Related Offences.* Vienna: United Nations Office on Drugs and Crime.

Anttila, Inkeri (1916–2013)

Inkeri Anttila was a Finnish academic and a world pioneer in criminology and victimology as well as a criminal justice reformer who promoted rational and humane criminal policy in her own country, across Europe, and around the world. For example, her work contributed to the world's first self-report studies and victim surveys and to a reassessment in many countries of their approach to crime prevention and sentencing.

Inkeri Anttila entered the Faculty of Law at the University of Helsinki in 1933, one of the first women to do so. She graduated three years later and served at a district court while continuing her academic studies, receiving her doctoral (JSD) degree in 1946. In 1949, she taught correctional science at the School of Social Sciences, and sociology merged with criminal law as her focus of interest. In 1954, she received academic degrees in sociology and soon after was appointed director of prison personnel training at the Department of Prison Administration. These first years in her professional career were emblematic of her life's work: she was cross-disciplinary, and she combined work in academia with work in government.

Anttila was appointed a professor of criminal law at the University of Helsinki in 1961, the first woman to hold a chair in law in Finland. She established the Institute of Criminology in 1963. In 1974, this was transferred to the Ministry of Justice to become the National Research Institute of Legal Policy. In 1981, Anttila became the director of the newly established European regional institute in the UN crime prevention and criminal justice program (HEUNI), a position that she held until her retirement in 1986.

Throughout her career, Anttila moved smoothly between criminal law and sociology. During the early 1950s, she introduced the new field of criminology to Finland. In 1962, she helped launch one of the world's first self-report studies of delinquency. She was also one of the first to realize the academic and practical importance of victimology, and her 1964 article "The Criminological Significance of Unregistered Criminality," in the journal *Excerpta Criminologica*, led to the first victim survey, which was carried out in the United States (Anttila 2011; Joutsen and Viljanen 2016).

Her experience in corrections and her wide contacts in academia led her to question received truths in criminal policy (Lahti 2013). Already during the 1960s, she challenged the prevailing belief that offenders should be "treated" to cure them of their criminality. She emphasized that situational factors contributed to crime and argued for more rational and humane approaches to both crime prevention and criminal justice (Anttila 2011). She was skeptical of punitive approaches and spoke out worldwide, for example, against capital punishment and long-term imprisonment. She laid out her ideas in hundreds of articles and papers, many of which were written in English, French, German, Danish, and Swedish, all languages in which she was fluent.

She briefly served as the minister of justice of Finland in 1975 and used this position to introduce several legislative bills, which were innovative in being based not solely on legal arguments but also on criminological research and cost-benefit analysis (Lahti 2013). She utilized this same approach when she was a driving force in the preparation of the total reform of Finland's criminal law from the 1970s to the end of the 1990s.

Anttila's international influence began with her first visits to Sweden and Denmark during the late 1940s. The Nordic countries were establishing national criminological associations, and she regularly participated at their joint Nordic meetings (Joutsen and Viljanen 2016). The Scandinavian Research Council of Criminology was established in 1962, and she served as its president from 1968 to 1973.

Anttila soon expanded her activity to the "Big Four" international organizations in criminal law and criminal policy, and she served as board member or vice-president in all four: the International Penal and Penitentiary Foundation, the International Association of Penal Law, the International Society for Criminology, and the International Society of Social Defence.

She was also active in the Council of Europe and in the United Nations in particular. She became a member of the select UN Committee on Crime Prevention and Control, serving as its vice-chairperson from 1972 to 1974. She was elected by acclamation as the president of the Fifth United Nations Crime Congress (1975). The establishment of HEUNI and her appointment as its first director were a logical extension of this activity, enabling her to organize major European expert meetings on crime prevention and criminal justice that for the first time brought together experts from both Western and Eastern Europe. This cross-fertilization of ideas had an impact in subsequent criminal policy, in particular in Eastern Europe, which underwent political and social upheaval during the 1990s.

In 1992, Inkeri Anttila received a testimonial from the secretary-general of the United Nations in recognition of her service to the UN program on crime prevention and criminal justice. In 1982, she received the Sellin-Glueck Award of the American Society of Criminology, and in 2011, she received the European Criminology Award of the European Society of Criminology in honor of her lifetime achievement. Anttila died on July 6, 2013, at the age of 96.

Matti Joutsen

See also: HEUNI; Transnational, Global, and International Crime

Further Reading

Anttila, Inkeri. 2011. Address to the ESC on the Occasion of the European Criminology Award 2011. *Criminology in Europe* 12: 8–10.

Joutsen, Matti, and Terhi Viljanen. 2016. "Inkeri Anttila's International Reach." In *Inkeri Anttila (1916–2013): Rikosoikeuden uudistajan ammatillinen ura ja vaikutus*,edited by Raimo Lahti, 207–226. Helsinki, Finland: University of Helsinki.

Lahti, Raimo, ed. 1996. *Towards a Rational and Humane Criminal Policy: Dedicated to Inkeri Anttila, 29 November 1996.* Helsinki, Finland: University of Helsinki.

Lahti, Raimo. 2013. "Inkeri Anttila in Memorium (Obituary)." *Annales internationales de Criminologie* 51 (1/2): 175–178.

Lahti, Raimo, and Patrik Törnudd, eds. 2001. *Inkeri Anttila, Ad Ius Criminale Humanius: Essays in Criminology, Criminal Justice and Criminal Policy.* Helsinki, Finland: Finnish Lawyers' Association.

Arms Brokers

Arms brokers are persons or entities acting as an intermediary to arrange or facilitate a transaction of small arms and light weapons in return for some form of financial or other type of benefit. Parties involved in an arms deal include buyers, sellers, transporters, financiers, and insurers. Brokers are often used to facilitate legitimate arms deals from the point at which the desired firearms are identified to their delivery to the final recipient. The brokers can be owners of the firearms they sell, but in the majority of cases, they are not. Their core activity consists of the mediation and arrangement of the firearms exchange, and for this reason, brokers are an intrinsic part of the legal trade in small arms and light weapons (Marsh 2002; SAS 2004).

However, brokers and their activities play a crucial role in the "gray area" of the firearms market, that is, the area among legal and illegal dealings. In particular, by exploiting their expertise, contacts, and knowledge of the market, they have been and are instrumental in transferring weapons and ammunitions to illegitimate users or destinations, including countries under UN arms embargo and conflict zones (Stohl 2005). Their centrality in the illicit trade has remained relatively unnoticed for decades, but in recent years, policy agendas and research have increasingly focused on the issue of illicit brokering activities.

HOW ILLICIT ARMS BROKERS OPERATE

Organizing illegal arms sales requires a large amount of skill, organization, preparation, and financial resources. A successful broker has to forge documents related to firearms transportation; bribe officials during the routine controls; interact with legitimate arms companies, persuading them to sell their weapons; launder money illicitly earned; and find efficient and trusty collaborators (Marsh 2002). Therefore, brokers are able to obtain the necessary official documentation (e.g., end-user certificates) through forgery or by exploiting the negligence or active complicity of state officials. They also establish their illicit activities in tax havens, countries with lax export or transit controls, and offshore banks to conceal the illicit financial transactions and launder the money (Naylor 2000; SAS 2001).

The brokering activities are facilitated by regulatory gaps or inadequate controls. In particular, these activities are often unregulated because they are not defined as a specific category under all national arms export laws (Wood and Peleman 2000). Brokers exploit the scarce and ineffective controls on firearms surplus and stockpiles, which are often used as the main source of illicitly brokered deals, as well as the difficulties of enforcement and monitoring in the transportation phase. Generally, they prefer to split the deliveries into many shorter trips and to disguise the content they are moving using a fast mode of transport (e.g., air freight) to reduce the chances of detection, making it harder to trace the exact route and to identify the party responsible for the shipment (Hogendoorn and Misol 2003; Wood and Peleman 2000; UNSC 2003, para. 104). Brokers also resort to the diversion of firearms from authorized routes with "emergency stops" that are used to load cargo different from that declared in the accompanying documentation or to offload concealed weapons to other means of transportation; the filing of false flight plans (SAS 2001; Wood and Peleman 2000); and the establishment of companies in countries with lax regulations. In most of the cases, transport agents take advantage of the difficulties in enforcing customs controls, especially in countries with long borders and few resources (SAS 2004).

INITIATIVES TO CONTROL THE BROKERING ACTIVITIES

In light of the high possibility that arms brokers are involved in illicit movements of firearms, since the mid-1990s, a series of multilateral initiatives has aimed to create a common understanding of illicit brokering and to develop the means for tackling it.

According to the UN Feasibility Study conducted in 1999, three key elements are essential to control brokering activities (United Nations 2001, para. 67):

1. Licensing systems—They ensure that only individuals or commercial entities that have received explicit consent by the relevant national authorities can legally engage in intermediary activities. Without this consent, the activity is automatically illicit and therefore liable to legal prosecution.
2. Registration of brokers—This records the number of individuals and companies that can legally trade firearms to supervise over and gather information about them. Without the registration, states cannot prevent the commission of illicit trade to those actors that have already committed this crime, and cannot exchange information on the brokers with other states.
3. Disclosure requirements—They ensure that the applicants requiring export licenses provide the states with all the details about any brokering agent involved.

Article 15 of the UN Protocol against the Illicit Manufacturing of and Trafficking in Firearms, Their Parts and Components and Ammunition, supplementing the

UN Convention against Transnational Organized Crime, fully accomplishes these requests. Also Article 1 of the Amended EU Directive 2017 stresses the relevance of these controls.

Besides these control activities, there are also some obligations for the brokers to better allow monitoring of their actions, that is, to keep records and to report their activities to national authorities.

In this regard, Article 1, Point 3 (b) of the Amended EU Directive 2017 asks for the maintenance of a register that dealers and brokers have to fill in with each firearm and each essential component that is received or disposed of by them, together with particulars enabling the firearm or essential component to be identified and traced (i.e., type, make, model, caliber, and serial number thereof and the names and addresses of the suppliers and of the persons acquiring it). The register has to be delivered to the national authorities responsible for the data-filing systems upon the cessation of their activities.

Due to the transnational nature of brokering activities, multilateral cooperation among states is becoming more essential: states are strongly encouraged to share information about arms brokers and their activities to limit the possibility that they will evade controls by acting in states with less rigorous controls or enforcement.

Marina Mancuso

See also: Arms Trade Treaty; Nuclear Weapons and Related Materials and Technologies, Trafficking in; Small Arms and Light Weapons, Trafficking in; Small Arms Survey; Weapons Sales

Further Reading

Hogendoorn, Ernst Jan, and Misol, Lisa. 2003. *The Role of Transport Agents in Illicit Arms Brokering and Prosecutions of Illicit Arms Brokers.* Background paper. Geneva, Switzerland: Small Arms Survey.

Marsh, Nicholas. 2002. "Two Sides of the Same Coin—The Legal and Illegal Trade in Small Arms." *Brown Journal of World Affairs* 9 (1): 217–228.

Naylor, Tom. 2000. "Gunsmoke and Mirrors: Financing the Illegal Trade." In *Running Guns: The Global Black Market in Small Arms*, edited by Lora Lumpe, 155–182. London: Zed Books.

O'Farrell, Kloé Tricot. 2013. *Arms Brokering Controls: How Are They Implemented in the EU?* Brussels, Belgium: Groupe de Recherche et D'Information sur la Paix et la Sécurité. Accessed January 21, 2019. http://www.grip.org/sites/grip.org/files/RAPPORTS/2013/Rapport_2013-2_EN.pdf.

Small Arms Survey (SAS). 2001. *Small Arms Survey 2001: Profiling the Problem.* Oxford: Oxford University Press.

Small Arms Survey (SAS). 2004. "Targeting the Middlemen: Controlling Brokering Activities." In *Small Arms Survey 2004: Rights at Risk*, edited by Small Arms Survey, 141–171. Geneva, Switzerland: Small Arms Survey.

Stohl, Rachel J. 2005. "Fighting the Illicit Trafficking of Small Arms." *SAIS Review of International Affairs* 25 (1): 59–68.

United Nations. 2001. *Report of the Group of Governmental Experts Established Pursuant to General Assembly Resolution 54/54 V of 15 December 1999, Entitled "Small Arm" ("UN Feasibility Study").* Reproduced in UN Document A/CONF.192/2, May 11.

United Nations Security Council (UNSC). 2003. *Report of the Panel of Experts Appointed Pursuant to Paragraph 4 of Security Council Resolution 1458 (2003), Concerning Liberia. S/2003/498 of 24 April.*

Wood, Brian, and Johan Peleman. 2000. "Making the Deal and Moving the Goods: The Role of Brokers and Shippers." In *Running Guns: The Global Black Market in Small Arms*, edited by Lora Lumpe, 129–154. London: Zed Books.

Arms Trade Treaty

The Arms Trade Treaty (ATT) is a multilateral treaty—a treaty to which three of more sovereign states are parties—that attempts to regulate the international trade market of conventional arms. The ATT establishes mutual standards for the international trade of conventional arms and seeks to reduce the illegal arms trade market. The ATT obligates parties to regulate the ammunition and munitions fired, launched, or delivered by conventional arms. These conventional arms include battle tanks, armored combat vehicles, missiles and missile launchers, large-caliber artillery systems, combat aircraft, warships, and small arms and light weapons. The ATT also calls for parties to regulate their states' export of parts that may be utilized in the construction of these conventional arms (NTI 2017). The ATT entered into force—or came to have legal force and effect—on December 24, 2014, and currently holds 130 signatories, representing 93 states parties, who have agreed to the treaty (UNODA n.d.).

HISTORY

In late 1995, Óscar Arias Sánchez, the former president of Costa Rica and Nobel Peace Prize laureate, called upon fellow Nobel laureates to encourage and champion an international agreement regulating the trade market of conventional arms (Arms Control Association 2016). In New York, in 1997, Arias Sánchez led a group of Nobel Peace Prize laureates in a conference that developed the Codes of Conduct to Control Arms Transfers (UNESCO 1998). This code of conduct created a set of common criteria for states to use when assessing arms exports and laid the foundation for a future arms trade treaty.

In 2006, the UN General Assembly passed Resolution 61/89, which instructed the UN secretary-general to undertake an exploration for a future arms trade treaty. In 2009, The UN General Assembly adopted Resolution 64/48, which established a treaty negotiating conference, to be held in 2012, to draft the text of a legally binding arms trade treaty. In 2012, the UN treaty negotiating conference failed to reach a consensus on the final treaty text; however, the UN General Assembly passed a resolution authorizing a second treaty negotiating conference to be convened in 2013. In early 2013, a final text was agreed upon for the ATT, and the UN General Assembly adopted the treaty by a vote of 153–3. The ATT entered into force on December 24, 2014, 90 days after the 50th ratification of the treaty (Arms Control Association 2016).

AIMS AND OBLIGATIONS

The ATT strives to establish the highest possible common international standards for the regulation of international trade in conventional arms. The ATT endeavors to prevent and eradicate the illicit trade market of conventional arms. The ATT undertook these aims to assist in the international and regional peace, security, and stability of the states parties as well as to reduce the overall human suffering at the hands of conventional arms. The ATT aims to promote cooperation, transparency, and responsible action by states parties in the international trade of conventional arms, thereby building confidence among states parties (United Nations 2013).

The ATT requires all states parties to adopt basic regulations and approval processes for the movement of conventional arms across international borders. Under the ATT, common international standards must be met before conventional arms exports are approved. Furthermore, the ATT declares that states parties must report annually on their imports and exports of conventional arms. Under the ATT, no state party is authorized to transfer conventional arms when an arms embargo is in place or if the state party has prior knowledge that the authorized conventional arms will be utilized to undermine the peace and security of an area. Additionally, authorization shall be denied if the state party has prior knowledge that the authorized conventional arms will, or could, be used to commit serious violations of international human rights law, acts of terrorism, or transnational organized crime. Finally, the ATT requires that states parties must take appropriate measures, pursuant to their own national laws, to regulate the illegal brokering of conventional arms taking place in their jurisdictions (NTI 2017).

Jessie L. Slepicka

See also: Arms Brokers; Small Arms and Light Weapons, Trafficking in; Small Arms Survey; Weapons Sales

Further Reading

Arms Control Association. 2016. "The Arms Trade Treaty at a Glance." Accessed March 15, 2018. https://www.armscontrol.org/factsheets/arms_trade_treaty.

Nuclear Threat Initiative (NTI). 2017. "Arms Trade Treaty (ATT)." Accessed March 15, 2018. http://www.nti.org/learn/treaties-and-regimes/arms-trade-treaty-att.

Parker, Sarah. 2016. *The Arms Trade Treaty: A Practical Guide to National Implementation.* Geneva, Switzerland: Small Arms Survey.

United Nations. 2013. "Arms Trade Treaty." Accessed March 15, 2018. https://unoda-web.s3.amazonaws.com/wp-content/uploads/2013/06/English7.pdf.

United Nations Educational, Scientific and Cultural Organization (UNESCO). 1998. "The Codes of Conduct to Control Arms Transfers." Accessed March 15, 2018. http://unesdoc.unesco.org/images/0011/001128/112830eo.pdf.

United Nations Office for Disarmament Affairs (UNODA). n.d. "The Arms Trade Treaty." Accessed March 15, 2018. https://www.un.org/disarmament/att.

United Nations Treaty Collection. 2018. "Arms Trade Treaty." Accessed March 15, 2018. https://treaties.un.org/Pages/ViewDetails.aspx?src=IND&mtdsg_no=XXVI-8&chapter=26&lang=en.

Aum Shinrikyō

Aum Shinrikyō, also known as Aum Supreme Truth or simply as Aum, is a religious group founded by Shoko Asahara (real name, Chizuo Matsumoto) in Japan in 1987. This group has been characterized as a doomsday cult and was designated by the U.S. Department of State as a foreign terrorist organization (U.S. Department of State 2011).

The leader of Aum, Chizuo, who was born with impaired vision, attended a boarding school for the blind, where his partial vision gave him an advantage over the other students (Kaplan and Marshall 1996). After graduating high school, Chizuo obtained a license as an acupuncturist and masseur. He married Tomoko Ishii, and with her family's money, he opened the Matsumoto Acupuncture Clinic. In June 1982, he was convicted of manufacturing and selling his own medicine (Kisala 1998). Following this conviction, Chizuo turned to religion.

In 1981, Chizuo began training in *Agonshu*, a Buddhist-based cult that promised psychic powers. After leaving this cult in 1984, Chizuo used Agonshu as a model in creating his own group, which he named Aum no Kai (Aum). Chizuo focused on teaching yoga, but he promised his followers that his instruction would lead to their development of psychic powers. Chizuo was featured in an article in *Twilight Zone* magazine in October 1985, in which a photograph showed him levitating above the ground. This article caused an increase in Aum's membership. As Aum membership grew, Chizuo opened new branches across Japan (Kaplan and Marshall 1996).

In 1987, Chizuo traveled to Tibet to find enlightenment. Despite failing to find an instructor in this quest, Chizuo claimed to have achieved enlightenment through self-study. Upon his return to Japan, Chizuo changed his name to Shoko Asahara. The newly enlightened Asahara claimed to have had a vision in which Japan went to war with the United States again. In his vision, this war would lead to Armageddon, and all would perish, except Aum members (Kaplan and Marshall 1996).

Aum recruited young intellectuals in their twenties and thirties, including members with science and engineering degrees. The Aum scientists and engineers would be important in the development of the Aum weapons program. The cult grew beyond the shores of Japan. It claimed an international membership as high as 65,000, of which most (30,000–50,000) were in Russia. As membership grew, so did Aum's wealth. Aum gained assets estimated at over $1 billion. This wealth would fund Aum's weapons program (Federation of American Scientists 1995).

Starting in 1989, the cult became dangerous. After joining Aum, new members were discouraged from staying in contact with their family members. This caused some families to make complaints to Japanese authorities concerning Aum's recruitment methods. The Aum Shinrikyō Victims Society was formed, and Yokohama lawyer Tsutsumi Sakamoto was retained to represent them. In November 1989, Aum members kidnapped and murdered Sakamoto and his family (Danzig et al. 2012).

In February 1990, 25 Aum members, including Asahara, unsuccessfully ran as candidates for the Japanese Diet. Following this, Asahara told his followers that the "only measure to save the world now is violence" (Hongo 2011). Aum increased the Armageddon rhetoric.

Aum started developing chemical and biological weapon programs. These weapons may have been to assist Aum in starting Armageddon or for use as weapons against Japanese government intervention. However, attempts at developing and deploying lethal forms of botulinum and anthrax proved too difficult for Aum scientists (Danzig et al. 2012).

Aum did succeed in producing sarin, an odorless, colorless lethal gas. Anticipating a loss in a civil trial against Aum in Matsumoto, Japan, Aum attempted to use sarin to assassinate the judges in the civil case in Matsumoto. On June 27, 1994, Aum deployed sarin from a vehicle parked near the homes of the judges, but a wind shift caused the sarin gas to blow into a nearby apartment complex. The sarin killed 8 and injured an additional 200 people (Danzig et al. 2012).

When Aum learned of Japanese police plans to raid their facilities, Asahara ordered members to use sarin against the Metropolitan Police. On March 20, 1995, five Aum members deployed sarin gas in the Tokyo subway, near the Metropolitan Police Headquarters. This attack resulted in 11 deaths and 3,796 injuries (Danzig et al. 2012).

After subsequent police investigation, on May 16, 1995, Asahara and 483 other Aum members were arrested, and 189 were indicted and tried. All but 1 of the 189 Aum members were convicted, and 13, to include Asahara, were sentenced to death by hanging. Asahara remains in prison.

Kenneth Gray

See also: Terrorism, Domestic; Tokyo Subway Sarin Attack (1994)

Further Reading

Danzig, Richard, Marc Sageman, Terrance Leighton, Lloyd Hough, Hidemi Yuki, Rui Kotani, and Zachary M. Hosford. 2012. *Aum Shinrikyo: Insights into How Terrorists Develop Biological and Chemical Weapons*. 2nd ed. Washington, D.C.: Center for a New American Security. Accessed January 21, 2019. https://www.cnas.org/publications/reports/aum-shinrikyo-second-edition-english.

Federation of American Scientists. 1995. "Global Proliferation of Weapons of Mass Destruction: A Case Study on the Aum Shinrikyo." Accessed January 13, 2019. https://fas.org/irp/congress/1995_rpt/aum/part04.htm.

Hongo, Jun. 2011. "Last Trial Brings Dark Aum Era to End." *Japan Times*, November 22. Accessed January 13, 2019. https://www.japantimes.co.jp/news/2011/11/22/reference/last-trial-brings-dark-aum-era-to-end/#.Wk-sVxM-dTY.

Kaplan, David E., and Andrew Marshall. 1996. *The Cult at the End of the World: The Terrifying Story of the Aum Doomsday Cult, from the Subways of Tokyo to the Nuclear Arsenals of Russia*. New York: Crown Publishers.

Kisala, Robert. 1998. "The AUM Spiritual Truth Church in Japan." In *Wolves within the Fold: Religious Leadership and Abuses of Power*, edited by Anson D. Shupe, 33–48. New Brunswick, NJ: Rutgers University Press.

Kristof, Nicholas D. 1995. "Japanese Arrest Cult Leader Blamed in Poison Gas Attack." *New York Times*, May 16. Accessed January 13, 2019. http://www.nytimes.com/1995/05/16/world/japanese-arrest-cult-leader-blamed-in-poison-gas-attacks.html.

U.S. Department of State. 2011. "Country Reports of Terrorism 2010." Office of Coordinator for Counterterrorism. Accessed January 21, 2019. https://www.state.gov/documents/organization/170479.pdf.

Australian Institute of Criminology

The Australian Institute of Criminology (AIC) is Australia's national research and knowledge center on crime and justice. It conducts and publishes research, including crime data and trend information, that informs crime and justice policy and practice in Australia. It is based in Canberra, Australia's capital city and home of the federal parliament.

HISTORY

Sir John Barry, a justice of the Supreme Court of the State of Victoria and a prominent supporter of prison and criminal justice reform, recommended that the Australian government establish an Australian Institute of Criminal and Penal Science, to be funded and maintained by the government. The legislation passed in 1971 and established the AIC to meet Barry's vision. After a period of intense lobbying and negotiation with the Australian states and territories, the federal government eventually heeded the concerns of government bureaucrats, academics, and criminal justice policy makers regarding the lack of national crime statistics and research, and it formed the institute (Smith 2017).

The AIC was created as an independent statutory research authority, with a small staff of academic researchers, a library—that became the J.V. Barry Memorial Library, one of the largest and most respected criminology libraries in the region—and a research fund that has provided grants for the conduct of criminological research in Australia.

In addition to addressing a wide variety of criminal justice topics, principally of relevance to federal government interests, the AIC has undertaken a number of studies in which statistics are regularly collected on criminal justice issues of national importance. These have included drug use among police detainees, homicides in Australia, armed robbery, deaths in custodial settings, firearms theft, young people in detention, fraud against Commonwealth entities, identity crime and misuse, consumer fraud, and anti–money laundering. Each of these monitoring programs aim to provide current statistics on the topic in question that include data on the types of crimes and criminals involved, trends over time, and how government agencies respond to emerging issues.

AIC EFFORTS ON GLOBAL CRIME

Although focusing principally on crime and criminal justice issues relevant to Australia, the AIC has had close ties with other international research bodies and forms one of the United Nations Crime Prevention and Criminal Justice

Programme Network of Institutes (the PNI), created by the Secretariat of the United Nations in the 1960s (UNODC 2018). The United Nations established this network in cooperation with the member states in recognition of the importance of regional and interregional cooperation in the field of criminal justice policy and crime prevention.

The AIC has always maintained an active interest in international criminology by conducting research into global crime problems such as cybercrime, human trafficking, intellectual property infringement, cross border fraud, and transnational organized crime. The AIC continues to share its research with other PNI members at meetings of the United Nations Congress on Crime Prevention and Criminal Justice and at annual meetings of the United Nations Commission on Crime Prevention and Criminal Justice, and it has contributed data to reports on transnational organized crime and most recently cybercrime, including the organization of the 2018 Workshop on Criminal Justice responses to prevent and counter cybercrime in all its forms, including through the strengthening of cooperation at the national and international levels.

The AIC's research staff has also participated in a wide variety of international conferences and research activities, including studies on anti–money laundering, online child exploitation, human trafficking, and the regulation of illicit drugs. The AIC has had a lengthy involvement in training and policy formation among criminal justice agencies, particularly in the Asia-Pacific region. Foremost among these is the Asian and Pacific Conference of Correctional Administrators that was established in 1980 through the efforts of a number of individuals, including Bill Clifford, who was the first permanent director of the AIC, having previously been a senior adviser to the Asia and Far East Institute for the Prevention of Crime and the Treatment of Offenders (UNAFEI) in Tokyo.

More recently, the AIC has undertaken and presented research for the Confederation of Asian and Pacific Accountants, the Asia/Pacific Group on Money Laundering, the International Association of Financial Crimes Investigators and the Association of Certified Fraud Examiners, the International Society for the Reform of Criminal Law, and the Asia-Pacific Association of Technology and Society. The institute's research is regularly sought-after by scholars and policy makers globally, with one of the institute's publications, *Cyber Criminals on Trial*, being awarded the American Society of Criminology's, Division of International Criminology, Distinguished Book Award in 2005 (Smith, Grabosky, and Urbas 2004).

Russell G. Smith

See also: HEUNI; National Institute of Justice; Raoul Wallenberg Institute of Humans Rights and Humanitarian Law; UN Office on Drugs and Crime; UN Program Network of Institutes

Further Reading

Finnane, Mark. 2006. "The ABC of Criminology: Anita Muhl, J. V. Barry, Norval Morris and the Making of a Discipline in Australia." *British Journal of Criminology* 46: 399–422.

Mayhew, Patricia. 2016. "In Defence of Administrative Criminology." *Crime Science* 5 (7): 1–10.

Smith, Russell G. 2017. "Public Sector Criminological Research." In *The Palgrave Handbook of Australian and New Zealand Criminology, Crime and Justice*, edited by Antje Deckert and Rick Sarre, 33–49. London: Palgrave Macmillan.

Smith, Russell G., Peter N. Grabosky, and Gregor F. Urbas. 2004. *Cyber Criminals on Trial.* Cambridge: Cambridge University Press.

United Nations Office on Drugs and Crime (UNODC). 2018. "Institutes of the UN Crime Prevention and Criminal Justice Programme Network (PNI)." Accessed April 3, 2018. https://www.unodc.org/unodc/en/commissions/CCPCJ/PNI/institutes.html.

B

Barcelona and Cambrils Terrorist Attacks (2017)

On the afternoon of August 17, 2017, a van driven at a high rate of speed plowed into throngs of pedestrians on Barcelona's Las Ramblas Boulevard, killing 14 people and injuring more than 100 others. On August 21, Spanish police apprehended and killed the assailant, a Moroccan-born Spanish national, in Subirats, Spain. Identified as Younes Abouyaaqoub, he was part of a larger jihadist group that had been operating out of a house in Alcanar, Spain. After Abouyaaqoub fled the scene in Barcelona, he hijacked a car, killed the driver, and drove out of the city. This incident brought the death toll in Barcelona to 15.

Just eight hours after the Barcelona attack, on August 18, five assailants affiliated with the same group—driving a black Audi—struck and killed a pedestrian in Cambrils, a seaside resort about 70 miles southwest of Barcelona. Police promptly killed the perpetrators. Although a news agency linked with the Islamic State of Iraq and Syria (ISIS) claimed that the Barcelona and Cambrils attacks had been carried out in its name, it is not clear whether the terrorist group actually planned or ordered the attacks.

On August 16, the day prior to the Barcelona attack, a house in Alcanar, situated about two hours south of Barcelona, had exploded. Initially, police thought it was a natural gas explosion. Upon further inspection, however, police found 120 gas canisters and bomb-making material. As it turned out, the house was the headquarters of the jihadist cell responsible for the car attacks in Barcelona and Cambrils. Two died in the explosion, including Imam Abdelbaki Es Satty, a Moroccan who had been previously convicted in Spain for drug trafficking. Spanish officials believe that the jihadists were planning much larger attacks, likely including bombings. Police took a survivor of the house explosion into custody, and he identified the imam as the leader of the terrorist cell.

Police have since made numerous arrests and have at least four individuals in custody. All of them have identified Es Satty as the ringleader of the Alcanar-based jihadist group. Most of the suspected terrorists killed or arrested were of Moroccan descent. Spain and Morocco have had a complicated and stormy relationship over the last century or so. Spain controlled large portions of the country beginning in the late 19th century and fought a vicious conflict with indigenous Berber tribes during the Rif War of the 1920s. Morocco did not completely throw off colonial rule until 1957.

By early 2018, there was still no concrete evidence showing that members of the jihadist cell were being coached from afar by Islamic State operatives, although authorities remain suspicious of trips cell members made to locations in France and Morocco, where they may have contacted ISIS operatives.

Paul G. Pierpaoli Jr.

See also: Islamic State of Iraq and Syria (ISIS); Terrorism, International

Further Reading

"Barcelona and Cambrils Attacks: What We Know So Far." *BBC News*, August 27, 2017. Accessed January 13, 2019. http://www.bbc.com/news/world-europe-40964242.

Burgen, Stephen. 2017. "Spanish Attacks Death Toll Rises to 16 after Woman Dies in Hospital." *The Guardian*, August 27. Accessed January 13, 2019. https://www.theguardian.com/world/2017/aug/27/death-toll-spain-terror-attacks-rises-barcelona.

Callimachi, Rukmini. 2018. "Cell behind Barcelona Attack May Have Had Sights on Eiffel Tower." *New York Times*, January 24. Accessed January 18, 2019. https://www.nytimes.com/2018/01/24/world/europe/isis-barcelona-attack.html.

Basel Convention on the Control of Transboundary Movements of Hazardous Wastes and Their Disposal

The Basel Convention on the Control of Transboundary Movements of Hazardous Wastes and Their Disposal, usually referred to simply as the Basel Convention, is the major international treaty that regulates the transboundary movements of hazardous waste. Hazardous waste is a waste with properties that make it dangerous or capable of having a harmful effect on human health or the environment. The convention was adopted on March 22, 1989, and entered into force on May 5, 1992. As of early 2018, there are 186 parties to the convention, including 185 states and the European Union. The United States is not currently a party, having signed the convention but not ratified it (EPA 2018). The Basel Convention is one of the few multilateral environmental agreements defining an illegal activity under the convention as a crime.

HISTORY

Between the 1970s and the 1980s, increased environmental awareness led to more stringent environmental regulations in the industrialized world, which in turn resulted in an escalation of disposal costs for hazardous waste. At the same time, globalization made transboundary shipments of waste more accessible, causing some operators to seek cheap waste disposal options in Eastern Europe and the developing world, where environmental regulations and enforcement mechanisms were lacking. During the 1980s, a public outcry followed the discovery, in Africa and other developing countries, of deposits of toxic wastes imported from abroad. In response to these events, the Governing Council of the United Nations Environment Programme (UNEP) mandated the drafting of a global convention to regulate transboundary waste shipments, which ultimately resulted in the adoption of the Basel Convention in 1989.

AIMS AND PROVISIONS

The Basel Convention aims to protect human health and the environment against the adverse effects of hazardous waste. To achieve this goal, the provisions of the convention follow three main directions. The first aim is to minimize hazardous waste generation and promote sound recycling methods. For this purpose, states are required to observe the fundamental principles of environmentally sound waste management. Second, the convention sets restrictions to the transboundary movements of waste, which are only allowed when in accordance with the principles of environmentally safe waste management. As a consequence, hazardous waste may not be exported to Antarctica, to a state not party to the Basel Convention, or to a party having banned the import of hazardous waste. Third, a regulatory system applies to cases where transboundary movements are permissible. The regulatory system is based on the concept of prior informed consent: an export of hazardous waste may take place only if the authorities of all involved states have given their written consent to the shipment.

Cecilia Meneghini

See also: Convention on the Prevention of Marine Pollution by Dumping Wastes and Other Matter; Waste Crime

Further Reading

European Commission. 2018. "Waste Shipments." Accessed February 16, 2018. http://ec.europa.eu/environment/waste/shipments/index.htm.

United Nations Environment Programme (UNEP). 1989. *Basel Convention on the Control of Transboundary Movements of Hazardous Wastes and Their Disposal.* January 21, 2019. http://www.basel.int/Portals/4/Basel%20Convention/docs/text/BaselConventionText-e.pdf.

United Nations Environment Programme (UNEP). 2018. "Basel Convention Overview." Accessed February 16, 2018. http://www.basel.int/TheConvention/Overview/tabid/1271/Default.aspx.

U.S. Environmental Protection Agency (EPA). 2018. "International Agreements on Transboundary Shipments of Hazardous Waste." Accessed February 16, 2018. https://www.epa.gov/hwgenerators/international-agreements-transboundary-shipments-hazardous-waste.

Bilateral Human Trafficking Enforcement Initiative

Under the U.S.-Mexico Bilateral Human Trafficking Enforcement Initiative, law enforcement authorities from the United States and Mexico conduct coordinated and bilateral law enforcement actions to dismantle human trafficking networks operating across their shared border. Mexico is the country of origin of the largest number of foreign-born human trafficking victims identified in the United States.

The initiative was launched by the U.S. Departments of Justice (DOJ) and Homeland Security (DHS) in 2009 to enhance the collaboration between both states' counterparts to more effectively combat transborder trafficking threats.

Through the bilateral initiative, which is under the leadership of the Civil Rights Division's Human Trafficking Prosecution Unit, U.S. and Mexican authorities exchange leads and intelligence to strengthen investigations and prosecutions and dismantle trafficking networks through high-impact prosecutions in both the United States and Mexico.

Furthermore, it also focuses on restoring victims and on recovering victims' children. The counterparts engage in extensive exchanges of expertise and case-based mentoring to advance best practices in victim-centered enforcement strategies. (DOJ n.d.).

In addition, the DOJ acknowledged the role played by victim service providers and advocates from nongovernmental organizations (NGOs) for their dedicated efforts to restore and improve the lives of survivors of trafficking and their families.

THE RESULTS

According to the DOJ's Office of Public Affairs, the U.S. Immigration and Customs Enforcement (ICE), and the U.S. District Court for the Southern District of New York, the U.S.-Mexico Bilateral Human Trafficking Enforcement Initiative has achieved significant results:

- U.S. federal prosecutions and indictments of over 170 defendants in multiple cases in Georgia, New York, Florida, and Texas;
- Mexican state and federal prosecution of over 30 associated defendants;
- Extradition of 8 defendants from Mexico to the United States to face charges;
- Rescue and assistance of over 200 victims, including 39 minors, and help in their recovery from the trafficking networks' control; and
- Reunion of 19 victims' children with their mothers and secured restitution orders of over $4 million on behalf of trafficking victims.

In November 2016, law enforcement authorities from the United States and Mexico also announced a bilateral operation that led to the arrest of a group of individuals who are allegedly part of an international criminal organization accused of smuggling women from Mexico into the United States for sex trafficking purposes.

Significant recent developments have included coordinated, bilateral enforcement actions to simultaneously apprehend charged coconspirators on both sides of the border in cases developed through this bilateral collaboration.

Ana Carolina Paci and Dafne Calderón Burgoa

See also: Human Trafficking; Human Trafficking and Sporting Events; Human Trafficking and Street Gangs; "Loverboy" Recruitment Approach to Human Trafficking

Further Reading

U.S. Department of Justice (DOJ). 2015. "Attorney General Loretta E. Lynch Announces Indictment of Eight Defendants in United States and Mexico on Sex Trafficking and Related Charges." Last modified November 20, 2015. Accessed January 18, 2019. https://www.justice.gov/opa/pr/attorney-general-loretta-e-lynch-announces-indictment-eight-defendants-united-states-and.

U.S. Department of Justice (DOJ). n.d. "Special Initiatives." Accessed January 21, 2018. https://www.justice.gov/humantrafficking/special-initiatives#bilateral.

U.S. Immigration and Customs Enforcement (ICE). 2016. "ICE HSI Investigation Leads to Arrest of 6 in US, Mexico in International Sex Trafficking Scheme." Last modified July 11, 2016. Accessed January 13, 2019. https://www.ice.gov/news/releases/ice-hsi-investigation-leads-arrest-6-us-mexico-international-sex-trafficking-scheme.

Bin Laden, Osama (1957/8–2011)

Osama bin Laden was an Islamic extremist who sought to bring the United States into a war and unite Muslims to create a single and "pure" Islamic state. Bin Laden's leadership of the terrorist group Al Qaeda and the terrorism activity claimed by them earned bin Laden the global status of the "most wanted" terrorist in the world. Terrorism, especially international terrorism, has been a defining factor in the present era of civilization, leading some people to call the most recent decades "the age of terror." This title constitutes both the threat and reality of international terrorism throughout the world. Terrorism consequently caused a shift in worldviews, international policy, and domestic organizations. Bin Laden was a key figure in this shift until his death in 2011.

BACKGROUND

Osama bin Laden was born Osama bin Mohammed bin Awad bin Laden in the year 1957 or 1958, in Riyadh, Saudi Arabia. He was born into an affluent household, allowing him to attend primary school, secondary school, and to go to a university. During his time in college in the late 1970s, he became a follower of Abdullah Azzam (1941–1989), a radical pan-Islamist scholar. Azzam believed that jihad, or a holy war, would allow all Muslims to create a single Islamic state. In addition, bin Laden followed the Muslim Brotherhood, which is a collection of Muslim scholars located in Jeddah and Mecca. These ideologies helped bin Laden shape his personal view that ultimately became his life's mission and the basis for Al Qaeda.

In 1979, bin Laden joined the Afghan resistance as a result of the Soviet Union invasion of Afghanistan, seeing it as his duty as a Muslim. In 1984, bin Laden began his leadership development by establishing a guest house/camp in Peshawar, allowing Arab mujahideen a place to go before training or fighting. Through the U.S. Central Intelligence Agency (CIA) program Operation Cyclone, the mujahideen were trained and eventually called "Freedom Fighters." Bin Laden started his own command and established six of his own camps inside Afghanistan between 1986 and 1988. Bin Laden saw the 1989 defeat of the Soviet Union and its retreat from Afghanistan as a turning point and an assertion of Muslim power and an opportunity to create an Islamic powerhouse via jihad.

GLOBAL TERRORISM: AL QAEDA

Osama bin Laden's fighting experience against the Soviet Union helped him establish the foundations for Al Qaeda, or "the base," in 1988. The creation and terrorist attacks of Al Qaeda led to bin Laden's notoriety. Over the development of the organization, Al Qaeda's focus shifted from military campaigns to committing symbolic acts of terrorism on a global scale. Inspired by bin Laden's early influences, Al Qaeda embodied the jihadist cause with the mission to correct wrongdoings according to Islamic law. Al Qaeda's terrorist acts became globally recognized by attacks in countries that included Somalia, Saudi Arabia, the United States, East Africa, Yemen, Dhahran, Kenya, and Tanzania, among others.

Bin Laden was believed to be behind the World Trade Center bombings in 1993 in New York City, and he was named the prime suspect in the terror attacks of September 11, 2001, in New York and Washington, D.C. Soon after the 9/11 attacks, Afghanistan's ruling Taliban government was believed to be harboring bin Laden. Many countries joined the United States in demanding that he be handed over. Operation Enduring Freedom was launched against the Taliban in October 2001, and U.S.-led forces quickly toppled the regime. Meanwhile, the Federal Bureau of Investigation (FBI) identified the 19 alleged hijackers, all Muslims from Middle Eastern countries. Bin Laden continued to be the prime suspect in the organization of the attacks.

Osama bin Laden transformed Al Qaeda into a multinational enterprise that took advantage of the development of technology and communication methods. Al Qaeda became a business that moved and obtained supplies, offered training camps, possessed a media base, and established various councils. This power, in conjunction with the acts of terrorism, made bin Laden a global enemy and ultimately led to the Saudi Arabian government revoking his citizenship, Sudan expelling him, and the United States having a federal grand jury indict him. These actions forced Osama bin Laden to seek refuge with the Taliban, the power occupant in Afghanistan. This mutually beneficial relationship allowed the Taliban to rise in power and provided bin Laden refuge and a base for jihad.

DEATH

Bin Laden constantly remained hidden, such as during his refuge with the Taliban, due to being a high-profile and highly sought-after criminal by multiple governments. In August 2010, this manhunt came to an end when the CIA tracked bin Laden to a compound in Abbottabad, Pakistan. On May 2, 2011 (May 1 in the United States), a team of U.S. Navy SEALs stormed the compound and killed bin Laden. The U.S. government buried bin Laden's body at sea.

GLOBAL IMPACT

Osama bin Laden's influence forever changed the face of society by instilling fear and immense terrorism on an international scale. Bin Laden led Al Qaeda for over two decades and managed to change multiple aspects of society. This is especially the case with airway travel as a result of the terrorist acts of September 11, 2001, in the United States. Though major indicators of his impact are notably seen, the true scope of his influence and residual power is unknown. The reach of his power spans the globe, but how many people and how many countries are involved will never be known. However, even though bin Laden terrorized people on a global scale, he also united countries all over the world by strengthening international counterterrorism efforts. He created a unified mission to end such acts of terrorism, solidifying the bonds between multiple nations.

Christina Lynn Richardson

See also: Al Qaeda; September 11 Terrorist Attacks (2001); Terrorism, International

Further Reading

Public Broadcasting Service. n.d. "Who Is Bin Laden?" Accessed January 13, 2019. https://www.pbs.org/wgbh/pages/frontline/shows/binladen/who/bio.html.

Zernike, Kate, and Michael T. Kaufman. 2011. "The Most Wanted Face of Terrorism." *New York Times*, May 2. Accessed January 13, 2019. https://www.nytimes.com/2011/05/02/world/02osama-bin-laden-obituary.html?mtrref=www.google.com.

Biometric Identification

Biometric identification is the practice of using biological information—the physical traits that are unique to an individual—as a method of verification. Physical characteristics, such as fingerprints, are very difficult to replicate, which contrasts with traditional forms of identification (e.g., identification cards, personal identification numbers, passwords) that are much easier to obtain (De Chant 2013). Therefore, a shift toward biometric identification benefits the security of individuals and societies alike.

Simple biometric identification is not new. Sir William Herschel used fingerprinting in the late Victorian era (19th century) as a way of identifying individuals during his governmental work in India. Subsequently, Sir Francis Galton, a relative of evolutionist Charles Darwin, created a classification method for fingerprints that was used to aid criminal analyses. Galton's method continues to be employed in criminal justice systems around the world. Technological advancements have enhanced the use of biometric identification in the last few decades, with law enforcement being the primary beneficiary (De Chant 2013).

TYPES

Biometric identification has been developed to focus on several different parts of the human body. Fingerprinting has been around since the late 19th century and is the most common type of biometric identification. The heavy reliance on fingerprinting by law enforcement has resulted in attempts to copy fingerprints, mar fingertips, or sever fingers. One recent alternative to fingerprinting uses veins; however, vein confirmation requires a living subject to work, while fingerprinting does not. The human eye has also been used as a means of identification. Both irises and retinas can be scanned as means for determining identity and permitting access. Another interesting approach tracks eye movements as an identification method (Moren 2014).

Larger body parts are possible biometric identification candidates, too. The human nose and human odors are emerging types of biometric identification. There are six common types of noses, but the human nose is considered unique, difficult to alter without surgery, and relatively easy to confirm (Moren 2014). Similarly, an individual's body aroma can be verified through sniff tests of an artificial nose. The human ear, like the nose, is a biometric that can be used to differentiate between two individuals. The human ear is so distinguishable that both ears on the same person are different. The human heart allows a person's identity to be verified through electronic monitoring of the heart's pulse (Moren 2014). Even "posterior analysis" allows researchers to identify the way the body makes contact with a seat as unique (Moren 2014). Finally, the way an individual walks is another unique way of distinguishing individuals from one another (De Chant 2013).

PRACTICAL USE

While there have been significant research contributions from academia, biometric identification has been heavily employed in the following sectors: business, law enforcement, and the military. The business uses for biometric identification have primarily centered on mobile phones and aviation security. In recent years, criminals have stolen many mobile phones and obtained linked authentication and payment data (Gofman and Mitra 2016). Many mobile phone developers have responded by developing ways to incorporate biometric identification. Samsung has incorporated face and voice recognition measures in its Galaxy S5 model as a way of improving authentication efficiency (Gofman and Mitra 2016). With the creation of new technology for iPhone X, Apple has employed facial recognition for the purposes of secure authorization and e-commerce (Metz 2017). The technology, known as Face ID, is so accurate that Apple boasts there is merely a one in a million chance that someone could successfully pose as another person (Metz 2017). The methodology behind the technology is that infrared sensors are used to make a three-dimensional mapping of the human face. Then, as an infrared light shines across the face, there is a camera that snaps an image. This process enables the phone to accurately authenticate whether the individual matches the identity of the owner of the phone (Metz 2017).

Aviation security has also benefited from the development of biometric identification. Several airports and airline companies around the world have incorporated facial and fingerprint verification technologies to authenticate passenger identification (Canaday 2017). For example, Spain has used the technology to improve verification efficiency for passport holders (Canaday 2017). For international flights, JetBlue Airways has tested facial recognition technology using images from border control databases (Canaday 2017). Delta Air Lines has incorporated a similar feature at select domestic airports. Moreover, Delta has created a frequent-flyer program where passengers use fingerprinting to authorize use of the company lounge at Ronald Reagan Washington National Airport (Canaday 2017).

The use of biometric identification by law enforcement and the military has greatly expanded since the September 11, 2001, terror attacks. Since 2001, the U.S. Departments of Homeland Security and Defense have spent more than a combined $3.6 billion on researching, developing, and acquiring biometric identification technologies (De Chant 2013). The Department of Homeland Security (DHS) has developed an intricate system of facial and fingerprint recognition for passport holders as they leave and reenter the United States (De Chant 2013). The Federal Bureau of Investigation (FBI) has enlarged its fingerprint database and has planned the addition of iris, palm, and facial scans to its investigative tools (De Chant 2013). The military has used biometrics frequently in military operations around the world. Specifically, the military has attempted to distinguish enemy combatants from civilians using fingerprinting, iris scans, and facial imagery in the Afghani and Iraqi operations (De Chant 2013).

LEGAL AND ETHICAL CONSIDERATIONS

Legally, there are several advantages of using biometric identification. For example, using biometric identification allows employers to adhere to immigration law and hire only those with valid credentials (Weinberg 2016). Biometrics is also another way of verifying that voter registration lists are accurate. Finally, it is a way of ensuring that government payments such as pensions and welfare are not abused through fraud.

However, there are also ethical issues, many involving privacy concerns, that have become the primary disadvantages in incorporating biometric identification. Private citizens are concerned about the implications of law enforcement stockpiling biometric information and whether that will put citizens at risk for abuse, data breaches, or identity theft (Weinberg 2016). Another concern is that using biometrics will lead to increased surveillance of daily activities as the use of biometrics spreads (Weinberg 2016).

FUTURE USE

While there are many legal and ethical considerations facing biometric identification, the future appears very bright. There is an industrial push for researchers to develop new methods of biometric identification. The automobile industry keenly awaits researchers developing car seats able to distinguish individuals (Moren 2014). The use of facial, fingerprint, and iris scanning for mobile phones may eventually become a universal feature (Metz 2017). The U.S. military is interested in developing odor biometrics that would help sniff out potential danger (Moren 2014). Most technology is still partially operated by human beings that manage the identification process. However, humans are slowly being replaced by cameras and computers, which may eventually supplant all human involvement in biometric identification (De Chant 2013).

Tamba Mondeh

See also: September 11 Terrorist Attacks (2001); Terrorism, Intelligence Gathering

Further Reading

Canaday, Henry. 2017. "Better Biometrics." *Air Transport World* 54 (7): 36. *MasterFILE Premier*, EBSCO*host*.

De Chant, Tim. 2013. "The Boring and Exciting World of Biometrics." *PBS*. Accessed December 06, 2017. http://www.pbs.org/wgbh/nova/next/tech/biometrics-and-the-future-of-identification.

Gofman, Mikhail I., and Sinjini Mitra. 2016. "Multimodal Biometrics for Enhanced Mobile Device Security." *Communications of the ACM* 59 (4) (April): 58–65. *Business Source Complete*, EBSCO*host*.

Metz, Rachel. 2017. "Face ID on the iPhone X Could Mean More Biometrics on Lots of Phones Soon." *MIT Technology Review*. Accessed December 13, 2017. https://www.technologyreview.com/s/608879/facial-recognition-is-only-the-beginning-heres-what-to-expect-next-in-biometrics-on-your.

Moren, Dan. 2014. "7 Surprising Biometric Identification Methods." *Popular Science*. Accessed December 6, 2017. https://www.popsci.com/seven-surprising-biometric-identification-methods#page-4.

Weinberg, Jonathan T. 2016. "Biometric Identity." *Communications of the ACM* 59 (1) (January): 30–32. *Business Source Complete*, EBSCO*host*.

Blanco, Griselda (1943–2012)

Griselda Blanco Restrepo was a high-profile drug trafficker of the Medellín Cartel and a notorious transnational crime figure. She is also known as *La Madrina*, Cocaine Godmother, Queen of Narco-Trafficking, *La Viuda Negra* ("the Black Widow"), and *La Dama de la Mafia*.

Blanco was born on February 15, 1943, to Ana Lucia Restrepo and Fernando Blanco in Cartagena, Colombia. Having been raised by an abusive mother, Blanco turned to a life of crime at an early age. She lived a very flamboyant and luxurious lifestyle of drug trafficking, drug use, and hedonistic parties. She was married three times, had three sons, and involved both her husbands and sons in the drug trade. To further establish her cocaine business, Blanco and her second husband, Alberto Bravo, immigrated to the United States in the 1970s (Siegel 2014).

DRUG BUSINESS

In 1971, along with Bravo, Blanco became the first Colombian drug lord to export the Medellín Cartel's product to the United States. During the cocaine boom in the United States from the mid-1970s to the 1980s, Blanco was one of the key managers of the routes used by the cartel to smuggle cocaine into Miami. She notoriously pioneered the use of young women as "drug mules" and also came up with the idea of creating customized underwear with hidden pockets and the use of fake breasts to smuggle cocaine (Axworthy 2017).

Blanco established a drug distribution network across the United States and made shipments of more than 1,500 kg of cocaine. Her distribution network brought in approximately $80,000,000 per month. She was a ruthless leader in the drug trade and the mastermind and instigator of several murders and drive-by shootings (Arsovska and Allum 2014). According to law enforcement, Blanco and her enforcers were responsible for the majority of homicides in South Florida from 1979 to 1982 (Ramsey 2012).

INVESTIGATION, CAPTURE, AND CONVICTION

In 1975, law enforcement linked Blanco to drug trafficking due to a joint New York Police Department and Drug Enforcement Administration (DEA) investigation called Operation Banshee, but she escaped any charges by fleeing to Colombia. Blanco later returned to Miami via Mexico using a Venezuelan passport provided by the full-time document forger on her payroll. In February 1985, she was finally captured and arrested on drug charges by DEA agents in California (Axworthy 2017).

Blanco's trial began in New York in June 1985, and it ended with a conviction on one count of conspiracy to manufacture, import into the United States, and distribute cocaine. Despite being accused of several Florida slayings, she escaped murder charges and was sentenced to 15 years in prison. In 1994, Blanco was transported back to Miami on three murder charges; however, the case was thrown out. The star witness in the case, a former hit man for Blanco named Jorge "Rivi" Ayala, became romantically involved with a secretary in the Florida State Attorney's Office, causing prosecutors to doubt the credibility of Ayala's testimony. Some speculated that Ayala botched the case on purpose, fearing retaliation from Blanco's cartel if he testified.

Blanco ended up pleading guilty to the three murder charges, and following a deal with prosecutors, she received a 10-year sentence. In June 2004, she was released from prison and deported back to Colombia. Once she returned to Colombia, Blanco lived a quiet life in poor health. On September 3, 2012, Blanco was shot by a motorcyclist in her hometown of Medellín in a manner similar to the execution-style shooting she had invented (Smith 2013).

BLANCO'S IMPACT

Griselda Blanco was one of the most prominent women involved with transnational organized crime and the Colombian drug trade. She was also the initiation godmother to several drug traffickers, most notably Pablo Escobar. She encouraged him to become a drug trafficker and helped him pursue independence in his criminal career. She was the one to receive Escobar's first drug cargo to the United States (Redacción 2012).

In the aftermath of Blanco's arrest, the seemingly untouchable Pablo Escobar was gunned down, and his cocaine trafficking empire splintered. This period also saw a U.S. law enforcement crackdown on smuggling routes through the Caribbean, ending Colombia's status as the primary transit point for cocaine headed north. This forced traffickers to turn to overland routes through Mexico and Central America, which contributed to the rise of powerful Mexican groups like the Beltran Leyva Organization and the Sinaloa Cartel (Ramsey 2012).

Griselda Blanco became one of the world's wealthiest and most successful drug traffickers. Her extraordinary and flamboyant lifestyle has inspired fashion, songs, books, movies, music videos, and documentaries (Brown 2017). The documentary *Cocaine Cowboys II: Hustlin' with the Godmother* focuses solely on the drug trafficker; in 2017 the song "Portland" by Drake mentions Blanco, and in 2018, the Lifetime TV network announced the release of the biographical movie *Cocaine Godmother* (Iannelli 2018). Her son, Michael Corleone Blanco, established a retail brand in her honor named "Puro Blanco" that sells Blanco-related merchandise (Redacción Actualidad 2018).

Aida Portillo and Fay V. Williams

See also: Escobar, Pablo; Medellín Cartel; Women and Transnational Crime

Further Reading

Arsovska, Jana, and Felia Allum. 2014. "Introduction: Women and Transnational Organized Crime." *Trends in Organized Crime* 17 (1): 1–15.

Axworthy, Jon. 2017. "The Godmother of Cocaine with Two A-List adaptations in the Pipeline, We Reveal the True Story of Griselda Blanco—the Woman Who Became Colombia's Cartel Queen." *Sun UK*, November 19. Accessed January 13, 2019. https://www.thesun.co.uk/fabulous/4908198/griselda-blanco-colombias-cartel-queen-godmother-of-cocaine.

Brown, Scott. 2017. "Hollywood North: Catherine Zeta-Jones Filming 'Cocaine Godmother' in Vancouver." *Vancouver Sun*, June 6. Accessed January 13, 2019. http://vancouversun.com/entertainment/movies/hollywood-north-catherine-zeta-jones-filming-cocaine-godmother-in-vancouver.

Iannelli, Jerry. 2018. "Who Was Griselda Blanco, the Miami Drug Queen Profiled in Lifetime's *Cocaine Godmother?*" *Miami New Times*, January 20. Accessed January 13, 2019. http://www.miaminewtimes.com/news/the-true-story-behind-cocaine-godmother-griselda-blanco-10010116.

Ramsey, Geoffrey. 2012. "The Rise and Fall of Colombia's 'Cocaine Queen.'" *InSight Crime*, September 4. Accessed January 13, 2019. https://www.insightcrime.org/news/analysis/colombias-cocaine-queen-griselda-blanco.

Siegel, Dina. 2014. "Women in Transnational Organized Crime." *Trends in Organized Crime* 17 (1-2): 52–65.

Smith, Jeannie Erin. 2013. *Cocaine Cowgirl: The Outrageous Life and Mysterious Death of Griselda Blanco, the Godmother of Medellín.* San Francisco: Byliner.

Bonded Labor

Bonded labor, also known as debt bondage, is today's most common form of contemporary slavery worldwide. Typically, it involves a person pledging to repay a loan when there is no hope of repaying the debt. Like many other forms of slavery, it exemplifies the negative effect of globalization caused by significant economic differences between varying regions of the world. Despite efforts by various institutions to conduct extensive analyses, the exact scale of the problem has not been determined. Estimates of various forms of slavery have increased from 12.3 million, as assessed by the International Labor Organization in 2005 (Belser, Cock, and Mehran 2005), to 45.8 million, as calculated by the Australian Walk Free Foundation in 2016 (*Global Slavery Index* 2016). One thing is certain, the problem is vast and continues to flourish. Although a ban on bonded labor was introduced more than a half century ago and is still considered the accepted international rule of law, enforcement is a complicated issue (IOM 2017).

Debt bondage has existed since the beginning of recorded history, and all cultures have demonstrated some form of bonded labor and economic exploitation. The ancient world was rife with examples of typical slavery, pawnship, and indentured service. From the Middle Ages to modern times, in many countries, people have been and still are subject to traditional slavery, serfdom, peonage, and sharecropping. For centuries, multiple methods have been used to trap indentured laborers: agricultural work in Europe, plantation work in Africa and the Americas, domestic slavery in the Caribbean, and working in the infamous brick kilns of Southeast Asia. Today, some such methods and forms of slavery have disappeared or changed, but debt bondage continues to occur worldwide, is not confined to any one country or region, and involves various sectors of the economy. Many victims of slavery do not consider themselves as such because the practices they are subject to are a traditional part of their local culture and economy (UN Human Rights Council 2016).

Bonded labor has been identified as a practice like slavery. According to Article 1a of the Supplementary Convention on the Abolition of Slavery, the Slave Trade, and Institutions and Practices Similar to Slavery, adopted in 1956, debt bondage means "the status or condition arising from a pledge by a debtor of his personal services or of those of a person under his control as security for a debt, if the value of those services as reasonably assessed is not applied towards the liquidation of the debt or the length and nature of those services are not respectively limited and defined." Bonded labor can be defined as a situation when a person borrows money, cannot repay it for some reason, is required to work to pay off the debt, and loses control over the conditions of their employment and the debt itself.

Debt bondage as thus described differs from forced labor as well as from human trafficking because debtors pledge to work and repay the debt without being required to perform certain forms of labor against their will. However, there are situations when the conditions are not so obvious. For example, persons who are unable to cover the agreed cost of smuggling them to another country accept work to pay off the debt. Such persons easily become victims of banned and forced labor, especially as their stay in the destination country is oftentimes clandestine and illegal. Difficulty in identifying such persons is one of the key obstacles to effective eradication of this practice.

Looking at the origins of debt bondage, it can be said that there are two mechanisms of establishing dependency. Some of the victims are people trapped in the traditional bonded labor system, which is characterized by feudal relationships in agriculture or economic dependence in other sectors of the economy. A typical element of this is an unequal power relation based on the caste system or any other traditional caste-like social order. This can be well illustrated by situations where sharecroppers took loans from their landlords to cover the costs of family needs or basic expenses related to health, marriages, or funerals. Such a loan was often too large for the debtor to pay off, and as a result, the relation of dependence became intergenerational, with children born into bondage and obliged to continue paying off the debt.

The second feature is related to working migrants. Opportunities for such persons to be exploited can include covering costs of expensive travel as well as a recruitment fee. In the case of Asians, costs can be significant for coming to Europe or the United States. Recruiters typically provide false promises about salaries, working conditions, or the nature of the job, which is often due to contracts being formulated in a language that is unfamiliar to the worker. This results in migrant workers being paid wages below national standards and employed under highly unacceptable working conditions (Lasocik, Rekosz-Cebula, and Wieczorek 2014). Employers can continue such unfair conditions due to immigrants' inability to receive visas in some countries.

Ann Jordan (2011) illustrates the process as follows: a person X agrees to work and to repay a debt of $5,000 for recruitment fees and travel costs allegedly paid by the employer or enforcer. Although the market wage for the work performed is $50 per day, the employer pays only $20, being aware that the worker is totally dependent on the employer. When a pledge to work and pay off the debt is made by person X, the employer often illegally inflates the interest rate to an unreasonable amount to make it impossible for the person to escape from debt bondage. Additionally, such employers constantly change the rules and conditions of employment to worsen them. The employer often imposes new obligations, increases the work hours, and manipulates wages to further entrap the worker; this is described as the continuum of exploitation (Andrees 2008). In many cases, the employer or trafficker intentionally imposes debt bondage to retain and exploit workers.

A UN special rapporteur (2016) informs that multiple forms of bonded labor are widespread around the world. In many African countries, such as the Democratic Republic of Congo, Mauritania, Zimbabwe, Malawi, and Zambia, adults and children are subjected to debt bondage or human trafficking in such work as mining, domestic services, and agriculture. This is more prevalent in South Asia, where India, Bangladesh, Pakistan, and Nepal face serious challenges to eradicate traditional ways of keeping people in different forms of dependency, such as work in brick kilns, agriculture, mills, mines, and factories. In India, which can serve as illustration for this region, debt bondage has also been reported in sectors such as stone quarries, cigarette manufacturing, carpet weaving, construction, fish processing, and work with looms. In some sectors, entire families are forced to work to pay off a debt taken by one of its members. Children can be held in bonded labor because of a loan their parents had taken decades ago.

A different situation exists in Latin America, where debt bondage mainly affects marginalized groups, including indigenous peoples, persons of African descent, the poor, and villagers. Sectors affected by bonded labor include agriculture, production of charcoal, pig iron production, and timber processing. Guatemala, Bolivia, and Peru are most often mentioned in this context.

In Europe, where one-third of victims of forced labor are in debt bondage, there is a greater share of male victims exploited than female victims. These sectors include construction, domestic services, agriculture, and factory work as well prostitution, where women are controlled through debt bondage or similar mechanisms. Dependence in Europe is often instigated by the illegal practice of recruiters and employers charging migrants recruitment fees.

According to the latest estimates prepared jointly by the ILO, the Walk Free Foundation, and the International Organization of Migration (IOM), 40.3 million people were victims of modern slavery in 2016 (ILO 2017). Of this number, approximately 24.9 million people were in forced labor, meaning being forced to work under threat or coercion, as described by ILO Convention, 1930 (No. 29). Over 4 million are victims of state-imposed forced labor, and almost 5 million are also subjected to other forms of exploitation, including sexual. The largest group is the 16 million men and women worldwide who are forced to work in the private sector. Approximately half of them are in debt bondage situations where personal debt was used to forcibly obtain their labor. The majority of persons held in debt bondage are forced to work in agriculture, domestic work, or different forms of manufacturing.

Zbigniew Lasocik

See also: Global Slavery Index; Labor Exploitation; U.K. Modern Slavery Act (2015)

Further Reading

Andrees, Beate. 2008. *Forced Labour and Trafficking in Europe: How People Are Trapped In, Live Through and Come Out.* Working Paper 57. Geneva, Switzerland: International Labour Office. Accessed January 19, 2019. http://lastradainternational.org/lsidocs/wcms_090548.pdf.

Belser, Patrick, Michaëlle de Cock, and Farhad Mehran. 2005. *ILO Minimum Estimate of Forced Labour in the World.* Geneva, Switzerland: International Labour Office. Accessed January 19, 2019. http://www.ilo.org/wcmsp5/groups/public/---ed_norm/---declaration/documents/publication/wcms_081913.pdf.

Global Slavery Index. 2016. Accessed January 13, 2019. https://www.globalslaveryindex.org/findings.

International Labour Organization (ILO). 2017. "Global Estimates of Modern Slavery: Forced Labour and Forced Marriage." Geneva, Switzerland: ILO. Accessed January 13, 2019. http://www.ilo.org/global/publications/books/WCMS_575479/lang--en/index.htm.

International Organization for Migration (IOM). 2017. "Combating Trafficking in Persons and Contemporary Forms of Slavery." Global Compact Thematic Paper. Accessed January 19, 2019. https://www.iom.int/sites/default/files/our_work/ODG/GCM/IOM-Thematic-Paper-Trafficking-in-persons.pdf.

Jordan, Ann. 2011. "Slavery, Forced Labor, Debt Bondage, and Human Trafficking: From Conceptional Confusion to Targeted Solutions." Issue Paper 2 (February). Program on Human Trafficking and Forced Labor, Center for Human Rights and Humanitarian Law, American University Washington College of Law. Accessed January 19, 2019. https://www.issuelab.org/resources/15356/15356.pdf.

Lasocik, Z., and E. Rekosz-Cebula, and L. Wieczorek. 2014. *Human Trafficking for Forced Labour in Poland—Effective Prevention and Diagnostics of Mechanisms.* Stockholm, Sweden: Council of the Baltic Sea States.

UN Human Rights Council. 2016. *Report of the Special Rapporteur on Contemporary Forms of Slavery, Including Its Causes and Consequences.* September 5, A/HRC/33/46. Accessed January 19, 2019. http://www.refworld.org/docid/57cd80554.html.

Boston Marathon Bombings (2013)

On April 15, 2013, two bombs made of pressure cookers filled with shrapnel hidden in backpacks were detonated on Boylston Street around 2:50 p.m. near the finish line of the 117th Boston Marathon, killing three people and wounding over 260. Brothers Tamerlan and Dzhokhar Tsarnaev were identified as the perpetrators (*United States v. Dzhokhar A. Tsarnaev* 2013a) and were allegedly motivated by radical Islamic views. Though inspired by radical Islamist groups such as the Islamic State of Iraq and Syria (ISIS), no evidence suggesting the attack was planned or supported by such groups was found (House Committee on Homeland Security 2014). At the time of the attack, the bombing was the deadliest terror attack inside the United States since September 11, 2001 (BBC 2015).

PERPETRATORS

Tamerlan, 26, and Dzhokhar, 19, are ethnic Avar-Chechens who immigrated to the United States from Kyrgyzstan in 2003 and 2002, respectively. Dzhokhar Tsarnaev arrived in the United States with his parents and applied for political asylum, which he received. He was followed by his brother, Tamerlan, and a sister in 2003. The family settled in Cambridge, Massachusetts. Dzhokar was naturalized on September 11, 2012. Tamerlan received a Green Card but did not become a citizen (House Committee on Homeland Security 2014).

Tamerlan Tsarnaev had already been under investigation for possible extremist tendencies prior to the bombing. In 2011, the Federal Bureau of Investigation (FBI) received a memo from the Russian Federal Security Service (FSB) stating that the Russian government had reason to believe Tamerlan Tsarnaev had been radicalized and might return to Russia with the intention of joining a radical Islamic group, without providing any further details. The FSB asked to be notified if Tamerlan Tsarnaev left the United States for Russia. The FBI opened an investigation on Tamerlan, which they closed on June 24, 2011, when they found no indication that he had become radicalized. However, Tamerlan was still entered into the TECS database (the Treasury Enforcement Communications System is the principal system used by officers at the border to assist with screening and determinations regarding admissibility of arriving persons). The FBI asked the FSB for more information, including the evidence suggesting radicalization, but received no reply.

Tamerlan did return to Russia in January of 2012 and then came back to the United States in July that same year. His departure was not flagged, despite his profile in TECS, and the Russian government was not notified. His movements during the seven-month period in Russia have not been completely accounted for, but he did spend some time in Makhachkala, Dagestan, with his family (House Committee on Homeland Security 2014). While in Dagestan, he prayed at the al-Nadira Mosque (Brooke 2013), whose founder, Nadirshakh Khachilaev, reportedly had contact with Al Qaeda leader Ayman Zawahiri (Cullison 2013). Tamerlan Tsarnaev was also thought to have been in contact with Mahmoud Mansour Nidal, a known local insurgent, while in Dagestan (Tapper, Metzger, and Pham 2013). Some news outlets reported that he attempted to join Chechen radical Islamist groups while in Russia, but federal investigators were unable to substantiate these reports (House Committee on Homeland Security 2014).

Dzhokhar Tsarnaev did not accompany his brother to Russia. When his brother and mother showed an increased religious devotion in 2010 or 2011, Dzhokhar reportedly rejected their renewed religious convictions. He did begin to pray five times a day, but he also smoked marijuana and drank. According to family friend Baudy Mazaev, also of Chechen descent, Tamerlan pushed his brother to become more religious and made him read books on Islamic fundamentalism. In the year before the bombing, Dzhokhar reportedly expressed only a minimal increase in religiosity (Wines and Lovett 2013). While he may have rapidly radicalized himself but not expressed much indication of his new views in public, Dzhokhar appears to have been heavily influenced by his brother, and his brother masterminded the entire plot. Based on reporting, including declassified government reports, exactly how the brothers were radicalized remains unclear.

INVESTIGATION AND MANHUNT

Shortly after the bombing, more than 1,000 law enforcement officials from local, state, and federal agencies were deployed to find and arrest the perpetrators. Within three days, the FBI had released stills from a surveillance camera of the Tsarnaev brothers, at that point still unidentified (House Committee on Homeland Security 2014).

Law enforcement was put on the trail of the brothers on April 18 after the killing of Massachusetts Institute of Technology campus police officer Sean Collier on the MIT campus, allegedly carried out by the brothers to take Collier's gun. Then, about a mile and a half from the MIT campus, Tamerlan Tsasrnaev threatened the driver of a Mercedes-Benz at gunpoint, reportedly saying, "Did you hear about the Boston explosion? I did that." The owner of the Mercedes-Benz later contacted the police, who tracked down the brothers in the stolen car and pursued them into Watertown, in Boston. During the chase, the brothers and police exchanged gunfire, and the brothers also threw explosives at the police ("The Hunt for the Boston Bombing Suspects," 2013). During the exchange, Tamerlan was shot and captured by the police. Dzhokhar escaped in the Mercedes, running over his brother in the process, and later abandoned the car to continue on foot (Hirsch 2013).

Tamerlan died at a Boston-area hospital on April 19 ("The Hunt for the Boston Bombing Suspects," 2013). Boston was put on lockdown at around 5:30 a.m. as the manhunt for Dzhokhar continued with a door-to-door search of the area. He was found that evening hiding in a boat parked in a yard in Watertown by police after they received a tip from a man who had spotted blood on the boat (Hirsch 2013). The police and Dzhokhar exchanged gunfire before he was finally taken into custody ("The Hunt for the Boston Bombing Suspects," 2013). Around 9:00 p.m., the Boston Police Department confirmed his capture through a tweet (Hirsch 2013). The manhunt was the largest in Massachusetts history (Wines and Lovett 2013).

TRIAL

On June 27, 2013, Dzhokhar Tsarnaev was indicted on all 30 counts he was charged with, including conspiracy to maliciously destroy property resulting in death, multiple counts of possession and use of a firearm during and in relation to a crime of violence resulting in death, and multiple counts of use of a weapon of mass destruction (*United States v. Dzhokhar A. Tsarnaev* 2013a). Tsarnaev was convicted of all 30 counts on April 8, 2015, and sentenced to death on June 24, 2015, following a recommendation of the death penalty by the jury (*United States v. Dzhokhar A. Tsarnaev* 2013b).

Three other people were charged with offenses related to the attack. Dias Kadyrbayev and Azamat Tazhayakov were charged with obstruction of justice for attempting to dispose of a backpack belonging to Dzhokhar Tsarnaev containing fireworks, a laptop, and a USB drive. Robel Phillipos was charged with making false statements to law enforcement. All three were convicted and sentenced to six, three and a half, and three years in prison, respectively (Sanchez 2015).

As of 2018, Dzhokhar was housed at the federal Supermax prison in Florence, Colorado, as his attorneys continue an appeals process through the U.S. court of appeals.

Lilla Heins

See also: Islamic State of Iraq and Syria (ISIS); Terrorism, Domestic

Further Reading

BBC. 2015. "Profile: Who Is Boston Bomber Dzhokhar Tsarnaev?" *BBC.com*, April 8. Accessed January 13, 2019. http://www.bbc.com/news/world-us-canada-31734557.

Brooke, James. 2013. "Boston Bomber Spent 6 Months in Russia's Most Violent Republic." *Voice of America*, May 20. Accessed January 13, 2019. https://www.voanews.com/a/tsarnaev-dagestan-russia-ties-may-hold-valuable-clues/1664419.html.

Cullison, Alan. 2013. "Dagestani Islamists Were Uneasy about Boston Bombing Suspect." *Wall Street Journal*, May 9. Accessed January 13, 2019. https://www.wsj.com/articles/SB10001424127887324059704578473160866108832.

Hirsch, J. M. 2013. "Boston: The unfolding of a 5-day manhunt for bomb suspects. *Daily Local News*, April 20, https://www.dailylocal.com/boston-the-unfolding-of-a--day-manhunt-for-bomb/article_c33e4a11-dfab-5ebb-adf2-bb2166022394.html.

House Committee on Homeland Security. 2014. "The Road to Boston: Counterterrorism Challenges and Lessons from the Marathon Bombings." Report, House Homeland Security Committee.

"The Hunt for the Boston Bombing Suspects." 2013. *New York Times*, April 19. Accessed January 13, 2019. http://www.nytimes.com/interactive/2013/04/19/us/boston-marathon-manhunt.html.

Sanchez, Ray. 2015. "Boston Marathon Bomber's Friends Sentenced to Prison." *CNN*, June 5. Accessed January 13, 2019. http://www.cnn.com/2015/06/05/us/boston-tsarnaev-friends-sentenced/index.html.

Tapper, Jake, Jessica Metzger, and Sherisse Pham. 2013. "Russian Sources Tell Congressman Boston Suspect Met with Two Chechen Extremists." "The Lead with Jake Tapper," CNN, May 9. Accessed January 13, 2019. http://thelead.blogs.cnn.com/2013/05/09/russian-sources-tell-congressman-boston-suspect-met-with-two-chechen-extremists.

United States v. Dzhokhar A. Tsarnaev. 2013a. "Indictment. No. 13-CR-10200-GAO (MBB)." Accessed January 13, 2019. https://www.justice.gov/sites/default/files/usao-ma/legacy/2013/06/27/Indictment1.pdf.

United States v. Dzhokhar A. Tsarnaev. 2013b. "Judgment. No. 13-CR-10200-GAO." Accessed January 13, 2019. https://www.justice.gov/usao-ma/file/643096/download.

Wines, Michael, and Ian Lovett. 2013. "The Dark Side, Carefully Masked." *New York Times*, May 4. Accessed January 13, 2019. http://www.nytimes.com/2013/05/05/us/dzhokhar-tsarnaevs-dark-side-carefully-masked.html.

Bout, Viktor (1967–)

Viktor Bout, who became known as the "Merchant of Death," was a former Soviet Air Force officer who ran an international arms trafficking network that he started after his air force unit disbanded with the breakup of the Soviet Union in 1991. U.S. officials believe that Bout ran an international arms trafficking network from 1995 until his arrest in 2008. In 2011, he was found guilty of conspiring to sell antiaircraft missiles and other weapons to men he believed were Colombian terrorists. At his sentencing hearing in 2012, he was sentenced to 25 years in prison, and he is currently serving that sentence.

BACKGROUND

Bout was born on January 13, 1967, reportedly in the Soviet republic of Tajikistan. After his service in the Soviet Air Force, in 1995, he founded an air freight company called Aircess that operated across Africa, and during the ensuing years, he came to control what U.S. officials said was the largest private fleet of Soviet-era cargo aircraft in the world (Johnston and Mydans 2008). During the Angolan Civil War (1995–2002), the company supplied weapons to the rebel group National Union for the Total Independence of Angola (UNITA) and to Liberia's Charles Taylor to help him fight two civil wars from 1995 to 2002. Eventually, Bout used his company and associates to sell guns, ammunition and even tanks and helicopters that U.S. Treasury officials said inflamed conflicts in Afghanistan, Congo, Rwanda, Sierra Leon, and Sudan. He is also believed to have furnished weapons to Al Qaeda and the Taliban in Afghanistan.

ARREST AND TRIAL

Agents from the U.S. Drug Enforcement Administration (DEA), who were posing as members of the Revolutionary Armed Forces of Colombia (FARC), arrested Bout in March 2008. The U.S. government identified FARC as a foreign terrorist group for its rebellion against Colombia's government—and because it was believed to finance its activities, in part, through cocaine trafficking. Bout was charged with conspiracy to provide material support to a foreign terrorist organization. Extradition proceedings from Thailand to the United States, which Russian officials vigorously opposed, took more than two and a half years but finally resulted in his extradition in November 2010.

Bout had always portrayed himself as an honest businessman operating as a traveling sales representative whose job was to shift products from seller to buyer. Moral questions, he suggested, would be left to others. Bout's attorney continued that portrayal during trial, claiming that Bout had simply gotten caught up in a plan to sell two cargo planes and that he had actually been quite skeptical that the buyers were members of FARC. The prosecution countered that Bout could have made a choice to withdraw from the agreement at any moment but chose instead to continue.

THE VERDICT

Following a three-week trial, Bout was found guilty in November 2011 of conspiring to kill American citizens, officers, and employees; conspiring to acquire and export surface-to-air antiaircraft missiles; and of conspiring to provide support or weapons to a foreign terrorist organization.

In addition to the 25-year prison sentence, Bout was given 5 years of supervised release and ordered to forfeit $15 million, which was the value of the goods he intended to deal. The judge rejected the prosecution's request of life imprisonment because she believed that Bout probably would not have committed the charged crimes had he not been ensnared in a sting operation (Rosenberg 2012). In 2016, the U.S. Court of Appeals rejected Bout's request for a retrial.

There have been several popular media accounts featuring Bout, including the books *Merchant of Death* (2007), which describes how Bout built up his global empire, and *Operations Relentless* (2017), which details the operation to catch him. Bout is also the subject of the documentary film *The Notorious Mr. Bout* (2014), and Nicholas Cage's character in the 2005 film *Lord of War* is said to have been inspired by Bout's career.

Philip L. Reichel

See also: Revolutionary Armed Forces of Colombia; Small Arms and Light Weapons, Trafficking in

Further Reading

Farah, Douglas, and Stephen Braun. 2007. *Merchant of Death: Money, Guns, Planes, and the Man Who Makes War Possible.* Hoboken, NJ: John Wiley & Sons.

Johnston, David, and Seth Mydans. 2008. "Russian Charged with Trying to Sell Arms." *New York Times*, March 7. Accessed January 19, 2019. https://www.nytimes.com/2008/03/07/world/europe/07dealer.html.

Lewis, Damien. 2017. *Operation Relentless.* London: Quercus.

Rosenberg, Noah. 2012. "Russian Weapons Trafficker Avoids Getting Life in Prison." *New York Times*, April 5. Accessed January 19, 2019. https://www.nytimes.com/2012/04/06/nyregion/russian-arms-dealer-is-sentenced-to-25-years.html.

Bribery

Bribery is the act of promising, offering, or giving, directly or indirectly, an undue advantage to a recipient so that this person acts or refrains from acting in a certain way (active bribery) or the solicitation or acceptance by such recipient of the undue advantage (passive bribery). Bribery is one form of corruption. Other forms of corruption include nepotism, patronage, and trading in influence. The undue advantage offered may be money, goods, property rights, or other things of value to the briber, such as a holiday trip, tickets to a highly coveted event, or privileges.

The action requested or hoped for by the briber is generally a decision granting the briber's request, such as deciding a court case in the briber's favor, granting their company a contract, or issuing them a license. The briber may also hope that the recipient will refrain from making a certain decision; a typical case is when a police officer stops a motorist who has been speeding, and a bribe is paid so that no summons or fine is issued to the motorist.

Typically, the bribe is offered to a public official. The recipient, however, need not have the status of a public official. Often, bribes are paid in a business context, in which "sweeteners" (in the form of facilitation payments, commissions, retainers, fees, gratuities, inducements, or irregular payments) are used to secure contracts. The recipient may also be an athlete (match fixing) or, for example, a member of an international organization (such as those that decide on where international athletic events are to be organized).

The extent of bribery varies across and within cultures. In some cultures, the giving of gifts is widespread, and it may be difficult to distinguish between culturally acceptable "tips" (such as to a doorman at the year-end holidays) and "gifts" that are routinely given in many countries to receive medical treatment, have a child accepted to school, pass an examination, or receive a permit or license.

A distinction is also made between "petty bribery" ("bribery/corruption in the streets") and "grand bribery" ("bribery/corruption in the suites"). Petty bribery refers to the everyday corruption that takes place between low-level public officials and members of the public. Grand bribery refers to bribery/corruption that involves higher levels of public officials and vast sums of money or other undue advantages. Grand bribery may be carried out to extract money for personal profit and also to maintain power. Heads of state that have been found to have been involved in such kleptocracy ("rule by thieves") include Mohamed Suharto (1921–2008) of Indonesia, Ferdinand Marcos (1917–1989) of the Philippines, Mobute Sese Seko (1930–1997) of Zaire, and Sani Abacha (1943–1998) of Nigeria.

Bribery can be found in both developed and developing countries. In the United States, petty bribery has been identified as a problem in law enforcement in many jurisdictions, in the form of shakedowns of motorists or of persons detained and threatened with arrest. Grand bribery, in turn, has been identified as a problem in such examples as the awarding of contracts in construction and waste management. A specific form of bribery is "pay to play," in which those wishing to submit tenders for government contracts are required to make (illegal) payments to those deciding on the contracts.

Persons from developed countries are also involved in bribery directed at developing countries, usually in connection with business transactions. In some countries, the cost of bribes can even be deducted as a business expense, although the taxpayer will generally refer to the bribes as commissions or other legally acceptable payments.

The response to bribery requires national and international action. The United States was the first country to adopt extensive legislation criminalizing the international aspects of corruption, in the form of the 1977 Foreign Corrupt Practices Act (FCPA). Although the FCPA was an important step toward decreasing commercial corruption in the United States, and the extent to which U.S. businesses engaged in corruption abroad, it did place U.S. businesses on unequal footing with other companies that could generally continue to pay bribes with relative impunity. The reduction in trade barriers during the 1980s and the 1990s increased the amount of competition in the search for business abroad.

The United States first worked for international measures against commercial bribery through the Organization for Economic Co-Operation and Development (OECD), an organization in which the United States has traditionally played a leading role. In 1994, the OECD adopted a recommendation on the criminalization of foreign bribery. This was followed in 1996 by the OECD recommendation on tax deductibility of bribes to foreign public officials.

At the same time, major political corruption scandals in a number of Latin American countries led to considerable discussion on the need to improve public ethics, also through legislative action. The United States sought to facilitate action by the Organization of American States, in which it was a member. The result was the first multilateral convention on corruption, the 1996 Inter-American Convention against Corruption of the Organization of American States. Only one year later, in 1997, this was followed by the adoption of the Convention on Combating Bribery of Foreign Public Officials in International Business Transactions. This convention was prepared within the framework of the OECD.

In very short order, these two conventions were following by several others:

- The 1998 Convention on the Fight against Corruption Involving Officials of the European Communities or Officials of Member States of the European Union;
- The 1999 Criminal Law Convention on Corruption and the 1999 Civil Law Convention on Corruption of the Council of Europe;
- The 2001 Southern African Development Community Protocol against Corruption; and
- The 2003 African Union Convention on Preventing and Combating Corruption.

The culmination of the series was the 2003 United Nations Convention against Corruption, which requires states parties to criminalize bribery of public officials and bribery of foreign public officials and officials of public international organizations. States parties are also required to take a number of other preventive measures, such as the adoption of codes of conduct and the improved regulation and monitoring of public procurement and managing of public finances.

The 2003 UN Convention against Corruption also urges states parties to consider what steps are necessary to deal with trading in influence, illicit enrichment, and bribery in the public sector.

Matti Joutsen

See also: Corruption; Foreign Corrupt Practices Act; UN Convention against Corruption

Further Reading

Organization for Economic Co-Operation and Development (OECD). n.d. "Bribery and Corruption." Accessed August 5, 2018. http://www.oecd.org/corruption.

United Nations Office on Drugs and Crime (UNODC). 2005. "United Nations Convention against Corruption." Accessed January 13, 2019. https://www.unodc.org/unodc/en/treaties/CAC.

Brussels Bombings (2016)

On March 22, 2016, a series of three coordinated suicide bombings killed 32 civilians and wounded 340 in two locations in Brussels. Two of the bombings took place at the Brussels Airport in Zaventem and one at the Maelbeek metro station in central Brussels, located very close to many of the European Union institutions. The attack on Brussels was the largest terrorist attack on Belgium soil and is symbolic because Brussels is frequently regarded as the heart of Europe, hosting major European Union institutions and the North Atlantic Treaty Organization (NATO). The Islamic State of Iraq and Syria (ISIS) claimed responsibility for the bombings, attributing them to a "security group from the soldiers of the caliphate" (Knoll, Chad, and Boyle 2016). ISIS warned of more attacks, which it said would be "worse and more bitter, God permitting" (Knoll, Chad, and Boyle 2016). The ISIS cell that committed the attack was the same cell that committed the 2015 Paris terror attacks, according to investigators (Miller 2016).

ATTACKS

Two men committed the bombing at Brussels airport: Ibrahim El Bakraoui and Najim Laachraoui. However, three men carried bombs hidden in large suitcases as they entered the airport. According to the federal prosecutor, they used shrapnel-type bombs that were very similar explosives to the ones used in the suicide bombings of the 2015 Paris attacks and the Manchester bombing that followed in 2017, using the trimer of acetone peroxide, called triacetone triperoxide, more commonly known as TATP, and a large number of nails and screws. At 7:58 a.m., there was a first massive blast at check-in row 2; this was followed nine seconds later by a second blast at check-in row 11. Both were places where people had gathered. Security camera footage shows that the two blasts pushed away the third bomber, Mohamed Abrini, from his bomb-laden suitcase. The man lay dazed on the floor for several seconds and then left the scene with the panicking crowd, leaving his bomb, the biggest of them all, behind (Miller 2016). The attack on the airport claimed 16 lives.

The second attack in the metro station took place at 9:10 a.m., during the height of the morning rush. When a three-carriage train of metro line 5 entered Maelbeek station, a suicide bomber, Khalid El Bakraoui, the brother of Ibrahim El Bakraoui (one of the airport bombers), detonated a bomb hidden in his backpack in the middle of the station. The blast claimed 16 lives. Just minutes before boarding his train, Khalid El Bakraoui was spotted on security cameras at the Pétillon metro station alongside another man, Osama Krayem, who carried an identical backpack filled with explosives. While Krayem traveled to an undisclosed location on the metro, he decided to back out at the last minute, according to the newspaper *De Standaard* (Kroet 2016).

AFTERMATH AND INVESTIGATION

Immediately after the attacks, Belgium raised its security threat level to the maximum of four, meaning the threat is "very serious," and announced three days of national mourning. Belgium security services launched a massive investigation, kicked off by a tip from a taxi driver who said he had driven three men with big bags to Brussels airport on the morning of the attack ("Brussels Explosions" 2016). When the police investigated the address where the taxi driver had picked up the three men, they found "a large nail bomb, along with 15kg of TATP high explosive, chemicals, detonators, bomb-making materials and an Islamic State flag" ("Brussels Explosions" 2016). During the raid, police also found fingerprints from the two suspects who failed to detonate their bombs during the attacks, Osama Krayem and Mohamed Abrini. Both suspects were apprehended on April 8, at separate locations in Belgium.

Krayem was charged with "criminal conspiracy in connection with a terrorist enterprise" and "complicity to murder" (Rankin 2018). Both suspects will also both be extradited to France, as they have been linked to the Paris attacks of 2015 (Rankin 2018; Garlindo 2018). As of June 2018, the overall investigation into the Brussels bombings, according to police records, involves 40 suspects, of whom 14 are dead; 16 are under arrest in France, Belgium, or elsewhere abroad; and two are still being sought (Schreuer 2018).

Wessel Groot

See also: Islamic State of Iraq and Syria (ISIS); Paris and *Charlie Hebdo* Terrorist Attacks

Further Reading

"Brussels Explosions: What We Know about Airport and Metro Attacks." 2016. BBC, April 9. Accessed May 30, 2018. http://www.bbc.com/news/world-europe-35869985.

Garlindo, Gabriela. 2018. "Brussels Terror Suspect to Be Extradited to France." *Politico*, June 8. Accessed June 12, 2018. https://www.politico.eu/article/brussels-bombing-terror-suspect-to-be-extradited-to-france.

Knoll, Corina, Sheldon Chad, and Christina Boyle. 2016. "Hunt Is on for Brussels Bombings Suspect; Islamic State Warns of More, Worse Attacks." *Los Angeles Times*, March 23. Accessed May 27, 2018. http://www.latimes.com/world/europe/la-fg-brussels-airport-explosion-20160322-story.html.

Kroet, Cynthia. 2016. "Osama Krayem 'Carried Explosives in Brussels Metro'—Report." *Politico*, April 15. Accessed June 1, 2018. https://www.politico.eu/article/osama-krayem-carried-explosives-in-brussels-metro-report.

Rankin, Jennifer. 2016. "Paris and Brussels Terror Suspect to Face Charges in France." *The Guardian*, June 9. Accessed June 11, 2018. https://www.theguardian.com/world/2016/jun/09/mohamed-abrini-paris-brussels-terror-suspect-france-man-in-the-hat.

Schreuer, Milan. 2018. "Associate of Paris Attacks Suspect Charged over Brussels Bombings." *New York Times*, June 1, 2018. Accessed June 12, 2018. https://www.nytimes.com/2018/06/01/world/europe/paris-brussels-attacks-sofien-ayari-salah-abdeslam.html.

C

Cali Cartel

The Cali Cartel was a drug syndicate based in Southern Colombia started by the Rodríguez Orejuela brothers, Gilbert, Miguel, and José Santacruz Londoño, known as "Chepe." The Cali Cartel is known to be one of the most powerful drug organizations in history, often referred to as the "Cali KGB," which at one point controlled more than 90 percent of the world's cocaine market and was widely credited for the rapid growth of Europe's cocaine market. At the height of its operation, revenue was suspected in the billions of dollars. The organization began to decline after successful raids by U.S. Customs Enforcement (DOJ 2006).

CALI CARTEL 1977

The Rodríguez Orejuela brothers had reputable social backgrounds as drug lords. Those who knew the Cali Cartel would often refer to the organization as *Los Caballeros de Cali* ("Gentlemen of Cali" or "Cali's Gentlemen") (Washington 2001). The organization initially started as a ring of kidnappers known as *Las Chemas*, led by Luis Fernando Tamayo Garcia. Notable kidnappings include two Swiss citizens, a diplomat (Herman Buff), and a student known as Zack Martin or "Jazz Mills." It is believed that the kidnappers received $700,000 in ransom, which in turn funded their drug trafficking operation.

The organization initially started by trafficking marijuana. At the time, marijuana had a low profit rate that did not meet the organization's resource needs. The group then decided to traffic cocaine, which was more profitable. Trafficking predominantly focused around Peru and Bolivia. The organization utilized new trafficking routes that eventually led to the drug being distributed in Panama. The organization also began trafficking opium and heroin, as many cartels did not traffic these narcotics.

The Cali Cartel eventually increased in influence as their organization grew by expanding internationally. One notable import and export was that of cocaine in Miami, Florida. The Cali Cartel was also involved in the trafficking and sale of narcotics in Liechtenstein, Germany, and the Ukraine.

REVOLT AGAINST PABLO ESCOBAR

The Cali Cartel gained credibility as an organization through the 1980s to 1990s. By the early 1990s, the Cali Cartel controlled over 90 percent of the world's cocaine trade. As their operation grew larger, the Cali Cartel saw the activities of Pablo Escobar as a direct threat against their organization. The Cali Cartel was instrumental in creating the group known as the People Persecuted by Pablo Escobar (Los Pepes), which specifically targeted Escobar's homes, businesses, and lieutenants (*PBS Frontline* n.d.). During the attempted capture and prosecution of Pablo Escobar, the U.S. counterterrorism unit, Delta Force, gave financial assistance to the Cali Cartel. As a crime syndicate, the Cali Cartel helped secretly supply information to the U.S. Drug Enforcement Administration (DEA) and the Colombian police (*PBS Frontline* n.d.). Los Pepes is also known for over 60 executions of the Medellín Cartel.

During the narco-terror wars and violence happening in Colombia, the Cali Cartel hired Jorge Salcedo. The Cali Cartel believed that Salcedo had been involved with a group of mercenaries that worked with a group of left-wing guerilla forces to deal with the problems of the narco-drug war. Due in part to the Cali Cartel's contributions, Pablo Escobar was eventually killed on December 2, 1993. The death of Pablo Escobar led to the downfall of the Medellín Cartel and led to the rise of the Cali Cartel.

FINANCIAL IMPACT

By 1996, the Cali Cartel was making as much as $7 billion per year (Moody 2001; Fedarko 1995). Apart from their trafficking operations, the Cali Cartel also funded numerous business ventures to mask the enormous revenue that they were bringing in. One notable organization that the Cali Cartel used was the Banco de Trabajadores, a local financial institution in the area. The Banco de Trabajadores is thought to have known about the money laundering operations of the Cali Cartel, but due to the enormous financial contributions of the organization, the bank did not report these funds to the authorities. With a successful front in place, it is believed that numerous members of the organization took out loans from the bank without any intent to repay the money.

Apart from the organization's banking operations, Gilberto Santacruz Londoño was also known to have started Grupo Radial Colombiano, a network of over 30 radio stations. He also started a pharmaceutical chain of over 400 stores in 28 cities, employing over 4,200 individuals. It is estimated that the pharmaceutical chain amassed a value of over $216 million at the height of its operation (Associated Press 2004).

SENTENCING OF CALI CARTEL LEADERS

In the early era of the Cali Cartel's operations, they operated with a large degree of immunity. However, this immunity did not prevent the eventual seizures of the organization's drug supply. In 1991, the organization had over 50 tons of its cocaine seized from them and over $15 million worth in assets.

In July 1990, Jorge Alberto Rodríguez was arrested after trying to import 100 kilos of cocaine into Tallahassee, Florida. Later in October 1990, he refused to testify or identify anyone he was criminally affiliated with. That same year, he was convicted and sentenced to 25 years in federal prison for his involvement (Chepesiuk 2003).

In June and July of 1995, six heads of the Cali Cartel were arrested. Gilberto Rodríguez Orejuela was arrested in his home along with other cartel heads. José Santacruz Londoño was arrested in a restaurant, and Miguel Rodríguez Orejuela was apprehended during a raid. Both Gilberto and Miguel were extradited to Florida on charges of conspiracy to export cocaine to the United States. They both later confessed and agreed to forfeit $2.1 billion in assets, but the agreement did not require them to cooperate with subsequent investigations (DOJ 2006). Following the arrests of Gilberto and Miguel, the Colombian government raided and seized their pharmacy chain, which ended in the replacement of 50 workers because of their contributions in serving the interests of the cartel.

Anthony Azari

See also: Colombian Drug Cartels; Escobar, Pablo; Medellín Cartel

Further Reading

Allum, Felia, and Renet Seibert, eds. 2008. *Organized Crime and the Challenge to Democracy.* New York: Routledge.

Associated Press. 2004. "Colombia Busts Store Chain for Cocaine Links." *NBC News,* September 17. http://www.nbcnews.com/id/6030868/ns/world_news/t/colombia-busts-store-chain-cocaine-links/

Belton, Catherine. 2003. "New Book Poses Question of Putin's Links with Underworld." *St. Petersburg Times,* October 7. https://www.tapatalk.com/groups/redcatsboards/new-book-poses-question-of-putin-s-links-with-unde-t9071.html

Chepesiuk, Ron. 2003. *The Bullet or the Bribe: Taking Down Colombia's Cali Drug Cartel.* Westport, CT: Praeger Publishers.

Dalton, Natalie. 2011. "Colombian Pharmacy Fueled by Cali Cartel Money." *Colombia Reports,* October 5.

Fedarko, Kevin. 1995. "Outwitting the Cali Cartels Professor Moriarty." *Time,* July 17, 1995.

Koshiw, J. V. 2007. "Kuchma's 'Parallel Cabinet': The Center of President Kuchma's Authoritarian Rule Based on the Melnychenko Recordings." Last Modified October 12, 2007. Accessed January 14, 2019. https://web.archive.org/web/20120120052247/http://www.ukrainianstudies.uottawa.ca/pdf/P_Koshiw_Danyliw07.pdf.

Moody, John. 1991. "A Day with the Chess Player." *Time,* July 1, p. 34..

PBS Frontline, n.d. "The Colombian Cartels." Accessed March 26, 2018. https://www.pbs.org/wgbh/pages/frontline/shows/drugs/business/inside/colombian.html.

Rempel, William. 2011. *At the Devils Table: The Untold Story of the Insider Who Brought Down the Cali Cartel.* New York: Random House Publishing

U.S. Department of Justice (DOJ). 2006. "Transcript of Press Conference Announcing Guilty Pleas by Cali Cartel." Last Modified 26, 2006. Accessed January 21, 2019. https://www.justice.gov/archive/ag/speeches/2006/ag_speech_060926.html.

Washington, Elaine. 2001. "New Kings of Coke." *Time,* June 24. Accessed January 14, 2019. http://content.time.com/time/magazine/article/0,9171,157350,00.html?artId=157350?contType=article?chn=world.

California Transparency in Supply Chains Act

Consumers of retail goods and manufactured products as well as businesses are often unaware that their purchases may be tainted by forced labor, which may inadvertently promote human trafficking through supply chains. To address this concern, the California Transparency in Supply Chains Act of 2010 (SB 657) was created, and it went into effect in the state of California on January 1, 2012. The act mandates companies disclose steps they have taken, if any, to address human trafficking and forced labor in their supply chains. Although this act is specific to California, it has national and global implications. California boasts the world's seventh-largest economy and the country's largest consumer base, which provided a unique opportunity to address the issue of human trafficking by requiring retail companies to manage their supply chains (ILO 2015). Many companies, such as Apple, Coca-Cola, Chevron, and General Mills, simply to name a few, have global operations. Given the global operations of various companies and California's large economy, this law can have far-reaching impacts.

Under the law, large manufacturers and retailers are required to disclose their efforts to eradicate slavery and human trafficking within their supply chains. If a business is found to violate the law, the attorney general has exclusive authority to enforce the Transparency in Supply Chains Act and may file a civil action for injunctive relief. The goal is to provide consumers with critical information about the efforts that companies are undertaking to prevent and root out human trafficking and slavery in their product supply chains, whether in the United States or overseas. The primary purpose of this law is to educate consumers, enable them to make informed decisions about goods they purchase, and encourage large manufacturers and retailers to responsibly manage their supply chains.

HISTORY

It is estimated that 21 million people are victims of forced labor around the globe, and victims can work in virtually every industry and across sectors, including manufacturing, agriculture, construction, entertainment, and domestic service. Additionally, in 2013, the International Labour Organization (ILO) identified 122 goods that were purchased from 72 different countries believed to be the product of forced or child labor. Oftentimes, the goods are regularly purchased in the United States by consumers, such as coffee, cotton, and shoes (ILO 2015). Prior to the establishment of the California Transparency in Supply Chains Act, consumers in California had demanded that producers provide greater transparency about goods brought to the market. Additionally, consumers' purchasing decisions were influenced by this information, and various indicators suggest that Californians are not alone. A recent survey of Western consumers revealed that people would be willing to pay extra for products they could identify as being made under good working conditions (Hiscox and Smyth 2015).

COMPLIANCE AND DISCLOSURE PRACTICES

The act requires large retailers and manufacturers doing business in California to disclose on their Web sites the efforts they are taking to eradicate slavery and human trafficking from their direct supply chain for tangible goods that will be sold in California. The law specifically applies to any company doing business in California, any business that has annual worldwide gross receipts of more than $100 million, and any business that identifies itself as a retail seller or manufacturer on its California tax return.

To comply with the act, companies must post disclosures on their Web sites covering five areas: verification, audits, certification, internal accountability, and training. First, verification requires the company confirm whether the company engages in verification activities to identify, assess, and manage the risks of human trafficking in its product supply chain. If the company conducts verifications, the business must additionally disclose whether the company uses a third-party verifier. Second, audits require the company to confirm whether the company audits suppliers in evaluating compliance with the company's standards for trafficking and slavery in its supply chains and if those audits are independent and unannounced. Third, certification makes the company state whether it requires direct suppliers to make the certification. Fourth, internal accountability requires companies to disclose whether the company has internal procedures for determining whether employees or contractors are complying with company standards regarding slavery and human trafficking. And fifth, training requires the company to confirm whether the company engages in the specified training (Harris 2015).

If a company takes no action related to these five disclosure categories, the company must disclose that it does not take any actions. To be accessible to consumers, businesses, retailers, and manufacturers must post online on their homepage. One option is to post a direct link disclosure on the business's homepage as well as posting it in a visible location that catches a reader's attention. Additionally, the disclosure should be easy to understand.

CRITICISMS

Businesses are not mandated to implement new measures to ensure that their product supply chains are free from human trafficking and slavery; it only requires they disclose this information to the public. Another criticism of the law's value and broader efforts to prevent the exploitation of human beings is that the state cannot disclose which companies are covered by the law. Furthermore, only the state attorney general is informed about which companies are covered under the law by the California Franchise Tax Board, and the list is not public. Simply put, the government is prohibited from being transparent about a law that requires transparency from businesses. This means the primary purpose of the law is not effective, and the public cannot make fully informed decisions or even determine which companies should be disclosing information (Todres 2015).

Shanell Sanchez

See also: Human Trafficking; Labor Exploitation

Further Reading

Harris, Kamala. 2015. "The California Transparency in Supply Chains Act: A Resource Guide." Attorney General, California Department of Justice. Accessed April 8, 2018. https://oag.ca.gov/sites/all/files/agweb/pdfs/sb657/resource-guide.pdf.

Hiscox, Michael J., and F. B. Smyth. 2011. "Is There Consumer Demand for Improved Labor Standards? Evidence from Field Experiments in Social Product Labeling." Accessed April 8, 2018. https://wcfia.harvard.edu/files/wcfia/files/hiscox_isthere.pdf.

International Labour Organization (ILO). 2015. "Forced Labour, Human Trafficking and Slavery." Accessed April 8, 2018. http://www.ilo.org/global/topics/forced-labour/policy-areas/statistics/lang--en/index.htm.

Todres, Jonathan. 2015. "Legal Glitch Means Trafficking Transparency Law Isn't So Transparent." *CNN*, June 16. Accessed April 8, 2018. https://www.cnn.com/2015/06/16/opinions/california-transparency-supply-chains-law-trafficking/index.html

Cambodian Statue Theft

The theft of a Khmer statue from Cambodia in the early 1970s provides an excellent case study of the transnational crime of antiquities theft. The sandstone statue of Duryodhana, an epic warrior in Hindu mythology, dated back to the 10th century and was illegally removed from the Prasat Chen Temple in the Cambodian city of Koh Ker. The statue was put up for auction in 2011 in the United States and was expected to sell for between $2 million and $3 million. It was proven stolen and was eventually returned to Cambodia.

Some millennia ago, the Khmer Empire, a people known for their stone temples and statues, ruled most of current-day Southeast Asia. Most of what is known today about these people has been learned through the temples and art they left behind, as there are no surviving written records. One large temple complex is in the city of Koh Ker, which remained mostly intact in the jungle until discovered by French explorers in the late 19th century. During a period of unrest and civil war in Cambodia in the 1960s and 1970s, during the Khmer Rouge's rule, Koh Ker and other temples were looted of many statues and other works of art.

One such looted statues was that of Duryodhana, a sandstone statue of a warrior that is over five feet tall and weighs 250 pounds. The statue had to be broken to be removed from the site, as its feet were part of a very large stone pedestal. Looters took the statue to middlemen in the northern Cambodian city of Sisophon and then trafficked the statue across the border into Thailand to a dealer in Bangkok (Mackenzie 2014, 729). The statue was sold at auction and resided in a private collection in Europe until 2010, when it was once again put up for sale at an auction.

The auction house Sotheby's prominently featured the statue in a 2011 catalog and anticipated a final sale price of $2–$3 million. Before the auction could take place, a Cambodian official requested that Sotheby's withdraw the statue from the auction, which it did. The statue was in limbo for a year while a court case over ownership of the statue proceeded.

It was proven that the statue was stolen from its original site in Koh Ker, as the feet that had remained behind matched the statue at Sotheby's. In late 2013, an agreement was reached for the statue to be returned to Cambodia. It turned out that this statue was part of a pair of statues, the other of which had also been stolen and was eventually returned to Cambodia.

This statue, its partner, and the temple they are from are a key part of understanding the Khmer Empire's culture and the cultural heritage of modern Cambodia. The statues were on display together at the National Museum of Cambodia, with hopes to one day return them to their original site.

Paula K. Priebe

See also: Antiquities and Cultural Objects, Theft of; Transnational, Global, and International Crime

Further Reading

Mackenzie, Simon, and Tess Davis. 2014. "Temple Looting in Cambodia: Anatomy of a Statue Trafficking Network." *British Journal of Criminology* 54 (5): 722–740.

Mashberg, Tom and Ralph Blumenthal. 2012. "Mythic Warrior Is Captive in Global Art Conflict." *New York Times*, February 28. Accessed January 21, 2019. https://www.nytimes.com/2012/02/29/arts/design/sothebys-caught-in-dispute-over-prized-cambodian-statue.html.

Velioglu, Ece, Anne Laure Bandle, and Marc-André Renold. 2014. *Khmer Statue—Cambodia and Sotheby's and the United States*. Geneva: Art-Law Centre, University of Geneva. Accessed January 14, 2019. https://plone.unige.ch/art-adr/cases-affaires/khmer-statue-2013-cambodia-and-sotheby2019s-and-the-united-states.

Camorra

Camorra is an Italian organized crime group (OCG) that originated in Campania, a region of Southern Italy, in the early 19th century. Since then, it has matured in terms of structural resilience, territorial control, and illegal profit making. Camorra has engaged in a variety of crimes, including but not limited to extortion, drug trafficking, and counterfeiting. It has used violence and bribery to further its criminal and legitimate activities.

In the 20th century, Camorra became active not only in Italy but also in other European countries and the Americas. The U.S. government identified Camorra as one of the four most threatening OCGs in 2011 (White House 2011). According to an Italian research center, Camorra's annual income was almost \$4.9 billion in 2013 (Transcrime 2013).

HISTORY

The origins of Camorra go back to 1863, when Marc Monnier, an Italian Swiss scholar, published the first historical-sociological analysis of the criminal organization. Camorra spread in Naples, Caserta, and other areas of the Campania region between 1800 and 1900, mostly recruiting members from the lower class.

Belonging to a lower class, members of Camorra were not only involved in illegal activities, but they also provided basic goods and services to the population, such as sharing stolen goods, redistributing illicit revenues, and administering justice when the state was either unable or unwilling to resolve disputes or sanction those who disturbed the public order. Through this fundamental community function, Camorra quickly became an integral part of the Italian society and gained public support and social respect.

During the Bourbon Restoration (1814–1830), Camorra assumed a fixed three-layered hierarchical structure. The first level was represented by *picciotto d'onore* who committed petty crime. After one year, *picciotto d'onore* could undergo a test of loyalty and courage and, if successfully passed, would be raised in the rank to *picciotto di sgarro*. After another examination of courage and service to the organization, *picciotto di sgarro* could be promoted to the leadership level and become a *camorrista* (Monnier 1863). Over time, this rigid hierarchy transformed into a more fluid and less centrally coordinated structure, which was in part an outcome of Camorra's expansion outside the Campania region.

Other changes took place after the defeat of the Liberal Party in the 1848 Spring of Nations, when the Liberals realized that they needed support of the masses to be able to overthrow the king. They established an agreement with Camorra, whereby camorristi would generate political support for the Liberal Party in exchange for political patronage and seats in the government.

Following the Italian unification in 1861, the government introduced repressive measures against Camorra, attempting to weaken its influence on the society. By doing so, in the 1901 Naples elections, Camorra-supported candidates were defeated. Losing power, many camorristi decided to leave for the United States.

During the era of fascism (1922–1943), as Camorra's influence on society was still strong, the Italian government implemented several attempts to suffocate it. Although some actions against Camorra were successful, the organization was not completely eradicated. The dramatic poverty conditions after World War II (1939–1945) affected the development of the black market, and many people's survival depended on it. Poverty and the power vacuum during these years created a favorable environment for Camorra's empowerment and enrichment. During the 1960s, Italy's rapid economic development further facilitated Camorra's business and trade. The growth of Camorra's power and influence continued through the 1970s as it launched international drug trafficking operations with a hub in Naples (Barbagallo 2010).

In 1982, the Rognoni-La Torre law considered only groups such as Cosa Nostra and 'Ndrangheta as organized crime. In 2010, however, the Italian government expanded the list to include Camorra as an organized crime group. Since then, the Italian government enacted the "anti-mafia package" in Decree Law no. 4 of February 4, 2010, to fight Italian criminal organizations more efficiently and established the National Agency for the Management and Use of the Assets Seized and Confiscated from Organized Crime. These steps allowed seizing illicit assets in the amount of €18.8 billion between 1992 and 2015 (Il Sole 24 ORE 2016), with over €1 billion worth of assets from Camorra during 2014 and 2015 (Barbagallo 2010).

ACTIVITIES AND ECONOMIC IMPACT

Contemporary Camorra is structured horizontally, with clans and families linked to each other in the form of alliances or cartels. The main feature of Camorra's structure is the flexibility of its clans and the violence with which they act to discipline members. As result of this fluid and highly coordinated structure, Camorra clans can act independently of each other.

Camorristi have been involved in a range of illegal activities, such as drug trafficking, arms trafficking, extortion and usury, prostitution, public procurement fraud, and money laundering, with a total business estimate of €12.5 billion per year (Eurispes 2008). These data are incomplete, however, because they exclude two other key sectors of Camorra's income, namely counterfeiting and illegal toxic waste. Furthermore, Camorra has infiltrated public institutions, municipalities, and health companies.

The huge amount of money derived mainly from drug trafficking and *pizzo* (extortion payments demanded from small businesses) is reinvested through their firms in other sectors, such as earthmoving services and concrete. Only in Italy, mafia revenues derived from money laundering, counterfeit and contraband cigarettes represent 12.4 percent of the country's GDP (U.S. Department of State 2016). Environmental crimes and the trafficking of toxic waste provide Camorra with additional profits. Given this magnitude of harm, Camorra, as well other Italian criminal organizations, have had a destructive effect on efficiency of governance and economic performance (Pinotti 2015).

The repertoire of Camorra's criminal activities is broad and transnational. Foreign countries provide logistics and transit bases to manage activities (Scaglione 2016). In the European Union (especially Spain and United Kingdom) and North and South America, Camorra has entered agreements with other criminal groups to facilitate cigarette smuggling, money laundering, and drug trafficking. Camorra clans have skillfully used the most advanced technologies and benefited from the free market and the global financial system. In doing so, the organization has posed serious risks to society's well-being and menaced international security.

Francesca M. Calamunci

See also: 'Ndrangheta; Organized Crime

Further Reading

Barbagallo, Francesco. 2010. *Storia della Camorra.* Roma and Bari: Editori Laterza.

Eurispes. 2008. *"Rapporto Italia 2008." Eurispes.* Rome: Institute of Political, Economic and Social Studies. Accessed January 14, 2019. http://www.eurispes.eu/content/rapporto-italia-2008.

Il Sole 24 ORE. 2016. "Un patrimonio nelle mani della Mafia. Dal 1992 al 2015 la DIA ha sequestrato oltre 18,8 miliardi." Il Sole 24 ORE, February 2. Accessed January 14, 2019. http://www.infodata.ilsole24ore.com/2016/02/02/un-patrimonio-nelle-mani-della-mafia-dal-1992-al-2015-la-dia-ha-sequestrato-oltre-188-miliardi.

Monnier, Marco.1863. *La Camorra. Notizie storiche raccolte e documentate.* Firenze: G. Barbèra Editore.

Pinotti, Paolo. 2015. "The Economic Costs of Organized Crime: Evidence from Southern Italy." *Economic Journal* 125 (586): 203–232.

Scaglione, Attilio. 2016. "Cosa Nostra and Camorra: Illegal Activities and Organizational Structures." *Global Crime* 17 (1): 60–78.

Transcrime. 2013. "Gli Investimenti delle Mafia." Transcrime for Ministry of Interior (PON sicurezza, 2007–2013), Milan: Transcrime. Accessed January 14, 2019. http://www.transcrime.it/pubblicazioni/progetto-pon-sicurezza-2007-2013.

U.S. Department of State. 2016. "Jurisdictions of Primary Concern: Italy." *2016 International Narcotics Control Strategy Report*. Vol. 2. Accessed January 14, 2019. https://www.state.gov/j/inl/rls/nrcrpt/2016/vol2/253411.htm.

White House. 2011. "Strategy to Combat Transnational Organized Crime." Washington, D.C. Accessed January 14, 2019. https://obamawhitehouse.archives.gov/administration/eop/nsc/transnational-crime.

Cartel Organization

When considering all distribution groups as part of a larger organization of drug smugglers, one finds an example of this formal hierarchy in the former Columbian trafficking groups of the Medellín and Cali Cartels. During this era, drug smuggling operations had clear leadership positions in charge of various functions in addition to a clearly defined area of control over which they ruled (Filippone 1994).

During the era of the Medellín and Cali Cartels, there was a formal hierarchy where there was a clear leadership in charge of various functions in addition to a clearly defined area of control over which they ruled. More recently, drug trafficking operates more as an organized network of connected units (Williams 1998). It is extraordinarily diffuse, much like Al Qaeda, which contributes to fear that the organization sows, as its power seems limitless due to the influence and prevalence of autonomous cells in different sectors of society. This also makes it difficult for authorities to identify and pursue them (Kuan 2010).

ORGANIZATIONAL STRUCTURE

Cartel Bosses

A cartel boss, drug lord, or kingpin is the person that controls and leads the network and operation, which is often divided by territory. In contrast to notorious drug lords such as Pablo Escobar and El Chapo, current cartel bosses control smaller operations to reduce the risk of apprehension and ensure the continuity of business over time.

External Connections

Drug cartels have been linked to organizations such as Hezbollah (Bargent 2016), the Revolutionary Armed Forces of Colombia (FARC), Central American gangs, and political parties in Latin America for different purposes, such as money laundering, financing, and protection.

Staff

In this respect, drug cartels operate like a regular enterprise and hire standard positions, such as accountants and legal advisers, and other specialty jobs, such as arms dealers, judges, policemen, and hit men, to carry out their operations.

Production Centers and Sales Channels

The drug cartels' supply chain is often compared to big box stores like Walmart, in the sense that they are a "monopsony," or the only buyers in the market. Drug cartels often have exclusive relationships with coca leaf farmers that allow them to maintain prices despite any disruption in the cultivation process (Narconomics 2016). Often, drug cartels either own or outsource clandestine laboratories to manufacture the drugs to be distributed. For distribution, drug cartels use different channels, such as gangs, mafias, and other criminal organizations, as well as small vendors that target both high-income and low-income markets.

Outsourced Services

Following a decentralized business model, drug cartels outsource many services needed for their operations, such as communication, private security and militias, and vehicles. At a local level, drug cartels use small cafeterias and produce stores to provide food for their personnel, which also generates a deeper connection with people and ensures protection in their territories.

CARTEL PROPAGANDA

As a result of governmental pressure, cartels evolved from criminal organizations to organizations with capabilities to conduct intelligence, enforcement, and propaganda operations. Propaganda is mostly associated with Mexican drug cartels, who have introduced the "narco" concept: the narco-culture, narco-saints, intimidation tactics, and intent to control the media. The use of propaganda is also intended to create fear among rivaling cartels and the state, to defend their plazas, and to provide a warning sign for those who cross their path (Guevara 2013).

An element that has highlighted narco-culture is the popularity of films, books, soap operas, and series dedicated to drug trafficking and notorious drug lords in the last decades. From Oscar-nominated movies like *Sicario*, Netflix series like *Narcos*, and best-seller novels like *The Cartel*, depictions of this trade have been mainstreamed around the world. In a recent case, Joaquín Guzmán Loera, known as "El Chapo," reached out to known actors such as Sean Penn and Kate del Castillo—who played a female drug boss in the series *La Reina del Sur*—to give an exclusive interviews to *Rolling Stone* magazine in an attempt to provide an insider look to his views on drug trafficking. It was also revealed that El Chapo promised the exclusive film rights of his story to Ms. del Castillo during this meeting—all of this while being on the run from the authorities (Penn 2016).

But drug cartels are most notorious for using the music industry for propaganda. The most common way is through "narcocorridos" (drug ballads), a widely known Mexican musical style that glamorizes the life and troubles of drug traffickers. Musicians in this genre have accounted for the common practice of cartels requesting and paying for this type of song to be written about them (Hastings 2013). Cartels also invest in the music industry by financing singers as a way to launder their money through their record production and sales. Singing narcocorridos from a rival cartel or the refusal to launder money has resulted in several singers of this genre to be killed under mysterious circumstances, often linked to drug trafficking (Burnett 2009).

Aida Portillo

See also: Cali Cartel; Central American Gangs; Colombian Drug Cartels; Gulf Cartel; Medellín Cartel; Sinaloa Cartel

Further Reading

Bargent, James. 2016. "DEA Operation Reveals Hezbollah-Colombia Connection." *InSight Crime*, October 12. Accessed January 13, 2019. https://www.insightcrime.org/news/brief/dea-operation-reveals-hezbollah-colombia-connection.

Burnett, John. 2009. "Narcocorridos: Ballads of the Mexican Cartels." NPR Music. October 10. Accessed January 13, 2019. https://www.npr.org/2009/10/10/113664067/narcocorridos-ballads-of-the-mexican-cartels.

Filippone, R. (1994). "The Medellín Cartel: Why We Can't Win the Drug War." *Studies in Conflict and Terrorism* 17: 323–344.

Guevara, America Y. 2013. "Propaganda in Mexico's Drug War." *Journal of Strategic Security* 6 (3 Suppl.): 131–151. Accessed January 14, 2019. https://scholarcommons.usf.edu/jss/vol6/iss5/17/.

Hastings, Deborah. 2013. " 'Narcocorridos,' the Popular Latin Music Styled After American Hip Hop, Bring About Bloodshed and Grammy Wins." *New York Daily News*, December 17. Accessed January 14, 2019. http://www.nydailynews.com/news/world/performers-narcocorridos-sell-arenas-u-s-mexico-generate-millions-sales-songs-romanticizing-drug-lords-beheadings-violent-drug-ballads-win-grammys-article-1.1536307.

Kuan, Cliff. 2010. "Infographic of the Day: The Power Structure of a Mexican Drug Cartel." *Fast Company*, May 11. Accessed January 14, 2019. https://www.fastcompany.com/1700431/infographic-day-power-structure-mexican-drug-cartel.

" 'Narconomics': How the Drug Cartels Operate Like Wal-Mart and McDonald's." 2016. *Fresh Air*. National Public Radio, February 15. Accessed January 14, 2019. https://www.npr.org/2016/02/15/466491812/narconomics-how-the-drug-cartels-operate-like-wal-mart-and-mcdonalds.

Penn, Sean. 2016. "El Chapo Speaks: A Secret Visit with the Most Wanted Man in the World." *Rolling Stone*, January 10. Accessed January 14, 2019. https://www.rollingstone.com/politics/politics-news/el-chapo-speaks-40784.

Williams, P. 1998. "The Nature of Drug-Trafficking Networks." *Current History* 97: 154–159.

Central American Gangs

Central American gangs, or *maras*, refers to the criminal organizations that operate in the territory of Guatemala, Honduras, and El Salvador, also known as the

"Northern Triangle." The reach of Central American gangs also extends to Mexico, the United States, and Italy. The current concept of maras differs from the youth gangs, or *pandillas*, that existed in the 1960s and 1970s in Central America because of its transnational origins and correlation with migratory patterns (Does 2013). The region's largest gangs are Mara Salvatrucha, or MS-13, and MS-18, or Barrio 18, which are estimated to have approximately 85,000 members in total.

ORIGIN

Guatemala and El Salvador experienced the longest and second-longest civil wars in Latin American history, from 1960 to 1996 and from 1980 to 1992, respectively, conflicts that caused thousands of Central Americans to leave their home countries, migrating up north, especially (but not exclusively) to Los Angeles in the United States.

The need to defend their territory and to feel included became the perfect environment for gangs to emerge and grow in size. M-18 was founded in 1960, initially by Mexican immigrants, but it developed due to the influx of migrants from El Salvador and Guatemala. The Mara Salvatrucha was created in the mid-1980s by another wave of Salvadoran migrants to compete with MS-18, and since then, the two gangs have become rivals. As a consequence of more restrictive immigration laws, such as the Illegal Immigration Reform and Immigrant Responsibility Act (IIRIRA) passed in 1996, the U.S. government has deported tens of thousands of gang members (Does 2013).

Many of the deported, who were born or brought up in United States, found it difficult to adjust in Central America and continued with their L.A. gang culture. The gangs evolved a culture of tattoos, brutal rites of initiation, extortion, crime, and drug trafficking. In contrast, Nicaragua has very little presence of gangs, despite being the poorest country in the region. This was partly because the Sandinista movement had better poverty policies, community, and national police programs. Also, Nicaragua did not receive as many deportees from the United States because most Nicaraguans immigrated to Miami, where most received refugee status (Viswanathan 2018).

ORGANIZATIONAL STRUCTURE AND OPERATIONS

Gangs concentrate and carry out their operations in low-income areas that are vulnerable due to poverty and lack of access to education and services. Their power is so great that those communities have become isolated and inaccessible even for police and military enforcement. After a wave of massive imprisonments in the 2000s, gang leaders were also running their businesses from prison.

The hierarchy is loosely divided into two levels, "Youngers" and "Olders." The lengths to which a potential new member is prepared to go to join the gang highlights their potential to climb the hierarchy. Initiation rituals to enter gangs are extreme and violent. Declarations from former gang members recount eating dog excrement and robbing or killing a person as some of the requirements to join a gang. Although poverty and the lack of opportunity are strong reasons why young people join gangs, the fear factor is another element to consider. In vulnerable areas, having no gang affiliation means a lack of protection that the gang offers and may be perceived as being untrustworthy ("Inside the Dark World" 2011). In some cases, the refusal to join a gang could mean death for the person or a family member.

Currently, 90 percent of the documented cocaine that flows into the United States passes through Central America. Drug cartels often partner with gangs to transport and distribute narcotics, which is one of the ways in which they finance their operations. In addition to the drug trade, gangs also profit from extortion, kidnapping, human trafficking, and smuggling.

The Northern Triangle has become the epicenter of extortions. Statistics show that Salvadorans pay an estimated $400 million annually in extortion fees; followed by Hondurans, who pay an estimated $200 million; and Guatemalans, who pay an estimated $61 million. These figures may be higher given that extortion is one of the most underreported crimes. Public transportation is one of the most affected sectors, with buses and taxis annually paying an estimated $25 million in Honduras and $34 million in El Salvador. Small businesses in El Salvador are also hard hit, paying $30 million monthly to criminal organizations in extortion payments (Dudley and Lohmuller 2015).

TURF WARS

The MS-13 and Barrio 18 gangs regularly fight over territorial control of cities, towns, and local drug markets in El Salvador to increase influence and profits, which causes a lot of violence. They fight for control of territory and of community members to extort. In this sense, killing both rival gang members and civilians with brutal methods is a way of communicating and reaffirming leadership. As of 2005, there are two factions of the Barrio 18 gang: the Revolucionarios and the Sureños. According to several interviews, as the smallest and weakest of the groups, the Revolucionarios are the most volatile, and they have ramped up violence to stake their place in the underworld (Kinosian, Albaladejo, and Haugaard 2016).

The other antagonists for gangs in the region are national governments and institutions. During the 2000s, all countries from the Northern Triangle opted for establishing "Iron Fist" policies against gangs, which resulted in mass incarcerations, prison overcrowding, and an increase in violence. In 2012, El Salvador's government negotiated a truce with gangs to reduce the homicide rates between 2012 and 2013. The truce was rejected by a later government, and all public officials that were part of the negotiations are now being prosecuted (Arce 2016).

Aida Portillo

See also: Mara Salvatrucha (MS-13) Organization

Further Reading

Arce, Alberto. 2016. "El Salvador Throws Out Gang Truce and Officials Who Put It in Place." *New York Times.* Last updated May 20, 2016. Accessed January 13, 2019.

https://www.nytimes.com/2016/05/21/world/americas/el-salvador-throws-out-gang-truce-and-officials-who-put-it-in-place.html.

Does, Antonia. 2013. "The Construction of the Maras: Between Politicization and Securitization." Geneva, Switzerland: Graduate Institute Publications. Accessed January 13, 2019. http://books.openedition.org/iheid/716.

Dudley, Steven, and Michael Lohmuller. 2015. "Northern Triangle Is World's Extortion Hotspot." *InSight Crime.* Last updated July 1, 2015. Accessed January 14, 2019. https://www.insightcrime.org/news/brief/northern-triangle-world-extortion-hotspot.

"Inside the Dark World of the Gang Initiation Ceremonies." 2011. *Independent UK.* Last updated August 13, 2011. Accessed January 14, 2019. https://www.independent.co.uk/news/uk/crime/inside-the-dark-world-of-the-gang-initiation-ceremonies-2336868.html.

Kinosian, Sarah, Angelika Albaladejo, and Lisa Haugaard. 2016. "El Salvador's Gang Violence: Turf Wars, Internal Battles and Life Defined by Invisible Borders." *Latin America Working Group.* Last updated February 10, 2016. Accessed January 14, 2019. http://www.lawg.org/action-center/lawg-blog/69-general/1579-el-salvadors-gang-violence-turf-wars-internal-battles-and-life-defined-by-invisible-borders.

Labrador, Rocio Clara, and Danielle Renwick. 2018. "Central America's Violent Northern Triangle." *Council of Foreign Relations.* Last updated on June 26, 2018. Accessed January 14, 2019. https://www.cfr.org/backgrounder/central-americas-violent-northern-triangle.

Viswanathan, R. 2018. "What Lies behind Central America's Gang Violence." *The Wire.* Last updated May 9, 2018. Accessed January 14, 2019. https://thewire.in/world/what-lies-behind-central-americas-gang-violence.

Charleston, South Carolina, Church Attack (2015)

On Wednesday evening, June 17, 2015, nine churchgoers attending a Bible study session at Emanuel African Methodist Episcopal (AME) Church in Charleston, South Carolina, were killed in an outburst of extremist violence. The assailant, Dylann Roof, became the first person to receive a death sentence for a federal hate crime.

The shooting occurred at a church that serves as a place of pride in Southern black history. Emanuel AME Church is one of the oldest black congregations in the South, dating back two centuries. Roof walked into Mother Emanuel, as the church is known, and asked for the preacher. He was directed to a room where Reverend Clementa Pinckney was holding a Bible study session. After sitting quietly with the group as they discussed the Gospel of Mark, Roof took advantage of the ending benediction when the parishioners' eyes were closed to pull from his fanny pack a .45-caliber Glock semiautomatic pistol. According to witnesses, he told the minister and parishioners, "You are raping our women and taking over our country" (Pérez-Peña 2017). Roof shot and killed nine people, including Rev. Pinckney, and then fled the church.

CHARGES AND TRIAL

The U.S. Department of Justice brought 33 charges against Roof—12 counts of committing a hate crime against black victims, 12 counts of obstructing the exercise of religion, and 9 counts of using a firearm to commit murder. The prosecution sought the death penalty in those charges due to Roof's lack of remorse and his animosity toward African Americans (Jarvie 2016). State charges of murder, attempted murder, and weapons violations were also filed, but the federal trial took place first.

Roof confessed to investigators soon after his arrest and claimed he wanted to start a race war, arguing that black corruption was taking over the United States and that there was an epidemic of black-on-white crime. The 21-year-old, ninth-grade dropout, who said his goal was the restoration of white power through violent subjugation, owned a Web site that included an essay on his belief in the danger and inferiority of blacks and the value of segregation (Blinder and Sack 2017; Pérez-Peña 2017). Authorities concluded that Roof's rampage was his own and not coordinated with any organized groups.

At the trial, prosecutors depicted Roof as a racist ideologue who had been radicalized on the Internet, had few friends, no steady work, and had been planning the assault for more than six months—waiting only until he was 21 and old enough to buy the gun.

Roof declined to testify or present any evidence in his defense. Instead, the jury heard Roof's own unapologetic words while watching his two-hour video confession and readings from his online essays and from a journal found in his jail cell.

A federal jury found Roof guilty of all 33 counts. Roof acted as his own lawyer during the penalty stage and denied any psychological incapacity—consistent with his journal comments that he was opposed to psychology as a Jewish invention. He also refused to offer other mitigating factors that might have encouraged jurors to decide on life in prison rather than the death penalty. The jury unanimously sentenced Roof to death, making him the first person in U.S. history to be sentenced to death under the 2009 federal Hate Crimes Prevention Act.

On April 10, 2017, Dylan Roof pleaded guilty to South Carolina state charges of nine counts of murder, three counts of attempted murder, and a related weapons charge in return for a life sentence. The state prosecutor explained that, rather than pursuing a state case after Roof had already been sentenced to death in federal court, it was better to accept his guilty plea to provide an insurance policy to the federal conviction and sentence. The deal had the added benefit, the prosecutor argued, of avoiding further participation in trials by the survivors and the victims' relatives (Zapotosky and Berman 2017). After accepting Roof's guilty plea, the judge imposed nine life sentences plus 90 years.

Philip L. Reichel

See also: Lone Wolf Terrorism; Terrorism, Domestic

Further Reading

Blinder, Alan, and Kevin Sack. 2017. "Dylann Roof Is Sentenced to Death in Charleston Church Massacre." *New York Times*, January 10. Accessed January 21, 2019. https://www.nytimes.com/2017/01/10/us/dylann-roof-trial-charleston.html.

Jarvie, Jenny. 2016. "Jurors Find Dylann Roof Guilty of All 33 Counts in Hate-Crime Shootings at South Carolina Church." *Los Angeles Times*, December 15. Accessed January 14, 2019. http://www.latimes.com/nation/la-na-south-carolina-dylann-roof-20161215-story.html.

Pérez-Peña, Richard. 2017. "Sentenced to Death: A Look at Dylann Roof's Rampage and Its Aftermath." *New York Times*, January 10. January 21, 2019. https://www.nytimes.com/2017/01/10/us/dylann-roof-trial-sentencing-verdict.html.

Zapotosky, Matt, and Mark Berman. 2017. "Charleston Church Shooter Dylann Roof Pleads Guilty in State Court, Avoids Second Death Penalty Trial." *Washington Post*, April 10. Accessed January 14, 2019. https://www.washingtonpost.com/news/post-nation/wp/2017/04/10/charleston-church-shooter-dylann-roof-pleads-guilty-in-state-court-avoids-second-death-penalty-trial.

Child Online Protection Act (COPA)

The Child Online Protection Act is often referred to as COPA. The purpose of COPA was to restrict Internet access to online material deemed harmful to minors. Congress passed COPA, and President Bill Clinton signed it into law in 1998 (H.R. 3783, 105th Cong. 1997–1998). In 2004, the U.S. Supreme Court upheld a lower court ruling that blocked enforcement of COPA, and the act ended without ever being in effect.

COPA was designed to require persons who are engaged in the business of selling or transferring harmful material to restrict its access to minors in various ways, such as requiring a credit card or other proof of age, to avoid government sanctions (Singel 2008). COPA punishments ranged from fines to prison sentences for placing harmful material on Web sites available to minors. COPA attempted to amend previous legislation by refining online content that is censored to minors. Three separate lawsuits led by the American Civil Liberties Union (ACLU) resulted in a permanent injunction against the law in 2009.

HISTORY

With the wide use and expansion of the Internet in the 1990s, Congress had concerns with accessibility of content for minors under age 17, particularly with exposure to sexually explicit materials. Prior to COPA, the Communications Decency Act (CDA) was the first attempt by Congress to regulate online pornography. In 1997, the CDA was found unconstitutional in a 9–0 decision (*Reno v. ACLU*). In that decision, the courts found "government interest in protecting children from harmful materials . . . does not justify an unnecessary broad suppression of speech addressed to adults" (S. Ct. at 2346 H.R. 3783). COPA was often referred to as CDA II and was a direct response to the 1997 decision.

HARMFUL TO MINORS

Though Congress recognized that parents and guardians are primarily responsible for their children, they acknowledged the availability of the Internet outside the home. Members of Congress stated that they were concerned parents would be unable to monitor materials accessed over the Internet. Congress suggested that protecting minors from harmful online materials that could impact their physical and psychological well-being should be a compelling government interest (Hailperin 1999). Therefore, harmful material was identified as anything that could violate contemporary community standards, which led to constitutional challenges from the ACLU. There was also a short-lived debate over whether the United States should implement a national standard following COPA challenges. Justice Kennedy said that even with such a standard, "the actual standard applied is bound to vary by community nevertheless" and to impose "a particular burden on Internet speech" (Greenhouse 2002, 1).

LITIGATION AND CONSTITUTIONAL CHALLENGES

COPA had a long history of litigation. The ACLU and other opponents of COPA claimed the law would lead to excessive self-censorship (Spinello 2013, chap. 3). The vague definition of what constitutes "harmful material" could allow for the exclusion of any material that appealed to the "prurient interest" and that showed sexual acts or nudity, limiting free speech of adults online. The ACLU won its first federal district court case in 1999, finding the law was too broad in using community standards as its measure of harmful materials. COPA was found to infringe on free speech rights. In 2002, the U.S. Supreme Court remanded the case to the Third Circuit, which stood by the decision that COPA was unconstitutional because it did not satisfy the First Amendment's "least restrictive means" test (*Aschcroft v. ACLU* 535 U.S. 564). Once again, this case was appealed to the Supreme Court.

FINAL COURT RULING

In 2004, the Supreme Court (*Ashcroft v. ACLU* 542 U.S. 656) upheld the district court's order blocking the enforcement of COPA and refused to hear the case again. On March 22, 2007, the district court issued a permanent injunction against COPA (*ACLU v. Gonzales* 2007 WL 861120). The Supreme Court concluded that COPA could inadvertently prevent adults from accessing legal pornography online and that minors could be adequately protected by Internet filtering software (Singel 2008). Ultimately, COPA was found to be a violation of the First Amendment; the debate between minimizing a risk to childhood's innocence and those who see a risk to free speech was decided in 2008 (Hailperin 1999).

Shanell Sanchez

See also: Child Protection and Sexual Predator Punishment Act; Children's Internet Protection Act (CIPA); Children's Online Privacy Protection Act (COPPA); PROTECT Act

Further Reading

Associated Press. 2007. "Judge Strikes Down '98 Law Aimed at Online." *Associated Press*, March 22. Accessed January 14, 2019. http://www.mercurynews.com/2007/03/22/judge-strikes-down-98-law-aimed-at-online-porn.

Greenhouse, Linda. 2002. "Justices Give Reprieve to an Internet Pornography Statute." *New York Times*, May 14. Accessed January 14, 2019. http://www.nytimes.com/2002/05/14/us/justices-give-reprieve-to-an-internet-pornography-statute.html.

Hailperin, Max. 1999. "The COPA Battle and the Future of Free Speech." *Communications of the ACM* 42 (1) (January): 24–25.

Singel, Ryan. 2008. "Child Online Protection Act Overturned." *ABC News*, July 23. Accessed January 14, 2019. http://abcnews.go.com/Technology/AheadoftheCurve/story?id=5428228&page=1.

Spinello, Richard. 2013. *Cyberethics: Morality and Law in Cyberspace*. 5th ed. Burlington, MA: Jones and Bartlett.

Child Pornography, *see* Child Sexual Abuse Material

Child Pornography Prevention Act (CPPA)

The Child Pornography Prevention Act of 1996 (CPPA) was enacted in an effort to protect minors against virtual child pornography and sexual exploitation. This act criminalized the use of computer technology to produce images or create visual depictions that look like children are engaged in sexual acts, even when no children are actually involved. CPPA punishments varied based on the number of offenses and ranged from fines to imprisonment, or both (Miranda 2000). The U.S. Supreme Court found CPPA to be unconstitutional in 2002.

FIRST AMENDMENT AND CHILD PORNOGRAPHY

In 1982, the U.S. Supreme Court held that child pornography is not entitled to protection under the First Amendment (*New York v. Ferber* 458 U.S. 747). This became referred to as the *Ferber* standard. Later, in 1990, *Osborne v. Ohio* (495 U.S. 103) extended the Ferber standard to individuals possessing child pornography. CPPA used similar arguments when creating the act in an attempt to exclude virtual child pornography from constitutional protections.

Arguments in favor of CPPA included concerns that virtual child pornography could be used to seduce children and could lend itself to easier access to children for pedophiles. The ultimate goal was to eliminate child pornography, and then law enforcement could effectively enforce laws and destroy the market (Miranda 2000).

CPPA FOUND UNCONSTITUTIONAL

The controversy before the courts in *Ashcroft v. Free Speech Coalition* was whether the CPPA's language criminalizing the production, distribution, or possession of images that "appear to be" of minors engaging in sexually explicit conduct inappropriately broadens this category of speech that is protected by *Ferber*. CPPA was a content-based restriction on speech, but because the CPPA criminalizes images that do not depict an identifiable child, the U.S. Supreme Court found CPPA to be a significant departure from *Ferber*. Additionally, there was a lack of evidence linking computer-generated images with real harm to children, thus challenging direct harm (Sternberg 2002).

CPPA was overturned by the U.S. Supreme Court in *Ashcroft v. Free Speech Coalition*, 535 US 234 (2002). The Free Speech Coalition argued provisions stated in CPPA were overbroad and vague, thus hindering First Amendment rights. CPPA lacked the link between its prohibitions and obscenity, which violated First Amendment rights.

In the words of one court, "the regulation . . . shifted from defining child pornography in terms of the harm inflicted upon real children to a determination that child pornography was evil in and of itself, whether it involved real children or not" (*Free Speech Coalition v. Reno* 198 F. 3d 1083, 1089 (9th Cir. 1999).

Shanell Sanchez and Christina Lynn Richardson

See also: Child Protection and Sexual Predator Punishment Act; Children's Internet Protection Act (CIPA); Children's Online Privacy Protection Act (COPPA); PROTECT Act

Further Reading

"Excerpts from Opinions in Ruling on the Child Pornography Prevention Act." 2002. *New York Times*, April 17. January 21, 2019. http://www.nytimes.com/2002/04/17/us/excerpts-from-opinions-in-ruling-on-the-child-pornography-prevention-act.html.

Miranda, Anthony. 2001. "Current Developments in the Law: A Survey of Federal Cases Involving the Child Pornography Prevention Act of 1996." *Boston University Publication International Law Journal* 9: 483.

Spinello, Richard. 2013. *Cyberethics: Morality and Law in Cyberspace*. 5th ed. Burlington, MA: Jones and Bartlett.

Sternberg, Sarah. 2001. "The Child Pornography Prevention Act of 1996 and the First Amendment: Virtual Antitheses." *Fordham Law Review* 69 (6) (May): 2783–2823.

Child Protection and Sexual Predator Punishment Act

The Child Protection and Sexual Predator Punishment Act of 1998, often referred to as the Sexual Predators Act (Public Law No: 105-314), prohibits knowingly contacting, or attempting to contact, minors over the Internet for illegal sexual activity, as well as knowingly sending obscene material to a minor over the Internet. This law increased prison sentences under the federal sentencing guidelines, expanded the definition of crimes counted as "prior sexual offenses," made convictions easier to obtain for crimes exploiting minors online, and severely punished an individual that used a computer to intentionally misrepresent one's identity (age, gender, or interests) online. The law has been modified in recent years to keep current with technological changes.

THE ACT

Based on a review of the legislative history, Congress argued the current guidelines were ill equipped to deal with technological advancements. The Sexual

Predators Act of 1998 was a bipartisan effort to increase the penalties for child pornography. The act specifically enhanced sentences if the defendant used a computer with the intent to "persuade, induce, entice, coerce, or facilitate the transport of a child," especially if there was a pattern of activity of predatory behavior. The act created several new crimes involving the distribution of obscenity to a minor, distribution of child pornography for nonfinancial gain, and the dissemination of identifying information about a minor, all in response to reports of previous abuses of the Internet by persons seeking sexual contact with children (Montgomery et al. 2000).

ENHANCED SENTENCES

The act took a "get tough" approach to child pornography, soliciting a minor, and predatory behavior on the Internet. New sanctions often included minimum sentences, with some sentences ranging from fines to life imprisonment. The use of a computer to "persuade, entice, coerce, or facilitate the transport of a child to engage in sexual activity" could be subjected to a fine and imprisonment with a minimum of three years. Additionally, pretrial detention of persons who commit specified sex offenses involving child pornography against a minor could be required. Tougher sentences were to be imposed for anyone found intentionally misrepresenting themselves to a minor or attempting to gain access to a minor via the Internet (Henderson 2005).

One of the amendments in the act instituted a zero-tolerance policy for child pornography, making the possession of any child pornography illegal. The law eliminated the provision that allowed individuals to possess up to two pictures of child pornography (Hutchinson 1998). These changes were important to the ongoing debate of protecting children online, and laws have been consistently revisited to keep current with technology.

Shanell Sanchez

See also: Children's Internet Protection Act (CIPA); PROTECT Act

Further Reading

Christensen, Korey. 2011. "Reforming Attempt Liability Under 18 U.S.C. § 2422(b): An Insubstantial Step Back from *United States v. Rothenberg*." *Duke Law Journal* 61: 693–730. Accessed January 14, 2019. https://scholarship.law.duke.edu/dlj/vol61/iss3/4.

Henderson, Harry. 2005. *Internet Predator*. New York: Facts on File.

Hutchinson, Asa. 1998. "Zero Tolerance for Child Predators." *Congressional Press Releases*, June 15.

Montgomery, Pamela, Kevin Blackwell, Keri Burchfield, John Butcher, Amie Clifford, Alan Dorhoffer, Paul Hofer, Krista Rubin, and Deborah Stevens-Panzer. 2000. "Sentencing Federal Sexual Offenders: Protection of Children from Sexual Predators Act of 1998." *United States Sentencing Commission Report*, February 17. Accessed January 14, 2019. https://www.ussc.gov/sites/default/files/pdf/research-and-publications/working-group-reports/sex-offenses/20000214-child-sex-offenses/SEXPREDRPT.pdf.

Child Sexual Abuse Material

Child sexual abuse material (CSAM) refers to any visual depiction (printed and digital) of sexually explicit conduct involving a minor (usually a person below the age of 18). Production and distribution of the CSAM is generally considered a form of sexual exploitation or sexual abuse of children.

While the term *child pornography* is commonly used in national legislation and the international policy discourse, there is a growing consensus among experts that the term *child sexual abuse material* reflects the harmful nature of pornographic content involving children and risks posed to them more accurately (UNODC 2015; Luxembourg Guidelines 2016). It implies the victimization that is faced by children as they are forced, threatened, or manipulated to participate in the production of pornographic content.

FORMS AND CRIMINALIZATION

The CSAM comes in many forms, ranging from still images (e.g., photographs, negatives, slides, magazines, drawings) to video records (e.g., movies, videotapes, computer disks or files). It depicts a child or children engaged in sexually explicit activity.

While there exists some consensus on criminalizing child pornography on the global level, individual states have adopted different legal positions on artificially generated images or virtual child pornography. Some countries prohibit simulated child pornography produced without the direct involvement of children. They ban modified images of real children, including nonminors made to look younger, and prohibit computer-generated imagery. In contrast, other countries debate on the minimal guarantees of freedom of expression and protection of artistic or scientific merit. From this perspective, freedom of expression may include subjects that can shock or go against established societal values.

For instance, Canadian laws (Canadian Code, Section 163.1) addressing child pornography define it as "a photographic, film, video or other visual representation, whether or not it was made by electronic or mechanical means," that "a person who is or is depicted as being under the age of eighteen years and is engaged in or is depicted as engaged in explicit sexual activity," or "the dominant characteristic of which is the depiction, for a sexual purpose, of a sexual organ or the anal region of a person under the age of eighteen years." In the 2001 case *R. v. Sharpe* (1 SCR 45; 2001), the Supreme Court of Canada interpreted the statute to also include purely fictional materials, which neither depicts real children nor involves them in the production process.

In the United States, pornographic materials are generally considered a form of personal expression and are governed by the First Amendment to the Constitution. Case law, however, suggests that the First Amendment does not apply to obscene materials (e.g., *Miller v. California*, 413 U.S. 15 (1973)). In *Ashcroft v. The Free Speech Coalition* (535 U.S. 234 (2002)), although the prosecutor argued that virtual child pornography could be used by pedophiles to encourage children to participate in sexual activity and "whet their own sexual appetites," thus facilitating the demand for the distribution in child pornography produced with the involvement of actual children, the Supreme Court did not support this position, recognizing that two provisions of the 1996 Child Pornography Prevention Act (CCPA) abridged "the freedom to engage in a substantial amount of lawful speech."

There has been increasing pressure on the Japanese government to regulate child pornography, particularly the popular purely fictional images, such as lolicon, amine, and manga that often feature cartoonlike animated characters that look like children in sexual and sometimes violent contexts.

OBSCENITY CATEGORIZATION

In the United States, the Miller test is often used in court to determine whether speech or expression can be interpreted as "obscene," in which case the First Amendment would not apply. The test includes three parts:

> (a) whether "the average person, applying contemporary community standards" would find that the work, taken as a whole, appeals to the prurient interest . . . ; (b) whether the work depicts or describes, in a patently offensive way, sexual conduct specifically defined by the applicable state law; and (c) whether the work, taken as a whole, lacks serious literary, artistic, political, or scientific value. (*Miller v. California*, 413 U.S. 15 (1973))

The Miller test requires all three elements to be present for finding an image to be falling into the "child pornography" category.

A California district court developed the six-factor Dost test in 1987 (*United States v. Dost*, 636 F. Supp. 828). It is used to distinguish between child pornography and child erotica (nonpornographic material used for sexual arousing that depicts a child) based on the following questions: (1) whether the focal point of the visual depiction is on the child's genitalia or pubic area; (2) whether the setting of the visual depiction is sexually suggestive, that is, in a place or pose generally associated with sexual activity; (3) whether the child is depicted in an unnatural pose, or in inappropriate attire, considering the age of the child; (4) whether the child is fully or partially clothed, or nude; (5) whether the visual depiction suggests sexual coyness or a willingness to engage in sexual activity; (6) whether the visual depiction is intended or designed to elicit a sexual response in the viewer.

In Europe, University College Cork, Ireland, developed the COPINE scale (Combating Paedophile Information Networks in Europe) in 1997. It is a rating system that categorizes the severity of images of child sex abuse. Its main objective is to create an objective measure of the different levels of sexual victimization and distinguish child pornography or CSAM from child erotica and other related images that do not meet the obscenity criteria. It has 10 levels that range from indicative and nudist images to erotic posing and explicit erotic posing to assault. The COPINE scale has been used by law enforcement (e.g., London Metropolitan Police) and in court. For instance, in the 2002 case *Regina v. Oliver*, the Court of Appeal of England and Wales (1 Cr App R 28 CA; 2003) adopted the SAP scale—a five-point scale based on the COPINE scale.

PRODUCTION AND DISTRIBUTION

The fast-paced expansion of the Internet and information communication technologies (ICTs) has considerably contributed to the growth and expansion of the CSAM. Child sexual abuse images are made available online through peer-to-peer networks (P2P) and social networking Web sites, gaming devices, and even mobile apps. Offenders of child pornography may also use the Internet to recruit victims, advertise to potential clients, and sell pornographic images. Organized criminal groups often use sophisticated technology, such as various encryption techniques and anonymous networks on the "darknet."

One of the most contentious trends in the production and distribution of the CSAM is user-generated child pornography, in other words, self-created and self-published sexually explicit materials, which are distributed online, often for free. "Sexting" is one of the forms of such content. It typically involves minors consensually producing and distributing (willingly or under psychological manipulation) sexually suggestive images or videos, often images of themselves. Common platforms where such content can be found include blogs, videos, podcasts, forums, and social media. Prosecution of young people under child pornography offenses has increasingly been the subject of public, media, and academic debates.

RESPONSES

Countries and international organizations have actively promoted universal criminalization of the production and distribution of the CSAM. Internationally, there are several UN conventions (e.g., United Nations Convention on the Rights of the Child and the Optional Protocol on the Sale of Children, Child Prostitution, and Child Pornography and the United Nations Convention against Transnational Organized Crime and the Protocol to Prevent, Suppress, and Punish Trafficking in Persons, Especially Women and Children) that were adopted by countries with the aim to protect children from exploitation and abuse.

On the national level, legal responses vary considerably in the way they address various forms of child abuse and exploitation (UNODC 2015). Although many states criminalize acts such as production and distribution of the CSAM, they may differ on the concrete elements of these crimes and definitions of a "child." Additionally, not all governments have provided the appropriate level of legal protection to children who are sexually abused online, such as "cyberenticement" and "online grooming," which often lead to the production of the CSAM.

INTERPOL's activities contributed to the capacity of law enforcement of member states to identify CSAM content and arrest offenders. For instance, INTERPOL's International Child Sexual Exploitation (ICSE) database works as an intelligence and investigative tool, allowing specialized law enforcement units to share data related to child sexual exploitation investigations with colleagues in other countries. This database is put together by experts who analyze the digital, visual, and audio content of photographs and videos with the aim to identify CSAM content and locate the victims.

The private sector often assists INTERPOL in developing advanced digital forensics and applying appropriate technologies to detect and investigate ICT-facilitated CSAM. Technologies such as Microsoft's PhotoDNA are vital in helping law enforcement quickly identify CSAM images. This tool computes hash values of images, video, and audio files to identify alike images and can be understood as "fingerprints for files" (INTERPOL 2018). Additionally, INTERPOL has developed a list of domains containing child pornography (the "Worst of" List) and shared it with ISPs, which could then block the images under concern and deny service to law-breaking customers. Thanks to ISPs joining forces with law enforcement, the filtering of the Internet from child pornography should become more feasible. In some jurisdictions (e.g., United States), ISPs and domain hosts are required to report any identified CSAM to the police, with noncompliance being a punishable offense.

Yuliya Zabyelina

See also: Child Pornography Prevention Act (CPPA); INTERPOL; UN Convention against Transnational Organized Crime; UN Protocol to Prevent, Suppress, and Punish Trafficking in Persons, Especially Women and Children

Further Reading

Crofts, Thomas, Murray Lee, Alyce McGovern, and Sanja Milivojevic. 2015. "Sexting as Child Pornography." In *Sexting and Young People*, edited by Thomas Croft et al., 45–55. London: Palgrave Macmillan.

INTERPOL. 2018. "Towards a Global Indicator: On Unidentified Victims in Child Sexual Exploitation Material." Technical Report. Accessed May 13, 2018. https://www.interpol.int/Media/Files/Crime-areas/Crimes-against-children/Technical-report-Towards-a-Global-Indicator-on-Unidentified-Victims-in-Child-Sexual-Exploitation-Material-February-2018

Luxembourg Guidelines. 2016. "Terminology Guidelines for the Protection of Children from Sexual Exploitation and Sexual Abuse." Interagency Working Group on Sexual Exploitation of Children. Accessed May 9, 2018. http://luxembourgguidelines.org/english-version.

United Nations Office on Drugs and Crime (UNODC). 2015. *Study on the Effects of New Information Technologies on the Abuse and Exploitation of Children.* Vienna: UNODC.

Children's Internet Protection Act (CIPA)

Enacted April 20, 2001, the Children's Internet Protection Act of 2001 (CIPA) is a Congressional bill that requires K–12 schools and public libraries to implement Internet safety policies and install Internet filtering software to remain eligible for government funding that discounts the cost of providing telecommunication services. The safety policies require that these public institutions must address a variety of topics, including how the institution will prevent access to obscene materials; the safety of minors when using electronic communication; minors disclosing, using, or sharing personal information about themselves and others; and how the institution will prevent users from accessing harmful material.

This bill was motivated by research conducted in the late 1990s that found children did not have the ability to understand the ramifications of revealing personal information online, the material they were accessing, or the concept of "stranger danger" via Internet communication. The research also highlighted parents' inability to successfully monitor their children's Internet usage due to a lack of computer skills, time, or awareness of potential dangers (Montgomery and Pasnik 1996). In 1996, both the Federal Trade Commission (FTC) and the Electronic Privacy Information Center (EPIC) testified in front of Congress in favor of enacting laws that protect children and their information while online.

In 2002, the American Library Association challenged the law, arguing that Congress does not have the authority to require institutions to censor Internet content to receive federal funding. The U.S. Supreme Court ruled in 2003, in *United States v. American Library Assn., Inc.* (539 US 194), that CIPA does not violate the First Amendment because the sites and material can be unblocked for authorized adult users.

COMPLIANCE

Schools or libraries that wish to receive funding from the Universal Service Discount Program, E-Rate, must be compliant to the six basic rules set out by the FCC: applicability, timing, filtering, Internet safety policy, certification, and enforcement:

- Applicability: CIPA compliance is required for any school or library that provides Internet access, Internet connections, and basic maintenance of Internet connections.
- Timing: Full CIPA compliance has been required since 2002 and is required by the second year of funding. Applicants applying for E-Rate funding for the first time do not have to be in full CIPA compliance when applying. However, the institution must prove they are "undertaking actions" to become compliant by the second year of their funding.
- Filtering: The institution must show that all computers with Internet access have a "technology protection measure" or Internet filter installed that does not allow access to pornography or images deemed obscene, harmful, or inappropriate for minors. The content of what is blocked is at the discretion of the school board, local education agency, library, or other authority.
- Internet Safety Policy: The policy must address the filtering methods described above and how the institution will supervise the online activities of minors, including direct electronic communications. This policy must then be publicly presented at least once to review the proposed new standards.
- Certification: Institutions must annually certify CIPA compliance during E-Rate funding applications by filing FCC Form 486. This form and the application documents must be kept by the institution for a minimum of five years after the end of the funding year.

- Enforcement: There is no specific enforcement rule. However, schools or libraries that do not prove certification are not eligible for funding. If the certification is found to be inaccurate, the funding will be reimbursed by the school or library.

CIPA does not apply to schools or libraries receiving discounts only for telecommunication services. Additionally, CIPA does not require institutions to track the Internet usage of minors, but simply to monitor it. Lastly, the filtering software may be disabled by an authorized adult for research purposes or other lawful reasons conducted by another legal adult.

CURRENT TRENDS

In the last decade, several additional bills have been proposed to Congress to further protect minors on the Internet. These include the Deleting Online Predators Act 2007 and the Protecting Children in the 21st Century Act. The second act was an amendment to CIPA that requires schools receiving E-Rate funding to provide students with education on appropriate online behavior via social media and cyberbullying awareness and response.

Cheyenne Reyes Selby

See also: Child Online Protection Act (COPA); Children's Online Privacy Protection Act (COPPA)

Further Reading

American Library Association. n.d. "The Children's Internet Protection Act (CIPA)." January 14, 2019. http://www.ala.org/advocacy/advleg/federallegislation/cipa.

Federal Communications Commission. 2001. "Children's Internet Protection Act (CIPA)." Last modified September 8, 2017. January 14, 2019. https://www.fcc.gov/consumers/guides/childrens-internet-protection-act.

Montgomery, Kathryn, and Shelley Pasnik. 1996. *Web of Deception: Threats to Children from Online Marketing.* Washington, D.C.: Center for Media Education

Children's Online Privacy Protection Act (COPPA)

The Children's Online Privacy Protection Act (COPPA) is a child protection statute for Internet sites and has provided the baseline for children's privacy in the United States since 1998. COPPA should not be confused with the Child Online Protection Act (COPA), which was introduced around the same time but failed to become law.

COPPA is meant to give parents control over the online collection, use, or disclosure of personal information given by their children. The law, enforced by the Federal Trade Commission (FTC), imposes strict parental notice and consent requirements for operators of Web sites or online services if they have actual knowledge that they are collecting personal information online from a child under 13 years of age. Children ages 13 and under were targeted because younger children are particularly vulnerable to overreaching by marketers and may not understand the safety and privacy issues created by the online collection of personal information. The commission issued an amended rule on December 19, 2012, and it took effect on July 1, 2013 (FTC 2015). If an organization or person was found in violation of COPPA, financial sanctions can be enforced.

GOALS

COPPA is designed to put parents and guardians in control of what information is shared by their children online. The law allows parents to access their child's personal information that is collected online and allows them to review or delete what they choose. Overall, COPPA's primary goal was to maintain confidentiality, security, and integrity of information online sources collected from children. The rationale behind enacting COPPA was that children may not be aware of potential repercussions of providing information to online sites. COPPA only applies to personal information collected from children, not from adults about children. This personal information can include information about themselves, parents, friends, or others. Information provided by children is required to have parental consent and is to remain confidential (64 Fed. Reg. 59888, 59902 n.213).

COPPA places restrictions on commercial Web sites and online services on items such as tablets and mobile applications. Specifically, COPPA directly prohibits unfair or deceptive acts or practices in connection with the collection, use, or disclosure of personal information about children on the Internet. Site operators are required to post a clear and comprehensive online privacy policy about personal information collected from children, provide direct notice to parents, and obtain verifiable parental consent prior to collecting information. Furthermore, site operators are prohibited from disclosing any personal information to third parties, unless it is integral to the site or service, and the disclosure is made clear to the parents.

COPPA REQUIREMENTS

Under COPPA, personal information can include the first and last name of the child; the child's home or physical address; telephone numbers; and online contact information, such as an e-mail address or Social Security number (FTC 2015). In 2000, the FTA amended the law to include four new categories. These included geolocational information; photos or videos containing a child's image or audio files with the child's voice, screen, or username; and other persistent identifiers that can be used to recognize a user over time and across different online services. These amendments went into effect in 2003. In 2018, the FTA updated COPPA rules to keep with technological changes. COPPA now applies to connected toys and other products intended for children. Further, COPPA has adapted to technological changes in the classroom, where teachers often rely upon technology (Yannella and Szewczyk 2018). Schools, acting in loco parentis, have long been able to provide such consent in educational contexts for children.

COPPA ENFORCEMENT

COPPA gives states and certain federal agencies the authority to enforce compliance with respect to entities over which they have jurisdiction. The FTA allows parents, consumer groups, industry members, and others to submit a complaint if they believe an operator is in violation. The court reserves the right to assess civil penalties, and if found guilty, and violators can be ordered to pay $41,484 per violation. The court can assess penalties based on previous offenses; the number of children involved; the amount and type of personal information collected; how they used the information, if information was shared; and the size of the company.

GLOBAL REQUIREMENTS

Due to the Internet being a global phenomenon, the jurisdiction of COPPA expands beyond the United States' borders. Foreign-based Web sites and online services must comply with COPPA if they are directed to children in the United States or if they knowingly collect personal information from children in the United States. In addition, U.S.-based online services are subject to COPPA jurisdiction, even when collecting information from foreign children (FTC 2015).

Shanell Sanchez and Christina Lynn Richardson

See also: Child Online Protection Act (COPA)

Further Reading

Federal Trade Commission (FTC). 2013. "COPPA Rules and Regulations." *Federal Register*, 78(12). Accessed March 15, 2018. https://www.ftc.gov/system/files/2012-31341.pdf.

Federal Trade Commission (FTC). 2015. "Complying with COPPA." Accessed March 15, 2018. https://www.ftc.gov/tips-advice/business-center/guidance/complying-coppa-frequently-asked-questions#General%20Questions.

Yannella, Philip, and Gregory Szewczyk. March 2018. "FTC Explains Evolution of COPPA in Live Twitter Chat." Accessed March 16, 2018. https://www.natlawreview.com/article/ftc-explains-evolution-coppa-live-twitter-chat.

Chinese Gangland Crime

In China, gangland crime is the most complicated type of organized crime. It has been referred to by various names, including black society organized crime, underworld, or mafia-style crime. During the 1997 revision of China's Criminal Law (People's Republic of China 1979), the basic traits of gangland or underworld organized crime were identified. In 2010, China's Supreme Court, the Supreme People's Procuratorate, and the Department of Public Safety jointly promulgated a memorandum on processing gangland organized crime that explained the basic traits of gangland crime in greater detail.

GANGLAND ORGANIZED CRIME TRAITS

On February 25, 2011, the Eighth Amendment of China's Criminal Law was enacted, and the 2010 memorandum of basic definitions were incorporated as the legal statute (People's Republic of China 1979, Item 294, Article 5). Accordingly, to be legally considered "organized crime," all of these characteristics must be present:

1. Organizational characteristics: the formation of relatively stabilized criminal organization; a certain number of members; clear/visible organizer; leadership; stabilized chief members;
2. Economic characteristics: attained economic benefits via organized criminal or other illegal activities; has strong economic backings and resources to support the organization's activities;
3. Behavioral characteristics: using violence, menacing, or other means; engaging in illegal activities multiple times in organized ways; atrocious bullying behaviors; intimidating civilians;
4. Illegal manipulation characteristics: engaging in illegal or criminal activities or having been harbored and connived under the shelter of governmental officials or employees; playing the tyrant in a certain locality or some particular business lines; forming a chain of illegal manipulation or tremendous negative ramifications; severely sabotaging economic, social, and daily life orders.

ORGANIZATIONAL CHARACTERISTICS

The criminal organizations are stable; have a certain number of participants (generally more than 10 members); have structured organizers, leaders, or backbone/chief members; and have specific division of labors. The organizer can also be the leader or the roles of organizer and leader can be assigned to different persons. There can be one organizer/leader or multiple organizers/leaders. The organizers and leaders are the ones who marshal illegal activities.

Generally, there are multiple numbers of backbone/chief members in this particular organization. They are responsible for routine activities, such as organizational staff management, or the actual commitment of illegal and criminal activities. Together with the organizers and the leaders, they have a high status in the upper tier of the organizational core. From this perspective, this hierarchical system is similar to the mafia-style groups, where the leader's identity is covert. In the implementation, it is usually the backbone/chief members that are the executors of all the specific organizational criminal activities. Those backbone/chief members are senior members of their organization, such as Liu Han, Liu Wei's underworld organization in Sichuan Province. Since 1993, they have established Sichuan Molong Group Company and other division companies. From that, they gradually formed a predominant underworld empire. After 20 years of evolvement, the organization's structure was stabilized, and the backbone/chief members were basically unchanged. That included Liu Han and Liu Wei as organizer and leader, respectively. Tang Xianbing and another eight members were mainstays; Zhang Donghua, Tian Xianwei, and 21 others were general members.

ECONOMIC CHARACTERISTICS

The organization needs economic resources to support its routine activities. The economic resources can be obtained by illegally possessing others' property, such as robbery, theft, extortion, kidnapping, and charging a "protection fee," to name but a few. They can also be achieved by providing illegal services and illicit merchandise trade for profiteering in the way of organizing gambling, drug trafficking, prostitution, smuggling, and other illegal activities. Another way of obtaining economic resources is to invest the illegal revenues into various legal trades, such as commodity wholesale, manufacturing, entertainment, transportation networks, construction, and the like. The illegal money is cleaned. This way, the organization can show evidence of legal income. This seemingly legal economic resource is also disguised and expanded with the advancement of new technology, such as credit card fraud, telecom fraud, Internet fraud, and other intelligent network–facilitated means of illegal activities. Meanwhile, with the money laundry agendas, the leader or organizer can easily escape criminal liability.

BEHAVIORAL CHARACTERISTICS

The underworld organization may have a variety of ways to implement illegal and criminal actions, such as organizing prostitution, trafficking women and children, kidnapping, smuggling, trafficking drugs, and intentional homicide.

ILLEGAL MANIPULATION CHARACTERISTICS

There are two types of illegal manipulations: one is to use the protection of government officials or state functionaries. It is also called "under the protection of umbrella." The other is to play the tyrant in a certain locality or some particular business lines through illegal criminal activities. For example, since 2007, in Henan province, Wei has invited Li, Xing, Liu, Guo, Zhou, and other social dispersers to engage in illegal activities. They gradually formed the gangland organized crime in that region. Whenever or wherever there is a conflict, either economic disputes or neighborhood tort disputes, even in the rural areas, Wei's organization would be there. They did bad things, whatever they wanted. They use these methods to obtain illegal economic benefits, thus maintaining the operation and development of the organization. Illegal manipulation is the most essential characteristic of Chinese gangland organized crime, which is an important aspect of distinction between the underworld organization and other organized crimes.

CONCLUSION

In the judicial practice, to decide whether a criminal organization is gangland organized crime or not, four characteristics are the essentials. The four characteristics are interrelated with each other, and all four must be present. First, no matter what illegal activities the organizations do, these activities must be premeditated. The other three characteristics of the organization are closely related to the first feature. Second, the economic benefits are used to maintain the survival and development of the organization and to support the daily expenditures of the organization, the violent activities and the illegal manipulation expenditures. Third, the commitment of illegal and criminal activities by means of threats and violence is an important manifestation of the illegal manipulation in a certain locality or some particular business lines. Fourth, by organizing illegal activities, the organizations get economic benefits to maintain survival and development issues and achieve the purpose of illegal control. Therefore, the four characteristics of the organization are interrelated and interdependent, which is a holistic entity. Only in the case of the four features mentioned above can a criminal organization be legally identified as a gangland organized crime.

Aili Miao and Qingli Meng

See also: Organized Crime; Transnational, Global, and International Crime

Further Reading

Antonopoulos, Georgios A. 2013. "The Dragon's Shadow: An Introduction to the Special Issue on 'Chinese Organized Crime.'" *Trends in Organized Crime* 16 (1): 1–12.

Lo, Shiu Hing. 2016. *The Politics of Controlling Organized Crime in Greater China.* New York: Routledge, Taylor & Francis Group.

People's Republic of China. 1979. "Criminal Law of the People's Republic of China." (2011 amended version). January 14, 2019. https://www.cecc.gov/resources/legal-provisions/criminal-law-of-the-peoples-republic-of-china.

Wang, Peng. 2013. "The Rise of the Red Mafia In China: A Case Study of Organised Crime and Corruption in Chongqing." *Trends in Organized Crime* 16 (1): 49–73.

Colombian Drug Cartels

Although there is not a single definition of "drug cartel," they can be considered to be organizations that promote, control, or be significantly involved in drug trafficking operations. Nonetheless, the United Nations Convention against Transnational Organized Crime defines an organized crime group as "a structured group of three or more persons, existing for a period of time and acting in concert with the aim of committing one or more serious or offenses . . . in order to obtain, directly or indirectly, a financial or other material benefit" (UNODC 2018).

HISTORY

Cartels are organized in many ways. For instance, in the 1990s, the first generation of Colombian drug cartels—the Medellín and Cali Cartels—followed a top-to-bottom model; they were hierarchical and vertically organized. When those cartels ended, drug organizations had to evolve, in part because of the changes in the global market and in part because of the pressure of the authorities, especially the coalition between the Columbian and U.S. governments.

The second generation was characterized by the remnants of the Cali and Medellín Cartels, the Norte del Valle Cartel, and the United Self-Defense Forces of Colombia (AUC). Federations and alliances were common among cartels after 1995; for instance, the Norte del Valle Cartel partnered with AUC for protection and to combat the Revolutionary Armed Forces of Colombia (FARC) after AUC emerged as a self-defense right-wing paramilitary group. Although FARC and AUC controlled the rural cultivation and production, there was not a single leader or group in control of every step of the trafficking process. Thus, "cartelitos" controlled some activities and worked with the larger groups.

The lack of leadership spread more violence in cities and rural areas; while the head of the cartels were being defined, sheer force of power and murders were the modus operandi of the criminals. The second generation not only expanded their activities—into robbery, extortion, and kidnapping—but they also increased their relationships with Colombian authorities and bureaucracy, helping in the expansion and safeguarding of their power. Criminal organizations funded political campaigns, creating a win-win situation: politicians would get into power, while drug traffickers would control the underworld and profit from the lack of control.

The third generation was defined by the demobilization of AUC and the capture of the Norte del Valle leaders, leading to the era of BACRIM (criminal bands). Similar to the second generation, there is not a single figure of leadership or a standardized process of trafficking. They are criminal networks composed of diverse independent cells, with almost no connections between each other, but part of a criminal syndicate—Rastrojos, Oficina de Envigado, or Urabeños. Thus, the removal of any of the cells would not imply the end of the network, as in the early generations. The business was also expanded to extortion, illegal gold mining, gambling, microtrafficking, and dealing marijuana and synthetic drugs for the local market.

CONTEMPORARY ISSUES

The tactics for illicit activities have changed to become more sophisticated. The third-generation cartels do not have open labs in the jungle. they have warehouses in urban areas. They do not use aircrafts and speedboats anymore; they have upgraded to semisubmersibles. Markets have also changed. Colombian drug traffickers have enlarged their market-developing networks to Europe and South America—especially Brazil and Argentina, but also Peru and Bolivia—or they have also exported the expertise to those regions. Furthermore, they stopped paying too much attention to the U.S. market, which is now dominated by the Mexican cartels—the closest structure to the Medellín cartel; nonetheless, they also work in federations. Likewise, Colombian cartels supply the Mexican cartels with the 35 percent of the cocaine they traffic.

The efforts of the authorities to stop drug trafficking have been undermined by the structure of the third-generation cartels. The cartels are not only organized in cells within Colombia; they also have an international federation with other regional cartels, such as Zetas, the Jalisco New Generation, and the Sinaloa Cartel. Central America, especially Honduras, has become the corridor for cocaine exported from Colombia to Mexico, with the United States as its destination.

Another strike inside the federation of cartels was the peace agreement between the Colombian government and FARC in 2016. The demobilization of the rebels is still an uncertain move in the underworld of drug trafficking between the two countries. First, the groups that could take the lead in the cocaine trade have been severely weakened—the Usugas and Urabeños—and the rebel National Liberation Army (ELN) started peace negotiations with the government in 2017. Second, the Colombian authorities claim that Mexican cartels are moving their way down to South America to fill in the partnership gap left by FARC; Colombia's general attorney has stated that Mexican cartels already have a presence in the departments of Antioquia, Cundinamarca, Norte de Santander, Valle del Cauca, Nariño, Meta, Guaviare, Vichada, and Córdoba. This does not mean that Mexican cartels would establish themselves in Colombia, but they are looking for new alliances to continue with cocaine exports from their country.

This shows how important it is to consider the transnational factor of organized crime activities and how a striking point in one place can have a domino effect. According to a 2017 UNODC report, although drug cartel structures have changed in the last 25 years, they have adapted to the new dynamics of the markets: "drug trafficking can serve as an incubator for the development of organize[d] crime groups" (UNODC 2018).

Mariana Cammisa and Jéssica Viales López

See also: Cali Cartel; Medellín Cartel; Revolutionary Armed Forces of Colombia

Further Reading

BBC. "The Colombian-Mexican Alliance." Accessed January 14, 2019. http://www.bbc.co.uk/worldservice/news/2008/11/081029_narcofight1.shtml.

CNN Library. 2018. "Mexico Drug War Fast Facts." *CNN*, March 21. Accessed January 14, 2019. https://edition.cnn.com/2013/09/02/world/americas/mexico-drug-war-fast-facts/index.html.

Dittmar, Victoria, and Salomón Josefina. 2018. "Mexican Cartels in Colombia: Setting Up Shop or Seeking New Partners." January 31. Accessed January 14, 2019. https://www.insightcrime.org/news/analysis/mexican-cartels-colombia-setting-up-shop-seeking-new-partners.

Manjoo, Farhad. 2017. "Snap Makes a Bet on the Cultural Supremacy of the Camera." *New York Times*, March 8. Accessed January 14, 2019. https://www.nytimes.com/2017/03/08/technology/snap-makes-a-bet-on-the-cultural-supremacy-of-the-camera.html.

McDermott, Jeremy. 2013. "20 Years after Pablo: The Evolution of Colombia's Drug Trade." *InSight Crime*, December 3. Accessed January 14, 2019. https://www.insightcrime.org/news/analysis/20-years-after-pablo-the-evolution-of-colombias-drug-trade.

United Nations Office on Drugs and Crime (UNODC). 2017. "Colombia-UNODC Sign Historic Agreement to Lead the Way in Tackling Country's Coca Cultivation."

November 3. Accessed January 14, 2019. https://www.unodc.org/unodc/en/press/releases/2017/November/colombia-unodc-sign-historical-agreement-to-lead-the-way-in-tackling-the-countrys-coca-cultivation.html.

United Nations Office on Drugs and Crime (UNODC). 2018. "Market Analysis of Plant-Based Drugs." Accessed January 14, 2019. https://www.unodc.org/wdr2017/field/Booklet_3_Plantbased.pdf.

United Nations Office on Drugs and Crime (UNODC). 2018. "The Drug Problem and Organized Crime, Illicit Financial Flows, Corruption and Terrorism." Accessed January 14, 2019. https://www.unodc.org/wdr2017/field/Booklet_5_NEXUS.pdf.

Wile, Rob. 2012. "How Mexicans Took Over the Drug Trade from Colombian Cartels." Business Insider, March 1. Accessed January 14, 2019. http://www.businessinsider.com/revealed-how-the-mexicans-took-over-the-drug-trade-from-the-colombians-2012-3.

Woody, Christopher. 2017. "Pablo Escobar's Death Cleared the Way for a Much More Sinister Kind of Criminal in Colombia." Business Insider, March 27. Accessed January 14, 2019. http://www.businessinsider.com/colombia-criminal-cartel-world-changes-after-pablo-escobar-was-killed-2017-2.

Commission on Narcotic Drugs

The Commission on Narcotic Drugs is a body within the United Nations that is responsible for creating and monitoring drug policies among UN member countries. It is one of the entities housed within the United Nations Economic and Social Council (ECOSOC) in New York City.

HISTORY

Inspired by the Advisory Committee on the Traffic in Opium and Other Dangerous Drugs of the League of Nations, the Commission on Narcotic Drugs was established by the United Nations in 1946 to supervise the implementation of international treaties focused on narcotics control (McAllister 2002). It initially served as a monitor for the ECOSOC but was expanded by the UN General Assembly in 1991 to function as the primary governing body of ECOSOC's drug control efforts. Per UN Resolution 1999/30, enacted in July 1999, the UN General Assembly strengthened the mandate of ECOSOC to address two key needs within its organizational composition: normative functioning and operational governance. The primary function of ECOSOC is to discharge tasks and support objectives outlined in narcotics treaties. In addition, the UN General Assembly affirmed the body's role as a governing body with binding outcomes.

FUNCTION

Extracting its authority from the 1961 Single Convention on Narcotic Drugs treaty, the commission is empowered to amend the schedules that define and classify narcotics, refer matters of concern to the International Narcotics Control Board for enforcement, and recommend certain scientific research be implemented into the considerations process for future United Nations action (Bewley-Taylor and Jelsma 2012).

Article 17 of the 1971 Convention on Psychotropic Substances treaty requires a two-thirds vote by the commission to reclassify a drug according to one of the four schedules, each with a varying level of control. In addition, any scheduling change must be in accordance with a recommendation from the World Health Organization (WHO), a separate UN agency. The UN General Assembly can make modifications to all decisions and outputs of the commission, except its actions in regard to narcotics scheduling. The ECOSOC does, however, have the ability to nullify any decision made by the commission.

MEMBERSHIP

Fifty-three UN member nations make up the commission, each serving a four-year term. There are three distinct criteria that are applied to a nation seeking membership:

1. A member must be a party to the 1961 Single Convention on Narcotic Drugs treaty.
2. Countries responsible for producing, manufacturing, and trafficking of drugs must be proportionally represented. Countries with a uniquely high drug addiction problem among its citizens are also eligible under this criterion.
3. There must be equitable distribution of members with regard to geography. Africa, Asia, Latin America and the Caribbean, Eastern Europe, and Western Europe are all regions that are represented on the commission. African states get 11 members, Eastern European states get 6, Western European states get 14, Asian states get 11, and Latin American and Caribbean states get 10. One seat rotates between the Asian and the Latin American and Caribbean states every four-year term.

CRITICISM

As is common with UN bodies, the Commission on Narcotic Drugs is criticized for lacking topical expertise due to its composition of political diplomats. This can also be a hindrance because drug policy recommendations that the commission produces can be viewed as a by-product of political gamesmanship rather than as a public health remedy based on scientific data. Finally, because the commission seeks consensus before recommending action, with the exception of scheduling classification, it can be difficult to navigate geopolitical biases that one member nation may have toward another with regard to a specific policy (Fazey 2003).

Corey B. Miles

See also: Global Drug Interdiction; International Narcotics Control Board; Single Convention on Narcotic Drugs; UN Convention against Illicit Traffic in Narcotic Drugs and Psychotropic Substances; UN Office on Drugs and Crime; UN World Drug Report

Further Reading

Bewley-Taylor, David, and Martin Jelsma. 2012. "Regime Change: Re-Visiting the 1961 Single Convention on Narcotic Drugs." *International Journal of Drug Policy* 23 (1): 72–81.

Fazey, Cindy S. J. 2003. "The Commission on Narcotic Drugs and the United Nations International Drug Control Programme: Politics, Policies and Prospect for Change." *International Journal of Drug Policy* 14 (2): 155–169.

McAllister, William B. 2002. *Drug Diplomacy in the Twentieth Century.* New York: Routledge.

Taylor, Allyn L. 2007. "Addressing the Global Tragedy of Needless Pain: Rethinking the United Nations Single Convention on Narcotic Drugs." *Journal of Law, Medicine & Ethics* 35 (4): 556–570.

United Nations Office on Drugs and Crime (UNODC). 2018. "World Drug Report 2017." United Nations Publications. Accessed January 14, 2019. https://www.unodc.org/wdr2017/index.html.

Controlled Delivery

Controlled delivery is used in law enforcement in the investigation of trafficking offenses, such as drug trafficking and trafficking in endangered species. An illegal or suspect consignment is allowed to proceed with the knowledge of, and under the supervision of, the law enforcement authorities to secure evidence against the entire network of traffickers, from source to intended destination.

RATIONALE

In traditional law enforcement, suspects are detained and arrested as soon as possible after a suspected offense is detected. In trafficking offenses, however, this would generally lead to the arrest of only the couriers, who do not necessarily know from where the consignment originated or its ultimate destination. It is also possible that the courier is not even aware of the illegal nature of the contents of the consignment. Allowing the consignment to proceed may make it possible to identify and bring to justice the persons directing and organizing the trafficking both "upstream" (production and processing) and "downstream" (distribution and retail), identify the modus operandi of the operation, and dismantle the entire operation. Controlled delivery may also facilitate the "following of the money," obtaining evidence of money laundering and other offenses involved in the trafficking (such as corruption of border enforcement and law enforcement agents), and seizing the proceeds of the crime.

LEGAL BASIS

Domestic controlled delivery (controlled delivery within national borders) has long been used extensively in the United States. The first significant convention to contain provisions on international controlled delivery is the 1988 United Nations Convention against Illicit Traffic in Narcotic Drugs and Psychotropic Substances, which requires state parties to take measures to allow for controlled delivery in drug trafficking cases, "if permitted by their respective domestic legal systems." The 2000 United Nations Convention against Transnational Organized Crime contains similar wording in respect to controlled delivery in general for serious offenses.

Controlled delivery is widely used within the European Union, on the basis of the Convention Implementing the Schengen Agreement (1985), the Convention on Mutual Assistance and Cooperation between Customs Administrations (1997), and the Convention on Mutual Assistance in Criminal Matters between the Member States of the European Union (2000). Countries that have extensive law enforcement cooperation with one another have entered into special agreements or arrangements regarding controlled delivery.

TYPES OF CONTROLLED DELIVERY

Investigations involving controlled delivery may involve different means of control and supervision of the consignment. In many cases, the consignment is transported by a package delivery service or transportation company, and the controlled delivery will take place with the cooperation of the service or company. If the consignment is in the possession of a suspected offender, several options are available. The courier may be placed under physical or technical surveillance (monitored delivery). Alternatively, the suspect may be detained and either encouraged to proceed under the control of the authorities or replaced with an undercover agent.

Ideally, the authorities may seek to replace the illicit consignment itself with a substitute while it is still in transit ("clean" controlled delivery), which lessens the negative results if the authorities lose track of the consignment and it proceeds unimpeded.

RISKS AND CHALLENGES

Despite the fact that the 1988 and the 2000 conventions have been widely ratified and implemented, national legislation on controlled delivery varies considerably from one country to the next. Responsibility for controlled delivery may be assigned to different agencies, and there may be different requirements in respect to judicial authorization and notification of prosecutors. Setting up an unbroken chain of controlled delivery across borders may thus require considerable bureaucratic procedures.

The risk of losing track of the consignment is particularly large at border crossings, especially if the courier is traveling by other than scheduled transport. The responsibility for supervision has to be passed on when the courier crosses a national border. Countries vary in respect to what extent foreign law enforcement agents may participate in controlled delivery. The basic principle is that foreign agents have no police powers and thus may not independently conduct surveillance. However, particularly if it is anticipated that the courier will cross a national border, an agent from the destination country may accompany the surveillance team so that responsibility for the case may be transferred smoothly at the border.

Matti Joutsen

See also: UN Convention against Illicit Traffic in Narcotic Drugs and Psychotropic Substances; UN Convention against Transnational Organized Crime; Wildlife and Forest Crime

Further Reading

Boister, Neil. 2012. *An Introduction to Transnational Criminal Law.* New York, NY: Oxford University Press.

Cutting, P. D. 1983. "The Technique of Controlled Delivery as a Weapon in Dealing with Illicit Traffic in Narcotic Drugs and Psychotropic Substances." *Bulletin on Narcotics* 35 (4): 15–22. Accessed January 14, 2019. https://www.unodc.org/unodc/en/data-and-analysis/bulletin/bulletin_1983-01-01_4_page003.html.

De Lucas, Martin, Ignacio Miguel, and Cristian-Eduard Stefan. 2016. *Transnational Controlled Deliveries in Drug Trafficking Investigations.* Brussels: European Commission. Accessed January 14, 2019. http://www.mpublic.ro/sites/default/files/PDF/manual_en_ump_ce_13.pdf.

Joubert, Chantal, and Hans Bevers. 1996. *Schengen Investigated: A Comparative Interpretation of the Schengen Provisions on International Police Cooperation in the Light of the European Convention on Human Rights.* The Hague, London, and Boston: Kluwer.

Convention on International Trade in Endangered Species of Wild Fauna and Flora

The Convention on International Trade in Endangered Species of Wild Fauna and Flora, also known as the Washington Convention or by its acronym, CITES, is an international treaty issued under the auspices of the International Union for Conservation of Nature. The convention's aim is to protect wild occurring populations of animal and plant species that are facing extinction (CITES n.d.-b). Each party to the convention is obliged to control, monitor, and limit international trade in those species and their recognizable parts or derivatives and to provide international cooperation for limiting illegal trade in endangered specimens. The convention is also designed to raise awareness about the impact humans have on wild species.

The convention includes three appendices that contain lists of approximately 5,300 species of animals and 30,000 species of plants. Appendix I identifies species that are in danger of extinction (for example, tigers and gorillas). Trade in those specimens is permitted only in exceptional circumstances, such as scientific research. Species listed in Appendix II are ones that are not yet threatened with extinction but that could become so through uncontrolled trade. For example, animals such as the hippopotamus and many corals can be traded internationally, but strict rules apply. Appendix III contains species protected in at least one country that has asked other countries for assistance in controlling trade of that species (CITES n.d.-a; World Wildlife Fund 2018).

The Washington Convention was opened for signature on March 3, 1973. There were 183 parties to the convention as of September 2018.

REGULATION OF TRADE

According to Article I of the convention, trade occurs in four forms: export, re-export (which is export of any specimen that was earlier imported), import, or introduction from the sea, which is the transportation into a country of specimens taken from international waters.

In principle, all kinds of trade require permits. The most restricted regulations concern trade of specimens listed in Appendix I of the convention. Usually a permit for trade of an Appendix I species is proceeded by issuing opinions and decisions that are made by authorized scientific and management organs. Authorities examine, among other things, whether trade would cause damage; whether conditions of transportation would minimize risk of injury, illness, or cruel treatment; and whether the recipient possesses suitable equipment to take care of the specimen. Each shipment requires a separate document.

The convention also provides exceptions from trade restrictions (Article VII). For example, regulations are not applied in case of (1) transit or transshipment during customs control, (2) trade of specimens that were acquired prior to their inclusion in the convention, (3) specimens designated for private purposes (with some reservations), (4) breeding of the specimen artificially or in captivity, (5) noncommercial donation or exchange between scientific institutions, and (6) transportation as a part of traveling zoos or exhibitions that meet certain requirements.

PREVENTIVE MEASURES

Some obligations are imposed on parties to bring domestic laws into compliance with provisions of the convention and to introduce bans on any trade that is contrary to those provisions. Primary among those obligations are that state parties should create criminal sanctions for violations of the convention and should confiscate and return the specimen to the country from which it was taken. Optionally, a country can establish its own domestic proceedings concerning confiscation fees. Moreover, countries should take appropriate steps to facilitate formalities, to provide care for specimens under customs, and to keep a data register, including lists of exporters and importers, and also to prepare periodic reports. To fulfill conventional commitments, countries should designate authorities responsible for issuing certificates or opinions and international contacts. One of the principles allows the existence of more restrictive domestic regulations.

INTERNATIONAL COOPERATION AND ORGANIZATION

The primary example of cooperation among countries is the opportunity they are given to make suggestions in the convention appendices. The management and coordination of initiatives and activities of the state parties is under the authority of the Secretariat, with offices located in Geneva, Switzerland, and under the administration of the United Nations Environment Programme. The Secretariat's basic functions include organizing conferences, conducting scientific and technical research, analyzing reports, and issuing current editions of appendices or making recommendations. It is also responsible for direct communication with a country in the case of acquiring knowledge about negative results of trade or the country not effectively obeying regulations.

Regular or extraordinary meetings of the state parties are held at least once every two years. At these meetings, representatives make decisions, approve or reject amendments to appendices, or review the level of enforcement the obligations set out in the convention. Countries that are not signatories of the convention as well as other authorities or institutions can be represented, but without a right to vote.

Besides the Secretariat, three committees make up CITES' organizational structure. The Plants Committee and the Animals Committee are responsible for technical and scientific support for their respective species and for drawing up nomenclature or providing consultancy services. The Standing Committee has the task of shaping policy, operating a budget, and coordinating the work of the Secretariat.

Starting in 2017, all state parties to the convention are asked to submit an annual illegal trade report that covers actions taken by the country in support of the convention's provisions. Data collected in the reports will be used for global research and analysis studies on wildlife and forest crime. The first such reports, covering the 2016 calendar year, were due to be filed by October 31, 2017.

Józef J. Doellinger

See also: International Consortium on Combating Wildlife Crime; UN Global Programme for Combating Wildlife and Forest Crime; Wildlife and Forest Crime

Further Reading

CITES. n.d.-a. "How CITES Works." Accessed September 26, 2018. https://www.cites.org/eng/disc/how.php.

CITES. n.d.-b. "What Is CITES?" Accessed September 26, 2018. https://www.cites.org/eng/disc/what.php.

Fuchs, Christine. 2008. "Convention on International Trade in Endangered Species of Wild Fauna and Flora (CITES)—Conservation Efforts Undermine the Legality Principle." *German Law Journal* 9 (11): 1565–1596.

Mahony, Dianne E. 1997. "The Convention on International Trade in Endangered Species of Wild Flora and Fauna: Addressing Problems in Global Wildlife Trade Enforcement." *New England International and Comparative Law Annual* 3: 1–24.

Schonfeld, Alan H. 1985. "International Trade in Wildlife: How Effective Is the Endangered Species Treaty." *California Western International Law Journal* 15: 111–160.

World Wildlife Fund. 2018. "Conservation Impacts." Accessed September 26, 2018. https://www.worldwildlife.org/pages/cites.

Young, Saskia. 2003. "Contemporary Issues of the Convention on International Trade in Endangered Species of Wild Fauna and Flora (CITES) and the Debate over Sustainable Use." *Colorado Journal of International Environmental Law and Policy* 14: 167–189.

Convention on the Means of Prohibiting and Preventing the Illicit Import, Export, and Transport of Ownership of Cultural Property

The Convention on the Means of Prohibiting and Preventing the Illicit Import, Export, and Transport of Ownership of Cultural Property is an international agreement written in 1970 at the General Conference of the United Nations Educational, Scientific and Cultural Organization (UNESCO). In this agreement, states can sign on to the convention, agreeing to actively take measures to prevent trade in illegal trade in cultural property, which the convention defines as "any property which, on religious or secular grounds, is specifically designated by each State as being of importance for archaeology, prehistory, history, literature, art or science" (UNESCO 1970). As of 2018, 134 countries have signed the treaty, which entered into force on April 24, 1972.

The text of the convention has several main parts. It opens with a preamble that describes the problem of the illicit trade in cultural property and the harm the loss of cultural property does to nations. Next, the body of the document contains 26 articles that describe the tasks state parties will take to address the problem. Some of these tasks include recognizing this illicit trade as a crime and prosecuting it within their jurisdiction, identifying within the state what it deems to be its own cultural property, setting up an international framework to deal with this crime across national boundaries, and establishing UNESCO as the central international agency regarding this problem, among other tasks. After the articles, the document closes with declarations and reservations from signatory states.

Despite being almost 50 years old, this convention continues to be important in combating the illegal trade in cultural property. The international frameworks for cooperation established in this agreement remain useful and strong. Periodic consultations are undertaken by UNESCO to check in with the convention, examine progress to date, and encourage more states to join the convention. The convention text does not require periodic monitoring, but it was deemed necessary by UNESCO and a meeting of state parties to the 1970 convention have taken place since 2003. These check-ins effectively keep the convention relevant and active over the decades.

While the UNESCO Convention of 1970 deals with the problem of the illegal trade in cultural property from the perspective of states, a complementary convention focusing on the recovery of cultural property was written at UNESCO's request in 1995 by the International Institute for the Unification of Private Law (UNIDROIT). The UNIDROIT Convention on Stolen or Illegally Exported Cultural Objects went into effect in 1998, and as of 2018, it has 28 member parties. Repatriation, or returning, of trafficked cultural objects to their original states was not thoroughly covered in the UNESCO Convention, and the UNIDROIT Convention seeks to address this weakness.

Paula K. Priebe

See also: Antiquities and Cultural Objects, Theft of; Cambodian Statue Theft

Further Reading

International Institute for the Unification of Private Law (UNIDROIT). 1995. *UNIDROIT Convention on Stolen or Illegally Exported Cultural Objects*. Rome: UNIDROIT.

Jowers, K. F. 2003. "International and National Legal Efforts to Protect Cultural Property: The 1970 UNESCO Convention, the United States, and Mexico." *Texas International Law Journal* 38: 145–172.

United Nations Educational, Scientific and Cultural Organization (UNESCO). 1970. *Convention on the Means of Prohibiting and Preventing the Illicit Import, Export and Transfer of Ownership of Cultural Property.* Paris: UNESCO. Accessed January 14, 2019. http://www.unesco.org/new/en/culture/themes/illicit-trafficking-of-cultural-property/1970-convention/text-of-the-convention.

United Nations Educational, Scientific and Cultural Organization (UNESCO). 2015. *Operational Guidelines for the Implementation of the Convention on the Means of Prohibiting and Preventing the Illicit Import, Export and Transfer of Ownership of Cultural Property (UNESCO, Paris, 1970).* Paris: UNESCO.

Convention on the Prevention of Marine Pollution by Dumping Wastes and Other Matter

The Convention on the Prevention of Marine Pollution by Dumping of Wastes and Other Matter of 1972 is often referred to as the "London Convention," and it went into force in 1975. This is not to be confused with the "London Protocol," which was established in 1996 and was intended to add further protections for the marine environment. The London Convention was one of the first global conventions to protect the marine environment from human activities. The primary goal was to promote the effective control of all sources of marine pollution and to take all practicable steps to prevent pollution of the sea by dumping of wastes and other matter worldwide. As of March 2018, 87 states are parties to the London Convention. In the United States, the Marine Protection, Research and Sanctuaries Act (MPRSA), also known as the Ocean Dumping Act, implements the requirements of the London Convention.

Beginning in the 1950s, there was worldwide concern about the environmental impacts of human activities on the marine environment, including the uncontrolled and unregulated disposal of wastes into the ocean (EPA 2018). The London Convention ensures that specific materials are permitted for ocean disposal and that they are carefully evaluated to make sure they will not pose a danger to human health and the environment. Additionally, the convention requires parties to determine whether there are more feasible alternatives for their reuse or disposal.

CONVENTION

Under Article I, parties that signed the convention agreed to recognize that the marine environment and the living organisms are of vital importance to all of humanity and that all people should have a vested interest in assuring that it is protected to ensure quality resources are not impaired. Article III outlines that "dumping" means any deliberate disposal at sea of wastes or other matter from vessels, aircraft, platforms, or other man-made structures at sea or any deliberate disposal at sea. Article III also includes the deliberate disposal of any man-made structures at sea. Lastly, the Charter of the United Nations and the principles of international law allow states the sovereign right to exploit their own resources pursuant to their own environmental policies, and they have responsibility to ensure that activities within their jurisdiction or control do not cause damage to the environment of other states or of areas beyond the limits of national jurisdiction (EPA 2018). This allows countries to develop policies that are specific to their country while also requiring states to not cross jurisdictional boundaries.

REGULATIONS

The London Convention initially required countries to control dumping by implementing regulatory programs to assess the need for, and the potential impact of, dumping. Additionally, countries were required to issue a permit for the dumping of wastes and other matter at sea, and that generally prohibits the dumping of certain hazardous materials. In recent years, amendments to the treaty have banned ocean dumping of certain wastes and promoted pollution prevention and sound waste management (EPA 2018). Lastly, the London Convention requires the submission of an annual report on all ocean dumping permits issued to monitor activities.

LONDON PROTOCOL

In 1996, the "London Protocol" was established to further modernize and replace the London Convention. Under the protocol, all dumping is prohibited, except for acceptable wastes on the "reverse list." The primary purpose of the London Protocol is similar to that of the convention, but the protocol is more restrictive. The protocol requires countries to take a "precautionary approach" as a general obligation. Further, the 1996 protocol prohibits the incineration of wastes at sea and the export of wastes for the purpose of dumping or incineration at sea. Lastly, the London Protocol extended compliance procedures, added technical assistance provisions, and allows for a transitional period for new parties to phase into compliance with the protocol over a period of five years, provided certain conditions are met (International Maritime Organization 2018). The protocol entered into force on March 24, 2006, and there are currently 50 parties to the protocol.

Shanell Sanchez

See also: Basel Convention on the Control of Transboundary Movements of Hazardous Wastes and Their Disposal; Environmental Crimes; Waste Crime

Further Reading

International Maritime Organization. 2018. "Convention on the Prevention of Marine Pollution by Dumping of Wastes and Other Matter." Accessed April 14, 2018. http://www.imo.org/en/OurWork/Environment/LCLP/Pages/default.aspx.

United Nations. 1977. "Convention on the Prevention of Marine Pollution by Dumping Wastes and Other Matter." Accessed April 14, 2018. https://treaties.un.org/doc/Publication/UNTS/Volume%201046/volume-1046-I-15749-English.pdf.

United States Environmental Protection Agency (EPA). 2018a. "Ocean Dumping: International Treaties." Accessed April 14, 2018. https://www.epa.gov/ocean-dumping/ocean-dumping-international-treaties.

United States Environmental Protection Agency (EPA). 2018b. "Convention on the Prevention of Marine Pollution by Dumping of Wastes and Other Matters." Accessed April 14, 2018. https://www.epa.gov/sites/production/files/2015-10/documents/lc1972.pdf.

Corruption

Nearly every country uses terms for corruption. "Greasing the wheels" in English has similarities to "*Spicken*" in German and "coming to an agreement" in Russian. In India, one does "the needful." Through language, cultures reflect the omnipresent nature of corruption. The most common definition is the use or abuse of one's power or position for personal gain, as corruption has usually focused on violations of public trust. Corruption within governmental institutions damages public trust because it undermines the rule of law. As corporations grow transnationally, private corruption, such as business-to-business bribes or consumer fraud, presents larger risks for the global economy (e.g., the 2008 world recession). Definitions of corruption have expanded from abusing one's assigned power for personal advantage to include public and private corrupt acts (Transparency International 2018). Corruption erodes legitimate governments, which provides fertile soil for other global crimes to proliferate, such as terrorism and organized crime.

SCOPE

Corruption exists across all sectors, public, private, and civil. Corruption within the public sector remains more pertinent of the three, given the state's role. Corruption affects many facets of safety, security, and legitimacy. Therefore, efforts to control corruption are critical to ensuring access to justice and equal treatment under the law. International efforts to strengthen the rule of law are critical to controlling corruption. Public corruption can affect the security of international borders, verdicts by the courts, and the upkeep of public infrastructure. It also takes a significant economic toll. Although it may seem that stable economies remained or even increased during times of corrupt practices, corruption may change the underlying nature of spending and economic activity, possibly deterring change (Wong 2017, 300). It also misuses public money meant to help the poor.

In addition to creating economic and internal threats, corruption also compromises national security agencies' ability to address external threats. Chokepoints of control provide fertile ground for corrupt acts. Military, police, intelligence organizations, and border guards face higher risks of corruption because of their authority and access. Understanding the types and effects of corrupt practices is important to thwarting corruption.

The World Justice Project (WJP) Rule of Law Index measures rule of law adherence across 8 different factors in 113 countries and jurisdictions worldwide based on more than 110,000 citizen and 3,000 expert surveys. One factor surveyed in this index measures the prevalence of bribery, informal payments, and other incentives in the delivery of public services and protections. After measuring all of the factors, countries were given scores. Only 11 countries scored above 80 percent, toward a strong rule of law. Two-thirds of countries scored 60 percent or below (World Justice Project 2018, 10).

According to Transparency International, the 2017 Corruption Perceptions Index highlights that the majority of countries are making little or no progress in ending corruption. The index ranks 180 countries and territories by their perceived levels of public-sector corruption and uses a scale of 0 to 100, where 0 is highly corrupt and 100 is not corrupt. In 2017, the index found that more than two-thirds of countries score below 50, with an average score of 43 (Transparency International 2018). As corruption grows, laws are ignored, and lawlessness becomes standard in many places, which may lead to human rights violations and further state deterioration (World Justice Project 2018, 2–154).

TYPES

Corruption has two major categories: public and commercial. Public corruption, often described as political corruption, consists of acts committed within the government that distort policies or the central functioning of the state. Examples include nepotism, cronyism, embezzlement, obstruction of justice, and official misconduct. Petty corruption refers to everyday abuse of entrusted power by low-level public officials in their interactions with ordinary citizens, often blocking public access to goods or services (Rose-Ackerman 1978, 33–34). For example, street-level bureaucrats act in their own best interest by directly disregarding their public duties (Fazekas 2017, 405).

Commercial corruption, the other major type, occurs more commonly and includes money laundering, business-on-business crimes, and consumer frauds. Money laundering, a conveyor belt for corruption, is the process in which criminals give their money a legitimate legal origin. Corrupt money is often laundered to legitimize it. Bribery, extortion, asset stripping, illicit influence, and embezzlement are the most common types of corruption.

ADVERSE EFFECTS

Generally, the rule of law applies to all citizens equally, from the top to the bottom. Effective rule of law reduces corruption, combats poverty and disease, and protects people from injustices and exploitation. It is the foundation for communities of peace, opportunity, and equity, underpinning development, accountable government, and respect for fundamental rights. Countries that have high ratings for the absence of corruption within the government also have high ratings of criminal and civil justice, constraints on the government, fundamental rights, and order and security.

Further analysis of those results indicated that countries with the least protection for press and nongovernmental organizations (NGOs) tend to have high rates of corruption (World Justice Project 2018). Government with high levels of corruption and distrust from its citizens erodes the rule of law, creating further opportunities for criminal behavior. As criminal behavior and corruption rise, the public loses confidence and further trust in the government, leading to a loss of state legitimacy. Measuring these factors, helps monitor the extent and effect of corruption.

INTERNATIONAL ANTICORRUPTION EFFORTS

Globally, no consensus has developed on how to deal with statewide corruption, in part because many international entities have framed the problem as the lack of state power rather than the states abusing their power. To outsiders, many states appear weak, fragile, overstretched, and underresourced. Anticorruption efforts need to eliminate opportunities for corruption, provide incentives for legal governing, encourage citizens to work with their governments, and find ways to hold corrupt entities accountable for their actions.

International organizations and conventions have tried to establish legally binding standards to criminalize many kinds of corruption. One of the first steps toward growing a global awareness of corruption was in 1977. The Foreign Corrupt Practices Act of 1977 (FCPA) was enacted for the purpose of making it unlawful for certain classes of persons and entities to make payments to foreign government officials to assist in obtaining or retaining business. In 1989, the United Nations Crime Prevention and Criminal Justice Program raised questions about whether action could be taken against corruption at the international level.

Governmental and nonprofit international organizations, including the United Nations, the Organization for Economic Co-Operation and Development (OECD), and Transparency International have created mechanisms to enhance anticorruption programs internationally. The signing of the OECD Anti-Bribery Convention in 1997 was the first international anticorruption instrument focused on the supply side of bribery. All countries that signed the convention agreed to make the bribery of public officials a criminal offense (OECD 2016). The OECD convention incited further action. Within the same year, the United Nations Declaration against Corruption and Bribery in International Commercial Transactions (UNDAC) was passed. This declaration underlines the need for responsibility and upholding of ethics on the part of companies and recognizes the link between corruption, fair but competitive business practices, and accountable governing bodies. Member states commit to criminalizing the bribery of foreign public officials.

The United Nations Convention against Corruption (UNCAC) was the first real global anticorruption treaty, presenting a common language for the international anticorruption movement (Wouters, Ryngaert, and Cloots, 2013, 216–219). The Group of States against Corruption (GRECO), the monitoring mechanism of the

Council of Europe (CoE), has also played a role in monitoring and fighting corruption on an international scale (Wouters, Ryngaert, and Cloots 2013, 216–219).

Kristine Artello and Hollie MacDonald

See also: Bribery; Corruption Measurements; Foreign Corrupt Practices Act

Further Reading

Chayes, Sarah. 2016. *Thieves of State: Why Corruption Threatens Global Security.* London: W. W. Norton & Co.

Fazekas, Mihály. 2017. "Red Tape, Bribery and Government Favouritism: Evidence from Europe." *Crime, Law and Social Change* 68 (4): 403–429.

Figueiredo, André T. D. 2017. *Corruption and Human Rights: Beyond the Link.* Tilburg, The Netherlands: Wolf Legal Publishers

Fisman, Raymond, and Miriam A. Golden. 2017. *Corruption: What Everyone Needs to Know.* Oxford: Oxford University Press.

Organization for Economic Co-Operation and Development (OECD). 2016. *The Fight against Corruption.* Accessed March 24, 2018. http://biac.org/focus-areas/the-fight-against-corruption.

Rose-Ackerman, Sarah. 1978. *Corruption: A Study in Political Economy.* New York: Academic Press.

Transparency International. 2018. *What Is Corruption?* Accessed March 24, 2018. https://www.transparency.org/what-is-corruptio.

Wong, Mathew. 2017. "Public Spending, Corruption, and Income Inequality: A Comparative Analysis of Asia and Latin America." *International Political Science Review* 38 (3): 298–315.

World Justice Project. 2018. *Rule of Law Index: 2017–2018.* Accessed March 24, 2018. https://worldjusticeproject.org/sites/default/files/documents/WJP_ROLI_2017-18_Online-Edition_0.pdf.

Wouters, Jan, Cedric Ryngeart, and Anne Sofia Cloots. 2013. "The International Legal Framework against Corruption: Achievements and Challenges." *Melbourne Journal of International Law* 14 (1): 205–280.

Corruption in China

In China, there are as many forms of corruption as there are rules forbidding such actions. Previous studies of corruption in China commonly used a general definition of corruption, such as "abuse of public office for private gains," while the body of research on Chinese corruption has since, conversely, highlighted unique features of Chinese corruption (Ko and Weng 2011, 361). As a transitional society, Chinese corruption is overall evident in five major categories: (1) crimes (especially economic crimes) committed by government officials while on duty; (2) a variety of malpractices in government agencies, where officials use public power for private gains; (3) malfeasance or dereliction of duty; (4) extravagant use of public funds; and (5) immoral conduct by party and government officials—acts not normally defined as corruption elsewhere.

Chinese corruption is a very comprehensive concept, and its definition varies during the developing process of Chinese transitional society. It has flourished since China's Reform and Opening policy in 1978. According to a Chinese official report, during the 1980s and early 1990s, corruption-related crimes referred to (1) embezzlement, theft, and fraud; (2) bribery; (3) extortion; (4) violation of codes of conduct; (5) exploiting a conflict of interest/insider trading; and (6) favoritism, nepotism, and clientelism. Actually, these activities were then collectively called "economic crimes" instead of corruption. In 1989, the term *misuse of public funds* first appeared as an official terminology for a new type of corruption. From 1990 to 1997, the official definition of corruption only included embezzlement, bribery, tax evasion, misuse of public funds, and official malfeasance of duty.

From 1998 to the present, there were considerable new elements in the official definition of corruption. Corruption was increasingly prevalent in China's political arena. During this period of time, two new major categories of corruption were brought to general attention, unexplained assets and official malfeasance of duty, which included three subdivisions: abuse of power, off-duty, and private gain using public power. There were three characteristics for official malfeasance of duty crimes: (1) public-sector employees who were found not qualified enough for their jobs or positions, which resulted in great loss of public assets, thereby negatively impacting the benefits of the citizens and the nation as a whole; (2) a huge loss of public funds used for business activities, often resulting from the head of a state-owned entity being cheated or swindled, resulting in a significant loss of taxpayers' money; and (3) financial and banking system employees who made loans to those who bribed them instead of making loans according to the regulations.

The ambiguous distinction among the public sector, private sector, and nonprofit sector of Chinese society makes the concept even more blurred as far as corruption is concerned. The difference between embezzlement and misuse of public funds is not entirely clear. It appears to be that if the misused public funds are returned, then only an administrative punishment or party discipline is stipulated. But, if the funds are not returned or if it amounts to a certain level, then the legal charge of misuse of public funds applies. The law, however, indicates that, in these circumstances, prosecutors may also level charges of embezzlement. The 1980 China Criminal Law defined embezzlement as illegally taking possession of public property. The offenders could be public-sector employees, employees of collective economic organizations, or other personnel in the position of handling or managing public property. Bribery is defined as when the related personnel take advantage of their positions to extort property from others or unlawfully receive property from others. Misuse of public funds is when the related personnel take advantage of their position to embezzle, steal, obtain by fraud, or by other means unlawfully take possession of public property and fail to return these funds within three months.

Other less legalistic definitions of corruption are part of the complete conceptualization of corruption in China. One example is what is called Unethical Issues or Bad Norms Issues. Overall, there are numerous variations among these types of cases. These are categorized as public fund/money consumption (mainly on three major categories: car, tour, and luxurious eating and drinking using taxpayers' money); gifting, gift offering, and gift giving; and public money hosting. Since 1979, the Chinese central government has been paying attention to this type of behavior. However, it was not until Xi Jinping's leadership took power in November 2012 that specific actions were taken against these misconducts.

Historically, corruption has been a sensitive political and public issue in China. China officially acknowledged the existence of a problem with corruption when the State Council Press Office released a white paper on "China's Efforts to Combat Corruption and Build a Clean Government." It was the first time that the Chinese central government officially acknowledged to the world that corruption was indeed a problem (Meng 2014, 3), though as early as 1984, the former general secretary Hu Yaobang predicted that "corruption is like cancer cells, if not curbed immediately and effectively, it will spread across all kinds of different aspects in Chinese Society" (Meng 2014, 3). The current corruption situation became worse, and the party general secretary Jinping said during the 18th Chinese Communist Party Congress on November 17, 2012, that it would kill the party and ruin the country if not curbed immediately. Corruption became so rampant that the current Chinese leadership made anticorruption a top priority. In a document prepared for the 18th Party Congress, the Central Commission of Disciplinary Inspection, the party's top antigraft agency in China, stated that punishing and preventing corruption is regarded as a serious political struggle for the sake of the party and the nation's future.

Since assuming power in 2012, the Xi Jinping government has prosecuted a number of very high-profile cases. According to a Chinese official source, from 2013 to 2018, 122 ministerial level officials were convicted of corruption-related crimes, a tremendous increase in comparison to the previous 10 years' convictions of the same type of crime (30 high-profile convictions during 2007–2012 and 35 high-profile convictions during 2001–2006).

Qingli Meng

See also: Corruption; Corruption Measurements

Further Reading

China Law Statistical Year Book. 1987. Accessed January 14, 2019. http://data.cnki.net/trade/Yearbook/Single/N2005110605?z=Z022.

China Supreme People's Procuratorate Annual Reports. 1988–2018. Accessed January 14, 2019. http://www.spp.gov.cn/spp/gzbg/index.shtml.

China Supreme People's Procuratorate Yearbooks. 1988–2018. Beijing: China Procuratorate Publisher.

Ko, Kilkon, and Cuifen Wenig. 2011. "Critical Review of Conceptual Definitions of Chinese Corruption: A Formal-Legal Perspective." *Journal of Contemporary China* 70 (20) (June): 359–378.

Meng, Qingli. 2014. *Corruption in Transitional China: A 33-year Study.* Tilburg, The Netherlands: Wolf Legal Publishers.

Corruption in Sub-Saharan Africa

Corruption refers to the abuse of entrusted power for private gain. Today, corruption is a serious problem in Africa. Taking place from the high level of government to the low and middle levels of the private and nonprofit sectors, corruption breeds inefficiency and waste and discourages foreign investment. Corruption also takes place at the political level through manipulation of policies, rules of procedure in the allocation of resources, and the electoral system.

ORIGINS OF CORRUPTION IN AFRICA

Some scholars argue that the traditional system in Africa was more accountable. Traditional African chiefs wielded vast power, yet they ensured a consultative process of governance that acted as a safeguard against corruption. Colonialism altered this system of governance as representative institutions replaced the tribal chiefs during and after colonial occupation. Corruption is a problem that has existed since the rise of organized states, and that is not likely to disappear anytime soon.

Incidences of rampant corruption in Africa are well-documented. Mobutu Sese Seko, the former military dictator and president of then Zaire (now the Democratic Republic of Congo), accumulated a fortune that was estimated at $5 billion. Sani Abacha, the military dictator and president of Nigeria between 1993 and 1998, is said to have stolen between $2 billion and $5 billion. Even democratically elected presidents in Africa have been implicated in corruption cases.

MEASURING CORRUPTION IN AFRICA

Measuring corruption is a difficult undertaking in Africa and the world over. It is estimated that corruption costs Africa roughly $150 billion a year. Because corruption takes place in secrecy, it is often hard to measure. The most popular measure of corruption is Transparency International's Corruption Perception Index (CPI). The CPI is a compilation of data from other sources that are merged to generate a single number for each country. From the time of its first publication in 1995, countries in Africa have been at the top of the list of the most corrupt countries. It can be argued that measuring perceptions is not an effective way to measure corruption, thus there is a need to come up with more robust and effective systems of measurement and strategies to combat corruption.

COMBATING CORRUPTION IN AFRICA

African countries actively combat corruption. Usually the publicity surrounding the levels of corruption, how much is perceived to have been embezzled, and who is responsible, overshadows the efforts in the corruption fight. There are country-specific efforts aimed at combating corruption, such as the establishment of anticorruption agencies aimed at preventing, investigating, and prosecuting corruption. Region-specific initiatives also exist. At the continental level, the African Union leads the corruption fight, guided by the Convention on Preventing and Combating Corruption adopted in 2003. To make substantial progress in the fight against corruption, Africa will need to do more than establishing institutions and developing laws. It will be important for the continent to embrace technology and the benefits it has to offer in addition to doubling up efforts in educating its citizens to get rid of the corruption culture.

Sombo Muzata Chunda

See also: Corruption; Corruption Measurements

Further Reading

African Union. 2003. "African Union Convention on Preventing and Combating Corruption." Accessed May 22, 2018. https://au.int/sites/default/files/treaties/7786-treaty-0028_-_african_union_convention_on_preventing_and_combating_corruption_e.pdf.

Ayittey, George B. N. 1994. *Africa Betrayed.* Houndmills, Basingstoke, Hampshire, UK: Palgrave Macmillan.

Hanson, Stephanie. 2009. "Corruption in Sub-Saharan Africa." Accessed May 22, 2018. https://www.cfr.org/backgrounder/corruption-sub-saharan-africa.

Rose-Ackerman, S., and B. J. Palifka. 2016. *Corruption and Government: Causes, Consequences, and Reform.* 2nd ed. New York: Cambridge University Press.

Transparency International. 2018. "What Is Corruption?" Accessed May 22, 2018. https://www.transparency.org/what-is-corruption.

Corruption Measurements

Corruption is a major transnational crime. Some observers call it the lubricant that allows the various aspects of transnational organized crime to operate smoothly. Although it is an unwieldy concept referring to a variety of actions, there have been attempts to determine its nature, extent, and seriousness. Most of those attempts have been based on perceptions of corruption rather than measurement of corruption itself. Transparency International, the most well-known anticorruption nongovernmental organization (NGO) in the world, provides one of the better corruption measurements in its annual Corruption Perception Index.

TRANSPARENCY INTERNATIONAL

Transparency International (TI) was created in 1983 and has its international headquarters (the Secretariat) in Berlin, Germany. The Secretariat provides leadership and support to more than 100 chapters, each of which is an independent organization, located around the world. The chapters are staffed with local experts who determine the priorities and approaches most appropriate for tackling corruption in their country. The TI mission is "to stop corruption and promote transparency, accountability and integrity at all levels and across all sectors of society" (Transparency International n.d.).

In 2012, the U.S. affiliate of TI gave Hillary Clinton an integrity award at the same time the U.S. State Department was issuing a subpoena to the Clinton Foundation. Transparency International believed the award was, at best, mistimed. In 2013, TI members called for the end of the prosecution of Edward Snowden (who released top secret documents about the U.S. government's domestic surveillance programs) as part of TI's demand for comprehensive protection for whistle-blowers

(Steinbock 2018). TI-USA rejected the idea, and by 2017, TI-USA had been renamed the Coalition for Integrity.

EXAMPLE MEASURES OF CORRUPTION

A key component of TI's work is its research and dissemination of information on the broad topic of corruption. TI provides national assessments and country-specific reports, and it supports an Anti-Corruption Helpdesk to facilitate the knowledge and research needs of practitioners and other stakeholders. But the most widely known endeavors by TI are the reports published on corruption around the world.

The Global Corruption Barometer is the world's largest survey asking citizens about their experience with corruption. Respondents are asked whether they had paid a bribe for a public service in the 12 months preceding the survey (e.g., to a teacher, school official, police officer, or court official). Additional questions asked people how well or badly they thought their government was doing at fighting corruption in their country. Recent results found that almost 1 in 4 said they had paid a bribe when accessing public services, with variation found across regions of the world. Further, 57 percent of the respondents said their government is doing badly, compared with 30 percent saying their government is doing well.

The Global Corruption Report is a periodic TI publication focusing on a specific corruption issue. Recent reports have focused on corruption in climate change, the private sector, water, and sport (e.g., match fixing). Each report highlights qualitative and quantitative research on the topic, showcases innovative tools, and seeks to provide practical and proven solutions for responding to corruption.

THE CORRUPTION PERCEPTIONS INDEX

The Corruption Perceptions Index (CPI) is TI's most well-known measure of corruption. Each year, when the newest version is released, media outlets around the world typically summarize the findings as they relate to their particular country or region.

The CPI, first published in 1995, is the leading global indicator of public-sector corruption—which TI defines as the misuse of public power for private benefit. Each year's index offers a snapshot of the relative degree of corruption by ranking countries from around the globe. The CPI uses a scale of zero (highly corrupt) to 100 (very clean). The 2017 CPI (released in February 2018) found that more than two-thirds of countries score below 50, with an average score of 43. Importantly, but also consistently and disappointingly, no country scores 100—indicating that corruption is everywhere.

The CPI score is based on opinion surveys and expert assessments from businesspeople and country experts—not from the general public. The actual score represents the average score from several polls and surveys within the past two years. For example, the 2017 CPI was based on 13 different data sources (e.g., African Development Bank, Economist Intelligence Unit, Freedom House, World Bank, World Justice Project).

Using the 2017 CPI as an example, the three least corrupt countries were New Zealand (89), Denmark (88), and Finland (85). The three most corrupt countries were Somalia (9), South Sudan (12), and Syria (14). The United States was 16th (tied with Austria and Belgium) with a score of 75. By world regions, countries in the European Union and Western Europe comprised the least corrupt region with an average score of 66, whereas the most corrupt region was sub-Saharan Africa with an average score of 32. Countries in the Americas and Asia Pacific had an average score of 44, the Middle East and North Africa an average of 38, and those in Eastern Europe and Central Asia an average of 34 (Transparency International 2018a).

USING MEASURES OF CORRUPTION WITH CAUTION

Aggregate measures of corruption may be nothing more than guesswork. Hough (2018) provides four reasons that indexes such as the CPI must be used with caution. First, indexes generally measure perceptions, rather than actual occurrences, of corruption. Perceptions can be quite different than reality and will occur within a particular cultural context. A bribe to one person may, for example, be perceived by another as no more than the proper way to make a deal. Second, because corruption is complex, multifaceted, and riddled with nuance, it is difficult to reduce the problem to a specific numerical value, as does the ranking provided by an index. Differences in two countries' population, demographics, development, and the like, can make it difficult to fairly compare their same index scores.

Third, the survey methodology is based on other surveys. The goal in doing this is to provide perceptions from a wide audience. However, most of the of the surveys come from the United States and a few European countries. Some of the sources, such as the World Bank, the Economist Intelligence Unit, and Freedom House have been criticized in emerging countries as having a pro-U.S. and pro-Western bias. In addition, some countries have so few data sources that it seems unlikely that a meaningful corruption table can be created. Fourth, it takes time for real-world events to be reflected in the indexes, resulting in what Steinbock (2018) calls "anomalies," wherein a country such as South Korea experienced improved rankings at the same time scandals associated with its president were rampant. Users should realize that a current index is best viewed as a snapshot of what was happening at a particular time in the past, not today.

Other methodological issues include problems associated with variation in the wording of the questions put to experts in different sources. The wording and changes in the questions from year to year make it difficult to estimate any actual net change in the level of perception of corruption. For example, one survey may ask to what extent public officeholders are prevented from abusing their position for private interests, whereas another survey asks to what extent public officeholders who abuse their position are prosecuted or penalized. These methodological challenges are important to keep in mind when evaluating the usefulness of the

CPI, and TI does an excellent job each year of clearly identifying the sources used and questions asked (Transparency International 2018b). Great care is taken by TI to ensure the highest possible quality of sources and methodology used. As a result, the CPI is a reputable index widely used by academics, economists, journalists, and business executives.

Philip L. Reichel

See also: Bribery; Corruption; Corruption in China; Corruption in Sub-Saharan Africa

Further Reading

Hough, Dan. 2017. *Analysing Corruption.* Newcastle upon Tyne: Agenda.

Hough, Dan. 2018. "The Yearly Corruption Perceptions Index Just Came Out. Who Got the Gold Medal?" *Washington Post*, Monkey Cage, February 21. Accessed January 14, 2019. https://www.washingtonpost.com/news/monkey-cage/wp/2018/02/21/the-yearly-corruption-perceptions-index-just-came-out-who-got-the-gold-medal/?utm_term=.2751267a6842.

Steinbock, Dan. 2018. "What Transparency International's Corruption Index Doesn't See." *South China Morning Post*, March 16. Accessed January 14, 2019. https://www.scmp.com/comment/insight-opinion/article/2137364/what-transparency-internationals-corruption-index-doesnt-see.

Transparency International. 2018a. "Corruption Perceptions Index 2017." Last Modified February 21, 2018. Accessed January 14, 2019. https://www.transparency.org/news/feature/corruption_perceptions_index_2017.

Transparency International. 2018b. "Resources and Downloads." Last Modified February 21, 2018. Accessed January 14, 2019. https://www.transparency.org/news/feature/corruption_perceptions_index_2017#resources.

Transparency International. n.d. "Who We Are." Accessed July 18, 2018. https://www.transparency.org/about.

Council of Europe Convention on Cybercrime

The Council of Europe Convention on Cybercrime, also known as the Budapest Convention or simply the Convention on Cybercrime, is an international treaty issued by the Council of Europe with the aim of creating common policy to protect society against cybercrime. The convention encourages international cooperation in criminal matters as well as adoption of appropriate legal solutions to combat criminal offenses against confidentiality, integrity, and availability of computer systems, networks, and data. However, all proceedings should obey fundamental human rights, including protection of personal data, freedom of expression, free transfer of information, and respect for privacy as well as dissimilarities that spring from domestic, federal, or state regulations.

The convention is the first international-scale treaty that concerns cybercrimes. It was opened for signature on November 23, 2001, in Budapest. As of March 2018, the convention had been ratified by 34 members of the Council of Europe and by 14 nonmembers, including the United States, Canada, and Australia. An additional part of the convention is formed by the protocol on xenophobia and racism, issued on January 28, 2003, in Strasbourg.

TYPES OF CRIMES

The Convention on Cybercrime obligates all signatories to introduce suitable measures to recognize some activities as crimes. It distinguishes four groups of cybercrimes. The first group is focused on confidentiality, integrity, and availability of data and systems, so all kinds of intentional access to a computer system, interception of nonpublic computer data, interference of data (e.g., damaging or alteration), serious hindering of the functioning of a computer system, and misuse of a device, computer program, or password with criminal intent are illegal. The second group refers to computer-related forgery and fraud. Forgery means input, alteration, or deletion of inauthentic data with the intent to be considered or used as authentic ones, while fraud is committed with the intent of fraud itself or reaping economic benefit. The third group places emphasis on offenses related to child pornography, producing, making available, distributing, procuring, and possessing materials in which the content presents the minor (those ages 16–18) during sexually explicit conduct. The last group discusses the sphere of intellectual property and contraventions of copyright or related rights.

PROCEEDINGS

The convention determines standards and proceedings that are desirable in matters of cybercrime. It outlines procedures on how to protect stored computer data and how to intercept data, which concerns serious offenses. The convention entitles proper authorities to secure those data and to disclose them in specific circumstances, to order specified data being in possession of a third party, to search and seize data or its storage, and to collect and record data in real time. It is also expected that the service provider (the entity enabling communication to users that processes or stores computer data) will keep confidential the fact that all rights arising out of this convention were carried out. Each party of the convention should also define its rights to hear and adjudicate cases (jurisdiction) of cybercrime, according to place of the offense and citizenship of the offender.

INTERNATIONAL COOPERATION

The primary aim of the convention is ensuring relevant instruments as well as incentives to their creation to increase international cooperation in criminal matters. Cooperation means mutual assistance, especially in a range of investigations, proceedings, and collections of evidence. In case of a lack of other treaties or arrangement about such cooperation, provisions of this convention could be applied. The main areas of cooperation concern conditions of exchanging information. The general principle requires a request for assistance, but particular cases may forward partial data spontaneously. The request may be executed completely, partially, with postponement, under special conditions, or be refused. Other spheres of cooperation concern preservation and disclosure of stored computer data, including access at the transborder level and the collection and interception of data. Each party is required to designate a point of contact (a 24/7 network) that will provide trained and equipped staff to ensure immediate and immanent assistance. Potential divergences and disputes in interpretation or application of conventional regulations should be presented to the European Committee on Crime Problems.

Józef J. Doellinger

See also: Cyberattack; Cybercrime; Cybercrime, Policing of; Cyberterrorism; Cyberwar and Cyber Warfare

Further Reading

Cangemi, Daniele. 2004. "Procedural Law Provisions of the Council of Europe Convention on Cybercrime." *International Review of Law Computers and Technology* 18 (2) (July): 165–171.

Keyser, Mike. 2003. "The Council of Europe Convention on Cybercrime." *Journal of Transnational Law and Policy* 12 (2): 287–326.

Moise, Adrian C. 2017. "A Few Comments on the Council of Europe Convention on Cybercrime" *Journal of Law and Administrative Studies* 28 (8): 28–38.

Venancio, Pedro D. 2013. "Similarity and Competition between Cybercrimes Related to Computer Data in the Council of Europe's Convention on Cybercrime" *Masaryk University Journal of Law and Technology* 7: 97–105.

Counterfeit Goods and Money

Counterfeiting refers to making an imitation of an item without authorization and with the intent to deceive others into believing it is genuine. The counterfeiting of goods or products and the counterfeiting of money are the two basic types of counterfeiting.

DECEPTIVE AND NONDECEPTIVE COUNTERFEITING

Counterfeit goods are fakes that are intended to deceive a buyer, but there are also examples of people who knowingly buy counterfeit items. The first instance is *deceptive counterfeiting* and refers to purchases made by a consumer who does not know the product is counterfeit. The second situation is a nondeceptive purchase of a counterfeit product, and this occurs when the consumer willingly and knowingly buys a fake item (Ali 2008).

A motivating factor in purchasing a known counterfeit item (that is, a nondeceptive purchase) is certainly a price that is lower than for the original, but it can also include curiosity about the product or an expression of negative attitudes toward big business. Some people who knowingly buy fake items argue it is an act of democratization by makings items available to everyone that would otherwise be available only to members of the economic elite. Regardless of the motive, nondeceptive purchases are illegal in most jurisdictions and do as much harm to society as deceptive counterfeiting.

Deceptive counterfeiting involves the production of unauthorized replicas of brands that consumers know and trust. The fake goods include clothes, accessories, music, toys, electronics, pharmaceuticals, and essential products from any industry. The global trade in illegitimate goods has increased since 1982 from $5.5 billion to about $600 billion annually. Just in the United States, counterfeiting costs businesses $200–$250 billion a year (McMahan 2015). The most counterfeited products in the world are leather goods (wallets and handbags), watches and jewelry, apparel and accessories, iPhones and consumer electronics, and footwear (McMahan 2015). The five most counterfeited brands in the world are Levi's, Hermes, The North Face, Ugg Boots, and Ray-Ban sunglasses (Straight off the Ledger 2018).

There are clear dangers to the buyer who does not understand that the item purchased is not genuine. Those dangers range from discomfort or displeasure when the item does not fit or work properly or quickly falls apart due to poor quality, to very serious problems of physical harm or death when the product fails to meet safety standards or does not include necessary ingredients. As U.S. Customs and Border Protection (2018) explains, counterfeiters do not care about the buyer's well-being. They only care about making a profit, and as a result, they produce products that can cause injury and pose health and safety risks.

In addition to dangers to the buyer, purchasing counterfeit goods—whether knowingly or not—also presents problems for local and national governments that are not getting expected taxes (meaning less money for schools, hospitals, parks, and so on). In addition, counterfeiters do not pay fair wages, often have poor working conditions, and may use forced or child labor. Profits from counterfeiting support organized crime and even terrorists (International AntiCounterfeiting Coalition n.d.).

COUNTERFEIT MONEY

The dangers of counterfeit currency include the threat it poses to national economies and also to financial institutions and consumers worldwide. INTERPOL (2018) points out that counterfeit money helps support the finances and activities of organized crime groups and terrorists.

Producing fake money has been around since currency was invented. Any country's money can be, and is, counterfeited, but currency such as the U.S. dollar, British pound, and the Euro are especially popular among counterfeiters. The most commonly counterfeited bills are the 20s, whether U.S. dollars, British pounds, Mexican pesos, or Euros (Kasperkevic 2017).

Although counterfeit $20 bills are the most common in the United States, fake $100 bills are the most widespread overseas. Most recently, the primary counterfeiter of those $100 bills is believed to be a government rather than an individual or a criminal enterprise. Specifically, North Korea is accused of making high-quality replicas of U.S. $100 bills and other foreign banknotes. Called "supernotes" by U.S. officials, the bills are so realistic they are indistinguishable from the real ones. Suspicion falls on North Korea because the country has a track record of forging foreign currency, and the country is in dire need of funds because of international sanctions that have been imposed on North Korea. In addition, it seems to many authorities that ordinary criminal organizations are unlikely to have the facilities needed to produce such high-quality forgeries (Ryall 2017).

TAKING ACTION

There are a variety of efforts being taken by government and business to fight against counterfeit goods and money. Two basic strategies being used by companies are tracking and marking (Sykes 2017). Tracking involves having a record or document attached to each branded item, so distributors, retailers, and law enforcement can determine whether a particular item is in the company database. Marking ensures that specific elements are integrated into the product so that the customer can differentiate the real from the fake. This assumes the buyer does not want to pay for a fake. The markings could be placed directly on the item, such as microparticles that look like metallic dust to the naked eye but can be seen as a shape or hologram with a closer look.

For online sales, digital stores such as Amazon and eBay provide opportunities for brands to sell their products directly on the Web site while simultaneously increasing scrutiny on third-party sellers. Online sales of counterfeit medicines are especially difficult to control because many of the fake drugs come from online pharmacies based in remote corners of the world and beyond the reach of regulators (Behner, Hecht, and Wahl 2017). But new technologies will allow more advanced anti-counterfeiting measures that use product codes and a unique serial number to track the movement of drugs from production through distribution to sale and includes automatic reporting of counterfeiting attempts.

Action to thwart counterfeit money is also relying on advanced technology. In 2013, the U.S. Federal Reserve began supplying banks with new $100 bills that include advanced anti-counterfeiting features. The redesigned bill has a blue three-dimensional security ribbon with images of bells and 100s and a color-changing bell in an inkwell (Simpson 2013). Other currencies use fluorescent fibers, microtext (text in tiny font that is legible only with a magnifying glass), colorized holographs, bill denomination numbers that change direction when tilted, properties revealed only by infrared light, watermarks, and raised print.

Counterfeit goods, products, and money continue to be a serious and large-scale problem around the world. Both governments and businesses seek new anti-counterfeiting attempts, but no one doubts that these illegal activities are so profitable that criminal networks will continue to try and find ways for them to stay engaged in these lucrative ventures.

Philip L. Reichel

See also: Counterfeit Medicine; Intellectual Property Crime; Movie Piracy; Music Piracy

Further Reading

Ali, Haider. 2008. "Why People Buy Counterfeit Brands." OpenLearn. Last updated February 14, 2008. January 14, 2019. http://www.open.edu/openlearn/society/the-law/criminology/why-people-buy-counterfeit-brands.

Behner, Peter, Marie-Lyn Hecht, and Fabian Wahl. 2017. "Fighting Counterfeit Pharmaceuticals: New Defenses for an Underestimated—and Growing—Menace." *Strategy&*. Last updated June 29, 2017. Accessed January 14, 2019. https://www.strategyand.pwc.com/reports/counterfeit-pharmaceuticals.

International AntiCounterfeiting Coalition. n.d. "Counterfeiting Costs Everyone." *What Is Counterfeiting?* Accessed October 6, 2018. https://www.iacc.org/resources/about/what-is-counterfeitin.

INTERPOL. 2018. "Counterfeit Currency and Security Documents." *Financial Crime.* Accessed January 14, 2019. https://www.interpol.int/Crime-areas/Financial-crime/Counterfeit-currency-and-security-documents/Counterfeit-currenc.

Kasperkevic, Jana. 2017. "7 Commonly Counterfeited Currencies." *Minnesota Public Radio Marketplace.* Last updated March 28, 2017. January 21, 2019. https://www.marketplace.org/2017/03/28/world/most-counterfeit-currencies.

McMahan, Elysia. 2015. "The 5 Most Counterfeited Products in the World." *First to Know.* Last updated September 30, 2015. Accessed January 14, 2019. https://firsttoknow.com/top-5-most-counterfeited-products-in-the-world.

Ryall, Julian. 2017. "Quality of Fake 'Supernotes' Found in Seoul Fan Suspicions That North Korea Is Forging $100 Bills." *The Telegraph*, December 11. Accessed January 14, 2019. https://www.telegraph.co.uk/news/2017/12/11/quality-fake-supernotes-found-seoul-fan-suspicions-north-korea.

Simpson, Ian. 2013. "U.S. Fed Ships New $100 Bills with Anti-Counterfeit Features." *Reuters.* Last updated October 8, 2013. Accessed January 14, 2019. https://www.reuters.com/article/us-usa-currency/u-s-fed-ships-new-100-bills-with-anti-counterfeit-features-idUSBRE9970IZ20131008.

Straight off the Ledger. 2018. "Top 10 Most Counterfeited Brands of the World." *Blockchain News Editorial.* Last updated March 7, 2018. Accessed January 14, 2019. https://straightofftheledger.com/editorial/top-10-counterfeited-brands-world.

Sykes, Tim. 2017. "Forming an Effective Anti-Counterfeiting Strategy." *Packaging Europe.* Last updated October 5, 2017. Accessed January 14, 2019. https://packagingeurope.com/anti-counterfeit-packaging-white-paper.

U.S. Customs and Border Protection. 2018. "The Truth behind Counterfeits." *Fake Goods, Real Dangers.* Last updated June 28, 2018. Accessed January 14, 2019. https://www.cbp.gov/FakeGoodsRealDangers.

Counterfeit Medicine

Counterfeit medicines are produced and marketed with the intention to make patients believe they are taking a genuine, approved medication of high quality. In reality, they are products that contain no medically beneficial, or even potentially harmful, substances. In cases when the correct medical ingredient is present, it is provided in an incorrect measure. By definition, falsified medicines cannot have a high standard of quality. Additionally, to the lack of drug effect or a dangerous effect, respectively, there is a high risk of insufficient hygienic standards during their concoctions under unsanitary and unregulated conditions, for example, in shacks, warehouses, or garages. These factors can cause several health dangers (illness, resistance to authentic medicines, disability) or, at worst, result in the consumer's coma or death. Hence, counterfeit drugs represent a serious threat to patient safety worldwide.

As a long-term effect, counterfeit drugs also undermine consumers' trust in health systems, government agencies, health care providers, and manufacturers of genuine medicines. Beside this global health issue, counterfeit drugs are also a challenge for law enforcement agencies. Organized criminal networks are involved in these actions, especially because of the huge profits to be gained with pharmaceutical crime. Therefore, this mostly cross border crime needs to be combated by transnational and international approaches.

THE SCOPE OF COUNTERFEIT MEDICINES

Regardless of its therapeutic category (brand name, generic, prescription, or over the counter) and its costs, almost every medical product is at risk of falsification. Antibiotics and anti-malaria medication are the most commonly counterfeited drugs worldwide; moreover, there is a growing trend in counterfeiting life-saving and so-called lifestyle medication (especially drugs against erectile dysfunction). Between 2014 and 2015, the Pharmaceutical Security Institute (PSI) documented a 34 percent increase in "counterfeit incidents" (IFPMA n.d.). It is estimated by the World Health Organization (2018) that 1 out of 10 medical products are not genuine medications. This is especially true for developing and low-income regions, where health systems are nonexistent or less pronounced and feature constrained access to (safe and quality) medications. Whereas this problem was limited to these countries in the past, today no country and no person remains untouched.

REASONS

This international trend is notably magnified by the exponential increase in the online drug market. Provoked by consumer forums and a culture of self-diagnosis and self-prescription, tens of thousands of unregulated and illegal online portals provide unsupervised access to counterfeit medication while pretending to be legitimate pharmacies. According to International Federation of Pharmaceutical Manufacturers and Associations (IFPMA n.d.), more than 50 percent of medicines purchased globally from illegal online sources that conceal their physical address are falsified; 96 percent of these Web sites delivering medications to Americans failed to live up to patient safety standards or pharmacy practice standards of U.S. state and federal laws.

Another main reason for (the rise of) the phenomenon of counterfeit medicine is the money that can be made by this kind of medical crime. Due to bypassing the complex and expensive system of production and licensing of pharmaceuticals or the nonuse or incorrect use of medical substances, the profit is very high and the risk of prosecution very low.

One further key factor that encourages the falsification of medicines is the lack of effective, well-developed drug regulation systems (especially in regard to production, license processes, and import). Currently, only 20 percent of WHO member states have effective rules and systems, whereas 30 percent have none or very limited ones (IFPMA n.d.). Even if a country has implemented a stable and well-working regulatory system, it can be endangered by its neighboring countries using a weak system, resulting in falsified medicines crossing national borders.

Additionally, for quite a long time, there was or (in some national laws) still is a lack of criminal sanctions for falsification of drugs. An important precondition for effective cross border criminal "responses" is a commonly agreed upon definition of counterfeit medicine.

DEFINITION

After an intense discussion about how to define counterfeit medical products, in 2017, the World Health Organization (2018) adopted the following definitions:

- Falsified medical products have had their identity, composition, or source fraudulently or deliberately misrepresented. As a result of this falsification, these products are considered a fraud crime.
- Substandard medical products (also called "out of specification") are authorized pharmaceutical products that fail to meet their quality standards or specifications, or both. Because substandard medicines have been legally approved and produced but do not meet the quality criteria, they are not considered to be falsified, even if they pose a substantial health risk.
- Unregistered or unlicensed medical products are those that have not undergone evaluation or approval by the national or regional regulatory authority for the market in which they are distributed or used.

COUNTERFEIT MEDICINES AND ORGANIZED CRIME

Typically, the crime of counterfeiting medicine is an organized one; only a few cases of individual perpetrators (e.g., in Germany a pharmacist falsified a cancer medicine) are known. The offenders operate across borders in activities that include production, distribution, import, and export. These illicit "pharmaceuticals" come from different countries and regions, under which Asia, Latin America, and China are the main sources.

According to a study by the Institute of Research against Counterfeit Medicines (IRACM), three categories of criminal organizations can be identified in this field: the "small-sizes organizations," operated by a few individuals to reach short-term gains; the "medium-sized transnational organizations," often consisting of groups of businessmen directly linked to the pharmaceutical industry and using sophisticated techniques; and the "large-scale and transnational organizations" (e.g., the "RxNorth case" or the "Jordanian-Syrian network") with complex systems of production and trade (e.g., with regional multiple subnetworks).

PREVENTING AND COMBATING COUNTERFEIT MEDICINE

Coordinated and cross border as well as cross sector actions are needed in the fight against the (organized) crime of counterfeit medicine. As demanded by international and supranational (binding) legal frameworks (e.g., the EU Falsified Medicines Directive or the Council of Europe MediCrime Convention), both practical measures and effective legal provisions (especially criminal law sanctions) are indispensable for a comprehensive strategy to ensure safe and authentic medicines and to rebuild consumers' full trust in the pharmaceutical system.

Criminal offenses with effective, proportionate, and dissuasive penalties for the falsification of drugs are vital in national legal frameworks to investigate and prosecute the criminals. Thereby a commonly agreed definition of counterfeit medicine, such as given by the WHO, should be used to facilitate a cross border law enforcement cooperation.

Additionally, agencies—such as law enforcement and border control agencies—must build international networks to identify the locations of manufacturing, the market roots, and the illegitimate online pharmacies as well as the criminals behind them. WHO supports networking with a collaboration platform for its member states and a monitoring system, which encourage countries to report cases of counterfeit medicines. The national authorities should also pursue a close collaboration, especially with pharmaceutical companies.

To succeed in an effective and comprehensive fight against counterfeit medicine, appropriate training for all agencies involved and all collaboration partners has to be offered. An important factor is raising awareness with consumers by calling patients' attention to the dangers of online purchases, accompanied by information on how to buy products from lawful sources (as realized by the Alliance for Safe Online Pharmacies in the European Union and the United States).

Karin Bruckmüller

See also: Counterfeit Goods and Money; Transnational, Global, and International Crime

Further Reading

International Federation of Pharmaceutical Manufacturers and Associations (IFPMA). n.d. "Falsified Medicines." Accessed January 30, 2019. https://www.ifpma.org/topics/falsified-medicines.

Lee, Kah Seng, et al. 2017. "Combating Sale of Counterfeit and Falsified Medicines Online: A Losing Battle." *Frontiers in Pharmacology* 8, Article 268. Accessed March 2018. https://www.frontiersin.org/articles/10.3389/fphar.2017.00268/full.

Mukhopadhyay, Rajendrani. 2007. "The Hunt for Counterfeit Medicine." *Analytical Chemistry, American Chemical Society* (April 1): 2623–2627.

Przyswa, Eric. 2013. "Counterfeit Medicines and Criminal Organizations." Accessed January 14, 2019. http://www.iracm.com/en/study-report-2013.

World Health Organization (WHO). 2017. *WHO Global Surveillance and Monitoring System for Substandard and Falsified Medical Products.* Geneva: World Health Organization. Accessed January 14, 2019. http://www.who.int/medicines/regulation/ssffc/publications/GSMS_executive_Summary.pdf?ua=1.

World Health Organization (WHO). 2018. "Substandard and Falsified Medical Products." Last modified January 31, 2018. Accessed January 14, 2019. http://www.who.int/mediacentre/factsheets/fs275/en/.

Counterterrorism

Counterterrorism refers to all activities and strategies, be it political, social, financial, or military, designed to prevent, thwart, or respond to—both real and imputed—acts of terrorism. While counterterrorism measures have been around for a long time, a major global increase and a paradigm shift came about as a result of the September 11, 2001, attacks (9/11) and the ensuing War on Terror (WoT). The start of the WoT brought about a dramatic change to the field of counterterrorism, which expanded rapidly.

HISTORY

Prior to 9/11, there was no clearly coordinated international response to terrorism. The existing prescriptions and frameworks were inadequate in dealing with the complex nature of the challenge (Ward 2003, 291). Even though the United Nations became involved in combating terrorism from 1972 onward, there was very little political commitment at the time. Despite quite a large number of international conventions prescribing instruments to support counterterrorism issues, none of these were universally applied, and ratification levels were staggeringly low (Ward 2003, 290–291).

Immediately after the 9/11 attacks, this changed dramatically. Through resolution 1368, the UN Security Council (UNSC) put into place the first universal measures to combat terrorism. These included measures to cut funding and other means of suppressing preparations of terrorist activities through all legal means available; a better exchange of information and judicial cooperation; measures to ensure asylum seekers are not terrorists; and preventing safe havens for terrorists through prosecution and extradition. Moreover, it referred to the right of individual or collective self-defense (in accordance with Article 51 in the charter), which meant that states are free to use violence against suspected terrorists. In doing so, it effectively bypassed one of the greatest achievements of the 20th century—the prohibition of the use of force as contained in the Charter of the United Nations.

The "1267 Sanctions Committee" was established just 17 days after the 9/11 attacks and tasked to combat Al Qaeda (United Nations 2001). Da'esh (also known as the Islamic State of Iraq and Syria, or ISIS) was later added to be targeted by sanctions. The committee had three main "weapons" to use to wit: asset freeze (freezing economic resources and funds of designated individuals or entities), travel ban (preventing entry and transit of designated individuals), and arms embargo. In the same year, the Counter Terrorism Committee (CTC) was created. The CTC can best be viewed as a support mechanism for member states as well as an observatory body monitoring the progress of the implementation of relevant counterterrorism resolutions, such as 1267 (1999), 1989 (2011), and 2253 (2015).

More recently, the UNSC expanded the obligations of states to comply with an even tougher counterterrorism policy, including stricter border control, criminal justice, information sharing and counterextremism, passenger name records (PNR), and other preventive efforts aimed at countering radicalization. Not only were the awareness, legislation, and administrative measures increased, but new forums such as the Global Counterterrorism Forum, the International Coalition against Da'esh, and think tanks were established to deal with the evolving threat of terrorism, particularly the rise of ISIS, whose brutality shocked the world.

APPROACHES AND HUMAN RIGHTS ISSUES

Current counterterrorism approaches can roughly be divided into two categories: "hard" and "soft" approaches. Both these approaches result in a wide variety of ethical, legal, and human rights challenges.

"Soft" measures "seek to undo the radicalization process by engineering the individual's return to moderate society, usually by providing them with a stable support network, probing their original reasons for radicalizing, and divorcing them from their extreme beliefs and social contacts" (Stern 2010, 108). This approach is commonly called the preventing and countering violent extremism approach (PCVE) and is noncoercive. Instead, it aims to build moral barriers, reduce recruitment, and facilitate exit from terrorist movements and tackle what the United Nations calls "conditions conducive to the spread of terrorism" (United Nations 2006). Examples are community promotion; addressing local grievances; youth programs, (online) counternarratives; economic development and inclusion; and encouraging tribal, local, religious, and young leaders to play a more active role in countering violent ideology.

While the upside is that PCVE tackles conditions conducive to terrorism, some major problems with PCVE efforts are that they require a long-term effort with no guarantees of success, and it is not easily measurable. It is, for instance, hard to measure how many attacks have been prevented or how many individuals abandoned their radical beliefs. Also, "hard" measures can easily disturb all the progress made by PCVE efforts. For example, drone strikes that kill innocent civilians while targeting terrorists can undermine the confidence that deradicalization program participants have in the government and the rule of law.

"Hard" measures take an enemy-centric doctrine consisting of primarily offensive, military hard power tactics such as drone strikes, Special Forces operations, and increased policing and intelligence operations (Rineheart 2010), which are aimed at neutralizing the threat. The advantage is that a threat can be effectively taken out, and results can easily be sold to the public in the form of immediate headlines with the illusion of measurable results. A major problem with this approach, however, is that it views terrorism as an event rather than a process, and it ignores that such actions can be conducive to radicalization and extremism (El-Said 2015, 4).

Implementing "hard" counterterrorist measures often results in reducing civil liberties, individual privacy, and sometimes even violations of human rights. Violations that have been flagged are violations to the right to life, the prohibition on torture or inhumane or degrading treatment, the right to liberty and security, the right to a fair trial, and respect for private and family life (Council of Europe 2018). According to many, forfeiting human rights in the fight against terrorism is counterproductive and could even inspire people to join the cause of the terrorists. These human rights advocates argue that human rights should be used as a "weapon" to isolate terrorists. By implementing counterterrorism policies that comply with human rights, one can preserve the values that terrorists are trying to destroy. Also, one can weaken the support base for radicalism among potential adherents while strengthening public confidence in the rule of law.

LEGAL CONTEXT

Although there is an international approach (United Nations Global Counter-terrorism Strategy), there is no legally binding international United Nations treaty on terrorism. A legal framework under construction (Comprehensive Convention on International Terrorism) has found itself in a deadlock since 1996. Thus, the applicable legal framework consists of a range of sources, including treaties, resolutions of the Security Council and the General Assembly, and jurisprudence. As mentioned, UNSC resolutions under Chapter VII impose legally binding obligations on member states to carry out these obligations.

A major prominent concern of many scholars is the lack of a common definition of *terrorism* by the international community. The absence of a definition for terrorism is what Adam Roberts calls confusing, dangerous, and indispensable (2005, 101). It is confusing because it does not mean the same to everyone, and the meaning can change over time (Roberts 2005, 101). It is dangerous, because "terrorism" can easily be used as a form of propaganda with the intention of avoiding debate on the many causes of political violence (Roberts 2005, 101). And it is indispensable because there is a real phenomenon out there that poses a serious threat (Roberts 2005, 101). The ambiguity of what constitutes terrorism may therefore lead to violations of human rights.

The United Nations was quick to recognize the potential harm that counterterrorism measures could do in terms of the violation of human rights. In a statement in the UNSC, Secretary-General Kofi Annan stated, "There is no trade-off between effective action against terrorism and the protection of human rights" (United Nations 2002). The UNSC took measures through resolution 1456 (2003), which reads, "States must ensure that any measure taken to combat terrorism comply with all their obligations under international law, and should adopt such measures in accordance with international law, in particular international human rights, refugee, and humanitarian law" (United Nations 2003). However, this has not always happened. Especially "in an environment in which terms such as 'terrorist' or 'war' can be used in an imprecise or loose manner, the risk of rendering [a] large number of people vulnerable increases, and the protective capacities of human rights organizations are thereby diminished" (Andreopoulos 2007, 20).

Wessel Groot

See also: Crime-Terrorism Nexus; Global Counterterrorism Forum; International Convention for the Suppression of the Financing of Terrorism; National Counterterrorism Center; Terrorism, Intelligence Gathering

Further Reading

Andreopoulos, George. 2007. "The Human Rights/Humanitarian Framework in the Age of Terror." *Zeitschrift für Menschenrechte, Menschenrechte und Terrorismus* 1: 19–36.

Council of Europe. n.d. *Counter Terrorism and Human Rights Protection.* Accessed April 4, 2018. https://www.coe.int/en/web/commissioner/thematic-work/counter-terrorism.

El-Said, Hamed. 2015. *New Approaches to Countering Terrorism: Designing and Evaluating Counter Radicalization and De-Radicalization Programs.* Houndmills, Basingstoke, Hampshire, UK: Palgrave Macmillan.

Rineheart, Jason. 2010. "Counterterrorism and Counterinsurgency." *Perspectives on Terrorism* 4 (5): 31–47.

Roberts, Adam. 2005. "The 'War on Terror' in historical perspective." *Survival* 47 (2): 101–130.

Samuel, Katja L. H. 2017. *Counter-Terrorism and International Law.* New York: Routledge.

Stern, Jessica. 2010. "Mind over Martyr: How to Deradicalize Islamist Extremists." *Foreign Affairs*, 95–108.

United Nations. 2002. "Document S/PV.4453." *Verbatim record of the 4453rd meeting of the Security Council*, January 18: 3. Accessed January 14, 2019. http://www.un.org/en/sc/meetings/records/2002.shtml.

United Nations. 2003. "Document S/RES/1456." Declaration attached to resolution 1456, January 20: para. 6. Accessed January 14, 2019. https://www.un.org/sc/ctc/news/keyword/1456.

United Nations. 2006. "Document A/RES/60/288." Annex. Plan of action attached to resolution 60/288, September 20. Accessed January 14, 2019. https://www.securitycouncilreport.org/un-documents/document/Terr%20ARES60288.php.

United Nations. 2018. *Counter-Terrorism Committee.* Accessed April 11, 2018. https://www.un.org/sc/ctc.

United Nations. n.d. *ISIL (Da'esh) & Al-Qaida Sanctions Committee.* Accessed April 11, 2018. https://www.un.org/sc/suborg/en/sanctions/1267.

Ward, Curtis A. 2003. "Building Capacity to Combat International Terrorism: The Role of the United Nations Security Council." *Journal of Conflict and Security Law* 8 (2): 289–305.

Crimes against Humanity

In a 1915 joint declaration, Great Britain, France, and Russia condemned the Turkish government for the massacres of Armenians in what was then the Ottoman Empire. With reference to the "crimes of Turkey against humanity and civilization," the declaration became the first international document to mention crimes against humanity.

Other landmarks in the concept's development include a 1966 decision by the UN General Assembly to condemn the apartheid policy of South Africa as a crime against humanity. And, in a 1992 declaration on enforced disappearance (an act by which a person, usually a political opponent, is arrested, detained, or abducted by government officials who refuse to disclose the fate or whereabouts of the persons), the United Nations announced that enforced disappearance is a crime against humanity because it undermines respect for the rule of law, human rights, and fundamental freedoms.

DISTINGUISHING AMONG INTERNATIONAL CRIMES

Today, the phrase "crimes against humanity" is considered one of the three core international crimes, along with genocide and war crimes. There is overlap among the terms, and legal distinctions are sometimes difficult to discern.

The term *genocide* was first used by the Polish Jewish lawyer Raphael Lemkin in reference to the destruction of a nation or of an ethnic group. As outlined in the 1948 UN Convention on the Prevention and Punishment of the Crime of Genocide, the crime of genocide is committed against a racial, religious, national, or ethnic group and is conducted with the specific intent of destroying the group in whole or in part. *War crimes* are serious violations of the laws and customs regulating armed conflict. Finally, *crimes against humanity* can be viewed as crimes deliberately committed against the most fundamental human rights of a civilian population in a targeted and systematic way.

Crimes against humanity differ from genocide in that they target a civilian population in general rather than a specific national, racial, or ethnic group. Also, in contrast to genocide, a crime against humanity does not require an intent to eliminate or destroy and entire group and can even be an act that targets the perpetrator's own population.

Unlike war crimes, crimes against humanity can be committed in a time of peace. However, the two types of international crime have much in common—with some people suggesting that both are serious violation of human rights with the only real difference being that war crimes occur during a time of declared war. Beyond that distinction, however, war crime victims can be both civilians and soldiers, but crimes against humanity are committed only against civilian populations. And war crimes can be isolated events, but crimes against humanity are part of widespread or systematic attacks.

LEGAL AUTHORITY

Only a few months after the end of World War II (1939–1945), the four Allied powers (France, the Soviet Union, the United Kingdom, and the United States) signed the London Agreement of 1945 with the purpose of organizing postwar trials through the establishment of the International Military Tribunal. During the conference at which the agreement was signed, the U.S. delegate, Robert Jackson, suggested the title "crimes against humanity" be given to what was a general category of atrocities, persecution, and deportations on political, racial, or religious grounds. As a result, Article VI of the Charter of the International Military Tribunal defined three categories of crimes over which the Nuremberg Tribunal would exercise jurisdiction: crimes against peace, war crimes, and crimes against humanity. Crimes against humanity were defined as being

> murder, extermination, enslavement, deportation, and other inhumane acts committed against any civilian population, before or during the war; or persecutions on political, racial or religious grounds in execution of or in connection with any crime within the jurisdiction of the Tribunal, whether or not in violation of the domestic law of the country where perpetrated. (Charter of the International Military Tribunal 1945, Article 6(c))

Although the Nuremberg Tribunal clearly envisioned crimes against humanity as acts committed in the context of war (even more specifically, in the context of World War II), the concept's application broadened rather quickly. For example, the Nuremberg Principles, as they are called, were formally adopted in 1950 by the UN International Law Commission for its definition of crimes against humanity, but a reference to "before or during the war" was excluded in favor of a "time of peace or war" (United Nations 1950).

Then, in 1993 and 1994, the UN Security Council included the concept of crimes against humanity in the statutes of two international tribunals that were established to prosecute the perpetrators of crimes during the war in former Yugoslavia (1991–1995) and during the Rwandan genocide in 1994. Most recently, in 1998, crimes against humanity were included in the Rome Statute that established the International Criminal Court (ICC). The definition of crimes against humanity found in the Rome Statute reflects the international community's current consensus and is considered the most authoritative definition.

Article 7 (1) of the Rome Statute provides a list of acts that, when committed as part of a widespread or systematic attack directed against a civilian population, constitute a crime against humanity (United Nations 2002):

- Murder
- Extermination
- Enslavement
- Deportation or forcible transfer of population
- Imprisonment or other severe deprivation of physical liberty in violation of fundamental rules of international law
- Torture
- Rape, sexual slavery, enforced prostitution, forced pregnancy, enforced sterilization, or any other form of sexual violence of comparable gravity
- Persecution against any identifiable group or collectivity on political, racial, national, ethnic, cultural, religious, gender, or other grounds that are universally recognized as impermissible under international law, in connection with any act referred to in this paragraph or any crime within the jurisdiction of the Court
- Enforced disappearance of persons
- The crime of apartheid
- Other inhumane acts of a similar character intentionally causing great suffering, or serious injury to body or to mental or physical health

The list is not exhaustive and presents definitional problems, but it does provide an idea of the acts that are believed to fall under the banner of crimes against humanity. And consistent with the interpretations since 1950, crimes against humanity need not be linked to an armed conflict and can also occur in peacetime.

The inclusion of various sex crimes as crimes against humanity was a direct consequence of nongovernmental organizations (NGOs) that advocated on behalf of women as frequent and persistent victims of crimes against humanity (Jackson 2006). In fact, prime examples of crimes against humanity, such as rape and sexual slavery, occur during periods of armed conflict. Wartime sexual violence can be perpetrated by individuals, or it can be more widespread and deliberate, even ordered from above as a war policy. That, for example, was the situation in the former Yugoslavia and Rwanda, where women and young girls were raped by enemy soldiers in the field or held in captivity and used as sex slaves. In Uganda, young girls have been abducted by the Lord's Resistance Army, a rebel group, and forced to "marry" rebel leaders (Smeulers 2013).

Crimes against humanity are identified as an international crime, so they are exempted from the general rule that states have a sovereign right to prosecute crimes committed within their own borders or by their own citizens. Instead, crimes against humanity may be punished by courts of countries other than where the crime took place and by international courts.

IS TERRORISM A CRIME AGAINST HUMANITY?

The terrorist attacks of September 11, 2001, were described by many observers, including the UN High Commissioner for Human Rights, as crimes against humanity. But if the meaning of crimes against humanity includes the actions of terrorist organizations, it becomes increasingly difficult to distinguish crimes against humanity from ordinary crimes punishable under domestic law. For example, authorities debate whether murder carried out as part of a widespread or systematic "attack against a civilian population" and is accomplished as part of a policy of a state or organized group to commit murder constitutes a crime against humanity. Using Boko Haram in Nigeria as an example, the Office of the Prosecutor of the International Criminal Court has concluded that there is a reasonable basis to believe that Boko Haram has committed acts that constitute crimes against humanity by committing murder and also persecution against an identifiable group or collectivity (Merkouris 2015).

Philip L. Reichel

See also: Genocide; International Criminal Court; International Criminal Tribunal for Rwanda; International Criminal Tribunal for the Former Yugoslavia; War Crimes

Further Reading

Bassiouni, M. Cherif. 2011. *Crimes against Humanity: Historical Evolution and Contemporary Application.* New York: Cambridge University Press.

Charter of the International Military Tribunal. 1945. "Nuremberg Trial Proceedings Vol. 1." Accessed July 15, 2018. http://avalon.law.yale.edu/imt/imtconst.asp.

Jackson, Donald W. 2006. "Crimes against Humanity." In *Governments of the World: A Global Guide to Citizens' Rights and Responsibilities*, edited by C. Neal Tate, 276–278. Detroit: Macmillan Reference USA.

Lerner, K. Lee, and Brenda Wilmoth Lerner, eds. 2006. "Introduction to Crimes against Humanity." In *Crime and Punishment: Essential Primary Sources*, 133. Detroit: Gale.

Luban, David. 2004. "A Theory of Crimes against Humanity." *Yale Journal of International Law* 29: 85–167.

Merkouris, Panos. 2015. "Q&A: Terrorist Acts—War Crimes, Crimes against Humanity, or Genocide? The Case of Nigeria." Accessed July 15, 2018. https://phap.org/questions/1202.

Robinson, Darryl. 1999. "Defining 'Crimes against Humanity' at the Rome Conference." *American Journal of International Law* 93 (1): 43–57.

"Rome Statute of the International Criminal Court (RSICC)." Adopted July 17, 1998; entered into force July 1, 2002. Accessed July 23, 2012. http://untreaty.un.org.unco.idm.oclc.org/cod/icc/statute/romefra.htm.

Smeulers, Alette. 2013. "Crimes against Humanity." In *Global Social Issues*, edited by Christopher G. Bates and James Ciment, 185–194. Armonk, NY: Sharpe Reference.

United Nations. 1950. "Yearbook of the International Law Commission." Accessed July 15, 2018. http://legal.un.org/docs/?path=../ilc/publications/yearbooks/english/ilc_1950_v2.pdf&lang=E.

United Nations. 2002. "Rome Statute of the International Criminal Court." Last modified January 16, 2002. Accessed January 21, 2019. http://legal.un.org/icc/statute/romefra.htm.

Vernon, Richard. 2002. "What Is Crime against Humanity?" *Journal of Political Philosophy* 10 (3): 231–149.

Crime-Terrorism Nexus

The crime-terrorism nexus is a controversial theoretical framework that stipulates that crime, especially organized crime, and terrorism are often highly intertwined. Some scholars, such as Louise Shelley, posit that all large-scale terrorist attacks have been facilitated by organized crime (Shelley 2014). Such interactions can take many forms: terrorist groups and organized crime groups can transact to provide each other with services that each cannot themselves perform. Terrorists can use traditional criminal enterprises to fund their terrorist activities, and organized crime groups may adopt terrorist strategies to protect their organizations and financial interests. This framework is based on the assumption that organized criminal groups are primarily motivated by profit and terrorist groups by some ideology.

Many scholars disagree about whether such interactions, when they occur, are impactful or relevant to the study of crime and terror and to security outcomes. Assuming such connections exist, any law enforcement strategy that does not incorporate a two-pronged approach targeting the subject of the investigation, be it an organized criminal or terrorist group, as well as the connections it has to groups of the opposite type, will most likely fail to incapacitate the organization.

TYPES OF INTERACTIONS

Scholars have identified three major ways that organized crime and terrorism can interact: alliances or simple transactional relationships, activity appropriation, and convergence. In alliances, organized criminal or terrorist groups will seek out specific expertise or operational support that the other type of group could supply. In such relationships, there is an exchange of goods and services, but each organization retains its organizational mandate (Makarenko 2004).

Alternatively, organized criminal or terrorist groups may take on qualities of the other by developing their own terrorist capabilities or engaging in organized crime by themselves. When such "activity appropriation" occurs, the groups will not lose their organizational mandate but rather adapt the methods of the other to fulfill some objective related to their primary goals: profit in the case of organized criminals and political change in the case of terrorists. In this stage, groups may or may not interact with each other as they borrow the methods of the other. Contact between organized criminal groups and terrorist groups is not necessary for one to appropriate the activity of the other, although such contact can and does occur (Shelley and Picarelli 2005).

Finally, groups may emerge that incorporate the methods and motivations of both organized crime and terrorism so that they cannot be reliably categorized as either an organized criminal group or a terrorist group, creating instead a "hybrid" group (Shelley and Picarelli 2005).

MAKARENKO'S CONTINUUM

Makarenko (2004) approaches the crime-terror nexus as a continuum, with pure organized crime and pure terrorism at either end. In the center of the continuum, there is complete convergence: an organization takes on enough characteristics from both ends of the spectrum that it can no longer reliably be called a terrorist organization or an organized crime group. Makarenko groups the type of interactions between organized criminal groups and terrorist organizations into four groups: alliances, operationally motivated unions, convergence, and the "black hole syndrome."

Alliances are the loosest of the associations in the sense that the groups involved in the alliance maintain their organizational mandates; terrorist groups remain committed to terrorism to achieve extremist ideological goals, and organized criminal groups retain a financial mandate. However, these alliances can range from one-time cooperations to short-term or even long-term relationships. These partnerships are largely transactional and are formed because one group lacks the technical knowledge or connections to accomplish an operational goal and are born out of convenience. However, such alliances come with considerable risk. Precisely because the groups do not share a common ideology, they have no great loyalties to each other. Therefore, if members of one group come under pressure from internal group politics or from law enforcement, they are not likely to protect the partner organization or its members.

Because of these risks, groups have a great incentive to undertake such tasks themselves, without involving another organization. Thus, organized criminal groups can perpetrate high-casualty attacks meant to intimidate and coerce a population to protect the organization or to secure some political outcome that would allow them to transact more safely, and terrorist groups can participate in profit-oriented crimes to finance their operations.

Alliances that involve an organized crime group and a terrorist group working closely with each other may result in members of one becoming members of the other and the gradual fusion of the two groups into one—that is, operationally motivated unions. This hybrid group would engage in the activities relating to both organized crime and terrorism. The tightening of the relationship between the two groups would be facilitated by the organized criminal group developing political motivations and the terrorist group becoming more interested in profit.

These hybrid groups thrive in areas outside state controls, and the absence of constraints from government facilitates the convergence of organized criminal groups and terrorist organizations. This is most noticeable in conflict-torn regions. As the conflict progresses and criminal groups can rapidly enrich themselves, terrorist groups that, at the start of the war, had strong ideological convictions can become more attracted to illicit profits. Alternatively, organized criminal groups may develop stronger ideological convictions and may join the hostilities as a hybrid organized criminal-terrorist group. A "black hole" scenario can refer to a situation in which formal state control is absent and convergence of organized criminal groups and terrorist organizations occurs. In such situations, the hybrid group or groups can assume control over the ungoverned area.

DISHMAN'S LEADERLESS NEXUS

Dishman (2005) identifies a crime-terror nexus as being particularly likely to emerge as hierarchies in organized criminal groups and terrorist groups flatten and organizations evolve from having strict command structures to being made up of networks in which a command structure, if it exists, exerts much less control over individual actors than in a traditional hierarchy. Sizeable organized criminal or terrorist groups are forced to flatten to avoid threats from law enforcement efforts or rivals. In a hierarchical structure, if the leader is arrested or killed, the entire organization is at risk of breaking down. In a networked structure, there may be a leader who sets a general agenda for the group, but day-to-day activity is run by members of each node of the network. If the leader of the organization or any one node is disrupted, the rest of the network can continue to operate.

Dishman argues that leaders of large organizations that are arranged in hierarchies often judge cooperation with either terrorist groups or organized criminal groups as being too risky and therefore prevent alliances from developing. Terrorist groups, because of their political agendas, draw attention to themselves. Organized criminal groups tend to avoid attention unless it benefits the earning power of the organization. As the control of such leaders weakens and networks develop, the members of a node have more autonomy in developing relationships with organized crime groups or terrorist organizations.

In addition, decentralized nodes often receive little financial or operational support from the organization at large. To fund day-to-day activities, including executing attacks or minimizing the threat of law enforcement, members might participate in activities outside the mandate of their organization.

PICARELLI'S TURBULENT NEXUS

Picarelli (2006) argues that cooperation between organized criminal and terrorist groups is based heavily on each group's relation to the state: whether the groups are "sovereign-free" or "sovereign-bound." Sovereign-free groups are those that are mostly concerned with transnational or international goals and are not particularly invested in the status and governance of one state in particular. These groups tend to be more networked than hierarchical and more adaptive to changing political and social climates. Sovereign-bound groups, on the other hand, are concerned with supplanting the state's control over one particular jurisdiction. These groups tend to be hierarchical, to mimic the organization of a legitimate state. Their behavior tends to be more habitual than adaptive. Organized criminal and terrorist groups can be either sovereign-free or sovereign-bound.

According to Picarelli, the attitude toward sovereignty must be similar between groups if a relationship is to form. Two forms of nexus can occur between organized criminal and terrorist groups: a state-centric nexus and a multicentric nexus. Which form a relationship takes depends on whether the groups are sovereign-free or sovereign-bound. A state-centric nexus is formed between sovereign-bound groups. These relationships tend to be purely transactional and relatively short-lived, having been formed to accomplish a specific short-term goal. Because such organizations want to supplant the state, autonomy is important, so these organizations tend to solve problems using exclusively internal resources if possible, rather than collaborating with another group. Because sovereign-bound groups tend to be hierarchical, collaborations often require permission from leaders who may be relatively risk-averse. Sovereign-free organizations, though, are generally not constrained by hierarchies or the need to gain legitimacy and solve problems internally. In addition, because of the global scope of such organizations, they are more likely to have needs that cannot be met by existing group members, such as money laundering or transnational smuggling operations. If these needs are recurring, groups may work together repeatedly and develop a bond of trust and a sustained partnership. Such a relationship constitutes a multicentric nexus.

Lilla Heins

See also: Counterterrorism; Organized Crime; Terrorism, International; Transnational, Global, and International Crime

Further Reading

Dishman, Chris. 2004. "The Leaderless Nexus: When Crime and Terror Converge." *Studies in Conflict and Terrorism* 28 (3) (September): 237–252.

Makarenko, Tamara. 2017. "The Crime-Terror Continuum: Tracing the Interplay between Transnational Organised Crime and Terrorism." *Global Crime* 6 (1) (February): 129–149.

Picarelli, John T. 2006. "The Turbulent Nexus of Transnational Organized Crime and Terrorism: A Theory of Malevolent International Relations." *Global Crime* 7 (1) (February): 1–24.

Shelley, Louise I. 2014. *Dirty Entanglements: Corruption, Crime, and Terrorism.* Cambridge: Cambridge University Press.

Shelley, Louise I., and John T. Picarelli. 2005. "Methods and Motives: Exploring Links between Transnational Organized Crime and International Terrorism." *Trends in Organized Crime* 9 (2) (Winter): 52–67.

Criminologists without Borders

Criminologists without Borders is a network of criminologists, researchers, professors, and those working in the field who seek to apply scientific findings and "best practices" to the policies and operations of crime prevention and criminal justice systems. Criminologists without Borders is a registered nonprofit organization that provides objective information and research to inform policy and programs dealing with crime and criminal justice. It offers a neutral forum for the pursuit of ideas and practices informed by evidence.

Criminologists without Borders has three objectives:

1) To provide up-to-date summaries of the scientific and evaluation literature to assist decision makers in considering alternative approaches to crime prevention and criminal justice issues.
2) To develop these up-to-date summaries of the scientific and evaluation literature on an ongoing basis through the contributions of the membership.
3) To offer technical assistance and training to requesting agencies (as funds to cover these costs become available).

The organization was founded in 2008 and has consultative status with the United Nations. In that capacity, Criminologists without Borders compiles and disseminates scientific literature syntheses and reading lists on themes covered by each session of Commission on Crime Prevention and Criminal Justice (CCPCJ) since 2009 and also the 59th, 60th, 61st and 62nd sessions of Commission on the Status of Women. The organization sponsored panels at the 26th and 27th sessions of CCPCJ and the 13th United Nations Congress on Crime Prevention and Criminal Justice.

Criminologists without Borders holds membership meetings at the American Society of Criminology conference in November of each year, where it raises awareness about its work and seeks membership support. The organization also held several information sessions at annual meetings of the Academy of Criminal Justice Sciences, a professional association of criminologists and instructors.

Representatives of Criminologists without Borders attended the 55th session of the Commission on Social Development and the 17th session of the United Nations Permanent Forum on Indigenous Issues. A statement was made at the 23rd session of the CCPCJ, and the literature synthesis compiled for the United Nations Congress on Crime Prevention and Criminal Justice was included as a document for Workshop 4.

Criminologists without Borders jointly sponsored a side event at the UN Headquarters in New York with the United Nations Interregional Crime and Justice Research Institute (UNICRI) at the 61st session of the Commission on the Status of Women entitled "Strengthening the Role of Women in Law Enforcement." The organization sponsored a side event at the 26th session of the Commission on Crime Prevention and Criminal Justice on a "Typology of Corruption Behaviors: Clues for Intervention and Prevention."

Criminologists without Borders works to achieve its objectives through its sponsoring of panels and dissemination of reading lists at the aforementioned sessions of the Commission on the Status of Women. The organization support its own and UN development goals through research literature syntheses, which were disseminated at every session of the Commission on Crime Prevention and Criminal Justice since 2009.

The role of civil society is vital to raise public awareness and inform policy decisions through active participation in UN meetings, professional conferences, and contributions through empirical scientific literature reviews, sponsoring of side events, and submission of documents. Criminologists without Borders has played an important role is raising public awareness and ensuring that scientific research is synthesized, available, and considered in policy discussions and debates.

Jay S. Albanese

See also: Transnational, Global, and International Crime; UN Commission on Crime Prevention and Criminal Justice; UN Congresses on Crime Prevention and Criminal Justice; UN Office on Drugs and Crime

Further Reading

Criminologists without Borders. 2018. *Criminal Justice Responses to Prevent and Counter Cybercrime in All Its Forms, Including through the Strengthening of Cooperation at the National and International Levels.* Accessed January 14, 2019. http://www.criminologistswithoutborders.org/services.

Criminologists without Borders. n.d. About Us. Accessed January 14, 2019. Criminologistswithoutborders.org/about_us.

Criminologists without Borders and United Nations Interregional Crime and Justice Research Institute. 2017. *Comprehensive and Integrated Crime Prevention Strategies: Public Participation, Social Policies, and Education in Support of the Rule of Law.* Accessed January 14, 2019. http://www.criminologistswithoutborders.org/services

Criminologists without Borders, International Sociological Association, and United Nations Interregional Crime and Justice Research Institute. 2016. *Preventing and Countering Terrorism: A Review of Recent Research.* Accessed January 14, 2019. http://www.criminologistswithoutborders.org/services.

Cryptocurrency

Cryptocurrency (i.e., virtual currency) is unregulated digital currency issued and (usually) controlled by its developers. The value of cryptocurrency is not set by a central bank or government authority, nor is it linked to a fiat currency (i.e., legal currency). Although members of the virtual community widely accept cryptocurrencies, they are less well-known to the public. In recent years, banks, businesses, and governments are recognizing the importance of cryptocurrency. There are more than 1,300 different types of cryptocurrencies in circulation, with the most common being Bitcoin, Litecoin, Rippel, Monero, Dash, Ethereum, and Zcash.

TYPES OF CRYPTOCURRENCY

The first cryptocurrency, Bitcoin, emerged in 2008. Its developer, Satoshi Nakamoto, proposed a peer-to-peer electronic cash system that would eliminate banks from transactions (Nakamoto 2008). Unlike fiat currency, Bitcoin's value is influenced by supply and demand. In addition, whereas no one knows how much fiat money is in circulation, the number of Bitcoins is capped at 21 million.

Initially valued at less than 1 cent to one Bitcoin in 2010, its value peaked to $14,670 per one Bitcoin in December 2017, surpassing the market cap of Goldman Sach's $92.9 billion and Morgan Stanley's $89.1 billion. Many experts fear that if Bitcoin's popularity increases, it could penetrate gold markets and offshore banking, resulting in a Bitcoin market cap of trillions of dollars, which would make it more dominant than fiat currency.

Although there are commonalities among cryptocurrencies, such as the encryption of transactions, which involves using cryptography where an owner of Bitcoin cryptographically signs a statement when Bitcoin is transferred to another recipient, after which the recipient posts the transaction on the global Bitcoin network so that the transferred Bitcoin coin will be accepted only from the new owner. Other things shared in common by cryptocurrencies are a lack of oversight by the government and peer-to-peer transactions involving the sharing of information, assets, or data between parties without a central authority. There are differences regarding the degree of privacy and anonymity offered to users, the speed of transactions, and technology.

Popular cryptocurrencies include the following:

- *Litecoin (LTC)*, launched in 2011, was among the first cryptocurrencies following Bitcoin. Although the maximum Bitcoins is set at 21 million, Litecoins can accommodate as high as 84 million. In addition, Litecoin has faster transaction confirmation, which means that a merchant has a wait time of only 2.5 minutes versus 9 minutes with Bitcoin.
- *Ripple (XRP)*, started in 2012, is a real-time global settlement network that offers instantaneous international payments. It uses a consensus ledger (a network that accepts and processes transactions) instead of mining (where miners compete to solve a difficult cryptographic puzzle, and the first one who solves the puzzle receives 12.5 newly minted bitcoins) and takes less time to produce transaction confirmations (Caster 2017). A ripple network can carry out foreign exchange conversions and calculate the cost of transactions to the nearest cent instantaneously.
- *Monero (XMR),* launched in 2014, creates private transactions known as "ring CT," which not only hides the sources of funds but also the amount of the transactions. Because of its enhanced privacy and anonymity, Monero has become popular in darknet markets.
- *Dash* (originally darkcoin), launched in 2014, offers more secrecy and anonymity than Bitcoins. Dash utilizes a decentralized masternode network, which allows the transactions to be almost nontraceable. The masternodes "represent a new layer of network servers that work in highly secure clusters"

to eliminate network attacks (Dash, n.d., para 2). It claims payment confirmation in seconds and over 4,500 servers around the world.

- *Ethereum (ETH)*, launched in 2015, runs on "smart contracts and distributed applications (ĐApps)." The smart contracts are scripts that allow any contract to be created between peers. It is unique in that it prevents any one entity to have complete control of the data: instead, the user maintains the control.
- *Zcash (ZEC)*, launched in 2016, uses advanced cryptographic methods, which shields transactions from being traced. As with a HyperText Transfer Protocol Secure (HTTPS), which uses encryption code for secure communication, Zcash hides the identity of the sender, the recipient, and the amount of the transaction.

CRIMINAL ACTIVITY AND CRYPTOCURRENCY

The rising popularity of cryptocurrencies has created opportunities for criminal enterprises, from Ponzi schemes to drug trafficking, money laundering, selling fake IDs and passports, and hackers for hire. The first major criminal case involving Bitcoins was Silk Road, an illegal online marketplace. Silk Road was an encrypted Web service that provided anonymity to its users. Using Bitcoin as a payment method, the Web site created a marketplace for illegal drugs, stolen goods, forged documents, and other services (Vigna and Casey 2017). In 2013, the Federal Bureau of Investigation (FBI) arrested the creator of the Web site, Ross Ulbricht, and in 2015, he was sentenced to life without the possibility of parole.

The popularity of cryptocurrency and its global outreach and decentralization concern many counterterrorism experts. However, there is only anecdotal evidence of the use of cryptocurrencies in terrorist operations. At present, most terrorist funding involves mechanisms such as the traditional *hawala* (informal cash transaction) system. Reports indicate that some technologically savvy terrorists groups are receptive to new technologies. Although the use of cryptocurrencies in terrorist activities is limited at present, some experts believe that financial regulatory committees should work to prevent this (Goldman et al. 2017).

Given their secrecy, the lack of a regulatory body, and cross border applications, cryptocurrencies also provide opportunities for Internet-based money laundering, for example, "online gambling, e-commerce transactions, online auctions or fake projects listed on foreign crowdfunding sites" (Virtual Currencies Work Group 2014, 7). Although experts agree on the need to regulate cryptocurrencies, they caution against government overreaction and misregulation. Enforcement entities should improve their own technology "to combat future crimes involving cryptocurrencies, while also allowing the technology room to evolve" to provide potential benefits to consumers (Carlisle 2017, ix).

Sesha Kethineni

See also: Cryptomarkets; Cybercrime; Dark Web/Deep Web

Further Reading

Carlisle, David. 2017. *Virtual Currencies and Financial Crime: Challenges and Opportunities*. London: Stephen Austin and Sons.

Caster, Amy. 2017. "A (Short) Guide to Blockchain Consensus Protocols." *Coindesk*, March 4. Accessed January 14, 2019. https://www.coindesk.com/short-guide-blockchain-consensus-protocols.

Dash. n.d. "Dash Is Digital Cash: A Revolutionary Digital Money System. Meet Digital Cash." *Dash Network*. Accessed January 14, 2019. https://www.dash.org.

Goldman, Zachary K., Ellie Maruyama, Elizabeth Rosenberg, Edoardo Saravalle, and Julia Solomon-Strauss. 2017. *Terrorists Use of Virtual Currencies: Containing the Potential Threat*. Washington, D.C.: Center for a New American Security. https://www.cnas.org/publications/reports/terrorist-use-of-virtual-currencies.

Nakamoto, S. 2008. "Bitcoin: A Peer-to-Peer Electronic Cash System." Accessed January 14, 2019. https://bitcoin.org/bitcoin.pdf.

Vigna, Paul, and Michael H. Casey. 2016. *The Age of Cryptocurrency: How Bitcoin and the Blockchain Are Challenging the Global Economic Order*. New York: St. Martin's Press.

Virtual Currencies Working Group. 2014. "Regulating Virtual Currencies: Recommendations to Prevent Virtual Currencies from Being Used for Fraudulent Purposes and Money Laundering." *TracFin*, June. Accessed January 14, 2019. https://www.economie.gouv.fr/files/regulatingvirtualcurrencies.pdf.

Cryptomarkets

Cryptomarkets are anonymous, encrypted marketplaces hosted on "Dark Web" platforms, such as Tor and I2P, where vendors can sell goods and services worldwide in exchange for cryptocurrency. Vendors post illicit goods that include drugs, pornography, weapons, hacking tips, counterfeits, and sometimes legal merchandise. Commonly referred to as "darknet markets" (DNMs), cryptomarkets can take on a wide range of possibilities, from hundreds of vendors and products to specialized personal vendor Web sites. Although anyone can use cryptomarkets, the community is made up of many crypto-libertarians who support personal freedoms and oppose censorship and regulation (Sotirakopoulos 2017).

FEATURES

Features and rules vary from marketplace to marketplace, but there are a few main characteristics that are common across sites. For example, one-way cryptomarkets enhance user satisfaction by acting as a third party during transactions through escrow services. By acting as a third party, marketplace administrators are able to handle disputes and act as mediators. Problems between buyers and vendors, or issues between parties and the marketplace itself, are taken to administrators who then attempt to remedy the situation.

Various ways to build trust and clientele are also important features for cryptomarkets. After a transaction is complete, buyers are often required to post feedback on the vendor's page. This rating includes stars (or similar rating system) and comments about the overall quality of the purchase. Positive feedback builds trust for a vendor. Higher trust levels indicate a better reputation, which means the vendor provides a quality product, reliable delivery, and friendly customer service. These key features have caused cryptomarkets to gain the comparison to clearnet sites (that is, unencrypted sites that can be accessed from any browser) such as eBay, Amazon, and Etsy, where the vendors are rated by buyers to signal to others their trustworthiness.

Forums are also a large aspect of cryptomarkets. Although separate sites, forums are places where any user can engage in open discussion about topics on discussion boards set up by the market administrators. The feedback feature can be extended to the forums, and vendors can also advertise or defend themselves. Additional topics include what listings buyers want to see posted, problems with administration, and other various topics. Not all cryptomarkets have a separate discussion forum, but larger markets utilize this feature to foster community among its users.

EVOLUTION

The premise of cryptomarkets was developed through the clearnet. Since the inception of the Internet, the trade of illegal items has been documented. In the late 1990s and into the early 2000s, items such as cannabis and information on drug synthesis were being sold via the Internet. By 2009, marketplaces began the transition to hosting on the darknet as opposed to the clearnet (Buxton and Bingham 2015).

Cryptomarkets had a breakthrough in February 2011 when Ross Ulbricht created Silk Road, the most famous of all cryptomarkets. Vendors could advertise many products, but drugs constituted 70 percent of the total listings. Approximately 1,229,465 transactions were successfully completed on the site, resulting in roughly $1.2 billion in revenue over two and a half years (Sealed Complaint 2013). The Federal Bureau of Investigation (FBI) shut down Silk Road in October 2013, and Ulbricht was sentenced to life without the possibility of parole (Weiser 2015).

After the Silk Road takedown, many smaller marketplaces emerged, but they did not have the longevity of business like their predecessor. Although cryptomarkets have increased in number, they typically have shorter life spans due to the possibilities of law enforcement seizures, hacks by outside parties, and exit scams when the administrators unexpectedly shut down the market and take user's cryptocurrency. In 2015, another wave of law enforcement takedowns forced market administrators to adopt stronger safety features, including multisignature escrow, two-factor authentication, more anonymous cryptocurrencies, and decentralization.

Despite claims of high security, paranoia began again in 2017 when an international effort to takedown the largest marketplaces, such as AlphaBay and Hansa, were successful. In the following months, other markets were plagued with seizures by law enforcement, exit scams, and unclaimed distributed denial-of-service (DDoS) attacks.

POLICING

There is an inherent distrust of law enforcement among users of cryptomarkets. National and international efforts to take down markets have been successful in the past, as shown with Silk Road, AlphaBay, and Hansa. On a smaller scale, law enforcement uses tactics to target buyers through postal interception and vendors through undercover stings. Nonetheless, law enforcement is constantly battling the paranoia of cryptomarket users, sophisticated anonymization techniques, and rapidly evolving technology.

Rachel Salter

See also: AlphaBay; Cryptocurrency; Cyberattack; Denial-of-Service Attacks; Tor (The Onion Router) Network

Further Reading

Buxton, Julia, and Tim Bingham. 2015. "The Rise and Challenge of Dark Net Drug Markets." *Policy Brief* 7: 1–24.

Sealed Complaint. 2013. *United States v. Ross William Ulbricht* (S.D.N.Y. 2013) (13 MAG 2328). Accessed January 14, 2019. https://web.archive.org/web/20140220003018/https://www.cs.columbia.edu/~smb/UlbrichtCriminalComplaint.pdf.

Sotirakopoulos, Nikos. 2017. "Cryptomarkets as a Libertarian Counter-Conduct of Resistance." *European Journal of Social Theory* (July): 1–18.

Weiser, Benjamin. 2015. "Ross Ulbricht, Creator of Silk Road Website, Is Sentenced to Life in Prison." *New York Times*, May 29. Accessed January 14, 2019. https://www.nytimes.com/2015/05/30/nyregion/ross-ulbricht-creator-of-silk-road-website-is-sentenced-to-life-in-prison.html.

Cyberattack

A cyberattack is a deliberate and malicious attempt by an individual, organization, or government to access or damage a computer system. The motive can be social, financial, or political, but there will be some benefit to the attacker. The attack is typically accomplished through the spread of malicious programs (viruses) and various means of stealing personal, institutional, or organizational information.

IMPACT OF CYBERATTACKS

Cyberattacks occur daily and are found everywhere computer systems are present. Or, as the former CEO of Cisco (a global communications and information technology company), John Chambers, explained, "There are two types of companies: those that have been hacked, and those who don't yet know they have been hacked" (Cisco n.d.).

Although cost varies depending on business or organization size, the average cost of a single cyberattack is estimated at $5 million, with the largest itemized cost being system downtime for the company. The variation is seen when comparing the $10 million estimated costs and three-month recovery time for a cyberattack at the Erie County (NY) Medical Center, the $300 million reported losses from cyberattacks in 2017 at global shipping giant Maersk, and a similar $300 million loss for the pharmaceutical company Merck (Crowe 2018).

There are both direct and hidden costs related to cyberattacks. For organizations, the direct costs include any money that may have been stolen as well as the costs related to notifying customers about any compromise to their personal information, costs associated with credit monitoring that the company may have offered customers, and money paid for legal judgments or regulatory penalties assessed to the company. Hidden costs can include damage to the business's reputation, loss of proprietary information, and changes to the business direction. The impact of a cyberattack can last for years after the actual attack occurred.

COMMON TYPES OF CYBERATTACKS

Cyberattacks take a variety of forms. Some of the more common include *phishing* (a form of identity theft that relies on fraudulent e-mail or Web sites to obtain users' personal information) and *ransomware*, which uses malicious software to prevent users from accessing their computer files until they pay a ransom to the criminals behind the attack. Less well-known attacks include *Structured Query Language injection* (SQLI or SQL injection), wherein the attack allows access to sensitive information (for example, company data or private customer details) not intended to be seen, and *man-in-the-middle* (MitM) attacks that occur when the attacker eavesdrops on a two-party transaction (for example, the victim provides personal credit card information to a merchant on an unsecure public Wi-Fi network).

TRENDS IN CYBERATTACKS

In 2017, 54 percent of companies experienced one or more successful cyberattacks, and most of those attacks used fileless techniques (Crowe 2018). The use of fileless techniques is a notable trend that presents new challenges for cybersecurity efforts. Fileless technologies are ones that effectively bypass security solutions because they avoid the use of executable files (files with an .exe extension that cause a computer to perform a task)—and it is those files that antivirus programs and other traditional security protections rely on to detect malware.

CYBERATTACKS ON CRITICAL NATIONAL INFRASTRUCTURE

A country's critical national infrastructure (CNI) refers to the essential facilities and services that are necessary for the country to function. The United States recognizes 16 CNI sectors that include the chemical sector, communications sector, emergency services sector, financial services sector, and the water and wastewater systems sector (see the complete list at DHS 2018). A cyberattack on any one of these sectors could have a debilitating effect on national security, the economy, or public health or safety.

Several incidents have occurred worldwide since 2015 that have led to increased media reporting on the dangers of cyberattacks on CNI. The *New York Times* reported that, in 2017, there have been cyberattack against several petrochemical plants in Saudi Arabia. One was intended to sabotage the plant's operations and to cause what could have been a deadly explosion (Perlroth and Krauss 2018). U.S. government officials were concerned that the culprits could repeat the attack in other industrial plants around the world, as so many plants use the same American-engineered computer systems that were compromised in at the Saudi plant.

In March 2018, the United States accused Russia of a cyberattack on operating systems of several U.S. energy companies in an attempt to compromise the energy grid. The Department of Homeland Security (DHS) said the cyberattack, which began in 2016, was coordinated and deliberate and showed attempts to collect information on industrial control systems (Borger 2018).

Attacks on CNI have raised alarms about CNI cybersecurity in countries around the world, and there are expectations among both business and government officials that action can be taken to lessen the likelihood that a country's essential services can be protected.

Philip L. Reichel

See also: Cybercrime; Phishing; Ransomware

Further Reading

Borger, Julian. 2018. "US Accuses Russia Of Cyber-Attack on Energy Sector and Imposes New Sanctions." *The Guardian*, March 15. Accessed January 14, 2019. https://www.theguardian.com/us-news/2018/mar/15/russia-sanctions-energy-sector-cyber-attack-us-election-interference.

Cisco. 2018. *Annual Cybersecurity Report*. San Jose, CA: Cisco Systems, Inc. Accessed January 14, 2019. https://www.cisco.com/c/en/us/products/security/security-reports.html#~download-the-report.

Cisco. n.d. "What Are the Most Common Cyberattacks?" *Security*. Accessed October 13, 2018. Accessed January 14, 2019. https://www.cisco.com/c/en/us/products/security/common-cyberattacks.html.

Crowe, Jonathan. 2018. "10 Must-Know Cybersecurity Statistics for 2018." Stats & Trends. Last updated February 2018. Accessed January 14, 2019. https://blog.barkly.com/2018-cybersecurity-statistics.

Fruhlinger, Josh. 2018. "Top Cybersecurity Facts, Figures and Statistics for 2018." *Cybersecurity Business Report*. Last updated October 14, 2018. Accessed January 14, 2019. https://www.csoonline.com/article/3153707/security/top-cybersecurity-facts-figures-and-statistics.html.

Perlroth, Nicole, and Clifford Krauss. 2018. "A Cyberattack in Saudi Arabia Had a Deadly Goal. Experts Fear Another Try." *New York Times*, March 15. Accessed January 14, 2019. https://www.nytimes.com/2018/03/15/technology/saudi-arabia-hacks-cyberattacks.html.

Techopedia. n.d. "Cyberattack." *Security*. Accessed October 13, 2018. https://www.techopedia.com/definition/24748/cyberattack.

U.S. Department of Homeland Security (DHS). 2018. "Critical Infrastructure Sectors." Office of Infrastructure Protection. Last updated August 22, 2018. Accessed January 14, 2019. https://www.dhs.gov/critical-infrastructure-sectors.

Cyberbullying

Cyberbullying is a term that refers to the harassment or bullying of another person through digital devices, such as a cell phone or a computer. The act of cyberbullying can occur through social media apps, texts, or forums, and it usually involves negative, harmful, or false content that is posted online. Oftentimes, personal or private information is used to humiliate or embarrass the target. There are reasons to study this phenomenon of online bullying. Because it can "cause embarrassment, invoke harassment and violence, and inflict psychological harm," it could lead to "severe and negative impacts on those victimized" (Solms and Niekerk 2013, 99).

TYPES

There are four main types of cyberbullying tactics that are used online: flaming, exclusion, outing, and masquerading. *Flaming* describes an online interaction where harsh language is used to intimidate a specific person. This is the most commonly reported method of cyberbullying due to the high amount of verbal abuse over the Internet There are often direct threats or images attached to the messages via e-mail, texts, or instant messaging. The bully is intentionally trying to evoke a certain emotion, whether that is anger, sadness, or shame (Mann 2008, 261). *Exclusion* involves an online group conversation, with multiple users, that intentionally excludes one person. The messages may ask for a specific individual to leave or may embarrass that individual to single him or her out (Mooren and Van Minnen 2014, 1–2).

Outing involves the distribution of personal images, information, or private videos to publicly humiliate a person (Vandebosch and Van Cleemput 2009, 1350–1351). Finally, *masquerading* refers to a situation where the bully makes a fake identity or profile online to impersonate someone else. This falsification allows the bully to send mean, insulting, or fake messages to the victim while keeping the bully's information unknown (Schenk and Fremouw 2012, 22).

LEGAL RAMIFICATIONS

These four forms of cyberbullying have been brought to the attention of the public and legislators and have resulted in new laws and regulations. Contrary to public belief, there is no federal law in place that universally challenges the act of cyberbullying. Instead, in the United States, each individual state attempts to address this issue separately. First, many Web sites have terms of use agreements that prohibit harmful speech and require users to confirm they are 13 years of age or older (Willard 2006). Second, freedom of speech as conveyed by the First Amendment of the U.S. Constitution must be preserved. Schools and other public institutions must follow specific standards to provide justice without infringing on the rights of the people involved (Willard 2006).

Anti-cyberbullying legislation is provided to the public schools in 21 states, which allows for persons to report "substantial disruption" to their learning environment or acts that cause a reasonable fear of harm for the student. Outside of the education system, there are 11 states that extend the reach of bullying to include disruption to school-related activities or the declaration that the place is not important but the action of communication over electronic means constitutes some legal pushback. Although the legal ramifications for cyberbullying differ, it is essential to be aware of what the law constitutes, depending on the state.

CASE EXAMPLES

In one case of masquerading, Lori Drew was accused of conspiring in a cyberbullying scheme against a 13-year old girl named Megan Meier. Drew created a fake MySpace account, acting as a man named "Josh Evans," and attempted to foster a relationship with Ms. Meier, a minor. Once consistent contact was established and personal information was being shared, the actor changed emotions toward Megan and sent malicious and degrading messages to her. Drew then decided to make a statement insisting that the world would be a better place without Ms. Meier. Later, the young girl committed suicide, and the situation resulted in legal proceedings. Lori Drew was charged with four felony counts of unauthorized computer access under the Computer Fraud and Abuse Act, but in 2008, a federal jury found her guilty of three misdemeanor charges instead. In 2009, a federal judge overturned the guilty verdicts and directed instead that she be acquitted on the three misdemeanor charges (Zetter 2009).

In a case of outing, 18-year-old Tyler Clementi was a victim of cyberbullying when his college roommate, Dharun Ravi, recorded Clementi engaging in sexual acts without Clementi's permission or knowledge. The recording was posted to Twitter to embarrass Clementi and expose his sexual orientation. Later, Clementi committed suicide by jumping off the George Washington State Bridge. Ravi was convicted on counts of bias intimidation, invasion of privacy, and tampering with evidence in 2012. In September 2016, a New Jersey appeals court threw out the conviction on bias intimidation and called for a new trial on the other charges. In October 2016, Ravi pleaded guilty to a charge of attempted invasion of privacy and was sentenced to time served and fines already paid (Schweber and Foderaro 2016).

In a case of flaming, 18-year-old Conrad Roy committed suicide in 2014 shortly after his girlfriend, Michelle Carter, suggested the taking of his own life through negative and verbally abusive text messages to Roy. Carter was sentenced to 15 months in a Massachusetts prison in 2017 and as of July 2018 was serving her sentence (Sullivan 2018).

PREVENTION

As more cyberbullying cases are being brought to the attention of the public and the criminal justice system, it is important to be aware of the safeguards for victims, the signs of abuse, and the ways to prevent this from happening in the future. Men and women who are using the Internet need to be aware of the risks. Often, suicidal thoughts, social isolation, depression, and anxiety may follow cyberattacks. Friends and family members are very crucial to this process. These people, closest to the victim, know the behaviors and attitudes of the person being harassed and should watch for changes. The victims of online harassment should document any threats sent to them via the Internet and take pictures for evidence. The individual should respond with a clear mind and know their rights and responsibilities. Also, due to the separation of authority in each state, the person being victimized should seek help through their school system or tell someone about the abuse to get the police involved.

No matter the state, it is necessary to ask for assistance. This way the correct steps can be followed to get justice for the wrongdoing. Cyberbullying prevention is becoming better known, and the impact can help save lives. The act of harassment online needs to stop, and the best way to do this is to inform people of their rights, keep men and women updated on how to document the abuse, and provide legal means of getting justice for themselves and others in need.

Sabrina Neimeister

See also: Internet Trolls

Further Reading

Mann, B. L. 2008. "Social Networking Websites—a Concatenation of Impersonation, Denigration, Sexual Aggressive Solicitation, Cyber-Bullying or Happy Slapping Videos." *International Journal of Law and Information Technology* 17 (3): 252–267.

Mooren, N., and A. Van Minnen. 2014. "Feeling Psychologically Restrained: The Effect of Social Exclusion on Tonic Immobility. *European Journal of Psychotraumatology 5* (1): 22928.

Schenk, A. M., and W. J. Fremouw. 2012. "Prevalence, Psychological Impact, and Coping of Cyberbully Victims among College Students. *Journal of School Violence 11* (1): 21–37.

Schweber, Nate, and Lisa Foderaro. 2016. "Roommate in Tyler Clementi Case Pleads Guilty to Attempted Invasion of Privacy." Last updated October 27, 2016. Accessed January 14, 2019. https://www.nytimes.com/2016/10/28/nyregion/dharun-ravi-tyler-clementi-case-guilty-plea.html.

Sullivan, Rebecca. n.d. "Michelle Carter and Conrad Roy Suicide Case: Carter's Lawyers Say Her Chilling Texts Were 'Cherry Picked' by Prosecution." *News*. Last updated July 28, 2018. Accessed January 14, 2019. https://www.news.com.au/lifestyle/real-life/news-life/michelle-carter-and-conrad-roy-suicide-case-carters-lawyers-say-her-chilling-texts-were-cherry-picked-by-prosecution/news-story/4f73d12fb3b5983c6749311867d3b235.

Vandebosch, H., and K. Van Cleemput. 2009. Cyberbullying among Youngsters: Profiles of Bullies and Victims. *New Media & Society* 11 (8): 1349–1371.

Willard, N. 2006. *Cyberbullying and Cyberthreats*. Eugene, OR: Center for Safe and Responsible Internet Use.

Zetter, Kim. 2009. "Cyber Bullying Case Officially Dismissed for Vagueness." *Wired*. Last updated August 31, 2009. Accessed January 14, 2019. https://www.wired.com/2009/08/lori-drew-ruling.

Cybercrime

The term *cybercrime* refers to a broad array of crimes committed using a computer and a computer network. A cybercrime can be the use of a computer and network to commit what is viewed as a more traditional crime, such as theft of personal information through hacking into a personal or organizational Web site. The use of a computer and network as a tool to commit crime has exploded in the last decade. Cybercriminals may be prosecuted domestically, even if living outside the United States, and in those countries in which they reside.

Computers and networks can also be the targets of crime, for example, disabling the entire computer network of a private company or a government agency, thereby causing significant financial or administrative damage. This kind of crime was relatively unheard of until the last two decades, and now it is a daily occurrence. Among other consequences, the surge in attacks on computers and computer networks has fostered an explosion of cybersecurity companies offering services to individuals and companies that help protect from such attacks. Educational institutions are now graduating students with bachelor's, master's, and doctoral degrees in cybersecurity.

Cybercrime causes significant damage in a number of ways. Identity theft or the hacking of an account by means of a cyberattack can result in large financial losses to an individual or organization in the form of either identity theft, account draining, unauthorized purchases, and recovery costs. In a 2014 study by the Center for Strategic & International Studies (CSIS), it was estimated that the global cost to individuals due to personal information loss was about $150 billion per year. CSIS estimated the overall loss to the global economy as around $445 billion every year.

PROSECUTION OF CYBERCRIME DOMESTICALLY

In theory, the instigators of a cyberattack might be charged with any number of crimes, ranging from theft, intellectual property piracy, identity theft, wire fraud, and espionage to criminal mischief and cybertrespassing under domestic criminal laws. These charges could be at the state or, more often, federal level.

Federal law is the most developed area of criminal laws targeted at cyberattacks. Examples include the Electronic Communications Privacy Act (ECPA), the Economic Espionage Act (EEA), the Computer Fraud and Abuse Act (CFAA), the Identity Theft and Assumption Deterrence Act (ITADA), and the USA PATRIOT Act.

The Electronic Communications Privacy Act (1986), which includes the Stored Wire Electronic Communications Act, is the omnibus federal wiretapping statute. It was passed well before the occurrence of cyberattacks, primarily to define the limits of intrusion on electronic privacy. Now, its coverage includes e-mails, telephone conversations, and data stored electronically, that is, wire oral and electronic communications and stored communications. ECPA bans the interception, acquisition, and disclosure of electronic communications and has both criminal and civil penalties. It focuses on communications in interstate and foreign commerce by corporations and individuals. The Stored Communications Act focuses on surreptitious access to communications "at rest" in electronic storage.

The Economic Espionage Act (1996) is a criminal statute concerning corporate espionage designed to protect the intellectual capital of private companies from cybertheft. One provision of the EEA punishes those who knowingly misappropriate trade secrets with the intent or knowledge that their offense will benefit a foreign government. The legislative history of that provision suggests that it is designed to apply only when there is "evidence of foreign government sponsored or coordinated intelligence activity."

The Computer Fraud and Abuse Act (1986) focuses less on communications and more on the computers themselves, effectively operating in part as an antihacking statute. The language states that only "protected computers" are covered. However, the definition of "protected computer" is broad. It includes any computer that affects interstate or foreign commerce. Therefore, most computers, including cell phones, are covered. The covered conduct includes computer trespassing; cyberespionage, including using viruses and worms; fraud; password trafficking to damage computers; and certain kinds of cyberthreats.

The Identity Theft and Assumption Deterrence Act (1998) focuses on identity theft and makes it a federal crime. It is a broad statute that covers other types of identity theft in addition to cyber identity theft, including the misuse of a broad array of information. It was passed in 1998 as the first federal statute to address the then growing phenomenon of identity theft. Interestingly, the "victims" are identified as banks, credit card companies, and merchants who suffered a direct economic loss rather than those whose identities have been hijacked.

Under the USA PATRIOT Act (2001), cyberconduct may also be charged as terrorism, either domestic or extraterritorial, depending on where the "acts" are said to have occurred and their purpose. Domestic terrorism requires a violation of a state or federal law and, in addition, a danger to human life.

The use of the domestic criminal justice system to prosecute cyberattacks as criminal acts also poses several significant procedural difficulties for such topics as jurisdiction, extradition, evidence collection, and witness immunity. Jurisdiction involves deciding whether U.S. domestic laws apply to cybercriminals overseas who attack a system in the United States. Some statutes treat this circumstance explicitly, and other statutes effectively allow for such extraterritorial reach via judicial interpretation. Thus, charges for cyberattacks based on extraterritorial conduct are possible, assuming the cyberattacker and that person's location can be identified.

The bigger problem often lies with extradition efforts in bringing the attacker to the United States. Once an individual who lives outside the United States is charged, that attacker must be brought to the United State for trial. The United States and the resident country must have an extradition treaty that provides procedurally for the resident country's legal system to enable the arrest and transfer of the individual to the United States. Many countries, including Russia, the Ukraine, North Korea, and China, do not have extradition treaties with the United States.

Further, to prosecute a criminal case effectively, one needs witnesses and other evidence. To do so in the context of a prosecution of extraterritorial conduct, the prosecuting authority needs evidence from the resident and possibly other countries. Without voluntary cooperation by witnesses or by resident country police, it is important that the two countries have a mutual legal assistance treaty or an executive agreement facilitating access to witnesses and evidence through agreed upon legal processes.

Often, the biggest problem is identifying who the cyberattacker is, particularly when the attacker is in a foreign state. Whether state-sponsored or an individual, the attacker is almost always very adept at disguising any presence. The veil of cyber anonymity is difficult to pierce. It is a veil more sophisticated than any veil of a noncyberattacker. And difficulty in piercing the veil is exacerbated when the attacker is tracked to a foreign state unsympathetic to the United States.

In sum, it is possible to charge a cyberattack from abroad under federal criminal statutes. Appropriate substantive statutes exist; they can be used extraterritorially; and, though often difficult, individual attackers may be brought to justice in the United States. No doubt, the coverage of domestic criminal statutes as to cyberattacks is still developing and likely remains behind the developments in cyberattack innovation.

PROSECUTION OF CYBERCRIME INTERNATIONALLY

A comprehensive international criminal justice system does not exist. Only a few targeted international law systems even exist for prosecuting crimes. Few of these systems allow for prosecution of cybercrime. The International Court of Justice, which is located in The Hague, in the Netherlands, operates in accordance with international law to settle legal disputes between states and those submitted to it by states. It is not a court with criminal jurisdiction, nor does it resolve disputes between a private entity or individual and a nation.

The International Criminal Court (ICC), which is also located in The Hague, prosecutes perpetrators of the most serious crimes of concern to the international community. Those crimes are identified as genocide, crimes against humanity, and war crimes. Thus, the ICC is not a viable international forum for seeking public accountability for cyberattacks within the United States.

Only a few international conventions or treaties exist that directly address the issue of cybercrime because cyberattacks themselves are a very new phenomenon. The most developed international agreement is the Council of Europe Convention on Cybercrime, signed by 48 countries in March 2016. It requires signatory countries to implement standardized laws and measures to combat the threat of cybercrime. That process is a slow one. As with domestic cybercrime, the approach operates through those signatory countries' criminal justice systems and with their attendant limits. Those countries may be able to prosecute an individual under their domestic law for a cyberattack that affected the United States.

Albert Scherr

See also: Economic Espionage Act of 1996; Identity Theft and Assumption Deterrence Act of 1998; International Court of Justice; International Criminal Court

Further Reading

Reuters Staff. 2014. "Cyber Crime Costs Global Economy $445 Billion a Year: Report." *Reuters*, June 9. Accessed January 14, 2019. https://www.reuters.com/article/us-cybersecurity-mcafee-csis/cyber-crime-costs-global-economy-445-billion-a-year-report-idUSKBN0EK0SV20140609.

Scherr, Albert. 2018. "Cyber Attacks: Cyber Crime or Cyber War?" In *Transnational Crime & Global Security*, edited by Philip Reichel and Ryan Randa, 105–126. Santa Barbara, CA: Praeger Security International.

Solow, Sara. 2011. "Prosecuting Terrorists as Criminals and the Limits of Extraterritorial Jurisdiction." *St. John's Law Review* 85: 1483–1545.

Cybercrime, Policing of

Cybercrime is defined as a crime that is directed at a technological device or a crime that is contingent on Internet access. Cybercrime takes the form of identity theft, child online sexual exploitation, blackmail, cyberbullying, cyberterrorism, hacking, fraud, and online scams (Nykodym, Taylor, and Vilela 2005, 408–414). The Internet has been integrated into everyday life, such as online shopping, academics, entertainment, and business. Digitalization has also made the functionality of society more efficient and reliable in such areas as finance, logistics, and manufacturing. With such convenience comes new challenges like cybercrime, which presents the need for cyber policing (Leppanen, Kiravuo, and Kajantie 2016, 291). It is imperative that cybercrime is properly combated for the Internet to properly serve its purpose.

Policing cybercrime has been a challenge for a number of reasons. First, there is no real data on cybercrimes. Most businesses are afraid to let the public know their system has been hacked and would rather settle with consumers than undermine consumer confidence; as such, they do not report the crime to the police. Uber was a recent hack victim, but the company hid it from the public to avoid bad publicity. Banks also prefer to reimburse customers their money when they have been hacked than let hundreds of other customers know there is a problem. With this trend, police have no real data on cybercrime cases that have actually been committed. The lack of knowledge regarding the prevalence of cybercrimes due to underreporting undermines the effort to fight the cause.

A second reason prosecution is difficult is prioritizing. Police departments in big jurisdictions are overwhelmed with violent crimes on the street and do not consider cybercrime a priority. There is also the issue of limited resources, which compels law enforcement to focus on conventional crimes where the community can see and feel the impact. But the truth remains that as society becomes more technologically advanced so does the vulnerability of citizens to cybercrimes. With more technological innovation emerging, law enforcement and the government must work to find ways to combat cybercrimes (Wexler 2014, 19–22).

Cybercrime being a faceless crime poses a challenge for law enforcement who seek to combat the problem with traditional crime-fighting methods. Law enforcement responds to conventional crimes using two approaches: problem-oriented policing and community-oriented policing; while this works for conventional crimes, it does not work for a faceless crime like cybercrime. For instance, it is easy for the police to apprehend a prostitute on the street for prostitution where the act is overt; however, if a prostitute utilizes the Internet for the same services, it will be difficult for law enforcement to use the traditional method to apprehend the prostitute. This is because the alleged crime and proof of compensation, which is a key element of the crime, cannot be easily proven. Someone can conveniently use the Internet for the same purpose and have customers pay for services rendered through a third-party vendor, thereby eluding law enforcement's effort to prove any evidence of wrongdoing.

Another challenge law enforcement faces with fighting cybercrime is tracking the criminal. With increased vigilance by law enforcement, instead of using stolen confidential information directly, criminals try to circumvent existing countermeasures by selling the information through the underworld to other criminals to reduce the risk of being caught. Such measures make it harder to effectively use traditional crime-fighting methods. Tracking users through their Internet service provider (ISP) is not the easiest task either, particularly if the type of ISP is dial-up. This is because, unlike ISP broadband providers that assign a customer an ISP that stays the same, dial-up providers assign random IP addresses each time a customer logs on to the service. This makes tracking criminals with random IP addresses as difficult as searching for a needle in a haystack (Hong 2012, 78).

The effort to fight cybercrime cannot be achieved by traditional policing agencies only; it has to be a collaborative approach on the part of the government at all levels (federal, state, territorial, county, and local) law enforcement at every level, private enterprises, and the general public (Huey, Nhan, and Broll 2012, 82). Since 2010, The Federal Bureau of Investigation (FBI) has been the primary agency in charge of investigating and combating cybercrime. The FBI has noted that cybercrimes are becoming more sophisticated and daring (2016, 1). The FBI has created an extensive Cybersecurity National Action Plan; the plan outlays a method that allows law enforcement officials to analyze all cybersecurity threats. In a 2016 policy directive, President Obama changed the way the federal government viewed cybercrime. For the first time in history, cybercrime was beginning to be viewed as an extensive crime that needs crime control and proper guidelines. The directive guides the federal government's response to cyber cases and assigns different agencies of the federal government to lead the three different response areas, namely, threat response, asset response, and intelligence support (White House 2016).

Today, the FBI has a cybercrime unit in all 56 of its field offices. The Department of Justice (DOJ) also collaborated with the FBI to create the National Cyber Investigative Joint Task Force; this allows the FBI to partner with any government agency to combat cybercrime. The FBI also has a Cyber Action Team that supports companies that have had their computer networks infiltrated. A 1997 FBI program called the National Cyber Forensics & Training Alliance has been revamped and restructured to keep cybersecurity agents updated on all of the latest trends in cybercrime (FBI 2016, 1).

Overall, the policing of cybercrime has changed tremendously to compete with the advancement of cybercriminality. Much work is still needed to keep abreast the trend of cybercrimes. As cybercrimes target the users, approaching the problem from a user's perspective will also be a beneficial technique. Proactive strategies such as training users to identify threats, emphasis on vigilance, installation of spam filters, use of firewalls and encryption, and blockages and taking down fake Web sites can be helpful.

Dorothy Kersha-Aerga

See also: Cyberattack; Cyberbullying; Cybercrime; Cyberterrorism

Further Reading

Federal Bureau of Investigation (FBI). 2016. "Addressing Threats to the Nation's Cybersecurity." Accessed December 28, 2017. https://www.fbi.gov/file-repository/addressing-threats-to-the-nations-cybersecurity-1.pdf/view.

Hong, Jason. 2012. "The State of Phishing Attacks." *Communications of the ACM* 55 (1): 74–81.

Huey, Lauren, Johnny Nhan, and Ryan Broll. 2012. "'Uppity Civilians' and 'Cyber-Vigilance': The Role of the General Public in Policing Cyber-Crime." *Criminology & Criminal Justice* 13 (1) 81–97.

Leppanen, Anna, Timo Kiravuo, and Sari Kajabtie. 2016. "Policing the Cyber-Physical Space." *The Police Journal* 89 (4) 290–310.

Nykodym, Nick, Robert Taylor, and Julia Vilela. 2005. "Criminal Profiling and Insider Cybercrime." *Computer Law & Security Review* 21 (5): 408–414. Accessed January 14, 2019. https://doi.org/10.1016/j.clsr.2005.07.001.

Walker, Darin, Deon Brock, and T. Ramon Stuart. 2006. "Faceless-Oriented Policing Traditional Policing Theories Are Not Adequate in a Cyber World." *The Police Journal* 79 (2): 169–309.

Wexler, Chuck. 2014. *The Role of Local Law Enforcement Agencies in Preventing and Investigation Cyber Crimes*. Washington, D.C.: Police Executive Research Forum. Accessed January 14, 2019. http://www.policeforum.org/assets/docs/Critical_Issues_Series_2/the%20role%20of%20local%20law%20enforcement%20agencies%20in%20preventing%20and%20investigating%20cybercrime%202014.pdf.

White House. 2016. "Presidential policy directive – United States cyber incident coordination." Accessed January 30, 2019. https://obamawhitehouse.archives.gov/the-press-office/2016/07/26/presidential-policy-directive-united-states-cyber-incident.

Cyberterrorism

Cyberterrorism describes terroristic acts commissioned through the use of technology instead of traditional means. While there is no universally accepted definition of *cyberterrorism*, most definitions of cyberterrorism are an extension of the definition of traditional terrorism. The U.S. Code of Federal Regulations defines terrorism as "the unlawful use of force and violence against persons or property to intimidate or coerce a government, the civilian population, or any segment thereof, in furtherance of political or social objectives" (*Code of Federal Regulations*, Title 28, sec. 0.85). Cyberterrorism shares these same goals but attempts to achieve them through the use of the Internet, computers, or other forms of information technology.

HISTORY

Barry Collin, a senior research fellow at the Institute for Security and Intelligence, first coined the term *cyberterrorism* in the 1980s (Collin 1997). However, public interest in cyberterrorism did not spike until the lead up to the year 2000, when concerns about "the millennium bug" began. The millennium bug, or Y2K bug, was a computer flaw that caused problems with formatting dates beginning in the year 2000. When computer programs were first being created, the dates were formatted as six digits (mm/dd/yy) instead of eight digits (mm/dd/yyyy), meaning the leading "19" in the dates 1900 through 1999 was excluded. Computer programmers were concerned that computers would interpret the "00" of 2000 as 1900 and cause a wide range of problems, including systems such as banks, transportation, and the power grid. Some experts expected a doomsday situation, fearing that computer systems would become so confused that they would completely shut down and thus end civilization. Ultimately, there were very few problems because most governments were able to implement updated solutions in time (Story and Crawford 2001). Although the millennium bug was not an act of cyberterrorism, it demonstrated to the average person how much his or her life relied on technology and served as an example of the extent to which a massive cyberterrorist attack could impact society.

DEFINITIONS

If the goals of cyberterrorism are the same as traditional terrorism (to cause damage, death, and instill fear), this would mean that there currently have been almost no actual incidents of cyberterrorism. There is a belief that cyberattacks should not be labeled as "terrorism" because of the unlikelihood that these attacks will cause significant property damage, physical harm, death, or instill fear in a population. Rather, cyberattacks should be categorized as "hacking" or "information warfare," meaning that information technology is simply a tool used to support traditional terrorism.

While computers cannot directly cause a death, altering critical systems, such as transportation schedules or nuclear centrifuges, can result in levels of property destruction that consequently cause death. All types of terrorism are committed through a weapon: bioterrorism uses tools like anthrax, nuclear terrorism uses nuclear weapons, and cyberterrorism uses technology. The way an attack is committed does not impact whether the act is considered "terrorism," so long as the attack causes damage, instills fear, and is for a political or ideological motive.

METHODS AND TOOLS

Successful cyberterrorism will utilize tools such as "off-the-shelf" malware, social engineering, and customized hacking suites designed to maliciously affect other networks and technology.

Cyberterrorism differs from traditional terrorism, as cyberattacks may disrupt or alter networks, hardware, and information without necessarily resulting in physical damage or violence. For example, denial-of-service (DoS) attacks or terrorist threats made through electronic communication may interrupt systems or create panic, but they do not always cause property damage.

PERPETRATORS

Cyberterrorism is committed by both state and nonstate actors and by both individuals and groups. The anonymity and interconnectivity of cyberspace enables many different types of individuals to commit acts of cybercrime and potentially cyberterrorism.

In September 2016, Ardit Ferizi, a citizen of Kosovo, was the first person to ever be convicted of cyberterrorism. Ferizi was sentenced to 20 years in prison for hacking crimes and providing material support to the foreign terrorist organization the Islamic State of Iraq and the Levant (ISIL, also known as the Islamic State of Iraq and Syria, or ISIS) (DOJ 2016). The information he provided was a "kill list" for ISIL that contained personally identifiable information on approximately 1,300 U.S. military members and government personnel.

Additionally, examples of other types of perpetrators include individual hackers, criminal organizations, cyber mercenaries, and hacktivists. All of these groups are capable of accomplishing acts of cyberterrorism; however, the motives behind each attack determine whether the groups are labeled as cyberterrorists. For instance, the hacktivist group Anonymous led a DoS attack against Israeli Defense Force officials by releasing over 5,000 of their names, identification numbers, and personal e-mail addresses. This attack was in response to a 2012 Israeli military operation in Gaza, Operation Pillar of Defense (Bussolati 2015). This attack is similar to the offenses committed by Ardit Ferizi and also had political and ideological motivations behind it. However, the Anonymous attack may be distinguished from cyberterrorism because the *intent* was not to cause harm or fear. Nevertheless, if the event does have indirect consequences, the affected party may still view it as cyberterrorism.

EXTENT OF DAMAGE AND FUTURE CONCERNS

Although unauthorized access of classified information and the disruption of networks and systems remain areas of great concern, the physical damage that cyberterrorism may cause is what worries government officials. There remains the possibility that computers will be used to damage critical government systems, national security programs, power grids, communication systems, or transportation controls. For example, loss of life is a real threat for compromised hospital systems and their many critical systems. Another major concern is that transportation systems could be hacked, causing traffic accidents or plane crashes. Many scholars have written about the possibility of a "digital Pearl Harbor."

The first cyberattack that caused significant property damage was Stuxnet, a cyber worm discovered in June 2010. Stuxnet is a malware suite that was specifically designed to target the industrial control systems used in Iran's nuclear-refinement centrifuges. The worm disrupted normal operation by causing the centrifuges' rotors to spin very rapidly, eventually destroying an estimated 10 percent of the centrifuges (Albright, Brannan, and Walrond 2010). Although neither country has taken credit, it is believed that Stuxnet was a joint American-Israeli effort.

The Stuxnet incident is a prime example of the problem of attribution in cybercrime. When an attack is conducted through the Internet, even though it is possible to find the country of origin, there is very little way of knowing whether the government mandated the act or it was the work of an independent hacker or a hacktivist group. Without definitively knowing who carried out the attack, it is difficult to respond, because incorrectly accusing or taking action against a nation could have severe consequences.

CURRENT PROTECTIONS

The United States has taken several precautionary measures to monitor and protect against potential cyber threats as well as execute missions that serve the interests of the United States. The Department of Defense (DOD), Central Intelligence Agency (CIA), Federal Bureau of Investigation (FBI), and National Security Agency (NSA) all currently have departments specializing in cybersecurity. As a precautionary measure against the increasing threat of cyberattacks, the U.S. government additionally established the United States Cyber Command (USCYBERCOM) and the Cyber Threat Intelligence Integration Center (CTIIC).

On June 23, 2009, the DOD instructed the United States Strategic Command (USSTRATCOM) to create the USCYBERCOM. The command became fully operational on October 31, 2010. USCYBERCOM's mission is to plan and coordinate measures to protect and promote the operations of certain DOD networks and to conduct military cyberspace missions when necessary (U.S. Strategic Command 2017).

In February 2015, as a response to the cyberattacks against Sony, Home Depot Inc., and Target, President Barack Obama created the CTIIC. The agency is structured similarly to the National Counterterrorism Center (NCTC) and has the goals of analyzing cyber threats and assisting other departments in coordinating strategic countermeasures (White House 2015).

On an international level, in 2008, members of the North Atlantic Treaty Organization (NATO) founded the Cooperative Cyber Defense Center of Excellence (CCDCOE), a facility that specializes in research, development, and training for cyber defense. In July 2016, NATO allies also made a Cyber Defense Pledge to prioritize the enhancement of cyber defenses. NATO recognizes cyberspace as a domain wherein it must protect itself and its assets with the same efficiency as it does on land, at sea, and in the air (NATO 2017).

Kleo McHugh

See also: Cyberattack; Cybercrime; Denial-of-Service Attacks

Further Reading

Albright, David, Paul Brannan, and Christina Walrond. 2010. *Did Stuxnet Take Out 1,000 Centrifuges at the Natanz Enrichment Plant?* Institute for Science and International Security. Accessed January 30, 2019. http://isis-online.org/isis-reports/detail/did-stuxnet-take-out-1000-centrifuges-at-the-natanz-enrichment-plant/

Bussolati, Nicolò. 2015. "The Rise of Non-State Actors in Cyberwarfare." In *Cyberwar: Law and ethics for virtual conflicts*, edited by Jens David Ohlin, Claire Finkelstein, and Kevin Govern, 102-126. Oxford, UK: Oxford University Press.

Collin, Barry C. 1997. "The Future of Cyberterrorism: Where the Physical and Virtual Worlds Converge." *Crime and Justice International* 13 (2): 14–18.

Department of Justice (DOJ). 2016. *ISIL-Linked Kosovo Hacker Sentenced to 20 Years in Prison.* Office of Public Affairs. Accessed December 5, 2017. https://www.justice.gov/opa/pr/isil-linked-kosovo-hacker-sentenced-20-years-prison.

North Atlantic Treaty Organization (NATO). 2017. *Cyber Defense.* Accessed: December 11, 2017. https://www.nato.int/cps/en/natohq/topics78170.htm.

Story, Jonathan, and Robert J. Crawford. 2001. "Y2K: The Bug That Failed to Bite." *Business and Politics* 3 (3): 269–296.

U.S. National Archives and Records Administration. 2010. *Code of Federal Regulations.* Title 28. Organization of the Department of Justice. Accessed January 30, 2019. https://www.archives.gov/federal-register/cfr/subject-title-28.html.

U.S. Strategic Command. 2016. *U.S. Cyber Command (USCYBERCOM).* Accessed December 5, 2017. http://www.stratcom.mil/Media/Factsheets/Factsheet-View/Article/960492/us-cyber-command-uscybercom.

White House. 2015. *Fact Sheet: Cyber Threat Intelligence Integration Center.* Office of the Press Secretary. Accessed December 11, 2017. https://obamawhitehouse.archives.gov/the-press-office/2015/02/25/fact-sheet-cyber-threat-intelligence-integration-center

Cyberwar and Cyber Warfare

Cyberwar and cyber warfare are terms with multiple meanings. Either one is sometimes used to describe a circumstance in which one country launches a cyberattack against another country, and the second country responds with its own cyberattack. Both terms are also used to refer to a situation in which one country attacks and the other responds with noncyber actions, such as economic sanctions or visa restrictions.

Many in the political arena use the terms to refer to any cyberattack by one country on another regardless of the existence of any response. The lack of a precise definition does not diminish the potential consequences of a cyberattack that may be cause for a serious international incident. That concern has fostered an intense focus by the Department of Defense and other government agencies in the

United States on cybersecurity. The same is true internationally, particularly in European countries

EXAMPLES

Examples of cyber warfare include a 2013 incident when a hacker affiliated with the Iranian government allegedly tried to access the controls of a small dam north of New York City. Though unsuccessful, the event provoked concerns about the vulnerability of other larger infrastructure in the United State—pipelines, mass transit, power grids, and the like. Also in 2013, an unauthorized user from China hacked into the U.S. Army Corps of Engineers' National Inventory of Dams, a database of information on the vulnerabilities of major dams in the United States. The database contains categories of dams based on the number of people who would be killed if a particular dam failed. No public evidence exists that the Chinese government was involved.

In 2014, British-owned BAE Systems reported that a "cyberespionage toolkit" known as Snake or Ouroboros had been found in the government computer networks of the Ukraine. The malware gave the hackers full remote access to the system, thereby enabling surveillance and data theft. Based on a measure of evidence, the suspicion was that the hackers were Russian. Similar evidence had been found in systems in Lithuania, Great Britain, and Georgia. Again, no public information exists that the Russian government was involved, though the hacking in the Ukraine became known as what appeared to be Russian-inspired unrest in the Ukraine was growing.

In his first term, President Obama authorized a cyberattack on Iran's computer systems that run Iranian nuclear-enrichment facilities. The operation, called Olympic Games, used a program named Stuxnet, developed in conjunction with Israel. The claim was that the computer worm temporarily disabled 1,000 of Iran's 5,000 nuclear centrifuges.

The Nuclear Threat Initiative (2016) identified countries with weapons-usable nuclear material or with nuclear facilities but no weapons-usable nuclear material. Of these countries, 20 do not yet have the laws and regulations needed to provide effective cybersecurity. Those 20 include several that are expanding their use of nuclear power.

WHEN DOES A CYBERATTACK CONSTITUTE WAR

Even the most technologically sophisticated governments around the world are beginning to confront the challenge of whether a cyberattack merits a response at all and what kind of response that should be, whether a cyberattack merits a response akin to a declaration, formal or otherwise, of war. Some of these circumstances are relatively easy. For example, a cyberattack that temporarily disables the functioning of a nonessential government computer will likely be charged as a cybercrime under a country's criminal code.

Going forward, the somewhat harder cases will be those in which significant financial damage is caused or in which death or serious bodily injury is caused. Those cases recall the damages that more traditional military attacks have caused, the difference lying in the antiseptic non-physically invasive nature of the cyberattack.

The hardest cases will be those attacks that do not cause personal or physical harm but do cause another kind of damage of an intangible but still serious nature. One example would be a cyberattack that gained access to the computers used to count votes in a country's election and successfully altered the outcome of that country's elections in some fashion. No physical invasion of the country would have occurred either by undercover operatives or by a military force. Yet, by virtue of a purely antiseptic attack, significant damage would be done to the integrity of that country's electoral process.

The core issue is what kind of cyberattack, if any, constitutes grounds for a retaliatory military attack of some sort. In the United States, the *Law of War Manual* of the Department of Defense, the most developed domestic operational version of the doctrine of the law of war, recently started to take that issue on directly. In its 2015 revision, the manual defines a cyber operation as the use of "computers to disrupt, deny, degrade or destroy information resident in computers and computer networks, or the computers and networks themselves" (DOD 2015, 995) and then describes the circumstances that may give rise to a use of force:

> Cyber operations may in certain circumstances constitute uses of force within the meaning of Article 2(4) of the Charter of the United Nations and customary international law. . . . For example, if cyber operations cause effects that, if caused by traditional physical means, would be regarded as a use of force under jus ad bellum, then such cyber operations would likely also be regarded as a use of force. Such operations may include cyber operations that: (1) trigger a nuclear plant meltdown; (2) open a dam above a populated area, causing destruction; or (3) disable air traffic control services, resulting in airplane crashes. [footnote omitted]. Similarly, cyber operations that cripple a military's logistics systems, and thus its ability to conduct and sustain military operations, might also be considered a use of force. (DOD 2015, 998–999)

DEFENDING THE CYBER DOMAIN

Recognizing that a cyber battlefield can be as lethal as the more traditional one, NATO has added "cyber" as the fourth domain of operation that must be defended along with air, land, and sea (NATO 2016). The U.S. Defense Department is also showing increased willingness to tackle the threat of cyberwar with the U.S. Cyber Command operating as of 2018 as an independent unit on equal basis with nine other U.S. warfighting commands (Strobel 2018). The Cyber Command, which includes military units trained to defend against cyberattacks as well as initiate them, is acknowledgment that a new warfighting domain has come of age.

Albert Scherr and Philip L. Reichel

See also: Cyberattack; Cybercrime; Russian Election Interference (2016)

Further Reading

Nakashima, Ellen. 2017a. "Russia Has Developed a Cyberweapon That Can Disrupt Power Grids, According to New Research." *Washington Post*, June 12. Accessed January 14, 2019. https://www.washingtonpost.com/world/national-security/russia-has-developed-a-cyber-weapon-that-can-disrupt-power-grids-according-to-new-research/2017/06/11/b91b773e-4eed-11e7-91eb-9611861a988f_story.html?noredirect=on&utm_term=.0fd8863aae0e.

Nakashima, Ellen. 2017b. "U.S. Officials Say Russian Government Hackers Have Penetrated Energy and Nuclear Company Business Networks." *Washington Post*, July 8. Accessed January 14, 2019. https://www.washingtonpost.com/world/national-security/us-officials-say-russian-government-hackers-have-penetrated-energy-and-nuclear-company-business-networks/2017/07/08/bbfde9a2-638b-11e7-8adc-fea80e32bf47_story.html?utm_term=.a064ed4ebcf1.

North Atlantic Treaty Organization (NATO). 2016. "NATO Recognises Cyberspace as a 'Domain of Operations' at Warsaw Summit." *Incyder News*, July 21. Accessed January 15, 2019. https://ccdcoe.org/nato-recognises-cyberspace-domain-operations-warsaw-summit.html.

Nuclear Threat Initiative. 2016. "2016 Findings." *NTI Nuclear Security Index*. Accessed January 14, 2019. http://www.ntiindex.org/findings-recommendations/findings.

Sanger, David E. 2015. "Cyberthreat Posed by China and Iran Confounds White House." *New York Times*, September 15. Accessed January 14, 2019. https://www.nytimes.com/2015/09/16/world/asia/cyberthreat-posed-by-china-and-iran-confounds-white-house.html.

Scherr, Albert. 2018. "Cyber Attacks: Cyber Crime or Cyber War?" In *Transnational Crime & Global Security*, edited by Philip Reichel and Ryan Randa, 105–125. Santa Barbara, CA: Praeger Security International.

Strobel, Warren. 2018. "Pentagon's Cyber Command Gets Upgraded Status, New Leader." *Reuters*, May 4. Accessed January 14, 2019. https://www.reuters.com/article/us-usa-defense-cyber/pentagons-cyber-command-gets-upgraded-status-new-leader-idUSKBN1I52MS.

U.S. Department of Defense (DOD). 2015. *Law of War Manual*. Accessed January 14, 2019. https://www.defense.gov/Portals/1/Documents/law_war_manual15.pdf.

D

Dark Web/Deep Web

The news media and law enforcement authorities are taking note of the online anonymity that the Deep Web and the Dark Web provide to consumers as well as related cybersecurity issues. Although many consumers have heard the terms *Deep Web* and *Dark Web*, there are still some misconceptions. People often equate the Deep Web and the Dark Web with the Internet and consider these sites hideaways for criminal activity. In reality, the Internet is much broader than just the servers and includes each server, computer, and device connected to different networks (Chertoff 2017). The Internet encompasses two elements: the Surface Web and the Deep Web. In general, the Surface Web is what users refer to as "the Internet." The Surface Web consists of a compilation of Web sites indexed by search engines such as Google, Yahoo, Bing, Ask, and Wikipedia. When a person conducts an online search, the search engines check billions of documents to find the most pertinent information and then orders the results by the popularity of the Web sites that offer the answer (Moz n.d.). Although search engines linked to the Surface Web are popular among users, the Surface Web makes up about 5 percent of the World Wide Web (WWW), and the remaining 95 percent is occupied by the Deep Web.

THE DEEP WEB

Unlike the Surface Web, Deep Web search engines are not indexed and require "a specific password encrypted browser or login details to access the sites" (Quinney 2016, para 5). Medical records, financial records, legal documents, organizational-specific repositories, and social media files (i.e., FaceBook, Twitter, and Snapchat) are securely stored on the Deep Web. A large part of the Deep Web also includes instant messaging and secure data and file sharing services such as Dropbox, Google Drive, and Syncplicity (Greenberg 2014; Chertoff 2017). Also, about 90 percent of the traffic on the Internet comes from the Deep Web, which is estimated to be considerably larger (4,000–5,000 times) than the Surface Web (Finklea 2015).

THE DARK WEB

Although the Web pages on the Deep Web are unidentifiable by such search engines as Google, Bing, or Yahoo, the majority of the Deep Web provides privacy and poses little or no threat to the safety of the devices. However, a small part of the Deep Web, known as the Dark Web, is inaccessible to ordinary Web users and hides the IP addresses of its servers, making it hard to identify where the servers are hosted or who is hosting (Greenberg 2015).

U.S. military researchers created the Dark Web technology. In 2002, the U.S. Naval Research Laboratories announced the project, known as "The Onion Routing" (Tor), to assist U.S. spies and the intelligence agencies in sending and receiving information anonymously (Quinney 2016). The intention for releasing Tor into the public domain was to use the software to hide messages from counterintelligence sources and help people voice their opinions freely without being persecuted, especially those living under oppressive regimes (Quinney 2016). Although the original purpose of the technology was for political purposes, it is now mostly used by criminals to carry out illegal activities with impunity.

In addition to Tor, a smaller number of the people use the I2P network, which offers anonymous communication and protects such communications from third-party surveillance. Although both Tor and I2P are used by people who want to protect their privacy and keep their communication confidential, such as activists, journalists, oppressed people, and whistle-blowers (I2P n.d.), Tor and I2P are often used by criminals to access the Dark Web. Both technologies encrypt Web traffic in multiple layers and pass it through randomly selected computers anywhere in the world, which makes it difficult for law enforcement to match the origin of the Web traffic with its destination. When a Web user runs Tor to access a site, the IP address is usually hidden. However, when a Web site itself runs Tor (i.e., Tor hidden services), it can only be accessed by Tor users (Greenberg 2014). Illegal Web sites such as Silk Road, Silk Road 2, Agora, AlphaBay, Hansa, and Evolution served as secure platforms for illegal drug markets, money laundering, credit card fraud and identity theft, hacking, arms trafficking, selling stolen goods, extortion, fund-raising to support terrorist activities, and Ponzi schemes. Among them, the most famous ones are Silk Road and AlphaBay.

Silk Road was owned and operated by Ross William Ulbricht from January 2011 until October 2013. He used aliases such as "Dread Pirate Roberts," "DPR," and "Silk Road" and carried out the most sophisticated and elaborate criminal marketplace on the Dark Web. It served as the primary platform for the purchase and sale of illegal narcotics, computer hacking, fake identification documents, and other illegal goods and services. Silk Road was accessible via the Tor network and only accepted Bitcoins as payment. By hosting the site, Ulbricht received a portion of the seller's revenue as a commission. After many months of investigation and surveillance, Ulbricht and his associates were arrested and charged with intent to distribute heroin, cocaine, LSD, and methamphetamine, conspiring to commit computer hacking, money laundering, and other charges (Weiser 2015). He was found guilty and sentenced to life imprisonment. Ulbricht was also ordered to pay a criminal monetary penalty as well as forfeiture of $183,961,921.

The second version of the Silk Road—Silk Road 2—came online within five weeks after the shutdown of Silk Road with a promise of reviving the drug trade on the Dark Web. With the coordination of U.S. and several international law enforcement agencies, Silk Road 2 was shut down. The operator of the site, 26-year-old Blake Benthall (using the name "Defcon"), was arrested and charged with trafficking of narcotics, money laundering, computer hacking, and trafficking of fraudulent identification documents. Although he initially denied the charges, he pleaded guilty to conspiracy to distribute heroin, cocaine, and methamphetamine and was sentenced to eight years in prison. During the short time the site was in operation, it is estimated that the site generated about $8 million sales per month with over 150,000 users (FBI 2014).

Another Dark Web illegal market site, AlphaBay, operated on the Tor network. AlphaBay launched its operations in December 2014 and was shut down on July 5, 2017. By many estimates, AlphaBay was one of the largest and most profitable underground marketplaces on the Dark Web and was known for illegal drugs and stolen credit cards (Statt 2017). The U.S. Department of Justice (DOJ) reported that the site was a marketplace for fentanyl and heroin as well as stolen and fraudulent identifications, counterfeit goods, computer hacking services, and firearms. By the time it was shut down, AlphaBay supposedly had over 200,000 users, about 40,000 vendors, over 200,000 listing of illegal drugs and harmful chemicals, and over 1,000 listings of other illegal goods and services. Silk Road, in comparison to AlphaBay, listed about 14,000 illegal goods and services (DOJ 2017).

The AlphaBay operator, Alexandre Cazes (or Alpha02), was a Canadian citizen living in Thailand at the time of his arrest. The U.S. government, with the help of law enforcement authorities from Thailand, the Netherlands, Lithuania, Canada, the United Kingdom, France, and Europol (European law enforcement), seized the Website. Cazes was arrested by Thai authorities and was reported to have committed suicide in jail. He and his wife's assets were located in Thailand, Cyprus, Lichtenstein, and Antigua and Barbuda and included cryptocurrencies, a hotel, residences, and luxury cars (DOJ 2017).

With the takedown of Silk Road 2, buyers and sellers of illegal drugs and services moved to other darknet Web sites, such as Hansa, Agora, and Evolution. Hansa was considered one of the largest European illegal drug operation sites on the Dark Web. Partners from 12 different enforcement agencies, including the FBI, the Drug Enforcement Agency (DEA), the Dutch police, and Europol, shut down Hansa at the same time that the authorities were taking down AlphaBay. Evolution (also known as Evo) attempted to fill some the vacuum left by the shutdowns of Silk Road and Silk Road 2. The site, launched in January 2014, went offline in March 2015 without any warning. It had a reputation for security, reliability, and professionalism, and its sudden disappearance resulted in panic among vendors and users (Greenburg 2015). With the sudden exit of Evolution, Agora became the largest darknet marketplace. Agora operated on the Tor network and was launched in 2013; the site is reported to be offline.

Many cybersecurity experts anticipate the continuing migration of cybercriminals to new sites that promise anonymity, security, quality products, and reliable services. The illegal activities on the Dark Web are challenging to control, given that the creators of these sites are hidden behind sophisticated software technology that ensures anonymity. Also, it takes enormous time, resources, and technical expertise to take down Dark Web sites. The recent arrests, rigorous prosecution, and severe sanctions of cybercriminals may serve as an example that law enforcement authorities are considering cybercrime a high priority.

Sesha Kethineni

See also: Cryptocurrency; Cryptomarkets; Cybercrime; Ulbricht, Ross

Further Reading

Chertoff, Michael. 2017. "A Public Policy Perspective of the Dark Web." *Journal of Cyber Security* 2 (1): 26–38.

Federal Bureau of Investigation (FBI). 2016. "Operator of Silk Road 2.0 Website Charged in Manhattan Federal Court." November 6. Accessed January 16, 2019. https://www.fbi.gov/contact-us/field-offices/newyork/news/press-releases/operator-of-silk-road-2.0-website-charged-in-manhattan-federal-court.

Finklea, Kristin. 2015. "Dark Web." *Congressional Research Services.* Accessed January 16, 2019. https://fas.org/sgp/crs/misc/R44101.pdf.

Greenburg, Andy. 2014. "Hacker Lexicon: What Is the Dark Web." *Wired*, December 19. Accessed January 16, 2019. https://www.wired.com/2014/11/hacker-lexicon-whats-dark-web.

Greenburg, Andy. 2015. "The Dark Web's Top Drug Market, Evolution, Just Vanished." *Wired*, March 18. Accessed January 16, 2019. https://www.wired.com/2015/03/evolution-disappeared-bitcoin-scam-dark-web.

I2P. n.d. "The Invisible Internet Project (I2P)." Accessed January 16, 2019. https://geti2p.net/en/about/intro.

Kushner, David. 2014. "Dead End on Silk Road: Internet Crime Kingpin Ross Ulbricht's Big Fall." *Rolling Stone*, February 4. Accessed January 16, 2019. http://www.rollingstone.com/culture/news/dead-end-on-silk-road-internet-crime-kingpin-ross-ulbrichts-big-fall-20140204.

Moz. n.d. *How Search Engines Work: The Beginners Guide to SEO.* Accessed January 16, 2019. https://moz.com/beginners-guide-to-seo.

Quinney, Andrew. 2016. "Surface Web vs. Deep Web vs. Dark Web," *Servicecare*, June 27. Accessed January 16, 2019. https://www.servicecare.org.uk/news/surface-web-vs-deep-web-vs-dark-web-61792715468.

Statt, Nick. 2017. "Dark Web Drug Marketplace AlphaBay Was Shut Down by Law Enforcement." *The Verge,* July 14. Accessed January 16, 2019. https://www.theverge.com/2017/7/14/15975140/alphabay-dark-web-drug-marketplace-police-shutdown-silk-road.

U.S. Department of Justice (DOJ). 2017. "AlphaBay, the Largest Online 'Dark Market,' Shut Down." July 20. Accessed January 16, 2019. https://www.justice.gov/opa/pr/alphabay-largest-online-dark-market-shut-down.

Debt Bondage, *see* Bonded Labor

Denial-of-Service Attacks

A denial-of-service (DoS) attack attempts to overload a Web site with requests to view its content; in some cases, the Web server hosting the site becomes inoperable while attempting to satisfy these requests and subsequently displays an error message to all legitimate users attempting to access the site. A distributed denial-of-service (DDoS) attack produces the same result as a DoS attack, but it emanates from many computers at once. Since DDoS attacks make blocking the involved IP addresses more difficult, DDoS attacks are implemented more often than single-device DoS attacks (Zetter 2016).

These types of attacks are used for a variety of reasons, from political schemes and extortion attempts to economic sabotage and distraction techniques. The term *hacktivism* is used when these attacks are carried out in an attempt to promote political change. Often, botnets are used to carry out DDoS attacks. A botnet is a collection of Internet-connected devices, or "bots," that have been infected by malware. The botnet's owner, or bot herder, then covertly commands the bots to initiate DDoS attacks. As normal services are not disrupted, users of the involved devices are typically unaware that their devices have been infected (Dariusz 2017).

SYMPTOMS AND EXAMPLES

The following symptoms may indicate a DoS or DDoS attack is in progress: unusually slow network performance (opening files or accessing Web sites); unavailability of a particular Web site; inability to access any Web site; or a dramatic increase in the amount of spam received (McDowell 2013).

Several DDoS attacks have become well known for their targets, objectives, and successes. The first DDoS attack took place in 1997 during DEF CON, a hacker convention held every year in Las Vegas, Nevada. Khan C. Smith, a well-known hacker, initiated a DDoS attack to disrupt Internet access on the entire Las Vegas strip.

In 2008, the hacktivist group Anonymous created Project Chanology after the Church of Scientology requested that YouTube take down a video of famous actor Tom Cruise praising Scientologists for their expertise on the mind. Anonymous declared its intent to expel the church from the Internet and launched DDoS attacks on the Church of Scientology's Web site. Project Chanology used the Low Orbit Ion Cannon (LOIC) tool to carry out the attacks; LOIC is a freely available application that allows many users to direct Internet traffic to a single network, server, or Web site. Users simply input a Web address, and the LOIC sends endless requests to overload the target system (Imperva 2017).

Later, in 2010, Anonymous launched DDoS attacks on several companies that had ceased their business support for WikiLeaks, an organization that publishes classified information provided by its anonymous sources, in an attack named Operation Payback. The originally targeted companies included PayPal, MasterCard, and Visa. After the file sharing site the Pirate Bay was taken down, Anonymous also attacked the Recording Industry Association of America (RIAA), the Motion Picture Association of America (MPAA), and the U.S. Copyright Office of the Library of Congress. Fourteen defendants, known as the "PayPal 14," reached plea deals in 2013 that delayed sentencing. In 2014, having demonstrated good behavior, during their time in the community, some of the group were sentenced to probation until their restitution was paid, while others were considered to have successfully completed their probation (RT 2014).

LEGALITY

According to the Computer Fraud and Abuse Act (CFAA) of 1986, the federal law that prohibits unauthorized or excessive access to a computer, DDoS attacks are illegal. However, hacktivists argue that these attacks are a form of protest and should be considered protected free speech under the First Amendment. Attorneys specializing in cybercrime cases coined the term *digital sit-in* to describe the essence of a DDoS attack. Hacktivists claim that a computer occupying a Web site is equivalent to protesters occupying physical space.

Amanda R. Graves

See also: Cyberattack; Cybercrime; Hackers

Further Reading

Dariusz. 2017. "What Is a Botnet?" *The Merkle*. Last modified April 9, 2017. Accessed January 16, 2019. https://themerkle.com/what-is-a-botnet.

Imperva. n.d. "Low Orbit Ion Cannon (LOIC)." Accessed December 5, 2017. https://www.incapsula.com/ddos/attack-glossary/low-orbit-ion-cannon.html.

McDowell, Mindi. 2013. "Understanding Denial-of-Service Attacks." Last modified February 6, 2013. Accessed January 16, 2019. https://www.us-cert.gov/ncas/tips/ST04-015.

RT. 2014. "Charges dropped for #PayPal14 hacktivists, company launches #PayPal15 trend." Last modified October 30, 2014. Accessed February 6, 2019. https://www.rt.com/usa/200667-paypal-hackers-anonymous-felony/

Vamosi, Robert. 2008. "Anonymous Hackers Take on the Church of Scientology." Last modified January 25, 2008. Accessed January 21, 2019. https://www.cnet.com/news/anonymous-hackers-take-on-the-church-of-scientology.

Zetter, Kim. 2016. "Hacker Lexicon: What Are the DoS and DDoS Attacks?" Last modified January 16, 2016. Accessed January 21, 2019. https://www.wired.com/2016/01/hacker-lexicon-what-are-dos-and-ddos-attacks.

Digital Forensics

Digital forensics is the process that uncovers, interprets, and collects electronic information as evidence for cases in the legal system. As technology advances, people store more and more personal information electronically on devices such as cell phones, computers, tablets, and smart watches. Living in a connected world has resulted in fewer physical records of a person's life, like paper bank statements and bills. These paper records have been the primary evidence used by law enforcement. With a shift from physical evidence-based cases to electronic cases, "digital forensics" has come into play.

The main goal of digital forensics is to ensure that the evidence remains intact and validated to reconstruct events. Digital forensics has existed for 40 years, and it experienced a golden age that lasted from 1994 to 2007 (Garfinkel 2010, s66). This era was a time of simplistic computer designs and file systems, during which the possession of a software install disk was all that was needed to bypass someone's password (Garfinkel 2010, s66). Historically, digital forensics involved computers, but the advent of smartphones necessitated the ability to retrieve data from these devices, too. Today, encryption threatens digital forensics and law enforcement's ability to access most electronic devices, which is compounded by a lack of standardization across platforms.

DEVICE FORENSICS

One subset of digital forensics is device forensics. Device forensics typically involves smartphones and tablets and the data collected from smartphones and other devices that can create a picture of someone's communication and travel history (Tassone et al. 2013, 1). Data pulled from these devices may include pictures, call history, text and e-mail messages, and events in the calendar application (Tassone et al. 2013, 1). Extraction techniques usually include making a "bit for bit" copy of the entire physical storage of a device, which aids in investigation. This copy, or disk image, can be manipulated, and if something were to happen to it, the investigator would still have the original. There are multiple techniques to extract data from a mobile device that range from basic manual extraction via simply looking through the phone to dumping, which is used to examine the raw data stored in the memory (Ayers, Brothers, and Jansen 2014, 17).

COMPUTER FORENSICS

While smartphones are the most commonly collected digital forensics target, personal computers are still incredibly common in the commission of crimes. It can be a challenge to investigate a computer for evidence, as there may be many different combinations of hardware and operating systems. Furthermore, experts must consider where the data they seek is stored; computer memory can be categorized into two types: volatile and involatile memory. Volatile memory refers to memory that is removed each time a computer's power supply is interrupted, including a reboot or shutdown. If something is stored in the volatile memory and the computer shuts off, the memory will be permanently lost, which can prove catastrophic to the data retrieval process. The most common type of volatile memory is random-access memory (RAM) found in nearly all PCs, smartphones, and tablets. Involatile memory is the type of storage that is permanent and will remain unaffected if the power supply is interrupted. Examples of this are mechanical hard drives (found in PCs) and solid-state drives (found in smartphones and tablets) that contain the operating system, files, data, and media saved to the device.

ENCRYPTION

The use of encryption has become popular to ensure the privacy and security of a documents, data, and e-mails. In the past 20 years, data encryption rates have exploded, making law enforcement's duties just that much more difficult. In 1997, the Federal Bureau of Investigation (FBI) computer analysis response team handled 500 cases where they were unable to perform decryption (Denning and

Baugh 1997). During the first nine months of 2017, the same response team had 7,000 cases that cannot yet be decrypted (Spadafora 2017).

The main advantages of encryption include ensuring confidentiality and controlled accessibility (Agrawal and Mishra 2012, 878). The encryption process uses an algorithm to convert a file from a readable format (plaintext) into something that is unreadable (ciphertext) by anyone who does not have the key. There are two common types of encryption: symmetric and asymmetric. Symmetric encryption involves a secret key in the possession of both the receiver and sender, which can be used to both encrypt and decrypt. Asymmetric encryption uses a key pair: one public key to encrypt data and one secret key to decrypt it (Microsoft n.d.). Popular programs such as Pretty Good Privacy and Vericrypt can be used to encrypt e-mails and files, respectively.

LEGAL AND TECHNICAL BARRIERS

There have been several recent legal challenges involving the use of digital forensics. On December 2, 2015, in San Bernardino, California, two perpetrators shot and killed 14 people outside a center geared to those suffering from a developmental disability. Both attackers were killed on scene, and there was a resulting legal battle when the FBI collected the main suspect's iPhone 5C and could not crack the passcode. As a result, the FBI attempted to force Apple to construct a workaround for their heavy phone encryption mechanisms (Rubin, Queally, and Dave 2016). Apple relented in court, and the FBI eventually relied on a third party to unlock the iPhone. After the months-long effort, there ended up being little to no valuable information regarding the motivation for the mass shooting.

Recently, cloud-based computing has grown in popularity, so instead of saving documents to a hard drive, users are saving them to the cloud. Popular cloud-based systems include Dropbox, Google Drive, and Apple's iCloud. The cloud promises large storage capability, but it has also made the process of digital forensic investigations harder to conduct. The problem exists due to a lack of clear boundaries (Jin, Guo, and Shang 2012, 250). For investigators, it is challenging to produce a warrant under the basis of probable cause, as investigators do not know where or if the data in question is in the cloud. Additionally, the cloud can make it difficult for forensics to process data if the service provider does not comply or takes ownership of the data via the terms of service (TOS) document (Wilson 2015).

Kaitlyn Hoover

See also: Cybercrime

Further Reading

Agrawal, Monika, and Pradeep Mishra. 2012. "A Comparative Survey on Symmetric Key Encryption Techniques." *International Journal on Computer Science and Engineering* 4 (5): 877–882. Accessed January 16, 2019. http://ieeexplore.ieee.org/document/7086640/?reload=true.

Almasy, Steve, Kyung Lah, and Alberto Moya. 2015. "At Least 14 Killed in Shooting in San Bernardino; Suspect Identified." CNN, December 3. Accessed January 16, 2019. http://www.cnn.com/2015/12/02/us/san-bernardino-shooting/index.html

Ayers, Rick, Sam Brothers, and Wayne Jansen. 2014. "Guidelines on Mobile Device Forensics." Accessed December 1, 2017 http://nvlpubs.nist.gov/nistpubs/SpecialPublications/NIST.SP.800-101r1.pdf.

Denning, Dorothy, and William Baugh. 1997. "Encryption and the Evolving Technologies: Tools of Organized Crime and Terrorism." *Trends in Organized Crime, 39*(1): 84–91.

Garfinkel, Simson. 2010. "Digital Forensics Research: The Next 10 Years." *Digital Investigation* 7: s64–s73.

Jin, Bo, Hong Guo, and Ting Shang. 2012. "Forensic Investigations in Cloud Environments." Presented at the *2012 International Conference on Computer Science and Information Processing Xi'an, Shaanxi, China*: 248–251. https://ieeexplore.ieee.org/abstract/document/6308841.

Microsoft. n.d. "Description of Symmetric and Asymmetric Encryption." Accessed November 28, 2017. https://support.microsoft.com/en-us/help/246071/description-of-symmetric-and-asymmetric-encryption.

Rubin, Joel, James Queally, and Paresh Dave. 2016. "FBI Unlocks San Bernardino Shooter's iPhone and Ends Legal Battle with Apple, for Now." *LA Times*, March 28. Accessed January 16, 2019. http://www.latimes.com/local/lanow/la-me-ln-fbi-drops-fight-to-force-apple-to-unlock-san-bernardino-terrorist-iphone-20160328-story.html.

Spadafora, Anthony. 2017. "Encryption Blocks the FBI from Accessing 7,000 Devices." *Beta News*, October 15. Accessed January 16, 2019. https://betanews.com/2017/10/25/fbi-struggles-to-decrypt-devices.

Tassone, Christopher, Ben Martini, Kim-Kwang Raymond Choo, and Jill Slay. 2013. "Mobile Device Forensics: A Snapshot." *Trends and Issues in Crime and Criminal Justice* 460: 1–7. Accessed January 17, 2019. http://aic.gov.au/publications/current%20series/tandi/441-460/tandi460.html.

Wilson, David. 2015. "Legal Issues in Cloud Forensics." Accessed December 13, 2017. https://www.forensicmag.com/article/2015/05/legal-issues-cloud-forensics.

Digital Piracy

Digital piracy is the unauthorized reproduction, trade, use, or distribution of a copyrighted work, such as software, music, movies, or other digital goods. Technological expansions have led to the proliferation of digital piracy among computer users. These advancements have influenced a modernized switch from consumer piracy to digital piracy, as digital piracy bypasses physical transactions and allows users to share electronic forms of media over the Internet.

METHODS OF FILE SHARING

Beginning in the mid-1990s, the first form of digital piracy was the "Sneakernet." A Sneakernet moves digital information through physical transportation, for example, giving a friend a copy of an album or film. Electronic information is copied and placed onto external hardware, such as floppy discs, USB flash drives, compact discs, or magnetic tape, and then physically transported to its destination. One of the biggest limitations of this type of distribution network was latency: physically transporting electronic information either by foot or by mail could take days to weeks.

As technology evolved, new forms of digital piracy emerged. By 1998, the wide use of the Internet largely replaced the need for the Sneakernet, as the Internet increased the accessibility of pirated media. In addition to pirating media, such as music and film, the Internet allowed the pirating of software or "warez." Warez is commercial software that has been stripped of its copyright protection and then posted online for distribution via the Internet. Popular forms of file sharing developed online, including File Transfer Protocol (FTP), instant messenger (IM), and electronic bulletin boards (BBS). Though these early Internet forms of piracy were greatly superior to the Sneakernet, most required communication through a centralized server, which meant that shutting them down was relatively trivial.

As the Internet became more widely accessible, the network's architecture began to change as well. Peer-to-peer (P2P) networking replaced the need for a centralized server and provided a way for users to communicate directly with one another and contribute both content and hardware resources. P2P networking permits a computer connected to the Internet to identify itself as both a client and server, thereby enabling the computer to communicate directly with any other computer on the Internet to exchange files, legitimate or otherwise.

Going public in 1999, Napster was one of the first P2P networks created. Though file transmission was P2P, Napster's search function operated on a centralized model. Napster was designed for users to share their local digital music files (MP3) with other compatible users. While Napster was never in possession of the media exchanged between users, it provided a search engine and database that allowed users to find one another and their file libraries to provide requested files. Though Napster had no control over what was being uploaded or distributed, with users injecting, storing, distributing, and consuming media (Biddle 2002), a legal injunction stopped Napster from providing the search function, and the software ceased to exist as a result.

Further technological advancements later permitted users to share information without the need for a centralized storage server. Gnutella, created in 2000, was one of the first P2P networks that operated on this new decentralized model. Gnutella users connect to a swarm of other users running Gnutella, which shares IP addresses of other peers in a blossoming chain that provides access to any host. Users connect to one another directly through this swarm model, so there is no supervision, restriction, or central search engine to block. Some of the most popular P2P file sharing programs to utilize the Gnutella network included LimeWire and Kazaa.

The most modern, and still widely utilized, decentralized P2P file sharing network is BitTorrent, which was created in 2001. BitTorrent was developed to share larger files at faster speeds than previous transmission methods. To join a BitTorrent network or swarm, a user must download a .torrent file from an index site, such as the popular "the Pirate Bay." Once a .torrent file is downloaded from the index site, the user needs a client (i.e., uTorrent or Transmission) to read the .torrent file, which connects the user to a "tracker" that directs the client software to the proper swarm. Each computer in the swarm has a partial or full copy of the desired file and is capable of sending small portions of a file to any user in the swarm without it. Once the client connects to multiple other users, it begins to download the different bits of the file simultaneously from various users and then reassembles them into the original file. As BitTorrent does not rely on a direct download server and instead operates purely P2P, the technology allows for many more users to download and share files at a faster rate than previous techniques. From a legal standpoint, the pure P2P nature of BitTorrent means there is no server to take offline or company to sue.

LEGAL CASES

A&M Records v. Napster (239 F.3d 1004; 9th Cir. 2001) was one of the first cases that applied copyright laws to P2P file sharing. As Napster was a P2P file-sharing network that allowed users to transmit MP3 music files, major record companies attempted to stop the company in court. The plaintiffs (multiple record companies) argued that Napster's users engaged in direct copyright infringement and wanted to sue Napster on the grounds of contributory infringement. Napster's defense was that the company could not be held liable for the copyright infringements its users engaged in. However, the plaintiffs were able to prove that Napster engaged in contributory infringement on the basis that Napster was aware that its users were sharing copyrighted files without permission and that Napster was supplying software to facilitate the copyright infringement. The court found Napster liable for contributory and vicarious infringement of copyright, which resulted in the end of services that facilitated copyright infringement (Washington University Law 2013).

In 2000, the band Metallica became the first artist or group to sue a P2P file-sharing network when they sued Napster. The dispute began when Metallica realized that their entire album was available for free download and was traced back to Napster. Metallica sought millions in damages due to the illegal downloading of their songs by Napster users. Metallica claimed that Napster enabled users to exchange copyrighted music files and demanded that all of their songs be removed (Marshall 2002). Metallica's attorneys also identified which Napster users were engaging in the illegal downloading and sharing of their music files and demanded that all of the users be banned from Napster. As a result, Napster was required to filter all copyrighted songs by Metallica from search results and banned over 300,000 users from using Napster (Borland 2002).

Thomas-Rasset v. Capitol Records (692 F.3d 899; 8th Cir. 2012) was the first file sharing copyright infringement case to be brought to court in the United States against an individual for digital piracy. The defendant, Jammie Thomas-Rasset, was held liable for the unauthorized downloading and sharing of 24 songs. The 24 songs on Thomas-Rasset's computer were made available to other users through Kazaa. Thomas-Rasset was originally awarded a $220,000 penalty, but he refused to pay the penalty and faced increased fines up to roughly $1.9 million (Electronic Frontier Foundation n.d.). The presiding judge, however, found the penalties to be too severe and reinstated the penalty of $220,000. Capitol Records was able to request such excessive penalties on the defendant because there was no limitation in regard to statutory penalties in copyright cases.

In 2009, the four Swedish creators of the Pirate Bay were arrested and accused of illegally hosting files. The prosecutor tried them on the notion of administering, hosting, and developing the site that is believed to facilitate other users' breach of copyright law. Though Pirate Bay does not host copyrighted files, the creators were charged with promoting the copyright infringement of users via their torrent tracking Web site. The founders were sentenced to one year in prison and charged with approximately $3.5 million in fines (Larsson 2008).

DIGITAL MILLENNIUM COPYRIGHT ACT (DMCA)

The Digital Millennium Copyright Act (DMCA), signed into law in 1998 by President Bill Clinton, declared any downloading or sharing of copyrighted digital media to be illegal. The DMCA protects against copying of copyrighted work. It also protects online service providers (OSP) and Internet service providers (ISP) from liability for copyright infringement by their users through the creation of a safe harbor. DMCA takedown notices are sent to Internet service providers when a copyright holder identifies unlawfully distributed copyrighted content. From there, the Internet service provider can locate where the copyrighted content is coming from and either cut services or block access to specific sites. Another provision under the DMCA includes anticircumvention, which bans any attempt to circumvent digital rights management, meaning that users are not allowed to bypass any technological measure (i.e., decrypting an encrypted work) without the authority of the copyright owner.

Amanda Rude

See also: Cybercrime; Intellectual Property Crime; Movie Piracy; Music Piracy

Further Reading

Biddle, Peter, Paul England, Marcus Peinado, and Bryan Willman. 2003. "The Darknet and the Future of Content Protection." In *Digital Rights Management*, edited by Joan Feigenbaum (155–176). Berlin: Springer. Accessed January 16, 2019. https://link.springer.com/chapter/10.1007/978-3-540-44993-5_10.

Borland, John. 2002. "Metallica Fingers 335,435 Napster Users." Last modified January 2, 2002. Accessed January 16, 2019. https://www.cnet.com/news/metallica-fingers-335435-napster-users.

Electronic Frontier Foundation. n.d. "*Capitol v. Thomas*." Accessed January 16, 2019. https://www.eff.org/cases/capitol-v-thomas.

Larsson, Linus. 2008. "Charges Filed against the Pirate Bay Four." *Computer Sweden*, January 31. Accessed January 16, 2019. https://computersweden.idg.se/2.2683/1.143146/charges-filed-against-the-pirate-bay-four.

Marshall, Lee. 2002. "Metallica and Morality: The Rhetorical Battleground of the Napster Wars." *Entertainment Law* 1 (1): 1–19.

Washington University Law. 2013. "*Case Study: A&M Records, Inc. v. Napster, Inc.*" Last modified August 1, 2013. Accessed January 16, 2019. https://onlinelaw.wustl.edu/blog/case-study-am-records-inc-v-napster-inc.

Double (Dual) Criminality

Double criminality (also referred to as dual criminality) is the term used in extradition and certain other forms of judicial cooperation (such as requests for the freezing of assets) to refer to the requirement that the conduct in question is recognized as an offense in the domestic law of both the requested and the requesting states. The issue becomes relevant when countries are cooperating in combating global crime. Although the requirement of double criminality is widely used, it can be waived by treaty or domestic law (Boister 2012, 218).

The requirement of double criminality rests on the view that no one should be prosecuted for conduct that is not recognized as an offense (the principle of *nullum crimen sine lege*, "no crime without law"). By extension, if the state in which the suspect is found does not consider the conduct to be an offense, this state should not contribute to the prosecution by, for example, extraditing the suspect to the requesting state.

STANDARDS USED IN ASSESSING DOUBLE CRIMINALITY

Two different standards are used in assessing whether double criminality exists: the concrete and the abstract. The concrete standard requires that the definition of the offense in the two jurisdictions uses the same essential elements and perhaps even the same title of the offense. For example, in the case of vandalism, this may require that the laws of the two jurisdictions use the elements of (1) willful or reckless (2) destruction of the property of another person (3) without a reasonable excuse. Problems with the concrete standard may arise if a new element is introduced that is not recognized by one of the jurisdictions, such as if the vandalism is committed in connection with the hacking of a computer system.

The abstract standard, which has gradually become the more widely applied standard, requires only that the underlying conduct is criminal in both jurisdictions, regardless of how it is defined or what the offense is called. To avoid having to provide assistance in petty cases, states generally require that the offense for which assistance is sought is punishable in the requested state by a certain minimum level of punishment, such as imprisonment for at least four years.

A special situation arises when the offense in question was not criminal in the requested state at the time of the conduct but is criminal at the time the request is made. The way in which this is resolved depends on national law.

WAIVER OF THE REQUIREMENT OF DOUBLE CRIMINALITY IN THE CASE OF MULTIPLE OFFENSES

In practice, it is possible that extradition is sought for several separate offenses, and some of these do not fulfill the conditions of double criminality. The general rule expressed in Article 2(2)(a) of the UN Model Treaty on Extradition is that the offenses in question must be criminal in both states; however, the condition of the minimum level of punishment may be waived for part of the offenses. Thus, for example, if extradition is sought for a bank robbery as well as for several less serious offenses for which the minimum punishment would not otherwise meet the conditions for extradition, all of them may nonetheless be included in the request.

JURISDICTIONAL DOUBLE CRIMINALITY

Jurisdictions may differ in the extent to which they apply extraterritoriality, which is the possibility of prosecuting conduct (such as terrorism or drug trafficking) that took place outside the territory of the state in question. Jurisdictional double criminality refers to the requirement that both states, under comparable situations, would allow their courts to establish jurisdiction.

Matti Joutsen

See also: Extradition

Further Reading

Boister, Neil. 2012. *An Introduction to Transnational Criminal Law*. Oxford, UK: Oxford University Press, 218–220.

Gardocki, Lech. 1993. "Double Criminality in Extradition Law." *Israel Law Review* 27 (1–2): 288–296.

Hafen, Jonathan O. 1992. "International Extradition: Issues Arising under the Dual Criminality Requirement." *Brigham Young University Law Review* 191: 191–230. Accessed January 16, 2019. https://digitalcommons.law.byu.edu/lawreview/vol1992/iss1/4.

Plachta, Michael. 1999. "The Role of Double Criminality in International Cooperation in Penal Matters." *Nordisk Tidskrift for Kriminalvidenskab, 76*(5): 84–134. Accessed January 16, 2019. https://tidsskrift.dk/NTfK/article/download/71233/103194

Williams, Sharon A. 1991. "The Double Criminality Rule and Extradition: A Comparative Analysis." *Nova Law Review* 15 (2): 581–623. Accessed January 16, 2019. https://nsuworks.nova.edu/nlr/vol15/iss2/9.

Dream Market

Dream Market, which was founded in 2013, operates on the Tor network (The Onion Router network) as a hidden online service that allows users to browse for and purchase a variety of content, including illegal items.

In July 2017, federal authorities shut down AlphaBay, which had been the largest online marketplace for illegal goods, and Hansa, the third largest. AlphaBay had flourished since 2014, when its predecessor, Silk Road, had been shut down. Critics and cynics suggest, and reality seems to support, that when one Dark Web market falls, buyers and sellers simply move to another. Or, more amusingly, shutting down these marketplaces is like playing whack-a-mole.

Some identified Dream Market as the successor to AlphaBay and Hansa—although other marketplaces such as Tochka and Valhalla were also mentioned. Like similar marketplaces, Dream Market provides opportunities to buy drugs, child pornography, stolen and fraudulent identification documents, counterfeit goods, malware and other computer hacking tools, firearms, and toxic chemicals.

As one example, a study by RAND Europe and the University of Manchester sought to estimate the size and scope of the illegal trade in firearms and found the United States to be the most common source country for arms being sold on the Dark Web and Europe the largest market (RAND Corporation 2017).

As early as 2017 and continuing into 2018, many people believed that the Federal Bureau of Investigation (FBI) controlled Dream Market. An April 2018 outage of the Dream Market Web site, and what appeared to some users as the loss of their Bitcoin or other cryptocurrency funds, encouraged speculation that Dream Market had become a captured site. Whether under federal government control or not, in February 2016, federal authorities were able to identify several drug dealers operating on Dream Market. One, French national Gal Vallerius ("OxyMonster" on Dream Market), was initially charged with conspiracy to distribute drugs and—as he was also identified as a Dream Market senior moderator—with conspiracy to facilitate the sale of illicit substances on Dream Market. He pleaded guilty to drug distribution and money laundering and was awaiting sentencing as of mid-2018.

Despite concerns and speculation, as of mid-2018, Dream Market was the sole remaining heavily populated darknet marketplace to trade goods or services over the Dark Web. In May 2018, Dream Market banned the sale of the opioid fentanyl and declared that no vendor would be allowed to sell the drug. As fentanyl and other opioids remain available from vendors on other Dark Web marketplaces, few people believe the Dream Market ban will have any effect on supply or demand of the product.

Philip L. Reichel

See also: AlphaBay; Dark Web/Deep Web; Tor (The Onion Router) Network

Further Reading

Aliens, C. 2018. " 'OxyMonster' Pleads Guilty to Drug and Money Laundering Charges." Last Modified June 25, 2018. Accessed January 16, 2019. https://www.deepdotweb.com/2018/06/25/oxymonster-pleads-guilty-to-drug-and-money-laundering-charges.

Ng, Alfred. 2017. "Buyers, Sellers and Cops on the Hunt for AlphaBay's Successor." Last Modified July 21, 2017. Accessed January 16, 2019. https://www.cnet.com/news/alphabay-hansa-silk-road-dream-market-dark-web-shuts-down.

RAND Corporation. 2017. "Behind the Curtain: The Illicit Trade of Firearms, Explosives and Ammunition on the Dark Web." Accessed July 12, 2018. https://www.rand.org/pubs/research_reports/RR2091.html.

E

Economic Espionage Act of 1996

President Bill Clinton signed the Economic Espionage Act (EEA, 18 U.S.C. § 1831–§ 1839) into law on October 11, 1996, criminalizing two types of trade secret misappropriations: economic espionage and theft of trade secrets. Economic espionage is defined as anyone stealing a trade secret with the intent or knowledge that the offense will benefit any foreign government, foreign instrumentality, or foreign agent. Individuals convicted of economic espionage can receive fines of up to $500,000 or be sentenced to up to 15 years in prison. Organizations convicted under this statute can receive fines of up to $10 million.

Theft of trade secrets is defined as anyone stealing a trade secret that is or will be produced and placed in commerce with the knowledge that their actions will injure the owner of the trade secret. Individuals convicted of the theft of trade secrets can receive prison sentences of up to 10 years and fines. Organizations convicted under this statute can receive fines of up to $5 million. Section 1834 of the EEA provides that the court in imposing sentencing shall order the forfeiture of any proceeds or property derived from violations of the EEA and may order the forfeiture of any property used to commit or to facilitate the commission of the crime (DOJ 2018).

CRIMINAL PROSECUTIONS

There are five elements that prosecutors must consider when charging individuals under §1831 and §1832: the scope of the criminal activity, including evidence of involvement by a foreign government, foreign agent, or foreign instrumentality; the degree of economic injury to the trade secret owner; the type of trade secret misappropriated; the effectiveness of available civil remedies; and the potential deterrent value of the prosecution (DOJ 2018). Since 1996, the Justice Department has secured approximately 231 indictments under the EEA, 20 percent of the cases appealing to the Courts of Appeals. Many cases came from the state of California, followed by Illinois, New York, and Virginia. Although not specified in the statute, independent development, reverse engineering, and lack of secrecy are defenses to EEA prosecutions in civil misappropriation cases and have been applied to EEA criminal prosecutions (Ryan et al. 2017, 1518).

AMENDMENTS

Recently, the Foreign and Economic Espionage Penalty Enhancement Act (FEEPEA) of 2012 and the Defend Trade Secrets Act (DTSA) of 2016 substantially amended the EEA. The FEEPEA increased the maximum fines for §1831 from $500,000 to not more than $5,000,000 for individuals and fines for organizations from $10 million to the greater of $10 million or three times the value of the stolen trade secret to the organization. The DTSA created a federal civil cause of action for trade secret misappropriation and legal immunity for corporate whistle-blowers.

David A. Rembert and Donna Ossorio

See also: Intellectual Property Crime

Further Reading

Defend Trade Secrets Act of 2016, Public Law 114-153, *U.S. Statutes at Large* 130 (2016): 376–386.

Economic Espionage Act, 18 U.S.C.A. § 1831–§ 1839 (1996).

Foreign and Economic Espionage Penalty Enhancement Act of 2012, Public Law 112-269, *U.S. Statutes at Large* 126 (2013): 2442–2443.

Krotoski, Mark L. 2009. "Common Issues and Challenges in Prosecuting Trade Secret and Economic Espionage Act Cases." *United States Attorneys Bulletin* 57: 2–23.

Ryan, Kevin, Destiny Howell, Melissa Keech, Yushan Luo, Brian Sperry, and Brittany Yantis. 2017. "Intellectual Property Crimes." *American Criminal Law Review* 54: 1509.

U.S. Department of Justice (DOJ). "United States Attorneys' Manual §9-59.100." Accessed March 4, 2018. https://www.justice.gov/usam/usam-9-59000-economic-espionage.

ECPAT International

ECPAT (End Child Prostitution in Asian Tourism) International is a global network of civil society organizations focused on ending sexual exploitation of children worldwide. According to its constitution, adopted in 1999, its vision is "to bring about the elimination of child prostitution, child pornography and the trafficking of children for sexual purposes, and to encourage the world community to ensure that children everywhere enjoy their fundamental rights free and secure from all forms of commercial sexual exploitation" (ECPAT International 2014). Based in Bangkok, Thailand, ECPAT International plays a key role in building awareness, setting standards, and providing advocacy and support for victims by initiating global mobilization of all potential actors (Steinmetz 2017). Currently there are 101 ECPAT members in 92 countries, including both large national coalitions and small grassroots organizations.

HISTORY

In 1990, a group of activists from several institutions established ECPAT International, including the Ecumenical Coalition of Third World Tourism, the Christian Conference of Asia (CCA), the Federation of Asian Bishops' Conference/Office for Human Development (FABC/OHD), the Third World European Ecumenical Network (TEN), and the North American Network on Tourism

(NANET). The organization's foundation was a response to a meeting of experts in Thailand where human rights activists expressed their common passion to end sexual exploitation of children worldwide. Thousands of people, including world leaders such as the prime ministers of Thailand and Vietnam, the Dalai Lama, and former U.S. president Jimmy Carter, signed a petition opposing child prostitution in March 1993 (ECPAT International 2015).

ECPAT International's terminology was first used and officially publicized at the First World Congress against the Commercial Sexual Exploitation of Children held in 1996. From 2001 to 2005, the network continued to progress by building partnerships and effectively responding to its worldwide goals. In 2008, in Rio di Janeiro, Brazil, together with the United Nations International Children's Emergency Fund (UNICEF) and the government of Brazil, ECPAT helped organize a World Congress where over 4,000 participants discussed the situation of children being potential victims of sex tourism and human trafficking. During the following years, ECPAT International continued to focus on sexual exploitation and trafficking of children as well as online safety of children. The organization also played a significant role in drafting and ratifying the Council of Europe Convention on Protection of Children against Sexual Exploitation and Sexual Abuse from 2007 to 2010. In 2016, ECPAT published the well-known Global Study on Sexual Exploitation of Children in Travel and Tourism (Hawke and Raphael 2016).

GOVERNANCE

ECPAT International is a nonprofit, nongovernmental organization registered as a foundation in the Netherlands in the year 2000. It is governed by an international board of trustees composed of eight regional representatives elected by member organizations in their local regions. The board and worldwide network are supported by a secretariat based in Bangkok and is registered with the Thai Ministry of Labor.

In 2002, ECPAT International established the Child and Youth Advisory Committee (EICYAC), which consists of 24 members, including children and young people from local organizations, who serve as a voice for those at risk.

ECPAT International has its own constitution, which was adopted by the ECPAT International General Assembly of September 1999 and amended in December 2014 (ECPAT International 2014).

ACTIONS

From its inception, ECPAT International has initiated numerous actions and initiatives that can be divided into three basic categories. The first can be traced back to the organization's roots, at which time advocacy and campaigns were the primary core of action. The second involves participation in child and survivor programs and is aimed at increasing the role of children in public debate and the decision-making process. Finally, ECPAT initiates and conducts research to better face challenges and identify problems.

Primarily, ECPAT works with governments and regional and international organizations to inform decision makers, the media, and civil society groups about special needs of the young generation as well as provide guidelines of how to eradicate sexual exploitation of children—both now and in the future.

From 2009 to 2011, ECPAT initiated the Global Youth Participation Project (YPP) that is aimed at actively involving children themselves in work against sexual exploitation. This project provided a voice to child survivors who also became involved as motivators, peer supporters, and advocates. ECPAT's Strategic Framework for 2015–2018 placed children at the heart of ECPAT's work, making them partners rather than just beneficiaries.

ECPAT's research places a priority on the creation of an accurate picture of sexual exploitation of children and explores methodologies that can improve estimation of the exact number of offenders and victims. As part of the mandate from the First World Congress, ECPAT produces Country Monitoring Reports (CMR) that are meant to monitor government's commitment to eradicate sexual exploitation of children. Also, more in-depth analysis of specific countries is provided in its Situational Analysis Reports (SITAN), which are based on multiple research tools. These include typical reporting methods created or specially designed to meet the needs of their specific research. The analytical tools are of such quality that the UN Special Rapporteur on the sale of children, child prostitution, and child pornography adopted them for use in its reports.

Relatively early, ECPAT focused on drafting and promoting legal regulations to enable law enforcement agencies to investigate and bring to justice persons perpetrating any form of sexual exploitation (especially of children) abroad.

One of ECPAT International's significant successes has been approval of the Code of Conduct for the Sexual Exploitation of Children in Travel and Tourism. The code was adopted in 1998 with the assistance of the United Nations World Tourism Organization. According to UNICEF, the code gained well over 1000 signatories in 42 counties and was highly successful in raising awareness of the issue of child sexual exploitation around the globe (UNICEF 2012).

Currently, ECPAT International's other programs focus on child sexual exploitation, exploitation of children in prostitution, trafficking of children, child and forced marriage, protection of legal regulations concerning children, and obviously sexual exploitation of children in travel and tourism.

Zbigniew Lasocik

See also: Human Trafficking; Sex Exploitation

Further Reading

ECPAT International. 2014. *ECPAT International Governance Documentation: Constitution.* Bangkok, Thailand: ECPAT International. Accessed January 17, 2019. http://www.ecpat.org/wp-content/uploads/legacy/ECPAT%20Governance%20Documentation%20(English)_Dec%202014_0.pdf.

ECPAT International. 2015. *ECPAT 25 Years: Rallying the World to the End Child Sexual Exploitation.* Bangkok, Thailand: ECPAT International. Accessed January 17, 2019. http://www.ecpat.org/wp-content/uploads/legacy/ECPAT%2025%20Years_FINAL.pdf.

Hawke, A., and A. Raphael. 2016. *Offenders on the Move. Global Study on Sexual Exploitation of Children in Travel and Tourism.* Bangkok, Thailand: ECPAT International.

Accessed January 17, 2019. http://cf.cdn.unwto.org/sites/all/files/docpdf/global-report-offenders-move-final.pdf.

Steinmetz, J. T. 2017. "Leaders Unite to Stop Global Sexual Exploitation of Children through Travel and Tourism." Accessed January 16, 2019. https://www.eturbonews.com/159723/leaders-unite-stop-global-sexual-exploitation-children-travel-tourism.

United Nations International Children's Emergency Fund (UNICEF). 2012. "Assessing the *Code of Conduct* for the Protection of Children from Sexual Exploitation in Travel and Tourism." *Innocenti Discussion Papers* no. 2012-01. UNICEF Innocenti Research Centre, Florence, Italy. Accessed January 17, 2019. https://www.unicef-irc.org/publications/662-assessing-the-code-of-conduct-for-the-protection-of-children-from-sexual-exploitation.html

18th Street Gang

The 18th Street gang is a transnational gang with members in Central America, Canada, and the United States. Mexican migrants from the Pico-Union neighborhood just west of Los Angeles formed the 18th Street in the 1960s because they were not allowed to join native-born Mexican American (Chicano) gangs in the area. As a result, the 18th Street gang recruited members from all racial and ethnic groups, which contributed to their growth, expansion, and becoming one of the first multiracial, multiethnic gangs in Los Angeles, California (Franco 2007, 24; Roumie 2017, 24–49). Recruitment of gang members involves forcing youth to join the gang through fear and intimidation.

ORGANIZATIONAL STRUCTURE

No international 18th Street gang leader has been identified; it is made up of independent neighborhood cliques (Moss 2012). Each clique has one leader, *primera palabra* ("shot caller"), who controls all the decisions of the gang and receives little input from individual gang members. Each clique also has a deputy, *segunda palabra*, who serves as the clique leader's right-hand man. The deputy is a trusted friend or relative of the leader who is responsible for advising the leader or representing the leader when he is absent from important meetings.

The next level in 18th Street gang's organizational hierarchy is standing committees, which are responsible for providing the leader with recommendations in the areas of discipline, logistics, enforcement, and surveillance. Finally, at the lowest level of 18th Street gang's organizational chart are soldiers and associates who are responsible for executing the leader's orders related to all operational functions and criminal activities. Each neighborhood clique operates independently and does not communicate with each other.

CRIMINAL ACTIVITIES

Analogous to many gangs, 18th Street gang members display a significant amount of criminal versatility. These crimes are motivated by profit, revenge, eliminating rival gangs, protecting turf, and maintaining gang rules. For example,

Griffin (2017) reported that 18th Street gang members murder their rivals, Mara Salvatrucha (MS-13), throughout South America and the United States. Further, three members of 18th Street gang were convicted of weapons trafficking and drug trafficking (U.S. Attorney's Office 2017). Finally, Markham (2015) reported that 18th Street gang members fired on buses in El Salvador, killing nine drivers and four citizens, in response to the government's crackdown on the gang.

Overall, the 18th Street gang is involved in various crimes that include petty, violent, organized, and transnational crimes. This organization has become one of the most notorious, ruthless, and violent organized crime units throughout North and South America.

ANTI-GANG TASK FORCES

The Federal Bureau of Investigation (FBI) is dedicated to eliminating transnational gangs that pose a significant threat to the United States through investigations and initiatives, such as the Safe Streets Violent Gang Task Force (SSVGTF), the National Gang Intelligence Center (NGIC), and Transnational Anti-Gang Task Forces (TAGTF). The SSVGTF is designed to expand collaboration and communication between all law enforcement agencies to address violent street gangs, drug-related violence, and the apprehension of violent fugitives. The NGIC is a fusion center responsible for providing all law enforcement agencies with educational resources on gang growth and migration, criminal networks, and patterns and trends of gangs. TAGTF are currently located in El Salvador, Guatemala, and Honduras. Each TAFTF is designed to investigate, disrupt, and dismantle gangs as well as to collect and disseminate intelligence to support U.S. investigations.

Justin Joseph and David A. Rembert

See also: Mara Salvatrucha (MS-13) Organization; Transnational Anti-Gang Task Forces

Further Reading

Franco, Celinda. 2007. *The MS 13 and 18th Street Gangs: Emerging Transnational Gang Threats?* CRS Report for Congress (RL 34233). Washington, D.C.: Congressional Research.

Griffin, Keith. 2017. "Barrio 18: Meet the Terrifying Gang with 50,000 Foot-Soldiers across the U.S. and So Unashamedly Violent It Rivals MS-13." *Daily Mail*, August 5. Accessed January 16, 2019. http://www.dailymail.co.uk/news/article-4764744/Barrio-18-Meet-terrifying-gang-rivals-MS-13.html

Markham, Lauren. 2015. "The 18th Street Gang Just Set Out to Prove It Runs El Salvador's Transport System." VICE News, August 5. Accessed January 17, 2019. https://news.vice.com/en_us/article/3kwq5n/the-18th-street-gang-just-set-out-to-prove-it-runs-el-salvadors-transport-system

Moss, Andrew. 2012. "Mara-18/M-18/18th Street Gang," Matthew B. Ridgway Center for International Security Studies. Accessed January 16, 2019. http://research.ridgway.pitt.edu/wp-content/uploads/2012/05/M-18PROFILEFINAL.pdf.

Roumie, Norma. 2017. "Gangs and the Culture of Violence in El Salvador (What Role Did the US Play?)." *Great Lakes Journal of Undergraduate History* 5 (1): 24–49.

U.S. Attorney's Office. 2017. "Three 18th Street Gang Members/Associates Plead Guilty to Gun Trafficking Charges." Accessed May 19, 2018. https://www.justice.gov

/usao-ma/pr/three-18th-street-gang-membersassociates-plead-guilty-gun-trafficking-charges.

U.S. Federal Bureau of Investigation (FBI). "Anti-Gang Initiatives." Accessed January 16, 2019. https://www.fbi.gov/investigate/violent-crime/gangs.

Environmental Crimes

Environmental crime takes many forms and can have either domestic or global consequences. The crimes include illegal dumping of toxic waste, illegal exploitation and trafficking of the world's flora and fauna, illegal fishing and logging, and many more.

ENVIRONMENTAL CRIME AND THE UNITED STATES

U.S. legislative action to protect the environment dates to the Refuse Act of 1899, which was the first environmental law to include criminal sanctions. It prohibited the discharge of refuse matter into navigable waters and made such dumping a criminal act regardless of the offender's intent. Despite that 19th-century start, environmental laws remained rare until the environmental movement of the 1960s and 1970s began influencing U.S. legislation. President Richard Nixon, declaring the 1970s as "the decade of the environment," established the Environmental Protection Agency (EPA), which is responsible for establishing environmental protections, conducting research, and investigating violations of environmental laws. It does not, however, have the power to shut down corporations that violate these laws. Laws passed in the 1970s to preserve the natural environment included the Clean Air Act (1970), the Federal Water Pollution Control Act (1972), and the Safe Drinking Water Act (1974).

One of the most infamous cases of environmental crime is referred to as Love Canal. Between 1942 and 1953, Hooker Chemical Corporation burned more than 20 million pounds of chemical waste in an abandoned waterway near Niagara Falls. As this was before the creation of the EPA or the Clean Water Act, the company simply abandoned the site. It was later sold to a local board of education, which built a school in the area. An entire community was built thereafter, but in 1977, residents began to notice a black sludgy substance in their basements. The community saw an unusually high number of miscarriages and stillbirths, and later studies found a disproportionately high number of children with learning disabilities, skin disorders, seizures, and other health problems. Internal documents show that Hooker leadership was aware of the problems and refused to do anything unless it was pushed. In 1995, Occidental Petroleum, the company that owned Hooker, agreed to reimburse the federal government $129 million for the cleanup of Love Canal.

Many of the biggest corporations in the United States have pleaded guilty to or been found guilty of committing environmental crimes. For instance, in 2013, Walmart pleaded guilty to violating the Clean Water Act and will pay more than $81 million. The company did not adequately train its employees on the storage and disposal of hazardous wastes.

A growing area of concern is the disposal of electronic waste (e-waste). Cellular phones, computers, televisions, and other technologies are made with toxic chemicals that cannot simply be dumped in landfills. Although people and corporations in the United States often do dump these items inappropriately, jeopardizing the safety of their communities, much of the e-waste generated in developed countries is shipped to developing ones, who are eager to take it for payment. There, poor individuals may sift through the dangerous rubble in search of items to recycle for precious funds, exposing themselves to a variety of toxins.

TRANSNATIONAL ENVIRONMENTAL CRIME

The United Nations Environment Program identifies transnational environmental crimes as being criminal activities undertaken by persons acting across national borders. Examples of such activities include illegal logging and timber smuggling, species smuggling, the black market in ozone-depleting substances, and the illegal movement of toxic and hazardous waste and other prohibited chemicals.

In addition to its serious environment consequences, transnational environmental crime also has significant economic impact—believed to only be behind drug trafficking and trade in counterfeit goods in terms of the global illicit economy. These crimes often involve corruption, loss of tax revenue, parallel trading with other forms of criminal activity, and distortion of the licit market. In addition, environmental crimes may be integrated into other transnational organized crime groups that deal in such activities as trafficking in drugs, weapons, and humans. Many terrorist groups engage in, and profit from, environmental crime (Stimson Center n.d.).

Although transnational environmental crime includes many different activities, there are five areas identified as being of major importance by the United Nations Environment Programme (2013):

1. Illegal logging and its associated timber trade that contribute to deforestation, deprive forest communities of vital livelihoods, cause ecological problems such as flooding, and are major contributors to climate change.
2. Illicit trade in ozone depleting substances that contribute to a thinning ozone layer that, in turn, causes human health problems such as skin cancer and cataracts.
3. Illegal, unreported, and unregulated (IUU) fishing that leads to lost revenue at national and individual levels.
4. Soil and water contamination from illegal hazardous waste dumping that not only damages ecosystems and human health but the illegal trade of which also undermines the legitimate waste treatment and disposal industries.
5. Poaching that has the greatest impact on species survival. For example, rhino, tiger, and elephant populations are today threatened with extinction due to poaching and illegal trade driven by growing demand, in particular from Southeast Asia and China.

The transnational nature of these crimes requires a coordinated response among countries. INTERPOL, for example, helps support states in curtailing global criminal networks involved in environmental crimes and helps shape new laws, practices, and training for law enforcement relevant to these issues. And the United Nations Environment Programme has implemented the Global Environmental Alert Service (GEAS), which uses the Internet to provide online access to information about environmental changes as they occur. The United Nations hopes that the GEAS platform becomes the standard delivery method for up-to-date information about any and all environment-related topics.

Philip L. Reichel and Laura Finley

See also: Basel Convention on the Control of Transboundary Movements of Hazardous Wastes and Their Disposal; Convention on International Trade in Endangered Species of Wild Fauna and Flora; Convention on the Prevention of Marine Pollution by Dumping Wastes and Other Matter; Green Criminology; Illicit Ivory Trade; International Consortium on Combating Wildlife Crime; International Union for Conservation of Nature; Metals and Minerals Smuggling; Nuclear Weapons and Related Materials and Technologies, Trafficking in; Poaching; UN Global Programme for Combating Wildlife and Forest Crime; Waste Crime; Wildlife and Forest Crime; World Wildlife Crime Report

Further Reading

"Environmental Crime." 2009. In *Environmental Science: In Context*, edited by Brenda Wilmoth Lerner and K. Lee Lerner, 279–281. Detroit: Gale.

Environmental Protection Agency. 2015. "Basic Information on Enforcement." October 22. Accessed December 31, 2015. http://www.epa.gov/enforcement/enforcement-basic-information.

INTERPOL. n.d. "Environmental Crime." Accessed July 14, 2018. http://www.interpol.int/Crime-areas/Environmental-crime/Environmental-crime.

Rosoff, S., H. Pontell, and R. Tillman. 2014. *Profit without Honor: White-Collar Crime and the Looting of America.* 6th ed. Boston: Pearson.

Stimson Center. n.d. "Environmental Crime." Accessed July 14, 2018. https://www.stimson.org/enviro-crime.

United Nations Environment Programme. 2013. "Transnational Environmental Crime—A Common Crime in Need of Better Enforcement." Global Environmental Alert Service (January). Accessed January 16, 2019. http://na.unep.net/geas/archive/pdfs/GEAS_Jan2013_EnvCrime.pdf.

United Nations Environment Programme. n.d. "Transnational Environmental Crime." Accessed July 12, 2018. http://web.unep.org/divisions/delc/transnational-environmental-crime.

Escobar, Pablo (1949–1993)

Pablo Emilio Escobar Gaviria rose from poverty to become one of the world's most ruthless and successful cocaine traffickers. His empire reached across the Western Hemisphere and Europe, and during the height of his power in the 1980s, he was one of the richest men in the world. During this period, Escobar's Medellín Cartel, in Colombia, was believed to be supplying 80 percent of the cocaine consumed annually in the United States.

Born in 1949 to a farmer father and teacher mother, Pablo and his brother Roberto were sent in the late-1950s to live with their grandparents in the city of Medellín, Colombia. As a teenager, Escobar engaged in petty theft and minor fraud, but in the early 1970s, he turned to more serious and profitable activities by purchasing cocaine paste in Peru and then driving it back to Colombia concealed in a car's wheel well. He set up a kitchen in Medellín to further refine the cocaine, and he soon replaced the single car with a fleet of trucks (Brennan 2009).

DRUG LORD

By the mid-1970s, Escobar had established himself as a major drug smuggler and an early prototype of the new international gangster. He learned to use the techniques of bribery and murder, which he relied upon to keep authorities at a distance. For example, after being caught with 39 pounds of cocaine in a pickup truck, Escobar walked out of jail three months later—his arrest mysteriously revoked. More ominous, both officers who arrested him were later killed (McFadden 1993).

When he began his operation, there was already an established marijuana business between Colombia and the United States, but cocaine was a new twist. Like the marijuana traffickers before him, Escobar started moving cocaine by using individual carriers ("mules") to transport the drug. But relying only on people transport limited the amount of drugs that could be smuggled. Escobar expanded his scale of operation by introducing speedboats and even custom-built submarines to deliver cocaine to Miami.

By the late 1970s, he was earning millions of U.S. dollars per week, but he wanted more. Escobar organized small-time smugglers and dealers into the criminal equivalent of a multinational corporation based in his hometown of Medellín. His new cartel built laboratories in the jungle to process cocaine paste, and the labs grew to the geographical equivalent of small cities. One "city" had a runway concealed by false homes built on wooden wheels. From there, Escobar could produce and fly out some 10,000 kilograms of cocaine every 15 days (Brennan 2009; Watson and Katel 1993).

Escobar enjoyed a lavish lifestyle and brought a level of attention to himself that some believe facilitated his eventual downfall. He owned a fleet of aircraft, a mansion in Miami Beach, apartments in Florida, hotels in Colombia and Venezuela, and a private zoo with kangaroos, hippos, camels, giraffes, and other exotic animals. The zoo provides an example of why some in Colombia considered Escobar to be a kind of Robin Hood figure—taking from the rich and giving to the poor. Locals, who were invited to enjoy Escobar's zoo, were also recipients of paved roads, jobs, housing projects, sports teams, and sports stadiums. The fact that the teams and stadiums were useful for laundering cocaine money did not lessen the esteem in which Colombia's poor held Escobar.

POLITICIAN

In 1979, Colombia signed a treaty with the United States that made drug traffickers eligible for extradition to the United States. Escobar decided to run for political office to take advantage of the immunity from extradition that was available to a member of congress. Drawing on his popularity, Escobar was elected in 1982 as a substitute deputy in Colombia's House of Representatives. Two years later, he was forced out of office when Justice Minister Rodrigo Lara Bonilla highlighted Escobar's criminal record as part of Lara Bonilla's anticorruption efforts.

In 1984, Lara Bonilla was assassinated on Escobar's orders. The high-profile killing forced Escobar underground as both Colombian and U.S. officials increased their efforts to find him. In 1989, those efforts intensified after Escobar arranged the killing of a presidential candidate, and he is believed to have ordered the blowing up of a Colombian jetliner that included among the passengers some informers from a rival cartel who were about to testify against the Medellín Cartel.

LA CATEDRAL

Escobar had essentially declared war on the Colombian government. On his orders, prosecutors, judges, lawyers, journalists, police officers, and ordinary Colombians were killed. He was being pursued by the Colombian and U.S. governments and by a vigilante group known by its Spanish acronym PEPES (People Persecuted by Pablo Escobar).

The intense manhunt caused Escobar to negotiate his surrender to Colombian authorities in 1991. Those negotiations included two conditions that would greatly benefit Escobar. First, Colombia had to ban the extradition of Colombian citizens to the United States, and, second, Escobar would be allowed to build his own prison.

Escobar's "prison," called *La Catedral*, was a lavish villa secured by guards that Escobar hired from his own hometown. The computers, cell phones, and boardroom tables allowed Escobar to continue running his criminal enterprise while in prison (McFadden 1993). When he was not "working," Escobar enjoyed the prison's stereo system, bar, color TV, whirlpool bath, and other luxuries.

As word spread of the extravagances he enjoyed, the government decided to move him to another location. Escobar got word of the planned transfer, and as it was ready to occur in July 1992, Escobar slipped away into the mountains. For more than a year, he eluded capture by moving among his supporters in Medellín and the surrounding countryside—often using disguises or traveling in coffins as a corpse.

DEATH

An elite police commando force, the *Bloque de Busqueda* ("Search Unit"), assigned the sole task of catching Escobar, killed him in December 1993. Aided by U.S. and British technology, calls that Escobar made while in hiding were traced and pinpointed to a house in Medellín. The Search Unit cut off telephones in the area to prevent lookouts from calling in a warning and sent a contingent to surround the house. Armed officers broke through the front and garage doors and killed Escobar as he attempted to escape across a rooftop. Because the fatal wound is believed to have been a shot to his ear, Roberto Escobar and other family members believe Pablo killed himself—doing what Roberto said his brother always planned to do if he ever found himself cornered (Fedarko and Caballero 1993).

Escobar's death is considered a symbolic victory for the Colombian and U.S. governments, and it badly damaged the Medellín Cartel. But all agree that it did nothing to reduce the flow of drugs to the United States.

Philip L. Reichel

See also: Cartel Organization; Medellín Cartel

Further Reading

Bowden, Mark. 2001. *Killing Pablo: The Hunt for the World's Greatest Outlaw.* New York: Atlantic Monthly Press.

Brennan, Zoe. 2009. "Cocaine Dreams: The Life of Pablo Escobar." *Sunday Independent (South Africa)*, April 12.

Escobar Gaviria, Roberto. 2010. *Escobar: The Inside Story of Pablo Escobar, the World's Most Powerful Criminal.* London: Hodder.

Fedarko, Kevin, and Maria Cristina Caballero. 1993. "Escobar's Dead End." *Time*, December 13.

McFadden, Robert D. 1993. "Head of Medellín Cocaine Cartel Is Killed by Troops in Colombia." *New York Times*, December 3. Accessed January 21, 2019. http://www.nytimes.com/1993/12/03/world/head-of-medellin-cocaine-cartel-is-killed-by-troops-in-colombia.html.

Watson, Russell, and Peter Katel. 1993. "Death on the Spot." *Newsweek*, December 12.

Eurojust

A European Union Council Decision established the European Union's Judicial Cooperation Unit (Eurojust) in 2002. Its mission is "to support and strengthen coordination and cooperation between national investigating and prosecuting authorities in relation to serious crime affecting two or more Member States" (Eurojust n.d.). Eurojust brings together prosecutors and judges from across Europe and is the world's first permanent network of judicial and prosecuting authorities.

EUROJUST IS ESTABLISHED

The idea of a unit dedicated to judicial cooperation had first been introduced in 1999, and in 2000, a provisional unit was formed under the name Pro-Eurojust. That unit, serving as the forerunner to Eurojust, provided an entity by which the principles that would eventually direct Eurojust could be tried and tested (Luchtman and Vervaele 2014).

After the September 11, 2001, terror attacks in the United States, the fight against terrorism was firmly placed in an international context, and the European Union Council believed that a judicial cooperation unit could be beneficial in the fight. In 2002, Eurojust was formalized, a budget assigned, and rules of procedures agreed upon. In 2003, Eurojust headquarters was moved to its current location in The Hague, Netherlands.

Since 2002, Eurojust has grown in size and power. All European Union (EU) countries are, of course, members of Eurojust, but so too are other countries. Cooperation agreements have been established with Norway, the United States, Iceland, Switzerland, Croatia, and the former Yugoslav Republic of Macedonia. In addition to cooperative agreements, Norway and the United States also have liaison prosecutors permanently based at Eurojust. Agreements also occur with other EU institutions and agencies, primary among them being an agreement with Europol, as close cooperation between Europol and Eurojust is essential to the two agencies being able to accomplish their shared task of fighting transnational crime.

EUROJUST OPERATION

Each EU member state sends a judge or prosecutor (termed the "national member") to work at Eurojust and operate as that country's "national desk" in the Eurojust building.

To accomplish its mission of coordinating the cooperation of investigating and prosecuting authorities as they respond to a serious crime that has affected two or more EU member states, Eurojust provides information and opportunities that allow more effective ways to deal with cross border crime. In addition, if a member state makes the request, there are conditions under which Eurojust can also assist with investigations and prosecutions between that member state and a nonmember state.

The crimes that are appropriate for Eurojust to handle are the same as those for which Europol has competence. That includes terrorism; drug trafficking; trafficking in human beings; counterfeiting; money laundering; computer crime; crime against property or public goods, including fraud and corruption; criminal offenses affecting the European Community's financial interests; environmental crime; and participation in a criminal organization.

Eurojust does not undertake investigations or prosecutions on its own. Instead, the national members working in the same building with offices near each other can communicate spontaneously and informally without bureaucratic obstacles. As each national member has expertise in the criminal law of their home country, a quick and nonbureaucratic exchange of information between the national members can occur. The ability to establish efficient information flows allows Eurojust to enhance the efficiency of the national investigating and prosecuting authorities as they deal with serious cross border crime (Helmberg 2007). For example, one national member might wonder about wiretap regulations in a different national member's country. A quick walk down the hallway may provide information that helps an investigation move forward with wiretap plans in accordance with relevant procedural law or could quickly provide warning that alternate methods might be needed.

JOINT INVESTIGATION TEAMS

An example of the way Eurojust can facilitate cooperation is with a joint investigation team (JIT). A JIT is set up for a specific purpose and for a limited period. It will be composed of law enforcement and other authorities from different member states who are jointly investigating a case of transnational or cross border crime. There are clear advantages for JITs, as the coordination of a case is possible at the start of the investigation, and it makes possible the coordination of investigating activities—avoiding, for example, duplicative or cross-purpose actions.

Despite what appear to be clear advantages of using JITs, member states have been slow to make use of them (Helmberg 2007). There are some unsurprising problems (for example, difference in language, culture, legal systems, and investigation strategies), but there are also some that are JIT specific. For example, those involved must agree on legal principles and procedures that may not always be reconcilable. Information and evidence must be collected with consideration to where (which country) the prosecution will occur so there will be compliance with admissibility of evidence. Even when agreement has been reached, problems may occur during the operation that require changes to the agreed upon procedures (for example, a new country becomes involved).

Understanding the difficulty of accomplishing cross-national cooperation when investigating and prosecuting transnational crime should not thwart such endeavors. Such problems can be frustrating, but many can be overcome. In the case of JITs, efforts have been undertaken to overcome many of the problems so that Eurojust can better meet its purpose of effectively coordinating investigation and prosecution efforts among EU countries.

Philip L. Reichel

See also: European Public Prosecutor's Office; Europol

Further Reading

Eurojust. n.d. "About Eurojust." Accessed July 16, 2018. http://www.eurojust.europa.eu/about/background/Pages/history.aspx.

Gutiérrez Zarza, Angeles, ed. 2015. *Exchange of Information and Data Protection in Cross-Border Criminal Proceedings in Europe*. Heidelberg: Springer.

Helmberg, Monika. 2007. "Eurojust and Joint Investigation Teams: How Eurojust Can Support JITs." *ERA Forum* 8 (2): 245–251.

Luchtman, Michiel, and John Vervaele. 2014. "European Agencies for Criminal Justice and Shared Enforcement (Eurojust and the European Public Prosecutor's Office)." *Utrecht Law Review* 10 (5): 132–150.

European Arrest Warrant

The European Arrest Warrant (EAW) is a writ issued by the competent judicial authority (court or prosecutor) of a European Union (EU) member state for the arrest and surrender of a suspect to stand trial, or a person convicted of a serious offense to serve his or her sentence. The EAW can be enforced as such in any of the other EU member states. The 2001 decision on the EAW was the first in a series of decisions on mutual recognition in criminal matters in the European Union.

EVOLUTION

The processing of requests for the extradition of a suspect or convicted offender from another jurisdiction is generally time-consuming, bureaucratic (burdened as it is with the possibility of different grounds for refusal of the request), and uncertain. Even where both the requesting and requested country are parties to an extradition treaty, such as the 1957 European Convention on Extradition negotiated within the framework of the Council of Europe, the process tends to be lengthy.

The situation in Europe has been made more complicated by the relative ease with which a person can move from one country to another. Unless the person wanted by the authorities of one country is taken into custody, he or she can readily move on to a third country before a request for extradition has been processed.

One solution that has been proposed to remedy this difficulty is mutual recognition of arrest warrants, along the line of the "backing of warrants" process (also referred to as "fast-track extradition") that was used between Ireland and the United Kingdom. In this process, a judge in one of the two countries would "endorse" an arrest warrant issued by a court of the other country, authorizing the execution of the warrant. This fast-track process did not require a formal request for extradition, which would go through the attorney-general.

Somewhat similarly, the five Nordic countries (Denmark, Finland, Iceland, Norway, and Sweden) have had a long-standing regional arrangement, whereby they recognize one another's judicial decisions and judgments in general, and refusals are almost unheard of. This system is based on the fact that the Nordic countries share very much the same legal system and also otherwise have long-standing cooperation with one another.

In 1999, the European Union agreed on the importance of mutual recognition of decisions and judgments, which, in its view, "should become the cornerstone of judicial co-operation in both civil and criminal matters within the Union" (European Parliament 2018). The argument was that the member states of the European Union share fundamental values and legal principles. The authorities of a member state should have confidence in the operation of the legal system of the other states and should therefore be prepared to give full faith and credence to any judicial decision or judgment handed down in other states. Accordingly, it should be possible for a decision or judgment handed down by a court in one member state to be immediately enforced as such in any of the other states. The European Council further identified arrest warrants as a priority area in which the principle of mutual recognition should be applied.

There was considerable opposition to mutual recognition (especially among the judiciary in many countries), and a number of technical and legal problems were raised. The terrorist attacks on New York and Washington, D.C., on September 11, 2001, changed the situation dramatically. Within only a few months, an agreement was reached on the European Arrest Warrant. Simply put, the new decision replaced extradition among the EU member states with a new system whereby suspects and convicted offenders are "surrendered" to the requesting state. The process no longer needs to go through diplomatic channels or the central authorities. An arrest warrant issued by a court in one state will be recognized as valid throughout the European Union and is to be enforced.

PROCEDURE AND GROUNDS FOR REFUSAL

A European Arrest Warrant may be issued only by a competent judicial authority and only for offenses punishable by the law of the issuing member state by a custodial sentence or a detention order for a maximum period of at least 12 months or, where a sentence has been passed or a detention order has been made, for sentences of at least 4 months.

The EAW may be transmitted to the central authority of the member state in which the person in question is known to be located. However, it may also be circulated through the European Judicial Network, the Schengen Information System, or INTERPOL.

There are certain grounds for refusal. The three mandatory grounds are cases in which the offense is covered by an amnesty in the requested state, *ne bis in idem* (double jeopardy), and the lack of criminal responsibility due to age.

The decision on the EAW lists several categories for which the absence of dual criminality is not grounds for refusal. For other offenses, the absence of dual criminality is discretionary (but not mandatory) grounds for refusal.

The fact that the person in question is a national of the requested state is not grounds for refusal. The requested state may require that, if the requested person is found guilty, he or she be returned to this state to serve any sentence imposed.

Matti Joutsen

See also: European Judicial Network; Extradition; Mutual Recognition in Criminal Matters; Schengen Cooperation

Further Reading

Boister, Neil. 2012. *An Introduction to Transnational Criminal Law.* Oxford, UK: Oxford University Press.

European Parliament. 2018. "Judicial Cooperation in Criminal Matters." Last updated May 2018. Accessed January 16, 2019. http://www.europarl.europa.eu/factsheets/en/sheet/155/judicial-cooperation-in-criminal-matters.

Geyer, Florian, and Elspeth Guild. 2008. *Security versus Justice? Police and Judicial Cooperation in the European Union.* Aldershot, UK: Ashgate.

"Handbook on How to Issue and Execute a European Arrest Warrant." 2017. Accessed January 17, 2019. https://www.ejn-crimjust.europa.eu/ejn/libdocumentproperties.aspx?Id=2023.

Klimek, Libor. 2017. *Mutual Recognition of Judicial Decisions in European Criminal Law.* Cham, Switzerland: Springer.

European Institute for Crime Prevention and Control, Affiliated with the United Nations, *see* HEUNI

European Judicial Network

The European Judicial Network (EJN) is a mechanism that was established by the European Union to provide practical support to EU judicial authorities in judicial cooperation in criminal matters in the form of training, the exchange of information, and the development of practical tools. (A separate network deals with civil and commercial matters: the European Judicial Network in Civil and Commercial Matters.)

ESTABLISHMENT

The European Union established the European Judicial Network in 1998. The basic structure of the EJN consists of a network of national contact points designated by each member state from among its central authorities responsible for judicial cooperation, judicial authorities, and other competent authorities. These national contact points, currently (2018) some 350 in number, are prosecutors, judges, or other officials. Furthermore, each EU state designates a national correspondent who is responsible for coordination as well as a "tool correspondent" who is responsible for ensuring that the information provided on the EJN Web site is up-to-date.

The role of the EJN contact points is to facilitate judicial cooperation among the EU states. On the general level, this is particularly done by ensuring that the available legal and practical information on their national law, system, and practice is up-to-date. In specific cases, the contact points help practitioners to establish direct contacts with one another and, if needed, to help practitioners in the proper formulation of requests for assistance. The EJN also has a secretariat, which is located in connection with Eurojust, in The Hague.

FORMS OF WORK OF THE EJN

The main forms of work of the EJN are its Web site (with a set of e-tools for formulating requests), the organization of training, and the holding of meetings. The EJN Web site, which is maintained by the secretariat, is designed to provide practical e-tools to practitioners involved in judicial cooperation in criminal matters: mutual legal assistance, European Arrest Warrants, and mutual recognition of financial penalties, freezing orders, confiscation orders, custodial sentences, probation decisions, supervision measures, protection orders, and investigation orders.

The Web site contains a "Judicial Atlas" (which identifies who the competent authority is in a country to receive requests for specific judicial cooperation), a "Compendium" (which is a tool to be used in writing the request for judicial cooperation), "Fiches Belges" (which contain legal and practical information on investigative measures in each country), the judicial library (which provides the texts of relevant EU, Council of Europe, and UN legal instruments), and a list of contact points. Of these categories, all except the list of contact points is open access.

Using the Web site, a practitioner in any EU country needing assistance from another country can identify who the competent authority would be and on what legal instrument to base the request. The Web site also provides needed background information on what specific types of assistance can be obtained and what requirements the country in question may have to fulfill the request. Finally, the practitioner can use the "compendium" section to generate and send the request in any of the languages accepted by the requested country. (These requests are generally sent through the secure telecommunication connection provided by the Web site.)

The EJN Web site provides a significant amount of other information, such as extensive background information on the legal system in the different EU countries and their regime for judicial cooperation as well as information on cooperation with other judicial networks and with countries outside of the European Union.

The EJN, either on its own or together, for example, with the European Judicial Training Network, organizes various training sessions that deal with the implementation of recent EU instruments (such as the European Investigation Order adopted in 2017) or with specific problem areas in judicial cooperation.

The EJN also holds regular meetings of the contact points. These serve several functions: substantive issues can be discussed, direct contacts can be formed, and the mutual trust that is necessary for effective judicial cooperation can be strengthened.

Matti Joutsen

See also: Eurojust; Mutual Legal Assistance

Further Reading

European Judicial Network. n.d. "About EJN." Accessed August 19, 2018. https://www.ejn-crimjust.europa.eu/ejn/EJN_StaticPage.aspx?Bread=2.

Guild, Elspeth, and Florian Geyer, eds. 2008. *Security versus Justice? Police and Judicial Cooperation in the European Union.* Hampshire, UK: Ashgate Publishing.

Jimeno Bulnes, Mar. 2003. "European Judicial Cooperation in Criminal Matters." *European Law Journal* 9 (5): 614–630.

Serzysko, Agnieszka. 2011. "Eurojust and the European Judicial Network on a New Legal Basis." *ERA Forum* 11 (4): 585–600.

European Public Prosecutor's Office

The European Public Prosecutor's Office (EPPO) is a body created by the European Union (EU) to investigate and prosecute offenses against the financial interests of the European Union. This marks a partial transfer of national competence to the supranational level. The EPPO is to be established on the basis of a decision taken in 2017 and will not be fully operational until 2021 at the earliest.

BACKGROUND

The annual EU budget is approaching $200 billion, and the bulk of this is used to provide subsidies and to pay for procurements. Some 80 percent of disbursements go through the member states. Various estimates have been made about the amount of "EU fraud" involved, but it is probably at least hundreds of millions of dollars annually.

Although the European Anti-Fraud Office (OLAF) is active in detecting and conducting administrative investigations into EU fraud, the responsibility for criminal investigations and prosecution lies with national authorities. Many types of large-scale fraud, in particular if they involve more than one country, are so complex that they have in practice been beyond the capacities of the national authorities of many EU member states. There have also been differences in the priorities and the responses of member states toward EU fraud, including their readiness to assume jurisdiction. OLAF, Europol, and Eurojust have no powers to require member states to act in a criminal investigation or prosecution.

The European Commission and some of the member states that pay large shares of the EU budget have, since the 1990s, called for the establishment of a European Public Prosecutor, but other member states have been reluctant to transfer national competence to such an EU body. When the basic EU treaty was renegotiated (the Treaty on the Functioning of the EU, 2007), supporters of the EPPO succeeded in inserting Article 86, which provides the legal basis for the EPPO and allows several member states to participate in "enhanced cooperation" in case not all member states agree to a proposal on the EPPO.

In 2013, the European Commission submitted its proposal for the establishment of the EPPO. As expected, this did not lead to unanimity. However, 20 member states (all with the exception of Denmark, Hungary, Ireland, Malta, the Netherlands, Poland, Sweden, and the United Kingdom) agreed in 2017 to "enhanced cooperation" on the EPPO.

ROLE AND STRUCTURE

The EPPO will be empowered to investigate and prosecute fraud against the financial interests of the EU, including fraud concerning EU funds of over €10,000 (ca. US$12,000) and cross border VAT fraud cases involving damages above €10 million (ca. US$12 million). In addition, national authorities may transfer other cases of EU fraud to the EPPO.

The EPPO will be located in Luxembourg. It will have a European chief prosecutor as well as one (or more) European delegated prosecutor sent by each of the 20 participating member states. The office will also have technical and investigative staff. The investigative measures that can be used are listed in the EPPO decision. Furthermore, the European Investigation Order in criminal matters, which entered into force in 2017, provides for the possibility of requests for investigative measures based on the principle of mutual recognition.

Prosecutions shall be undertaken by the European delegated prosecutors in the competent national courts, in accordance with national law, and with the procedural safeguards of suspects and defendants noted in the Charter of Fundamental Rights. In their capacity as delegated prosecutors, they are independent of their national prosecution bodies.

The EPPO shall work in close cooperation with OLAF, Europol (the European Police Office), and EUROJUST (the EU agency dealing with judicial cooperation in criminal matters) as well as with the national authorities of the participating states.

POSSIBLE EXTENSION OF MANDATE

The nonparticipating states have the option of joining the EPPO. It is possible that some of these states may do so already before the EPPO becomes operational in 2021. (The United Kingdom is withdrawing from the European Union, and

Denmark has opted out of cooperation in criminal matters.) The commission may submit a proposal expanding the mandate of the EPPO to terrorism and serious cross border crime.

Matti Joutsen

See also: Eurojust; Europol; Mutual Recognition in Criminal Matters

Further Reading

Council Regulation (EU) 2017/1939 of 12 October 2017 Implementing Enhanced Cooperation on the Establishment of the European Public Prosecutor's Office ('the EPPO') OJ L 283, 31.10.2017, 1–71. Accessed January 17, 2019. https://eur-lex.europa.eu/eli/reg/2017/1939/oj.

Erkelens, L. H., A. W. H. Meij, and M. Pawlik, eds. 2015. *The European Public Prosecutor's Office: An Extended Arm or a Two-Headed Dragon?* The Hague: T.M.C. Asser Press.

Ligeti, Katalin. 2013. *Toward a Prosecutor for the European Union.* Oxford: Hart.

Mitsilegas, Valsamis. 2013. The Future of Prosecution after Lisbon: Special Edition. *New Journal of European Criminal Law* 4 (1): 1–198.

Monar, Jörg 2013. Eurojust and the European Public Prosecutor Perspective: From Cooperation to Integration in EU Criminal Justice? *Perspectives on European Politics and Society* 14 (3): 339–356.

Europol

The European Union Agency for Law Enforcement Cooperation (Europol) is the primary organization for cooperation among the various law enforcement agencies of the 28-member states of the European Union (EU). Its main purpose is to assist the member states in combating serious transnational crimes, such as organized crime, terrorism, and cybercrime. It also works alongside other European and international organizations, such as the Organization for Security and Co-Operation in Europe (OSCE) and the European Union Agency for Law Enforcement Training (CEPOL), for a more capable and efficient response in the mandated areas.

HISTORY AND MANDATE

While previously playing a minor role compared with other policies of the European Union, it has been since the mid-1990s that the European criminal justice policies became focused on developing a more coordinated response to transnational organized crime. Since then, this problem has been dealt with on an EU-wide level and relied heavily on EU institutions. The EU strategies against organized crime were developed as part of the European Council programs adopted at Tampere, Finland (1999–2004); The Hague, Netherlands (2005–2009): Stockholm, Sweden (2010–2014); and Ypres/Brussels, Belgium (2015–2020). The legal basis for the EU counterorganized crime policy also developed through several EU treaties.

At the meeting in Tampere in 1999, it was recognized that to create "a union of freedom, security and justice," EU citizens had the right to expect the European

Union to protect them from serious crime. Having a joint police force (Europol) and integrated judicial resources (Eurojust) were discussed as priorities to achieve this goal. The Maastricht Treaty of February 7, 1992, established Europol as a response to the growing problem of drug trafficking. Its first manifestation of joint work started in the form of the Europol Drugs Unit (EDU) in January 1994. Since then, Europol has occupied a central position in the European security architecture, offering a unique range of expertise, including support for law enforcement operations on the ground and collecting, analyzing, and disseminating information and intelligence, among other vital tasks.

The Treaty of Lisbon (2009) introduced a "new era" for cooperation in the Area of Freedom, Security and Justice (AFSJ), reaffirmed by the Stockholm Programme (2010–2014). The Lisbon Treaty abolished the pillar structure but left serious and organized crime to be perceived as a severe threat to EU security. Importantly, following the Treaty of Lisbon, Europol's mission was reinforced with the focus on collecting, sorting, processing, analyzing, and exchanging information and findings (intelligence) to support the responsible authority in the member states (Hecker 2016). Although Europol has no independent executive or investigatory power set in Article 88(III) TFEU that authorizes the organization to take operational measures only in connection and consultation of the authority of the affected member state, the European Parliament and the Council reinforced Europol's response in efforts against terrorism, cybercrime, and other serious and organized forms of crime. More specifically, the regulation calls for Europol to "evolve and become a hub for information exchange between the law enforcement authorities of the Member States, a service provider and a platform for law enforcement services" (European Parliament 2016).

Following the Treaty of Lisbon, the Stockholm Programme developments touched upon areas of homeland and public security, migration, and organized crime. They also brought some expansion of Europol and Eurojust, including the establishment of interoperability of police databases, advanced satellite surveillance, usage of the military against immigration, police intervention outside of EU territory, and intensified cooperation across borders, including non-EU countries. The program, more than its predecessors, illustrates a shift toward comprehensive approaches to security, such as by merging internal and external security strategies and cooperation. In particular, the program states,

> Europol should work more closely with European Security and Defence Policy (ESDP) police missions and help promote standards and good practice for European law enforcement cooperation in countries outside the EU. Cooperation with Interpol should be stepped up with a view to creating synergies and avoiding duplication. . . . Pilot projects in cross-border regional cooperation dealing with joint operational activities and/or cross-border risk assessments, such as Joint Police and Customs Centres, should be promoted by the Union, inter alia, through financing programmes (Council of the European Union 2009, 41–42).

Europol serves three main purposes for the EU community as per its mandate, which include (1) a support center for law enforcement operations; (2) a hub for information on criminal activities; and (3) a center for law enforcement expertise (Europol 2018). These functions include operational activities in certain mandated areas, including, but not limited to, illicit drugs, trafficking in human beings, cybercrime, intellectual property crime, euro counterfeiting, money laundering and asset tracing, mobile organized crime groups, and terrorism.

Europol focuses on crime analysis and collecting data on crime trends, including terrorism. It produces regular assessments, including the EU Serious and Organised Crime Threat Assessment (SOCTA), which informs EU's law enforcement community and decision makers on developments in serious and organized crime and the threats it poses; the EU Terrorism Situation and Trend Report (TE-SAT), which updates EU member states on the state of the terrorism threat; the Internet Organised Crime Threat Assessment (iOCTA), which reports on key findings and emerging threats related to cybercrime; and the *Europol Review*, an annual publication that covers the progress achieved in combating crimes in Europol's mandated areas.

STRUCTURE

Europol is accountable at the EU level to the Council of Ministers for Justice and Home Affairs and the European Parliament. Together with the European Parliament, the Council approves Europol's budget (which is part of the EU's general budget) and adopts regulations related to Europol's activities.

The Management Board of Europol is the main administrative and management body of Europol. It is composed of one representative from each EU member state taking part in the Europol Regulation and one representative from the European Commission. The Management Board sets the budget, verifies its execution, and adopts the appropriate financial rules and planning documents, and it adopts rules for the prevention and management of conflicts of interest in respect of its members and establishes transparent working procedures for decision making by the executive director of Europol.

Europol's executive director is appointed by the Council of Ministers upon recommendation of the Management Board. The executive director is appointed for a four-year term with a possibility of extension for the second term. The executive director is also the head of Europol's Directorate, which deals with the everyday functions of Europol. Additionally, law enforcement agencies of the EU member states have liaison officers stationed at Europol's headquarters at The Hague.

PARTNERSHIPS

Given the nature of its mandate that incorporates transnational and cross border crimes, Europol maintains productive relationships with various regional and international organizations. It has partnered with INTERPOL, the international law enforcement agency based in Lyon, France. Working in tandem, these organizations have signed the agreement that allows both parties to establish and maintain cooperation in

> combating serious forms of organized international crime within the field of competence of each Party. . . . In particular, this will be achieved through the exchange of operational, strategic, and technical information, the co-ordination of activities,

including the development of common standards, action plans, training and scientific research and the secondment of liaison officers. (Europol-INTERPOL Agreement 2001)

Additionally, Europol has strategic agreements with the United Nations Office on Drugs and Crime (UNODC) and the World Customs Organizations (WCO). Its liaison officers are posted in non-EU states, including the United States and its agencies (e.g., Bureau of Alcohol, Tobacco, Firearms and Explosives; Customs and Border Protection; and the Drug Enforcement Administration).

Daniel Braslavsky and Yuliya Zabyelina

See also: Eurojust; INTERPOL

Further Reading

Council of the European Union. 2009. "The Stockholm Programme—An Open and Secure Europe Serving and Protecting the Citizens." Accessed February 15, 2019. https://ec.europa.eu/anti-trafficking/eu-policy/stockholm-programme-open-and-secure-europe-serving-and-protecting-citizens-0_en.

European Parliament. 2016. "Regulation (EU) 2016/794 of the European Parliament and of the Council of 11 May 2016 on the European Union Agency for Law Enforcement Cooperation (Europol) and replacing and repealing Council Decisions 2009/371/JHA, 2009/934/JHA, 2009/935/JHA, 2009/936/JHA and 2009/968/JHA." https://eur-lex.europa.eu/legal-content/EN/TXT/?uri=celex%3A32016R0794

Europol. 2018. "About Europol." Accessed January 17, 2019. https://www.europol.europa.eu/about-europol.

Hecker, Bernd. 2016. "The EU and the Fight against Organised Crime." In *International Law and Transnational Organized Crime*, edited by Pierre Hauck and Sven Peterke, 63–84. Oxford: Oxford University Press.

INTERPOL and Europol. 2001. "Agreement between Interpol and Europol." Accessed January 16, 2019. https://www.europol.europa.eu/sites/default/files/documents/agreement_between_Interpol_and_Europol.pdf.

Joutsen, M. 2014. "The European Union and Judicial Cooperation." *International Crime and Justice*, 430–435). Cambridge: Cambridge University Press.

The Stockholm Programme—An Open and Secure Europe Serving and Protecting Citizens. OJ C 115/01 of 4 May 2010, 1–38. Accessed January 17, 2019. https://eur-lex.europa.eu/legal-content/EN/ALL/?uri=CELEX:52010XG0504(01)&qid=1547789629038.

Extradition

Extradition is the process by which the competent authorities of a jurisdiction forcibly transfer a person to another jurisdiction, generally for this person to stand trial for an offense or to serve a sentence.

THE BASIS FOR EXTRADITION

Under international law, countries are sovereign and decide on their own whether, and to what extent, to cooperate with other countries in the administration of justice. Traditionally, in the very rare cases that a suspect has been extradited from one sovereign country to another, this was largely a matter of courtesy between rulers. (If one country was politically dependent on another country, or felt threatened, extradition could also have been due to subservience.)

With some individual and short-lived exceptions in ancient times, bilateral extradition treaties did not begin to emerge until the 1800s. Such bilateral treaties continue to be in wide use. The first multilateral convention (the Organization of American States Convention on Extradition) was completed in 1933. It was followed by the Arab Extradition Agreement in 1952, the European Convention on Extradition in 1957, and the British Commonwealth scheme for the "rendition of fugitives" in 1966. Within the European Union, extradition has been replaced by the use of the European arrest warrant.

In addition to general treaties on extradition, provisions on extradition have also been included in several international conventions that deal with specific subjects. The most important such conventions are the 1988 UN Convention against Illicit Traffic in Narcotic Drugs and Psychotropic Substances, the 2000 UN Convention against Transnational Organized Crime, and the 2003 UN Convention against Corruption.

In 1990, the UN General Assembly adopted a Model Treaty on Extradition, which countries are encouraged to use as a point of reference when negotiating new bilateral and multilateral extradition treaties.

GROUNDS FOR REFUSAL OF A REQUEST FOR EXTRADITION

The most common grounds for refusing a request for extradition are the absence of double criminality, the person in question is a national of the requested state, and the offense is deemed a "political offense."

The Principle of Double Criminality

The great majority of extradition treaties require that the offense in question is criminal in both the requesting and the requested state, and, that it is often subject to a certain minimum punishment, such as imprisonment, for at least four year. Even where a state allows extradition in the absence of an extradition treaty, this principle of double criminality is generally applied.

The principle of double criminality has caused problems of interpretation, as countries define criminal conduct in very different ways. A recent trend in extradition has been to seek to ease difficulties with double criminality by inserting general provisions into agreements, either listing acts and requiring only that they be punished as crimes or offenses by the laws of both states or simply allowing extradition for *any* conduct subject to a certain level of punishment by each state (Blakesley and Lagodny 1992, 87–88).

The Nonextradition of Nationals

States have generally not been willing to extradite their own citizens. Some states have even incorporated such a prohibition into their constitutions.

Furthermore, the principle of the nonextradition of nationals is often expressly provided for in international instruments. The rationale is a mixture of the obligation of a state to protect its citizens, a lack of confidence in the fairness of foreign legal proceedings, the many disadvantages that defendants face when defending themselves in a foreign legal system, and the many disadvantages of being in custody in a foreign state (Nadelmann 1993, 427).

In cases where the requested state does refuse to extradite on the grounds that the fugitive is its own national, the state is generally seen to have an obligation to bring the person to trial. This is an illustration of the principle of *aut dedere aut judicare* ("extradite or adjudicate").

The reluctance to extradite one's own nationals appears to be lessening in many states. The 2000 UN Convention against Transnational Organized Crime, for example, encourages extradition of nationals on the condition that he or she be returned to serve out the possible sentence.

The Political Offense Exception

During the early 1800s, the view began to emerge that suspects should not be extradited for politically motivated offenses (Nadelmann 1993, 419). Although there is no universally accepted definition of what constitutes a "political offense," reference is generally made to the motive and purpose of the offense, the circumstances in which it was committed, and the character of the offense as treason or sedition under domestic law.

Recent developments have been along the lines of restricting the scope of the political offense exception or even abolishing it. The 2000 UN Convention against Transnational Organized Crime does not make specific reference to political offenses as grounds for refusal.

One factor behind the restriction or abolition of the political offense exception is the growth of terrorism. A distinction is commonly made between "pure" political offenses (such as unlawful speech and assembly) and politically motivated violence (*Restatement of the Law* 1990, 558). If the offense is serious—such as murder, political terrorism, or genocide—courts in different states have (to varying degrees) tended not to apply the political offense exception and granted extradition. Other common grounds for refusal to extradition include the danger that the suspect would be persecuted or have an unfair trial in the requesting country, the expected punishment would be excessive (in particular if capital punishment is possible), and the possibility of double jeopardy (*non bis in idem*).

EXTRAORDINARY RENDITION

The term *extraordinary rendition* has both a narrow legal sense and a popular sense. In the strict legal sense, it refers to the extradition (rendition) of a person to another jurisdiction for a purpose other than to stand trial or serve a sentence. For example, a convicted offender may be transferred to another jurisdiction to be heard by the police or by the court as a witness, after which he or she will be returned to continue serving his or her sentence. In the popular sense, as used in the media, the term refers to an alleged (and under international law unlawful) practice whereby a person suspected of having information about terrorism cases or other serious offenses is transferred to a jurisdiction where that person may be subjected to torture to extract this information.

Matti Joutsen

See also: Mutual Legal Assistance

Further Reading

Bassiouni, M. Cherif. 1974. *International Extradition and World Public Order.* Leiden: A. W. Sijthoff.

Blakesley, Christopher, and Otto Lagodny. 1992. "Competing National Laws: Network or Jungle?" In *Principles and Procedures for a New Transnational Criminal Law: Documentation of an International Workshop 1991*, edited by Albin Eser and Otto Lagodny, 47–100. Freiburg im Breisgau, Germany: Max Planck Society.

Boister, Neil. 2012. *An Introduction to Transnational Criminal Law.* Oxford, UK: Oxford University Press, 214–234.

Restatement of the Law, Third, Foreign Relations Law of the United States. 1990. 2 Vols. St. Paul, MN: American Law Institute.

Shearer, Ivan Anthony. *Extradition in International Law.* 1971. Manchester, UK: Manchester University Press.

United Nations Model Treaty on Extradition. General Assembly Resolution 45/116 of December 14, 1990.

F

Failed State

The relationship between the state and society is governed by an informal agreement, whereby individuals surrender some rights and liberties to recognize the authority of the state in exchange for the latter's protection and provision of basic social services. When states collapse, they lose their ability to provide these services, are no longer capable of controlling their territories, and fail to exercise the monopoly on the legitimate use of physical force therein. As a result, the erosion of governance facilitates the formation of a political vacuum, which is often exploited by illicit actors, such as organized crime groups and terrorist organizations. Politically abandoned, economically stagnated, and often conflict-torn, failing states turn into criminal havens. The conditions that limit economic development and diminish the state's incentives to develop the infrastructure necessary to maintain a robust state presence lead to the emergence of illicit economies.

ORIGINS OF SOVEREIGN STATEHOOD

The 1648 Treaty of Westphalia that ended the Thirty Years' War (1618–1648) laid the foundations of the international system based on sovereign statehood. The treaty recognized the exclusive sovereignty of each party over its lands and people and established the principle of noninterference into the domestic affairs of the parties. However, the specific characteristics, rights, and duties of modern statehood would not be codified until the 1933 Montevideo Convention on Statehood. The convention recognized that as a person of international law the state must possess the following qualifications: (1) a permanent population; (2) a defined territory; (3) government; and (4) the capacity to enter into relations with other states (Montevideo Convention 1933).

Since then, sovereign states have been widely recognized for securing the provision of public goods (e.g., education, roads, health care), safeguarding the interests common to all persons under their jurisdiction, and providing mechanisms for resolving disputes. States are also expected to maintain control over their territories, police their borders, and protect the interests of their constituents. Sometimes, however, governments fail to fulfill these traditional obligations due to the existence of internal war and insurgencies, ethnic or religious conflicts, corrupt government, or economic underdevelopment. Confronted with these challenges, states are no longer able to secure their borders and provide for the population. As conditions worsen, weakened states are exploited through their porous borders by organized syndicates and terrorist organizations. These nonstate actors often choose to fill the governance void, allowing for criminal organizations to gain legitimacy and support of the population, alienated from the formal government.

DEFINING AND MEASURING FAILED STATEHOOD

Although there is no universal definition for failed states, failing states are most commonly defined according to their inability to perform basic functions (Di John 2008). There have been various attempts to measure the degree of state failure along several dimensions, such as governance, territorial control, and management of public goods (Foreign Policy 2010; WGI 2010). These indicators are condensed into multiple indices to best suit the needs of policy makers. The Fund for Peace, for instance, runs the Fragile States Index (FSI) (originally named the Failed States Index) that evaluates state performance annually. More specifically, the FSI developed 12 indicators to gauge a country's status on a scale from zero (sustainable states) to 120 (states on alert). These indicators are grouped into four dimensions (cohesion, economic, political, and social) and typically showcase the status of a given country. The FSI measures state fragility by analyzing the quality of public services, group grievance, state legitimacy, and other sociopolitical factors that impact statehood (Fund for Peace 2017).

The Political Stability and Absence of Violence/Terrorism Index, the Bertelsmann Transformation Index, the Country Indicator Foreign Policy (CIFP) Fragility Index, and the World Governance Indicators (WGI) are other indices for measuring state failure. Similar to the FSI, these indices compile data based on sociopolitical factors, such as the perceptions of civil society, the prevalence of corruption, the ability of a state to provide protection and services to the population, the ability to guard its territories and institutions, and whether it cooperates with the international community.

While identifying states in danger is an important task, the FSI and similar indices have been criticized for creating a false dichotomy between failed states and sustainable states. Concerns have also been raised related to the methodology, which is often based on perceptions. Additionally, the raw data is not accessible to the public.

STATE FAILURE AND ILLICIT NONSTATE ACTORS

When states are nearing collapse and their borders and infrastructure are heavily weakened, organized groups and terrorist organizations can take advantage of state failure. In many cases, these illicit armed groups challenge the state either by violating the rule of law or by employing violence to dominate local communities. Despite their divergent agendas, roles, organization structures, and the relationship with state authorities, each of them represents a common challenge to the state monopoly of force and violence (Williams 2008). They may provide alternative governance, "offering services and supplying collective goods that the state is unable or unwilling to offer and provide" (Williams 2008; Rabasa et al 2007). Sullivan (2009) suggests that, in some cases, they can even transform into "war-making entities capable of the challenging the legitimacy and even the solvency of nation-states." Therefore, they may threaten the balance of power and stability within the international community.

As nonstate actors infiltrate state institutions, they garner illicit profits from transnational crimes. When illicit profits increase and integrate into legitimate economies, they make up larger portions within failing states than in countries that are economically prosperous. The illicit profits outweigh regular job prospects and promote the expansion of a criminogenic environment. Once legal institutions are permeated, criminal groups may cement their influence both on the government and the general population, rendering state-building initiatives, whether local or international, difficult if not completely useless.

FROM STATE FAILURE TO SUSTAINABLE STATEHOOD

The focal point of the crime, terror, and failed state nexus is centered on institutional and infrastructural permeability, or, in other words, the ability for nonstate actors to infiltrate legitimate institutions and recruit from the impoverished and alienated population (Hansen 2011). Using the United Nations 17 Sustainable Development Goals (SDGs) as a global blueprint for the safeguarding of institutions as well as the prevention of state failure may allow states to effectively mitigate and prevent the expansion of criminal groups (United Nations 2017). More specifically, states that make sufficient progress toward the SDGs may be able to provide a better safety net that may discourage criminal and terrorist pursuits before they originate. Additionally, utilizing the SDGs in this manner allows states to dispel environments conducive of corruption before they turn into state failure or collapse.

Nicole Kalczynski

See also: Globalization; UN Sustainable Development Goals

Further Reading

Di John, Jonathan. 2008. "Conceptualising the Causes and Consequences of Failed States: A Critical Review of the Literature." Working Paper No. 25. Crisis States Research Center, London School of Economics.

Fund for Peace. 2017. "Indicators Fragile States Index." Accessed January 16, 2019. http://fundforpeace.org/fsi.

Hansen, Wibke. 2011. "The Failed State–Organized Crime–Terrorism Nexus." Berlin: German Institute for International and Security Affairs (SWP).

Montevideo Convention on the Rights and Duties of States. Signed at Montevideo, December 26, 1933. https://www.jus.uio.no/english/services/library/treaties/01/1-02/rights-duties-states.xml

Rabasa, Angel, Steven Boraz, Peter Chalk, Kim Cragin, Theodore W. Karasik, Jennifer D. P. Moroney, Kevin A. O'Brien, and John E. Peters, eds. 2007. *Ungoverned Territories: Understanding and Reducing Terrorism Risks*. 1st ed. Santa Monica, CA: Rand Publishing.

Sullivan, John P. 2009. "Future Conflict: Criminal Insurgencies, Gangs and Intelligence." *Small Wars Journal* 248, May 9. http://www.academia.edu/1113574/Future_Conflict_Criminal_Insurgencies_Gangs_and_Intelligence

United Nations. 2017. "SDGs: Sustainable Development Knowledge Platform." Accessed January 21, 2019. https://sustainabledevelopment.un.org/sdgs.

Williams, Phil, 2008. *Violent Non-State Actors and National and International Security.* Zurich, Switzerland: ETH Zurich, International Relations and Security Network.

Fatwa

A fatwa is a legal opinion issued by an Islamic scholar on a specific issue. The word is known to many non-Muslims because of media coverage on sensational fatwas, such as the destruction of Buddhist statues or the fatwas endorsed by Osama bin Laden and Ayman al- Zawahiri stating that Muslims should kill Americans—including civilians—anywhere in the world (CNN Wire Staff 2011). However, for Muslims, fatwas are mostly a positive aspect of Islamic law that provide guidance on what is permitted and what is forbidden. Fatwas are also important for Muslims living in non-Muslim countries, as they can provide guidance through the challenge of adhering to two sets of laws: those of Islam and the enacted national laws—with the recognition that the country's national laws take precedence (Black, Esmaeili, and Hosen 2013).

THE NEED FOR FATWAS

Islam recognizes no distinction between a legal system and other prescriptions for a person's behavior. Muslims believe their religion provides all answers to questions about appropriate behavior in any sphere of life. However, given the complexity of the law and the variety of cases and new circumstances presenting themselves, the need for consultation and clarification on points of doctrine often becomes apparent. Islam has no centralized hierarchy, so there is no controlling authority stipulating who should provide the requested clarification. Instead, Muslims turn to legal scholars who have met certain qualifications. A jurist qualified to give such an opinion is a *mufti* who, ruling through an understanding of Islamic law and following the correct procedures, states what should be the correct procedure according to a particular school of Islamic law.

PROCEDURES FOR ISSUING A FATWA

A fatwa is issued in response to a question asked by a person (e.g., individual, judge, government official) or an entity (e.g., corporation, institution, organization). Islam identifies for Muslims their religious duties, what is pure and impure, what one can eat and drink, what can be legitimately acquired or possessed, what transactions and sales can occur, what are the laws of war, and essentially all aspects of life. All these topics, regardless of one's position, status, or occupation, can be the object of legal consultations in case of doubt or necessity.

Fatwas provide flexibility in Islamic law in terms of contemporary social and economic practices. Many modern topics are not addressed in the Koran, so fatwas provide a means by which those problems can be addressed. For example, in 1727, a fatwa authorized the printing of nonreligious books, and in 1845, a fatwa declared vaccination to be legitimate. Importantly, fatwas not only provide a mechanism for growth and change in Islamic law, but they are adaptable and can be revised when they are deemed no longer suitable to the situation to be contrary to Islam. Thus, fatwa makes Islamic law adaptable to social change (Reichel 2018).

FATWAS TODAY

As predominantly Muslim countries adopt secular legal systems, fatwas are increasingly issued on a personal basis or for political reasons. The legitimacy of a particular fatwa may be recognized by the followers of the person making the pronouncement, but that same fatwa may not be considered a legitimate juristic opinion by the rest of the Muslim community. This is consistent with the tradition of fatwas being nonbinding and compliance being voluntary. The person making the inquiry is free to go to a different mufti to seek another opinion, but once a convincing opinion is found, it should be obeyed. However, in some countries today, fatwas can be given legal force when issued by state jurists or by sanctioning the enforcement of those that are published in an official journal (Masud, Brinkley, and Powers 1996).

Philip L. Reichel

See also: Al Qaeda; Bin Laden, Osama; Jihad

Further Reading

Black, Ann, Hossein Esmaeili, and Nadirsyah Hosen. 2013. *Modern Perspectives on Islamic Law.* Northampton, MA: Edward Elgar.

CNN Wire Staff. 2011. "Timeline: Osama bin Laden, over the Years." Accessed March 16, 2018. http://www.cnn.com/2011/WORLD/asiapcf/05/02/osama.timeline/index.html.

Kamali, Mohammad Hashim. 2008. *Shari'ah law: An Introduction.* Oxford, UK: Oneworld Publications.

Masud, Muhammad Khalid, Brinkley Morris Messick, and David Stephan Powers. 1996. "Muftis, Fatwas, and Islamic Legal Interpretation." In *Islamic Legal Interpretation: Muftis and Their Fatwas*, edited by Muhammad Khalid Masud, Brinkley Morris Messick and David Stephan Powers, 3–32. Cambridge, MA: Harvard University Press.

Reichel, Philip L. 2018. *Comparative Criminal Justice Systems: A Topical Approach.* 7th ed. New York: Pearson.

Financial Action Task Force

The Financial Action Task Force (FATF) is an intergovernmental organization concerned with the establishment of international standards that combat terrorism financing, money laundering, the financing of proliferation of weapons of mass destruction, and other threats to the global financial system. Established in 1989, the FATF designs, promotes, and implements legal, regulatory, and operational measures that endeavor to protect the integrity of the international financial system. Deemed a policy-making body, the FATF strives to generate the necessary political resolve to bring about national regulatory and legislative reforms in the previously mentioned financial areas (FATF n.d.-c). To this end, the FATF has established international standards, or Recommendations, centered around combating these threats to the integrity of the global financial system. These Recommendations have been recognized internationally as the global policy benchmarks for antiterrorist, anti–money laundering, and antiproliferation financing measures by the United Nations, the World Bank, the International Monetary Fund (IMF), the Asian Development Bank, and many other international organizations and bodies (Asia Pacific Group n.d.).

HISTORY

The FATF was established in 1989 during the G-7 Summit in Paris. During the summit, the mounting concern surrounding money laundering influenced the G-7 heads of state or government as well as the president of the European Commission to convene the FATF Task Force, which was originally composed of the European Commission, the G-7 member states, and eight other countries (FATF n.d.-a). The task force was charged with examining previous money laundering techniques and trends as well as reviewing the actions that had already been taken at a national or international level. Furthermore, the task force was responsible for theorizing and relaying the measures that still needed to be taken to combat money laundering. Toward this latter goal, the FATF issued a report containing Forty Recommendations constituting a comprehensive strategy to contest money laundering.

In 2001, the FATF broadened its operation to include the fight against terrorist financing. The FATF sought to establish comparable standards to combat terrorist financing, to which Eight Special Recommendations were championed by the FATF. In 2003, the FATF revised its comprehensive recommendations due to the increasing levels of sophistication used in money laundering techniques. In 2004, the FATF published a Ninth Special Recommendation, which sought to solidify the agreed upon international standards for combating money laundering and terrorist financing. Finally, in February of 2012, the FATF completed an extensive review of its recommendations and standards and subsequently issued the revised FATF Recommendations. These revisions issued by the FATF provided governments with stronger tools to act against financial crime and included new financial threats surrounding the financing of the proliferation of weapons of mass destruction (FATF n.d.-a). Additionally, the Nine Special Recommendations on terrorist financing were fully integrated with the procedures against money laundering.

ORGANIZATION

The FATF is currently composed of 35 member jurisdictions and 2 regional organizations, representing most of the major financial centers in the world.

In addition to these FATF members, 3 FATF observers, 9 FATF associate members, and 28 observer organizations constitute the entirety of the FATF. The FATF membership policy establishes that to become a FATF member, a country must be considered strategically important. The strategical importance of the prospective member is measured both quantitatively (the country's gross domestic product, population, and size of banking, insurance, and securities sectors) as well as qualitatively (the country's impact on the global financial system, the openness of its financial sector, its interaction with international markets, and the level of commitment to anti–money laundering and counterterrorism financing efforts) (FATF n.d.-b). Furthermore, the strategic importance of the prospective member is determined based on its willingness to adhere to globally recognized financial standards as well as its previous participation in other international organizations.

Once a country or organization becomes a member of the FATF, it must advocate for and support the most recent FATF recommendations. Additionally, the member must commit to being evaluated by other members of the FATF to assess the member's compliance with FATF membership criteria. Finally, the member must agree to actively participate in the FATF's development of future recommendations (FATF n.d.-b). These assessments are carried out by the FATF's decision-making body, the FATF Plenary, which meets three times per year to discuss relevant FATF matters (FATF n.d.-c).

RECOMMENDATIONS

The Forty FATF Recommendations, as well as the Nine Special Recommendations, necessitate that countries, territories, and regions actively criminalize money laundering, terrorist financing, and proliferation financing. Furthermore, the Recommendations dictate that all terrorist assets should be frozen by countries, territories, and regions and that the proceeds of these acts should be confiscated. The FATF further recommends that each country, territory, and region should establish a financial intelligence unit that collects, analyzes, evaluates, and disseminates any suspicious transaction report that comes across its jurisdiction. Finally, the FATF Recommendations specify that each country, territory, and region must ensure that effective mechanisms are in place that allow for these entities to cooperate efficiently, on the global level, if any financial-related crimes should arise (FATF 2012).

Jessie L. Slepicka

See also: Financial Crimes Enforcement Network; Intergovernmental Organization; Money Laundering

Further Reading

Asia Pacific Group. n.d. "Financial Action Task Force on Money Laundering (FATF)." Accessed August 22, 2018. http://www.apgml.org/fatf-and-fsrb/page.aspx?p=a8c3a23c-df6c-41c5-b8f9-b40cd8220df0.

De Nederlandsche Bank. 2013. "Financial Action Task Force on Money Laundering." Accessed August 22, 2018. http://www.toezicht.dnb.nl/en/2/51-202292.jsp.

Financial Action Task Force (FATF). 2012. "International Standards on Combating Money Laundering and the Financing of Terrorism & Proliferation: The FATF Recommendations." Accessed August 22, 2018. http://www.fatf-gafi.org/media/fatf/documents/recommendations/pdfs/FATF_Recommendations.pdf.

Financial Action Task Force (FATF). n.d.-a. "About: History of the FATF." Accessed August 22, 2018. http://www.fatf-gafi.org/about/historyofthefatf.

Financial Action Task Force (FATF). n.d.-b. "FATF Members and Observers." Accessed August 22, 2018. http://www.fatf-gafi.org/about/membersandobservers.

Financial Action Task Force (FATF). n.d.-c. "About: Who We Are." Accessed August 22, 2018. http://www.fatf-gafi.org/about/whoweare.

Financial Crimes Enforcement Network (FinCEN). n.d. "The Financial Action Task Force." Accessed August 22, 2018. https://www.fincen.gov/resources/international/financial-action-task-force.

Financial Crimes Enforcement Network

The Financial Crimes Enforcement Network (FinCEN) is a U.S. government bureau that safeguards the financial system from illicit use, combats money laundering, and promotes national security. Under the oversight of the U.S. Department of the Treasury, FinCEN collects, analyzes, and disseminates financial-based intelligence as well as information surrounding the strategic use of financial authorities. FinCEN achieves these strategic goals by receiving and maintaining financial transactions data and subsequently analyzing and disseminating said data for law enforcement purposes. Furthermore, FinCEN strives to build global cooperation with other countries' counterpart organizations as well as with various international bodies to combat domestic and international money laundering, terrorist financing, and other financial crimes.

HISTORY

Secretary of the Treasury Nicholas Brady established FinCEN on April 25, 1990, through the enactment of Treasury Order Number 105-08. FinCEN's original mission was to provide a multisource, government-wide financial intelligence and analytical network. Additionally, FinCEN's original undertaking was to assist the detection, investigation, and prosecution of domestic and international money laundering as well as other financial-based crimes. In October 1994, the Office of Financial Enforcement—the Treasury Department's precursor of FinCEN—merged with FinCEN. Correspondingly, in 1994, FinCEN's authority was broadened to exercise regulatory responsibilities for administering the Bank Secrecy Act (BSA). The BSA was the nation's first anti–money laundering and counterterrorism financing statute—known as AML/CFT efforts—as well as required U.S. financial institutions to collaborate with the state in cases of suspected fraud and money laundering. On September 26, 2002, Treasury Order 180-01 established FinCEN as an official bureau in the Department of the Treasury, subsequently following the passage of Title III of the 2001 Patriot Act.

MONEY LAUNDERING

Money laundering is the undertaking of making illegally gained proceeds appear legal. A three-step process of placement, layering, and integration is generally attempted to clean these illegitimate funds. First, placement of the illegitimate funds involves secretively introducing the funds into a legitimate financial system. Second, layering of the illegitimate funds involves transferring, or wiring, the funds through numerous accounts to create a sense of confusion surrounding the funds. Third, integration of the illegitimate funds involves incorporating the funds into a legitimate financial system through various additional transactions until the funds appear clean (FinCEN n.d.-a).

FinCEN combats this illegal activity by following the inevitable money trail. Various counter–money laundering laws, such as the BSA, require banks and financial institutions to keep records and reports of all financial transactions conducted within their organizations. This detailed record keeping allows FinCEN officials to trace the preserved financial trail left by offenders. Under the BSA, banks and financial institutions are also required to report suspicious currency transactions, giving the FinCEN another avenue to launch investigations into alleged money laundering occurrences.

CONGRESSIONAL DUTIES

Congress has charged FinCEN with certain duties and responsibilities for the central collection, analysis, and dissemination of financial-based intelligence. This financial-based intelligence is critical in the support of FinCEN's government and financial industry partners at the international, federal, state, and local levels. To accomplish their responsibilities of detecting and deterring financial crime, FinCEN issues and interprets various financial regulations entitled by statue. Concurrently, FinCEN actively supports and enforces compliance with those statute-mandated regulations. As FinCEN's main responsibilities revolve around the collection, processing, storage, dissemination, and protection of financial-based intelligence data, FinCEN proactively uses this data to recommend internal and external allocation of resources to areas of the suspected greatest financial crime risk. Further, tasks undertaken by FinCEN include the maintenance of an effective and efficient government-wide access service to all FinCEN data. Finally, FinCEN supports various law enforcement investigations and prosecutions related to specific financial-based offenses (FinCEN n.d.-c).

As operations are conducted on the international level as well, FinCEN serves as the foreign financial intelligence unit (FIU)—a central national agency responsible for receiving, requesting, analyzing, and disseminating disclosures of financial information to combat money laundering and terrorism financing—for the United States. FinCEN is one of more than 100 FIUs comprising the Egmont Group—an informal international association focused on the cooperation and effective information sharing of FIUs—and it receives information on suspicious or unusual financial activity from the group. The Egmont Group offers united body members an opportunity for the secure exchange of expertise and financial intelligence used in the fight to combat money laundering and terrorist financing. Serving as the FIU for the United States, FinCEN shares information regarding AML/CFT efforts with FIU counterparts. FinCEN also coordinates with FIU counterparts on proposed AML/CFT efforts.

Jessie L. Slepicka

See also: Financial Action Task Force; Money Laundering; U.S. International Money Laundering Abatement and Anti-Terrorist Financing Act

Further Reading

Computer Services Incorporated. n.d. "Federal Regulations: FinCEN Regulations." Accessed June 9, 2018. https://www.csiweb.com/industries-we-serve/financial-institutions/regulatory-compliance/federal-regulations/fincen.

Federal Register. n.d. "Financial Crimes Enforcement Network." Accessed June 9, 2018. https://www.federalregister.gov/agencies/financial-crimes-enforcement-network.

FinCEN. n.d.-a. "History of Anti-Money Laundering Laws." Accessed June 9, 2018. https://www.fincen.gov/history-anti-money-laundering-laws.

FinCEN. n.d.-b. "1997–2002: Strategic Plan." Accessed June 9, 2018. https://www.fincen.gov/sites/default/files/shared/strategic_plan_1997.pdf.

FinCEN. n.d.-c. "What We Do." Accessed June 9, 2018. https://www.fincen.gov/what-we-do.

U.S. Department of the Treasury. 2007. "About: Financial Crimes Enforcement Network." Accessed June 9, 2018. https://www.treasury.gov/about/history/Pages/fincen.aspx.

Forced Marriage

A forced marriage is one that takes place without the full and free consent of one or both parties. When the marriage occurs in the context of force, fraud, or coercion, it can be a type of human trafficking. Even when force, fraud, or coercion does not seem to be present, if one of the marriage partners is a minor (usually defined as under age 18), an argument is made that it is still a human trafficking crime because the minor was not old enough to have informed consent.

ASPECTS OF FORCED MARRIAGE

A forced marriage is one in which a person feels that he or she essentially has no meaningful way to say no to the marriage. It is important to distinguish forced marriage from an arranged marriage, wherein the families of both parties (or religious leaders or others) take the lead, but the choice ultimately remains with each individual. It is, of course, always difficult to assess the presence of compulsion, so arranged marriages can also be suspect.

The International Labour Organization (ILO) estimates that about 15 million people live in a forced marriage (2017). Men and boys can be victims of forced marriage, but most victims are women and girls (84%). Further, more than one-third of the victims were under age 18 at the time of the marriage(37%).

Examples of forced marriage are found everywhere, but the highest prevalence is in Africa (4.8 per 1,000 persons) and Asia and the Pacific (2.0 per 1,000 persons). More than 90 percent of all forced marriages took place in those two regions. But examples are also found in Western countries. A survey by the Tahirih Justice Center (2011) determined there were about 3,000 known and suspected cases of forced marriage in immigrant communities of the United States. Examples of forced marriage were reported in U.S. immigrant communities representing 56 different countries and among people of different faiths. Many victims had Muslim family backgrounds, but victims of Christian, Hindu, and Buddhist backgrounds were also reported. Freely given consent is a prerequisite of Christian, Jewish, Hindu, Muslim, and other major faiths. In fact, no major faith advocates forced marriage.

In the United Kingdom, forced marriage is a crime of violence against women and men. A case of forced marriage occurs when one or both people do not consent to the marriage and pressure or abuse has been used to accomplish the marriage. That pressure to marry can be physical (threats and actual violence), emotional, and psychological (the person has been made to feel he or she is bringing shame of the family) or financial (wages are taken).

The Forced Marriage Unit (FMU) has operated in the United Kingdom and abroad since 2005 to provide assistance in the United Kingdom and to British nationals living overseas. That assistance ranges from providing simple safety advice to helping a victim prevent their unwanted spouse from moving to the United Kingdom. In extreme circumstances, the FMU could help rescue victims held against their will overseas.

CHILD MARRIAGE AS FORCED MARRIAGE

The United Nations International Children's Emergency Fund (UNICEF) considers any formal marriage or informal union before the age of 18 to be child marriage and a human rights violation (UNICEF 2018). UNICEF estimates that approximately 650 million girls and women alive today were married before their 18th birthday.

Child marriage is considered a human rights violation because it can lead to a lifetime of disadvantage and deprivation. For example, child brides are less likely to remain in school and more likely to experience domestic violence.

Some jurisdictions allow persons under the age of 18 to marry (sometimes, but not always, needing parental permission) so cases of child marriage may not involve force, fraud, or coercion. But, much like human trafficking statutes that define any instance of a minor being persuaded to perform a commercial sex act as still being human trafficking, UNICEF takes the approach that a person under age 18 is not old enough to give informed consent.

TACTICS USED

Conditions of force, fraud, or coercion take many forms as applied to forced or child marriages. The person may be pressured or bullied (that is, coerced) into believing that the marriage is required to comply with custom or tradition (for example, to ensure that a daughter will adhere to conservative morals and gender roles), or that the marriage is necessary to honor a contract or arrangement between families. In some instances, such as an individual becoming pregnant outside of marriage, the person might be convinced that the marriage is needed to protect family honor.

But there can also be more obvious examples of force, fraud, and coercion—both for entering and continuing in the marriage. Economic threats (against the person or their family), emotional blackmail (parent threatens self-harm), social ostracization (the person will be a community outcast), isolation tactics (the ability to leave home is limited), and threats of and actual physical violence have all been used against victims of forced marriage.

SHAM MARRIAGE

Sham marriage, also exploitative sham marriage, is a phrase currently used in the European Union that refers to a phenomenon where an EU citizen becomes exploited or even a victim of human trafficking in the context of a bogus, fake, or sham marriage with a non-EU citizen. A study by the European Institute for Crime Prevention and Control, affiliated with the United Nations (HEUNI), found three types of exploitative marriage scenarios—all of which were designed to have the groom receive an EU residence permit (Viuhko et al. 2016).

Philip L. Reichel

See also: Human Trafficking; Sex Exploitation; U.K. Modern Slavery Act (2015)

Further Reading

International Labour Organization (ILO). 2017. "Global Estimates of Modern Slavery: Forced Labour and Forced Marriage." Accessed July 20, 2018. https://www.ilo.org/global/publications/books/WCMS_575479/lang--en/index.htm.

Tahirih Justice Center. 2011. "Forced Marriage in Immigrant Communities in the United States." Accessed July 24, 2018. https://www.tahirih.org/pubs/forced-marriage-in-immigrant-communities-in-the-united-states.

United Kingdom. 2018. "Forced Marriage." Last Modified May 10, 2018. Accessed January 16, 2019. https://www.gov.uk/guidance/forced-marriage.

United Nations International Children's Emergency Fund (UNICEF). 2018. "Child Marriage: Latest Trends and Future Prospects." Last Modified June 26, 2018. Accessed January 16, 2019. http://data.unicef.org/resources/child-marriage-latest-trends-and-future-prospects.

Viuhko, Minna, Anni Lietonen, Anniina Jokinen, and Matti Joutsen. 2016. "Exploitative Sham Marriages: Exploring the Links between Human Trafficking and Sham Marriages in Estonia, Ireland, Latvia, Lithuania and Slovakia." Last Modified November 7, 2017. Accessed January 21, 2019. http://heuni.fi/en/index/publications/heunireports/reportseries82.exploitativeshammarriages.html.

Foreign Corrupt Practices Act

The Foreign Corrupt Practices Act of 1977 (FCPA), is a U.S. federal law enacted in response to U.S. companies' widespread bribery of high foreign officials to secure business (15 U.S.C. §§ 78dd-1, et seq.). This act prohibits individuals and entities from influencing the acts or decisions of foreign government officials through payments or other kinds of rewards to secure improper business advantages. It also requires issuers to maintain an adequate internal accounting control system and to keep accurate and fair records of their business transactions and asset dispositions. All U.S. individuals and entities are subjected to this act whether they act inside or outside the United States. FCPA is also applicable to certain foreign individuals and businesses while they act in the territory of the United States (DOJ n.d.).

HISTORY

In the 1970s, the Securities and Exchange Commission (SEC) initiated an extensive investigation into payments to domestic and foreign political officials by corporations after discovering unreported campaign contributions. This investigation revealed that an estimated 400 U.S. companies reported that they had made questionable or illegal payments, totaling over $300 million, in bribes to foreign officials, politicians, and political parties to secure business. To restore the public confidence in U.S. companies, Congress passed the FCPA in 1977 to prevent corporate bribery of foreign officials. This act also required corporations to keep accurate records and books about transactions and maintain a responsible system for internal accounting control (Coleman 2017, 1382–1385).

In 1988, the FCPA was first amended by the Omnibus Trade and Competitiveness Act of 1988. Some of the major amendments included no criminal penalties for commissions or omission in keeping records or maintaining an accounting control system if a person does not knowingly and purposely do so and limited influence of a minority owner holding 50 percent or less of the voting power in a company on the accounting practices of a subsidiary. It also retained the "knowing" standard for finding violation of the act, encompassing "conscious disregard" and "willful blindness." The amendment provided affirmative defenses against finding violations of FCPA: The local law defense and the reasonable and bona fide expense defense (Seitzinger 2016). For example, a payment or gift is lawful if it is written in the laws of the foreign country or if it is a reasonable and bona fide expenditure or is necessary for the performance or implementation of a contract with the foreign country.

In 1998, the second amendment was made to the FCPA. This amendment extended the scope of the coverage to payments for any improper business advantage, added public international organizations to the category of foreign official, and extended the jurisdiction beyond the borders of the United States. Under this amendment, all U.S. individuals and companies are subjected to FCPA, even if they act outside the United States, and certain foreign individuals or companies are also subjected to the act if they act inside the United States.

PROVISIONS

The FCPA uses two main provisions to regulate international corruption: the anti-bribery provisions and the accounting provisions. The antibribery provisions prohibit any payments, including intent, promise, offer, and authorization of payments in money or anything of value to foreign officials and political actors to obtain or retain business or direct business to any person. Under the FCPA, the intent for corruption is sufficient to constitute a violation of the act, even if no corrupt payment is actually paid or no benefit has ultimately been obtained by the company. And it is unlawful to make improper payments to political officials through a third party under the FCPA. These provisions apply to all U.S. citizens and entities inside and outside the United States as well as certain foreign nationals and entities acting within the territory of the United States.

Accounting provisions of FCPA require issuers to make and keep books and records that accurately and fairly reflect the transactions and asset dispositions of their companies to prevent concealment and falsification of bribes. The provisions also require issuers to maintain a responsible internal accounting controls system to ensure reasonable and proper transactions in their corporations. The FCPA accounting provisions apply to issuers under the Exchange Act, including publicly held companies and companies with American Depository Receipts. Private companies are not subjected to the accounting provisions.

ENFORCEMENT, PENALTIES, SANCTIONS, AND REMEDIES

Both the Department of Justice (DOJ) and the Securities and Exchange Commission (SEC) share enforcement authority of the FCPA. The DOJ primarily enforces criminal provisions, while the SEC primarily enforces civil provisions. Both entities and individuals violating FCPA are subject to criminal penalties imposed by the DOJ. Corporations and business entities are subject to a penalty of up to $2 million for each violation of the antibribery provisions and up to $25 million for each violation of the accounting provisions. Individuals are subject to a fine of up to $250,000 and imprisonment of up to five years for each violation of the antibribery provisions and up to $5 million and imprisonment for up to 20 years for each violation of the accounting provisions. Significantly higher fines may be imposed by the courts under the Alternative Fines Act, 18 U.S.C. § 3571(d) (DOJ and SEC 2012).

Entities and individuals may also be subject to civil penalties enforced by the DOJ and SEC for violations of the FCPA. Corporations, other business entities, and individuals are subject to a civil penalty of up to $16,000 per violation of the antibribery provisions. The civil penalties of individuals may not be paid directly or indirectly by their employer or principal. For violations of accounting provisions, the SEC may seek a civil penalty of up to the gross amount of the pecuniary gain to the defendant or a specified dollar limitation based on the egregiousness of the violation. This limitation ranges from $7,500 to $150,000 for an individual and $75,000 to $725,000 for a company.

In addition to the criminal and civil penalties discussed above, corporations, other business entities, and individuals may also face collateral consequences, including suspension or debarment from doing business with the federal government, cross-debarment by multilateral development banks such as the World

Bank, and the loss of certain export privileges for their violations of FCPA (DOJ and SEC 2012).

Yali Pang

See also: Anticorruption Efforts; Corruption; Corruption Measurements

Further Reading

Coleman, Sean. 2017. "Foreign Corrupt Practices Act." *American Criminal Law Review* 54 (4): 1381–1442. http://link.galegroup.com.proxy.library.vcu.edu/apps/doc/A503310704/OVIC?u=viva_vcu&sid=OVIC&xid=24058b35.

Koehler, Mike. 2014. *The Foreign Corrupt Practices Act in a New Era.* Cheltenham, UK: Edward Elgar Publishing.

Seitzinger, Michael V. 2016. "Foreign Corrupt Practices Act (FCPA): Congressional Interest and Executive Enforcement, in Brief." Accessed January 16, 2019. https://fas.org/sgp/crs/misc/R41466.pdf.

U.S. Department of Justice (DOJ). n.d. "Foreign Corrupt Practices Act." Accessed April 15, 2018. https://www.justice.gov/criminal-fraud/foreign-corrupt-practices-act.

U.S. Department of Justice (DOJ) and U.S. Securities and Exchange Commission (SEC). 2012. "A Resource Guide to the U.S. Foreign Corrupt Practices Act." Accessed April 15, 2018. https://www.justice.gov/sites/default/files/criminal-fraud/legacy/2015/01/16/guide.pdf.

Forest Crime, *see* Wildlife and Forest Crime

Fuerzas Armadas Revolucionarios de Colombia (FARC), see Revolutionary Armed Forces of Colombia (FARC)

G

Gender-Based Violence

Gender-based violence is often present in many transnational organized crimes, such as human trafficking and smuggling. According to United Nations High Commissioner for Refugees (UNHCR), gender-based violence "refers to any act that is perpetrated against a person's will and is based on gender norms and unequal power relationship" (UNHCR 2018). It is important to note that violence does not only mean physical violence; it also encompasses the threat of using violence and coercion. The harm inflicted on women and girls—the most common targets—can also be emotional, psychological, sexual, economic harm, or a denial to resources or access to services, for example, denying the access to gynecological assistance. Likewise, it also refers to other forms of violence related to exploitation, forced prostitution, and trafficking.

GENDER VIOLENCE IN CONFLICT AND WAR ZONES

Regardless of the form it takes, gender-based violence expresses the power inequalities between women and men. In addition, it is a human rights violation and a form of discrimination against the victims. Conflict or war zones are environments where gender-based violence is a common occurrence. Gender-based violence, especially sexual violence, is often used as a tactic of war, and the perpetrators are state and nonstate actors. The UN secretary-general has stated that sexual gender-based violence "refers to rape, sexual slavery, forced prostitution, forced pregnancy, forced abortion, enforced sterilization, forced marriage, and any other forms of sexual violence of comparable gravity perpetrated against women, men, girls or boys that is directly or indirectly linked to a conflict" (United Nations 2018).

In this climate of impunity, characterized by the lack of state control or total collapse, the victims are perceived to be or are actual members of a persecuted minority (either political, ethnic, religious, or in terms of sexual orientation or gender identity). The objective of using gender-based violence in conflict zones serves as incentives for recruitment, to terrorize populations into compliance, to displace civilians strategically, for intelligence purposes, to suppress women's rights, and to control sexuality and reproduction. It also serves economic purposes: in sex trafficking networks, sexual slavery and forced prostitution may be payment for soldiers' or combatants' services.

Due to the lack of opportunities and the high intensity of violence in some places, people are often forced to flee their homes in the pursuit of a better life.

The victims affected by conflicts are more vulnerable to criminal networks, such as smuggling or human trafficking. All those crimes are possible where the political, legal, economic, and social systems have collapsed.

HUMAN TRAFFICKING AND GENDER VIOLENCE

The United Nations Office on Drugs and Crime (UNODC) reports that two-thirds of human trafficking victims are women. Throughout the trafficking process, women and girls experience some type of gender-based violence: (1) they are subdued or intimidated; (2) during recruitment, their freedoms and rights are curtailed; and (3) they may suffer extreme physical, psychological, and reproductive violence, such as rape, imprisonment, forced abortions, or isolation. It is important to mention that human trafficking can occur across borders or within a country; the purpose of the trafficking can be any kind of exploitation—forced labor, reproductive exploitation, forced prostitution or other sexual exploitation, slavery or similar practices, and organ removal, among others—and it can take place with or without organized crime groups.

FEMICIDE

The most extreme form of gender-based violence is femicide, which refers to the intentional murder of women because of their gender. Types of femicide include the murder of women as a result of intimate partner violence, the killing of women and girls in the name of "honor," dowry-related killings of women, the killing of women and girls because of their sexual orientation and gender identity, genital mutilation–related deaths, accusations of witchcraft, and other gender-based murders connected with gangs, organized crime, drug dealers, human trafficking, and the proliferation of small arms (UNODC 2012).

Crimes of femicide are rarely investigated and prosecuted, especially because so many of them take place in a domestic context. The United Nations is taking a leadership role in bringing femicide to the forefront in international discussions with the Vienna Declaration on Femicide and the Femicide Watch Platform. These and other initiatives are important because violence against women and girls is too often an invisible aspect of cultures around the world. Combating femicide requires the systematic collection and documentation of these killings, and the Global Knowledge Hub on Femicide plans to provide key information and data that will allow informed action by policy and decision makers.

PREVENTION

There are many actions that can be taken to prevent gender-based violence, such as countering harmful attitudes and gender stereotypes, enhancing safety and protection, encouraging reporting and early detection of violence, prohibiting and criminalizing violence against women, providing adequate resources, and evaluating already existing prevention programs. The importance of national and international criminal systems to acknowledge femicides is imperative, as well. In many countries, femicide is not even present in the penal codes, nor in the Declaration on the Elimination of Violence against Women.

Indications of change are found in the efforts against femicide as well as in broader initiatives directed at all types of gender violence. Violence against women does not only concern women. As is true when combating transnational organized crime, eradicating gender-based violence must be a collective effort. Everyone can contribute by creating awareness and safe places for victims, building partnerships, providing information, reporting, and protecting the victims.

Mariana Cammisa and Jéssica Viales López

See also: Forced Marriage; Granados Sex Trafficking Organization; Human Trafficking; "Loverboy" Recruitment Approach to Human Trafficking; Sex Exploitation; Sex Tourism; Trafficking Victim Identification Tools; UN Protocol to Prevent, Suppress, and Punish Trafficking in Persons, Especially Women and Children; U.S. Trafficking Victims Protection Act

Further Reading

European Institute for Gender Equality. 2018. "What Is Gender-Based Violence?" Accessed January 16, 2019. http://eige.europa.eu/gender-based-violence/what-is-gender-based-violence

Femicide Watch. 2018. "About." Accessed January 16, 2019. http://femicide-watch.org/about.

United Nations. 2018. "Report of the Secretary-General on Conflict-Related Sexual Violence." Last updated March 23, 2018. Accessed January 16, 2019. https://reliefweb.int/sites/reliefweb.int/files/resources/N1808325-1.pdf.

United Nations High Commissioner for Refugees (UNHCR). 2018. "Sexual and Gender Based Violence." Accessed January 16, 2019. http://www.unhcr.org/sexual-and-gender-based-violence.html.

United Nations Office on Drugs and Crime (UNODC). 2009. "Human Trafficking Fuels Violence against Women." Last updated November 25, 2009. Accessed January 16, 2019. https://www.unodc.org/unodc/en/frontpage/2009/November/human-trafficking-fuels-violence-against-women.html.

United Nations Office on Drugs and Crime (UNODC). 2012. "Symposium on Femicide: A Global Issue That Demands Action!" Accessed January 16, 2019. https://www.unodc.org/unodc/en/ngos/DCN5-Symposium-on-femicide-a-global-issue-that-demands-action.html.

Genocide

The term *genocide* comes from the Greek word *genos* (race, tribe) and the Latin verb *cide* (killing). In 1944, it appeared for the first time in the publication "Axis Rule in Occupied Europe" by Polish lawyer Raphael Lemkin; he described it as "the destruction of a nation or of an ethnic group" (Lemkin 1944, 79). Lemkin's work was a response to Adolf Hitler's German Nazi regime and the atrocities that occurred during the World War II (1939–1945), which led to the systematic persecution and murder of millions of Jews and other vulnerable groups. In later years, genocide was identified as a crime under international law by the UN General Assembly and other international entities, such as the International Criminal

Court (ICC). Known examples of genocide in modern history are the Holocaust, the mass slaughter of Tutsis in Rwanda (1994), the persecution and execution of Muslim Bosnians in Srebrenica (1995), and the genocide being carried out by Sudanese government forces in Darfur (2003 and ongoing as of 2018).

GENOCIDE IN LEGAL DOCUMENTS

In addition to coining the term *genocide*, Lemkin also led a campaign urging the international community to take action against the atrocities that had been committed during World War II and to recognize and codify genocide under international law regulations. This became a reality in 1946, when the UN General Assembly recognized genocide as a specific crime, later codified in the 1948 Convention on the Prevention and Punishment of the Crime of Genocide (the Genocide Convention). As of 2018, the Genocide Convention has been ratified by 149 countries, and the many international organizations consider genocide to be an example of general customary international law and a crime that should be prohibited by all countries.

In 2002, when the Rome Statute of the International Criminal Court (ICC) came into force, it established core international crimes that represent the most serious violations of human rights and humanitarian law. Genocide is recognized in this document, along with crimes against humanity, war crimes, and crimes of aggression.

The definition of genocide that was established in the Genocide Convention, and also used for the Rome Statute of the ICC, defines the crime as any and all acts carried out with the intent to destroy a national, religious, racial, or ethnical group, whether in whole or in part. Be it by killing members of said group, causing serious physical or mental damage to its members, perpetrating actions with the intent to bring about the destruction of the group, preventing births, or forcibly transferring members of the group, including children, to other groups. "Genocide is a denial of the right of existence of entire human groups, as homicide is the denial of the right to live of individual human beings; such denial of the right of existence shocks the conscience of mankind" (UN General Assembly 1946, 188–189).

By codifying genocide as a specific crime, the international community provided the term with a definition, specific acts to be committed, and types of perpetrators, making it punishable under international law. However, it is important to note that the efforts made to penalize such wrongdoings have not been completely successful in preventing similar events from occurring again. After 1945, there have been several instances classified as genocide, tragedies that have left nations with deep wounds and thousands of lives lost.

GENOCIDE EXAMPLES IN SREBRENICA AND RWANDA

Two of the most infamous cases of recent genocide took place in Rwanda and in Srebrenica, a city of the newly independent Bosnia and Herzegovina. In 1992, the republic of Bosnia and Herzegovina declared its independence from Yugoslavia. A retaliatory offense was launched in Bosnia's capital of Sarajevo by Bosnia Serb forces with the backing of the Serb-dominated Yugoslav army. By 1995, three towns in eastern Bosnia—Srebrenica, Zepa, and Gorazde—were under control of the Bosnian government and had been declared by the United Nations to be safe havens protected by international peacekeeping forces. In July 1995, Bosnian Serb forces overwhelmed the UN peacekeeping force and women and girls in Srebrenica were put on buses and sent to Bosnian-held territory. Some of the women were raped or sexually assaulted, and the men and boys who remained in Srebrenica were immediately killed or bused to mass killing sites. Estimates of Bosniaks killed by Serb forces at Srebrenica range from 7,000 to more than 8,000 (History .com Editors 2009a).

The genocide in Rwanda must be understood in the context of ethnic differences that were deeply embedded within the culture since the colonization period in 1916, when the Belgians arrived and started separating the population according to their ethnic groups. The Tutsis, who were believed to be superior by the Belgian colonists, were given political control over the country, and for the next 20 years, they enjoyed the better jobs and educational opportunities. Resentment among the Hutus, who composed the statistical majority (85%) of the Rwanda population, resulted in a series of riots in 1959, and when Belgium granted Rwanda independence in 1962, the Hutus took political control of the country. Over the following three decades, Rwanda witnessed violent encounters between Tutsis and Hutus.

In April 1994, sparked by the death of Hutu president Juvenal Habyarimana, the genocide began. For 100 days, Tutsis, as well as moderate Hutus who refused to take part in the violence, were persecuted, slaughtered, and forced to flee the country. Rape was used as weapon of war against Tutsi women, who were later left to die by the militias. The mass killings started within hours of the president's death, as organized gangs of government soldiers and militias moved through the Tutsi population bringing death and destruction at each step (BBC News 2011). In early July 1994, the Tutsi-led Rwandese Patriotic Front used a military offensive to gain control of the country—but not until more than 800,000 people, mostly Tutsi, had been murdered. The 2004 film *Hotel Rwanda* (directed by Terry George) tells the story of a hotel manager who sheltered more than 1,000 people inside his hotel during the genocide.

GENOCIDE TRIALS

In 1993, the International Criminal Tribunal for the former Yugoslavia (ICTY) was established at The Hague, Netherlands. Over the next 24 years, 161 people were indicted on charges that included genocide, crimes against humanity, violations of the laws or customs of war, and grave breaches of the Geneva Conventions. In 2017, the ICTY's last major prosecution resulted in the conviction and sentencing to life imprisonment of army general Ratko Mladic, who had been dubbed the "Butcher of Bosnia" for directing his troops in acts of genocide and crimes against humanity—including the massacre at Srebrenica (Gunter 2017).

In 1994 the International Criminal Tribunal for Rwanda (ICTR) was established in Tanzania as an extension of the ICTY, and in 1995, the court began indicting and trying people for their roles in the Rwandan genocide. Trials continued through 2012, and of the 93 individuals indicted, 63 were sentenced in connection with the 1994 genocide (United Nations n.d.).

Mariana Cammisa and Jéssica Viales López

See also: International Criminal Tribunal for Rwanda; International Criminal Tribunal for the Former Yugoslavia (ICTY); International Military Tribunal at Nuremberg; UN Convention on the Prevention and Punishment of the Crime of Genocide

Further Reading

BBC News. 2011. "Rwanda: How the Genocide Happened." Last updated May 17, 2011. Accessed January 16, 2019. https://www.bbc.com/news/world-africa-13431486.

Gunter, Joel. 2017. "Ratko Mladic, the 'Butcher of Bosnia.'" *BBC News*. Last updated November 22, 2017. https://www.bbc.com/news/world-europe-13559597

History.com Editors. 2009a. "Bosnian Genocide." Last updated August 21, 2018. Accessed January 16, 2019. https://www.history.com/topics/1990s/bosnian-genocide.

History.com Editors. 2009b. "Rwandan Genocide." Last updated August 21, 2018. Accessed January 16, 2019. https://www.history.com/topics/africa/rwandan-genocide.

Lemkin, Raphaël. 1944. *Axis Rule in Occupied Europe*. Washington, D.C.: Carnegie Endowment for International Peace.

UN General Assembly. 1946. "The Crime of Genocide." A/RES/96(I). United Nations Publications.

United Nations. n.d. "The ICTR in Brief." International Residual Mechanism for International Criminal Tribunals. Accessed September 18, 2018. http://unictr.unmict.org/en/tribunal.

Global Counterterrorism Forum

The Global Counterterrorism Forum (GCTF) is an informal, civilian-led, action-oriented, and pragmatic forum that aims to reduce the vulnerability of people to terrorism by effectively preventing, combating, and prosecuting terrorist acts and countering incitement and recruitment to terrorism (GCTF 2011). It is set up to complement and reinforce existing counterterrorism (CT) practices employed by both the United Nations and existing regional bodies. The primary activity of the multilateral forum is to function as a platform for senior policy makers and practitioners from different regions to share experience, best practices, and work on solutions and to assess and act upon gaps in CT. Furthermore, to build capacity, coordinate CT efforts, and build, develop, and promote the implementation of the comprehensive CT strategies in line with the UN Global Counter-Terrorism Strategy at all levels. The main focus is on civilian capacity building in areas such as rule of law, border management, and countering violent extremism.

The GCTF was founded on September 22, 2011, by its 30 founding members in New York through a political declaration. These 30 founding members are Algeria, Australia, Canada, China, Colombia, Denmark, Egypt, the European

Union (EU), France, Germany, India, Indonesia, Italy, Japan, Jordan, Morocco, the Netherlands, New Zealand, Nigeria, Pakistan, Qatar, Russia, Saudi Arabia, South Africa, Spain, Switzerland, Turkey, the United Arab Emirates, the United Kingdom, and the United States. Additionally, some 40 nonmember states and dozens of nonmember international, regional, subregional, and nongovernmental organizations have participated in GCTF activities (U.S. Department of State, 2015).

The GCTF has broad political support, considering that all five of the permanent members of the UN Security Council are among the founding members, as well as the European Union as a separate member.

ORGANIZATION

The GCTF is always cochaired by two countries. They propose a plan of action and strategic priorities. Operationally, the GCTF, as of 2018, has five Working Groups. The way the GCTF is set up, however, the organization can quickly adapt to trends in the dynamics of terrorist threats and violent extremism by setting up new working groups or initiatives.

From the five current working groups, three are thematic: Countering Violent Extremism, Foreign Terrorist Fighters, and Criminal Justice and the Rule of Law. The two remaining working groups have a regional focus and work on capacity building: capacity building in the East Africa region and capacity-building in the West Africa region (GCTF 2018d). The working groups are mainly involved with identifying "relevant civilian CT challenges and capacity gaps or needs; consider activities to address these gaps or needs; and mobilize political will, financial resources, and expertise to implement those activities" (GCTF 2018d).

Twice every year, the GCTF Coordinating Committee (COCO) meets to oversee the activities of the working groups. The COCO comprises all GCTF members, generally represented by their national CT coordinator or any other senior CT policy maker (GCTF 2018a). The goal of these meetings is to provide the working groups with strategic advice and prioritizations to most effectively address the evolving threat of terrorism (GCTF 2018a).

In September, the GCTF also organizes the GCTF Ministerial Plenary Meeting, where the forum releases a ministerial statement, reveals new initiatives, and individual countries announce their priorities.

The GCTF has also employed various initiatives. They are intended to focus on a number of cross-cutting and overarching issues. As of 2018 these are the following:

- Initiative to address the Life Cycle of Radicalization to Violence: from prevention to intervention to rehabilitation and reintegration;
- Border security and the challenges posed by permeable borders;
- Preventing and responding to kidnapping for ransom;
- Supporting victims of terrorism; and
- Developing a worldwide network of civilian CT practitioners. (GCTF 2018b)

During the GCTF Ministerial Plenary Meeting of 2017, three new initiatives were announced: homegrown violent extremists, the nexus between transnational organized crime and terrorism, and the challenge to address returning families of foreign terrorist fighters (GCTF 2017).

The GCTF also has an administrative unit, which has a coordinating and support function. For instance, the unit prepares framework documents and organizes and facilitates the workshops and other meetings. It also provides the necessary analytical, administrative, and logistical support for the COCO, working groups, and initiatives (GCTF 2018a). Besides, it fulfills a critical role in the information management of the organization and finally coordinates the promotion of GCTF tools with the three GCTF-inspired institutions.

TOOLS

The GCTF has developed various tools and mechanisms to deal with a host of CT issues, in line with the facilitating role it plays. One of these is the "Life Cycle" tool kit. This tool kit consists of a large number of existing and new tools that address the life cycle of radicalization to violence, such as programming options and GCTF memoranda. The tool kit is available as a Web-based instrument (both Web site and mobile application). The tool kit is essentially built with the idea in mind that radicalization is part of an ongoing cycle. Interventions thus need to happen in any phase during this cycle, from prevention to detection and intervention to rehabilitation and reintegration (GCTF 2018c).

The GCTF has also inspired three institutions: the Global Community Engagement and Resilience Fund (GCERF), Hedayah, and the International Institute for Justice and the Rule of Law (IIJ). GCERF is a public-private partnership that supports "local, community-level initiatives aimed at strengthening resilience against violent extremism in states where support is most needed" (GCTF 2018a). Hedayah, the International Center of Excellence for Countering Violent Extremism, is a key operational delivery arm for the forum's CVE efforts (GCTF 2018a). Lastly, the IIJ develops, implements, and promotes GCTF good practices and memoranda and other initiatives with criminal justice practitioners and experts, and it also trains judges and prosecutors on how to address terrorism-related activities within a rule of law framework (GCTF 2018a).

GCTF also set up various mechanisms, such as the International Counterterrorism and Countering Violent Extremism Capacity-Building Clearinghouse Mechanism (ICCM), the Foreign Terrorist Fighters Knowledge Hub, and the Catalogue of Foreign Terrorist Fighters (FTF)-Related Countering Violent Extremism (CVE) and Returnee Programs. The ICCM is concerned with developing "an up-to-date database of recent and ongoing CT and CVE capacity-building assistance, identifying gaps in programming, de-conflicting overlapping programs, and helping to mobilize and guide donor resources through non-binding recommendations"; the Knowledge Hub is a platform only accessible for GCTF members that can be used for data sharing and experience sharing good practices exchanges (GCTF 2018c). Finally, the Catalogue, lists all "existing programs sponsored or led by countries that all UN member states may find useful or appropriate for their particular national context" (GCTF 2018c).

Wessel Groot

See also: Counterterrorism; Crime-Terrorism Nexus; National Counterterrorism Center; Rule of Law

Further Reading

Global Counterterrorism Forum. 2011. "Political Declaration." Accessed April 17, 2018. https://www.thegctf.org/Portals/1/Documents/Foundational%20Documents/GCTF-Political-Declaration_ENG.pdf.

Global Counterterrorism Forum. 2017. "Eighth GCTF Ministerial Plenary Meeting and Delivered Statements." Last Modified September 20, 2017. Accessed April 24, 2018. https://www.thegctf.org/Home/ArtMID/491/ArticleID/46/Eighth-GCTF-Ministerial-Plenary-Meeting-and-delivered-Statements.

Global Counterterrorism Forum. 2018a. "About—Structure." Accessed April 19, 2018. https://www.thegctf.org/About-us/Structure.

Global Counterterrorism Forum. 2018b. "Cross-Cutting Initiatives." Accessed April 19, 2018. https://www.thegctf.org/Cross-Cutting-Initiatives.

Global Counterterrorism Forum. 2018c. Toolkit." Accessed May 9, 2018. https://www.thegctf.org/Tools/Overview.

Global Counterterrorism Forum. 2018d. "Working Groups—Structure." Accessed April 19, 2018. https://www.thegctf.org/Working-Groups/Structure.

U.S. Department of State. 2018. "Global Counterterrorism Forum Co-Chairs' Fact Sheet: About the GCTF." Last Modified September 27, 2015. Accessed January 16, 2019. https://2009-2017.state.gov/r/pa/prs/ps/2015/09/247369.htm.

Global Crime, *see* Transnational, Global, and International Crime

Global Drug Interdiction

Global drug interdiction is an important component of the international drug control regime. Traditional antidrug policies can be divided into supply-oriented and demand-oriented strategies that focus on reducing the supply of and the demand for illicit drugs, respectively. Drug interdiction is a supply-oriented complex of measures aimed at "interrupting illegal drugs smuggled by air, sea, or land" (U.S. Department of Defense 2017, 71). It is a law enforcement strategy rooted in the assumption that stopping illegal drugs from crossing the border of source or transit countries will help solve the problem of drug use in final market countries. The rationale behind this assumption is that limiting drug supply will raise the price of the drugs available on the market and will deter consumers from buying them. Interdiction efforts involve such activities as blocking shipment of precursor chemicals, destroying processing and shipping facilities, and seizing illicit drugs. The inspection of goods crossing the border and the seizure of any illicit substances in the air, on land, and on the sea requires effective cooperation between law enforcement authorities of different countries. Thus, international antinarcotic policies are usually coordinated and regulated within the framework of international organizations, especially the United Nations.

THE ROLE OF THE UNITED STATES

The United States has been an undisputable leader of global antinarcotic efforts throughout the 20th century, playing a significant role within the UN drug control treaties and allocating more than any other country to the fight against drugs (Nadelmann 1990). In doing so, the U.S. government has been an ardent proponent of a hard-line approach to drug control, dedicating most of its resources to attacking the supply of illicit drugs through crop eradication, drug interdiction, and military assistance to source and transit countries.

Since 1971, when President Richard Nixon declared a "war on drugs," a variety of agencies, such as the U.S. Customs and Border Protection Agency, the Drug Enforcement Administration (DEA), the Bureau of International Narcotics and Law Enforcement Affairs (INL), and the Department of Defense, have been involved in disrupting the flow of drugs into the U.S. territory. Some of these agencies also operate abroad, providing technical and military assistance to the countries where drugs are cultivated, manufactured, or smuggled. For example, the U.S. military has actively participated in drug-related activities in the source countries of Central and South America and Afghanistan.

GLOBAL TRENDS

According to the World Drug Report 2017 issued by the United Nations Office on Drugs and Crime (UNODC), as of 2015, cannabis remained the most seized drug worldwide, in terms of quantities. The second most seized drug was cocaine; its estimated interception rate (based on cocaine production estimates and quantities of cocaine seized) reached a record level of 55 percent (UNODC 2017, 17). In other words, almost half of all cocaine produced in clandestine laboratories remained in the hands of law enforcement. The third-largest quantities seized were those of opioids; their estimated global interception rate constituted 30 percent in 2015. The traditional drugs were followed by the new psychoactive substances (NPS), both synthetic and plant-based, and by the amphetamine-type stimulants (ATS) (UNODC 2017, 40–42). Overall, official data shows that higher quantities of illicit drugs have been seized worldwide, partly due to the rising effectiveness of the international law enforcement cooperation (UNODC 2017, 17).

CRITICISM

The heavy focus on militarized drug interdiction within the global prohibition framework has been an object of criticism by experts and civil society. First, it has not achieved its goal of decreasing the retail price of drugs and curbing the demand (Drug Policy Alliance n.d.). Second, when interdiction efforts succeed in disrupting a trafficking route, the corridor tends to shift to another location as traffickers search for alternative routes. This "balloon effect" occurred in the late 1980s after the disruption of the Caribbean route for the Andean cocaine. Instead of South Florida, the drug's primary entry point to the United States shifted to the U.S.-Mexico border (Bagley 2015; UNODC 2016, 35).

Yulia Vorobyeva

See also: Commission on Narcotic Drugs; International Drug Trafficking; International Narcotics Control Board; UN Office on Drugs and Crime; UN World Drug Report

Further Reading

Bagley, Bruce M. 2015. "Introduction." In *Drug Trafficking, Organized Crime, and Violence in the Americas Today*, edited by Bruce M. Bagley and Jonathan D. Rosen, 1–24. Gainesville: University Press of Florida.

Buxton, Julia. 2006. *The Political Economy of Narcotics: Production, Consumption and Global Markets*. London: Zed Books.

Drug Policy Alliance. n.d. "Making Economic Sense." Accessed January 5, 2018. http://www.drugpolicy.org/issues/making-economic-sense.

Musto, David. 1987. *The American Disease: Origins of Narcotic Control*. New York: Oxford University Press.

Nadelmann, Ethan. 1990. "Global Prohibition Regimes: The Evolution of Norms in International Society." *International Organization* 44 (4): 479–526.

United Nations Office on Drugs and Crime (UNODC). 2016. *World Drug Report 2016*. Vienna: United Nations publication.

United Nations Office on Drugs and Crime (UNODC). 2017. *World Drug Report 2017*. Vienna: United Nations publication.

U.S. Department of Defense. 2017. *DOD Dictionary of Military and Associated Terms*. Military Studies Press. Accessed January 16, 2019. http://www.jcs.mil/Doctrine.

Global Slavery Index

The *Global Slavery Index* (GSI) is a report issued by the Walk Free Foundation, which is a nongovernmental organization (NGO) founded in 2012 by the Australian philanthropists Andrew and Grace Forrest. The GSI ranks countries based on the prevalence of modern slavery, which encompasses activities that comprise human trafficking. The GSI is presented as a way to provide benchmark figures that can be used in the coming years to measure global efforts to eliminate modern slavery.

The first GSI was issued in 2013, with subsequent reports in 2014, 2016, and 2018. A 2017 report made use of data from the International Labour Organization (ILO) and received support from the International Organization for Migration (IOM). The collaboration resulted in a joint publication titled the *Global Estimates of Modern Slavery*.

THE IMPORTANCE OF COUNTING

Determining, or even estimating, the extent of human trafficking is very difficult. The problems of labor and sex exploitation clearly exist, but the number of people involved in these forms of human slavery is unknown. As is true when trying to research other hidden or hard-to-reach populations where illegal or stigmatized activity may be involved (for example, drug addicts or gang members), human trafficking victims, perpetrators, and clients are difficult to sample.

The inability to estimate the size of a population presents problems for researchers as well as legislators, policy makers, practitioners, victim advocates, and others hoping to understand and do something about a problem. Motivation to pass laws, provide funding, and simply to take action is hindered when there are no or unreliable counts of the number of people affected. The GSI is designed to provide those numbers and to encourage action.

2018 REPORT HIGHLIGHTS

As was done in the previous GSIs, the 2018 report (Walk Free Foundation 2018) continues to provide country-by-country measures of where modern slavery occurs and how governments respond to it. New to the 2018 report is information about the factors allowing modern slavery to prosper and data on where the products of the crime are sold and consumed.

The 2018 report uses information from the *Global Estimates of Modern Slavery* (ILO 2017) as a starting point to provide estimates of modern slavery in countries around the world and to identify factors that contribute to modern slavery. For example, GSI 2018 (Walk Free Foundation 2018, 2–3) shows a connection between modern slavery and two major external drivers: (1) highly repressive regimes with state-imposed forced labor (for example, Burundi, Eritrea, and North Korea) and (2) conflict situations that result in the breakdown of rule of law, social structures, and social institutions (for example, Afghanistan, the Central African Republic, Pakistan, and South Sudan).

CRITICISM OF THE INDEX

Although acknowledging the need for improved methods of determining the extent of modern slavery, critics found fault with the GSI on several levels. The first GSI (2013) grew harsh methodological criticism. Gallagher (2014) cited inconsistently applied methodology, unverified assumptions, and changing definitions of "modern slavery" to be especially problematic. But, critics argued, an especially serious problem was the extrapolation from random surveys in only 19 countries to estimates of modern slavery for 148 other countries.

Mügge (2017) writes that the global acceptance and growing use of the GSI/GEMS as a guide for international policy requires a close look at its data limitations. The empirical base for the GSI was broadened in the 2014 and 2016 editions, but Mügge argues that the key weaknesses remained: (1) there are surveys on the prevalence of modern slavery in only a minority of countries, and (2) the GSI simply extrapolates from those to the rest of the world.

Philip L. Reichel

See also: Human Trafficking; Labor Exploitation; Sex Exploitation

Further Reading

Gallagher, Anne. 2014. "The *Global Slavery Index* Is Based on Flawed Data—Why Does No One Say So?" *The Guardian*, November 28. Accessed January 19, 2019. https://www.theguardian.com/global-development/poverty-matters/2014/nov/28/global-slavery-index-walk-free-human-trafficking-anne-gallagher.

International Labour Organization (ILO). 2017. *Global Estimates of Modern Slavery: Forced Labour and Forced Marriage*. Accessed January 16, 2019. https://www.ilo.org/global/publications/books/WCMS_575479/lang--en/index.htm.

Mügge, Daniel. 2017. "40.3 Million Slaves? Four Reasons to Question the New Global Estimates of Modern Slavery." openDemocracy, October 17. Accessed January 19, 2019. https://www.opendemocracy.net/beyondslavery/daniel-m-gge/403-million-slaves-four-reasons-to-question-new-global-estimates-of-moder.

Walk Free Foundation. 2018. *Global Slavery Index 2018*. Accessed January 16, 2019. https://www.globalslaveryindex.org/resources/downloads.

Globalization

Globalization describes the growing interconnectedness of countries and peoples. These interconnections have been enhanced through technological advances that have, in effect, compressed time and space. The compression of space refers to the exponential growth in the movement of peoples, goods, services, information, and culture across national boundaries. The compression of time refers to the unprecedented speed at which these interactions occur across the globe. Globalization is a dynamic social process that gradually transforms society from a national perspective to a broader global consciousness (Steger 2013, 9–10). This process occurs in economic, political, cultural, and ecological dimensions. Globalization is uneven; the effects are not felt uniformly around the globe.

The impacts of globalization are multifaceted, having both positive and negative outcomes. For example, the Internet facilitates the global distribution of information that enables the collective production of knowledge, but it also enables hackers, pirates, smugglers, and others to inflict widespread damage more quickly than in the past (Gilman, Goldhammer, and Weber 2013). Or, as the United Nations explains, the process of globalization has outpaced mechanisms for global governance, and a result is a type of regulation vacuum in which transnational organized crime can thrive. People and goods can move more cheaply and broadly than ever before, and both human and commercial flows are too intense to easily distinguish the licit from the illicit (Studies and Threat Analysis Section 2010).

HISTORY OF GLOBALIZATION

Tracing the origins of globalization depends on how far the chain of causation is extended. Looking across human history, globalization can be separated into distinct stages (Steger 2013, 20–36). The global dispersion of the human species across five continents in the prehistoric period can be seen as an early form of globalization. Each stage has provided the current epoch of globalization with structural context and operational tools. Inventions in Asia and Africa (such as writing, mathematics, the wheel, the calendar, the compass, paper, printing, metallurgy, hydraulic engineering, tapping of natural gas, etc.) serve as essential tools of modern-day globalization. Similarly, the trade routes established by Asian, African, and European empires established the basis for modern-day international trade. European imperialism was the foundation for a capitalist world system, which set the structural stage for the current form of globalization.

Contemporary globalization, which began in the 1980s, distinguishes itself from all previous stages in the development and use of technology, which has made the globalization process faster and more intense than any period before. Technological advances have stimulated industrialization at an unprecedented scale, combining older models of exploitation with the realities of global competition (Franko Aas 2013, 9). This is exemplified by the pervasive practice of multinational corporations to produce goods in countries with cheap, underregulated labor for international markets. Simultaneously, contemporary globalization is marked with an exceptional concern by the international community for human rights. This is evident from the various international conventions that have codified international standards to be ratified into national laws (on subjects ranging from human trafficking to corruption and terrorist financing) and the establishment of a series of ad hoc tribunals in response to grave violations of human rights. Perhaps one of the most distinctive features of our current phase of globalization is its contradiction between the global promise of democracy and universal protection of human rights and its entrenchment of an uncompromising free market economy that has upheld global hierarchies of power.

GLOBALIZATION AND NEOLIBERALIZATION

The motor of economic globalization in the cotemporary period has been neoliberalization. Neoliberalization refers to the opening up of national borders to promote unfettered international trade and financial flows, also known as the free market. This is combined with policies privatizing state assets, deregulation, austerity, and reduction of the welfare state to reduce the interference of national governments while expanding the social and economic role of the private sector (Twyman-Ghoshal and Passas 2015, 106). These policies have been instrumental in the erosion of laws that control harmful human behaviors. Labor standards, health and safety regulations, and environmental protection laws have been reduced or thwarted in an effort to stimulate international trade and investment. State welfare programs have simultaneously been shrunk to reduce governmental spending. These policies have been implemented vigorously in the developing nations by international financial institutions such as the World Bank and the International Monetary Fund (IMF), resulting in increasing economic inequality both within and across countries.

The effect has been to render large segments of the population vulnerable and destitute (Oxfam International 2014, 2). Economic inequality, particularly when it is highly visible due to an increasingly connected and mediated society, has consequences on population health. Unequal societies have been found to have increased social health problems, including mental illness, violence, imprisonment, lack of trust, teenage births, obesity, drug abuse, and poor educational performance (Wilkinson and Pickett 2009, 495).

GLOBALIZATION, CRIME, AND CRIMINOLOGY

At the most basic level, free market globalization has allowed for global trade in goods and services, but it has also stimulated a rising number of illicit transactions. Transnational crimes, that is, criminal behaviors that have a cross border element (criminalized in the countries concerned or in international law), have been emboldened by the increased opportunities presented by a free market. This includes activities such as human trafficking, fraud, and trade in narcotics. The impact is not limited to transnational crimes. International crimes, which include genocide, crimes against humanity, war crimes, and the crime of aggression (as proscribed by the 1998 Rome Statute of the International Criminal Court), have also been affected by globalization. As the world has become more interconnected, so has the concern over gross human rights violations that occur within territorial boundaries of a sovereign nation. This concern resulted in the establishment of the first permanent International Criminal Court (ICC) in 2002.

Beyond traditional notions of transnational and international crime, globalization has demanded a rethinking of the concept of crime itself (Friedrichs 2007, 11). In a rapidly globalizing environment where organizations and behaviors are not restricted to one jurisdiction, the use of a legalistic definition of crime is of limited value. This has meant a broadening of global criminology to incorporate willful social harms within its ambit, including deviant activities by corporations, states, and international financial institutions. Global criminology studies criminality beyond individual agency, exploring the criminogenic effects of a social structure and its normative effect on the individuals within that system. Globalization, in its current neoliberal form, has created large-scale asymmetries: a system that gives rise to demands and incentives for deviance while simultaneously reducing the ability to control crime (Twyman-Ghoshal and Passas 2015, 106).

Anamika A. Twyman-Ghoshal

See also: Bonded Labor; Failed State; International Drug Trafficking

Further Reading

Franko Aas, Katja. 2013. *Globalization and Crime*. London: Sage.

Friedrichs, David. 2007. "Transnational Crime and Global Criminology: Definitional, Typological, and Contextual Conundrums." *Social Justice* 34 (2): 4–18.

Gilman, Nils, Jesse Goldhammer, and Steven Weber. 2013. "Deviant Globalization." In *Convergence: Illicit Networks and National Security in the Age of Globalization*, edited by Michael Miklaucic and Jacqueline Brewer, 3–13. Washington, D.C.: National Defense University Press.

Held, David. 2000. "The Changing Contours of Political Community." In *Governing Modern Societies,* edited by Richard Ericson and Nico Stehr, 42–59. Toronto: University of Toronto Press.

Oxfam. 2014. *Working for the Few*. Oxfam Briefing Paper 178. Accessed January 16, 2019. https://www.oxfam.org/en/research/working-few.

Steger, Manfred. 2013. *Globalization: A Very Short Introduction.* Oxford: Oxford University Press.

Studies and Threat Analysis Section. 2010. "The Threat of Transnational Organized Crime." In *The Globalization of Crime: A Transnational Organized Crime Threat Assessment*, edited by UNODC, 25–39. Vienna: United Nations Office on Drugs and Crime.

Twyman-Ghoshal, Anamika, and Nikos Passas. 2015. "State and Corporate Drivers of Global Dysnomie: Horrendous Crimes and the Law." In *The Routledge International Handbook of the Crimes of the Powerful*, edited by Gregg Barak, 105–120. London: Routledge.

Wilkinson, Richard, and Kate Pickett. 2009. "Income inequality and social dysfunction." *Annual Review of Sociology* 35: 493–511.

Golden Triangle

The area known as the Golden Triangle is the source for much of the world's opium. With an area of 367,000 square miles along the Mekong River, the area has become a dominant player in the worldwide opium trade and is the world's second-largest producer of illicit opium behind Afghanistan. The Golden Triangle consists of the countries of Myanmar, Laos, and Thailand. The largest opium-producing country within the Golden Triangle is Myanmar. Today, the Golden Triangle provides illicit opium and other opioids throughout the entire world. In recent years, China, the United States, and the United Nations have tried to curtail the production of the illicit substance, but the production and distribution of illegal substances is still profitable. Today, opium remains one of the most profitable crops of the area.

The growing of opium in the Golden Triangle began in the early colonial years of these countries. With the influence of global colonialism, the cultivation and harvesting of the substance was widely encouraged. The early roots were further promulgated by China when opium use and production were banned in 1946. With enormous profits and a growing demand, production substantially increased in the area. Today, much of the people in the area are in severe poverty. Lack of infrastructure has left many to live off the cultivation of these substances. Due to their status at the bottom of the chain of distribution, drug lords and other officials exploit the labor for the product to remain profitable.

While opium is still the largest product of the Golden Triangle, the production of opiates has also increased. The production and distribution of opioids appear to be as large as all other legal exports from the area. According to recent estimates, 731–823 metric tons of opium are grown each year (United Nations News 2015). With the increase in exportation of opiates, the drug market continues to be a major economical supplier for the area. Today, not only is opium and heroin grown, but a new substance known as "Yaba," otherwise known as methamphetamine, is also being grown in the area.

TRAFFICKING AND LAUNDERING

Drug producers in the Golden Triangle utilized numerous means to traffic and launder their money to avoid detection. One of the biggest traffickers was the Myanmar Oil and Gas Enterprise (MOGE), under the control of the Myanmar Army. Business deals were signed between French oil giant Total Unocal that helped mask the laundering. At the conclusion of a four-year investigation, MOGE was found to have laundered over $60 million through investments in the company. It was later found that Khun Sa, who was a renowned drug lord in the area, was a key player in the operation. Through the use of other banks and public entities, the money brought into the community helped provide significant financial assets. Due to financial constraints from the Myanmar government, infrastructure had been largely abandoned. Drug lords and other producers from the area filled this need and have provided financial support for the area through these excessive profits. Big community players included the State Law and Order Restoration Council (SLORC) and other community banks that would charge a 40 percent commission for holding and managing the funds (Voice of America 2009).

Another key player to the trafficking operation was the United Wa State Army (UWSA). In collusion with local area drug lords, UWSA helped traffic opium and opioids between Thailand and Myanmar, allowing for an open channel of access. Utilizing these open channels, couriers moved product grown in the area through mountains, river channels, and commercial airlines (Yong-an 2012).

Smugglers are now adopting new methods of exporting and distributing the substances through international networks. The most recent adaptation is the use of the 14K triad, which is a drug trading route that can move drugs into Southeast Asia and China by utilizing multiple drug networks.

ENFORCEMENT

Numerous entities are becoming involved to curtail the production efforts of the Golden Triangle. Citing internal concerns, the government of Myanmar has stepped up enforcement and had the goal in 2014 to end all production within the area. These efforts, however, are still ongoing.

Anthony Azari

See also: Global Drug Interdiction; International Drug Trafficking

Further Reading

The Golden Triangle: Forbidden Land of Opium. 2006. Directed by Neil Hollander. New York: Filmakers Library, Video.

United Nations News. 2015. "Opium Production in Myanmar and Laos Are Stable at High Levels New UN Report Shows." Last modified December 16, 2015. Accessed January 16, 2019. https://news.un.org/en/story/2015/12/518342-opium-production-myanmar-and-laos-are-stable-high-levels-new-un-report-shows.

Voice of America. 2009. "Opium Cultivation and Blossoms in Myanmar." Last Modified November 1, 2009. Accessed January 16, 2019. https://www.voanews.com/a/a-13-2007-10-12-voa10/406999.html.

Yong-an, Zhang. 2012. "Asia, International Drug Trafficking, and U.S.-China Counternarcotics Cooperation." Brookings Institution. Accessed January 20, 2019. https://www.brookings.edu/wp-content/uploads/2016/06/02_drug_trafficking_zhang_paper.pdf.

Granados Sex Trafficking Organization

Since at least 1998, members of the Granados sex trafficking organization (the STO) have trafficked young women from Mexico into the United States. Several members of the STO are related (mostly brothers, uncles, or cousins) through the Granados family, and as of 2018, five have been convicted in U.S. District Court (Eastern District of New York) on international sex trafficking charges. Most of those convicted received prison sentences of about 15 years, plus another 5 years of supervised release.

THE CRIMES

U.S. federal authorities say that the Mexican town of Tenancingo, 80 miles southwest of Mexico City, is that country's sex trafficking capital—and has been since the 1960s. Members of the Granados family have been especially active in the sex trafficking trade, as they used threats and actual acts of physical and sexual violence to force and coerce minor and adult women to engage in commercial sex in both Mexico and the United States. The male members of the STO were especially likely to rely on false promises of romance and marriage as they lured victims into relationships and convinced the women to travel to the United States with false promises of a better life.

With minimal variation in technique, the operation would start in Mexico with the traffickers using multiple means of isolating victims from their families. The trafficker might use romantic promises to convince the victim to leave her family and live with him. Or, the trafficker might rape the victim, making it difficult for her to return to her family due to the associated stigma of rape.

Once separated from her family, the victim would often be taken to a Mexico City neighborhood, where she was kept in a locked apartment, subjected to continued physical and sexual abuse, and forced to work in prostitution, seeing as many as 20–40 customers per day. The traffickers would make the women turn over all proceeds from the prostitution with a claim that it was payment toward a debt owed the traffickers by the victim.

Eventually, the victims would be smuggled to the United States and housed in shared apartments under continual threat of violence. They typically operated in Queens, New York, and along that borough's streets; the sex ring handed out pamphlets in Spanish called "Chica cards" that advertised a phone number to call for cheap sex (Bello 2015).

BILATERAL HUMAN TRAFFICKING ENFORCEMENT INITIATIVE

Of particular help in bringing members of the Granados sex trafficking organization was the U.S.-Mexico Bilateral Human Trafficking Enforcement Initiative. The Department of Justice and Homeland Security Investigations have collaborated with Mexican law enforcement counterparts to more effectively combat transborder trafficking threats and to strengthen high-impact prosecutions under both U.S. and Mexican law. The initiative is aimed at dismantling human trafficking networks operating across the U.S.-Mexico border, bringing human traffickers to justice, reuniting victims with their children, and restoring the rights and dignity of human trafficking victims. These efforts have resulted in successful prosecutions in both Mexico and the United States and numerous Mexican federal and state prosecutions of associated sex traffickers.

ARRESTS AND SENTENCES

Federal authorities, primarily from Homeland Security Investigations (a component of U.S. Immigration and Customs Enforcement (ICE) and the principal investigative component of the Department of Homeland Security (DHS)), have been acting to disrupt the Granados sex trafficking organization for many years.

In some cases, the traffickers had returned to Mexico, and U.S. authorities had to initiate extradition proceedings to get the defendants back to New York. In 2018, for example, four Mexican nationals were extradited to the United States to face international sex trafficking charges, including Efrain Granados-Corona ("Chavito") and Alan Romero-Granados ("El Flaco").

Arrests and indictments of the traffickers found in the United States began in 2011. For example, Eleuterio Granados-Hernandez and his brother Samuel were among the Granados family members arrested for smuggling victims, including one minor, from Mexico illegally into the United States and forcing them to engage in prostitution. Eleuterio was sentenced to 22 years in prison and Samuel to 15 years. Convictions continued into 2017, when Paulino Ramirez-Granados was sentenced in February 2017 to 188 months in prison and 5 years supervised release after pleading guilty to trafficking young Mexican women into the United State. and forcing them into prostitution. As of 2018, he was the most recent member of the Granados organization to be sentenced since 2013.

Philip L. Reichel

See also: Bilateral Human Trafficking Enforcement Initiative; Human Trafficking; "Loverboy" Recruitment Approach to Human Trafficking

Further Reading

Bello, Marisol. 2015. "Sex Traffickers Are among ICE's Most Wanted." *USA Today*, January 27. Accessed January 16, 2019. https://www.usatoday.com/story/news/nation/2015/01/27/human-trafficking-most-wanted-fugitives/22358301.

Rosenberg, Eli. 2016. "7 Men Accused in Sex-Trafficking Ring in U.S. and Mexico." *New York Times*, November 1. Accessed January 21, 2019. https://www.nytimes.com/2016/11/02/nyregion/7-men-accused-in-sex-trafficking-ring-in-us-and-mexico.html.

U.S. Department of Justice (DOJ). 2017. "Member of Mexican Sex Trafficking Ring Sentenced to 188 Months in Prison." Last Modified February 24, 2017. Accessed January 21, 2019. https://www.justice.gov/usao-edny/pr/member-mexican-sex-trafficking-ring-sentenced-188-months-prison-term.

U.S. Immigration and Customs Enforcement (ICE). 2018. "4 Mexican Nationals Extradited to US for International Sex Trafficking Offenses." Last Modified May 11, 2018. Accessed January 16, 2019. https://www.ice.gov/news/releases/4-mexican-nationals-extradited-us-international-sex-trafficking-offenses.

Green Criminology

Criminologists have long been concerned with crime that directly affects humans, but in the 1990s, a new interdisciplinary approach emerged, often referred to as "green criminology." In its broadest sense, green criminology is the convergence of criminology and environmental issues. Michael Lynch and Paul Stretesky are known as the pioneers in the field of green criminology, and they ultimately helped to expand the scope of crimes that are concerning to the global community to include environmental crimes and injustices toward the environment (Lynch 1990). As of 2018, a handful of criminologists have focused their research on environmental justice. Green criminology studies and examines environmental crime, policy toward environmental harms, ecological justice, and environmental laws (Nurse 2017).

"Green" often refers to the inclusion of the natural environment, which can also include wildlife, climate change, habitat loss, pollution, destruction of plants, and depletion of natural resources, to name a few (Potter 2010). Green criminology is the analysis of environmental harms from a criminological perspective. At the theoretical level, green criminology explores the social, political, and economic conditions that lead to environmental crimes. However, on a philosophical level the main concerns are which types of harms should be considered crimes and who classifies as a victim of green crime (Green Criminology 2012). Primary goals of green criminology are to examine and analyze the causes of environmental harm and to develop policies to protect the environment both locally and globally (Nurse 2017).

AREAS OF STUDY

Taking a green criminological approach requires researchers and theorists to think about how and why crimes are inflicted on the environment, who commits crimes against the environment and why, who suffers as a result of environmental damage, and how the suffering occurs. Green criminology also heavily involves responses to environmental crimes by examining policing practices, punishments, and crime prevention (Green Criminology 2012).

The areas of study in green criminology are constantly evolving. A primary area of study is "green" crimes, which have included pollution, crimes of overproduction and overconsumption, wildlife trafficking, smuggling and poaching, and biopiracy (Lynch, Stretesky, and Long 2017). Another is the reaction to green crimes, which can come in the form of protests about environmental issues, such as marches and public rallies. Additionally, criminologists are interested in the criminal justice system's reaction in such areas as policing and the courts (Potter 2010). Green criminologists also study the impact on victims of environmental harm, which can include wildlife, animals, plants, bodies of water, or people (Lynch, Stretesky, and Long 2017). Additionally, some study activities that are legal, such as fishing, deforestation, and pollution, are deemed harmful to the environment despite being legal.

GLOBAL APPROACH

Environmental protection is one of the fastest-growing areas of both international law and justice. A green approach to criminology requires dialogue to occur at both the national and global levels. Global talks about environmental issues with global leaders demonstrate that green criminology is firmly on the international political agenda and of public concern.

The concern with green issues has been led by scientific research highlighting world problems to various forms of environmental degradation (Potter 2010). Rob White coined "eco-global criminology" to suggest that it is necessary to employ a critical analysis of environmental crime as it occurs in its global content (White 2011). Criminologists who take an eco-global approach recognize that environmental harms incorporate global harms to individuals and social groups that may entail human rights abuses toward the most impoverished or vulnerable nations and people. Additionally, they recognize the millions of deaths that occur around the globe that could be prevented through changes in punishment and policy toward environmental problems (Potter 2010). The eco-global approach focuses on green crimes that are global, cross-national, and intrinsically transnational in nature. Additionally, this approach recognizes the need for collaboration with individuals and countries.

Shanell Sanchez

See also: Basel Convention on the Control of Transboundary Movements of Hazardous Wastes and Their Disposal; Convention on the Prevention of Marine Pollution by Dumping Wastes and Other Matter; Environmental Crimes; Waste Crime; Wildlife and Forest Crime

Further Reading

Green Criminology. 2012. "What Is Green Criminology?" Accessed February 21, 2018. http://greencriminology.org/about-green-criminology.

Lynch, Michael. 1990. "The Greening of Criminology: A Perspective for the 1990s." *Critical Criminologist* 2 (3): 11–12.

Lynch, Michael, Michael Long, Paul Stretesky, and Kimberly Barrett. 2017. *Green Criminology: Crime, Justice, and the Environment.* Oakland: California Press.

Nurse, Angus. 2017. "Green Criminology: Shining a Critical Lens on Environmental Harm." *Palgrave Communications* 3 (10): 1–4.

Potter, Gary. 2010. "What Is Green Criminology?" *Sociology Review, 20*(2): 8–12.

White, Rob. 2011. *Transnational Environmental Crime: Toward an Eco-Global Criminology.* London: Routledge.

Guantánamo Bay Prison Camp

The Guantánamo Bay prison camp is a military prison at the U.S. naval facility at Guantánamo Bay in Cuba. In one of the most controversial aspects of what has been termed the U.S. War on Terror, prisoners held at the camp have been denied the legal protections afforded to citizens of any nationality under U.S. and international law. Legally classified as "enemy combatants," prisoners may be detained indefinitely. An estimated 780 people from more than 35 nations have been kept prisoner at the camp since 2002.

Guantánamo came under intense international scrutiny when the George W. Bush administration began holding enemy combatants there after the September 11, 2001, terrorist attacks. The U.S. military moved its first detainees from Afghanistan there on January 11, 2002. By the beginning of Bush's second term, in 2005, there were more than 500 individuals from more than 35 nations being held there without formal charges and with no access to lawyers or contact with their families, diplomats, or national government officials. The Guantánamo Bay detainees were also denied the rights accorded to prisoners of war under the Geneva Conventions.

The Bush administration contended that detainees at Guantánamo Bay fall into the legal category of "unlawful enemy combatants" and therefore must be assumed to be guilty until proven innocent, though precisely what evidentiary or legal avenues remain open to detainees has been unclear. The administration also argued that, as unlawful combatants, the prisoners do not fall within the scope of the Geneva Convention.

Such human rights organizations as Amnesty International and the International Committee of the Red Cross, as well as former military officials working at Guantánamo Bay, have described the conditions of prison life there. Prisoners are alleged to have been kept in isolation cells for many days at a time; been beaten and otherwise physically harmed; been exposed to aggressive dogs, loud music, and strobe lights; and been kept caged and exposed in outdoor cells during violent tropical weather. Prisoners are also alleged to have been subjected to extremely hot and cold temperatures, been chained in uncomfortable or strenuous positions, and been denied food and water. Other allegations claim that prisoners have had their religious beliefs ridiculed.

One of the most controversial allegations was that U.S. forces abducted foreign nationals, tortured the captives in their native countries with U.S. assistance and instruction, and then sent them to Guantánamo Bay for further persecution and detention. Evidence was presented to Amnesty International, the Red Cross, and the British government that nationals of Pakistani, Chinese, Afghan, Egyptian, Syrian, Canadian, and Iraqi descent, among others, had been detained in this way.

Those known to be held at Guantánamo Bay were denied access to lawyers, and non-U.S. detainees were not given the right to be charged and tried in courts where appeals are possible. Further, coerced testimony and admissions were said to have been accepted as valid evidence against them. A variety of legal rulings by U.S. courts, including by the U.S. Supreme Court, have asserted that Guantánamo Bay detainees have the right to military tribunals as prisoners of war, and even to U.S. military or criminal courts in some cases. Nevertheless, the Bush administration unilaterally declared that any trials of camp detainees would be conducted by a board directly responsible only to the executive branch of the government, with no appeals process available. The board operated from 2004 to 2007.

During his 2008 presidential campaign, Senator Barack Obama campaigned on closing the Guantánamo facility. On January 22, 2009, just two days after taking office, President Obama signed several executive orders relevant to Guantánamo.

Executive Order 13491, Ensuring Lawful Interrogations, banned torture and other forms of excessive interrogations. The order removed measures enacted during the Bush administration and instead required all interrogations to be conducted following the guidelines in the Army Field Manual, which conforms to the Geneva Conventions.

Executive Order 13493, Review of Detention Policy Operations, ordered Guantanamo Bay to be closed within one year and a review of the legal status of the remaining detainees. The order also required the operation of prisoner facilities and the treatment of prisoners to conform to existing international law, including the Geneva Conventions. In addition, the order suspended the use of military tribunals.

The Obama plan for dealing with the Guantánamo prisoners included transferring many to foreign countries, with the remaining prisoners going to maximum security prisons on U.S. soil. However, much of the public and many members of Congress objected to moving prisoners to the United States. As a result, Congress took steps to deny the funding that would be required to close the Guantánamo Bay prison and transfer prisoners. In November 2009, Obama announced that the prison at Guantánamo would not be shut down within the one-year deadline. In 2011, Congress passed a defense spending bill that blocked the funding required to close Guantánamo or transfer prisoners. A few months later, Obama allowed military tribunals of Guantánamo prisoners to resume.

In 2013, more than half of the approximately 160 detainees still at the prison participated in a hunger strike, with about a third of the participants being force-fed through tubes. On May 23, when the hunger strike had been going on for more than 100 days, Obama renewed efforts to shut the facility down. He also announced that he would appoint a senior envoy at the State Department and Department of Defense (DOD) whose sole responsibility would be to accomplish the transfer of detainees to third countries. Finally, Obama indicated that many of the detainees could be dealt with through the U.S. justice system.

As had been the case in the past, that suggestion was met with resistance from Congress, with bills introduced that would bar the DOD from spending money on U.S. facilities to house the Guantánamo detainees or for the transfer of prisoners out of Guantánamo. Some congress members said they would be willing to consider closing Guantánamo if Obama came up with a comprehensive plan for dealing with the detainees. Meanwhile, other congress members objected outright to closing Guantánamo.

Between the arrival of the first detainees at Guantánamo in January 2002 and Obama's 2013 announcement, nearly 800 prisoners were held there; the number had dropped to about 160 by the time of Obama's announcement and was down to 41 when Obama left office. Of the nearly 800 prisoners, 532 were released under the Bush administration and 72 under the Obama administration. Since his 2016 election, President Donald Trump—who had vowed during campaign speeches to fill the prison camp back to capacity—has overseen a continued reduction in its population. As of July 2018, 40 detainees remain, more than 730 have been transferred to other countries, and 9 died in custody (Bowers and Williams 2018).

Nancy L. Stockdale and Philip L. Reichel

See also: September 11 Terrorist Attacks (2001); Terrorism, International

Further Reading

American Civil Liberties Union. 2018. "Guantánamo by the Numbers." Last Modified May 2018. Accessed January 16, 2019. https://www.aclu.org/issues/national-security/detention/guantanamo-numbers?redirect=national-security/guantanamo-numbers.

Bowers, Jeremy, and Margot Williams. 2018. "The Guantánamo Docket." *New York Times*, May 2. Accessed January 21, 2019. https://www.nytimes.com/interactive/projects/guantanamo.

Finley, Laura L. 2008. *The Torture and Prisoner Abuse Debate*. Santa Barbara, CA: Greenwood.

Fogarty, Gerard P. 2005. *Guantánamo Bay—Undermining the Global War on Terror*. Carlisle Barracks, PA: U.S. Army War College. Accessed January 16, 2019. http://www.dtic.mil/dtic/tr/fulltext/u2/a434467.pdf.

Lansford, Tom. 2011. *9/11 and the Wars in Afghanistan and Iraq: A Chronology and Reference Guide*. Santa Barbara, CA: ABC-CLIO.

Saar, Erik, and Viveca Novak. 2005. *Inside the Wire: A Military Intelligence Soldier's Eyewitness Account of Life at Guantánamo*. New York: Penguin.

Strauss, Michael J. 2009. *The Leasing of Guantánamo Bay*. Santa Barbara, CA: Praeger.

Gulf Cartel

The Gulf Cartel is widely recognized as one of Mexico's original and oldest drug trafficking organizations. It is a Mexican transnational criminal organization (TCO) with a diversified illicit portfolio. The Gulf Cartel is primarily engaged in cocaine and marijuana trafficking, as well as money smuggling in the Southern region of the United States. The TCO is also involved in weapons trafficking, human smuggling, human trafficking, oil theft, corruption, disappearances, and assassinations (Beittel 2017). The Gulf Cartel extends from its central hub of Matamoros, located in the northeastern state of Tamaulipas, Mexico, across into the United States, Central America, parts of Europe, and Africa.

ORGANIZATION

The Gulf Cartel operates in a hierarchical structure. At the top of the corporate ladder is the drug lord, followed by the right-hand man and treasurer, and then by a set number of key operators acting as managers in charge of municipal plazas, cities, states, and countries.

While originally destined to be a family dynasty, the group has undergone a high turnover rate of leaders due to intracartel and intercartel fighting. In its original formation in the 1980s, Juan Garcia Abrego succeeded his uncle, Juan Nepomuceno Guerra. Garcia Abrego was to be succeeded by Salvador Gomez; however, Osiel Cardenas Guillen assassinated Salvador Gomez. Cardenas Guillen created the first known armed faction of a TCO.

In 1999, Osiel Cardenas recruited former members of the Grupo Aeromovil de Fuerzas Especiales (Special Airforce Group; GAFES is its Spanish acronym) and created Los Zetas. A total of 32 former GAFES were recruited to carry out assassinations, extortions, bribery, and kidnappings. The Gulf Cartel, along with Los Zetas, perfected a process dubbed "levantones," in which individuals are kidnapped and typically killed afterward. A notable example of the use of violence to exhort control was in May 2002, when the leader and second-in-command of "Los Chachos," a subgroup of the Juarez Cartel, were killed while the Gulf Cartel was effectively taking control of the Nuevo Laredo plaza (Proceso 2003).

HISTORY

The Gulf Cartel originated during the U.S. Prohibition era (1920–1933). Juan Nepomuceno Guerra founded what is now known as the Gulf Cartel. Its proximity to the United States enabled the organization to hold strategic control of a close and direct route into the United States. During the Prohibition era, Nepomuceno Guerra smuggled alcohol into the United States; at the end of Prohibition, Nepomuceno Guerra shifted from smuggling alcohol to narcotics. The strategic control of the smuggling corridors made the Gulf Cartel the de facto TCO in charge of the northeastern corridor and point of entry into the United States, allowing the group to charge nonmembers a fee known as "derecho de piso" (right of usage). A method enforced using the Gulf Cartel's armed wing, Los Zetas.

Although it has lost its place as a power player in the narcotics world, the Gulf Cartel still maintains a strong distribution base in northeast Mexico and has cells out of southern Texas, the Southeastern United States, and part of the Midwestern United States. The Drug Enforcement Administration (DEA) still considers the Gulf Cartel as a great drug threat in the United States (DOJ and DEA 2017). In its current state, the Gulf Cartel has been involved in numerous violent battles vying for control of key routes.

DRUG TRAFFICKING ROUTES

There are three primary routes used to traffic narcotics, air, land, and sea, with each using unique tactics to transport narcotics from point A to point B. The quantity of narcotics trafficked influences the types of route used. It is worth noting that the three routes are not mutually exclusive. While quantity dictates the method of transporting, it does not dictate the route being used. A general example of using small carriers or smaller aspects of a vehicle/aircraft is as follows. If less than a kilogram of cocaine is being smuggled, the TCO has several options. First, they may use a human carrier, known as a "drug mule," who will either swallow the drug in several latex capsules, strap it to their body, or carry it in suitcase. Second, the TCO will use hidden compartments within a vehicle, such as the center console. And third, the TCO will launch the narcotics over the border with a recipient awaiting the small quantity of narcotics in the United States using legitimate border entry points, porous border points, or airline routes.

In a similar fashion, the cartel utilizes porous and nonporous entry points that extend from South America into Mexico and then into the United States. The Gulf

Cartel engages in bribery of airline officials and border patrol officials to ensure that narcotics are not seized. Cessnas and other aircrafts are used to transport large quantities of cocaine that are delivered through traditional means (i.e., retrieving narcotics at the airport's terminal) and unconventional means (i.e., dropping of narcotics in the Gulf of Mexico or in rural uninhabited areas of Mexico, subsequently transported into the United States along the Texas southern coast or southern border.

WEAPONS TRAFFICKING FUELING CARTEL VIOLENCE

In a process dubbed "reverse trafficking" (the same routes that are used for trafficking narcotics into the United States are used to traffic weapons and money back into Mexico), straw buyers are utilized by the Gulf Cartel to legally purchase weapons at gun stores in the United States. Once purchased, the weapons are then sent through the same smuggling routes into Mexico. Weapons are also obtained from military installations in Mexico and Guatemala. They are often purchased from corrupt officers and smuggled to various Gulf Cartel locations. Such weapons include high-powered rifles, bazookas, grenade launchers, and rocket launchers (Pachico 2011). These weapons are used to fuel the intra- and intercartel violence for strategic smuggling routes and key plazas. As a result, it has been speculated that the contraband has increased the number of victims. Indeed, social media platforms have often described active shootings and shown the aftermath of the violent incidents that have unfolded in territories where the Gulf Cartel has attempted to gain control or maintain their ground.

Jairo Patiño

See also: Jalisco New Generation Cartel; Juárez Cartel; Los Zetas; Sinaloa Cartel; Tijuana Cartel

Further Reading

Beittel, June S. 2017. *Mexico: Organized Crime and Drug Trafficking Organizations.* CRS Report No. R41576. Washington, D.C.: Congressional Research Service. Accessed January 21, 2019. https://fas.org/sgp/crs/row/R41576.pdf.

Pachico, Elyssa. 2011. "How Much Is Guatemala Arming the Zetas?" *InSight Crime.* Last modified April 8, 2011. Accessed January 16, 2019. https://www.insightcrime.org/news/analysis/how-much-is-guatemala-arming-the-zetas.

Proceso. 2003. "Tamaulipas: las narco desapariciones." Proceso. Last modified January 18, 2003. Accessed January 16, 2019. http://www.proceso.com.mx/188930/tamaulipas-las-narco-desapariciones.

U.S. Department of Justice (DOJ) and Drug Enforcement Administration (DEA). 2017. *2017 National Drug Threat Assessment.* Washington, D.C.: DEA. Accessed January 19, 2019. https://www.dea.gov/sites/default/files/2018-07/DIR-040-17_2017-NDTA.pdf

Guzmán Loera, Joaquín (El Chapo) (1957–)

Joaquin Archivaldo Guzmán Loera, or El Chapo ("Shorty" in English), became one of the most infamous drug lords in the world. El Chapo came from a small town in Mexico and through the years came to be the head of one of the most powerful drug cartels ever—the Sinaloa Cartel. In 2009, he was named to the *Forbes* billionaires list. He has also earned the distinction of being named "Public Enemy Number One" in Chicago, the first since Al Capone, making him one of the most powerful drug lords since Pablo Escobar (1949–1993).

Guzman Loera was born in La Tuna, Badiraguato, in the Mexican State of Sinaloa, in 1957. His parents, Consuelo and Emilio, were farmers and had 11 children. Although some sources say his father was a cattle rancher, locals in La Tuna believe that he was an opium poppy farmer. His father was also believed to be a relative of Pedro Aviles Perez, a well-known drug trafficker in Sinaloa. With little opportunity in the area, El Chapo began working in the drug trade as a youth. Over the next several decades, he grew to become one of the most prominent drug lords.

RISE TO POWER

In the 1970s, El Chapo began working for a local drug trafficker, Hector Luis "El Guera" Palma Salazar. Throughout the 1970s, El Chapo became more prominent himself, garnering the attention of other cartels. In the early 1980s, he was introduced to Miguel Angel Felix Gallardo, "El Padrino" ("the Godfather"), who was the leader of the Guadalajara Cartel. During this time, Colombian drug cartels were the primary providers of drugs in the United States, but the growing pressure on Colombian groups had increased the number of drugs entering the United States through Mexico. In 1985, Felix Gallardo and his associates, including Rafael Caro Quintero, were linked to the kidnapping and murder of U.S. Drug Enforcement Administration (DEA) agent Enrique "Kiki" Camerena in Mexico. This led to Felix Gallardo's arrest in 1989, which opened the door for El Chapo to grow his own empire.

FIRST ESCAPE

On May 24, 1993, some rivals planned to assassinate El Chapo, who would be at the Guadalajara Airport on that day. Instead, a shootout ensued that led to the death of Cardinal Posadas Ocampo, which was declared by the FBI to be a case of mistaken identity (Saviano 2015). A month later, El Chapo was arrested, and in 1995, he was transferred to the Puente Grande prison, where he spent the next eight years running his operations safely from behind bars. In the early 2000s, however, the Mexican Supreme Court upheld a law that made it easier to extradite individuals from Mexico to the United States. This prompted El Chapo to take action. On the evening of January 19, 2001, El Chapo escaped from prison after stowing away in a cart of dirty laundry.

SECOND ESCAPE

After his escape from the maximum-security prison, El Chapo continued running his empire with close associates Ismael Zambada Garcia, "El Mayo"; Juan Jose Esparragoza Moreno, "El Azul"; and Ignacio Coronel Villarreal, "Nacho." By 2005–2006, Mexican cartels surpassed the Colombian groups with the quantity of drugs being trafficked into the United States. The targeted source control in Colombia led to the increased drug flow through the Mexican-U.S. border.

The Mexican Drug war that began in 2006 led to unprecedented levels of violence near the northern border with groups fighting to control the smuggling routes (Freeman 2006). The number of drug-related murders in Mexico skyrocketed during this time. By 2009, El Chapo had made the *Forbes* Billionaires list and earned a ranking of 41st on the *Forbes* Most Powerful People in the World list.

In February 2014, Joaquín Guzmán Loera was arrested in his beach condo in Mazatlan, Mexico, in a predawn raid. He had escaped 13 years prior and was now arrested for a second time. He was serving his sentence in the Altiplano Federal prison outside of Mexico City, which is famous for having a long list of drug lords held there, including leaders of the Tijuana Cartel, Beltran-Leyva, Gulf Cartel, Los Zetas, and more. On the evening of Saturday July 11, 2015, El Chapo went into the shower in his cell and escaped by crawling through a hole in the shower and through a tunnel that was dug out under the prison.

COMING TO AMERICA

This second escape just showed the power of El Chapo in escaping from a maximum-security prison. Mexican authorities found a well-lit and ventilated tunnel. The tunnel began with a 20-inch by 20-inch opening inside the shower of El Chapo's cell and led to a passage, equipped with a ladder, descending 33 feet underground. This led to a tunnel that was 5 feet 6 inches tall, 28 inches wide, and more than a mile long that ended in a half-built home in Almoloya de Juarez (Shoichet 2015).

In October 2015, El Chapo sat down for an interview with Mexican actress Kate Del Castillo and American actor Sean Penn, which appeared in *Rolling Stone* magazine. Then, on January 8, 2016, El Chapo was arrested in Los Mochis, Sinaloa, after a shootout with Mexican authorities. Initially, he was sent to Altiplano, the same prison he had escaped from in 2015, but he was subsequently transferred to a prison near the U.S. border in Ciudad de Juarez to help facilitate extradition. On January 19, 2017, El Chapo was extradited to the United States to stand trial in New York for drug trafficking. On February 12, 2019, El Chapo was convicted of drug conspiracy and now faces a sentencing hearing at which he could receive up to life in prison (Feuer 2019).

Vesna Markovic

See also: Colombian Drug Cartels; Escobar, Pablo; Gulf Cartel; International Drug Trafficking; Los Zetas; Sinaloa Cartel; Tijuana Cartel

Further Reading

Beith, Malcom. 2010. *The Last Narco: Inside the Hunt for El Chapo, the World's Most Wanted Drug Lord.* New York: Grove Press.

Feuer, Alan. 2019. "El Chapo Found Guilty on All Counts; Faces Life in Prison." New York Times, February 12. Accessed February 12, 2019. https://www.nytimes.com/2019/02/12/nyregion/el-chapo-verdict.html.

Freeman, Laurie. 2006. "State of Siege: Drug-Related Violence and Corruption in Mexico; Unintended Consequences of the Drug War." Advocacy for Human Rights in the Americas, June. Accessed January 19, 2019. https://www.wola.org/sites/default/files/downloadable/Mexico/past/state_of_siege_06.06.pdf

Hernández, Anabel. 2014. *Narcoland: The Mexican Drug Lords and Their Godfathers.* London: Verso.

Hogan, Andrew, and Douglas Century. 2018. *Hunting El Chapo: The Inside Story of the American Lawman Who Captured the World's Most-Wanted Drug Lord.* New York: Harper Collins.

Penn, Sean. 2016. "El Chapo Speaks." *Rolling Stone*, January 9. Accessed January 16, 2019. http://www.rollingstone.com/culture/features/el-chapo-speaks-20160109.

Shoichet, Catherine E. 2015. "Tunnel Vision: A Look Inside El Chapo's Underground Hideaways." CNN, July 14. Accessed January 16, 2019. https://www.cnn.com/2015/07/12/americas/mexico-el-chapo-escape-sinaloa-cartel-tunnels/index.html

H

Hackers

As everyday use of technology has increased, hackers have become a dangerous and permanent part of society today. A *hack* is the alteration or modification of computer software or hardware to use the technology, either legitimately or illegitimately, in new ways (Holt, Bossler, and Seigfried-Spellar 2015, 35). Hackers are individuals with skills beyond those of average computer users, who may use these skills to explore programmable systems and expand their capabilities. Since the 1980s, the hacker community has grown, leading to an expansive subculture that has wide implications for computer security and society as a whole.

A BRIEF HISTORY

Hacking first emerged at the Massachusetts Institute of Technology (MIT) in the 1950s, where engineering students found innovative and unconventional means to solve computer issues through "hacks." As the number of hackers expanded throughout the next decade and the subculture was further defined, a code of hacker "ethics" emerged. Six criteria were defined: access to computers should be unlimited and total; all information should be free; decentralization should be promoted; hackers should be judged by their hacking and not by any other means (race, gender, etc.); art and beauty can be created on a computer; and computers can change lives for the better (Holt, Bossler, and Seigfried-Spellar 2015, 46). At this time, phreakers, or telecommunications system hackers, also emerged and became the first form of hacking to gain a widespread audience outside of computer programming. Phreaking was also the first form of hacking to garner a response from law enforcement and encourage legislation on computer crimes.

In 1983, the arrest of hacker group "414" marked the transition of hacking from computer innovation to criminal deviance. The break from traditional hacking was also emphasized by the Hacker Manifesto, which deviated from the broader hacker ethics, encouraged phreaking, and encouraged hackers to seek knowledge at any cost. Today, hacker subculture has rapidly expanded to include a wide variety of hackers with differing motives. The current hacking culture is generally defined by three norms: technology, the appreciation of computer hardware and software, and the intent to explore and expand the limits of computers; knowledge, the intimate understanding and mastery of computer hardware and software; and secrecy, the use of various techniques to conceal one's identity due to the criminal nature of hacking (Holt, Bossler, and Seigfried-Spellar 2015, 41–62).

HACKER TYPOLOGY

Three types of hackers are defined by today's culture: white hat hackers, black hat hackers, and gray hat hackers. White hat hackers are defined as ethical hackers who legally and legitimately find weaknesses in systems to benefit computer security. Black hat hackers are defined as hackers who have more malicious motivations and use vulnerabilities to illegally gain access to information or to harm systems. Black hat hackers were previously known as "crackers," a term developed to separate criminal hackers from ethical hackers; however, this term is outdated and rarely used today. Gray hat hackers fall in between the two aforementioned hacker groups, as they do not consistently align with the motives of either group. Rather, their motives shift depending on the situation, emphasizing the ethical flexibility of hackers and the ambiguity of the hacker ethics (Holt, Bossler, and Seigfried-Spellar 2015, 60; Lemos 2002).

IMPLICATIONS

Hackers pose a unique problem to society for a number of reasons. First, hacking has presented several obstacles to the criminal justice system. In the United States, the Computer Fraud and Abuse Act of 1986 is the primary law used to prosecute hackers. This act criminalizes attacks against "protected computers," which includes "any computer used exclusively or non-exclusively by a financial institution or the federal government, as well as any computer used to engage in interstate commerce" (Holt, Bossler, and Seigfried-Spellar 2015, 62); this last stipulation realistically includes any computer connected to the Internet, including smartphones and tablets. Several sections defined in this law criminalized hacking, defined as "knowingly accessing a computer without authorization or by exceeding authorized access" (Holt, Bossler, and Seigfried-Spellar 2015, 63). However, the interpretation of unauthorized access or exceeding unauthorized access is hotly contested, resulting in conflicting case law and further disruptions in prosecuting computer crimes.

Second, hackers remain a constant security threat for governments, corporations, and individuals alike. As hackers become more skilled, organizations need to be able to protect their assets and defend information from those who attempt to steal or alter it. To provide the best defense, many have encouraged hiring friendly hackers to defend their organizations, as those who actively participate in hacking are the most knowledgeable in the field. The private sector has more readily accepted this proposal and has hired hackers to protect their organizations; however, government agencies have not followed suit. Some of the most talented hackers may not have a clean criminal record and are therefore passed over for positions. Therefore, the government is left more vulnerable by not hiring the best in the field (Roose 2017; Symantec n.d.).

Lyn LaFave

See also: Cyberattack; Cybercrime; Phreaking

Further Reading

Holt, Thomas, Adam Bossler, and Kathryn Seigfried-Spellar. 2015. *Cybercrime and Digital Forensics: An Introduction*. New York: Taylor and Francis Group.

Lemos, Robert. 2002. "The Thin Gray Line." Cnet.com, September 25. Accessed January 16, 2019. https://www.cnet.com/news/the-thin-gray-line.

Roose, Kevin. 2017. "A Solution to Hackers? More Hackers." *New York Times*, August 2. Accessed January 16, 2019. https://www.nytimes.com/2017/08/02/technology/a-solution-to-hackers-more-hackers.html.

Symantec. n.d. "What Is the Difference between Black, White and Grey Hat Hackers?" Norton. Accessed November 7, 2017. https://us.norton.com/internetsecurity-emerging-threats-what-is-the-difference-between-black-white-and-grey-hat-hackers.html.

Hamas

Hamas (in Arabic, *Harakat al-Muqawama al-Islamiya*; in English, the Islamic Resistance Movement) is a Palestinian terrorist organization that operates in the Palestinian territories of the West Bank and Gaza. Hamas considers itself to be a "national Palestinian movement that works . . . on resisting the Israeli occupation as well as liberating the Palestinian land" (Hamas Islamic Resistance 2017). Hamas does not recognize the existence of Israel as a sovereign state and claims Israel's occupation of Palestinian territories unlawful. The organization is divided into two branches: its military wing *Izz ad-Din al-Qassam Brigade* and its political bureau *Hamas*. Hamas emerged as a spinoff organization of the Muslim Brotherhood in 1987 during the First Intifada. Sheikh Ahmed Yassin, a well-known Palestinian cleric and activist in the Muslim Brotherhood during the 1980s to 1990s, founded the group.

FIRST INTIFADA (1987–1993)

The First Intifada began in December 1987 as a result of the deaths of four Palestinians by Israeli Defense Forces (IDF). The intifada (in Arabic, "shaking off") consisted of a strategy of resistance using boycotts and protests to defy Israeli occupations in Gaza, the West Bank, and East Jerusalem. The main resistance consisted of Palestinians throwing rocks and Molotov cocktails at IDF soldiers. Hamas initially acted as a grassroots social activism group that promoted resistance against Israeli occupation of the Palestinian territories. Additionally, Hamas operated charity organizations worldwide that provided social services to Palestinians, such as food distribution, opening schools, and running medical clinics.

Hamas originated as a charitable organization but transitioned into militant group with the formation of the al-Qassam Brigade in 1991. The brigade's objective was changed to forcibly oppose the political dialogue between the Palestinian Liberation Organization (PLO) and Israel. Hamas first implemented its tactic of suicide bombings in April 1993, in the waning months of the First Intifada (Laub 2014). The fighting ended with the signing of the Oslo Accords, which included the creation of the Palestinian Authority, a self-governing body for Palestinian territories, and recognition of the State of Israel.

SECOND INTIFADA (2000–2005)

The Second Intifada, also referred to as the Al-Aqsa Intifada, started on September 28, 2000, when Israeli politician Ariel Sharon visited the Al-Aqsa Mosque, the third holiest site in Islam. Contrary to the actions of Hamas during the First Intifada, the Second Intifada became synonymous with Hamas's military actions against Israel. Hamas engaged in a campaign of suicide bombings, shootings, stabbings, and rocket attacks against Israeli soldiers and civilians. Israel responded with military incursions into the West Bank and Gaza and air strikes that killed Hamas fighters. International criminal enterprises funded Hamas's military activity during the Second Intifada, and the organization used weapons funneled from international arms traffickers.

TERRORIST ACTIVITY

Hamas has conducted various terrorist activities, including suicide bombings, kidnappings of Israeli soldiers, rocket and mortar attacks on Israeli civilians, and ambushes of Israeli soldiers. The United States declared Hamas a terrorist organization on October 7, 1997, in accordance with Section 219 of the Immigration and Nationality Act of 1965. The European Union, Israel, Australia, Japan, New Zealand, and several Middle Eastern countries also designate the military wing of Hamas as a terrorist organization. Both Jordan and Egypt banned the political party of Hamas from operating in their countries.

TRANSNATIONAL CRIMINAL ACTIVITY

Financing for Hamas's terrorist activity comes from various criminal enterprises, such as smuggling of illicit goods and money laundering. Its smuggling enterprises operate worldwide in funneling financial support to Hamas. The United States is one of the largest markets for the illicit sale of untaxed cigarettes. The smuggling of cigarettes by Hamas sympathizers occurs domestically from low-tax states to higher-tax states. States with high tobacco sales taxes, such as New York and California, create a lucrative opportunity for criminal activity. Applying fake tax-compliance stickers on untaxed cigarettes and distributing them to small businesses for commercial sale is one of the most common tactics used by Hamas.

Charity organizations act as front organizations to launder illicit revenue from criminal activity to Hamas. The money is claimed as charitable donations for Palestinian refugees and for humanitarian aid that is instead used to fund terrorist operations (DOJ 2009). Contributors to the charities can often be unaware of the criminal intent of the organization. Charitable donations to Hamas also originate in Middle Eastern countries as a form of *zakat*, or an obligatory religious contribution.

Besides the smuggling of cigarettes, Hamas also partakes in transnational arms smuggling. The weapons are provided from the Iranian Revolutionary Guard Corps and transit through the Eastern African states of Ethiopia, Sudan, and Egypt before entering Gaza (Cohen and Levitt 2009). Arms are smuggled through a complex set of subterranean tunnels across the Egyptian and Gaza border in the area known as the "Philadelphi Route."

JohnMichael Da Silva

See also: Illicit Trade; Suicide Bombings; Terrorism, International

Further Reading

Bureau of Counterterrorism. 2017. "Foreign Terrorist Organizations." U.S. Department of State. Accessed December 10, 2017. https://www.state.gov/j/ct/rls/other/des/123085.htm.

Cohen, Yoram, and Matthew Levitt. 2009. "Hamas Arms Smuggling: Egypt's Challenge." Washington Institute. Accessed December 23, 2017. http://www.washingtoninstitute.org/policy-analysis/view/hamas-arms-smuggling-egypts-challenge.

Counter Extremism Project. 2017. "Hamas." Accessed December 10, 2017. https://www.counterextremism.com/threat/hamas.

Ehrenfeld, Rachel. 2009. "Where Hamas Gets Its Money." *Forbes*, January 16. Accessed December 10, 2017. https://www.forbes.com/2009/01/16/gaza-hamas-funding-oped-cx_re_0116ehrenfeld.html#530065077afb.

Hamas Islamic Resistance. 2017. "About Hamas." Accessed December 10, 2017. http://hamas.ps/en/page/2.

Laub, Zachary. 2014. "Hamas." Council on Foreign Relations. Accessed December 10, 2017. https://www.cfr.org/backgrounder/hamas.

U.S. Department of Justice (DOJ), Office of Public Affairs. 2009. "Federal Judge Hands Downs Sentences in Holy Land Foundation Case." Accessed December 23, 2017. https://www.justice.gov/opa/pr/federal-judge-hands-downs-sentences-holy-land-foundation-case.

Harmonization of Laws

Harmonization of laws (also referred to as approximation of laws) refers to a process by which the laws, regulations, and legal standards of different states are brought into closer alignment. Harmonization has long taken place in legal sectors such as trade law and contract law. In transnational criminal justice, the primary areas of focus in harmonization are substantive criminal law (ensuring that certain forms of conduct are criminalized and thus punishable) and procedural law (ensuring that differences in how offenses are investigated and how suspects are dealt with do not hamper law enforcement, customs, and judicial cooperation and that human standards and good practice are followed in dealing with suspects and victims).

Harmonization of laws is not intended to make laws uniform. This may be difficult if not impossible, especially if countries belong to different legal traditions, with different approaches to the drafting of law. For the purpose of international cooperation, what is generally sufficient is that countries share a similar approach, major differences or legal gaps are eliminated, and minimum requirements or standards are established and followed.

HARMONIZATION OF SUBSTANTIVE CRIMINAL LAW

The way in which even the basic types of offenses are defined in different legal systems varies considerably. In the day-to-day administration of justice, these differences may give rise to curiosity, but they do not cause particular difficulties.

Difficulties can and do arise, however, in transnational criminal justice. Extradition or mutual legal assistance may be refused if the conduct in question is not criminalized in the requested state or if the expected punishment is below a certain minimum. This is particularly a problem in the case of newly emerging forms of crime, such as money laundering or cybercrime, which may not be criminalized at all in the requested state or only certain aspects may be criminalized. Offenders may deliberately take advantage of differences in laws, by using as their base of operations jurisdictions that lack the criminalization in question (as is widely the case with money laundering).

Harmonization of substantive law is also sought when changing circumstances or changing perceptions lead to international efforts to give a higher priority to preventing and responding to certain types of crime. This has been the case for issues such as terrorism, trafficking in persons, corruption, exploitation of children and child pornography, environmental crime, and racist and xenophobic crimes.

HARMONIZATION OF PROCEDURAL CRIMINAL LAW

In the investigation of offenses, new techniques, such as undercover operations and electronic surveillance, have been developed. Countries that have already adopted them may request mutual legal assistance in other countries that would require use of these techniques, thus leading to efforts to get these countries to update their legislation. The United States, in particular, has been active in this regard.

More widely, international law enforcement and judicial cooperation requires a certain level of harmonization, for example, in respect to what forms of assistance can be provided.

While harmonization of legislation and standards in respect to investigative techniques and international cooperation is intended to expedite and increase the effectiveness of such cooperation, other harmonization is designed to strengthen internationally recognized human rights standards and good practice in the areas of individual rights and equality of treatment. Furthermore, with increasing international mobility, differences between laws can create difficulties for suspects and for victims when they come into contact with the criminal justice system of another country. The problems include lack of transparency, difficulties in access to justice, and diminished legal certainty.

FORMAL AND INFORMAL HARMONIZATION OF LAWS

Harmonization can be achieved both formally (primarily through binding international agreements) and informally (for example, through the adoption of international standards and norms and model codes as well as through regular coordination).

Of these, the negotiation and adoption of international agreements is the most direct route. Over the past century, a growing number of international treaties have given basic definitions for various transnational crimes, and since World War II (1939–1945), many such instruments have sought to raise the standard of human rights and access to justice. Especially in the area of human rights, different monitoring bodies have been established with a view to ensuring more uniform implementation.

The informal harmonization involves, for example, various standards and norms, resolutions, and other so-called soft law instruments. As they are not binding, they cannot have a direct impact on harmonization. However, they can influence the work of practitioners and serve as arguments on the national level to develop new policy, and in this way, they bring different legal systems and criminal justice systems into closer alignment with one another. Soft law instruments may also affect court practice.

REGIONAL HARMONIZATION

In addition to the global instruments, many regions, in particular Europe and Latin America, have adopted a number of regional instruments that have contributed to harmonization. The European Union in particular, with its supranational level of government, has moved very rapidly in the direction of harmonization of many aspects of criminal justice.

Matti Joutsen

See also: Extradition; Mutual Legal Assistance

Further Reading

Colson, Renaud, and Stewart Field. 2016. *EU Criminal Justice and the Challenges of Diversity: Legal Cultures in the Area of Freedom, Security and Justice.* New York: Cambridge University Press.

Gierczyk, Yvonne N. 2005. "The Evolution of the European Legal System: The European Court of Justice's Role in the Harmonization of Laws." *ILSA Journal of International and Comparative Law* 12: 153–182.

Kaiafa-Gbandi, Maria. 2001. "The Development towards Harmonization within Criminal Law in the European Union—A Citizen's Perspective." *European Journal of Crime Criminal Law and Criminal Justice* 9 (4): 239–263.

Weyembergh, Anne. 2005. "The Functions of Approximation of Penal Legislation within the European Union." *Journal of European and Comparative Law* 12 (2): 155–170.

Hawala

Hawala refers to an ancient informal banking and money remittance system. It originated in the Middle East and South Asia in the 10th century in response to increased trading between the two regions. Interregional trade created demand for a safe way to settle transactions across great distances that was also compliant with Islamic law regarding usury. Although hawala banking was primarily created to serve Muslim customers, it is just one of several similar remittance systems and is not necessarily an Islamic institution (Razavy 2006). Some hawala systems have evolved past being just remittance services and offer other financial services, such as short-term lending, currency exchange, and funds management. *Hawaladars*, agents who operate within hawala networks, often use legitimate business to conceal and facilitate the money transfers. Though hawala is most often used to remit licit funds, its existence parallel to the formal banking system and outside of global anti–money laundering laws makes it an attractive system through which to launder money or finance terror (FATF 2013).

HOW IT WORKS

When completing transactions through a hawala network, funds "sent" rarely physically travel to their intended destination. Rather, hawaladars operate with a "two-pot system." In a simple transaction, a customer pays a hawala agent in their location, and that agent calls an associate in the receiving location to pay out that amount, minus the commission fee, to the intended recipient (Razavy 2006). Periodically, the two agents will reconcile their ledgers through net settlement or value settlement. Settlements generally take one of four forms: a "reverse hawala," triangular settlement, value settlement, or cash transport (FATF 2013).

In a reverse hawala transaction, the agent in location X who requested their partner to disburse a payment in location Y would then fulfill a request from the agent in location Y to disburse a payment in his location, X. Because money flows are often not equal in both directions, as greater amounts of money move from areas with strong economies to those with weak economies than from weak to strong, lasting deficits may be settled with wire transfers between the two agents (FATF 2013).

Triangular settlements are used across networks of hawaladars when an agent does not have a direct contact with an agent in a country that a customer wants to send money to. For example, an agent in the United Kingdom has a client that wants to send money to Pakistan. The U.K.-based agent asks a Pakistani associate to disburse money to the local recipient of their client's remittance. The U.K.-based agent now owes a debt to the Pakistani agent. The agent in Pakistan also has a client wishing to send money to Egypt but has no contact there. However, the British agent has a contact in Egypt that owes a debt to him or her. In exchange for settling the debt between the Pakistani and British agents, the British agent will ask the Egyptian contact to disburse the money from the Pakistani client. The Egyptian agent will agree to pay the debt to the British agent. In this transaction, the two debts, that owed to the Pakistani agent by the British agent and that owed to the British agent by the Egyptian, are both settled (FATF 2013).

In value settlements and cash settlements, payment instruments travel from one hawaladar to another. In value settlements, debts are paid not by currency but through an exchange of commodities. Because some hawala agencies are operated by shopkeepers alongside their retail businesses, debts are often paid by waiving payment on goods sold in the store by the supplier. Additionally, debts could be paid by the transport of gold, art, or currency from one hawaladar to another.

In cash settlements, hard currency can be carried from one agent to another or sent electronically. Some hawaladars use the formal banking system to settle debts by wire transfer (FATF 2013).

USES

Hawala networks can be used to remit funds for both licit and illicit purposes. Expatriates often send money to their families in their home countries through hawaladars to avoid exorbitant fees levied on transactions by formal remitters or because formal remitters do not operate in their home country due to underdeveloped formal banking systems in that country (Razavy 2006).

Because hawala banking is often unregulated, it is not subject to anti–money laundering laws, such as customer due diligence (CDD). Ledgers kept by the networks are often inaccessible or indecipherable to law enforcement (FATF 2013). These features make it particularly vulnerable to money laundering and terrorist financing. The 9/11 Commission, based on classified reports created by the CIA, claims that since their move to Afghanistan in 1996, Al Qaeda has heavily relied on hawala networks to transport money between nodes of the operation because the Afghan banking system was so underdeveloped and unreliable (Roth, Greenburg, and Wille 2004).

ENFORCEMENT AND REGULATORY RESPONSES

Law enforcement must be particularly careful when investigating and prosecuting potential terrorist financing or money laundering through hawala networks as illicit funds are often intermingled with licit funds; disrupting networks may have great unanticipated consequences for underdeveloped countries that are reliant on remittances. When the U.S. government shut down the Al Barakaat hawala network in 2001 following claims that the organization was transmitting funds and intelligence to Al Qaeda, the Somali economy collapsed. Wracked by years of war, the Somali economy was heavily reliant on remittances, and Al Barakaat was the largest remittance service operating in the country. It was so large that the United Nations used it to distribute aid because no functional formal banking system existed (Salam 2009).

Hawala networks are largely criminalized if they are not registered or licensed in the country or countries they operate in. Increasingly, countries are allowing hawala networks to operate as long as hawaladars register as money service businesses and follow anti–money laundering measures, especially CDD and suspicious transaction reporting.

Lilla Heins

See also: Al Qaeda; Money Laundering

Further Reading

Financial Action Task Force (FATF). 2013. *The Role of Hawala and Other Similar Service Providers in Money Laundering and Terrorist Financing.* Paris: Financial Action Task Force. http://www.fatf-gafi.org/media/fatf/documents/reports/Role-of-hawala-and-similar-in-ml-tf.pdf

Razavy, Maryam. 2005. "Hawala: An Underground Haven for Terrorists or a Social Phenomenon?" *Crime, Law and Social Change* 44 (3): 277–299.

Roth, John, Douglas Greenburg, and Serena Wille. 2004. *Monograph on Terrorist Financing.* National Commission on Terrorist Attacks upon the United States. Washington, D.C.: Government Printing Office.

Salam, El-Fatih Abdel A. 2009. "War on Terror: Fantasy and Fiction behind the Mythology of Terrorist Financing." *Intellectual Discourse* 17 (1): 1–23.

HEUNI

HEUNI (the European Institute for Crime Prevention and Control, affiliated with the United Nations) is the European regional institute in the UN Crime Prevention and Criminal Justice Program Network of Institutes. It is located in Helsinki, Finland. HEUNI was established in 1981 through an agreement between the United Nations and Finland as one of the regional institutes in the UN Crime Prevention and Criminal Justice Program Network. At the time, corresponding regional institutes had already been established for Asia and the Far East and for Latin America and the Caribbean. Subsequently, institutes were established to serve the African region and the Arab countries.

As the European regional institute, HEUNI has a profile somewhat different from the others, which seek to provide training to practitioners and to conduct basic research. HEUNI serves a region with an exceptionally active criminological community, with a number of different legal systems, and with governments that are relatively receptive to research and innovation in criminal justice. HEUNI also serves a region that has two major intergovernmental organizations that have also fostered international cooperation in crime prevention and criminal justice: the Council of Europe and the European Union.

Europe thus forms a hotbed for innovation in national and international criminal justice and for innovation in research. The lessons learned in Europe, and the good practice developed there, may have wider application. HEUNI has sought to identify these and, through the UN Crime Prevention and Criminal Justice Program, bring them to the attention of the world community.

HEUNI's primary form of activity is the conduct of research projects, either independently or in cooperation with other institutions and individual researchers. HEUNI also organizes international seminars at times as well as smaller expert meetings on specific themes. The longer term research activities include crime statistics (including work on the European Sourcebook on comparative crime and criminal justice statistics) and trafficking in persons.

HEUNI has also assisted the UN Secretariat in the drafting of various documents for submission to the policy-making bodies of the United Nations, including the Crime Commission and the quinquennial UN Congresses on Crime Prevention and Criminal Justice.

Similarly, HEUNI has been actively working on the development of the United Nations' structure for international cooperation and in assisting the Crime Commission with its work. For many years, for example, HEUNI has coordinated cooperation within the United Nations' Programme Network of Institutes, which has expanded to include 18 entities around the world.

HEUNI also seeks to strengthen the ties between the work of the United Nations and other intergovernmental and nongovernmental organizations, such as the European Union, the Council of Europe, the Organisation for Economic Co-Operation and Development (OECD), the Organization for Security and Co-operation in Europe (OSCE), and the Council of Baltic Sea States, as well as various national agencies in this field.

Matti Joutsen

See also: UN Office on Drugs and Crime; UN Program Network of Institutes

Further Reading

European Institute for Crime Prevention and Control, affiliated with the United Nations (HEUNI). 2017. "Publications." Last updated March 2, 2017. Accessed January 16, 2019. http://www.heuni.fi/en/index/publications.html.

European Institute for Crime Prevention and Control, affiliated with the United Nations (HEUNI). n.d. "Entry Page." Accessed August 20, 2018. http://www.heuni.fi/en/index.html.

Joutsen, Matti. 1993. "Crime Institute's Profile." *European Journal on Criminal Policy & Research* 1 (1):115–122.

Hezbollah

Hezbollah is a Shiite Muslim political party and militant group, with its base of operations located in Lebanon. Hezbollah, which translates to "Party of God" or "Party of Allah" in English, originated in 1982 following the Israeli invasion of Lebanon, which instigated the First Lebanon War—also known as Operation Peace for Galilee. Conceived by a group of Muslim clerics, Hezbollah was primarily formed to help Lebanon expel the Israeli occupation and to subsequently establish an Iranian-style clerical regime in the country (Masters and Laub 2014). Currently headed by Secretary General Hassan Nasrallah, Hezbollah retains close political and military ties with the sovereign states of Iran and Syria. On October 8, 1997, the U.S. State Department designated the entire Hezbollah organization as a foreign terrorist organization. Since then, 13 other nations, or entities, have listed Hezbollah, or certain aspects of it, as a terrorist group.

HISTORY

Following the attempted assassination in 1982 of the Israeli ambassador to the United Kingdom, Shlomo Argov, the Israeli Defense Forces (IDF) launched an assault on Palestinian terrorists based in southern Lebanon. Attempting to expel the Palestinian militants, the IDF occupied a strip of South Lebanon, along with the South Lebanon Army (SLA), a Lebanese militia dominated by Christians and supported by Israel. The occupation galvanized Muslim clerics to devise the Hezbollah organization, which was originally organized and trained by a contingent of 1,500 Iranian Revolutionary Guards (Shatz 2004). After receiving funding, training, and personnel from Iran, Hezbollah was charged with disrupting the Israeli occupation of Lebanon.

In October 1983, Hezbollah suicide attacks killed 258 Americans in Beirut, Lebanon, with the U.S. embassy and the Marine Corps barracks being the primary targets. These attacks helped enforce the narrative that the Hezbollah organization was an effective leader of the Shiite resistance (Masters and Laub 2014). On February 16, 1985, Hezbollah issued its open letter, founding manifesto—a public declaration of policy and aims—which vowed the organization's loyalty to Ayatollah Ruhollah Khomeini, Iran's supreme leader at the time. The manifesto continued by calling for the expulsion of the United States, Israel, and France from Lebanese territory. Lastly, the manifesto advocated for the creation of an Islamic regime within the region as well as the complete destruction of the Israeli state (Jerusalem: Middle East Institute 1988).

In the 1990s, Hezbollah began its transformation from a revolutionary faction to a political party. Described as the Lebanonization of Hezbollah, the organization began participating in elections during the 1992 general election cycle, ultimately winning 12 out of 128 seats in parliament during the election (Ranstorp 1998; Alagha 2011). Hezbollah's participation in the general election cycle received endorsement from the supreme leader of Iran at the time, Ali Khamenei.

DOCTRINE

Hezbollah's ideology emerges from the Iranian Revolution (January 1978–February 1979), which called for a religious Muslim government to represent the downtrodden and oppressed (Jewish Virtual Library n.d.). Following the Israeli invasion of Lebanon, and the subsequent occupation by Israeli forces, Lebanon existed in a space ideal for Iranian diplomats to unify the Hezbollah force while discreetly extending Iran's influence in the region (Counter Extremism Project n.d.). As an instrument of the Iranian regime, Hezbollah strived to adopt an Iranian-style doctrine to expel the Israeli presence in the Lebanese political sphere, a style that often included the use of terror to obtain a political objective (Jewish Virtual Library n.d.).

CONTROVERSY

Classification of Hezbollah as a terrorist group has been met with some resistance from various countries and entities, with some bodies choosing to commit to the notion that Hezbollah manages separate terrorist, military, and political wings of their organization. The United Kingdom is one sovereign country that holds this perspective, with bans on both the terrorist (2001) and military (2008) wings of Hezbollah, but not the political wing (Levitt 2018). This ideological stance is often met with dismay from lawmakers and citizens, undoubtedly reinforced by Naim Qassem, Hezbollah's deputy secretary general, asserting that Hezbollah's operation does not unfold under three separate wings (Levitt 2018). Naim Qassem alluded to Hezbollah operating under one complete wing, succinctly affirming that all wings are geared toward the resistance fight. Confounding this issue are the statements of Secretary General Hassan Nasrallah, who expressed concerns surrounding a European designation of all of Hezbollah as a terror group. If that designation were to occur, Hassan Nasrallah claimed that organizational finances would dry up and moral, political, and material support for the organization would run dry (Levitt 2018).

Jessie L. Slepicka

See also: Crime-Terrorism Nexus; Terrorism, International

Further Reading

Alagha, Joseph. 2011. *Hizbullah's Documents: From the 1985 Open Letter to the 2009 Manifesto.* Amsterdam, Netherlands: Amsterdam University Press.

BBC News. 2010. "Who Are Hezbollah?" Accessed June 10, 2018. http://news.bbc.co.uk/2/hi/middle_east/4314423.stm.

Counter Extremism Project. n.d. "Hezbollah." Accessed June 10, 2018. https://www.counterextremism.com/threat/hezbollah.

Jerusalem: Middle East Institute. 1988. "An Open Letter: The Hizballah Program." *Jerusalem Quarterly* 48 (Fall): 1–5.

Jewish Virtual Library. n.d. "Hezbollah: History & Overview." Accessed June 10, 2018. http://www.jewishvirtuallibrary.org/history-and-overview-of-hezbollah.

Levitt, Matthew. 2018. "Hezbollah Is a Terrorist Group in Its Entirety; UK Must Recognize That." Accessed June 10, 2018. http://thehill.com/opinion/finance/370533-hezbollah-is-a-terrorist-group-in-its-entirety-uk-must-recognize-that.

Masters, Johnathan, and Zachary Laub. 2014. "Hezbollah." Accessed June 10, 2018. https://www.cfr.org/backgrounder/hezbollah.

Ranstorp, Magnus. 1998. "The Strategy and Tactics of Hizballah's Current 'Lebanonization Process.'" *Mediterranean Politics* 3 (1): 103–134.

Shatz, Adam. 2004. "In Search of Hezbollah." Accessed June 10, 2018. http://www.nybooks.com/articles/2004/04/29/in-search-of-hezbollah.

Hot Pursuit, International

The concept of hot pursuit (fresh pursuit) is usually associated with the domestic law of common law countries. It allows a law enforcement officer (1) to pursue a suspected felon into private premises without the need for a search warrant, or (2) to pursue a suspected felon who has fled outside the jurisdiction of the officer. In transnational criminal justice, the concept of hot pursuit is used in two contexts: (1) the law enforcement authorities of one state follow a fleeing suspect across international borders, and (2) the authorities of a coastal state pursue and detain a vessel that has fled into international waters. The first is generally considered a violation of international law. However, a number of member states of the European Union have agreed to its use under certain conditions. The second is a maritime version of hot pursuit that is allowed under international law.

HOT PURSUIT ACROSS INTERNATIONAL BORDERS

One of the basic principles of international law is that no state may violate the territorial sovereignty of another state. In line with this, if law enforcement authorities are in pursuit of a fleeing felon, and the felon crosses into the territory of a foreign state, the authorities must break off their pursuit and at the most contact the competent authorities of the foreign state to request that the felon be detained and extradited.

Within the European Union, the 1985 Schengen Agreement and the 1990 Schengen Convention eliminated internal border controls among most European Union member states (all except Bulgaria, Croatia, Ireland, Romania, and the United Kingdom) as well as with the territorially contiguous Switzerland, Liechtenstein, Norway, and Iceland. The ease with which borders can be crossed has led these so-called Schengen countries to agree to allow international hot pursuit.

Article 41 of the Schengen Convention provides that an officer of one state party (state A) who is pursuing an individual caught in the commission of a serious offense is authorized to continue the uninterrupted pursuit into the territory of another state party (state B) without the latter's prior authorization. The same possibility applies when an officer is in pursuit of a person who has escaped provisional custody or who has escaped while serving a custodial sentence.

The conditions for hot pursuit are that, given the particular urgency of the situation, it is not possible to notify the competent authorities of state B of the hot pursuit prior to entry into the territory of state B, or where the authorities of state B are unable to reach the scene in time to take over the pursuit.

The pursuing officer is required to contact the competent authorities of state B no later than when crossing the border. The right of hot pursuit ends as soon as the authorities of state B request this. The pursuing officer has no right, in state B, to enter into private premises or any other places not accessible to the general public.

The pursuing officer may detain the person being pursued, but may not seek to establish his or her identity or make an arrest. These measures can be done only by the competent authorities of state B.

HOT PURSUIT INTO INTERNATIONAL WATERS

In international maritime law, the doctrine of hot pursuit refers to the right of the competent authorities of a coastal state to pursue a vessel that the authorities have sufficient and valid reason to believe has violated any law within its territorial waters (such as drug trafficking, environmental pollution, or illegal fishing). The vessel may be pursued outside the territorial limits into the open sea and be stopped and taken into custody. In this way, hot pursuit is an exception to the principle that a vessel on the open sea is subject to the exclusive jurisdiction of the flag state.

This doctrine has been long established. It has been codified as article 23 of the Geneva Convention on the High Seas (1958) and subsequently incorporated as Article 111 into the United Nations Law of the Sea Convention (1982), which replaced, among others, the Geneva Convention.

The pursuit must have commenced immediately after the offense was committed or attempted, and the pursuit must be continuous. For example, an interruption due to a mechanical or technical failure of the pursuing vessel, or to natural causes such as darkness or bad weather, does not void the continuity of the pursuit.

The right can be exercised only by authorized government vessels or warships that are identifiable and clearly marked. The pursuit may be commenced only after the foreign vessel has been given a signal to stop that has been heard or seen by the foreign vessel. The right of hot pursuit ends if the vessel being pursued enters the territorial sea of another state.

Matti Joutsen

See also: Schengen Cooperation; Transnational, Global, and International Crime

Further Reading

Boister, Neil. 2012. *An Introduction to Transnational Criminal Law.* Oxford, UK: Oxford University Press

Daman, Maarten. 2008. "Cross-Border Hot Pursuit in the EU." *European Journal for Crime, Criminal Law and Criminal Justice* 16: 171–207.

Kleiven, Maren Eline. 2012. "Nordic Police Cooperation." In *Cross-Border Law Enforcement: Regional Law Enforcement Cooperation—European, Australian and Asian-Pacific Perspectives,* edited by Saskia Hufnagel, Clive Harfield, and Simon Bronitt, 63–73. London and New York: Routledge.

Poulantzas, Nicholas M. 2002. *The Right of Hot Pursuit in International Law.* 2nd ed. The Hague: Martinus Nijhoff Publications.

Human Trafficking

Human trafficking, also called trafficking in persons or modern slavery, occurs when a person has been recruited or is kept by means of force, fraud, or coercion with the aim of exploiting him or her. Although there is no universally agreed upon definition, the one provided in the UN Protocol to Prevent, Suppress and Punish Trafficking in Persons, Especially Women and Children (UN Protocol) and the one in the U.S. Trafficking Victims Protection Act (TVPA) are frequently relied upon:

> Human trafficking is the recruitment, transportation, transfer, harboring, or receipt of persons by improper means (such as force, abduction, fraud, or coercion) for an improper purpose including forced labor or sexual exploitation. (UN Protocol)
>
> Human trafficking is the recruitment, harboring, transportation, provision, or obtaining of a person for labor or services, through the use of force, fraud, or coercion for the purpose of subjection to involuntary servitude, peonage, debt bondage, or slavery. (TVPA)

Under either definition, it is clear that human trafficking involves an act of recruiting, harboring, or transporting a person for labor, services, or commercial sex acts by means of force, fraud, or coercion, for the purposes of exploitation, involuntary servitude, debt bondage, or slavery (UNODC 2018). Importantly, any minor who has been persuaded to perform a commercial sex act is a human trafficking victim, even if there has been no force, fraud, or coercion.

Traffickers use a variety of techniques to instill fear in victims and to keep them enslaved. Being kept under lock and key is among them, but methods used more frequently include isolating them from the public by limiting and monitoring contact with outsiders, confiscating passports and other identification documents, using threats of violence against the victims or their families, and controlling the victim's money.

HUMAN TRAFFICKING VERSUS HUMAN SMUGGLING

Unfortunately, the concepts of human trafficking and human smuggling are too often confused, and the distinctions between the two are left unclear. In neither the UN nor the U.S. definition must a victim be physically transported from one location to another for the crime to be an example of human trafficking. On the other hand, transportation—specifically illegal national border crossing—is a required component of human smuggling. There are other distinctions as well. Trafficking, but not smuggling, requires force, fraud, or coercion. Trafficking is a crime against an individual, but smuggling is a crime against the state. The trafficked person is a victim, whereas the smuggled person is a law violator. Smuggling typically involves migrants who have consented to the smuggling.

An act may start as an example of smuggling but become one of trafficking. If a migrant pays to be illegally transported from Mexico across the U.S. border, an instance of smuggling occurs. But if, upon arrival in the United States, the migrant is forced to stay and work without pay, what started as smuggling has become trafficking. In other words, even though trafficking victims may have initially consented, that consent is rendered meaningless by coercive, deceptive, or abusive action of the traffickers.

These distinctions are important for political and public relations reasons. When politicians and the general public confuse trafficked persons with smuggled persons, the reaction is often less supportive toward the trafficked person who is a victim.

EXTENT AND DISTRIBUTION

Trafficking in persons is a multibillion-dollar form of transnational organized crime. Estimates of the extent of human trafficking are inexact due to the clandestine nature of the enterprise, but the International Labour Organization (2017) indicates about 25 million people are in situations of forced labor around the world, including 5 million in forced sexual exploitation.

Women and girls are disproportionately represented among trafficking victims, accounting for 99 percent of the victims in the commercial sex industry and 58 percent in other types of forced labor. Children (persons under age 18) were 18 percent of those subjected to forced labor exploitation and 21 percent of the total victims of commercial sex exploitation.

Instances of human trafficking are found all around the world. Some countries are more likely to be countries of origin, whereas others are countries of destination; but no country is without examples of modern slavery. According to the International Labour Organization (ILO), human trafficking is most prevalent in Africa, followed by Asia and the Pacific, then Europe and Central Asia. When forced labor is specifically considered, Asia and the Pacific have the highest prevalence, followed by Europe and Central Asia, then Africa.

TYPES OF HUMAN TRAFFICKING

Agencies, organizations, and governments may differ in how types of human trafficking are categorized. Technically, all categories of human trafficking are subsets of forced labor, but there is usually a distinction within that category. For example, the organization End Slavery Now (2018) distinguishes among sex trafficking, domestic servitude, bonded labor, child labor, and forced (sham) marriages.

Sex Trafficking

Forced sex trafficking refers to instances when women, men, or children are forcefully involved in commercial sex acts. In many jurisdictions, including the United States, any minor engaged in commercial sex acts is automatically considered a victim of sex trafficking under the law. Sex trafficking often overlaps with other types of trafficking as the victim may be forced to perform sex acts while also in a situation of debt bondage, involuntary domestic servitude, or others. Because they are engaged in commercial sex acts, these trafficking victims are often arrested and charged as criminals rather than being recognized as victims. Efforts are ongoing to find ways to help law enforcement and prosecutors identify, early and accurately, victims of sexual exploitation.

Domestic Servitude

Involuntary domestic servitude often involves foreign migrants, usually women, who were recruited from less developed countries to work as nannies, domestic servants, and caretakers in more developed countries. But as their workplaces are often private homes, authorities cannot provide oversight regarding the work conditions, and too often the result is exploitation of the workers.

Confined to the home, either because of physical restraint or through confiscation of identity and travel documents, the workers may find it difficult to make others aware of their situation. Domestic servitude can also be a form of debt bondage if the person initially agreed to the employment, but the employer adds on fees for recruitment, travel, housing, food, or other items, making the debt one that can never be repaid.

Bonded Labor

Bonded labor (also called debt bondage or peonage) refers to situations wherein persons are forced to work to pay off their own or even their family members' or ancestors' debts. Initially, it might look like an employment agreement wherein work will repay the debt, but it becomes enslavement when repayment becomes impossible. For example, the worker may begin with a $200 debt (a loan, for example) that he or she has agreed to pay through labor. While working, often in brutal conditions and unable to leave, the worker needs shelter, food, and water. The employer tacks on an amount each day to cover these expenses, and the debt grows at a more rapid rate than the worker's pay can cover. It would not be unusual for the debt to be handed down from generation to generation, with children being forced to work under the same circumstances to pay off their parents' or even their grandparents' debt.

Child Labor

Child labor is present in many industries and takes many forms. For some industries, there may be a need for workers that are agile and small of stature. For others, the need may simply be linked to cheap, unskilled labor. A job may be accepted because of the child's poverty, or possibly because the child was encouraged by his or her parents to accept the job to supplement the family income.

Victims of child labor may be forced to commit commercial sex acts; required to do work that is mentally, physically, socially, or morally harmful; or even to be an armed soldier. Child soldiers are trafficking victims when force, fraud, or coercion has been used to recruit or use them. Perpetrators can be government armed forces, but more often they are paramilitary organizations or rebel groups.

Forced Marriage

Forced marriage is one that takes place without the full and free consent of one or both parties, and it typically involves an element of force, fraud, or coercion. The key is that at least one of the marrying partners has not given consent or is too young to knowingly consent. It can happen to either gender at any age, but most victims are women and girls; more than one-third were under age 18 at the time of the marriage (ILO 2017).

RESOURCES

International organizations, national and local governments, and nongovernmental organizations (NGOs) have all been involved in efforts to prevent and combat human trafficking. Especially notable among them are the United Nations Office on Drugs and Crime (UNODC), the U.S. Department of State, and the Polaris Project. A few organizations provide particularly unique information, especially the U.S. Department of Labor, which raises public awareness about forced labor and child labor through an interactive Web page that identifies specific goods that are believed to be produced by child or forced labor within a particular country. For example, blueberries from Argentina are likely to have been provided by child labor and fish from Thailand by forced labor. Organizations such as Slavery Footprint allow consumers to estimate the number of slaves involved in producing materials and products that they use on a daily basis.

Philip L. Reichel

See also: Forced Marriage; *Global Slavery Index*; Labor Exploitation; Sex Exploitation; UN Protocol to Prevent, Suppress, and Punish Trafficking in Persons, Especially Women and Children; U.S. Trafficking Victims Protection Act

Further Reading

End Slavery Now. 2018. "Slavery Today." Accessed July 20, 2018. http://www.endslaverynow.org/learn/slavery-today.

Farrell, Amy, Rebecca Pfeffer, Meredith Dank, and Colleen Owens. 2018. "Human Trafficking for Labor Exploitation." In *Transnational Crime and Global Security*, edited by Philip Reichel and Ryan Randa, 233–250. Santa Barbara, CA: Praeger.

International Labour Organization (ILO). 2017. "Global Estimates of Modern Slavery: Forced Labour and Forced Marriage." Accessed July 20, 2018. https://www.ilo.org/global/publications/books/WCMS_575479/lang--en/index.htm.

Lugo, Kristina. 2018. "Transnational Sex Trafficking: An Issue of State and Human Security." In *Transnational Crime and Global Security*, edited by Philip Reichel and Ryan Randa, 207–231. Santa Barbara, CA: Praeger.

United Nations Office on Drugs and Crime (UNODC). 2018. "Human Trafficking." Accessed July 20, 2018. https://www.unodc.org/unodc/en/human-trafficking/what-is-human-trafficking.html.

U.S. Department of State. n.d. "Trafficking in Persons Report." Accessed July 20, 2018. https://www.state.gov/j/tip/rls/tiprpt.

Human Trafficking and Sporting Events

Human trafficking is the recruitment of persons through means of force, fraud, or coercion for purposes of labor or sexual exploitation (TVPA 2000). Though estimates are notoriously unreliable, some suggest that more than 800,000 people are trafficked across international borders each year (Wright 2013). Eighty percent of trafficked persons are female, and 70 percent of those females are trafficked for the purposes of sexual exploitation (Rieger 2007). Human trafficking is presumed to be one of the fastest-growing businesses of organized crime and the third-largest criminal enterprise in the world, generating nearly $32 billion per year (Finkel and Finkel 2015; Wright 2013). Sex trafficking specifically generates an estimated $12 billion each year.

Global and large-scale sporting events, such as the Olympic games, the FIFA World Cup, and the NFL Super Bowl in the United States, have been labeled magnets for human trafficking, especially sex trafficking (Finkel and Finkel 2015). However, researchers have admittedly not been able to document a consistent, clear link between sporting events and a concomitant increase in sex trafficking. This is due in part to the clandestine nature of sex trafficking as well as differences in how each host country views or legislates sex work and human trafficking. For instance, researchers have noted that there was no significant increase in sex trafficking at the 2006 FIFA World Cup in Germany, partially because sex work is legal there (though trafficking is not). Regardless, no evidence does not necessarily mean the activity is not taking place.

What has been established in the research is that sexual exploitation is perpetuated by the cycle of supply and demand—the demand is largely generated by men looking to buy commercial sex acts. However, these men are often unaware of, or unwilling to recognize, the coercion and involuntary circumstances under which the acts are performed (Wright 2013). High attendance at world sporting events increases the demand for prostitution in host cities and makes recruitment easier for traffickers (Hayes 2010). Traffickers are able to take advantage of travel visas issued for the games by posing their victims as spectators.

THE SUPER BOWL

The crime of human trafficking is often stigmatized as an issue affecting foreign, often Third World, countries. However, the problem is widespread throughout the United States and in all cities. The Super Bowl is the largest annual sporting event in the United States and also "the single largest magnet for sex trafficking [and] child sex work in the U.S. and possibly the world" (Finkel and Finkel 2015). Research has found evidence for this increase in trafficking activity: in 2010, during the Super Bowl in Dallas, Texas, researchers documented a 136 percent increase in the number of online advertisements for female escort services in the adult section of the Web site Backpage.

The Super Bowl draws hundreds of thousands of spectators, and it is estimated that "tens of thousands of women and children are brought to the event to meet the demand for commercial sex" (Wright 2013, 110). In response to the growing concern of human trafficking in the United States, Congress passed the Trafficking Victims Protection Act (TVPA) of 2000, which provides tools to contest the trafficking of persons domestically and worldwide.

THE FIFA WORLD CUP

Around the world, it is generally accepted that "soccer is a male dominated arena with masculine identified constructed areas" (Gould 2010, 31). Not only are the majority of spectators at the World Cup male (Agence-France Presse 2014), the game itself illustrates stereotypical masculine values while indirectly implying that women encompass the opposite stereotypes. These masculine stereotypes present men as strong, dominant, competitive, and active, which suggests that women are weak, submissive, and vulnerable (Gould 2010). Women, in relation to soccer, are portrayed as being attracted to the game only because of the physical attraction they feel for players. Therefore, the only way in which women are accepted at soccer events is in a sexualized manner, not as fans but as objects of male sexual desire (Gould 2010).

This was particularly evident at the most recent World Cup in Russia (2018). While over the past 20 years World Cup tournaments in countries such as South Africa (2010) and Germany (2006) have each held widespread anti-trafficking campaigns, no such campaign existed in Russia (Dean 2018). In Russia, there are no legal protections or services for victims of sex or labor trafficking at the national level. The lack of support or provision for anti-trafficking awareness during this highly publicized global event was in contrast to those campaigns seen at recent World Cup events.

While most researchers agree that there is a significant uptick in prostitution and trafficking during high-profile sporting events, the pro–sex work side of the debate has been unsuccessful during World Cup tournaments. In 2014, the Brazilian government supported the "Happy Being a Prostitute" campaign, which encouraged prostitutes to use protection and obtain medical services. Yet, in the year preceding the World Cup in Brazil, officials claim sex trafficking peaked as young girls from impoverished areas of Brazil were abducted and taken to construction sites where the stadiums were being built (Lillie 2014). This increase in trafficking and prostitution continued through the tournament itself, with the government minimally supporting anti-trafficking campaigns.

Most recent anti-trafficking messages have played off the "red card" that players receive during soccer matches by featuring awareness messages on red cards distributed to travelers and attendees. Officials claim that anti-trafficking campaigns are effective if done correctly (Dean 2018). During the 2006 tournament in Germany, travelers were made aware of Web sites where they could anonymously report human trafficking. In 2010, South African police increased investigations of brothels and other reports due to increased activity leading up to the tournament.

OLYMPIC GAMES

Context is key when interpreting the available data on Olympic games and the presence of sex trafficking. As an example, according to some estimates, the Greek Olympic games in 2004 witnessed a 95 percent increase in the number of victims of human trafficking (Matheson and Finkel 2013). Though controversy surrounds how these statistics are interpreted (e.g., whether the increase accompanied better awareness campaigns, improved methods of identification and reporting), the increase is still notable.

Similar conflicting estimates plagues research on the 2010 Vancouver Olympic games. Matheson and Finkel (2013) reported that the perceived prevalence of sex trafficking depended on whom you asked; sex worker rights' advocates argued that there was no increase, and others—sex workers, frontline workers, and investigators—suggested the games were definitely a catalyst for increased trafficking. More recent Olympic games held in locales like Russia necessitate a broader understanding of the country's perception of sex work. In Russia, sex work is illegal but not considered a major offense (Finkel and Finkel 2015). Because of this, it is unlikely that reliable statistics on sex trafficking are available.

SITES FOR AWARENESS

Although world sporting events are sites for escalated rates of human trafficking, they also provide opportunities to increase global awareness about the issue and prevalence of the problem. Events such as the Super Bowl or the FIFA World

Cup enable host cities and countries the opportunity to showcase their commitment to, and strategy for, combating human trafficking (Hayes 2010). Global sporting events also provide incentives for countries to review and improve their anti-trafficking legislation.

Lauren M. Guyer and Angie Henderson

See also: Human Trafficking; Sex Exploitation; U.S. Trafficking Victims Protection Act

Further Reading

Agence-France Press. 2014. "Brazil's World Cup Crown Mostly White, Wealthy: Survey." *NDTV Sports*. Accessed January 21, 2019. https://sports.ndtv.com/fifa-world-cup-2014/brazil-s-world-cup-crowd-mostly-white-wealthy-survey-1516475.

Dean, Laura. 2018. "A Stage for Human Trafficking: The World Cup in Russia." *Wilson Center*. Accessed January 16, 2019. https://www.wilsoncenter.org/blog-post/stage-for-human-trafficking-the-world-cup-russia.

Finkel, Rebecca, and M. L. Finkel. 2015. "The 'Dirty Downside' of Global Sporting Events: Focus on Human Trafficking for Sexual Exploitation." *Public Health* 129 (1): 17–22.

Gould, Chandre. 2010. "Moral Panic, Human Trafficking and the 2010 Soccer World Cup." *Agenda* 24 (85): 31–44.

Hayes, Victoria. 2010. "Human Trafficking for Sexual Exploitation at World Sporting events." *Chicago-Kent Law Review* 85: 1105.

Lillie. Michelle. 2014. "Sex Trafficking at the FIFA World Cup in Brazil." *Human Trafficking Search*. Accessed January 16, 2019. http://humantraffickingsearch.org/sex-trafficking-at-the-fifa-world-cup-in-brazil.

Matheson, Catherine M., and Rebecca Finkel. 2013. "Sex Trafficking and the Vancouver Winter Olympic Games: Perceptions and Preventative Measures." *Tourism Management* 36: 613–628.

Perrin, Benjamin. 2007. "Faster, Higher, Stronger: Preventing Human Trafficking at the 2010 Olympics." Calgary: Future Group.

Riegler, April. 2007. "Missing the Mark: Why the Trafficking Victims Protection Act Fails to Protect Sex Trafficking Victims in the United States." *Harvard Journal of Law and Gender* 30: 231.

Trafficking Victims Protection Act. 2000. "Victims of Trafficking and Violence Protection Act of 2000."

Wright, Abbey L. 2013. "Cleaning up the Blood, Sweat, and Tears of the Super Bowl [Sex Trade]: What Host Cities Must Do in Preparation for Major Sporting Events to Combat Sex Trafficking." *Virginia Sports and Entertainment Law Journal* 13: 97.

Human Trafficking and Street Gangs

Neither street gangs nor human trafficking are new phenomena. What is new is the perpetration of human trafficking by criminal street gangs. As both street gangs and human trafficking evolve, and as gangs begin the trafficking of persons, unique challenges are presented to policy makers, law enforcement, victims, and communities.

STREET GANGS

Gangs can be found in many forms throughout the world, including street gangs, cartels, prison gangs, and outlaw motorcycle gangs. Essentially, street gangs are a form of criminal association, traditionally composed of young people, who commit illegal activity to the benefit of the gang. Street gangs are different from other criminal organizations in that the processes inherent within their activities enhance criminal involvement and bolster the reputation of the gang. Gangs function and thrive through the use of power, respect, and violence to bolster criminal activity.

In the United States, and throughout the world, immigration, social disadvantage, and victimization often contribute to the emergence of street gangs. As such, gangs use the disadvantaged as a recruitment ground, promising protection, economic opportunities, and a sense of belonging. Gang members and victims of gang violence vary from state to state and country to country, but no race, ethnicity, sex, or national origin is immune from gang recruitment or victimization. In addition to varying in makeup and partnerships, street gangs diverge in level of organization, with few obtaining the organizational levels of established organized crime syndicates or drug cartels.

As gangs age and evolve, many aim to commit less "loud" and more diverse criminal activities. This evolution complements a gang's power and respect and elevates money to the prime motivator for gangs. With the focus on financial success, evolved street gangs often look for new business opportunities that provide cover from law enforcement and an easy profit margin. As a low-risk, high-reward crime, gangs have flocked to human trafficking, particularly sex trafficking, as the crime provides easy monetary gains for the gang (Stearns 2014). Although not a new crime, the involvement of street gangs in human trafficking has increased exponentially both domestically and internationally. As gangs evolve and increase their organizational structures, the opportunities for transnational and global crimes, such as human trafficking, expand.

HUMAN TRAFFICKING

Although most nations legally abolished slavery in the 19th century, slavery continues to exist today. Human trafficking, or modern-day slavery, features persons forced through sexual, physical, or psychological violence to perform such acts as sexual activity, labor, and domestic servitude. International organizations estimate that close to 21 million people have been trafficked, resulting in billions of dollars in revenue to criminal organizations (Ventura 2016). Though the majority of human trafficking victims are adult females or minors, no ethnicity, sex, or nation is immune from victimization. Although human trafficking has existed for centuries, attempts to define and codify human trafficking is a recent development. In 2000, the Convention against Transnational Organized Crime was adopted by the United Nations and included a protocol to prevent, suppress, and punish trafficking in persons. The protocol was the first to establish a definition of trafficking—the recruitment, transportation, or receipt of persons through threats or use of force, to include coercion, abduction, deception, or abuse of power—and has been adopted by 147 countries.

Similarly, in 2000, the United States enacted the Trafficking Victims Protection Act (TVPA) and established a U.S. definition of severe forms of human trafficking and labor trafficking. In the years since the enactment of the TVPA, every state in the United States has created its own version of anti-trafficking laws. Victim advocates have questioned the intent of some states in passing trafficking laws because they are written to curb immigrant migration instead of focusing on protecting victims. Domestically, however, state and federal prosecutors have used the statutes to investigate and prosecute traffickers. The most common form of prosecutions related to trafficking are the use of the federal statues related to child sex trafficking. Federally, and in the majority of states, any prostitution of a minor is considered human trafficking.

As a crime, human trafficking itself is a process. Victims are recruited in their communities and exploited by traffickers for an array of purposes through coercion and control. Human trafficking includes three elements: the act, the means, and the purpose. The act includes the recruitment and movement of persons, the means includes the force or coercion of victims, and the purpose includes the profit from exploitation through compelled servitude. While most envision sex trafficking when considering human trafficking, forced labor and domestic servitude are equally problematic. With the increase in migratory populations, nations in crisis, and economic downturn, opportunities to recruit and exploit victims has increased profits for human traffickers.

STREET GANGS IN HUMAN TRAFFICKING

With an estimated annual global profit in the billions, human trafficking offers a ripe market through the exploitation of vulnerable people. The crime of human trafficking attracts gangs through the consistent stream of revenue, less chance of detection, and the ability to intimidate victims into silence. Trafficking by street gangs takes many forms, including transnational labor or sex trafficking and domestic sex trafficking. The high-profit, low-risk nature of sex trafficking offers gangs a safer business opportunity as opposed to drug trafficking, which can attract more attention from law enforcement and community members. In recent years, human trafficking emerged as the crime of choice for many street gangs. Arguably the fastest-growing business for street gangs, the majority of sex trafficking is international—moving victims across country or continent lines—but also present as a homegrown problem in many nations. Most street gangs use human trafficking for the purposes of sex work.

Similar to street gangs, the first stage of human trafficking is recruitment. Like gang recruiters, traffickers often prey on vulnerable members of a community with promises of lucrative financial opportunities and protection that are ultimately methods of coercion, fraud, and deception. Targets of human trafficking display similar risk factors as targets for gang recruitment, including unemployment, lack of education, substance abuse, abuse or neglect in the home, or lack of supervision. Many street gangs prey on undocumented immigrants and foreign-born victims with promises of transport, jobs, or safety, only to later compel the victim into servitude via threats and violence and the exploitation of fears of being detained and deported.

Street gangs engaging in sex trafficking seek to recruit vulnerable youth, isolate them from the world in rooms or brothels, and subject them to brutal gang rapes and violence. Gangs use drugs, financial tactics, and emotional and physical controls to keep victims subject to traffickers' control. Part of this control includes taking victims' forms of identification and denying all contact to the outside world. Concerning sex trafficking, street gangs utilize the same strategies as "pimps" or other sex traffickers, including using physical violence, initiating a faux romance, or offering a sense of belonging or protection. While some victims initially consent to the trafficking as sex workers or laborers, gangs will increase their control over the victim through threats, coercion, or fraud to continue victimization and exploitation.

Another intersection of street gangs and human trafficking is the ability of the gang to transport victims. Traffickers often rely of extensive means and structured practices to transport victims. Gangs, using drug and weapon networks, often exploit the same connections for the trafficking of persons. These networks can include entertainment networks—nightclubs, bars, motels, and massage parlors—or tourism and domestic networks. Evolved street gangs with stronger organization structures are particularly effective at committing human trafficking as their informal networks, highly structured organizations, access to drugs and weapons, and use of violence provide easily assessable tools to commit the act of trafficking and for the components of force or coercion. Several studies have found that the more structured the gang is, the more likely the members are to participate in drug and weapons trafficking and violent offending. Similarly, the more structured and organized the gang, the more likely the gang is to participate in human trafficking.

CONCLUSION

Evolved street gangs, with highly structured organizations and informal networks, exploit vulnerable populations for recruitment for street gangs and human trafficking. Emerging as one of the fastest-growing criminal enterprises, human trafficking touches every nation through global crime. Armed with reputations for extreme violence and driven by financial motivations, gangs are engaging in human trafficking through the exploitation of victims for the sex industry, domestic servitude, and forced labor.

Jessica C. Smith

See also: Human Trafficking; Sex Exploitation; UN Protocol to Prevent, Suppress, and Punish Trafficking in Persons, Especially Women and Children; U.S. Trafficking Victims Protection Act

Further Reading

Chacón, Jennifer M. 2017. "Human Trafficking, Immigration Regulation, and Subfederal Criminalization." *New Criminal Law Review: In International and Interdisciplinary Journal* 20 (1): 96–129.

Decker, Scott H., and David C. Pyrooz, eds. 2015. "Street Gangs, Terrorists, Drug Smugglers, and Organized Crime: What's the Difference?" In *The Handbook of Gangs*, edited by Scott Decker and David Pyrooz, 294–308. West Sussex, UK: John Wiley & Sons.

Stearns, Joseph. 2014. "Street Gangs and Human Trafficking." In *Combating Human Trafficking: A Multidisciplinary Approach*, edited by Michael J. Palmiotto, 149–156, Boca Raton, FL: CRC Press.

Terwilliger, G. Zachary, Michael J. Frank, and Taryn A. Merkl. 2017. "Human Trafficking and Organized Crime: Combating Trafficking Perpetrated by Gangs, Enterprises, and Criminal Organizations." *United States Attorneys' Bulletin* 65 (6): 123–138.

Ventura, Iris. 2016. "The Rise of Human Trafficking in Central America." *Law School Student Scholarship*. Paper 739. Accessed January 16, 2019. http://scholarship.shu.edu/student_scholarship/739.

Walker-Rodriguez, Amanda, and Rodney Hill. 2011. "Human Sex Trafficking." *FBI Law Enforcement Bulletin* 80 (3): 1–9. Accessed January 16, 2019. https://leb.fbi.gov/articles/featured-articles/human-sex-trafficking.

Humanitarian Law

Humanitarian law refers to the rules designed to limit the effects of armed conflict, whether within or among countries. The rules are designed to protect people during hostilities and to restrict how warfare is conducted. More commonly called international humanitarian law (IHL) to emphasize its global nature, IHL is also known as the law of armed conflict or the law of war. As the International Committee of the Red Cross (n.d.) puts it, "Even wars have rules."

Rather than being based in a single document, IHL is considered to be part of international law and finds legitimacy in several documents. Primary among those are the four 1949 Geneva Conventions for the Protection of War Victims (Geneva Law) and the treaties, declarations, and a convention adopted in The Hague, the Netherlands (Hague Law).

RULES PROTECTING INDIVIDUALS (GENEVA LAW)

Geneva, Switzerland, has been the site for many treaties and conventions related to IHL. One of the first was the 1864 convention dealing with wounded combatants of war. The rules of that original Geneva Convention have been revised, and protections have been expanded to a variety of people. The four Geneva Conventions for the Protection of War Victims adopted in 1949 specifically declare that IHL applies to all cases of declared war or other armed conflict between two or more countries and to conflicts arising within the territory of a state. The Geneva Conventions identify protected persons as including prisoners of war, members of the armed forces who no longer take part in the hostilities, medical and religious personnel, and civilians who find themselves in the custody of a combatant state of which they are not nationals (International Committee of the Red Cross 2018a).

In 1977, two protocols were added to the Geneva Conventions. Those protocols strengthened the protection of victims of international armed conflicts (Protocol I) and noninternational armed conflict (Protocol II). Both protocols also regulated the conduct of hostilities during armed conflict, and in doing so, the protocols are considered to have united Geneva Law and Hague Law. However, it is still instructive to discuss Hague Law separately to have proper context.

RULES REGULATING WARFARE (HAGUE LAW)

Supporting the Geneva Law, which protects individuals from violence during war, is the Hague Law, which limits the right to use certain methods of warfare. Hague Law comes from treaties and declarations adopted in The Hague during peace conferences in 1890 and 1907 and also from the 1954 Hague Convention on the Protection of Cultural Property in the event of armed conflict (International Committee of the Red Cross 2018b). The resulting rules govern the means and methods of warfare and the rights and duties of occupying forces.

Although not part of Hague Law in the sense of their location, several treaties since the 1970s were designed to regulate warfare as an aspect of IHL. In 1975, the Convention on the Prohibition of the Development, Production and Stockpiling of Bacteriological (Biological) and Toxin Weapons and on Their Destruction entered into force. This biological weapons convention was the first multilateral disarmament treaty to ban the development, production, and stockpiling of an entire category of weapons of mass destruction.

The 1980 Convention on Certain Conventional Weapons is also known as the Inhumane Weapons Convention and bans or restricts the use of specific types of weapons that are considered to cause unnecessary or unjustifiable suffering to combatants or to affect civilians indiscriminately. Examples of such weapons include land mines, booby traps, incendiary weapons, and blinding laser weapons. Land mines were also addressed by the 1997 Convention on the Prohibition of the Use, Stockpiling, Production and Transfer of Anti-Personnel Mines and on Their Destruction (typically referred to as the Ottawa Convention or Mine Ban Treaty), seeking to end the use of anti-personnel land mines worldwide. States parties to the Ottawa Convention commit to not using, developing, producing, acquiring, retaining, stockpiling, or transferring anti-personnel land mines (defined as mines designed to explode in the presence of a person and to incapacitate, injure, or kill one or more persons).

The Chemical Weapons Convention (CWC) is a multilateral treaty that bans chemical weapons and requires their destruction within a specified period of time. The CWC prohibits developing, producing, acquiring, stockpiling, retaining, transferring, or using chemical weapons.

POLITICAL IMPLICATIONS

IHL results in political stability especially when other countries intervene in both external and internal conflicts. A good relationship is established whereby a country feels secure when there are universal laws that protect its sovereignty in regard to armed conflict. In regard to the political environment, the major issue is on countries being able to store nuclear weapons as a way of protecting themselves. The decision to use nuclear weapons is viewed as coming from the political environment rather than the military (Fleck 2008).

Melanie Prud'homme

See also: Crimes against Humanity; Transnational, Global, and International Crime

Further Reading

Dinstein, Y. 2016. *The Conduct of Hostilities under the Law of International Armed Conflict.* Cambridge: Cambridge University Press.

Fleck, D. 2008. *The Handbook of International Humanitarian Law.* Oxford: Oxford University.

International Committee of the Red Cross. 2018a. "Geneva Conventions." Accessed September 25, 2018. https://casebook.icrc.org/glossary/geneva-conventions.

International Committee of the Red Cross. 2018b. "Hague Conventions." Accessed September 25, 2018. https://casebook.icrc.org/glossary/hague-conventions.

International Committee of the Red Cross. n.d. "War & Law." Accessed September 21, 2018. https://www.icrc.org/en/war-and-law.

Solis, G. D. 2016. The Law of Armed Conflict: International Humanitarian Law in War. Cambridge: Cambridge University Press.

I

Identity Theft and Assumption Deterrence Act of 1998

President Bill Clinton signed the Identity Theft and Assumption Deterrence Act of 1998 (ITADA) into law on October 30, 1998. The ITADA defines identity theft as any person "knowingly transferring or using, without lawful authority, a means of identification of another person with the intent to commit, or to aid or abet, any unlawful activity that constitutes a violation of Federal law, or that constitutes a felony under any applicable State or local law" (18 U.S.C. § 1028 (1998)). ITADA imposes penalties of up to 15 years' imprisonment and a maximum fine of $250,000 upon any person who (1) steals the victim's identifying information to represent oneself as the victim and opening new accounts in the victim's name, (2) steals and spends money from victim's financial account, and (3) combines the victim's stolen identifying information with fictional information to create fake identities (Sabol 1998). The ITADA also directs the United States Sentencing Commission to provide sentencing enhancements for defendants who are convicted for offenses based on the number of victims involved; whether the offense involves the stealing or destroying of a quantity of undelivered U.S. mail; and the potential loss that could have resulted from such offense. In addition, any equipment used to commit identity theft can be subject to forfeiture. Additionally, the ITADA established the rights to restitution for victims of identity theft (i.e., make amends to or reward someone for (loss, harm, or effort)) (Trost 2017).

The passage of the ITADA authorized the Federal Trade Commission (FTC) to create a centralized repository for consumer complaints, maintain and promote the Consumer Sentinel Network database for law enforcement agencies, and provide educational resources for consumers and businesses (Anderson, Durbin, and Salinger 2008). Victims of identity theft are encouraged to report it at IdentityTheft.gov, which is used to create a report and personal recovery plan based on the individual's financial situation. While the FTC does not investigate or prosecute individual identity theft cases, it only supports federal, state, and local law enforcement efforts to investigate consumer fraud through its Consumer Sentinel Network secure online database. The FTC provides educational resources that include active duty military alerts, information on how to secure personal information, identity theft protection services, and advice on understanding warning signs of business and consumer risk (Milne, Rohm, and Bahl 2004).

David A. Rembert

See also: Cybercrime; Identity-Related Crimes; Phishing; Vishing

Further Reading

Anderson, Keith B., Erik Durbin, and Michael A. Salinger. 2008. "Identity Theft." *Journal of Economic Perspectives* 22 (2): 171–192.

Federal Trade Commission (FTC). 2017. *Consumer Sentinel Network Data Book For January-December 2016*. Washington, D.C.: Federal Trade Commission.

Milne, George R., Andrew J. Rohm, and Shalini Bahl. 2004. "Consumers' Protection of Online Privacy and Identity." *Journal of Consumer Affairs* 38 (2): 217–232.

Sabol, Martha A. 1998. "Identity Theft and Assumption Deterrence Act of 1998—Do Individual Victims Finally Get Their Day in Court." *Loyola Consumer Law Review* 11: 165.

Trost, Jennifer. 2017. "The Impostor Rule and Identity Theft in America." Law and History Review 35 (2): 433-459.

Identity-Related Crimes

Identity-related crimes are those that involve the acquisition or misuse of individuals' identifying information (e.g., personal attributes, distinguishing characteristics) for criminal purposes. Names, as well as Social Security, driver's license, bank account, and credit card numbers are some of the pieces of personal identifying information that are exploited by criminals to commit crimes. There are several types of identity-related crimes, but scholarly attention into the extent and nature of these offenses has mostly focused on identity theft. Criminal justice responses to identity-related crimes have likewise primarily targeted identity theft. Research into identity theft suggests that it is prevalent and that the consequences for victims of these crimes can be, but are not always, severe.

TYPES OF IDENTITY-RELATED CRIME

Crimes in which identity is used as either a target or tool to commit a crime are referred to as "identity-related crimes." From a social science perspective, there are several types of criminal behaviors within this broad classification, including identity delegation, identity exchange, and identity creation, which are each classified as forms of identity fraud. Each of these involves changing identifying information in some way for criminal purposes. Other identity-related offenses include identity restoration, identity obstruction, and identity erasure. There may also be counterparts to each of these behaviors that do not rise to the level of crimes. However, the most researched, investigated, legislated, prevalent, and serious identity-related crime is identity theft.

Identity theft entails the takeover of another's identity, and in the United States, it is defined by the Federal Trade Commission (FTC) as "a fraud that is committed or attempted, using a person's identifying information without authority." The criteria used to identify a crime as identity theft are threefold and include using an actual person's identity, rather than a fictitious one; fraudulently obtaining the victim's information without his or her consent; and using this information to commit a crime, such as a fraud involving a new or existing bank or credit card account. There are some differences in how identity-related crimes—and identity theft specifically—are defined legally from state to state and country to country, but laws against identity theft generally include these criteria and often subsume the other identity-related offenses. The Identity Theft and Assumption Act of 1998 (ITADA) makes identity theft a federal crime in the United States.

LEGAL ASPECTS OF IDENTITY-RELATED CRIME

Both federal and state laws exist to combat identity-related crimes. The main federal statute dealing with identity-related crimes is ITADA. This act is quite expansive, adopting 10 federal criminal prohibitions that extend beyond merely identity theft as defined above. The act includes prohibitions on the production of false or unauthorized identification documents and the transfer of stolen or false identification documents as well as the knowing use or transfer, without legal authority, of identification documents of another person with the intent to commit or aid and abet a violation of any federal or state law a felony. It also criminalizes attempts to do any of these prohibited acts.

ITADA defines "identification documents" broadly to include not only government-produced identification cards but also passwords, account numbers, Social Security numbers and unique biometric data used to identify individuals, such as fingerprints, voice prints, and retinal images. This act provides some protections for victims, authorizing courts to award restitution for attorney's fees, lost time from work for court appearances, damages for denial of credit, and expenses related to correcting a victim's credit history. The act is limited, however, by the fact that legal actions must be initiated following a law enforcement investigation and may not be brought by an individual civil suit. ITADA also directs the FTC to serve as a central clearinghouse for identity theft complaints. The FTC has established the Consumer Sentinel Network, made up of qualifying law enforcement agencies in the United States and around the world, to collect information and coordinate law enforcement activities over what are frequently multijurisdictional crimes.

Most states have their own state identity theft statutes, which generally track many of the same prohibitions as ITADA but vary in their particulars. This makes the accurate collection and comparison of crime data relating to identity theft crimes a challenge. There is also a fair degree of disagreement between states as to the appropriate punishment of identity theft, with some states defining such crimes as misdemeanors and others states categorizing them as felonies. Most identity-related crimes across the nation are prosecuted under these state identity theft statutes. Prosecutions under these state statutes frequently suffer complications stemming from the multijurisdictional nature of many of these crimes. Prosecutions under these statutes also frequently suffer from limited state and local resources directed to nonviolent crimes.

EXTENT AND NATURE OF IDENTITY-RELATED CRIME

The most timely and methodologically rigorous estimates of the extent of identity-related crimes in the United States are published by the Bureau of Justice Statistics and generated through the National Crime Victimization Survey

(NCVS). The NCVS collects information on identity theft victimization, which it defines as unauthorized use or attempted use of an existing account, unauthorized or attempted use of personal information to open a new account, or other misuse of personal information for a fraudulent purpose.

According to the NCVS, identity theft affected 17.6 million, or 7 percent, of U.S. residents 16 or older in 2014. Further, the NCVS suggests that the majority of these identity thefts (86%) involved fraudulent use of existing accounts, such as credit card or bank information; the remainder of identity thefts were composed of misuse of other existing accounts, new accounts, or some other fraudulent use of personal information. Findings from the NCVS also include victimization rates, which indicate that females, persons of two or more races, those age 25–34, and those with annual household incomes of $75,000 or greater have the highest victimization rates. However, identity theft victimization spans all demographic groups.

Although identity-related crimes can be quite distressing for victims in a number of ways, including financially, emotionally (e.g., anxiety, depression), and physically (e.g., poor health), findings from the NCVS indicate that only about 14 percent of victims experienced a loss of greater than $1 as a result of the crime. Of these victims, almost half suffered out-of-pocket costs of $100 or less. This suggests that while identity theft is a prevalent crime and an apparently growing problem, it is often entities other than the individual whose information was appropriated (e.g., stores, banks, credit card companies) that are ultimately financially harmed by identity theft. This may account for the low rates of victim reporting for identity-related crimes; instead, research suggests that victims often opt to resolve the incident with their credit card company or other appropriate entity rather than by contacting law enforcement. According to the NCVS, victims report that most problems of this nature are resolved in a day or less.

The NCVS does not collect information on identity-related fraudsters, nor do other publicly available official sources of crime statistics in the United States. However, scholarly research has investigated the characteristics and tactics of offenders and identified some general patterns. Among published studies, findings suggest that offenders are most often female, African American, and older than the average "street offender" (e.g., in their thirties). It is also not uncommon for offenders to work together in the perpetration of identity-related crimes. Research further suggests that identity thieves often obtain victims' personal information by buying it from other thieves or simply by stealing it from available sources (e.g., mailboxes, trash).

CONCLUSION

Identity-related crimes—particularly identity theft—are a worldwide problem. Broadly speaking, patterns in identity theft reported in other Western industrialized nations (e.g., Australia, England, and Wales) closely parallel those reported in the United States. Overall, this suggests that not only do identity-related offenses impact a substantial number of individuals, businesses, and organizations globally, but given the remote nature of many of these offenses, identity-related crimes are also transnational in nature. Yet, the state of knowledge on identity-related crimes outside these countries is all but unknown. Effectively responding to identity-related crimes will require innovation and cooperation among international law enforcement agencies as well as partnerships with corporations and other stakeholders.

Bradford W. Reyns and Mark W. Denniston

See also: Cybercrime; Identity Theft and Assumption Deterrence Act of 1998; Phishing; Vishing

Further Reading

Copes, Heith, Kent R. Kerley, Rodney Huff, and John Kane. 2010. "Differentiating Identity Theft: An Exploratory Study of Victims Using a National Victimization Survey." *Journal of Criminal Justice* 38 (5): 1045–1052.

Golladay, Katelyn, and Kristy Holtfreter. 2017. "The Consequences of Identity Theft Victimization: An Examination of Emotional and Physical Health Outcomes." *Victims and Offenders* 12 (5): 741–760.

Koops, Bert-Jaap, Ronald Leenes, Martin Meints, Nicole van der Meulen, and David-Olivier Jaquet-Chiffelle. 2009. "A Typology of Identity-Related Crime: Conceptual, Technical, and Legal Issues." *Information, Communication & Society* 12 (1): 1–24.

Rebovich, Donald J. 2009. "Examining Identity Theft: Empirical Explorations of the Offense and the Offender." *Victims and Offenders* 4 (4): 357–364.

Reyns, Bradford W. 2013. "Online Routines and Identity Theft Victimization: Further Expanding Routine Activity Theory beyond Direct-Contact Offenses." *Journal of Research in Crime and Delinquency* 50 (2): 216–238.

Reyns, Bradford W., and Billy Henson. 2016. "The Thief with a Thousand Faces and the Victim with None: Identifying Determinants for Online Identity Theft Victimization with Routine Activity Theory." *International Journal of Offender Therapy and Comparative Criminology* 60 (10): 1119–1139.

Illegal Gambling

Gambling, where something of value is wagered on the outcome of a game of chance, can be either legal or illegal. Depending on jurisdiction, a person can openly walk into a room and bet on a roll of the dice or turn of a numbered wheel. In another jurisdiction, maybe even in the same state or country, such a bet would have to take place secretly and without the knowledge of authorities. How gambling is regulated at the national, state/province, and local levels determines whether it is legal or illegal.

The various iterations of how gambling is regulated by jurisdictions are too numerous to review. For example, it is possible that playing the lottery can be legal gambling when the numbers are purchased in a government-approved store, but illegal when purchased secretly in the back room of a Laundromat next door to the official store. Such differences in regulation make it difficult to define illegal gambling, and, in fact, there is no agreed upon definition that would be accurate internationally or even regionally.

Activities constituting illegal gambling depend on domestic regulations rather than agreed upon standards at international or multinational levels. As a result, there are countries where gambling is strictly forbidden, such as China and in Muslim countries, and there are countries recognized as gambling havens, such as Macau and Singapore. Similarly, in a single country, one can find cities like Las Vegas, Nevada, where many types of gambling are legal in approved settings, but the same activities are illegal in other U.S. cities.

THE ROLE OF ORGANIZED CRIME

When gambling is made legal, a compelling argument is often one based in economics. State-run lotteries, for example, are presented as an opportunity to boost government funds that can be used for projects benefiting the entire community. Illegal gambling operations can also have an economic benefit to the community by providing employment opportunities, supplemental income, and allowing small businesses to survive.

The potential for economic benefit is the primary motivator for illegal gambling—for both the gambler hoping to win and for criminals looking to make a profit. The gambler's demand for game-of-chance opportunities has been met for decades by organized crime networks that are happy to provide illicit services. Albanese (2015) notes that even where gambling is legal, criminals can thrive by offering credit (not available in legal operations) and by providing better odds.

INTERNATIONAL ASPECTS

Traditionally, until the mid-1990s, illegal gambling was mostly a local and regional issue. Because of technological development, gambling opportunities today extend around the globe to places where it might be legal, illegal, or not even yet thought about by authorities. Technological advancement brought transactions faster, easier, and more intensive transfer of money and information. Because of the Internet, it is possible to gamble online without geographic limitations. As a result, the effectiveness of current regulations has decreased, which develops new opportunities for committing crimes. Human card dealers in traditional casinos have been supplemented by electronic dealing on monitors. The borderless illegal gambling world allows the electronic devices in places outside of recognized jurisdictions, such as ships on exterritorial seas or drilling platforms. Growth in cryptocurrency, such as Bitcoins, also makes illegal gambling easier to provide, as this allows gamblers and criminals to engage in the activity anonymously.

The aim of modern illegal gambling is the same as the traditional one: provide a service that people want but cannot otherwise legally get. The difference lies in the more sophisticated tools and measures used today as criminals meet the demand.

Józef J. Doellinger

See also: Cryptocurrency; Dark Web/Deep Web; Organized Crime

Further Reading

Albanese, Jay S. 2015. *Organized Crime: From the Mob to Transnational Organized Crime*. 7th ed. New York: Routledge.

Anon. 2000. Internet Gambling and Crime. 2000. *The Police Journal* 73(1): 25–30.

Carnelley, Marita. 2000. "Illegal Gambling." *South African Journal of Criminal Justice* 13: 106–111.

Dunphy, Kaitlyn. 2014. "Following Suit with the Second Circuit: Defining Gambling in the Illegal Gambling Business Act." *Brooklyn Law Review* 79 (3): 1295–1331.

Harris, Julian. 2017. *Gaming Law: Jurisdictional Comparisons*. London: Sweet & Maxwell.

Holleman, M. Christine. 2006. "Fantasy Football: Illegal Gambling or Legal Game of Skill." *North Carolina Journal of Law and Technology* 8 (1) (Fall): 59–80.

Royce Fichtner, J. 2011. "Carnival Games: Walking the Line between Illegal Gambling and Amusement." *Drake Law Review* 60: 41–66.

Illicit Ivory Trade

The ivory trade is the commercial, and illegal, trade of ivory tusks. This phenomenon affects mostly elephants and rhinos in Africa and Asia and is globally known because of the danger that illicit trade represents for both species, which are also endangered animals. The process that follows this activity usually originates in Africa, where poaching is most common. From there, the ivory is transported to Asia, to the factories, and then to stores. The United States and other countries take part in the final part of the process, buying the ivory at an incredibly high cost. This of course makes the ivory trade extremely lucrative and therefore fuels poaching and other illicit activities in the heart of Africa.

Today, ivory trade is illegal, but it was not until 2018 that China, the world's largest market of ivory, put a ban on the trade. In the 1970s, the ivory trade was legal and became such a profitable activity that, in a decade's time, the elephant population dropped from 1.3 million to roughly 600,000. To regulate trade and protect the species, in 1988, the Convention on International Trade in Endangered Species of Wild Fauna and Flora (CITES) approved the African Elephant Conservation Act, banning the import of ivory into the United States. Even with the ban in place, it has been difficult to control the market, and the high demand of ivory continued to push forward until further action needed to be taken. CITES approved one-off sales of government-held ivory stockpiles in Africa in 1997 and 2008, with the hope of reducing illegal poaching. The reality of the matter is that illicit trade continues and keeps getting worse with every passing year. "Things turned particularly ugly in 2013, when more than 300 fell victim to cyanide poisoning by poachers in Zimbabwe. If things continue at this rate, African elephants may be extinct in as few as 15 years" (Humane Society International n.d.).

In Africa, most of the elephant and rhino populations can be found in Botswana, Kenya, Uganda, Zimbabwe, Sudan, and South Africa; these are also where most poaching takes place. Most of these countries are also home to regimes that fuel their wars and other illicit activities, such as arms trading, through the ivory trade. Because of this, ivory is commonly known as the currency that finances terror in

Africa. Several insurgent groups, such as the Janjaweed from Sudan and others from Central Africa, are known for transporting ivory to the Sudanese border to trade for weapons and ammunition with the government forces of Sudan's president, Omar al-Bashir.

Once the animals are poached, an important part of the process is the correct extraction of the tusks and their transportation. The tusks must be transferred from one place or country to another in full pieces to maintain high prices for selling. From the sources (countries mostly in Africa), the ivory goes to the carving centers. These facilities are mostly in China and other Asian countries, such as Thailand, Malaysia, and India. The tusks are transported mostly by sea from African ports into the carving centers. Carving ivory is considered a form of art in Asia; working on one single piece can take years from the moment it arrives to the factory until it is complete.

Once the pieces were ready to be sold out, the ivory was infiltrated into China's legal market to be offered in stores. This was before 2018. As of now, and thanks to international pressure, the ivory trade is illegal in China. Presently, with the newly implemented Chinese ban on ivory, the situation is taking a turn for the better. Organizations such as Save the Elephants have reported important drops on ivory prices. Looking back to 2014, the cost of purchasing 1kg of ivory was approximately $2,000; in late 2017, the price has lowered to roughly $700. "The 130 licensed outlets in China have been gradually reducing the quantity of ivory items on display for sale, and recently have been cutting prices to improve sales" (Save The Elephants 2017).

With the ban in place and the international community more aware than ever before on the very real threat that this market has set upon elephants and rhinos, today there are higher hopes for the preservation of the species.

Mariana Cammisa and Jéssica Viales López

See also: Convention on International Trade in Endangered Species of Wild Fauna and Flora; Wildlife and Forest Crime

Further Reading

Christy, Bryan. 2015. "How Killing Elephants Finances Terror in Africa." *National Geographic.* Last updated August 12, 2015. Accessed January 16, 2019. https://www.nationalgeographic.com/tracking-ivory/article.html.

Humane Society International. n.d. "Ivory Trade and CITES." Accessed August 20, 2018. http://www.hsi.org/campaigns/dont_buy_wild/african_ivory_trade.html.

Levin, Dan. 2013. "An Illicit Trail of African Ivory to China." *New York Times.* Last updated March 1, 2013. Accessed January 16, 2019. https://www.nytimes.com/2013/03/02/world/asia/an-illicit-trail-of-african-ivory-to-china.html.

Save the Elephants. 2017. "Press and Media." Accessed August 20, 2018. http://www.savetheelephants.org/about-ste-2/press-media.

World Wildlife Fund. n.d. "Illegal Wildlife Trade." Accessed August 20, 2018. https://www.worldwildlife.org/threats/illegal-wildlife-trade.

Illicit Trade

Illicit trade is the movement of illegal goods and services from the producer of the good in question to the final consumer. In an increasingly globalized world, the movement of illicit goods and services has also become global, where demand in one country is met by supply from another. Illicit goods are illegal goods that are freely chosen by a consumer. An illicit purchase is one where the good or service purchased is offered illegally and the buyer can freely accept or reject the product in question (Albers-Miller 1999). Buying a knockoff designer bag is an example of an illicit purchase, because that product has not met the legal copyright and quality standards necessary and the person buying the bag did so knowingly and freely.

Illicit trade is not limited to physical goods; it can also include services such as money laundering and smuggling. These are services that are considered illegal in most countries and are consumed freely by the customers in question. In addition, illicit trade does not only refer to the trade of illegal goods but can also mean the illegal trade of legal goods. For example, if one is smuggling natural resources through containers into other countries to trade, the items being traded are not necessarily illegal; however, the way in which they are transported and delivered to the final consumer is illegal.

TYPES OF ILLICIT GOODS AND SERVICES

Illicit trade has become increasingly global in recent times, partially due to the growth of organized crime. Illicit goods and services can now be collected in one continent, smuggled to another, and marketed in a third (UNODC 2010). Included among the types of illicit goods and services are drugs, humans, wildlife, various consumer goods, and medicines.

Drug Trafficking

Drug trafficking includes the cultivation, manufacturing, distribution, and sale of illegal substances, such as cocaine and heroin. The supply of illegal drugs tends to originate from developing countries and regions, and it travels to more economically developed countries where the majority of demand for these goods lies.

According to 2009 records, the general trend for the flow of heroin largely originated in Afghanistan and surrounding regions and was trafficked to end users in the Russian Federation and Western and Central Europe. The heroin was smuggled to these locations using two main smuggling routes. When being transported to the Russian Federation, the heroin was smuggled through Central Asia, and when transported to Western and Central Europe, the heroin was smuggled across a longer route that crossed the Caspian Sea and Southeastern Europe into the Western and Central nations (UNODC 2010). The smuggling of heroin reflects a trend where illicit demand, which is the demand for illegal goods and services, originates in more economically developed nations, and people in less economically developed nations attempt to improve their standard of living by supplying the illicit goods in question.

Human Trafficking and Human Smuggling

Human trafficking is the recruitment, transportation, transfer, harboring, or receipt of people, by means of threat or use of force, deception, abuse of power, coercion, or giving payment or benefits in control of the victim all for the purpose of exploitation. Some examples of the exploitation that occurs when a person is trafficked include but are not limited to prostitution, forced labor, slavery, and the removal of organs (UNODC 2010). Two key features of human trafficking are the victim's inability to make an informed decision or choice to be transported to another location and their exploitation at the final location. An example of this is when a person is told that they will have the opportunity to work freely in another country, but once they arrive they are forced into work without any compensation in poor conditions.

Human smuggling deals with the illegal entry of a person into a country to obtain, directly or indirectly, a financial or other material benefit. Both smugglers and traffickers move people across borders illegally; however, in the case of smugglers, clients agree to pay to be transported, understand the risks involved, and are free to continue their journey once they arrive at the new location (HRW 2015). An example of human smuggling is paying a person to drive a group of people across a national border illegally, with those people being free to go once they arrived at the desired country.

The global flow of female trafficking victims typically originated in Brazil and Eastern Europe. These victims were then transported to Western and Central Europe as their final destinations. In regard to smuggling, a significant proportion of migrants originated in North, West, and East Africa and were transported to Western and Central Europe as their final destinations (UNODC 2010). In this context, it is interesting to note that the final destination for people transported without their consent, in this case the female trafficking victims, and those transported willingly is the same. The trafficking of female victims is driven by illicit demand in more economically developed nations, but smuggling of migrants reveals a type of illicit services that is demanded in developing nations; that demand is based on a desire of some members of the population to leave the country in question.

Wildlife Trafficking

Wildlife trafficking is the poaching or taking of protected or managed species and the illegal trade of their related parts and products (FWS n.d.). Wildlife trafficking can mean the illegal sale and purchase of protected animals, such as lions and giraffes, or their body parts, such as elephant tusks. The illegal wildlife industry generates between $5 million and $62 million depending on the wildlife parts sold. Most of this money is collected by transnational organized crime groups. These groups help coordinate the procurement, transportation, and sale of illegal wildlife products (UNODC 2010). Two key drivers of demand for wildlife products are status and wealth and the perceived medicinal or health value of the wildlife goods (USAID 2017).

In the early- to mid-2000s, wildlife products were generally smuggled from Central and Southern African to Southeast Asia, China, and Japan (UNODC 2010). In this case, it is possible to see how the convergence of cultural norms, such as the use of certain wildlife products for medicinal purposes and status symbols, can drive illicit trade throughout a fairly large geographical region.

Counterfeit Consumer Goods

Counterfeit consumer goods are goods of usually inferior quality that are made or sold under another brand's name without authorization from the brand owner. In many cases, the sellers of counterfeit consumer goods do not align with the trademark, copyright, and patents of the brand owner, resulting in consumer fraud (Chaudhry and Zimmerman 2009). A common example of a counterfeit consumer good would be fake designer bags, but counterfeiting is not limited to only these types of products. The National Hockey League (NHL) is a company that has had its fair share of experience with counterfeit consumer goods. Between the years 1992 and 2014, the NHL seized more than 10.6 million counterfeit items carrying the logos of its hockey teams. The retail value for the counterfeit items was estimated at $405 million (Balde 2014).

The general movement of counterfeit consumer goods originated in China and was smuggled across the Russian Federation and into Western and Central Europe (UNODC 2010). The desire for counterfeit consumer goods in a more economically developed region of the world reflects a pressure to present wealth that not all citizens of the region are necessarily able to meet. This type of illicit trade is also differentiated by the fact that there is demand and supply by two economically developed regions of the world.

Counterfeit Drugs and Medicines

Counterfeit drugs are medicines that either contain the wrong active ingredient or no active ingredient at all, making them ineffective when taken. These fake medications imitate the brand names and packaging of legitimate medications but often do not meet the legal requirements necessary (FDA n.d.). It is estimated that 1 in 10 medical products circulating in middle- or low-income countries does not meet legal standards or is fake (WHO 2017). The distribution of counterfeit drugs is especially concerning because people in less economically developed countries tend to have less access to health care. Counterfeit drugs make this issue worse because not only do people have to worry about gaining access to health care but they must now determine whether the medication they have access to will actually treat their condition or illness.

The movement of counterfeit drugs generally originated in China from where counterfeit pharmaceuticals were smuggled to countries in Eastern, Southern and Western Africa (UNODC 2010). In prior forms of illicit trades mentioned in this section, the consumer is fully aware of the product or service they are purchasing and its legality. This is not always the case with illicit drugs because the industry is based on allowing a consumer to believe that they are purchasing the legal and effective form of that medication for a lower price.

ILLICIT FLOWS

Illicit flows are the general paths that illicit goods and services move along from the producer to the final consumer. Many illicit goods and services move from developing countries in the southern region of the world to more economically developed countries in the northern region of the world. Illicit goods and services that follow this trend include, but are not limited to, cocaine, gold, and people trafficked for forced labor. Therefore, one can see that the Global North seems to demand a significant proportion of illicit goods and services, and the Global South meets this demand by supplying the illicit goods and services in question. However, this is not always the case. Counterfeit pharmaceuticals are an example of an illicit good being supplied in the Global North with the majority of its demand lying in the Global South. Understanding the movement of illicit goods also offers the opportunity to understand how these flows impact current events as well (UNODC 2010).

Kandyl Kotta

See also: Counterfeit Goods and Money; Counterfeit Medicine; Human Trafficking; Wildlife and Forest Crime

Further Reading

Albers Miller, Nancy D. 1999. "Consumer Misbehavior: Why People Buy Illicit Goods." *Journal of Consumer Marketing* 16 (3): 273–287.

Balde, Lisa. 2014. "NHL Warns Blackhawks Fans of Counterfeit Merchandise." NBC Chicago, May 19. Accessed April 16, 2018. https://www.nbcchicago.com/blogs/madhouse-enforcer/nhl-warns-blackhawks-fans-of-counterfeit-merchandise-259816561.html.

Chaudhry, Peggy E., and Alan Zimmerman. 2009. *The Economics of Counterfeit Trade: Governments, Consumers, Pirates, and Intellectual Property Rights*. Verlag Berlin Heidelberg: Springer.

Human Rights Watch (HRW). 2015. "Smuggling and Trafficking Human Beings." September 17. Accessed April 16, 2018. https://www.hrw.org/news/2015/07/07/smuggling-and-trafficking-human-beings.

United Nations Office of Drugs and Crime (UNODC). 2010. "The Globalization of Crime: A Transnational Organized Crime Threat Assessment." Accessed April 16, 2018. https://www.unodc.org/unodc/en/data-and-analysis/tocta-2010.html.

United States Agency for International Development (USAID). 2017. "What Drives Demand for Wildlife? A Situation Analysis of Consumer Demand for Wildlife Parts and Products in China, Thailand and Vietnam Based on a Literature Review." Accessed April 16, 2018. http://www.usaidwildlifeasia.org/resources/reports/what-drives-demand-for-wildlife.

U.S. Fish and Wildlife Service (FWS). n.d. "Wildlife Trafficking." Accessed April 16, 2018. https://www.fws.gov/international/wildlife-trafficking.

U.S. Food and Drug Administration (FDA). n.d. "Counterfeit Medicine." Accessed April 16, 2018. https://www.fda.gov/drugs/resourcesforyou/consumers/buyingusingmedicinesafely/counterfeitmedicine.

World Health Organization (WHO). 2017. "1 In 10 Medical Products in Developing Countries Is Substandard or Falsified." November 29. Accessed April 16, 2018. http://www.who.int/mediacentre/news/releases/2017/substandard-falsified-products/en.

Immigration, *see* Migrant Smuggling

Intellectual Property Crime

Intellectual property refers to intangible creations of the mind. Those can include inventions, designs, literary and artistic works, and names and images used in commerce. Intellectual property is divided into the two categories of "industrial property" (for example, patents, trademarks, industrial designs, trade secrets) and "copyright" (for example, novels, plays, films, music, paintings, computer programs). There are rights attached to both categories of intellectual property, and those intellectual property rights allow inventors, creators, and owners to benefit from their work or investment (WIPO n.d.).

Intellectual property crime occurs when intellectual property rights are violated. That is, when someone manufactures, sells, or distributes counterfeit or pirated goods for commercial gain, they are committing intellectual property crime (Europol 2018).

IMPACT OF INTELLECTUAL PROPERTY CRIME

In addition to depriving the inventors, creators, and owners of their rightful benefits, intellectual property crime also results in more negative social and economic effects, which include loss of jobs and possible health and safety issues (for example, when unregulated items, such as fraudulent medicine, are illegally introduced into the marketplace). Also, the criminal groups involved will use the profits to finance other illegal activities (Europol 2018).

The economic impact is easier to measure than the impact on consumer health and safety. Europol estimates that IPC was involved in 2.5 percent of world trade in 2013 (about $461 billion), and counterfeit clothing alone cost businesses in the European Union about $49 billion in lost sales.

In the United States, U.S. Customs and Border Patrol (2018) seized 34,000 products in 2017 that infringed on U.S. trademarks and copyrights, threatened the health and safety of Americans, or posed risks to national interests. The estimated retail price of the seized goods, had they been genuine, was more than $1.2 billion. Most of the products seized were wearing apparel/accessories (15% of the total), watches/jewelry (13%), footwear (12%), and consumer electronics (12%). More than 75 percent of the products seized had either China or Hong Kong as the reported country of origin—which may or may not be where the seized goods were actually produced.

TYPES OF INTELLECTUAL PROPERTY

Although intellectual property is conveniently divided into the categories of copyright and industrial property, it is helpful to understand some specific examples that fall into the industrial property category. *Copyright*, *patents*, and *trademarks* are common terms. Two other types of industrial property, *industrial designs* and *geographical indications* may be less familiar. *Industrial designs*, which can be two-dimensional drawings or three-dimensional shapes and models, help make an object attractive or appealing. In doing so, the object's usefulness, marketability, and commercial value is increased. Examples of industrial designs range from the safety pin and Swiss army knife to Band-Aid bandages and Chinese food take-out containers.

The term *geographical indications* (GIs) refers to an intellectual property right that identifies where a product comes from, but it also recognizes the product's special characteristics that are the result of its origins. Examples include "Champagne" being used only when the product comes from the Champagne region of France or a spirit being called "Tequila" only when it has been made in the Mexican state of Jalisco or in specific regions of three neighboring states. Other well-known examples protected by geographical indication include Asiago (Italy) cheese, Darjeeling (India) tea, Pinggu (China) peaches, and Roquefort (France) cheese.

What copyright and the four examples of intellectual property have in common is that each is used by criminals for illegal purposes. An intellectual property crime occurs when an unauthorized person, company, or government produces an item without the permission of the patent holder (a patent violation); reproduces a painting, film, poem, or other literary or artistic work without permission of the work's creator (a copyright violation); or illegally uses an identifying mark in an attempt to convince others that a product is the original (a trademark violation); or makes an item with specific features so that it looks similar to a genuine item (an industrial design violation); or sells something as being from a specific locale even though it is not. It is for these reasons that laws are passed and agreements made in attempts to protect intellectual property.

PROTECTING INTELLECTUAL PROPERTY

There are more than 20 treaties and conventions relevant to intellectual property (WIPO 2004, 241–366). Some of those are administered by the World Trade Organization (WTO) and some others by the World Intellectual Property Organization (WIPO).

A few of the more important agreements include the Paris Convention for the Protection of Industrial Property (adopted in 1883), which applies to industrial property and was the first attempt to help creators and inventors ensure that their intellectual property was being protected in other countries. The Berne Convention for the Protection of Literary and Artistic Work (adopted in 1886) does for copyright what the Paris Convention did for industrial property. That is, the Berne

Convention established a system that gave artistic creators (such as authors, musicians, and painters) the right to control and receive compensation for their creative works on an international level (Gordon n.d.). Other agreements are more focused. For example, the WIPO Copyright Treaty (1996) is a special agreement under the Berne Convention that protects the works and rights in the digital environment, such as information technology, computer software, and program design.

The most widely recognized agreement among countries regarding the recognition and protection of intellectual property rights is the Agreement on Trade-Related Aspects of Intellectual Property Rights (TRIPS). TRIPS is a model agreement that was negotiated from 1986 to 1994 and is administrated by the WTO. TRIPS provides common international rules for the protection and enforcement of intellectual property rights around the world by establishing minimum standards that governments must give to intellectual property rights (WTO n.d.).

THE IMPORTANCE OF PROTECTING INTELLECTUAL PROPERTY

Human progress and well-being depend, in part, on the ability to create and invent new works in areas of technology and culture. In turn, legal protection for the works of those creators and inventors must be provided to encourage their continued innovation. By promoting and protecting intellectual property, economic growth is supported, new jobs and industries are created, and the quality of life is enhanced (WIPO n.d., 3).

Philip L. Reichel

See also: Counterfeit Goods and Money; Movie Piracy; Music Piracy; World Intellectual Property Organization

Further Reading

Europol. 2018. "Intellectual Property Crime." *Crime Areas.* Accessed October 8, 2018. https://www.europol.europa.eu/crime-areas-and-trends/crime-areas/intellectual-property-crime.

Gordon, Jason M. n.d. "International Protection of Intellectual Property." *Business Professor.* Accessed October 10, 2018. https://thebusinessprofessor.com/knowledge-base/international-protection-of-intellectual-property.

U.S. Customs and Border Protection. 2018. "Intellectual Property Rights Seizure Statistics, Fiscal Year 2017." Accessed January 16, 2019. https://www.cbp.gov/trade/priority-issues/ipr/statistics.

World Intellectual Property Organization (WIPO). 2004. *WIPO Intellectual Property Handbook.* 2nd ed. Reprinted 2008. Geneva, Switzerland: World Intellectual Property Organization.

World Intellectual Property Organization (WIPO). n.d. *What Is Intellectual Property?* Accessed October 8, 2018. http://www.wipo.int/edocs/pubdocs/en/intproperty/450/wipo_pub_450.pdf.

World Trade Organization (WTO). n.d. "Intellectual Property: Protection and Enforcement." *Understanding the WTO: The Agreements.* Accessed October 10, 2018. https://www.wto.org/english/thewto_e/whatis_e/tif_e/agrm7_e.htm.

Intergovernmental Organization

An intergovernmental organization (IGO) is an organization that has been formally established by national governments, and its primary membership consists of sovereign states. The treaty that establishes the IGO generally sets out its mandate (purpose), membership criteria, structure, decision-making process, and budget. The treaty (charter) of the IGO provides it with an international legal personality, as a result of which it can establish its own administration (secretariat) and conduct activities on behalf of its member states.

IGOs can have a widely defined mandate (such as with the United Nations), or they can focus on specific issues, such as trade and economic development (examples include the World Bank, the International Monetary Foundation (IMF), the World Trade Organization (WTO), and the Organization of Economic Co-Operation and Development (OECD)). They may also be global (the United Nations), regional (the African Union, the Association of Southeast Asian Nations), or be based on historical, cultural, linguistic, or other ties (the Arab League, the Commonwealth of Independent States).

IGOs provide a framework for the exchange of experience and the formulation of a common policy on issues within the mandate of the organization. All of the examples of IGOs noted above have formulated policy and adopted decisions that relate in some way to the prevention and response of global crime. In this area, the exchange of experience and formulation of common policy can lead to the identification of various aspects of global crime as a threat and to agreement among the member states on what action can be taken. The decisions may take the form of nonbinding statements of principle (resolutions, declarations, recommendations, standards; collectively referred to as "soft law") or decisions that are deemed to be binding on the member states that have specifically agreed to them, for example, through ratification or accession of a treaty drafted by the IGO in question ("hard law").

The United Nations, with its global and general mandate, is the most visible and active IGO in preventing and responding to global crime. It has produced a number of treaties related to drug trafficking, transnational organized crime, and corruption as well as many standards and norms related to crime prevention and criminal justice, and the United Nations Office on Drugs and Crime (UNODC), through its network of field offices and affiliated institutes, provides technical assistance to member states.

Many of the regional IGOs, and in particular the Council of Europe and the Organizations of American States, have adopted regional treaties that deal with specific forms of global crime, such as trafficking in persons and corruption. The European Union, in turn, has pioneered many structures for, and forms of, cross border cooperation in responding to crime. Examples include mutual recognition of decisions, cross border surveillance, the Schengen Information System, Europol, and Eurojust.

Matti Joutsen

See also: International Organization for Migration; Nongovernmental Organization; UN Office on Drugs and Crime; World Bank

Further Reading

Aspremont, Jean. 2013. *Participants in The International Legal System: Multiple Perspectives on Non-State Actors in International Law*. London: Routledge.

Beckfield, Jason. 2008. "The Dual World Polity: Fragmentation and Integration in the Network of Intergovernmental Organizations." *Social Problems* 55 (3): 419–442.

Boehmer, Charles, Erik Gartzke, and Timothy Nordstrom. 2004. "Do Intergovernmental Organizations Promote Peace?" *World Politics* 57 (1): 1–38.

Virzo, Roberto, and Ivan Ingravallo. 2015. *Evolutions in the Law of International Organizations: Legal Aspects of International Organizations*. Leiden: Brill Nijhoff.

International Consortium on Combating Wildlife Crime

The International Consortium on Combating Wildlife Crime (ICCWC) is a cooperative effort between five intergovernmental organizations to bring organized and coordinated support to wildlife law enforcement agencies around the world. Additionally, the ICCWC provides aid, expertise, and assistance to regional and subregional wildlife networks, which act in the defense of natural resources on a daily basis. Established in 2010, ICCWC's mission is to strengthen criminal justice systems while providing coordinated support at the national, regional, and international level, all in the effort to combat wildlife and forest crime. The ICCWC champions an ethos where perpetrators of serious wildlife crimes will face a formidable and coordinated, response to their illicit activities. Following this ethos, the ICCWC works for, and with, the wildlife law enforcement community, aiding the frontline officers who bring wildlife criminals to justice (CITES n.d.-a).

HISTORY AND UNDERSTANDING

In November 2009, five international organizations—the Convention on International Trade in Endangered Species of Wild Fauna and Flora (CITES), the International Criminal Police Organization (INTERPOL), the United Nations Office on Drugs and Crime (UNODC), the World Bank, and the World Customs Organization (WCO)—held a joint meeting in Vienna to design and implement a coordinated approach to combat the flourishing illegal trade of wild plants and animals (UNODC n.d.). During this meeting, these organizations collectively formed the ICCWC, which would help deliver multiagency support to countries combating wildlife and forest crime. On November 23, 2010, during the International Tiger Forum in St. Petersburg, Russia, all five organizations signed a Letter of Understanding and formally launched the ICCWC.

This Letter of Understanding—which is a formal document that sums up the specifics of a partnership being mutually agreed upon—detailed the dangers associated with the illicit harvesting and trade of protected fauna and flora. The ICCWC, through the Letter of Understanding, delineated that harvesting and overexploitation could prompt extinction of these specimens, which would detrimentally impact the livelihood of the communities adjoining these protected fauna and flora. Moreover, the ICCWC outlined the impact that harvesting and trading these protected specimens would have on food security within these adjoining communities as well as upon the inhabited ecosystems. The Letter of Understanding described that the introduction of invasive alien species increased the risk to the inhabited ecosystems because it reduces the ecosystems' natural biodiversity, representing a real threat to the national security and biosecurity of these regions. Finally, the Letter of Understanding discussed the dangers to human health at the hands of cross border smuggling of various flora and fauna, mainly detailing the increased risk of invasive disease spreading because of smuggling activities, which could be life-threatening to humans (ICCWC 2010).

GOALS

Following the ratification of this Letter of Understanding, the ICCWC vowed to cooperate closely with fellow organizations within the consortium while simultaneously promoting several goals for the organization. First, the ICCWC strived to highlight the importance for the fight against wildlife crimes while simultaneously promoting the ICCWC and its goals among governments of states. Further goals included collaboratively supporting national law enforcement agencies, and regional wildlife law enforcement agreements in their response to transnational wildlife crimes. Finally, the ICCWC strived to undertake research into the causes, nature, scale, and value of wildlife crimes and, using those findings, to propose innovative ways to prevent future crimes and violations (ICCWC 2010).

THE WILDLIFE AND FOREST CRIME ANALYTIC TOOLKIT

One such research product is the Wildlife and Forest Crime Analytic Toolkit, which serves as an entry point for national governments, international actors, and practitioners to better understand the complexity of wildlife and forest crime. This tool, built on the technical expertise of all ICCWC partners, serves as a framework for future prevention and response strategies to be developed around. The tool kit includes relevant legislation on wildlife offenses, applicable law enforcement responses to wildlife offenses, judicial capacities to respond to wildlife offenses, and relevant data surrounding wildlife offenses and previously implemented preventative strategies (CITES n.d.-b).

Jessie L. Slepicka

See also: Convention on International Trade in Endangered Species of Wild Fauna and Flora; UN Global Programme for Combating Wildlife and Forest Crime; Wildlife and Forest Crime; World Wildlife Crime Report

Further Reading

Action Guide. n.d. "International Consortium on Combating Wildlife Crime (ICCWC)." Accessed May 15, 2018. http://actionguide.info/m/inits/134.

CITES. n.d.-a. "International Consortium on Combating Wildlife Crime." Accessed May 15, 2018. https://cites.org/eng/prog/iccwc.php.

CITES. n.d.-b. "Tools: The Wildlife and Forest Crime Analytic Toolkit." Accessed May 15, 2018. https://cites.org/eng/prog/iccwc.php/Tools.

ICCWC. 2010. "Letter of Understanding: Establishing the International Consortium on Combating Wildlife Crime." Accessed May 15, 2018. https://cites.org/sites/default/files/i/iccwc/mou_0.pdf.

Scanlon, John E., and Lisa Farroway. 2016. "Organisational Consortiums: The International Consortium on Combating Wildlife Crime (ICCWC)." In *Environmental Crime and Collaborative State Intervention*, edited by Grant Pink and Robert Douglas White, 77–99. London: Palgrave Macmillan.

United Nations Office on Drugs and Crime (UNODC). n.d. "Wildlife and Forest Crime: ICCWC." Accessed May 15, 2018. https://www.unodc.org/unodc/en/wildlife-and-forest-crime/iccwc.html.

International Convention for the Suppression of the Financing of Terrorism

The International Convention for the Suppression of the Financing of Terrorism, also known as the Terrorist Financing Convention, is an international treaty issued under the auspices of the United Nations. The main aim in creating the instrument is to help states prevent and counteract the financing of terrorists and terrorist organizations. The source of the financing is a side issue. It does not matter whether money comes directly or indirectly from other organizations or private entities or whether financing activity is primary, subsidiary, or only incidental. All domestic or international tools should respect legal and free capital transfers, with control of dubious fund movements at the same time. The incentives to issue this convention were an increasing number of terrorist attacks, lack of appropriate regulations in relation to financing of terrorism in current legal systems, and an awareness of how financial resources affected the number of attacks that could be carried out. The convention was adopted by the UN General Assembly on December 9, 1999, and as of 2018, it had 188 parties. The inherent part of this treaty is the annex, which contains a list of nine international conventions concerning various aspects of terrorism.

CHARACTERISTIC OF CRIME AND PERPETRATOR

The convention does not define terrorism; however, the annex lists the specific terrorist crimes, while the assumption of this treaty is penalization of financing of terrorism itself. First, Article 2 of the convention, in a very detailed way, describes what kinds of activities should be recognized as offenses. The crime is committed when the perpetrator illegally and intentionally provides or collects funds that are intended to be used for the activities mentioned in the convention, as well as other acts that are committed to intimidate a society, to blackmail the government or organization, or to cause death or serious injuries. Second, offense is also committed by an entity that is a coperpetrator, instigator, or accessory. Third, the convention also takes into consideration cases where crime is committed by a representative of a legal person, but that does not exclude their individual responsibility at the same time on a criminal, civil, or administrative level. When the suspect is going to be transferred or extradited to another country, they should be provided rights to contact (or visit) with the representative of the country of their citizenship. Any kind of the offense cannot be justified by political, philosophical, ideological, racial, ethnic, religious, or other views.

PRECAUTIONARY MEASURES

According to conventional guidelines, all state parties are obliged to apply some measures to standardize proceedings and to coordinate actions. All parties have to inform the secretary-general of the United Nations about the situation, when they are competent to examine the particular case. Measures to be taken are divided into those that concern the object of the crime and those that concern the subject of the crime. The first group includes instruments to identify, detect, and freeze funds that were used to commit crimes and can be forfeitable or partially used as compensation for victims. The second group contains conditions of taking the suspect into custody (temporarily) as well as regulation of extradition.

INTERNATIONAL COOPERATION

The basic and main indication of international cooperation is assistance. The widest scope of assistance concerns legal aspects. Parties should support each other both in the investigative stage and during trial, especially in the matter of collecting evidence and information exchange (also through INTERPOL). Article 18 of the convention enumerates in detail spheres of cooperation. States are obliged to forbid all kind of activities that lead to encouraging, instigating, or organizing any offenses mentioned above. Financial institutions are entitled to verify their clients and fund movements when they seem to be unusual or suspect. The same applies to bank accounts, which cannot be opened if the owner is unidentified, as well as to money transactions, which should be controlled and reported in the case of unusual amounts or proceedings. Moreover, those institutions have to store at least five years of financial documentation. Additional protection requires some limitation (by licensing, for example) of subjects able to deal with money transactions as well as cash or securities tracking (including cross border transportation).

Józef J. Doellinger

See also: Crime-Terrorism Nexus; Global Counterterrorism Forum; National Counterterrorism Center; U.S. International Money Laundering Abatement and Anti-Terrorist Financing Act

Further Reading

Barrett, Richard. 2011. "Preventing the Financing of Terrorism." *Case Western Reserve Journal of International Law* 44: 719–736.

Gardella, Anna. 2003–2004. "The Fight against the Financing of Terrorism between Judicial and Regulatory Cooperation." *Studies in International Financial, Economic and Technology Law* 6: 109–147.

McCulloch, Jude, Sharon Pickering, Rob McQueen, and Joo-Cheong Tham. 2004. "Suppressing the Financing of Terrorism." *Current Issues in Criminal Justice* 16: 71–78.

Pieth, Mark. 2006. "Criminalizing the Financing of Terrorism." *Journal of International Criminal Justice* 4: 1074–1086.

Smallwood, Joy. 2005. "Combating the Financing of Terrorism: The Roles of the IMF." *Villanova Law Review* 50: 645–654.

International Court of Justice

Established in June 1945 by the United Nations Charter, the International Court of Justice (ICJ) is the main judicial organ of the United Nations. It is responsible for the settlement of legal disputes between member states in accordance with international law and for providing legal guidance to the various UN organs and specialized agencies. The court is based in The Hague, in the Netherlands, and is composed of 15 judges, each elected for a nine-year term by the UN General Assembly and the UN Security Council. The work of the court is supported by a Registry, which acts as its Secretariat. Its official languages are English and French. Because the statute of the ICJ is part of the UN Charter, all member states of the United Nations are parties to the statute.

HISTORY

The Permanent Court of International Justice (PCIJ), the predecessor to the ICJ, was created in December 1920 to resolve conflicts between states. The PCIJ was based in The Hague and was initially well received. However, with increasing international tensions during the 1930s and the ultimate outbreak of World War II in 1939, the PCIJ became obsolete. Upon the conclusion of World War II in 1945, and the creation of the United Nations that same year, the founding members of the United Nations decided to replace the PCIJ to dissociate it from the reputation of inactivity that it had gained. The PCIJ was officially dissolved in April 1946.

The UN Charter, the founding document of the United Nations, entered into force on October 24, 1945, and concurrently created the ICJ. The ICJ was established as one of the six principal organs of the United Nations, with the intent to give willing states a platform to resolve disputes peacefully and avoid violent conflict.

STRUCTURE

The ICJ consists of 15 judges, otherwise referred to as "members," all of whom must be nationals of different states. The judges must individually possess the highest moral character and qualifications and collectively represent the diversity of global legal systems. Upon request by the UN secretary-general, the judges are nominated by national groups of the Permanent Court of Arbitration, an intergovernmental organization that serves as a registry for international arbitration. The names of the judges are then sent to the UN General Assembly and UN Security Council, where judges must obtain an absolute majority to be considered elected. If two judges of the same nationality are considered elected, only the eldest of the two is elected. A judge may be dismissed only by a unanimous decision by the other judges.

Every three years, the judges elect the president and vice-president of the court by absolute majority through a secret ballot. All hearings at the court are presided over by the president. The president is also responsible for directing and supervising the court's budget. The vice-president performs the duties of the president whenever the president is unable to do so. Both the president and vice-president are eligible for reelection.

The Registrar is elected for a seven-year term by the court. The Registrar's duties are split into three categories: judicial, diplomatic, and administrative duties. Judicially, the Registrar oversees all documents relating to a case, manages the proceedings in the case, signs documents produced by the court, and supervises the translating and publishing of court documents. Diplomatically, the Registrar manages all external communication, including correspondence with case parties, member states of the United Nations, and the press. In terms of administration, the Registrar prepares and implements the court's budget and oversees all administrative tasks within the court.

BUDGET

The expenses of the court are paid for by the United Nations, which is funded by contributions from member states. If a state that is not member to the United Nations is party to a case at the ICJ, the court fixes the amount that the state must contribute toward the expenses of the court.

JURISDICTION

The court exercises consensual jurisdiction, which means that the court can only undertake cases where all parties agree to refer the case to the court and accept the court's jurisdiction. In these conditions, the court undertakes all cases that relate to legal disputes over interpretations of a treaty, international law, and international obligations. The court bases its decisions on international conventions, international custom, widely accepted general principles of law, and treaties.

COURT PROCEEDINGS

Cases are brought before the court by written notifications to the Registrar by states to appear before the court or by the UN secretary-general, who notifies members of the United Nations. The trial consists of written and oral parts. In the written part, the court and parties exchange memorials, countermemorials, replies, papers, and documents through the Registrar. The oral part consists of the court's hearing of witnesses, experts, agents, counsel, and advocates. If the president is unable to preside over the hearing, the vice-president presides; if they are unable, the senior judge presides. The hearings are public unless the case parties request otherwise.

Decisions in the court are made by majority vote by those judges present. If the result is a tie, the presiding judge will cast the deciding vote. Decisions made by the court are not legally binding, meaning that the case parties are not obligated to carry out the decisions unless they so choose. Decisions by the court cannot be appealed.

ADVISORY OPINIONS

Upon request of the United Nations or its agencies, the court may provide advisory opinions to legal questions. The Registrar is responsible for notifying all relevant states entitled to appear before court. After notifying the UN secretary-general, member states of the United Nations, and any other concerned parties, the court delivers its advisory opinion in open court.

Ariun Enkhsaikhan

See also: International Criminal Court

Further Reading

Bordin, Fernando Lusa. 2015. "Procedural Developments at the International Court of Justice." *Law & Practice of International Courts & Tribunals* 14 (2): 340–364.

Jennings, Robert Y. 1995. "The International Court of Justice after Fifty Years." *American Journal of Law* 89 (3): 493–505.

Thirlway, Hugh. 2016. "The International Court of Justice: Cruising Ahead at 70." *Leiden Journal of International Law* 29 (4): 1103–1119.

United Nations. 1945. Charter of the United Nations. http://www.un.org/en/charter-united-nations/

International Crime, *see* Transnational, Global, and International Crime

International Criminal Court

The International Criminal Court (ICC) continues a tradition in international criminal justice to form courts to prosecute violations of international criminal law. The Nuremburg Tribunals, established after World War II (1939–1945), were the first instance of such courts in the 20th century, followed by the ad hoc international tribunals established by the United Nations after conflicts in the former Yugoslavia and Rwanda. The ICC differs from its forerunners by being the first permanent international tribunal.

Originally established by the Rome Statute on July 17, 1998, the ICC was officially ratified in April 2002 and entered into force in July of that same year. As of

2018, there were 123 countries that had ratified or acceded the treaty and are therefore legally bound by its provisions. The United States has not signed the Rome Statute and, therefore, is not subject to its provisions.

An independent, international organization, the ICC is located at The Hague, in the Netherlands. It is not part of the United Nations, but it is linked, as the UN Security Council may refer cases to the ICC or ask it to defer investigation or prosecution. The ICC comprises four organs: the presidency, which includes the president, first vice president, and second vice president; the Chambers, which is divided into the appeals division, trial division, and pretrial division; the Office of the Prosecutor, which holds the responsibility of obtaining referrals of situations and crimes within the scope of the ICC; and the Registry, which is responsible for all nonjudicial aspects of the ICC. Eighteen judges preside over the ICC. Judges can hold office for a term of nine years, after which time they are not eligible for reelection. However, judges may alternatively be elected for three- and six-year terms and in these cases are eligible for reelection as long as the total time served is not more than nine years.

INVESTIGATIONS

The ICC prosecutes genocide, crimes against humanity, and war crimes based on the complementarity principle—that is, it only intervenes in such cases when the signing countries are unable or unwilling to intervene. Since its inception, 32 arrest warrants have been issued, and 26 cases have come before the court. Among the early cases were inquiries into war crimes committed in the Democratic Republic of Congo, Uganda, and the Central African Republic. Each of those were referred to the court by the governments of the states in question. In July 2005, the ICC controversially opened a fourth investigation into war crimes committed in Darfur, Sudan, at the behest of the UN Security Council, but to the vehement objection of the Sudanese government. Other crimes under investigation include those committed in Kenya, Libya, Cote D'Ivoire, Mali, Georgia, and Burundi. The court has issued verdicts in 6 cases (some with more than one defendant), with 8 convictions and 2 acquittals.

During the height of the Iraq War (2003–2011), some people suggested that the ICC should investigate war crimes committed in Iraq. However, such an investigation was not initiated and likely never will be because the United States has no involvement with the ICC. Although former U.S. president Bill Clinton, in 2000, authorized the United States to sign the Rome Treaty establishing the ICC, the George W. Bush administration withdrew U.S. support for the organization in 2002 and disavowed all legal obligations to cooperate with the court. Because of the lack of U.S. support for the court, critics argue that the ICC lacks credibility and will not be effective in bringing war criminals to justice.

PROCEDURES

The ICC operates with a combination of adversarial and inquisitorial procedures. Although its structure includes prosecutors, judges, investigators, and other staff, there is no international police system nor an international prison system. As such, the ICC depends on its signatory countries for assistance in detecting and apprehending offenders as well as for housing those it convicts and sentences. As of 2018, the ICC has over 900 staff members from 100 countries. Its working languages are French and English. It has an annual budget of €147 million. The work of the court is arduous and painstaking, as the strategy of the court is to prosecute major figures, not minor offenders, and the cases undertaken by the court are at the forefront of international politics.

The ICC differs from the UN International Court of Justice (ICJ) in that, although the ICC was established by the United Nations, it is a separate entity and is independent of the United Nations, whereas the ICJ is the principal judicial organ of the United Nations. Additionally, the ICJ is a civil tribunal that deals with such matters between nations as border disputes; it does not, however, have the jurisdiction to try individuals.

Tamar Burris and Philip L. Reichel

See also: Crimes against Humanity; Genocide; International Court of Justice; International Criminal Tribunal for Rwanda; International Criminal Tribunal for the Former Yugoslavia (ICTY); International Military Tribunal at Nuremberg; International Military Tribunal for the Far East

Further Reading

Harrington, Joanna, ed. 2006. *Bringing Power to Justice?: The Prospects of the International Criminal Court.* Montreal, Canada: McGill-Queen University Press.

International Criminal Court. n.d. "About." http://www.icc-cpi.int/about.

Roach, Steven. 2006. *Politicizing the International Criminal Court: The Convergence of Politics, Ethics, and Law.* Lanham, MD: Rowman and Littlefield Publishers.

Schabas, William A. 2004. *An Introduction to the International Criminal Court.* 2nd ed. Cambridge: Cambridge University Press.

Sewall, Saray, and Carl Kaysen. 2000. *The United States and the International Criminal Court.* Lanham, MD: Rowman and Littlefield Publishers.

United Nations. 1998. "Rome Statute of the International Criminal Court." Last Modified March 7, 2018. Accessed January 16, 2019. https://treaties.un.org/pages/ViewDetails.aspx?src=IND&mtdsg_no=XVIII-10&chapter=18&lang=en.

International Criminal Tribunal for Rwanda

In August 1994, the Rwandan government agreed to hold trials for the genocide before an international tribunal, at which time the UN Security Council passed Resolution 955. Prior to this, a total of 135,000 genocide suspects were held in custody awaiting their trial in Rwanda, leaving the system overwhelmed and unable to hold individuals accountable for crimes (Banks and Baker 2016). The main purpose of the UN Security Council is to help maintain peace and security throughout the world. The council established the International Criminal Tribunals for Rwanda (ICTR) to prosecute high-ranking individuals in Rwanda and neighboring states responsible for human rights violations, with specific focus on genocide.

The ICTR was the first international tribunal to punish and deliver verdicts for the crime of genocide, which was set forth in the 1948 Geneva Conventions. Individuals found guilty could be sentenced to life imprisonment. Additionally, the ICTR was significant because it was the first international tribunal that defined rape as violation of international criminal law and recognized rape as a means of perpetrating genocide. Finally, the ICTR was the first international tribunal to hold members of the media responsible for propaganda to inflame the public to commit acts of genocide (UNMICT 2017).

The tribunal was located in Arusha, Tanzania, and had offices in Kigali, Rwanda. Overall 93 individuals were indicted for serious violations of international humanitarian law committed in Rwanda during 1994. The individuals indicted included high-ranking military and government officials, politicians, and businessmen, as well as religious, militia, and media leaders. The ICTR delivered its first trial judgment in 1998 and its last on December 20, 2012 (UNMICT 2017). Since the formation of the ICTR, Rwandans and the international community have heavily criticized the ICTR.

HISTORY

Two ethnic groups, the Hutu and Tutsi, had had long tensions since before World War II (1939–1945), when Rwanda was under Belgian rule. In Rwanda, on April 6, 1994, Hutu president Juvenal Habyarimana was assassinated, at which point radical Hutu extremists replaced the government (Fichtelberg 2008). Hutu extremists in the National Republican Movement for Development and Democracy (MRND) and the Rwandan Armed Forces (RAF), fueled by propaganda, set out to murder and exterminate moderate Hutus and the entire Tutsi ethnic minority (Scharf 2008). The Rwandan genocide also included systematic rape and sexual violence against countless Tutsi women and children (U.S. Department of State 2017). The genocide, largely carried out with machetes, ended on July 19, 1994, when the rebel Tutsi Rwandese Patriotic Front (RPF) overthrew the Hutu regime (Fichtelberg 2008). It is estimated between 800,000 and 950,000 Rwandans were murdered (UNMICT 2017).

Globally, the world refused to help the Tutsis, holding to the belief it was too dangerous because of the recent killings of Belgian peacekeepers in Rwanda. Therefore, the UN Security Council refused to send needed peacekeepers into the region at the start of the genocide and quickly withdrew most help from the region (Fichtelberg 2008).

INTERNATIONAL JUSTICE

The International Criminal Tribunal for Rwanda's mission was to promote justice and accountability for crimes committed in Rwanda and neighboring countries in 1994. The ICTR was one of the first attempts to develop international courts and expand on the principles of international criminal law. The goal was to hold high-ranking individuals accountable in the hopes of deterring other countries from perpetrating similar crimes and to end impunity for serious violations of international humanitarian law. Persons were assigned to categories according to the seriousness of the crime they were charged with (UNMICT 2017).

According to Chapter VII Security Council resolution, the ICTR had the ability to force the surrender of an accused, be they a Rwandan citizen or not, located in Rwanda or any third state (UNMICT 2017). The first genocide trial before the ICTR was in 1997, Jean-Paul Akayesu, a local government official, who was found guilty of ordering mass killings in his area. His conviction was the first conviction by an international court for the crime of genocide and where rape was recognized as a means of perpetuating genocide and as a crime against humanity (Gahima 2013).

In September 2000, the ICTR created the Support Programme for Witnesses and Potential Witnesses, often referred to as the Victim and Witness Support Unit. Its goals were to engage the community and provide support and care to the victims of the genocide. Additionally, Operation NAKI (Nairobi-Kigali) was developed to work with other countries to find individuals who had fled prosecution, which helped detain seven suspects, including the former prime minister of the Rwandan interim government, who was the first person in global history to plead guilty to genocide. Countries agreeing to ensure enforcement of ICTR sentences were Mali, Benin, France, Italy, Rwanda, Senegal, Swaziland, and Sweden. This was important because it illustrated the role national authorities play in ensuring that those convicted of serious violations of international law serve their sentences in compliance with international detention standards (UNMICT 2017).

The ICTR was the first to hold members of the media responsible for their role in perpetuating propaganda. The trial of Jean Bosco Barayagwiza, Ferdinand Nahimana, and Hassan Ngeze resulted in the first verdict by an international tribunal holding members of the media responsible for broadcasts intended to inflame the public to commit acts of genocide (UNMICT 2017), setting a global standard for the role of propaganda in the commission of war crimes such as genocide.

The UN Security Council adopted Resolution 1503, requiring the ICTR to develop a strategy to complete its work. The ICTR concluded as of June 30, 2012, with estimated costs around $2 billion. Of the 93 individuals indicted, 61 individuals were sentenced, and 14 were acquitted, with more than 3,000 witnesses testifying in court (Leithead 2015). After 2012, any trials or appeals started after that date are to be handled by the Mechanism for the International Criminal Tribunals (MICT). As of April 2014, only three fugitives remained at large to be tried by the MICT (UNMICT 2017). The ICTR Appeals Chamber officially took judicial notice that a genocide against the Tutsi ethnic group took place in Rwanda in 1994, which recognized the genocide as an established fact that cannot be disputed.

CRITICISMS

The ICTR was heavily criticized since its formation for inaction, delay, and poor management. Additionally, Rwandan citizens were unable to attend hearings because it was located in Tanzania, trials were not translated into the local

Rwandan languages, and it was not until four years into the ICTR that the Victim and Witness Support Unit was established. Rwandans criticized the ICTR for its acquittal of several notorious defendants and the leniency of the sentences. In the eyes of many survivors, a life sentence was lenient relative to the crimes committed (Gahima 2013).

Shanell Sanchez

See also: Crimes against Humanity; Genocide; International Criminal Court; UN Convention on the Prevention and Punishment of the Crime of Genocide

Further Reading

Banks, C. and J. Baker. 2016. *Comparative International, and Global Justice: Perspectives from Criminology and Criminal Justice.* Thousand Oaks, CA: Sage.

Fichtelberg, Aaron. 2008. *Crime without Borders: An Introduction to International Criminal Justice.* Upper Saddle River, NJ: Pearson Education.

Gahima, G. 2013. *Transnational Justice in Rwanda: Accountability for Atrocity.* Abingdon, UK: Routledge.

Leithead, A. 2015. "Rwanda Genocide: International Criminal Tribunal Closes." BBC, December 14. Accessed January 16, 2019. http://www.bbc.com/news/world-africa-35070220.

United Nations Mechanism for International Criminal Tribunals (UNMICT). 2017. "The ICTR in Brief." Accessed January 4, 2018. http://unictr.unmict.org/en/tribunal.

U.S. Department of State. 2017. "International Criminal Tribunal for Rwanda." Accessed January 2, 2018. https://www.state.gov/j/gcj/ictr.

International Criminal Tribunal for the Former Yugoslavia (ICTY)

The International Criminal Tribunal for the Former Yugoslavia (ICTY) was a United Nations court of law that dealt with war crimes that took place during the conflicts in the Balkans during the 1990s. Resolution 827 was passed in The Hague, Netherlands, in May 1993, before the war had even ended. The United Nations was briefed on reports of massacres, rape and torture, extreme violence in the cities, and the massive suffering of the hundreds of thousands who had been expelled from their homes. The ICTY lasted from 1993 to 2017. The tribunal was the first court to prosecute and adjudicate an international crime since the post–World War II Nuremberg and Tokyo trials. It was ruled in 2001 that genocide occurred in Srebrenica, and in 2007, the International Court of Justice (ICJ) stated that Serbia had violated the Genocide Convention by not doing enough to prevent it.

The tribunal helped outline current accepted norms and practices for conflict resolution and postconflict development across the globe. The ICTY was groundbreaking for international humanitarian law because it provided victims the opportunity to voice the horrors they had witnessed and experienced. Additionally, it demonstrated that those suspected of bearing the greatest responsibility for atrocities committed during armed conflicts can be held accountable. The ICTY set a clear precedent that an individual's senior position in a country will not protect them from prosecution and that guilt would be individualized, ultimately protecting entire communities from being labeled "collectively responsible." The ICTY demonstrated that efficient and transparent international justice is possible.

HISTORY

Yugoslavia began to collapse in 1991, and a clear division along ethnic lines formed. During this time, the largest massacre in Europe after the Holocaust occurred. The Bosnian War marked the fall of communism in Europe, and there was a long, and particularly awful, genocide. In 1991, Bosnia and Herzegovina joined several republics of the former Yugoslavia and declared independence, ultimately triggering a civil war. Prior to the war, Bosnia's population consisted of a multiethnic mix of Muslim Bosniaks (44%), Orthodox Serbs (31%), and Catholic Croats (17%) (Taylor 2012).

The height of the killings took place in July 1995, when Serbs killed 8,000 Bosniaks in what is now known as the Srebrenica genocide. Supported and heavily armed by Serbia, the Bosnian Serbs sieged the city of Sarajevo in early April 1992. The Bosnian War lasted approximately four years and was deemed an ethnic cleansing because the Serbs primarily targeted the Muslim Bosniak population. In 1995, UN air strikes and sanctions helped create a peace agreement. It is estimated that 90,000–300,000 individuals were murdered during the course of the war (Taylor 2012). In August 1992, the UN Commission on Human Rights started an investigation into the alleged human rights abuses in the former Yugoslavia.

INTERNATIONAL JUSTICE

The ICTY was known for legal expertise and testimonies as well as for producing an archive of evidence that can serve future historians well. Prosecutors in the ICTY pioneered the legal concept of "joint criminal enterprise," which is a doctrine that ties defendants to a common plan for genocide or crimes against humanity (Bowcott 2017). The ICTY was marked by 24 years of investigations, with court proceedings that lasted 10,800 days, and contained over 2.5 million pages of transcripts. Leaders of the war were put on trial, such as the former Yugoslav president Slobodan Milosevic, the Bosnian Serb leader Radovan Karadzic, and General Ratko Mladic (Bowcott 2017).

The ICTY ultimately indicted 161 individuals, with over 90 individuals being sentenced. Individuals had various charges, but four specific war crimes were prosecuted during the ICTY: genocide, crimes against humanity, violations of the laws or customs of war, and grave breaches of the Geneva Conventions. Of the 161 individuals indicted, 13 individuals were referred to countries in the former Yugoslavia for trial. As of July 2011, there were no fugitives reported and more than 4,650 witnesses to the atrocities that took place (UNMICT n.d.).

RAPE AS TORTURE AND GENOCIDE

Additionally, the tribunal played a historic role in the prosecution of wartime sexual violence in the former Yugoslavia, with extensive investigations conducted on systematic detention and rape of women, men, and children. In *Prosecutor v. Kunarac* (2001), the Trial Chamber of the ICTY held that mass rape, torture, and enslavement of Muslim women amounted to a crime against humanity (Banks and Baker 2016). In fact, more than one-third of those convicted were guilty of crimes involving sexual violence (UNICTY n.d.). A team of medical experts investigated rape allegations in Bosnia and Herzegovina. This team, referred to as the Experts Commission, found that Muslim women composed most of the victims from Bosnia and Herzegovina, and that Serbian men had raped them. Additionally, they found a pattern to the rapes: Serbian men committed rape before outbreaks of fighting, concurrently with invasion and capture of towns and villages, against women held in detention and against women in so-called rape camps; Serbian men also forced women to work in brothels to service soldiers.

Genocide, as defined by Article 2 of the Convention on the Prevention and Punishment of the Crime of Genocide 1948, is intending to destroy a national, ethnic, racial, or religious group. Rape is not specifically mentioned in genocide, but the ICTY showed the systematic nature of rape and the intention to destroy a group. Thus, rape can fall under genocide. Ultimately, "rapes indicated adherence to a policy and plan of ethnic cleansing," where rape was used to terrorize and displace the community, to force the birth of children of mixed descent, and generally to demoralize" (Niarchos 1995, 653). Women were targeted because they were women, not because they were the enemy.

CRITICISMS

Many criticized the ICTY's delayed response to prosecuting those responsible, especially as the body did not name a prosecutor until 1994. Once the ICTY began, Serbia and Croatia refused to turn over their war criminal suspects or share information with the tribunal. This decision jeopardized their membership in the European Union (United to End Genocide 2016). In addition, critics claim that the tribunal represented victor's justice and thus was biased, as about two-thirds of all those charged were Serbs. However, supporters of the indictments said the convictions were justified, given the worst atrocities of the conflict were inflicted by Serb forces on Bosnian civilians (Bowcott 2017).

The ICTY helped create the shift away from discrete tribunals, which were seen in the Balkans, Rwanda, and Sierra Leone. This shift moved the world toward the goal of universal jurisdiction under the international criminal court (ICC). The ICC is the first permanent international criminal court with "global jurisdiction and it departs from the practice of establishing ad hoc tribunals as instruments to ensure accountability for war crimes and atrocities committed anywhere in the world" (Banks and Baker 2016, 267).

Shanell Sanchez and Christina Lynn Richardson

See also: Crimes against Humanity; Genocide; International Criminal Court; International Criminal Tribunal for Rwanda; International Military Tribunal at Nuremberg; International Military Tribunal for the Far East

Further Reading

Banks, Cyndi, and James Baker. 2016. *Comparative International, and Global Justice: Perspectives from Criminology and Criminal Justice.* Thousand Oaks, CA: Sage Publications.

Bowcott, Owen. 2017. "Yugoslavia Tribunal Closes, Leaving a Powerful Legacy of War Crimes Justice." *The Guardian*, December 20. Accessed March 16, 2018. https://www.theguardian.com/law/2017/dec/20/former-yugoslavia-war-crimes-tribunal-leaves-powerful-legacy-milosevic-karadzic-mladic.

Niarchos, Catherine. 1995. "Women, War, and Rape: Challenges Facing the International Tribunal for the Former Yugoslavia." *Human Rights Quarterly* 17 (4): 649–690.

Taylor, Alan. 2012. "20 Years since the Bosnian War." *The Atlantic*, April 13, Accessed March 16, 2018. https://www.theatlantic.com/photo/2012/04/20-years-since-the-bosnian-war/100278.

United Nations International Criminal Tribunal for the former Yugoslavia (UNICTY). n.d. "Crimes of Sexual Violence." Accessed February 9, 2019. http://www.icty.org/en/features/crimes-sexual-violence

United Nations Mechanism for International Criminal Tribunals (UNMICT). n.d. Accessed March 16, 2018. http://www.icty.org.

United to End Genocide. 2016. "The Bosnian War and Srebrenica Genocide." Accessed March 16, 2018. http://endgenocide.org/learn/past-genocides/the-bosnian-war-and-srebrenica-genocide.

International Drug Trafficking

International drug trafficking is one of the world's largest and most profitable illicit businesses. Every day, tons of illicit drugs cross national borders hidden among licit goods. In a broader sense, as defined by the United Nations Office of Drugs and Crime (UNODC), drug trafficking refers to "a global illicit trade involving the cultivation, manufacture, distribution and sale of substances which are subject to drug prohibition laws" (UNODC 2017a). According to this definition, the trafficking of drugs involves a broad range of interconnected actors that operate at different stages of the process. Illicit crops are cultivated in drug-producing countries and refined in clandestine laboratories, sometimes located in a different country. The drugs are then illegally transported to a consumer country, where they are distributed by drug dealers and consumed by drug users. Finally, the illegal proceeds from the drug trade are laundered by money launderers.

In the narrower sense, the term *drug trafficking* refers only to the stage that involves transportation of drugs from one point to another. Traffickers use shipping companies to smuggle illicit drugs by land, sea, or air alongside trafficking routes and bribe customs officials and police to avoid detection and arrest. They are an essential part of the drug trade process, as they make the international movement of drugs possible by linking drug suppliers to drug consumers. While illicit drug trade brings enormous profits to the traffickers, its social costs are extremely high, and it often results in violence that affects the communities along the supply chain.

TYPES OF DRUGS AND MAIN TRAFFICKING ROUTES

Illicit drugs can be divided into two major groups: plant-based and synthetic drugs. Cannabis (marijuana), opiates, and cocaine are the most widespread naturally grown drugs, and the amphetamine-type substances are the most common synthetic narcotics. As with other illicit activities, drug flows are in constant flux and adapt to the shifts in economic incentives and interdiction efforts.

The most widely used drug globally is cannabis, which can grow in a variety of climates and is cultivated in almost every country in the world. Therefore, trafficking of the cannabis herb is largely intraregional and aimed at local consumers. In contrast, the cannabis resin, produced by processing cannabis flowers, is widely trafficked between regions. Two major routes of cannabis resin are from Morocco to Europe and other North African countries and from Afghanistan to Pakistan and Iran (UNODC 2017b, 40).

Opiates, such as heroine and morphine, are produced from the opium poppy plant. Its cultivation is mainly concentrated in three countries—Afghanistan, Myanmar, and Mexico—with Afghanistan accounting for roughly 80 percent of the world's heroin supply. Afghan opiates are trafficked along three major routes: the Balkan route is used to smuggle the drugs into Western and Central Europe; the southern route via Pakistan serves markets in South Asia, the Gulf countries, the Middle East, and Africa; and the northern route through Central Asia supplies the vast heroin market in Russia. Myanmar- and Mexico-grown opiates cater the markets of Southeast Asia and the Americas, respectively (UNODC 2017b, 16–18).

Cocaine is produced from the coca leaf grown in the Andean region of South America, specifically in Colombia, Peru, and Bolivia. The drug is then trafficked to North America, the largest cocaine consumer in the world (33% of cocaine consumers worldwide); to Western and Central Europe (20% of world cocaine consumption); or remains in South America, together with the Caribbean and Central America (17% of world cocaine consumption) (UNODC 2017b, 28). Among the three South American cocaine producers, Colombia is the largest. Ninety percent of the cocaine entering the United States is of Colombian origin. Most of the cocaine enters the United States via Central America and Mexico. As for the European market, its major hubs for cocaine shipments are the seaports of the Iberian Peninsula and the Netherlands (UNODC 2017b, 31).

Besides the traditional plant-based drugs, there is a rapidly growing global market for synthetic drugs, such as methamphetamine, amphetamine, and "ecstasy," as well as new psychoactive substances. Unlike plant-based drugs, synthetic drugs are produced in laboratories from precursor chemicals, and their manufacture is relatively easy, as it is not limited by geographic conditions. Precursor chemicals required for the manufacture of synthetic drugs often originate in China and India and are shipped to the manufacturing points worldwide. For example, major manufacturing locations of methamphetamine include Mexico, the United States and East and Southeast Asia. Manufactured synthetic drugs tend to be distributed to consumers within the same regions where they are produced (UNODC 2017b).

EVOLUTION OF DRUG TRAFFICKING

Mind-altering substances have been used in different civilizations for thousands of years for ceremonial, recreational, and medicinal purposes. In the 19th century, with the expansion of international trade, drugs started crossing national borders. However, it was not until the early 20th century that the drug trade became regulated by some countries, paving the way to the international drug control regime that developed over the 20th century. International drug trade experienced a boom in 1960s, when the demand for drugs skyrocketed in the United States and spread to Western Europe. Further, globalization created conditions for the explosion of the global drug trade. As a result, more criminal organizations turned to illicit drugs as their main source of revenue.

Due to the global scale and the diversity of market for illicit drugs, there is a large variety of actors who serve as intermediaries between the producers and the consumers of drugs. Although drug trafficking is usually associated with hierarchically structured criminal syndicates that control the whole process from crop cultivation to retail drug sales, this activity is often carried out by rather disorganized networks coming together on an ad hoc basis at different stages (Paoli 2001; Mares 2006, 85). Large criminal organizations may become easy targets for governmental efforts aimed at disrupting their power, as illustrated by the recent tendency toward fragmentation and dispersion among drug cartels in Latin America (Bagley 2015). For example, after major Colombian trafficking organizations were dismantled in the late 1980s and the early 1990s by the Colombian government's law enforcement efforts, they were replaced by numerous criminal gangs and paramilitaries in the cocaine smuggling business. Mexico's major drug cartels have followed a similar path of splitting into numerous factions since the 1990s (Mares 2006; Bagley 2015).

Moreover, insurgent groups and other nonstate violent actors often use drug trafficking as a source of funding. For example, the Taliban in Afghanistan and the Revolutionary Armed Forces of Colombia (FARC) are known to have been involved in illicit drug trade. There are also reports of the Islamic State terrorist organization (ISIS) participating in drug trafficking after its main financing sources were cut off (Clarke 2017).

In recent years, a new way of drug trafficking, via the Internet, has been growing at an alarming pace. Every year, more drug users are willing to purchase illicit drugs using cryptocurrencies, such as Bitcoins, over the Dark Web. Individual vendors and drug users are attracted to the Internet-facilitated drug trade because it is perceived as being safer than offline drug markets (Kruithof et al. 2016). The most common drugs sold on the Dark Web are recreational drugs, such as cannabis, "ecstasy," cocaine, and hallucinogens (UNODC 2017b). The online drug market represents a major challenge for the international drug control regime, as its regulation remains at early stage.

Yulia Vorobyeva

See also: Cali Cartel; Colombian Drug Cartels; Dark Web/Deep Web; Golden Triangle; Gulf Cartel; Juárez Cartel; Los Zetas; Medellín Cartel; Sinaloa Cartel; Tijuana Cartel; UN Office on Drugs and Crime; UN World Drug Report

Further Reading

Bagley, Bruce M. 2015. "Introduction." In *Drug Trafficking, Organized Crime, and Violence in the Americas Today*, edited by Bruce M. Bagley and Jonathan D. Rosen, 1–24. Gainesville: University Press of Florida.

Buxton, Julia. 2006. *The Political Economy of Narcotics: Production, Consumption and Global Markets.* London: Zed Books.

Clarke, Colin P. 2017. "ISIS Is So Desperate It's Turning to the Drug Trade." *RAND Blog.* Last modified July 25, 2017. Accessed January 16, 2019. https://www.rand.org/blog/2017/07/isis-is-so-desperate-its-turning-to-the-drug-trade.html.

Kruithof, Kristy, Judith Aldridge, David Décary-Hétu, Megan Sim, Elma Dujso, and Stijn Hoorens. 2016. *Internet-Facilitated Drugs Trade: An Analysis of the Size, Scope and the Role of the Netherlands.* RAND Corporation. Accessed January 16, 2019. https://www.rand.org/pubs/research_reports/RR1607.html.

Mares, David. 2006. *Drug Wars and Coffeehouses: The Political Economy of the International Drug Trade.* Washington, D.C.: CQ Press.

Paoli, Letizia. 2001. "Drug Trafficking in Russia: A Form of Organized Crime?" *Journal of Drug Issues* 31 (4): 1007–1038.

United Nations Office on Drugs and Crime (UNODC). 2017a. "Drug Trafficking." Last modified 2017. Accessed January 21, 2019. https://www.unodc.org/unodc/en/drug-trafficking/index.html.

United Nations Office on Drugs and Crime (UNODC). 2017b. *World Drug Report 2017: Market Analysis of Plant-Based Drugs (Booklet 3).* Vienna: United Nations publication. Accessed February 9, 2019. https://www.unodc.org/wdr2017/field/Booklet_3_Plantbased.pdf.

International Forum on Globalization

The International Forum on Globalization (IFG) was founded in 1994 and is a nonprofit advocacy and action organization. The IFG is an educational group that conducts global research and is composed of activists, economists, scholars, and researchers who analyze and critique the various impacts of globalization. The forum is led by an international board of scholars and citizens dedicated to the movement and currently spans 10 countries. The primary purpose of IFG is to focus on the impacts of dominant economic and geopolitical policies. This is done by collaborating with environmental, social justice, and antimilitarism activists to create secure models of democracy and sustainability, both locally and globally (IFG 2018c). The main goals of the IFG are to expose the multiple effects of economic globalization to stimulate debate and illuminate issues with the globalization process by encouraging ideas and activities that revitalize local economies and communities and ensure long-term ecological stability (IFG 2018a).

HISTORY

The first IFG meeting was in San Francisco in January 1994 after the passage of the North American Free Trade Agreement (NAFTA) and the conclusion of the Uruguay Round of the General Agreement on Tariffs and Trade (GATT). The goal of IFG was to continue global activism and understand it systematically as a global process. IFG originally functioned as a think tank that aimed at discussing the issues and developing alternative strategies that might reverse the globalization trend and redirect actions toward revitalizing local economies. Additionally, discussions were centered on the different views of environmental and labor issues within trade agreements, the role of globalization on technology, and how to gain control of resources at the local level. These meetings were a starting point to discuss economic globalization and propose viable alternatives (IFG 2018a).

The IFG works to examine how globalization can be improved to bring numerous diverse groups and perspectives into the discussion with union members, farmers, women's organizations, youth organizations, environmentalists, and various others and is focusing efforts on being a citizen movement. The IFG produces publications, organizes events, hosts seminars, and participates in various activities to demonstrate the failure of current globalization measures and "free trade" policies. Some of the issues the IFG has taken up since its creation are loss of jobs and livelihoods, displacement of indigenous peoples, massive immigration, rapid environmental devastation and loss of biodiversity, increases in poverty and hunger, and many additional negative effects (IFG 2018b).

Today, the IFG continues to critique globalization by examining how current policies may benefit transnational corporations over workers, foreign investors over local businesses, and wealthy countries over developing nations, which has typically been a widely accepted global model.

Shanell Sanchez

See also: Globalization; Transnational, Global, and International Crime

Further Reading

CSPAN. 2018. "International Forum on Globalization." Accessed June 9, 2018. https://www.c-span.org/organization/?42406/International-Forum-Globalization.

International Forum on Globalization (IFG). 2018a. "History." Accessed June 9, 2018. http://ifg.org/about/history.

International Forum on Globalization (IFG). 2018b. "Position Statement." Accessed June 9, 2018. http://ifg.org/about/position-statement.

International Forum on Globalization (IFG). 2018c. "Who We Are." Accessed June 9, 2018. http://ifg.org/about.

International Law, *see* Crimes against Humanity

International Maritime Bureau Piracy Reporting Center

The International Maritime Bureau Piracy Reporting Center is an independent nongovernmental agency that provides two key services to mariners: a maritime security hotline for seafarers under attack and daily status reports on attacks to the shipping community. In addition, the agency is also the internationally recognized collection point for both piracy reports and statistics.

HISTORY

The International Maritime Bureau (IMB) was established in 1981 as a specialized division of the International Chamber of Commerce (ICC). It is one of three specialized bureau of the ICC's anticrime unit, the Commercial Crime Services. The IMB is a nonprofit organization tasked with reducing and preventing various forms of maritime crime and misconduct. As part of this mandate, it has also become the principal international organization dealing with maritime piracy. In 1983, the IMB began systematically collecting accounts of piracy attacks in Southeast Asia and compiling these into annual reports for the United Nations' International Maritime Organization (Hyslop 1989, 3).

The increase in the number of maritime piracy attacks led the IMB to establish what is now known as the Piracy Reporting Center (PRC) on October 1, 1992, in Kuala Lumpur, Malaysia. The PRC was established with the intention of being a single point of contact for actual, attempted, and suspected attacks. Its maritime security hotline is used to report any attacks of piracy, armed robbery against ships, or other maritime crime. It is staffed 24 hours a day and facilitates the process of initiating a response.

Once a report is received by the PRC, it passes the information from the victimized vessels to the appropriate authorities for further action. The PRC does not conduct investigations of these attacks, nor does it track the progress of any investigations (Murphy 2009, 60). The agency broadcasts warnings of attacks using global satellite communication services (Inmarsat) and their live online piracy map. The agency is funded through voluntary contributions and industry sponsors, allowing all services to be provided free of charge.

PIRACY DATA

The IMB issues worldwide annual (and quarterly since 1995) piracy reports detailing the attacks recorded by the PRC. These reports are available for free upon request. The IMB published its first annual report in 1992. Over the years, IMB reports have provided improved data and geographic coverage of piracy and other types of attacks on ships (Twyman-Ghoshal and Pierce 2014, 653). The PRC attack reports, received from captains or owners/operators of victimized vessels, are firsthand self-reports that are logged using a standard report template that provides both consistency and reliability.

Attacks that are listed in the IMB Piracy Reports include a variety of harmful behaviors without application of a specific juridical definition. This is a consequence of the PRC fundamentally being a support service for seafarers rather than a data collection agency. However, despite the broad ambit of the piracy reports, the IMB estimates that about 40–60 percent of attacks go unreported (Ong-Webb

2007, 40). Various reasons contribute to the underreporting of attacks, including the cost of staying in port during investigations (a burden on the ship owner or charterer) and the fear of increases in insurance premiums (Chalk 2008, 7). Fishing vessels are also less likely to report attacks. Traditionally, the focus of the IMB since its inception has been on merchant shipping; however, this has been broadened over time, increasing their capacity as the key piracy data collection point.

Anamika A. Twyman-Ghoshal

See also: Maersk Alabama Pirate Attack (2009); Sea Piracy

Further Reading

Chalk, Peter. 2008. *The Maritime Dimension of International Security: Terrorism, Piracy and Challenges for the United States.* Santa Monica, CA: RAND.

Hyslop, Ian. 1989. "Contemporary Piracy." In *Piracy at Sea*, edited by Eric Ellen, 3–40. Paris: ICC Publishing.

International Chamber of Commerce, Commercial Crime Services. 2018a. "IMB Piracy Reporting Center." Accessed January 16, 2019. https://www.icc-ccs.org/index.php/piracy-reporting-centre.

International Chamber of Commerce, Commercial Crime Services. 2018b. "Request Piracy and Armed Robbery Report." Accessed January 16, 2019. https://www.icc-ccs.org/index.php/piracy-reporting-centre/request-piracy-report.

International Chamber of Commerce, Commercial Crime Services. 2018c. "24-hour Maritime Security Hotline." Accessed January 16, 2019. https://www.icc-ccs.org/index.php/piracy-reporting-centre/24-hour-maritime-security-hotline.

Murphy, Martin. 2009. *Small Boat, Weak States Dirty Money: Piracy and Maritime Terrorism in the Modern World.* New York: Columbia University Press.

Ong-Webb, Graham. 2007. "Piracy in Maritime Asia: Current Trends." In *Violence at Sea: Piracy in the Age of Global Terrorism*, edited by Peter Lehr, 37–94. London: Routledge.

Twyman-Ghoshal, Anamika, and Glenn Pierce. 2014. "The Changing Nature of Contemporary Maritime Piracy: Results from the Contemporary Maritime Piracy Database 2001–2010." *British Journal of Criminology* 54 (4): 652–672.

International Military Tribunal at Nuremberg

The International Military Tribunal (IMT) was held in Nuremberg (also spelled Nürnberg), Germany, from 1945 to 1949. It was the first international tribunal authorized to hold state authorities personally accountable for crimes under international law. The main Nuremberg trial and the follow-up trials after World War II dealt with crimes committed by leaders and organizations of the Nazi Regime. The IMT and its charter are still a guidepost for international criminal tribunals and the international criminal law for dealing with perpetrators of genocide or other crimes against humanity.

BACKGROUND

At the conclusion of World War II (1939–1945), the four Allied forces of Great Britain, France, the Union of Soviet Socialist Republics (USSR), and the United

States declared their intention to bring to justice Nazi war criminals for crimes and massacres carried out during the war. The formal statement of this intention was provided in the Moscow Declaration, which was signed by President Franklin D. Roosevelt, Soviet Premier Joseph Stalin, and British Prime Minister Winston Churchill in October 1943. Different legal systems in each country made it difficult to agree on the specific trial procedures to be used; but a mixed process was finally agreed upon that relied on aspects of both Anglo-American (British and American) and Continental (France and USSR) systems. After deciding on the procedures to be followed by the court, the IMT was established as an annex to the London Agreement, signed on August 8, 1945, by the Allied powers.

THE CRIMES—ARTICLE 6

Article 6 of the IMT Charter determined the crimes for which the defendants should be held accountable. The first, crimes against peace, referred to the planning, initiating, and waging of wars of aggression in violation of international treaties and agreements. The second, war crimes, were violations of the laws or customs of war as practiced around the world. These included, but were not limited to, murder or the deportation to slave labor of a civilian population; wanton destruction of cities, towns, or villages; and any devastation not justified by military necessity. The final category, crimes against humanity, included murder, extermination, enslavement, and other inhumane acts committed against civilian populations. In addition, every form of political, racial, and religious persecution carried out in furtherance of a crime punishable by the IMT was considered a crime against humanity.

THE IMT'S COMPOSITION

The tribunals' organization was also determined by the charter (Articles 2, 14, and 15). The IMT was composed of four judges, each with an alternate. Each signatory country appointed one judge and one alternate. From among their members, the four judges selected a president to hold office during the trial.

In addition to the four member of the tribunal, four chief prosecutors—one appointed by each of the four signatory countries—composed the IMT. The chief prosecutors acted as a committee to agree on a work plan for each chief prosecutor, to determine which major war criminals would be tried by the tribunal, to approve and file indictments, and to recommend to the tribunal the rules of procedures that would be followed. Also, acting individually or in collaboration with others, each chief prosecutor was responsible for the investigation, collection, and production of evidence to be used at trial.

THE DEFENDANTS AND THEIR VERDICTS

At the first trial, in Berlin, on October 18, 1945, 24 former Nazi leaders were charged with war crimes. Starting on November 20, 1945, all IMT sessions were held in Nuremberg. Of the original 24 defendants, a verdict was given for 22 of them on October 1, 1946. One of the remaining 2 had committed suicide in prison, and the mental and physical condition of the other prevented him from being tried. Some of the most infamous Nazi leaders, Adolf Hitler, Joseph Goebbels, and Heinrich Himmler, had avoided eventual trial by committing suicide before the war ended.

Of the 22 defendants for whom verdicts were given, 3 were acquitted, 4 were sentenced to prison terms of 10–20 years, and 3 were sentenced to life imprisonment (including Rudolf Hess, Hitler's deputy minister). Sentences of death by hanging were given to 12 defendants, and 10 of them were hanged on October 16, 1946. One of those sentenced to death had been condemned in absentia, and the other, Hermann Göring (considered the most influential person after Hitler in the Nazi organization), committed suicide before he could be executed (Austin n.d.).

CONTINUED INFLUENCE

The legal justification for the trials and the procedures followed were controversial at the time, but the Nuremberg trials now stand as the landmark event in the growth of international law and toward establishment of international courts to deal with acts of genocide and other crimes against humanity (History.com Editors 2010). The United Nations Convention on the Prevention and Punishment of the Crime of Genocide (1948), the Universal Declaration of Human Rights (1948), and the Geneva Convention on the Laws and Customs of War (1949) are examples of international law developed from the IMT. In addition, the IMT served as the primary example for the establishment of the International Criminal Tribunal for the Former Yugoslavia (1993), the International Criminal Tribunal for Rwanda (1994), and for the International Criminal Court (1998). The 1961 film *Judgment at Nuremberg* (directed by Stanley Kramer) is a dramatized version of the proceedings at one of the IMT trials.

Karin Bruckmüller and Julia Kellner

See also: Crimes against Humanity; Genocide; International Criminal Court; International Criminal Tribunal for Rwanda; International Criminal Tribunal for the Former Yugoslavia (ICTY)

Further Reading

Austin, Ben S. n.d. *The Nuremberg Trials: Brief Overview of Defendants & Verdicts.* Jewish Virtual Library. Accessed September 18, 2018. https://www.jewishvirtuallibrary.org/brief-overview-of-defendants-and-verdicts-at-nuremberg-trials.

Constitution of the International Military Tribunal. 1945. *Nuremberg Trial Proceedings.* Vol. 1. Accessed September 18, 2018. http://avalon.law.yale.edu/imt/imtconst.asp.

History.com Editors. 2010. "Nuremberg Trials." Last updated August 21, 2018. Accessed January 16, 2019. https://www.history.com/topics/world-war-ii/nuremberg-trials.

Loyola Law School Los Angeles. 2017. "Special Edition: The Nuremberg Laws and the Nuremberg Trials." *International and Comparative Law Review* 39 (1). Accessed February 9, 2019. https://digitalcommons.lmu.edu/ilr/vol39/iss1/.

Memorium Nuremberg Trials. n.d. "The International Military Tribunal (1945–1946)." Accessed September 18, 2018. https://museums.nuernberg.de/memorium-nuremberg-trials/the-nuremberg-trials/the-international-military-tribunal.

Telford Tylor. 1992. *The Anatomy of the Nuremberg Trials*. New York: Knopf.

United States Holocaust Museum. "International Military Tribunal at Nuremberg." Accessed December 2017. https://www.ushmm.org/wlc/en/article.php?ModuleId=10007069.

International Military Tribunal for the Far East

In the aftermath of World War II (1939–1945), 11 countries convened the International Military Tribunal for the Far East (IMTFE), informally known as the Tokyo War Crimes trial, to try Imperial Japanese leaders for conspiracy to start and wage war, for conventional war crimes, and for crimes against humanity. The IMTFE began on April 29, 1946, and ended on November 12, 1948. The IMTFE set a precedent for international law and the future development of the International Criminal Court. During the 20th century, the IMTFE is most notably recognized alongside the Nuremberg trials, also created by Allied powers to try leadership of the Nazi regime in Germany. International tribunals were a temporary yet organized way to judge persons for their behavior during a specific time for a specific event. The need for the tribunals arose from the states' failure to punish individuals for the crimes committed during World War II (Reichel and Albanese 2014).

THE TRIBUNAL

Australia, Canada, China, France, India, the Netherlands, New Zealand, the Philippines, the Soviet Union, the United Kingdom, and the United States provided judges and prosecutors for the court. The IMTFE was unique because the Tokyo trial featured only one chief prosecutor, Joseph B. Keenan, an American who was a former assistant to the U.S. attorney general. Japanese and American lawyers comprised the defense team. This was in contrast to the Nuremberg trials, where there were four chief prosecutors who represented Great Britain, France, the USSR, and the United States. The main tribunal was held in Tokyo, but there were various other tribunals that happened outside of Japan that heard around 5,000 cases regarding the Japanese civilians accused of committing war crimes.

Some of the troops were charged with committing atrocities at Nanking, which included raping 20,000 women and murdering 300,000 people, as well as being informed that these crimes were occurring and doing nothing to stop it. One example was the foreign minister, Koki Hirota, who was well informed the massacre was going on. The smaller tribunals heard around 5,000 cases, and it is estimated that 900 individuals were executed following sentencing.

OUTCOME

The main tribunal in Tokyo concluded on November 4, 1948, with 25 of 28 Japanese defendants being found guilty, two dying of natural causes during the trial, and one declared insane. All the defendants tried in the tribunal were found guilty on at least one count, with sentences ranging from seven years of imprisonment to execution. A total of seven men were executed, which included high-ranking officials such as General Hideki Tojo, who served as Japanese premier during the war; Iwane Matsui, who organized the Rape of Nanking; and Heitaro Kimura, who brutalized Allied prisoners of war. The executions took place on December 23, 1948, in Tokyo in an attempt to provide swift justice and set a clear precedence on war crimes.

A major criticism of the IMTFE was that the Emperor Hirohito was not tried for his tacit approval of policy during the war. The United States saw the emperor as a symbol of potential unity and conservatism and protected him from prosecution. This decision did not go without criticism, but, overall, the IMTFE tribunals were seen as successful for holding war criminals accountable, delivering swift punishments, and setting international precedence.

Shanell Sanchez

See also: Crimes against Humanity; International Military Tribunal at Nuremberg

Further Reading

Banks, Cyndi, and James Baker. 2016. *Comparative International, and Global Justice: Perspectives from Criminology and Criminal Justice.* Thousand Oaks, CA: Sage Publications.

Dammer, Harry, and Jay Albanese. 2014. *Comparative Criminal Justice Systems.* 5th ed. Belmont, CA: Wadsworth Cengage Learning.

Reichel, Philip, and Jay Albanese. 2014. *Handbook of Transnational Crime and Justice.* 2nd ed. Sage Publications.

United Nations. 1946. International Military Tribunal for the Far East. Accessed June 7, 2018. http://www.un.org/en/genocideprevention/documents/atrocity-crimes/Doc.3_1946%20Tokyo%20Charter.pdf.

International Narcotics Control Board

The International Narcotics Control Board (INCB) is an independent agency of the United Nations responsible for monitoring and enforcing international restrictions on narcotics, along with the Commission on Narcotic Drugs (CND).

HISTORY

The INCB was commissioned by the 1961 Single Convention on Narcotic Drugs, which was designed to consolidate and organize the various multilateral drug treaties that had been in effect since the 1909 International Opium Commission in Shanghai, China. After that conference, the League of Nations became the governing umbrella organization under which several boards and commissions were created to address the international narcotics industry. Following the League of Nations' dissolution, the 1946 Protocol Amending the Agreements, Conventions, and Protocols on Narcotic Drugs held several meetings to create drug control bodies under the new United Nations model. These efforts culminated in the joint designation of the International Narcotics Control Board and the Commission on Narcotic Drugs as the United Nations' governing bodies of international narcotics policy.

In its origins, the INCB focused on drugs such as cannabis and opium; however, the 1971 Convention on Psychotropic Substances expanded the power of the INCB to address narcotics such as amphetamines, barbiturates, and psychedelics (Bayer 1999).

MEMBERSHIP

Article 9 of the 1961 Single Convention on Narcotic Drugs outlines that the INCB will have 13 members—3 to be chosen from a list of 5 medical professionals, nominated by the World Health Organization, and 10 to be nominated by the United Nations—elected by the UN Economic and Social Council (ECOSOC), with respect given to geographic equity. Article 10 states that the board members are to serve renewable five-year terms.

FUNCTION

Although it shares governance of UN drug control policies with the Commission on Narcotic Drugs, which serves as an advisory body issuing recommendations, the INCB is charged with enforcing UN conventions.

The INCB has the authority to investigate a country's alleged failure to comply with UN drug policy, to question a country's government and request explanation, and to recommend appropriate remediation by the government. If a government does not comply with these measures, the INCB is empowered to notify other parties to the 1961 convention and to bring it to the attention of the CND and ECOSOC. The INCB has the authority to recommend the seizure of all importing and exporting of narcotics from a country in question, although this is an exceptional measure that requires a two-thirds vote of INCB board members.

In addition to enforcing violations of the 1961 treaty, the INCB is also responsible for monitoring the availability and distribution of legal drugs. It publishes data in a variety of reports that attempt to capture the state of narcotics flows, both legal and illegal, among differing global regions.

CRITICISM

The INCB has come under continued criticism due to its lack of action to ensure more accessibility to pain medication in developing countries (Taylor 2007). Human rights advocates suggest that pharmaceutical manufacturers lack financial incentive to distribute controlled, but legal, narcotics into underdeveloped economies, therefore resulting in a concentration of pain medication in more developed societies. Critics denounce the INCB's efforts to protect equitable distribution of opiates. In its annual report, released in March 2008, the INCB called on governments to support a new program of the World Health Organization designed to increase the availability of opiates.

The INCB has also experienced recent criticism regarding its attitude toward cannabis usage. Its interjection and commentary on the actions of sovereign national governments in amending national drug laws has sparked backlash from otherwise friendly parties. In its 2002 annual report, the INCB has publicly shamed countries such as Canada and the United Kingdom for exploring legalization of cannabis or, at least, the lessening of its severity as a controlled substance (Carstairs 2005).

Corey B. Miles

See also: Global Drug Interdiction; International Drug Trafficking; Single Convention on Narcotic Drugs; UN Convention against Illicit Traffic in Narcotic Drugs and Psychotropic Substances; UN Convention on Psychotropic Substances

Further Reading

Bayer, Istvan, and Hamid Ghodse. 1999. "Evolution of International Drug Control, 1945–1995." *Bulletin on Narcotics* 51 (1): 1–17.

Bewley-Taylor, David, and Martin Jelsma. 2012. "Regime Change: Re-Visiting the 1961 Single Convention on Narcotic Drugs." *International Journal of Drug Policy* 23 (1): 72–81.

Carstairs, Catherine. 2005. "The Stages of the International Drug Control System." *Drug and Alcohol Review* 24 (1): 57–65.

International Narcotics Control Board. 2018. "Annual Reports." Last updated August 20, 2018. Accessed January 16, 2019. https://www.incb.org/incb/en/publications/annual-reports/annual-report.html.

Taylor, Allyn L. 2007. "Addressing the Global Tragedy of Needless Pain: Rethinking the United Nations Single Convention on Narcotic Drugs." *Journal of Law, Medicine & Ethics* 35 (4): 556–570.

International Organization for Migration

The International Organization for Migration, officially abbreviated as IOM, is the leading intergovernmental organization focused on migration-related issues. It is characterized by its close working cooperation with governmental, intergovernmental, and nongovernmental partners to find practical solutions to migration problems. Migration and development, facilitating migration, regulating migration, and forced migration are the IOM's main fields of activity.

IOM offers advice, services, and assistance not only to the mentioned cooperation partners but also to migrants. Staff members provide for humanitarian support for migrants in need (including refugees and internally displaced persons). They are also engaged to prevent and combat human trafficking and smuggling. For the benefit of all, including its 169 member states, the 8 observer states, and the migrants, the IOM's mission is to encourage humane and well-ordered migration.

MISSION

Following the principle that humane and orderly migration benefits both migrants and society, the IOM and its international partners are committed to assisting the operational challenges of migration and to encouraging social and economic development through migration while upholding the human dignity and well-being of migrants (IOM n.d.-a).

These goals are accomplished by focusing on such issues as providing secure, reliable, flexible, and cost-effective services for persons requiring migration assistance. The IOM also offers expert advice, research, and technical cooperation to governments and to intergovernmental and nongovernmental agencies.

HISTORY

Over the last 50 years, the organization has evolved from a regionally focused logistics agency to a globally oriented network. In 1951, the Provisional Intergovernmental Committee for the Movement of Migrants from Europe (PICMME) was established, which one year later, in 1952, was transformed into the International Committee for European Migration (ICEM). After the latter was renamed in 1980 as the Intergovernmental Committee for Migration, the International Organization for Migration finally emerged in 1989.

IOM helped to manage a wide range of voluntary and forced migration scenarios, including those in Hungary (1956), Czechoslovakia (1968), Chile (1973), the Vietnamese Boat People (1975), Kuwait (1990), Kosovo and Timor (1999), and the Pakistan earthquake of 2004–2005. Since 2015, IOM has been engaged in the "refugee crisis," especially in Europe.

Helping migrants while cooperating with governments and civil societies resulted in an international acceptance of IOM, and it has become the head of debate on the far-reaching impacts of migration in the 21st century. Along with its growing engagement and the continuing increase of memberships from 67 states in 1998 to 169 in 2017, the organization has expanded not only its annual operating budget from $242.2 million in 1998 to $1.4 billion in 2016, but also its operational staff, located in more than 150 countries around the world, from approximately 1,100 in 1998 to over 9,000 people in 2017.

ORGANIZATIONAL STRUCTURE

The IOM's structure is vastly decentralized. This is necessary to ensure the increasing number and diversity of projects requested by the cooperation partners. There are 22 special offices plus the African Capacity Building Centre (ACBC) and the Global Migration Data Analysis Centre (GMDAC), as well as country offices and sub offices, treating all the projects concerning specific migration needs.

The nine regional offices develop regional strategies plus action plans and are offering support wherever needed by the countries. On a higher level, the two Special Liaison offices situated in New York and Addis Ababa focus on consolidating relations with multilateral bodies, diplomatic missions, and nongovernmental organizations.

In addition, two Administrative Centers (Panama and Manila) manage the whole technical as well as administrative support, whereas further Country Offices with Coordinating Functions have the extra responsibility to ensure the implementation of data analysis of the migratory reality in each country, and Country Offices with Resources Mobilization Functions have added responsibility for the whole budget. It is worth knowing that over 97 percent of the IOM's funding is voluntary contributions, which is completed by funding of the member states.

Apart from its decentralized organization due to various offices all over the world, the IOM coordinates all its projects while assigning each activity a distinct project code as well as a project manager, guaranteeing that the projects are directed in a responsible, transparent, and efficient manner.

CONSTITUTION AND ORGANS OF IOM

After the establishment of the Intergovernmental Committee for European Migration in 1951, its constitution was adopted on October 19, 1953, and became effective on November 30, 1954. On November 14, 1989, amendments, which were adopted by the 55th Session of the Council, entered into force, which resulted in the name change to the International Organization for Migration. Recently, on November 21, 2013, another amendment, adopted by the 76th session of the Council, became effective; it resulted in the abolishment of the Executive Committee.

All those enumerated texts are part of the present constitution, which stipulates a framework for all important issues concerning the functioning of the organization, including the purposes, function, finance, legal status, and membership.

The full juridical personality of the IOM is established by its two organs, the Administration and the Council. The Administration includes the leading executive officials of the IOM, called the director general (presently Ambassador William Lacy Swing) and the deputy director general (presently Ambassador Laura Thompson). It is its function to lead the organization in accordance with the constitution and the other two organs.

The Council, consisting of one representative per member state, with one vote each, is the highest entity of the IOM and establishes its policy. Furthermore, it independently elects the director general and the deputy director general for a period of five years. The Standing Committee on Programs and Finance (SCPF) is a subcommittee of the Council, which meets twice per year and is open to all member states, and operates in a support function. It reviews and discusses all activities, programs, and policies elaborated by the Council in administrative, financial, and budgetary issues and can also be called upon by the Council to examine specific matters.

Karin Bruckmüller

See also: Intergovernmental Organization; Migrant Smuggling; UN Protocol against the Smuggling of Migrants by Land, Air, and Sea

Further Reading

Appleyard, Reginald T. 1991. *International Migration: Challenge for the Nineties.* Geneva: International Organisation for Migration.

Bradley, Megan. 2017. "The International Organization for Migration (IOM): Gaining Power in the Forced Migration Regime." *Refuge: Canada's Journal on Refugees*

33 (1). Accessed February 15, 2019. https://refuge.journals.yorku.ca/index.php/refuge/article/view/40452

Geiger, Martin, and Antoine Pécoud, eds. 2010. *The Politics of International Migration Management*. Houndsmills, Basingstoke, Hampshire, UK: Palgrave Macmillan.

International Organisation for Migration. n.d.-a. "Mission." Accessed August 17, 2018. https://www.iom.int/mission.

International Organisation for Migration. n.d.-b. "The UN Migration Agency." Accessed August 17, 2018. https://www.iom.int.

International Police Cooperation

Investigations of transnational crime and terrorism can be complex and thus require cross-border police cooperation. International police cooperation facilitates investigations and intelligence gathering, sharing, and analysis. It regularizes bilateral and multilateral operations with the engagement of different parties, helping them to form and disseminate internationally acceptable norms, standards, and best practices.

Despite multiple benefits of international police cooperation, some governments nevertheless discourage direct contact between investigators and limit the sharing of sensitive information. This is often done due to political reasons or because governments are more interested in empowering domestic criminal justice institutions than international collaborative projects. Differences in legal systems and institutional structures, language and cultural barriers, asymmetrical levels of professionalism and training of police cadres, corruption and lack of trust are also importance obstacles to international police cooperation.

FORMS OF COOPERATION

International police cooperation can take several forms. It can be informal and formal. Informal police cooperation on an international level can be illustrated with unofficial fraternal police exchanges and the development of intentional working relationships within specialized areas of policing. Official agreements do not support this form of collaboration between law enforcement agencies. Instead, it is based on semiconfidential protocols or memoranda of understanding (MoUs), which despite allowing for some reliable channels of cooperation between the parties do not impose any legal commitments.

Another example of informal law enforcement cooperation is assigning liaison officers abroad with a host government's law enforcement agency. Overseas liaison officers (OLOs) are not permitted to carry out any law enforcement activities (e.g., arrests or interrogations). Yet, they act as contact persons and facilitate intelligence gathering and performance of law enforcement operations that require cross border coordination.

Formal international police cooperation arrangements vary too. They may be governed by bilateral agreements, multilateral treaties, or both. Whereas bilateral arrangements are tailored to the specific needs of the parties and are usually adaptable to their specific interests and needs, multilateral treaties are more resource intensive. They take a long time to draft and amend and often require a permanent infrastructure or secretariat. Additionally, they usually presuppose a greater degree of commitment from states parties. For instance, the United Nations Convention against Transnational Organized Crime (UNTOC) is one of the most important global instruments to promote international cooperation against transnational organized crime. The importance given to cooperation in the convention is reflected in Article 1, which states that the convention's purpose is "to promote cooperation to prevent and combat transnational organized crime more effectively." Article 18 calls for states parties to "afford one another the widest measure of mutual legal assistance in investigations, prosecutions and judicial proceedings." Different forms of international cooperation are encompassed by the mutual legal assistance provision, including (a) taking evidence or statements from persons to effecting service of judicial documents; (b) executing searches and seizures and freezing; (c) examining objects and sites; (d) providing information, evidentiary items, and expert evaluations; (e) identifying or tracing proceeds of crime, property, instrumentalities, or other things for evidentiary purposes; and (f) facilitating the voluntary appearance of persons in the requesting state party (UNODC 2012).

Law enforcement agencies from different states can also benefit from the use of special investigative techniques provided for in Article 20 of the UNTOC. This provision encourages states parties to conclude bilateral or multilateral agreements to make appropriate use of special investigative techniques (e.g., undercover operations, controlled delivery, and physical and electronic surveillance) to the extent that allows for "full compliance with the principle of sovereign equality of States."

INTERPOL

The International Criminal Police Organization (INTERPOL) is the largest intergovernmental organization for international police cooperation. It was created in 1923 in Vienna, Austria, as the International Criminal Police Commission. With the name change to INTERPOL in 1956, the organization has since then enlarged to 192 member states in 2018.

From the legal point of view, INTERPOL is a self-organization of police forces around the world. It is not based on a treaty or convention. Instead, INTERPOL is governed by a constitution drawn up by its members. INTERPOL is recognized as an international organization by the United Nations. The two organizations have worked together on multiple occasions, establishing a close partnership in the areas of common interest. One of INTERPOL's most active partners is the United Nations Office on Drugs and Crime (UNODC). Having worked closely for many years, the two organizations signed a formal cooperation agreement focusing on operations against organized crime and terrorism in 2016.

INTERPOL provides secure communication channels, trainings, and expert investigative support to the police and other relevant parties. Any action is taken within the limits of existing national laws and in accordance with the Universal Declaration of Human Rights. INTERPOL's constitution prohibits the organization to interfere with the domestic affairs of member states or engage in any activities of a political, military, religious, or racial character.

REGIONAL POLICE ORGANIZATIONS

Since its creation in the beginning of the 20th century, INTERPOL has served as a model for regional police organizations. Almost all regions of the world have created regional police bodies. These include the European Union's Europol, the African Union's Afripol, the Americas and the Caribbean's Ameripol, ASEANAPOL represents countries in Asia, and the Gulf Cooperation Council's GCCPOL. What unites all these regional police organizations is that they work to identify areas for collaboration and encourage greater information exchange within their organizations, among regional police organizations, and with INTERPOL and other relevant international bodies. Neither INTERPOL nor regional police organizations, however, constitute supranational police agencies with far-reaching executive powers. Secretariats of these organizations do not send officers to countries to arrest individuals. All investigations and arrests are carried out by the national police and comply with relevant national laws.

Regional police organizations vary with regards to their legal status. Some regional police organizations are independent organizations of police forces. Similar to INTERPOL, they are not based on a treaty or convention. National police forces apply for membership, appoint delegates, and contribute to the organization's budget. For instance, the Police Community of the Americas (Ameripol), founded in 2007, offers a mechanism of cooperation for police agencies in the Americas. Ameripol's Secretariat is located in Bogota, Colombia. It coordinates regional efforts in criminal investigations and judicial assistance. Ameripol has concluded partnerships with up to about 20 external organizations, including law enforcement agencies from other parts of the world (e.g., Civil Guard and National Police Corps of Spain, Italy's Guardia di Finanza and Carabinieri) and international organizations (e.g., INTERPOL, the Organization of American States).

In contrast to Ameripol, some regional police organizations are embedded in larger regional political and economic bodies and do not have complete decision-making and budgetary independence. For instance, the European Union Agency for Law Enforcement Cooperation (Europol) was created by the European Union's 1992 Maastricht Treaty. It is tasked to manage criminal intelligence and combat organized crime and terrorism. Europol is thus accountable to EU justice and interior ministers, members of the European Parliament, and a Europol Management Board drawn from all 28 EU member states. From its headquarters in The Hague, Europol supports various EU bodies working in the area of freedom, security, and justice, including the European Union Agency for Law Enforcement Training (CEPOL) and the European Anti-Fraud Office (OLAF). Its budget consists of allocations from the EU general budget.

The "shrinking" of the world brought by globalization has facilitated transnational crime. Greater international police cooperation is thus necessary for states to be able to respond to the risks posed by transnational treats. Building an effective international police relationship is important and can merit not only law enforcement activities, such as by saving time, effort, and resources, but also improve short- and long-term enmity and rivalry between countries.

Yuliya Zabyelina

See also: Europol; Hot Pursuit, International; INTERPOL; UN Convention against Transnational Organized Crime

Further Reading

Brown, Steven D. 2008. *Combating International Crime: The Longer Arm of the Law.* Abingdon, UK: Routledge-Cavendish.

Casey, John. 2010. *Policing the World: The Practice of International and Transnational Policing.* Durham, NC: Carolina Academic Press.

Madsen, Frank. 2016. "Policing Transnational Organised Crime: The International Perspective." In *International Law and Transnational Organised Crime,* edited by P. Hauck and S. Peterke, 494–509. New York: Oxford University Press.

United Nations Office on Drugs and Crime (UNODC). 2009. *International Cooperation in Trafficking in Persons Cases (Module 6). Anti-Human Trafficking Manual for Criminal Justice Practitioners.* Vienna: UNODC. Accessed March 14, 2018. http://www.unodc.org/documents/human-trafficking/TIP_module6_Ebook.pdf

United Nations Office on Drugs and Crime (UNODC). 2012. *Manual on Mutual Legal Assistance and Extradition.* Vienna: UNODC. Accessed March 14, 2018. https://www.unodc.org/documents/organized-crime/Publications/Mutual_Legal_Assistance_Ebook_E.pdf.

International Union for Conservation of Nature

The International Union for Conservation of Nature (IUCN), officially known as the International Union for Conservation of Nature and Natural Resources, is an international organization that operates to conserve the integrity and diversity of nature and attempts to ensure that any use of natural resources is equitable and sustainable. The IUCN has played a crucial role in the creation and development of major environmental conventions and international agreements, such as the Convention on International Trade in Endangered Species (CITES). Through these conventions and agreements, the IUCN plays a key role in the global movement to tackle the illegal trade of wildlife. The IUCN provides information and advice on illegal wildlife trade to coalition partners, environmental organizations, and local communities proximate to illegal wildlife hunting. Furthermore, the IUCN engages in field-based projects aimed at reducing the swelling business of illegal wildlife trade.

The IUCN provides public, private, and nongovernmental organizations with the information necessary to empower human progress, economic development, and nature conservation collectively. The IUCN's 1,300 member organizations, comprising over 10,000 conservation experts, develop, support, and lobby for the use of cutting-edge conservation science, particularly in the subject areas of species, ecosystems, and biodiversity (UNESCO n.d.). The IUCN also educates and champions the impact that these scientific achievements will have on human livelihoods. The IUCN operates in over 150 countries, with a strong presence being applied to countries who are currently in transition, the least developed countries, and small island developing states (Green Climate Fund 2016).

HISTORY

Following an international conference in Fontainebleau, France, the International Union for the Protection of Nature (IUPN) was founded in October 1948. This conference was the first global environmental union, and its goal was to bring together governments and civil society organizations under a common banner of protecting nature. The original aim was to encourage international cooperation on the conservation subject while also providing scientific knowledge and tools to guide subsequent conservation action. The organization changed its name to the International Union for Conservation of Nature and Natural Resources in 1956 and continued its work by examining the impact that specific human activities had on nature.

Beginning in the 1960s, the IUCN began work on the protection of species and the habitats necessary for their survival. In 1980, the IUCN published the *World Conservation Strategy*, which helped define the concept of sustainable development, while also assisting in the global conservation and sustainable development agenda. This preceding work, coupled with efforts throughout the 1990s, led the IUCN to be granted official observer status to the United Nations, where it remains today as the only environmental organization with such status (IUCN n.d.-b.).

ORGANIZATION

IUCN experts are organized into six branches dedicated to conservation issues that include species survival, environmental law, protected areas, social and economic policy, ecosystem management, and education and communication (IUCN n.d.-a). Each branch of investigation is tasked with upholding the IUCN's values of respecting and conserving nature, ensuring effective and equitable governance of its use, and deploying nature-based solutions to global challenges. The IUCN undertakes and supports scientific research, manages and implements various field projects on the ground, and brings together various stakeholders to develop and improve policies, laws, and best practices. These various field projects are implemented all over the world, with some projects occurring at a local level and some involving several countries. All these conservation projects are aimed at the sustainable management of biodiversity and natural resources (Green Climate Fund 2016).

The IUCN operates as a democratic organization, where voting occurs on various resolutions that will drive the conservation agenda. Meetings occur every four years at the IUCN World Conservation Congress, which calls for all parts of society to share the responsibilities and benefits of conservation (IUCN n.d.-d.).

WILDLIFE CRIME

The IUCN takes a frontline approach when challenging the illegal wildlife trade, which is assessed to be worth \$50–\$150 billion per year (IUCN n.d.-c). One such approach is through the IUCN's Environmental Law Centre (ELC), which provides environmentalist, conservationist, and legal practitioners around the world with support and legal advice to help combat poaching and illegal wildlife trade. Since its establishment in 1970, the ELC has worked in conjunction with the IUCN and the World Commission on Environmental Law (WCEL) to conceptualize, develop, and implement environmental law. The ELC is also charged with maintaining WILDLEX, a free legal database that presents relevant legislation, literature, court decisions, and training materials related to wildlife law.

IUCN RED LIST

Established in 1964, the IUCN Red List of Threatened Species is a comprehensive assessment of the present risk of extinction for thousands of animal, plant, and fungi species across the globe. The Red List is utilized as a tool to inform and spark action for conservation and policy changes critical to the protection of the natural areas inhabited by the listed species. The Red List provides information about the range, population size, habitat and ecology, use or trade, threats, and conservation actions tied to the threatened species. The goal of the Red List is to inform various entities on the necessary conservation decisions relating to the listed species as well as the global environment where the listed species inhabit. The Red List is utilized by several different entities, including government agencies, wildlife departments, conservation-related nongovernmental organizations, natural resource planners, educational organizations, students, and the business community (IUCN Red List 2017).

Jessie L. Slepicka

See also: Convention on International Trade in Endangered Species of Wild Fauna and Flora; Environmental Crimes; UN Global Programme for Combating Wildlife and Forest Crime; Wildlife and Forest Crime

Further Reading

Green Climate Fund. 2016. "IUCN—International Union for Conservation of Nature." Accessed March 14, 2018. https://www.greenclimate.fund/-/international-union-for-conservation-of-nature.

International Union for Conservation of Nature (IUCN). 2018. "IUCN 2017—International Union for Conservation of Nature Annual Report 2017." Accessed March 14, 2018. https://portals.iucn.org/library/sites/library/files/documents/Rep-2018-003-En.pdf.

International Union for Conservation of Nature (IUCN). n.d.-a. "About." Accessed March 14, 2018. https://www.iucn.org/about.

International Union for Conservation of Nature (IUCN). n.d.-b. "IUCN—A Brief History." Accessed March 14, 2018. https://www.iucn.org/about/iucn-brief-history.

International Union for Conservation of Nature (IUCN). n.d.-c. "Sustainable Use and Trade." Accessed August 22, 2018. https://www.iucn.org/theme/species/our-work/sustainable-use-and-trade.

International Union for Conservation of Nature (IUCN). n.d.-d. "World Conservation Congress." Accessed March 14, 2018. https://www.iucn.org/about/world-conservation-congress.

International Union for Conservation of Nature (IUCN) Red List. 2017. "The IUCN Red List of Threatened Species." Accessed March 14, 2018. http://www.iucnredlist.org

United Nations Educational, Scientific and Cultural Organization (UNESCO). n.d. "International Union for Conservation of Nature." Accessed March 14, 2018. https://en.unesco.org/partnerships/non-governmental-organizations/international-union-conservation-nature.

Internet Trolls

An Internet troll is an individual who engages in verbal harassment via the Internet. Hardaker (2013) defines a *troll* as "being deliberately antagonistic online, usually for amusement's sake" and *Internet trolling* as the practice of behaving in a deceptive, destructive, or disruptive manner in a social setting on the Internet with no apparent instrumental purpose. This mischievousness is what differentiates the behavior of trolls from that of malicious cyberbullies (Buckels, Trapnell, and Paulhus 2014).

Trolls can appear in many forms. Insult trolls look to post hateful comments with no true purpose. Grammar trolls comment with "**you're" to remind users that they struggle with the English language. Spammer trolls let a person know about new media releases and encourage people to purchase them (Moreau 2017). A more aggressive troll might take to obituaries or memorial pages and post inappropriate or derogatory comments about the deceased and their family in an attempt to interrupt the grieving process. The lack of committing a crime makes trolls so difficult to deal with in highly emotional situations (Phillips 2011).

WHAT MAKES A TROLL A TROLL?

Studies have found that Internet trolls have sometimes differed in their psychological makeup from other users on the Internet. Internet users that self-identified as trolls scored higher on measures of narcissism, psychopathy, and sadism (Buckels, Trapnell, and Paulhus 2014). Buckels, Trapnell, and Paulhus argue that a troll's ultimate aim is to disrupt the original post and upset the poster to fulfill the sadist mentality. Other researchers believe that trolling behaviors are about the "gaining of negative power and influence over others" (Craker and March 2016).

Internet trolls sometimes follow a pattern of behavior that stems from psychological traits; yet others are born out of individual mood and context. For instance, one study found that "mood and discussion context" are strong indicators of trolling. They believe that trolling is more situational and that any person having a bad day could become a troll with one poorly worded post by an outsider (Cheng et al. 2017). Without knowing exactly what causes the behavior of trolls, situational or psychological, Internet users are left to fend for themselves against the irritation of such posts.

LEGALITY OF TROLLING—IS IT JUST FREE SPEECH?

The *Elonis v. United States* case was a landmark case for freedom of speech online. The case involved a man who posted threats to his Facebook account aimed at his family, coworkers, and a Federal Bureau of Investigation (FBI) agent. He claimed that he was an artist, the threats were simply lyrics, and that the claims should not be taken seriously. The U.S. Supreme Court agreed and stated that there needed to be a reasonable standard of "victim," which required that those who were targeted believe the threat of violence to be more than just words on a screen (Roark 2015).

ANONYMOUS GAINS TROLLING NOTORIETY

Trolling incidents have increased in recent years. The group Anonymous is notorious for carrying out large-scale trolling events, such as the Habbo Hotel "Pool's Closed" incident in 2006. When rumors of racist policies within the online world spread, users began changing their avatars to suit-wearing, dark-skinned men with afros and formed human shields blocking other users from the pool, responding with simply "Pool's Closed due to AIDS." While immature, this event marks the beginning of many similar online trolling events (YF 2017).

Taylor S. Fisher

See also: Cyberbullying; Hackers

Further Reading

Buckels, Erin E., Paul D. Trapnell, and Delroy L. Paulhus. 2014. "Trolls Just Want to Have Fun." Personality and Individual Differences 67: 97–102.

Cheng, Justin, Michael Bernstein, Cristian Danescu-Niculescu-Mizil, and Jure Leskovec. 2017. "Anyone Can Become a Troll: Causes of Trolling Behavior in Online Discussions." https://files.clr3.com/papers/2017_anyone.pdf.

Craker, Naomi, and Evita March. 2016. "The Dark Side of Facebook: The Dark Tetrad, Negative Social Potency, and Trolling Behaviours." *Personality and Individual Differences* 102: 79–84.

Hardaker, Claire. 2013. "'Uh . . . . Not to Be Nitpicky, but . . . the Past Tense of Drag Is Dragged, Not Drug': An Overview of Trolling Strategies." *Journal of Language Aggression and Conflict* 1 (1): 58–86.

Moreau, Elise. 2017. "10 Types of Internet Trolls You'll Meet Online." Lifewire, May 19. Accessed November 16, 2017. https://www.lifewire.com/types-of-internet-trolls-3485894.

Phillips, Whitney. 2011. "LOLing at Tragedy: Facebook Trolls, Memorial Pages and Resistance to Grief Online." *First Monday* 16 (12). https://firstmonday.org/article/view/3168/3115

Roark, Mary Margaret. 2015. "*Elonis v. United States*: The Doctrine of True Threats: Protecting Our Ever-Shrinking First Amendment Rights in the New Era of Communication." *Pittsburgh Journal of Technology Law and Policy* 15 (2): 197–223.

YF. 2017. "Pool's Closed" Know Your Meme, September 27. Accessed November 16, 2017. http://knowyourmeme.com/memes/pools-closed.

INTERPOL

The International Criminal Police Organization, officially abbreviated to ICPO-INTERPOL, is widely recognized as simply INTERPOL. INTERPOL is not an international police or detective force with worldwide jurisdiction. It does not have the power to investigate crimes, arrest individuals, or interrogate suspects. Instead, it is an information clearinghouse that enables the investigation of transnational crime among member countries by facilitating the mutual exchange of information among police agencies. Investigations are conducted by the national police forces of member nations under their own sovereign laws. INTERPOL's role is to supply information to these national police forces.

HISTORY

The idea of international cooperation in police activities was introduced in 1914 at the International Criminal Police Congress held in Monaco. World War I (1914–1918) postponed action, but in 1923, the International Criminal Police Commission (ICPC) was established in Vienna, Austria. World War II (1939–1945) caused suspension of activities until 1946, when Belgium led the organization's rebuilding. The ICPC continued to grow, and in 1956, it was renamed the International Criminal Police Organization (INTERPOL).

In 1989, INTERPOL moved its General Secretariat from Paris to Lyon, France, where it continues to operate. Growth and expansion endures, and in 2015, the Global Complex for Innovation was opened in Singapore, where INTERPOL works to combat cybercrime by providing police around the world with innovative techniques and training to address emerging threats of cybercrime (INTERPOL 2017a; Reichel 2018).

INTERPOL is not based on an international treaty, convention, or any similar document. Nonetheless, it is treated as a legitimate organization by most governments of the world, is recognized as an intergovernmental organization by the United Nations, and has Special Representative offices at the African Union and the European Union. Member nations must apply for membership, appoint delegates, pay an annual contribution, and abide by the INTERPOL rules.

ORGANIZATION

INTERPOL operates with two interrelated governing bodies, the General Assembly and the Executive Committee. The General Assembly, composed of delegates appointed by each member country, meets annually on issues related to policy, resources, working methods, finances, activities, and programs. The Executive Committee, elected by the General Assembly, provides guidance and direction and oversees the implementation of General Assembly decisions. Actual implementation of those decisions falls to the General Secretariat in Lyon and through seven regional offices around the world.

The specific point of contact for any member country is the Command and Coordination Centre (CCC), which operates from the General Secretariat in Lyon and, to provide better support across time zones, at additional sites in Buenos Aires, Argentina, and Singapore. The CCC is in continuous operation and has staff members from various backgrounds and nationalities who are fluent in several different languages. All incoming communication is assessed by the CCC to determine what priority level it should be assigned. The CCC also issues warnings to police and the public regarding potential threats, coordinates the exchange of intelligence and information, and monitors open sources to assess threats and to ensure INTERPOL resources are ready and available whenever and wherever they may be needed.

NATIONAL CENTRAL BUREAUS

The structure of policing varies considerably around the world. Some countries have a single national police force, others organize policing at the state or province level, and still others, such as the United States, have thousands of police organizations at local, state, and federal jurisdictions. Given that diversity, it can be difficult for police in one country to know what agency to contact in another. For INTERPOL member countries, the system of National Central Bureaus (NCBs) assists in this communication between law enforcement agencies in different countries.

Each INTERPOL member country maintains an NCB, staffed by the country's own law enforcement officers, linking the country's police to INTERPOL's global network. The NCBs provide information for INTERPOL's criminal databases and facilitate cooperation on cross border investigations, operations, and arrests. Because each country controls its own NCB, they differ widely in size, personnel, and level of activity. However, each NCB is responsible for: (1) maintaining open channels to all police units in its own country; (2) maintaining connections with the NCBs of all other member countries; and (3) maintaining a liaison with the General Secretariat. In this manner, the NCBs provide a contact point in each member nation to allow the coordination of international criminal investigations (Reichel 2018).

Determining which police agency will serve as a country's NCB is not difficult in countries with centralized systems. In Austria, for example, where policing is provided by a department of the Federal Ministry of the Interior, the NCB is part of the Austrian Criminal Intelligence Service (CIS). In countries with greater decentralization of policing, determining the placement of the NCB is more difficult. In the extremely decentralized United States, with nearly 18,000 different police agencies, it would be practically and politically unsuitable to name a state or local police department as the country's representative to INTERPOL. Instead, the NCB of the United States (INTERPOL Washington) is in Washington, D.C., where it operates under the Department of Justice in conjunction with the Department of Homeland Security. It serves as the official U.S. point of contact with INTERPOL and supports local, state, federal, and tribal law enforcement agencies in the United States—as well as any foreign counterparts—that seek assistance in criminal investigations extending beyond national borders.

SPECIFIC TOOLS

Facilitation of global communication by INTERPOL occurs primarily with databases of international criminals and criminal activity. Member countries are provided with instant direct access to multiple databases that contain millions of records on fingerprints, DNA, stolen motor vehicles, firearms, stolen and lost travel documents, suspected foreign terrorist fighters, a criminal's modus operandi, and more. These databases share information that has been contributed to daily by member countries. Access to most of the databases is provided to frontline law enforcement officers, such as border guards, without having to make a request through the country's NCB. This allows the officer to simultaneously submit a query to a national database and an INTERPOL database for information on wanted persons, stolen and lost travel documents, and stolen motor vehicles.

A primary way INTERPOL tracks international criminals is by sending out notices to police forces around the world. These notices are requests for cooperation or alerts that allow police in member countries to share crime-related information. They serve to warn police about criminals or about other issues relevant to the global law enforcement community. For example, at the request of a member country, the General Secretariat can issue a "Red Notice" to all members. That notice, which may contain details of the case, criminal history, photographs, and fingerprints of an internationally wanted criminal, asks for assistance in the location and arrest of wanted persons. Member nations use that information to locate, arrest, and detain the suspect pending an extradition application.

Upon request, INTERPOL will provide member countries with specialized teams to assist the national police. Incident Response Teams (IRTs) are deployed during a crisis—either disaster (such as a large-scale accident or natural disaster) or a serious police issue (for example, a terrorist attack). An IRT, composed of highly specialized and trained personnel relevant to the disaster or crime, can be briefed, equipped, and deployed within 12–24 hours of an incident. The team provides on-site investigative and analytical support.

The INTERPOL Major Events Support Teams (IMESTs) are deployed to assist in the preparation, coordination, and implementation of security arrangements for major events. Since events that attract large crowds or intense media coverage also attract individuals or groups seeking criminal gain or intent on gaining attention through disruption, an IMEST can assist national police in making efficient use of INTERPOL's array of databases. The first IMEST was deployed in 2002 to the Winter Olympics in Salt Lake City, Utah.

Cooperation with INTERPOL is completely voluntary, even among member countries. Requests for assistance or information may be accommodated or ignored by an NCB. Issues of sovereignty require that INTERPOL allow countries to pursue their own criminal justice policies as they deem appropriate (Fichtelberg 2008). Further, INTERPOL's constitution, through its neutrality clause, forbids INTERPOL from undertaking any intervention or activities of a political, military, religious, or racial character. These limits help INTERPOL avoid being used as a tool by governments wishing to carry out oppressive policies under the guise of law enforcement.

Philip L. Reichel

See also: Eurojust; Europol; International Police Cooperation; INTERPOL Notices System

Further Reading

Fichtelberg, Aaron. 2008. *Crimes without Borders: An Introduction to International Criminal Justice.* Upper Saddle River, NJ: Pearson/Prentice Hall.

Haberfeld, Maria, William McDonald, and Agostino von Hassell. 2008. "International Cooperation in Policing." In *Comparative Policing: The Struggle for Democratization*, edited by Maria R. Haberfeld and Ibrahim Cerrah, 341–375. Los Angeles: SAGE Publications.

INTERPOL. 2017a. "Overview." Accessed January 21, 2019. https://www.interpol.int/About-INTERPOL/Overview.

INTERPOL. 2017b. "Response Teams." Accessed January 21, 2019. https://www.interpol.int/INTERPOL-expertise/Response-teams/Incident-Response-Teams.

Reichel, Philip L. 2018. *Comparative Criminal Justice Systems: A Topical Approach.* 7th ed. New York: Pearson.

U.S. Department of Justice (DOJ). 2017. "About INTERPOL Washington." Last Modified February 2, 2017. Accessed January 21, 2019. https://www.justice.gov/interpol-washington/about-interpol-washington.

INTERPOL Notices System

The International Criminal Police Organization (known as INTERPOL) is an information clearinghouse that enables the investigation of transnational crime among its 192-member countries. INTERPOL tracks international criminals by sending out notices to police forces around the world. These notices are requests for cooperation or alerts that allow police in member countries to share crime-related information.

PROCEDURES

Notices are international requests for cooperation that allow police in member countries to share critical crime-related information. They are used to alert police around the world about crimes, criminals, and threats to safety and also to request assistance in solving crimes. They are published by INTERPOL's General Secretariat at the request of National Central Bureaus (NCBs). An NCB is the organizational entity that allows a member country to interact with INTERPOL's global network. The NCB is made up of the member country's own law enforcement officers and the NCB.

When a member country believes the international community can be of assistance in locating a suspect, the member country's NCB issues a notice that alerts all the other member countries about the suspect and requests their assistance in a potential arrest and extradition. For example, in 2015, authorities in Nepal issued a Red Notice, discussed later, for a fugitive wanted in Nepal for rape and multiple murders. In 2018, police authorities in Qatar located the fugitive working as a laborer in Doha. The fugitive was arrested and deported by Qatari authorities to Nepal, where he was awaiting trial in 2018 (INTERPOL 2018b).

TYPES OF NOTICES

INTERPOL uses seven color-coded notices for a variety of situations. Of the color-coded notices, the most important and well-known is the Red Notice. It is a request by one country for other countries to help locate and potentially extradite a suspect sought by the requesting country. As such, persons for whom a Red Notice has been issued are not wanted by INTERPOL but by a specific country. Although it is not an international arrest warrant, a Red Notice is considered by many of INTERPOL's member countries to be a valid request for provisional arrest. In 2017 and 2018, for example, Red Notices were issued for a suspected ivory smuggler (by Malawi), for a tiger trafficker (by Nepal), and for a leader of one of the largest drug cartels (by Russia).

A Blue Notice is issued when a member country wants to collect information about a person's identity, location, or activities regarding a particular crime. Green Notices, on the other hand, provide warnings and intelligence about persons who have committed crimes and are believed likely to continue doing so in other countries. A Yellow Notice attempts to locate missing persons or to identify persons who are unable to identify themselves. They are also issued for victims of parental abductions, kidnappings, or unexplained disappearances. A Black Notice seeks information on unidentified bodies, and a Purple Notice is either looking for or providing information about a criminal's methods of operation. The last of the color-coded notices, an Orange Notice, warns about an event, person, object, or development presenting a serious and imminent threat to public safety (INTERPOL 2108b).

In addition to the seven color-coded notices, INTERPOL also issues Special Notices and diffusions. The Special Notices (formally, INTERPOL—United Nations Security Council Special Notices) are issued for persons and entities subject to sanctions by the UN Security Council. For example, if a person or entity is under a travel ban or has had their assets frozen, the Special Notices alert law enforcement agencies worldwide about these sanctions.

Similar to the various notices, diffusions are also alerts or requests for cooperation, but they are less formal and are circulated directly by an NCB rather than through the INTERPOL General Secretariat.

ABUSE OF THE SYSTEM

According to the INTERPOL constitution, notices are not to be issued if they are of a political, military, religious, or racial character. That prohibition has not stopped some countries from using notices to seek the arrest and extradition of dissidents who are considered a political problem by the issuing country. For example, in 2017, Human Rights Watch (HRW) accused China of misusing the Red Notice system to have other countries arrest and extradite persons living abroad who China considers to be politically problematic (HRW 2017). Also, several times in recent years, Russia has tried to use the notice system (especially diffusion notices) to have antigovernment activists arrested and extradited. INTERPOL repeatedly rejects the Russian requests, but there have been times when an arrest was already made—as happened in Spain, in 2017, when the Spanish National Police arrested but then released a critic of Russian president Putin after deciding the request from Russia was politically motivated (Gilsinan 2018).

TOOLS IN FIGHTING GLOBAL CRIME

The diffusion and INTERPOL notice system are tools that encourage and support international cooperation in combating transnational crime. As member countries work together to inform one another about people and events threatening domestic and international security, the ability of law enforcement to counter the cross border movements of criminals is enhanced.

Sergio Yépez Cordero and Philip L. Reichel

See also: International Police Cooperation; INTERPOL

Further Reading

Gilsinan, Kathy. 2018. "How Russia Tries to Catch Its 'Criminals' by Abusing Interpol." *The Atlantic*, May 30. Last modified May 30, 2018. Accessed January 16, 2019. https://www.theatlantic.com/international/archive/2018/05/russia-interpol-abuse/561539.

Human Rights Watch (HRW). 2017. "Interpol: Address China's 'Red Notice' Abuses." Last modified September 25, 2017. Accessed January 16, 2019. https://www.hrw.org/news/2017/09/25/interpol-address-chinas-red-notice-abuses.

INTERPOL. 2018a. "About INTERPOL." Accessed August 17, 2018. https://www.interpol.int/About-INTERPOL/Overview

INTERPOL. 2018b. "Notices." Accessed August 17, 2018. https://www.interpol.int/INTERPOL-expertise/Notices

Reichel, Philip L. 2018. *Comparative Criminal Justice Systems: A Topical Approach*. 7th ed. New York: Pearson.

Islamic State of Iraq and Syria (ISIS)

The Islamic State of Iraq and Syria (ISIS) is a militant Islamist organization. Though based primarily in Iraq and Syria, ISIS has as many as 25 affiliates in as many as 21 countries (TRAC n.d.). The group operates in the Middle East with a loose network of other militant Islamist groups, and it aims to overthrow local governments and replace them with an Islamic caliphate. The group is opposed militarily by the Assad regime in Syria, Russia, and the Global Coalition, a group of 75 partners of countries and intergovernmental organizations led primarily by the United States.

CONFUSION OF WORDING

The group most widely known as ISIS has changed its own name several times, and it has also been referred to by different names by the media and governments, leading to some confusion about the name of the group.

When the group first gained notoriety in the 2014, when it officially entered the Syrian Civil War, it called itself *al Dawla al-Islamiyya fi al-Iraq wa-al-Sham*, which translates to "the Islamic State of Iraq and al-Sham." Arabic-language media decided to use the acronym *Daesh* (Reynolds 2016), which sounds similar to the word *daes*, or "to crush underfoot," and is often used pejoratively (Bilefsky 2014). Western media and governments had trouble translating the word *al-Sham*. Classically, al-Sham has referred to a large area known also as the Levant, which includes modern-day Syria, Lebanon, and Jordan. This is the source of the name ISIL, or "the Islamic State of Iraq and the Levant." Al-Sham, however, has also historically referred to just Syria, so many just substituted *al-Sham* with *Syria* and kept the acronym, ISIS, the same. The choice of title is largely political. The use of the word *Levant* in the name was more accurate to the group's goals, as it accounts for a larger territory than just Syria. "Daesh" became popular among Western governments toward the end of 2014 after it gained traction in Arabic media, largely because of the negative connotations associated with the term (Reynolds 2016).

FUNDING WITH TRANSNATIONAL CRIME

In addition to taxation, ISIS has relied on transnational organized crime for funding, including through kidnapping for ransom and the trafficking of antiquities, oil, narcotics, and humans (Tierney 2017). Oil trafficking was initially the largest source of income for ISIS, producing an estimated annual profit of between $730 million and $1,460 million. Sanctions placed on buyers of the oil were difficult to enforce and generally unsuccessful at preventing trade from happening. To make up for the potential risks to buyers, ISIS sold their oil at deeply discounted prices (Martin and Solomon 2017). To get the oil to market, the group often used the same routes that Saddam Hussein had used in the 1990s to circumvent international sanctions (Ryder 2018). However, this funding source proved to be highly insecure, as coalition forces began targeted strikes on oil fields under the control of the group. As oil revenues declined, the group expedited sales of antiquities stolen from museums, cultural heritage sites, and private collections to dealers worldwide. The group reportedly set up an office to handle the extraction and trafficking of antiquities, which garnered as much as $200 million per year.

The second-largest source of revenue, and the most stable, came from illegal taxation of the populations living under the group's control, which produced about $360 million per year. ISIS justifies these taxes under the principle of *zakat*, or alms, found in Islam. The group taxes everything from commercial activity to imports and exports into controlled territories, to utility provision, to school attendance.

Finally, ISIS uses a mixture of other illegal activities such as narcotics smuggling, human trafficking, and kidnapping for ransom, to finance itself. Heroin in particular has been a stable source of revenue for the group and is smuggled to European and African markets. Human trafficking is used by the group both as a recruitment strategy and a source of revenue. Women and children from religious minorities, particularly Yazidis, are kidnapped and then sold at auction for relatively low prices so that male fighters can buy them to marry or just to use them as sex slaves. In addition, the group has capitalized on the migrant crisis that they in part created, smuggling people from North Africa and the Middle East into Europe (Martin and Solomon 2017). ISIS often kidnaps foreigners and demands ransoms from their families, insurance companies, or governments. A number of European countries, including Germany, France, Italy, and Spain, have all paid out ransoms for the return of their citizens, though a UN Security Council resolution has called this practice counterproductive (Ryder 2018).

IDEOLOGY

ISIS selects ideological tenets from various strains of Islam, especially Salafism. Salafis seek to strip Islam of its cultural trappings and revert the religion to the form practiced by the Prophet Muhammad and the generation that directly followed him (Hassan 2016).

The justification for the founding of an Islamic state comes from an extreme interpretation of a core principle of Islam, *tawhid*, or monotheism. In this interpretation, living in a state in which *sharia* is not the basis of national law constitutes serving something before Allah and is therefore polytheistic. Under this strict definition of *tawhid*, Shia and Sufi practices are polytheistic, as they place imams and ritual between themselves and Allah.

ISIS also borrows from Wahhabism, a subset of Salafism, the principle of *wala wal bara*, an extension of *tawhid*. *Wala wal bara* states that Muslims must not only practice monotheism but also must wholeheartedly reject anything un-Islamic. ISIS also borrows the broadened practice of *takfir*, excommunication of other Muslims branded as infidels for disagreement over religious practice, from Sayyid Qutb (1906–1966), one of the leaders of the Muslim Brotherhood during the 1950s. The combination of *tawhid*, *wala wal bara*, and *takfir* provide the justification for the creation of an Islamic state and the use of violence against anyone in opposition in service of that goal, even if they self-identify as Muslim (Hassan 2016).

ORIGINS

ISIS started as an offshoot of the local terrorist organization Al Qaeda in Iraq (AQI). The group that later became AQI started as Jamaat al-Tawhid wal-Jihad (JTJ) by Abu-Musab al Zarqawi (1966–2006) in 2000 with funding from Osama bin Laden (1957–2011), who wanted to strengthen Al Qaeda's reach in Iraq. By 2003, ahead of the American invasion of Iraq, Zarqawi had assembled a sizeable group. In 2004, the group pledged allegiance to Al Qaeda and bin Laden and formally became AQI (Byman 2016).

It was not until after Zarqawi's death in 2006 that AQI, under the leadership of Abu Ayub al-Masri (1968–2010) and later Abu Omar al-Baghdadi (1959–2010), declared its intentions of building a Sunni state in the Levant, the Islamic State of Iraq (ISI) (Hashim 2014).

AQI/ISI alienated many Sunni tribes by trying to force participation in the newly declared state and, when faced with reluctance, killed the family members of the leaders of the tribes. This violence drove many Sunni tribes to seek a deal with the U.S. forces, promising intelligence support in exchange for protection from AQI/ISI (Byman 2016), involvement of Sunnis in Iraqi security forces, and financial aid for Sunni areas under severe economic hardship. Over the next four years, the U.S. military heavily targeted AQI/ISI, and ultimately, in April 2010, U.S.-Iraqi coalition forces killed both Ayub al-Masri and Omar al-Baghdadi.

After the death of the core leadership, Ibrahim Awwad Ibrahim Ali al-Badri Al-Samarri, also known as Abu Bakr al-Baghdadi, assumed control of the organization. At this point, AQI/ISI was all but dissolved. Previously, al-Baghdadi created his own militant Islamist group, Jaish ahl-Sunnah wal-Jamaah (Army of the People of Tradition and Unification), operating in Samarra, Diyala, and Baghdad. When American troops jailed al-Baghdadi in February 2004, his group folded into AQI. After his release around 11 months later, he also joined AQI (Hashim 2014).

After the start of the Syrian Civil War in 2011, AQ/ISI sent representatives to join diverse, fragmented, and expanding anti-Assad forces. These representatives, mostly Syrians that had fought American and Iraqi forces in Iraq, joined a group being formed by Abu Muhammad al-Jawlani known as Jabhat al-Nusra. In April 2013, al-Baghdadi claimed Jabhat al-Nusra as an agent of ISI and announced a formal merger of the two groups.

Al-Baghdadi moved more forces into Syria and set about taking control of territory, including the city of Raqqa in northeastern Syria, with the intent of establishing a functioning state. Al-Jawlani rejected the merger declaration and appealed to Al Qaeda central leadership to prevent AQI/ISI from pursuing the merger. Ayman al-Zawahiri released a statement ordering AQI to limit the scope of its operation to Iraq. After al-Baghdadi refused to give up his claim on Jabhat al-Nusra, Zawahiri ordered that AQI be dissolved. After an 8-month-long dispute between al-Baghdadi and Zawahiri, Al Qaeda formally severed ties with ISI, now rebranded as the Islamic State in Iraq and Syria (ISIS), and in 2014 staged a rapid offensive to gain more territory in Iraq (Hashim 2014).

BUILDING THE CALIPHATE

On June 29, 2014, al-Baghdadi declared the territory the group controlled in Syria and Iraq to be a caliphate and himself the caliph. He also began to refer to the group as simply "the Islamic State," dropping mention of territorial bounds. In the early period of territorial growth, much of the additions came from peaceful surrenders of villages in the Deir ez-Zour province of Syria (Hashim 2014). At that point, ISIS already controlled Fallujah, Mosul, Tikrit, and parts of Ramadi in Iraq and Raqqa and Deir ez-Zour in Syria (Glenn 2016).

In early August 2014, ISIS captured two Kurdish towns, Sinjar and Zumar, and began killing the Yazidi population in the area (Glenn 2016). The attempted genocide of the Yazidis prompted the Barack Obama administration to authorize air strikes on the ISIS forces (Byman 2016). These air strikes began on September 23, 2014. In between the announcement of the air strikes and the first strike, ISIS beheaded two American journalists, James Foley and Steven Sotloff, and a British aid worker, David Haines. ISIS filmed the executions and posted the videos online.

In 2015, while battling the Syrian government, Kurdish Peshmerga, the United States, and other Syrian rebel forces, ISIS gained more territory in Syria and Iraq, including the rest of Ramadi, Palmyra, and villages on the outskirts of Aleppo. ISIS-affiliated militants also seized the town of Sirte in Libya, Muammar Ghaddafi's hometown (Glenn 2016).

The tide in the war against ISIS began to turn against the group in late 2015, when it lost control of a number of key cities, including Ramadi, Fallujah, and Sirte, and the symbolic town of Dabiq. At the same time, ISIS faced serious pressure from U.S.-led coalition forces in Mosul (Glenn 2016).

Governance

In 2016, ISIS released a video detailing the structure of the provincial governments they claimed to have established. The video showed that ISIS central leadership divided the territory gained into different provinces and appointed a governor, a deputy governor, and an Islamic legal scholar to run each province. Each province was to have a series of bureaus, or *diwawin*, including the *diwan* of education, *hisba* (morality enforcement), soldiery, health, treasury, *zakat* (taxation) and agriculture, proselytizing and mosques, public services, resources, and of *fay'* and *ghana'im* (war spoils) (Raqqa Is Being Slaughtered Silently 2016).

In all of the cities controlled, local ISIS administrations levied harsh taxation structures, heavily enforced strict social codes with strict penalties, and ruled through intimidation. The government institutions ISIS set up varied in efficiency among territories. In cities that were relatively safe from attack, authorities could use more of the tax money earned to support economic growth, and government institutions functioned reasonably well, continuing to provide utilities and repairing and updating infrastructure. However, in cities that were vulnerable to attack, including Tikrit and Deir ez-Zour, ISIS did not provide even a minimum standard of governance (Robinson et al. 2017).

The Foreign Fighter Phenomenon

Due in part to a highly sophisticated propaganda machine making use of social network platforms such as Twitter, Facebook, Telegram, and WhatsApp, ISIS inspired an unprecedented number of foreign fighters and others to travel to Syria and Iraq to join the organization. At ISIS's peak in 2015, it had attracted as many as 31,000 people (Barrett et al. 2015). After ISIS began to lose territory in 2016, the flow of foreign fighters was significantly reduced. However, the number of women and children traveling to the region increased (Barrett et al. 2017). Initially, the greatest number of fighters were arriving from neighboring Muslim countries. The three largest sources of fighters were Tunisia, Saudi Arabia, and Morocco, and they accounted for over half of the total fighters in the country prior to 2014 (Barrett 2014). However, between 2014 and 2017, former Soviet republics and Western Europe provided growing percentages of foreign fighters. Though other militant Islamist groups attracted foreign fighters, ISIS was the most popular of the groups joined (Barrett et al. 2017).

Lilla Heins

See also: Al Qaeda; Barcelona and Cambrils Terrorist Attacks (2017); Brussels Bombings (2016); Crime-Terrorism Nexus; Manchester Arena Terrorist Attack (2017); Manhattan Truck Attack (2017); Paris and *Charlie Hebdo* Terrorist Attacks (2015); Returning Foreign Terrorist Fighters; Terrorism, International; Terrorism, Online Propaganda; Terrorism, Vehicle Ramming Attacks

Further Reading

Barrett, Richard. 2014. "Foreign Fighters in Syria." The Soufan Group. Accessed January 17, 2019. http://soufangroup.com/wp-content/uploads/2014/06/TSG-Foreign-Fighters-in-Syria.pdf.

Barrett, Richard, Jack Berger, Lila Ghosh, Daniel Schoenfeld, Mohamed el-Shawesh, Patrick M. Skinner, Susan Sim, and Ali Soufan. 2015. "Foreign Fighters: An Updated Assessment of the Flow of Foreign Fighters into Syria and Iraq." The Soufan Group. http://soufangroup.com/wp-content/uploads/2015/12/TSG_ForeignFightersUpdate_FINAL3.pdf

Barrett, Richard, Stephanie Foggett, Melissa Salyk-Virk, Marie Siegel, Meredith Stricker, and Ali Soufan. 2017. "Beyond the Caliphate: Foreign Fighters and the Threat of Returnees." The Soufan Group. https://thesoufancenter.org/wp-content/uploads/2017/11/Beyond-the-Caliphate-Foreign-Fighters-and-the-Threat-of-Returnees-TSC-Report-October-2017-v3.pdf

Bilefsky, Dan. 2014. "In New Front against Islamic State, Dictionary Becomes a Weapon." *New York Times*, October 2, sec. World. Accessed January 21, 2019. https://www.nytimes.com/2014/10/03/world/europe/islamic-state-isis-muslims-term.html.

Byman, Daniel. 2016. "Understanding the Islamic State—A Review Essay." *International Security* 40 (4): 127–165.

Glenn, Cameron. 2016. "Timeline: The Rise, Spread and Fall of the Islamic State." Wilson Center, July 5. Accessed January 17, 2019. https://www.wilsoncenter.org/article/timeline-the-rise-spread-and-fall-the-islamic-state.

Hashim, Ahmed S. 2014. "The Islamic State: From Al-Qaeda Affiliate to Caliphate." *Middle East Policy* 21 (4): 69–83.

Hassan, Hassan. 2016. "The Sectarianism of the Islamic State: Ideological Roots and Political Context." Carnegie Endowment for International Peace. https://carnegieendowment.org/2016/06/13/sectarianism-of-islamic-state-ideological-roots-and-political-context-pub-63746Martin, Michaela and Hussein Solomon. 2017. "Islamic State: Understanding the Nature of the Beast and Its Funding." *Contemporary Review of the Middle East* 4 (1): 18–49.

Raqqa Is Being Slaughtered Silently. 2016. "The Truth of the Islamic State's Governance." *Atlantic Council*, July 28. Last updated July 28, 2016. Accessed January 17, 2019. http://www.atlanticcouncil.org/blogs/syriasource/the-truth-of-the-islamic-state-s-governance.

Reynolds, Gabriel Said. 2016. "Naming an Enemy: Islamic State, IS, ISIL, ISIS, or Daesh?" *Huffington Post* (blog), June 3. Accessed January 21, 2019. https://www.huffingtonpost.com/gabriel-said-reynolds/naming-an-enemy-islamic-s_b_10217768.html.

Robinson, Eric, Daniel Egel, Patrick B. Johnston, Sean Mann, Alexander D. Rothenberg, and David Stebbins. 2017. *When the Islamic State Comes to Town.* RAND

Corporation. Accessed January 16, 2019. https://www.rand.org/pubs/research_reports/RR1970.html.

Ryder, Nicholas. 2018. "Out with the Old and . . . in with the Old? A Critical Review of the Financial War on Terrorism on the Islamic State in the Levant." *Studies in Conflict & Terrorism* 41 (2): 79–95.

Tierney, Michael. 2017. "Well-Funded and Dangerous: Assessing the Islamic State's Financing Operations." *Journal of Money Laundering Control; London* 20 (2): 159–171.

TRAC. n.d. "Islamic State (IS)." Accessed April 29, 2018. https://www.trackingterrorism.org/group/islamic-state-islamic-state-iraq-and-ash-sham-isis-islamic-state-iraq-isis-or-isil.

J

Jalisco New Generation Cartel (Cartel de Jalisco Nueva Generación)

The Cartel de Jalisco Nueva Generación (CJNG) is a transnational criminal organization that developed in response to the widespread use of armed groups, such as Los Zetas and La Linea. Under the leadership of the Sinaloa Cartel, the group was known as "Los Matazetas" (literally, "Zeta Killers"). The CJNG developed circa 2007 as a response to Los Zetas' widespread acts of violence throughout Mexico (Flores 2018). In its formative years, the CJNG was involved in the killing of rival armed wing members in the state of Veracruz, located southeast of the rival territory of the Gulf Cartel's/Los Zetas' armed wing faction, Tamaulipas. Between 2010 and 2011, Los Matazetas splintered from the Sinaloa Cartel and changed its name to the CJNG, with its headquarters in the state of Jalisco, Mexico (Cartel 2017; Flores 2018). The CJNG rapidly expanded its areas of operations and has a presence in 14 Mexican states and the United States and is considered to have surpassed its rival cartels in smuggling cocaine, heroin, synthetic drugs, and marijuana into the United States (Flores 2018). With a global presence on six continents, the cartel obtains cocaine from Colombia, ephedrine for processing methamphetamine from China, and opium from Guerrero, Mexico, to process heroin ("Jalisco Cartel New Generation" 2018; "Mexican Authorities" 2018).

ORGANIZATION

The CJNG is a violent organization led by Ruben Osegura Cervantes, also known as Nemesio Oseguera Cervantes, "El Mencho." The group operates in cells throughout Mexico, and its henchman have been trained in tactics used by the Revolutionary Armed Forces of Colombia (FARC) and the Kaibiles of Guatemala, a special forces group from the military (Flores 2018). The arrest of a CJNG boss in Tijuana, Baja California, revealed that hitmen are paid $15,000 Mexican pesos for each execution of a rival member (R 2016). In certain instances, the CJNG has reportedly been using social media to further its recruitment efforts (Gallegos 2017). Such was the case in the state of Jalisco, where it was alleged that the CJNG set up fake job advertisements via Facebook to recruit 16- to 35-year-olds, who were then forced to attend the group's training camps (Gallegos 2017).

The online presence of the CJNG, however, predates its recruitment efforts. In the early stages of the CJNG's development, and continuously, its online presence was used for waging war against rival cartels, denouncing military actions and law enforcement personnel, and torturing its victims before killing them (Dittmar

2018). The typical modus operandi of the CJNG using the social media platform YouTube involves having their victims answer questions, such as who they work for, what their role was, who they are denouncing, and why they are about to be killed, while a group of CJNG members stand behind them in ski masks and armed with weapons. Another scenario shows a group of CJNG members either standing or sitting down and more CJNG members standing or kneeling in the background while the spokesmen denounce government actions and promote their own agenda (Redaccion 2018). In the early days of February 2018, the CJNG kidnapped two agents from the organized crime unit of the Attorney General's Office (SEIDO, its Spanish acronym) and uploaded the video of the interrogation onto YouTube. The two agents were later found dead in Xalisco, Nayarit (Dittmar 2018).

TURF WARS

The CJNG wages war against rival cartels for the control of viable routes and key strategic ports of entry throughout Mexico. The use of social media has been one method of demonstrating their brute and violent actions as a method to control or win an area in dispute. In the state of Michoacán, the CJNG has been involved in a turf war with the Viagras and fragments of La Familia Michoacana and the Knights Templar. And in the states of Baja California, Jalisco, Nayarit, and Sinaloa, it has been waging a bloody battle with the Sinaloa Cartel (Woody 2016). The level of violence for the key routes and control of the zones led to a 20 percent increase in homicides for the year 2016 (Garcia Ramos 2017).

NOTABLE EVENTS

The CJNG has been involved in numerous high-profile attacks against rival members and law enforcement. Some of the most notable were the May 2015 downing of a military Blackhawk helicopter with a rocket-propelled grenade in the state of Jalisco, the massacre of 35 people in Veracruz in 2011, and an April 2015 attack that left 15 police officers dead (Nemesio 2018).

On May 23, 2018, it was reported that, in an attempt to sway the 2018 elections, a CJNG commando unit of approximately 20 men attacked the candidate for governor, leaving a baby dead and 15 other wounded. The CJNG members set fire to vehicles and public transportation sites (Ortega, Ibal, and Chavez 2018).

Jairo Patiño

See also: Los Zetas; Sinaloa Cartel

Further Reading

Dittmar, Victoria. 2018. "Is Mexico's CJNG Following in the Footsteps of the Zetas?" *InSight Crime.* Last modified February 19, 2018. Accessed January 17, 2019. https://www.insightcrime.org/news/analysis/mexicos-cjng-following-footsteps-zetas.

Flores, Raul. 2018. "CJNG Lidera Trasiego de Drogas a EU; Nació como Los Matazetas." Excelsior. Last modified February 2, 2018. Accessed January 17, 2019. http://www.excelsior.com.mx/nacional/2018/02/10/1219402.

Gallegos, Zorayda. 2017. "Mexico's Jalisco Drug Cartel Uses Facebook to Recruit New Hitmen." El Pais. Last modified August 3, 2017. Accessed January 17, 2019. https://elpais.com/elpais/2017/08/01/inenglish/1501585590_499112.html.

Garcia Ramos, Ines. 2017. "De la Pax Sinaloa al Empoderamiento del CJNG." Zeta Tijuana, Last modified April 24, 2017. Accessed January 17, 2019. http://zetatijuana.com/2017/04/de-la-pax-sinaloa-al-empoderamiento-del-cjng.

"Jalisco Cartel New Generation (CJNG)." 2018. *InSight Crime*. Last modified March 30, 2018. Accessed February 9, 2019. https://www.insightcrime.org/mexico-organized-crime-news/jalisco-cartel-new-generation/

Lucio, R. 2016. "After His Arrest, "El Peter" Reveals CJNG Structure in Tijuana." *Borderland Beat*, May 26. Accessed January 19, 2019. http://www.borderlandbeat.com/2016/05/after-his-arrest-el-peter-reveals-cjng.html.

"Mexican Authorities Arrest Wife of Drug Kingpin 'El Mencho.'" 2018. *ABC 7 News*. Last modified May 27, 2018. Accessed January 17, 2019. http://abc7chicago.com/mexican-authorities-arrest-wife-of-drug-kingpin-el-mencho-/3527940.

"Nemesio Oseguera Cervantes, Alias 'El Mencho.'" n.d. *InSight Crime*. Last modified March 30, 2018. Accessed January 17, 2019. https://www.insightcrime.org/mexico-organized-crime-news/nemesio-oseguera-ramos-alias-el-mencho.

Ortega, Román, Elizabeth Ibal, and Victor Chávez. 2018. "Ataque del CJNG es Violencia Electoral, dice Exfiscal de Jalisco, Luis Carlos Najera." El Sol del Centro. Last modified May 23, 2018. https://www.elsoldelcentro.com.mx/republica/justicia/ataque-del-cjng-es-violencia-electoral-dice-exfiscal-de-jalisco-luis-carlos-najera-1707484.html

Redaccion. 2018. "Asi es como el Cartel Jalisco Nueva Generacion se esta expandiendo en Mexico." *Huffington Post*. Last modified February 12, 2018. Accessed January 17, 2019. https://www.huffingtonpost.com.mx/2018/02/12/asi-es-como-el-cartel-jalisco-nueva-generacion-se-esta-expandiendo-en-mexico_a_23358887.

Woody, Christopher. 2016. "Mexico's Biggest Cartel Is Leaderless, and Drug Violence May Be about to Intensify." Business Insider. Last modified October 29, 2016. Accessed January 17, 2019. http://www.businessinsider.com/mexico-fighting-between-sinaloa-cartel-jalisco-cartel-getting-worse-2016-10.

Japanese Yakuza

Yakuza is a blanket term for Japan's organized crime groups. There are 21 major yakuza groups with some 53,000 members—the largest being the Yamaguchi-gumi, which numbers more than 23,000 (Adelstein 2015). The yakuza run legitimate businesses—often having offices and business cards—but many of their money-making activities are illegal. Although they are not officially outlawed, they are regulated and monitored. Traditionally known for their arresting full-body tattoos and severed fingertips, yakuza members today are less likely to favor tattoos or to chop off a finger, as both bring unwanted attention by authorities.

Yakuza are involved in the construction, real estate, currency exchange, and financial industries, and they even supply much of the labor for Japan's nuclear industry. Their criminal activities include extortion rackets, drug smuggling, money laundering, illegal gambling, the sex trade, and wildlife crime. Such activities have resulted in the U.S. Treasury Department labeling them a transcontinental organized crime group. Those transnational crime activities are conducted via relationships with criminal affiliates in Asia, Europe, and the Americas (Adelstein 2015).

Unlike the loose-knit Chinese triads, Japanese yakuza are organized into monolithic criminal organizations whose power is diffused from a central core through an *oyabun-kobun* ("father-child") chain of command. Despite their criminal activities, up until 1992, the yakuza were widely accepted in Japanese society. Unlike other organized crime groups, which conduct largely clandestine operations, the yakuza seem to have no interest in keeping a low profile. They are easily identifiable by their shiny, tight-fitting suits, pointy-toed shoes, and long pomaded hair. In fact, yakuza social clubs and gang headquarters are clearly marked with signs and logos.

Yakuza members see themselves as social misfits or losers, and, in fact, they come from marginalized groups, such as the Korean Japanese whose parents came to Japan as slave laborers or the former outcast class of Japan (the *burakumin*). Moreover, in parsing the syllables in the word *yakuza*, "ya" means 8, "ku" means 9, and "sa" means 3. These numbers add up to 20, which represents a losing hand in Oicho-Kabu (a game played with *hanafudaor kabufuda* cards).

Some sources contend the yakuza trace their origins back to 1612, when *kabuki-mono* ("crazy ones") or *hatamoto-yakko* ("servants of the shogun"), who reveled in outlandish clothing and bizarre hairstyles, spoke in elaborate slang, and tucked elongated swords in their belts, attracted attention. Modern yakuza members, however, maintain they are actually descendants of the *machi-yokko* ("servants of the town"), who safeguarded their villages from the unmanageable kabuki-mono or hatamoto-yakko.

During the Tokugawa age (1668–1868), an extended period of peace in Japan, the services of the machi-yokko were no longer required. They became leaderless *ronin* ("wave men"), who shifted their focus from community service to theft and mayhem. They divided themselves into *bakuto* (traditional "gamblers"), who originated the yakuza's traditional *Yubitsume* (finger-cutting ceremony), and *tekiya* (street peddlers), who evolved into protection racketeers.

As Japan began to industrialize, the bakuto and tekiya were joined by the *gurentai* ("hoodlums" and black marketeers) who modeled themselves after Al Capone–era bootleggers. Gurentai also enjoyed harassing unions and other workers' organizations, which made them terribly attractive to the conservative element of the Japanese power structure. During the militarization of Japan, gurentai became the enforcement arm of Japanese politicos known as *uyoku*, or ultranationalists. In 1987, when Noboru Takeshita was elected Japan's prime minister, there were suspicions of ties between Takeshita and the yakuza.

Membership in yakuza groups has declined in recent years, with core members standing at about 17,000 in 2017 according to the National Police Agency (Ryall 2018). The decline has been attributed to a general decline in Japan's economy, leaving the low-level street yakuza scrabbling to make ends meet. Japan's underworld is feeling the same pinches as the legitimate businesses.

Beverly Merrill Kelley and Philip L. Reichel

See also: Organized Crime; Yamaguchi-Gumi

Further Reading

Adelstein, Jake. 2015. "The Yakuza: Inside Japan's Murky Criminal Underworld." *CNN*: Asia, December 16. Accessed January 21, 2019. https://www.cnn.com/2015/09/15/asia/yakuza-yamaguchi-gumi-explainer/index.html.

Bester, John. 1995. *Confessions of a Yakuza: A Life in Japan's Underworld.* New York: Kodansha International.

Hill, Peter B. E. 2003. *The Japanese Mafia: Yakuza, Law, and the State.* Oxford: Oxford University Press.

Johnson, David T. 2001. *The Japanese Way of Justice: Prosecuting Crime in Japan.* Oxford: Oxford University Press.

Kaplan, David E., and Alec Dubro. 2003. *Yakuza: Japan's Criminal Underworld.* Berkeley: University of California Press.

Ryall, Julian. 2018. "Times Are Tough for Japan's Poor Yakuza." *South China Morning Post*, July 2. Accessed January 21, 2019. http://www.scmp.com/news/asia/east-asia/article/2153401/times-are-tough-japans-poor-yakuza-gangs-theyre-stealing-melons.

Jihad

Although the word is used by terrorists to describe their extremist agenda, *jihad* is more accurately an Arabic word meaning "striving" and refers to the duty of Muslims to know and do the will of Allah and to strive in the way of Allah. The concept is a central tenet of Islam that encourages Muslims to do what is right and good.

JIHAD IN SUPPORT OF ISLAM

In addition to referring to the internal struggle to do what is right (the *greater jihad*), the term is also used to mean the outward defense of Islam. This external or *lesser jihad* explains that Muslims should support the spread of Islam and be prepared to defend Islam when it is under attack. Efforts at support and defense can be peaceful (jihad of the tongue or jihad of the pen) in accordance with such Koranic verses as Sūrah 16:125 ("Call to the way of your Lord with wisdom and goodly exhortation, and have disputations with them in the best manner"), or they can involve the use of force (jihad of the sword) as in Sūrah 9:5 ("So when the sacred months have passed away, then slay the idolaters wherever you find them, and take them captives and besiege them and lie in wait for them in every ambush"). In this way, waging war to defend the faith can be viewed as not only permissible but even a duty.

Aggressive jihad is justified for many reasons, but most Islamic scholars believe that the Koran is clear that self-defense is always the underlying cause. In that context, jihad may be permissible to strengthen Islam, to protect the freedom of Muslims to practice their faith, to protect Muslims against oppression, or to right a wrong. Jihad can be accomplished using legal, diplomatic, economic, political, or other peaceful means, but force is also allowed under strict rules of engagement. For example, military jihad must be declared by a proper authority. It should be defensive, and innocents should not be harmed. Difficulties arise in achieving agreement over who is a proper authority, when an action is defensive, and who counts as an innocent.

JIHAD AND TERRORISTS

In the 19th and 20th centuries, jihad came to be associated with Muslim resistance to European and North American imperialism. One example is the Muslim action in 1912 that was a failed attempt to thwart the French bid for control in southern Morocco. More recently, jihad has been associated with groups who consider armed force as a necessary means for Muslims to resist the encroachment of Western values. The spread of such practices as democracy, capitalism, and the equality of men and women are believed by these groups to violate divine law and constitute an emergency condition for Muslims. In response, fighting becomes an obligation for every Muslim.

Terrorists exploit the word *jihad* to create the false impression that the Koran supports their violence. The majority of Koranic verses that reference jihad make no mention of fighting, and the other verses instruct Muslims to take up arms only against an aggressor (Kirchner 2010). In addition, a jihad of the sword can traditionally only be declared through a religious authority, such as a widely recognized Muslim scholar or judge. And, contemporary Muslim scholars agree, such a jihad is only permissible for the purposes of defense. But what must be defended can be a broad category (Lawrence 1991). An argument that oppressed Muslims anywhere can be defended by Muslims everywhere could provide a rationale for taking action in locations beyond the geographical boundaries of, for example, the Israeli-Palestinian conflict.

Any purported link between terrorism and jihad—at least as it is understood by mainstream Muslims—is tenuous at best. First, most respected Islamic scholars contend that the concept of jihad has been hijacked by extremist groups to justify various forms of violence. Second, even if a group claims to be engaged in jihad, it seems that individual terrorists may not have that motivation. In an attempt to find out why terrorists commit terrorism, Peter Bergen reviewed court records and spoke with terrorists and the friends and families of terrorists. He found that the terrorists were motivated by a mix of factors. For some, it was their understanding of jihad, but for others, it was a response to personal loss, hatred of a country, admiration or fear of someone else, or even an attempt to become heroes of their own story (Bergen 2016).

Terrorists gain a strategic advantage when linking jihad to terrorism and by spreading the belief that Islam and the West are at war. If terrorists convince Muslims that the United States and other countries are not fighting a war on terrorism but are instead waging a war against Islam, the terrorists believe they can benefit from the resulting anti-American and anti-West sentiments. But mainstream Muslims continue to argue that jihad is not a justification for terrorism, and it seems many of the terrorists themselves would agree. For these reasons, many Muslims today are trying to reclaim jihad in its sense of striving to do what is right and good.

Philip L. Reichel

See also: Al Qaeda; Fatwa; Hamas; Hezbollah; Islamic State of Iraq and Syria (ISIS); Terrorism, International

Further Reading

Bergen, Peter. 2016. "Why Do Terrorists Commit Terrorism?" *New York Times*, June 14. Accessed January 21, 2019. https://www.nytimes.com/2016/06/15/opinion/why-do-terrorists-commit-terrorism.html.

Cook, David. 2015. *Understanding Jihad.* 2nd ed. Oakland: University of California Press.

Kirchner, Allie. 2010. "Losing the Meaning of Jihad: Terrorism and the US Media." Stimson, December 27. Accessed January 21, 2019. https://www.stimson.org/content/losing-meaning-jihad-terrorism-and-us-media.

Lawrence, Bruce. 1991. "Holy War (Jihad) in Islamic Religion and Nation-State Ideologies." In *Just War and Jihad: Historical and Theoretical Perspectives on War and Peace in Western and Islamic Traditions*, edited by John Kelsay and James Turner Johnson, 141–160. New York: Greenwood Press.

Joint Investigation Teams

A joint investigation team (JIT) is a tool used in the conduct of investigations of complex crimes that have links to two or more countries in which coordination appears to be required. A JIT consists of representatives of law enforcement authorities (and possibly also prosecutorial and judicial authorities) from the two or more countries affected by the investigation in question, with all the members of the team sharing information on the progress of the investigation in the different countries. It is set up for a specific purpose (the investigation of a specific case or related cases) and for a defined period.

Article 11 of the 1988 UN Convention against Illicit Traffic in Narcotic Drugs and Psychotropic Substances and Article 19 of the UN Convention against Transnational Organized Crime encourage the establishment of "joint investigative bodies." The United States has long engaged in ad hoc practices of establishing joint investigative teams with law enforcement agencies of other countries.

The use of JITs has seen its greatest use in the European Union (EU), where the teams are regulated by a Framework Decision adopted in 2002 (2002/465/JHA), in the aftermath of the terrorist attacks of September 11, 2001, in the United States. The Framework Decision was subsequently replaced by the entry into force in 2005 of the EU Convention on Mutual Assistance in Criminal Matters.

RATIONALE

In traditional international investigations, the law enforcement agencies of different countries act independently of one another in the conduct of the investigation in their respective jurisdictions, under the control (as required) of national prosecutorial and judicial authorities. Information is exchanged across borders only sporadically, generally on specific request, and through cumbersome and time-consuming procedures. If investigations in one jurisdiction appear to require investigative measures in another jurisdiction, this requires its own procedures.

By establishing a JIT, the law enforcement agencies are able to cooperate closely in the planning and the conduct of the investigation. Information can be shared directly without the need for formal cross border requests. Investigative measures can be directly requested among JIT members without the need for traditional letters of request (Mesko and Furnam 2014, 339). This can be facilitated, as needed, by including representatives of the relevant prosecutorial or judicial authorities in the JIT, who can decide directly on the use of investigative measures in their own jurisdiction.

Even as members of a JIT, law enforcement agents acting outside of their jurisdictions ("seconded members") have no police powers and may not independently conduct investigations. However, as members of a JIT, they may be present when coercive measures are being used (such as house searches) and during the questioning of suspects and witnesses. This allows them to follow the progress of the investigation in real time and to suggest further questions as needed that duly authorized local colleagues may ask, or they may suggest further investigative measures to be taken. Having representatives of different law enforcement agencies present may also help in overcoming linguistic and cultural barriers to investigations.

PROCEDURE FOR THE ESTABLISHMENT OF A JIT

Within the European Union, the establishment of a JIT requires a specific agreement between the competent authorities of the states concerned for a specific purpose and for a limited period of time. In 2017, the European Union adopted a resolution that contains a model agreement on setting up a JIT. The composition of the JIT must be defined, and the proposing country may invite Europol or Eurojust to participate in the JIT.

The leader of the JIT must be a representative of the state in which the team operates. (The team may have different leaders when operating in different countries.) The leader and all the members of the team must respect the national law of the state in question. "Seconded members" may be entrusted with certain investigative duties, in accordance with the national law of the state in question and with the approval of the competent authorities of both this state and of the seconding state.

Matti Joutsen

See also: Eurojust; Europol; Mutual Legal Assistance; UN Convention against Illicit Traffic in Narcotic Drugs and Psychotropic Substances; UN Convention against Transnational Organized Crime

Further Reading

Boister, Neil. 2012. *An Introduction to Transnational Criminal Law.* Oxford, UK: Oxford University Press.

Council of the European Union. 2017. *Joint Investigation Teams Practical Guide.* Accessed January 17, 2019. https://www.ejn-crimjust.europa.eu/ejn/libdocumentproperties.aspx?Id=1949.

Mesko, Goarzd, and Robert Furnam. 2014. "Police and Prosecutorial Cooperation in Responding to Transnational Crime." In *Handbook of Transnational Crime and*

Justice, edited by Philip Reichel and Jay Albanese, 323–353. Los Angeles, London, New Delhi, Singapore and Washington, D.C.: Sage.

Plachta, Michael 2005. "Joint Investigation Teams: A New Form of International Cooperation in Criminal Matters." *European Journal of Crime, Criminal Law and Criminal Justice* 13 (2): 284–302.

Rijken, C., and G. Vermeulen. 2006. *Joint Investigation Teams in the European Union: From Theory to Practice.* The Hague: Asser Press.

Joutsen, Matti (1951–)

Matti Joutsen is a Finnish criminologist, lawyer, and civil servant who has combined academic work with hands-on involvement in the formulation of intergovernmental policy on criminal justice. He has played a key role in particular in negotiations within the framework of the United Nations as well as the European Union and the Council of Europe.

Joutsen has degrees in political science (1974), law (1977), and a J.S.D. degree (1987), all from the University of Helsinki. He was drawn into criminology and international cooperation by Inkeri Anttila (1974–1982), who was one of the pioneers in combining sociological research and criminal law and in advocating for a rational, effective, and humane criminal policy. He began his career at the Research Institute of Legal Policy established by Anttila, and he followed her when she established the European Institute for Crime Prevention and Control, (HEUNI), first as its senior researcher (1982–1987) and then, upon Anttila's retirement, he became HEUNI's director (1987–1999 and 2012–2017). At various times, he also served as a court clerk and judge in Finland (1980–1981), as an interregional adviser to the United Nations (1993), and as the director of International Affairs at the Ministry of Justice of Finland (1999–2011). He also spent extended periods as a visiting professor at the University of Illinois at Chicago (1992) and at the John Jay College of Criminal Justice, City University of New York (1997, 2007–2008, and 2013–2014), teaching comparative and transnational criminal justice.

Joutsen has described the trajectory of his career in transnational criminal justice as having been the result of several coincidences, beginning with his first years under Anttila. Anttila introduced him to other key figures in the field, including Professors Gerhard Mueller, Freda Adler, and Cherif Bassiouni. Since 1974, he has accompanied Anttila to Council of Europe meetings, UN Crime Congresses, and meetings of the UN Committee on Crime Prevention and Criminal Justice, of which she was a member, and he later replaced her in this select body.

When Finland joined the European Union in 1995, in the same year the European Union expanded its activities into crime and criminal justice, Joutsen became involved in the rapid evolution of European cooperation in this field. He had a hand in the drafting of many EU decisions, including the European Arrest Warrant, in the immediate aftermath of the September 11, 2001, terrorist attacks as well as in the negotiations of EU and U.S. treaties on extradition and mutual legal assistance.

His main impact has been in the UN Crime Programme. Beginning with the drafting of the 1985 UN Declaration on Basic Principles of Justice for Victims of Crime and Abuse of Power, he played a role in many key UN negotiations over the years. He was one of the architects of the restructuring of the UN Crime Program, which culminated in 1991 with the replacement of the committee by the UN Commission on Crime Prevention and Criminal Justice. Several years later, he played an instrumental role in the drafting of the UN Convention on Transnational Organized Crime. Joutsen's influence can be seen by the fact that he was elected to several key positions, including rapporteur-general at the Tenth UN Crime Congress (Vienna 2000) and vice-chairperson of all subsequent UN Crime Congresses (Bangkok in 2005; Salvador de Bahia, Brazil, in 2010; and Doha in 2015).

In UN connections, he is most noted for having been a tenacious negotiator on the mechanism for the review of implementation of the UN Convention on Corruption, which incorporated the concept of peer review for the first time in connection with any UN treaty (Joutsen and Graycar 2012). Subsequently, he has been at the forefront of the continuing UN debate over the involvement of civil society in crime prevention and criminal justice. In recent years, he has used his insider's access to document the evolution of the UN Crime Programme and to provide an (at times somewhat sardonic) analysis of how intergovernmental negotiations and transnational criminal justice are conducted.

In the field of research, Joutsen contributed to the development of Europe-wide comparative analyses of crime trends and the operation of criminal justice systems, which served as the template for subsequent global analysis within the United Nations. He has also prepared a European comparative survey of victim policy and been involved in research on a wide range of topics, from procedural justice to noncustodial sanctions.

Joutsen has served as an expert to the Council of Europe and the European Union, dealing with such topics as corruption, organized crime, money laundering, and trafficking in persons. He has in addition lectured widely around the world on such subjects as noncustodial sanctions, the prevention and control of economic crime, extradition and mutual legal assistance, and the national and international response to organized crime.

In 2004, he received the Distinguished International Scholar award from the Division of International Criminology of the American Society of Criminology.

Natalia Ollus

See also: Anttila, Inkeri; HEUNI

Further Reading

Joutsen, Matti. 1991. "Changing Victim Policy: International Dimensions." In *Victims and Criminal Justice*, edited by Günther Kaiser, Helmut Kury, and Hans-Jörg Albrecht, 765–797. Vol. 52/2. Freiburg im Breisgau: Max-Planck Institute for Foreign and International Law.

Joutsen, Matti. 2004. "Confessions of a Peripatetic Comparativist." In *Lessons from Comparative/International Criminology/Criminal Justice*, edited by John Winterdyk and Liqun Cao, 259–274. Whitby, Ontario: de Sitter Publications.

Joutsen, Matti. 2006. *The European Union and Cooperation in Criminal Matters: The Search for Balance*. Helsinki, Finland: HEUNI.

Joutsen, Matti. 2011. "The Impact of United Nations Crime Conventions on International Cooperation." In *Routledge Handbook of International Criminology*, edited by Cindy Smith, Sheldon X. Shang, and Rosemary Barberet, 112–124. New York, NY: Routledge.

Joutsen, Matti. 2012a. "International Instruments on Cooperation in Responding to Transnational Crime." In *Handbook of Transnational Crime and Justice*, edited by Philip Reichel and Jay Albanese, 303–322. 2nd ed. Thousand Oaks, CA: Sage.

Joutsen, Matti. 2012b. "Negotiating Conventions in the United Nations: Ten Rules to Follow." In KLM *Van Dijk. Liber amicorum prof.dr.mr. J.J.M. van Dijk*, edited by Marc Groenhuijsen, Rianne Letschert, and Sylvia Hazenbroek, 177–190. Nijmegen, Netherlands: Wolf Legal Publishers.

Joutsen, Matti. 2012c. "A View from the Trenches: The Reality of International Cooperation." In *Handbook of Transnational Crime and Justice*, edited by Philip Reichel and Jay Albanese, 419–423. 2nd ed. Thousand Oaks, CA: Sage.

Joutsen, Matti. 2016. "International Standards and Norms as Guidance in the Criminal Justice System." Resource Material Series No. 98. Tokyo: UNAFEI, 54–67.

Joutsen, Matti. 2017a. *Four Transitions in the United Nations Crime Programme*. Helsinki, Finland: HEUNI.

Joutsen, Matti. 2017b. *How to Survive UN Crime Programme Meetings*. Helsinki, Finland: HEUNI.

Joutsen, Matti, and Adam Graycar. 2012. "When Experts and Diplomats Agree: Negotiating Peer Review of the UN Convention against Corruption" *Journal of Global Governance: A Review of Multilateralism and International Organizations* 18 (4): 425–439.

Juárez Cartel

Pablo Acosta Villarreal informally created the Juárez Cartel in the 1980s. During its early years, the cartel primarily smuggled marijuana and heroin from its home base in Ojinaga, Chihuahua, using aircraft to smuggle the narcotics. Due to the increased pressure by the Drug Enforcement Administration (DEA) on the Colombian cartels in Florida, cocaine smuggling was outsourced to Mexican drug trafficking organizations (DTOs) in the mid to late 1980s. The Juárez Cartel's proximity to the United States facilitated the group to smuggle cocaine for the Colombian cartels, a relationship that endured through the 1990s, 2000s, and the present day. The Juárez Cartel's headquarters shifted to its namesake location, Ciudad Juárez, Chihuahua, after the death of Pablo Acosta Villarreal and the subsequent dismantling of the Guadalajara DTO. The present-day Juárez Cartel was created circa 1989–1992 and expanded throughout the Americas, with a reach extending through Central America and as far as Chile. Under various leaders, the Juárez Cartel made a name for itself in smuggling multiton shipments of cocaine, the use of street gangs for protection and smuggling in Mexico and the United States, and for their corruption and bribery tactics.

ORGANIZATION

The Juárez Cartel operates under a business structure, which largely followed the use of bribes to operate throughout Mexico and Central and South America. Under the leadership of Amado Carrillo Fuentes, alias "El Señor de los Cielos" ("the Lord of the Skies"), multiton shipments of cocaine were being smuggled from Colombia to Mexico using Boeing 727s, a feat that was facilitated by corrupting law enforcement officials in the 1990s up to 1997, the year Amado Carrillo Fuentes died.

DTOs in the early 2000s underwent a change in tactics for gaining ground, one that the Juárez Cartel was not immune to, the use of armed groups to further their goals. The Juárez Cartel employed members of the U.S. gang "Barrio Azteca" for its U.S.-Mexico operations. A unique characteristic of the Juárez Cartel as the Barrio Azteca gang was used on the U.S. and Mexican side. In addition to the Barrio Azteca gang, the Juárez Cartel also employed "La Lina" gang as its armed wing to expand its operations and protect its organization in Chihuahua, Mexico. However, due to power struggles and disputes for the territory and high-profile arrests, such as Vicente Carrillo Fuentes, alias "El Viceroy," the former leader of the Juárez Cartel, the cartel has undergone a restructuration that has had its armed wing splintered off into its own organization as of 2015 (Fregoso 2017).

TURF WARS

The turf wars in which the Juárez Cartel has been involved are primarily associated with its strategic location, Ciudad Juárez, Chihuahua, across from El Paso, Texas. For 2015, the El Paso crossing accounted for the crossings of 758,074 trucks, 12,247,409 personal vehicles, and 6,847,689 pedestrians into the United States for a total of 38.1 percent of pedestrians who crossed into the United States through Texan points of entry (Texas Comptroller of Public Accounts 2016). Indeed, the number of individuals and vehicles that cross into the United States via Ciudad Juárez is a significant point of entry for many DTOs, and many organizations have fought over the territory for three decades.

Prior to the arrest of Vicente Carrillo Fuentes, the Juárez Cartel engaged in a turf war against the Sinaloa Cartel. In a pact between the Tijuana Cartel, Los Zetas, and the Juárez Cartel, violence in Ciudad Juárez and its surrounding towns, cities, and villages increased. Violence became a main staple in Ciudad Juárez, and in 2010, it was named the most violent city in the world, comparable to war-torn countries such as Syria and Afghanistan (O'Connor 2012). The use of car bombs began to emerge as a tactic against law enforcement and other rivals (Dulin and Patiño 2014).

NOTABLE EVENTS

The associates of the Juárez Cartel, that is, the Barrio Azteca, are allegedly believed to have been involved in the assassination of U.S. embassy employees. In

March 13, 2010, it was reported that the Barrio Azteca gang had acted in retaliation against a U.S. embassy employee who allegedly worked for a rival gang, thus leading to the assassination of the employee (Associated Press 2010).

In 2010, the first use of a car bomb was reported in Ciudad Juárez, Chihuahua, on July 15, 2010, in which four individuals were killed (Cardona 2010). It is believed that La Linea was responsible for the attack in retaliation for the arrest of a Juárez Cartel member (Cardona 2010).

Jairo Patiño

See also: Gulf Cartel; Jalisco New Generation Cartel; Los Zetas; Sinaloa Cartel; Tijuana Cartel

Further Reading

Associated Press. 2010. "Drug Cartel Enforcer Confesses to Killing U.S. Consulate Employee Who Reportedly Helped Rival Gang." *Daily News*, July 2. Accessed January 17, 2019. http://www.nydailynews.com/news/national/drug-cartel-enforcer-confesses-killing-u-s-consulate-employee-reportedly-helped-rival-gang-article-1.464723.

Cardona, Julian. 2010. "Deadly Cartel Responsible for Deadly Mexico Car Bomb." *Reuters*, July 15. Accessed January 17, 2019. https://www.reuters.com/article/us-mexico-bomb/drug-cartel-responsible-for-deadly-mexico-car-bomb-idUSTRE66F50G20100716.

Dulin, Adam L., and Jairo Patiño. 2014 "The Logic of Cartel Car Bombings in Mexico." *Trends in Organized Crime* 17 (4): 271–289.

Fregoso, Juliana. 2017. "La Linea el Nuevo Grupo Criminal que se Perfila como el Modelo de los Carteles Mexicanos del Futuro." Infobae, July 6. Accessed January 17, 2019. https://www.infobae.com/america/mexico/2017/07/06/la-linea-el-nuevo-grupo-criminal-que-se-perfila-como-el-modelo-de-los-carteles-mexicanos-del-futuro.

O'Connor, Emma. 2012. "Mexico's Ciudad Juárez Is No Longer the Most Violent City in the World." News Feed, October 15. Accessed January 17, 2019. http://newsfeed.time.com/2012/10/15/mexicos-ciudad-juarez-is-no-longer-the-most-violent-city-in-the-world.

Texas Comptroller of Public Accounts. 2016. *Port of Entry: El Paso Economic Impact, 2015.* Texas Comptroller. https://comptroller.texas.gov/economy/economic-data/ports/el-paso.php.

Junger-Tas, Josine (1929–2011)

Josine Junger-Tas was a Dutch-born criminologist, civil servant, and university professor, who inspired many criminologists in Europe and beyond through her belief in the roles of reason and science being firmly grounded in the need for empathy for the most vulnerable youth in society. She started her career as a criminologist rather late, at age 42, with her PhD dissertation *Characteristics and Social Integration of Juvenile Delinquents*, and throughout her work life, she passionately championed for the interests of youth, the marginalized, and the powerless. As director of the Research and Documentation Centre (1990–1994) of the Dutch Ministry of Justice, she emphasized the need for translational (i.e., applied) research, and she became a crucial central figure in the internationalization of Dutch criminology and criminal justice. Josine was a prolific writer, with publications written in Dutch, French, German, and English.

EARLY BELIEVER IN COMPARATIVE CRIMINOLOGY

Junger-Tas initiated the International Self-Report Delinquency Study (ISRD) in 1990, when under her leadership a working group of international researchers developed a common questionnaire and research protocol aimed at achieving a comparable way of measuring delinquency among 13 participating countries. Between 2005 and 2007, the international Self-Report Delinquency Study (ISRD) developed into a much expanded project in which more than 30 countries participated. The fieldwork for ISRD3 started in 2012, and now over 35 countries have contributed their data on delinquency and victimization.

The ISRD combined Josine Junger-Tas's belief in empirical research on youth, the value-added contributions of comparative work, and the methodology of self-report, on which she was considered an international expert (Junger-Tas and Haen-Marshall 1999). In addition to her leading role in the first large-scale international collaborative study of delinquency and victimization (ISRD), she also published a number of comparative volumes on juvenile delinquency and juvenile justice.

INSTITUTIONALIZATION OF EUROPEAN CRIMINOLOGY

Junger-Tas contributed to the institutionalization of European criminology through her work as the founder of the European Journal on Criminal Policy and Research and as one of the founders of the European Society of Criminology. In 2000, together with several European colleagues, Josine took the initiative to establish the European Society of Criminology (ESC). This was a crucial turning point in European criminology. She became the second president of the ESC (2001–2002).

She regarded the ESC as a catalyst for the development of European criminology independent from American traditions. She envisioned the development of the ESC based on European principles, namely "those of the Enlightenment—emphasizing reason, empiricism, and human rights—and those of social care and support for the losers in our society" (Levay 2011, 3–4).

A COMPASSIONATE CRIMINOLOGIST

Josine Junger-Tas was a "public criminologist" and never afraid to speak her mind. She was a fervent and compassionate believer in prevention rather than punishment, and she often spoke out publicly against the repressive and hard-line policies that have emerged in the Netherlands since the early 2000s. She questioned the "hype" about alleged rising crime rates, and she never hesitated to express her indignation about the increasing repressive nature of youth policy.

Josine Junger-Tas's view on the role of criminology may be best captured by the concept of "compassionate criminology" (Marshall and Boutellier 2013). Compassionate criminology not only means that one speaks one's mind (publicly), but also that one has true empathy for the suffering of others. Josine believed in "empirical criminology with a heart." However, as a compassionate criminologist, she also embraced policy-relevant research as well as the value of insights derived from careful cross-national research.

Ineke Haen Marshall

See also: Transnational, Global, and International Crime

Further Reading

Enzmann, D., J. Kivivuori, I. H. Marshall, M. Steketee, M. Hough, and M. Killias. 2018. *A Global Perspective on Young People as Offenders and Victims: First Results from the ISRD3 Study*. New York: Springer.

Enzmann, D., I. H. Marshall, M. Killias, J. Junger-Tas, M. Steketee, and B. Gruszczynska. 2010. "Self-Reported Youth Delinquency in Europe and Beyond: First Results of the Second ISRD (International Self-Report Study) in the Context of Police and Victimization Data." *European Journal of Criminology* 7 (2): 159–183.

Junger-Tas, J. and I. H. Marshall. 1999. "The Self-Report Methodology in Crime Research: Strengths and Weaknesses." In *Crime and Justice*, edited by M. Tonry. Vol. 25, pp. 291–367. Chicago: University of Chicago Press.

Junger-Tas, J., I. H. Marshall, D. Enzmann, D. Killias, M. Steketee, and B. Gruszcynska, eds. 2010. *Juvenile Delinquency in Europe and Beyond: Results of the Second International Self-Report Delinquency Study*. New York: Springer.

Junger-Tas, J., I. H. Marshall, D. Enzmann, M. Killias, M. Steketee, and B. Gruszczynska. 2012. *The Many Faces of Youth Crime: Contrasting Theoretical Perspectives on Juvenile Delinquency across Countries and Cultures*. New York: Springer.

Levay, Miklos. 2011. "Josine Junger-Tas and the European Society of Criminology." *Criminology in Europe* 10 (1): 3–4. Accessed January 17, 2019. https://escnewsletter.org/sites/escnewsletter.org/files/newsletter/2016/may2011_1_10escnewsletter.pdf.

Marshall, I. H., and H. Boutellier. 2013. "Josine Junger-Tas: The Life and Works of a Compassionate Criminologist." *European Journal on Criminal Policy and Research* 19 (3): 71–84.

L

Labor Exploitation

Human trafficking occurs when a person has been recruited or is kept by means of force, fraud, or coercion with the aim of exploiting the person. Technically, all categories of human trafficking are subsets of forced labor, but typically there is a distinction made between labor trafficking and sex trafficking. The U.S. Victims of Trafficking and Violence Protection Act of 2000 (Public Law 106-386) defines severe forms of human trafficking as including "sex trafficking in which a commercial sex act is induced by force, fraud, or coercion, or in which the person induced to perform such as act has not attained 18 years of age" (Section 103(8)(A)). Labor trafficking occurs with the "recruitment, harboring, transportation, provision, or obtaining of a person for labor or services, through the use of force, fraud, or coercion for the purpose of subjection to involuntary servitude, peonage, debt bondage, or slavery" (Section 103(8)(B)). A point of confusion is how human trafficking differs from migrant smuggling. An increasingly agreed upon distinction is that trafficking, but not smuggling, requires deception or coercion.

One of the earliest definitions of forced labor is found in the *Forced Labour Convention of 1930* (ILO 1930), which declared that "forced or compulsory labour shall mean all work or service which is exacted from any person under the menace of any penalty and for which the said person has not offered himself voluntarily" (Article 2(1)). For clarity, the convention also identifies situations that are, under certain circumstances, exceptions to forced labor. For example, compulsory military service, prison labor, and required work during an emergency, such as war or earthquake.

TYPES OF LABOR TRAFFICKING

From the definitions provided by U.S. law and an international convention, there are several types of labor trafficking: involuntary domestic servitude, bonded labor, child labor, child soldiers, and forced labor imposed by state authorities.

Involuntary Domestic Servitude

Involuntary domestic servitude is a form of human trafficking found in distinct circumstances—work in a private residence. It is a crime in which a domestic worker is not free to leave his or her employment and is abused and underpaid, if paid at all. These workers are often foreigners who were recruited from less developed countries. Because they work in a private home, isolation and vulnerability is increased because authorities generally do not have the authority to inspect employment conditions in private homes. Confined to the home, either because of physical restraint or through confiscation of identity and travel documents, the workers may find it difficult to make others aware of their situation. In addition, domestic workers, especially women, confront various forms of abuse, harassment, and exploitation, including sexual and gender-based violence.

Bonded Labor

Bonded labor (also called debt bondage or peonage), involves a form of coercion wherein persons are forced to work to pay off a debt. The debt could be their own or even that of a relative. In South Asia, for example, it is estimated that there are millions of trafficking victims working to pay off their ancestors' debts. Debts that are not inherited may have been incurred as part of the recruitment process or as a condition of employment. Traffickers, labor agencies, recruiters, and employers in both the country of origin and the destination country can contribute to debt bondage by charging workers recruitment fees and exorbitant interest rates, making it difficult, if not impossible, to pay off the debt.

Child Labor

Child labor is work performed by a child under coercion applied by a third party (other than the child's parents) either to the child or to the child's parents. As it is possible for children to legally do some kinds of work, it is important to be able to distinguish legal types of work from conditions of forced child labor. For example, indicators of forced child labor include situations in which the child appears to be in the custody of a non–family member who requires the child to perform work that financially benefits someone outside the child's family and does not offer the child the option of leaving, such as forced begging.

Child Soldiers

Child soldiers are a specific example of human trafficking in both the recruitment and use of children for government, paramilitary, or rebel armed groups. Some children are forcibly abducted to be used as combatants, whereas others are made to work as porters, cooks, guards, servants, messengers, or spies. Young girls may be forced to "marry" or be raped by commanders and male combatants. Both male and female child soldiers are often sexually abused or exploited by armed groups, and such children are subject to the same types of devastating physical and psychological consequences associated with child sex trafficking (U.S. Department of State 2018).

Forced Labor Imposed by State Authorities

Forced labor imposed by state authorities includes instances where the coercion comes from the government rather than from private individuals and groups. The International Labour Organization (ILO) identifies five situations of forced labor imposed by state authorities—and each is considered inappropriate and something that should be abolished: "(1) as punishment for the expression of political views, (2) for the purposes of economic development, (3) as a means of labour discipline, (4) as a punishment for participation in strikes, and (5) as a means of racial, religious or other discrimination" (ILO n.d.).

Examples vary widely and range from picking cotton to building roads. Sometimes such work is assigned by the government under the guise of community work, but the work does not in fact benefit the community and has not been decided upon by members of the community. In North Korea, for example, children are forced, as part of their schooling, to do work that is very demanding and far exceeds the goals of vocational education (ILO 2017).

EXTENT AND DISTRIBUTION

The ILO provides one of the most extensive and widely cited reports on how much forced labor occurs in the world. The *Global Estimates of Modern Slavery* has based its estimates on a variety of respected sources, but it especially draws from extensive surveys, administrative data, and International Organization for Migration (IOM) databases.

According to ILO estimates, 25 million people are in situations of forced labor around the world. They were working under threat or coercion as domestic workers, on construction sites, on farms, in mines and quarries, and on fishing boats—as just some examples. The ILO separates that broad category into those experiencing forced labor exploitation (16 million), those under forced sexual exploitation (5 million), and those under state-imposed forced labor (4 million).

Women and girls are disproportionately affected by modern slavery in both the forced labor category (58% female) and forced sexual exploitation (99% female). The only category with males comprising the majority is state-imposed forced labor (84% male). Age is another key factor, with about 80 percent or more of the people in all three categories being adults.

Interesting regional variation occurs with, for example, debt bondage being most common in Asia, Africa, and the Arab States and least common in the Americas and in Europe and Central Asia. More than 70 percent of victims under forced sexual exploitation were in the Asia Pacific region compared with about 1 percent in the Arab States.

Philip L. Reichel

See also: Bonded Labor; Human Trafficking; Sex Exploitation; UN Protocol to Prevent, Suppress, and Punish Trafficking in Persons, Especially Women and Children; U.S. Trafficking Victims Protection Act

Further Reading

Farrell, Amy, Rebecca Pfeffer, Meredith Dank, and Colleen Owens. 2018. "Human Trafficking for Labor Exploitation." In *Transnational Crime and Global Security*, edited by Philip Reichel and Ryan Randa, 233–250. Santa Barbara, CA: Praeger.

International Labour Organization (ILO). 1930. "C029—Forced Labour Convention, 1930." Accessed July 21, 2018. http://www.ilo.org/dyn/normlex/en/f?p=NORMLEXPUB:12100:0::NO::P12100_ILO_CODE:C029.

International Labour Organization (ILO). 2017. "Global Estimates of Modern Slavery: Forced Labour and Forced Marriage." Accessed July 20, 2018. https://www.ilo.org/global/publications/books/WCMS_575479/lang--en/index.htm.

International Labour Organization (ILO). n.d. "What Is Forced Labour, Modern Slavery and Human Trafficking." Accessed July 21, 2018. http://www.ilo.org/global/topics/forced-labour/definition/lang--en/index.htm.

U.S. Department of State. 2018. "Trafficking in Persons Report 2018." Accessed July 21, 2018. https://www.state.gov/j/tip/rls/tiprpt/2018/index.htm.

Legal Attachés

Legal attachés ("legats," also referred to internationally as liaison officers) are law enforcement agents who are posted abroad to promote law enforcement cooperation. Although they have no police powers in the host country, they can and do promote the exchange of information between, and coordinate the activities of, the law enforcement and security agencies of the two countries in question.

THE ROLE OF LEGAL ATTACHÉS

Legal attachés are generally posted in countries that have extensive cooperation with the sending country or have been identified as significant source or transit countries for drug trafficking, other forms of trafficking, terrorism, or other crimes of concern to the sending country. They seek to encourage the law enforcement and security agencies in the host country to investigate cases of interest to the sending country and can in turn advise the host country's agencies on how to request assistance from the sending country. Legal attachés may also provide training (for example, in crime scene investigation, other investigative techniques, or counterterrorism) and otherwise facilitate the provision of technical assistance to the law enforcement and security agencies of the host country.

THE STATUS OF LEGAL ATTACHÉS

Two major global conventions, the UN Convention on Illicit Trafficking in Narcotic Drugs and Psychotropic Substances (1988) and the UN Convention on Transnational Organized Crime (2000) encourage states to facilitate effective coordination between their competent authorities, agencies, and services by the posting of liaison officers "subject to bilateral agreements or arrangements between the States Parties concerned."

Such bilateral agreements or arrangements outline the duties and rights of legal attachés, providing them with the official status that is necessary to establish a working relationship with the law enforcement and security agencies of the host country. Although they may not independently carry out investigations or intelligence-gathering operations in the host country, these bilateral agreements or arrangements may open up the possibility of sharing intelligence and other sensitive information. Depending on the arrangements with the host country, legal attachés may also accompany host country agents in actual investigations.

THE POSTING OF LEGAL ATTACHÉS

The United States has been an early proponent of the use of legal attachés. These were first deployed by the Federal Bureau of Investigation (FBI) during the World War II (1939–1945) in Bogota, Colombia; Mexico City, Mexico; Ottawa, Ontario, Canada; and London to gather intelligence on the threat posed by the Axis powers. Currently, the FBI has over 60 legal attaché offices and several sub-offices around the world. The legal attachés are generally posted at the respective U.S. embassy or consulate. The FBI has also posted an agent at INTERPOL headquarters in Lyon, THE Europol headquarters in the Hague, and at the United Nations.

Legal attachés can and do offer forensic and other assistance on request to the law enforcement and security agencies of the host country. In this way, FBI legal attachés have been directly involved in the investigation of many cases, such as the terrorist bombings in Bali in 2002 and the London bombings in 2005. The FBI also assisted in the identification of victims of the tsunami that struck Thailand and many other countries around the Indian Ocean in 2004. In addition to the FBI, other U.S. law enforcement agencies, such as the Drug Enforcement Administration (DEA), also make extensive use of posted legal attachés.

The European Union has also been active in the posting of legal attachés (liaison officers). The 1990 Schengen Convention defines the task of law enforcement liaison officers as providing assistance in the exchange of information for the purposes of both prevention and law enforcement, executing requests for mutual police and judicial assistance in criminal matters, and assisting in tasks carried out by the authorities responsible for external borders. Although several EU member states initially posted their own liaison officers in other EU states as well as in, for example, Washington, D.C., and Bangkok, currently the posting of liaison officers from the European Union is largely coordinated through Europol, which has posted some 160 liaison officers both in EU states and outside the European Union.

Matti Joutsen

See also: Joint Investigation Teams

Further Reading

Boister, Neil. 2012. *An Introduction to Transnational Criminal Law.* Oxford, UK. Oxford University Press

Council of the European Union. 2008. "Compendium on Law Enforcement Liaison Officers." Accessed January 17, 2019. https://www.eumonitor.eu/9353000/1/j9vvik7m1c3gyxp/vi7jgtcch6zv.

Federal Bureau of Investigation (FBI). 2004. "Legal Attaché Program." U.S. Department of Justice. Accessed January 17, 2019. https://oig.justice.gov/reports/FBI/a0418/final.pdf.

Federal Bureau of Investigation (FBI). n.d. "International Operations." Accessed January 17, 2019. https://www.fbi.gov/about/leadership-and-structure/international-operations.

Fuentes, Thomas V. 2007. "The Legal Attaché Program." Statement before the Subcommittee on Border, Maritime and Global Counterterrorism of the House Homeland Security Committee. Accessed January 17, 2019. https://archives.fbi.gov/archives/news/testimony/the-fbis-legal-attache-program.

Nadelmann, E. A. 1993. *Cops across Borders: The Internationalization of U.S. Criminal Law Enforcement*. University Park: Pennsylvania State University Press.

Lone Wolf Terrorism

Lone wolf terrorism is not a new type of criminality but rather a new phrase assigned to a certain group of terrorists. Previous phrases used in lieu of the modern term included "homegrowns," "cleanskins," "freelancers," and "unaffiliated" (Burke 2017). Lone wolf terrorists commit acts of terrorism to accomplish larger goals that align with their political, ideological, or religious beliefs. The violence associated with their terrorism is not solely for personal endeavors, such as finances and revenge. Despite the emphasized association with terrorism, lone wolf terrorism intermixes personal frustrations with religious, political, or ideological beliefs. This blend of motivation not only creates a lack of consistency within this subfield but difficulty with establishing who qualifies as a lone wolf.

HISTORY

Lone wolf terrorism, as a concept, originated around the 19th century with ties to anarchism and the anti-state motivations surrounding it. In the 20th century, this ideology evolved and developed into the idea of "leaderless resistance." Leaderless resistance emphasized violence directed toward anti-state movements and was characterized by individuals that were separate from a group or movement (Spaaij 2010).

Jihadi groups, dating back to the 1990s with Al Qaeda, took on an ideology similar to the leaderless resistance movement. In an attempt to decentralize the jihadi cause, Mustafa Setmariam Nasar, also known as Abu Musab al-Suri, a Syrian influential, strategized an organizational structure similar to the concept of leaderless resistance. He based attacks predominantly on principles and called for them to be committed by individuals. Such attacks would be guided and published via online sources, thus allowing for global attacks (Burke 2017).

Though these groups further developed the idea that helped influence the rise of lone wolf terrorism, they are not solely responsible for such actions. Main ideological doctrines associated with lone wolf terrorism include white supremacism, Islamism, nationalism and separatism, and anti-abortion activism (Spaaij 2010). Lone wolf terrorism has the potential to apply to any extremist viewpoint.

DIFFERING DEFINITIONS

The definition of lone wolf terrorism lacks agreement among sources as to what actually constitutes this behavior. Many media sources even argue that lone wolf terrorism is nonexistent due to the globalization and influence of the Internet. Organized terrorist groups utilize the Internet to broadcast their ideology, specifically on social media sites. As a result, the "no such thing" argument asserts that even if a person acts alone, he or she was persuaded by others and cannot be considered "lone." The focus of this perspective is on the connection to and power of terrorist organizations over the individual via virtual sources, which has widely expanded since the 1990s (Easterly and Geltzer 2017).

Other media sources echo this view by placing single-person terrorists into different categories that are dictated by varying degrees of the individual's relationship with those of extremist mind-sets. The differences between such groups rely on whether the connection was face-to-face or online and whether such connection was from an organized terrorist group or individuals with similar extremist beliefs (Burke 2017).

In contrast to the media approach, the working definition of most academic studies defines lone wolf terrorists as those individuals who commit the terrorist act individually, who do not belong to an organized terrorist group, and whose method of terrorism does not originate or is directed by someone other than the lone wolf (Saaij 2010). However, some research includes isolated dyads as persons who qualify as lone wolf terrorists (Gill, Horgan, and Deckert 2014). Despite such differences, the definitions used in research have the most validity due to the consensus surrounding such definitions and the results produced from their usage.

Such varying definitions of who is labeled a lone wolf terrorist affect research and, consequently, government policies and procedures as well as the public's view on such individuals. Though media and the general populace lack a solid definition of who a lone wolf terrorist is, researchers are generally in consensus.

CRIMINALITY COMPARISON OF LONE WOLF TERRORISM

Criminality comparisons of lone wolf terrorism are paradoxical due to the complexity of the definition. Lone wolves are considered terrorists due to their acts falling within the definition of terrorism. Some have argued that having a single definition of each type of terrorism is best (Laqueur 1999), while others have advocated having a consensus definition that uses the key elements of a number of definitions (Schmid and Lonman 2005).

The most prominent definition of terrorism is "the use or threat [that] is designed to influence the government or to intimidate the public . . . and/or . . . is made for the purpose of advancing a political, religious, or ideological cause"

(Gill, Horgan, and Deckert 2014). However, terrorism, and consequently the lone wolf, often becomes associated with organized terrorist groups due to media outlets. This is despite the lack of membership a lone wolf has with such terrorist organizations.

Rather, it is estimated that lone wolf terrorists have more similarities with mass murderers than those in an organized terrorist group. A mass murderer is defined as an individual who has killed at least four people in a 24-hour period (Horgan et al. 2016). Both groups commit acts that are public and publicized and use similar weapons to commit such acts. In addition, there are few differences in regards to sociodemographics and behaviors, such as types of targets, stressors, and having verbalized their intent. Despite the general similarities, a significant difference between the groups is the motivation behind the act, with the lone wolf having an ideology in correspondence with a personal motive (Horgan et al. 2016).

Due to the overall similarities between mass murderers and lone wolf terrorists, there is speculation that these individuals may be grouped together to form a new subcategory of criminality (Worth 2016). The call for change is also a by-product of terrorism being seen as predominantly a social activity due to it mostly being collectivized.

LONE WOLF PROFILE

Lone wolf terrorists lack consistent psychological markers to permit the establishment of a subject profile. Such inconsistencies include age, education level, and marital status. A major source of the inconsistencies originates with how lone wolf terrorists create their own views through a lens that blends their personal grievances with broader social aims (Gill, Horgan, and Deckert 2014).

Despite the inconsistencies, there are general similarities that constitute the majority. Lone wolves are predominantly males, socially isolated, rarely impulsive (in regard to their terrorist act), and are engaged with a wider group that shares similar ideologies. In addition, other people know about the lone wolf's ideologies, views, grievances, or intent to be violent (Gill, Horgan, and Deckert 2014; Saaij 2010). The acts of violence are typically completed via firearms, explosives, or armed hijackings (Saaij 2010). Less frequently, approximately a third of lone wolf terrorists have a history of mental illness or a personality disorder (Gill, Horgan, and Deckert 2014). Though significant, the influence of their mental condition in regard to their terrorist acts is unknown and cannot be explained as the primary cause, despite media accusations.

When subgroups are established based on ideology, the number of similarities between individuals increases. Three dominant subgroups include Al Qaeda–related offenders, right-wing offenders, and single-issue offenders. Al Qaeda–related offenders tend to be younger, to learn virally, and to seek legitimization from authority. Right-wing offenders are less likely to share their ideologies and engage in "dry runs." Single-issue offenders are more likely to have a criminal history and a history of mental illness, and they often give warnings before the event (Gill, Horgan, and Deckert 2014).

"LONE WOLF PROVISION"

The U.S. Foreign Intelligence Surveillance Act of 1978 (FISA) (50 U.S.C. § 1801) established protocols for electronic surveillance (and later physical surveillance) and collection of foreign intelligence. In 2004, the Intelligence Reform and Terrorism Prevention Act, P.L. 108-458, amended FISA to include those that are considered lone wolves under "agents of a foreign power." Via this provision, those who act alone and engage in international terrorist activities fall within FISA. This is significant because it acknowledges the impact of lone wolf terrorists and recognizes that they are unique in their motivations and overall psychology.

GOING FORWARD

The prevalence of lone wolf terrorism has increased within the past three decades, though more so in the United States than in other countries. However, the true figures of international lone wolf terrorism are unknown due to the discontinuation of RAND-MIPT, a terrorism database (Saaij 2010). Despite the overall increase, casualties remain low. The increase in recognition of lone wolves has sparked the interest of media outlets, bringing more light to such individuals.

Christina Lynn Richardson

See also: Islamic State of Iraq and Syria (ISIS); Terrorism, Domestic

Further Reading

Borum, Randy, Robert Fein, and Bryan Vossekuil. 2012. "A Dimensional Approach to Analyzing Lone Offender Terrorism." *Aggression and Violent Behavior* 17 (5): 389–396.

Gill, Paul, John Horgan, and Paige Deckert. 2014. "Bombing Alone: Tracing the Motivations and Antecedent Behaviors of Lone-Actor Terrorists." *Journal of Forensic Sciences* 59 (2): 425–435.

Horgan, John G., Paul Gill, Noemie Bouhana, James Silver, and Emily Corner. 2016. *Across the Universe? A Comparative Analysis of Violent Behavior and Radicalization across Three Offender Types with Implications for Criminal Justice Training and Education.* Report no. 249937 (June). Accessed January 17, 2019. https://www.ncjrs.gov/pdffiles1/nij/grants/249937.pdf.

Spaaij, Ramón. 2010. "The Enigma of Lone Wolf Terrorism: An Assessment." *Studies in Conflict and Terrorism* 33 (9): 854–870.

Los Zetas

The Los Zetas transnational criminal organization (TCO) is largely considered to be one of the most violent and bloodthirsty groups that has developed in the past 20 years (Dulin and Patino 2014). Los Zetas is recognized as one of Mexico's fastest-growing TCOs. While originally founded as an enforcement arm of the Gulf Cartel, Los Zetas split from the Gulf Cartel and has grown as a feared and respected TCO in its own right. Los Zetas' reach extends from South America

(Colombia), through Central America (primarily Guatemala and El Salvador), to Europe (Italy) and across the United Sates and throughout Mexico. Los Zetas is primarily headquartered in Nuevo Laredo, Tamaulipas, in the northeastern part of Mexico. Its central hub is situated directly across from Laredo, Texas, giving it an advantage in directly smuggling narcotics into the United States and then smuggling money back. Los Zetas also controls the points of entry for human smuggling by charging a fee for the right of usage.

While Los Zetas has lost its powerful status due to intracartel fighting, it remains on the Drug Enforcement Administration's list as a TCO that is a great drug threat to the United States (DOJ and DEA 2017).

HISTORY

Osiel Cardenas Guillen (a former drug lord and leader of the Gulf Cartel) founded Los Zetas in 1999. Cardenas Guillen adopted the use of an armed enforcement group to carry out violent operations for the Gulf Cartel. Cardenas Guillen created Los Zetas after offering Arturo Guzman Decena, then a member of the Grupo Aeromovil de Fuerzas Especiales (Special Airforce Group; GAFES is its Spanish acronym), several hundred thousand dollars to work for the Gulf Cartel as the head of the enforcement arm of the TCO. Guzman Decena was tasked with recruiting other GAFES members. A total of 32 former and current GAFES members deserted the military and formed Los Zetas. The group was called Los Zetas because of its military affiliations. Each original founding member was dubbed Zeta 1 up to Zeta 32.

Throughout the early part of the 2000s, Los Zetas was used to enforce and expand the size of the Gulf Cartel. However, in late 2009 and early 2010, after a series of leadership turnovers within Los Zetas and the Gulf Cartel, Los Zetas officially split from the Gulf Cartel. The split generated an unprecedent level of cartel violence vying for control for the lucrative entry point of the Mexican northeastern corridor.

ORGANIZATION

Los Zetas primarily operated in a mixed model hierarchy structure; that is, it incorporated its military background into the structure of the group as well as using a business structure model. The group is believed to be the first and only group to use a military chain of command to carry out drug trafficking and other illicit activities. Each member and group operates in a hierarchical structure.

"Halcones" (literally "Falcons," but they are considered informants, or the eyes of the group) are at the bottom of the structure, these members are used to identify enemies, law enforcement, or military personnel and to pass along the information to higher members of the group. In a similar fashion, the "Panteras" are composed of all females. The Panteras are used to gather intelligence from rivals, law enforcement, and politicians. These lower members pass along information to the next group, known as Cobras. Cobras are in charge of the informants, and they carry out executions and kidnappings. Next are the Zetas Nuevos (New Zetas), which are composed of former or current law enforcement as well as military personnel, to include Guatemalan special forces, known as Kaibiles (Gomez 2008). Lastly, are the Zetas Viejos ("Old Zetas"), the 32 original founding members (Gomez 2008).

NATIONAL AND INTERNATIONAL PRESENCE

Los Zetas made international headlines through their violent tactics in targeting innocent bystanders and killing scores of individuals. Numerous massacres have been attributed to Los Zetas, in particular the killing of 72 migrants in San Fernando, Tamaulipas, Mexico. Indeed, their violent tactics and disregard for life enabled the organization to expand throughout Northwestern, Southern, and Central Mexico. Los Zetas engaged in numerous incidents of intercartel violence while vying for control of key plazas and drug trafficking routes.

At an international level, Los Zetas has utilized social media outlets such as YouTube and Twitter to display gruesome acts of violence. Numerous videos show how members of Los Zetas have tortured and killed competitors. Graphic images display beheaded enemies, tortured individuals left hanging from bridges, and threatening messages for other potential victims to establish dominance of the routes and plazas they aim to control. The aforementioned tactics are the epitome of the modus operandi that launched Los Zetas in the spotlight as one of the most fearsome TCOs in Mexico's war on drugs, at home and abroad. The latter is perhaps best exemplified when Los Zetas was allegedly involved in the murder of an American on Falcon Lake along the Texas-Mexico border and the murder of Immigration and Customs Enforcement (ICE) agent Jaime Zapata in 2011 in the central state of San Luis Potosi, Mexico (Suspect 2012; Univision 2016).

Jairo Patiño

See also: Gulf Cartel; Jalisco New Generation Cartel; Juárez Cartel; Sinaloa Cartel; Tijuana Cartel

Further Reading

Dulin, Adam L., and Jairo Patiño. 2014. "The Logic of Cartel Car Bombings in Mexico." *Trends in Organized Crime* 17 (4): 271–289.

Gomez, Francisco. 2008. "Los Zetas por Dentro." El Universal. Last modified December 31, 2008. Accessed January 21, 2019. http://archivo.eluniversal.com.mx/nacion/164819.html.

"Suspect Arrested in Case of American Killed on Border Lake while Riding Jet Ski in 2010." Fox News. Last modified October 09, 2012. Accessed January 21, 2019. http://www.foxnews.com/us/2012/10/09/wife-murdered-colorado-man-hopeful-mexico-will-try-cartel-leader.html.

Univision y agencias. 2016. "México Extradita a Dos Acusados de Asesinar a Jaime Zapata, Agente de ICE." Univision. Last modified May 17, 2016. Accessed January 17, 2019. https://www.univision.com/dallas/kuvn/noticias/asesinatos/mexico-extradita-a-dos-acusados-de-asesinar-a-jaime-zapata-agente-de-ice.

U.S. Department of Justice (DOJ) and Drug Enforcement Administration (DEA). 2017. *2017 National Drug Threat Assessment.* Washington, D.C.: DEA. Accessed January 17, 2019. https://www.dea.gov/docs/DIR-040-17_2017-NDTA.pdf.

Love Virus

The Love Virus, sometimes referred to as the Love Letter Virus, Love Bug Virus, or ILOVEYOU Virus, was a computer worm that originated in the Philippines. On May 5, 2000, the Love Virus began infecting tens of millions of Windows personal computers worldwide via the computer operator's e-mail. The computer worm originated in an e-mail with the subject line "ILOVEYOU," under the guise of a secret admirer of the operator (Strickland n.d.). The e-mail contained the attachment "LOVE-LETTER-FOR-YOU.txt.vbs." If the operator opened this attachment, a Visual Basic script—a computer language with a series of commands within a file—was executed, and the computer was subsequently infected. Once infected, the computer worm utilized the operator's e-mail contacts and e-mail itself to everyone within that operator's contact list. The Love Virus spread rapidly and was estimated to have reached over 45 million users in the first day (Rouse 2006). Within the first 10 days, the virus was estimated to have infected 10 percent of all the networked computers in the world, costing an estimated $5.5 billion to $8.7 billion in damages (Garza n.d.).

VIRUS DESIGN

The attachment "LOVE-LETTER-FOR-YOU.txt.vbs" contained a vbs interpreted file, which fooled Microsoft Windows into concealing the interpreted file as a simple text file. Once activated, the interpreted file e-mailed itself to everyone in the operator's contact list and then edited the operator's Windows Registry so that the worm could establish itself during startup. The Love Virus then began replacing the existing data in the operator's computer files, including JPEG images and Word Documents, with copies of itself (Computer Hope 2017). These copies of the Love Virus were hidden in several different folders on the operator's hard drive, often adding new files to the victim's registry keys in the process. Finally, the Love Virus downloaded a file called "WIN-BUGSFIX.EXE," which was a password-stealing application that e-mailed passwords and secret information to the creator's e-mail address (Strickland n.d.).

SPREAD

The Love Virus was first reported on May 5, 2000, in Hong Kong, and it began to spread westward through corporate e-mail systems. The Love Virus spread quickly among users of Microsoft Outlook as well as corporate networks that utilized the Microsoft Exchange e-mail server. The Love Virus was efficient because it sent a copy of itself to every e-mail address in a recipient's Outlook address book (Kleinbard and Richtmyer 2000). The worm's use of mailing lists as its source of targets made the subsequent e-mails appear to come from acquaintances, and it was therefore often regarded as safe by recipients.

The Love Virus swept through banks, securities firms, and online companies in the United States and spawned several copycat viruses. The Love Virus caused companies, governments, and end users extreme grief and temporarily forced mailing systems, mail servers, and bank systems to shut down (Computer Hope 2017). The virus caused extensive damage at companies that made heavy use of multimedia files, such as magazines and advertising agencies; however, the Love Virus proved in large part to be more of an annoyance than a costly disruption of business. The reported monetary loss associated with the Love Virus was tied to a loss of productivity during removal of the virus from corporate systems (Kleinbard and Richtmyer 2000).

SUSPECT

Onel de Guzman, a Filipino hacker, had been the individual subject to multiple criminal investigations by the Philippines' National Bureau of Investigation in relation to the Love Virus. A local Internet service provider traced an unusually heavy volume of data traffic to the home of de Guzman's sister in the hours leading up to the release of the Love Virus. The Philippine authorities filed theft and other charges against de Guzman; however, the authorities dropped the charges because of insufficient evidence. The case against de Guzman was weakened because of a lack of laws governing computer espionage in the Philippines.

Just two months after the worm outbreak, the Philippine Congress enacted Republic Act No. 8792, which is otherwise known as the E-Commerce Law, in July 2000, to address this legislative deficiency. Under its provisions, the legislation enabled the Philippine government to bring charges against future hackers; however, it did not allow for charges to be filed against de Guzman for his alleged involvement in the Love Virus (Lander 2000).

Jessie L. Slepicka

See also: Cyberattack; Cybercrime

Further Reading

Computer Hope. 2017. "Love Letter Virus." Accessed March 16, 2018. https://www.computerhope.com/vinfo/iloveyou.htm.

Denning, Dorothy E. 2000. "Cyberterrorism." *Focus on Terrorism* 9: 1–10. Accessed January 17, 2019. https://calhoun.nps.edu/bitstream/handle/10945/55351/Denning_Dorothy_2000_cyberterrorism.pdf?sequence=1&isAllowed=y.

Garza, George. n.d. "Top 10 Worst Computer Viruses." Accessed March 16, 2018. https://www.catalogs.com/info/travel-vacations/top-10-worst-computer-viruses.html.

Kleinbard, David, and Richard Richtmyer. 2000. "U.S. Catches 'Love' Virus." Accessed March 16, 2018. http://money.cnn.com/2000/05/05/technology/loveyou.

Lander, Mark. 2000. "A Filipino Linked to 'Love Bug' Talks about His License to Hack." Accessed March 16, 2018. http://www.nytimes.com/2000/10/21/business/a-filipino-linked-to-love-bug-talks-about-his-license-to-hack.html.

Rouse, Margaret. 2006. "ILOVEYOU virus." Accessed March 16, 2018. http://searchsecurity.techtarget.com/definition/ILOVEYOU-virus.

Strickland, Jonathan. n.d. "10 Worst Computer Viruses of All Time." Accessed March 16, 2018. https://computer.howstuffworks.com/worst-computer-viruses2.htm.

"Loverboy" Recruitment Approach to Human Trafficking

"Loverboys" are human traffickers that promise men or women a love relationship but subsequently use coercion, violence (or the threat of it), extortion, fraud, deception, or abuse of circumstances to exploit the victim's vulnerability (Myria 2016). The term *loverboy* is especially used in the Netherlands and Belgium to display the love relationship that is being promised by human traffickers to young boys and girls. However, this method takes place all over the world to force people into human trafficking (Siegel 2012). Victims of loverboys can be sexually exploited both nationally and transnationally. Moreover, loverboys often do not have the local ethnicity or nationality. Also, clients that visit the victims of loverboys, forced prostitutes, predominantly come from other countries. This makes the local problem of loverboys an international problem, supporting transnational organized crime related to human trafficking and drugs trafficking. The latter is supported by this crime, as many prostitutes become highly dependent on drugs (Myria 2016).

VICTIMS

Anyone who can fall in love can become a loverboy's victim, independent of sex, age, race, education, or social class. However, the majority of victims are young girls between 14 and 23 years of age, which makes teenage and adolescent girls a vulnerable group. Although, historically, mostly girls become victims of loverboys, in recent years, more and more boys fall for loverboys, and lovergirls as well. Apart from sex and age, there are other factors that increase the vulnerability of young people for loverboys. Young adults that cope with problems at home are more receptive to attention in general and from loverboys in particular. Examples of these problems are (sexual) abuse, (emotional) neglect, bullying, and broken families. Moreover, impactful events such as the death of a relative can make young people more vulnerable and receptive for attention (Bock and Archer 2016).

THE METHOD

Loverboys generally make use of a vast pattern of recruitment. The traditional "loverboy method" has four phases and makes use of the physical recruitment of victims: (1) recruiting; (2) influencing/making someone dependent and in love; (3) Cutting off social network/isolating; and (4) exploiting.

In the first phase, the loverboy recruits girls at schools, in parks, in community centers, and at other places. He finds a vulnerable teenager and overloads her with attention and love. When a person is receptive to it, the loverboy tries to make the victim fall in love with him by being a listener, giving presents, and being nice. Once the targeted victim is in love, the loverboy starts setting the victim up against family and friends and making her socially and economically dependent on him. The boy starts to change his behavior and switches between hate and love. He starts spying and demands justification for everything the potential victim does. The victim is in love and very dependent on him, which results in justifying the "few" bad moments. Partly, this happens because the victim has no one to talk to about the situation. Later in this phase, violence or drugs can be used to make the victim dependent.

Ultimately, the exploiting phase takes place in which it is time to pay back the presents, the guy has a financial problem and needs the victim's help to quickly pay back the money. Other options are that he promises to leave the country with the victim, and they need money. Or one of his friends needs company after his girlfriend broke up with him. This often results in (group) raping, and the victim is forced into prostitution. Once the victim is in prostitution, the loverboy blackmails the victim with naked pictures or videos or threatens to tell the victim's family. There now seems no way out, and the victim stays in sex work, with the risk of being trafficked abroad (Myria 2016).

Due to the important role of Internet and social media in the recruitment of victims, a new method called "loverboy method 2.0" has been identified (Myria 2016): (1) grooming and hawking; (2) influencing or making someone dependent; (3) incorporating; and (4) exploiting.

The first phase changes from physically recruiting victims to recruiting them via the Internet and social media. This can not only be done by peers but also by adults targeting minors (grooming). The selection of a victim often takes place by scanning profiles on age, educational level, hobbies, and a seductive profile picture.

The second phase can be the same as in the classical loverboy method. However, the Internet makes it easier for the loverboys, as trust can be built up easily, and it becomes possible to talk about secrets and make the victim answer sexual questions and respond to sexual requests. Generally, teenagers do not realize that their actions are being recorded and that those recordings are easily spread.

The third phase usually contains a meeting with the loverboy. Making use of the gathered material and secrets, the loverboy often forces the targeted victim to carry out sexual acts or rapes the victim. Hereafter, the exploitation phase starts, which is similar to the traditional method. (Naturally, it is not necessary that all phases take place for every case, and it is even possible to mix phases from both methods).

In various cases, a victim gets transnationally trafficked during or as a consequence of the loverboy methods. This is a demonstration of involvement in transnational organized crime. However, also when trafficked in their own country, victims often become subject to transnational organized crime due to the international backgrounds of loverboys and customers of their prostitution. There are also links to other forms of transnational organized crime, as the trafficking routes and tools can be shared with others, for example, human trafficking networks. Furthermore, many victims become dependent on drugs, enforcing this network.

COUNTERACTIONS TAKEN

Even though loverboys recruit many young people for human (sex) trafficking, there is little international counteraction against loverboys. However, there are many local and national programs that focus on improving prevention to stop people from falling victim to loverboys, improving the investigation and prosecution of loverboys, and providing victims with services and protection (Dettmeijer-Vermeulen 2012).

An example of such a national program is the Web site and movie *My Dangerous Loverboy*, created by Eyes Open Creative. This organization seeks to eliminate sexual exploitation of children by alerting people, both victims and social workers, to the signs of sexual exploitation and loverboys specifically (Eyes Open Creative 2012).

Despite these local and national efforts, loverboys continue to carry out their jobs. Young boys and girls fall into the hands of loverboys every day, and human trafficking is one of the biggest forms of transnational organized crime.

Puck van Eijk

See also: Gender-Based Violence; Granados Sex Trafficking Organization; Human Trafficking; Sex Exploitation

Further Reading

Bock, L. and C. Archer. 2016. "Sex Trafficking an International and Local Problem." *BlueDevilHUB*, March 9. Accessed January 17, 2019. http://www.bluedevilhub.com/2016/03/09/sex-trafficking-an-international-and-local-problem.

Bovenkerk, F., and M. van San. 2011. "Loverboys in the Amsterdam Red Light District: A Realist Approach to the Study of a Moral Panic." *Crime, Media, Culture* 7 (2): 185–199.

Dettmeijer-Vermeulen, C. 2012. "Trafficking in Human Beings. Ten Years of Independent Monitoring by the Dutch Rapporteur on Trafficking in Human Beings. *European Journal on Criminal Policy and Research* 18 (3): 283–302.

Eyes Open Creative. 2012. "My Dangerous Loverboy." Accessed July 25, 2018. http://mydangerousloverboy.com.

Myria. 2016. *Annual Report 2015: Trafficking and Smuggling in Human Beings: Tightening the Links.* Brussels, Belgium: Myria, 23–48.

Siegel, D. 2012. "Mobility of Sex Workers in European Cities." *European Journal on Criminal Policy and Research* 18 (3): 255–268.

Lula da Silva, Luiz Inácio (1945–)

Luiz Inácio Lula da Silva, referred to as "Lula," became Brazil's first working-class president. He was one of the most popular politicians in Brazil and the world until he became entwined in a corruption scandal that began in 2014. Following a bribery investigation, Operation Car Wash, he was found guilty in 2017 of money laundering and corruption and sentenced to over 12 years in prison.

Da Silva, who was born on October 27, 1945, in Garanhuns, Permambuco, Brazil, formally added "Lula" to his name in 1982. His mother, Euridice Ferreira de Mello, was a seamstress, and his father, Aristedes Inacio da Silva, was an agriculture worker. Da Silva's father believed it was more important to support the family than pursue an education, so da Silva only learned to read by age 10 and began working full-time by age 12.

Da Silva became a metal worker in the 1960s, and shortly after, he lost the little finger on his left hand due to a work incident. He was diagnosed with throat cancer on October 29, 2011, but by February 17, 2012, his cancer was in full remission. He has been married twice—first to Maria de Lourdes, who died in 1971 from hepatitis during pregnancy, and then to Marisa Leticia Lula da Silva, who died in February 2017.

RISE TO PRESIDENCY

After the death of his first wife, Maria, da Silva developed an interest in activism. His speeches often focused on the needs of the working class and developing nations. In 1975, he became the president of the Metal Workers' Union, which he helped to transform into a powerful movement. By 1980, along with members of the union, intellectuals, and activists, he had established Brazil's Socialist Political Party, also known as Partidos dos Trabalhadores ("the Workers' Party"). In 1986, he was elected federal deputy to the Chambers of Deputies, which is a legislative branch of the government.

After three failed presidential attempts, he was elected president of Brazil on October 27, 2002. He then won the next presidential election on October 29, 2006, to serve another four-year term in office. On January 1, 2010, a biographical film called *Lula, Son of Brazil*, which captured da Silva's early life, was released. In April of the same year, he was voted the most influential person in the world, according to *Time* magazine. By the time he left office on January 1, 2011, he had an approval rating of nearly 90 percent (Phillips 2010). When Rio de Janeiro was chosen as the venue for the 2016 Summer Olympics, he was credited with helping the city become the first in South America to host the Olympics.

CORRUPTION SCANDAL

Operation Car Wash was considered a straightforward corruption scandal at the start, but during the investigation, other scandals emerged. The investigation began in 2014 with allegations that executives from Petrobras, the state oil company, had accepted bribes in return for awarding contracts to certain construction firms at inflated prices. As the investigation progressed, there were further allegations that some of the bribery money had been funneled to political parties and politicians. The Workers' Party and Da Silva were among those accused (BBC News 2018).

Da Silva was defiant during the investigation and vowed to run for president again. On March 16, 2016, however, he accepted an offer from President Dilma Rousseff, his protégé and presidential successor, to become Rousseff's chief of staff. He was sworn in the following day. The appointment would have provided legal protection from the corruption case pending against him, but it also led to divisions and political tensions in Brazil. An injunction filed by a judge from Brazil's Supreme Federal Court a day after he was sworn in prevented him from becoming the chief of staff to Rousseff because the appointment would have limited legal actions against him. By September 14, 2016, corruption charges against both da Silva and his wife were filed after it was ruled that there was enough evidence to bring the case to trial.

On July 12, 2017, da Silva was found guilty of money laundering and corruption charges related to the benefits and bribes he reportedly received from Petrobas, an oil company controlled by the state and whose chairpersons are chosen by the government. During the trial, photographic evidence emerged showing an OAS (a Brazilian multinational conglomerate) executive with da Silva inside the latter's infamous apartment property. According to the executive, who cooperated with investigators, the apartment was financed by OAS for da Silva. In return, OAS received lucrative contracts from Petrobas. Petrobas was then overcharged for contracts, and the profit was shared among politicians and Petrobas chairpersons. Investigators revealed that evidence indicated that da Silva received improvements and furniture for the apartment valued at more than a quarter million dollars. At the conclusion of the case, da Silva was sentenced to nine and a half years in prison, but he was allowed to remain free pending appeals. He also faced money laundering, obstruction of justice and corruption charges in other court cases.

On September 5, 2017, da Silva, Dilma Rousseff, and several members from the Workers' Party faced further charges of money laundering and corruption. They denied the charges. Evidence suggests neither da Silva nor his wife utilized the apartment, and no official document connecting da Silva to the apartment was found. The testimony hinged on the executive's statements. Nevertheless, on January 24, 2018, in a subsequent appeal, his conviction was upheld in a unanimous ruling, and his original sentence was increased by two and half years by three appellate court judges. He remains free pending the outcome of any additional appeals, and he could appeal to the Supreme Court to hear his case.

Marika Dawkins

See also: Bribery; Corruption

Further Reading

BBC News. 2018. "Brazil Corruption Scandals: All You Need to Know." Last modified April 8, 2018. Accessed January 17, 2019. https://www.bbc.com/news/world-latin-america-35810578.

Bourne, Richard. 2008. *Lula of Brazil: The Story So Far.* London: Zed Books Limited.

Brooks, Brad. 2017. "Ex-Brazil President Lula Sentenced to Nearly 10 Years for Corruption." *Reuters*, July 12. Accessed January 3, 2018. https://www.reuters.com/article/us-brazil-corruption-lula-idUSKBN19X2FO.

Cuadros, Alex. "The Most Important Criminal Conviction in Brazil's History." *The New Yorker*, July 13. Accessed November 22, 2017. https://www.newyorker.com/news/news-desk/the-most-important-criminal-conviction-in-brazils-history.

Leahy, Joe, and Andres Schipani. 2017. "Lula da Silva Jail Sentence Divides Brazil." *Financial Times*, July 13. Accessed December 14, 2017. https://www.ft.com/content/062b00fe-677a-11e7-8526-7b38dcaef614.

Londoño, Ernesto. 2017. "Ex-President of Brazil Sentenced to Nearly 10 Years in Prison for Corruption." *New York Times*, July 12. Accessed December 13, 2017. https://www.nytimes.com/2017/07/12/world/americas/brazil-lula-da-silva-corruption.html.

Phillips, Tom. 2010. "Lula Era Comes to an End in Brazil." *The Guardian*, December 13. Accessed February 5, 2018. https://www.theguardian.com/world/2010/dec/31/brazil-lula-era-ends.

Global Crime

Global Crime

An Encyclopedia of Cyber Theft, Weapons Sales, and Other Illegal Activities

VOLUME 2: M–Z

Philip L. Reichel, Editor

ABC-CLIO™

An Imprint of ABC-CLIO, LLC
Santa Barbara, California • Denver, Colorado

Library of Congress Cataloging-in-Publication Data

Names: Reichel, Philip L., editor.
Title: Global crime : an encyclopedia of cyber theft, weapons sales, and other illegal activities / Philip L. Reichel, editor.
Description: Santa Barbara, CA : ABC-CLIO, [2019] | Includes bibliographical references and index.
Identifiers: LCCN 2018054480 (print) | LCCN 2019011370 (ebook) | ISBN 9781440860157 (eBook) | ISBN 9781440860140 (set : alk. paper) | ISBN 9781440860164 (volume 1) | ISBN 9781440860171 (volume 2)
Subjects: LCSH: Transnational crime—Encyclopedias. | International crimes—Encyclopedias.
Classification: LCC HV6252 (ebook) | LCC HV6252 .G5553 2019 (print) | DDC 364.1/3503—dc23
LC record available at https://lccn.loc.gov/2018054480

ISBN: 978-1-4408-6014-0 (set)
978-1-4408-6016-4 (vol. 1)
978-1-4408-6017-1 (vol. 2)
978-1-4408-6015-7 (ebook)

23 22 21 20 19 1 2 3 4 5

This book is also available as an eBook.

ABC-CLIO
An Imprint of ABC-CLIO, LLC

ABC-CLIO, LLC
147 Castilian Drive
Santa Barbara, California 93117
www.abc-clio.com

This book is printed on acid-free paper ∞

Manufactured in the United States of America

Dedicated to my friends and colleagues who graciously volunteered or agreed to provide one or more entries for this encyclopedia. And to Eva Jewell and Jay Albanese, who provide counsel and advice that I should more often follow.

Contents

M

Madrid Train Bombing (2004)

The terrorist bombing attacks in Madrid, Spain, on March 11, 2004 (also known in Spain as 11-M), were the deadliest terrorist attacks in Spain's history. The nearly simultaneous coordinated bombings were launched in the morning against the city's commuter train system, killing 191 people and injuring about 1,700 others. The victims included citizens of 17 countries.

The attacks took place during the morning rush hour on four commuter trains traveling between Alcala des Henares and the Atocha Station in Madrid in an obvious effort to inflict the greatest number of casualties possible. Thirteen bombs, hidden in backpacks, were placed on the trains, and 10 of these exploded within a two-minute period, beginning at 7:37 a.m. Two of the three additional bombs were detonated by a police bomb squad, as was a suspicious package found near the Atocha Station. An additional unexploded bomb was brought intact to a police facility and later dismantled. This unexploded bomb provided evidence for the investigation and subsequent trial of the terrorists.

In the immediate aftermath of the attacks, the Spanish government blamed the attacks on Euskadi Ta Askatasuna (Basque Homeland and Freedom, or ETA), the Basque separatist movement that had launched terrorist attacks in the past. Investigators quickly absolved ETA of the attacks, however, and the blame shifted to the terrorist group Al Qaeda, which had perpetrated the September 11, 2001, terrorist attacks against the United States. Spanish authorities have claimed that the attackers were a loose-knit group of radical Muslims, primarily from Morocco, Syria, and Algeria. Several Spanish nationals were also involved, mainly by selling the explosives to the terrorists.

On April 2, 2004, an additional explosive device, which appeared to have been made of the same explosives as those from March 11, was found on the tracks of a high-speed rail line. The explosives had been prepared for detonation but were not connected to any detonating device. Following this further discovery, new investigations were launched, and Spanish police tracked down suspects in an area south of Madrid. During the raid to apprehend them, an explosion, apparently caused by a suicide bomb, killed seven suspects. Security officials believe that between five and eight suspects managed to escape the police that day. As of 2018, they had not yet been apprehended.

In all, 29 suspects, 20 Moroccans and 9 Spaniards, were apprehended and charged for involvement in the attacks. Their trial began on February 15, 2007, and lasted four and a half months. The verdict, handed down on October 31, 2007, found 21 guilty of various crimes, ranging from forgery to murder. Two of the convicted terrorists were sentenced to prison terms that added up to 42,924 years, but Spanish law limits actual imprisonment to 40 years.

The court sentences did not mention any direct links between the convicted terrorists and Al Qaeda. Al Qaeda may have inspired the Madrid terrorists, and a connection cannot be ruled out; however, no irrefutable evidence has been found to connect it with the planning, financing, or execution of the Madrid attacks.

Nevertheless, the Madrid attacks may well have been the first major success for an Al Qaeda–type terrorist organization in Europe. The attacks did lead to greater cooperation between West European security services in an attempt to prevent further attacks.

On the three-year anniversary of the attacks, the Atocha Train Station Memorial was dedicated in memory of those killed. It is a 36-foot-high cylinder of glass bricks that rises from the ground to form a tower that is illuminated at night by lights from its base. Floating inside the cylinder is a balloon-like membrane inscribed with thousands of messages of condolence sent from around the world after the attacks.

Elliot P. Chodoff and Philip L. Reichel

See also: Al Qaeda; Terrorism, International

Further Reading

CNN Library. 2018. "Spain Train Bombings Fast Facts." Last modified April 2, 2018. Accessed January 2, 2019. https://www.cnn.com/2013/11/04/world/europe/spain-train-bombings-fast-facts.

Puniyani, Ram. 2007. *Terrorism: Facts versus Myths*. New Delhi: Pharos Media.

Von Hippel, Karin. 2005. *Europe Confronts Terrorism*. New York: Palgrave Macmillan.

Maersk Alabama Pirate Attack (2009)

On April 8, 2009, four Somali pirates, armed with AK-47s, attacked and hijacked the 508-foot (155-meter) *Maersk Alabama*, a U.S.-flagged cargo ship roughly 240 nautical miles off the Somalian coastline. The attack was the first pirate attack on a U.S.-flagged vessel in roughly 200 years. The ship was on its way from Ṣalālah, Oman, to Mombasa, Kenya, to deliver humanitarian aid. Aboard the ship were 21 American crew members, including the ship's captain, Richard Phillips. A movie about the hijacking, *Captain Phillips*, was released in 2013.

THE ATTACK

In the early morning of April 8, the crew sighted the approach of a small skiff and quickly notified the captain. In an attempt to fend off the attack, the crew used the ship's fire hoses and shot flares. After having eluded the pirates for nearly three hours, two pirates managed to board the ship. In response to the threat, 16 crew members fled to the fortified steering room, which served as a safe room. Phillips and several crew members did not make it and were captured on the ship's bridge. In a bid to shake off the two remaining pirates still on the skiff, the

Alabama's chief engineer, Mike Perry, swung the rudder. It did not prevent the remaining pirates from boarding the *Maersk Alabama*, but it did scuttle and capsize the pirate's skiff. Afterward, the crew successfully disabled the ship, which slowly came to a complete halt.

The pirates sent one of the captured crewmen to find the others and bring them to the bridge. After the third mate, Collin Wright, did not return and instead hid with the others, the pirates sent the helmsman and one of their own. The crew ambushed and gagged the pirate and dragged him into the safe room. Not much later, over the radio, Captain Phillips urged the crewmen to show themselves, as the pirates were getting desperate and had threatened to kill some of the captured crewmembers if their companion was not returned.

In the meantime, the ship's chief mate, Shane Murphy, managed to obtain a very high frequency (VHF) radio from the captain's hut and set off the emergency position-indicating radio beacons. The pirates could overhear the Mayday calls on the VHF radio on the bridge as well as Murphy's faked conversation with the U.S. Navy (Murphy 2009).

The pirates decided to leave, and the captured crew members helped them prepare the ship's lifeboat for their departure. The pirates' only demand was to get their friend back in an exchange of hostages. A failed exchange followed, and Phillips was taken aboard the rescue pod by the pirates.

In the meantime, the USS *Bainbridge*, a guided-missile destroyer, had arrived at the scene and started chasing the lifeboat. A four-day standoff followed, and FBI hostage negotiators as well as Navy SEAL snipers were flown to the scene (BBC 2009). One of the pirates, Abduwali Abdukhadir Muse, boarded the *Bainbridge* to negotiate. This saved his life, as the other three pirates were simultaneously killed by the SEAL snipers. President Barack Obama had authorized lethal action in the event Phillips's life was in imminent danger. When all three pirates were exposed and one aimed his AK-47 at Phillips, the snipers opened fire.

The *Bainbridge* then provided the *Maersk Alabama* a security detail, and the *Maersk Alabama* made it safely into the port of Mombasa and celebrated the release of its captain.

TRIAL

The captured pirate, Abduwali Muse, was taken into custody aboard the *Bainbridge* and tried in the United States. The prosecutor accused Muse of the hijacking of the *Maersk Alabama* as well as two other incidents.

Through an interpreter, Muse apologized for the incident, blamed the Somalia government for his actions, and asked for forgiveness. "What we did was wrong. I am very sorry for all of this. . . . All of this happened because of the government in Somalia" (Robinson 2010). Muse further said, "I ask for forgiveness from all the people I harmed, including the U.S. government" (Richardson 2011).

Muse pleaded guilty to six felony counts of kidnapping, hostage taking, and hijacking maritime vessels (Richardson 2011). Despite his apologies, he was eventually indicted on 10 counts of piracy under the law of nations, conspiracy, hostage taking, kidnapping, and possession of a machine gun while seizing a ship by force. He received the maximum sentence of 33 years and 9 months in prison (Richardson 2011).

LAWSUIT

Not long after the pirate attack, nine crew members filed a lawsuit against the shipowner, Maersk Line Limited, and the crew's employer, Waterman Steamship Corporation (Collins 2013). According to the plaintiff's attorney, Captain Phillips had decided to sail through an area roughly 250 nautical miles off Somalia despite seven formal warnings from maritime authorities (Collins 2013) and the fact that 39 pirate attacks had taken place the previous week in that area (Casey-Maslen and Connolly 2017). The plaintiffs also alleged the captain did not order the crew to practice any pirate attack safety drills prior to the trip (Casey-Maslen and Connolly 2017). The attorney also countered the claims made in the movie *Captain Phillips*, which portrayed the captain as a hero. Ultimately, Maersk Line Limited reached a confidential out-of-court settlement for each client after having denied any negligence or responsibility for years (VB Attorneys 2017).

Wessel Groot

See also: International Maritime Bureau Piracy Reporting Center; Sea Piracy

Further Reading

BBC. 2009. "FBI in Hostage Talks with Somalis." April 9. Accessed April 15, 2018. http://news.bbc.co.uk/2/hi/africa/7991114.stm.

Casey-Maslen, Stuart, and Sean Connolly. 2017. *Police Use of Force under International Law.* Cambridge, UK: Cambridge University Press.

Collins, Laura. 2013. "A New Tom Hanks Movie Says Captain Phillips Is the Hero Who Saved His Men when Pirates Attacked . . . but Now a $50 million Lawsuit Says He Risked Their Lives." *Daily Mail*, October 1. Accessed April 15, 2018. http://www.dailymail.co.uk/news/article-2439561/Captain-Phillips-lawsuit-says-risked-Maersk-Alabama-crews-lives.html.

McFadden, Robert D., and Scott Shane. 2009. "In Rescue of Captain, Navy Kills 3 Pirates." *New York Times*, April 12. Accessed April 15, 2018. https://www.nytimes.com/2009/04/13/world/africa/13pirates.html.

Murphy, Shane. 2009. "'I'm Your Worst F**king Nightmare.'" *GQ*, November 17. Accessed April 14, 2018. https://www.gq.com/story/shane-murphy-maersk-alabama-somali-pirates.

Richardson, Jerika. 2011. "Somali Pirate Asks Forgiveness, Sentenced to Nearly 34 Years in Prison." *ABC News*, February 16. Accessed April 15, 2018. http://abcnews.go.com/Blotter/somali-pirate-muse-sentenced-34-years/story?id=12930166.

Robinson, Cheryl. 2010. "Somali Pirate Pleads Guilty in *Maersk Alabama* Hijacking." *CNN*, May 19. Accessed April 15, 2018. http://edition.cnn.com/2010/CRIME/05/18/new.york.pirate.plea/index.html.

Sanders, Edmund, and Julian E. Barnes. 2009. "Somalia Pirates Hold U.S. Captain." *Los Angeles Times*, April 9. Accessed April 14, 2018. http://articles.latimes.com/2009/apr/09/world/fg-somali-pirates9.

VB Attorneys. 2017. "Maersk Settles Lawsuit Brought by Victims of Somali Piracy." October 31. Accessed January 18, 2019. https://www.vbattorneys.com/case-results/maersk-settles-lawsuit-piracy.

Manchester Arena Terrorist Attack (2017)

On May 22, 2017, a terrorist attack at American singer Ariana Grande's concert killed 22 people at the Manchester Arena in Manchester, United Kingdom. The assailant, Salman Ramadan Abedi, detonated a shrapnel-type nail bomb in the foyer of the concert hall as people gathered to leave the venue. The terrorist organization the Islamic State of Iraq and Syria (ISIS) claimed responsibility for the attack and warned that the Manchester attack would be "the first of many," that all efforts showing defiance against them had been a "complete failure," and, lastly, that "the focus of its followers ha[d] shifted to carrying out attacks on 'Crusader soil' " (Burke 2018).

According to Detective Superintendent Jonathan Chadwick of the Greater Manchester Police, the senior identification manager for the attack, Abedi had awaited the crowd in the foyer after the concert ended, carrying a rucksack with an improvised explosive device (IED) filled with metal fragments and holding a detonator in his left hand (Enoch 2017). When Abedi detonated the bomb, the blast that followed was so powerful that it killed victims as far as 60 feet (20 meters) away. Chadwick added that some 220 people received medical attention as a result of the explosion (Enoch 2017). It was further reported that around 800 people are known to have suffered physical and psychological injuries after the Manchester bombing (BBC 2018).

AFTERMATH AND INVESTIGATION

Immediately after the attacks, Great Britain set its threat level to "critical," but it was lowered back to "severe" a week later. At the same time, the police opened a massive investigation into the crime that involved 1,000 investigators. Despite referencing 7,000 people in the inquiry, taking 2,000 witness statements, combing 11,000 tons of trash on the lookout for a suitcase allegedly dumped by Abedi, arresting (and later releasing) 23 people, and spending some £4 million, no one had been charged with the crime almost a year later (Pidd 2018).

The only person that the police have linked to the crime is Hashem Abedi, a brother of the perpetrator, for whom the Greater Manchester Police believes to "have enough evidence to charge him with the murder of 22 people, the attempted murder of others who were injured and conspiracy to cause an explosion" (Osborne 2018). A month before the attack, Hashem had traveled with his brother to Libya; Hashem then stayed in Libya while Salman returned to Manchester to carry out the bombing (Osborne 2018).

Two days after the attack, Libyan authorities arrested Hashem because he was, according to Libya's chief investigator, Asadiq al-Sour, suspected of having helped his brother and of collecting materials for the attack (Osborne 2018). He has since been in the custody of a militia group in Tripoli (Lockwood 2018).

Since October 2017, the U.K. government has repeatedly requested Hashem's extradition. This has not yet happened, but the issue is "under review pending verification of Hashem Abedi's legal citizenship status" (Osborne 2018). According to the former head of the U.K. National Counter Terrorism Security Office, Chris Philips, issues with extradition are more of a political and policing issue: "They are dealing with terrorism of their own, there are different factions in charge of different parts of the country and to get a stable answer has proved difficult or else they would have brought him here by now" (Lockwood 2018).

Wessel Groot

See also: Islamic State of Iraq and Syria (ISIS); Suicide Bombings; Terrorism, International

Further Reading

BBC. 2018. "Manchester Arena Attack: Bomb 'Injured More Than 800.'" May 16. Accessed May 25, 2018. http://www.bbc.com/news/uk-england-manchester-44129386.

Burke, Dave. 2017. "ISIS Warns That the Manchester Bombing Is a Preview of What Is to Come as It 'Shifts Its Focus to Carrying Out Attacks on Crusader Soil.'" *Mail Online*, June 8. Accessed May 25, 2018. http://www.dailymail.co.uk/news/article-4583668/ISIS-warns-Manchester-bombing-preview-s-come.html.

Enoch, Nick. 2017. "Manchester Attacker 'Detonated Rucksack Bomb Packed with Shrapnel Just Five Yards from His Nearest Innocent Victim." *Mail Online*, June 9. Accessed May 23, 2018. http://www.dailymail.co.uk/news/article-4588550/Manchester-rucksack-bomb-massive-metal.html.

Lockwood, Sally. 2018. "Manchester Arena Bomber 'Definitely Had Help,' Says Man Who Knew Attacker." *Sky News*, May 22. https://news.sky.com/story/manchester-arena-bomber-definitely-had-help-says-man-who-knew-attacker-11382269.

Osborne, Simon. 2018. "Manchester Suicide Bomber's Brother Could REFUSE to Face Trial before British Court." *Express*, May 22. Accessed May 25, 2018. https://www.express.co.uk/news/uk/963511/manchester-bombing-salman-abedi-brother-hashem-abedi-manchester-arena-attack-ariane-grande.

Pidd, Helen. 2018. "Cost of Police Inquiry into Manchester Arena Bombing Rises to £4m." *The Guardian*, May 16. Accessed May 25, 2018. https://www.theguardian.com/uk-news/2018/may/16/cost-of-police-inquiry-into-manchester-arena-bombing-rises-to-4m.

Manhattan Truck Attack (2017)

On October 31, 2017, Sayfullo Habibullaevic Saipov drove a flatbed truck down a bike path in New York City, killing 8 people and injuring at least 12 others. Media outlets have called this attack "New York's deadliest terror attack since 9/11." Despite being shot by police, Saipov survived and was taken into custody. Saipov told officials that he had been heavily influenced by the Islamic State of Iraq and Syria (ISIS) and that he was proud to commit such an attack in its name. Saipov was indicted on 22 counts, including providing material support and resources to a designated foreign terrorist organization and murder in aid of racketeering. The case against Saipov began in November 2017 and is continuing into 2019.

Sayfullo Habibullaevic Saipov is a 29-year-old from Uzbekistan. He came to the United States in 2010 with a green card, allowing him to maintain permanent legal residence. During his time in the United States, Saipov lived in multiple states, including Ohio and New Jersey. In these states, Saipov received traffic citations and was issued a warrant for failure to appear in court. The October 2017 attack was not his first encounter with the criminal justice system (Prokupecz et al. 2017).

THE ATTACK

On October 31, 2017, at approximately 3:00 p.m., Saipov drove a rented flatbed truck onto the bike lane and pedestrian walkway of the West Side Highway in New York City. Saipov drove down the path for several blocks before crashing into a school bus that was carrying special needs children. He then exited the truck with what appeared to be firearms, later identified as a paintball gun and a pellet gun, and yelled "Allahu Akbar," an Arabic phrase meaning "God is great." Saipov was shot by law enforcement officers in the abdomen and taken into custody. The attack ended with 8 people killed and at least 12 injured (Sealed Complaint 2017).

At the crime scene, law enforcement officers recovered a black bag (later found to contain three knives and Saipov's wallet), two cell phones, a stun gun, and a document written by Saipov in Arabic and English. The Arabic sections of the document read "No God but God and Muhammad is his Prophet" and "Islamic Supplication, It will endure." "It will endure" is a common phrase used in reference to ISIS. In addition, one of the cell phones contained approximately 90 videos and 3,800 images of ISIS-related propaganda (Sealed Complaint 2017).

CONNECTION TO ISIS

ISIS is a terrorist organization that recruits individuals internationally in a mission to expand its caliphate in Africa and the Middle East. Its methods of recruitment include pictures, videos, video lectures, and updates of its attacks. The development of the Internet, and especially social media, has globalized ISIS's outreach and influence.

On September 21, 2014, Abu Muhammad al-Adnani, an ISIS spokesperson, called for attacks against citizens of countries that participate in a coalition aimed to end ISIS, of which the United States is a member. The November 2016 issue of *Rumiyah*, ISIS's magazine, includes an article entitled "Just Terror Tactics." This article focuses on a vehicle attack as a primary attack, followed by a secondary attack using a knife or gun (Sealed Complaint 2017).

Though Saipov's attack seemingly followed the guidelines in the article, he stated in Bellevue Hospital that he had been motivated to commit the attack after viewing a video by Abu Bakr al-Baghdadi, the leader of ISIS. This video questioned what Muslims were doing in response to the killings of Muslims in Iraq, and it inspired Saipov to begin planning the attack approximately a year in advance. Two months prior to the attack, he decided to use a truck as his main method of violence. Saipov chose this modus operandi, in conjunction with doing it on Halloween, to cause the maximum number of casualties (Sealed Complaint 2017).

COURT ACTIONS

The U.S. Attorneys' Terrorism and International Narcotics Unit prosecuted Saipov, and on November 21, 2017, a federal grand jury returned a 22-count indictment that included 8 counts of murder in aid of racketeering, 12 counts of attempted murder in aid of racketeering, 1 count of providing and attempting to provide material support to ISIS, and 1 count of violence and destruction of a motor vehicle (Criminal Indictment 2017). The penalties Saipov can receive include time in prison, life in prison, and the death penalty (U.S. Department of Justice 2017).

Christina Lynn Richardson

See also: Islamic State of Iraq and Syria (ISIS); Terrorism, Vehicle Ramming Attacks

Further Reading

Almukhtar, Sarah, Troy Griggs, Jasmine C. Lee, Ford Fessenden, K. K. Rebecca, Jugal Patel, Bedel Saget, and Anjali Singhvi. 2017. "Trail of Terror in the Manhattan Truck Attack." *New York Times*, October 31. Accessed January 3, 2019. https://www.nytimes.com/interactive/2017/10/31/nyregion/manhattan-truck-attack.html?_r=0.

Criminal Indictment. 2017. *United States v. Sayfullo Habibullaevic Saipov* (S.D.N.Y. 2017) (17CRIM722). Accessed January 3, 2019. https://www.justice.gov/usao-sdny/press-release/file/1013346/download.

Prokupecz, Shimon, Eric Levenson, Brynn Gingras, and Steve Almasy. 2017. "Note found near truck claims Manhattan attack done for ISIS, source says." CNN. Last updated November 6, 2017. Accessed February 9, 2019. https://www.cnn.com/2017/10/31/us/new-york-shots-fired/index.html.

Sealed Complaint. 2017. *United States v. Sayfullo Habibullaevic Saipov* (S.D.N.Y. 2017) (17MAG8177). https://assets.documentcloud.org/documents/4165614/U-S-v-Sayfullo-Saipov-Complaint.pdf.

U.S. Department of Justice. 2017. "Sayfullo Saipov Indicted on Terrorism and Murder in Aid of Racketeering Charges in Connection with Lower Manhattan Truck Attack." News release, November 21. U.S. Attorney's Office, Southern District of New York. Accessed January 3, 2019. https://www.justice.gov/usao-sdny/pr/sayfullo-saipov-indicted-terrorism-and-murder-aid-racketeering-charges-connection-lower.

Yan, Holly, and Dakin Andone. 2017. "Who Is New York Terror Suspect Sayfullo Saipov?" CNN, November 2. Accessed January 3, 2019. http://www.cnn.com/2017/11/01/us/sayfullo-saipov-new-york-attack/index.html.

Mara Salvatrucha (MS-13) Organization

The Mara Salvatrucha, commonly known as MS-13, is one of the largest street gangs in the Western Hemisphere. Although it originated in Los Angeles in the

1980s, MS-13 is currently based mainly in Central America's Northern Triangle countries (El Salvador, Honduras, and Guatemala). It also continues operating in Los Angeles, and its presence has been detected in other major U.S. cities. The gang operates in marginal neighborhoods, where it extorts small and medium businesses, provides hitmen services for larger criminal organizations, controls markets for illegal drugs and weapons, and intimidates communities. Although youth gangs are often seen as the main drivers of violence in the Northern Triangle countries, there are deeper socioeconomic causes—such as poverty, inequality, lack of educational and job opportunities, and social marginalization—that underlie their persistence. Gang warfare accounts for a significant portion of the deaths in the Northern Triangle, which consistently ranks as the most violent region in the world.

HISTORY

The origins of MS-13 can be traced to poor neighborhoods of Los Angeles, where many Salvadorans had fled because of their country's civil war during the early 1980s. Many of the refugees were children who had witnessed war atrocities at an early age and then endured the hardships of a long trip to the United States, guided by human smugglers. In Los Angeles, newly arrived refugee youth faced another series of challenges, such as a new language, a new culture, and bullying at schools.

Coming from dysfunctional families with a lack of adult supervision, these youngsters united in neighborhood-based groups, or gangs, to deal with the numerous challenges of immigrant life and to protect themselves from other gangs, mostly of Mexican origin. The largest of these newly established gangs was Mara Salvatrucha. "Mara" is a Central American slang term for any group of people. Early youth gangs adopted this term to distinguish themselves from other social groups, and the term came to designate all street gangs in the region. "Salva" refers to El Salvador, and "trucha" is a Central American slang term for "smart." Later, the gang added 13 to its name, "M" being the 13th letter in the alphabet.

Although it started as a nonviolent stoner gang whose main activities were hanging out together and listening to heavy metal music, the gang members eventually socialized with more serious street gangs in prisons and adopted the violent style of a criminal enterprise (Savenije 2009; Ward 2013). By 1990, two major Latin American gangs in Los Angeles, MS-13 and the 18th Street Gang, had become sworn enemies, creating a rise in violence in the city's underprivileged communities.

After the end of the civil war in El Salvador in 1992, the U.S. government assumed a tougher stance on immigration and began a program of mass deportation of foreign-born residents with criminal histories through the Illegal Immigration Reform and Immigrant Responsibility Act (IIRIRA), passed in 1995. As a result, tens of thousands of gang members that had served prison sentences in the United States were returned to their countries of origin (mainly El Salvador, Honduras, and Guatemala).

There, they did not form new gangs but joined the already existing myriad of *maras*, bringing with them their U.S. gang experience and culture and transforming the local criminal landscape. As a result, the multiple small local gangs, mainly dedicated to petty crime and hanging out on the street corners, evolved into more violent criminal groups with a marked sense of identity based on the rivalry with their archenemy. Eventually, almost all existing gangs in Central America became integrated into two major rival gangs, the MS-13 and the 18th Street Gang.

STRUCTURE AND ACTIVITIES

Like most street gangs, MS-13 does not have a well-defined single leader. However, it is the largest and most organized gang in Central America. It also possesses higher levels of territorial control than other street gangs (Cruz et al. 2016). The gang consists of a network of multiple cliques (*clicas*), turf-based cells typically organized around specific neighborhoods. Each clique has its own leader and hierarchy. Some larger cliques, called *sectores*, control more than one neighborhood. The regional-level management is called *programas*. The top organizational level is composed of *ranfla*, a group of leaders that control the national operation of the gang and serves as a decision-making board (Cruz et al. 2016).

The media's depiction of MS-13 as an evil, highly structured criminal organization, supported by its designation as a transnational criminal organization by the U.S. Treasury Department, is criticized by some experts as misleading. Indeed, most of MS-13's activities are locally oriented, and its profits are relatively low (Martínez et al. 2016; Wolf 2012).

MS-13 has its own subculture manifested in the use of tattoos, hand signals, slang, and a code of conduct. Defending the neighborhood (*barrio*) from rival gangs is an essential part of this culture. Within MS-13, numerous assassinations and the capability to control new territories through extortions, threats, and murders are critical strategies for ascending within the gang structure.

Although not all gang members take part in violent activities, those who do give the gang its reputation of ruthlessness. Disenfranchised youth join the gang for numerous reasons, including easy access to alcohol, drugs, and women, as well as the search for respect and identity (Cruz et al. 2016).

PUBLIC POLICY RESPONSES

The governments of the Northern Triangle did not have institutional mechanisms to deal with the growing influx of deportees during the 1990s. Their response has been predominantly repressive, with little, if any, attention to deeper causes of the phenomenon, such as inequality, unemployment, poor education, and a lack of basic human services within deprivileged communities.

In 2003, the Salvadoran and Honduran governments launched *Mano Dura* ("Iron Fist") policies that enabled police to arrest suspected gang members based on their physical appearance (such as having tattoos). As a result, already overcrowded Central American prisons saw a drastic overflow of gang members. At the same time, repressive policies triggered the adaptation mechanism among the gangs; they became more isolated from society, more sophisticated in their organization, and more professionalized in their criminal activities (Wolf 2012).

In recent years, increasing police abuse and extrajudicial killings as part of the state's hard-line approach to the gang problem led to an all-out war between the gangs and the police and soldiers. El Salvador, where the state's public security strategy has been particularly repressive, has witnessed a sharp increase in homicide rates since the turn of the century. An exception of this trend was in 2013, when an ill-fated truce between major gangs and the government caused the murder rate to drop dramatically.

Yulia Vorobyeva

See also: Central American Gangs; 18th Street Gang; Transnational Anti-Gang Task Forces

Further Reading

Cruz, José Miguel, Jonathan D. Rosen, Luis Enrique Amaya, and Yulia Vorobyeva. 2017. *The New Face of Street Gangs: The Gang Phenomenon in El Salvador.* Miami: Florida International University. http://lacc.fiu.edu/research/the-new-face-of-street-gangs_final-report_eng.pdf.

Martínez, Óscar, Efren Lemus, Carlos Martinez, and Deborah Sontag. 2016. "Killers on a Shoestring: Inside the Gangs of El Salvador." *New York Times*, November 20. Accessed January 4, 2019. https://www.nytimes.com/2016/11/21/world/americas/el-salvador-drugs-gang-ms-13.html.

Seelke, Clare Ribando. 2016. Gangs in Central America. Congressional Research Service. August 29. Accessed January 4, 2019. https://fas.org/sgp/crs/row/RL34112.pdf.

Ward, Thomas. 2013. *Gangsters without Borders: An Ethnography of a Salvadoran Street Gang.* New York: Oxford University Press.

Wolf, Sonja. 2012. "Mara Salvatrucha: The Most Dangerous Street Gang in the Americas?" *Latin American Politics and Society* 54: 65–99.

Maritime Piracy, *see* Sea Piracy

McVeigh, Timothy (1968–2001)

Timothy James McVeigh was the mastermind of the 1995 bombing of the Alfred P. Murrah Federal Building in Oklahoma City, Oklahoma—the worst act of terrorism on American soil prior to the September 11, 2001, attacks in New York City and Washington, D.C.

FORMATIVE AND MILITARY YEARS

McVeigh was born in Pendleton, New York, on April 23, 1968. His parents divorced in 1978, and while his sisters went to live with their mother, McVeigh chose to live with his father. After graduating from high school, he was hired as a guard by an armored car company. In 1988, he and a friend bought 10 acres of rural land, where he was able to enjoy shooting his guns. That same year, he enlisted in the U.S. Army and was eventually assigned to the 1st Infantry Division, based in Fort Riley, Kansas.

McVeigh had a successful army career, moving up the ranks from private to platoon leader. He reenlisted at the end of his initial term and applied for the Special Forces, but before he could begin that training, he was sent to Saudi Arabia in 1991, where he saw some combat in the Persian Gulf War (May, Outman, and Outman 2003). After completing his time in the Middle East, he began Special Forces assessment. He quickly realized that he was not in good enough physical condition and dropped out two days later. He applied for, and was granted, discharge from the army in 1991.

INFLUENCES

During his military service, McVeigh read and apparently liked *The Turner Diaries*, a novel supportive of far-right extremism. He was also influenced by the growing militia movement in the United States, wherein various armed citizen groups had banded together in opposition to what they believed was too much government control over their personal lives (May, Outman, and Outman 2003). An incident in 1992 at Ruby Ridge, Idaho (federal agents shot and killed the son and wife of Randy Weaver, a white supremacist accused of selling weapons illegally), and another incident in 1993 in Waco, Texas (federal agents tried to take the compound of the Branch Davidians religious sect and the siege ended with a fire—later determined to have been set by the Branch Davidians—killing 81 people), are believed to have been motivating factors developing McVeigh's antigovernment views. Militia groups viewed both incidents as evidence that the U.S. government was trying to take firearms from its citizens (Applebome 1995).

McVeigh was upset by the government raids, and although he did not join any of the militia groups, he began planning revenge for the raid at Waco—especially against the Bureau of Alcohol, Tobacco, and Firearms (ATF), whose agents had played a role at both Ruby Ridge and Waco. The date April 19 came to have special importance for McVeigh, as it was not only the date of the Waco fire (April 19, 1993) but also marked the start of the American Revolutionary War, when patriots had their first military engagement with the British troops (April 19, 1775).

In 1995, with the assistance of Terry Nichols—a friend he met during army basic training—McVeigh combined fertilizer and diesel fuel to make a bomb. McVeigh rented a Ryder truck, loaded it with about 5,000 pounds of the fertilizer-fuel mixture in the back, and drove it to Oklahoma City. On the morning of April 19 (the two-year anniversary of the siege in Waco), he parked the truck outside the Alfred P. Murrah Federal Building (which he mistakenly believed held an ATF office) and walked away. At 9:02 a.m., the truck bomb exploded. One-third of the building was destroyed, 168 people were killed, and hundreds more were injured—some many blocks away.

A little over an hour later, McVeigh was pulled over by an Oklahoma Highway Patrol officer who had noticed that McVeigh's car had no license plates. McVeigh tried to explain that he had just bought the car and had no plates or documentation. The officer noticed a gun on McVeigh and arrested him for driving without a license plate, no proof of car insurance, unlawful possession of a weapon, and carrying a loaded gun in a car. While McVeigh was being held in jail to await a bail hearing, the FBI identified McVeigh as a suspect in the bombing. He was released from jail into the custody of the FBI on April 21, 1995.

MCVEIGH'S TRIAL

Federal authorities put McVeigh on trial at the federal courthouse in Denver, Colorado, on April 25, 1997. The trial location had been moved out of Oklahoma after a federal judge ruled that McVeigh could not receive a fair trial in Oklahoma due to the extensive publicity that had effectively demonized McVeigh.

The government presented 141 witnesses against McVeigh, including two friends who testified that McVeigh had told them of his plans to bomb the Murrah building. On June 2, 1997, after three days of deliberation, the jury found McVeigh guilty of murder and conspiracy charges, and he was sentenced to death by lethal injection. McVeigh was then transferred to a federal prison in Terre Haute, Indiana, where he was executed on June 11, 2001.

Philip L. Reichel

See also: Nichols, Terry; Oklahoma City Bombing (1995); Terrorism, Domestic

Further Reading

Applebome, Peter. 1995. "Terror in Oklahoma: The Extremists: Radical Right's Fury Boiling Over." *New York Times*, April 23. Accessed January 4, 2019. https://www.nytimes.com/1995/04/23/us/terror-in-oklahoma-the-extremists-radical-right-s-fury-boiling-over.html.

Constantakis, Sara, ed. 2016. "Alfred P. Murrah Federal Building Bombing, 1995." In *World of Forensic Science*, 21–23. Farmington Hills, MI: Gale.

May, Matthew, James L. Outman, and Elisabeth M. Outman, eds. 2003. "McVeigh, Timothy." In *Terrorism Reference Library*, 182–189. Detroit: UXL.

Michel, Lou. 2002. *American Terrorist: Timothy McVeigh and the Tragedy at Oklahoma City*. New York: Avon Books.

Medellín Cartel

The Medellín Cartel, which operated primarily in the 1970s and 1980s, was a transnational criminal network of drug producers and smugglers that originated in the city of Medellín, Colombia. The cartel operated in Colombia, Bolivia, Peru, Central America, the United States, Canada, and Europe. It was founded in 1976 by a group of small-scale drug traffickers that obtained coca paste from Peru to be processed in Medellín (*EcuRed* 2018).

The notable head of the organization was Pablo Escobar Gaviria, known as "El Patrón" ("the Boss"). Other key members included José Gonzalo Rodríguez Gacha, "El Mexicano" ("the Mexican"), the cartel's military leader, and Fabio, Jorge Luis, and Juan David Ochoa, also known as "the Ochoa Brothers," the main financial contributors. Other notable members included Carlos Lehder, "El Loco" ("the Crazy Man"), who opened routes to the Caribbean through his U.S. connections; Gustavo Gaviria, "El Leon" ("the Lion"), Pablo's cousin and second-in-command; and Roberto Escobar, "El Osito" ("the Little Bear"), Pablo's brother and accountant. Other active members were Luis Fernando Gaviria, "Abraham," Pablo's cousin and the logistics and military leader; Mario Henao Vallejo, "Paco," Pablo's brother-in-law and the business manager; and Griselda Blanco, "La Reina de la Coca" (the Queen of Cocaine), who was the first to receive the cartel's shipments in Miami. There were also paramilitary leaders and hit men who became renowned by their aliases: "Rambo," "Popeye," "Tyson," "Pinina," "El Chopo," and "El Titi." By the late 1980s, the cartel had more than 2,000 men just in their military organization (Bowden 2001; Woody 2016).

The organization grew exponentially due to the Colombian phenomenon known as the *Bonanza Marimbera*, in which national policies and legislation allowed the exchange of dollars for pesos with no origin justification, boosting money laundering of drug trafficking earnings (*Verdad Abierta* 2008). At the height of their operations, the cartel moved tons of cocaine and earned $4 billion a year (Cordero 2017). The number of victims attributed to the cartel ranges from 20,000 to 40,000; the cartel was also responsible for killing 550 policemen and detonating approximately 250 car bombs (*20 minutos* n.d.).

TURF WARS

The Medellín Cartel had a very complex history of turf wars fought on different fronts: paramilitary leftist groups, the Cali Cartel, and most notably the Colombian government. In 1981, several members of the Medellín Cartel created the group called *Muerte a los Secuestradores*, or MAS ("Death to the Kidnappers"), a private army of 2,230 men and a budget of 446 million Colombian pesos with the purpose of counteracting the operations and exterminating any suspected members of guerrilla groups in Colombia (*Verdad Abierta* 2011).

There are several theories about the origin of the animosity between the Medellín and Cali Cartels, ranging from personal vendettas to whistle-blowing and control of the U.S. market. The war against the Cali Cartel involved murder attempts against both cartels' bosses and selective killings, mainly in Medellín but also in Cali and in New York. These attacks included such events as the bombings of several locations of the pharmacy chain *Drogas La Rebaja* and an intentional fire to a radio station of *Grupo Radial Colombiano*, both owned by the Cali Cartel, and the 1988 car bomb attack at the Monaco Building in Medellín, a property of Pablo Escobar (Sabogal 1988).

The main contention between the Medellín Cartel and the Colombian government was the issue of extradition, which became the focus of intermittent periods of dialogue and attacks between the two sides. This resulted in the period known as "Narco-Terrorism." During this time, the Medellín Cartel associated with other drug cartels to avoid the ratification of the extradition treaty that would allow the United States to extradite from Colombia any person related to drug trafficking, to be judged, convicted, and imprisoned in their territory. This group was known as *Los Extraditables* ("the Extraditables"), whose motto was "We prefer a Colombian grave, than a dungeon in the United States" (Associated Foreign Press 1999).

During this period, any person that spoke in favor of extradition became a target, which resulted in the murder of journalists, judges, public officers, and their family members. These efforts reached their highest levels during *La Ofensiva* ("the Offensive"), which lasted from 1989 to 1993. The government eventually negotiated national trials and the reduction of sentences in exchange for the cartels' bosses surrendering voluntarily to the authorities. The Ochoa Brothers were among the first members of the Medellín Cartel to be imprisoned under this deal (Redacción 1993).

Through violence, Pablo Escobar secured a better deal. In June 1991, Parliament voted to have extradition prohibited, and Escobar surrendered to serve his sentence in *La Catedral*, a prison built by him, from which he escaped in July 1992 (Escobar and Fisher 2009). The operations of the Medellín Cartel ended with the death of Pablo Escobar on December 2, 1993 ("La Sangrienta" 1999).

NOTABLE EVENTS

The Medellín Cartel participated in Colombian politics in the early 1980s. Carlos Lehder created the *Movimiento Nacional Latino* ("National Latino Movement"), and Pablo Escobar even held a position in the Senate with his party *Civismo en March* ("Civics in Action"). Escobar's political career ended because of the accusations and criticism received from such conservative leaders as Rodrigo Lara Bonilla and Luis Carlos Galán (Fernandez 2002, 104).

The main attacks attributed to the Medellín Cartel include the assassinations of Minister Rodrigo Lara Bonilla in 1984 and journalist Guillermo Cano in 1986 and, in 1989, the assassination of presidential candidate Luis Carlos Galán; the attack on Avianca Flight 203, in which 107 people died; and the bombing of the Administrative Security Department (DAS), in which 63 perished (Redacción 1993).

The Medellín Cartel has been the subject of many books, such as *The Accountant's Story: Inside the Violent World of the Medellín Cartel*, written by Escobar's brother, Roberto Escobar; TV shows, such as *Narcos* and *El Patron del Mal*; and movies, such as *Blow* and *Escobar: Paradise Lost*. In 2014, after serving 23 years in prison, John Jairo Velásquez, "Popeye," the last living hit man from the cartel, became a famous public figure with two books published, a series, a movie, and a successful YouTube channel (*20 minutos* n.d.). In 2018, Popeye was sent back to prison on extortion charges.

Aida Portillo

See also: Blanco, Griselda; Cali Cartel; Escobar, Pablo

Further Reading

Associated Foreign Press. 1999. "La explosión de un coche bomba en Bogotá causa siete muertos y 30 heridos." *El Mundo*, November 11. Accessed January 5, 2019. http://www.elmundo.es/elmundo/1999/noviembre/11/internacional/colombia.html.

Bowden, Mark. 2001. *Killing Pablo: The Hunt for the World's Greatest Outlaw*. New York: Atlantic Monthly Press.

Cordero, Gonzalo. 2017. "Cartel de Medellín vs Cartel de Cali: la delgada línea (blanca) que los separa." *Esquire*, September 17. Accessed January 5, 2019. https://www.esquire.com/es/adv/a12158026/diferencia-cartel-medellin-cartel-cali-narcos.

EcuRed. 2018. "Cartel de Medellín." Last updated on July 22, 2018. Accessed January 4, 2019. https://www.ecured.cu/Cartel_de_Medell%C3%ADn.

Escobar, Roberto, and David Fisher. 2009. "The Accountant's Story: Inside the Violent World of the Medellín Cartel." Author's Note. New York, NY: Grand Central Publishing, Hachette Book Group.

Fernandez Andrade, Elsa Maria. 2002. "El narcotrafico y la decomposicion politica y social: el caso de Colombia." San Rafael, Mexico: Plaza y Valdés.

"La sangrienta historia del poderoso Cartel del Medellín." 1999. *El día*. November 18, 2009. Accessed January 5, 2019. https://www.eldia.com/nota/1999-11-18-la-sangrienta-historia-del-poderoso-cartel-de-medellin.

Redacción. 1993. "Escobar: 17 años de Historia del Criminal." *El Tiempo*, December 2. Accessed January 5, 2019. http://www.eltiempo.com/archivo/documento/MAM-270722.

Sabogal, Hugo. 1988. "Lucha a muerte de los cárteles colombianos de Cali y Medellín por el control del narcotráfico en Nueva York." *El País*, August 29. Accessed January 5, 2019. https://elpais.com/diario/1988/08/29/internacional/588808815_850215.html.

20 minutos. n.d. "Pablo Escobar y el Cártel de Medellín: 40 años de dolor y narcoculture." Accessed January 5, 2019. https://www.20minutos.es/especial/narcos-pablo-escobar.

Verdad Abierta. 2008. "Bonanza Marimbera 1976–1985." October 29. Accessed January 4, 2019. https://verdadabierta.com/bonanza-marimbera-1976-1985.

Verdad Abierta. 2011. "Muerte a secuestradores MAS: Los orígenes del paramilitarismo." September 23. Accessed January 5, 2019. https://verdadabierta.com/muerte-a-secuestradores-mas-los-origenes-del-paramilitarismo.

Woody, Christopher. 2016. "Meet the Cocaine-addled, Hitler-obsessed Drug Smuggler Who Tried to Take Down Pablo Escobar." *Business Insider*. August 21. Accessed February 15, 2019. https://www.businessinsider.com/carlos-lehder-pablo-escobar-and-the-history-of-the-medellin-cartel-2016-8.

Metals and Minerals Smuggling

Illicit mining and smuggling of high-value-added metals and minerals endanger peace, bring instability, and cause human suffering. They undermine investment climate and contribute to social insecurity of local communities. In conflict-affected and high-risk states, the illegal extraction and trade in metals and minerals contribute to violence, boost crime and corruption, and stagnate economic and social development. They also finance illegal armed formations and criminal organizations.

Metals and materials that come from conflict-affected regions are usually called "conflict minerals." This term has traditionally been used in policy and academic circles to emphasize the negative consequences of the illegal extraction and trade in diamonds or to label individual diamonds that originate from conflict zones. For instance, the revenues from the illicit trade in diamonds mined during civil wars in Angola (1975–2002), Côte d'Ivoire (2002–2007), and Sierra Leone (1991–2002), to name a few, went to the armed groups. Rebel forces used coercion and slave labor, exploited children, and caused continuous armed violence, human rights violations, and socioeconomic underdevelopment.

The Kimberley Process started in 2000, following South Africa's call to stop the trade in illicit diamonds mined on the African continent and to prevent diamond purchases from funding armed conflicts. The proposal was supported by the United Nations and the World Diamond Council. Through the Kimberley Process, the international community developed mechanisms to track diamonds from the mine to consumers. The Kimberley Process Certification Scheme (KPCS) established by the 2001 United Nations General Assembly Resolution 55/56 requires diamond producers to certify that all unpolished diamond exports were produced through responsible mining and distributed through legitimate sales and that they were not used to undermine legitimate governments or to finance conflict.

Whereas "conflict diamonds" were the most typical conflict minerals in the 1990s and 2000s, illicit extraction and smuggling in 3TGs—terminology commonly used to refer to four minerals, namely, tungsten, tantalum, tin, and gold, mined in the African Great Lakes region (Angola, Burundi, Central African Republic, Republic of Congo, Democratic Republic of Congo, Kenya, Rwanda, Sudan, Tanzania, Uganda, and Zambia)—has been of growing international concern (UNODC 2011). These metals are commonly used in the production of electronics (e.g., cell phones, batteries, LED lights) and are in large industry demand today.

SMUGGLING NETWORKS

The illicit trafficking in minerals and metals usually involves complex smuggling operations. In one case, the Chamber of Mines of South Africa identified up to five clearly distinguishable levels of operation. The group, known as the Mountain Boys, acted as a highly organized criminal syndicate dealing in unwrought precious metals. According to the UNODC SHERLOC Database, the syndicate committed serious offenses under South African law, engaging in racketeering activities and related categories of offenses, including money laundering, theft, and fraud, and other offenses under the provisions of the South African Mining Rights Act and the Precious Metals Act.

The hierarchy of criminal operations perpetrated by the Mountain Boys started with "runners," who were typically employees of the gold mines. They stole gold from mines and used smelters to conceal the origins of the stolen metals. As soon as the stolen gold was melted with gold sourced elsewhere, it became almost impossible to ascertain the mine of origin. After being smelted, the stolen gold was divided into smaller pieces and transported to intermediaries across South Africa. The intermediaries were well connected to transnational syndicates and independent global couriers. They registered shell companies, often scrap metal dealers, and used them as fronts to export the illicit gold out of the country, supplying international firms dealing in platinum-group metals (PGMs). Refiners in Western Europe, the United Kingdom, Canada, and other countries sourced their PGMs from them and then prepared products for global commercial use.

PROMOTING RESPONSIBLE SOURCING

In April 2013, South Africa—one of the countries deeply concerned with illegal mining—initiated a resolution to combat transnational organized crime and possible links to the illegal mining of precious metals. In 2013, the United Nations Economic and Social Council (ECOSOC) reaffirmed the need to develop an international response to the growing involvement of organized criminal groups in illegal mining and cross border smuggling of illegally mined metals and minerals.

ECOSOC's activities against illegal mining and smuggling in metals and minerals were supported by other international organizations. With the focus on 3TGs, the Organization for Economic Cooperation and Development (OECD), in collaboration with 11 countries of the International Conference on the Great Lakes Region and industry and civil society groups, developed a set of due diligence guidelines for responsible supply chains of minerals from conflict-affected and high-risk areas (OECD 2013). The objective of the guidance is to "help companies respect human rights and avoid contributing to conflict through their mineral sourcing practices" (OECD 2013, 3). It is meant to ensure transparent mineral supply chains and sustainable corporate engagement in the mineral sector.

On the national level, several countries took action against the smuggling of metals and minerals. In 2010, the United States passed the Dodd-Frank Act. It requires that companies using 3TGs make efforts to determine that their materials are conflict-free and carry out a due diligence review of their supply chain. Such companies must file a report with the U.S. Securities and Exchange Commission (SEC) and go through an independent audit of the supply chain due diligence.

The European Union (EU) has also attempted to stem the trade in conflict minerals, such as bypassing Regulation 2017/821. It aims to stop conflict minerals and metals from being exported to the EU, laying down supply chain due diligence obligations for EU importers of tin, tantalum, and tungsten; their ores; and gold originating from conflict-affected and high-risk areas. The regulation applies to global and EU smelters and refiners, mine workers, and relevant EU companies. It requires that only "conflict-free" minerals and metals extracted from responsible sources enter the EU.

Yuliya Zabyelina

See also: Failed State; SHERLOC; Transnational, Global, and International Crime

Further Reading

ECOSOC. 2013. Resolution E/RES/2013/38, October 7. Accessed July 1, 2018. https://www.unodc.org/documents/commissions/CCPCJ/Crime_Resolutions/2010-2019/2013/ECOSOC/Resolution_2013-38.pdf.

European Parliament. 2017. Regulation (EU) 2017/821 of the European Parliament and of the Council of 17 May 2017. Accessed June 23, 2018. https://eur-lex.europa.eu/legal-content/EN/TXT/PDF/?uri=OJ:C:2017:158:FULL&from=EN.

OECD. 2013. *OECD Due Diligence Guidance for Responsible Supply Chains of Minerals from Conflict-Affected and High-Risk Areas: Second Edition.* Paris: OECD Publishing. Accessed June 24, 2018. https://www.oecd.org/corporate/mne/GuidanceEdition2.pdf.

United Nations General Assembly. 2001. Resolution A/RES/55/56. Accessed July 27. https://undocs.org/en/A/RES/55/56.

UNODC. 2011. *Organized Crime and Instability in Central Africa: A Threat Assessment.* United Nations Office on Drugs and Crime. Accessed June 13, 2018. https://www.unodc.org/documents/data-and-analysis/Studies/Central_Africa_Report_2011_web.pdf.

UNODC SHERLOC Case Law Database. "Project Yield: South Africa." UNODC No.: ZAFx003. United Nations Office on Drugs and Crime. Accessed July 13, 2018. https://www.unodc.org/cld/case-law-doc/corruptioncrimetype/zaf/project_yield.html?lng=en&tmpl=sherloc.

Migrant Smuggling

Migrant smuggling is a crime committed against a state that involves the transportation and facilitation of the irregular entry and permanence of a person(s) in a country other than the one of origin. It is carried out by individuals (known as smugglers) and organized networks that operate across borders for purely material gains. The most common definition of migrant smuggling is the one adopted by the United Nations in the 2000 Convention against Transnational Organized Crime and the subsequent Protocol against the Smuggling of Migrants by Land, Sea and Air, which states (Article 3) that migrant smuggling consists of the "procurement in order to obtain, directly or indirectly, a financial or other material benefit, of the illegal entry of a person into a State Party of which the person is not a national or a permanent resident" (United Nations 2000, 2).

Improvements in communications, technology, and transportation have significantly contributed to the increase in, and sophistication of, migrant smuggling, to the point that it affects the lives of millions of people in the migrants' communities of origin, transit, and destination.

Human smuggling is closely connected to and sometimes overlaps with irregular migration, human trafficking, and asylum seeking, as people who wish to move to a different country (in a forced or voluntary way) may contact and hire a smuggling network to achieve this aim. However, irregular migration can happen without smuggling, and a person who is smuggled into a country is not necessarily an irregular migrant, as he or she may be fleeing persecution and, therefore, be entitled to asylum upon arrival.

Asylum seekers and irregular migrants share many of the vulnerabilities and risks associated with dangerous journeys, especially sexual abuse and other forms of human rights violations and deprivation of basic needs. Thousands of people have lost their lives as a result of smugglers' negligence, unsafe transport, violent treatment, and exposure to harsh conditions.

DISTINCTION BETWEEN MIGRANT SMUGGLING AND HUMAN TRAFFICKING

Because smugglers and human traffickers frequently use the same routes and means to transport people from origin to destination, these two phenomena have usually been treated indistinctively by policy makers, advocacy groups, politicians, and the media. Nevertheless, there are important features that distinguish them.

First, although migrant smuggling and human trafficking share a similar modus operandi (including recruitment, transportation, harboring, and reception of irregular migrants), they differ greatly in their intention and purpose. While migrant smuggling is driven by the profit associated with transporting irregular migrants and asylum seekers, human traffickers do so with the purpose of exploiting these persons, mostly through sex work and forced labor.

Another important distinction refers to the individual's agency: a potential migrant enters into an informal contract with the smuggler in a voluntary way and has some scope for changing his or her mind during the journey or for renegotiating the terms of transportation in the event of a failed entry attempt. The level of agency depends on the negotiated deal between the smuggled person and the smuggler. By contrast, a trafficked person has very limited agency, as most of the time the person is kept in isolation and forced to work for the traffickers via coercion, deception, and abuse. This person generally lacks freedom and mobility.

Finally, a person who has been smuggled into a country is considered an offender (depending on the country's legislation) and cannot be referred to as a "victim" because unauthorized entry into a country is a criminal offense committed against the receiving state rather than the person per se. By contrast, people who have been trafficked are considered "victims" because of the coercion, exploitation, and restrictions on freedom suffered at the hands of traffickers.

In many cases, the relationship between the smuggler and the person who was smuggled ends when the latter reaches the destination country. However, in some cases, their contact may continue for several months or years due to debt bondage, shared nationality, or cultural ties at origin or destination; indeed, informal and often illegal work arrangements may end up reaching levels of exploitation similar to those experienced by trafficking victims. The lack of legal and psychological support mechanisms for irregular migrants in destination countries may contribute to perpetuating and exacerbating this situation.

FACTORS THAT CONTRIBUTE TO MIGRANT SMUGGLING

There are several factors that influence a person's decision to migrate and to hire a smuggler to help him or her reach the country of destination. Poverty, deprivation of basic human needs and rights, the desire for a better life, violent conflict, and environmental catastrophes are among the main motivations that people have to migrate. Indirect factors can also trigger an increase in migrant smuggling to a specific destination, for example, changes in labor markets that may demand more "unskilled" workers; family and coethnic networks that push for and facilitate family reunification through informal channels; and the profitability of the "business model" of many smuggling networks. The proliferation of smuggling networks is closely connected to the implementation of restrictions on regular migratory channels, the tightening of migration policies in destination countries, the geographic distance between countries of origin and destination, and the complexity of the trip, among other factors.

APPROACHES TO ANALYZE MIGRANT SMUGGLING

There are two main approaches to analyzing migrant smuggling from a theoretical perspective. On the one hand, smuggling is seen as a purely economic transaction between the migrant and the smuggler, whose relationship ends when the migrant enters the destination country or when the money for facilitating the journey is paid. According to this perspective, the migrant's consent to being smuggled is a rational choice decision based on a cost-benefit analysis (the cost of the trip, risks in transit, effectiveness, etc.) (Tamuray 2007). This is a purely economic analysis that does not consider the social, ethnic, or other factors that may inform a person's decision to migrate in an irregular way.

Another approach recognizes that migrant smuggling involves social and cultural networks at origin, transit, and destination that enable the migrant's journey and facilitate the arrival and integration processes. Family, friendship, and coethnic ties are critical to understanding human smuggling (Herman 2006).The socioeconomic perspective also pays attention to the organization of smuggling networks (hierarchies, financing model, organizing principles, etc.) (Triandafyllidou and Maroukis 2012). According to this approach, the composition of smuggling networks and their modus operandi resemble the organization of human trafficking networks in many ways (shared routes, organization, logistical arrangements in transit, and the dependency created among the migrants) but differ greatly in their intent (transportation of migrants versus exploitation of migrants).

Adriana Salcedo

See also: Human Trafficking; UN Protocol against the Smuggling of Migrants by Land, Air, and Sea

Further Reading

Herman, Emma. 2006. "Migration as a Family Business: The Role of Personal Networks in the Mobility Phase of Migration." *International Migration* 44: 191–230.

Tamuray, Yuji. 2007. "Migrant Smuggling." *Warwick Economic Research Papers*, No. 791: 1–46. Accessed May 30, 2018. http://wrap.warwick.ac.uk/1414/1/WRAP_Tamura_twerp_791.pdf.

Triandafyllidou, Anna, and Thanos Maroukis. 2012. *Migrant Smuggling: Irregular Migration from Asia and Africa to Europe*. London: Palgrave Macmillan UK.

United Nations. 2000. Protocol against the Smuggling of Migrants by Land, Sea and Air, Supplementing the United Nations Convention against Transnational Organized

Crime. New York. Accessed May 29, 2018. https://treaties.un.org/doc/Treaties/2000/11/20001115%2011-21%20AM/Ch_XVIII_12_bp.pdf.

United Nations Office on Drugs and Crime (UNODC). 2011. *Smuggling of Migrants. A Global Review and Annotated Bibliography of Recent Publications.* Vienna: UNODC. Accessed on May 29, 2018. https://www.unodc.org/documents/human-trafficking/Migrant-Smuggling/Smuggling_of_Migrants_A_Global_Review.pdf.

Mitnick, Kevin (1963–)

In the 1990s, Kevin Mitnick was the Federal Bureau of Investigation's (FBI) most wanted computer hacker. He began hacking as a teenager and was accused of causing millions of dollars in damage by hacking into the computers of major companies and stealing software, product plans, and other data. Mitnick's crimes occurred at a time when Internet technology and security brought new challenges for law enforcement and prosecution. These high-tech crimes were often too complex for police and prosecutors to handle. In fact, the defendant in such cases was often the only person who could really understand and explain the technical aspects of the crime (Baughman et al. 2001).

In 1988, the FBI arrested Mitnick for invading Digital Equipment Corporation systems and allegedly stealing software. Mitnick's defense team convinced the prosecution that Mitnick was addicted or psychologically compelled to hack, and he was sentenced to a relatively lenient 12 months in prison followed by 3 years of supervised release.

During his time on supervised release, Mitnick focused on telephone-related computer crimes, and a warrant was issued for his arrest in 1989. Mitnick fled, and he stayed on the run for two and a half years. Part of that time was spent in Denver, Colorado, where he got a job with a local law firm, helping with computer security and even suggesting the firm switch to what has come to be called two-factor authentication for greater security (Chuang 2018).

The beginning of the end came in 1994 when Mitnick broke into the home computer of Tsutomu Shimomura, a computer security expert at the San Diego Supercomputer Center. Shimomura joined forces with the FBI and helped find Mitnick, who was living in Raleigh, North Carolina. Mitnick was arrested in 1995 at his Raleigh apartment, with more than 100 cloned cell phones and 20,000 credit card numbers on his computer. He had not used any of the accounts. He was kept in jail while awaiting trial, and in 1999 he pleaded guilty to wire fraud, computer fraud, and to illegally intercepting a wire communication. He was sentenced to five years in prison, but with credit for time served while awaiting trial, he was released in 2000 and began a period of supervised release that ended in 2003.

Mitnick's notoriety has resulted in a variety of opportunities, ranging from television roles as a hacker to public speaking engagements and book author. He now uses his hacking skills for good purposes as a consultant for a cybersecurity firm that works to prevent the crimes Mitnick once committed.

Philip L. Reichel

See also: Cybercrime; Hackers

Further Reading

Baughman, Judith S., Victor Bondi, Richard Layman, Tandy McConnell, and Vincent Tompkins, eds. 2001. "Internet and Digital Citizens." In *American Decades*, Vol. 10, pp. 1990–1999. Detroit: Gale.

Chuang, Tamara. 2018. "The Magician's Transformation." *Denver Post*, March 16: 9A & 11A.

Petruso, A. 2012. "Mitnick, Kevin." In *Newsmakers 2012 Cumulation*, edited by Laura Avery, 314–317. Detroit: Gale.

Shimomura, Tsutomu, and John Markoff. 1996. *Take-Down: The Pursuit and Capture of Kevin Mitnick, America's Most Wanted Computer Outlaw—By the Man Who Did It*. New York: Hyperion.

Money Laundering

Money laundering is the process in which perpetrators attempt to disguise the illicit origins of funds. It includes three stages: (1) placement or integration of ill-gotten gains into legitimate financial systems; (2) layering or disguising of the origin of the proceeds through the use of numerous accounts, shell companies, and the like, to make them more difficult to trace; and (3) integration or transfer of the "clean" money to financial institutions where it can be made available for legal use (UNODC 2011).

First and foremost, money laundering facilitates the operations of organized criminal groups. As McClean (2002) bluntly stated, "It is no use making a large profit out of criminal activity if that profit cannot be put to use" (p. 261). While this statement highlights the importance of money laundering for organized crime, money laundering is a critical element of operations of terrorist organizations, which are dependent on secure channels of financing.

The United Nations Convention against the Illicit Traffic in Narcotic Drugs and Psychotropic Substances, specifically Article 3(b), was the first international legal instrument to criminalize money laundering. Without mentioning the offense by name, the 1988 convention criminalized the "concealment or disguise of the true nature, source, location, disposition, movement, rights with respect to, or ownership of property, knowing that such property is derived from an offence or offences established [in this Convention]" (United Nations 2013, 128).

Article 6 of the United Nations Convention against Transnational Organized Crime requires that each state party criminalize money laundering, and Article 7 requires them to put into place adequate regulatory framework domestically to combat money laundering (UNODC 2000). The 2003 United Nations Convention against Corruption (UNODC 2003) also covers money laundering. Article 14 calls states parties to "institute a comprehensive domestic regulatory and supervisory regime for banks and non-bank financial institutions" and to cooperate and exchange information at the national and international levels. In addition, the convention also criminalizes the laundering of criminal proceeds derived from corruption (Article 23).

In the 1990s, the Financial Action Task Force (FATF), an intergovernmental body that aims to promote the effective implementation of legal, regulatory, and operational measures for combating money laundering, issued its 40 recommendations on money laundering control and counterterrorism financing. These recommendations constitute the international standard for combating money laundering and the financing of terrorism.

FORMS OF MONEY LAUNDERING

There are many forms of money laundering. They range from simple transfers via formal banking institutions and shell companies to more complex operations that may go through informal banking agencies and unregistered intermediaries.

One of the most common forms of money laundering is through a legitimate cash-based business owned by a criminal organization. For instance, if an organized criminal group owns a restaurant, it might report an inflated daily cash income and save it at the bank. Cash-intensive businesses used by criminal organizations to launder illicit funds are often called "fronts."

Another common practice is "smurfing," whereby a person divides a large sum of illicit cash into multiple small deposits, often spread out over many different accounts. Doing so helps the money launderer to avoid detection.

The Internet and the expanding availability of information communication technologies have revolutionized how official banking institutions work and caused a change in money laundering strategies as well. The emerging trends in money laundering in the form of new payment technologies (NPMs) are increasingly rendering traditional anti–money laundering (AML) systems obsolete.

The rise of online banking institutions, anonymous online payment systems, peer-to-peer transfers using mobile phones and apps, and the use of digital currencies such as Bitcoin have made identifying illicit financial flow more difficult. In addition, the use of proxy servers and anonymizing software, such as Tor, make money laundering almost untraceable to the ultimate beneficiary of ill-gotten funds.

Although owners of certain digital currencies require formal registration and can be traced, those who specifically possess cryptocurrencies (Bitcoin, Ethereum, etc.) do not need to demonstrate documents issued by a public institution. Registration for cryptocurrencies contains no confidential information. While not totally anonymous, these forms of currencies are increasingly being used in currency blackmailing schemes, the drug trade, and other criminal activities due to their anonymity compared to other forms of currency.

Although the traditional financial system seems to be unnecessarily riskier for money launderers than some of the emerging cryptocurrency markets, traditional methods remain popular. Until there becomes a point where countries either cannot or do not feel they have to generate their wealth from offering relaxed banking laws, there will always be the opportunity to move illicit funds through traditional systems in ways that AML systems are still not equipped to track.

RESPONSES TO MONEY LAUNDERING

The UNODC identifies three primary actions to tackle money laundering:

1. supporting regional networks
2. providing technical assistance and capacity building programs
3. deploying in-country mentors to directly assist states

Training has become one of the most important tools, if not the most important, at the disposal of nations and international organizations alike. In 2016, the UNODC provided tailor-made training to focus on the specific needs of particular states. The success of this approach is displayed in the increase of trained professionals from approximately 1,000 in previous years to 4,400 in 2016 (UNODC 2017). Going forward, an emphasis on training authorities to effectively recognize, prevent, and counter money laundering activities to introduce effective domestic regulatory and supervisory regimes will be critical to limit the regularity in which this crime occurs (UNODC 2017).

To keep pace with this ever-evolving crime, the FATF has made efforts to refine its mutual evaluation and assessment process to ensure that members are truly adhering to the necessary standards that have been established. And in addition to this change, the FATF has strengthened its relationship with Financial Intelligence Units (FIUs) to optimize their ability to investigate and identify new money laundering as well as terrorist financing trends. This has been done in combination with a renewed drive to enhance their relationship with the private sector. The establishment of a more cooperative relationship will enhance the level of information sharing to best support investigations and identify when unusual events occur (FATF 2018).

Connor Rutherford

See also: Counterfeit Goods and Money; Cryptocurrency; Organized Crime; UN Convention against Illicit Traffic in Narcotic Drugs and Psychotropic Substances

Further Reading

FATF. 2018. *FATF Annual Report 2016–2017.* Paris: FATF. Accessed January 6, 2019. http://www.fatf-gafi.org/media/fatf/documents/reports/FATF-annual-report-2016-2017.pdf.

Gilmore, W. 2014. "Money Laundering" In *Routledge Handbook of Transnational Criminal Law,* edited by N. Boister and R. J. Currie, 331–346. London: Routledge.

McClean, J. 2002. *International Cooperation in Civil and Criminal Matters.* Oxford: Oxford University Press.

United Nations. 2013. "Part Three: United Nations Convention Against Illicit Traffic in Narcotic Drugs and Psychotropic Substances of 1988." In *The International Drug Control Conventions.* New York; United Nations. Accessed February 9, 2019. https://www.unodc.org/documents/commissions/CND/Int_Drug_Control_Conventions/Ebook/The_International_Drug_Control_Conventions_E.pdf.

UNODC. 2000. United Nations Convention Against Transnational Organized Crime and the Protocols Thereto. Vienna: UNODC. Accessed February 9, 2019. https://www.unodc.org/unodc/en/organized-crime/intro/UNTOC.html

UNODC. 2003. United Nations Convention Against Corruption. Vienna: UNODC. Accessed February 9, 2019. https://www.unodc.org/unodc/en/treaties/CAC/.

UNODC. 2011. *Estimating Illicit Financial Flows Resulting from Drug Trafficking and Other Transnational Organized Crime.* Vienna: UNODC. Accessed January 6, 2019. http://www.unodc.org/documents/data-and-analysis/Studies/Illicit_financial_flows_2011_web.pdf.

UNODC. 2017. *UNODC Annual Report: Covering Activities during 2016.* Vienna: UNODC. Accessed January 6, 2019. https://www.unodc.org/documents/AnnualReport2016/2016_UNODC_Annual_Report.pdf.

Morris, Robert Tappan, Jr. (1965–)

In 1988, as a graduate student at Cornell University, Robert Morris created and unleashed the first Internet virus—designated the "Morris worm." He claims the event was an unintentional coding mistake that was intended to be harmless. It was not harmless but resulted in extensive damage to computers at universities, research centers, and military installations. The cost of removing the worm from each computer ranged from $200 to $53,000, with an additional cost of up to $10 million lost due to lack of access to the Internet. In 1989, Morris became the first person indicted under the Computer Fraud and Abuse Act of 1986 (CFAA).

THE WORM

Morris explained that he was trying to show the weakness of computer security measures by inserting a worm into as many computers as he could access; however, his plan was to have the worm replicate itself slowly enough that it would not cause the computers to slow down or crash. He miscalculated how quickly the worm would replicate, and although he tried to release a message explaining how to kill the worm, the damage was done: some 6,000 computers crashed or were slowed down to such a speed that they were virtually unusable. Although 6,000 may not sound like many computers, it was about 6 percent of all Internet-connected computers worldwide at the time (Murphy 2017).

Some computer experts suggest that the Morris worm was less newsworthy for what it did than for what it could have done. If Morris had acted with a plan to damage as many computers as he could, the harm would have been considerably greater.

THE AFTERMATH

Morris was convicted of violating a provision of the CFAA that prohibits anyone from intentionally accessing, without authorization, a "federal interest computer" and damages or prevents authorized use of information in such a computer, causing losses of $1,000 or more.

Although the CFAA at the time allowed a sentence of up to five years in prison, Morris was sentenced to three years of probation, a $10,500 fine, and 400 hours of community service. Many people saw that sentence as little more than a slap on the wrist and regretted that the judge had not sent a stronger message to hackers, even those without evil intent. Others found the sentence to be perfectly appropriate, arguing that Morris did the world a favor by serving as a wake-up call that showed the risk of software bugs and the Internet's vulnerability to the attention of the Internet engineering community. It set the stage for computer security to become a valid area of research and development.

Morris received his doctorate from Harvard in 1999 and was given the status of Fellow of Association for Computing Machinery (ACM) in 2014 for outstanding accomplishments in computing and information technology. As of 2018, Morris was a tenured professor in the Department of Electrical Engineering and Computer Science at the Massachusetts Institute of Technology.

Philip L. Reichel

See also: Cybercrime; Hackers

Further Reading

Lerner, K. Lee, and Brenda Wilmoth Lerner, eds. 2013. "Computer Fraud and Abuse Act of 1986." In *Computer Sciences*, 42–46. Detroit: Macmillan.

Marsan, Carolyn Duffy. 2008. "Morris Worm Turns 20." *Network World* 25 (43): 10. Accessed January 6, 2019. https://www.networkworld.com/article/2268919/lan-wan/morris-worm-turns-20--look-what-it-s-done.html.

Murphy, Katherine. 2017. "The Morris Worm and Robert T. Morris Jr." Last Modified August 3, 2017. Accessed January 6, 2019. http://blog.cybertraining365.com/2017/08/03/hacking-history-morris-worm-robert-t-morris-jr.

Movie Piracy

Movie piracy can be defined as the unauthorized reproduction, showing, or distribution of copyrighted motion pictures. It includes copying, downloading, selling, acquiring, or distributing copyrighted movies and films without permission. Mediums can include VHS tapes, DVDs, Blu-ray discs, or compressed files. As technology has improved and people have increased access to the Internet, movie piracy has blossomed as an international crime. The movie industry has adapted, like the music industry, with authorized streaming Web sites and channels.

HISTORY

Vaudevillian entertainers often included other entertainers' acts or characters in their own live shows. According to Segrave (2003), W.C. Fields, Harry Houdini, Bob Hope, Jack Benny, and George Burns were among the more famous names who stole parts of other acts, had parts of their own acts stolen from them, or both. Although this was legal, many entertainers applied peer pressure or tried judicial measures to stop the use of their material by other artists.

When motion pictures appeared on the scene, so did thieves. "Bicycling" was the first type of movie piracy. "An exhibitor who had rented a film legitimately for a period of time, say, one week at a fixed sum of dollars, would try to screen the print for an extra day or two at the beginning or end of his run. Or the cinema owner would rent the movie for one of his theatres and then screen it illegally at another theater he owned" (Segrave 2003, 42). Additionally, other theater owners traded or shared each other's rented films and showed illegal screenings.

While there were some issues with movie piracy during the beginnings of television, namely, television networks "hacking" original motion pictures to fit in an allotted time slot for television viewing, the nightmare scenario for the film industry began in the late 1970s and boomed during the 1980s with the invention of videotapes and camcorders. Some movie patrons purchased a ticket and then illegally filmed the movie with a handheld camera. It could then be recopied and sold all over the world. The evolution of videocassette piracy and camcorder piracy has morphed in the past two decades.

During the Internet age, movies, like music, have been subjected to data compression files and then shared through peer-to-peer (P2P) Web sites. Illegal downloads, file sharing, pirate servers, illegal Web sites selling counterfeit movies, and hacked computers created a dearth of possibilities for online movie piracy. Anyone with Internet access and a computer had the ability to illegally download or upload unauthorized movie files through P2P Web sites. Ultimately, the primary source of newly released pirated movies was individuals who had used handheld cameras to record movies in a theater. They then illegally sold them to other individuals who distributed them throughout the world (MPAA 2009). Eventually, file sharing Web sites such as Megaupload and Grokster were shut down. The founders of these Web sites were sued for assisting in copyright infringement.

If there were no movie piracy, it is estimated that box-office revenues would increase 15 percent, or $1.3 billion per year (Ma, Montgomery, and Smith 2016). However, many consumers of pirated content do not care. When informed that pirated movies hurt studios' ability to create new content, 39 percent said it had no effect on the number of pirated films they wanted to watch (Spangler 2017).

LAWS

Copyright laws protect creative work, and each country creates its own copyright laws to protect its citizens' works. Like other laws, there are international copyright treaties and conventions that protect foreign works. The Berne Convention, first established in 1896, set a minimum standard of protection for authors, inventors, and creators internationally. The World Intellectual Property Organization (WIPO) administers the treaty, which has been signed by nearly 180 countries (WIPO n.d.). In the United States, the Copyright Office is responsible for regulating intellectual property under Title 17 of the U.S. Code. The first Copyright Act occurred in 1790, with revisions occurring in 1831, 1870, 1909, and 1976 (Cummins 2013).

Starting in 2003, the Federal Bureau of Investigation authorized the Anti-Piracy Warning Seal. Most movies produced feature the seal, which states, "The unauthorized reproduction or distribution of this copyrighted work is illegal. Criminal copyright infringement, including infringement without monetary gain, is investigated by the FBI and is punishable by fines and federal imprisonment (FBI 2017).

Brian Fedorek

See also: Digital Piracy; Intellectual Property Crime; Music Piracy; World Intellectual Property Organization

Further Reading

Cummings, Alex Sayf. 2013. *Democracy of Sound: Music Piracy and the Remaking of American Copyright in the Twentieth Century.* New York: Oxford University Press.

FBI. 2017. "FBI Anti-Piracy Warning Seal." Accessed December 30, 2017. https://www.fbi.gov/investigate/white-collar-crime/piracy-ip-theft/fbi-anti-piracy-warning-seal.

Ma, Liye, Alan Montgomery, and Michael D. Smith. 2016. "The Dual Impact of Movie Piracy on Box-Office Revenue: Cannibalization and Promotion." Accessed January 6, 2019. https://ssrn.com/abstract=2736946.

Motion Picture Association of America (MPAA). 2009. "Movie Piracy Is Copyright Infringement." In *Copyright Infringement*, edited by Roman Espejo, 134–140. Farmington Hills, MI: Greenhaven Press.

Segrave, Kerry. 2003. *Piracy in the Motion Picture Industry.* Jefferson, NC: McFarland & Co.

Siwek, Stephen E. 2009. "Copyright Infringement of Movies Hurts the Economy." In *Copyright Infringement*, edited by Roman Espejo, 134–140. Farmington Hills, MI: Greenhaven Press.

Spangler, Todd. 2017. "Piracy Survey: 39% of U.S. Consumers Don't Care That Studios Lose Money From Illegal Sharing." *Variety*, January 18. Accessed January 6, 2019. http://variety.com/2017/digital/news/piracy-survey-consumers-studios-lose-money-1201961634.

World Intellectual Property Organization. n.d. "Berne Convention for the Protection of Literary and Artistic Works." Accessed on December 27, 2017. http://www.wipo.int/treaties/en/ip/berne.

Mueller, Gerhard O. W. (1926–2006)

Gerhard O. W. Mueller was born in Germany and is considered one of the foremost scholars in the areas of international law and transnational crime. He came to the United States to earn a law degree at the University of Chicago (1953) and LL.M. at Columbia University (1955). He began his academic career at West Virginia University (1955–1958). He followed this with a long tenure at New York University Law School beginning in 1958 and into the 1970s, serving as a professor of law and director of the Comparative Criminal Law Project and Criminal Law Education and Research Center. His longest appointment occurred when he joined the founding faculty at the Rutgers University School of Criminal Justice in 1974, where he was promoted to distinguished professor in 1982. He retired from Rutgers in 2005.

During his academic tenure, Gerhard Mueller served in a large number of visiting faculty positions throughout the world and, most notably, served as chief of the United Nations Crime Prevention and Criminal Justice Branch from 1974 to 1982 (since renamed the United Nations Office on Drugs and Crime (UNODC)).In that capacity, he was responsible for all UN initiatives and programs addressing problems of crime and justice globally. Among the initiatives he led was the development of a world survey of crime and criminal justice systems, which the United Nations continues today. He also led the effort to assess the implementation of Minimum Rules for the Treatment of Prisoners worldwide. Gerhard Mueller served as executive secretary to the global United Nations Congresses for the Prevention of Crime and Treatment of Offenders in 1975 (Geneva) and 1980 (Caracas).

Professor Mueller was a prolific scholar, serving as author or editor of more than 50 books and several hundred journal and law review articles. He was an expert on criminal law and procedure, writing several standard texts in the field.

His expertise in international legal issues was vast and pioneering. He will be most remembered for his contributions to international criminal law and procedure. Mueller introduced the concept of international criminal law to the English-speaking world (Wise 1994). He emphasized its connection to the protection of human rights, and the book he coauthored in 1965 on international law was the first book on the subject in the English language (Mueller and Wise 1965). Mueller's work was revolutionary because there were many skeptics at the time who claimed international criminal law was impossible because it could never be enforced and sovereign nations would never agree on jurisdiction or adjudication (Wise 1994).

Mueller was an early advocate for enforcement of international law, an international criminal court, supranational courts, and law enforcement education and training. Remarkably, all these ideas came to be established in subsequent years. The present-day existence of transnational and international crimes, extradition, mutual legal assistance, multijurisdictional law enforcement task forces, European arrest warrants, and an international criminal court all operate as viable methods to respond to multinational crimes. It has been demonstrated through multinational negotiation over many years, largely under the auspices of the United Nations, that global consensus can be reached to respond effectively to crimes across borders. This worldwide movement may be the most significant development in criminal law and criminal justice over the last century, and Gerhard Mueller was a prime mover in this effort.

Professor Mueller's influence can be inferred by the respect accorded him by his professional colleagues. Thirteen books have been dedicated to him as well as a collection of writings in his honor (Wise 1994).The Academy of Criminal Justice Sciences International Section's Outstanding Scholar Award for contributions to comparative and international criminal justice was named after G. O. W. Mueller. He was elected president of the American Society of Criminology (1968) and vice president of the Association International de Droit Pénal. He was chair of the International Scientific and Professional Advisory Council of the United Nations and a member of the board of directors of the International Institute of Higher Studies in Criminal Sciences in Siracusa, Italy.

Professor Mueller received many awards over his long career. The doctor of law honoris causa by the University of Uppsala, the Order of Knights of the Lions of Finland, and the Order of Merit of Venezuela are among his many awards, including the Bruce Smith Sr. Award from the Academy of Criminal Justice Sciences for outstanding contributions to criminal justice.

Professor Mueller was a gifted speaker, and his students marveled at his ability to deliver a perfect lecture, complete with illustrations and historic asides, without glancing at his notes. He was charismatic and generous, unselfishly providing assistance to students and colleagues all over world. There are many stories of his ability as a speaker, a diplomat, and as a scholar in which his knowledge of law, criminal justice, and foreign language came together in a captivating way. In one instance recounted by James Finckenauer (distinguished professor emeritus at Rutgers University), Gerhard Mueller was with him as part of a small U.S. delegation to Russia when they realized they were going to receive gifts from their hosts but had no gifts with them to present in return. When the moment came, Gerhard took off the United Nations tie that he was wearing, and he presented it to the host as a symbol of their international cooperation—using a number of Russian language phrases to do it—making a potentially embarrassing situation into a diplomatic victory. That kind of gesture was typical of Gerhard Mueller, who was also a sharp dresser and rarely seen without wearing a three-piece suit.

Gerhard Mueller had four children and was married in 1976 to noted criminologist Freda Adler until his death in 2006.

Jay S. Albanese

See also: Adler, Freda; European Arrest Warrant; International Criminal Court; Transnational, Global, and International Crime; UN Congresses on Crime Prevention and Criminal Justice; UN Office on Drugs and Crime

Further Reading

Mueller, G. O. W. 1977. *Sentencing: Process and Purpose.* Springfield, IL: Charles Thomas.

Mueller, G. O. W. 1998. *Oral History: G.O.W. Mueller.* Interviewed by James Finckenauer. Accessed January 6, 2019. www.oralhistoryofcriminology.org.

Mueller, G. O. W., and F. Adler. 1985. *Outlaws of the Ocean: The Complete Book of Contemporary Crime on the High Seas.* New York: Hearst Marine.

Mueller, G. O. W., and F. L. Griffith. 1969. *Comparative Criminal Procedure.* New York: New York University Press.

Mueller, G. O. W., and J. Hall. 1965. *Criminal Law and Procedure.* 2nd. ed. Indianapolis: Bobbs-Merrill.

Mueller, G. O. W., and E. Wise. 1965. *International Criminal Law.* South Hackensack, NJ: Rothman.

Wise, E. W. 1994. *Criminal Science in a Global Society: Essays in Honor of G .O. W. Mueller.* Littleton, CO: Rothman.

Music Piracy

Listening to music is a social activity—people want to experience music together and share those experiences with one another. Thus, it can be difficult to ascertain what is legal sharing and what is illegal sharing. According to the Recording Industry Association of America (RIAA), "Many different actions qualify as piracy, from downloading unauthorized versions of copyrighted music from a file-sharing service to illegally copying music using a streamripping software or mobile apps" (2017). Music piracy is the illegal downloading, copying, manufacturing, and distributing of a piece of music. In general, music piracy is theft and violates copyright laws. Although music piracy has occurred in various forms for over a century, such as the copying of musical sheets, bootlegging, mixtapes, and sampling, the invention of computers and the Internet has made music piracy more prominent than ever before.

HISTORY

Since the invention of the printing press, copying content has vexed governments and citizens. The ideas of "ownership" and "authorship" of a string of words, images, and drawings led to the creation the first copyright laws in Europe.

Copyright laws have continued to evolve as technology evolves. With the creation of new technologies, copying becomes easier, more efficient, and harder to detect. When Thomas Edison invented the gramophone in 1877, the music recording industry changed forever. For the first time, people could record and play back sounds. During the 1930s, citizens in the United States began to "bootleg" music. Bootlegging is making, distributing, or selling material. Instead of buying records, some people would make recordings of live performances or copy records. Theses bootlegs were then shared.

However, bootlegging, which is one form of music piracy, became ubiquitous during the 1960s and 1970s. Although many concertgoers recorded live performances, the Grateful Dead fans were most synonymous with bootlegging. The Grateful Dead even encouraged and incorporated bootlegging into their business ventures.

Starting in the late 1970s and continuing into the 1980s, another type of piracy known as the hip-hop "mixtape" began. "The tapes documented the performance of the DJs who played records at parties and the emcees who rhymed over the music—but they were also copies of the artists whose recordings were chopped up and recombined by the DJ" (Cummings 2013, 164). These chopped up pieces of music are known as "sampling," which can also be a form of music piracy. Although the mixtape started as cassette tapes, technological advances in music recording rendered compact discs, or CDs, a better and cheaper alternative.

In the early 1990s, another musical format changed the game. The creation of MP3s, a type of audio data compression file, enabled the digitization of music to be much smaller. Online peer-to-peer (P2P) file sharing network services such as Napster, eDonkey2000, and LimeWire allowed users to share music files with one another. On August 10, 1996, Metallica's "Until It Sleeps" became the world's first pirated MP3 (Witt 2015). These services facilitated illegal downloading of music files on a massive scale. As a result, it disrupted the music industry and forced it to change.

LAWS

Each country creates its own copyright laws to protect musicians' creative work. Like other laws, there are international copyright treaties and conventions that protect foreign works. The Berne Convention, first established in 1896, set a minimum standard of protection for authors, inventors, and creators internationally. To date, 175 countries have signed the convention (World Intellectual Property Organization n.d.).

In the United States, the Copyright Office is responsible for regulating intellectual property under Title 17 of the U.S. Code. The first Copyright Act occurred in 1790, with revisions occurring in 1831, 1870, 1909, and 1976 (Cummings 2013). Simply put, music sound recordings, regardless of format, may not be copied or distributed without the owner's permission.

Through a series of judicial decisions, the following behaviors are considered illegal piracy: stripping music from music videos and permanently keeping it, making an MP3 copy from a purchased CD and then putting your MP3 copy on the Internet for others to download, downloading unauthorized music from P2P servers, joining unauthorized P2P services, and using a CD burner to make copies of music for friends.

Brian Fedorek

See also: Digital Piracy; Intellectual Property Crime; Movie Piracy; World Intellectual Property Organization

Further Reading

Bonner, Steven, and Eleanor O'Higgins. 2010. "Music Piracy: Ethical Perspectives." *Management Decision* 48 (9): 1341–1354.

Chiou, Jyh-Shen, Chien-yi Huang, and Hsin-hui Lee. 2005. "The Antecedents of Music Piracy Attitudes and Intentions." *Journal of Business Ethics* 57: 161–174.

Cummings, Alex Sayf. 2013. *Democracy of Sound: Music Piracy and the Remaking of American Copyright in the Twentieth Century.* New York: Oxford University Press.

Recording Industry Association of America. 2017. "About Piracy." Accessed December 27, 2017. https://www.riaa.com/resources-learning/about-piracy.

Witt, Stephen. 2015. *How Music Got Free: A Story of Obsession and Invention.* New York: Penguin Books.

World Intellectual Property Organization. n.d. "Berne Convention for the Protection of Literary and Artistic Works." Accessed February 5, 2018. http://www.wipo.int/treaties/en/ip/berne.

Mutual Legal Assistance

Mutual legal assistance in criminal matters (also referred to as MLA, legal assistance, mutual assistance, and mutual assistance in criminal matters) is the process by which the judicial authorities of one state obtain the assistance of judicial authorities of another state in the investigation or prosecution of a criminal case. It is used, for example, in securing the testimony of victims, witnesses, or expert witnesses; in obtaining other forms of evidence; in obtaining copies of judicial or other official records; and in tracing the proceeds of crime.

THE BASIS FOR MUTUAL LEGAL ASSISTANCE

MLA is a very recent development. As recently as the middle of the 1900s, the prevailing attitude was that the courts of one country should not give effect to the criminal law of another country—and therefore they should not provide mutual legal assistance in criminal cases.

Despite this prevailing attitude, over time the tool of letters rogatory was developed. A letter rogatory is a formal request from the judicial authority of one state to the judicial authority of another state to perform one or more specified actions on behalf of the first judicial authority. This request would be conveyed through diplomatic channels. Whether or not the requested country would provide such assistance was entirely at its discretion. The process was lengthy and bureaucratic, and the outcome was quite uncertain. Furthermore, letters rogatory were primarily used in civil cases, not criminal cases.

During the late 1800s, the first bilateral MLA treaties to emerge provided a framework for MLA and thus a greater expectation of success. The first multilateral treaty did not emerge until 1959, the Convention on Mutual Assistance in Criminal Matters, prepared within the framework of the Council of Europe. The 1986 British Commonwealth Scheme for Mutual Assistance in Criminal Matters (the Harare Scheme), while not an international binding treaty, represents an agreed set of recommendations that continues to be in wide use.

The United States used the 1959 Council of Europe convention as a frame of reference in negotiating its first bilateral MLA treaty, which was with Switzerland (Ellis and Pisani 1985, 196–198). This was signed in 1973. Since then, the United States has negotiated a total of some 60 such treaties.

This growing U.S. interest in negotiating bilateral MLA treaties was not shared by many other countries. They preferred multilateral treaties as being less resource-intensive to negotiate and in providing a more consistent framework for judicial cooperation with a number of countries. Within the framework of the United Nations, three major conventions were negotiated on specific types of crime: illicit trafficking in narcotic drugs and psychotropic substances (1988, referred to below as the 1988 Drug Convention), transnational organized crime (2000, the Palermo Convention), and corruption (2003). These three conventions differed from earlier crime-specific instruments in one notable respect: they contained detailed provisions on MLA.

The earliest MLA treaties primarily referred to the hearing of witnesses, other taking of evidence, and the service of documents. Over the past 50 years, the scope has been constantly expanded. The Palermo Convention, for example, also includes provisions on searches and seizures, the tracing of the proceeds of crime and the freezing of assets, the provision of originals or copies of documents or records, the facilitation of the voluntary appearance of persons in the requesting state party, and in general any other type of assistance that is not contrary to the domestic law of the requested state party.

The most common grounds for refusal to grant a request for MLA noted in the treaties are the absence of double criminality, the offense is a political offense or a fiscal offense, bank secrecy, and violation of vital interests of the requested state. In general, the scope of these grounds for refusal has been restricted.

Other grounds for refusal generally found in MLA treaties that can be interpreted quite expansively is that the requested state can refuse assistance that it deems might endanger its sovereignty, security, law and order, or other vital interests.

IMPROVING THE EFFICIENCY OF THE MLA PROCEDURE

The general trend is toward more extensive treaties globally on mutual legal assistance, a wider scope of assistance, fewer grounds for refusal, and various ways of making the process more efficient and rapid.

For example, the traditional diplomatic channels are being replaced by reliance on central authorities or even by direct contacts between courts. Increasingly,

MLA treaties require that states parties designate a central authority (generally, the ministry of justice) to which the requests can be sent directly, thus providing a quicker alternative to diplomatic channels. Today, even more direct channels are being used, in that an official in the requesting state sends the request directly to the appropriate official in the other state.

Another trend is toward overcoming differences between the procedural laws of states, for example, when the requesting state requires special procedures (such as notarized affidavits) that are not recognized under the law of the requested state. Traditionally, the requested state always followed its own procedural law and would refuse assistance if unknown procedures were required. Already the 1988 Drug Convention, while not requiring that the requested state comply with the procedural form required by the requesting state, clearly urged the requested state to do so. A corresponding provision was taken into of the Palermo Convention.

Matti Joutsen

See also: Double (Dual) Criminality; Extradition

Further Reading

American Law Institute. 1990. *Restatement of the Law, Third, Foreign Relations Law of the United States*. 2 vols. 1990. St. Paul, MN: American Law Institute.

Boister, Neil. 2012. *An Introduction to Transnational Criminal Law*. Oxford, UK. Oxford University Press.

Ellis, Alan, and Robert L. Pisani. 1985. "The United States Treaties on Mutual Assistance in Criminal Matters: A Comparative Analysis." *The International Lawyer* 19 (1): 189–223.

Joutsen, Matti. 2014. "International Instruments on Cooperation in Responding to Transnational Crime." In *Handbook of Transnational Crime and Justice*, edited by Philip Reichel and Jay Albanese, 303–322. 2nd ed. Los Angeles, London, and New Delhi: Sage.

McClean, D. 1992. *International Judicial Assistance*. Oxford, UK: Clarendon.

Mutual Recognition in Criminal Matters

Mutual recognition in criminal matters refers to an agreement among states that a judicial decision made in one state may be enforced directly, as such, in another state, without the need to have it confirmed by a domestic court. (This should be kept distinct from "recognition of a foreign judgment," which is a unilateral decision by a court to give force to a foreign judgment.) Mutual recognition is possible on the basis of certain international conventions. Since 2001, it has been increasingly used among European Union member states.

EVOLUTION OF THE CONCEPT OF MUTUAL RECOGNITION

Mutual recognition of judicial decisions and judgments has traditionally been almost nonexistent in international cooperation. Courts have been reluctant to give effect to the criminal law of another country. If a court in one country orders that a suspect who has fled abroad be arrested, that his or her assets be frozen, or that his or her house be searched for evidence, the authorities of that country generally have to use mutual legal assistance and request that the decision be carried out abroad. This process is slow, bureaucratic, and uncertain.

A few bilateral and multilateral treaties have been formulated on mutual recognition. The foremost such treaty is the European Convention on the International Validity of Criminal Judgments, prepared within the framework of the Council of Europe in 1970. However, even this treaty has very few signatories, and even fewer ratifications. The convention only applies to legally final judgments and not, for example, to decisions made in the course of an investigation (such as arrest warrants).

Bilateral arrangements for mutual recognition include the "backing of warrants" process (also referred to as "fast-track extradition") that is used between Australia and New Zealand (and had been used between Ireland and the United Kingdom before the introduction of the European Arrest Warrant). In this process, a judge in one of the two countries would "endorse" an arrest warrant issued by a court of the other country, authorizing the execution of the warrant. This fast-track process thus does not require a formal request for extradition, which would go through the attorney general.

Somewhat similarly, the five Nordic countries (Denmark, Finland, Iceland, Norway, and Sweden) have a long-standing regional arrangement, whereby they recognize one another's judicial decisions and judgments, and refusals are almost unheard of. This system is based on the fact that the Nordic countries have legal systems that are quite similar and also otherwise have long-standing cooperation with one another.

EVOLUTION OF MUTUAL RECOGNITION IN THE EUROPEAN UNION

In 1999, the European Union agreed on the importance of mutual recognition of decisions and judgments, which, in its view, "should become the cornerstone of judicial co-operation in both civil and criminal matters within the Union." The argument was that the member states of the European Union share fundamental values and legal principles. The authorities of a member state should have confidence in the operation of the legal system of the other states and should therefore be prepared to give full faith and credence to any judicial decision or judgment handed down in other states. Accordingly, it should be possible for a decision or judgment handed down by a court in one member state to be immediately enforced as such in any of the other states.

The European Council further identified two priority areas in criminal law where the principle of mutual recognition should be applied, arrest warrants and pretrial orders, in particular those that would enable competent authorities to quickly secure evidence and to seize assets that are easily movable.

Work proceeded slowly. For a time, it seemed as if work on mutual recognition would be buried by the many technical and legal problems involved. The terrorist attacks on New York and Washington, D.C., on September 11, 2001, changed the situation dramatically. Within only a few months, agreement was reached on an EU arrest warrant. Simply put, the new decision replaced extradition among the EU member states with a new system whereby suspects and convicted offenders are "surrendered" to the requesting state. The process no longer needs to go through diplomatic channels or the central authorities. An arrest warrant issued by a court in one state will be recognized as valid throughout the European Union and is to be enforced.

A European arrest warrant may be issued for offenses punishable by the law of the issuing member state by a custodial sentence or a detention order for a maximum period of at least 12 months or, where a sentence has been passed or a detention order has been made, for sentences of at least 4 months. There are certain grounds for refusal: cases where the offense is covered by an amnesty in the requested state, *ne bis in idem* (double jeopardy), and the lack of criminal responsibility due to age.

A second framework decision was adopted soon afterward (also in 2002) on the mutual recognition of decisions on the freezing of property and evidence. (This second decision was replaced by the updated directive on the European Investigation Order issued in 2017.) The framework decision makes it possible, for example, for the decision of a court in one member state on the freezing of the accounts of a suspect to be enforced immediately in any and all of the other member states. Subsequently, several other decisions on mutual recognition were given on financial penalties, on confiscation orders, on pre- and posttrial measures, and on protection orders. (A somewhat related decision applies to the exchange of information on convictions and criminal records.)

Matti Joutsen

See also: European Arrest Warrant; Mutual Legal Assistance

Further Reading

Boister, Neil. 2012. *An Introduction to Transnational Criminal Law.* Oxford, UK: Oxford University Press.

Geyer, Florian, and Elspeth Guild. 2008. *Security versus Justice? Police and Judicial Cooperation in the European Union.* Aldershot, UK, and Burlington, Ontario: Ashgate Publishing.

Klimek, Libor. 2017. *Mutual Recognition of Judicial Decisions in European Criminal Law.* Cham, Switzerland: Springer.

N

National Counterterrorism Center

The National Counterterrorism Center (NCTC) is an organ of the Office of the Director of National Intelligence (ODNI) intended to coordinate the efforts of the U.S. intelligence community to facilitate the sharing of information and coordination of counterterrorism policy related to counterterrorism. The center was created to address the lack of interagency communication that allowed key intelligence findings that could have been used to predict and possibly prevent the September 11, 2001, terrorist attacks that were overlooked by the web of numerous government agencies that collect intelligence (Best 2011).

The NCTC's mandate is laid out in United States Public Law 108-458. Its mandate includes analysis of terror threat based on intelligence received from different government intelligence agencies, dissemination of intelligence and analysis products to relevant parties, and formulation of operations for military and civilian counterterrorism efforts. Relevant parties include the director of national intelligence (DNI), the president and other executive branch members, select congressional committees, and state, local, and foreign governments (Best 2011).

Few assessments of the effectiveness of the NCTC have been conducted. The largest to date, commissioned by Congress, found that the NCTC operated almost exclusively as a think tank for the intelligence community, and its mandate for coordinating counterterrorism operations was not being fulfilled. This failure was explained by continued lack of involvement of member agencies and the inability to maintain a committed workforce representative of all agencies, as positions in the NCTC have little room for mobility and therefore have high turnover (Kravinsky et al. 2010).

HISTORY

The NCTC began in part as the Terrorist Threat Integration Center (TTIC). On January 28, 2003, during his State of the Union address, President George W. Bush announced his intent to instruct the four largest intelligence agencies in the U.S. government, namely the Federal Bureau of Investigation (FBI), the Central Intelligence Agency (CIA), the Department of Homeland Security (DHS), and the Department of Defense (DoD), to jointly develop a project to share and synthesize the intelligence collected by each individual agency pertaining to terrorist threats. This project, the TTIC, began operation on May 1, 2003, under the direction of John Brennan.

However, around this time, a number of agencies were being created to fulfill the same or similar functions, including the DHS. The National Commission on Terrorist Attacks upon the United States (more commonly known as the 9/11 Commission) recognized this problem, and in July 2004, it recommended that the TTIC be provided a statutory mandate that included not only the transfer of intelligence products but also the responsibility for the coordination of strategies for disrupting terrorist plots identified in the intelligence (Best 2011). Following the 9/11 Commission's report (2004), which included the recommendation for the expansion of the TTIC, President Bush issued Executive Order 13354, which created the NCTC out of the TTIC, placing it under the director of central intelligence (DCI) and including the broadened mandate.

Under Executive Order 13354, the NCTC would store collective information gathered on all identified and potential or suspected terrorists, with the exception of terrorists acting exclusively domestically. Using this analysis, the NCTC would advise the president, Congress, government bodies, and law enforcement when appropriate. The president would appoint the DCI, who would be responsible for appointing the director of the NCTC.

Congress became concerned that the center was too far beyond the reach of congressional oversight. As a result, Congress passed the Intelligence Reform and Terrorism Prevention Act (IRTPA), or Public Law 108-458, in December 2004. IRTPA has three main provisions: (1) establishing a statutory mandate for the NCTC; (2) creating the ODNI, which would fall under the oversight of Congress; and (3) moving the NCTC from under the control of the DCI to the DNI (Best 2011).

In 2005, following a recommendation from the Weapons of Mass Destruction Commission, the system of National Intelligence Managers (NIM) was established as another attempt to consolidate and organize the U.S. intelligence system. As a result, the director of the NCTC (D/NCTC) was given the additional responsibility of being the NIM for counterterrorism (NIM-CT) (National Counterterrorism Center 2017b).

STRUCTURE

The NCTC falls under the direct control of the Office of the Director of National Intelligence (ODNI), an organization dedicated to coordinating intelligence operations across the intelligence community in different fields. NCTC is one of six organs within the ODNI.

Of the over 1,000 staff members of the NCTC, around 40 percent are primarily employed by another intelligence agency and act as a liaison between the NCTC and their agency. Around 20 intelligence agencies are represented on the NCTC's staff.

The position of the director of the NCTC (D/NCTC) is filled by appointment by the president and is subject to Senate confirmation. The D/NCTC reports directly to both the president and the DNI. The D/NCTC, with the deputy and executive directors, oversees four directorates that comprise the organs of the center: the Directorates of Strategic and Operations Planning, Intelligence, Terrorist Identities, and Operations Support.

The Directorate of the Strategic and Operations Planning coordinates and plans the entirety of the U.S. government's counterterrorism missions, but it does not have any operational personnel responsible for implementing the plans. Implementation is solely carried out by law enforcement personnel with jurisdiction in a case.

The structure of the NCTC therefore makes it accountable to both the executive and legislative branches, and it works to centralize the efforts and products of the large and sometimes unwieldy U.S. intelligence apparatus.

Lilla Heins

See also: Counterterrorism; Crime-Terrorism Nexus; Global Counterterrorism Forum

Further Reading

Best, Richard A. 2011. "The National Counterterrorism Center (NCTC)—Responsibilities and Potential Congressional Concerns." Report, Congressional Research Service. Accessed January 6, 2019. https://fas.org/sgp/crs/intel/R41022.pdf.

Bloy, Natalie, and Heidi M. Peters. 2018. "National Counterterrorism Center (NCTC)." Congressional Research Service, July 11. Accessed January 6, 2019. https://fas.org/sgp/crs/intel/IF10709.pdf.

Kravinksy, Robert S., Daniel R. Landberg, Creighton Visack, and Cody M. Brown. 2010. "Toward Integrating Complex National Missions: Lessons from the National Counterterrorism Center's Directorate of Strategic Operational Planning." Project on National Security Reform.

National Counterterrorism Center. 2017a. "NCTC Organizational Chart." April 10. Accessed January 6, 2019. https://www.dni.gov/files/NCTC/documents/RelatedContent_documents/NCTC_Org_Chart_April2017_UNCLASS.pdf.

National Counterterrorism Center. 2017b. "History." Accessed December 10, 2017. https://www.dni.gov/index.php/nctc-who-we-are/history.

Office of the Director of National Intelligence. 2017. "Organization." Accessed December 10, 2017. https://www.dni.gov/index.php/who-we-are/organizations.

National Institute of Justice

The National Institute of Justice, NIJ, is the research and evaluation agency of the United States Department of Justice. NIJ funds research and conducts other activities across a broad spectrum of criminal justice issues, ranging from DNA analysis and forensics, to violence against women, human trafficking, and prison reform. Although it is a federal agency, NIJ's primary stakeholders are state and local criminal justice practitioners, including law enforcement, courts, and corrections. NIJ is based in Washington, D.C., but works with criminal justice practitioners and researchers across the United States of America and has a long history of global engagement, dating back nearly to its inception in 1968.

HISTORY

In the early 1960s, President Lyndon B. Johnson tasked a commission to examine the state of law enforcement in the country and put forward recommendations for criminal justice reform and tackling crime. The commission published its final report in 1967, *The Challenge of Crime in a Free Society*. The Department of Justice had begun to provide grants to state and local law enforcement agencies in 1965, and the commission's report strongly endorsed this support, calling for additional efforts: "[The Commission] believes further that the Federal Government can make a dramatic new contribution to the national effort against crime by greatly expanding its support of the agencies of justice in the States and in the cities" (President's Commission 1967).

In the wake of this presidential impetus for reform and change, the United States Congress passed the Omnibus Crime Control and Safe Streets Act of 1968, which President Johnson signed into law. This act established the Law Enforcement Assistance Administration, which allocated federal funding for criminal justice research, in addition to a number of other activities. Under the direction of the Law Enforcement Assistance Administration, the act also established the National Institute of Law Enforcement and Criminal Justice, which was renamed the National Institute of Justice in 1978.

ORGANIZATION AND FUNDING

Unlike many federal government research agencies, NIJ is directed by a presidential appointee. NIJ receives all of its funding from U.S. congressional appropriations. NIJ's funding includes both designated funds for specific subject areas and "base funds," which the institute has discretion in allocating.

NIJ conducts research and provides grants for research on topics related to criminal justice. This includes an extremely broad range of topics, encompassing crime prevention and control, law enforcement, victim services, human trafficking, domestic radicalization and terrorism, drugs, school safety, violence against women, forensics, protective equipment, prisoner reentry, broadband communications, unmanned aviation, digital evidence, and other areas.

The institute has three sciences offices—the Office of Investigative and Forensic Sciences, the Office of Research and Evaluation, and the Office of Science and Technology—which oversee research grants and maintain a small intramural research program. NIJ also maintains a standards and conformity assessment program for body armor and supports programs to improve the capacity and infrastructure of the justice system, including the National Missing and Unidentified Persons System database.

In addition to conducting and supporting research, NIJ has independent authority to disseminate research findings. The institute produces print and electronic media, including the award-winning *NIJ Journal*. NIJ's CrimeSolutions.gov is a Web-based clearinghouse that rates the effectiveness of criminal justice programs. NIJ supports the professional development of criminal justice practitioners committed to integrating research into policies and practice, and it often partners with sister agencies to ensure that program development reflects the latest understanding of what works and what matters for the field. All NIJ-funded research is publicly available through the National Criminal Justice Service Reference Service, and datasets are available through the National Archive of Criminal Justice Data.

A GLOBAL SCOPE

An International History

NIJ has a long history of international work, dating back nearly five decades. The Omnibus Crime Control and Safe Street Acts, NIJ's founding legislation, gives the institute statutory authority to serve as a national and international clearinghouse for the exchange of criminal justice information. The institute's international authority was further expanded under the Homeland Security Act of 2002.

Although NIJ conducted some international activities in its early years, the political will to expand this work came under Jeremy Travis, the NIJ director from 1995 to 2002. Under Director Travis's leadership, the institute established an International Center, which housed all of NIJ's international activities from 1997 through 2010. In 2010, the International Center was replaced with a designated research portfolio on transnational crime and a portfolio manager who also coordinated most of the institute's nonresearch international activities. The transnational crime research portfolio was dissolved in 2016, but NIJ continues to conduct research on issues with an international nexus, including human trafficking, domestic radicalization, terrorism, and transnational crime.

International Activities

NIJ's international work has included a wide range of activities. From its earliest days, NIJ hosted international fellows, delegations, and other visitors. NIJ grants do not directly fund international entities, but they have funded U.S. researcher partnerships with Canadian, Chinese, German, Mexican, and Ukrainian researchers to study the causes and correlates of juvenile delinquency, criminal career trajectories, human trafficking, the commercial exploitation of children, and other issues.

True to its mandate as a clearinghouse of international criminal justice research, NIJ has established and maintained a number of online criminal justice research networks and founded a network of directors of government research institutes in more than two dozen countries. NIJ organized a conference on international forensic radiology research in 2016, held in the Netherlands, and has certified law enforcement body armor manufactured in more than a dozen countries.

NIJ established and coordinated the International Arrestee Drug Abuse Monitoring Program (I-ADAM), an international drug surveillance system for arrestees that was also used to study the consequences of drug abuse within and across national boundaries. Although I-ADAM is no longer active, it included collaboration with a dozen countries and built international dialogue about the links between drug use and crime.

The institute has also pursued formal partnerships with governments of other countries, including Australia, Israel, New Zealand, the Netherlands, and the United Kingdom, in the form of Memorandums of Understanding. NIJ is one of 17 United Nations Program Network Institute (PNI) sites worldwide, part of a network developed to promote international cooperation regarding crime prevention and criminal justice. In 2017, NIJ director David Muhlhausen attended a PNI summit in Seoul, South Korea.

Criminal justice issues in the United States are inextricably linked to international issues. NIJ's key stakeholders—state and local criminal justice practitioners—face many problems similar to their counterparts across the world. NIJ's international work draws on this work to help U.S. criminal justice practitioners learn from relevant international research and best practices.

Rianna P. Starheim

See also: Human Trafficking; Terrorism, Domestic; Terrorism, International; Transnational, Global, and International Crime; UN Program Network of Institutes

Further Reading

Kennedy, John F. 1960. "Address of Senator John F. Kennedy Accepting the Democratic Party Nomination for the Presidency of the United States." Los Angeles, July 15. Accessed January 6, 2019. http://www.presidency.ucsb.edu/ws/index.php?pid=25966.

National Archive of Criminal Justice Data. 2018. "About NACJD." Accessed April 19, 2018. https://www.icpsr.umich.edu/icpsrweb/content/NACJD/about.html.

National Institute of Justice. 1995–2015. "National Institute of Justice Annual Reports." Accessed January 6, 2019. https://nij.gov/publications/pages/annual-reports.aspx.

National Institute of Justice. 2018a. "About CrimeSolutions.gov." Accessed April 19, 2018. https://crimesolutions.gov/about.aspx.

National Institute of Justice. 2018b. "About NIJ." Last Modified January 22, 2018. Accessed April 19, 2018. https://www.nij.gov/about/pages/welcome.aspx.

Office of Justice Programs. 2018. "About NCJRS." Accessed April 19, 2018. https://www.ncjrs.gov/whatsncjrs.html.

President's Commission on Law Enforcement and Administration of Justice. 1967. *The Challenge of Crime in a Free Society.* Washington, D.C.: Government Printing Office. Accessed January 18, 2019. https://www.ncjrs.gov/pdffiles1/nij/42.pdf.

'Ndrangheta

The 'Ndrangheta (believed to be from the Greek for "courageous man") is an Italian Mafia organization that originated in Southern Italy. There are two explanations that trace its historical origins, both claiming to play an influential role in the organization's culture and ideology. The first is mythical and begins in the 15th century with three Spanish knights creating a secret society built on honor, family, and rules. The second explanation places the origin of 'Ndrangheta during the Italian unification of 1861, a political-social movement unifying all regions of the Italian peninsula into a single state called the Kingdom of Italy (Sergi and Lavorgna 2016). 'Ndranghetistas consider their stronghold to be in San Luca, a municipality in the Province of Reggio Calabria in the Italian region of Calabria. Many of the male residents of San Luca are members of 'Ndrangheta, and the Sanctuary of Polsi is their meeting place, which is located in the heart of the Aspromonte Mountains (Varese 2006).

'Ndrangheta has managed to remain under the radar from many criminal justice agencies around the world for many years. Criminal justice personnel in Italy argued that 'Ndrangheta managed to make themselves invisible, both informationally and in an investigative manner, due to their law enforcement efforts focusing on Camorra and Sicilian Mafia organizations (Ciconte 2014). As a result, it was not until the late 20th century that 'Ndrangheta rose to the top of international crime syndicates and law enforcement agencies began to investigate and prosecute its members.

ORGANIZATIONAL STRUCTURE

Family is the foundation for the success of 'Ndrangheta. The 'ndrine is a unit of the 'Ndrangheta that is formed by members of the same family that cover a specific geographical territory. The fact that members of the 'ndrine are connected by family ties guarantees their secrecy and trust and a high level of unity among its members, and it decreases the risk of deserters (Dickie 2014). The *Padrino*, "Godfather," is the highest-ranking member of the 'ndrine, followed by the *Quarlino* and then *Treuarlino*, which are the most senior positions. The next tier consists of *Vangelista*, or "gospelist," and *Santista*, or "saintist." This level is considered the major society. The next tier consists of *Camorrista di sgarro* (*camorrista*, "who is up for a fight," also known as *sgarrista*), *Camorrista*, and *Picciotto*, "lad." This level is considered the minor society. The last tier is the *Giovane d'onore* ("honored youth") who are being prepared to enter the organization.

ACTIVITIES

The Council on Hemispheric Affairs estimated that 'Ndrangheta made most of their money through drug trafficking, commercial enterprise and public contracts, extortion, arms trafficking, prostitution, and human trafficking, with a net worth of €44 billion ($60 billion) in 2014. They also use extortion and violence to infiltrate local and national politics around the world (Calderoni 2012).The Federal Bureau of Investigations estimates that there are 160 'Ndrangheta cells with 4,000 to 10,000 members impacting communities in Europe, North and South America, Africa, and Australia. In the United States, it is estimated that 200 'Ndrangheta members and associates reside primarily in New York and Florida.

JOINT LAW ENFORCEMENT OPERATIONS

In 2010, German and Italian police arrested 305 members of 'Ndrangheta for various crimes in Operation Crimine, which revealed that the 'Ndrangheta was extremely "hierarchical, united and pyramidal" and not just clan-based as previously believed. In 2014, the FBI and Italian police arrested members of both the Gambino and Bonanno families in the United States as well as 10 members of

'Ndrangheta in Italy to disrupt the international trade of drugs, weapons, and laundered money between Italy, the United States, Canada, and Latin America in Operation New Bridge. In 2018, police in Italy and Germany arrested 169 'Ndrangheta mafia members and 3 Italian mayors for exploiting business owners to buy products made in Southern Italy.

Tina Fowler and David A. Rembert

See also: Organized Crime; UN Convention against Transnational Organized Crime

Further Reading

Calderoni, Francesco. 2012. "The Structure of Drug Trafficking Mafias: The 'Ndrangheta and Cocaine." *Crime, Law and Social Change* 58 (3): 321–349.

Ciconte, Enzo. 2014. "Origins and Development of the 'Ndrangheta." In *The 'Ndrangheta and Sacra Corona Unita: The History, Organization and Operations of Two Unknown Mafia Groups*, edited by Nicoletta Serenata, 33–50. 1st ed. Vol. 12. Cham, Switzerland: Springer International Publishing.

Dickie, John. 2014. *Blood Brotherhoods: A History of Italy's Three Mafias*. New York: PublicAffairs.

Sergi, Anna, and Anita Lavorgna. 2016. *'Ndrangheta: The Glocal Dimensions of the Most Powerful Italian Mafia*. Cham, Switzerland: Palgrave Macmillan.

Varese, Federico. 2006. "How Mafias Migrate: The Case of the 'Ndrangheta in Northern Italy." *Law & Society Review* 40 (2): 411–444.

Newman, Graeme (1939–)

Graeme Newman is a world-renowned criminologist. He was born and raised in Australia, where he studied education, psychology, and criminology at the University of Melbourne before enrolling for his PhD at the University of Pennsylvania to study under Professor Marvin Wolfgang, himself a giant on the subject of culture and violence. Newman has enjoyed a long career at State University of New York (SUNY) Albany's School of Criminal Justice, where he is distinguished professor emeritus. He has made enduring contributions to criminology and criminal justice through more than 20 books, some written with his students. These books cover sentencing and punishment, violence and terrorism, crime prevention, identity theft, cybercrime, and more. Each of his publications are relevant to understanding crime from an international perspective.

Professor Newman's first major international work was *Comparative Deviance*, published in 1976, based on a United Nations study directed by Professor Franco Ferracuti, a renowned Italian criminologist. Although first published more than 40 years ago, the book remains a classic resource for anyone seeking to undertake cross-cultural empirical research—as indicated by its republishing in 2008 and in 2017. It is the first systematic attempt to survey public perceptions of deviant behavior across cultures, including India, Indonesia, Iran, Italy, Yugoslavia, and the United States. This book helps in designing research that avoids pitfalls, in analyzing quantitative data with appropriate theoretical interpretation, and in drawing accurate and clearly stated conclusions.

In the 1990s, Newman produced two reports that together serve as major sources on international crime and justice issues. For the first, he served as project manager to coordinate narrative descriptions of the criminal justice systems of countries around the world. The resulting *World Factbook of Criminal Justice Systems* included 42 country descriptions (Bureau of Justice Statistics 2017). A 2002 update by William McDonald added three new countries and amended two of the originals. His second edited report, *Global Report on Crime and Justice*, was published by the United Nations Centre for International Crime Prevention (Newman 1999). The report presents a variety of data collected from the United Nations and its ancillary bodies over a period of 25 years. The result is a collection of cross-national data on such topics as police records of crime, comparative justice systems, and transnational crime and its control.

In 2000, Newman and his coauthors produced a report for the National Institute of Justice (NIJ). It emphasizes the need for theory building and testing, particularly to prevent and control the burgeoning variety of transnational crimes. The book's message to the fields of criminology and criminal justice is this: "Expand curricular offerings to support such comparative practices. But such offerings must extend beyond survey courses or a smattering of specialty seminars. Those activities will surely help the current state of affairs, but for comparative criminology to truly bear fruit and achieve its potential, we must deepen the repertoire of skills, talent, and knowledge that its practitioners command" (Howard, Newman, and Pridemore 2000, 191).

In 2010, Newman edited a four-volume encyclopedia on *Crime and Punishment around the World*. Each volume was edited by former students and colleagues trained in comparative criminological/criminal justice research. The four volumes (*Africa and the Middle East*, *The Americas*, *Asia and Pacific*, *Europe*) are important additions to the global understanding of crime and justice around the world and reflect Newman's insistence that international crime statistics be supported by as much qualitative data as possible.

Of necessity when studying international crime and justice, Professor Newman became an early and expert user of the Internet. In the 1980s, he established the United Nations Crime and Justice Information Network. This was the first criminal justice presence on the Web. Soon after, he set up the World Criminal Justice Library Network with Phyllis Schultz in association with the Criminal Justice Library at Rutgers University. And in 1999, together with Mike Scott and Ron Clarke, he set up an award-winning Web site for the Center for Problem-Oriented Policing, an international resource on policing and crime prevention that many thousands of police professionals, researchers, and students around the world access daily.

Mangai Natarajan

See also: Identity Theft and Assumption Deterrence Act of 1998; National Institute of Justice; Transnational, Global, and International Crime

Further Reading

Bureau of Justice Statistics. 2017. *World Factbook of Criminal Justice Systems*. Last modified December 30, 2017. Accessed January 6, 2019. https://www.bjs.gov/content/pub/html/wfcj.cfm.

Howard, Gregory J., Graeme Newman, and William A. Pridemore. 2000. "Theory, Method, and Data in Comparative Criminology." *Criminal Justice 2000*, Vol. 4,

139–211. Washington, D.C.: National Institute of Justice. Accessed January 6, 2019. https://www.ncjrs.gov/App/publications/Abstract.aspx?id=185540.

Newman, Graeme. 1976. *Comparative Deviance: Law and Perception in Six Cultures.* New York: Elsevier.

Newman, Graeme, ed. 1999. *Global Report on Crime and Justice.* New York: Oxford University Press.

Newman, Graeme, ed. 2010. *Crime and Punishment around the World*, Vol. 4. Santa Barbara: ABC-CLIO.

Nichols, Terry (1955–)

Terry Lynn Nichols conspired with Timothy McVeigh to commit what was at the time the deadliest act of terrorism in the United States when they detonated a homemade bomb on April 19, 1995, outside the Alfred P. Murrah Federal Building in Oklahoma City, Oklahoma.

LINK TO MCVEIGH

Nichols first met McVeigh when they were both in U.S. Army basic training at Fort Benning, Georgia, in 1988. Nichols received a hardship discharge from the army in 1989 so he could go home to take care of his son. In 1994, after McVeigh's discharge from the army in 1991, Nichols and McVeigh went into business together selling guns and military supplies (CNN Library 2018).

Nichols and McVeigh shared antigovernment sentiments—strong enough that Nichols tried to relinquish his citizenship in 1992. Those sentiments were intensified for both men after the government's siege of the Branch Davidian compound near Waco, Texas, in 1993.

LINK TO THE BOMBING

Nichols was at home in Kansas, not in Oklahoma City, at the time of the bombing. However, prosecutors said he had helped McVeigh make the bomb and transfer the materials to a Ryder truck the day before in a park near Junction City, Kansas. Nichols knew how to make fertilizer and fuel bombs when growing up on a farm where his father had prepared fertilizer and fuel mixes to blow up tree stumps (CNN Library 2018).

Two days after the bombing, Nichols heard he was under suspicion and surrendered to police in Kansas. During a search of his Kansas home, authorities found a receipt for 2,000 pounds of fertilizer, blasting caps, and plastic barrels like those used in the bombing. Prosecutors linked Nichols to various elements of the explosive device, although there were no witnesses who could identify him as the man who bought the fertilizer. However, Michael Fortier, a friend of McVeigh, testified that Nichols had a role in assembling the bomb materials and that McVeigh had told Fortier that Nichols was heavily involved in the plot (PBS News Hour 2004).

After his federal conviction, evidence continues to support Nichols's involvement in the bombing. In 2005, the Federal Bureau of Investigation (FBI) found previously undetected residual bomb-making material in Nichols's former residence, and in 2011, in letters written by Nichols in prison and published in *The Oklahoman*, he admitted to knowing there would be a bombing but denied knowing the Murrah building was the target or that the building would be occupied (CNN Library 2018).

FEDERAL AND STATE TRIALS

On December 23, 1997, Nichols was found guilty of conspiracy to use a weapon of mass destruction and on eight counts of involuntary manslaughter. On June 4, 1988, he was sentenced to life in prison without parole.

In 2001, fearing that the federal conviction may be overturned, an Oklahoma district attorney brought state charges against Nichols for his role in the bombing. The state trial began in March 2004, and two months later, Nichols was found guilty on 161 counts of murder. However, the jury was unable to decide on a sentence of life in prison or death by lethal injection. With the jury deadlocked, the decision fell to the judge, and in August 2004, Nichols was sentenced to 161 consecutive life terms without the possibility of parole.

As of 2018, Nichols was serving his federal life sentence at the United States Penitentiary, Administrative Maximum Unit, in Florence, Colorado.

Philip L. Reichel

See also: McVeigh, Timothy; Oklahoma City Bombing (1995); Terrorism, Domestic

Further Reading

A&E Television Networks. 2016. "Terry Nichols Biography." Last Modified October 24, 2016. Accessed January 7, 2019. https://www.biography.com/people/terry-nichols-236030.

CNN Library. 2018. "Terry Nichols Fast Facts." Last Modified March 8, 2018. Accessed January 7, 2019. https://www.cnn.com/2013/03/25/us/terry-nichols-fast-facts/index.html.

PBS News Hour. 2004. "Nichols Guilty on All Charges in Oklahoma City Bombing Trial." Accessed July 6, 2018. https://www.pbs.org/newshour/politics/law-jan-june04-nichols_05-26.

Nongovernmental Organization

A nongovernmental organization (NGO) is an organization voluntarily established by people with a common interest to perform certain functions. They are formally independent of national or local governments.

The term *nongovernmental organization* has a specific legal meaning in the United Nations. It is an entity that has a recognized legal structure and purpose, and its representatives may act on its behalf (locally, nationally, and internationally). In this sense, NGOs have a legal personality recognized by law. Such nongovernmental organizations may apply for consultative status with the Economic and Social Council, and a large number have done so.

In a wider sense, however, the term *NGO* is commonly used to refer to any association established for a certain purpose, whether or not they are recognized by law to have a legal personality. In areas related to global crime, the purpose may, for example, be the raising of public awareness, the mobilization of resources, the provision of services (such as to victims of crime), promotion of human rights, advocacy for certain policies, monitoring of the response of local or national government, and encouragement of political participation. In this wider sense, synonyms for NGOs include "civil society organizations" and "third sector organizations."

NGOs are generally nonprofit, and much of their work is based on the voluntary input of members. NGOs may also raise money for their activities through membership fees as well as through donations from the public, from governments, or from the private sector. Governments may support NGOs by registering them as charities or by granting them tax exempt status. Governments may also establish NGOs for specific purposes, in which case reference is made to "government-organized NGOs," "government-operated NGOs," or "quasi-autonomous NGOs."

NGOs may act on the international, regional, national, or local level. The United Nations recognizes the formal category of an "international non-governmental organization" (not to be confused with an intergovernmental organization), which is an NGO that functions in more than one country. The United Nations also has the formal category of a "national NGO," which, as the term implies, is an NGO that is based in one country.

In the area of the prevention of and response to global crime, many examples can be given of influential NGOs. International academic NGOs include the International Association of Penal Law, the International Penal and Penitentiary Foundation, the International Society of Criminology, and the World Society of Victimology. International professional NGOs include the International Police Association, the International Prison Chaplains Association, and the International Association of Prosecutors. Other prominent international NGOs include the International Organization for Victim Assistance, Penal Reform International, and Transparency International.

The activity of NGOs in supplementing the efforts of governments to prevent and control global crime is widely regarded as critically important. On the local level, for example, NGOs provide advice to citizens on crime prevention, assistance to victims, legal advice and support to suspects, assistance to different elements of the criminal justice system, and help in the reintegration of offenders into society.

The work of NGOs in general has also created controversy, especially within the framework of the United Nations Crime Prevention and Criminal Justice Programme. Although the large majority of member states of the United Nations support the mobilization of the public through the work of NGOs as part of participatory democracy, and as providing welcome support to the formal criminal justice system, some governments have expressed concerns that NGOs could serve as fronts for foreign governments seeking to influence policy and public opinion, in violation of local values and even laws. Some of these governments that are concerned with NGO activity have required that all NGOs report on their membership, funding, and activity and that NGOs receiving foreign funding formally register as "foreign agents." The activity of NGOs that do not comply with these requirements has often been hampered or even proscribed.

Matti Joutsen

See also: Alliance of NGOs on Crime Prevention and Criminal Justice; Corruption Measurements; Criminologists without Borders; ECPAT International; *Global Slavery Index*; Intergovernmental Organization; Polaris Project

Further Reading

Clark, Ann Marie. 1995. "Non-Governmental Organizations and Their Influence on International Society." *Journal of International Affairs* 48 (2): 507–525.

Lewis, David, and Nazneen Kanji. 2009. *Non-Governmental Organizations and Development*. New York: Routledge.

Ripinsky, Sergey, Peter van den Bossche, and British Institute of International and Comparative Law. 2007. *NGO Involvement in International Organizations: A Legal Analysis*. London: British Institute of International and Comparative Law.

Nuclear Weapons and Related Materials and Technologies, Trafficking in

Nuclear trafficking is the illegal movement, removal, theft, sale, or transfer of nuclear materials, including highly enriched uranium (HEU) with 20 percent enrichment or higher and plutonium, and nuclear technologies. Theft, misappropriation, and trafficking in nuclear materials and technology constitute a global risk to security and public health.

A nuclear weapon is a device that derives its explosive energy from fission or through the combination of fission and fusion processes. The energy is produced by splitting the nucleus of an atom, which results in a sustained chain reaction. Fission weapons are often referred to as *atomic bombs*, whereas fusion bombs are commonly known as *hydrogen bombs*. Similar to conventional bombs, nuclear weapons are designed to cause damage through an explosion that is caused by the release of a significant amount of energy in a short period of time. The nuclear explosion produces distinct forms of energy that may have serious effects, such as blast, thermal radiation, electromagnetic pulse, direct nuclear radiation, and fallout.

NUCLEAR TRAFFICKING

The availability of nuclear materials and technologies on the black market is dangerous, as they may be used for malicious purposes, such as for the development of a radiological dispersal device (RDD). An RDD, also known as a "dirty bomb," is a product of the combination of radioactive materials with conventional explosives, and when detonated, there is a high possibility of the dispersion of radioactive material over an area, which may contaminate persons, property, and the environment. Dirty bombs can combine conventional explosives (e.g., dynamite) with radioactive materials (e.g., bomb-grade uranium or plutonium). Although dirty bombs are technically difficult to make and require hard-to-obtain materials, many governments acknowledge the important security risks posed by trafficking and illicit trade in nuclear materials and technologies, particularly in cases where they are acquired by organized criminal groups and terrorist organizations.

Some of the main perpetrators providing HEU or plutonium on the black market are insiders or former employees of nuclear facilities. Usually, insiders are motivated by profit from selling nuclear materials and technologies. Insiders are often contacted by intermediaries, who seek out potential customers of nuclear materials and technologies.

In the 1990s, experts reported that much of the known cases of smuggled nuclear material were traceable to stockpiles in Russia and other former Soviet republics (Armitage and Squassoni 2015). As the Soviet Union collapsed, nuclear facilities became poorly maintained and guarded, thus presenting multiple opportunities for corruption and theft. According to the European Union Non-Proliferation Consortium, "Over 630 nuclear trafficking incidents were recorded in the Black Sea states between 1991 and 2012, almost half of them in Russia. Five of the recorded incidents involved highly enriched uranium (HEU), raising concerns about the region's use as a transit route for nuclear material smuggled from the former Soviet Union to the Middle East" (Zaitseva and Steinhausler 2014, 1).

One of the largest and publicly known cases of nuclear trafficking to date is the Kintsagov case. In February 2006, Oleg Khintsagov, Revaz Kurkumuli, Henry Sujashvili, and Vaja Chikhasvili were arrested while attempting to smuggle approximately 100 grams of 89 percent enriched HEU. The arrests, a culmination of a weekslong effort by the U.S. Central Intelligence Agency (CIA) and the Georgian Ministry of Internal Affairs (MIA), were made after the suspects met with an undercover Georgian agent posing as a prospective Turkish buyer of the nuclear materials (Bronner 2008). Government corruption played an important role in enabling the nuclear material to flow through the Khintsagov group. According to the Russian State Security Services (FSB), Khintsagov used his family connections, namely his cousin Miron Garabaev, a former Russian customs officer, to secure unchecked travel through the Russian-Georgian border (Bronner 2008).

The evidence connecting nuclear smuggling with terrorist groups is more obscure. According to some documents, Al Qaeda and the Islamic State of Iraq and Syria (ISIS) had interest in acquiring nuclear weapons and radiological materials. Yet, there is no concrete evidence on the probability of their success (Armitage and Squassoni 2015).

RESPONSES TO THE NUCLEAR AND RADIOLOGICAL THREAT

Nuclear energy can be used for civilian purposes, such as producing electricity. There is a possibility, however, that criminally motivated individuals could abuse nuclear technology. If not controlled and utilized appropriately, nuclear and radioactive materials can pose serious risks to public health and the environment.

The International Atomic Energy Agency (IAEA) came into force in 1957 in response to the fears associated with the unauthorized use of nuclear materials and technology. The IAEA cooperates with its 170-member states and multiple partners to promote security, safety, and the peaceful use of nuclear technologies. Its main objective is to accelerate and enlarge the contribution of atomic energy to peace, health, and prosperity throughout the world.

In the 46th IAEA general conference in September 2002, protection against nuclear terrorism was adopted, and activities concerned with the physical protection of nuclear materials and nuclear installations were established. Additionally, the IAEA offers nuclear material accountancy, detection of and response to trafficking of nuclear and radioactive materials, security of radioactive sources, security in the transport of nuclear and other radioactive material, and emergency response and preparedness measures to the member states.

The treaties administered by the IAEA, such as the Convention of the Physical Protection of Nuclear Material (CPPNM) and the Treaty on the Non-Proliferation of Nuclear Weapons (NPT), play an important role in establishing legal rules. They promote international cooperation and safety standards against nuclear misuse and sabotage. The IAEA provides assistance to member states through Advisory Service Missions, training courses, and the publication of guidance documents and reference materials. These materials are used by states, regional authorities, facility operators, and other relevant stakeholders.

The IAEA's Nuclear Security plan develops nuclear security requirements and guidance for the prevention and detection of and responses to acts and threats of nuclear terrorism. It is not only responsible for dealing with nuclear threats and trafficking, but it also helps member states in the management of relevant data. For instance, the IAEA collects data on incidents of theft and diversion of nuclear materials reported or confirmed by governments.

In addition to the IAEA's Incident and Trafficking Database (ITDB), other organizations help to access the scope of trafficking nuclear materials. The University of Salzburg runs the Database on Nuclear Smuggling, Theft, and Orphan Radiation Sources (DSTO), which includes incidents reported by governments as well as in the open-source. The DSTO is only accessible to authorized users. The CNS Global Incidents and Trafficking Database, launched in 2013 for the Nuclear Threat Initiative, also collects official and media-reported incidents, and it is freely accessible to the public. These databases aim to record nuclear materials that fall out of regulatory control and could be available to criminals and terrorists. Understanding how any nuclear or other radioactive material falls out of regulatory control can illuminate gaps in the global nuclear security architecture and inform preventive and protecting actions.

Mariana Kakarakis and Yuliya Zabyelina

See also: Al Qaeda; Islamic State of Iraq and Syria (ISIS)

Further Reading

Armitage, Amelia, and Sharon Squassoni. 2015. "Nuclear Smuggling: From Moldova to ISIS?" Center for Strategic and International Studies (CSIS). Accessed June 30, 2018. https://www.csis.org/analysis/nuclear-smuggling-moldova-isis.

Bronner, Michael. 2008. "100 Grams (and Counting . . .): Notes from the Nuclear Underworld." Belfer Center for Science and International Affairs, Harvard Kennedy School. Accessed June 5, 2018. https://www.belfercenter.org/sites/default/files/legacy/files/100-Grams-Final-Color.pdf.

CNS Global Incidents and Trafficking Database. "The Nuclear Threat Initiative (NTI)." Accessed June 30, 2018. http://www.nti.org/analysis/reports/cns-global-incidents-and-trafficking-database.

Golovnina, Maria. 2012. "Nuclear Trafficking Getting More Professional: IAEA Chief." *Reuters*, October 17. Accessed July 15, 2018. https://www.reuters.com/article/us-nuclear-security-extremists-idUSBRE89G1AN20121017.

International Atomic Energy Agency. 2007. "Combating Illicit Trafficking in Nuclear and Other Radioactive Material." Accessed June 15, 2018. https://www-pub.iaea.org/mtcd/publications/pdf/pub1309_web.pdf.

Zaitseva, Lyudmila, and Friedrich Steinhäusler. 2014. "Nuclear Trafficking Issues in the Black Sea Region." Non-Proliferation Papers, EU Non-Proliferation Consortium, No. 39, April. Accessed July 13, 2018. https://www.files.ethz.ch/isn/187240/April_2014_39.pdf.

O

Oklahoma City Bombing (1995)

At 9:02 a.m., on April 19, 1995, a massive explosion caused by the detonation of homemade explosives left in a parked truck tore apart the Alfred P. Murrah Federal Building in Oklahoma City, Oklahoma. The final death toll counted 168 people killed in the blast, including 19 children who were being cared for at a daycare center. More than 500 others were injured in the blast, some of them blocks away. The bombing was the worst act of terrorism in U.S. history until the World Trade Center and Pentagon attacks of September 11, 2001. It underscored the vulnerability of the nation to terrorist acts and led to increased attention on the risk of homegrown or domestic terrorism. Following the explosion, a nationwide manhunt was launched to search for the person or persons responsible for the bombing. Two men, Timothy McVeigh, a veteran of the Persian Gulf War, and his army friend Terry Nichols were ultimately charged and convicted.

BACKGROUND

The Oklahoma City bombing is believed to have been carried out in revenge for the 1993 government siege of the Branch Davidian compound near Waco, Texas. The Branch Davidians, a religious sect, was a rather typical doomsday cult that had accumulated a large arsenal at their compound in Waco. The cache of weapons, along with accusations of physical and sexual abuse of children by members of the group, drew the attention of federal authorities. On February 28, 1993, agents from the Bureau of Alcohol, Tobacco, and Firearms (BATF) approached the Davidian compound to arrest its leader, David Koresh. A gun battle ensued, resulting in the deaths of four BATF agents and six Davidians.

The Federal Bureau of Investigation took charge of the situation, and a 51-day siege began. On April 19, 1993, BATF and FBI agents attempted to take the compound using tanks and large quantities of military-grade tear gas. Fires, which independent investigators later determined to have been set by the Davidians, engulfed the compound, and shooting could be heard inside. In the end, 75 people were dead, including 21 children (Haberman 2015). Militia members contended that the deaths of the Branch Davidians in the FBI- and BATF-led assault was a taste of what lay ahead for similar antigovernment dissidents. A growth of the militia movement was sparked, and the bombing of the Murrah building occurred on the second anniversary of the Branch Davidian siege.

THE INVESTIGATION AND TRIAL

In the hours after the bombing, media reports suggested the terrorists were likely Muslim extremists, and in the following days, Muslims across the United States were harassed, even beaten, in retaliation for the bombing (Constantakis 2016). However, less than an hour after the attack, an Oklahoma Highway Patrol officer had stopped and arrested Timothy McVeigh for driving without a license plate. By April 21, 1995, the FBI investigation had identified McVeigh as a prime suspect, and the federal authorities learned that he was already in the custody of the Oklahoma Highway Patrol. The investigation also began focusing on Terry Nichols, who McVeigh first met during their U.S. Army basic training in 1988.

McVeigh and Nichols began planning the bombing of the Murrah building in 1994—having chosen the building as a symbol of their opposition to the federal government. The two worked together to acquire fertilizer, fuel, blasting caps, and other necessary supplies. On April 19, McVeigh parked a rented Ryder truck in front of the Murrah building and walked to his getaway car.

At a trial held in Denver, Colorado, McVeigh was found guilty by a federal jury on counts of murder, conspiracy, and using a weapon of mass destruction. He was sentenced to death on August 14, 1997, and was executed by lethal injection on June 11, 2001. Nichols was found guilty of federal involuntary manslaughter and conspiracy for the deaths of eight federal law enforcement officials. He was sentenced to life imprisonment on June 4, 1998. As of 2018, Nichols remains in federal prison at the super-secure United States Penitentiary ADMAX, in Florence, Colorado. USP ADMAX is an administrative security prison housing the country's most dangerous federal prisoners.

The Murrah building, half-destroyed by the bombing, was demolished in May 1995 and replaced in 2000 (on the fifth anniversary of the bombing) by the Oklahoma City National Memorial and Museum, a unit of the National Park System.

Philip L. Reichel and Steven Strom

See also: McVeigh, Timothy; Nichols, Terry; Terrorism, Domestic

Further Reading

Constantakis, Sara, ed. 2016. "Alfred P. Murrah Federal Building Bombing, 1995." In *World of Forensic Science*, 21–23. Farmington Hills, MI: Gale.

Haberman, Clyde. 2015. "Retro Report: Memories of Waco Siege Continue to Fuel Far-Right Groups." *New York Times*, July 12. https://www.nytimes.com/2015/07/13/us/memories-of-waco-siege-continue-to-fuel-far-right-groups.html.

Hamm, Mark S. 1997. *Apocalypse in Oklahoma: Waco and Ruby Ridge Revenged.* Boston, MA: Northeastern University Press.

Kight, Marsha, ed. 1998. *Forever Changed: Remembering Oklahoma City, April 19, 1995.* New York: Prometheus Books.

Stock, Jennifer, ed. 2014. "The Oklahoma City Bombing Claims 168 Lives." In *Global Events: Milestone Events throughout History*, 429–432. Farmington Hills, MI: Gale.

Wright, Stuart A. 2007. *Patriots, Politics, and the Oklahoma City Bombing.* Cambridge, UK: Cambridge University Press.

Online Child Sexual Abuse

Online child sexual abuse is also described as sexual grooming and includes a series of activities undertaken by an adult to make friends with a child to establish a close emotional relationship with him or her. The ultimate purpose of such action is to reduce the child's resistance to engage in a potential sexual relation. The same method is used to induce child prostitution or to engage a child in pornography (Ost 2009).

Two categories of adults undertake sexual grooming: persons with a sexual dysfunction (pedophiles) and persons who are not interested in having sex with the child but rather intend to use the child to meet the sexual needs of others (recruiters). According to worldwide reports, victims of groomers are most often between the ages of 13 and 17 (Choo 2009).

Oxford Living Dictionaries define grooming as "the action by a paedophile of preparing a child for a meeting, especially via an Internet chat room, with the intention of committing a sexual offence." Terms such as *grooming, online grooming*, and *sexual grooming* are synonymous and refer to the same process of establishing a relationship with a child through the Internet or in person to facilitate either online or offline sexual contact.

The perpetrator attempts to become friends with the child and lures him or her into a closer relationship (eventually sexual). Grooming always involves some form of psychological manipulation. Most often, the groomer misinforms the child about his or her own age and attempts to befriend the child by sharing common interests or empathizing with difficulties the child might be experiencing with family members or friends. In short, grooming "is the act of befriending and influencing a child, and sometimes the child's family as well, for the purpose of preparing the child for sexual activity" (Randhawa and Jacobs 2013).

STAGES OF CHILD GROOMING

The process of a child becoming a victim is gradual. A common approach is for the adult perpetrator to make initial acquaintance with the child, with the content of the first interaction being relatively "innocent." The next steps involve building a relationship with the child and pretending to be his or her friend, often by establishing a rapport with the child, which often includes the groomer referring to his or her similar life experiences. Once the child's trust is gained, the pedophile or recruiter checks whether an adult (parent) can learn about their contact or whether someone oversees the child (Welner 2010).

Once a child becomes emotionally involved with such a stranger as a "friend" from the Internet and the adult knows no one is controlling the child's contacts, the predator attempts to initiate a meeting to have a sexual interaction. If the pedophile or recruiter realizes he or she has moved too fast or the child raises objections, he or she pretends to be understanding and stops the offending activity. Such encounters can end the relationship, and, if not, the predator simply waits for a better opportunity and continues to try to win the child's confidence and trust. Once the relationship becomes stronger, another attempt is made.

Oftentimes, a child can become emotionally dependent on such an adult, and it becomes increasingly difficult for the child to refuse requests for favors. Such illicit requests may include sexually oriented acts, such as showing the child nude pictures, introducing masturbation, or proposing secret meetings. The perpetrator often creates a mysterious or secretive atmosphere, which can make it difficult for the child to discern whether such activities are acceptable or not. To avoid the risk of the child reporting or seeking help from other adults, the perpetrator attempts to develop a bond of secret trust with the child.

According to research studies, a list of common characteristics of children susceptible to grooming may include the following elements:

- Emotional deprivation
- Lack of strong relationships in real life, with both adults and friends
- Rejection by other children
- Low self-esteem and trustfulness
- The desire to be important
- A tendency to keep everything secret
- Naivete and susceptibility to manipulation
- A dysfunctional family (Perry 2008)

SCALE OF THE PROBLEM

The problem of online child sexual abuse is massive and on a scale that is almost impossible to determine, as illustrated by two examples. In 2009, the U.S.-based National Center for Missing and Exploited Children (NCMEC) identified 1,591 suspected IP (Internet protocol) addresses in the United Kingdom, and by 2016, there was a nearly twentyfold increase to 30,661 suspected addresses. In 2018, the British National Crime Agency (NCA) reported that during a weeklong operation, 131 people were arrested on suspicion of online child sex offenses. This was being reported at the same time the U.K. home secretary revealed that at least 80,000 people in the United Kingdom are believed to pose a sexual threat to children online (Gabbatiss 2018).

LEGAL ACTS AND PREVENTION OF SEXUAL GROOMING

International documents provide a solid legal foundation for protection of children from sexual grooming. The three most prominent are the 2000 Optional Protocol on the Sale of Children, Child Prostitution and Child Pornography (attached to the Convention on the Rights of the Child); the Council of Europe's Convention on the Protection of Children against Sexual Exploitation and Sexual Abuse, known also as the Lanzarote Convention (2007); and EU Directive 2011/93/EU on combating sexual abuse and sexual exploitation of children and child pornography (2011).

A legal response to online sexual child abuse must combine provisions determining grooming as a criminal offense as well as other regulations regarding Internet safety, child protection, and care for victims. Legal definitions must cover all forms of grooming, committed both by words as well as physical actions. The construction of the wording of legal statutes of such offenses should also take into account the harm caused to the victim.

Penal law provisions regarding grooming are rarely used, as in most cases the crime is detected only after abuse has taken place. Therefore, it is imperative that effective preventive measures are set in place and widely used (Global Alliance 2015). Among the most important are

- Campaigns to raise public awareness
- Programs to educate parents, teachers, social workers, etc.
- Special training programs for law enforcement
- Information available for the prosecutors and the judiciary

Victims of online sexual abuse often need intensive care, support, and understanding. The effects can be traumatizing, and victims may require some form of professional therapy.

Zbigniew Lasocik

See also: Child Online Protection Act; Child Pornography Prevention Act; Child Protection and Sexual Predator Punishment Act; Child Sexual Abuse Material; Children's Internet Protection Act; Children's Online Privacy Protection Act

Further Reading

Bowcott, Owen. 2018. "Online Child Sex Abuse Referred to Met Increased by 700% since 2014." *The Guardian*, January 22. Accessed January 7, 2019. https://www.theguardian.com/uk-news/2018/jan/22/online-child-sex-abuse-referred-to-met-increased-by-700-since-2014.

Choo, K.-K. R. 2009. *Online Child Grooming: A Literature Review on the Misuse of Social Networking Sites for Grooming Children for Sexual Offences*. Research and Public Policy Series 103. Canberra: Australian Institute of Criminology.

Department of Justice. 2015. *Global Alliance against Child Sexual Abuse Online: 2015 Report*. Accessed January 7, 2019. https://ec.europa.eu/home-affairs/sites/homeaffairs/files/what-we-do/policies/organized-crime-and-human-trafficking/global-alliance-against-child-abuse/docs/global_alliance_2015_report_en.pdf.

Gabbatiss, Josh. 2018. "Over 130 Suspected Child Sex Offenders Arrested in Police Raids." *Independent*. Last updated September 3, 2018. Accessed January 7, 2019. https://www.independent.co.uk/news/uk/crime/police-raids-paedophiles-child-sex-offenders-national-crime-agency-nca-a8519886.html.

Ost, Suzanne. 2009. *Child Pornography and Sexual Grooming: Legal and Societal Responses*. Cambridge, UK: Cambridge University Press.

Perry, Bruce D. 2008. "Child Maltreatment: A Neurodevelopmental Perspective on the Role of Trauma and Neglect in Psychopathology." In *Child and Adolescent Psychopathology*, edited by Theodore P. Beauchaine, Stephen P. Hinshaw, 93–128. New York: Wiley New York.

Randhawa, Trisha, and Scott Jacobs. 2013. *Child Grooming: "Offending All the Way Through from the Start": Exploring the Call for Law Reform*. n.d.: Child Wise.

Accessed January 7, 2019. http://childwise.blob.core.windows.net/assets/uploads/files/Grooming%20-%20Exploring%20the%20call%20for%20law%20reform%20-%20Child%20Wise%20%28Web%29.pdf.

Welner, Michael. 2010. "Child Sexual Abuse: 6 Stages of Grooming." Oprah.com, October 18. http://www.oprah.com/oprahshow/child-sexual-abuse-6-stages-of-grooming/all#ixzz5CHKo6Qa9.

Operation Sunflower

Operation Sunflower was an international effort in November and December 2012 that led by the federal entity Homeland Security Investigations within Immigration and Customs Enforcement (ICE) to identify and hold accountable persons who produce, trade, or possess child pornography. In partnership with other federal, state, and local law enforcement in 47 states and 6 countries, plus the National Center for Missing and Exploited Children's Child Victim Identification Program, 245 persons were arrested, with 222 of these arrests occurring in the United States. The operation's name, "sunflower," refers to the shape of a highway sign that was instrumental in rescuing an 11-year-old girl from an adolescent pedophile a year before the operation.

Operation Sunflower was part of a victim-focused agenda that prioritized identifying the persons in child pornography online; 123 sexually victimized minors were identified across 19 states. Tourist-friendly states with high immigrant populations had more arrests than other states; 37 arrests in California, 29 in Texas, 19 in New York, 17 in Florida (most in the Cocoa Beach and Orlando areas), and 11 arrests in New Mexico. Only 13 of the children who were rescued were outside of the United States. The foreign source countries of child pornography included Ukraine, Russia, and Thailand. In the operation, 44 victims were removed from their abusers with whom they lived, and 79 had been victimized by persons outside of their homes. Fifty-three victims were male, and 70 were female; 24 were adults at the time of identification. Fifteen of the victims were ages 16–17, 38 were ages 13–15, 11 were ages 10–12, 21 were ages 7–9, 9 were ages 4–6, and 5 were less than 3 years old.

After these initial rescues, a Los Angeles woman, Letha Mae Montemayor, was also arrested after several photographs emerged online of her abusing a 13-year-old girl. The woman had been wanted since at least 2007, when photos going back to 2001 (as determined by a wall calendar in some of the images) had been found by immigration authorities in Chicago. Her identification was established after her tattoos were run through a database.

Another female arrested in the operation was Corine Danielle Gillreath (née Motley) of Okaloosa County, Florida. She had made a long video of herself abusing a minor believed to be as young as 4 years old. Danish National Police discovered the video and then notified U.S. law enforcement. Further investigation revealed that Corine and her husband, Brandon C. Gillreath, had actually victimized several children for over a year. She was eventually sentenced to 29 and a half years for her offenses, and he was sentenced to 35 years for his role in the crimes.

The Danish police were also instrumental in the capture of Stephen Keating, of Jesup, Georgia, for pornography in which he sexually abused two girls. Three children were removed from his custody.

Another case was that of Lance Robert Fries, of Tucson, Arizona, who was sentenced to over 24 years for repeatedly sexually abusing a male toddler in a video. Law enforcement had been after him since 2006, when the materials were first discovered. In yet another case, Ann Piper, of Peoria, Illinois, was arrested after child pornography images of her with a girl, discovered in 2011, were matched to her vacation photographs online. After the Minnesota lakeside vacation resort was identified, resort staff were able to identify the woman. Piper was sentenced to 25 years.

The success of Operation Sunflower was largely a matter of cooperation between authorities in determining what minute details in the online materials revealed about the identity of persons in the images and their locations. The image analyses were often with the assistance of software programs and knowledge of general predator profiles. In many cases, the images of perpetrators were publicized on the Internet and social media sites, soliciting the public's help in identifying the predators.

Operation Sunflower was a part of a larger effort called Operation Predator, which continued after Sunflower. Besides tracking child pornography cases, Operation Predator includes arresting those who traffic children for sex or who travel overseas to engage in child sex tourism.

Camille Gibson

See also: Child Online Protection Act; Child Pornography Prevention Act; Child Protection and Sexual Predator Punishment Act; Child Sexual Abuse Material; Human Trafficking; Sex Exploitation; Sex Tourism; Trafficking Victim Identification Tools; U.S. Trafficking Victims Protection Act

Further Reading

Guarino, Mark. 2013. "Child Sex Abuse: Operation Sunflower Highlights New Efforts to Get Predators." *Christian Science Monitor*, January 5. Accessed December 28, 2017. https://www.csmonitor.com/USA/Justice/2013/0105/Child-sex-abuse-Operation-Sunflower-highlights-new-efforts-to-get-predators.

U.S. Department of Homeland Security. 2013. "123 Sexually Exploited Children Identified by HS during 'Operation Sunflower.'" Last modified April 3, 2015. Accessed December 28, 2017. https://www.ice.gov/news/releases/123-sexually-exploited-children-identified-hsi-during-operation-sunflower.

U.S. Immigration and Customs Enforcement. 2012. "Operation Predator—Targeting Child Exploitation and Sexual Crimes." Last modified August 17, 2017. Accessed December 28, 2017. https://www.ice.gov/factsheets/predator.

Organ Trafficking

More than 110,000 people in the United States need a lifesaving organ transplant, but only 30,000–35,000 organ transplants are performed each year. International estimates show there were more than 126,000 organ transplantations worldwide in

2015, an increase of almost 6 percent from 2014 (Global Observatory on Donation and Transplantation 2017). But, as in the United States, the need for healthy organs exceeds the supply (Levitt 2015). The discrepancy between supply and demand creates opportunities for illegal behavior. In this instance, the crime filling the void is the illegal sale or trafficking of organs. "Illegal sale" refers to a person who knowingly acquires, receives, or transfers a human organ in exchange for something of value. A transaction of this type could be between a willing donor and willing recipient, but it would still be illegal in jurisdictions with such laws. Organ trafficking refers to a type of organized crime wherein people are victims of human trafficking for the specific purpose of organ removal and sale. The organs most frequently transplanted are kidney, liver, heart, lungs, pancreas, and small bowel. However, the kidney makes up the majority of the transplantations, followed by the liver.

BACKGROUND

In the 1980s, speculations about organ theft by prostitutes surfaced. News media accounts of prostitutes drugging unsuspecting clients and removing their kidneys created panic among travelers (Emery 2017). There were also reports of the forcible removal of eyes from children that were sold to private eye banks (Columb 2017). Although many of these claims were dismissed as myths, the United Nations is investigating recent reports that the Islamic State of Iraq and Syria (ISIS) may be involved in harvesting organs from slain civilians to finance their terrorist activities (Sanchez 2015).

The limited supply of organs, the willingness of recipients to pay high prices, and the financial desperation of donors created an ideal situation for international organ trafficking syndicates. The terms " 'organ trafficking,' 'illegal organ trade,' 'transplant tourism,' 'organ purchase' and others are often used interchangeably" to identify trafficking a person for removal of organs (UNODC 2015, 5). Organ trafficking is now considered an organized crime, and the participants include recruiters; transporters; doctors, nurses, and other health care professionals; intermediaries; and contractors. The traffickers exploit donors by promising a better economic opportunity for them and their families, and they also exploit recipients who are willing to pay any price to improve their chance of living or making their life better.

The recruiters look for vulnerable people from impoverished neighborhoods, such as migrant workers, the homeless, runaways, and uneducated people. In other situations, organs are taken out of the victims without their knowledge, after stating that they need some medical treatment for an illness. Although some traffickers are part of criminal syndicates, others are legitimate health care professionals, such as doctors, nurses, ambulance drivers, and hospital administrators, who perform legitimate activities while also participating in trafficking activities (UNODC 2018).

When the supply of legal organ donors is less than the demand, recipients travel to other countries to look for a potential donor who would be willing to sell his or her organ. Most of the demand comes from developed countries, and potential recipients often seek an intermediary to find a potential donor from a developing nation (e.g., India, Pakistan, Afghanistan, South Africa, Brazil, and Indonesia). Countries such as China were accused of harvesting organs from deceased prisoners and making them available to hospitals to meet the demand. In 2015, the Chinese government banned the practice of harvesting organs from executed prisoners. The law increased the demand for organs, which precipitated kidnappings and harvesting organs from victims, and there are suspicions that China now claims prisoners are volunteering (PBS News Hour 2017).

In Cairo, Egypt, migrant Sudanese are reported to be heavily involved in the organ trade. Although the government of Eygpt passed legislation in 2010 making it illegal to buy or sell organs (the Transplantation of Human Organs and Tissues Act), the demand for organs continues to rise. Significant cultural resistance to organ donation and the lack of infrastructure to monitor the national organ donation program have put heavy reliance on live donors. Many migrant workers have become live kidney donors. The government does not identify donors as victims, and the donors do not admit to being victims of organ trafficking. "Rather their exploitation is bound up in their migrant status and a lack of opportunities to generate income" (Columb 2017, 1306).

MEDICAL TOURISM

In recent years, there has been an increase in "medical tourism," where patients travel from their home country to another country for medical treatment. In 2005, an estimated 400,000 people (including about 55,000 Americans) were reported to have traveled to Thailand for medical treatment. India, Malaysia, Singapore, and Mexico have also become destinations for medical tourism. Many people go to these countries because they are uninsured or underinsured. There are benefits and disadvantages of medical tourism. For example, patients get affordable treatment, but there are concerns about the quality of care and what happens if there is a medical error. Another concern is what effect it will have on a country's health care industry if people start seeking care outside their home country. Finally, there are concerns about how medical tourism affects the access to health care in the destination country (Cohen 2010).

ETHICAL CONCERNS

Professional, ethical, and legal guidelines govern organ transplantation from deceased donors. Organs from deceased donors occur "after brain death and circulatory death" (UNODC 2015, 7). There are two ways consent is obtained for procuring organs from a deceased donor—explicit and implicit consent. Explicit consent (i.e., an "opt in") is where a donor or his family members make a conscious decision to donate. Implied consent ("opt out") is where a donor does not explicitly refuse to donate. Countries such as Spain, Belgium, and Austria recognize implied or presumed consent, whereas the Netherlands, Germany, the United States, and Switzerland require explicit consent (UNODC 2015).

Live donations, especially of kidneys, have become a critical alternative to deceased organs due to their limited availability. Also, the advancement in transplant technology has improved the safety of live donors. However, in 2010, the World Health Organization provided guidelines stating that a living donor should be related to the recipient genetically, legally, and emotionally (UNODC 2015). There are other international guidelines, such as the Declaration of Istanbul on Organ Trafficking and Transplant Tourism, which is intended to combat unethical practices and offers recommendations for the care of living and deceased donors (Delmonico 2008).

At present, all countries except Iran prohibit harvesting or selling organs illegally. (The organ trade in Iran is, however, regulated by nongovernmental organizations.) Brazil, for example, prohibits selling and soliciting the sale of organs or tissues, and offenders can be punished for up to eight years. The country passed a law in 1998 requiring every citizen to donate organs after death, but only with permission from relatives. In response to increased trafficking in organs, India recently approved new legislation increasing penalties for illegal organ trafficking to up to 10 years in prison and a substantial fine (Carvalho 2011). In 1984, the U.S. Congress passed the National Organ Transplant Act (NOTA), which prohibits the sale of human organs.

Despite national and international efforts to curb illegal organ harvesting and trafficking, the demand for organs is at an all-time high. Lax enforcement of these crimes and the cultural barriers that prevent legal organ donations continue to hinder efforts to curtail the problem. For example, the United States prosecuted the first organ trafficking case in 2011. Levy Izhak Rosenbaum, who claimed to be in the business of matchmaking, was brokering deals involving kidneys from vulnerable people in Israel. He would pay $10,000 per kidney and sell them for $160,000. He was charged with organ trafficking and one count of conspiracy (Porter and Johnson 2009). Unless the most vulnerable population is protected from victimization, the trade in illegal organs will continue.

Sesha Kethineni

See also: Human Trafficking; Organ Trafficking, the Medicus Case of

Further Reading

Carvalho, Nirmala. 2011. "Law against Organ Trafficking Approved." *AsiaNews.it*, August 29. Accessed January 7, 2019. http://www.asianews.it/news-en/Law-against-organ-trafficking-approved-22490.html.

Cohen, Glenn. 2010. "Medical Tourism: The View from Ten Thousand Feet." *Hasting Center Report* 40 (2): 11–12.

Columb, Sean. 2017. "Excavating the Organ Trade: An Empirical Study of Organ Trading Networks in Cairo, Egypt." *British Journal of Criminology* 57: 1301–1321.

Delmonico, Francis L. 2008. "The Development of the Declaration of Istanbul on Organ Trafficking and Transplant Tourism." *Nephrology Dialysis Transplantation* 23: 3381–3382.

Emery, David. 2017. "The Kidney Thieves: An Urban Legend Causes Real World Crisis." *ThoughtCo*, March 18. Accessed January 7, 2019. https://www.thoughtco.com/kidney-thieves-3299488.

Global Observatory on Donation and Transplantation. 2017. *Organ Donation and Transplantation Activities: 2015 Report*. Accessed January 7, 2019. http://www.transplant-observatory.org/download/report-2015-activity.

Levitt, Mairi. 2015. "Could the Organ Shortage Ever Be Met?" *Life Sciences, Society and Policy* 11 (1): 6.

PBS News Hour. 2017. "Has China really stopped obtaining organs from executed prisoners?" Accessed February 15, 2019. https://www.pbs.org/newshour/show/china-still-gathering-organs-executed-prisoners.

Porter, David, and Carla K. Johnson. 2009. "First Case of Organ Trafficking in U.S.: NYC Man Accused of Buying Kidneys Abroad, Selling at Hefty Profit." NBCNews.com, July 24. Accessed January 7, 2019. http://www.nbcnews.com/id/32132371/ns/us_news-crime_and_courts/t/first-case-organ-trafficking-us/#.WvKOT2rwZyw.

Sanchez, Ray. 2015. "United Nations Investigates Claim of ISIS Organ Theft." *CNN*, February 19. Accessed January 7, 2019. https://www.cnn.com/2015/02/18/middleeast/isis-organ-harvesting-claim/index.html.

United Nations Office on Drugs and Crime (UNODC). 2015. *Trafficking in Persons for the Purpose of Organ Removal*. Vienna: UNODC. Accessed January 7, 2019. http://www.unodc.org/documents/human-trafficking/2015/UNODC_Assessment_Toolkit_TIP_for_the_Purpose_of_Organ_Removal.pdf.

United Nations Office on Drugs and Crime (UNODC). 2018. "Organ Trafficking." Accessed January 7, 2019. https://www.unodc.org/unodc/en/organized-crime/intro/emerging-crimes/organ-trafficking.html.

Organ Trafficking, the Medicus Case of

Trade in human organs is a large-scale form of transnational crime that generates between $600 million and $1.2 billion in illicit revenue each year and results in severe health issues for both donors and recipients (Kelly 2013). One of the most recent and best-known cases of illegal organ transplantation is the Medicus case in Pristina, Kosovo. It includes all aspects of illicit organ trade and involved the recruiting of donors from Moldova, Russia, Ukraine, Kazakhstan, and Belarus and recipients primarily from Israel, Turkey, Poland, Canada, and Germany (Salcedo-Albaran and Santos 2017).

HUMAN ORGAN TRAFFICKING

The trafficking of human organs, tissues, and cells involves a variety of illegal activities that usually converge during a transplant surgery. When considered together, organ sales, organ harvesting (removal of organs), and transplant tourism (traveling across state borders to purchase organs) form the basics of transnational crime of organ trade.

There are three primary options for the surgery. The recipient can travel to the surgery location, the donor can travel, or both donor and recipient can travel. Organs that are regularly being traded illegally include the pancreas, liver, lung, kidney, and even heart. Furthermore, not only is organ trade itself a transnational crime, it can also be linked to other transnational criminal networks, including human trafficking—making use of similar resources and routes. Organ trafficking is recognized as the second largest form of transnational crime, and the revenues are extremely high (Kelly 2013).

THE MEDICUS CASE

Kosovan immigration authorities discovered illegal transplantation activities in 2008 after seeing an increased number of patients visiting the Medicus Clinic for heart disease treatment. The immigration authorities became suspicious because heart disease is not a medical condition for which the clinic is especially known. Three of the patients questioned were allowed to enter, but authorities discovered that one of them had donated a kidney in exchange for money. The investigation resulted in the arrests of three men: an Israeli organ trafficking broker, a Turkish organ supplier, and the brother of a recipient of unknown nationality. Additional investigation found that the Medicus Clinic had performed 24 illegal organ transplantations in three years (Salcedo-Albaran and Santos 2017).

Lutfi Dervishi, the owner and director of the Medicus Clinic, started preparing the illegal organ trade in 2005 with his son, Arban Dervishi. They approached a Turkish doctor, Yusuf Somnez, to carry out the illegal surgeries as the lead surgeon. They also hired an anesthesiologist and a broker. Lastly, they approached doctors to set up the network. These doctors carried out all necessary blood tests and scans in the home country so the donors and recipients would only have to travel to Kosovo for the surgery.

Dervishi and his recruited team decided on only trading kidneys and started performing surgeries in 2006. In total, the clinic derived 24 kidneys from international donors and sold them to recipients. It is known that nine recipients paid a total of $700,000 for their kidneys. Despite the large amount of money that recipients paid for their kidneys, donors often received very little to no money for their donated organ. Donors were promised $30,000 by recruiters but would only receive a part of this amount until they had recruited new donors. If the donor declined the recruiting job, he or she was often threatened for weeks. In other cases, the donors were promised the money when they returned to their home countries, but they never saw or heard from the recruiter or clinic again.

Apart from failing to comply with the original financial promises, the Medicus Clinic also spread false information about the surgery, the needed treatment, and the seriousness of the surgery. After just a few days, patients were sent back to their home countries with false information. Donors, who had received limited or incorrect information to encourage them to donate, continued to receive incorrect information after the surgery. This resulted in more complications after returning home. As most donors agreed to the process because of their poor financial status, they did not have good access to health care in their home countries, and this resulted in a higher degree of after-surgery complications. Moreover, recipients were also sent home too soon. They received false information to give to their doctors to lessen the likelihood that the Medicus Clinic's crimes would be discovered (Salcedo-Albaran and Santos 2017).

NATIONAL AND INTERNATIONAL REACTION

Globally, human organ trafficking is seen as a victimless crime. Donors receive remuneration, and in many cases, donors, recipients, and doctors are in their positions voluntarily. However, due to the misinformation, health consequences, and insufficient payments, some argue it is not a victimless crime. In the Medicus case, owner Lutfi Dervishi was sentenced to eight years in prison and an $80,000 fine, and he lost his medical license for two years. His son, Arban, was convicted and sentenced to seven years in prison and a fine of $2,500. The anesthesiologist, Sokol Hajdini, was sentenced to three years in prison, and he lost his license for one year. Lead surgeon Yusuf Somnez and broker Moshe Harel are still fugitives in 2018. Furthermore, father and son Dervishi had to pay $15,000 to all victims as compensation (Salcedo-Albaran and Santos 2017).

With the Medicus Clinic and other internationally placed hospitals carrying out illegal organ transplantations, the international attention on this crime is growing. Several nonbinding documents have been created, such as the World Health Organization's (WHO) guiding principles and the Declaration of Istanbul. This declaration was created in 2008, during the Summit on Organ Trafficking and Transplant Tourism. It defines such issues as organ trade and transplant tourism and provides ethical principles. Even though it is a nonbinding document, it has led to the strengthening of laws in several countries and is endorsed by over 100 countries.

Furthermore, there are some binding documents about organ trafficking, such as the Council of Europe Anti-Trafficking Convention, the UN Trafficking in Persons Protocol, and a study carried out by the United Nations in cooperation with the Council of Europe. In addition, a clause was added to the UN Convention on the Rights of the Child. In addition to fighting the illegal organ trade, national responses consist out of the reduction of the existing organ shortage. When a balance is created between the organ demand and supply, countries hope to reduce the need for recipients to turn to the illegal market (Kelly 2013).

Apart from the direct health consequences for donors and recipients, illegal organ transplantations also affect national health care systems and policies by impeding the local legal organ market. Additionally, it might affect the insurance recommendations and the availability of regular health care and increase the risk of antibiotic resistance due to traveling between hospitals (Kelly 2013). Also, it might discourage donors from altruistic donation because of their fear of exploitation (Hippen 2005).

Puck van Eijk

See also: Organ Trafficking

Further Reading

Columb, S. 2015. "Beneath the Organ Trade: A Critical Analysis of the Organ Trafficking Discourse." *Crime, Law and Social Change* 63 (1–2): 21–47.

Hippen, B. E. 2005. "In Defense of a Regulated Market in Kidneys from Living Vendors." *Journal of Medicine and Philosophy* 30 (6): 593–626.

Kelly, E. 2013. "International Organ Trafficking Crisis: Solutions Addressing the Heart of the Matter." *Boston College Law Review* 54: 1317.

Salcedo-Albarán, E, and D. Santos. 2017. "The 'Medicus Case': Organ Trafficking in Kosovo." *Global Observatory of Transnational Criminal Networks* 14: 6–19.

Shimazono, Y. 2007. "The State of the International Organ Trade: A Provisional Picture Based on Integration of Available Information." *Bulletin of the World Health Organization* 85: 955–962.

Organization for Security and Co-operation in Europe

The Organization for Security and Co-operation in Europe (OSCE), which plays a significant role in combating global crime, is the world's largest regional security organization. The OSCE traces its origin to the early 1990s, when the Conference on Security and Cooperation in Europe (CSCE) was created to serve as a multilateral forum for dialogue and negotiation between East and West. Its name changed to the OSCE in 1994, and as of 2018, OSCE had 57 participating states from Europe, Asia, and North America (OSCE 2018).

In the late 1980s, with the impending collapse of the Soviet Union, it became clear that a new framework for European security was needed. So in November 1990, delegates from 34 countries signed the Charter of Paris for a New Europe, which expanded the organization's mandate and created an institutional framework. Also in Paris, delegates signed the Treaty on Conventional Armed Forces in Europe (CFE), which declared an official end to the Cold War. In July 1992, the organization declared itself the principal European authority regarding security threats in or to Europe and claimed the power to direct the military responses of the European Union, the North Atlantic Treaty Organization, and the Western European Union to such threats.

ORGANIZATIONAL STRUCTURE

The OSCE is an intergovernmental organization with 57 participating states working together as equals in all decision-making bodies. The OSCE Secretariat, located in Vienna, Austria, cooperates with partner countries and organizations on such issues as antiterrorism, border management, policing reform, and other transnational concerns.

Operating as institutions within the OSCE are the Office for Democratic Institutions and Human Rights (promoting democratic development and human rights through election observation and the promotion of tolerance and nondiscrimination), the Representative on Freedom of the Media (providing warning on violations of freedom of expression), and the High Commissioner on National Minorities (seeking resolution of ethnic tensions). Also, the Parliamentary Assembly brings together more than 300 legislators from the parliaments of OSCE participating states to facilitate dialogue and cooperation on the various OSCE initiatives.

In addition to its 57 participating states, OSCE maintains relations with 11 Asian and Mediterranean countries to better address shared security challenges. These "Partners for Co-operation" are kept informed of the full range of OSCE activities, but each group of partners also engages in cooperative endeavors on specific issues. For example, the Mediterranean partners focus on such issues as antiterrorism, border security, tolerance, and nondiscrimination, whereas the Asian partners share experiences on combating human trafficking, responding to transnational threats, and building democratic institutions.

ADDRESSING SECURITY CHALLENGES ACROSS BORDERS

Terrorist attacks in the early 21st century highlighted the new complexity of security issues facing OSCE member states. In December 2001, the organization adopted the Decision on Combating Terrorism and the more detailed Bucharest Plan of Action for Combating Terrorism. A year later, the OSCE Charter on Preventing and Combating Terrorism was adopted. The charter suggested that participating states "reaffirm their commitment to take the measures needed to protect human rights and fundamental freedoms, especially the right to life, of everyone within their jurisdiction against terrorist acts" (OSCE 2002, 1) This new focus also led the OSCE to analyze its effectiveness as an international organization. A seven-member panel was appointed to review the OSCE's work, and in June 2005, it released a report with recommendations for revitalizing the organization and strengthening its effectiveness.

Continuing its attention on security challenges at the broadest level, the OSCE addresses such issues as radicalization and violent extremism, organized crime, cybercrime, trafficking in drugs and weapons, and human trafficking. Specific efforts are conducted through field operations, established at the invitation of a host country, wherein OSCE staff and resources are deployed. The purpose of field operations, which are currently found in Southeastern Europe, Eastern Europe, the South Caucasus, and Central Asia, is to assist host countries in implementing concrete projects that respond to the country's needs in a way that fosters partnerships with local and national authorities, agencies and institutions, civil society, and international organizations.

As one example, OSCE takes a victim-centric, human rights approach to combat human trafficking. Understanding that all OSCE participating states are affected by human trafficking—as a country of origin, transport, or destination—the post of special representative and coordinator for combating trafficking in human beings was established in 2003. Through the Office of the Special Representative, OSCE has developed an action plan to combat human trafficking that includes core recommendations for action at the national level to address the "3 Ps" of prevention, prosecution, and protection. In addition to those concerns of awareness raising and addressing root causes of human trafficking (prevention), investigation and cooperation with international law enforcement (prosecution), and addressing victims' rights (protection), a fourth "P," partnership, was added in 2013 to highlight the need for cooperation with international organizations to include public institutions and the private sector.

Philip L. Reichel

See also: Human Trafficking; Intergovernmental Organization; Terrorism, Domestic; Terrorism, International

Further Reading

Organization for Security and Co-Operation in Europe. 2000. "OSCE Charter on Preventing and Combatting Terrorism." Last Modified December 7, 2002. Accessed February 11, 2019. https://www.osce.org/odihr/16609?download=true

Organization for Security and Co-Operation in Europe. 2003. "OSCE Action Plan to Combat Trafficking in Human Beings." Last Modified July 24, 2003. Accessed January 7, 2019. https://www.osce.org/actionplan.

Organization for Security and Co-Operation in Europe. 2018. "Factsheet: What Is the OSCE?" Last Modified September 21, 2018. Accessed January 7, 2019. https://www.osce.org/whatistheosce/factsheet.

Organized Crime

Organized crime—a self-perpetuating enterprise that profits from public demand for illegal products or services—originated within the immigrant populations pouring into the United States during the 19th century. The word *mafia* found its way into the American lexicon in 1891. While investigating the murder of an Italian immigrant, David C. Hennessy, the police superintendent of New Orleans, stumbled across a secret association that had established a stranglehold on the waterfront. No boat could unload its cargo until "dues" had been paid to the *La Cosa Nostra* (roughly translated as "this thing of ours"). Anyone who refused to "do business" with this group was found brutally slaughtered and floating facedown in one of the murky canals. This was law enforcement's first encounter with the Mafia, but it would not be the last.

RISE OF ORGANIZED CRIME

Large immigrant populations entered the United States in the 19th century. During this time, young Irish, Italians, and Jews, among others, often found themselves targets of anti-immigrant prejudice. Not only were they denied employment and housing, but they often found themselves in physical danger. Seeking safety in numbers and the opportunity to realize the American dream, they formed gangs that profited from extorting "protection" money from legitimate businesses. As the organizations grew in power and sophistication, they evolved into tightly knit "families" of criminals.

Organized crime took off during Prohibition, the period between 1920 and 1933, when liquor sales were outlawed in the United States. The efforts of federal officials to enforce the highly unpopular Volstead Act generated a spectacular surge in illegal liquor sales (bootlegging) and propelled the rise of such gangsters as Al Capone.

It was also during Prohibition that organized crime first gained a reputation for bloodthirsty violence. In an attempt to monopolize the marketplace, organized criminals waged war on each other in broad daylight and on crowded city streets. The 1927 St. Valentine's Day Massacre, when Capone's men executed seven associates of his major rival, Bugsy Moran, shocked the nation into a public outcry against gangsters.

MOBSTERS AND THE LAW

American mobsters realized that their underworld depended on the complicity of an upper world of corrupt politicos, police, and prosecutors. No gangland leader could operate for long in a vacuum. As a result, many were forced to find a way to merge with the machinery of power, often through bribery (if intimidation or blackmail failed). Ultimately, public revulsion, initially ignited by the 1930 Wickersham Commission investigation (a federal committee tasked with auditing law enforcement), led to a crackdown on law enforcement corruption. However, mobsters remained in business after the 1933 repeal of Prohibition by shifting to prostitution, labor racketeering, gambling, and narcotics. During the early 1940s, when wartime rationing made consumer goods scarce, crime families quietly engaged in black market capitalism.

In 1950, *Life* magazine reported that crooked cops, sheriffs, and prosecuting attorneys were accepting bribes from mobsters. That same year, a Senate investigating committee chaired by Senator Estes Kefauver turned the spotlight on organized crime's involvement in interstate gambling. The televised hearings introduced 20–30 million Americans to a century of organized crime and allowed viewers to gawk at such infamous figures as Joe Adonis, Albert Anastasia, and Meyer Lansky. The committee and the TV audience sat transfixed as they became acquainted with an invisible government of crime families who apportioned territorial boundaries, allocated profits, and punished those who violated syndicate decisions.

By the 1960s, the U.S. government was determined to break up organized crime, which, until then, had been dealt with by local police, who were easily corrupted. The Federal Bureau of Investigation (FBI) was put in charge and armed with the Racketeer Influenced and Corrupt Organizations Act (RICO), passed in 1962 and enacted in 1970, which is still used today. RICO was designed to end "racketeering" by the Mob, an ongoing pattern of criminal activities that included extortion, bribery, loan-sharking, murder, attempted murder, illegal drug sales, prostitution, gambling, and theft rings. RICO, which put such gangland notables as John Gotti behind bars, is the U.S. government's biggest bludgeon in the battle against organized crime.

RISE OF TRANSNATIONAL CRIME

In the 1980s, law enforcement seriously crippled American underworld activities—due in large part to a relaxation of constitutional safeguards for criminals. The 1990s, however, witnessed a global transformation in political and economic life as well as the ascendance of revolutionary technologies that were now in the hands of ordinary civilians. In the post–Cold War world, such technologies as the Internet and advances in telecommunications and transportation erased once-secure borders in most regions of the world.

As trade and travel restrictions between countries disappear and world economies become increasingly interdependent, so do international crime syndicates. In the clamor attributable to globalization, cyberspace, and the information superhighway, organized crime continues to defy definition. What has become increasingly clear is that today's groups do not conform to the traditional paradigm exemplified by the Italian Mafia. Rather, organized crime groups have evolved into amorphous enterprises, shifting from one activity to another, depending on geopolitics and changing markets—both legitimate and illegitimate in nature.

Beverly Merrill Kelley and Mitchel P. Roth

See also: Camorra; Chinese Gangland Crime; Japanese Yakuza; 'Ndrangheta; Racketeer Influenced and Corrupt Organizations Act (RICO); Racketeering; Russian Organized Crime; Solntsevskaya Bratva; Transnational, Global, and International Crime; Yamaguchi-Gumi

Further Reading

Abadinsky, Howard. 2010. *Organized Crime.* 9th ed. Belmont, CA: Wadsworth Publishing.

Dickie, John. 2004. *Cosa Nostra: A History of the Sicilian Mafia.* New York: Palgrave Macmillan.

Lunde, Paul. 2004. *Organized Crime: An Inside Guide to the World's Most Successful Industry.* New York: DK Adult.

Lyman, Michael D., and Gary W. Potter. 2003. *Organized Crime.* Englewood Cliffs, NJ: Prentice Hall.

Robinson, Jeffrey. 2000. *The Merger: The Conglomeration of International Organized Crime.* New York: Overlook Hardcover.

P

Panama Papers

The Panama Papers are 11.5 million documents that were leaked from the database of the Panama-based offshore law firm Mossack Fonseca. The documents, which include such items as financial spreadsheets, corporate records, and e-mails, represent the largest leak of private information in history. The files were obtained by the German newspaper *Süddeutsche Zeitung* from an anonymous source, possibly through the hacking of Mossack Fonseca's servers. The newspaper first reported the documents in April 2016. The files were then shared with the International Consortium of Investigative Journalists, which, in turn, shared them with other media outlets in more than 70 countries.

The publication of the files resulted in wide-ranging political and business scandals in numerous countries. The documents revealed how government and business leaders and other wealthy, powerful people used secret offshore tax havens and shell companies to hide their wealth. The use of these tax havens and shell companies was legal in some cases and illegal in other cases. The illegal cases involved such crimes as money laundering, fraudulent ownership records to evade taxes or sanctions, looting of national treasuries, and scamming of investors. Moreover, records indicated that some of this "dark money" was used to finance drug trafficking, terrorism, and other illegal activities.

The revelations led to the ousters of some government leaders, numerous prosecutions of public and private figures, and the closure of tens of thousands of companies. In addition, new laws were passed in some countries to require greater transparency regarding offshore companies and tax shelters.

POWERFUL PEOPLE AROUND THE WORLD

The Panama Papers implicated about 140 politicians in more than 50 countries in financial schemes involving Mossack Fonseca, including more than a dozen current or former heads of state and government. Also implicated were thousands of business executives as well as some celebrities, such as sports stars. More than 14,000 banks, law firms, and other middlemen entities worked with Mossack Fonseca to help these clients establish and manage sham companies, foundations, and trusts. The activities described in the files occurred during a period ranging from 1977 through 2015.

Among the European government leaders caught up in the vast scandal was Iceland's prime minister, Sigmundur David Gunnlaugsson. He resigned in April 2016 after it was revealed that he had an undeclared interest in his wife's offshore company. The president and former prime minister of Ukraine, the former prime minister of Georgia, and the prime minister of Australia were also tied to business deals with Mossack Fonseca. Relatives and friends of leaders were named in the scandal, including the late father of British prime minister David Cameron, the sister of former king Juan Carlos of Spain, and several close associates of Russian leader Vladimir Putin.

Pakistan's prime minister, Nawaz Sharif, and three of his children were linked to illegal activities. In July 2017, the Pakistani Supreme Court removed Shariff from office, and he was indicted and banned from politics for life. The former prime minister of Mongolia was also named in the scandal, as were the brother-in-law of Chinese president Xi Jinping and the daughter of Chinese premier Li Peng.

Eastern leaders were linked to questionable activities involving Mossack Fonseca. These included the king of Saudi Arabia, the president of the United Arab Emirates, the vice president of Iraq, the former prime minister of Jordan, and the former prime minister and ruling emir of Qatar. Also named in the scandal were the son of former Egyptian president Hosni Mubarak and cousins of Syrian president Bashar Assad. African nations were touched by the scandal, too. Among those named in the Panama Papers were the former president of Sudan and the nephew of the South African president.

Several political leaders in Brazil were implicated in the Panama Papers scandal as well as another scandal related to the state oil company, Petrobras. In this mix of corruption, Eduardo Cunha was suspended as the speaker of the lower chamber of Congress in May 2016. Brazilian president Dilma Rousseff was impeached and removed from office in August 2016. Argentine president Mauricio Macri was acquitted of money laundering charges in August 2017, but he remained under investigation for tax evasion.

In the United States, there were more than 2,000 wealthy clients of Mossack Fonseca, including bankers, real estate developers, celebrities, and others. Mossack Fonseca managed complex arrangements of shell companies and foundations for these clients, moving money through banks in different countries to avoid taxes and financial disclosures. This hidden money was believed to represent lost revenue to the U.S. government of as much as $70 billion per year.

Also implicated in questionable dealings with Mossack Fonseca were prominent figures with the Fédération Internationale de Football Association (FIFA), the international governing organization for soccer. The Panama Papers further revealed the names of entities illegally doing business with Mexican drug cartels, Hezbollah and other terrorist organizations, and nations under international sanctions, including Iran and North Korea.

FALLOUT FROM REVELATIONS

The revelations from the Panama Papers led to more than 150 investigations into corporations and individuals in more than 70 countries, including numerous criminal prosecutions. Moreover, government legislators and regulators in certain countries took action to address the problems highlighted by the revelations. In

Panama, authorities closed down more than 275,000 offshore companies and required the sharing of more financial information with other governments. Regulations enacted in the United Kingdom in 2018 required the names of the true owners of offshore companies and tax shelters to be divulged. As a result of the disclosures, investigations, and audits related to the Panama Papers, government tax authorities around the world recovered more than $500 million by the beginning of 2018.

In February 2017, Jurgen Mossack and Ramon Fonseca—the founders of Mossack Fonseca—were arrested by Panamanian police on money laundering charges. Mossack Fonseca went out of business in March 2018. In August 2018, the International Consortium of Investigative Journalists reported a second leak of documents from Mossack Fonseca that exposed more details about illicit campaign funding and about the activities of the world's rich, famous, and nefarious.

A. J. Smuskiewicz

See also: Bribery; Corruption

Further Reading

Bernstein, Jack. 2017. *Secrecy World: Inside the Panama Papers Investigation of Illicit Money Networks and the Global Elite.* New York: Henry Holt and Co.

Fitzgibbon, Will. 2018. "Second Panama Papers Leak: Findings from around the World." International Consortium of Investigative Journalists, August 16. Accessed January 8, 2019. https://www.icij.org/investigations/panama-papers/second-panama-papers-leak-findings-from-around-the-world.

"The Panama Papers: Leaders, Criminals, Celebrities." n.d. International Consortium of Investigative Journalists. Accessed September 14, 2018. https://www.icij.org/investigations/panama-papers.

Paris and *Charlie Hebdo* Terrorist Attacks (2015)

In January 2015, two gunmen opened fire in the offices of the satirical French magazine *Charlie Hebdo*. In the same day, another gunman shot a police officer and bystander in another area of Paris. Then, in November, terrorists carried out a series of highly coordinated, near simultaneous attacks aimed at multiple civilian targets in and around Paris on Friday, November 13. Gunmen and suicide bombers, armed with Kalashnikov-type machine guns, hand grenades, and suicide vests, attacked six targets, causing the deaths of 130 people and leading to over 413 injuries. Seven of the attackers were also killed. The attacks, claimed by the Islamic State of Iraq and Syria (ISIS), counts as the deadliest attacks that have taken place on French soil since World War II and the deadliest in Europe since the 2004 train bombings in Madrid, Spain.

CHARLIE HEBDO ATTACK

On January 7, 2015, at 11:30 a.m. local time, two brothers, Chérif and Saïd Kouachi, armed with Kalashnikov-type machine guns, made their way into the offices of the satirical magazine *Charlie Hebdo*. Upon entering, they shot a maintenance worker who was sitting by the reception desk. To access the newsroom of the magazine, the assailants threatened one of the staff members to enter the keypad's code. They stormed in during the magazine's editorial meeting, attended by 15 people, and killed 8 of the magazine's journalists/cartoonists, a police bodyguard, and a visitor. Witnesses heard the attackers scream "We have avenged the Prophet Muhammad" and "God is Great" in Arabic while they were calling out the names of the journalists they murdered ("Charlie Hebdo Attack" 2015). They then fled, and during their escape, they killed a police officer. A massive manhunt commenced.

The following day, while police searched for the *Charlie Hebdo* attackers, another gunman opened fire with a machine gun and pistol in the southern Parisian suburb of Montrouge. The assailant, Amedy Coulibaly, killed a police officer and injured a bystander before fleeing the scene.

On January 9, the Kouachi brothers hijacked a car in the town of Montagny Sainte Felicite, about 30 miles northeast of Paris. Police pursued the brothers in a high-speed chase, during which Said Kouachi was wounded in the neck by gunfire. The chase ended as the brothers hid in a printworks in Dammartin-en-Goele, 22 miles from Paris. For eight hours, the brothers hid in the business, which was occupied at the time by owner Michel Castalano and a graphic designer, Lilian Lepere. The brothers later emerged from the printworks, firing at police officers and injuring two; police shot and killed both Kouachi brothers.

That same day, Coulibaly had taken several people hostage in a kosher supermarket at Porte de Vincennes, in eastern Paris. Coulibaly demanded the release of the Kouachi brothers and threatened to kill hostages if the demand was not met. Minutes after the Kouachi brothers were killed in Dammartin-en-Goele, French authorities stormed the supermarket. Reports indicated that "Coulibaly had just knelt for evening prayers when elite commandos stormed the supermarket, shooting the gunman dead and freeing 15 hostages from the store" ("Charlie Hebdo Attack" 2015). They found the bodies of four other hostages.

In response to these attacks, France raised its security level to the highest state and deployed soldiers in Paris to monitor the transport system, media offices, places of worship, and the Eiffel Tower. Massive protests in solidarity with *Charlie Hebdo* were held on the evening of the attacks, and the slogan "Je suis Charlie" (I am Charlie) became a worldwide sign of solidarity against the attacks. The magazine would not much later sell a record publication of nearly 8 million copies, much more than the regular 35,000 copies. In addition, a number of mosques around France were attacked in right-wing violence.

NOVEMBER ATTACKS

Ten months later, a group of terrorists carried out coordinated attacks at multiple locations in Paris. The first attack took place at the French national stadium, Stade de France, in Saint-Denis, where a friendly soccer match was taking place between France and Germany. Three suicide bombers, Bilal Hadfi and two other individuals whose identities cannot be verified but are believed to be Iraqis ("Paris Attacks" 2016), attempted to inflict as many casualties as possible. Around 9:20 p.m., the first suicide bomber attempted to enter the stadium but was discovered during a routine security check. The attacker then stepped back and detonated, killing himself and a bystander. Two other suicide bombers detonated themselves 10 to 23 minutes after the initial bombing, respectively, in the perimeter of the stadium without killing anyone but themselves (De la Hamaide 2015).

The second attack occurred in the 10th district of Paris, around 9:25 p.m. At the crossroads of Rue Bichat and Rue Alibert, two gunmen, Abdelhamid Abaaoud, the group's ringleader, and a man who the police believe to be Chakib Akrouh, opened fire at unsuspecting patrons sitting at the terraces of Le Carillon bar and Le Petit Cambodge restaurant, which are located on opposite sides of the street. The shootout resulted in 15 deaths and 10 injuries (De la Hamaide 2015). The assailants fled the scene some 10 seconds after launching their attack.

A third attack took place at 9:32 p.m., in the 11th district, at the intersection of Rue Fontaine au Roi and Rue Faubourg du Temple. Two gunmen opened fire at people in front of a bar called A La Bonne Bière and a pizzeria called La Casa Nostra. This attack killed five and wounded eight ("Paris Attacks" 2015).

Some four minutes later, the fourth attack and second deadliest took place in Rue de Charonne, also in the 11th district, on the terrace of restaurant La Belle Equipe. Abaaoud and Akrouh, who had earlier attacked Le Carillon bar and Le Petit Cambodge restaurant, killed 19 people and left 9 severely injured.

Again, four minutes later, at 9:40 p.m., a suicide bomber, Brahim Abdeslam, blew himself up inside of Le Comptoir Voltaire restaurant on boulevard Voltaire, injuring one person severely (De la Hamaide 2015).

The deadliest attack occurred at the Bataclan concert hall at 9:40 p.m., during a performance by the Eagles of Death Metal rock group. Three gunmen wearing suicide vests stormed the hall where 1,500 people were attending the sold-out concert. The assailants, Omar Ismail Mostefai, Samy Animour, and Foued Mohamed-Aggad, immediately began shooting indiscriminately at the crowd while shouting Arabic phrases such as "God is great" and blaming President Francois Hollande for intervening in Syria (De la Hamaide 2015). The attack and siege of the Bataclan ended shortly after midnight when elite security forces stormed the concert hall. Police shot one of the gunmen, after which the remaining two detonated their suicide vests ("Paris Attacks" 2015). The attackers killed 89 concertgoers and severely wounded 99 others.

AFTERMATH AND RESPONSE

On November 14, a day after the attack, ISIS claimed responsibility for the attacks. Not much later, France conducted the heaviest air raids thus far on ISIS targets in the then ISIS-controlled city of Raqqa, Syria. In the meantime, French authorities determined that seven of nine Paris attackers had been killed.

President Hollande announced three days of national mourning and declared war on ISIS. Furthermore, he declared a state of emergency shortly after the attacks, adding sweeping new powers for the state to take measures against ISIS. The French police started combing operations across Paris, and tactical police units conducted some 168 raids across the country (*Financial Times* Reporters 2015). This led to many arrests and seizures of weapons and ammunition.

On November 18, police forces identified the terrorists' ringleader, Abaaoud, to be sheltering in an apartment in Saint Denis, a northern suburb of Paris. He was located in the presence of another man by shadowing Abaaoud's cousin, Hasna Aitboulahcen. The suspects resisted when the police tried to arrest them, eventually leading to a five-hour long shootout in which the police fired over 5,000 bullets and many grenades were thrown ("Paris Attacks" 2016). Abdelhamid Abaaoud, Chakib Akrouh, and Hasna Aitboulahcen were killed. Seven police officers were wounded.

In November 2016, a last accomplice, Salah Abdeslam, who had helped facilitate the attacks, was arrested in Brussels. In 2018, he was convicted in Belgium and sentenced to 20 years in prison for terror-related attempt to murder. A separate trial is expected to take place in 2019 in Paris regarding the attacks there.

Wessel Groot

See also: Islamic State of Iraq and Syria (ISIS); Terrorism, International

Further Reading

Callimachi, Rukmini, and Andrew Higgins. 2015. "Video Shows a Paris Gunman Declaring His Loyalty to the Islamic State." *New York Times*, January 11. Accessed June 20, 2018. https://www.nytimes.com/2015/01/12/world/europe/amedy-coulibaly-video-islamic-state.html?mtrref=www.google.nl&assetType=nyt_now.

"*Charlie Hebdo* Attack: Three Days of Terror." 2015. *BBC*, January 14. Accessed June 25, 2018. www.bbc.com/news/world-europe-30708237.

De la Hamaide, Sybille. 2015. "Timeline of Paris Attacks According to Public Prosecutor." *Reuters*, November 14. Accessed January 8, 2019. https://www.reuters.com/article/us-france-shooting-timeline/timeline-of-paris-attacks-according-to-public-prosecutor-idUSKCN0T31BS20151114#h8KRqimXftutLeR3.97.

Financial Times Reporters. 2015. "Paris Attacks: Hollande Says France Is at 'War' with Isis." *Financial Times*, November 16. Accessed January 8, 2019. https://www.ft.com/content/560804dc-8c34-11e5-a549-b89a1dfede9b.

"Paris Attacks: What Happened on the Night." 2015. *BBC*, November 9. Accessed May 22, 2018. http://www.bbc.com/news/world-europe-34818994.

"Paris Attacks: Who Were the Attackers?" 2016. *BBC*, April 27. Accessed May 23, 2018. http://www.bbc.com/news/world-europe-34832512.

Sawer, Patrick, David Barrett, and Lexi Finnigan. 2015. "Paris Terror Attack: Diners Gunned Down in Their Favourite Restaurants." *The Telegraph*, November 14. Accessed May 23, 2018. https://www.telegraph.co.uk/news/11996468/Paris-terror-attack-Diners-gunned-down-in-their-favourite-restaurants.html.

Shoichet, Catherine E., and Josh Levs. 2015. "Al Qaeda Branch Claims *Charlie Hebdo* Attack Was Years in the Making." *CNN*, January 21. Accessed June 20, 2018. https://edition.cnn.com/2015/01/14/europe/charlie-hebdo-france-attacks.

Phishing

Phishing is a form of identity theft used by scammers to obtain personal information from unsuspecting Internet users. Scammers use fraudulent e-mail or Web sites that appear authentic to unsuspecting users and lure them into divulging their personal information (Russell 2004, 44). Phishing is not a new phenomenon;

for decades, malicious hackers had utilized phones to scam consumers and called it "social engineering." What is new about the scam is the delivery style, which now involves spam and fake Web pages. In 1998, Congress passed the Identity Theft and Assumption Deterrence Act, which made identity theft a federal crime with a penalty of up to 15 years in prison. Despite the law, identity theft has continued to flourish (Hong 2012, 76). To support the theory that identity theft is not new, the director of the Federal Trade Commission's (FTC) Bureau of Consumers Protection, J. Howard Beales, indicated in an interview in 2006 that identity theft accounts for 43 percent of the calls the agency receives. The FTC report of September 2003 indicated that about 9.9 million U.S. residents had been victims of identity theft the previous year (Russell 2004, 44).

PHASES OF PHISHING

Scammers target device users and not the system, as all it takes is for the unsuspecting user to click and open a link, regardless of how well an individual or institution has secured the system with firewalls, encryption software, and the like. There are three phases of phishing: (1) receipt of the phish, (2) disclosure of information, and (3) acquisition of sensitive information by the scammer. A key component of phishing is to convey a sense of urgency that requires immediate action. Common examples are a request from a loved one supposedly in dire stress and in need of urgent financial assistance; a complaint of multiple failed attempts at logging into an account and the need to verify personal details for security; a notice that one's device is at risk and there is an urgent need for protection; or, better yet, taking advantage of a distressed situation and disguising it as part of a relief effort.

The more sophisticated method is the selective target of victims (spear phishing). Scammers use contextual information targeting specific individuals based on specific information. For instance, a scammer may use a company e-mail address and send an e-mail purportedly from the CEO of a business demanding the employee wire money to a specific account. Alternatively, the scam might be in form of a notice of an urgent meeting with important documents to review prior to the meeting, causing an unsuspecting employee to open the file. Scammers are using spear phishing more because consumers who are less likely to be victims of phishing scams are more likely to fall for it due to the context (Hong 2012, 76).

The second step is creating the fake Web site. Using free Web space, scammers impersonate legitimate sites with slight variations and register the new domain. The difference might be as minor as using two *V*s, which at a glance might appear to be a *W* to an unsuspecting user who lacks understanding of the URLs. Once an unsuspecting consumer falls victim to the phishing scam and divulges their information, they are at the mercy of the scammers.

Scammers monetize the stolen information either directly or indirectly. For instance, if the stolen information is account credentials, they can make transfers directly. If its phishing on a social network, scammers utilize the stolen information indirectly by compromising an individual's account to spread malware by sending e-mails to contacts requiring them to visit an infected site. The more recent and sophisticated approach in monetizing stolen information is to sell the information through underground network to avoid detection (Hong 2012, 76–80).

COUNTER PHISHING MEASURES

Phishing is a scam that costs organizations, institutions, businesses, and individuals billions of dollars each year. Research suggests a number of reasons why consumers are vulnerable to phishing: greed, gullibility, but most of all ignorance. In an investigation of why people fall victims to phishing, Dhamija, Tygar, and Hearest (2006) found that 90 percent of participants were fooled by phishing sites due to their content and professionalism. In a complementary study, Downs, Holbrook, and Cranor (2006) found that participants used incorrect heuristic in making decisions on responding to such e-mails. For instance, a spear phishing e-mail targets selective individuals, and those individuals might believe they are only verifying information their company already has and so there is no harm. In their study of demographic and phishing susceptibility, Sheng, Holbrook, Kumaraguru, and Cranor found younger people (ages 18–25) and women to be more susceptibility to phishing than men (2010). Young people were more susceptible than women for a number of reasons: less aversion to risk, less experience with the online environment, and less exposure to training materials (Arachchilage and Love 2014).

Countermeasures from a user's perspective can be addressed using three strategies: using filters or blockages that prevent the user from being exposed to the threats; providing better interface that offers additional security or makes threats more obvious; and using a proactive approach by training users to identify potential threats and avoiding them (Hong 2012). As phishing targets users, training users makes logical sense, but training does not guarantee total protection. In 2010, Kumaraguru, Sheng, Aquist, and Cranor found that simply e-mailing anti-phishing information to users was not effective, as most people ignored it because they believed they already knew how to protect themselves. A more effective approach was the embedded training approach, typically in a classroom setting, which taught people in the specific context in which they might be attacked and provided them with the opportunity to test what they have learned (Hong 2012, 80).

Phishing is a prevalent and ever-growing threat, with irreparable damage to a user's credit, loss of intellectual property, financial loss, and compromise of security—the list is endless. While no one is immune, users can reduce their vulnerability by being vigilant. Upon receipt of an e-mail that requires verification of personal information, simple steps such as calling the institution to verify the authenticity of the e-mail, checking the legitimacy of the Web site, checking for obvious spelling mistakes, and carefully examining the URL link can help reduce susceptibility to phishing.

Dorothy Kersha-Aerga

See also: Cyberattack; Cybercrime; Identity Theft and Assumption Deterrence Act of 1998; Identity-Related Crimes; Smishing; Vishing

Further Reading

Arachchilage, Nalin Asanka Gamagedara, and Steve Love. 2014. "Security Awareness of Computer Users: A Phishing Threat Avoidance Perspective." *Computers in Human Behavior* 38: 304–312.

Dhamija, Rachna, J. D. Tygar, and Marti Hearst. 2006. "Why Phishing Works." In *Proceedings of the SIGCHI Conference on Human Factors in Computing Systems*, edited by Rebecca Grinter, Thomas Rodden, Paul Aoki, Ed Cutrell, Robin Jeffries, and Gary Olson, 581–590. New York: ACM Press.

Downs, Julie S., Mandy B. Holbrook, and Lorrie F. Cranor. 2006. "Decision Strategies and Susceptibility to Phishing." In *Proceedings of the SOUPS Symposium on Usable Privacy and Security*, Pittsburgh, July 12–14. New York: ACM Press.

Hong, Jason. 2012. "The State of Phishing Attacks." *Communications of the ACM* 55 (1): 74–81.

Kumaraguru, Ponnurangam, Steve Sheng, Alessandro Acquisti, Lorrie Faith Cranor, and Jason Hong. 2010. "Teaching Johnny Not to Fall for Phish." *ACM Transactions on Internet Technology* 10 (2): 1–31.

Russell, Kay. 2004. "Phishing." *Computerworld*, Last Modified January 19. Accessed February 11, 2019. https://www.computerworld.com/article/2575156/security0/phishing.html.

Sheng, Steve, Mandy Holbrook, Ponnurangam Kumaraguru, Lorrie Cranor, and Julie Downs. 2010. "Who Falls for Phish?: A Demographic Analysis of Phishing Susceptibility and Effectiveness of Interventions." In *28th International Conference on Human Factors in Computing Systems*, Atlanta, GA, April 10–15.

Phreaking

Phreaking is the practice of the experimentation, exploration, and study of telecommunication systems (Enzweiler 2014). In the 1950s and 1960s, phone phreaking developed out of curiosity, and the exploration and manipulation of these systems were motivated by the mere fascination of exploring the bounds of the new communication systems. In the 1970s, phone phreaking reached its peak, developing into a subset of computer hacking that involved the hacking of telephone systems to make fraudulent phone calls (Lee et al. 1999). No one knows for sure how many people utilized the vulnerabilities in the telephone system to make these free calls, as records were only kept of billable calls, something the phreaks were able to avoid.

Though phreaks viewed their actions as innocent exploration, telephone companies such as American Telephone and Telegraph (AT&T) viewed their actions as criminal and sought to have them prosecuted. At the time, no law made phreaking illegal, though Title 18, Section 1343, of the U.S. Code, "Fraud by Wire," made it illegal to transmit over a wire and across state lines "writings, signs, signals, pictures, or sounds" for the purpose of fraud (Lapsley 2013). The Justice Department determined this law was meant to protect individuals from others seeking to defraud them, not to protect the telephone company itself. AT&T resorted to stern talks with the young phreaks they caught and prosecution of those using phreaking "boxes" to participate in organized crime. Phone phreaking declined in the

1980s and 1990s before becoming nearly impossible after phone companies switched from multifrequency to digital call switching in the 1990s.

DEVICES USED

Phreaks used a series of color-coded "boxes" to perform specific tasks. Some of the most common boxes are referred to by color: blue, red, and black. Blue boxes provide complete control by convincing the telephone system that the user is a telephone operator. Blue boxes simulated the tones that the system used, such as single-frequency (SF) and multifrequency (MF) tones, as well as the 2,600 Hz tone used to signal when a telephone had been answered.

A red box allowed the person to make free calls on a pay phone by imitating the tones made when coins have been deposited in the phone. A black box, on the other hand, allows free calls from a home phone. Also called a "mute," the black box was built from a 10k ohm resistor. Black boxes prevented phone company equipment from detecting that the user has answered an incoming phone call by blocking the 2,600 Hz signal used to signify that the phone had been answered. Black boxes were created so the system would not realize that the user had answered the phone, and the person who called the user's number would not be billed for the call. This solved the issue of being able to make free calls but not receive them from others.

PROMINENT PHREAKS

Bill Acker, who was born blind in New York, took an interest in technology from a very young age. His interests stemmed from playing with radio and television signals, and they grew to include the telephone system. At age 14, Acker took it upon himself to figure out the location of every area code. In doing so, he discovered the differences in tones throughout the system. Using a toy flute called a Tonette, Acker was able to disconnect a call that was in progress and later discovered how to give the system a new number to dial by whistling. This realization led him to create his first blue box.

Steve Jobs and Steve Wozniak discovered phreaking and blue boxes from an article in 1971, when Wozniak was 20 and Jobs was 17. The duo immediately learned everything they possibly could about phreaking and built their first blue box. Wozniak, with previous knowledge of electrical circuits, developed a digital blue box that he and Jobs eventually began selling. Both Wozniak and the late Jobs contributed the development of Apple Computer, Inc., to their partnership designing and selling blue boxes.

From a small town in northern California, John Draper served four years of active duty as a technician in the U.S. Air Force. At age 26, he received a wrong call that ended up exposing him to the world of phreaking. Intrigued, Draper sought to learn more about the inner operation of the phone system and how it could be manipulated. His use of a Cap'n Crunch cereal whistle to replicate the important 2,600 Hz tone earned him the nickname "Captain Crunch." Draper became an icon among phreaks and was arrested in 1972 for the use of his blue box. In 2017, Draper was accused of sexual misconduct at various hacking conventions between 1999 and 2007 and is banned from attending future conferences.

Kristina Nicole Van Wyk

See also: Hackers; Phishing; Smishing; Vishing

Further Reading

Enzweiler, Matthew James. 2014. "Swatting Political Discourse: A Domestic Terrorism Threat." *Notre Dame Law Review* 90 (5): 2001–2038.

Lapsley, Phillip. 2013. *Exploding the Phone.* New York: Grove Press.

Lee, Michael, Sean Pak, David Lee, and Aaron Schapiro. 1999. "Electronic Commerce, Hackers, and the Search for Legitimacy: A Regulatory Proposal." *Berkeley Technology Law Journal* 14 (2): 839–886.

Linder, Courtney. 2017. "Hacker Culture Traces Back to an Illegal Device Made by Apple's Co-Founder. Now It's for Sale." *Pittsburgh Post-Gazette,* December 4. Accessed January 8, 2019. http://www.post-gazette.com/business/tech-news/2017/12/04/Phreaking-Hacker-culture-Blue-Box-Steve-Jobs-Steve-Wozniak-Apple-phone/stories/201712060002.

Williams, Hayley. 2015. "The Hacker Who Inspired Apple: John 'Captain Crunch' Draper." Life Hacker, November 17. Accessed January 8, 2019. https://www.lifehacker.com.au/2015/11/the-hacker-who-inspired-apple-john-captain-crunch-draper.

Poaching

Poaching is the illegal hunting of animals through violation of government-established regulations. Rudimentarily, hunting is regulated via permits and the authorization of the location, type of weapon, and species of animal that can be killed. Poaching is when someone goes outside these requirements. Though poaching is known for being unlawful, it has implications in every facet of society, including having economic and environmental consequences. Due to the congruence of these aspects, poaching has become an international concern that has sprouted several international projects that focus on law enforcement and conservation.

HISTORY

The origins of poaching span back to the Late Middle Ages, when hunting was reserved for landowners and nobility. Punishment was applied to those who went outside these regulations. Thus, the reservation of hunting became a motivation and a catalyst for poaching to be a means of rebelling against poverty. The definition of *poaching* has since expanded to include any illegal hunting of animals, without limitations to societal standing.

Though poaching occurs on every continent, legislation varies, thus, deregulating the punishment of offenders. Even within the United States, poaching legislation varies by state (Shadow 2008). In addition to formal mechanisms of control, a grassroots movement has been prominent in recent decades. Multiple nonprofit organizations, supplemented with support from citizens, have formed to both raise awareness and actively help the animals being poached. This shift in activism shows the increasing responsibility citizens are taking on. Such efforts, both informal and formal, have extended past national borders to become a globalized phenomenon.

TYPES OF POACHERS

Poaching is characterized by a positive feedback loop that accompanies the illicit sector of wildlife trade. The closer a species is to extinction, the greater in value their parts are worth, thus creating a positive relationship that enables poaching. This, in conjunction with the increase in legislation, has created an inverse effect by making both wildlife poaching and wildlife trafficking more lucrative. Though there are different categories of poachers, all types of poaching affects this.

Poachers do not fit in a singular group or fit a certain profile. The majority of poachers illegally hunt for monetary gain, and subcategories of this type include commercial poachers, insurgent militias, corrupt government officials, and criminal syndicates. Commercial poachers hunt wildlife to sell the meat at markets. Rebel militias poach as a source of income and predominantly hunt elephant and rhino populations. Corrupt officials accept bribery from poachers and partake in wildlife trafficking to supplement their income. This bribery is predominately committed by criminal organizations. These syndicates connect poachers and buyers, both internationally and at all levels of government. Contrary to the majority, subsistence poachers only illegally hunt in an effort to have food. Unlike big-game hunters, these poachers coexist with wildlife and only kill as a means of survival (Poaching Facts n.d.).

EFFECTS OF POACHING

The effects of poaching have regulatory, criminal, economic, environmental, and international consequences. Poaching violates government regulations, and if it is carried into the realm of wildlife trafficking, it has criminal implications. Though poaching is known for its unlawful behavior, it also has significant economic and environmental implications. Poaching hinders a country's tourism industry and sustainable trade, affecting the overall economic status of the country. It is this aspect of sustainability that is the most critical aspect that characterizes poaching. Due to poaching, the sustainability threshold of various species is affected, and populations are in a decline. This is especially the case when specific sexes are targeted by poachers. This targeting causes a shortage in males and, consequently, a shortage in genetic variation (CITES 2016). In addition, the effects of this are seen throughout the animal kingdom, not just in the most notable species, such as big cats, elephants, and rhinoceros. Thus, the effects of poaching can be seen on any continent and with the majority of wildlife. It is this aspect, in conjunction with violating international treaties, that makes it a global concern.

GLOBAL ATTEMPTS TO COMBAT POACHING

The militarization of wildlife trade has led to more substantive governmental means of control, including international programs. The Convention on International Trade in Endangered Species of Wild Fauna and Flora (CITES) allied 179 countries, standardized regulation, and organized means of increased communication between countries. Such effort is highlighted with the International Consortium on Combating Wildlife Crime (ICCWC), a multidepartmental force established with the intent to increase law enforcement and prosecution. ICCWC is composed of CITES Secretariat, INTERPOL, the United Nations Office on Drugs and Crime (UNODC), the World Bank, and the World Customs Organization (WCO) (USFWS n.d.).

Specific programs created to target poaching include conservation patrols. These patrols fight poaching by providing regional training workshops, increasing fines and jail time, building private-sector partnerships, and creating campaigns aimed at reducing the market. A part of these patrols includes the Spatial Monitoring and Reporting Tool (SMART), a program that provides near real-time data to rangers, allowing them to mobilize to those areas more effectively (USAID and CARPE n.d.).

These specific programs, along with standardizing regulation, allow for a globalized and significant effort to reduce poaching and increase the sustainability of species. Efforts to stop poaching and raise awareness lie on both a citizen and governmental level as well as on national and global scales. The increase in recognition has created a positive feedback loop with increased regulation, creating a solid backing aimed at stopping poaching.

Christina Lynn Richardson

See also: Convention on International Trade in Endangered Species of Wild Fauna and Flora; International Consortium on Combating Wildlife Crime; UN Global Programme for Combating Wildlife and Forest Crime; Wildlife and Forest Crime; World Wildlife Crime Report

Further Reading

CITES. 2016. "African Elephants Still in Decline due to High Levels of Poaching." March 3. Accessed January 8, 2019. https://www.cites.org/eng/news/pr/african_elephants_still_in_decline_due_to_high_levels_of_poaching_03032016.

Poaching Facts. n.d. "Faces of the Poachers Overview." Poaching Facts: Truth from the Front-Line. Accessed January 8, 2019. http://www.poachingfacts.com/faces-of-the-poachers.

Shadow, Simon. 2008. "How Poaching Works." HowStuffWorks, December 9. Accessed January 8, 2019. https://adventure.howstuffworks.com/outdoor-activities/hunting/traditional-methods/poaching1.htm.

United States Agency for International Development (USAID) and Central Africa Regional Program for the Environment (CARPE). n.d. *Getting SMART about Combating Wildlife Trafficking.* Accessed February 11, 2019. https://carpe.umd.edu/sites/default/files/documentsarchive/USAID_SMART.pdf

U.S. Fish and Wildlife Service (USFWS). n.d. "Illegal Wildlife Trade." Accessed January 8, 2019. https://www.fws.gov/international/travel-and-trade/illegal-wildlife-trade.html.

Polaris Project

The Polaris Project was founded in 2002 and is a nonprofit, nongovernmental organization (NGO) with the mission of combating modern-day slavery and human trafficking. Since 2014, the organization is known simply as Polaris. Polaris is one of the largest anti-trafficking organizations in the United States and Japan and currently has local projects in Washington, D.C., Colorado, New Jersey, and Tokyo. The goal of the organization is to take a comprehensive approach to combating human trafficking by conducting research, helping identify victims, and providing an array of services to victims. Polaris also provides training and technical assistance through the National Training and Technical Assistance Program (NTTAP) and operates the National Human Trafficking Resource Center (NHTRC). Polaris advocates for anti-trafficking legislation, both at the state and federal levels, as well as grassroots movement and local community involvement (Polaris 2019b).

HUMAN TRAFFICKING AND MODERN-DAY SLAVERY

Polaris' mission is to spread awareness that slavery is not a thing of the past by focusing on human trafficking issues throughout the world. Trafficking is a multibillion-dollar illegal trade that traps people in sex slavery and forced labor. Traffickers use violence, threats, deception, debt bondage, and other manipulative tactics to force people to engage in commercial sex, forced labor, or other means of slavery.

Two pieces of legislation have been significant in combating human trafficking in the United States and global world. The United Nations Protocol to Prevent, Suppress, and Punish Trafficking in Persons (UN Human Rights 2000, Article 3), commonly referred to as the Palermo Protocol, is the voluntary international law that lays the foundation for nations to develop their own laws. That same year, the United States developed federal legislation, the Trafficking Victims Protection Act (TVPA), that is aimed to address both labor and sex trafficking specific to the United States (Sections 8a and 8b).

HISTORY

The Polaris Project, named for the North Star, was started in 2002 by Kathern Chon and Derek Ellerman. "Polaris" is meant to symbolize when slaves in the United States were guided to freedom in the North in the 19th century through what is known today as the Underground Railroad. During their senior year at Brown University, a newspaper reported on a brothel located near the college apartments and detailed horrific conditions and abuse that was occurring. This inspired Chon and Ellerman to create a nonprofit organization aimed at combating human trafficking and modern-day slavery. Together they developed a business plan for an Internet Web site that would offer immediate and practical help to victims of human trafficking and submitted that plan to Brown University's annual entrepreneurship competition. Their second place prize ($12,500) allowed them to immediately relocate to Washington, D.C., and launch Polaris Project, which is still housed in Washington, D.C.

PRIMARY GOALS AND VALUES

Polaris aims to fight underlying causes of trafficking and create long-term solutions for victims, communities, and the world. They do this by providing an effective and immediate response to victims of human trafficking, enabling stakeholders and communities to address and prevent human trafficking, and using targeted campaigns to disrupt the business of human trafficking. The values underlying those efforts include working with humility and a spirit of service, with their work being grounded in victims' and survivors' experiences (Polaris 2019a).

PROGRAMS

Polaris has established direct outreach and victim identification, including multilingual and global crisis hotlines; provided nationally renowned sources of information on trafficking; and offered services to victims, including transitional housing for victims (Jacobson 2006). Perhaps most notably, Polaris operates the National Human Trafficking Resource Center (NHTRC), which serves as the central hotline on human trafficking for the United States. The primary goal of NHTRC is to improve responses across the country to protect victims. The hotline is toll-free, available to answer calls from anywhere in the country, and is available 24-hours a day, 7 days a week, every day of the year. The NHTRC hotline handles calls from all regions of the United States from a wide range of callers, including, but not limited to, potential trafficking victims, community members, law enforcement, medical professionals, legal professionals, service providers, researchers, students, and policy makers.

In addition to NHTRC, Polaris operates BeFree Textline as a service to survivors to receive help and ensure their safety. Polaris also offers advisory services that provide recommendations and solutions to support individuals and institutions in the public and private sectors working to combat human trafficking based upon research (Polaris 2019c).

POLICY AND LEGISLATION

Perhaps what makes Polaris unique in its approach to protecting victims is the organization's work to ensure that the U.S. government prioritizes efforts to eradicate all forms of human trafficking, both nationally and internationally. Their public policy focus "drives legal and regulatory changes that enable the United States and international governments to better protect victim populations, reduce worker vulnerability, increase support to survivors and increase human trafficking investigations" (Polaris 2019b). Polaris focuses on legislative changes at various levels to ensure protection and progress.

Polaris works closely with the government and various agencies to ensure support and inform policy and legislation. Additionally, Polaris shares the development of data standards and data-sharing practices and protection. This is seen in the various global hotlines operated as a form of multinational collaboration to provide services to governments and law enforcement to eradicate flows of trafficking that cross borders. Lastly, Polaris is often seen as an excellent source of policy expertise, often because of their use of data to find out where and how traffickers operate (Polaris 2019c).

Shanell Sanchez

See also: Human Trafficking; UN Protocol to Prevent, Suppress, and Punish Trafficking in Persons, Especially Women and Children; U.S. Trafficking Victims Protection Act

Further Reading

Jacobson, Rebecca. 2006. "Two Alums Fight Modern-Day Slavery: Polaris Project Identifies Trafficking Victims and Seeks Policy Reform." *Brown Daily Herald*, March 7. Accessed January 8, 2019. http://www.browndailyherald.com/2006/03/07/two-alums-fight-modernday-slavery.

Nichols, Andrea. 2016. *Sex Trafficking in the United States: Theory, Research, Policy, and Practice*. New York: Colombia University Press.

Polaris. 2019a. "Our Values." Accessed February 11, 2019. https://polarisproject.org/about/our-values

Polaris. 2019b. "Policy & Legislation." Accessed February 11, 2019. https://polarisproject.org/policy-legislation.

Polaris. 2019c. "Resources." Accessed February 11, 2019. https://polarisproject.org/resources.

UN Human Rights. 2000. *Protocol to Prevent, Suppress, and Punish Trafficking in Persons*. Accessed January 8, 2019. http://www.ohchr.org/EN/ProfessionalInterest/Pages/ProtocolTraffickingInPersons.aspx.

Poulsen, Kevin (1965–)

Kevin Poulsen is a hacker who built his reputation as a black hat hacker who notoriously breached telephone communication lines to win different radio stations' giveaways and contests Now, however, he is a well-respected cybersecurity journalist for *Wired* magazine. During his mischievous years, Poulsen used his hacking skills to win over $20,000 and a Porsche 944 S2 Cabriolet. These exploits resulted in an investigation by the Federal Bureau of Investigation (FBI). Due to the investigation, Poulson went on the run. The case aired on NBC's *Unsolved Mysteries*, and Poulsen was later arrested, tried, and convicted of espionage. He was sentenced to over 50 months in prison; at the time, this was the longest sentence a person had served in prison for computer hacking. Along with the sentence, he was ordered to pay $56,000 in restitution to the companies he had breached.

POULSEN'S CASE

Kevin Poulsen had been on the run for months by the time NBC aired an episode of *Unsolved Mysteries* that covered his case. Poulsen found a telephone number for the ARPANET computer network at the Pentagon. Using this information, Poulsen used his modem to connect to the military research center at the University of California, Berkeley. He guessed passwords until he successfully entered the classified military network using the password "UCB." After Berkeley administrators detected an intrusion, an investigation was opened.

Investigators were able to find Poulsen easily, as he had used his real name while on the network. On September 22, 1983, the Los Angeles district attorney obtained a search warrant for Poulsen's computer and seized it. Poulsen was still a minor, 17 years old, so police officials did not arrest him and, instead, informed him to stop hacking. After a months-long pause, Poulsen returned to hacking by logging into the classified network.

Poulsen decided that continued hacking could be educational but that he needed to be smarter about it. He rented a storage unit to hide his stolen telephone equipment. After months of unpaid rent, the unit was opened to remove the things inside. Workers found the large amount of stolen telephone equipment and contacted the local police department. During the resulting search, detectives found Poulsen's name on documents and obtained a search warrant for his house.

The search of Poulsen's house revealed a complete wiretapping enterprise in one of his bedrooms. Poulsen possessed equipment that allowed him to both enter federal computer databases and listen to phone conversations. The local police contacted the FBI to help determine which systems were hacked and what information was stolen. Investigators ultimately charged Poulsen and two cohorts with 19 counts of piracy, hacking, and theft of property.

MYSPACE INVESTIGATION

Upon Poulsen's release from prison, he used his skills to catch convicted sex offenders who preyed on underage victims via the social networking site MySpace. According to an article written by Poulsen (2006), a registered sex offender named Andrew Lubrano, with three prior sexual offense convictions, created a MySpace account and began adding teenagers to his friends list. Lubrano made sexual advances toward the underaged teens that accepted his friend request.

To find predators like Lubrano, Kevin Poulsen wrote a script that sought the names of convicted sex offenders on MySpace. Poulsen found 744 confirmed sex offenders, 492 convicted of sex crimes against children. Lubrano's activities were detected by Poulsen, and he notified the police of a possible sexual recidivist on MySpace's social media site. The police department opened an investigation into Lubrano's sexual advances toward underage children, which resulted in Lubrano's arrest and charges of endangering the welfare of a child. In 2017, the U.S. Supreme Court unanimously overturned North Carolina's ban on sex offenders using social media platforms in *Packingham v. North Carolina*, 582 U.S.

KEVIN POULSEN TODAY

Today, Kevin Poulsen is an editor at *Wired* magazine, an industry-leading publication with numerous awards. He also worked with Aaron Swartz to create a program that allows for private and personal communication between journalists and inside sources. Allowing for private communication between the two has become essential over the past decade. He is also the author of *Kingpin: How One Hacker Took Over the Billion-Dollar Cybercrime Underground.* The book is a biography of Max Butler ("Max Vision"), who is most well-known for stealing the information of over 2 million credit cards users. Butler started off as a "white hat" hacker hired by companies to penetrate their security lines. After years of hacking, his expertise gave him the ability to hack into major banks throughout the United States (Burrough 2011). Though Kevin Poulsen is considered an old-school hacker, he will be forever known as one of the best cybercriminals ever to enter the Internet.

Stephen Komisarjevsky

See also: Cybercrime; Hackers; Mitnick, Kevin; Morris, Robert Tappin, Jr.

Further Reading

"About the Author: Kingpin: How One Hacker Took Over the Billion-Dollar Cybercrime Underground." KINGPIN How One Hacker Took Over the Billion Dollar Cybercrime Underground. Accessed January 8, 2019. https://www.kingpin.cc/about.

Burrough, Bryan. 2011. "Behind a Coup of Cybercrime." *New York Times*, March 19. Accessed January 8, 2019. http://www.nytimes.com/2011/03/20/business/20shelves.html?_r=0.

Markoff, John. 1992. "Hacker Indicted on Spy Charges." *New York Times*, December 7. Accessed January 8, 2019. http://www.nytimes.com/1992/12/08/us/hacker-indicted-on-spy-charges.html.

NBC. 1990. *Unsolved Mysteries: Kevin Poulsen*, October 10.

Poulsen, Kevin. 2006. "MySpace Predator Caught by Code." Wired, October 16. Accessed January 8, 2019. https://www.wired.com/2006/10/myspace-predator-caught-by-code.

Project VIC

Project VIC provides information to investigators, victim identification specialists, application developers, scientists, and strategic partners dedicated to developing and delivering the newest technologies and victim-centric methods of investigation. In championing a new approach to child exploitation and the human trafficking industry, Project VIC provides law enforcement agencies worldwide with technology that enables the rescue of child victims and the apprehension of offenders. Project VIC views child sexual abuse as a global problem that requires global strategies (Project VIC 2019b).

Project VIC improved and standardized resources available to law enforcement when reviewing images of child sexual exploitation to save victims and prosecute offenders. Project VIC partnered with the Organization for the Advancement of Structured Information Standards (OASIS), who developed technology to get streamlined worldwide to better fight child sexual exploitation and trafficking. OASIS ensures providers can use technology to simplify information sharing. The primary goals of Project VIC are to help identify new abuse victims abuse, secure crime scenes, locate perpetrators, and assist law enforcement in rescuing victims and suspects. Project VIC works with law enforcement agencies across 40 countries.

HISTORY

With the 1990s Internet expansion, the proliferation of online child pornography created unique challenges for law enforcement. Since individual offenders have extensive collections, terabytes or petabytes of data, it is difficult for law enforcement to sift through, thus leaving victims undetected. Project VIC's philosophy, "Victims First: No Child Left Behind," is reinforced by the goal to develop an efficient technological system to share information and filter images (Project VIC 2019a).

PROJECT VIC CLOUD

Project VIC approached Internet child sexual exploitation in a unique way. First, they recognized and encouraged discussion at a global level and offered their technological platform to over 40 countries by creating a cloud. Second, they compiled all existing online child abuse stills and videos into a single repository referred to as the Project VIC data model, Video Image Classification Standard, or VICS (Brown, Oldenburg, and Cole 2018). Each video has a unique identifier, referred to as a "hash value," which allows investigators to quickly rule images out of their searches (Magnet Forensics 2018). Project VIC also proposed the creation of an "image hash cloud," which will be shared globally in hopes of saving victims quicker and earlier. Lastly, they created a "master image list," which contains the identifiers of highly vetted and popular images of child sexual exploitation that are frequently updated and expanded by law enforcement.

PHOTO DNA

In the mid-2000s, Microsoft developed photo DNA, which compiles a digital signature of images known as a *digital fingerprint*. This fingerprint will be matched against a more extensive database of known child pornography images, which will minimize the time law enforcement officers have to spend sifting through images to determine danger. Microsoft made this service free in their attempt to protect children from online victimization (Project VIC 2019c).

GLOBAL IMPACTS

It can be challenging for countries to determine whether a child is being sexually assaulted or it is a simulated encounter. In 2018, Project VIC launched the Global Alerts System, which is an international system designed to help in cases where the victim is difficult to identify or where investigators are trying to determine if there is other material that might lead to identification of a victim. It is through efforts such as these that Project VIC works with law enforcement and other partners around the world to rescue child victims (Brown, Oldenburg, and Cole 2018).

Shanell Sanchez and Hena Mustafa

See also: Child Sexual Abuse Material; Sex Exploitation

Further Reading

Brown, Richard, Eric Oldenburg, and Jim Cole. 2018. "Project VIC: Helping to Identify and Rescue Children from Sexual Exploitation." Police Chief online. Last updated June 6, 2018. Accessed February 11, 2019. http://www.policechiefmagazine.org/project-vic.

Magnet Forensics. 2014. "Using Common Hashing Algorithms to Identify and Categorize Pictures." February 5. Accessed January 10, 2018. https://www.magnetforensics.com/computer-forensics/using-hashing-algorithms-to-identify-and-categorize-pictures.

"Microsoft and National Center for Missing & Exploited Children Push for Action to Fight Child Pornography." 2009. Microsoft, December 15. Accessed January 14, 2018. https://news.microsoft.com/2009/12/15/microsoft-and-national-center-for-missing-exploited-children-push-for-action-to-fight-child-pornography.

"Microsoft Releases Tool to Spot Abuse Images." 2015. *BBC*, July 17. Accessed January 10, 2018. http://www.bbc.com/news/technology-3356798. https://www.bbc.com/news/technology-33567981

Project VIC. 2019a. "About Us." Accessed February 11, 2019. http://projectvic.org/about-2/.

Project VIC. 2019b. "Law Enforcement Agencies Worldwide Use the Technology in Project VIC's Ecosystem." Accessed February 11, 2019. http://projectvic.org/.

Project VIC. 2019c. "PhotoDNA." Accessed February 11, 2019. http://projectvic.org/technology/photodna/.

PROTECT Act

In 2003, the U.S. Congress passed the PROTECT Act, which stands for Prosecutorial Remedies and Other Tools to End the Exploitation of Children Today Act (18 U.S.C. § 2252), in an effort to prevent child abduction and the sexual exploitation of children. The PROTECT Act had three broad goals: to expand previous offenses that can be prosecuted for sexual exploitation of children and enhance sentences, to provide more resources to prosecute offenders, and to provide support for public outreach. The PROTECT Act was a direct response to previous acts attempting to criminalize online virtual child pornography that were found unconstitutional. In 2008, the U.S. Supreme Court sided in favor of the PROTECT Act in *United States v. Williams* (553 US 285). The court deemed the law constitutional, effectively allowing for the elimination of the "real" children requirement in online child pornography.

HISTORY

The Internet poses unique challenges for regulation due to the anonymity, availability and the affordability of the Web. The federal effort to protect minors online began with the passage of the Protection of Children against Sexual Exploitation Act of 1977 and continued throughout the 2000s. The PROTECT Act was a direct response to the 2002 ruling by the Supreme Court (*Ashcroft v. Free Speech Coalition*), which held the overbroad definition of child pornography was unconstitutional in two provisions of the Child Pornography Prevention Act of 1996 (CPPA).

The First Amendment to the U.S. Constitution provides that "Congress shall make no law . . . abridging the freedom of speech." However, some categories of speech may be regulated and restricted despite the protections of the First Amendment, such as obscenity (*Miller v. California*) and child pornography (*New York v. Ferber*). Then in *Ashcroft v. Free Speech Coalition*, the Supreme Court found the overbroad definition of virtual child pornography unconstitutional, which led Congress to pass the PROTECT Act of 2003.

The PROTECT Act revised the definition of child pornography to include digital images that are indistinguishable of a minor engaging in sexually explicit conduct (Dugan 2004). This did not include any depictions that could infringe on artistic creations, such as drawings, cartoons, sculptures, or paintings depicting minors. The act made it illegal to make computer-generated images or digitally altered photos, often referred to as *virtual child pornography* (18 U.S.C. 2252A).

TITLE I: SANCTIONS AND OFFENSES

Title I of the PROTECT Act focused on enhancing sentences for current crimes that sexually exploit minors or involve child abductions. The PROTECT Act established a get-tough approach that implemented a two-strikes law for repeat sexual offenders that required a mandatory sentence of life imprisonment. Furthermore, mandatory minimums were extended to several crimes involving sexual exploitation of a minor and stricter penalties for sexual abuse and kidnapping. Specifically, Title I required mandatory supervised release terms for sex offense cases that involved a minor. Additionally, first-degree murder could be given for child abuse and child torture murders.

The PROTECT Act also strengthened penalties for sex tourism, both nationally and internationally, especially for Americans that traveled with the intent to engage in illicit sexual conduct with children. The PROTECT Act also allowed for attempt liability for international parental kidnapping. Lastly, Title I provided funds for a pilot program that would create a national criminal history background checks for child safety.

TITLE II: INVESTIGATIONS AND PROSECUTIONS

The PROTECT Act provided more discretionary tools to investigate and prosecute the sexual exploitation of children and child abduction. It expanded communication for sex crime investigations and eliminated the statute of limitations in place for child abductions and sex crimes. The act also mandated there would not be pretrial release for anyone charged with the rape or kidnapping of a child, ultimately allowing for constant supervision of offenders. Lastly, *Suzanne's Law* was created, which provides there will be no waiting period before an investigation is initiated by law enforcement of a person under the age of 21, and the National Crime Information Center of the Department of Justice is notified immediately if someone goes missing.

TITLE III: PUBLIC OUTREACH

Title III was directed at public outreach to prevent child abductions and sexual exploitations of children. Most notable for public outreach are the funds allocated toward implementing Amber Alerts in all states, including training, with minimum standards and expectations for reporting, and the creation of a national coordination network. The second area of public outreach was to provide increased financial support, forensic and investigative support, and the creation of a cyber tip line for the National Center of Missing & Exploited Children. Lastly, funds and training were provided for Sex Offender Apprehension Programs and procedures for missing children in public buildings (Public Law No: 108-21).

The PROTECT Act responded to the U.S. Supreme Court's concerns in previous legislation and, in 2008, was deemed constitutional (*United States v. Williams*) and allowed for the inclusion of virtual child pornography to be excluded from First Amendment protections.

Shanell Sanchez

See also: Child Online Prevention Act; Child Protection and Sexual Predator Punishment Act; Children's Internet Protection Act

Further Reading

Dugan, Kate. 2004. "Regulating What's Not Real: Federal Regulation in the Aftermath of *Ashcroft v. Free Speech Coalition.*" *St. Louis University Law Journal* 48 (1063): 1090–1099.

Greenhouse, Linda. 2002. "Justices Give Reprieve to an Internet Pornography Statute." *New York Times*, May 14. Accessed January 8, 2019. http://www.nytimes.com/2002/05/14/us/justices-give-reprieve-to-an-internet-pornography-statute.html.

Kornegay, James. 2006. "Protecting Our Children and the Constitution: An Analysis of the 'Virtual' Child Pornography Provisions of the Protect Act of 2003." *College of William & Mary Law Review* 47: 2129.

Spinello, Richard. 2013. *Cyberethics: Morality and Law in Cyberspace*. 5th ed. Burlington: Jones and Bartlett.

R

Racketeer Influenced and Corrupt Organizations Act (RICO)

The Racketeer Influenced and Corrupt Organizations Act (RICO) is a U.S. federal law implemented to target organized and white-collar crimes. Encompassed in the Organized Crime Control Act—a congressional act signed into law by President Richard Nixon on October 15, 1970—RICO calls for the prosecution of, and possible civil penalties for, racketeering activity that is performed in conjunction with an ongoing criminal enterprise. To achieve a criminal conviction under the RICO statute, the state is tasked with establishing that a defendant was associated with, or employed by, an enterprise—any group with associated members striving to achieve a common purpose, provided that their relationship lasts long enough to pursue that purpose—and that that enterprise affected interstate or foreign commerce (U.S. DOJ 2016). Furthermore, the state is charged with establishing that the defendant engaged in a pattern of racketeering activity or a collection of unlawful debt. Finally, the state must establish that the defendant conducted, or participated in, at least two acts of racketeering activity within 10 years of each other.

HISTORY

In the early 1950s, Tennessee senator Estes Kefauver chaired a special committee—the Special Senate Committee to Investigate Organized Crime in Interstate Commerce—of the U.S. Senate that investigated organized crime in the United States. Following Senate Resolution 202, the special committee concluded that organized crime was a palpable threat to the United States' economy and security. This effort, in conjunction with the creation of the American Bar Association's Commission on Organized Crime, as well as the President's Commission on Law Enforcement and the Administration of Justice final report, led to the passage of the Organized Crime Control Act of 1970. Through the U.S. Senate Government Operations Committee, advisor George Robert Blakey drafted the act, and chairman John Little McClellan sponsored the act. On October 15, 1970, President Nixon signed the act into law. Since 1972, the RICO statute, which is conveyed in Title IX of the Organized Crime Control Act, has been adopted by 33 states, the Territory of the United States Virgin Islands, and the Commonwealth of Puerto Rico.

CRIMINAL RICO

Under the RICO statute, racketeering activities include a long list of both state and federal offenses, with the repeated commission of these offenses establishing the basis for a RICO claim. Racketeering activities include state offenses involving murder, robbery, kidnapping, arson, bribery, extortion, dealing in obscene matter, gambling, or dealing in a controlled substance or listed chemical. These offenses must be chargeable under state law as well as be punishable by imprisonment for greater than one year. Racketeering activities also include over 100 federal offenses, with terrorism, counterfeiting, fraud, human trafficking, narcotics violations, interstate transportation of stolen property, and certain immigration offenses constituting some of these offenses. Additionally, under the RICO statute, the collection of unlawful debt includes any debt incurred or contracted in an illegal gambling activity or business as well as any debt incurred in connection with the business of lending money. A criminal RICO conviction is punishable by a fine of $25,000 or less, imprisonment of 20 years or less, or both (Legal Information Institute. n.d.). A criminal RICO conviction can also result in the defendant forfeiting property to the state (Blakey and Gettings 1980).

CIVIL RICO

Civil RICO is the process of the state or any person injured at the hands of the RICO enterprise bringing a civil suit in federal court against the RICO offender. Under Civil RICO statutes, a successful civil suit of a RICO defendant would result in the defendant being awarded threefold the sustained damages as well as the cost of the suit, which includes a reasonable attorney's fee (Legal Information Institute. n.d.).

Jessie L. Slepicka

See also: Organized Crime; Racketeering

Further Reading

Blakey, Robert, and Brian Gettings. 1980. "Racketeer Influenced and Corrupt Organizations (RICO): Basic Concepts—Criminal and Civil Remedies." *Temple Law Quarterly* 53: 1009–1048.

Floyd, John E. 2012. "Introduction: RICO State by State: A Guide to Litigation under the State Racketeering Statutes, Second Edition." Accessed June 8, 2018. https://www.americanbar.org/groups/gpsolo/publications/gpsolo_ereport/2012/november_2012/introduction_rico_state_by_state.html.

Legal Information Institute. n.d. "18 U.S. Code Chapter 96—Racketeer Influenced and Corrupt Organizations." Accessed June 8, 2018. https://www.law.cornell.edu/uscode/text/18/part-I/chapter-96.

U.S. Department of Justice. 2016. "Criminal RICO-18 U.S.C. §§1961-1968: A Manual for Federal Prosecutors." Accessed June 8, 2018. https://www.justice.gov/usam/file/870856/download.

U.S. Department of Justice. n.d. "Offices of the United States Attorneys: 109. RICO Charges." Accessed June 8, 2018. https://www.justice.gov/usam/criminal-resource-manual-109-rico-charges.

U.S. Senate. n.d. "Special Committee on Organized Crime in Interstate Commerce." Accessed June 8, 2018. https://www.senate.gov/artandhistory/history/common/investigations/Kefauver.htm.

Racketeering

Racketeering refers to criminal involvement in the legal economy through domination of certain territories or economic sectors by organized crime groups. It is a loose term that implies any dishonest or fraudulent activity, usually perpetrated by members of organized crime to extract profit. The definition of racketeering encompasses a lengthy list of felonies, all of which are part of criminal infiltration in legitimate business, such as provision of illegal goods or services, protection racket, extortion, money laundering, illegal gambling, loan-sharking, obstruction of justice, and bribery. Racketeering also involves a collusive relationship between businessmen, state officials, and criminal groups.

ORIGINS OF THE TERM

The term *racketeering* comes from *racket*, a loud noise or disturbance. In the 19th century, English pickpockets used the ploy of producing cracking sounds to distract their victims. Due to this practice, the word *racket* acquired a meaning of "a scheme, a dodge, illicit criminal activity" (Hendrickson 1997). The term was introduced into popular usage in the United States during the Prohibition era, which lasted from 1920 to 1933. In that stage, *racketeering* was used to describe a new form of crime in which businessmen, labor union leaders, underworld figures, and politicians formed criminal conspiracies (Hostetter and Quinn Beesley 1929). The Employers' Association of Chicago coined the term in 1927 in a denunciation of organized crime influence on the Teamsters union (Witwer 2004).

It was then used in the Anti-Racketeering Act enacted by Congress in 1934 and designed to prevent labor unions from criminal gangs' infiltration. The act provided punishment for obtaining material profit by the "use or threat to use force, violence or coercion, in connection with or in relation to any act in any way or in any degree affecting trade or commerce" (Boudin 1943, 261). Nowadays, the term is used in the Racketeer Influenced and Corrupt Organizations (RICO) Act, a part of the Organized Crime Control Act that became U.S. law in 1970.

HISTORY OF RACKETEERING IN THE UNITED STATES

In the 1920s, "labor racketeering" spread in the United States in the wake of increasing involvement of organized crime in disputes between labor unions and employers, each of whom resorted to gangsters' help. Business owners hired thugs to suppress the unions by policing strikes and controlling workers through violence and intimidation. They also countered militant labor unions by colluding with corrupt labor leadership.

Labor union officials, in turn, hired members of the underworld to prolong strikes, to protect strikers, or to extort employers by imposing union sanctions (Jacobs and Peters 2003). Thus, criminals were functioning as intermediaries between both sides in favor of industries and corrupt union officials. This collusive relationship eventually led some members of organized crime or their associates to occupy influential positions within labor unions' themselves. This allowed them to extort employers and unions through embezzlement of welfare and pension funds.

Besides infiltration in labor unions, organized crime members may become actively involved in legitimate business enterprises with the purpose of controlling entire business sectors. Throughout most of the 20th century, "business racketeering" plagued certain industries in the U.S. main economic centers, especially Chicago and New York. Initially, racketeers were invited by business owners to help organize a market. Business competitors sought collusive price arrangements and invited racketeers to create cartels to coordinate their actions and restrain competition. Racketeers used violence or threat of violence to coerce outsiders to join the cartel or they drove them out of business. This allowed business-criminal alliances to establish monopoly over an entire industry in such sectors as cleaning, garbage collection, textiles, trucking, and food supply, among others (Gambetta and Reuter 1995). In the 1980s, the United States became known as the period of active prosecution of organized crime figures, especially Italian Americans associated with La Cosa Nostra mafia organization. Many of these sentences were racketeering cases, in which the RICO Act was used as the main instrument of prosecution.

RACKETEERING TODAY

Modern-day racketeers continue to infiltrate legitimate businesses by obtaining a share of business or regular payoffs. In the United States, the RICO Act remains a major legal instrument used against organized crime activities. Racketeering, however, is not exclusive to the United States; it takes place around the globe in the forms of extortion, protection rackets, gambling, and loan-sharking, wherever organized crime dominates a certain territory or an economic sector. Be it Russian, Chinese, or Italian organized crime, the techniques of violence, intimidation, corruption, and fraud remain distinctive features of racketeering activity today.

Yulia Vorobyeva

See also: Chinese Gangland Crime; Illegal Gambling; Illicit Trade; Money Laundering; 'Ndrangheta; Racketeer Influenced and Corrupt Organizations Act (RICO); Russian Organized Crime

Further Reading

Boudin, Louis. 1943. "Place of the Anti-Racketeering Act in Our Constitutional Legal System." *Cornell Law Review* 28 (3): 261–285.

Gambetta, Diego, and Peter Reuter. 1995. "Conspiracy among the Many: The Mafia in Legitimate Industries." In *The Economics of Organised Crime*, edited by Gianluca Fiorentini and Sam Peltzman, 116–142. Cambridge: Cambridge University Press.

Hendrickson, Robert. 1997. *The Facts on File: Encyclopedia of Word and Phrase Origins*. 3rd ed. New York: Facts on File, Inc.

Hostetter, Gordon, and Thomas Quinn Beesley. 1929. *It's a Racket!* Chicago: Les Quin Books Inc.

Jacobs, James, and Ellen Peters. 2003. "Labor Racketeering: The Mafia and the Unions." *Crime and Justice: A Review of Research* 30: 229–282.

Kelly, Robert. 1999. *The Upperworld and the Underworld: Case Studies of Racketeering and Business Infiltrations in the United States*. New York: Kluwer Academic/Plenum.

Witwer, David. 2004. "'The Most Racketeer-Ridden Union in America': The Problem of Corruption in the Teamsters Union during the 1930s." In *Corrupt Histories*, edited by Emmanuel Kreike and William Chester Jordan, 197–238. Rochester, NY: University of Rochester Press.

Ransomware

Ransomware is a type of malicious software (malware) that takes over the victim's computer and prevents access to computer data and personal files or threatens to publish the victim's data until a ransom payment is made to the criminals behind the attack. This technique has been very profitable for cybercriminals, who took an estimated $1 billion in 2016 using ransomware attacks (Morgan 2016). According to Europol (2018), ransomware holds the dominant position among global cybercriminal threats in both law enforcement and industry reporting.

HISTORY OF RANSOMWARE

The first instance of what is today known as ransomware occurred in 1989 with a trojan called PC Cyborg. After infecting a vulnerable computer, all folders were hidden, and file names were encrypted. A dialog box opened on the monitor and instructed the victim to send a cashier's check, bank draft, or international money order in the amount of $189 to the PC Cyborg Corporation at a post office box in Panama. Upon receipt of the money, the victim's computer would be returned to working order. Fortunately, the trojan had a weakness that allowed experts to reverse the malware effects and also to identify the creator of the ransomware—Dr. Joseph Popp. Popp, who was eventually declared mentally unfit, said at his trial that the ransom money would be used for AIDS research—leading some to call this the AIDS trojan rather than PC Cyborg (Kassner 2010).

In the mid-1990s, public-key cryptography—wherein a random number is used to generate a pair of keys (one known only to the owner) that makes reverse engineering of the malware virtually impossible—started being used in ransomware. The victim's files are encrypted using one key, and the key needed to decrypt the files is provided only after the victim pays the ransom.

Even with advancements in cryptography, ransomware did not become the malware of choice because cybercriminals were concerned about the money trail created when ransom payments were made. Victims were told to make payments via Western Union accounts or by purchasing something from a specified Web site, often in Russia (Kassner 2010). But with the advent of cryptocurrency such as Bitcoin in the late 2000s, tracking ransom payments became more difficult. Now, the cybercriminal has the advantage of receiving funds via an unregulated digital currency that provides a level of anonymity. The result has been unprecedented growth of ransomware among cybercrime threats.

RANSOMWARE EXAMPLES

Although ransomware is constantly evolving, certain types have been more successful than others. Palmer (2018) explains that Locky and Cerber have been especially active and long-lasting. Locky, first seen in early 2016, holds users' files hostage until payment in Bitcoin ($400–$800 in value) is made. It quickly grew in functionality (for example, displaying ransom requests in 30 different languages) and seems to be used by several different groups. With its constantly changing techniques and anti-analysis tricks, Locky was still one of the most dangerous forms of ransomware in 2018.

Cerber is one of the most active ransomware rings operating today, with estimates of 150,000 Windows computers infected in July 2016 alone. A primary reason for its widespread use is the decision by its original creators to sell Cerber on the dark web (Palmer 2016). For a 40 percent cut in their customers' illicit earnings, Cerber creators make the ransomware available to anyone (even technically illiterate cybercriminals) who wants to pay for it—leading some pundits to call Cerber "ransomware for dummies." With this distribution technique, Cerber spreads quickly and widely and was accounting for 90 percent of ransomware attacks on Windows computers as of mid-2017 (Palmer 2018). Because Cerber is found most everywhere, except in Russian-speaking countries (it's encoded with an instruction to not run when it finds a machine configured for Russian language), it is commonly believed that the creators are of Russian origin (Palmer 2016).

WANNACRY RANSOMWARE

Although ransomware incidents had been active for several years, it was brought to the general public's attention in May 2017 when the WannaCry ransomware attack hit organizations around the world. After the malware encrypts files and makes them inaccessible to the user, a ransom notice is displayed that demands $300 in Bitcoin to make the files accessible. Health care offices and organizations across the United Kingdom were especially hurt in the attack, with hospitals and doctors' surgeries knocked offline, patient appointments cancelled, and people being told to avoid visiting emergency departments unless it was absolutely necessary (Palmer 2018). Mistakes in the virus code allowed many victims to unlock their systems without giving into the hackers' demands.

The malware infected more than 300,000 PCs and crippled Windows systems across the Americas, Europe, Russia, and China. Global coverage by mainstream media outlets reported on the attack, as the malware locked governments, hospitals, public transport networks, factories, and other organizations out of their computer systems. Using worm-like features, WannaCry quickly spreads across an infected network.

Organizations continued to report infections for several months after the initial outbreak. Honda was forced to shut down a factory, traffic cameras in Australia fell victim, and banks in Russia crashed. In March 2018, Boeing was hit with a suspected WannaCry attack (apparently doing little damage before being stopped). Australia was still reporting WannaCry incidents in September 2018.

Private cybersecurity firms and government investigating agencies (including those in the United States, the United Kingdom, and Australia) have linked WannaCry to the Lazarus Group, which is a cybercrime organization suspected of being connected to the North Korean government (Fruhlinger 2018).

PREVENTING A RANSOMWARE ATTACK

The most popular access point for ransomware is through e-mail, so individuals and employees are encouraged to take training on how to spot an incoming malware attack, and some businesses are restricting what employees can access or enable on their computers.

In 2016, Europol and the Dutch National Police collaborated with cybersecurity companies such as McAfee to launch the "No More Ransom" initiative (Palmer 2018). Free decryption tools for several ransomware versions help victims retrieve their encrypted data without having to pay the ransom. The portal (www.nomoreransom.org) is available in more than 29 languages with partners across the public and private sectors.

Philip L. Reichel

See also: Cryptocurrency; Cyberattack; Cybercrime

Further Reading

Europol. 2018. *Internet Organised Crime Threat Assessment 2018.* Accessed January 20, 2019. https://www.europol.europa.eu/internet-organised-crime-threat-assessment-2018.

Fruhlinger, Josh. 2018. "What Is WannaCry Ransomware, How Does It Infect, and Who Was Responsible?" CSO from IDG. Last updated August 30, 2018. Accessed January 20, 2019. https://www.csoonline.com/article/3227906/ransomware/what-is-wannacry-ransomware-how-does-it-infect-and-who-was-responsible.html.

Kassner, Michael. 2010. "Ransomware: Extortion Via the Internet." *TechRepublic.* Last updated January 11, 2010. Accessed January 20, 2019. https://www.techrepublic.com/blog/it-security/ransomware-extortion-via-the-internet.

Morgan, Steve. 2016. "Hackerpocalypse: A Cybercrime Revelation." Herjavec Group. Last updated August 17, 2016. Accessed January 20, 2019. https://www.herjavecgroup.com/hackerpocalypse-cybercrime-report.

Palmer, Danny. 2016. "Ransomware-as-a-Service Allows Wannabe Hackers to Cash-In on Cyber Extortion." ZDNet. Last updated August 16, 2016. Accessed January 20, 2019. https://www.zdnet.com/article/ransomware-as-a-service-for-allows-wannabe-hackers-to-cash-in-on-cyber-extortion.

Palmer, Danny. 2017. "WannaCry Ransomware: Hackers behind Global Cyberattack Finally Cash Out Bitcoin Windfall." ZDNet. Last updated August 3, 2017. Accessed January 20, 2019. https://www.zdnet.com/article/wannacry-ransomware-hackers-behind-global-cyberattack-finally-cash-out-bitcoin-windfall.

Palmer, Danny. 2018. "What Is Ransomware? Everything You Need to Know about One of the Biggest Menaces on the Web." *ZDNet*. Last updated August 22, 2018. Accessed January 20, 2019. https://www.zdnet.com/article/ransomware-an-executive-guide-to-one-of-the-biggest-menaces-on-the-web.

Raoul Wallenberg Institute of Human Rights and Humanitarian Law

The Raoul Wallenberg Institute of Human Rights and Humanitarian Law is an independent academic institution. It was founded in 1984 and is affiliated with Lund University. Its headquarters is in Lund, Sweden. In legal terms, the institute is a charitable trust under Swedish private law and governed by a board of trustees. It is named after Raoul Wallenberg, a Swedish diplomat, to pay homage to his well-known humanitarian work in Hungary at the end of the World War II.

The institute operates worldwide through its four regional offices in Amman, Jakarta, Nairobi, and Lund (Europe) and four bilateral offices in Beijing, Istanbul, Phnom Penh, and Stockholm, and it maintains activities in approximately 45 countries. Hosting one of the largest human rights libraries in Northern Europe and engaged in numerous research and publication activities, the institute provides a conducive environment for studies, research, and direct engagement.

In addition to the close cooperation with Lund University, the institute maintains close relations with other academic institutions, international organizations, government agencies, and civil society organizations throughout the world.

VISION, MISSION, AND WORK METHOD

The mission of the institute is to "contribute to a wider understanding of, and respect for, human rights and international humanitarian law," and its vision is "just and inclusive societies with effective realisation of human rights for all" (Raoul Wallenberg Institute n.d.). In light of this, the institute contributes to strengthening structures, systems, and mechanisms for the promotion and protection of human rights at all levels in society by

- Conducting innovative and multidisciplinary human rights research to support relevant policy processes, education, and the practical application of human rights law
- implementing and supporting human rights education, primarily in cooperation with academic institutions and human rights centers around the world.
- Directly engaging and cooperating with government institutions, national human rights institutions, international organizations, universities, civil society, and the business sector to improve the practical application of human

rights, through advice, professional training, curricula development, establishment of resource centers, exchange programs, and the like.

- Being a human rights forum, bringing together policy makers, academia, civil society, and other stakeholders to roundtables, conferences, and expert meetings to engage in solution-oriented dialogue to advance human rights.

THEMATIC PRIORITIES

The institute's thematic priority areas are (1) inclusive societies, meaning to promote the development of societies that are open and inclusive to all; (2) people on the move, enhancing the rights and protection of refugees and migrants at risk; (3) fair and efficient justice, ensuring that justice is accessible and administered to all equally; and (4) economic globalization and human rights, contributing to a fair and socially sustainable global economy where human rights, in particular economic, social, and cultural rights, are key building blocks for development, business, and environmental governance (Raoul Wallenberg Institute n.d.). While providing a special focus on these areas, anticorruption and gender perspectives form an integrated part of all the institute's programs.

THE FAIR AND EFFICIENT JUSTICE PROGRAMME

Through its Fair and Efficient Justice program, the Raoul Wallenberg Institute has, since the early 1990s, promoted fair, efficient, humane, and accountable justice for everyone, attempting to ensure that justice is accessed, delivered, and administered in accordance with international human rights standards.

The institute has provided support to strengthening the capacity of justice systems all over the world through different programs and partnerships, including in countries such as Cambodia, China, Colombia, Guatemala, Indonesia, Jordan, Kenya, Laos, Mongolia, Myanmar, South Africa, Tanzania, Uganda, Zambia, and Zimbabwe. For example, the institute has been working with national, regional, and international courts and tribunals, police, prosecutors, lawyers, judicial training institutions, national human rights institutions, correctional services, and traditional leadership with the view to ensure that justice is accessible and administered equally to all. The actions that have been undertaken have varied depending on the region, country, and context and have always been demand-driven, with local ownership as one of the cornerstones.

Throughout the years, the institute's programs have, among others, resulted in

- Strengthened operational and human rights capacity of over 25 national human rights institutions in Africa and Asia, to promote and protect human rights, by providing staff training, infrastructural support, and advice.
- The implementation of a nationwide prison auditing system based on the United Nations Standard Minimum Rules for the Treatment of Prisoners (SMR) in Indonesia.

- Improved knowledge and skills regarding human rights and methodologies for teaching human rights and criminal justice among National Prosecutor colleges in China.
- The development and implementation of the first compulsory and credited human rights course for future prosecutors and judges in Cambodia, in cooperation with the Royal Academy for Judicial Professions.
- Strengthened capacity of human rights officers at each level of the Kenyan Prisons Service to conduct human rights assessments, deliver relevant training, and advise on compliance with international standards.
- Action-oriented studies on juvenile justice reform in Southeast Asia.
- Enhanced knowledge and skills with judicial training institutes in the Middle East and North Africa region (Algeria, Iraq, Jordan, Lebanon, Morocco, the State of Palestine, and Tunisia), to mainstream human rights in teaching and enhance intraregional cooperation.
- Strengthened human rights knowledge and skills with judges of the East African Court of Justice and improved awareness of and information on the court's cases and proceedings with regional stakeholders.
- Increased knowledge and exchange on contemporary approaches, and development of strategies, regarding capacity development for correctional reform from a human rights perspective among East African correctional services.
- Development of training modules, for example, for correctional officers and judges/prosecutors, respectively, on the United Nations Rules for the Treatment of Women Prisoners and Non-custodial Measures for Women Offenders.

The institute is network based and is a member of several European and international networks within the framework of its mandate, including the United Nations Crime Prevention and Criminal Justice Program Network of Institutes, to which the institute has belonged since 1994.

Mikael Johansson

See also: UN Office on Drugs and Crime; UN Program Network of Institutes

Further Reading

International Raoul Wallenberg Foundation. n.d. "About Us." Accessed August 23, 2018. http://www.raoulwallenberg.net.

Raoul Wallenberg Institute. n.d. "About Us." Accessed August 23, 2018. http://rwi.lu.se/about.

University of Michigan. n.d. "Raoul Wallenberg." Wallenberg Legacy. Accessed August 23, 2018. http://wallenberg.umich.edu/raoul-wallenberg.

Returning Foreign Terrorist Fighters

The rise of the Islamic State of Iraq and Syria (ISIS) caused an unprecedented flow of foreign individuals moving to combat areas in Syria and Iraq. This led to a noteworthy predicament for countries whose nationals had traveled to participate in this conflict and now wished to return home. In 2014, the UN Security Council Resolution 2178 defined *foreign terrorist fighters* (FTF) as "individuals who travel to a State other than their states of residence or nationality for the purpose of the perpetration, planning, or preparation of, or participation in, terrorist acts or the providing or receiving of terrorist training, including in connection with armed conflict." Correspondingly, returning foreign terrorist fighters (RFTF) are those who, for a variety of different reasons, are able or express their willingness to return to their respective state of residence or nationality.

While the concept of RFTFs is nothing new, it has gained attention among policy makers since the collapse of ISIS's "caliphate." With ISIS continuing to lose ground in Syria and Iraq, foreign terrorist fighters started returning home, sometimes accompanied by family members. Although estimates vary, it is commonly agreed that roughly 30,000 people from over 100 countries have traveled to Iraq and Syria to join the fighting. While a large number of these people died or fled elsewhere, at least 5,600 are reported to have returned to their home countries, and it is expected that many more will follow (Barrett 2017, 5). With this, a number of policy challenges and dilemmas quickly emerged.

HISTORY

As mentioned, the phenomenon of RFTFs is not new. There are examples where individuals traveled to conflict areas and later returned. In the late 1980s, individuals went to Afghanistan to fight the Soviet Union, to Bosnia in the early 1990s in support of Muslim minorities, and to Somalia during the UN-backed Ethiopian intervention in 2006 (de Roy van Zuijdewijn and Bakker 2014). When these conflicts ended, many of the fighters returned home. The majority of these RFTFs did not engage in terrorist activity. Some however did, the most notable example is an American national named Clement Hampton-El, one of the key figures in the 1993 World Trade Center Bombing (de Roy van Zuijdewijn and Bakker 2014, 4).

MOTIVATIONS AND THREAT

There are a number of reasons for RFTFs to return. While some may return on their own free will, others may be forced to return. Independent of their motivations, these individuals undoubtedly witnessed or may have participated in traumatic events and, hence, are likely to hold more extreme views. The motivations for returnees can be roughly divided into five categories, as outlined by Barrett (2017, 18–19), presenting various levels of risk:

(i) those who left early or after only a short stay and were never particularly integrated with ISIS;
(ii) those who stayed longer, but did not agree with everything that IS was doing;
(iii) those who had no qualms about their role or IS tactics and strategy, but decided to move on;

(iv) those who were fully committed to IS but forced out by circumstances, such as the loss of territory, or were captured and sent to their home countries; and
(v) those who were sent abroad by IS to fight for the caliphate elsewhere.

In addition, some also choose to return due to health issues or the pressures of family. Because of their unknown motives and volatile nature, RFTFs pose serious challenges for the international community. While relatively few attacks take place (contrasted to the number of returnees), atrocities have happened that, to a degree, were perpetrated by RFTFs, such as the 2014 and 2016 terrorist attacks in Brussels and the 2015 Paris attacks (European Commission 2017, 15). Moreover, German research has shown that almost 50 percent of these returnees stay loyal or active members in extremist networks at home (Flade and Bewarder 2016) and therefore demand the full attention of governments.

APPROACHES

Initially, many states attempted to tackle the issue of RFTFs by trying to prevent their return in the first place. When the flow increased, states realized they had to find ways to start addressing RFTFs. From this, two approaches emerged generally referred to as the "hard" and "soft" approaches (Reed and Pohl 2017, par. 2).

Under the so-called hard approach, the criminal justice system (court sentencing) and administrative measures (e.g., blocking bank accounts or revoking citizenship) are generally favored. However, problems may arise that impede the use of hard approaches. In the case of prosecution, there may be lack of evidence against the suspect. Moreover, incarceration does not necessarily tackle the issue of radicalization.

As a result of these complications, "soft approaches," or countering violent extremism (CVE) approaches, were quickly added to the toolbox of policy makers. For this approach, measures such as prevention and rehabilitation are common. This proposes a more case-by-case look at the RFTFs, which is, of course, costly—the major drawback.

RETURNING FAMILIES OF FOREIGN TERRORIST FIGHTERS

A specific group that only recently received a lot of attention is the returning families of FTFs. In attracting many individuals for its cause, ISIS also attracted individuals who took on support roles. Women were no exception to this rule and sometimes took on the role of "jihadi bride," coming alongside their husbands or finding husbands in ISIS territory. While exact numbers are not available, many children with a wide variety of foreign identities have been born or brought to this area. Now many of them have returned or expressed their willingness to return home. These returning families, and particularly the returning children, pose major additional challenges for states. Children have often been indoctrinated or witnessed atrocities; in the worst case, they were forced to commit them.

Wessel Groot

See also: Islamic State of Iraq and Syria (ISIS); Terrorism, International

Further Reading

Barrett, Richard. 2017. "Beyond the Caliphate: Foreign Fighters and the Threat of Returnees." New York: *Soufan Center*. Accessed February 11, 2019. https://thesoufancenter.org/wp-content/uploads/2017/11/Beyond-the-Caliphate-Foreign-Fighters-and-the-Threat-of-Returnees-TSC-Report-October-2017-v3.pdf.

European Commission. 2017. Responses to Returnees: "Foreign Terrorist Fighters and Their Families." *Radicalisation Awareness Network (RAN)*. Accessed January 10, 2019. https://ec.europa.eu/home-affairs/sites/homeaffairs/files/ran_br_a4_m10_en.pdf.

Flade, Florian, and Manuel Bewarder. 2016. "Manche kommen zurueck um sich zu erholen." *Welt*, November 28. Accessed January 28, 2018. https://www.welt.de/politik/deutschland/article159797782/Manche-kommen-zurueck-um-sich-zu-erholen.html.

Kohlmann, Evan. 2004. *Al Qaida's Jihad in Europe: The Afghan-Bosnian Network*. Oxford: Oxford University Press.

Reed, Alastair, and Johanna Pohl. 2017. "Tackling the Surge of Returning Foreign Fighters." *NATO Review*, July 14. Accessed January 20, 2019. https://www.nato.int/docu/review/2017/Also-in-2017/daesh-tackling-surge-returning-foreign-fighters-prevention-denmark-rehabilitation-programmes/EN/index.htm.

UN Security Council. 2014. "Resolution 2178 (2014)." Accessed January 20, 2019. http://www.un.org/en/sc/ctc/docs/2015/SCR%202178_2014_EN.pdf. http://www.un.org/ga/search/view_doc.asp?symbol=S/RES/2178%20%282014%29

Van Zuijdewijn, Jeanine de Roy, and Edwin Bakker. 2014. *Returning Western Foreign Fighters: The Case of Afghanistan, Bosnia and Somalia*. The Hague: International Centre for Counter-Terrorism.

Revolutionary Armed Forces of Colombia

The Revolutionary Armed Forces of Colombia (Fuerzas Armadas Revolucionarios de Colombia, or FARC) was a left-wing terrorist organization that operated in rural Colombia from 1964 until its disintegration in 2016. FARC emerged as a result of *La Violencia*, a 10-year civil war between the Colombian Conservative Party and the Colombian Liberal Party between 1948 and 1958. The founders, Manuel Marulanda and Jacobo Arenas, formed FARC as a communist guerilla force called Southern Bloc after the Colombian Communist Party (PCC) was excluded from peace accords between the Liberal Party and Conservative Party. The Southern Bloc "called for land reform [and] better conditions for those in the countryside, and [it] vowed to defend the communities of followers in the countryside from the Colombian government" (Stanford University 2015). FARC members followed a Marxist-Leninist ideology of economic class conflict and the struggles of proletarian workers, especially rural farmers, against capitalist elites in urban Colombia.

The U.S. government designated FARC as a foreign terrorist organization. The European Union had an analogous designation until September 2016, when it removed the designation to promote peace negotiations. In November 2016, FARC reached a peace accord with the Colombian government and disbanded and reintegrated into formal politics by forming a political party: the Common Alternative Revolutionary Force. It nonviolently advocates FARC's left-wing political ideology.

STRUCTURE

FARC had a hierarchical structure with a single leader holding the rank of commander in chief. Below this rank existed the leadership council known as "the Secretariat," which consisted of seven military commanders who directed military strategy for the organization. These seven members held dual roles, as 7 of the 25 members of the Central High Command. The Central High Command was the organization's highest political body and made up of military commanders from all regions of Colombia and political bureaucrats. The Central High Command was responsible for the overall planning and implementation of political and economic objectives of FARC.

Militarily, the organization was divided into seven blocs, or regions, each with a bloc commander. The seven blocs were the Caribbean Bloc, the Northwestern Bloc, the Middle Magdalena Bloc, the Central Bloc, the Southern Bloc, the Western Bloc, and the Eastern Bloc. Estimates for FARC's military division vary from 8,000 to 18,000 fighters. FARC used to recruit children to fight in its ranks. According to some estimates, child soldiers constituted up to approximately 25 percent of FARC's military force (Human Rights Watch 2015).

ILLEGAL SOURCES OF FUNDING

To fund their guerilla war with the Colombian government, FARC relied on illicit sources of income. In the initial years of the fight, FARC derived its finances entirely from a targeted campaign of kidnapping politicians and businessmen for ransom. Extortion, or "taxation," of rural communities was a common way to supplement its income as well. A major development occurred in the 1970s when cocaine became Colombia's and FARC's major illicit export. The prevalence of cocaine production increased the annual income of the group and spurred an increase of fighters.

The rebels exploited the illicit trade by taxing coca farmers who cultivated on the territory under FARC's control. FARC also set up cocaine manufacturing sites throughout the Colombian jungles and partnered with the Sinaloa Cartel to transport the cocaine into the United States (Woody 2015). In 2009, the U.S. Senate estimated that FARC was responsible for 60 percent of all cocaine shipments from Colombia to the United States (U.S. Senate 2009).

By 2012, illegal gold mining had become a lucrative source of income for FARC (McDermott 2012). In addition to running illegal mines, FARC charged companies and individuals to pay a "heavy machinery tax" on all equipment. Smaller illegal mines of tungsten and coltan were also run by FARC. Illegal mining became the preferred source of income, as the United States had no jurisdiction over criminal prosecution and could not extradite FARC members (Otis 2014).

JohnMichael Da Silva

See also: International Drug Trafficking; Metals and Minerals Smuggling; Sinaloa Cartel

Further Reading

Felter, Claire, and Danielle Renwick. 2017. "Colombia's Civil Conflict." *Council on Foreign Relations*. Accessed December 17, 2017. Accessed January 20, 2019. https://www.cfr.org/backgrounder/colombias-civil-conflict.

Human Rights Watch. 2015. "Colombia: Armed Groups Send Children to War." *Human Rights Watch*, April 17. Accessed December 17, 2017. https://www.hrw.org/news/2005/02/21/colombia-armed-groups-send-children-war.

McDermott, Jeremy. 2012. "Gold Overtakes Drugs as Source of Colombia Rebel Funds." *BBC News*. Accessed December 17, 2017. http://www.bbc.com/news/world-latin-america-18396920.

Otis, John. 2014. "The FARC and Colombia's Illegal Drug Trade." *Wilson Center*. Accessed December 17, 2017. https://www.wilsoncenter.org/publication/the-farc-and-colombias-illegal-drug-trade.

Stanford University. 2015. "Revolutionary Armed Forces of Colombia—People's Army." *Mapping Militant Organizations*. Accessed December 17, 2017. http://web.stanford.edu/group/mappingmilitants/cgi-bin/groups/view/89.

U.S. Senate, Committee on Foreign Relations. 2009. "Drug Control: U.S. Counternarcotics Cooperation with Venezuela Has Declined: Report to the Ranking Member, Committee on Foreign Relations, U.S. Senate." 111th Congress, 1st sess. Rept. GAO-09-806. Washington, D.C.: U.S. Government Accountability Office: 1–34.

Woody, Christopher. 2015. "'El Chapo' Guzmán's Key Role in the Global Cocaine Trade Is Becoming Clearer." *Business Insider*. Accessed December 23, 2017. http://www.businessinsider.com/the-sinaloa-cartel-and-colombian-cocaine-2015-8.

Rome Statute of the International Criminal Court

The Rome Statute is an international treaty signed in 1998 that established the International Criminal Court (ICC), the first permanent international criminal tribunal. The statute laid the foundations for the ICC to prosecute individuals accused of committing international crimes. These crimes include genocide, war crimes, crimes against humanity, and crimes of aggression. The ICC does not prosecute countries or organizations but only establishes individual criminal liability of perpetrators of the crimes in its mandate. The statute entered into force on July 1, 2002, and as of August 2018, 123 countries have ratified the treaty.

HISTORY

The Rome Statute was drafted at the request of the UN General Assembly, recognizing the need for a permanent international criminal tribunal. Previous international tribunals had been established ad hoc, meaning that their jurisdiction was limited to a specific time frame and event. For instance, the International Criminal Tribunal for Rwanda prosecuted individuals involved in the Rwandan genocide, and the Nuremberg trials prosecuted the individuals responsible for planning or carrying out the Holocaust. Many controversies arose in the drafting process of the statute. A crucial point of disagreement was the list of crimes under the jurisdiction of the statute as well as their definitions. For instance, permanent members of the UN Security Council, all of whom possess nuclear weapons, insisted that nuclear weapons not be included in the list of weapons in the statute (Kirsch and Holmes 1999).

After years of drafting and reviewing the statute, representatives from countries, intergovernmental organizations, and nongovernmental organizations gathered in Rome. The United Nations Diplomatic Conference of Plenipotentiaries on the Establishment of an International Criminal Court was funded by the Italian Ministry of Foreign Affairs and lasted from June 15 to July 17, 1998. On the last day of the conference, the Rome Statute was adopted; 120 countries voted in favor of the treaty, 7 countries opposed, and 21 countries abstained (Scharf 1998). According to Article 126 of the statute, the treaty would come into effect after the 60th country ratified it. This occurred in early 2002, after which the statute entered into force on July 1, 2002. The ICC is funded by contributions from states parties, the United Nations, and voluntary contributions from governments, organizations, and individuals.

CONTENTS

The ICC is based in The Hague in the Netherlands and is permitted to act on the territory of states party to the statute. The statute gives the ICC international legal personality. The ICC may prosecute individuals—not states or organizations—over the age of 18 who knowingly or intentionally commit, order, or facilitate international crimes. An individual may be excluded if he or she has a mental disease, was severely intoxicated at the time of the crime, or acted in self-defense. The ICC exercises jurisdiction over crimes that were either committed on the territory of a state party or perpetrated by a national of a state party. The ICC is a court of last resort, acting only if the country itself is unable to prosecute the individual. The ICC's jurisdiction is limited to four international crimes committed after July 1, 2002: genocide, crimes against humanity, war crimes, and crimes of aggression.

Genocide is the attempt to entirely or partially destroy a racial, ethnic, or religious group. Genocide does not only involve killings. It can also include injuring people within the group, preventing them from giving birth, or forcibly relocating them.

The statute defines "crimes against humanity" as the conscious and widespread or systematic attack against a particular population. Crimes against humanity include crimes such as murder, enslavement, torture, and rape, so long as it is part of a wider practice or pattern. Committing these crimes on an individual basis is a criminal offense but would not reach the threshold to be defined as a crime against humanity.

War crimes, in short, are crimes committed against a civilian population during wartime. Under the Geneva Conventions—a series of international treaties that established the laws of war—civilians are protected against targeted attacks, such as killings and torture. Any breach of these laws is considered a war crime. War crimes also include the intentional destruction of or attack on hospitals, schools, churches, and charitable buildings, as long as they are not military objectives.

Although the statute has jurisdiction over crimes against aggression, it is not defined in the treaty itself because representatives at the 1998 conference in Rome could not agree on a definition. The article defining crimes of aggression was later inserted in 2010. In essence, a crime of aggression is the use of military force by a country to offensively—not defensively—attack another country.

Composition and Administration of the Court

The ICC has 18 judges, of which no 2 may be nationals of the same country. Judges hold a term of 9 years. The ICC has four organs: the Presidency, the Chambers, the Office of the Prosecutor, and the Registry. The Presidency is composed of the president and vice-presidents of the ICC and is responsible for the overall administration of the ICC. The Chambers is composed of the Appeals Division, Trial Division, and Pre-Trial Division. In the Chambers, judges are responsible for various stages of a case. The Office of the Prosecutor receives and examines referrals and information on crimes within the jurisdiction of the ICC. The Prosecutor also conducts investigations and prosecutions. The Registry oversees all nonjudicial administration.

Investigation and Prosecution

Investigations at the ICC can be initiated through one of three ways: (1) through referral by a state party to the prosecutor of the ICC; (2) through referral by the UN Security Council; or (3) through the request of the prosecutor of the ICC, if he or she believes there is enough evidence to proceed with an investigation. The second and third options of starting an investigation can oblige countries that are not parties of the treaty to cooperate with the ICC.

The UN Security Council has the authority to determine a threat to international peace and security under Chapter VII of the UN Charter. The statute states that, under Chapter VII, the Security Council may extend the jurisdiction of the statute to countries that are not party to the treaty. The prosecutor of the ICC can also instigate an investigation by requesting the authority from the Pre-Trial Chamber of the ICC. If the Pre-Trial Chamber believes there is enough grounds to proceed with an investigation, the jurisdiction of the statute may also be extended to countries that are not party to the treaty.

Once there is a charge, the Pre-Trial Chamber holds a hearing in the presence of the prosecutor and the person charged to confirm the charges. At this time, the person charged may challenge or object to the charges. If the charges are confirmed, the case proceeds to trial.

Trial, Penalties, and Appeal or Revision

Unless otherwise specified by the Trial Chamber, the trial is held in public. The trial is held in a timely, transparent manner. The ICC operates on the presumption that the person charged is innocent until proven guilty by the prosecutor. A conviction is made only when the majority of judges are convinced of the guilt beyond reasonable doubt. The ICC takes measures to provide all necessary protections for victims and witnesses. Convicted persons are imprisoned in a state party that has agreed to accept sentenced persons.

The ICC may penalize the convicted persons with a fine, forfeiture of assets, or a sentence of up to 30 years or life imprisonment. The prosecutor or convicted persons may appeal the ICC's sentence or decision. The appeal is considered by the Appeals Chamber, which may order a new trial or reverse or amend the sentence or decision.

International Cooperation and Judicial Assistance

The ICC may call upon states parties for cooperation. This includes providing documents, protecting witnesses or victims, and surrendering persons with an arrest warrant. This provision of the statute has not always been successful. The ICC called for the arrest of the current president of Sudan, Omar al-Bashir, in 2009. Al-Bashir has since traveled to countries that have ratified the statute without being arrested, including a trip in 2017 to South Africa.

The statute establishes an Assembly of State Parties, in which each state party has one representative. The purpose of the Assembly is to oversee the ICC, including its organs and budget.

SIGNATURE AND RATIFICATION

The statute is currently signed by 139 countries, of which 123 have ratified the treaty. Countries that are signatories but have not ratified the Rome Statute include the United States and Russia. Being a signatory but not a state party means that the ICC cannot exercise jurisdiction over the country, except in the circumstances previously mentioned. The remaining countries, including China, are neither a state party nor a signatory of the Rome Statute. The statute's ratification, acceptance, and accession processes are deposited with the UN Secretary General.

RESERVATION AND WITHDRAWAL

States parties may withdraw from the statute by a written notification to the UN secretary-general. Withdrawing from the Rome Statute does not remove the statute's jurisdiction from the period during which the state was party to the treaty, nor does it absolve jurisdiction from the one-year withdrawal period. In 2016, several countries signaled their withdrawal from the Rome Statute, including South Africa and Gambia. Although Russia is a signatory, not a state party, it has also announced its withdrawal. Burundi is the first country to withdraw from the ICC, effective as of October 27, 2017.

Ariun Enkhsaikhan

See also: Crimes against Humanity; Genocide; International Criminal Court

Further Reading

Arsanjani, Mahnoush H. 1999. "The Rome Statute of the International Criminal Court." *American Journal of International Law* 93 (1): 22–43.

International Criminal Court. 2011. "The Rome Statute of the International Criminal Court." Accessed January 20, 2019. https://www.icc-cpi.int/NR/rdonlyres/ADD16852-AEE9-4757-ABE7-9CDC7CF02886/283503/RomeStatutEng1.pdf.

Kirsch, Philippe, and John T. Holmes. 1999. "The Rome Conference on an International Criminal Court: The Negotiating Process." *American Journal of International Law* 93 (1): 2–12.

Scharf, Michael P. 1998. "Results of the Rome Conference for an International Criminal Court." *American Society of International Law* 3 (10): 167–200.

United Nations. 2002. "United Nations Diplomatic Conference of Plenipotentiaries on the Establishment of an International Criminal Court." Accessed January 20, 2019. http://legal.un.org/icc/rome/proceedings/E/Rome%20Proceedings_v1_e.pdf.

Rule of Law

The concept called *rule of law* is often used in reference to transnational organized crime and how the rule of law is undermined by those criminal activities. Despite its use in that context, what the rule of law actually means is more elusive than might first appear. Nachbar considers it "an inherently vague term meaning different things to different people" (2009, 303). Kleinfeld (2006) compares it with the proverbial blind man's elephant—like a rope to one and a wall to another. For some, rule of law is simply the principle that both government and the governed are subject to law. As authors get more specific, reference is made to a dependence on norms and rules that are deemed lawful and legitimate to establish and preserve a community (Belz 2016). Or, the concept might be defined by what it is not: government operating with wide, arbitrary, or discretionary powers.

THE MANY ASPECTS OF THE RULE OF LAW

Absent an agreed-upon definition of the rule of law, Kleinfeld suggests that the concept should be viewed as having at least five separate meanings: (1) a government abides by standing laws and respects judicial rules; (2) law and order exists in a society; (3) human rights are enforced; (4) justice is efficient and predictable; and (5) a contrarian view that sees rule of law as meaning a lack of equality before the law (Kleinfeld 2006, 32).

Fuller also believes there are a variety of elements to consider when deciding whether rule of law has been achieved. For example, he argues that the elements necessary for aspiring to institute the rule of law should include the points that laws must be published, clearly written, and obeyed by all (Fuller 1977). Those elements are compatible with ones believing that rule of law elements must include a way to protect human rights, encourage public confidence in the police and courts, and allow for economic development.

The complex nature of what rule of law means is especially apparent when considering the World Justice Project's approach, which defines the rule of law as consisting of 16 factors and 68 subfactors organized under the following set of four principles (World Justice Project 2009):

1. The government and its officials and agents are accountable under the law;
2. The laws are clear, publicized, stable, and fair and they protect fundamental rights, including the security of persons and property;
3. The process by which the laws are enacted, administered, and enforced is accessible, fair, and efficient;
4. Access to justice is provided by competent, independent, and ethical adjudicators, attorneys, or representatives and judicial officers who are of sufficient number, have adequate resources, and reflect the makeup of the communities they serve.

The confusion, Kleinfeld (2006) suggests, is that two very different ways of defining rule of law are often discussed in parallel. The first, which Kleinfeld calls "ends-based definitions," refers to the ends to be achieved through rule of law (for example, law and order, a government bound by law, conditions in which human rights are protected). The second, the institutional approach, refers to the social institutions needed for a society to possess the rule of law (for example, published laws, a noncorrupt police force, and an independent judiciary). When the two ways of defining rule of law are conflated, it is unlikely that either rule of law outcomes or institutional reform will occur. This is because achieving "rule of law ends" requires reform across social institutions, but institutional reform is typically carried out within single institutions. As a result, institutional reform can be undertaken with no significant effect on rule of law ends. We must, Kleinfeld argues, improve our definitions to understand what we are trying to accomplish and how reforms should be implemented. Treating the rule of law from only the institutional approach (especially one institution at a time) will make it difficult to achieve rule of law end goals, as those require reform across institutions as well as cultural and political changes apart from the institutions.

HOW IS RULE OF LAW ACHIEVED?

Three steps are needed for a country to achieve a rule of law in the sense of that country having its law, rather than its government, being supreme (Reichel 2018). First, the nation must recognize the supremacy of certain fundamental values. Those values, which can have either secular or divine origin, must reflect basic and ultimate principles. For example, basic principles regarding a right to assemble, universal access to justice, and equality before the law can provide the needed fundamental values.

After being recognized, the second step requires that the core values be reduced to written form. In the United States, the Bill of Rights (1791) provides one such document, as does the Magna Carta (1215) for the British and the Declaration of the Rights of Man and the Citizen (1789) for the French.

The third step to rule of law requires a nation to provide procedures that hold its government to the core principles. If citizens cannot challenge laws made by the country's legislature or ruler, the concept of a higher law is lost. For example, consider a situation wherein a law is passed that prohibits followers of a particular religion from operating a place of worship. If the country's constitution ensures freedom of religion, citizens must be able to challenge the substance of such a law as violating fundamental values that are recorded in the constitution. If that challenge cannot occur, the concept of rule of law is without power.

JUDICIAL REVIEW

Of the three steps to a rule of law (that is, recognizing supremacy of certain values, reducing them to writing, and providing a way to hold the government to those laws), the third is often accomplished through the process of judicial review. This term refers to the power of a court to hold unconstitutional, and therefore unenforceable, any law or action by a public official that the courts deem in conflict with the country's basic law.

In the United States, this is accomplished in a way that allows the entire judiciary to exercise constitutional control. Even lower-level state and federal courts can rule that a law violates the U.S. Constitution. The U.S. Supreme Court always has the final say, but judges and courts across the country have the authority to rule that a law or act is unconstitutional. For example, in 1984, Texas had a law that prohibited the desecration of a venerated object. A protestor (Gregory Johnson) at the 1984 Republican National Convention was charged with violating that law when he burned the American flag to protest the policies of President Ronald Reagan. In 1989, the U.S. Supreme Court (*Texas v. Johnson*, 491 U.S. 397) ruled that the Texas law was unconstitutional because burning the flag is an act of symbolic speech protected by the First Amendment. That is, burning the flag in protest is an act that is consistent with a core American value.

Philip L. Reichel

See also: Corruption; Failed State; Global Counterterrorism Forum; Globalization

Further Reading

Belz, Herman J. 2016. "Rule of Law." In *American Governance*, edited by Stephen Schechter, Thomas S. Vontz, Thomas A. Birkland, Mark A. Graber, and John J. Patrick, 330–332. Vol. 4. Farmington Hills, MI: Macmillan Reference.

Fuller, L. L. 1977. *The Morality of Law*. Rev. ed. New Haven, CT: Yale University Press.

Kleinfeld, R. 2006. Competing Definitions of the Rule of Law. In *Promoting the Rule of Law Abroad: In Search of Knowledge*, edited by T. Carothers, 31–74. Washington, D.C.: Carnegie Endowment for International Peace.

Nachbar, T. 2009. "Defining the Rule of Law Problem." University of Virginia Public Law and Legal Theory Working Paper Series, Working Paper 125. Accessed January 10, 2019. http://law.bepress.com/cgi/viewcontent.cgi?article=1194&context=uvalwps.

Reichel, Philip L. 2018. *Comparative Criminal Justice Systems: A Topical Approach*. 7th ed. New York: Pearson.

World Justice Project. 2009. "Rule of Law Index." Accessed February 17, 2010. http://www.worldjusticeproject.org/rule-of-law-index.

Russian Election Interference (2016)

Independent and state-sponsored Russian hackers allegedly used various online means to interfere with the 2016 U.S. presidential election. Hacks were targeted at the computer systems of the Democratic National Committee (DNC), while propaganda targeted the social media accounts of millions of users. Due to the inherent anonymity provided by the Internet's structure, it can be difficult to determine responsibility for hacking attempts. In this case, however, several factors pointed to the involvement of Russian hackers. First, Russian hackers have been committing cyberattacks and interfering in elections in various countries for over 20 years and have gained unauthorized access in U.S. governmental e-mail systems in the past (Lipton, Sanger, and Shane 2016). Second, the Intelligence Community Assessment (ICA), an agency that includes members from the Central Intelligence Agency (CIA), Federal Bureau of Investigation (FBI), and National Security Agency (NSA), officially concluded that Russian president Vladimir Putin and the Russian government had extensively interfered in the 2016 presidential election (Borger 2017). Though the group maintains there was widespread interference in the 2016 election, they have concluded that this interference did not affect the results of the election.

HACKS

According to the FBI, in the summer of 2015, the Russian group "Cozy Bear" hacked into the DNC system using phishing e-mails (Borger 2017). As the DNC is a nonprofit organization, their budget at the time only allowed for "a standard email spam-filtering service," and this system was not advanced enough to track suspicious activity (Lipton, Sanger, and Shane 2016).

Over the following year, Russian hackers continued to collect data inside the DNC system and remained mostly undetected. In September 2015, the FBI attempted to alert the DNC of a cyberattack that they had been tracking for several months, but the DNC had no way to verify the legitimacy of this warning; therefore, no serious action was taken to protect their computer system (Lipton, Sanger, and Shane 2016). The following spring, a second wave of hackers, known as "Fancy Bear," continued work on the DNC system.

Seven months later, the DNC hired CrowdStrike, a cybersecurity company, to investigate further and install more advanced monitoring software. However, the damage had already been done. In June 2016, an individual or group, self-named "Guccifer 2.0," released a spreadsheet of over 10,000 DNC names, the information of more than 20,000 Republican donors, and research conducted by the DNC against the Republican presidential candidate, Donald Trump. The following month, WikiLeaks released 40,000 e-mails from the servers of several DNC officials; the DNC publicly accused Russian hackers of providing this information to WikiLeaks (Lipton, Sanger, and Shane 2016).

PROPAGANDA

In January 2017, the Office of the Director of National Intelligence released a report explaining that hackers had not breached voting machines or computers tallying election results, but Russians were believed to have meddled in other ways, for example, by creating paid advertisements and fake accounts to spread propaganda and instill chaos and confusion on American social media Web sites. The advertisements and accounts were particularly pronounced in electoral swing states and often presented polarizing ideas about topics of political debate. Facebook reported receiving $150,000 from over 3,000 paid political ads linked to Russia's Internet Research Agency (IRA); more than 10 million users viewed these ads (Glaser 2017). Google reported receiving approximately $5,000 in political ads linked to the IRA and an additional $53,000 in political ads purchased from Russian IP addresses.

Russians organized political rallies on U.S. soil through event pages (Borger 2017). On Facebook, groups linked to Russian IP addresses posted memes that stirred opposing political sentiments. The media Web site has reported 470 Russian-linked groups; posts from these groups were shared more than 340 million times (Lapowsky 2017). Additionally, the IRA has been connected to a large number of fake Twitter accounts that posted praise for Donald Trump and disparaged Democratic candidate Hillary Clinton during the election season. Twitter revealed that 22 of the 470 Russian Facebook pages were linked to fake Twitter accounts, and it found an additional 179 Russian-linked accounts (Glaser 2017). Researchers have found hundreds more Twitter accounts tied to Russia.

Due to Russian interference, the integrity of the 2016 presidential election has been questioned. Although hacking and propaganda were not shown to have affected the election, confidence in social media campaigning has been violated, and a collective sense of security has been lost. Continued ramifications of this security breach remain unclear as further evidence of interference is uncovered. It is assured this event will shape future election processes and cybersecurity measures.

Abbey Harbert

See also: Cyberattack; Cybercrime; Hackers; Phishing

Further Reading

Borger, Julian. 2017. "Top Senate Intelligence Duo: Russia Did Interfere in 2016 Election." *The Guardian*, October 4. Accessed January 21, 2019. https://www.theguardian.com/world/2017/oct/04/senate-intelligence-committee-russia-election-interference.

Glaser, April. 2017. "Here's What We Know about Russia's Use of American Social Media to Sway the Election." *Slate*, October 11. Accessed January 11, 2019. http://www.slate.com/articles/technology/future_tense/2017/10/what_we_know_about_russia_s_use_of_american_facebook_twitter_and_google.html.

Lapowsky, Issie. 2017. "Everything We Know about Facebook, Trump, and Russia." *Wired*, October 24. Accessed January 20, 2019. https://www.wired.com/story/what-we-know-and-dont-know-about-facebook-trump-and-russia.

Lipton, Eric, David E. Sanger, and Scott Shane. 2016. "The Perfect Weapon: How Russian Cyberpower Invaded the U.S." *New York Times*, December 13. Accessed January 20, 2019. https://www.nytimes.com/2016/12/13/us/politics/russia-hack-election-dnc.html.

Russian Organized Crime

Known under different terms, such as thieves-in-law (*vory-v-zakone*) and *bratva*, and tapping into essentially every criminal market, Russian organized crime

(ROC) is composed of various transnational criminal groups operating not only in Russia and post-Soviet states but also worldwide. ROC is often understood as Russian-speaking organized crime, whereby criminal organizations from different parts of the former Soviet Union use the Russian language as their lingua franca. This broader term incorporates criminal organizations of ethnic descent other than Russian (e.g., Chechen, Jewish), citizens of countries of the former Soviet Union and the Soviet bloc (e.g., Poland, Serbia), and countries with a large Russian minority (e.g., Germany).

It should also be noted that "Russian mafia"—another popular and commonly used term to refer to ROC—is widely considered by scholars to be a misnomer produced by the mass media and authors of fiction who draw parallels between Italian Mafia families and ROC. "Mafia," however, is not a suitable term to use in the context of ROC because it creates a certain image of conservative, hierarchical, and hereditary families led by a single don. "Russian mafia" is a hyperbolic and misunderstood term that distorts the nature of ROC, which is usually not based on kinship or bloodlines and is maintained by a network of *avtoritety* (bosses), hitmen, bookkeepers, and street thugs.

HISTORY

Although the origins of ROC are often argued to go back to Imperial Russia, whereby peasants revolting against the czar committed crimes against imperial property and then created a fund and shared it with one another, it is more common to relate the formation of ROC to the early Soviet penal system. As soon as Joseph Stalin took power following Vladimir Lenin's death in 1924, many of professional thieves (*vory*) were thrown into *gulags* (labor camps), where Russia's criminal underworld truly shaped and matured.

The *vory* developed a code of conduct grounded in traditional criminal customs and rituals (e.g., forsake relatives, never work but live only on means gained from crime, never cooperate with authorities, help other thieves and provide them with both moral and material support). During that period, the Russian criminal community (*vorovskoy mir*) used to create a common fund (*obshchak*) that was used primarily to provide mutual aid to support imprisoned members, bribe public officials, and mastermind new crimes.

During Gorbachev's *perestroika* (a series of political and economic reforms in the Soviet Union during the 1980s and 1990s) and even more so after the collapse of the Soviet Union in 1991, ROC groups were able to exploit the opportunities provided by a free market economy and the general degeneration of governance and social alienation caused by systemic political and socioeconomic perturbations. "The privatization of state property that began in Russia in 1992—when public property began to be sold to private investors—both expanded and solidified the complex relationship that had developed between the state and organized crime" (Finckenauer and Voronin 2001, 7). Many ROC groups successfully managed to take over a considerable section of post-Soviet economies, establishing control over both illegal activities and legitimate business.

During this time, they were also rapidly expanding outside post-Soviet countries, namely in North America. Within just a couple of years, various ROC groups were able to arrange international operations, including narcotics trafficking, arms trafficking, human trafficking and prostitution, and other criminal activities. According to some sources, ROC groups were even able to strike deals with the American Italian mafia and Colombian drug cartels (Shelly and Cornell 2006). The 2011 White House Strategy to Combat Transnational Organized Crime acknowledged the importance of Russian and Eurasian organized crime networks that were described to pose "significant threat to economic growth and democratic institutions." In 2012, the Brothers' Circle was sanctioned under the U.S. Department of the Treasury Executive Order 13581, along with Camorra, Yakuza, Los Zetas, and MS-13.

ROC groups have also reportedly established their presence in Hungary and the Czech Republic, the French Riviera, and the Spanish coastline. They have also emerged in the organized crime scene in South Africa and have occupied one of the central positions in cybercrime.

UNIQUE FEATURES AND SIGNIFICANCE

ROC represents a network of loose criminal groups from the post-Soviet space. Unlike Colombian, Italian, or Mexican organized crime groups, ROC is not primarily based on either ethnic or family structures. Some of its most profitable activities include extortion rackets, drug trafficking, arms trafficking, financial fraud, and money laundering. In addition, ROC has gained a reputation for being skillful cybercriminals.

The danger emanating from ROC is usually associated with their use of corruption and violence to influence state officials, law enforcement agencies, and private companies. ROC has demonstrated that they can use the state apparatus and legal businesses to advance and protect illicit revenues as well as uphold immunity from arrest and prosecution.

It is therefore reasonable to conclude that the fight against the ROC is complicated and cannot be achieved over a short period of time. Any activities to counter ROC must not only be legislative but also provide the law enforcement with sufficient instruments and tools. Given ROC's global outreach, countermeasures should also be undertaken at national, regional, and international levels, allowing for law enforcement coordination across borders and efficient and expeditious mutual legal assistance.

Yuliya Zabyelina

See also: Organized Crime; Solntsevskaya Bratva; Transnational, Global, and International Crime

Further Reading

Finckenauer, James, O., Alexander Sukharenko, and Eric G. Lesneskie. 2011. "Russian Organized Crime." In *International Crime and Justice*, edited by Mangai Natarajan, 247–254. New York: Cambridge University Press.

Finckenauer, James O., and Yuri A. Voronin. 2001. *The Threat of Russian Organized Crime*. Washington, D.C.: National Institute of Justice.

Kegö, Walter, and Alexandru Molcean. 2011. *Russian Speaking Organized Crime Groups in the EU*. Stockholm Paper (March), Institute for Security and Development Policy (ISDP).

Shelley, Louise, and Svante E. Cornell. 2006. "The Drug Trade in Russia." In *Russian Business Power: The Role of Russian Business in Foreign and Security Relations*, edited by Andreas Wenger, Jeronim Perović, and Robert W. Orttung, 196–216. New York: Routledge.

U.S. Department of the Treasury. 2012. "Press Release: Treasury Designates Key Members of the Brothers' Circle Criminal Organization." December 20. Accessed December 1, 2017. https://www.treasury.gov/press-center/press-releases/Pages/tg1811.aspx.

Volkov, Vadim. 2014. "The Russian Mafia, Rise and Extinction." In *The Oxford Handbook of Organized Crime*, edited by Letizia Paoli, 159–176. New York: Oxford University Press.

White House. 2011. *Strategy to Combat Transnational Organized Crime*. Washington, D.C. Accessed February 11, 2019. https://obamawhitehouse.archives.gov/administration/eop/nsc/transnational-crime.

S

Saferworld

Saferworld is an independent international organization that operates to prevent violent conflicts as well as to build safer lives for individuals around the world. Saferworld works globally to promote regional, national, and international peace and security policies. These policies are geared toward people affected by violent conflicts and helps establish conditions for peace worldwide. These policies impact regions such as East and North Africa, the Middle East, Europe, and multiple geographic regions within Central, South, and Southeast Asia. Policy centers established in China, the European Union, the United Kingdom, the United States, the United Nations, and Vienna, Austria, incorporate evidence and experience from Saferworld partners, programs, and communities to advocate for changes that favor conflict-ravaged areas.

HISTORY

Saferworld was pioneered in Bristol, England, in 1989. The original purpose of Saferworld was to become a politically independent research organization that focused on violence prevention throughout the world. Original work for the organization centered on arms control and other violence-prevention strategies; however, the research focus shifted more toward the theoretical elements associated with global conflict. Saferworld focused on topics such as governance, power, marginalization, access to resources, and development of certain geographical areas.

As Saferworld progressed, in-country programming became a forefront of the organization's mission, with focus being placed on community security, gender, peace and security, justice, and development of these areas. These topics were addressed at the local, regional, national, and international level. In 2000, Kenya was the first country where Saferworld conducted in-country programming; however, Saferworld is currently conducting in-country programming in 20 different countries.

The original guiding principle of Saferworld was the call for individuals to be at the heart of the response to violent conflict, and that guiding principle is still employed by Saferworld today. Saferworld has expanded its focus to include issues surrounding gender, terrorism, migration, arms control, power structures, security, and justice. All these topics are addressed by Saferworld in their efforts to facilitate long-lasting global peace.

OPERATION

Saferworld maintains that for long-term peace to be attainable, individuals require access to fair and effective avenues to address the inequalities that lead to violent conflict. Saferworld advocates that all individuals within a society must take an active role in the pursuit of long-term peace. Furthermore, Saferworld believes that influential individuals have a duty to exercise their power in the sponsorship of just and equitable societies. Saferworld believes in the equality of every person and respects the richness of social and cultural diversity. To maintain these beliefs, Saferworld uses expertise and tested methodologies to improve the safety and sense of security of individuals affected by conflict.

At the community level, Saferworld utilizes community programming to bring people together across various divides while facilitating an atmosphere of cooperation to find solutions, overcome division, and promote peace. All sectors of society are included in this discussion to receive a well-rounded approach to future violence prevention. Saferworld establishes, and maintains, effective partnerships with organizations embedded in these violent conflict regions. These organizations are fundamental in the implementation of violence-prevention policies due to their expertise and experience regarding the context-specific conflict.

Saferworld provides peace-building resources, offers technical expertise, and brings communities' concerns to these organizations and the decision makers involved in setting peace and security policies. These organizations then incorporate the concerns of the communities when discussing and implementing future solutions. The amplification of community voices allows for accountability on the part of the various organizations and decision makers. Saferworld also forms relations with development actors, business leaders, elected representatives, academics, international and multilateral bodies, and other various entities to ensure that ample pressure is placed on decision makers in their quest to build sustainable peace and security.

At the international level, Saferworld advocates for changes that favor conflict-affected communities. Utilizing the partnerships and experience gained by taking an active involvement in these communities, Saferworld coordinates and meets with international policy makers and peace-building practitioners to confront the underlying motivators of violent conflict. Better informed policies, due to the community involvement and problem relaying done by Saferworld, is the goal of these practitioners and policy makers.

Jessie L. Slepicka

See also: Failed State; Globalization; Transnational, Global, and International Crime

Further Reading

Joachim, Jutta, and Matthias Dembinski. 2011. "A Contradiction in Terms? NGOs, Democracy, and European Foreign and Security Policy." *Journal of European Public Policy* 18 (8): 1151–1168.

Saferworld. 2017. "Saferworld's Annual Review 2016-17." Organisational Communications. Accessed March 12, 2018. https://www.saferworld.org.uk/resources/publications/1145-saferworlds-annual-review-2016-17.

Saferworld. n.d.-a. "Issues: Saferworld Works on a Range of Issues Relating to Conflict and Peace." *News and Resources*. Accessed August 22, 2018. https://www.saferworld.org.uk/issues/issues.

Saferworld. n.d.-b. "Who We Are." News and Resources. Accessed August 22, 2018. https://www.saferworld.org.uk/who-we-are/who-we-are.

San Bernardino Terrorist Attack (2015)

On December 2, 2015, Syed Rizwan Farook and his wife, Tashfeen Malik, killed 14 employees of the San Bernardino, California, Public Health Department at the Inland Regional Center and injured another 22 people. Police killed both assailants during a shootout following a car chase. The Federal Bureau of Investigation (FBI) concluded the perpetrators' act was an act of terrorism and that the couple was self-radicalized "homegrown violent extremists" inspired by foreign terrorist organizations, but they did not receive any funding from those organizations (Winton 2016).

The shooting occurred during a training session and holiday party for the employees of the Public Health Department at the Inland Regional Center. Farook, who worked at the Public Health Department, attended the training but suddenly left and then returned with his wife, Malik. Both wore load-bearing vests and ski masks and carried two rifles, a .223-caliber Smith & Wesson M&P15 and a .223-caliber DPMS A-15, as well as some pistols and a large number of rounds (Berman 2016). After killing two people outside the building, Farook and Malik entered the center and opened fire at the crowd, firing over 100 rounds in total (Braziel et al. 2016).

Many people managed to escape by fleeing deeper into the building, the bathroom, or any place they could find cover. Visibility was decreased as a stray bullet had hit the sprinkler system, causing a cloud of water to gush down on the room. Despite law enforcement units responding to the attack 3 minutes and 32 seconds after the shooting had commenced and arriving on scene not much later, they were unable to neutralize the assailants (Braziel et al. 2016). Farook and Malik quickly fled the scene and announced their loyalty to the leadership of the Islamic State of Iraq and Syria (ISIS) via a post on social media not much later (Braziel et al. 2016).

THE CHASE

After law enforcement secured the perimeter, they began a broad search for the suspects. Information provided by witnesses led law enforcement to believe Farook was involved. Some four hours after the initial shooting, police identified Farook and Malik leaving their residence in a black SUV with Utah plates, the same vehicle that was seen fleeing the scene earlier (Rubin et al. 2015). Ignoring police emergency lights and sirens, Malik opened fire at police units in pursuit.

Eventually, on Richardson Street, some 1.7 miles from the Inland Regional Center, Farook and Malik pulled over, and a massive shootout started (Rubin et al. 2015).

Police killed Farook and Malik, and the suspects wounded two officers. In the perpetrators' vehicle, law enforcement found almost 2,500 rounds of .223-caliber and 9mm ammunition, medical supplies, and a detonator for three pipe bombs left behind at the Inland Regional Center, which had failed to detonate (Braziel et al. 2016).

INVESTIGATION

The subsequent investigation resulted in other arrests, including ones for immigration violations by family members of Farook and Malik and of Enrique Marquez, one of their neighbors. In 2011, Marquez and Farook had plotted an attack together, but the plans were abandoned in 2012. Marquez had however purchased and sold guns to Farook that were used during the attack, and he never reported this to authorities. Neither did Marquez report about Farook's terrorist ideology. Marquez, who had abandoned his former terrorist plotting, expressed remorse for his former deeds and fully cooperated with authorities during and after the attack ("25 Years Urged for Buyer of Rifles Used in Terror Attack" 2018).

On February 16, 2017, Marquez pleaded guilty to conspiring with Farook to provide material support to terrorists and with making false statements regarding the rifles he had purchased in his own name and supplied to Farook ("25 Years Urged for Buyer of Rifles Used in Terror Attack" 2018). The U.S. attorney urged a 25-year sentence for Marquez. All court cases were still ongoing as of 2018.

Wessel Groot

See also: Lone Wolf Terrorism; Terrorism, Domestic

Further Reading

Berman, Mark. 2016. "One Year after the San Bernardino Attack, Police Offer a Possible Motive as Questions Still Linger." *Washington Post*, December 2. Accessed May 9, 2018. https://www.washingtonpost.com/news/post-nation/wp/2016/12/02/one-year-after-san-bernardino-police-offer-a-possible-motive-as-questions-still-linger.

Braziel, Rick, Frank Straub, George Watson, and Rod Hoops. 2016. "Bringing Calm to Chaos: A Critical Incident Review of the San Bernardino Public Safety Response to the December 2, 2015, Terrorist Shooting Incident at the Inland Regional Center." *Critical Response Initiative*. Washington, D.C.: Office of Community Oriented Policing Services.

Rokos, Brian. 2017. "Tatiana Farook, Sister-in-Law of Dec. 2 Shooter, Pleads Guilty in Marriage-Fraud Case." *Press-Enterprise*, February 9. Accessed May 19, 2018. https://www.pe.com/2017/02/09/tatiana-farook-sister-in-law-of-dec-2-shooter-pleads-guilty-in-marriage-fraud-case.

Rubin, Joel, Richard Winton, Brittny Mejia, and Joseph Serna. 2015. "'All Hell Broke Loose' as Police Chased the San Bernardino Shooters." *Los Angeles Times*, December 13. Accessed 17 May 2018. graphics.latimes.com/san-bernardino-chase.

"25 Years Urged for Buyer of Rifles Used in Terror Attack." 2018. *AP News*, April 10. Accessed May 19, 2018. https://apnews.com/cea2b7c35cda4a9b8e45dd5d6764dd4c.

Winton, Richard. 2016. "A Year after the San Bernardino Terror Attack, the FBI Is Still Struggling to Answer Key Questions." *Los Angeles Times*, December 1. Accessed May 22, 2018. http://www.latimes.com/local/lanow/la-me-san-bernardino-terror-probe-20161130-story.html.

Savona, Ernesto (1943–)

Ernesto Savona, a leading authority on organized crime, is the director of the Transcrime Institute at the Università Cattolica del Sacro Cuore in Milan, Italy. Professor Savona's career began after graduating with a degree in law in 1965 in Palermo, Sicily. In the mid-1980s, he trained as a quantitative sociologist, which was unusual for a lawyer. In 1986, he became a professor of criminology at Trento University's Law School, and in 2002, he became a professor of criminology at the Università Cattolica del Sacro Cuore in Milan.

Transcrime offers a master's in security and a PhD in criminology and has produced a series of accomplished young scholars trained in studying, teaching, and producing policy relevant research that is of vital interest to local, national, and international agencies in fighting crime (Savona and Leclerc 2016; Savona, Berlusconi, and Riccardi 2016). Transcrime's success relies heavily on external grants. Dr. Savona is a recipient of more than 20 large grants from the European Commission and several from the Italian government to undertake research on corruption, business and corporate crime, cybercrime, organized crime, insecurity and urban crime, immigration, fraud, child pornography, money laundering, terrorism, human trafficking, urban security, crime proofing of legislation, situational crime prevention, risk management, seizure and confiscation of crime proceeds, and maritime piracy. Transcrime also provides high-level training courses for law enforcement agencies and security professionals in the private sector.

During the 1990s, Dr. Savona was invited to spend several extended periods of time at the National Institute of Justice, the research center of the U.S. Department of Justice in Washington, D.C., to undertake studies on organized crime and international money laundering. Consequently, he became very familiar with U.S. policies directed at dismantling organized crime. During that time, he also worked closely with Giovanni Falcone, the famous Italian judge who was later assassinated by the Sicilian mafia. That event led to the adoption of the "Palermo Convention," the landmark UN Convention against Transnational Organized Crime.

Savona has made many contributions to the study of organized crime, but perhaps his most significant and original work relates to extortion. According to the U.S. Code 18 U.S.C. § 1951(b)(2)), extortion is "the obtaining of property from another, with his consent, induced by wrongful use of actual or threatened force, violence, or fear, or under color of official right." The legal definitions of extortion in other countries, including those in the Europe, are similar to the U.S. definition. Dr. Savona's study for the European Commission is the leading publication on understanding and combating extortion. According to the study, there are two different types of extortion racketeering (systemic and casual) linked to three main variables: (1) the organizational structure of the criminal crime group that engages in extortion racketeering; (2) its presence at the local territorial level; and (3) the victim-offender relationship (Savona and Zanella 2019). Based on this typology, the vulnerability to extortion racketeering index was created that assisted in identifying which of the EU member states were particularly vulnerable to extortion.

Savona is a consultant to the United Nations, the Council of Europe, the European Union, and several national governments. He also served as the president of the European Society of Criminology in 2003–2004. Since 2003, he has been editor-in-chief of the *European Journal on Criminal Policy and Research*. In 2010–2011, he chaired of the Global Agenda Council on Organized Crime of the World Economic Forum.

Professor Ernesto Savona has influenced many scholars around the world, and in 2014, a Festschrift for him was prepared by two of his closest students, Stefano Caneppele and Francesco Calderoni (2014), documenting the extent of his world renown. Despite the many demands on him resulting from this fame, Ernesto Savona is also a remarkable teacher and mentor (Clarke 2014). Whenever seen in public, he is surrounded by his young colleagues and students and engaged in lively and animated discussions.

Mangai Natarajan

See also: Racketeering; Transcrime; Transnational, Global, and International Crime

Further Reading

Caneppele, Stefano, and Francesco Calderoni, eds. 2014. *Organized Crime, Corruption and Crime Prevention: Essays in Honor of Ernesto U. Savona*. New York: Springer.

Clarke, R. V. 2014. Foreword to *Organized Crime, Corruption and Crime Prevention: Essays in Honor of Ernesto U. Savona*, ix–xi edited by Stefano Caneppele and Francesco Calderoni. New York: Springer.

Savona, E. U., G. Berlusconi, and M. Riccardi, eds. 2016. *Organized Crime in European Businesses*. London: Routledge.

Savona, E. U., and B. Leclerc, eds. 2016. *Crime Prevention in the XXI Century*. New York: Springer.

Savona, E. U., and M. Zanella. 2019. "Extortion and Organized Crime." In *International and Transnational Crime and Justice: An Anthology*, edited by M. Natarajan. 2nd ed. New York: Cambridge University Press.

Transcrime, Joint Research Centre on Transnational Crime. 2008. *Study on Extortion Racketeering the Need for an Instrument to Combat Activities of Organized Crime*. Brussels: European Commission.

Schengen Cooperation

A number of European Union (EU) member states (referred to as the "Schengen states") have eliminated internal border controls. The ease with which borders can be crossed has led these countries, along with some contiguous countries that are not EU members, to agree on special border control and law enforcement arrangements to better respond to crime and security concerns in a "borderless Europe." These arrangements consist in particular of the Schengen Information System, controlled delivery, hot pursuit, and cross border surveillance.

THE SCHENGEN AGREEMENTS

One of the principles of the European Union is freedom of movement. After prolonged discussions over the gradual elimination of internal border controls throughout the European Union failed to lead to consensus, Belgium, the Federal

Republic of Germany, France, Luxembourg, and the Netherlands negotiated such an agreement among themselves: the 1985 Schengen Agreement. This was followed by the 1990 Schengen Convention, which included provisions not only on the elimination of internal border controls and a common visa policy but also on police cooperation.

When the fundamental EU treaty was renegotiated (the 1997 Treaty of Amsterdam), the substance of the two Schengen agreements was incorporated. In the meantime, all EU member states, with the exception of Ireland and the United Kingdom, had signed the Schengen Convention. (In signing the Treaty of Amsterdam, Ireland and the United Kingdom maintained their "opt out" from the Schengen cooperation.) Iceland, Liechtenstein, Norway, and Switzerland, while not EU members, have made separate agreements on joining the Schengen cooperation.

Bulgaria, Croatia, Cyprus, and Romania, although EU members and signatories of the Schengen Convention, have not yet been certified "Schengen ready" in respect to their air borders, visa arrangements, police cooperation, and personal data protection. Until they do so, they can only participate in the Schengen cooperation to a limited extent.

To ordinary citizens, the practical impact of the Schengen area is that they can travel throughout much of continental Europe without needing to show a passport at any of the internal borders. (Some countries have since temporarily reintroduced internal border controls, in particular as a response to the migrant crisis in 2016.)

Such free movement, however, opens up the risk that offenders might take advantage of the territorial nature of law enforcement or that persons refused entry into the Schengen area by one country may seek to enter the area through another country. The Schengen arrangements are designed to counter this risk.

THE SCHENGEN INFORMATION SYSTEM

The Schengen Information System (SIS) is used for cooperation among law enforcement, judicial, border control, and migration authorities of the Schengen countries. The SIS contains data on, for example, arrest warrants; missing persons; lost or stolen firearms, identity documents and motor vehicles; and third-state nationals refused entry into or the right to stay in the Schengen area. The SIS can be consulted by any competent law enforcement or border agent in any of the participating states.

The SIS consists of a central system (maintained by France), national systems, and a communications infrastructure connecting these systems. Each Schengen country is responsible for maintaining its national system and its national SIRENE bureau. Both EU and national data protection regimes apply. Every person has the right to access his or her personal data in the SIS and ask, as needed, for its correction or deletion.

Although Ireland and the United Kingdom are not a party to the Schengen Convention, they do use the SIS for law enforcement purposes. Bulgaria, Croatia, Cyprus, and Romania, which intend to join Schengen cooperation, also use the SIS for law enforcement cooperation. None of these six countries have access to

SIS data on third-state persons who have been refused entry into the Schengen area or who are staying in the Schengen area.

OTHER SCHENGEN LAW ENFORCEMENT COOPERATION

In addition to SIS, the Schengen Convention contains provisions on controlled delivery, cross border surveillance, and hot pursuit across borders. Controlled delivery, in the Schengen context, refers to cases in which the authorities allow an illegal or suspect consignment to proceed across internal borders under the cover supervision of the respective law enforcement authorities to secure evidence against the entire network of traffickers.

Cross border surveillance refers to the possibility that law enforcement and security agencies may continue their surveillance of suspects or persons of interest even if these persons cross an internal border. Similarly, hot pursuit involves the pursuit of a fleeing suspect caught in a serious offence or a person escaping from custody across an internal border. In both cases, the authorities of the country in question are to be notified so that they can take over the surveillance or the hot pursuit.

Matti Joutsen

See also: Controlled Delivery; Hot Pursuit, International; International Police Cooperation

Further Reading

De Capitano, Emilio. 2014. "The Schengen System after Lisbon: From Cooperation to Integration." *ERA Forum* 15 (1): 101–118.

Den Boer, Monica. 2017. "Policing Schengen." In *A Threat against Europe? Security, Migration and Integration,* edited by J. Peter Burgess, 191–210. Brussels: Brussels University Press.

European Commission. n.d. "Schengen Area." Accessed January 21, 2019. https://ec.europa.eu/home-affairs/what-we-do/policies/borders-and-visas/schengen_en.

Zaiotti, Ruben. 2011. *Cultures of Border Control: Schengen and the Evolution of European Frontiers.* Chicago and London: University of Chicago Press.

Sea Piracy

Sea piracy (Maritime piracy) is considered one of the oldest international crimes. In the 17th century, pirates were classified as *hostis humani generis* ("enemies of mankind"). This granted ships universal jurisdiction over pirate vessels regardless of location or nationality of the vessel or persons therein. This legal principle was maintained in the current international law of piracy (United Nations Convention on the Law of the Sea 1982, Article 103).

DEFINITIONS

The international definition of "piracy" is listed in Article 101 of the 1982 United Nations Convention on the Law of the Sea (UNCLOS). A relic of historical piracy, the UNCLOS definition is a facsimile of the piracy clause in the 1958 Convention on the High Seas, stating that piracy consists of

> a) Any illegal acts of violence, detention, or any act of depredation committed for private ends by the crew or the passengers of a private ship or a private aircraft, and directed:
>
> i. On the high seas, against another ship or aircraft, or against persons or property on board such ship or aircraft;
> ii. Against a ship, aircraft, persons or property in a place outside the jurisdiction of any State;
>
> b) Any act of voluntary participation in the operation of a ship or of an aircraft with knowledge of facts making it a pirate ship or aircraft.

Based on this international definition, piracy is limited to acts that occur in international waters, in a ship-to-ship conflict, and for private ends. These legal limitations have meant that acts of violence, detention, or depredation are only labeled "piracy" if they occur outside of territorial waters (i.e., beyond 12 nautical miles from the coast of a nation-state). Therefore, under international law, a vessel that is attacked while in port or waiting at anchorage will not be seen as a victim of piracy. This is reinforced by the two-ship requirement that excludes cases that are initiated from a dock. The private ends limitation excludes acts that are organized or condoned by states as well as any acts that are committed by organized subnational groups with a political motive (Twyman-Ghoshal 2018, 137).

The consequence of this narrow definition of piracy is that de facto piracy attacks are excluded if the location of the incident is in territorial waters or if the attack was not launched from another ship. In an effort to address this issue, the International Maritime Organization (IMO), a specialized agency of the United Nations tasked with maritime issues, added "armed robbery against ships" as a separate but related category. The new category was added in the 1995 Code of Practice for the Investigation for the Crime of Piracy and Armed Robbery against Ships, laying out identical guidelines for investigation and information sharing for both piracy and armed robbery (Twyman-Ghoshal 2018, 137).

Another concern of the piracy provision has been its exclusion of politically motivated acts. This issue was highlighted in the 1985 seizure of the cruise ship *Achille Lauro* by the Palestinian Liberation Front. The incident resulted in the killing of a passenger when demands were not met. The incident laid bare the limitations of UNCLOS piracy provision, which did not apply to the case due to the political motive and the lack of a second ship. The 1988 Convention for the Suppression of Unlawful Acts against the Safety of Maritime Navigation (SUA) was drafted with the intention of resolving these limitations. The broad scope of the convention has seen a move away from the term *piracy*; instead, the language includes any form of unlawful and intentional seizure, control, act of violence, or threat thereof that endangers the safe navigation of a vessel (Article 3). SUA does not distinguish between the location at sea of the attack, nor does it require a ship-to-ship conflict. Moreover, SUA does not consider the purpose or motivation of the act (Twyman-Ghoshal 2018, 139). However, despite these amendments, the convention has a major drawback that has limited its use: it does not have universal jurisdiction.

Due to the limitations of the legal definition of "sea piracy," an alternative that has been used for research purposes has been that of the International Maritime Bureau (IMB), a nongovernmental agency. In their piracy reports, the IMB includes "any act of boarding or attempting to board any ship with the apparent intent or capability to use force in the furtherance of the act" (IMB 1992, 2). The benefit of this broad definition is that it captures a variety of piratical acts.

TYPES OF PIRACY

The IMO classifies piracy into three distinct types: low-level armed robbery, medium-level armed assault and robbery, and major criminal hijack (Murphy 2009, 129). This simple typology acknowledges that a range of behaviors are classified as piracy. These include boarding a vessel clandestinely to appropriate items from a ship's storage; robbery that includes interpersonal violence and targets the belongings of the crew; and boardings that are directed at stealing some of the ship's cargo. More complex attacks may involve short- and long-term vessel seizures that can be motivated by theft of the cargo or obtaining a ransom in exchange for releasing the vessel.

HISTORY OF CONTEMPORARY PIRACY

Despite its long heritage, contemporary piracy has some notable distinctions from its historical predecessor. Historical forms of piracy navigated in a world without sovereign territorial boundaries and at a time when not all piracies were seen as unlawful (with distinctions made between privateers, buccaneers, and pirates) (Young 2005, 16). With the advent of the 20th century, piracy had all but disappeared. However, in the late 1970s, incidents of piracy began to be reemerge.

In this early phase of contemporary piracy, most of the recorded attacks were concentrated in the Malacca Straits, a busy 500-mile shipping lane that connects parts of Southeast Asia and the Pacific to South Asia, the Middle East, and Europe. However, piracy was not unique to this part of the world; incidents of contemporary piracy have been recorded in Asia, Africa, North and South America, and Europe (Twyman-Ghoshal and Pierce 2014, 657).

The majority of piracy involves petty sea robbery, with low levels of violence, organization, and sophistication. These incidents usually occur at night, close to shore, and target ship equipment (Twyman-Ghoshal and Pierce 2014, 664). A more serious form of these low-level crimes includes a short-term seizure of the vessel where the crew members are held hostage while their valuables or the ship's high-value goods (such as electronics or money) are pilfered.

In the 1990s, the number and scale of attacks in Southeast Asia increased. More sophisticated cases involved the partial or complete appropriation of a vessel's cargo. Particularly notable at the time were phantom ship cases. These involved the theft of entire ships and their cargoes, jettisoning of their crews, rebranding the vessels, reregistering the vessels under new names, and using the vessels and cargoes for fraud.

With the dawn of the new century, global piracy trends changed again. From 2001 to 2010, the five highest piracy incident countries (HPICs) that accounted for nearly 70 percent of all recorded piracies were Indonesia (24.8%), Somalia (24.2%), Nigeria (8.3%), Bangladesh (7.5%), and India (3.8%) (Twyman-Ghoshal and Pierce 2014, 656). While most piracy around the world was motivated by theft and occurred in territorial seas, Somali piracy was characterized by highly organized seizures for ransom in international waters (Twyman-Ghoshal 2018, 144). Somali attacks occurred during the day, using sophisticated weaponry, but were less likely to successfully board a ship than the other HPICs (Twyman-Ghoshal and Pierce 2014, 667). Nigerian piracy, which was also highly armed, exhibited more violence and lethality than the other HPICs (Twyman-Ghoshal and Pierce 2014, 661, 667).

RESPONSE TO PIRACY

Much of the focus in responding to maritime piracy has been on using a law enforcement model (Murphy 2009, 24). This has included understanding factors that create opportunities for piracy, such as favorable ocean geography, legal and jurisdictional weaknesses, and inadequate policing and maritime security. Although these are important factors, they are limited in applicability in the vast ocean environment. Alternative models have focused on addressing the root causes of piracy, which stems from societal precursors on land that ultimately explain the changing trends and patterns seen in contemporary piracy (Twyman-Ghoshal 2018, 155).

Anamika A. Twyman-Ghoshal

See also: Maersk Alabama Pirate Attack; Transnational, Global, and International Crime; UN Convention on the Law of the Sea

Further Reading

International Maritime Bureau. 1992. *IMB Annual Piracy Report.* Kuala Lumpur: IMB Regional Piracy Center.

Murphy, Martin. 2009. *Small Boat, Weak States, Dirty Money: Piracy and Maritime Terrorism in the Modern World.* New York: Columbia University Press.

Twyman-Ghoshal, Anamika. 2018. "Somali Maritime Predation: Traditional Piracy or a New Form of Terrorism?" In *Historical Perspectives on Organised Crime and Terrorism*, edited by James Windle, John Morrison, Aaron Winter, and Andrew Silke, 135–156. Abington, UK: Routledge.

Twyman-Ghoshal, Anamika, and Glenn Pierce. 2014. "The Changing Nature of Contemporary Maritime Piracy: Results from the Contemporary Maritime Piracy Database 2001–2010." *British Journal of Criminology* 54 (4): 652–672.

United Nations. 1982. Convention of the Law of the Sea. Accessed February 11, 2019. http://www.un.org/depts/los/convention_agreements/convention_overview_convention.htm.

Young, Adam. 2005. "Roots of Contemporary Maritime Piracy in Southeast Asia." In *Piracy in Southeast Asia: Status, Issues and Responses*, edited by Derek Johnson and Mark Valencia, 1–22. Singapore: International Institute for Asian Studies.

September 11 Terrorist Attacks (2001)

On September 11, 2001, the worst act of terrorism in the history of the United States destroyed the Twin Towers of the World Trade Center in New York City and part of the Pentagon in Washington, D.C. The attacks killed nearly 3,000 people at the World Trade Center and almost 200 at the Pentagon. In an intricate plot, terrorists hijacked four planes and crashed one into each tower of the World Trade Center and one into the Pentagon. The fourth plane crashed into a field in western Pennsylvania after its passengers attempted to overtake the hijackers. All aboard were killed. Officials believe that the fourth aircraft was headed for the White House or the U.S. Capitol in Washington, D.C.

EVENTS OF 9/11

American Airlines Flight 11 from Boston was the first plane to crash, hitting the North Tower of the World Trade Center at 8:45 a.m. At 9:03 a.m., United Airlines Flight 175 from Boston hit the South Tower. At 9:40 a.m., the Federal Aviation Administration (FAA) stopped all air traffic nationwide for the first time in history. The FAA also diverted all incoming international flights to Canada. However, the order came too late. At 9:43 a.m., American Airlines Flight 77 from Dulles Airport in Washington, D.C., crashed into the Pentagon, and at 10:10 a.m., United Airlines Flight 93 crashed near Shanksville, Pennsylvania. All were cross-country flights carrying full loads of fuel.

Both towers of the World Trade Center eventually collapsed, the South Tower at 10:05 a.m. and the North Tower at 10:28 a.m. The collapse killed thousands of people who were attempting to evacuate the buildings, including several hundred New York City firefighters that had been dispatched after the first plane hit), as well as other firefighters at the scene, police officers, rescue workers, and onlookers outside the buildings.

The chaotic day included evacuations at the White House, the U.S. State Department, and the U.S. Capitol Building. President George W. Bush was flown from Florida to a bunker at a U.S. Air Force base in Nebraska, the Canadian and Mexican borders were put on the highest state of alert, and all U.S. military personnel around the world were placed on high alert. All potential targets around the United States were evacuated (including airports); all nonessential employees at the North Atlantic Treaty Organization (NATO) headquarters in Brussels, Belgium, were sent home; and Israel evacuated all its diplomatic missions.

IMMEDIATE AFTERMATH OF ATTACKS

In the initial days after the attacks, the full extent of the damage was still unclear. Rescue crews continued their search and rescue missions at the World Trade Center and the Pentagon, digging through millions of tons of rubble. The stock market remained closed until September 17, sending the already lagging U.S. economy into further distress. Airlines announced layoffs, as consumers expressed fears of flying. To help offset this, the U.S. government quickly established the September 11th Victim Compensation Fund, which provided monetary compensation to the families of victims who agreed not to file any lawsuits related to the attacks. There were only 80 lawsuits filed, making the fund a success in shielding the airlines. In addition, the world rallied in support, and for the first time in history, NATO invoked Article 5 of the North Atlantic Treaty (1949), which states that an attack on one member of the alliance is an attack on all members and calls for the implementation of collective self-defense. Donations to such charities as the Red Cross and the United Way reached unprecedented heights.

On September 20, Bush became the first president to address an emergency joint session of the U.S. Congress since Franklin D. Roosevelt gave his "Day of Infamy" speech to Congress on December 8, 1941, after the Japanese attack on Pearl Harbor. During Bush's speech, he pledged that justice would be done to those responsible and announced the creation of the Office of Homeland Security. Bush appointed Pennsylvania governor Tom Ridge as the first director of the cabinet-level office responsible for a federal plan to combat domestic terrorism (the office later became part of the Department of Homeland Security). Bush also used the speech to condemn domestic hate crimes against Arab Americans, who suffered from scattered violence throughout the United States after the attacks.

In the aftermath of the World Trade Center and Pentagon attacks, the U.S. government called for the implementation of an overall strategy of vigilance to deter terrorism. Bush underlined the particular need for international cooperation. Indeed, the tragedy had not only claimed American lives; the victims originated from more than 100 different countries. The international response showed that many countries understood the tragedy was theirs as well.

U.S. RESPONSE TO TERRORISM

Unlike most previous terrorist attacks, there were no credible claims of responsibility. However, Saudi millionaire Osama bin Laden, the leader of Al Qaeda, was named the prime suspect. He was also believed to have been behind the World Trade Center bombing in 1993, the U.S. Embassy bombings in Africa in 1998, and the USS *Cole* bombing in 2000. Soon after the attacks, all nations cut diplomatic ties with Afghanistan's ruling Taliban government, which was said to be harboring bin Laden, and many demanded that bin Laden be handed over. On October 7, Operation Enduring Freedom was launched against the Taliban. U.S.-led forces quickly toppled the regime, and Afghanistan began a new government with the support of the United States and United Nations. Meanwhile, the Federal Bureau of Investigation (FBI) quickly identified 19 alleged hijackers, all Muslims from Middle Eastern countries. Hundreds of people believed to be linked to or to have information about the hijackers were detained or arrested in the United States and throughout the world.

For nearly a decade, Osama bin Laden, the prime suspect in the attacks, eluded capture. On May 2, 2011, he was killed in Pakistan in a raid by U.S. Navy SEALs. In announcing bin Laden's death, President Barack Obama called it the most significant achievement to date in America's effort to defeat Al Qaeda, but he also noted that bin Laden's death did not mark the end of America's action, as there was no doubt that Al Qaeda would continue to pursue attacks.

9/11 COMMISSION REPORT

In September 2002, Bush created the National Commission on Terrorist Attacks upon the United States, which was charged with investigating the events leading up to the attacks, including any intelligence failures that may have occurred. After more than a year of hearings and inquiries, the commission concluded that though the attacks certainly came as a shock, they should not have come as a surprise. The commission reported that the U.S. intelligence community was poorly organized, and the country was ill prepared to react to the attacks. In light of the failures of the intelligence and defense communities, the commission recommended several sweeping reforms. These included creating a national counterterrorism center and "unifying the intelligence community with a new National Intelligence Director." In addition, the commission recommended enhancing diplomatic relationships in the Middle East, particularly with certain Islamic groups that may have been alienated by the War on Terror. The overhaul of the intelligence and defense communities took years to accomplish, though Congress quickly created legislation based on the 9/11 Commission Report.

9/11 MEMORIAL

The National September 11 Memorial is a tribute to the nearly 3,000 people killed in the terror attacks at the World Trade Center, the Pentagon, and near Shanksville, Pennsylvania, and also the 6 people killed in the 1993 World Trade Center bombing. Twin reflecting pools, each nearly an acre in size, feature the largest manmade waterfalls in North America. The pools sit within the footprints where the Twin Towers stood. Bronze panels, inscribed with the names of each person who died in 2001 and 1993, edge the memorial pools.

Philip J. MacFarlane and Philip L. Reichel

See also: Al Qaeda; Bin Laden, Osama; Terrorism, International

Further Reading

Baker, Peter, Helene Cooper, and Mark Mazzetti. 2011. "Bin Laden Is Dead, Obama Says." *New York Times*, May 1. Accessed January 11, 2019. https://www.nytimes.com/2011/05/02/world/asia/osama-bin-laden-is-killed.html?mtrref=undefined&gwh=CE49F978A9BCD738455B5C839E00B380&gwt=pay.

Dudley, William, ed. 2002. *The Attack on America, September 11, 2001.* San Diego, CA: Greenhaven Press.

Halliday, Fred. 2002. *Two Hours That Shook the World: September 11, 2001: Causes and Consequences.* London: Saqi Books.

National Commission on Terrorist Attacks upon the United States. 2004. "The 9/11 Commission Report." Accessed January 11, 2019. https://www.9-11commission.gov.

Villemez, Jason. 2011. "9/11 to Now: Ways We Have Changed." *PBS NewsHour*, September 14. Accessed January 11, 2019. https://www.pbs.org/newshour/world/911-to-now-ways-we-have-changed.

Sex Exploitation

Sex trafficking refers to individuals forced, defrauded, or coerced to perform commercial sex. This includes women, men, and children who have involuntarily entered the sex industry. It is the second most common form of modern slavery after forced labor exploitation (ILO and Walk Free Foundation 2017).

Minors under the age of 18 engaging in commercial sex are considered to be victims of human trafficking, regardless of the use of force, fraud, or coercion. Nonetheless, according to UNICEF (2005), every two minutes a child is being prepared for sexual exploitation.

There is a great gender bias among victims of sex trafficking. Women and girls are disproportionately affected by the illegal commercial sex industry, accounting for 99 percent of the victims (ILO and Walk Free Foundation 2017) In other types of human trafficking, such as labor exploitation, this number drops to 58 percent. Furthermore, the trafficking of women and children for sexual exploitation is the fastest-growing criminal enterprise in the world (Equality Now n.d.).

Regarding geographical distribution, the International Labour Organization and Walk Free Foundation (2017) report that more than 70 percent of victims of forced sexual exploitation were in the Asia Pacific region, followed by Europe and Central Asia (14%), Africa (8%), the Americas (4%), and the Arab States (1%). This refers to the regions where the victims came from, but being a transnational crime, they can be taken to another state.

DATA ON SEX TRAFFICKING

As sexual exploitation is more frequently reported or detected by authorities than other forms of human trafficking, it has become the most statistically documented type of trafficking (Chamie 2015). However, the amount of data are still not sufficient nor totally reliable. Trafficking statistics are underreported to government authorities, and as trafficking can often overlap with other crimes, such as illegal immigration, child abuse, prostitution, and forced labor, it can end up being recorded as something other than sex exploitation.

SEX TRAFFICKERS

Sex traffickers employ the means of force, fraud, or coercion to compel the victim to provide commercial sexual acts. This means that the victim has not consented in free will, although he or she may be colluded to do so. It is common for sex traffickers to lie, make false promises, or use threats or violence, and they may also make use of debt bondages and other forms of control and manipulation.

A diverse set of venues and business are trespassed by sex trafficking, such as escort services, brothels, truck shops, strip clubs, hostess clubs, and hotels and motels, among others. Major sporting events are also characterized by the presence of sex trafficking.

Just as there is a gender bias in terms of trafficking victims, there is also one regarding the traffickers. Compared to other crimes, there is a major involvement of women in the recruitment for sexual exploitation and in the trafficking of girls. Some studies have found that woman traffickers are typically in low-level positions of human trafficking networks, but they tend, nonetheless, to be more exposed to being detected and prosecuted than men (Chamie 2015).

It is also important to highlight that, as other criminal gangs, sex traffickers have adapted to globalization and modern technology to set up networks for a wide range of criminal enterprises (Katel 2014). This means that the criminals might also be involved in drug trafficking, weapons, extortion, and other misconducts.

DEMAND

There are three primary components to the demand for sexual exploitation: the exploiters who make up the sex industry, the culture that tolerates or promotes sexual exploitation, and the men who buy commercial sex acts (Hughes 2005). Sex trafficking is a market-driven criminal industry that is based on the principles of supply and demand. Therefore, buyers of commercial sex increase the demand and might likewise provide a trafficking incentive for traffickers.

People trafficked for sexual exploitation have to compete with voluntary sex workers, whose numbers can be expected to swell if economic conditions worsen. The growth in supply is likely to cause a drop in price, chasing what is likely to be a declining demand from the cash-strapped population. The net result would be smaller incentives for trafficking.

Global Centurion (n.d.) mapped major hubs for sex trafficking around the world. The United States, Mexico, Brazil, Germany, the Netherlands, Israel, the Gulf States, South Africa, India, Sri Lanka, and China are the countries that push the demand. The mapping results found that major sporting events (for example, the Super Bowl or World Cup), the presence of military bases, politically unstable countries, and countries in economic crisis create demand hubs.

VICTIMS AND SURVIVORS

According to the International Labour Organization (ILO) and Walk Free Foundation (2017), victims of sexual exploitation remain in this situation for an average of about two years (23.1 months) before being freed or managing to escape. As mentioned, women and children are the main victims of sex trafficking. Vulnerable populations, from developing countries or from poorer parts of society in developed countries, are frequently targeted by traffickers, including runaway and homeless youth and victims of domestic violence, sexual assault, war, and social discrimination (Polaris Project n.d.).

Many are lured in with the false promise of a job, such as modeling or dancing, and they become victims of a complex and organized criminal network. Some are even forced by family members. The victims may suffer physical and mental consequences that are even more severe in children, such as sleeping and eating disorders, sexually transmitted diseases, drug addiction, guilt and shame, fear, anxiety, and depression. For those taken to a new country, there may be shock from finding themselves in a strange country. There can also be trauma associated with bonding with the trafficker.

ENDING SEX TRAFFICKING

Attempts to combat trafficking were addressed by the United Nations Convention against Transnational Organized Crime, but its eradication requires international, regional, and national cooperation. Poverty, discrimination, exclusion, and violence are the root causes and need to be addressed along with the demand side (UNICEF 2006).

At the international level, the UN General Assembly adopted the Global Plan of Action to Combat Trafficking in Persons in 2010. It calls on governments, UN bodies, international organizations, and civil society to work together to integrate the fight against human trafficking into the UN's broader programs on global development.

Civil society and nongovernmental organizations (NGOs) have launched campaigns to ensure that sex trafficking is addressed as its own distinct form of human trafficking in its review of the Global Plan of Action.

Dafne Calderón Burgoa and Ana Carolina Paci

See also: Gender-Based Violence; Granados Sex Trafficking Organization; Human Trafficking; Human Trafficking and Sporting Events; Labor Exploitation; Sex Tourism

Further Reading

Chamie, Joseph. 2015. "Human Trafficking: A Serious Challenge to Humanity." In *Great Decisions 2015*, edited by the Foreign Policy Association, 77–88. New York: Foreign Policy Association.

Equality Now. n.d. "Sex Trafficking Fact Sheets." Accessed August 20, 2018. https://www.equalitynow.org/sex-trafficking-fact-sheet.

Global Centurion. n.d. "Mapping Human Trafficking." Accessed August 20, 2018. https://www.globalcenturion.org/archived-workpages/mapping-hubs-of-demand.

Hughes, Donna M. 2005. "The Demand for Victims of Sex Trafficking." http://www.academia.edu/download/31193909/demand_for_victims.pdf

International Labour Organization (ILO) and Walk Free Foundation. 2017. "Global Estimates of Modern Slavery: Forced Labour and Forced Marriage." Accessed January 21, 2019. http://www.ilo.org/wcmsp5/groups/public/---dgreports/---dcomm/documents/publication/wcms_575479.pdf.

Katel, Peter. 2014. "Transnational Crime." *CQ Researcher* 24 (30): 697–720.

Polaris Project. n.d. "Sex Trafficking." Accessed August 20, 2018. https://polarisproject.org/human-trafficking/sex-trafficking.

United Nations International Children's Emergency Fund (UNICEF). 2005. "Children Out of Sight, Out of Mind, Out of Reach." Press release, December 14. Accessed January 11, 2019. https://www.unicef.org/sowc06/press/release.php.

United Nations International Children's Emergency Fund (UNICEF). 2006. "Child Protection Information Sheet: Trafficking." Last modified May 2006. Accessed January 11, 2019. https://www.unicef.org/people/files/Trafficking.pdf.

United Nations Office on Drugs and Crime (UNODC). 2010. *The Globalization of Crime: A Transnational Organized Crime Threat Assessment*. Vienna: UNODC.

Sex Tourism

Sex tourism is travel planned with the intent to engage in sex with a child or adult in a foreign country where prostitution may be legal or illegal (CDC 2013). Sex tourism occurs in developed and developing nations but is most visible in Southeast Asia, Latin America, and the Caribbean. Sex tourism supports global human trafficking because tour operators in developed countries can organize tours to other parts of the world to engage buyers in sexual relations with trafficked people (Banks and Baker 2016). Furthermore, children and trafficked adults are unable to consent to sex or pornography. Whether the aim is to have sex with children or adults, the sex tourist believes the exchange is voluntary or accepted by local value systems (Ryan and Hall 2001, 56).

Even when prostitution is legal in a specific country, human trafficking, sex with children, and child pornography are typically crimes in every country, and someone who engages in these activities in a foreign country can still be prosecuted under U.S. law upon return (Andrews 2004; CDC 2013). Two laws have been signed in the United States that are aimed at combating sex tourism. In June 2002, the U.S. House of Representatives passed the Sex Tourism Prohibition Improvement Act of 2002. Later, in April 2003, the PROTECT Act was signed into law, outlining specific provisions and punishments for sex tourism (Andrews 2004).

TOURISM AND THE SEX INDUSTRY

Tourism is one of the fastest-growing global industries, and it has become central to economic development for countries experiencing poverty, high rates of unemployment, and international debt. Sex tourism is a part of the informal tourism economy, but it can involve individuals employed in the formal tourism sector that are attempting to supplement low wages in exchange for sex with tourists (Sanchez Taylor 2006).

The tourism industry has continued to grow since the 1970s, and sex tourism is estimated to be a multibillion-dollar industry. Currently, it is the third most lucrative illegal industry in the world. According to the International Labour Organization (ILO), about 21 million people are sold into the commercial sex trade worldwide, approximately 1 million being children (U.S. Department of State 2006). For many traveling abroad from more industrialized nations to less developed ones, paying for sex is integral to the travel experience (Ryan and Hall 2001). The financial disparities between these customers and those who service them result in a heightened imbalance of power, and they create challenges in prosecuting perpetrators (Andrews 2004).

Sex tourism can include engaging in such activities as purchasing pornography, visiting brothels and strip clubs, watching peep shows, receiving sexual massages, going on sex tours, hiring escorts, having sex with minors, or paying for any form of sex while traveling (Bender and Furman 2004). In the tourism sector, commercial sex can be a consensual trade or a form of global human trafficking, but it is often challenging to distinguish. Commercial sex workers are made up primarily of vulnerable populations, such as migrant women, victims of trafficking, or exploited children (ECPAT International 2008). Globally, a focus has been placed on protecting children and punishing offenders who seek out sex with children in foreign countries.

CHILD SEX TOURISM

Technological changes made global travel more accessible, which created new challenges to protect children from sexual exploitation. Whether by preference or circumstance, children are frequently targeted by sex tourists (Andrews 2004). The United Nations defined "child sex tourism" as tourism that is organized with the primary purpose of facilitating a commercial-sexual relationship with a child and involves anyone below the age of 18, which is stated in the United Nations Convention on the Rights of the Child.

It is estimated that 2 million children are victimized every year worldwide (CDC 2013). Nearly 250,000 people travel annually to have sex with children, referred to as "child sex tourists" (ECPAT International 2008). Children exploited by sex tourists suffer sexual abuse, poverty, homelessness, and physical, emotional, and psychological abuse. Additionally, exploited children suffer from various health problems, including illnesses, addictions, malnourishment, infections, injuries, and sexually transmitted infections (CDC 2013).

CHILD SEXUAL ABUSE PREVENTION ACT

In the 1990s, child advocates, nongovernmental organizations (NGOs), the United Nations, and the media applied pressure to have "consumer" countries of sex tourism develop laws to combat the commercial sexual exploitation of children (Andrews 2004). In 1994, President Bill Clinton signed into law the Violent Crime Control and Law Enforcement Act, often referred to as the "Crime Bill" (Andrews 2004). The bill included a provision, the Child Sexual Abuse Prevention Act, which made it illegal to travel abroad to engage in sexual activity with a minor.

In December 2002, the United States became the 42nd country to ratify the Optional Protocol to the United Nations Convention on the Rights of the Child on the Sale of Children, Child Prostitution, and Child Pornography (Articles 34 and 35), which provided a framework for international law to criminalize actions of child sex abusers on a global level (UNICEF 2005). Approximately 45 countries have implemented laws to allow for the prosecution of any child sex tourism abroad, and they created a global Code of Conduct for the Protection of Children from Sexual Exploitation in Travel and Tourism to protect children from sex tourism (UNICEF 2005).

OPERATION PREDATOR

In 2003, U.S. Immigration and Customs Enforcement (ICE) began Operation Predator. Operation Predator is an international initiative that collaborates with law enforcement agencies around the world in the attempt to identify, investigate, and arrest child predators who engage in the sex trafficking of children. Additionally, Operation Predator works with foreign governments to track American child sex tourists. Traveling to have sex with a minor is illegal, and offenders can be fined and prosecuted to the fullest extent. So far, ICE agents have arrested and convicted 99 U.S. child sex tourists, with many more cases currently under investigation (ICE 2012).

Shanell Sanchez and Hena Mustafa

See also: Gender-Based Violence; Human Trafficking; Human Trafficking and Sporting Events; Labor Exploitation; Sex Exploitation

Further Reading

Andrews, Sarah. 2004. "Domestic Prosecution of the American International Sex Tourist: Efforts to Protect Children from Sexual Exploitation." *Journal of Criminal Law & Criminology* 94 (2): 415–454.

Banks, C., and J. Baker. 2016. *Comparative International, and Global Justice: Perspectives from Criminology and Criminal Justice.* Thousand Oaks, CA: Sage.

Bender, Kimberly, and Rich Furman. 2004. "The Implications of Sex Tourism on Men's Social, Psychological, and Physical Health." *Qualitative Report* 9 (2): 176–191.

Centers for Disease Control and Prevention (CDC). 2013. "Travelers' Health." Accessed January 21, 2019. https://wwwnc.cdc.gov/travel/page/sex-tourism.

ECPAT International. 2008. "Combating Child Sex Tourism: Questions and Answers." Accessed January 21, 2019. http://www.ecpat.org/wp-content/uploads/legacy/cst_faq_eng.pdf.

Immigration Customs Enforcement (ICE). 2012. "Operation Predator: Targeting Child Exploitation and Sexual Crimes." Accessed January 21, 2019. https://www.ice.gov/factsheets/predator.

Lichtblau, Eric, and James Dao. 2004. "U.S. Is Now Pursuing Americans Who Commit Sex Crimes Overseas." *New York Times*, February 11. Accessed January 21, 2019. http://www.nytimes.com/2004/06/08/us/us-is-now-pursuing-americans-who-commit-sex-crimes-overseas.html.

Ryan, Chris, and Michael Hall. 2001. *Sex Tourism: Marginal People and Liminalities.* Abingdon, UK: Routledge.

Sanchez Taylor, Jacqueline. 2006. "Female Sex Tourism: A Contradiction in Terms?" *Feminist Review* 83 (1): 42–59.

United Nations International Children's Emergency Fund (UNICEF). 2005. "Convention on the Rights of a Child." Accessed January 21, 2019. https://www.unicef.org/crc/index_30204.html.

Sex Trafficking, *see* Sex Exploitation

SHERLOC (Sharing Electronic Resources and Laws on Crime)

The SHERLOC (Sharing Electronic Resources and Laws On Crime) knowledge management portal is an initiative developed by the United Nations Office on Drugs and Crimes (UNODC) to facilitate the dissemination of information regarding the implementation of the UN Convention against Transnational Organized Crime (UNTOC) and its three protocols, for which UNODC is the guardian.

The SHERLOC portal currently hosts five databases: the Case Law Database, the Database of Legislation, the Bibliographic Database, a database on treaties, and a database on strategies. Moreover, it also hosts the Legislative Guide that supports users in better understanding the scope of the legislative provisions of UNTOC and the protocols thereto. SHERLOC has a broad geographical scope, and it includes resources from over 190 countries. It contains a wide range of legal resources: more than 7,000 legal provisions and 3,000 cases of jurisprudence. Finally, it is a multilingual platform available in the six official languages of the United Nations (Arabic, Chinese, English, French, Russian, and Spanish).

SCOPE

The resources hosted on SHERLOC cover a wide range of topics amounting to 15 different crime types, namely participation in an organized criminal group, corruption, counterfeiting, drug trafficking, money laundering, obstruction of justice, cybercrime, piracy and maritime crimes, smuggling of migrants, trafficking in persons, trafficking in cultural property, wildlife (including forest and fisheries) crimes, falsified medical products, trafficking in firearms, and terrorism. These crime types represent the different mandated areas of work of the UNODC, and states should consider criminalizing them as serious crimes, as defined in UNTOC, Article 2.

All databases are searchable by country or region, relevant UNTOC article(s), and relevance to specific crime types. Further, resources can be also filtered by additional keywords and crosscutting issues. Crosscutting issues include special procedures and provisions of the convention that facilitate international cooperation in the effective prosecution and adjudication of transnational organized crime, such as extradition, mutual legal assistance, joint investigations, or special investigative techniques, but also broader issues such as crime prevention and the protection of victims and witnesses. Moreover, crosscutting issues also include additional categories of trend topics in the discussion of organized crime, such as the gender dimension and the use of electronic evidence.

USE IN RESEARCH

The Case Law Database is a comprehensive database that allows users to see how member states are tackling organized crime cases both operationally and in their courts. It contains jurisprudence as well as records of successful law enforcement operations on the above-mentioned crime types. It provides users with a generic overview of the facts and main legal proceedings and provides details on specific aspects mentioned by the convention. The structure of this database provides users with a user-friendly overview of the main legal issues of each case, ranging from aspects of the investigation, international cooperation, and the core legal reasoning, together with the possibility to also access the full text of the original court documents.

The Database of Legislation is an electronic repository of laws relevant to the provisions of UNTOC and its protocols. It is searchable by country, UNTOC article, crime type, and crosscutting issue. While also enabling access to full legislation documents, the Database of Legislation provides extracts of laws relevant to specific UNTOC articles and crime types, allowing the user to quickly find provisions relating to their search query. This database collects relevant laws adopted at the domestic level to implement UNTOC. In doing so, it provides users with an overview of the key legal provisions of a domestic law as well as access to the full law. Through this database, users can get acquainted with the different measures taken by states parties in implementing UNTOC. Similarly, it can also be instrumental for a comparative study of laws adopted in a given region or between two or more specific countries.

The Bibliographic Database is an annotated bibliography that provides a synopsis of key articles that are searchable by country, research method, and keywords. This database contains both UNODC's and other international and regional organization's more relevant publications as well as articles from academia. The resources hosted in this database cover a wide geographical scope and are of global, regional, and country-specific relevance. Part of the articles and publications collected in this database are open resource. This database contributes to the general understanding of organized crime or of specific aspects related to the 15 crime types covered by SHERLOC.

The Strategies Database is a collection of strategic instruments adopted at regional and national levels to implement the Organized Crime Convention and the protocols thereto. It collects different types of documents, mainly strategies and plans of actions, adopted by states to tackle issues related to the 15 crime types covered by SHERLOC. This database can be used to assess the policy implications of specific laws adopted at the national level by member states. It provides an additional complementary type of resource, that is, the policy perspective of how international treaties are translated into policy.

The Treaties Database contains the ratification status of the UNTOC and its protocols. It can be searched by type of treaty and by country. It also provides a historical overview of the ratification status of those instruments by providing users with a timeline, illustrating who ratified or acceded UNTOC or other instruments and at what time. This database can be used to get a more exhaustive understanding of the different legal instruments negotiated and adopted by states to combat organized crime and related issues. Users can consult different categories of treaties (bilateral, regional, or international) to get a more comprehensive understanding of the existing treaty framework.

GLOBAL COVERAGE AND MULTILINGUALISM

One of the key principles of the portal is multilingualism, as resources hosted on the databases are related to more than 190 countries. Hence, the portal can be navigated in the six official languages of the United Nations (Arabic, Chinese, English, French, Russian, and Spanish) and is adaptable to mobile devices.

The portal plays a significant role in research, which is reflected in the large number of users from academia, including students. The portal enables researchers to learn from practices in other states and regions and different legal and political systems and not only from an academic perspective but from practical examples stemming from jurisprudence and legislative frameworks.

Maria Cristina Montefusco and Riikka Puttonen

See also: Transnational, Global, and International Crime; UN Convention against Transnational Organized Crime; UN Office on Drugs and Crime

Further Reading

United Nations. 2000. *United Nations Convention against Transnational Organized Crime and the Protocols Thereto.* Accessed January 21, 2019. https://www.unodc.org/unodc/en/organized-crime/intro/UNTOC.html.

United Nations Office on Drugs and Crime (UNODC). 2018. "About Us." Sharing Electronic Resources and Laws on Crime (SHERLOC). Accessed January 21, 2019. https://www.unodc.org/cld/about-us/index.html?lng=en.

Sinaloa Cartel

The Sinaloa Cartel has long been recognized as one of Mexico's original drug trafficking organizations. Pedro Aviles Perez, a pioneer in using aircrafts to smuggle narcotics into the United States, founded the cartel. In its formative years, the Sinaloa Cartel primarily focused on trafficking marijuana and heroin. Much of the cartel's success as a transnational criminal organization was rooted in its ability to engage in political corruption and having key members in law enforcement, such as Miguel Angel Felix Gallardo, dubbed the "Padrino" (the "Godfather"), who was a member of the Federal Judicial Police in Sinaloa and acted as family bodyguard to Sinaloa governor Leopoldo Sanchez Celis in the 1960s. However, the group has since expanded into smuggling cocaine, crystal methamphetamine, human smuggling, corruption, money laundering, disappearances, assassinations, and turf disputes with other trafficking organizations. The Sinaloa Cartel is regarded as the largest and most powerful drug trafficking organization (DTO) in the Western Hemisphere ("Sinaloa Cartel" 2018). Its headquarters are based in Culiacan, Sinaloa, and it has cells and reach in as many as 50 countries, including northern Mexico, the United States, Colombia, and Peru ("Sinaloa Cartel" 2018).

HISTORY

The present state of the Sinaloa Cartel owes its formation to the fall of the Guadalajara DTO in the 1980s, formerly led by Miguel Angel Felix Gallardo, Ernesto

Fonseca Carrillo, and Rafael Caro Quintero. After the assassination of Drug Enforcement Administration (DEA) Special Agent Enrique "Kiki" Camarena by the Guadalajara DTO in 1985, and subsequent arrests of the leaders of the DTO, Gallardo splintered the Guadalajara DTO ("The Felix Gallardo Organization" n.d.). In doing so, Joaquin Archivaldo "El Chapo" Guzmán and Ismael "El Mayo" Zambada Garcia commanded the Sinaloa Cartel, while the Tijuana Cartel went to the Arellano Felix siblings and the Juarez Cartel to Rafael Aguilar Guajardo ("The Felix Gallardo Organization" n.d.).

In the early 1990s and throughout the 2000s, the Sinaloa Cartel under Guzman's leadership continued to pioneer its tactics in smuggling narcotics into the United States. The most notably strategies were shipping cocaine in hidden compartments, such as jalapeño pepper cans and fake bananas, and through elaborate underground tunnels originating in Baja California Norte and Sonora, Mexico, with exit openings in U.S. cities such as Otay Mesa and Calexico, California, as well as Douglas, Arizona (Woody 2016).

ORGANIZATION

The Sinaloa Cartel operates under a business structure. Although it has been involved in disputes involving assassinations, its principal tactic that allows it to dominate the drug trafficking world and reign as the most powerful DTO in the world is centered on bribing officers and making alliances with other DTOs rather than going to war. Turf wars and disputes have been inevitable since the dissolvement of the Guadalajara DTO, with the most notable being the Sinaloa Cartel against the Tijuana Cartel in the 1990s and up to the early 2010s and then again in the mid to late 2010s.

The process of *plata o plomo* ("silver or lead"), whereby a DTO offers money to cooperate, join forces, or turn the other cheek (this being the silver approach), versus killing an individual who refused to cooperate (this being the lead approach) was tactfully mastered by Juan Jose Esparragoza Moreno, alias "El Azul." El Azul served as the dealmaker between the DTO factions of the Sinaloa Cartel, Tijuana Cartel, and Juarez Cartel to prevent violence ("Juan Jose Esparragoza Moreno" 2017).

TURF WARS

Although the Sinaloa Cartel handles its business transactions in a bribery manner, turf wars have been an inevitable part of its history and present-day dealings. After the dismantling of the Guadalajara Cartel, the Tijuana Cartel was authorized as the only cartel that would charge a quota for using the Tijuana border entry into the United States to other cartels, thus initiating a turf war between the Tijuana Cartel and the Sinaloa Cartel, as the leading members of the Sinaloa Cartel opposed a tax for using the border. This set off a bloody dispute for the free rite of passage over the Tijuana border that has been ongoing since circa 1990 to circa 2012 with intermediary alliances ("Tijuana Cartel" 2018). Alliances have been disrupted by new groups, such as the Cartel de Jalisco Nueva Generación engaging in an alliance with the Tijuana Cartel to fight against the Sinaloa Cartel since 2016 (Redaccion 2018).

GLOBAL EMPIRE

The Sinaloa Cartel is believed to be a multibillion-dollar operation with strong presence in numerous U.S. cities, such as Chicago, Illinois, where the Sinaloa Cartel controls as much as 80 percent of the cocaine market. Other U.S. cities, such as Los Angeles, California, are used as money laundering hubs. In one notable case, the Federal Bureau of Investigation (FBI) agents netted $90 million in the Los Angeles fashion district (Mozingo, Hsu, and Kim 2014).

Members of the Sinaloa Cartel have been arrested or detained in countries such as Colombia, where the Sinaloa Cartel had a direct connection for purchasing cocaine from the Revolutionary Armed Forces of Colombia (FARC), reducing the cost of cocaine. Other links to the Sinaloa Cartel have been reported in Malaysia and Australia, where the cartel has a direct connection for precursor chemicals and a new market for selling cocaine and a kilogram can exceed $200 million, respectively (Stewart 2016). Indeed, the Sinaloa Cartel has established itself as a dominant organization in the global drug trade that takes its share of $19 billion to $29 billion from the United States to Mexico per year, excluding the European, African, and Australian markets (Castillo 2017).

Jairo Patiño

See also: Cartel Organization; Guzman Loera, Joaquin; Jalisco New Generation Cartel; Los Zetas

Further Reading

Castillo, Mariano. 2017. "Drugs, Money and Violence: The Toll in Mexico." *CNN*. Last modified March 27, 2017. Accessed January 21, 2019. https://www.cnn.com/2016/02/15/world/mexico-drug-graphics/index.html.

"The Felix Gallardo Organization (Guadalajara OCG)." Wilson Center. Accessed May 8, 2018. https://www.wilsoncenter.org/the-felix-gallardo-organization-guadalajara-ocg.

"Juan Jose Esparragoza Moreno, alias 'El Azul.'" InSight Crime. Last modified March 10, 2017. Accessed January 21, 2019. https://www.insightcrime.org/mexico-organized-crime-news/juan-jose-esparragoza-moreno-el-azul.

Mozingo, Joe, Tiffany Hsu, and Victoria Kim. 2014. "L.A. Fashion District Firms Raided in Cartel Money Laundering Probe." *Los Angeles Times*. Last modified September 10, 2014. Accessed January 21, 2019. http://www.latimes.com/local/crime/la-me-fashion-district-raids-20140911-story.html.

Redaccion. 2018. "Asi es como el Cartel Jalisco Nueva Generacion se esta expandiendo en Mexico." *Huffington Post*, Last modified February 12, 2018. Accessed January 12, 2019. https://www.huffingtonpost.com.mx/2018/02/12/asi-es-como-el-cartel-jalisco-nueva-generacion-se-esta-expandiendo-en-mexico_a_23358887.

"Sinaloa Cartel." InSight Crime. Last modified January 24, 2018. Accessed January 12, 2019. https://www.insightcrime.org/mexico-organized-crime-news/sinaloa-cartel-profile.

Stewart, Scott. 2016. "From Colombia to New York City: The Narconomics of Cocaine." Business Insider. Last modified June 27, 2016. Accessed January 21, 2019. http://www.businessinsider.com/from-colombia-to-new-york-city-the-economics-of-cocaine-2015-7.

"Tijuana Cartel." InSight Crime. Last modified February 13, 2018. Accessed January 21, 2019. https://www.insightcrime.org/mexico-organized-crime-news/tijuana-cartel-profile.

Woody, Christopher. 2016. " 'A Candy Store for Smugglers': Step Inside the Billion-Dollar Drug Tunnels That 'Riddle' the US-Mexico Border." Business Insider. Last modified April 3, 2016. Accessed January 21, 2019. http://www.businessinsider.com/inside-mexican-drug-cartel-narco-tunnels-on-the-us-border-2016-4.

Single Convention on Narcotic Drugs

The Economic and Social Council of the United Nations held a conference in 1949 that laid the foundation to adopt the Single Convention of Narcotic Drugs of 1961 and develop global policy for drug control. The United Nations Conference for the Adoption of a Single Convention on Narcotic Drugs met in 1961 with 73 countries represented in New York. The treaty had three core objectives: replace existing multilateral treaties by creating a unified treaty and reducing the number of international treaties that focused on controlling narcotic drugs, limit the production of raw materials, and codify existing conventions into one to make drug control easier. The convention applies to more than 116 narcotic drugs and divides them into four groups with varying standards of control. The primary purpose of the Single Convention on Narcotic Drugs of 1961 was to secure an adequate narcotic drug supply for licit purposes, including medical and research needs, while also preventing the illicit drug trade (UNODC 2018). The Single Convention on Narcotic Drugs of 1961 entered into force on December 13, 1964, having met the requirement of 40 state ratifications.

HISTORY

The United States was a major force in developing the Single Convention, especially since its emerging role as a superpower following the World Wars and its unique involvement with the drug trade. The United States has historically imported more illicit narcotic drugs than any other country in the world, which makes the role of U.S. support for international drug control and treaties extremely important from a global context. The three international drug agreements currently in place resulted from intense and long-term U.S. pressure toward the international community. The shift from the focus on multilateral drug control to a more prohibitionist approach for nonmedical and nonscientific use of substances, including plant-based substances, such as cannabis, opium, and the coca leaf, was a drastic change with heavy U.S. influence. In fact, the final form of the convention was an initiative launched by the longtime head of the U.S. delegation, Harry J. Anslinger (Bewley-Taylor and Jelsma 2011).

Earlier treaties had focused on controlling opium, coca, and derivatives such as morphine, heroine, and cocaine and did not include cannabis. The Single Convention on Narcotic Drugs included cannabis and expanded the focus on other illicit drugs. The three drug agreements that are currently in place are the Single Convention on Narcotic Drugs of 1961, which was amended by a 1972 protocol; the Convention on Psychotropic Substances of 1971; and the United Nations Convention against Illicit Traffic in Narcotic Drugs and Psychotropic Substances of 1988. The vast majority of anti–drug trafficking strategies have focused on stopping the supply of drugs into the United States, but they have rarely focused on the demand side (Banks and Baker 2016). In fact, the three international drug agreements currently adopted by the United Nations attempt to regulate and control drug distribution throughout the world.

GOALS

The Single Convention on Narcotic Drugs of 1961 merged all other treaties that existed before 1961 in the attempt to have a "unified" treaty and also created the International Narcotics Control Board (INCB). The INCB was put in charge of administering controls on drug production, international trade, and dispensation. Further, this convention focused on combating drug abuse by coordinated international action. There are two forms of intervention and control that work together. First, it seeks to limit the possession, use, trade in, distribution, import, export, manufacture, and production of drugs exclusively to medical and scientific purposes. Specifically, serious concern of drug addiction was noted throughout the convention, and the need to control nonmedicinal drug use was a top priority. However, the recognition that drugs are a tool to relieve pain and that research should continue to be conducted was also recognized when writing the convention. Second, the convention attempts to combat drug trafficking through international cooperation to deter and discourage drug traffickers (Banks and Baker 2016).

PENAL PROVISIONS

Widely accepted penal obligations were introduced that could criminalize drug use under domestic law and also extend the preexisting controls put in place for the cultivation of plant-based drugs. The convention required countries that were less developed to abolish all nonmedical and nonscientific uses of plant-based drugs that had been used for centuries. Article 36 required the adoption of measures against such things as cultivating, producing, manufacturing, possessing, offering for sale, or importing or exporting drugs. Additionally, it allowed for drug offenders to be extradited. Article 37 states that any drugs, substances, and equipment used in or intended for the commission of any offenses in Article 36 are liable to seizure and confiscation. Article 38 required measures be taken against the abuse of drugs, but a 1971 amendment said criminal penalties could be substituted for "treatment, education, after-care, rehabilitation and social reintegration" if the offender is a drug abuser (UNODC 2018). The treaty allows for discretion toward drug enforcement across nations.

Shanell Sanchez

See also: International Narcotics Control Board; UN Convention against Illicit Traffic in Narcotic Drugs and Psychotropic Substances; UN Convention on Psychotropic Substances (1971)

Further Reading

Banks, Cyndi, and James Baker. 2016. *Comparative International, and Global Justice: Perspectives from Criminology and Criminal Justice.* Thousand Oaks, CA: Sage Publications.

Bewley-Taylor, David, and Martin Jelsma. 2011. "Fifty Years of the 1961 Single Convention of Narcotic Drugs: A Reinterpretation. Series on Legislative Reform of Drug Policies." *Transnational Institute* 12 (23): 72–81.

Single Convention on Narcotic Drugs. 1961. Accessed April 14, 2018. https://www.unodc.org/pdf/convention_1961_en.pdf.

United Nations Office on Drugs Crime (UNODC). 2018. *Single Convention on Narcotic Drugs.* New York: United Nations. Accessed April 14, 2018. https://www.unodc.org/unodc/en/treaties/single-convention.html.

Small Arms and Light Weapons, Trafficking in

Small arms and light weapons (SALW) consist of all lethal man-portable military equipment. SALW may include assault rifles, pistols, machine guns, grenades, landmines, anti-tank weapons, and their respective ammunition. The categories of weapons included in SALW encompass most weapons seen on the modern battlefield as well as those in the hands of criminal organizations and insurgencies worldwide. SALW excludes heavy weapons such as tanks, artillery, aircraft, and any other weapon that must be transported in a vehicle (Small Arms Survey n.d.).

SALW are often legally traded between states in accordance with international regulations. In some jurisdictions, SALW may be traded between citizens. However, trafficking in SALW is a criminal offense that involves illicit transfer of SALW between states, groups, or individuals. Those who are often interested in procuring illicit SALW are terrorist organizations, insurgencies and rebel formations, and other organized criminal groups. In some cases, states also are complicit in SALW trafficking.

SOURCES OF ILLICIT SALW

The SALW black market is deeply rooted with a large demand. During the Cold War, the United States, the Soviet Union, and their respective allies were active in the SALW trade during their proxy wars. However, the illicit trade in SALW was not a primary concern for states until the fall of the Soviet bloc in 1989. Following the fall of the Soviet Union, former Soviet military installations, such as arms depots, were left nearly unguarded for years (Martyniuk 2017). Lack of employment and the disenfranchisement of military members acted as a catalyst for the increase in the SALW trade during the 1990s, as these military members were easily bribed or recruited into organized criminal networks. Through a process called "diversion" of SALW, many of these military weapons could easily be stolen or procured illicitly with the assistance of corrupt employees by criminals and insurgent organizations.

There are two types of diversion: criminal and accidental. Criminal diversion is the process in which weapons are diverted from their original destination or owner by criminal means. This can include the bribery of military officials to buy weapons from military stockpiles and sell on the black market. Criminal diversion is also seen through more elaborate schemes to gather SALW, such as the forgery of end-user certificates, which are designed to certify the intended user of the weapons. Accidental diversion occurs when states or individuals lose SALW. Accidental diversion may be as simple as a weapon falling off a truck or as complex as the coordinated attack by insurgents on a military installation for the purpose of procuring weapons. Regardless of how the weapons are diverted from legal trade to the black market, trafficking in SALW is a top concern of the international community, and there exists a range of laws and countermeasures in place today.

A large case of accidental diversion was the loss of an arms depot to Chechen rebels in 1991. In this instance, over 42,000 SALW were stolen from a lightly guarded former Soviet military installation. There were no casualties reported as the Soviet troops either took economic advantage of the situation or were too disenfranchised to mount a resistance (Arsovka and Zabyelina 2014).

INTERNATIONAL LEGAL INSTRUMENTS

There were few international regulations on the illicit trade in SALW until the 2001 adoption of the United Nations Programme of Action to Prevent, Combat, and Eradicate the Illicit Trade in Small Arms and Light Weapons in All Its Aspects (PoA). As stated by its title, the primary directive of the PoA is to combat the illicit trade of SALW. The PoA combats trafficking in SALW with many different efforts; however, transparency, stockpile management, and agreements on the production and sale of SALW by states are the most prominent.

Transparency is one of the most important aspects of the PoA and is primarily achieved in two ways. First, states are encouraged to cooperate both regionally and with INTERPOL through information sharing on the illicit transfer of SALW. Second, transparency is established by encouraging states to voluntarily report to the UN Office for Disarmament Affairs on SALW data (e.g., seizures, legal sales, exports and imports of SALW, and weapon markings) with the objective of recording the SALW trafficking patterns, trends, and strategies.

States party to the UN PoA are also concerned with stockpile management. States are encouraged to reduce national stockpiles in to prevent the diversion of weapons from the stockpiles to the black market. Large and poorly guarded stockpiles may pose a security and safety risk. To best combat diversion, states are expected to partake in stockpile destruction of unused SALW.

The PoA was the basis for legislation regarding SALW that followed its adoption. While not legally binding, PoA provided states an outline to combat trafficking in SALW. Prior to the adoption of the PoA, the only international regulations on the trade in SALW, aside from comparatively small agreements, were arms embargoes. Arms embargoes regulate how states may trade with the targeted state.

As the PoA is not legally binding, the treaties that followed, such as the Arms Trade Treaty, the Firearms Protocol to the UN Convention against Transnational Organized Crime (CTOC), and the European Union's regulations on arms trade, can be important for combating the illicit trafficking in SALW, as states may face repercussions from their partners should such agreements be violated.

The Protocol against the Illicit Manufacturing and Trafficking in Firearms, Their Parts and Components and Ammunition (Firearms Protocol) of CTOC entered into force in 2005. The goal of the Firearms Protocol was to "prevent, investigate and prosecute the offences stemming from the illicit manufacturing of and trafficking in firearms" (UNODC n.d.). One of the main effects that the Firearms Protocol had was the establishment of the trafficking in firearms as an offense specifically outlined in CTOC. This means that such an offense can be applicable to CTOC regardless of whether the offense is considered to be a serious crime (United Nations 2005).

On the international level, the primary agreement that governs SALW transfer and sale is the Arms Trade Treaty (ATT), which is administered by the United Nations Office for Disarmament Affairs (UNODA). The ATT is one of the largest multilateral treaties regulating the trade in SALW and other conventional weapons. There are 130 signatories and 96 states parties to the treaty. The ATT includes several reporting requirements similar to those in the PoA, with the distinction that the ATT is legally binding. These reports are written to increase transparency in the arms trade and close loopholes for diversion of SALW into conflict zones or in the hands of insurgent organizations and criminal groups. States are required by the ATT to report measurers implemented to decrease diversion (UNODA n.d.).

The ATT also has specific measures in place to prevent and combat diversion. Diversion can be combated in many different ways, but certifying the end user and adopting national legislation are both ways of responsible SALW trade (UNODA n.d.). Certifying the end user can be as simple as using postdelivery certificates to confirm which states or nonstate actors received SALW. Another technique used to prevent diversion through the end user is to not trade with users that have a known history of diverting SALW to the black market.

COUNTER–SALW TRAFFICKING ACTIVITIES

Both the UN General Assembly and the UN Security Council have expressed concern with SALW trafficking. To address it, international arms embargoes are enacted by both organs. International arms embargos are generally enacted against states complicit in crimes against humanity. Such embargoes are usually mandatory, and states may face repercussions for trading weapons with an embargoed state.

The first UN arms embargo was Security Council Resolution 232 in 1966, which prevented the sale of military equipment to Rhodesia. Security Council

Resolution 232 was in response to the humanitarian crimes committed by the Rhodesian government (United Nations 1966). This embargo was only lifted in 1979 when the Rhodesian government capitulated and the government of Zimbabwe was established.

Marking and recording weapons is seen by the United Nations as an important way to counter SALW diversion globally. In 2005, the United Nations facilitated the development of the International Tracing Instrument (ITI) as part of the PoA. The ITI was created to combat diversion of SALW, primarily by decreasing complexity associated with record keeping. Included in the ITI is the requirement for states to both permanently mark weapons as well as keep detailed records about SALW imports, exports, and stockpiles.

Also observable on states' own accord are the actions of states with global and regional police organizations such as INTERPOL. Being an information-sharing organization, INTERPOL has created two large databases, the INTERPOL Firearms Reference Table (IFRT) and the INTERPOL Illicit Records and Tracing Management System (iARMS), to identify trafficked SALW and firearms that were used during a crime. The IFRT consists of the unique identifiers seen on over 250,000 different weapons and is regularly updated (INTERPOL n.d.-b). Using the IFRT allows law enforcement to identify such characteristics as the country of manufacture of a weapon and to later send a trace request to that country to identify global arms flows. The use of iARMS allows for the weapons to be logged and to see if such weapons have been used in any other crimes worldwide, also helping to identify illicit arms flows (INTERPOL n.d.-a).

Daniel Brendan Hughes

See also: Arms Brokers; Arms Trade Treaty; Small Arms Survey; UN Convention against Transnational Organized Crime; Weapons Sales

Further Reading

Arsovska, J., and Y. Zabyelina. 2014. "Irrationality, Liminality and the Demand for Illicit Firearms in the Balkans and the North Caucasus." *European Journal on Criminal Policy and Research* 20 (3): 399–420.

Department of State. n.d. "Iran Sanctions." Accessed January 21, 2019. https://www.state.gov/e/eb/tfs/spi/iran/index.htm.

INTERPOL. n.d.-a. "INTERPOL Firearms Reference Table (IFRT)." Accessed January 12, 2019. https://www.interpol.int/Crime-areas/Firearms-trafficking/INTERPOL-Firearms-Reference-Table-IFRT.

INTERPOL. n.d.-b. "INTERPOL Illicit Arms Records and Tracing Management System (iARMS)." Accessed January 12, 2019. https://www.interpol.int/Crime-areas/Firearms-trafficking/INTERPOL-Illicit-Arms-Records-and-tracing-Management-System-iARMS.

Martyniuk, A. 2017. *Measuring Illicit Arms Flow: Ukraine.* Small Arms Survey, 1–8. http://www.smallarmssurvey.org/fileadmin/docs/T-Briefing-Papers/SAS-BP3-Ukraine.pdf.

Small Arms Survey. n.d. "Definitions of Small Arms and Light Weapons." Accessed February 12, 2019. http://www.smallarmssurvey.org/weapons-and-markets/definitions.html.

United Nations. 1966. "Security Council Resolution 232." Accessed January 21, 2019. http://unscr.com/en/resolutions/232.

United Nations. 1994. "Security Council Resolution 919." Accessed January 21, 2019. http://unscr.com/en/resolutions/919.

United Nations. 2001. *Programme of Action to Prevent, Combat and Eradicate the Illicit Trade in Small Arms and Light Weapons in All Its Aspects: Adopted by the United Nations Conference on the Illicit Trade in Small Arms and Light Weapons in All Its Aspects*, New York, 9–20 July 2001. New York: United Nations.

United Nations. 2005. *U.N. Convention against Transnational Organized Crime (Treaty Doc. 108-16): Report (to Accompany Treaty Doc. 108-16)*. Washington, D.C.: U.S. GPO.

United Nations Office for Disarmament Affairs (UNODA). n.d. *Arms Trade Treaty*. https://www.un.org/disarmament/convarms/arms-trade-treaty-2/.

United Nations Office on Drug and Crime (UNODC). n.d. *United Nations Convention against Transnational Organized Crime and the Protocols Thereto*. https://www.unodc.org/unodc/en/organized-crime/intro/UNTOC.html.

Small Arms Survey

The Small Arms Survey is a global center of excellence providing expertise on small arms and armed violence, including evidence-based, impartial, and policy-relevant knowledge and analysis for governments, policy makers, researchers, and civil society. Established in 1999 by the Swiss government in conjunction with other states, the Small Arms Survey is a project of the Graduate Institute of International and Development Studies and is based at Maison de la Paix in Geneva, Switzerland. The Small Arms Survey's staff is composed of an international team with backgrounds in security studies, political science, law, economics, development studies, sociology, and criminology.

The main oversight body of the Small Arms Survey is the International Programme Council. It includes representatives from governments, research institutes, and nongovernmental organizations (NGOs). It meets twice a year and is responsible for approving the broad strategic direction, administration, and budget of the project. It also offers advice and counsel to the director and the director of programs.

MISSION

Effective governmental or nongovernmental action depends on a correct diagnosis of the problem; yet, policy makers, analysts, and activists around the world often lack basic information concerning the production, transfer, stockpiling, and use of small arms. The strengths and weaknesses of various policy instruments (such as weapons surrender or collection programs) also need to be assessed on an ongoing basis so that best practices can be shared between countries, states, and regions.

To address these complex issues, the survey provides research, analysis, resources, and services to aid decision makers to make progress toward the overall objectives of significantly reducing illicit arms flows, in line with the United Nations Sustainable Development and Goal (SDG) Target 16.4, and reducing armed violence, thus contributing to SDG Target 16.1.

RESEARCH AREAS

The Small Arms Survey conducts research in five overarching small arms–related fields, namely weapons and markets, armed violence, armed actors, regulations and controls, and security programs.

Within weapons and markets, the survey provides knowledge on definitions, producers, product categories, transfers, stockpiles, and tools. As part of its armed violence portfolio, it looks at social and economic costs, conflict and nonconflict armed violence, gender aspects of armed violence, armed violence assessments, urban violence, and issues of measuring armed violence. Under the armed actors umbrella, the Small Arms Survey researches state security forces, civilians, private security companies, armed groups, and gangs.

Noting the different levels of action on regulations and controls (national, regional, and international), the organization provides analyses on manufacturing controls, regulations of civilian possession, stockpile management and security, international transfer controls, brokering controls, weapons collection and destruction, and marking, record keeping, and tracing. Its work on security programs involves research on disarmament, demobilization, and reintegration, security sector reform, and armed violence prevention and reduction. The organization incorporates a crosscutting gender lens through all its research areas.

All Small Arms Survey findings in these areas are available for free online on the organization's Web site. Where findings are likely to have specific regional interest, publications are translated into other languages to increase their accessibility, with publications in over 20 languages available online.

PROJECTS AND NOTABLE PUBLICATIONS

As of April 2018, the Small Arms Survey is implementing over 20 single- and multiyear projects on all aspects of the life cycle of small arms and light weapons to prevent their diversion to the illicit market as well as for use in armed violence and conflict. These projects provide research, resources, trainings, and targeted assistance.

The survey has published extensively on international control measures, such as the UN Programme of Action on small arms and its International Tracing Instrument; new technologies and developments in illicit proliferation of small arms, including research on illicit online arms markets, converted firearms, and craft production; and physical security and stockpile management.

One of the Small Arms Survey's longest-running projects is the Human Security Baseline Assessment for Sudan and South Sudan (HSBA), which has produced research and analysis since 2006 on armed actors, weapons flows, and conflict dynamics in support of violence reduction in Sudan and South Sudan. The Security Assessment in North Africa (SANA) project has researched and analyzed small arms availability and circulation, armed groups, and conflict dynamics and assessed related insecurity in North Africa and the Sahel-Sahara region since 2012. The Making Peace Operations More Effective (MPOME) project, active since 2017, focuses on the scale, causes, and impacts of weapons and ammunition losses from peace operations, and it provides support for the development of mechanisms that strengthen weapons and ammunitions management in peace operations.

In addition, the Small Arms Survey hosted the Secretariat of the Geneva Declaration on Armed Violence and Development—a diplomatic initiative launched by Switzerland and the United Nations Development Programme (UNDP) in 2006 to address the interrelations between armed violence and development. With the adoption of the 2030 Agenda for SDG 16 on peaceful and inclusive societies, the Geneva Declaration accomplished its main mission and ceased to be an active political process at the end of 2015. In line with its previous commitment, the Small Arms Survey continues work on supporting the measurement and implementation of the 2030 Agenda, in particular SDGs 5 and 16.

To provide practitioners with concrete, policy-relevant reference material, the Small Arms Survey produces handbooks on specific key issues, including the life cycle management of ammunition, regional organizations and the UN Programme of Action, the UN small arms process, unplanned explosions at munitions sites, and the Arms Trade Treaty.

The *Small Arms Survey Yearbook* was published every year between 2001 and 2015, but the organization has since discontinued this publication, an annual review of global small arms issues and themes, instead focusing on shorter reports and briefing papers. Since its inception, the organization has also published annual analyses on the authorized global small arms trade, analyzing states' exports and imports as well as ranking the transparency of these. The *Trade Update 2017* ranked Germany as the most transparent small arms exporter and Iran, Israel, North Korea, Saudi Arabia, and the United Arab Emirates as the least transparent with a shared score of zero.

In 2007, the Small Arms Survey—as the only organization to ever do so—presented an estimate of the number of guns in the world at 875 million, three-quarters of which were approximated to be in civilian hands. This estimate will be revised, and a new number is to be published in mid-2018. In late 2017, the report *Global Violent Deaths 2017: Time to Decide* estimated the number of violent deaths globally in 2016 at 560,000. The report also presented a number of violent death scenarios by 2030 based on government action, or lack thereof. In these scenarios, the Small Arms Survey found that if current trends continue, the annual number of violent deaths is likely to increase to approximately 610,000 by 2030, mostly due to population growth. However, the organization notes in its report that if states were to replicate the results of the countries that have been most successful at preventing and controlling violence in their respective world regions, the number could drop to about 408,000. This would mean that 1.35 million lives could be saved by 2030.

DONORS AND PARTNERS

As of April 2018, the Small Arms Survey was receiving financial support primarily from the following governments and organizations: Australia, Belgium, Canada, Denmark, Finland, France, Germany, Japan, the Netherlands, New

Zealand, Nigeria, Norway, Sweden, Switzerland, the United Kingdom, the United States, as well as the European Union and the United Nations.

In addition, the Small Arms Survey works extensively with regional organizations such as the African Union, the Commonwealth Secretariat, the Economic Community of West African States (ECOWAS), the Intergovernmental Authority on Development (IGAD), the Organization of American States (OAS), the Organization for Security and Co-Operation in Europe (OSCE), and the Regional Centre on Small Arms (RECSA).

Emilia Dungel

See also: Arms Brokers; Arms Trade Treaty; Small Arms and Light Weapons, Trafficking in; UN Sustainable Development Goals; Weapons Sales

Further Reading

"Geneva Declaration on Armed Violence and Development." Accessed April 13, 2018. http://www.genevadeclaration.org http://www.genevadeclaration.org/the-geneva-declaration/what-is-the-declaration.html.

Holtom, Paul, and Irene Pavesi. 2017. *Trade Update 2017: Out of the Shadows.* Geneva: Small Arms Survey. Accessed January 21, 2019. http://www.smallarmssurvey.org/fileadmin/docs/S-Trade-Update/SAS-Trade-Update-2017.pdf.

Mc Evoy, Claire, and Gergely Hideg. 2017. *Global Violent Deaths 2017: Time to Decide.* Geneva: Small Arms Survey. Accessed January 21, 2019. http://www.smallarmssurvey.org/fileadmin/docs/U-Reports/SAS-Report-GVD2017.pdf.

Small Arms Survey. 2018a. "About the Small Arms Survey." Accessed April 13, 2018. http://www.smallarmssurvey.org/about-us/mission.html.

Small Arms Survey. 2018b. "Focus Projects." Accessed April 13, 2018. http://www.smallarmssurvey.org/de/focus-projects.html.

Smishing

Smishing, short for "SMS phishing," is a security attack through SMS text messages in which a user is tricked into clicking a malicious link that contains a Trojan horse, virus, or other form of malware (Dunham 2009). Smishing is a direct variation of the larger hacking practice of "phishing." Phishing utilizes e-mail to accomplish the same goal of uploading malware to a user's device. Smishing attacks usually attempt to steal the victim's personal information, including credit card numbers, usernames, and passwords. As these attacks are directed at mobile devices, smishing is extremely difficult to stop and prosecute (Gilmore 2017).

Smishing began in 2006 and has continued to expand throughout the growth of the smartphone revolution. Phone-based cybercrime, including phishing, has grown exponentially as technology has become a more integral part of society. Smishing occurs globally, but it is a larger issue in developing nations with less legal regulation and technology access (Gilmore 2017). A typical smishing attempt will bait the user into clicking the link via social engineering techniques. Social engineering is a "meat hack" that relies on the beliefs that people can be manipulated to obtain information through interaction and that human beings are the weakest point in security systems (Kent, Cheang, and Newcomb 2017).

COMMON ATTACKS

A social-engineered smishing attack is typically performed in one of three ways. The first method begins with the target receiving a text message that confirms the target's enrollment in a subscription service or with a bank that requires a hyperlink to be clicked to cancel the paid monetary subscription or to review financial records. This method utilizes fear or worry to pressure the target into clicking the malicious link. The second method is through a "You're a WINNER!" text message that requires a link to be activated to claim the available prize. This strategy utilizes curiosity and greed in an effort to compromise the target's common sense. The final method works through friendly or flirtatious dialogue that may get the user to click a link that seems either believable or enticing. This dialogue typically relies on aspects of loneliness or mystery (Kent, Cheang, and Newcomb 2017).

While all attacks differ, there are some common indicators of an attempted smishing attack ("What Is a 'Smishing' Scam" 2017). First, SMS that originate from a phone will consist of at least seven digits (area code + phone number), but messages that originate from numbers with less than seven digits (such as "5050") are sent from computers. SMS sent via computer are more difficult to trace to a source, so this is a preferred method for smishers. Second, many smish attacks will begin in a different country with possible operating system and language differences. These may manifest through incorrect formatting within the message or non-ASCII characters (gibberish).

Unfortunately, neither of these indicators are ironclad, and smishers appear to be evolving. As of 2018, some smish attacks in developed countries have begun to not only come from full seven-digit numbers, but also from the same area code as the target number! For example, a target in San Francisco may receive a smish attempt from a number beginning with 415, the area code for the city. Finally, another new tactic is to incorporate the imagery, iconography, or mention of commonly used apps such as Snapchat, Instagram, or Facebook. Users may see and click these "familiar" links with much less scrutiny ("What Is a 'Smishing' Scam" 2017).

PREVENTION

The easiest way to prevent a smishing attack is to simply not click links in text messages from unknown phone numbers. Frequently, dangerous text messages will come from numbers that do not resemble the typical phone number format; messages from a phone number with more or less digits than expected should be considered as unknown and possibly dangerous sources. Though this may appear simple to do, smishing attempts are designed to override the victim's logical thoughts by creating a sense of doubt, fear, or excitement in an effort to distract the target from commonsense security awareness.

Adam K. Ghazi-Tehrani and Greyson Smith

See also: Cyberattack; Cybercrime; Identity-Related Crimes; Phishing; Vishing

Further Reading

Dunham, Ken. 2009. "Phishing, SMishing, and Vishing." In *Mobile Malware Attacks and Defense*, edited by Ken Dunham, 125–196. Burlington, MA: Syngress.

Gilmore, Courtney. 2017. "Smishing: New Cyber Scam Targets Text Messages." NBC 5 Dallas–Fort Worth, July 5. Accessed December 9, 2017. https://www.nbcdfw.com/news/local/Smishing-is-the-New-Cyber-Scam-that-Targets-Your-Text-Messages-432634773.html.

Kent, Jo Ling, John Cheang, and Alyssa Newcomb. 2017. "How Cyber Criminals Are Targeting You through Text Messages." *NBCNews.com*, July 20. Accessed December 9, 2017. https://www.nbcnews.com/tech/security/how-cyber-criminals-are-targeting-you-through-text-messages-n782671.

"What Is a 'Smishing' Scam?" 2017. *USA Today*, July 4. Accessed December 9, 2017. https://www.usatoday.com/videos/news/2017/07/04/what-smishing-scam/103415334.

Software Piracy

Compared to music, movie, and literature piracies, software piracy is a relatively new type of global intellectual property crime. Since the mid to late 1970s, the concept of software piracy has been ubiquitous. Intellectual property arguments ask questions about ownership versus use, open-source software, property of software coding, and other cultural, social, and economic issues. Software, or data, piracy "refers to the reproduction, distribution, and use of software without the permission or authorization of the owner of copyright" (Britz 2009, 69). Perhaps the most confounding issue is "use." Consumers purchase the ability to "use" software rather than "own" it. Furthermore, some software has confusing monikers like "shareware" or "freeware." Shareware is copyrighted software, but it is distributed for the purpose of testing or review. Once the user decides to use the software, payment to the copyright owner is expected. Freeware allows individuals and nonprofit organizations to use the software at no charge. However, there is usually a user license agreement that prohibits the copying, sale, or distribution of the freeware. "Crippleware" software allows users limited functions, or pieces, of software. If the user decides that he or she wants full access, the user must purchase the code to activate all features of the software.

TYPES

According to the Software & Information Industry Association (2009), there are many types of software piracy, but nine are especially common: softlifting, unrestricted client access, hard-disk loading, OEM piracy/unbundling, commercial use of noncommercial software, counterfeiting, CD-R piracy, Internet piracy, and renting.

Softlifting happens when consumers legally purchase software but install it on multiple machines. This behavior violates the license agreement. Most softlifting occurs when friends share software at home or at work. This is the most common type of software piracy in corporations. Unrestricted client access is when "a copy of a software program is copied onto an organization's servers, and the organization's network 'clients' are allowed to freely access the software in violation of the terms of the license agreement" (SIIA 2009, 62). What separates softlifting from unrestricted client access is not volume or quantity; rather, it is where the software is loaded. Softlifting occurs on individuals' computers, but unrestricted client access occurs when software is loaded onto the company's servers, which allows many to possible violate the license.

Hard-disk loading happens when unscrupulous vendors sell computers with illegal or unlicensed preloaded software. When consumers purchase or rent computers, vendors are required to list preloaded software that is legal and official copies. Another type of piracy is OEM piracy/unbundling. Sometimes certain software is sold strictly with specific hardware. When this software is copied, sold, or distributed with other hardware, it violates the distribution agreement. Additionally, some software is bundled together for sale. When these software programs are "unbundled" and sold, it becomes a form of piracy. Most "Not for Resale" software programs are examples of bundled applications. At times, some software companies will make two different versions of the same software. One is marketed to normal consumers, and the other is marketed toward a specific audience, such as schools and universities, at a greatly reduced price.

Commercial use of noncommercial software is "using educational or other commercial-use-restricted software in violation of the software license [and] is a form of software piracy" (SIIA 2009, 63). Computer shows are notorious for counterfeit software. Counterfeiting is the process of duplicating and selling software and then passing it off as if it were legal and authorized. Similarly, CD-R piracy is the duplication and sale of pirated software onto a CD-R disc without attempting to make the disc look authorized or official. Most times, the CD-R disc has handwriting on it. This technology has created a robust black market. Many CD-R discs can hold multiple software programs. Additionally, CD-R discs are inexpensive and ubiquitous.

The Internet has also facilitated software piracy. Internet piracy is the most rapidly growing type of piracy and one of the most difficult for law enforcement to combat because of its many manifestations. Through auction sites, peer-to-peer file sharing sites, Internet relay chats, warez (illegally copied software), and other malicious sites, illegally uploaded software can be illegally downloaded by anyone. Some software companies continue to manufacture CD-ROM versions of their software so their authorized vendors can sell these copies to the public. However, piracy can happen at the manufacturing plant when employees steal licensed CD-ROM discs from the plant or plant officials illegally "sell" those discs destined to be destroyed or scrapped.

HISTORY

Great Britain issued the first software patent in 1966 for "A Computer Arranged for the Automatic Solution of Linear Programming Problems." In the mid-1970s, the American electronics company Micro Instrumentation and Telemetry Systems (MITS) released the first BASIC interpreter software on 4k cards. Eventually, copies were made by the infamous Homebrew Computer Club, which quickly became the first software piracy group of hackers in the United States. During the 1980s, Internet relay chats (IRC) sprung up to connect people and their ideas. It also served as an avenue to share files between users. In 1981, the U.S. Supreme Court case *Diamond v. Diehr* (450 U.S. 175) upheld the idea that a programmed computer, which physically transformed materials, could be patentable. Thus, programs, or software, were considered intellectual property.

The Business Software Alliance was established in 1988 as the first group funded to examine issues of software piracy. Currently, BSA has operations in more than 60 countries (Business Software Alliance 2017). The Federal Bureau of Investigation (FBI) raided Rusty n Edie's BBS (bulletin board system) in 1993. Approximately 14,000 subscribers had paid $89 per year to access 100,000 files over the Internet. Russ and Edwina (Rusty n Edie) Hardenburgh were two of the first people arrested for committing large-scale software piracy. In August 2001, the FBI arrested four men in connection to over $10 million in software counterfeiting of Microsoft (Britz 2009). Chinese law enforcement officials raided two separate criminal organizations for counterfeiting over $500 million in software. The results demonstrate the working relationship between the United States and China in antipiracy efforts. Collectively, there were 25 arrests between the two countries.

DIMENSIONS OF SOFTWARE PIRACY

On average, the software industry loses upward of $12 billion per year to software pirates (SIIA 2009). The biggest offenders occur in China and Indonesia. However, software piracy is a significant problem in Western Europe, Latin America, Central Europe, and North America. Obviously, software piracy directly impacts financial losses of software companies; as a result, companies have less money to invest in further research and development. There are issues for users too. For example, there is an increased probability that pirated software will not perform correctly or will fail completely. Additionally, there is no warranty, no ongoing support, and no bug fixes. There is also an increase of viruses and the possibility of facing fines for copyright infringement.

Brian Fedorek

See also: Digital Piracy; Intellectual Property Crime; Movie Piracy; Music Piracy

Further Reading

Britz, Margie T. 2009. *Computer Forensics and Cyber Crime*. Upper Saddle River, NJ: Prentice Hall.

Business Software Alliance. 2017. "About BSA & Members." Accessed on January 8, 2018. http://www.bsa.org/about-bsa.

Johns, Adrian. 2009. *Piracy: The Intellectual Property Wars from Gutenberg to Gates*. Chicago: University of Chicago Press.

Software & Information Industry Association (SIIA). 2009. "Software Piracy Is Copyright Infringement." In *Copyright Infringement*, edited by Roman Espejo, 57–69. New York: Greenhaven Press.

Washkuch, Frank. 2009. "Copyright Infringement of Software Has Serious Consequences." In *Copyright Infringement*, edited by Roman Espejo, 166–171. New York: Greenhaven Press.

World Intellectual Property Organization. n.d. "Berne Convention for the Protection of Literary and Artistic Works." Accessed on December 27, 2017. http://www.wipo.int/treaties/en/ip/berne.

Solntsevskaya Bratva

Solntsevskaya Bratva, or "Brotherhood," is one of the most famous Russian organized crime groups. It was formed in the 1980s in Solntsevo, a district of Moscow, Russia. Over several decades, the group managed to accumulate considerable assets in different regions of the Russian Federation, post-Soviet states, and more remote countries, such as Italy, Spain, and the United States (Siegel 2003).

At the origins of the organization were former waiters with prison experience. Sergei Mikhailov (or Mikhas) and Viktor Averin (or Avera) chose to lead the criminal gang away from the traditional criminal code of professional criminals that demanded noncooperation with authorities and a life of crime. On the contrary, Mikhas and Avera wanted to create a criminal organization that would cooperate with authorities when it was good for the criminal brotherhood. Initially the group ran extortion rackets against street trades and small businesses. Soon, they expanded into protection rackets and gambling (i.e., thimble rigging—a sleight-of-hand swindling game also known as a shell game).

By the early 1990s, the Solntsevo organized crime group (OCG) was challenged by Chechen crime groups led by Nikolay Suleimanov, which took control of some parts of Moscow, in part due to their excessive use of violence. Together with the Orekhovskaya gang and other Slavic OCGs, the Solntsevo created an alliance that aimed to remove the Chechens from the capital. They also sought collaboration with law enforcement against Chechen OCGs. This turf war brought many casualties but allowed the Solntsevo OCG to consolidate their forces in Moscow and expand to other lucrative locations in the country. In the mid-1990s, the group was weakened again by another confrontation with other criminal groups and the arrest of its leader, Sergei Mikhailov, in Switzerland in 1998 on charges of using forged documents and breaking a Swiss law restricting foreigners from buying property (BBC 1998; Abadinsky 2010). Due to lack of evidence, Mikhailov was acquitted and returned to Russia.

According to some sources, in the early days of the organizations, the Solntsevo OCG had up to 300 members. By the end of the 1990s, they had expanded from low-skilled street crime and extortion rackets to more sophisticated crimes, including those in the banking sector (e.g., money laundering, ponzi schemes), and they were able to recruit more than a thousand members. Despite the dearth of information about the criminal group, its nearly global activities and sophistication of operations certainly indicate that the size of the group remains significant. The Solntsevo OCG displays some degree of hierarchy, but as a whole, it functions as a flexible network. The cells of the group are loosely affiliated with the core and as a rule make independent decisions on matters of its operations and management.

In the United States, Solntsevskaya OCG is known for both illicit and legitimate activities. The OCG is known to operate extensively in New York, particularly in Brighton Beach and Brooklyn, and the tristate area of Pennsylvania, New Jersey, and New York. The group has established partnerships with Mexican and Colombian criminal organizations, among others, enhancing its power and capabilities.

In addition, the Solntsevskaya OCG has had ties with renowned Russian criminal bosses (*avtoritety*), Vyacheslav Ivankov ("Yaponchik") and Sergei Mogilevich. Some scholars allege that Yaponchik traveled to the United States to represent the interests of the Solntsevskaya OCG in New York (Abadinsky 2010). Mogilevich was once associated with the Solntsevskaya OCG as well. He acted as the key money laundering contact person for the group in Moscow and the European Union, namely Hungary.

Since the 2000s, there has been very little information about the leadership and activities of the Solntsevskaya OCG. According to some analysts, the criminal group has been under close scrutiny of the FSB and other Russian intelligence and law enforcement agencies and suffered considerable human and financial losses (Volkov 2014). Those members of the Solntsevo OCG who survived interdiction and turf wars succeeded in consolidating a considerable amount of legitimate assets. This ability made them legitimate businessmen in Russia and elsewhere. Sergei Mikhailov, for instance, is considered one of the most influential entrepreneurs in Russia. He has never been convicted on charges related to organized crime.

Yuliya Zabyelina

See also: Organized Crime; Russian Organized Crime; UN Convention against Transnational Organized Crime

Further Reading

Abadinsky, Howard. 2010. *Organized Crime.* 9th ed. Belmont, CA: Wadsworth Cengage Learning.

BBC. 1998. "Swiss Try Alleged Russian Mafia Boss." *BBC*, November 30. Accessed January 21, 2019. http://news.bbc.co.uk/2/hi/europe/224430.stm.

Siegel, Dina. 2003. "The Transnational Russian Mafia." In *Global Organized Crime: Trends and Developments*, edited by Dina Siegel, Henk van de Bunt, and Damian Zaitch, 51–53. London: Springer.

Volkov, Vadim. 2014. "The Russian Mafia, Rise and Extinction." In *The Oxford Handbook of Organized Crime*, edited by Letizia Paoli, 159–176. New York: Oxford University Press.

Sport Corruption and Match Fixing

Sport corruption is not new. However, in recent years, it has taken sport from the back pages of newspapers to front page headlines as the criminality involved expands into the daily lives of athletes, coaches, administrators, and fans. Corruption in sport can be broadly defined as the deviation from public expectations that sport will be played and administered in an honest manner (Masters 2015). This encompasses many behaviors that remove the element of chance and fair competition from sporting events.

There are many reasons why sport corruption occurs: money, fame, and power are major reasons, but external pressure and threats can also corrupt those involved in sport. Over the past century, key trends have emerged in sports that have led to the growth in doping: sport has been de-amateurized, with an emphasis on winning at any costs over simple participation; medicalization has opened up far more sophisticated means of ensuring peak performance through licit and illicit means; politicization, particularly during the Cold War, placed the expectations of society on athletes competing from different ends of the political spectrum; and commercialization—especially through mass media—vastly expanded the profitability of sport (Paoli and Donati 2013, 2).

SPORT CORRUPTION

With the rise of broadcasting and the Internet has come a growth in the global popularity of sports. Concurrent with this has been a growth in both legal and illegal betting markets. It is estimated the sport betting market is worth $1.5 trillion (Jay 2015). Gambling has long been associated with sport. The thrill of winning a bet can complement a gambler's satisfaction of knowing his or her team has won. However, corrupting sport is not always about winning; sometimes it is about losing.

Most research in the field focuses on match fixing or doping. The former involves practices to alter the outcome of a match, with athletes performing below standard to the advantage of gamblers in on the fix. The Black Sox scandal of 1919, where players for the Chicago White Sox baseball team took bribes from organized crime figures to throw the World Series, provides a memorable example of match fixing. Doping involves athletes using performance-enhancing drugs (PEDs) to obtain an unfair advantage over other competitors. The American Olympic sprinter Marion Jones was stripped of her gold medals for such an offense.

These cases involving athletes represent only part of the broader problem. Doping and match fixing often combine in sport and can involve animals, when match fixers administer drugs to racing animals—predominantly horses or dogs—to either improve their performance with stimulants or to nobble champion animals so they underperform. Historically, match fixing via doping has also occurred with unwitting humans—notably the anecdotes concerning the doping regime within East German athletics and swimming during the Cold War.

In recent years, world soccer has been the subject of an ongoing investigation into bribes received by Fédération Internationale de Football Association (FIFA) officials. The bribes have been paid to secure a variety of unfair advantages to the bribed payers, but importantly, they often reverse the standard transactional arrangements associated with bribery: public officials becoming the payers of the bribe and private officials the recipients.

FIFA officials enriched themselves by selling what should have been their impartial votes on important issues such as television rights, endorsements, and host rights for the World Cup. The U.S. Department of Justice (DOJ) laid charges under the Racketeer Influenced and Corrupt Organizations Act of 1970 (RICO) against nine FIFA officials and five corporate executives for "conspiracy, wire fraud conspiracy, wire fraud, money laundering conspiracy, money laundering and obstruction of justice charges" (DOJ 2015).

While doping and the FIFA scandal are important aspects of sport corruption, they are essentially administrative problems within sport. Match fixing is the form of sport corruption most commonly associated with criminality. Match fixing creates a profitable pastime for organized crime and is a drain on law enforcement resources.

MATCH FIXING

In plain terms, match fixing is an act committed by an athlete, official, or sport administrator to remove or alter the uncertainties associated with a sporting competition. Often, those with insider knowledge that a match has been fixed are in a position to take financial advantage through either legal or illegal betting. For example, jockeys hold back their horses; footballers give away penalties; pitchers deliberately throw balls instead of strikes; tennis players fail to return serves; referees ensure marginal calls favor one team over another; coaches place players in unfamiliar positions; owners direct teams to underperform; and the list goes on.

The criminality associated with gambling goes beyond the laying of illegal bets. Match fixers will as easily rely on violence as bribery to ensure the desired outcome. Players and officials have been intimidated, threatened, assaulted, hospitalized, and murdered by criminal syndicates involved in match fixing (Hill 2008). Match fixing is not isolated by sport or locality (Haberfeld and Sheehan 2013). While the examples given affect the outcome of a play or a match in any sport, soccer is deeply affected by match fixing.

THE WORLD GAME

Soccer is played in 211 states and territories worldwide by millions of registered and unregistered players. For many, soccer is far more important than politics. FIFA's 211 member associations outnumber the member states of the United Nations. Of the millions of games played annually, many are affected by gambling-related and non-gambling-related match fixing.

Non-gambling-related match fixing is often strategically gaming the system to prevent relegation or ensure promotion to or from the lower divisions of the sport. While this remains corrupt in terms of the above definition, it is not necessarily criminal. In Italy, for example, coaches and owners pressured referees to ensure the final ranking for *Serie A* (the Italian premier league) were determined according to the clubs' wishes (Boeri and Severgnini 2011). Known as the *Calciopoli* (football city) scandal, it primarily revolved around the manipulation of league tables; some of those involved took the opportunity to bet on the fixed results. More often than not, when match fixing in soccer is revealed, it is gambling related and linked to organized criminal groups (Hill 2008). Within clubs and teams, a high level of organization is also required to ensure the fix goes as planned.

Guaranteeing an outcome in a soccer match is not necessarily easy. With 22 players, referees, officials, and millions of fans scrutinizing high-profile matches, fixers often turn to lower league matches (Hill 2008). Even then, it takes more than one player to ensure the desired result.

Since 2007, INTERPOL has coordinated Operations SOGA (short for "soccer gambling") and SOGA II–VI among mainly Asian member states. By 2016, this series of operations had raided more than 6,000 gambling dens and seized more than $53 million. Records indicated these dens had processed more than $6.4 billion worth of illegal bets.

Asian gambling syndicates involved themselves in fixing the seemingly obscure matches. An investigation by Europol linked Asian betting syndicates to an A League match in Australia on which AU$40 million had been gambled (Misra, Anderson, and Saunders 2013, 140). While Australian football authorities denied any match fixing had occurred on this occasion, within two years, players from a second-level team had confessed to match fixing in connection to Asian gambling (McKenzie, Bucci, and Baker 2013). The rise in arrests and the broad spread of police action demonstrate that, despite the best efforts of law enforcement, corruption in sport and match fixing are likely to remain a common feature of sports around the globe for the foreseeable future.

Adam B. Masters

See also: Corruption; Europol; INTERPOL; Racketeer Influenced and Corrupt Organizations Act (RICO)

Further Reading

Boeri, Tito, and Battista Severgnini. 2011. "Match Rigging and the Career Concerns of Referees." *Labour Economics* 18 (3): 349–359.

Department of Justice (DOJ). 2015. "Nine FIFA Officials and Five Corporate Executives Indicted for Racketeering Conspiracy and Corruption." Department of Justice News Release, May 27. Accessed January 12, 2019. http://www.justice.gov/opa/pr/nine-fifa-officials-and-five-corporate-executives-indicted-racketeering-conspiracy-and.

Haberfeld, M. R., and Dale Sheehan, eds. 2013. *Match-Fixing in International Sports: Existing Processes, Law Enforcement, and Prevention Strategies.* New York: Springer.

Hill, Declan. 2008. *The Fix: Soccer and Organised Crime.* Toronto: McLelland and Stewart.

Jay, Patrick. 2015. "Data Sharing Mechanisms." *Sport Integrity: Global Data Sharing for Effective Investigation and Prosecution in Match Fixing Cases.* Doha, Qatar, April 15, 2015.

Masters, Adam. 2015. "Corruption in Sport: From the Playing Field to the Field of Policy." *Policy and Society* 34 (2): 111–123.

McKenzie, Nick, Nino Bucci, and Richard Baker. 2013. "Victorian Detectives Bust Alleged Soccer match-Fixing Syndicate." *Sydney Morning Herald*, September 15. Accessed January 21, 2019. http://www.smh.com.au/sport/soccer/victorian-detectives-bust-alleged-soccer-matchfixing-syndicate-20130915-2tsh5.html.

Misra, Ashutosh, Jack Anderson, and Jason Saunders. 2013. "Safeguarding Sports Integrity Against Crime and Corruption: An Australian Perspective." In *Match-Fixing in International Sports: Existing Processes, Law Enforcement, and Prevention Strategies,* edited by M. R. Haberfeld and Dale Sheehan, 135–156. New York: Springer.

Paoli, Letizia, and Alessandro Donati. 2013. *The Sports Doping Market: Understanding Supply and Demand, and the Challenges of Their Control.* New York: Springer.

Stolen Motor Vehicle Database

The International Criminal Police Organization's (INTERPOL) Automated Search Facility-Stolen Motor Vehicle Database (ASF-SMV) is used by INTERPOL member countries' police departments to see whether suspicious vehicles have been reported stolen. The database brings together various national databases on vehicles to make the possible reconciliation of vehicle and owner as fast as possible. INTERPOL has over 120 member countries. The database, which is managed by a General Secretariat is frequently used by INTERPOL's own Stolen Motor Vehicle Task Force and its Integrated Border Management Task Force to combat international vehicle trafficking, often at ports and border crossings. The database is instrumental, as stolen vehicles are commonly moved across national borders. Transnational crime gangs are frequently behind these vehicle thefts, and they are sometimes connected to terrorism, human trafficking, or weapons trafficking.

In 2015, the database included 7.4 million vehicles. That year, 123,000 vehicles were identified as stolen through use of the database for 150 million searches. Database summaries are shared at conferences and in occasional analytical reports. Of particular concern are vehicles moved from North America to Central and South America and from Western Europe, such as the United Kingdom, to Africa and Eastern and Southern Europe. Communications about the database tend to be via INTERPOL-provided secure communication channels.

The accuracy of the database is crucial to its effectiveness. Project INVEX is an investigative effort utilizing the database in a partnership with specific member counties and car manufacturers such as Volkswagen, BMW, Porsche, and Audi. The project is to enhance database accuracy and to offer investigative assistance. The increased technology in vehicles makes them vulnerable to interference by criminals. This technology, however, can also be utilized for investigations. Project Formatrain is another effort that utilizes the database in partnership with relevant private-sector entities to develop investigative training materials and tools with adherence to varying laws by regions.

The Stolen Motor Vehicle Database offers insights on the illicit trade in used car parts, car trafficking routes, and the connections with cybercrime. The database is helpful in addressing VIN number fraud that accompanies motor vehicle theft. VIN fraud largely involves altering a VIN number by changing digits in the number or cloning the VIN (replacing the true VIN with that of another legally registered vehicle). The cloned VIN might come from recently salvaged vehicles, those in dealerships or parked in public places, or numbers that are visible online.

Camille Gibson

See also: Illicit Trade; INTERPOL; UN Convention against Transnational Organized Crime

Further Reading

INTERPOL. 2014. "Analytical Report: Motor Vehicle Crime in Global Perspective." Accessed January 1, 2018. https://www.interpol.int/Media/Files/Crime-areas/Vehicle-crime/Vehicle-crime-a-global-perspective.

Stauffer, Eric, and Monica S. Bonfanti. 2006. *Forensic Investigation of Stolen-Recovered and Other Crime-Related Vehicles.* Oxford, UK: Academic Press, Elsevier.

Suicide Bombings

A suicide attack is any type of terrorist attack in which there is a high likelihood the perpetrator will die during the commission of the attack. A suicide bombing, however, is a specific type of attack involving the taking of one's own life while targeting others, by carrying a bomb—generally on one's person or in a vehicle—and killing others in the process. The death of the perpetrator is expected in a suicide bombing for the attack to be successful. This is oftentimes carried out by a willing perpetrator, although there have been many instances where the bomber is somehow forced or coerced to carry out an attack. The first modern suicide bombing occurred in 1981 in Lebanon, when an attacker detonated a car bomb targeting the Iraqi Embassy in Beirut. From that point forward, the tactic began to be used by groups more frequently.

HISTORY OF THE MODERN SUICIDE BOMBER

In the 1980s, there were over 50 suicide bombings carried out in three countries. There was one bombing in Sri Lanka in 1987, two in Kuwait, and the rest were in Lebanon. One of those attacks was the suicide bombing targeting the U.S. Embassy in Beirut in 1983. Later that year, the terrorist group Hezbollah carried out a suicide truck bombing targeting the U.S. Marine barracks and French Paratrooper barracks, killing over 300. This became a watershed event, not only because of the large number of casualties, but because the United States and France pulled their troops out of Lebanon. This proved that the tactic of suicide bombings worked.

By the 1990s, the tactic had spread to over 10 countries, but a majority of the attacks were occurring in Sri Lanka, Israel/Palestine, and Turkey. Over 100 suicide bombings were carried out worldwide in the 1990s, but the most prominent were the simultaneous attacks on the U.S. Embassies in Dar es Salaam, Tanzania, and Nairobi, Kenya, in 1998. The attacks, perpetrated by Al Qaeda, claimed over 230 lives.

Although the September 11, 2001, terrorist attacks were suicide attacks rather than suicide bombings, they led to many changes to global terrorism. By the end of 2017, there had been thousands of suicide bombings carried out in over 50 countries around the world, a majority of them occurring in Iraq, Afghanistan, Pakistan, and Syria. The tactic of suicide bombings was adopted by many groups, including Al Shabaab in Somalia and Boko Haram in Nigeria. Some groups, such as Boko Haram, have used young children, some as young as seven or eight years old, to carry out these attacks.

MOTIVATION

There are various reasons why individuals engage in suicide bombings. Some carry out the attacks for nationalist reasons, doing it for the greater good, for their country, or for their people. Some are religiously motivated. Others have carried out the attacks as a method of revenge in response to a real or perceived injustice. Some individuals are coerced or forced into carrying out the attacks. Boko Haram, for example, kidnapped 276 schoolgirls in 2014 from Chibok, in Nigeria, and began using female suicide bombers shortly after. Many of the girls were forced to carry out the bombings.

The first female suicide bombing took place in Lebanon in April 1985. Using female suicide bombers also has had an added impact for groups. These attacks gained more attention in the media. Although the overwhelming majority of suicide bombers are male, there are some regions that see high numbers of female bombers. The method of suicide bombings has provided groups with a tactical advantage, and because of that, its use is expected to continue.

Group motives are also very important. It is rare to see an individual accomplish a suicide bombing without any group support. If a group is willing to conduct a suicide bombing, they will be able to find willing or unwilling participants. Groups have viewed suicide bombings as a tactic that has worked. Suicide bombings generally account for a larger number of casualties when compared to any other form of terrorism. They also provide the groups with strategic and tactical advantages. Suicide bombers are considered a "smart" bomb. They can change the time and location of the detonation to inflict mass casualties.

Vesna Markovic

See also: Al Qaeda; Brussels Bombings (2016); Hamas; Hezbollah; Islamic State of Iraq and Syria (ISIS); Jihad; Manchester Arena Terrorist Attack (2017); Terrorism, International

Further Reading

Bloom, Mia. 2005. *Dying to Kill: The Allure of Suicide Terror.* New York: Columbia University Press.

Hafez, Mohammed M. 2007. *Suicide Bombers in Iraq: The Strategy and Ideology of Martyrdom.* Washington, D.C.: U.S. Institute of Peace Press.

Markovic, Vesna. 2017. "Terrorism and the Female Suicide Bomber." In *Across the Spectrum of Women and Crime*, edited by Susan F. Sharp, Susan Marcus-Mendoza, Kathleen A. Cameron, and Elycia S. Daniel-Roberson, 143–161. Durham, NC: Carolina Academic Press.

Moghadam, Assaf. 2008. *The Globalization of Martyrdom: Al Qaeda, Salafi Jihad, and the Diffusion of Suicide Attacks.* Baltimore: Johns Hopkins University Press.

Pape, Robert. 2005. *Dying to Win: The Strategic Logic of Suicide Terrorism.* New York: Random House.

Pedahzur, Ami. 2007. *Suicide Terrorism.* Cambridge: Polity.

T

T Visa

T Nonimmigrant Status (T visa) is provided by U.S. Citizenship and Immigration Services (USCIS) for persons who are or have been victims of human trafficking. The status was authorized in 2000 when Congress passed the Victims of Trafficking and Violence Protection Act (commonly, the Trafficking Victims Protection Act, or TVPA). The trafficking (T) visa protects victims and survivors of human trafficking by allowing them to become temporary U.S. residents and eligible to become permanent residents after three years.

Human trafficking is the acquisition of people through such improper means as force, fraud, or deception for purposes of labor or sexual exploitation. Although there is no requirement that a victim be taken across national borders, some of them are. When victims have been taken to a new country, they are often isolated or given limited opportunities to leave a restricted area. Of the many methods used by traffickers to detain and control the victim, threats that the victim will be arrested for illegal entry to the country and imprisoned or deported are among the more effective. The T visa allows immigration relief to foreign nationals trafficked into the United States while they assist authorities in an investigation or prosecution of human trafficking cases.

ELIGIBILITY

To qualify for a T visa, the applicant must

- Be or have been a victim of severe trafficking in persons.
- Be physically present in the United States, American Samoa, or the Commonwealth of the Northern Mariana Islands, or at a port of entry due to trafficking.
- Comply with any reasonable request from a law enforcement agency for assistance in the investigation or prosecution of human trafficking.
- Demonstrate that he or she would suffer extreme hardship involving severe and unusual harm if he or she were removed from the United States.
- Be admissible to the United States or obtain a waiver of admissibility. (U.S. Citizenship and Immigration Services 2014)

The requirement that the victim assist in the investigation or prosecution of the trafficker has been controversial. Victim advocates argue that forcing the victim to provide such assistance may prolong the victimization. Criminal justice authorities argue that human trafficking can be efficiently combated only with effective prosecution—and victim cooperation is typically required for that to happen.

The TVPA has been reauthorized in 2003, 2005, 2008, and 2013 (U.S. Department of State n.d.). Because of revisions during the 2003 and 2008 reauthorizations, victims under the age of 18 at the time of the victimization, or victims who are unable to cooperate with a law enforcement request due to physical or psychological trauma, can still qualify for the T nonimmigrant visa without having to assist in investigation or prosecution (DHS 2016).

Trafficking victims may also be eligible for U nonimmigrant status (U visa). The U visa is for victims of certain crimes (for example, domestic violence, sexual assault, rape, stalking, and human trafficking) who have suffered mental or physical abuse (U.S. Citizenship and Immigration Services 2017). The U visa allows for legal immigration status for up to four years for victims who cooperate or are willing to cooperate with reasonable law enforcement requests in the investigation or prosecution of the qualifying criminal activity. An arrest, prosecution, or conviction is not required, and U visa holders and their family members are authorized to work and, after three years, are eligible for permanent residence status and eventual citizenship.

APPLICATION PROCESS

Persons seeking a T visa must complete (no fee is required) an application that requests information regarding their eligibility to T nonimmigrant status and their admissibility to the United States. A statement, in the applicant's own words, about their victimization must also be included. To demonstrate cooperation with law enforcement, a signed statement from law enforcement can be included as part of the application as well as such items as court documents, police reports, news articles, and affidavits.

Persons receiving a T visa are granted an Employment Authorization Document at the same time, so they are legally able to work in the United States during the three years for which the T visa is valid. After three years in T nonimmigrant status, the visa holder can apply for permanent residence.

USE OF T VISAS

Congress limits the number of T visas that can be granted each year to 5,000. Once the cap is reached, applicants are placed on a waiting list, and their application will receive priority the following year. However, unlike the U visa, which is capped at 10,000 per year and typically has a waiting list, the number of T visas granted is far below the annual cap. Since 2012, fewer than 1,000 T visas per year have been granted to victims (U.S. Department of State 2017).

Federal agencies open about 3,000 human trafficking investigations each year. With fewer than 1,000 T visas being granted, there is concern that trafficking victims are not being informed about the availability of the T visa program. In 2017, the U.S. Department of Homeland Security (DHS) issued a resource guide for federal, state, local, tribal, and territorial law enforcement officers, prosecutors, and judges (DHS 2017). A goal of the guide is to provide justice personnel with more information about the T visa program so they can help stabilize the victims' legal status—providing trafficking victims a greater sense of security and making it easier for them to assist law enforcement and prosecutorial efforts.

Philip L. Reichel

See also: Human Trafficking; U.S. Trafficking Victims Protection Act

Further Reading

U.S. Citizenship and Immigration Services. 2014. "Questions and Answers: Victims of Human Trafficking, T Nonimmigrant Status." Last Modified December 29, 2014. Accessed January 21, 2019. https://www.uscis.gov/humanitarian/victims-human-trafficking-other-crimes/victims-human-trafficking-t-nonimmigrant-status/questions-and-answers-victims-human-trafficking-t-nonimmigrant-status.

U.S. Citizenship and Immigration Services. 2017. "Victims of Criminal Activity: U Nonimmigrant Status." Last Modified August 25, 2017. Accessed January 21, 2019. https://www.uscis.gov/humanitarian/victims-human-trafficking-other-crimes/victims-criminal-activity-u-nonimmigrant-status/victims-criminal-activity-u-nonimmigrant-status.

U.S. Department of Homeland Security (DHS). 2016. "Classification for Victims of Severe Forms of Trafficking In Persons; Eligibility for 'T' Nonimmigrant Status." In *Federal Register, 12/19/2016*. Accessed January 21, 2019. https://www.federalregister.gov/documents/2016/12/19/2016-29900/classification-for-victims-of-severe-forms-of-trafficking-in-persons-eligibility-for-t-nonimmigrant.

U.S. Department of Homeland Security (DHS). 2017. "U and T Visa Law Enforcement Resources." Accessed January 21, 2019. https://www.dhs.gov/publication/u-visa-law-enforcement-certification-resource-guide.

U.S. Department of State. 2017. "Trafficking in Persons Report." Accessed January 21, 2019. https://www.state.gov/j/tip/rls/tiprpt/index.htm.

U.S. Department of State. n.d. "U.S. Laws on Trafficking in Persons." Accessed September 23, 2017. https://www.state.gov/j/tip/laws.

Target Stores Data Breach (2013)

The Target Corporation suffered one of the most widespread hacks of customer financial information in late 2013. A third-party investigator claimed that Target's breach "will put its mark up there with some of the largest retail breaches to date" (Krebs 2013b). Due to the breach, Target laid off 475 employees who worked at their headquarters in Minneapolis and another 700 positions worldwide. By February 18, 2014, the cost of Target's breach exceeded $200 million, and the company announced it would provide one year of free credit monitoring and identity theft protection for its shoppers in the United States.

Between the dates of November 27 and December 15, 2013, hackers accessed and stole the credit card information of 70 million Target customers. The unusual source of the breach was Fazio Mechanical, a small heating and air conditioning firm based in Pennsylvania, and the HVAC company used by Target in all of its stores. Fazio Mechanical was the victim of its own breach from malware sent by an e-mail (Krebs 2015). This initial malware allowed the attackers to steal the virtual private network credentials that Fazio's technicians used to connect to Target's network.

On December 15, Target confirmed internally that their stores had been hacked and that hackers had gained access to its point-of-sale network. To help find out the extent of the damage, the United States asked for permission from the Brazilian authorities to receive the data that was on their server (Krebs 2014). Four days later, Target announced to the public that they had been hacked and that the incident was now under investigation. The next day, December 20, Target stated that the breach was limited to credit card information and that there was no evidence that information such as birth dates or Social Security numbers had been stolen. A third-party forensics unit announced on December 27 that encrypted debit card PIN information had also been stolen.

VULNERABILITIES

Target needed to fail best security practices at multiple levels for this attack to have occurred. First, Target used Microsoft's virtualization software, centralized name resolution, and Microsoft System Center Configuration Manager for their system updates and security patches (Kassner 2015). Attackers were able to discover the systems that Target used and the vendors that they were connected to by searching the detailed case study on Microsoft's Web site. Second, as Target allowed vendors to connect to their internal network, when the Fazio employee accepted the e-mailed Trojan virus, named Citadel, hackers now had the ability to access Target's system (Kassner 2015). Third, Fazio's network was so easily compromised because the company used a free version of anti-malware instead of opting for a high-quality, and costlier, defense. Fourth, instead of using separate systems for HVAC, inventory, payroll, and point-of-sale systems, Target chose to host all store software on one machine per store. So, hackers gained entry through the Ariba system, used for air conditioning, and subsequently found access to the more desirable payment information hosted on the same machine (Krebs 2015).

Once the hackers found the information that they were searching for, the malware sent the information to a secure "dump server" and sent a confirmation notification to the thieves (Kassner 2015). The dump shop that the hackers used to sell the cards had been given the base name Tortuga, the Spanish word for "tortoise" or "turtle" (Krebs 2013a). Fifth, due to Target's single-server-per-store policy, the hackers had the ability to steal the data from software portals that had been designed to lack Internet connectivity! The information that had been stolen was sold on digital black markets, which ruined some Target shoppers' credit. With this information stolen, hackers had the ability to produce counterfeit credit cards and debit cards and withdraw cash from others' bank accounts. The counterfeit cards were found to be sold on the black markets for $20 to more than $100 (Kreb 2013a).

LESSONS

The Target breach provides a number of important cybersecurity lessons. First, Target needed to limit access that certain vendors had to its system. By permitting many vendors to have access, it allowed for hackers to get into its network through many different portals. Second, Target should not have had all its internal networks managed by one server. Having the point-of-sale systems and HVAC systems on the same machine may have made access easier for employees, but it also made it easier for the hackers to get into the system and control everything. In response, Target began training its employers to rotate and change passwords, and it hired new cybersecurity teams (Kassner 2015).

Alexis S. Lemanski

See also: Cyberattack; Cybercrime; Hackers

Further Reading

Kassner, Michael. 2015. "Anatomy of the Target Data Breach: Missed Opportunities and Lessons Learned." ZDNet, Last updated February 2, 2015. Accessed January 21, 2019. http://www.zdnet.com/article/anatomy-of-the-target-data-breach-missed-opportunities-and-lessons-learned.

Krebs, Brian. 2013a. "Cards Stolen in Target Breach Flood Underground Markets." Last Updated December 20, 2013. Accessed January 21, 2019. https://krebsonsecurity.com/2013/12/cards-stolen-in-target-breach-flood-underground-markets.

Krebs, Brian. 2013b. "Sources: Target Investigating Data Breach." Last updated December 13, 2013. Accessed January 21, 2019. https://krebsonsecurity.com/2013/12/sources-target-investigating-data-breach.

Krebs, Brian. 2014. "Target Hackers Broke in via HVAC Company." Last updated February 5, 2014. Accessed January 21, 2019. https://krebsonsecurity.com/2014/02/target-hackers-broke-in-via-hvac-company.

Krebs, Brian. 2015. "Inside Target Corp., Days after 2013 Breach." September 21. Accessed January 21, 2019. https://krebsonsecurity.com/2015/09/inside-target-corp-days-after-2013-breach.

Tax Havens and Grand Corruption

While it remains true that many tax havens fulfill the fantasy image of a tropical island with governance structures designed to attract foreign business, many havens are more mundane. In 1981, the U.S. Internal Revenue Service (IRS) defined *tax havens* as "any country having a low or zero rate of tax on all or certain categories of income, and offering a certain level of banking or commercial secrecy" (cited in Findley, Nielson, and Sharman 2014, 70). To this day, Tax havens remain jurisdictions that structure their tax and corporate laws to attract foreign or interstate financial flows, allowing corporations and criminal enterprises to disguise either taxable profits or proceeds of crime.

More recently, researchers have begun to refer to tax havens as offshore financial centers (OFCs). Some OFCs act as conduits between clients wishing to disguise their income or illicit wealth from domestic tax and law enforcement authorities, and other OFCs are where the wealth is deposited (Garcia-Bernardo et al. 2017). The conduit-OFCs—predominantly the Netherlands, the United Kingdom, Singapore, Switzerland, and Ireland—represent the mundane. Whereas the top 25 sink-OFCs include both the exotic—Bermuda, the Cayman Islands, and eight other island states—as well as small or micro European states, such as

Cyprus, Liechtenstein, Luxembourg, Monaco, and Malta. The more mundane sink-OFCs are current or former U.K. territories—Gibraltar, Jersey, and Hong Kong. In most cases, the tax havens/OFCs themselves are not the site of either licit or illicit economic activity of a significant scale; corporations do not usually use tax havens as manufacturing centers, and criminals use tax havens to unlink their crimes from their profits.

Tax havens have long associations with grand corruption, which is defined as the abuse of public office for private gain by national leaders. Such leaders engaged in grand corruption are often referred to as "kleptocrats" (Andreski 1968, 92–109). National leaders include not only presidents and prime ministers but members of their cabinets or senior political officials, family and friends, business associates, and other close associates of the ruling regime. The UN Convention against Corruption (UNCAC) and the UN Convention against Transnational Organized Crime (UNTOC) have both outlawed grand corruption. But in reality, the existence of tax havens as part of the international system enables unscrupulous national leaders to enrich themselves.

In 2016, investigative journalists in Germany were provided with millions of documents from the Panamanian law firm Mossack Fonseca. This enormous leak, referred to as the "Panama Papers," has been made available in a searchable database to the public (International Consortium of Investigative Journalists 2017). Journalists from Africa who had early access to this database discovered evidence of grand corruption with links to multiple scandals involving leaders from African nations (Obermayer and Obermaier 2016, 192–198). The president of the Democratic Republic of Congo; children and relatives of current or former leaders of Equatorial Guinea, Mozambique, and Malawi; and former ministers from Malawi and Angola provide a representative sample of links found to the offshore companies set up by Mossack Fonseca.

Such abuses by national leaders were not limited to Africa. Strong connections in the Panama Papers were found between multimillion-dollar transactions and close friends of Russian president Vladimir Putin. While many of those named have denied any wrongdoing, the level of enrichment revealed by the Panama Papers goes well beyond what can be explained through public income. Furthermore, the use of tax havens reflects either a distrust by national leaders of the integrity of their own national institutions or a deliberate attempt to conceal wrongdoing on their part. The latter is more likely, as kleptocrats and their relatives use shell companies to disguise both ownership and origin of their ill-gotten wealth.

Shell companies provide legal protection to kleptocrats, as such companies are legal persons created under the relevant national law (Panamanian law in the case of Mossack Fonseca) as a means to transfer and hide wealth (Findley, Nielson, and Sharman 2014, 31). Short of a leak such as the Panama Papers, investigators and anticorruption agencies have little hope of identifying links between the grand corruption of kleptocrats and the billions they have hidden in tax havens.

Adam B. Masters

See also: Corruption; Money Laundering; UN Convention against Corruption; UN Convention against Transnational Organized Crime

Further Reading

Andreski, Stanislav. 1968. *The African Predicament: A Study in the Pathology of Modernisation.* New York: Atherton.

Findley, Michael G., Daniel L. Nielson, and Jason C. Sharman. 2014. *Global Shell Games: Experiments in Transnational Relations, Crime and Terrorism.* Edited by Christian Reus-Smit and Nicholas J. Wheeler. Vol. 128, *Cambridge Studies in International Relations.* Cambridge: Cambridge University Press.

Garcia-Bernardo, Javier, Jan Fichtner, Frank W. Takes, and Eelke M. Heemskerk. 2017. "Uncovering Offshore Financial Centers: Conduits and Sinks in the Global Corporate Ownership Network." *Scientific Reports* 7 (1): 6246.

International Consortium of Investigative Journalists. 2017. "The Panama Papers." International Consortium of Investigative Journalists. Accessed January 21, 2019. https://panamapapers.icij.org.

Obermayer, Bastian, and Frederik Obermaier. 2016. *The Panama Papers: Breaking the Story of How the Rich & Powerful Hide Their Money.* Translated by Simon Pare, Seiriol Dafydd, Alice Paul, and Jackie Smith. London: Oneworld.

Terrorism, Domestic

Domestic terrorism is defined in Chapter 113B of the U.S. Code as activities that occur primarily in the territorial jurisdiction of the United States that involve acts dangerous to human life that are a violation of federal or state law and that appear to be intended to intimidate or coerce a civilian population; to influence the policy of a government by intimidation or coercion; or to affect the conduct of a government by mass destruction, assassination, or kidnapping (18 U.S. Code § 2331 (5)). International terrorism has essentially the same definition in the U.S. Code, but it refers to acts that "occur primarily outside the territorial jurisdiction of the United States, or transcend national boundaries in terms of the means by which they are accomplished, the persons they appear intended to intimidate or coerce, or the locale in which their perpetrators operate or seek asylum" (18 U.S. Code § 2331 (1)).

Key words in the definition include the intention to intimidate or coerce and to influence government policy. Prior to the 21st century, the goal of influencing policy was usually rather specific (for example political, social, or economic in nature), and the complaints could potentially be resolved by negotiation. In the 21st century, religious beliefs are more common motivators than political, social, or economic factors. This becomes important because negotiated resolutions for religious disputes are less likely to be found than is true for political, social, and economic disputes.

HISTORY

Using the definition of the U.S. Code, many violent events in American history could be described as terrorist acts. Indeed, in many efforts to create political or social change, some actors have become disenchanted with mainstream political processes and sought more dramatic tactics. Many of the early incidents of domestic terrorism emerged from disagreements over racial issues. In one of the first acts of terrorism, colonial Puritans ransacked a Native American Pequot village in Connecticut in 1637. The Puritans burned the village and killed many fleeing residents in an effort to convince the tribe to leave the area. During the heated political debate over slavery in the mid-19th century, proslavery forces murdered an abolitionist newspaper editor and sacked the town of Lawrence, Kansas, killing nearly all of the men in the town. In response, abolitionist John Brown led a raid on a proslavery group in which several individuals were murdered. In the 1870s, the Ku Klux Klan (KKK) tried to overturn the gains made by African Americans and convince the South to return to pre–Civil War social and political arrangements through coordinated attacks on black communities.

The targets of domestic terrorism evolved in the late 19th and early 20th centuries. Most terrorist acts resulted from conflict between labor and business. Such groups as the Molly Maguires and the International Workers of the World (IWW) committed acts of arson, bombings, and murder in an effort to change business or government policies. By the mid-20th century, domestic terrorist attacks had become more antigovernment. In the 1960s, the Cold War gave rise to debates over national security. Left- and right-wing groups both engaged in terrorism. On the left, antiwar groups such as the Weather Underground bombed university facilities in an effort to end the war in Vietnam. On the right, such groups as the Minutemen engaged in terrorist activity to protect the United States from the perceived Soviet threat. In the 1990s, antiabortion activists increasingly turned to violent criminal activity in their attempts to end abortion. Meanwhile, in response to federal government excesses at Ruby Ridge (1992) and Waco (1993), some newly formed citizen militia groups planned violent attacks against the U.S. government. At the dawn of the 21st century, threats of domestic terrorism came largely from racist neo-Nazi groups and radical animal rights and environmental groups engaging in large-scale property destruction.

TYPES OF DOMESTIC TERRORISM

A variety domestic terrorism types have been described, typically under the categories of left-wing terrorism and right-wing terrorism. Left-wing terrorism often incudes extremist groups within social and political movements that were not themselves fundamentally violent. Examples might include violent extremists among communist or socialist groups, antiwhite racists, animal rights activists, and LGBTQ extremists. Far-left extremists were particularly active during the 1960s and 1970s as young people rallied around the antiwar movement, the civil rights movement, women's rights, and other political and social causes. Since 2016, loosely affiliated groups called Antifa (short for anti-fascists) have received considerable media attention. Composed mostly of young people, initially on the West Coast but spreading across the country, Antifa members dress in black and wear masks when they confront right-wing groups (Kaste and Siegler 2017).

Right-wing terrorism often includes white nationalists, neo-Confederates, anti-communists, fascists, anti-Muslim attackers, anti-immigration extremists, and abortion clinic bombers. Since the 1990s, far-right extremism has been especially active with such examples as abortion clinic bombings, a racially motivated attack in 2012 at a Sikh temple in Wisconsin, and the Oklahoma City bombing in 1995. Martin (2019) explains that right-wing extremism is rooted in such trends as anti-government and evangelical religious activism. The Patriot movement that came into prominence in the early 1990s is an example of right-wing extremism, with their belief that non-American interests are taking over key government centers of authority.

RESPONSES TO DOMESTIC TERRORISM

The government response to domestic terrorism has taken many forms and has often led to abuses by law enforcement and intelligence agencies. For example, early responses to the Ku Klux Klan included President Ulysses S. Grant's suspension of habeas corpus to pursue suspected Klan members in several areas of South Carolina. In the early 20th century, extremists associated with socialist and anarchist groups often faced sedition charges under constitutionally questionable laws. The FBI used illegal tactics to crack down on extremists—or alleged extremists—in the 1960s and 1970s. The crackdown included unlawful surveillance, incitement of violence between groups, and questionable associations with criminal informants. These tactics even included illegal wiretaps of phone conversations involving civil rights leader Dr. Martin Luther King Jr., who was wrongly suspected of harboring communist sentiments simply because he was challenging the status quo in U.S. race relations.

In the 1980s and 1990s, state and federal officials adopted a number of new policies to address domestic terrorism. In response to rising violence around abortion clinics, governments adopted restrictions on protests around the clinics. In reaction to right-wing paramilitary groups, including citizen militia groups, many state governments adopted laws that made most types of paramilitary group activities illegal.

But significant changes to federal law and law enforcement policies regarding terrorism did not occur until the Oklahoma City bombing in 1996 and again in 2001 following the September 11, 2001, attacks. In 1996, the federal government significantly expanded its domestic counterterrorism efforts and developed new law enforcement tools for preventing terrorism through the Antiterrorism and Effective Death Penalty Act. In September 2001, President George W. Bush signed the USA PATRIOT Act, which greatly increased the government's authority to respond to domestic and international terrorism. The act expanded the power and authority of law enforcement and intelligence agencies. It also established a series of terrorism-related crimes and created the basis for the creation of the Department of Homeland Security (DHS), which would eventually house nearly all government agencies tasked with preventing and responding to terrorism.

Most government efforts to address domestic terrorism have been successful in that perpetrators have been captured and convicted of crimes. However, the success of preventive efforts is difficult to assess because most government efforts to address the problem are a reaction to a significant terrorist event. Given that we still know so little about the causes of terrorism, perhaps it is not surprising that those prevention efforts will only achieve limited success.

Donald P. Haider-Markel and Philip L. Reichel

See also: Charleston, South Carolina, Church Attack; Lone Wolf Terrorism; Oklahoma City Bombing (1995); September 11 Terrorist Attacks (2001); Terrorism, International; Tokyo Subway Sarin Attack (1994)

Further Reading

Hewitt, Christopher. 2002. *Understanding Terrorism in America (Extremism and Democracy).* London: Routledge.

Kaste, Martin, and Kirk Siegler. 2017. "Fact Check: Is Left-Wing Violence Rising?" NPR All Things Considered. Last updated, June 16, 2017. Accessed January 21, 2019. https://www.npr.org/2017/06/16/533255619/fact-check-is-left-wing-violence-rising.

Martin, Gus. 2019. *Essentials of Terrorism: Concepts and Controversies.* 5th ed. Thousand Oaks, CA: Sage.

Spindlove, Jeremy R., and Clifford E. Simonsen. 2018. *Terrorism Today: The Past, the Players, the Future.* 6th ed. Hoboken: Pearson.

Vohryzek-Bolden, Miki, Gayle Olson-Raymer, and Jeffrey O. Whamond. 2001. *Domestic Terrorism and Incident Management: Issues and Tactics.* Springfield, IL: Charles C. Thomas, Publishers LTD.

Terrorism, Intelligence Gathering

Maintaining national security is reliant on gathering and analyzing intelligence. This has been further emphasized in the recent century by the globalization of communication and the increased frequency of international threats, specifically ones relating to terrorism. Overall, intelligence is information gathered either within or outside a nation's borders that involves threats to the country, people, property, or interests, and thus posing a danger to homeland security. The methods for gathering intelligence has grown immensely due to the expansion of technology and increased collaboration within the intelligence community. Such forms for acquisition include human intelligence, signals intelligence, open-source intelligence, imagery intelligence, measurement and signature intelligence, and geospatial intelligence. The increased need for intelligence has globalized the effort to protect national security and strengthen counterterrorism and counterintelligence programs.

INTELLIGENCE COMMUNITY

Specifically regarding the United States, the U.S. Intelligence Community has a main focus on gathering and analyzing such information from intelligence sources. This community is composed of 17 executive branch agencies and organizations that are administered by the Office of the Director of National Intelligence. These agencies collect information and compose it to be used by Intelligence Community customers. The National Security Act of 1947 defined customers as the president, the National Security Council, the heads of departments and agencies of the executive branch, the chairman of the Joint Chiefs of Staff and senior military commanders, and Congress (Office of the Director of National Intelligence n.d.).

The number of agencies involved is to help ensure the raw data obtained for the initial collection is easily understood and corroborated by other sources as to help with the final decisions regarding national and homeland security. This is especially the case in regard to protecting threats against terrorist groups. Since the Cold War, and especially since the September 11, 2001, terrorist attacks, terrorism has been a main priority for the Intelligence Community. This shift in priorities has made intelligence gathering an active field rather one that passively obtains information (Dahl and Viola 2017). The importance of intelligence gathering in regard to terrorism is due to the increased threat of such attacks as well as the increased challenges terrorist groups hold in regard to intelligence gathering. Despite such threats, intelligence is an ever-evolving field with multiple types of methods and the dedicated backing of the Intelligence Community.

HUMAN INTELLIGENCE

One of the main types of intelligence that is collected is human intelligence (HUMINT), which is gathered from human sources rather than technology alone. The main purpose of HUMINT is to fill in missing information gathered from other intelligence methods. The information gathered via HUMINT is used when there is no other way to obtain such intelligence. Due to the inverted nature of terrorist groups, HUMINT has been argued to be the most important source of intelligence with regard to combating terrorism (Dahl and Viola 2017). In addition, HUMINT is multifaceted by including the services of clandestine acquisition of photography, documents, and other such material; overt collection internationally by people; debriefing foreign nationals or citizens that travel internationally; and contact with foreign governments. Due to the range of tasks associated with HUMINT operations, missions can vary tremendously in duration and can be continued for years at a time (CIA 2013a).

Due to the human component of HUMINT, such intelligence attainment can be more complex than other methods. The collection of information via HUMINT is to identify elements, intentions, composition, strength, dispositions, tactics, equipment, personnel, and capabilities of the target. To obtain such information, the collection process involves screening, planning and preparation, approach and termination, questioning, and reporting. This process is complex and thus requires prioritization and specificity when collecting the intelligence. This helps maintain the goal of HUMINT, which is to obtain the maximum amount of accurate information in the least amount of time possible. The duality of accuracy and quantity is imperative when it comes to reporting, as these elements are key in sorting through national security threats (U.S. Department of the Army 2006).

This process of HUMINT collection is complex and high stakes, making it a very specialized field of intelligence. The collector must be a specialized individual with key characteristics that include initiative, interpersonal skills, ability to manage multiple perspectives, alertness, and adaptability. These skills are imperative because of the nature of the work. Human nature is extremely dynamic due to an influx of emotions, intentions, and motivations. These factors, in conjunction with the significance of intelligence in general, allows for HUMINT to be a unique and imperative aspect of intelligence gathering.

SIGNAL INTELLIGENCE

Signal intelligence (SIGINT) is another imperative method of gathering intelligence. SIGINT is the collection of foreign intelligence via communication systems. Signals are transmitted when an electronic form of communication is sent. SIGINT entails a wide array of communication methods, and thus it is further split into the subfields of communications intelligence, the interception of foreign communications; electronic intelligence, the collection from radars and weapon systems; and foreign instrumental signals intelligence, gathered from weapons under development (CIA 2013c).

In regard to the United States, SIGINT processes are regulated by the Constitution, federal law, executive orders, and other such regulations from the executive branch. The National Security Agency (NSA) is predominantly responsible for the collection and processing of SIGINT data. The data that is collected is specifically raw, and thus it is further sent on to the Intelligence Community as a whole, with special regards to the Central Intelligence Agency (CIA 2013c). SIGINT is beneficial in complementing other intelligence gathered via other methods. All of the raw intelligence is thus combined to form what is known as "finished intelligence," which can be relayed to the Intelligence Community customers. SIGINT examines the international impact of intelligence gathering, it predominantly involves foreign communication. The globalization of technology, and consequently communication as a whole, has expanded the popularity and importance of SIGINT as a method of maintaining national security.

OPEN-SOURCE INTELLIGENCE

Though open-source intelligence (OSINT) is a more contemporary form of intelligence gathering, it is still just as complex as other methods. OSINT is collected via publicly available material, such as the Internet, mass media, journals, conferences, photos, and geospatial information. OSINT expands on intelligence gathering in covert operations of human intelligence, overhead imagery, and signals intelligence. This intersection of methods allows OSINT to create a foundation to build other intelligence upon. However, there are some situations where OSINT is the only type of intelligence, such as when there is a lack of accessibility or when opportunities are limited (CIA 2013b).

Due to the nature of OSINT, pertinent challenges and criticism accompany it. By using open-source media and public information, there is a sheer volume of data to sort through. This has made the need for coordinated efforts imperative, as there is a probable chance of duplication and, thus, inaccurate information. A major criticism of OSINT is that it is less reliable than other methods, especially with the possibility of including insignificant information. This has led some people in this community to suggest that OSINT is not a true form of intelligence, and some reject it altogether. Such opinions have created polarized views of OSINT, making it a further complicated method of raw intelligence.

GLOBAL IMPORTANCE

Intelligence gathering is a significant and complex necessity to maintain national security. This complexity is shown through several ways, including the number of agencies involved in the Intelligence Community and how many different ways intelligence can be gathered. By compiling information from a range of sources, gaps of information can be filled in, thus increasing the accuracy of the intelligence. This accuracy is crucial because most intelligence is of foreign relations. Inaccurate information can strain foreign policy and affect global communication. This is especially the case in regard to intelligence and counterterrorism efforts. Terrorism is an international threat as well as a reality and has consequently shifted methods of intelligence gathering. The increased pressure associated with terrorism has unified national intelligence agencies in an effort to not only protect the nation but also international relations.

Christina Lynn Richardson

See also: Terrorism, Domestic; Terrorism, International; Terrorism, Online Propaganda; Terrorism, State-Sponsored; Terrorism, Vehicle Ramming Attacks

Further Reading

Central Intelligence Agency (CIA). 2013a. "INTelligence: Human Intelligence." April 30. Accessed January 21, 2019. https://www.cia.gov/news-information/featured-story-archive/2010-featured-story-archive/intelligence-human-intelligence.html.

Central Intelligence Agency (CIA). 2013b. "INTellingence: Open Source Intelligence." April 30. Accessed January 21, 2019. https://www.cia.gov/news-information/featured-story-archive/2010-featured-story-archive/open-source-intelligence.html.

Central Intelligence Agency (CIA). 2013c. "INTelligence: Signals Intelligence." April 30. Accessed January 21, 2019. https://www.cia.gov/news-information/featured-story-archive/2010-featured-story-archive/intelligence-signals-intelligence-1.html.

Dahl, Erik J., and David Viola. 2017. "Intelligence and Terrorism." *Oxford Research Encyclopedia of International Studies*. November 29, 2017. Accessed January 21, 2019. http://internationalstudies.oxfordre.com/view/10.1093/acrefore/9780190846626.001.0001/acrefore-9780190846626-e-91.

Office of the Director of National Intelligence. n.d. "What Is Intelligence." Accessed January 21, 2019. https://www.dni.gov/index.php/what-we-do/what-is-intelligence.

U.S. Department of the Army, Headquarters. 2006. *Human Intelligence Collector Operations*. Washington, D.C.

Terrorism, International

The word *terror* originates from the Latin *terrere*, meaning to scare, terrify, or frighten. Referring to a state of mind, it denotes a psychological rather than a physical effect. Although the use of terror as a form of coercion dates back to early civilizations, "terrorism," describing a conscious practice, first emerged in France in the 14th century. Terrorism is a politicized term that is selectively applied to certain criminal acts. Although there are over 250 academic, governmental, and intergovernmental definitions of terrorism, there is no international consensus (Schmid 2013, 99).

Nations use their position of authority to designate a subnational group as terrorist. In the United States, there are over 20 definitions of domestic and international terrorism that have changed over time to reflect current concerns. The U.S. State Department definition, for instance, has changed seven times between 1982 and 2004 (Schmid 2013, 44). State definitions are often accompanied by lists of subnational groups that are designated as terrorist organization. These lists vary between nations in the groups and the numbers of organizations included.

Reviewing the many definitions provides insight into some central elements of terrorism. Beyond the underlying illegal violent acts, terrorism is the communication of a political motive that is intended to impact a larger audience than the immediate victims. This process of terrorism includes seizing attention (a provocation through shock, horror, fear, revulsion), conveying a message (a political objective that may be expressed in tandem to the act or through the act itself), and eliciting a response (in the form of a concessions, a violent retaliation, or a public reaction) (Townshend 2011, 8).

TYPES OF TERRORISM

A common distinction is made between domestic and international terrorism. Domestic terrorism is defined as incidents that are perpetrated by local nationals against a purely domestic target on a national stage (Schmid 2013, 184). The concept of international terrorism emerged after the airliner hijackings of the 1970s broadened the geographic scope of attacks. These distinctions are increasingly blurred. For instance, the 2011 attacks of Anders Behring Breivik in Norway could be deemed domestic terrorism (location, offender, and victims were all Norwegian); however, Breivik's motivation had emerged from a globalized world and anti-Islamic sentiments.

A more nuanced approach contrasts international and transnational terrorism (Schmid 2013, 184). International terrorism refers to groups pursuing nationalist goals operating domestically and across national boundaries, such as in the assassination of Prime Minister Rajiv Gandhi in India by the Sri Lankan Liberation Tigers of Tamil Eelam in 1991. Transnational terrorism refers to group actions that operate on an international stage in pursuit of a goal that transcends any single nation. This was illustrated by the attacks of Al Qaeda in various locations around the globe in the quest of establishing a pan-Islamist caliphate (Hoffman 2004, 550).

Another means of categorizing terrorism has been by distinguishing between state and nonstate actors (Townshend 2011, 37). State terrorism describes a government that oppresses its citizens, such as through the use of disappearances, mass terror, or genocide, as seen in Hitler's Germany, Pol Pot's Cambodia, or Guatemala's 36-year civil conflict (Wilkinson 2006, 8–17; Schmid 2013, 203). Nonstate terrorism refers to violence perpetrated by an entity that does not have governing force that uses "a strategy of assault on the state" (Townshend 2011, 54).

Nonstate terrorist movements have been further characterized by four types of political motivation: ethnonationalist, religiopolitical, ideological, and single-issue groups (Wilkinson 2006, 4). Ethnonationalist groups are motivated by the creation of an independent state along an ethnic identity, such as the Basque National Liberation Movement (Euskadi Ta Askatasuna) in northern Spain, whose goal was to gain independence for the Basque Country. Irredentism is another form of ethnonationalism, as seen in the ambitions of the Irish Republican Army (IRA) that wanted to not only separate Northern Ireland from Great Britain but also to unite with the Republic of Ireland. Religiopolitical groups seek political independence; however, the quest for independence is coupled with religious doctrine. Hamas in Palestine identifies itself as a resistance movement focused on creating an independent Islamist Palestine. In contrast, the objective of ideological groups is to bring about political and social change through revolution. The Weather Underground Organization that operated in the United States in the early 1970s sought to overthrow U.S. imperialism by advancing Marxism, opposing the Vietnam War, and liberating African Americans.

It is important to note that these categories, as any, are mere guides rather than definitive motivational distinctions. A case in point is the Algerian National Liberation Front (Front de Liberation Nationale) that was a both an ideological and an ethnonationalist group seeking independence from France while espousing socialism. Finally, single-issue groups refer to organizations that are focused on one particular concern rather than wholesale social change. One such example is the Animal Liberation Front, which has been motivated by the pursuit of animal rights.

All of the above organizations have at some point been labeled a terrorist organization; however, the designation has been contested by the groups themselves. What these groups have in common is that they have all used violence, in some form, in furtherance of their goals. Some have used a campaign of terror exclusively in the pursuit of their objectives, while others have relied on it only partially.

HISTORY

Terrorism changes over time. There have been three distinct phases since World War II (1939–1945): anticolonial-nationalist, ideological, and religious or new terrorism (White 2005, 69). In the aftermath of World War II, revolutionaries in European colonies used terrorism as a tool to oust occupying powers by mimicking asymmetrical warfare methods used during the war. The tactic relied on killing "one enemy soldier in front of the world's media [rather] than . . . kill ten of them in a forsaken dessert" (White 2005, 70). The goal was to seize the attention of the world by laying bare the plight of colonized peoples.

The 1960s saw an evolution of terrorism from anticolonial-nationalist to ideological motivations that sought to galvanize social change. The targets were largely symbols of Western capitalist democracies, and although many of these movements were operating domestically, the left-wing ideologies connected the various movements in the Middle East, Asia, Latin America, and the West.

More recently, terrorism has again morphed to what some refer to as religious terrorism (White 2005, 71; Townshend 2011, 97) and others as new terrorism (Schmid 2013, 232). The more recent manifestation of terrorism is a reaction to a globalized world. Common to these fundamentalist groups is a rejection of multiculturalism, progressive movements, and social change. It is a quest for a reversion to more traditional ideals and values. Boko Haram in Nigeria, the Lord's Resistance Army in Uganda, and the American Front in the United States are all examples of reversionist groups. Interestingly, although many of these groups have religious undertones, these groups are better described as united by a belief rather than a religion.

Even "domestic" forms of terrorism have some international elements, whether this is in the global publicity, the transference of ideology, or in the supranational motivations.

RESPONSE

The response to terrorism is a core element of the process of terror; eliciting a reaction is built into the provocation (Townshend 2011, 14). Although concession to demands may be the objective, a major purpose of terror is to delegitimize the opposition. Two key methods have been used in responding to terrorism, either combating the manifestations or by addressing the root causes (Schmid 2005, 223). The former is more common. It is intended to pacify public sentiment for vengeance and usually involves the use of extralegal measures (Schmid 2013, 30). Evidence suggests that a symptoms-based approach and reactive policies are not productive. In fact, such tactics serve to intensify violence through increasing popular support for the movement and motivating new recruits (Silke 2005, 253). The root causes approach, on the other hand, requires understanding the underlying grievances and formulating a strategy that addresses grievances. An effective terrorism strategy needs a scaffolded approach that protects civilians without compromising the integrity of democracy and challenging the hatred politically.

Anamika A. Twyman-Ghoshal

See also: Al Qaeda; Barcelona and Cambrils Terrorist Attacks (2017); Islamic State of Iraq and Syria (ISIS); *Maersk Alabama* Pirate Attack (2009); Manchester Arena Terrorist Attack; Paris and *Charlie Hebdo* Terrorist Attack (2015); September 11, 2001, Terrorist Attacks

Further Reading

Hoffman, Bruce. 2004. "The Changing Face of Al Qaeda and the Global War on Terrorism." *Studies in Conflict & Terrorism* 27 (6): 549–560.

Schmid, Alex. 2013. *The Routledge Handbook of Terrorism Research.* Abington, UK: Routledge.

Silke, Andrew. 2005. "Fire of Iolaus: The Role of State Countermeasures in Causing Terrorism and What Needs to Be Done." In *Root Causes of Terrorism: Myths, Realities and Ways Forward,* edited by Tore Bjorgo, 241–255. Abington, UK: Routledge.

Townshend, Charles. 2011. *Terrorism: A Very Short Introduction.* 2nd ed. Oxford: Oxford University Press.

White, Jonathan. 2005. "Terrorism in Transition." In *Handbook of Transnational Crime & Justice*, edited by Philip Reichel, 65–78. Thousand Oaks, CA: Sage Publications.

Wilkinson, Paul. 2006. *Terrorism versus Democracy: The Liberal State Response.* Abington, UK: Routledge.

Terrorism, Online Propaganda

Terrorists spread their propaganda (i.e., misleading and biased information) online to promote a specific ideological view of reality or to instill fear and anxiety among wide circles of a population. Terrorist groups from all over the world professing various ideologies maintain a Web presence. Terrorist groups have traditionally taken advantage of various media to spread their propaganda messages as a strategy of psychological warfare (Weimann 2015). For example, terrorist attacks inflicting serious damage could be planned to ensure visibility on TV media outlets and newspapers. However, in the past, terrorists could not retain full control over the coverage of traditional media.

The emergence of information and communications technologies (ICTs) has provided them with new and effective channels for garnering publicity. Social media, forums, blogs, and Web sites allow terrorists to retain the control over their messages by overcoming physical and social barriers. They can effectively manipulate their own image and that of their enemy and shape how they are perceived by audiences (Weimann 2015). Since the September 11, 2001, terrorist attacks, jihadist terrorists have gained growing public attention, and over the last few years, their online presence has become the most visible and advanced (Calderoni et al. 2017).

MESSAGES AND PURPOSE

Online propaganda of terrorist networks pursues various objectives. On one side, the messages aim to generate support from local communities or specific target populations of supporters. For example, they could present terrorist activities as patriotic and religious duties, and they frequently exaggerate the power of the organization. These messages try to connect emotionally with the audience, as is the case of battle reporting by Western foreign fighters in Syria and Iraq (Klausen 2015). Western jihadist foreign fighters are particularly active in creating propaganda content to convince others of their beliefs or to indicate their commitment to the cause (Gill and Corner 2015).

Terrorists also promote collective identity by building narratives upon a "them vs. us" rhetoric. For example, the Taliban in Afghanistan during the first half of 2012 based their rhetoric on a culture-based "clash of civilizations" between "the civilized Islamic world vs. the West" (Drissel 2015). They claimed a "global justice" against intervention, colonialism, and economic inequality, blaming the "Western occupation" for civilian causalities and destruction of infrastructures

(Drissel 2015). ISIS rhetoric tries to balance between showing violent images and themes of ideology and pragmatism as a reflection of their offline strategy (Derrick et al. 2016).

Religious teaching materials and quotes are shared by jihadist radicals to pursue indoctrination and radicalization (Weimann 2015). On the other side, messages could aim at engaging the wider audience and shifting perspectives of society at large. For example, some groups avert the image projected by traditional media by embracing a nonviolent rhetoric (Tsfati and Weimann 2002). Messages also strive to morally legitimize terrorism and the use of violence, as in the case of terror presented within the "no other choice" narrative. The enemy is then demonized in contrast to the heroes, the freedom fighters (Tsfati and Weimann 2002).

TARGET AUDIENCE

Terrorist online propaganda can address both insiders, such as operative terrorists, lone wolves, and nonactive supporters, and outsiders, such as uninvolved people and the general population. Terrorists' content shared online is shaped according to four recurrent types of audiences (Tsfati and Weimann 2002). The content targeting local supporters is characterized by the use of local languages and the spread of detailed descriptions of internal politics. The content targeting the international public is shared in a widely spoken language, and it often explains basic facts on the organization and its mission. The content targeting traditional media outlets is often distributed in the form of press releases. Finally, content targeting enemy audiences usually aims at demoralizing the enemy. The target population could further determine the form and content of the information. For example, multimedia content often addresses younger audiences.

Martina E. Marchesi

See also: Al Qaeda; Islamic State of Iraq and Syria (ISIS); Returning Foreign Terrorist Fighters

Further Reading

Calderoni, Francesco, Martina Marchesi, and Mariya Karayotova. 2017. "Systematic Review of Cyber-Related OC and Terrorist Activities, and Technological Means for Their Study." In *Report on OC and Terrorism in Cyberspace*, edited by Stefan Rilling, Jingquan Xie, Michael Osborne, Michael Baentsch, Axel Tanner, Francesco Calderoni, Martina Elena Marchesi, Valentina Calcagno, Michael Wolfowicz, and Simon Perry, 13–65. Milan, Italy: Project PROTON. Accessed February 15, 2019. https://www.projectproton.eu/wp-content/uploads/2018/01/Deliverable-D3.1.pdf.

Derrick, Douglas C., Karyn Sporer, Sam Church, and Gina Scott Ligon. 2016. "Ideological Rationality and Violence: An Exploratory Study of ISIL's Cyber Profile." *Dynamics of Asymmetric Conflict* 9 (1–3): 57–81.

Drissel, David. 2015. "Reframing the Taliban Insurgency in Afghanistan: New Communication and Mobilization Strategies for the Twitter Generation." *Behavioral Sciences of Terrorism and Political Aggression* 7 (2): 97–128.

Gill, Paul, and Emily Corner. 2015. "Lone Actor Terrorist Use of the Internet and Behavioural Correlates." In *Terrorism Online: Politics, Law and Technology*, edited by Lee Jarvis, Stuart MacDonald, and Thomas M. Chen, 35–54. London and New York: Routledge.

Klausen, Jytte. 2015. "Tweeting the Jihad: Social Media Networks of Western Foreign Fighters in Syria and Iraq." *Studies in Conflict & Terrorism* 38 (1): 1–22.

Tsfati, Yariv, and Gabriel Weimann. 2002. "Www.Terrorism.Com: Terror on the Internet." *Studies in Conflict & Terrorism* 25 (5): 317–332.

Weimann, Gabriel. 2015. *Terrorism in Cyberspace: The Next Generation*. Washington, D.C.: Woodrow Wilson Center Press, Columbia University.

Terrorism, State-Sponsored

State-sponsored terrorism is when a government supports violent, independent actors that engage in terrorism. This support can be given in a multitude of ways, which is dependent on the state, the terrorist organization, and the motivations behind the sponsorship. Such variation is echoed in every aspect of said partnership, making state-sponsored terrorism unique and complex. This partnership shifts the dynamic of the state itself, both in the introduction to the sponsorship and alleviation of it, thus affecting global governance. This change in foreign relations, in conjunction with the global impact of terrorism in general, makes state-sponsored terrorism of international significance. These factors compound to create the complexity associated with state-sponsored terrorism and allude to the challenges associated with combating it.

HISTORY

Modern-day state-sponsored terrorism has implications as both domestic policy and international policy. Domestic state sponsorship has been a reality since the existence of nation-states and was especially prominent in the 17th century. States commonly tried to repress revolutionaries and demonstrate the state's power. Domestic application of sponsorship has kept its origins by focusing on intimidating and repressing those who are in opposition to the government.

Meanwhile, international state sponsorship has been a more recent development, with its prevalence in the 20th century. Military forces engaged in acts of aggression, conquest, or cultural or ethnic cleansing. This led states to begin using terrorism as an instrument, especially when governments could not ensure the deployment of armed forces. Consequently, state sponsorship of terrorism became an acceptable method of enhancing foreign policy. This dichotomy is still applicable today and is affecting both domestic and foreign policy (Martin 2018).

However, a significant historical shift lies with the term *state*. Though "state" typically refers to the central government as a whole, modern sponsorships have evolved to also mean independent bureaucracies and key figures, both of which are associated with the government. This expansion of sponsors exemplifies the complexity associated with state-sponsored terrorism and how it is an evolving type of criminality.

TYPES OF SPONSORSHIPS

The diversity of sponsors is echoed in every facet of the sponsorship, from the motivations behind said sponsorship to how the sponsorship is conducted. The motivations of the sponsorship vary based on whether it is for domestic acts or international acts of terror. In regard to international endeavors, motivations include ones that are political, economic, or ideological. Though domestic sponsorships have been reminiscent of these, the prominent motivation is maintaining security and control over citizens. However, no matter what soil the acts of terror are committed on, the modes of violence can include warfare, genocide, assassination, and torture (Martin 2018).

In addition to motivations, there is variance in the type of sponsorship the state gives the terrorist group. The connotation of "support" can vary tremendously, but initial research focused on states that actively aided the growth and functioning of terrorist groups, most notably through money, propaganda, and providing a safe base. However, some have argued for an expansion of the definition of "support" to include acts that are both active and passive in nature. While active sponsorship is a deliberate state decision to provide support to a terrorist organization, passive sponsorship is a state's deliberate nonintervention of such terrorist activities (Byman 2008).

Active sponsorship via state support can take form through means of control, coordination, and contact. This type of sponsorship can be divided into acts of state patronage and acts of state assistance. State patronage requires active participation in the terrorist activity, most notably through policies, arming and training, and providing a safe haven. The state rationalizes such activism through denial or seeing it as a necessity. On the other hand, state assistance uses indirect and more ambiguous means to encourage terrorist activity. Like state patronage, the state wants to enable the terrorist group, but state assistance limits the formal associations and connections the state has with the group. This distance makes denial, of either connections or specific operations, more feasible (Martin 2018). Both state patronage and state assistance differ from passive sponsorship due to the conscious decision to aid terrorism. Contrarily, the inaction of passive sponsorship is most notably shown through knowing toleration, unconcern or ignorance, and having an incapacity to act otherwise.

DANGERS ASSOCIATED WITH STATE-SPONSORED TERRORISM

States partake in sponsorships for a multitude of reasons. Some examples of such motivation include the terrorist group having unconventional military skills, which may be better than the state's military; a possibility of increasing credibility of commitments; and reinforcement of the state's influence on domestic soil. Despite these projected benefits, it is often the case that terrorist groups deviate from the initial agreement. This deviance provides unknown consequences by enabling the terrorist group.

A distinguishing factor of such divergence is different motivations of the state and the sponsored group in regard to the sponsorship. This can either be the result of initial deception on behalf of the terrorist group to gain the sponsorship, of having a different perspective on developing events, or the group striving for additional power. By sponsoring a terrorist group, the state creates a competitor that is less willing to compromise. This change in power dynamics lends itself to danger in terms of an international conflict, an external conflict with a specific target country, or an internal conflict between the terrorist organization and the state (Bapat 2012).

This change, specifically with a change in partnership dynamics, ultimately affects the likelihood that the state can repress the terrorist organization. As the terrorist group's goals are successfully accomplished because of the sponsorship, they have more bargaining power in negotiations with the state. Furthermore, due to increasing the power and status of the terrorist organization, the sponsorship decreases the likelihood that the state can negotiate the end of the relationship (Bapat 2012).

Sponsor states try to avoid such consequences by enacting specific controls, each of which is determined by the sponsorship and the behaviors of the terrorist organization. Initially, states pull together resources to monitor the behavior of the terrorist group's autonomy and, if needed, to try to modify such unsanctioned behavior. When these controls fail and the group diverges from the state's agreement, additional controls are put in place that try to limit the authority of the group. This is further coupled with enhanced monitoring and reporting of the group (Byman and Kreps 2010). However, these means of control often fail due to the said change in the power dynamic. This lack of control on behalf of the state thus transfers responsibility to international entities, as terrorism has a global impact.

COMBATING STATE-SPONSORED TERRORISM

Generally, specific efforts for combating state-sponsored terrorism are limited. Foreign policy typically dictates enacting generalized measures, such as invading the accused state and increasing counterterrorism efforts in general. However, some public and private organizations specifically monitor and compile data of acts of state-sponsored terrorism. Due to the scope of state-sponsored terrorism, such entities tend to focus on either domestic or international acts. Human Rights Watch and Amnesty International are the main proponents looking at domestically sponsored acts, while the U.S. State Department is a key player in looking at internationally sponsored terror attacks (Martin 2018).

Due to the U.S. State Department's analysis, the U.S. government has enacted sanctions that include a ban on arms-related exports and sales, controls over exports of dual-use materials, and limitations on economic assistance and financial means. In addition, the United States has passed laws that reprimand people and countries that engage in trade with countries that are determined sponsors (U.S. Department of State n.d.). These sanctions show that the development of state-sponsored terrorism affects countries all over the world, whether they are directly involved with the terrorism or not.

Such legislation has encouraged states to stop said sponsorship and thus rid themselves from the title of being a terrorist sponsor. To accomplish such, the states are required to take substantial efforts to separate themselves from the terrorist group. These efforts include, but are not limited to, a significant change in leadership and policies, not supporting international terrorism, providing assurances, sharing intelligence on terrorist groups, and resolving outstanding claims of terrorist acts (U.S. Department of State 2004). The communication of critical information and taking substantial steps in counterterrorism are essential to alleviate the sanctions. The opportunity to nullify sponsorships reflects a unified global effort against terrorism as a whole and how global governance is always subject to change.

Christina Lynn Richardson and Brian Fedorek

See also: Cybercrime; Ransomware; Small Arms and Light Weapons, Trafficking in; Terrorism, Domestic; Terrorism, International

Further Reading

Bapat, Navin A. 2012. "Understanding State Sponsorship of Militant Groups." *British Journal of Political Science* 42 (1) (January), 1–29.

Byman, Daniel L. 2008. *The Changing Nature of State Sponsorship of Terrorism.* Washington, D.C.: The Saban Center for Middle East Policy, the Brookings Institution. Accessed January 21, 2019. https://www.brookings.edu/research/the-changing-nature-of-state-sponsorship-of-terrorism/

Byman, Daniel, and Sarah E. Kreps. 2010. "Agents of Destruction? Applying Principal-Agent Analysis to State-Sponsored Terrorism." *International Studies Perspectives* 11 (1): 1–18.

Martin, Gus. 2018. *Understanding Terrorism: Challenges, Perspectives, and Issues.* 4th ed. Los Angeles, London, New Delhi, Singapore, Washington, D.C.: Sage.

U.S. Department of State. n.d. "State Sponsors of Terrorism." Accessed January 21, 2019. https://www.state.gov/j/ct/list/c14151.htm.

U.S. Department of State, Office of the Coordination for Counterterrorism. 2004. "Patterns of Global Terrorism." *News Release*, April 29.

Terrorism, Vehicle Ramming Attacks

A vehicle ramming attack is a type of attack in which an individual purposefully rams a vehicle into a target. The target can be a crowd of people, a building, or another vehicle. Vehicle ramming attacks have become more common in recent years. The attacks are easier to carry out than other types of terrorist attacks. Due to the low-tech nature of these attacks, which require little to no planning, they are becoming a method of choice for some terrorists.

Although the first vehicle ramming did not occur recently, there have been numerous attacks since the July 14, 2016, vehicle ramming attack in Nice, France, during a Bastille Day event that killed 86 people. Since that attack, there have been various attacks carried out by individuals claiming allegiance to the Islamic State of Iraq and Syria (ISIS). Also in 2016, there was an attack at a Christmas Market in Berlin. In 2017, there were three separate attacks in London; one in Sweden; attacks in Barcelona and Cambrils, Spain; one in Canada; and one in New York City. The New York attack occurred on Halloween. A terrorist claiming allegiance to ISIS drove a rented vehicle into a crowded bike path in lower Manhattan, killing 8 and wounding 12.

The 2017 New York City attack shows the influence of ISIS. In November 2016, ISIS released its third issue of *Rumiyah Magazine* (online), which includes an article entitled “Just Terror Tactics.” The article solely focuses on vehicle attacks and discusses which vehicles to use, which vehicles to avoid, ideal targets for the attacks (outdoor markets, festivals, parades, etc.), and some tips on preparation and planning—including the use of a secondary weapon if possible. In the New York attack, the attacker followed the described methods. The attacker rented a truck from Home Depot. He practiced driving the vehicle, and then he drove the vehicle along his selected route prior to the day of the attack. After crashing the vehicle, the driver emerged holding both a pellet and a paintball gun. The driver was shot and captured by a New York police officer. During the subsequent search, an ISIS flag and several knives were found in the vehicle.

In the March 2017 attack in London, England, a lone attacker ran down pedestrians on the Westminster Bridge (killing 5 and injuring 49) until he crashed his rental car. He then continued on foot to the gate of the Palace of Westminster, where he stabbed an unarmed guard. In the June 2017 vehicle attack in London, England, the driver ran over pedestrians on the London Bridge (killing 7 and injuring 48), and then the driver and several passengers continued the attack on foot after their vehicle crashed. The vehicle ramming attack method appears to be changing. The attacks continue with knives or other weapons following the initial vehicle attack, which was outlined in the *Rumiyah* article.

Following the two vehicle ramming attacks, movable barriers were installed throughout London to separate vehicles from pedestrians. In New York City, dump trucks and snowplows have been used as temporary barriers to protect crowds during the Thanksgiving parade and the New Year’s Eve celebration in Times Square. On January 2, 2018, New York City mayor Bill de Blasio announced that the city would spend $50 million to secure the city from future vehicle attacks, to include installing 1,500 metal bollards in popular locations and placing large planters at vulnerable spots.

Any vehicle can be used as a weapon. Vehicle ramming attacks have used personally owned vehicles, rented vehicles, rented trucks, work trucks, and stolen tractor trailers. The attacks have involved lone drivers and vehicles with multiple attackers. As many of the vehicle ramming attacks have involved rental vehicles, one potential way of countering this method is to alert and seek assistance from rental agencies, similar to “see something, say something.” Despite these efforts, the ability to counter the unconventional use of vehicles as weapons will continue to be difficult. As long as pedestrians and vehicles share the same space, vehicles will remain a potential threat as a weapon.

Vesna Markovic and Kenneth Gray

See also: Barcelona and Cambrils Terrorist Attacks; Islamic State of Iraq and Syria (ISIS); Lone Wolf Terrorism; Manhattan Truck Attack (2017); Terrorism, International

Further Reading

Clark, Colin, and Louis Klarevas. 2017. "London and the Mainstreaming of Vehicular Terrorism: Is There a Way to Prevent It?" *The Atlantic*, June 4. Accessed January 21, 2019. https://www.theatlantic.com/international/archive/2017/06/london-bridge-terrorism-attack/529116.

Malsin, Jared. 2017. "Terrorists Have a Long, Grim History of Using Cars as Weapons." *Time*, November 1. Accessed January 21, 2019. http://time.com/5005604/new-york-car-truck-attacks-isis.

Shvetsov, Alexey V., Victor A. Sharov, and Svetlana V. Shvetsova. 2017. "Method of Protection of Pedestrian Zone against the Terrorist Attacks Made by Means of Cars Including Off-Road Vehicles and Trucks." *European Journal for Security Research* 2 (2) (November): 119–129.

Tijuana Cartel

The Tijuana Cartel was originally known as the Arellano Félix Organization. The Arellano Félix family, seven brothers and four sisters, inherited the organization from Miguel Ángel Félix Gallardo upon his incarceration in Mexico in 1989 for his complicity in the murder of Drug Enforcement Administration (DEA) Special Agent Enrique Camarena. Arrests and deaths of family members negatively affected the Arellano Félix cartel during the 2000s, but the organization survived. Today the group is led by Arellano's nephew, Luis Fernando Sánchez Arellano (Dibble 2018).

The Tijuana Cartel is notorious for being one of the most well-known groups in Mexico to traffic drugs into the United States. The city of Tijuana is home of roughly 2 million people. Criminal activities include drug trafficking, money laundering, people smuggling, murder, arms trafficking, and bribery. The original drug cartel was formed in the 1960s in Sinola, Mexico, primarily distributing heroin and marijuana from Sinola to the United States. After the 1980s, members of the cartel moved from Sinola to Guadalajara and joined with Colombian drug traffickers to move massive amounts of cocaine. When the cartel grew, members were established in Juárez, Mexico, and Tijuana, Mexico. Murders in Tijuana from the cartel are malicious. For instance, the mangled dead bodies of people whom the cartel murdered are left visible for the community to see as a threat and as a sign of the power that the Tijuana Cartel possesses. Mexico's three main drug-smuggling routes are controlled by three major cartels: Tijuana, Sinola, and Gulf.

A key function to organized crime like the Tijuana Cartel is corruption within the police force.

> Police officers can provide key information and services. In Mexico, they often moonlight for the cartels as drivers, bodyguards, kidnappers, hit men, drug runners, lookouts, thieves, corpse-disposal experts, and extortionists; Cops can also be useful simply by hearing and seeing no evil, or by directing the law-enforcement efforts of more gung-ho colleagues toward the operations of rivals. (Finnegan 2010)

The Tijuana cartel is known to intimidate government officials and police officials by brutally attacking the noncorrupt officials.

In 2012, one of the last original members of the Tijuana Cartel, Eduardo Felix, was arrested and extradited to the United States and sentenced to 15 years in prison. Although the original leaders and members may not be present, the Tijuana Cartel is alive and well, with continued bloodshed and drug distribution at a rapid pace. For instance, "Tijuana registered one of the steepest increases in the country. The tally for the year was record 1,744 homicides almost double the record of 910 homicides set in 2016, according to figures from the Baja California Attorney General's Office" (Dibble 2018, 2).

Mexico's stability is of critical importance to the United States, and the nature and intensity of violence in Mexico has been of concern to the U.S. Congress. Mexico shares a nearly 2,000-mile border with the United States, and the two countries have close trade and cultural and demographic ties. In addition to U.S. concerns about this strategic partner and close neighbor, policy makers have expressed concern that the violence in Mexico could spill over into U.S. border states (or further inland), despite beefed-up security measures. Mexico's brutal drug trafficking–related violence has been dramatically punctuated by beheadings, public hanging of corpses, car bombs, and the murders of dozens of journalists and government officials. Beyond these brazen crimes, violence has spread from the border with the United States to Mexico's interior, flaring in the Pacific states of Michoacán and Guerrero in recent years, in the border state of Tamaulipas, and in Chihuahua and Baja California, where Mexico's largest border-region cities of Tijuana and Juárez are located and where violence spiked between 2009 and 2011. Organized crime groups have splintered and diversified their crime activities, turning to extortion, kidnapping, auto theft, human smuggling, retail drug sales, and other illicit enterprises. These crimes are often described as more "parasitic" for local populations inside Mexico.

Violence is an intrinsic feature of the trade in illicit drugs. Violence is used by traffickers to settle disputes, and a credible threat of violence maintains employee discipline and a semblance of order with suppliers, creditors, and buyers. This type of drug trafficking–related violence has occurred routinely and intermittently in U.S. cities since the early 1980s. The violence now associated with drug trafficking organizations (DTO) in Mexico is of an entirely different scale. In Mexico, the violence is not only associated with resolving disputes or maintaining discipline but also has been directed toward the government, political candidates, and the news media.

Based on different drug trafficking organizations, the Tijuana Cartel and the Juárez Cartel are considered Toll-Collector Cartels. These are drug trafficking organizations whose main income comes from toll fees received from other organizations that convey drug shipments through their controlled municipalities along the northern border. Given that these cartels are largely confined to some border municipalities, they cannot diversify their illegal activities as actively as other DTOs. If these DTOs eventually lose control of their respective border areas, they will probably disappear.

Examples of other DTOs are national cartels, such as the Sinola and Los Zetas. These DTOs control or maintain presence on numerous drug routes, including points of entry and exit along the northern and southern borders. Also, they operate major international routes to and from the country. Regardless of their wide territorial presence, they actively seek to expand control over new routes that lead to the north. These organizations have sought to build upon the profits they receive from drug trafficking to diversify their illegal portfolios, mainly toward oil theft, which is a highly lucrative and low-risk activity.

Serita Whiting

See also: Cartel Organization; Gulf Cartel; Los Zetas; Sinaloa Cartel

Further Reading

Beittel, J. 2015. *Mexico: Organized Crime and Drug Trafficking Organizations. Congressional Research Service*, July 22: 1–33. Accessed January 21, 2019. https://fas.org/sgp/crs/row/R41576.pdf.

Dibble, S. 2018. "Control for Street Drug Trade Pushes Tijuana to Grisly New Record: 1,744 Homicides." *San Diego Union Tribune*, January 14. https://www.sandiegouniontribune.com/news/border-baja-california/sd-me-homicides-tijuana-20180102-story.html

Finnegan, W. 2010. "In the Name of the Law." *New Yorker* 86 (32): 62–71.

Tokyo Subway Sarin Attack (1994)

In June 1994, the religious group known as Aum Shinrikyō (also known as Aum Supreme Truth or simply as Aum) carried out a sarin gas attack against the Tokyo subway system. The Tokyo subway sarin attack was the culmination of a series of events involving the development and use of chemical and biological weapons programs by Aum Shinrikyō. The decision to develop and deploy these weapons was at the direction of Shoko Asahara.

Founded in 1984 by Shoko Asahara (real name Chizuo Matsumoto), Aum has been characterized as a doomsday cult and has also been described as "a case study of what can happen when a fanatical group with financial resources obtains sophisticated technical abilities and decide[s] to utilize weapons of mass destruction in furthering its goals" (Sopko and Edelman 1995).

Aum was granted legal status as a religious organization in 1989 by the Tokyo government, but by the early 1990s, Asahara's followers, believing the end of the world was coming, had begun gathering firearms, developing biological weapons, and obtaining supplies for sarin nerve gas.

The sarin was first used in 1994, when Aum attempted to kill three judges who were presiding over a case that had been brought against Aum. The judges survived, but 8 other people were killed and some 500 injured. Then, upon learning about planned police raids on Aum facilities scheduled for March 22, 1995, Aum countered with a preemptive attack on March 20 against Tokyo subway lines near the Metropolitan Police Headquarters (Danzig et al. 2012).

Japanese police reports described the attack as involving a team of five Aum members carrying a total of 11 bags of sarin. The attackers also carried sharpened umbrellas to puncture the bags. The attackers boarded different trains in the Tokyo subway system and successfully punctured 8 bags. This attack resulted in 11 deaths and 3,796 injuries. In addition to the casualties, hospitals in Japan were overwhelmed with the "worried well," or those who were not affected, but feared exposure to sarin (Danzig et al. 2012).

Prior police investigation led to the identification of Aum as the source of the attack. On May 16, 1995, police raided Aum headquarters and arrested Asahara. The police obtained arrest warrants for Asahara and 40 of his followers for murder and attempted murder charges. Japan mobilized 80,000 police officers due to fears of additional sarin gas attacks (Kristof 1995).

After subsequent police investigation, Asahara and 483 other Aum members were arrested, and 189 were indicted and tried. All but one of the 189 Aum members were convicted, and 13, to include Asahara, were sentenced to death by hanging. Asahara remains in prison (Kristof 1995).

Kenneth Gray

See also: Aum Shinrikyō; Terrorism, Domestic

Further Reading

Danzig, Richard, Marc Sageman, Terrance Leighton, Lloyd Hough, Hidemi Yuki, Rui Kotani, and Zachary M. Hosford. 2012. *Aum Shinrikyo: Insights into How Terrorists Develop Biological and Chemical Weapons.* Washington, D.C.: Center for a New American Security.

Kaplan, David E., and Andrew Marshall. 1996. *The Cult at the End of the World: The Terrifying Story of Aum Doomsday Cult, from the Subways of Tokyo to the Nuclear Arsenals of Russia.* New York: Crown Publishers.

Kisala, Robert. 1998. "The AUM Spiritual Truth Church in Japan." In *Wolves within the Fold: Religious Leadership and Abuses of Power*, edited by Anson D. Shupe, 33–48. New Brunswick, NJ: Rutgers University Press.

Kristof, Nicholas D. 1995. Japanese Arrest Cult Leader Blamed in Poison Gas Attacks. *New York Times*, May 16. Accessed January 21, 2019. http://www.nytimes.com/1995/05/16/world/japanese-arrest-cult-leader-blamed-in-poison-gas-attacks.html.

Sopko, John, and Alan Edelman. 1995. "Introduction." In *A Case Study on the Aum Shinrikyo*, edited by Senate Government Affairs Permanent Subcommittee on Investigations. Accessed February 12, 2019. https://fas.org/irp/congress/1995_rpt/aum/part01.htm.

Tor (The Onion Router) Network

The onion router (referred to as Tor) network is a computer software tool that is commonly used to access the Dark Web, the part of the Internet that is inaccessible via normal Web browsers and search engines. The technology was created by the U.S. military and was subsequently released as open source for users around the world to take advantage of its anonymous Web browsing. By offering anonymous browsing, however, the Tor network presents a unique challenge to authorities seeking to prosecute those who use the network for illegal activities.

DEVELOPMENT

The technology that forms the basis of Tor, known as onion routing, was originally developed by the U.S. Naval Research Laboratory in the mid-1990s. Its original purpose was to conceal covert U.S. military and government communications.

The government released the onion routing system to civilian users under a free license in 2004 so that these covert military communications would be better hidden among the traffic of everyday users. During this same year, Roger Dingledine and Nick Mathewson presented a proposal for "Tor: The Second-Generation Onion Router." Following this, the Electronic Frontier Foundation funded the project so it could be further developed. In 2006, seven individuals, including Mathewson and Dingledine, founded the Tor Project to facilitate maintenance of the network. A majority of the funding for the network would continue to be provided by the U.S. government (Levine 2014).

In 2014, an international law enforcement campaign called "Operation Onymous" targeted various sites and marketplaces across the network (Everett 2015). Several marketplaces, which were targeted for soliciting drugs and weapons, were shut down and their cryptocurrency seized. Silk Road 2.0 was a notable marketplace that was taken down in the operation. Following the campaign, law enforcement boasted that they had identified a method by which they could de-anonymize Tor users. In 2016, a judge confirmed that the U.S. Department of Defense (DOD) had paid Carnegie Mellon University $1 million to take advantage of the vulnerability and identify users (Cox 2016). After the incident, the Tor Project changed leadership and hired Shari Steele as executive director.

HOW IT WORKS

The Tor network is open-source software available to anyone to download. Sites that are only accessible through the Tor network end in ".onion." The infrastructure of the Tor network is hosted entirely by volunteers who configure their machines to operate as "nodes," which are the points at which the network traffic is processed and passed along. Using layered encryption, a Tor user's traffic is routed through three types of nodes: an entrance node, a middle node, and an exit node. These nodes are identified via a directory server, and the traffic between each node is encrypted. In doing this, the system makes a user's data anonymous, as data can only be tracked back to the last node through which it was routed, not to the source machine making the request. Only the entrance node can identify where the traffic originated from, and only the exit node can decrypt the packet to send it to its destination. As anonymity can only be guaranteed by the system during the transport of the data, protocol-specific support software must be used to prevent sites from seeing one's identifying information. Additionally, if a user provides any of his or her own identifying information, just as on the clear Web, it can be linked back to them.

USE OF THE TOR NETWORK

Due to the network's anonymizing properties, it is difficult to tell exactly where the traffic is coming from as well as who is using it. Research has attributed traffic to at least 126 countries, including the United States, Germany, and China (McCoy et al. 2008). The Tor network is used by citizens of countries with strict Internet censorship, as its infrastructure allows users to bypass the government's restrictions. For example, Tor traffic originating from Egypt sharply increased during the Egyptian Revolution of 2011, during which Egyptian citizens used the network to organize their protests (Watson 2012).

The legality of using the Tor network depends on a country's respective Internet use laws. Using Tor in the United States is legal, although there are legal issues with some of the content accessed through the network. In China, not only is using Tor expressly prohibited by law, the government additionally takes efforts to prevent citizens from accessing it (Watson 2012).

Though the network's anonymity allows for unmonitored browsing and the circumvention of government regulations, it also provides a secure way for individuals to operate illicit online marketplaces. Silk Road, Dream Market, and RS Club are just three of the many marketplaces hosted on Tor. Here, vendors advertise and sell goods ranging from drugs and weapons to hitmen and personal services. Additionally, child pornography is often hosted and distributed on Dark Web sites accessible through Tor.

CHALLENGES TO LAW ENFORCEMENT

Although Tor's anonymous browsing is advantageous to its users, it creates a unique challenge for law enforcement. Finding illegal activities on the network is not difficult, as any Tor user can access most marketplaces and their listed goods. However, the anonymity of users makes the identification and apprehension of illicit vendors exceptionally difficult. Due to Tor's infrastructure and encryption, traffic from an exit node cannot be traced back to its origin. The traffic can be traced backward from its destination to its exit node, but no further. This is because during each "hop" between nodes, the traffic is encrypted. Users' own additional protections further complicate the attribution of any collected information. Thus, identifying who exactly is engaging in illegal activities via the Tor network is nearly impossible for law enforcement.

Jurisdiction presents another hurdle concerning crimes within Tor. This issue is not unique to Tor, as law enforcement has struggled with jurisdictional issues of clear net criminal activity in recent years. The nodes that constitute the Tor network are scattered across the world and operated by civilian volunteers and researchers. When illegal activity is captured, it can only be traced back to its exit node. Because of this, questions have been raised as to whether the operator of an exit node can be held liable for traffic that passes through his or her node. If the node is operated outside of a law enforcement agency's respective country, the cooperation of foreign agencies is then required to address it. This issue is especially pertinent regarding drug and weapon marketplaces, as vendors have been identified from the United Kingdom, the Netherlands, Germany, and more (Dolliver 2015).

Rachel L. McNealey

See also: AlphaBay; Cryptocurrency; Cryptomarkets; Dark Web/Deep Web; Dream Market; Ulbricht, Ross

Further Reading

Cox, Joseph. 2016. "Confirmed: Carnegie Mellon University Attacked Tor, Was Subpoenaed by Feds." *Motherboard*, February 24. Accessed January 21, 2019. https://motherboard.vice.com/en_us/article/d7yp5a/carnegie-mellon-university-attacked-tor-was-subpoenaed-by-feds.

Dolliver, Diana S. 2015. "Evaluating Drug Trafficking on the Tor Network: Silk Road 2, the Sequel." *International Journal of Drug Policy* 26 (11) (November): 1113–1123.

Everett, Cath. 2015. "Should the Dark Net Be Taken Out?" *Network Security* 3 (March): 10–13.

Levine, Yasha. 2014. "Privacy Spooks: Almost Everyone Involved in Developing Tor Was (or Is) Funded by the US Government." Last updated July 16, 2014. Accessed January 21, 2019. https://yashalevine.com/articles/tor-spooks.

McCoy, D., K. Bauer, D. Grunwald, T. Kohno, and D. Sicker. 2008. "Shining Light in Dark Places: Understanding the Tor Network." Paper presented at the International symposium on privacy enhancing technologies symposium. Accessed June 3, 2019. https://homes.cs.washington.edu/~yoshi/papers/Tor/PETS2008_37.pdf.

Watson, Keith D. 2012. "The Tor Network: A Global Inquiry into the Legal Status of Anonymity Networks." *Washington University Global Studies Law Review* 11 (3): 715–737.

Trafficking Victim Identification Tools

The identification of victims of human trafficking is a major practical problem. These victims are afraid of calling attention to their situation or of disclosing all the information about their exploitation upon request (e.g., of authorities) because they are under permanent pressure, mostly triggered by threats, and continuous control of the traffickers.

This problem is further aggravated by two issues: (1) language and cultural barriers and (2) previous negative experiences with public authorities in their states of origin. Prevailing corruption of law enforcement officials in these countries not only results in the loss of confidence by the victims but also in a general fear of public authorities. Consequently, they generally avoid going to the police or other relevant authorities in the country of destination.

In many cases, a victim of human trafficking is initially considered (only) as an offender of a typical migration crime (e.g., illegal entry into the country, falsification of a document, or illegal employment) by customs authority or the police before they are correctly identified as a victim.

IMPORTANCE OF IDENTIFICATION

Although it is often difficult to recognize victims of human trafficking, their identification needs to occur as early as possible. Identification is a precondition for the recognition as a victim and, consequently, the access to their rights as victims to comprehensive assistance as well as protection measures. Staff members who often come in contact with victims, such as the police, law enforcement officers, border and immigration officers, the staff of health and social services, and nongovernmental organizations (NGOs), should be aware of this issue. However, this is not enough; they also need measures of support. Therefore, organizations and research institutes developed identification tools to facilitate the identification process.

UNODC TOOL

To increase the chances to indicate victims of trafficking in human beings, the UN Office on Drugs and Crime (UNODC) elaborated a more general tool on victim identification with fundamental recommendations and guidelines for the whole identifications process in its "Online Toolkit to Combat Trafficking in Persons." It is intended for use in dealings with all kinds of trafficking victims.

To cover the topic comprehensively, the identification process itself is described as well as the issues that have to be considered before and after the identification of a victim. Additionally, basics are addressed, such as the principle that the victim has to be in the focus as a human being with special needs (for protection and assistance) and not just as a helpful witness for the criminal justice proceedings. Hence, it is underlined that the potential victim has to be treated with full respect (also in case the victim is a suspect at the same time), and the identification conversation has to be conducted in an ethical and safe way for the interviewees (also for children). Thus, it is also important to stress the need for victims of human trafficking, who are or have to be offenders at the same time, should not be criminalized.

At the core of the tool are the guidelines on victim identification, including an overview for the initial interview (e.g., how to open the interview in the best way: they recommend making clear what the interviewer is doing and what the potential victim can expect). One tool presents the International Organization for Migration (IOM) victim-screening form with detailed questions and provides examples of checklists for the interviewer.

VERA TOOL

Especially notable is the first statistically validated and science-based screening tool created by the Vera Institute of Justice in the United States. It aims to simplify the human trafficking victim identification process by providing a detailed questionnaire, which helps to identify adult and minor victims, especially of sex and labor trafficking. This interview guide should be used by victim service agency staff, social service providers, law enforcement, and health care and shelter workers.

In 2006, Vera started with researching and developing effective and reliable identification practices. To achieve their aim, the institute collaborated with 11 experienced victim service organizations in the United States and asked (potential) victims of trafficking in human beings about working and living conditions as well as migration to elicit any indication of trafficking victimization experiences, such as physical harm or violence, isolation, abusive labor experiences, force, fraud, coercion, or sexual exploitation. These interviews with 180 (potential) victims also helped Vera to get a better understanding of cultural nuances that need to be considered during an interview and how victims respond to different types of questions.

Another research focus is on the victims' fear and distrust of law enforcement as a barrier of victim identification. Vera wanted to find out the best way to conduct interviews to facilitate trust between interviewers and respondents. With this approach of the screening tool, two objectives can be accomplished: the victim is able to speak in a safe and confident atmosphere about his or her situation, and the law enforcement agency also gets useful information for collecting evidence for the human traffickers' prosecution.

Additionally, in this research, different statistical analysis demonstrated which questions best predicted trafficking outcomes, and it also determined how well the tool worked in distinguishing trafficking victims from other crime victims and to differ between victims of labor and sex trafficking or between foreign- and U.S.-born victims. The tool's validity and reliability were finally confirmed by several statistical methods.

Finally, a 30-topic, or in a briefer version 16-topic, questionnaire in English and Spanish was devised by Vera. Given the fact that the shortened 16 questions version is a combination of the questions with the strongest predictors of all types of trafficking, it is only a small decline in predicative power compared to the larger 30-question tool. Therefore, depending on the situation and purpose of screening, both versions can be used equally to identify victims of trafficking in human beings.

Karin Bruckmüller

See also: Human Trafficking; UN Office on Drugs and Crime

Further Reading

International Organization for Migration (IOM). n.d. "UN Migration Agency in Finland Releases Guidelines for Identifying Victims of Human Trafficking." Accessed February 12, 2019. https://www.iom.int/news/un-migration-agency-finland-releases-guidelines-identifying-victims-human-trafficking.

United Nations Office on Drugs and Crime (UNODC). n.d. "Online Toolkit to Combat Trafficking in Persons, Chapter 6: Victim Identification." Accessed May 2018. https://www.unodc.org/unodc/en/human-trafficking/2008/electronic-toolkit/electronic-toolkit-chapter-6-victim-identification.html.

Vera. n.d.-a. "Out of the Shadows: A Tool for the Identification of Victims of Human Trafficking." Accessed May 2018. https://storage.googleapis.com/vera-web-assets/downloads/Publications/out-of-the-shadows-identification-of-victims-of-human-trafficking/legacy_downloads/human-trafficking-identification-tool-summary-v2.pdf.

Vera. n.d.-b. "Screening for Human Trafficking—Guidelines for Administering the Trafficking Victim Identification Tool (TVIT)." Accessed May 2018. https://storage.googleapis.com/vera-web-assets/downloads/Publications/out-of-the-shadows-identification-of-victims-of-human-trafficking/legacy_downloads/human-trafficking-identification-tool-and-user-guidelines.pdf.

Transcrime

In 1994, the University of Trento School of Law in Trento, Italy, established Transcrime (Joint Research Centre on Transnational Crime) as a research group. In 2000, it became an interdepartmental center (law, economics, and sociology) of the same university. After its founder and director, Professor Ernesto Savona, transferred to the Università Cattolica in Milan (2002), Transcrime became an interuniversity center between the Università Cattolica and the University of Trento, and in 2016, with the exit of the University of Trento, the Universities of Bologna and Perugia joined the center.

VISION

The birth of Transcrime is connected to the development of the 2000 UN Convention against Transnational Organized Crime. Williams and Savona (1996) prepared some documents that contributed to the establishment of this convention. In a time when the violence of organized crime was spread across borders and combated by law and criminal justice, Transcrime suggested preventative policies focusing on the reduction of opportunity approach. Research on crime dynamics, its opportunities, and its policy implications have been the recurring theme of the work carried by Transcrime during its life, with more than 100 research projects funded by international organizations, governments (national and local), and private companies across the following topics:

- Analysis of criminal phenomena (organized crime, economic crime, money laundering, illegal markets, urban crime);
- Evaluation of crime prevention policies;
- Analysis and identification of criminogenic opportunities in legislation (crime proofing analysis); and
- Development of risk-assessment models and crime-prevention strategies for public (e.g., law enforcement, public entities) and private actors (e.g., banks, professionals, companies).

ACTIVITIES

The integrated approach (criminology, law, economics, statistics, sociology, and forensic accounting) of its 25 senior and junior researchers has driven the center through the mix of academic and policy relevant research, listening, discussing, and contributing to the debate in many different fora on transnational crime and its consequences. A recent focus was on the measurement of illicit financial flows as a main indicator of Sustainable Development Goal 16.4 of the 2030 United Nations Agenda for Social Development.

Since 2003, the center has been the site of the European Journal on Criminal Policy and Research, and Professor Savona is its editor-in-chief. He is also the editor of the Springer Brief Series on international and comparative criminology.

In 2015, Transcrime, together with the Università Cattolica, founded the academic spin-off Crime&Tech. It is the point of contact between the needs of the business world and the long-standing experience of Transcrime in the field of criminological research.

Transcrime is also a key supporting body of the education activities provided by the Università Cattolica del Sacro Cuore, Milan. In particular, the center coordinates the master's degree in security policy within the framework of the master's program in political and social sciences and the international PhD in criminology.

FOCUS ON EUROPE

When Transcrime was born, European institutions dealing with crime were in their infancy. Europol had a staff of approximately 50 officers, and today it has more than 1,000; UCLAF, the antifraud unit (today Olaf), had less than 50, and today it has almost 1,000. The directorate for internal affairs was a task force of around 10 people (today around 500). The booming of these institutions corresponds to the priorities the European Union has attributed to the security issues. The many research programs and, more recently, the Horizon 2020 Secure Society program have fertilized the research in the field, putting law enforcement agencies and policy makers in the pivotal position of demanding more research oriented to practical solutions. Results are coming, and they will improve in quality and quantity if researchers, policy makers and practitioners will understand each other's languages despite the many geopolitical and cultural differences that characterize the European member states and their internal regimes. With its work, Transcrime aims to add an Italian flavor to this European and international approach, helping to make the different languages understandable.

Ernesto Ugo Savona

See also: Savona, Ernesto; Transnational, Global, and International Crime; UN Convention against Transnational Organized Crime

Further Reading

Crime&Tech. n.d. "About the Company." Accessed August 22, 2018. https://www.crimetech.it/index.php?file=page&id_page=2.

Transcrime. n.d.-a "About Transcrime." Joint Research Centre on Transnational Crime. Accessed August 21, 2018. http://www.transcrime.it/en/about.

Transcrime. n.d.-b "Publications." Joint Research Centre on Transnational Crime. Accessed August 21, 2018. http://www.transcrime.it/en/transcrime-pubblicazioni.

Williams, P., and Ernesto U. Savona, eds. 1996. *The United Nations and Transnational Organized Crime.* London: Frank Cass & Co.

Transnational, Global, and International Crime

The terms *transnational crime*, *global crime*, and *international crime* are often used interchangeably. In fact, still other terms might be presented as referring to similar phenomenon: *multinational crime*, *cross-national crime*, and *cross border* or *transboundary criminality.* There are, however, important—if not always clear—distinctions to be made. The first three terms are more frequently used in academic and media accounts.

TRANSNATIONAL CRIME

At the simplest level, transnational crime refers to criminal acts involving more than one country. A more complex definition refers to activities that occur across national borders, violate the criminal law of at least one country, and whose resolution requires the cooperation of two or more countries.

Prior to the 1970s most people thought of crime in a domestic context. Drug trafficking, for example, was understood as possibly having a foreign link regarding the drug's origin, but the "problem" was typically thought of in terms of the seller on the street rather than in its broader context. Roth (2014) explains that the term *transnational crime* began appearing in the mid-1970s in some UN documents and then more frequently in the 1990s as INTERPOL officials and academics began using it.

Some of the early sources listed specific examples of transnational crime (for example, money laundering, illicit arms trafficking, illegal drug trafficking, sea piracy, and theft of art and cultural objects). As the concept of transnational crime has become more widely used in the 21st century, there has been less interest in simply listing examples (which were becoming rather extensive) and greater interest in providing types or categories within which specific examples of transnational crime can fit.

One example of categorizing transnational crime to make the study and discussion more manageable is offered by Albanese (2011, 3). He groups transnational crimes into three broad categories that are identified as provision of illicit goods, provision of illicit services, and infiltration of business or government. Each category has general examples, such as drug trafficking and counterfeiting under provision of illicit goods; human trafficking and commercial vices under provision of illicit services; and extortion and corruption under infiltration of business or government. In this manner, it is not necessary to list all examples of transnational crime because specific offenses that are not mentioned can be easily placed within its broader category. For example, theft of intellectual property is a form of counterfeiting, so we know it belongs in the provision of illicit goods category, whereas sea piracy is an example of extortion, so we know it is a type of extortion.

Transnational crime is considered to have considerable complexity not only because of the requirement of multiple countries but also because the crimes cannot be effectively carried out by lone offenders or even by multiple offenders who are not organized (Albanese 2011, 4). As a result, the concept of transnational organized crime, rather than just transnational crime, is increasingly used by scholars and practitioners to reflect the central role of organized crime in any discussion of transnational crime generally.

GLOBAL CRIME

The concept of global crime is often used in two contexts. In one sense, global crime is used to explain a crime's distribution around the world. That is, some crimes, such as cybercrime or sea piracy, are best understood and discussed in the context of the world community rather than a particular region or country. Other than for purposes of prosecution (still an important concern), it makes little sense to study or come to understand cybercrime only as it occurs in the United States or some other country. The global nature of cybercrime requires that it be understood in a worldwide context.

A second use of global crime is through its link to globalization. Reference is made to the globalization of crime to show that free market globalization for trade in goods and services has also increased opportunities for illicit transactions. That is, globalization allows or even encourages crime to move from a location-specific activity to a worldwide or global activity. This aspect of globalization has been called "deviant globalization" (Gilman, Goldhammer, and Weber 2013) in reference to how the global economy meets the demand for goods and services that are considered illegal in one place by using a supply from another part of the world where morals differ or law enforcement in less effective.

Finally, it can be argued that globalization has increased inequality around the world, and its disruptive effect has forced people into crime as a means of coping with that disruption. In this sense, globalization can be considered a cause of criminal behavior.

INTERNATIONAL CRIME

Of the three concepts, international crime is most clearly distinguished from the others. International crime is generally used to refer to activities that threaten world order and security. Such crimes include war crimes, crimes against humanity, and genocide. These are offenses that are universally considered so reprehensible that the international community is obliged to investigate and prosecute when they are believed to have occurred.

The Charter of the International Military Tribunal at Nuremberg (Constitution of the International Military Tribunal 1945) identifies war crimes as violations of the laws or customs of war as practiced around the world. Examples of such violations include murder or the deportation to slave labor of a civilian population; wanton destruction of cities, towns, or villages; and any devastation not justified by military necessity.

The charter also addresses crimes against humanity, which are said to include murder, extermination, enslavement, and other inhumane acts committed against civilian populations. In addition, the Rome Statute of the International Criminal Court (1998) defines crimes against humanity as acts committed as part of a widespread or systematic attack directed against any civilian population. Examples of such acts include murder, extermination, torture, sexual slavery, and inhumane acts intentionally causing great suffering or serious bodily or mental injury (International Criminal Court 2011, 3–4). Some have argued that because terrorism includes murders committed as part of a widespread or systematic attack against a civilian population, terrorism is a crime against humanity and should be included along with war crimes and genocide as an international crime (Cryer 2003). That view is not yet widespread, and most authorities do not currently include terrorism as an example of international crime.

Genocide was recognized as a specific international crime by the UN General Assembly in the 1948 Convention on the Prevention and Punishment of the Crime of Genocide (the Genocide Convention). The crime involves acts that are intended to partially or entirely destroy a national, ethnic, racial, or religious group. The specific acts referred to include murder, but also the mental or physical harm of group members, preventing births, forcibly transferring children to another group, and imposing living conditions that would bring destruction to the group. In addition, acts of rape and enslavement can constitute genocide as long as there is intent to destroy the group.

Philip L. Reichel

See also: Globalization; International Law; International Military Tribunal at Nuremberg; Rome Statute of the International Criminal Court; UN Convention on the Prevention and Punishment of the Crime of Genocide

Further Reading

Albanese, Jay S. 2011. *Transnational Crime and the 21st Century: Criminal Enterprise, Corruption, and Opportunity.* New York: Oxford University Press.

Constitution of the International Military Tribunal. 1945. *Nuremberg Trial Proceedings.* Vol. 1. Accessed September 18, 2018. http://avalon.law.yale.edu/imt/imtconst.asp.

Cryer, Robert. 2003. "Terrorism and the International Criminal Court." *Australian Law Reform Commission Reform Journal* 82: 14–16, 70. Accessed January 21, 2019. http://classic.austlii.edu.au/au/journals/ALRCRefJl/2003/4.html.

Gilman, Nils, Jesse Goldhammer, and Steven Weber. 2013. "Deviant Globalization." In *Convergence: Illicit Networks and National Security in the Age of Globalization,* edited by Michael Miklaucic and Jacqueline Brewer, 3–14. Washington, D.C.: National Defense University Press.

International Criminal Court. 2011. "The Rome Statute of the International Criminal Court." Accessed September 20, 2018. https://www.icc-cpi.int/NR/rdonlyres/ADD16852-AEE9-4757-ABE7-9CDC7CF02886/283503/RomeStatutEng1.pdf.

Roth, Mitchel P. 2014. "Historical Overview of Transnational Crime." In *Handbook of Transnational Crime and Justice,* edited by Philip L. Reichel and Jay S. Albanese, 5–22. Los Angeles: Sage.

Transnational Anti-Gang Task Forces

In an effort to combat Central American gangs, mainly Mara Salvatrucha (MS-13) and the 18th Street gangs, the Federal Bureau of Investigation (FBI), U.S. Department of Justice (DOJ), and U.S. Department of State (DOS) have established and sponsored Transnational Anti-Gang Task Forces (TAGs) since 2007. Gangs and gang violence have been increasing in the United States and Central America. Most gang-related investigations have slowed to a halt, but TAG provides the ability for law enforcement to cooperate with each other. TAG's mission is to investigate, disrupt, and dismantle transnational gangs by collecting, investigating, and sharing intelligence and to coordinate programs countering gang activities. Since the establishment of TAG, the FBI has built partnerships in Central American countries and managed to launch TAG units outside the United States, namely in El Salvador (since 2007), Guatemala (since 2009), and Honduras (since 2011).

TAG PERSONNEL

Each TAG unit is staffed with FBI agents and law enforcement officers from Central America. Collectively, TAG personnel investigate transnational gang cases and share intelligence by identifying gang members, their cliques, and their leadership structures. To be eligible to work for TAG, candidates must undergo a careful clearance process, which includes passing a thorough background screening and a polygraph test every six months. In the case of failing a polygraph test, candidates are usually disqualified from the selection process, and those who are already employed in TAG must terminate their involvement with the unit. The screening process is essential because there are ongoing investigations with confidential information, so disclosure of information may negatively impact cases and delay the investigation.

INTERAGENCY COLLABORATION

To maximize its effectiveness, TAG cooperates with two FBI anti-gang initiative programs in the United States: Safe Streets Gang Unit (SSGU) and Central American Law Enforcement Exchange (CALEE). These anti-gang interagency efforts provide a platform for FBI agents, U.S. law enforcement, and Central American law enforcement to share intelligence about investigations, to exchange information, and to facilitate the prosecution of gang members in their respective states. TAG is the primary anti-gang initiative program that investigates gang organizations on a regional level, and it attempts to do so in a coordinated way. Because of the anti-gang interagency efforts, investigating cases has become more successful because prosecutions and convictions have occurred in the program's participating countries.

The SSGU was established in 1992 with the mission to increase collaboration, cooperation, and communication between local, state, and federal law enforcement agencies on issues related to gang-related crimes and violence. Since then, there have been more than 150 SSGU units founded across the United States. SSGU units only operate and investigate in the United States.

Since 2009, CALEE is an exchange program for U.S. and Central American law enforcement, with the mission to facilitate interagency intelligence sharing, expand law enforcement contacts, provide access to intelligence about gang related investigations, and explore new techniques and prevention strategies to combat gangs and gang violence. In Central American states, the judicial systems are not well developed. To strengthen their judicial systems and effectively investigate cases, CALEE provides training to law enforcement agencies, judges, and prosecutors from Mexico, El Salvador, Honduras, Guatemala, Belize, and Panama.

LEGAL ASPECTS OF TAG ACTIVITIES OUTSIDE THE UNITED STATES

Within the United States, the FBI has the authority to investigate any federal crime that is not being investigated by another federal agency. Federal law gives the FBI authority to investigate threats to the national security pursuant to presidential executive orders, attorney general authorities, and various statutory sources (Title II of the Intelligence Reform and Terrorism Prevention Act of 2004; Public Law 108-458, 118 Stat. 3638; Executive Order 12333; 50 U.S.C. 401 et seq.; 50 U.S.C. 1801 et seq.). Outside the United States, the FBI has no powers of arrest, and its investigative authorities are limited by the national laws of the country in which they operate. FBI operations outside the United States thus depend on cooperation with the host nation's counterparts, and this includes TAG.

TAG is effective because of cooperation between the United States and Central America, but it is voluntary cooperation because there are no formal mutual legal assistance treaties (MLAT). MLAT is the exchange of evidence and information about criminal investigations. Thus, it can limit potential operations because El Salvador, Guatemala, and Honduras have no binding treaties with the United States or TAG.

Lorena Villavicencio

See also: Central American Gangs; 18th Street Gang; Human Trafficking and Street Gangs; International Police Cooperation; Mara Salvatrucha (MS-13) Organization

Further Reading

Federal Bureau of Investigation (FBI). n.d.-a. "Gangs." Accessed December 3, 2017. https://www.fbi.gov/investigate/violent-crime/gangs.

Federal Bureau of Investigation (FBI). n.d.-b. "International Operations." Accessed December 8, 2017. https://www.fbi.gov/about/leadership-and-structure/international-operations.

Federal Bureau of Investigation (FBI). n.d.-c. "Where Is the FBI's Authority Written Down." Accessed December 8, 2017. https://www.fbi.gov/about/faqs/where-is-the-fbis-authority-written-down.

Franco, Celinda. 2007. "The MS-13 and 18th Gangs: Emerging Transnational Gang Threats?" *Congressional Research Service* (November): 1–20.

U.S. Department of Justice (DOJ) and Federal Bureau of Investigation (FBI). 2016. "The FBI Story." Accessed December 30, 2017. https://www.fbi.gov/file-repository/the-fbi-story-2016.pdf/view.

U.S. Department of State: Diplomacy in Action. 2012. "Bureau of International Narcotics and Law Enforcement Affairs." Accessed December 30, 2017. https://www.state.gov/j/inl/rls/nrcrpt/2012/vol2/184110.htm.

U.S. Government Accountability Office. 2017. "Combating Gangs: Federal Agencies Have Implemented a Central American Gang Strategy, but Could Strengthen Oversight and Measurement of Efforts." Accessed December 3, 2017. http://www.gao.gov/assets/310/303539.pdf.

U

U.K. Border Force

The United Kingdom Border Force, commonly referred to as simply Border Force, is a law enforcement command responsible for the border security of the United Kingdom. The Border Force is parented by the Home Office, and its 7,500 employees are tasked with carrying out the immigration and custom controls of the United Kingdom. The Border Force is charged with monitoring both individuals and goods requesting to enter or leave the United Kingdom. Immigration and custom checks are administered by the Border Force at 140 seaports, rail stations, and airports across the United Kingdom and overseas.

HISTORY

In 2006, former Home Office secretary John Reid introduced the idea of a uniformed border control force at ports and airports for the first time in U.K. history. This uniformed border control force was created and housed under the Border and Immigration Agency in 2007, until its dismantling after only one year of operation (BBC News 2006). The Border and Immigration Agency was replaced by the U.K. Border Agency in 2008, and it parented this uniformed border control force until 2012.

The U.K. Border Agency was placed under investigation by the Independent Chief Inspector of Borders and Immigration in 2010, following allegations that hundreds of thousands of people were let into the country without appropriate checks. These allegations led former Home Office secretary Theresa May to dissolve the U.K. Border Agency, which was subsequently replaced by two separate entities, one being the Border Force that is known today (BBC News 2012).

ORGANIZATION

The Border Force is housed under the Home Office of the United Kingdom. The Home Office was established in 1782, and it plays a fundamental role in the security and economic prosperity of the United Kingdom. The Home Office is the lead government department for issues such as immigration and passports, drug policy, crime, fire, counterterrorism, and police. The Home Office responsibilities include curbing problems associated with illegal drug use, keeping the United Kingdom safe from the threat of terrorism, issuing passports and visas, securing the U.K. border, and controlling immigration.

The Independent Chief Inspector of Borders and Immigration monitors the operation of the Border Force. The Independent Chief Inspector of Borders and

Immigration is a public-appointed official responsible for scrutinizing and reporting the efficiency of the immigration and customs functions carried out by the United Kingdom, with one of those immigration and custom functions being the Border Force. The Independent Chief Inspector of Borders and Immigration is independent from the government and lays out reports before the Parliament of the United Kingdom (United Kingdom Legislation 2007).

OPERATION

The Border Force assists the Home Office in the security and containment of the U.K. borders. The Border Force is primarily responsible for checking the immigration status of people arriving in and departing the United Kingdom. In conjunction with this, the Border Force searches baggage, vehicles, and cargo entering the United Kingdom for illicit goods or undocumented immigrants. Furthermore, the Border Force is responsible for patrolling the U.K. coastline and searching vessels for previously mentioned illegal goods or individuals.

The Border Force also assists in the gathering of intelligence related to people of interest and alerts the police and security services to potential threats. The Border Force makes it a priority to deter and prevent individuals and goods from entering the United Kingdom that would harm the national interests. The Border Force does this by facilitating the legitimate movement of individuals and trade to and from the United Kingdom. Finally, the Border Force protects and collects customs revenues for trade crossing the border.

At an operational level, the Border Force ports have arrangements with the local police to increase joint activity and cooperation at the border. Representatives from the Border Force regions will also either sit on or participate in Regional Intelligence Units, which are generally made up of the police and other crime prevention organizations. The Border Force believes that a collaborative approach to crime prevention assists in the security and containment of the United Kingdom's borders (Home Office 2016).

Jessie L. Slepicka

See also: Counterfeit Goods and Money; Human Trafficking; Migrant Smuggling

Further Reading

BBC News. 2006. "Reid Plans Border-Control Force." Accessed March 13, 2018. http://news.bbc.co.uk/2/hi/uk_news/politics/5207112.stm.

BBC News. 2012. "Theresa May to Split Up UK Border Agency." Accessed March 13, 2018. http://www.bbc.com/news/uk-politics-17099143.

GOV.UK. n.d.-a. "Border Force—About Us." Accessed March 13, 2018. https://www.gov.uk/government/organisations/border-force/about.

GOV.UK. n.d.-b. "Home Office—About Us." Accessed March 13, 2018. https://www.gov.uk/government/organisations/home-office/about.

Home Office. 2016. "Have You Got What It Takes? Working with the UK Border Agency and Border Force." Accessed March 13, 2018. https://www.gov.uk/government/uploads/system/uploads/attachment_data/file/512416/ukba-and-border-force.pdf.

United Kingdom Government Legislation. 2007. "UK Borders Act 2007." Accessed March 13, 2018. http://www.legislation.gov.uk/ukpga/2007/30/pdfs/ukpga_2007 0030_en.pdf.

U.K. Modern Slavery Act (2015)

The Modern Slavery Act 2015 (MSA) is an act of the Parliament of the United Kingdom that covers slavery in the United Kingdom, ties together previous legislation, and defines specific criminal offenses of slavery and human trafficking. MSA is a significant step forward in defining, preventing, and criminalizing both slavery and human trafficking.

HISTORY

The United Kingdom ratified the Protocol to Prevent, Suppress and Punish Trafficking in Persons, Especially Women and Children, Supplementing the United Nations Convention against Transnational Organized Crime (Palermo Protocol) in February 2006. Nevertheless, its effectiveness for combating slavery and human trafficking in the United Kingdom was questioned. According to numerous reports, including the 2005 and 2013 reports by the Centre for Social Justice (CSJ), it was obvious that the scale of the problem was much greater than expected. Thousands of adults and children were reportedly being trafficked into or within the United Kingdom. The government was heavily criticized for its inadequate response to the issues of slavery, sexual exploitation, and forced labor (Mantouvalou 2015). A new bill of legislation was drafted and introduced to the House of Commons in October 2013.

STRUCTURE OF THE ACT

The Modern Slavery Act is divided into seven parts. Part 1, entitled "Offences," contains definitions of key offenses, such as slavery, servitude, forced or compulsory labor, and human trafficking, and the notion of "exploitation," which is crucial to understanding all such definitions, is defined. Provisions of this part describe penalties and explain sentencing rules and procedure of reparation orders. Part 2 contains regulations regarding preventive orders, including sentencing, regulations on prohibition of foreign travel, risk orders, appeals, and cross border enforcement. Part 3 contains provisions related to maritime enforcement, mostly in relation to ships in U.K. territory.

Part 4 regulates the position, authority and obligations of the United Kingdom's newly established Independent Anti-Slavery Commissioner. According to the MSA, "The Commissioner must encourage good practice in the prevention, detection, investigation and prosecution of slavery and human trafficking offences and identification of victims of those offences." Part 5 sets out rules regarding protection of victims of slavery and human trafficking. The act establishes a defense clause for victims of any form of slavery who committed an offense as well as a system of advocates for child victims of human trafficking.

Part 6 contains the well-known Section 54 regarding transparency in supply chains. It states that "a commercial organization . . . must prepare a slavery and human trafficking statement for each financial year of the organization . . . of the steps the organisation has taken . . . to ensure that slavery and human trafficking is not taking place." The business community has positively responded to this section, resulting in many discussions and programs focusing on trafficking/slavery free supply chains (Co-Op Modern Slavery and Human Trafficking Statement 2016; Home Office 2017). Part 7 consists of miscellaneous, general regulations, rules of interpretation, financial provisions, and schedules.

CRITICISM

Despite its positive features, the MSA is not without fault and has been subject to much criticism. Experts claim it focuses too much on law enforcement as opposed to being a victim-oriented piece of legislation (Analysis of Modern Slavery Act 2015). According to critics, the rights of victims of slavery and overseas domestic workers were not well protected. There were some reservations to the "non-punishment clause" (Article 8 of the EU Directive 2011/36), as this clause can be used only when the victim of human trafficking is compelled to commit a crime and when the compulsion is attributable to slavery or to relevant exploitation (Muraszkiewicz 2015). Moreover, the 37 paragraphs of Schedule 4 significantly dilute the defense clause and include crimes such as robbery, burglary, and manslaughter, to name a few. Critics have argued that many of the offenses are nonapplicable. Nevertheless, the Independent Anti-Slavery Commissioner is looked at as a promising step forward to combating modern slavery (Analysis of Modern Slavery Act 2015).

Zbigniew Lasocik

See also: Bonded Labor; *Global Slavery Index*; Labor Exploitation; UN Protocol to Prevent, Suppress, and Punish Trafficking in Persons, Especially Women and Children

Further Reading

Analysis of Modern Slavery Act. 2015. "Anti-Slavery's Europe Programme and Advocacy Co-Ordinator Klara Skrivankova Analyses the Modern Slavery Act." https://www.antislavery.org/analysis-modern-slavery-act.

Co-operative Group. n.d. "Co-Op Modern Slavery and Human Trafficking Statement." 2016. Accessed January 21, 2019. https://www.co-operative.coop/ethics/modern-slavery.

Home Office. 2017. "Transparency in Supply Chains etc.: A Practical Guide." Accessed January 21, 2019. https://www.gov.uk/government/uploads/system/uploads/attachment_data/file/649906/Transparency_in_Supply_Chains_A_Practical_Guide_2017.pdf.

Mantouvalou, Virginia, 2015. "Am I Free Now? Overseas Domestic Workers in Slavery." *Journal of Law and Society* 42 (3): 329–357.

Muraszkiewicz, Julia. 2015. "Non-Prosecution or Non-Punishment of the Victims of Human Trafficking: Case Study of England and Wales." In *Niekaralność ofiar handlu ludźmi – nowe perspektywy (On Non-Punishment Clause)*, edited by Z. Lasocik, 81–90. Warsaw, Poland: Human Trafficking Studies Center.

Ulbricht, Ross (1984–)

Ross William Ulbricht is best known for developing and operating the darknet market Web site Silk Road. Using the pseudonym "Dread Pirate Roberts," a character from the movie *The Princess Bride*, Ulbricht created an online market for illegal drugs, such as heroin, cocaine, and LSD, in 2011. Silk Road also offered services that included selling fake IDs, counterfeit passports, driver's licenses, and Social Security cards to hackers for hire.

Many members of Ulbricht's inner circle explained his online drug market as "an experiment in victimless crime and a nonviolent alternative to the bloody turf wars of the streets" (Greenburg 2015, para. 1). After infiltrating the Web site, the Federal Bureau of Investigation (FBI) shut down Silk Road on October 1, 2013. In the two and half years, Ulbricht reportedly made a half billion dollars from his criminal enterprise (Kushner 2014).

Born in 1984 in Austin, Texas, Ulbricht graduated from the University of Texas at Dallas with a bachelor's degree in physics. In 2009, he received a master's degree in materials science and engineering from the University of Pennsylvania. After graduation, Ulbricht returned to Austin and worked as a day trader, and he later started an online used book company. However, he found regular employment uninteresting and wanted to venture into an online black market. He sought a lucrative business venture that fit with his beliefs in libertarian political principles and a free market economy (Munksgaard and Demant 2016).

Ulbricht found the Dark Web site "Tor" (The Onion Router) to be an ideal site to launch his business, as it provided anonymity to users through encrypted data and hidden IP addresses. Also, Bitcoins were the only method of payment on Silk Road, which allowed users to avoid linking identities to the transactions (Bradbury 2014; Weiser 2015). However, Ulbricht did not realize he was under FBI watch, and on October 1, 2013, he was arrested by the FBI while using his laptop at the San Francisco Public Library.

Ulbricht was indicted on charges of narcotics trafficking, money laundering, computer hacking, and conspiracy to commit murder, although the conspiracy to commit murder charge was later dropped. On February 2015, Ulbricht was convicted of all charges and given a life sentence without parole (Weiser 2015). The defense appealed the sentence on the ground that Ulbricht had been deprived of a fair trial, but the federal appellate court denied the appeal.

Sesha Kethineni

See also: Cryptocurrency; Cybercrime; Dark Web/Deep Web; Tor (The Onion Router) Network

Further Reading

Bradbury, Danny. 2014. "Unveiling the Dark Web." *Network Security* 14 (4): 14–17.

Greenburg, Andy. 2015. "Read the Transcript of Silk Road's Boss Ordering 5 Assassinations." *Security*, February 2. Accessed January 21, 2019. https://www.wired.com/2015/02/read-transcript-silk-roads-boss-ordering-5-assassinations.

Kushner, David. 2014. "Dead End on Silk Road: Internet Crime Kingpin Ross Ulbricht's Big Fall." *Rolling Stone*, February 4. http://www.rollingstone.com/culture/news/dead-end-on-silk-road-internet-crime-kingpin-ross-ulbrichts-big-fall-20140204.

Munksgaard, Rasmus, and Jacob Demant. 2016. "Missing Politics and Crime: The Prevalence and Decline of Political Discourse on the Cryptomarket." *International Journal of Drug Policy* 35: 77–83.

Weiser, Benjamin. 2015. "Ross Ulbricht, Creator of Silk Road Website, Is Sentenced to Life in Prison." *New York Times*, May 29. Accessed January 21, 2019. https://www.nytimes.com/2015/05/30/nyregion/ross-ulbricht-creator-of-silk-road-website-is-sentenced-to-life-in-prison.html.

UN Commission on Crime Prevention and Criminal Justice

The Commission on Crime Prevention and Criminal Justice (CCPCJ) is "the principal policymaking body of the United Nations in the field of crime prevention and criminal justice" (UNODC n.d.). Established in 1992 as part of the Economic and Social Council (ECOSOC), the CCPCJ guides international action against drugs and crime. It emerged from a ministerial meeting held in Versailles in 1991 and replaced the Committee on Crime Prevention and Control formed in 1971.

MANDATE AND FUNCTIONS

The CCPCJ guides the activities of the United Nations in the field of crime prevention and criminal justice. Since 2006, its mandate has expanded to function as a governing body of the UN Office on Drugs and Crime (UNODC). Now the commission approves the budget of the UN Crime Prevention and Criminal Justice Fund, which provides resources for technical assistance in the field of crime prevention and criminal justice worldwide. The commission also serves as a preparatory body for the quinquennial (every five years) UN Congress on Crime Prevention and Criminal Justice, for which it provides substantive and organizational direction. The CCPCJ implements the outcome of the congresses into concrete action through decisions and resolutions. The commission coordinates with other UN bodies that have specific mandates in the areas of crime prevention and criminal justice, such as the UN Security Council, the Conference of the Parties to the United Nations Convention against Transnational Organized Crime, and the Conference of the States Parties to the United Nations Convention against Corruption.

The CCPCJ also leads international efforts in developing and reviewing UN standards and norms in the fields of crime prevention and criminal justice. These standards and norms cover such issues as access to justice, treatment of offenders, justice for children, victim protection, and violence against women, among others. The commission serves as a forum for member states to discuss and develop strategies that promote effective and fair criminal justice structures. At the same time, the CCPCJ reviews the use and application of these guiding principles by member states.

MEETINGS

The CCPCJ meets annually in Vienna, Austria, for one week in the first half of the year and has a reconvened session at the end of each year to discuss budgetary and administrative matters. Each meeting is devoted to a specific theme determined by the ECOSOC in advance. The aim of the meetings is to coordinate international responses to trafficking, corruption, terrorism, and other organized crime. The 2010–2020 themes on the CCPCJ agenda have included human trafficking, cybercrime, terrorism, and crime prevention strategies, among others.

During its regular sessions, the commission holds multiple side events that regularly bring together up to 1,000 participants representing member states, civil society, academia, and international organizations (UNIS 2017). The CCPCJ also organizes annual intersessional meetings to finalize its agenda and to provide policy guidance to the UNODC. During a session, the CCPCJ may set up committees or working groups composed of members of the commission that study and report on a particular issue of the agenda. As of 2018, the CCPCJ has nine open-ended intergovernmental expert and working groups on issues ranging from financial situation of the UNODC to treatment of prisoners and cybercrime.

MEMBERSHIP

The CCPCJ is composed of 40 member states, whose term of office is three years. The commission members are elected by the Economic and Social Council on the basis of equitable geographical distribution, with the following distribution of seats among the regional groups: 12 for African states, 9 for Asian states, 8 for Latin American and Caribbean states, 4 for Eastern European states, and 7 for Western European and other states. Among the "other" countries are the United States and Canada, with the current U.S. three-year term ending in December 2018. Canada was not serving a three-year term as of January 2018.

Yulia Vorobyeva

See also: UN Congresses on Crime Prevention and Criminal Justice; UN Office on Drugs and Crime; UN Program Network of Institutes

Further Reading

Economic and Social Council. 1992. "Implementation of General Assembly Resolution 46/152 Concerning Operational Activities and Coordination in the Field of Crime Prevention and Criminal Justice." Resolution 1992/22, July 30. Accessed on May 1, 2018. http://www.unodc.org/documents/commissions/CCPCJ/ECOSOC_Resolution-1992-22_E.pdf.

United Nations Information Service (UNIS). 2017. "26th Session of the Commission on Crime Prevention and Criminal Justice Starts on Monday in Vienna." Press Release UNIS/CP/968, May 19. Accessed May 1, 2018. http://www.unis.unvienna.org/unis/en/pressrels/2017/uniscp968.html.

United Nations Office on Drugs and Crime (UNODC). 2016. *Compendium of United Nations Standards and Norms in Crime Prevention and Criminal Justice.* New York: United Nations.

United Nations Office on Drugs and Crime (UNODC). 2018. "Commission on Crime Prevention and Criminal Justice." Accessed January 21, 2019. http://www.unodc.org/unodc/en/commissions/CCPCJ.

UN Congresses on Crime Prevention and Criminal Justice

The UN Congresses on Crime Prevention and Criminal Justice have been organized at five-year intervals since 1955, when the first such UN Crime Congress was organized in Geneva. Subsequent Crime Congresses were held in London (1960), Stockholm (1965), Kyoto (1970), Geneva (1975), Caracas (1980), Milan (1985), Havana (1995), Cairo (1995), Vienna (2000), Bangkok (2005), Bahia de Salvador (2010), and Doha (2015). The 14th UN Crime Congress is to be organized in Kyoto, Japan, in 2020.

The congresses continue the tradition of the International Penal and Penitentiary Foundation (IPPF), which began organizing international congresses at the end of the 1800s. With the establishment of the United Nations, this work was transferred to the United Nations, and the scope of the discussions widened to deal with crime prevention and criminal justice in general. They bring together national delegations, representatives of intergovernmental and nongovernmental organizations, UN agencies and other entities, and individual experts. The total number of participants at recent Crime Congresses has been about 4,000–5,000 people.

The basic role and function of the UN Crime Congresses is defined in General Assembly resolution 46/152, adopted in 1991. The congress is a consultative body that provides a forum for the exchange of views and experience, the identification of emerging trends and issues, the provision of advice and comments to the UN Commission on Crime Prevention and Criminal Justice on selected matters submitted to the congress by the commission, and the submission of suggestions to the commission regarding possible subjects for the program of work.

Over the years, the UN Crime Congresses have adopted a large number of resolutions, including on international standards and norms. Beginning with the 2000 Congress in Vienna, the formal output of the Crime Congresses has been consolidated into a single Congress Declaration, which provides a general framework for the subsequent work of the UN Crime Prevention and Criminal Justice Programme.

The work of the UN Crime Congresses takes place within formal structures (the plenary session, and during recent congresses, two committees sitting in parallel with the plenary) and in more informal ancillary sessions. The formal sessions deal with four or five general topics, along with four or five "workshops" that focus on technical or practical issues. The ancillary sessions, which are organized by member states, intergovernmental organizations, and nongovernmental organizations (NGOs), provide an opportunity to discuss a wide variety of more specific issues.

The overall theme of the 2020 Congress in Kyoto, Japan, will be "Advancing Crime Prevention, Criminal Justice and the Rule of Law: Towards the Achievement of the 2030 Agenda" and will include among its agenda items comprehensive crime prevention strategies and multidimensional approaches to promoting the rule of law. In addition, delegates are asked to address terrorism in all its forms and new and emerging forms of crime (UN General Assembly 2018).

Matti Joutsen

See also: UN Commission on Crime Prevention and Criminal Justice; UN Office on Drugs and Crime; UN Program Network of Institutes

Further Reading

UN General Assembly. 2018. "Follow-Up to the Thirteenth United Nations Congress on Crime Prevention and Criminal Justice and Preparations for the Fourteenth United Nations Congress on Crime Prevention and Criminal Justice." Resolution adopted by the General Assembly. Last updated December 19, 2017. Accessed January 21, 2019. http://www.un.org/en/ga/search/view_doc.asp?symbol=A/RES/70/174.

United Nations Office on Drugs and Crime (UNODC). n.d.-a. "About." The Fourteenth United Nations Congress on Crime Prevention and Criminal Justice. Accessed August 21, 2018. https://www.unodc.org/congress/en/about.html.

United Nations Office on Drugs and Crime (UNODC). n.d.-b. "Previous Congresses." The Fourteenth United Nations Congress on Crime Prevention and Criminal Justice. Accessed August 21, 2018. https://www.unodc.org/congress/en/previous-congresses.html.

UN Convention against Corruption

The UN Convention against Corruption (UNCAC), also known as the Merida Convention, is a multilateral treaty binding signatories to implement policies that protect against public- and private-sector corruption. UNCAC was adopted by the UN General Assembly on October 31, 2003, and it entered into force on December 14, 2005. Initial signees included 140 nations, and there are 186 parties to the treaty as of July 2018.

HISTORY

On October 31, 2003, the UN General Assembly voted to adopt the UNCAC as a measure to prevent corruption between governments and private interests, which it recognized as a key factor in weakening democratic governance based upon the rule of law and sustainable economic development focused on minimizing poverty. The treaty was initially accepting signatories on December 9, 2003, in Merida, Mexico, and at the UN headquarters in New York City after the initial signing period (Buscaglia 2011). States party to the agreement regularly meet at a Conference of the States Parties (CoSP) to review the treaty's implementation and to adopt resolutions that can help strengthen the purpose of the convention. One of the outputs of the CoSP is the creation of various internal subgroups, each tasked with supervising different aspects of the treaty. The CoSP meetings have been in Jordan (2006), Indonesia (2008), Qatar (2009), Morocco (2011), Panama (2013), Russia (2015), and Austria (2017). The UN Office on Drugs and Crime (UNODC) is the secretariat responsible for monitoring the treaty's implementation and compliance among parties.

CONTENT

UNCAC's purpose is stated as being (a) the promotion and strengthening of measures to prevent and combat corruption more efficiently and effectively; (b) to promote, facilitate, and support international cooperation and assistance in the prevention of, and fight against, corruption; and (c) to promote integrity, accountability, and proper management of public affairs and public property.

The convention outlines preventive measures that states should adopt in coordination with one another. These might include the creation of separate domestic bodies to monitor implementation of the treaty or measures that promote public-sector employment based on merit and equity. Other suggested preventive measures are ones that address conflict of interest issues arising with public-sector officials and that guarantee an auditing system that is enforced by an independent judiciary.

Member states are required to create law enforcement agencies that focus on financial crimes such as bribery, embezzlement, obstruction of justice, and using governmental stature to distribute unfair influence over private-sector practices. In addition, parties are required to simplify their national laws governing corrupt behavior so that the exploitation of loopholes and technicalities are prevented.

The convention also creates a system of international cooperation in the efforts to prevent corruption. Each party to the convention is bound to assist another with the investigation and prosecution of alleged offenses. This assistance comes via extradition, legal aid, and shared law enforcement resources. To help expedite and streamline cooperation, each party must empower a central authority to receive and process requests for mutual legal assistance (MLA) from coparty nations.

The recovery of assets lost to corrupt practices is a defining characteristic of the UNCAC. This provision motivated many developing countries to sign on to the treaty because it enables them to utilize a variety of financial measures—including tracing, freezing, and recouping—to pursue lost assets that may be hidden in a nation more powerful than their own. Article 60 of Chapter 5 identifies experts who can assist developing countries with asset recovery.

An infrastructure for technical assistance aimed at treaty enforcement is also described. Guidelines are offered on strategic training, staffing, research, and information sharing. Included is a recommendation for parties of greater capability to share their resources with coparties with underdeveloped and transitioning economies.

Conference of State Parties (CoSP) is established as a meeting to review implementation of the UNCAC and to recommend future measures. It also commissions the UN Secretariat to provide internal support services and operational governance to the UNCAC. The UNCAC framework is finalized by stating that it creates a minimum common standard and that states are encouraged to create internal mechanisms for more stringent enforcement of corrupt practices.

IMPLEMENTATION

Although each party to the treaty is responsible for how its measures are implemented within its own government, the UNCAC coalition was created to bolster multilateral cooperation. Through a network of civil society organizations, such as nonprofit centers and academic institutions, a coordinated effort is made to increase treaty compliance by facilitating information exchanges among UNCAC members.

Corey B. Miles

See also: Bribery; Corruption; Corruption in China; Corruption in Sub-Saharan Africa; Corruption Measurements; Failed State

Further Reading

Buscaglia, Edgardo. 2011. "On Best and Not So Good Practices for Addressing High-Level Corruption Worldwide: An Empirical Assessment." In *International Handbook on the Economics of Corruption*, edited by Rose Rose-Ackerman and Tina Soreide, 453–477. Northampton, MA: Edward Elgar.

Hechler, Hannes, Gretta Fenner Zinkernagel, Lucy Koechlin, and Dominic Morris. 2011. "Can UNCAC Address Grand Corruption?" U4 Report 2011, no. 2.

Hussmann, Karen, Hannes Hechler, and Miguel Peñailillo. 2009. "Institutional Arrangements for Corruption Prevention: Considerations for the Implementation of the United Nations Convention against Corruption Article 6." U4 Issue.

Kubiciel, Michael. 2009. "Core Criminal Law Provisions in the United Nations Convention against Corruption." *International Criminal Law Review* 9 (1): 139–155.

United Nations Office on Drug and Crime (UNODC). 2004. *United Nations Convention against Corruption.* Vienna: UNODC. Accessed January 19, 2019. https://www.unodc.org/documents/brussels/UN_Convention_Against_Corruption.pdf.

Webb, Philippa. 2005. "The United Nations Convention against Corruption: Global Achievement or Missed Opportunity?" *Journal of International Economic Law* 8 (1): 191–229.

UN Convention against Illicit Traffic in Narcotic Drugs and Psychotropic Substances

The Convention against Illicit Traffic in Narcotic Drugs and Psychotropic Substances was adopted by the UN General Assembly on December 20, 1988, and entered into force on November 11, 1990. As of 2018, 190 member states are party to the convention. The treaty builds on two former conventions (the 1961 Single Convention on Narcotic Drugs and the 1971 Convention on Psychotropic Substances) by adding specific provisions to facilitate international cooperation and aid in the prosecution of transnational organized crimes.

ORIGINS

Throughout the 1970s and 1980s, demand for narcotics such as cocaine, cannabis, and heroin triggered increases in drug cultivation. As the narcotics supply increased in less developed countries, organized crime groups capitalized on the opportunity to export narcotics to consumers in developed countries. The increase in drug consumption and production directly influenced the well-being of individuals, prompted the spread of criminogenic factors like corruption, and generally deteriorated social order. As the drug epidemic advanced, the economic condition of states worsened, prompting the international community to recognize the growing dangers of drug abuse and transnational organized crime as a threat to state security.

CONTENTS AND IMPLICATIONS

The magnitude of the drug epidemic forced an international response, as, individually, states could not successfully combat crimes of a transnational nature. The 1988 convention filled the gaps in previous treaties by introducing provisions addressing mutual legal assistance, controlled deliveries, and the transfer of proceedings, which enhanced interstate cooperation in the prosecution of transnational crime and organized criminal groups. Moreover, the convention criminalized and defined money laundering, established mechanisms for states to confiscate the illicit proceeds of crime, and prompted states to create national frameworks for the prosecution of illicit drug trafficking (Bewley-Taylor 2003).

Article 7 of the convention established mutual legal assistance between nations, which would facilitate the extradition of criminals and create a set protocol for member states to follow when prosecuting transnational organized crime. Controlled deliveries, as discussed in Article 11, allowed for law enforcement officers to secure, identify, and track illicit drug shipments as they made their way between borders. Article 8 addressed the transfer of proceedings and provided states with a blueprint for transferring cases from one to another. Moreover, Articles 2 and 3 of the convention focus on the individual drug user and prompt states to criminalize the personal consumption of illicit substances (United Nations 1988)

Additionally, the 1988 treaty included provisions to limit the availability of precursors, or chemicals that can be readily bought in legitimate markets to use in the production of narcotics. The provisions within the 1988 convention allowed for the prosecution of transnational organized crime to become synonymous with its prevention. Beyond the scope of drug trafficking, the convention also defined money laundering and obligated state parties to create mechanisms that recognized and criminalized the act. The convention also laid the foundation for the UN Convention against Transnational Organized Crime (UNTOC), which would replace the 1988 treaty as the go-to legislation for dealing with transnational threats (Drugs and Democracy 2006).

CHALLENGES AND LIMITATIONS

The challenges posed to international law usually revolve around state sovereignty, or the ability of a state to voluntarily execute or refute any given legislation within its territory. Essentially, this prevented some states from passing articles if the provisions contradicted their national legislation or constitution. Austria, Bolivia, and the United States cited reservations stemming from these concerns. In Bolivia, the coca leaf has been traditionally and legally used for centuries prior to the convention. Under Article 3 of the 1988 convention, states are prompted to criminalize the entire chain of drug production, which includes personal drug usage (Lines 2017).

The 1988 convention has been likened to a globalization of the war on drugs, as states are expected to turn international obligations into a uniform system of drug controls driven by punitive approaches. When states fail to fulfill their obligations under the 1988 convention, the International Narcotics Control Board is tasked with overseeing their progress with international drug control treaties. However, the organization holds few enforcement powers and is limited to issuing investigations, annual reports, and recommendations.

Nicole Kalczynski

See also: Commission on Narcotic Drugs; International Narcotics Control Board; UN Convention on Psychotropic Substances (1971); UN Office on Drugs and Crime

Further Reading

Bewley-Taylor, David R. 2003. "Challenging the UN Drug Control Conventions: Problems and Possibilities." *International Journal of Drug Policy* 14 (2) (April): 171–179.

Drugs and Democracy. 2006. "Bolivia's Reservations to the 1988 Convention." *Transnational Institute.* Accessed January 21, 2019. https://www.tni.org/en/article/bolivias-reservations-to-the-1988-convention.

Lines, Richard. 2017. *Drug Control and Human Rights in International Law.* Cambridge: Cambridge University Press.

United Nations. 1988a. "Commentary on the UN Convention against Illicit Traffic in Narcotic Drugs and Psychotropic Substances." Accessed January 21, 2019. https://www.unodc.org/documents/treaties/organized_crime/Drug%20Convention/Commentary_on_the_united_nations_convention_1988_E.pdf.

United Nations. 1988b. "UN Convention against Illicit Traffic in Narcotic Drugs and Psychotropic Substances." Accessed January 21, 2019. https://www.unodc.org/pdf/convention_1988_en.pdf.

UN Convention against Transnational Organized Crime

The UN General Assembly adopted the UN Convention against Transnational Organized Crime (UNTOC) in 2000, and the convention entered into force in 2003. UNTOC, often called the Palermo Convention, for the Italian city where it was signed, is the primary international instrument in the fight against transnational organized crime. It is a legally binding instrument through which signing state parties (189 as of August 2018) commit to taking a series of measures against transnational organized crime. In his foreword to the convention, UN Secretary-General Kofi Annan noted that if crime crosses borders, so too should law enforcement. The convention, he explained, demonstrates the political will of countries to provide a global response to a global challenge.

KEY ASPECTS OF THE CONVENTION

The Palermo Convention does not provide a clear definition of what constitutes transnational organized crime. It describes an "organized criminal group" as being a structured group of three or more persons acting in concert to commit a transnational crime for financial or material benefit, but it does not define transnational organized crime itself. Instead, the convention and its protocols offer examples of activities that can be considered core transnational crimes. Those include money laundering, corruption, trafficking in humans, and all serious offenses committed by organized crime groups.

The measures that nations ratifying UNTOC agree to take include

> (a) the creation of domestic criminal offences to combat the problem; (b) international cooperation through the adoption of new and sweeping frameworks for mutual legal assistance, extradition, and law enforcement cooperation; and (c) domestic measures such as the promotion of training and technical assistance for building or upgrading the country's capacity to combat transnational organized crime. (United Nations 2000)

The convention requires ratifying countries to enact legislation making four specific activities domestic crimes if such laws do not already exist in the country. Those crimes are participation in organized criminal groups (Article 5), money laundering (Article 6), corruption (Article 8), and obstruction of justice (Article 23). Additional crimes are identified by the protocols (for example, trafficking in persons, smuggling of migrants, smuggling or illicit manufacture of firearms).

Realizing that cooperation by law enforcement and other agencies is necessary to deal effectively with organized crime groups, the ratifying countries are expected to assist each other in dealing with transnational organized crime as a general problem but also on specific cases. Examples include mechanisms for extradition and mutual legal assistance and for measures that allow the collection and exchange of information that can be helpful for law enforcement and prosecution purposes.

Countries are also expected to adopt laws and practices that prevent or suppress organized crime–related activities. For money laundering, for example, countries should require banks to keep accurate records and make them available for inspection by law enforcement officials. In addition, countries able to do so should assist developing countries in their efforts to build domestic capacity to combat transnational organized crime.

UNTOC PROTOCOLS

Three protocols (termed the Palermo Protocols) are attached to UNTOC. The Protocol to Prevent, Suppress and Punish Trafficking in Persons, Especially Women and Children entered into force in 2003. The second, the Protocol against the Smuggling of Migrants by Land, Sea and Air, was added in 2004. The following year, the Protocol against the Illicit Manufacturing of and Trafficking in Firearms, Their Parts, and Components and Ammunition was added. Each protocol addresses a particular type of transnational organized crime and includes specific obligations for those countries choosing to ratify the protocol.

The Protocol to Prevent, Suppress and Punish Trafficking in Persons, Especially Women and Children is the first global, legally binding instrument with an agreed upon definition of trafficking in persons. Specifically, "'trafficking in persons' shall mean the recruitment, transportation, transfer, harbouring or receipt of persons, by means of the threat or use of force or other forms of coercion, of abduction, of fraud, of deception, of the abuse of power or of a position of vulnerability or of the giving or receiving of payments or benefits to achieve the consent of a person having control over another person, for the purpose of exploitation" (Protocol Article 3).

The intention for providing this definition was to facilitate convergence in national approaches in terms of establishing domestic criminal offenses that would support international cooperation in investigating and prosecuting trafficking in persons cases. An additional objective of the protocol was to protect and assist the victims of trafficking in persons with full respect for their human rights.

The impact of this protocol is seen in steps taken by various nations to combat human trafficking domestically and internationally and to protect victims. For example, in the United States, the Trafficking Victims Protection Act of 2000 includes definitions consistent with those found in the protocol. And, as an example of regional cooperation, the Council of Europe, in 2005, took action that requires nations to adopt policies intended to reduce human trafficking, to increase penalties for human smugglers, and to provide for the basic needs, medical assistance, and safety of trafficked persons.

The Protocol against the Smuggling of Migrants by Land, Sea and Air deals with the problem of organized criminal groups who smuggle migrants, often at high risk to the migrants and at great profit for the offenders. As with the human trafficking protocol, a major achievement of this protocol was creation of an agreed upon definition of smuggling of migrants: "'Smuggling of migrants' shall mean the procurement, in order to obtain, directly or indirectly, a financial or other material benefit, of the illegal entry of a person into a State Party of which the person is not a national or a permanent resident" (Protocol Article 3).

The protocol aims to prevent and combat the smuggling of migrants and to promote cooperation among countries. Also, recognizing that the smuggling process is often dangerous, the protocol seeks to protect the rights of smuggled migrants and prevent the worst forms of their exploitation.

The objective of the Protocol against the Illicit Manufacturing of and Trafficking in Firearms, Their Parts and Components and Ammunition, which is the first legally binding instrument on small arms that has been adopted at the global level, is to promote, facilitate, and strengthen cooperation among ratifying countries to prevent, combat, and eradicate the illicit manufacturing of and trafficking in firearms. By ratifying the protocol, states make a commitment to adopt a series of crime-control measures and implement domestically three provisions: (1) the establishment of criminal offenses related to illegal manufacturing of, and trafficking in, firearms on the basis of the protocol requirements and definitions; (2) a system of government authorizations or licensing intending to ensure legitimate manufacturing of, and trafficking in, firearms; and (3) the marking and tracing of firearms.

UNTOC and its protocols have become important documents in both domestic and international efforts to define and combat transnational organized crimes. Because of the provisions to which ratifying countries are obligated, there have been increased and more effective efforts throughout the world to respond to the activities of transnational organized crime groups.

Philip L. Reichel

See also: UN Protocol against the Smuggling of Migrants by Land, Air, and Sea; UN Protocol to Prevent, Suppress, and Punish Trafficking in Persons, Especially Women and Children.

Further Reading

"Summary of the United Nations Convention against Transnational Organized Crime and Protocols Thereto." 2000. *Trends in Organized Crime* 5 (4): 11–21.

United Nations. 2000. "United Nations Convention against Transnational Organized Crime and the Protocols Thereto." Accessed July 16, 2018. https://www.unodc.org/unodc/en/organized-crime/intro/UNTOC.html.

UN Convention on Psychotropic Substances (1971)

The 1971 Convention on Psychotropic Substances is a UN treaty that became effective on August 16, 1976. It was created to control the dissemination of narcotics and psychotropic drugs internationally. The convention addressed the expansion and diversification of psychotropic substances and their precursors, therapeutic value, and abuse potential, which may lead to social or public health concerns. The goal was to limit the use of psychotropic substances and their precursors to medical and scientific purposes.

BACKGROUND

The Convention of 1971 is based primarily on the Single Convention on Narcotic Drugs of 1961 and includes 33 articles. Countries were supportive of the 1971 convention after a rise in the use of methamphetamine following World War II became an international problem. The convention was not without challenges, however, as interest groups and pharmaceutical companies lobbied to minimize regulatory control of psychotropic substances.

Seventy-one countries had signatories at the UN meeting in Vienna, Austria, for the adoption of the protocol on psychotropic substances. According to the convention, participating countries are required to provide statistics on the imports, exports, and manufacture of these psychotropic substances to the International Narcotics Control Board (INCB) and make these substances available only for scientific and medical purposes. The statistical returns system of the 1971 convention is identical to that of the 1961 single convention.

Over 130 psychotropic substances are under the control of the 1971 convention. Psychotropic substances are classified into four different schedules based on the risk of abuse, which may lead to social or public health concerns, and the potential therapeutic value of these substances. Schedule I is the most restrictive of the four schedules and includes substances such as lysergide (LSD), MMDA, rolicyclidine (PCPY, PHP), and tenamefetamine (MDA). Substances included in Schedule I are identified as posing serious public health risk and possessing virtually no therapeutic value. Those under Schedule II are also identified as posing a great risk to public health and have low therapeutic value. Some examples of these substances include phencyclidine (PCP), amphetamine, methamphetamine, and dronabinol (delta-9-tetrahydrocannabinol and stereochemical variants). Schedule III substances also pose a great risk to public health but have moderate therapeutic value, while Schedule IV substances pose a small risk to public health and have higher therapeutic value. Schedule IV is the least restrictive classification and includes substances such as barbital, diazepam, and ethyl loflazepate.

The convention also specified the roles of the Secretariat and INCB. The Secretariat, via the UN Office on Drugs and Crime (UNODC), mainly focuses on the illegal trade of psychotropic substances, while the INCB focuses on both the trade and manufacture of legal psychotropic substances.

Marika Dawkins

See also: International Drug Trafficking; International Narcotics Control Board; Single Convention on Narcotic Drugs; UN Convention against Illicit Traffic in Narcotic Drugs and Psychotropic Substances

Further Reading

Bayer, István. 1989. "Development of the Convention on Psychotropic Substances, 1971." Budapest, Hungary: Unpublished Manuscript. Accessed December 13, 2017. https://www.tni.org/files/publication-downloads/bayer-1971convention.pdf.

International Narcotics Board. 2018. "Psychotropic Substances." Accessed January 4, 2018. https://www.unodc.org/pdf/convention_1971_en.pdf.

United Nations Office on Drugs and Crime (UNODC). "Convention on Psychotropic Substances, 1971." Accessed December 13, 2017. https://www.unodc.org/pdf/convention_1971_en.pdf.

United Nations Treaty Collection. 2017. "Chapter VI: Narcotic Drugs and Psychotropic Substances." Convention on Psychotropic Substances. Vienna, February 21, 1971. Accessed December 13, 2017. https://treaties.un.org/Pages/ViewDetails.aspx?src=IND&mtdsg_no=VI-16&chapter=6&clang=_en.

World Health Organization (WHO). 2017. "Management of Substance Abuse: United Nations Drug Conventions." Accessed December 13, 2017. http://www.who.int/substance_abuse/right_conventions/en.

UN Convention on the Law of the Sea

The UN Convention on the Law of the Sea (1982) was a landmark agreement that endeavored to standardize international maritime law and was seen as the "Constitution for the oceans" (Freestone 2012, 672). The convention regulates the use of the oceans, the rights to natural resources therein, and maritime piracy.

HISTORY

The UN Convention on the Law of the Sea (UNCLOS) was a replacement of a 300-year-old legal doctrine called the 'freedom of the seas' (Mare Liberum). This doctrine restricted the territorial sea of a nation to three nautical miles (nm) from the shoreline. The first major challenge to this principle occurred in 1945 with the

Truman Doctrine, which unilaterally declared jurisdiction over the resources of the continental shelf of the United States, which exceeded the three nm limit. When the first of three UN conferences tasked with drafting UNCLOS convened in 1958, 81 countries had claimed an extended territorial sea limit, and eight states claimed a 200 nm sea limit. Maritime nations (countries with large merchant navies) were looking to preserve the right of passage and freedom of navigation and to limit the size of territorial seas; coastal nations (countries that depend on sea resources) were more concerned with establishing maritime sovereignty and limiting the depletion of fish stocks in local seas.

UNCLOS was adopted in 1982 and came into force in 1994 after negotiations, which included 100 countries and three conferences (in 1958, 1960, and 1973). The convention compelled nations to adopt it in its entirety, without reservations (DOALOS 2012). UNCLOS provided each coastal nation with territorial waters that extended 12 nm from the coast and an exclusive economic zone (EEZ) stretching 200 nm, granting states exploitation rights over the natural resources therein. Other key provisions of UNCLOS included navigation rights, legal status of resources on the seabed in the high seas, conservation and management of living marine resources, marine research regimes, dispute settlement mechanisms, and piracy laws.

MARITIME PIRACY

Of the 327 articles in UNCLOS, only seven dealt with piracy. The UN conferences on the Law of the Sea were primarily concerned with redistribution of resources to postcolonial nations, while also ensuring freedom of navigation for the established fleets of former colonial powers (Anderson 1995, 178). The first international codification of piracy occurred in the 1958 Geneva Convention on the High Seas (Article 15); UNCLOS replicated its piracy clause verbatim in Article 101. Piracy is defined as "any illegal acts of violence, detention, or any act of depredation committed for private ends by the crew or the passengers of a private ship or a private aircraft, and directed on the high seas, against another ship or aircraft, or against persons or property on board such ship or aircraft" (DOALOS 2001). The convention limits acts of piracy to those for private ends, to incidents that occur outside the jurisdiction of any nation, and to a conflict between two ships (or aircraft).

LIMITATIONS

UNCLOS has been criticized for its restricted definition of piracy, its lack of definitional clarity, its lack of dealing with other forms of maritime crime, its failure to set any requirements for nations to legislate comparable domestic piracy legislation, and its neglect to require cooperation between nations (Passas and Twyman-Ghoshal 2012, 69). The environmental protections in UNCLOS are seen as inadequate, reflecting a time when the ocean's resources were believed to be inexhaustible (Nyman 2017, 643). Furthermore, the convention is seen as an aging document that struggles to keep up with changing technology.

Anamika A. Twyman-Ghoshal

See also: International Maritime Bureau Piracy Reporting Center; *Maersk Alabama* Pirate Attack; Sea Piracy

Further Reading

Anderson, John. 1995. "Piracy and World History: An Economic Perspective of Maritime Predation." *Journal of World History* 6 (2): 175–199.

Freestone, David. 2012. "The Law of the Sea Convention at 30: Success, Challenges, and New Agendas." *International Journal of Marine and Coastal Law* 27 (4): 675–682.

Nyman, Elizabeth. 2017. "Outpaced by Events: Our Ageing Law of the Sea." *International Journal of Maritime History* 29 (3): 636–644.

Passas, Nikos, and Anamika Twyman-Ghoshal. 2012. "Controlling Piracy in Southeast Asia—Thinking Outside the Box." In *Piracy and International Maritime Crimes in ASEAN: Prospects for Cooperation*, edited by Robert Beckman and Ashley Roach, 130–175. Cheltenham, U.K.: Edward Elgar Publishing.

United Nations Division for Ocean Affairs and the Law of the Sea (DOALOS). 2001. "United Nations Convention on the Law of the Sea." Accessed February 21, 2018. http://www.un.org/depts/los/convention_agreements/texts/unclos/UNCLOS-TOC.htm.

United Nations Division for Ocean Affairs and the Law of the Sea (DOALOS). 2012. "UNCLOS: A Historical Perspective." Accessed February 21, 2018. http://www.un.org/depts/los/convention_agreements/convention_historical_perspective.htm.

UN Convention on the Prevention and Punishment of the Crime of Genocide

The Convention on the Prevention and Punishment of the Crime of Genocide (otherwise referred to as the Genocide Convention) is an international agreement between countries to adopt laws to prevent and punish genocide. The convention defines genocide as the act of killing, mentally or physically harming, or creating conditions with the intent to destroy, in whole or in part, a national, ethnic, racial, or religious group. The United Nations adopted the Convention on December 9, 1948, and to date, 149 countries are party to the convention.

HISTORY

During World War II (1939–1945), Jewish lawyer Rafael Lemkin coined the term *genocide* in his 1944 book *Axis Rule in Occupied Europe: Laws of Occupation, Analysis of Government, Proposals for Redress.* The term is a combination of the Greek word for race, *genos*, and the Latin word for killing, *cide*. He defined genocide as the "destruction of a nation or of an ethnic group," either directly or through a "coordinated plan of different actions" (Lemkin 1944). He used this term to describe the actions of the Nazi government against his race and others that he had witnessed throughout the war.

On August 8, 1945, following the end of World War II and the defeat of the Nazi regime, the Nuremberg Charter was issued to prosecute individuals who had committed crimes against peace, war crimes, and crimes against humanity during wartime. Although the term *genocide* was not included in the charter, it addressed genocide through crimes against humanity, which included "murder, extermination, enslavement, deportation and other inhumane acts committed against any civilian population, before or during the war." Because the charter was limited to crimes committed during wartime, the charter did not allow prosecution of crimes committed, for example, by the Nazi regime before 1939, when the war officially started (Schabas 2005). Thus, there was public demand to create a mechanism to acknowledge and prosecute these crimes when committed during peacetime to prevent such atrocities occurring in the future.

Recognizing this shortfall, Lemkin drafted a resolution in 1946 for the UN General Assembly, which would become the foundation for the Genocide Convention. After some amendments, the UN General Assembly unanimously adopted the resolution. The resolution accomplished three goals: (1) it recognized genocide as a crime under international law; (2) it called on member states to enact national laws to prevent and punish genocide; and (3) it requested the UN Economic and Social Council—one of the six principal organs of the United Nations—to draft a convention on this matter to submit to the UN General Assembly.

The UN General Assembly unanimously adopted the Convention on the Prevention and Punishment of the Crime of Genocide on December 9, 1948. It became the first human rights instrument adopted by the United Nations. Signatories to the convention agreed to take measures to prevent genocides and adopt laws within their countries to prosecute and punish the crime.

CONTENTS OF THE CONVENTION

Definition and Scope

The crime of genocide includes several types of acts intended to partially or entirely destroy a national, ethnic, racial, or religious group. These acts include killing or mentally or physically harming group members, preventing births, forcibly transferring children to another group, and imposing living conditions that would bring destruction to the group. A wide range of acts, such as damaging a group's living environment so that they can no longer survive, rape, and enslavement, could also constitute genocide as long as there is intent to destroy the group. It is not considered genocide if these acts are committed randomly, without the intent to destroy a group.

In addition to criminalizing the act of genocide, the convention criminalizes the conspiracy and attempt to commit genocide, complicity in genocide, and direct and public incitement to commit genocide. The convention states that anyone, even heads of state and public officials, can be punished for the crime of genocide.

Jurisdiction

Genocide is tried in the courts of the country in which the crime is committed or in an international court. The convention does not recognize universal jurisdiction for genocide, meaning that the jurisdiction for genocide does not go beyond what is stipulated in the convention. If there are any disputes between countries regarding the convention, the countries can request the International Court of Justice (ICJ)—the principal judicial organ of the United Nations—to settle the dispute. The convention also grants signatories the right to call upon the United Nations to take action to prevent and suppress genocide.

Signature and Ratification

The convention enters into force 90 days after it is signed by 20 countries. Once the convention enters into force, it is in effect for 10 years. After the first 10 years, the convention is renewed for periods of 5 years, unless a country notifies the UN secretary-general otherwise in writing within 6 months of its expiry. Any country can extend the application of the convention to its territories by notifying the UN secretary-general. The convention is no longer in effect if it has less than 16 signatories at any given time.

Revisions

Countries can submit a request for revision to the UN secretary-general, after which the UN General Assembly decides whether to take action.

DRAFTING PROCESS

To ensure that the convention was adopted, drafters of the convention had to make certain concessions to gain the votes it needed. The convention maintains a very narrow definition of the crime of genocide and excludes political, social, and economic groups. For instance, it does not account for groups based on sexual orientation, gender, or profession. The convention is also not legally binding, meaning that signatories pledge to uphold the convention but are not obligated to do so. Making the convention legally binding would, to a certain extent, permit international forces such as the United Nations to intervene in a country's domestic matters (Lippman 2002). This would not be popular among the voting member states, as it runs contrary to the United Nations' principle of respecting the sovereign equality of all its members.

Despite the significance of the crimes committed by the Nazi regime and its role in highlighting the need for the convention, the drafters of the convention further agreed to not specify any particular groups or historical events within the convention. Mentioning specific groups as perpetrators or victims or tying genocide to a historical event, the drafters argued, would limit the scope of the convention.

Although there were no international criminal courts at the time of drafting the convention, the drafters recognized that genocide could not be left only to domestic courts. Historically, governments often acted as sponsors or perpetrators of genocide. In these cases, its courts could not reasonably be expected to prevent or punish the crime of genocide.

DEVELOPMENT

The Convention on the Prevention and Punishment of Genocide remained the prevailing document on international crimes until the adoption of the Rome Statute in 1998. The Rome Statute established the International Criminal Court (ICC), which prosecutes, among other international crimes, the crime of genocide.

In the 1990s, the International Criminal Tribunal for the former Yugoslavia and the International Criminal Tribunal for Rwanda were established to prosecute individuals responsible for the mass atrocities that occurred in those countries. The ICC and these tribunals—the three most formative bodies of international criminal law to date—employ the definition of genocide as first set out in the Genocide Convention. Thus, despite its shortcomings and limitations, the Convention on the Prevention and Punishment of the Crime of Genocide has withstood the test of time and was fundamental in shaping the international criminal justice system.

Ariun Enkhsaikhan

See also: Crimes against Humanity; Genocide; International Criminal Tribunal for Rwanda; International Criminal Tribunal for the Former Yugoslavia (ICTY); International Military Tribunal at Nuremberg; International Military Tribunal for the Far East

Further Reading

Lemkin, Raphael. 1944. *Axis Rule in Occupied Europe: Laws of Occupation, Analysis of Government, Proposals for Redress.* Washington, DC: Carnegie Endowment for International Peace, Division of International Law.

Lippman, Matthew. 1994. "The 1948 Convention on the Prevention and Punishment of the Crime of Genocide: Forty-Five Years Later." *Temple International and Comparative Law Journal* 8 (1): 1–84.

Lippman, Matthew. 2002. "A Road Map to the 1948 Convention on the Prevention and Punishment of the Crime of Genocide." *Journal of Genocide Research* 4 (2): 177–195.

Schabas, William A. 2005. "Convention on the Prevention and Punishment of Genocide." In *Encyclopedia of Genocide and Crimes against Humanity,* edited by Dinah L. Shelton, 204–205. Vol. 1. Detroit: Macmillan Reference USA.

United Nations. 1945. "Charter of the International Military Tribunal—Annex to the Agreement for the Prosecution and Punishment of the Major War Criminals of the European Axis." https://www.legal-tools.org/en/doc/64ffdd/.

UN Global Programme for Combating Wildlife and Forest Crime

The Global Programme for Combating Wildlife and Forest Crime (GP) is a global response to wildlife and forest crime led by the UN Office on Drugs and Crime (UNODC). It is a four-year program that delivers technical assistance to prevent and combat wildlife and forest crime on a local, regional, and national basis.

Since 2014, it aims to enhance capacity-building and wildlife law enforcement networks, linking existing regional efforts in a global system. It works for and with the wildlife law enforcement community to ensure that wildlife crime, illegal logging, and related crimes are treated as serious transnational organized crimes

(UNODC 2018), which is a challenge and a barrier to combat them. Until recently, wildlife crime was mostly seen as an environmental issue rather than a transnational criminal activity.

Illicit trafficking and other illegal activities related to wild fauna and flora (that is, wildlife and forest crime) occurs across borders, and the various products taken often end up thousands of miles from the source and having passed through several countries in transit. That is why a global response, as the one brought by GP, is necessary.

The GP also raises awareness of wildlife and forest crime among different stakeholders around the globe, which includes international organizations and civil society. It contributes, therefore, to the reduction of the demand of illicit wildlife and flora. UNODC, through the GP, also provides technical assistance activities that can strengthen the ability of UN member states to prevent, investigate, prosecute, and adjudicate wildlife and forest crimes.

OBJECTIVES AND AREAS

The Global Programme acts as the overarching umbrella program for UNODC activities on wildlife and forest crime. It involves liaising closely with UNODC Country and Regional Offices to ensure appropriate support for the design and delivery of wildlife and forest crime projects and activities.

The GP delivers a range of technical assistance activities within several thematic areas toward achieving the key project objective of strengthening capacity to prevent and combat wildlife and forest crime on a regional, national, and local basis. It also serves to raise awareness of wildlife and forest crime among different stakeholders, including civil society, and aims to contribute to the reduction of demand for wild fauna and flora.

Additionally, the GP improves cooperation and capacity of member states to work, locally, nationally and internationally, to address wildlife and forest crime as well as other forms of serious and organized crime.

Within each of the six thematic areas, focus is being placed on delivering a range of evidence-based good practices, technical assistance measures to support national law enforcement, customs, border control, and criminal justice agencies, as well as regional wildlife law enforcement agencies and networks, in their efforts to respond to wildlife and forest crime.

THE WILDLIFE AND FOREST CRIME ANALYTIC TOOLKIT

The Global Programme for Combating Wildlife and Forest Crime/Sustainable Livelihoods Unit (GP/SLU) provides advice and assistance at the country and regional levels and will at times engage in specific activities, such as training. The *Wildlife and Forest Crime Analytic Toolkit*, prepared in conjunction with the International Consortium on Combating Wildlife Crime (ICCWC), is one of those resources.

The toolkit (ICCWC 2012) is a technical resource designed to help government wildlife and forestry officials analyze the strengths and weaknesses of preventive and criminal justice responses to the protection and monitoring of those products that are vital to limiting a wildlife and forest crime both nationally and internationally. The toolkit is available to all governments interested in taking action regarding the protection of wildlife and the forest in their country (ICCWC 2012).

Users of the toolkit are provided with assistance in identifying current patterns of wildlife and forest offenses, analyzing the current criminal justice response in their country, understanding the different links and actors in the wildlife and forest offenses chain, and implementing measures, including alternative incentives, that will address and prevent the commission of wildlife offenses (ICCWC 2012).

The GP/SLU team works on developing close partnerships and coordinates with other UN agencies and international organizations that focus on wildlife and forest crime, including, among others, the Convention on International Trade in Endangered Species of Wild Fauna and Flora (CITES), INTERPOL, the World Wide Fund for Nature (WWF), and nongovernmental organizations (NGOs). In addition, the team works with other agencies and regional organizations to establish new partnerships and cooperation as the GP continues to expand its influence.

Ana Carolina Paci and Dafne Calderón Burgoa

See also: UN Office on Drugs and Crime; Wildlife and Forest Crime

Further Reading

International Consortium on Combating Wildlife Crime (ICCWC). 2012. *Wildlife and Forest Crime Analytic Toolkit.* Rev. ed. Vienna: United Nations Office on Drugs and Crime. Accessed January 21, 2019. http://www.unodc.org/unodc/en/wildlife-and-forest-crime/wildlife-and-forest-crime-analytic-toolkit.html.

Lale-Demoz, Aldo. 2015. "Speech by the Deputy Executive Director of UNODC Mr. Aldo Lale-Demoz." UN World Wildlife Day. Last modified March 4, 2015. Accessed January 21, 2019. http://www.wildlifeday.org/content/speech-deputy-executive-director-unodc-mr-mr-aldo-lale-demoz-2015.

United Nations Office on Drugs and Crime (UNODC). 2018. "Global Programme." Wildlife and Forest Crime. Accessed January 21, 2019. https://www.unodc.org/unodc/en/wildlife-and-forest-crime/global-programme.html.

UN Office on Drugs and Crime

The UN Office on Drugs and Crime (UNODC) is the UN Secretariat unit responsible for administration of the UN drug control program and the UN crime prevention and criminal justice program.

ORGANIZATION

The UNODC is headed by an executive director appointed by the UN secretary-general. Its headquarters are located at the Vienna International Centre, in Vienna, Austria. The UNODC also operates through 21 field offices, and it has liaison offices in Brussels and New York. Its total staff consists of between 1,500 and 2,000 people.

A large majority of the UNODC staff members deal with the UN drug program, in the form of the Commission on Narcotic Drugs and the International Narcotics Control Board. In so doing, the UNODC serves as the Secretariat for the various drug conventions: the Single Convention on Narcotic Drugs (1961, amended by a 1972 Protocol), the 1971 Convention on Psychotropic Substances, and the 1988 Convention against Illicit Traffic in Narcotic Drugs and Psychotropic Substances. The 1988 Drug Convention marked a considerable improvement in several respects. Not only did it consolidate and bring international hard law up to date in respect of the definition of drug-related crime, but it included, for the first time in a multilateral agreement, provisions on international law enforcement cooperation and judicial cooperation—all activities that require an extensive administrative structure on the international level.

Throughout much of its existence, the UN Secretariat unit responsible for crime prevention and criminal justice issues remained in comparison rather small, with less than a dozen professional staff members. This unit also serviced the UN Committee on Crime Prevention and Control, which in 1991 was reconstituted as the UN Commission on Crime Prevention and Criminal Justice. In recent years, largely as a consequence of the adoption of the two UN crime conventions (transnational organized crime and corruption), with their extensive sets of provisions on international law enforcement and judicial cooperation (largely modeled on the 1988 Drug Convention), the number of persons dealing with substantive crime issues in the UNODC has increased to about 40.

The two separate units were merged to form the UNODC in 1997. This was largely a result of the growing realization of the interrelationship between drug and crime issues as well as the need to also prevent and respond to terrorism and corruption.

ACTIVITIES

The work of the UNODC takes the form of research, policy guidance, and technical assistance to member states on request. Regularly updated publications include the *World Drug Report* and the *Global Report on Trafficking in Persons*. Numerous research reports have been prepared on global and regional issues, such as wildlife and forest crime, maritime crime, violent crime, and prison issues.

Policy guidance is provided, for example, in the form of model laws and treaties on drug control, organized crime, trafficking in persons, the smuggling of migrants, firearms, money laundering and the financing of terrorism, international cooperation in criminal matters, assistance to child victims and witnesses of crime, and witness protection. In the drug control sector, the UNODC also provides extensive laboratory and forensic services to member states on request.

Matti Joutsen

See also: Commission on Narcotic Drugs; International Narcotics Control Board; UN Commission on Crime Prevention and Criminal Justice; UN Congresses on Crime

Prevention and Criminal Justice; UN Convention against Illicit Traffic in Narcotic Drugs and Psychotropic Substances; UN Convention against Transnational Organized Crime; UN Convention on Psychotropic Substances (1971); UN Program Network of Institutes

Further Reading

United Nations Office on Drug and Crime (UNODC). 2018. "World Drug Report 2018." Accessed January 21, 2019. http://www.unodc.org/wdr2018.

United Nations Office on Drug and Crime (UNODC). n.d.-a. "About UNODC." Accessed August 21, 2018. https://www.unodc.org/unodc/en/about-unodc/index.html?ref=menutop.

United Nations Office on Drug and Crime (UNODC). n.d.-b. "Global Report on Trafficking in Persons." Accessed August 21, 2018. https://www.unodc.org/unodc/en/data-and-analysis/glotip.html.

United Nations Office on Drug and Crime (UNODC). n.d.-c. "Research Publications." Accessed August 21, 2018. https://www.unodc.org/unodc/en/data-and-analysis/publications.html.

UN Program Network of Institutes

The UN Crime Prevention and Criminal Justice Program Network of Institutes (PNI) consists of a number of research and training institutes and other entities around the world that cooperate with the UN Office on Drug and Crime (UNODC) in activities promoting the UN Crime Program, including cooperative efforts in combating global crime.

MEMBERS OF THE PNI

The PNI was originally envisaged as a network consisting of the UN Interregional Crime and Justice Research Institute (established in 1968 and located in Italy) and four regional institutes that are affiliated with the United Nations: the Asia and Far East Institute for the Prevention of Crime and the Treatment of Offenders (Japan, the first PNI to be established, in 1962); the Latin American Institute for the Prevention of Crime and the Treatment of Offenders (Costa Rica); the European Institute for Crime Prevention and Control, affiliated with the United Nations (Finland); and the African Institute for the Prevention of Crime and the Treatment of Offenders (Uganda). The regional institutes were established on the basis of agreements between the United Nations and the host government, and the institutes were specifically mandated to cooperate with the UN Secretariat on crime prevention and criminal justice issues. A fifth regional institute, the Naif Arab University for Security Sciences, serving the Arab region, subsequently joined the network.

Over time, more institutes and one organization joined the network. These include four governmental research institutes (the Australian Institute of Criminology, the Korean Institute of Criminology, the Thailand Institute of Justice, and, in the United States, the National Institute of Justice) as well as institutes that have specific focuses: the Siracusa International Institute for Criminal Justice and Human Rights (located in Italy), the International Centre for Criminal Law Reform and Criminal Justice Policy and the International Centre for the Prevention of Crime (both located in Canada), the Institute for Security Studies (located in South Africa), the Raoul Wallenberg Institute of Human Rights and Humanitarian Law (located in Sweden), the International Centre for Asset Recovery (ICAR), which was established by the Basel Institute on Governance (both in Switzerland), and the College for Criminal Law Science at the Beijing Normal University (located in China). In addition, the International Scientific and Professional Advisory Council (ISPAC) joined the PNI as a structure for cooperation between the Secretariat and those nongovernmental organizations (NGOs) and academic institutions that are involved in crime prevention and criminal justice issues.

ACTIVITIES OF THE PNI

The institutes vary considerably in respect to their size, structure, mandate, priorities, capacity, and funding basis. Only the interregional and the regional institutes have been specifically established to contribute to the UN Crime Prevention and Criminal Justice Program. The other institutes must remain mindful of their original mandate, which, for example, in the case of the national institutes in Australia, South Korea, Thailand, and the United States, is understandably focused on national priorities in crime and justice.

Some of the institutes focus on research and others on training. Some of the institutes (such as the national institutes as well as the regional institutes for Asia and the Pacific and for Europe, which are funded primarily by their host governments) have a relatively stable funding base, allowing them some flexibility when deciding whether to assist the Secretariat.

These limits notwithstanding, a significant amount of cooperation takes place between the Secretariat and the institutes. This cooperation has been fostered by regular coordination meetings, a tradition dating back to 1984 (at the initiative of the institute in Saudi Arabia). The PNI has organized, since 1985, one or more of the workshops at each of the quinquennial UN Congresses as well as several other events. Since 2001, the PNI has organized practical workshops and other events during the annual sessions of the UN Commission on Crime Prevention and Criminal Justice, focusing on the theme of the annual session in question.

In addition to the cooperation with and among the institutes, individual institutes have given their own contributions to the program. This takes the form, for example, of research and the organization of expert meetings and training activities related to UN priorities. The interregional and the regional institutes have assisted in developing the UN surveys on crime and criminal justice, on victimization, and on violence against women. They as well as several of the specialized institutes have also contributed to work on the implementation of UN standards and norms.

Matti Joutsen

See also: Australian Institute of Criminology; HEUNI; National Institute of Justice; Raoul Wallenberg Institute of Human Rights and Humanitarian Law; UN Office on Drugs and Crime

Further Reading

United Nations Interregional Crime and Justice Research Institute (UNICRI). n.d. "The Institutes Comprising the United Nations Crime Prevention and Criminal Justice Programme Network (PNI)." Accessed August 21, 2018. http://www.unicri.it/information/partners_donors/crime_prevention_network.

United Nations Office on Drug and Crime (UNODC). n.d. "Institutes of the UN Crime Prevention and Criminal Justice Programme Network (PNI)." Commission on Crime Prevention and Criminal Justice. Accessed August 21, 2018. https://www.unodc.org/unodc/en/commissions/CCPCJ/PNI/institutes.html.

UN Protocol against the Smuggling of Migrants by Land, Air, and Sea

The Protocol against the Smuggling of Migrants by Land, Air, and Sea, often referred to as the Anti-Smuggling Protocol or Smuggling Protocol, was adopted by the UN General Assembly in 2000 to produce a multidisciplinary and global response to migrant smuggling by providing a treaty framework to help states combat transnational crime. This protocol was one of three Palermo protocols adopted by the United Nations to supplement the Convention against Transnational Organized Crime.

The Anti-Smuggling Protocol entered into force on January 28, 2004, and as of August 2018, it had 146 state parties. This protocol aimed to prevent and combat the smuggling of migrants, to protect the rights of smuggled migrants, and to promote global cooperation between states via information sharing. Additionally, it provided an internationally recognized definition of human smuggling by focusing on illegal entry of foreign nationals in exchange for financial and other material benefit.

HISTORY

During the late 1990s, organized crime was becoming a global issue as the world continued to expand through globalization. At this same time, Italy appealed for an international legal instrument to be created to deal specifically with smuggling people by sea, which was in direct response to the unprecedented number of people arriving in Italy from Turkey by sea (Brolan 2002). Additionally, the global community became concerned with organized crime and human smuggling rings. The United Nations came together to make smuggling an international organized crime that provided a framework for an international response.

SMUGGLING OF MIGRANTS

Smuggling of migrants and trafficking in persons are by nature interlinked with migration and are often perpetrated by individuals attempting to profit. According to Article 3 in the Anti-Smuggling protocol, people smuggling involves the illegal movement of people across borders to gain financial or other material benefits. This protocol recognized smuggling as a form of illegal immigration, whether voluntary or involuntary. Migration may occur for various reasons, such as social and economic hardship, lack of educational or job opportunities in the home country, and discrimination, among others (Brolan 2002).

PROVISIONS

The protocol is unique because it ensured humane treatment and full protection of migrant rights as well as increased global dialogue, strengthened international cooperation for migrant smuggling, and developed strategies to effectively deter the crime by addressing root causes such as poverty. Article 2 outlined the purpose of the Anti-Smuggling Protocol, which is threefold: first, it is to prevent and combat the smuggling of migrants; second, it is to promote cooperation between states; and third, it is to protect the rights of smuggled migrants by providing assistance and protection (UN General Assembly 2000).

To comply with the protocol, Article 6 requires states to criminalize both the smuggling of migrants and the enabling of a person to remain in a country illegally, as well as aggravating circumstances that endanger lives or safety or entail inhumane or degrading treatment of migrants. However, the protocol does not aim to punish or criminalize persons who are being smuggled (as specified in Article 5), nor does it intend to criminalize migration itself. Smuggled migrants and trafficked persons are particularly vulnerable to experiencing human rights violations at all stages of the migration process through exploitation, physical and emotional abuse, inhumane treatment, or lack of access to justice. This protocol attempts to protect and punish all those involved in the smuggling of migrants.

Shanell Sanchez

See also: Human Trafficking; Migrant Smuggling; UN Convention against Transnational Organized Crime

Further Reading

Brolan, Claire. 2002. "An Analysis of the Human Smuggling Trade and the Protocol against the Smuggling of Migrants by Land, Air and Sea (2000) from a Refugee Protection Perspective." *International Journal of Refugee Law* 14 (4): 561.

Gallagher, Anne T., and Fiona David. 2014. *The International Law of Migrant Smuggling.* New York: Cambridge University Press.

Gualtieri, Claudia. 2018. *Migration and the Contemporary Mediterranean: Shifting Cultures in Twenty-First-Century Italy and Beyond.* Oxford: Peter Lang.

UN General Assembly. 2000. "Protocol against the Smuggling of Migrants by Land, Sea and Air." Accessed January 21, 2019. http://www.unodc.org/documents/treaties/UNTOC/Publications/TOC%20Convention/TOCebook-e.pdf (see Annex III).

UN Protocol to Prevent, Suppress, and Punish Trafficking in Persons, Especially Women and Children

The Protocol to Prevent, Suppress and Punish Trafficking in Persons, Especially Women and Children is one of three supplementing protocols of the UN Convention against Transnational Organized Crime (UNTOC), which is the main international instrument in the fight against transnational organized crime. It is also called the "Palermo Protocol," because the documents were first opened for signature in Palermo, Italy, after its adoption together with the convention by the General Assembly resolution 55/25 of November 15, 2000. On December 25, 2003, the protocol entered into force. A vast majority of states has now signed and ratified the protocol; as of March 2018, it counts 117 signatories and 173 parties.

As outlined in Article 2, the protocol has three main aims (the so called "3 Ps"): preventing and combating trafficking, protecting and assisting the trafficking victims with full respect for their human rights, and promoting cooperation among state parties. To best reach these, partly conflicting, goals, attempts were made to create a balanced system between law enforcement—the prosecution and sanctioning of the perpetrators—and the protection and support of the victims.

The protocol is the first legally binding global instrument with an agreed definition of human trafficking as a crime that facilitates international law enforcement cooperation. The offense is structured by three main elements: the act, which includes the entire process, from the recruitment to the receipt of the trafficked person; the means, for example, by using threat, force, or fraud; and the purpose of exploitation.

HISTORY AND BACKGROUND

To combat trafficking in persons, which is an organized crime dramatically rising on a global scale, in April 1998, at the UN Commission for Crime Prevention and Criminal Justice, the United States introduced a resolution on trafficking in women and children that calls for the development of a protocol under the UN Convention against Transnational Organized Crime. The following factors were the background for this requirement and at the same time the reasons for the development of the protocol.

NGOs made their governments aware of the issue of human trafficking as a grave human rights violation with reference to the procedures used by human traffickers to control and thereby traumatize their victims. Additionally, this crime is mostly linked to migration, because traffickers make use of migration crises and economic as well as social disadvantages to recruit the victims in their home countries. Therefore, it was and is not only an increasing phenomenon, but also a transnational and organized one that needs to be combated by a criminalizing approach toward investigation, prosecution, and punishment of traffickers by intensifying international police and judicial cooperation across borders.

However, the absence of national trafficking laws or different and inconsistent definitions of the offense of "human trafficking" in domestic laws avoided an effective transnational law enforcement process against the perpetrators. In former (international) trafficking agreements, no definition of trafficking was involved, or the agreements were limited to the act of recruiting and the exploitation of women for prostitution while omitting unnoticed children or men as victims as well as other exploitation situations.

LEGAL SCOPE

The (mandatory) rules of the protocol, as an international (or rather transnational) framework, have to be implemented into national law by the ratified states.

The domestic legislator does not have to follow the language of the protocol precisely, but it should be adapted in accordance with the national legal system. It must be noted that the protocol contains several additional provisions to the convention and therefore must be interpreted together with the latter, while the provisions of the convention shall apply, mutatis mutandis, to the protocol (unless otherwise is provided). The protocol also stressed that human trafficking should be an independent crime in national criminal codes rather than simply an aspect of some other criminal act.

The UN Office on Drugs and Crime (UNODC) offers to support states in drafting an effective national anti-trafficking law when implementing the protocol. It also helps states and organizations to find the best (regional) practical measures to criminalize the offenders and to protect the victims.

CONTENT

The protocol is primarily a law enforcement framework; the traffickers should be prosecuted and sanctioned. At the same time, the victims of human trafficking should be protected and assisted comprehensively by (national) support organizations; therefore, rules on victim support measures are included.

To reach the goal of criminalization (part I of the protocol), the definition of trafficking is a very broad one, including a variety of practices and offenders that can be involved in the process of human trafficking and exploitation. It is also clarified that the consent of a victim is irrelevant to the criminal proceedings against the offender. Thereby, the vulnerable situation of victims, who are aware of a (possible) exploitation in the destination country, is considered. Such a circumstance should not dispense the offender from legal responsibility.

Widespread legal and practical protection measures for victims are stated in part II of the protocol and include such items as counseling and information for the victim regarding his or her legal rights; the obligation of providing the victim with appropriate and safe housing; medical as well as psychosocial support; special care and education for children; victim compensation possibilities; repatriation possibilities; and the question of permanent residency or a safe return.

Part II covers the prevention aspect of trafficking and demands the implementation of appropriate programs, explicitly citing mass media awareness-raising campaigns and educational, social, or cultural measures, also through collaboration with relevant (nongovernmental) organizations. Further, likely causes such as "poverty, underdevelopment and lack of opportunity," which can make people vulnerable to traffickers, shall be alleviated by state parties a well as by bilateral or multilateral cooperation. These measures and policies should not only prevent and combat trafficking but also protect victims, especially women and children, from revictimization.

Additionally, information exchange—for example, concerning transportation routes, fraudulent documents, and potential traffickers—among law enforcement and immigration authorities and intensified border control measures should help to reduce human trafficking. All these policies, programs, and measures can only be effective if staff members of the relevant offices are trained in prevention, prosecution, and victims' protection issues, taking human rights as well as child- and gender-sensitive issues into account.

Although the protocol is a significant milestone in international efforts to stop human trafficking, its implementation into reality remains problematic. Only a few traffickers have been convicted, and most of the victims are still hard to identify.

Karin Bruckmüller

See also: Granados Sex Trafficking Organization; Human Trafficking; Labor Exploitation; Migrant Smuggling; Sex Exploitation; Trafficking Victim Identification Tools; U.S. Trafficking Victims Protection Act

Further Reading

Hyland, Kelly E. 2001. "The Impact of the Protocol to Prevent, Suppress and Punish Trafficking in Persons, Especially Women and Children." *Human Rights Brief* 8 (2): 30–31, 38.

Ollus, Natalia. 2004. "The United Nations Protocol to Prevent, Suppress and Punish Trafficking in Persons, Especially Women and Children: A Tool for Criminal Justice Personnel." UNAFI International Training Course Resource Material Series No. 62: 31–43. Accessed January 21, 2019. https://www.peacepalacelibrary.nl/ebooks/files/no62.pdf.

United Nations Office on Drugs and Crime (UNODC). 2018. "Human Trafficking." Accessed January 21, 2019. https://www.unodc.org/unodc/en/human-trafficking/what-is-human-trafficking.html.

UN Sustainable Development Goals

In September 2015, the UN General Assembly formally adopted the 2030 Agenda for Sustainable Development (the 2030 Agenda) along with a set of 17 Sustainable Development Goals (SDGs). The agenda itself is a plan of action designed to bring prosperity, peace, and freedom to humans everywhere. The 17 SDGs provide focus and guidance in reaching the goals.

HISTORY AND CONTEXT

More than 150 world leaders attended the UN Sustainable Development Summit that took place at the UN Headquarters in New York City in September 2015. Together they adopted the 2030 Agenda and its 17 SDGs. The overall objective of the SDGs is to mobilize efforts that will end all forms of poverty, fight inequalities, and tackle climate change, while ensuring that no one is left behind (United Nations 2015).

The Millennium Development Goals (MDGs), which were identified in the 2000 UN Millennium Declaration, preceded the SDGs. The United Nations developed a total of eight MDGs with the objective to promote extreme poverty eradication. The MDGs placed top priority on fostering the development of the least developed countries (LDCs), among other relevant objectives. Although the results of the MDGs are hard to estimate, the final report on the MDGs notes many successes, including a decline by more than half in the number of people living in extreme poverty from 1990 to 2015, 2.1 billion people gaining access to improved sanitation, and a drop by almost half in the number of undernourished people since 1990 (UNDP 2015).

THE SDGs

The General Assembly designed the SDGs to replicate the progress achieved by the MDGs and to expand that progress beyond the LDCs to promote sustainable development throughout the world. The SDGs cover a broad range of socio-economic development and environmental issues, including ending poverty and hunger, improving health and education, achieving gender equality, making cities more sustainable, combating climate change, protecting oceans and forests, promoting peace and justice, and strengthening partnerships between nations to accomplish these goals. The complete list of 17 SDGs is as follows:

1. No poverty—End poverty in all its forms.
2. Zero hunger—End hunger, achieve food security and improved nutrition, and promote sustainable agriculture.
3. Good health and well-being—Ensure healthy lives and promote well-being for all at all ages. This SDG includes targets related to global crime, such as strengthening the prevention and treatment of substance abuse and reducing deaths and illnesses from environmental crime.
4. Quality education—Ensure inclusive and equitable quality education and promote lifelong learning opportunities for all.
5. Gender equality—Achieve gender equality and empower all women and girls. This SDG makes specific reference in its targets to eliminating all forms of violence, including human trafficking and other types of exploitation.
6. Clean water and sanitation—Ensure availability and sustainable management of water and sanitation for all.
7. Affordable and clean energy—Ensure access to affordable, reliable, sustainable, and modern energy for all.
8. Decent work and economic growth—Promote sustained, inclusive, and sustainable economic growth; full and productive employment; and decent work for all.
9. Industry, innovation, and infrastructure—Build resilient infrastructure, promote inclusive and sustainable industrialization, and foster innovation.
10. Reduced inequalities—Reduce inequality within and among countries.
11. Sustainable cities and communities—Ensure sustainable consumption and production patterns.
12. Responsible consumption and production—Ensure sustainable consumption and production patterns
13. Climate action—Take urgent action to combat climate change and its impacts.

14. Life below water—Conserve and sustainably use the oceans, seas, and marine resources for sustainable development. This SDG includes a target specifically related to fisheries crime and to illegal, unreported, and unregulated fishing.
15. Life on land—Protect, restore, and promote sustainable use of terrestrial ecosystems; sustainably manage forests; combat desertification; halt and reverse land degradation; and halt biodiversity loss. Wildlife and forest crime are targeted in this SDG.
16. Peace, justice, and strong institutions—Promote peaceful and inclusive societies for sustainable development; provide access to justice for all; and build effective, accountable, and inclusive institutions at all levels. This goal is elaborated upon later, as it is directly related to global crime issues.
17. Partnerships for the goals—Strengthen the means of implementation and revitalize the global partnership for sustainable development. (United Nations 2018a)

Neither MDGs nor SDGs are legally binding. National governments are expected to take ownership of their commitment to the implementation of the SDGs and are responsible for evaluating their progress toward realization of the sustainable development agenda.

SDG 16: PEACE, JUSTICE, AND STRONG INSTITUTIONS

Several of the SDGs are important for impacting global crime, but SDG 16: Peace, Justice and Strong Institutions is especially relevant and is the focus here. SDG 16 is designed to promote peaceful and inclusive societies, to provide everyone with access to justice, and to build effective institutions. It is based on the rationale that people everywhere in the world need to be free from all forms of violence and that it is important that governments and communities work together to achieve rule of law, justice, and accountability. SDG 16 also aims to help governments enforce laws indiscriminately and deliver basic services to the communities equally.

The UN Office on Drugs and Crime (UNODC) is the central institution that provides normative, analytical, and operational assistance to member states as it relates to strengthening the effectiveness, fairness, and accountability of their criminal justice institutions and the policies adopted to tackle crime, corruption, and terrorism. In doing so, the UNODC has exercised leadership in the attainment of SDG 16, and in particular the areas that are identified as targets within the general goal. There are 10 such targets, but these 5 provide examples of ones geared specifically to global crime (UNODC n.d.):

- [16.1] *Significantly reduce all forms of violence and related death rates everywhere* by promoting access to legal aid; alternatives to imprisonment; youth crime prevention programs; offenders' rehabilitation; social reintegration measures; etc.
- [16.2] *End abuse, exploitation, trafficking and all forms of violence against and torture of children* by providing countries assistance in ensuring that children are better served and protected by justice systems.

- [16.3] *Promote the rule of law at the national and international levels and ensure equal access to justice for all* by supporting the monitoring of the exploitation and trafficking of children.
- [16.4] *By 2030, significantly reduce the illicit financial and arms flows, strengthening the recovery and return of stolen assets and combat all forms of organized crime* by providing a full spectrum of tools to strengthen anti–money laundering legal frameworks and develop capacities of national agencies to investigate money laundering and terrorism financing, disrupt illicit financial flows, and support the recovery of stolen assets.
- [16.5] *Substantially reduce the corruption and bribery in all their forms* by assisting countries in preventing, detecting, investigating, and sanctioning corruption, and in promoting international cooperation against corruption as well as the recovery of proceeds of corruption.

PROGRESS TOWARD SDG 16

Each year, an assessment is provided regarding progress toward each of the 17 SDGs. SDG 16 will be reviewed in-depth in 2019, but the report on progress toward SDG 16 in 2017 shows promise but still much work being needed (United Nations 2018b). For example, the share of victims trafficked for sexual exploitation has declined, but the proportion of those trafficked for forced labor has increased. And whereas the homicide rate declined over the past decade, people in some Latin American, sub-Saharan African, and Asian countries face increased risk of intentional murder.

Christine Marie Gancayco and Yuliya Zabyelina

See also: Failed State; Small Arms Survey; UN Office on Drugs and Crime; van Dijk, Jan

Further Reading

United Nations. 2015. "Transforming Our World: The 2030 Agenda for Sustainable Development." New York City, NY. Accessed June 10, 2018. https://sustainabledevelopment.un.org/content/documents/21252030%20Agenda%20for%20Sustainable%20Development%20web.pdf.

United Nations. 2018a. "Sustainable Development Goals." *Sustainable Development Knowledge Platform.* Accessed July 25, 2018. https://sustainabledevelopment.un.org/sdgs.

United Nations. 2018b. "Sustainable Development Knowledge Platform." Sustainable Development Goal 16: Progress of Goal 16 in 2017. Accessed July 25, 2018. https://sustainabledevelopment.un.org/sdg16.

United Nations Development Programme (UNDP). 2015. "The Millennium Development Goals Report." Accessed June 10, 2018. http://www.undp.org/content/undp/en/home/librarypage/mdg/the-millennium-development-goals-report-2015.html.

United Nations Office on Drugs and Crime (UNODC). n.d. "SDG 16: Promote Peaceful and Inclusive Societies for Sustainable Development, Provide Access to Justice for All and Build Effective, Accountable and Inclusive Institutions at All Levels." *About UNODC, Sustainable Development Goals.* Accessed September 26, 2018. https://www.unodc.org/unodc/en/about-unodc/sustainable-development-goals/sdg16_-peace-and-justice.html.

UN War Crimes Commission (1943–1948)

The United Nations was founded after the close of World War II (1939–1945), when Nazi Germany and Imperial Japan had waged aggressive wars. It was at this time the international community set out to create an organization that would serve as a "forum for debating issues of global concern, but also have the power to enforce its will when a state or group of states refused to behave properly" while still respecting sovereign states (Fichtelberg 2008, 19). The UN War Crimes Commission (UNWCC) was created in 1943 and was initially called the UN Commission for the Investigation of War Crimes.

The primary purpose of the UNWCC was to create a multilateral organization to mobilize international retributive justice efforts for offenders of war crimes (Plesch and Sattler 2013). The UNWCC was a fact-finding body that helped ensure the detection, apprehension, trial, and punishment of persons accused of war crimes in Europe and Asia during World War II. Additionally, the commission performed advisory functions for the development of principles of international law and planning for international tribunals. Lastly, the UNWCC set out to promote justice for survivors of war crimes. The UNWCC had its first official meeting on January 11, 1944, and it actively continued its work until the end of March 31, 1948 (Plesch and Sattler 2014).

WAR CRIMES

The UNWCC was created prior to the development of the International Criminal Court (ICC) and the tribunals in Rwanda and Yugoslavia, which were later formal ways to punish war criminals and promote justice for survivors. The first question the commission had to determine was what constituted a war crime, but as no agreed upon definition existed, it decided to adopt the list of war crimes prepared by a 1919 commission. This definition was used because it was a previously agreed upon definition of war crimes by Japan and Germany. Ultimately, the definition of a war crime did not come until the end of the war.

Today, war crimes are defined as a "grave breach of the laws of war in an attempt to regulate the behavior of soldiers and civilians both on and off the battlefield" (Fichtelberg 2008, 123). The rules set forth are designed to govern the conduct of warfare and are often referred to as international humanitarian law (Fichtelberg 2008). The creation of the war crime commission allowed for both a legal and military response to unprecedented atrocities being committed against the military and civilian populations of the countries during World War II (Plesch and Sattler 2014).

UNWCC COMMITTEES

The UNWCC member states that actively participated were Australia, Belgium, Canada, China, Czechoslovakia, France, Greece, India, Luxemburg, the Netherlands, New Zealand, Norway, Poland, the United Kingdom, the United States, and Yugoslavia. The UNWCC had three specific duties. The first was to investigate and record the evidence of war crimes and identify any individuals to be held responsible, referred to as Committee I dedicated to facts and evidence. Second, the commission was to report to the governments any cases that appeared to be concerning in which adequate evidence would be forthcoming on individuals, referred to as Committee II dedicated to matters of enforcement. The emphasis was placed on maintaining constant dialogue with member states and the global community. And third, the commission made recommendations to member governments concerning questions of law and procedure as necessary for them to be able to fulfill their role of conducting trials, referred to as Committee III committed to creating dialogue on legal affairs. This last duty was what made the UNWCC an advisory tool for creating laws and rules at the international level for World War II war crimes and future atrocities (Plash and Sattler 2013).

COMMISSION PROCEEDINGS

During UNWCC's four-and-a-half years, over 8,178 classified files were created that represented over 36,810 war criminals, with the vast majority being German and Italian. The UNWCC was responsible for making judgments on 36,000 cases put to the commission by member states, which resulted in over 2,000 trials. Additionally, the UNWCC completed a list of German and Italian war criminals that included 712 names. There were 49 high-ranking Nazi officials that consisted of generals, administrators of occupied regions, and political appointees. The commission rejected the idea that heads of state or members of government would be immune to punishment.

The UNWCC's collaborative multilateral efforts generated a significant contribution to the development of customary international criminal law, legal standards, and proceedings to combat impunity and promote justice. It was not until the fall of 2011 that the UN Archives Records Management Section (UNARMS) agreed to allow access to researchers to review the majority of the archives. The section that remains closed to the general public includes 36,000 pretrial charge files that detail various charges, witness statements, and testimonies (Plesch and Sattler 2014).

Shanell Sanchez

See also: Crimes against Humanity; Genocide; International Criminal Tribunal for the Former Yugoslavia (ICTY); International Military Tribunal at Nuremberg; International Military Tribunal for the Far East

Further Reading

Fichtelberg, Aaron. 2008. *Crime without Borders: An Introduction to International Criminal Justice.* Upper Saddle River, NJ: Pearson Education, Inc.

Plesch, Dan, and Shanti Sattler. 2013. "Changing the Paradigm of International Criminal Law: Considering the Work of the United Nations War Crimes Commission of 1943–1948." *International Community Law Review* 15, 203–223.

Plesch, Dan, and Shanti Sattler. 2014. "A New Paradigm of Customary International Criminal Law: The UN War Crimes Commission of 1943–1948 and Its Associated Courts and Tribunals." *Criminal Law Forum* 25: 17–43.

Schabas, William, Carsten Stahn, Joseph Powderly, Dan Pleschand, and Shanti Sattler. 2014. "The United Nations War Crimes Commission and the Origins of International Criminal Justice." *Criminal Law Forum* 25 (1–2): 1–7.

UN World Drug Report

The UN Office on Drugs and Crime (UNODC) annually publishes the UN World Drug Report to articulate a constant analysis of the effects of drugs on populations around the world and to make necessary recommendations for governmental remedies. As a publication of the United Nations, and not one that is attributed disproportionately to any specific member nation, the World Drug Report is able to appropriately examine global drug trends without biased emphasis on any one geographic region. A challenge of the World Drug Report, however, is that the illicit nature of drug production, trafficking, sales, and usage create an environment that is not conducive for accurate data collection. As a result, there is some dispute regarding its effectiveness (Reuter and Greenfield 2001).

HISTORY

The UNODC published the first World Drug Report in 1997, the same year the United Nations established the UNODC. Originally named the Office for Drug Control and Crime Prevention, the UNODC combined the UN International Drug Control Program and the UN Crime Prevention and Criminal Justice Division. UN secretary-general Kofi Annan stated in the first World Drug Report that the proliferation of worldwide drug usage in the latter half of the 20th century required a coordinated response, and that the 1997 report was the first attempt at such a measure:

> Illicit drugs destroy innumerable individual lives and undermine our societies. Confronting the illicit trade in drugs and its effects remains a major challenge for the international community. Although the consumption of drugs has been a fact of life for centuries, addiction has mushroomed over the last five decades. It now demands a determined and international response. (UNODC 1997)

USAGE

Data compiled within the report is widely cited in articles and reports by media outlets, political think tanks, universities, nonprofit groups, and government agencies. Despite the United Nations' intention to utilize the data to support its own recommendations, secondary analysis of the data can be critical to contextualizing or informing other projects undertaken by external researchers (Irvine et al. 2011). While the recommendations of the World Drug Report are not binding for governments, many do utilize the recommendations to inform their own national policies to prevent additional drug use (Li et al. 2010).

STRUCTURE

The content and format of the report changes annually, depending on the theme adopted by the UN Office on Drugs and Crime, but it does consistently follow a loose structure that includes nine different components: preface, explanatory notes, executive summary, statistics, trend analyses, summary, conclusion, annex, and glossary. The preface serves as an introductory insight into the rationale and theme behind configuring the report in the way it is written. It typically includes messages from the UN secretary-general and the executive director of the UN Office of Drugs and Crime. The explanatory notes contain explanations for the abbreviations, symbols, and semantic ambiguities within the report. The executive summary is a brief synopsis of the report's content and serves as a way to quickly inform the reader; it is typically only 4–6 pages of text.

The statistics section of the report is where most of the data collected is communicated in charts and graphs relating to various topic areas, usually accompanied by a textual explanation. The trend analyses is a section dedicated to synthesizing the material from the statistics section into topical trends that are more easily digestible for the reader. The conclusion serves as a capstone to discuss the implications and relevance of the content from the report. The annex is similar to the appendix of a book, where supporting documentation is published. The glossary attempts to further define any uncommon words or new ideas that were introduced in the report.

LIMITATIONS

The data showcased in the UN World Drug Report is submitted by member states of the United Nations via its Annual Reports Questionnaire. This reliance on member state participation creates limitations in the research because there is not 100 percent participation by members in completing the Annual Reports Questionnaire, nor is the data provided fully reliable. A member state can manipulate or omit certain pieces of data that it does not want to be published by the United Nations. For example, of the 207 questionnaires sent to 192 member states and 15 territories by the United Nations in 2014 for information relating to the 2015 World Drug Report, only 36 percent of American nations and 22 percent of African nations had responded with data (UNODC 2015).

Corey B. Miles

See also: International Drug Trafficking; UN Office on Drugs and Crime

Further Reading

Irvine, Rodney J., Chris Kostakis, Peter D. Felgate, Emily J. Jaehne, Chang Chen, and Jason M. White. 2011. "Population Drug Use in Australia: A Wastewater Analysis." *Forensic Science International* 210 (1–3): 69–73.

Li, Jianhua, Toan H. Ha, Cunmin Zhang, and Hongjie Liu. 2010. "The Chinese Government's Response to Drug Use and HIV/AIDS: A Review of Policies and Programs." *Harm Reduction Journal* 7 (1): 4. https://harmreductionjournal.biomedcentral.com/articles/10.1186/1477-7517-7-4.

Reuter, Peter, and Victoria Greenfield. 2001. "Measuring Global Drug Markets." *World Economics* 2 (4): 159–173.

United Nations Office on Drug and Crime (UNODC). 1997. "World Drug Report 1997." United Nations. Accessed January 21, 2019. http://www.unodc.org/unodc/en/data-and-analysis/WDR-1997.html.

United Nations Office on Drug and Crime (UNODC). 2015. "World Drug Report 2015." United Nations. Accessed January 21, 2019. https://www.unodc.org/wdr2015.

United Nations Office on Drug and Crime (UNODC). 2018. "World Drug Report 2018." United Nations. Accessed January 21, 2019. https://www.unodc.org/wdr2018.

U.S. Currency and Foreign Transactions Reporting Act

The U.S. Currency and Foreign Transaction Reporting Act, also referred to as the Bank Secrecy Act (BSA), is an anti–money laundering law issued by the U.S. government in 1970. The law requires individuals, banks, and other financial institutions to identify persons conducting suspicious transactions, to keep a proper record of these transactions, and to file currency reports with the U.S. Department of the Treasury. It also requires domestic financial institutions to file a report on single or multiple transactions of funds in currency of $10,000 or more in a single day. Adopted to assist the U.S. government in preventing criminals from hiding their illicit gains, this law has been used in criminal, tax, and regulatory investigations and proceedings. The BSA, with its later amendments, imposes penalties on financial institutions for failing to properly comply with its regulations.

BACKGROUND

An intention to create the BSA was announced during an investigative hearing of the House Committee on Banking and Currency in 1968. It was highlighted how the U.S. financial system was misused by organized crime to hide the sources of profits from illegal activities and how U.S. residents used secret foreign bank accounts in violation of domestic law. The BSA was designed to help U.S. Treasury agencies, such as the Financial Crimes Enforcement Network (FinCEN), in detecting money laundering and fraud by tracing the movement of currency and other monetary instruments deposited in financial institutions. Through its reporting requirements, the BSA aims at attacking a money laundering operation at its earlier stage (the placement of illicit proceeds into a banking system) and creating a paper trail for any suspicious financial transaction. The initial BSA, however, did not make money laundering a federal crime, and in the first decade of its existence, the act's rules were not clearly defined. The act was often met with resistance from some financial institutions on the grounds of its constitutionality and confusion over the responsibility for filing reports. As a result, very few prosecutions were made during the 1970s, and compliance levels were low (Grosse 2001; Meltzer 1991).

Until the mid-1980s, money launderers were able to circumvent the BSA regulations by making multiple deposits of less than $10,000 (for example, of $9,900) by one customer in one or several banks to avoid reporting requirements ("structuring"). Money launderers also actively resorted to "smurfing," hiring people to deposit less than $10,000 over short periods of time in multiple banks. These practices led to the adoption of a new legislation in 1986, the Money Laundering

Control Act, as part of the Anti-Drug Abuse Act. The new legislation made money laundering—including related activities such as structuring—a criminal offense; toughened penalties for failing to comply with the BSA; and allowed U.S. law enforcement agencies to prosecute such crimes.

REPORTING REQUIREMENTS

There are several types of reports that are required to be filed by financial institutions and individuals under the BSA. First, a Currency Transaction Report (CTR) must be filed when a domestic currency transaction involves $10,000 or more. Second, institutions and individuals must file a Currency and Monetary Instrument Report (CMIR) with the U.S. Customs Service when they move $10,000 or more in currency or monetary instruments into or out of the United States. Third, individuals must file Reports of Foreign Bank and Financial Accounts (FBARs) annually if they have overseas financial accounts of $5,000 or more. In addition, a 1996 regulation introduced a Suspicious Activity Report (SAR) to be used by all banks in the United States. A bank is required to file a SAR whenever it detects a possible money laundering activity or a violation of the BSA requirements.

Legal businesses are often used to hide funds of illicit origin or funds aimed at financing illegal activity. Therefore, regulators have placed special emphasis on the "know your customer" policy, the backbone of the BSA. Financial institutions are required to have standardized programs of customer identity verification and investigation of business entities. Within the framework of the "know your customer" principle, and based on a bank's reasonable judgment, banks may exempt certain types of customers from reporting requirements. Such exemptions include transactions between financial institutions and transactions related to established retail and cash businesses operated by a known customer.

Yulia Vorobyeva

See also: Financial Action Task Force; Financial Crimes Enforcement Network; Money Laundering; U.S. International Money Laundering Abatement and Anti-Terrorist Financing Act; U.S. Money Laundering Control Act of 1986

Further Reading

Grosse, Robert E. 2001. *Drugs and Money: Laundering Latin America's Cocaine Dollars.* Westport, CT: Praeger.

Meltzer, Peter. 1991. "Keeping Drug Money from Reaching the Wash Cycle: A Guide to the Bank Secrecy Act." *Banking Law Journal* 108: 230–255.

U.S. Government. 1970. Public Law 91-508, October 26. Accessed on June 6, 2018. https://www.gpo.gov/fdsys/pkg/STATUTE-84/pdf/STATUTE-84-Pg1114-2.pdf.

U.S. Department of the Treasury. n.d.-a "Bank Secrecy Act Forms and Filing Requirements." Financial Crimes Enforcement Network (FinCEN). Accessed on June 6, 2018. https://www.fincen.gov/resources/filing-information.

U.S. Department of the Treasury. n.d.-b "Bank Secrecy Act (BSA)." Office of the Comptroller of the Currency. Accessed on June 6, 2018. https://www.occ.treas.gov/topics/compliance-bsa/bsa/index-bsa.html.

U.S. International Money Laundering Abatement and Anti-Terrorist Financing Act

The U.S. International Money Laundering Abatement and Anti-Terrorist Financing Act is one of the most significant anti–money laundering legislations since the Bank Secrecy Act (BSA). It is the Title III of the USA PATRIOT Act passed by Congress on October 26, 2001, in response to the September 11, 2001, terrorist attacks. The act is aimed at preventing terrorists and other illegal actors from using U.S. financial institutions to obtain funds from or to finance terrorism and other illegal activities. It introduced sweeping measures to prevent, detect, and prosecute terrorism and international money laundering.

BACKGROUND

Prior to the 9/11 attacks, several counterterrorism financial regulations already existed in the United States, and many provisions that would become part of the PATRIOT Act were in their draft form. Still, terrorist financing was not a priority in policy-making circles, and there was little interagency cooperation on this matter. The money laundering regulations in place primarily focused on drug trafficking and large-scale financial fraud. September 11, however, put a sense of urgency on the issue of terrorist financing by shedding light on how terrorists used U.S. financial institutions to sponsor their activities. Investigations into the 9/11 attacks revealed that the hijackers financed their plot mainly by moving funds from abroad into U.S. accounts through wire transfers and deposits of cash or traveler's checks. It also came to light that terrorist groups diverted funds from charity donations or used entirely corrupt charity organizations to finance their activities (Roth, Greenberg, and Wille 2004).

Although the hijackers did not use sophisticated money laundering schemes, the existing controls could not have detected their activity prior to the attacks (Roth, Greenberg, and Wille, 2004). Within two weeks after the 9/11 attacks, the U.S. government made an unprecedented use of a previously little-known policy of the terrorist designations and asset freezes. Subsequently, the George W. Bush administration focused its attention on gathering financial information to better understand terrorist networks (Eckert 2007). These efforts culminated in the new legislation, Title III of the PATRIOT Act, which tightened domestic anti–money laundering controls and expanded the jurisdiction of the secretary of the treasury to regulate financial activities involving foreign jurisdictions.

SCOPE

The act is far-reaching in scope and contains over 40 substantial provisions that cover a broad range of financial activities and institutions. Among new regulatory measures, the act amends the BSA by expanding its requirements to all financial institutions, including securities brokers and dealers; money transmitters; travel agencies; credit card operators; insurance companies; currency exchangers; dealers in precious metals, stones, and jewels; and casinos and gambling establishments.

Through this provision, the act introduced the first attempt by U.S. legislators to regulate informal money-transfer systems, such as *hawala*, popular among Middle Eastern, African, and South Asian migrants.

The act also increases the powers of the Department of the Treasury to impose measures against noncooperating foreign financial institutions for failure to take steps to stop money laundering and terrorist financing. The act permits forfeiture of proceeds of crime transferred or invested in the United States, even if the crime occurred on foreign soil. In addition, it prohibits U.S. financial institutions from engaging in business with foreign "shell banks" and requires them to ensure that foreign correspondent accounts are not used indirectly by "shell banks."

The act strengthens customer identification procedures by requiring financial institutions to identify and verify the identity of new customers. The customer identification programs allow for creation of paper trails that may assist law enforcement officials in investigations of money laundering and terrorist financing. Finally, the act facilitates the sharing of information between the government and financial institutions and between financial institutions regarding possible terrorist or money laundering activity.

Yulia Vorobyeva

See also: Financial Action Task Force; International Convention for the Suppression of the Financing of Terrorism; Money Laundering; Terrorism, International; U.S. Currency and Foreign Transactions Reporting Act; U.S. Money Laundering Control Act of 1986

Further Reading

Baldwin, Fletcher, Jr. 2003. "Money Laundering Countermeasures with Primary Focus upon Terrorism and the USA Patriot Act 2001." *Journal of Money Laundering Control* 6 (2): 105–136.

Eckert, Sue. 2007. "The US Regulatory Approach to Terrorist Financing." In *Countering the Financing of Terrorism*, edited by Thomas Biersteker and Sue Eckert, 209–233. New York: Routledge.

Murphy, Maureen. 2001. "International Money Laundering Abatement and Anti-Terrorist Financing Act of 2001, Title III of P.L. 107-56." *Congressional Research Service*, Library of Congress, December 4. Accessed on June 7, 2018. https://www.epic.org/privacy/financial/RL31208.pdf.

Roth, J., D. Greenberg, and S. Wille. 2004. *Monograph on Terrorist Financing (Staff Report to the Commission)*. National Commission on Terrorist Attacks upon the United States. Accessed on June 9, 2018. https://govinfo.library.unt.edu/911/staff_statements/911_TerrFin_Monograph.pdf.

U.S. Department of the Treasury. "USA PATRIOT Act." Financial Crimes Enforcement Network (FinCEN). Accessed on June 10, 2018. https://www.fincen.gov/resources/statutes-regulations/usa-patriot-act.

U.S. Money Laundering Control Act of 1986

The U.S. Money Laundering Control Act of 1986 is the federal law that made money laundering a crime in the United States. Money laundering refers to efforts to make funds gained illegally, such as via embezzlement, terrorism, and drug trafficking, appear to have been acquired by legal means. Suspected violations are often investigated by the U.S. Department of Treasury and prosecuted under U.S. Code: Title 18, Sections 1956 and 1957. In addition to fines and imprisonment, the act allows the possibility of asset forfeiture of anything acquired with illicit gains. The law also increased sanctions for violation of the related Bank Secrecy Act (BSA) of 1970, which requires banks to report transactions of certain amounts.

Money laundering often begins with identifying financial institutions over which large sums of money are structured, that is, broken into smaller amounts to evade bank reporting requirements. The funds are then moved between financial institutions to make them difficult to trace over time. These now “clean” funds are then reintroduced into the mainstream economy as if they were legitimate.

Under 18 U.S. Code § 1956, it explains that anyone who knowingly engages in activities to disguise in whole or in part money’s unlawful source, ownership, or control has committed money laundering. Further, the section addresses any related activities to avoid required reporting laws. The second part of Section 1956 addresses efforts to move the funds in or outside of the United States in support of lawful activity and to avoid required reporting. The sanctions for any of these actions are a fine of up to a half million dollars or twice the amount of the transaction funds involved and/or imprisonment for up to 20 years.

Section 1956 also authorizes U.S. authorities to pursue foreign agents and institutions in money laundering activities. This is according to Federal Rules of Civil Procedure with consideration of the laws in the foreign country. A foreign person would be of interest for participating in an illicit financial transaction that involves the United States in whole or in part, if the person converts for personal use property to which the United States has ownership or a forfeiture interest. The law also applies if, instead of a person, the offending party is a financial institution with an account at a financial entity in the United States.

Regarding forfeiture, Section 1956 allows a judge to issue a restraining order pretrial to access related property in the United States for legal action. The court may appoint a federal receiver to seize all of a defendant’s assets for a civil judgment or civil forfeiture per Section 981 (of assets foreign or domestic traceable to a list of offenses). In contrast, Section 1957 forfeitures are for criminal judgments per Section 982, which involves criminal forfeiture for the imposition of a sanction in violation of Sections 1956, 1957 or 1960. The forfeiture may also be for restitution purposes. The federal receiver, as an officer of the court, has powers similar to that of a federal prosecutor to submit information requests to affect the forfeiture to foreign countries per agreements with those countries and to the Financial Crimes Enforcement Network of the U.S. Department of Treasury. Agreements with foreign countries may include an exchange of law enforcement assistance.

The other important section, 18 U.S. Code § 1957, addresses monetary transactions in property valued at over $10,000 connected to illicit activities. Prosecution does not require proving knowledge of the illicit activities behind the property involved. The criminal activities, however, must occur in the United States or its maritime areas or territories. The law also applies to instances outside of the United States when the defendant is a United States person. A “United States person,” per 18 U.S. Code § 3077, refers to U.S. citizens, a permanent resident of the United States, a person within the United States, and U.S. government employees or contractors regardless of country of origin. The identity also includes a company with a majority of U.S. persons or a corporation set up under U.S. laws. Section 1957 crimes are investigated by the U.S. Department of Justice (DOJ), Department of the Treasury, Department of Homeland Security (DHS), or the United States Postal Service, depending on which has jurisdiction for the alleged offenses. The sanction for persons convicted of a Section 1957 offense could be imprisonment of up to 10 years or a fine of up to twice the value of the property involved.

Camille Gibson

See also: Counterfeit Goods and Money; Money Laundering; U.S. International Money Laundering Abatement and Anti-Terrorist Financing Act

Further Reading

Madinger, John. 2012. *Money Laundering: A Guide for Criminal Investigat*ors. 3rd ed. Boca Raton, FL: CRC Press.

Sullivan, Kevin. 2015. *Anti-Money Laundering in a Nutshell: Awareness and Compliance for Financial Personnel and Business.* New York: Apress/Springer.

U.S. Code. n.d. Title 18 Part I Crimes and Part II Criminal Procedure.

Weismann, Miriam F. 2015. *Money Laundering: Legislation, Regulation and Enforcement.* Chicago: American Bar Association.

U.S. Trafficking Victims Protection Act

The Trafficking Victims Protection Act of 2000 (TVPA) was passed by the U.S. Congress and signed by President Bill Clinton in 2000. The TVPA was one of three divisions of the Victims of Trafficking and Violence Protection Act of 2000 (Public Law No: 106-386). The second division was the Violence against Women Act of 2000, and the third division contained miscellaneous provisions.

The TVPA provides the legislative foundation to combat human trafficking at the federal level. It was the United States' response to the UN Protocol to Prevent, Suppress and Punish Trafficking in Persons, Especially Women and Children (the Trafficking Protocol), in which ratifying countries (including the United States) agreed to prosecute traffickers, protect victims and survivors of trafficking, and cooperate on a global level to eliminate human trafficking. With the TVPA, the United States fulfilled several obligations under the Trafficking Protocol, including the criminalization of human trafficking.

The primary goals of TVPA were to combat trafficking in persons, specifically targeting the illicit sex trade, slavery, and involuntary servitude, as well as to reauthorize certain federal programs to prevent violence against women. TVPA was both a reactive and proactive response to trafficking that established several methods to prosecute traffickers, prevent human trafficking, and protect victims and survivors of trafficking (Polaris Project 2017). Additionally, TVPA created measures to monitor global trafficking and assess individual country reports. The TVPA was reauthorized in 2003, 2005, 2008, and 2013 through Trafficking Victims Protection Reauthorization Acts (TVPRA).

FORMS OF TRAFFICKING

TVPA was written in response to concerns that existing criminal law was ineffective and insufficient at protecting survivors and prosecuting traffickers and was the first comprehensive federal law to address trafficking in persons (Albonetti 2014). TVPA focused efforts on two forms of trafficking: sex trafficking and labor trafficking. Sex and labor trafficking are the "recruitment, harboring, transportation, provision, obtaining, patronizing, or soliciting of a person for the purposes of a commercial sex act, labor or services, in which the act is induced by force, fraud, or coercion, or in which the person induced to perform such an act has not attained 18 years of age" (22 USC § 7102). Both emphasize the individual is held against his or her will in involuntary servitude, often with debt bondage and coercion, but for different purposes of exploitation.

GOALS

Prevention

TVPA approached prevention in two ways: to prevent sex trafficking from occurring and to prevent further trafficking of a person that was previously trafficked. Prevention services largely come in the form of outreach, education, training, and hotline use. The act created penalties against buyers and traffickers to strengthen prevention efforts such as mandating sex offenses be treated as federal offenses.

TVPA provides funding for the development of 42 interagency state task forces to educate communities and provide awareness. The act also works to provide a federal-level interagency task force, the Interagency Task Force to Monitor and Combat Trafficking in Persons, which publishes a trafficking in persons report each year (Nichols 2016). Additionally, the act established the Office to Monitor and Combat Trafficking in Persons, which is required to publish a Trafficking in Persons (TIP) report each year. This report allows for global comparison to describe and rank the efforts of countries to combat human trafficking (Polaris Project Current Federal Laws 2017). The United States has the ability to provide assistance to foreign countries, through nongovernmental and multilateral organizations, to eliminate trafficking. If a country fails to meet the minimum standards agreed upon, actions can be taken toward them, such as withholding of nonhumanitarian and non-trade-related assistance (H.R. 3244). Lastly, prevention efforts have focused on at-risk groups of sex trafficking, such as American Indian and Alaskan Native populations (Nichols 2016).

Protection

The TVPA aims to provide protection and assistance to survivors of trafficking through funding for aftercare services and temporary immigration status to protect survivors who hold undocumented status rather than punishing them. TVPA recognizes that many undocumented immigrants may need extra protections and services. The act established the T visa, which allows victims and survivors to become temporary U.S. residents and the opportunity to become permanent citizens after three years (Polaris Project Current Federal Laws 2017). The goal is to prevent deportation so survivors can be witnesses for prosecution (Nichols 2016). Lastly, the act mandates that restitution be paid to survivors.

Prosecution

The third "prong" to TVPA is prosecution. Most prosecutions occur at the federal rather than the state level, if there is "a strong case with sufficient evidence of force, fraud, or coercion, or if the case involves a minor, and if there is a cooperating victim" (Nichols 2016, 180). TVPA helped adopt victim-centered techniques to minimize revictimizing experiences by the courts, such as the use of closed-circuit television for testimony.

The Trafficking Victims Protection Act of 2000 provides the tools to combat trafficking in persons both worldwide and domestically. Currently, the TVPA is considered one of the most effective and comprehensive systems to monitor human trafficking globally.

REAUTHORIZATIONS

The TVPA was reauthorized in 2003, 2005, 2008, and 2013. Each reauthorization provided additional protections and services for victims, tools for prosecution, and expanded sanctions. The first reauthorization in 2003 established the right for victims of trafficking to sue their traffickers, added human trafficking to the list of crimes that can be charged under the Racketeer Influenced and Corrupt Organizations Act (RICO), and included additional provisions to protect victims from deportation.

In 2005, the TVPRA reauthorization expanded financial resources, both nationally and internationally, to continue to combat trafficking and provide services to victims. The TVPRA of 2005 included specific provisions designed to fight sex tourism, directed money to provide treatment of trafficking victims abroad, and strengthened regulations over government contracts to ensure products are not made by individuals or organizations that promote or engage in human trafficking. The TVPRA of 2008 primarily focused on new prevention strategies and enhanced criminal sanctions. Some of the more notable parts of the 2008 reauthorization are the systems that were put in place to gather and report human trafficking data, the expanded protections available with the T visa, and expanded definitions of various types of trafficking to make prosecution easier.

The 2013 reauthorization was passed as an amendment to the Violence against Women Act. This reauthorization placed an emphasis on strengthening programs to ensure that U.S. citizens do not purchase products made by victims of human trafficking, strengthening policy to prevent child marriage, and providing resources for areas where people are particularly susceptible to being trafficked (Nichols 2016; Polaris Project 2017).

In January 2019, President Trump signed the Trafficking Victims Protection Reauthorization Act of 2017 (the year the act technically expired), becoming Public Law No: 115–427.

Shanell Sanchez

See also: Human Trafficking; Racketeer Influenced and Corrupt Organizations Act (RICO); T Visa; UN Protocol to Prevent, Suppress, and Punish Trafficking in Persons, Especially Women and Children

Further Reading

Albonetti, Celesta. 2014. "Changes in Federal Sentencing for Forced Labor Trafficking and for Sex Trafficking: A Ten Year Assessment." *Crime, Law and Social Change* 61 (2): 179–204.

Nichols, Andrea. 2016. *Sex Trafficking in the United States: Theory, Research, Policy, and Practice.* New York: Colombia University Press.

Polaris Project. 2017. "Polaris Project Current Federal Laws." Accessed January 21, 2019. https://polarisproject.org/current-federal-laws.

Trafficking Victims Violence Protection Act of 2000 (TVPA), Pub. L. 106-386, Statues at Large, 114 (2000), Section 103, 8a and 8b.

V

van Dijk, Jan (1947–)

Criminology and criminal justice mainly focus on offenders, the perpetrators of crime, while frequently neglecting its targets, the crime victims. Jan van Dijk has orchestrated detailed research on victims and has also played a leading role in developing programs of victim assistance. During the 1980s and 1990s, he helped to determine policies of the Dutch government on crime prevention, victim assistance, organized crime, and drug control. Four of his major contributions include the International Crime Victimization Survey (ICVS), his lifetime work on victim assistance, his work at the United Nations on organized crime and human trafficking, and his recent, groundbreaking work on the international crime drop.

Jan van Dijk is emeritus professor of victimology at the International Victimology Institute of the University of Tilburg, the Netherlands, which he helped found. He obtained a law degree from Leiden University in 1970 and a PhD in criminology from the University of Nijmegen in 1977. He was also awarded an honorary doctorate from the Manonmaniam Sundaranar University, Tirunelveli, India. Apart from numerous books and articles in literary magazines and the popular press, he has authored more than 200 articles on crime and criminal justice in academic journals.

In 1987, van Dijk started the ICVS with Patricia Mayhew and Martin Killias. Under his leadership, five waves of data have been collected (1989, 1992, 1995, 2000, and 2005) covering over 80 countries. The ICVS is unsurpassed as a source of cross-cultural comparative data on victimization, and the information it provides not only brings attention to the neglected role of victims in the criminal justice system but also assists governments in making provisions to assist victims. In 2012, van Dijk received the Stockholm Prize in Criminology for his enduring work on the International Crime Victims Survey.

Van Dijk cofounded the National Organization of Victim Assistance in the Netherlands, which he also chaired. He was president of the World Society of Victimology (1997–2000) and president of the Ninth International World Symposium on Victimology (1997). In his book with Rianne Letschert, *New Faces of Criminal Victimhood* (2014), he articulated the need for global action against the increasing number of victims of old and new forms of transnational and international crimes, specifically to include legal aid for victims.

He extended his advocacy for victims in 1998 when he became Officer-in-Charge of the United Nations Centre for International Crime Prevention in Vienna. He launched the UN Global Program against Human Trafficking, and he played a major role in developing the 2000 Palermo Protocol to Prevent, Suppress and Punish Trafficking in Persons, Especially Women and Children. To date, a large majority of countries have ratified the instrument, and many have incorporated it into their domestic legislation. Van Dijk's book *The World of Crime* (2007) strongly emphasizes that rampant crime hampers sustainable development, and due to his influence, the United Nations has adopted Sustainable Development Goal 16, SDG16, on gender equality to eliminate all forms of exploitation, human trafficking, and modern slavery.

Jan van Dijk has played a major role in expanding U.S.-centric explanations for the crime drop by showing in his 2012 book with Tseloni and Farrell, *The International Crime Drop: New Directions in Research*, that the crime drop was not confined to the United States but was also evident from police statistics and victimization surveys undertaken in many other developed countries. The book shows that many explanations for the crime drop favored by U.S. authors (such as COMPSTAT policing, the heavy use of imprisonment, and changes in demography) could not explain crime drops in other countries. It goes on to promote the "security hypothesis" that holds that crime has fallen as a result of an avalanche of security measures introduced in these countries.

Mangai Natarajan

See also: Organized Crime; UN Protocol to Prevent, Suppress, and Punish Trafficking in Persons, Especially Women and Children; UN Sustainable Development Goals

Further Reading

Letschert, R., and J. J. M. van Dijk. 2011. *The New Faces of Victimhood.* London: Springer.

van Dijk, J. J. M. 2007. *The World of Crime: Breaking the Silence on Issues of Security, Justice and Development.* Thousand Oaks, CA: Sage Publications.

van Dijk, J. J. M, A. Tseloni, and G. Farrell. 2012. *The International Crime Drop: New Directions in Research.* Basingstoke, UK: Palgrave Macmillan.

van Dijk, J. J. M., and P. G. M. van der Heijden. 2016. *Research Brief: Multiple Systems Estimation for Estimating the Number of Victims of Human Trafficking across the World.* Vienna: UNODC.

Vishing

Vishing refers to an identity theft scam that uses a phone call to convince victims to give up personal information. It is also called *voice phishing* because it shares characteristics with *phishing*, which is a form of identity theft that relies on fraudulent e-mail or Web sites to obtain users' personal information. Vishing scams over mobile phones are expected to increase in number and sophistication as consumers get wiser about e-mail phishing and fake Web sites (Cook 2018). Although vishing scams typically target individuals, the victims can also be banks and other businesses whose employees are tricked into providing the scammer with the personal information of customers or valuable data about the business itself.

TECHNIQUES USED

Vishing attempts may be placed by a real human or be in the form of voice-to-text synthesizers using a recorded message. Using autogenerated phone numbers or phone information the scammer bought on the dark web, the criminal places calls and tries to get the victim to give up a personal identification number (PIN), Social Security number, bank account number, credit card security code, password, or other personal identifiers (Cook 2018). As the calling number is often from the victim's own area code or shows in the caller ID as a recognizable or reasonable name or business, the victim's guard is lowered. The provided information is then used by the criminal to engage in an identity crime or to steal money from the victim's financial account.

Common types of vishing include calls alerting the victim to suspicious activity on a bank account, overdue or unpaid taxes, offers from companies the victim recognizes or does business with, prize or contest winnings, or computer tech support asking to remotely access a personal computer to fix a problem. Those tactics are worrisomely effective, but Cook (2018) also describes a strategy called the "no hang up" that can entrap even careful and suspicious victims. Using this approach, the scammer calls the victim using any of the standard methods, but then the scammer advises the victim to call his or her bank, or other business or government agency being impersonated, to be assured that the call is legitimate. When the victim thinks the call has ended, the criminal instead stays on the line and produces a fake dial tone to indicate a disconnection. The victim then calls the given number, and instead of speaking with the intended business or agency, he or she is talking to another scammer.

COUNTERMEASURES

In July 2018, the U.S. Justice Department announced it had broken up a large-scale multinational vishing operation. Between 2012 and 2016, more than 15,000 victims in the United States lost hundreds of millions of dollars to the scam, and more than 50,000 people had their personal information misused (Hauser 2018). During the fraudulent calls, a person posing as an IRS or immigration official threatened the victim with arrest, deportation, or other penalties if the victim's debts were not immediately paid. The 21 defendants, who were of Indian origin living in the United States, coordinated with call centers in India. Sentences ranging from probation to 20 years in prison were handed down by a federal judge in Houston, who also ordered about $8.9 million to those victims who could be identified.

Unfortunately, victims cannon count on law enforcement officials to protect them from vishing scams. Nothing can be done to protect oneself against successful vishing attacks against businesses holding private information. However, there are steps individuals can take to reduce the likelihood of falling prey to scams. Commonly noted ones include not answering calls from unknown numbers, never giving personal information over the phone, never paying fees for prizes or rewards, and using (but not completely trusting) caller ID. Additional suggestions and information on reporting suspected fraud are provided by the Federal Trade Commission (n.d.).

Philip L. Reichel

See also: Cyberattack; Dark Web/Deep Web; Identity-Related Crimes; Phishing

Further Reading

Cook, Sam. 2018. "What Is Vishing (with Example Scams) and How to Recognize and Avoid It." *Comparitech.* Last updated July 24, 2018. Accessed January 21, 2019. https://www.comparitech.com/blog/information-security/what-is-vishing-how-to-avoid.

Federal Trade Commission (FTC). n.d. "Identity Theft." Consumer Information. Accessed October 12, 2018. https://www.consumer.ftc.gov/topics/identity-theft.

Hauser, Christine. 2018. "U.S. Breaks Up Vast I.R.S. Phone Scam." *New York Times*, July 23. Accessed January 21, 2019. https://www.nytimes.com/2018/07/23/business/irs-phone-scams-jeff-sessions.html.

W

War Crimes

The term *war crimes* can include many different types of crimes that occur during war or armed conflict. The conflict can be both of an international nature or non-international in character, such as a civil war. In the strictest sense, war crimes are violations of treaties or international customary law that relate to the manner in which war is carried out and the criminalization of certain activities that go beyond the authorized license to engage in violent or belligerent acts toward enemy combatants. War crimes also consist of acts that are directed at harming or killing civilians or attacking and destroying civilian objects.

Some of the better-known treaties that relate to war crimes include The Hague Conventions of 1899 and 1907, both of which deal with respecting the laws and customs of war. Following World War II, the Geneva Conventions of 1949 were adopted. As relates to grave breaches (serious crimes), the third and fourth conventions are the most relevant. For example, Geneva Convention III serves to protect prisoners of war, and Geneva Convention IV relates to the protection of civilian persons in times of war. Consequently, these "protected persons" cannot be assaulted, tortured, murdered, raped, or mishandled.

There are other crimes outside of the Geneva Conventions, which are often brought under the overall category of war crimes. These are crimes against humanity and genocide. The elements of these offenses do not require that they be perpetrated within the context of war, but for crimes against humanity, the acts must be to such a degree as to be considered widespread and systematic and must be directed toward civilian populations.

Specific offenses include murder, extermination, enslavement, forced deportation, torture, rape, and sexual slavery. There is a requirement to prove that the prohibited conduct included the multiple commission of prohibited acts, and each of the crimes have specific elements of the offense that must be proved. For example, the crime of torture requires not only the intentional infliction of severe pain or suffering, but under the Convention against Torture, for example, the act must be done for the purpose of obtaining a confession, intimidation, or punishment.

Genocide involves acts that are specifically intended to destroy a national, ethnical, racial, or political group. This crime is typically carried out by committing homicide, but it can include other means, such as imposing methods to prevent births within the group or forcibly transferring children of one group to another. The crime does not require that the entire group be destroyed.

WAR CRIMES INVESTIGATIONS

Before any accused war criminal can be brought to court, there must be a criminal investigation. After World War II (1939–1945), war crimes investigations were largely carried out by legal officers, intelligence agents, and ordinary soldiers. No professional criminal investigation unit was brought in to undertake investigations despite repeated requests for agencies like Scotland Yard (United Kingdom) or the Federal Bureau of Investigation (FBI) to do so.

Contemporary war crimes investigations are different, however, and the difficult task is to prove the individual criminal responsibility of persons alleged to have committed war crimes. This begins with what is known as the *crime base investigation*, which means investigating the killers and rapists on the ground who physically perpetrated the acts. The work gets even more complicated as war crimes investigators attempt to work their way up to senior-level political, military, intelligence, and security personnel. Consequently, multidisciplinary investigation teams are led by a senior criminal investigations officer and include homicide detectives, sex crimes investigators, legal officers, anthropologists, and crime scene officers.

There are always two main questions for any prosecution, whether national or international, and those relate to venue and jurisdiction. Venue mostly relates to the place where the case may be heard, such as a military court martial, a civilian court, or an international tribunal. Jurisdiction is related to the power of the court over the crimes and power over the accused. Many national governments have passed legislation that incorporates international war crimes laws into domestic law to enable a flexible scheme toward war crimes prosecution. For example, the United States has codified The Hague Conventions and the Geneva Conventions into its criminal laws, and this accordingly covers circumstances under which the person committing the war crime or is the victim of the war crime is a member of the U.S. armed forces or a citizen of the United States.

DEFENSES

Many of the standard defenses in criminal trials are available to those who stand accused on charges of war crimes, both at the national and international levels. At the International Criminal Court (ICC), for example, an accused can successfully plead insanity, duress, self-defense, or mistake of fact. The defense of superior orders, however, is very limited. This was made clear during the post–World War II trials. Orders given by superiors that are "manifestly" unlawful, such as murdering prisoners of war or sexually assaulting civilians, must be refused.

It is also important to point out that all deaths of civilians during armed conflict are not necessarily criminal. The Geneva Conventions of 1949 and other aspects of customary international law recognize the conception of "collateral damage." This means it is not a crime to kill civilians—even intentionally—as long as the primary objective of the attack was a legitimate military target and the civilian deaths were not disproportional.

John R. Cencich

See also: Genocide; Humanitarian Law; International Criminal Court; International Criminal Tribunal for Rwanda; International Criminal Tribunal for the Former Yugoslavia (ICTY); International Military Tribunal at Nuremberg; International Military Tribunal for the Far East; UN War Crimes Commission; War Criminals

Further Reading

Cencich, John. 2013. *The Devil's Garden: A War Crimes Investigator's Story.* Washington, D.C.: Potomac Books.

Internal Committee of the Red Cross. 2007. *The Geneva Conventions of August 12, 1949.* Geneva, Switzerland: ICRC.

Meron, Theodor. 1999. *War Crimes Law Comes of Age: Essays.* Oxford: Clarendon Press.

Rome Statute of the International Criminal Court. 1998. Accessed January 12, 2019. https://www.icc-cpi.int/nr/rdonlyres/ea9aeff7-5752-4f84-be94-0a655eb30e16/0/rome_statute_english.pdf.

Waterlow, Jonathan, and Jacques Schuhmacher. 2018. *War Crimes Trials and Investigations: A Multi-Disciplinary Introduction.* Basingstoke, UK: Palgrave Macmillan.

War Criminals

War criminals are individuals who commit crimes during international or internal armed conflicts as well as perpetrators of crimes against humanity and genocide, even if the latter are not committed in conjunction with a technical or declared armed conflict. War criminals are involved in some of the most serious crimes in the world, including grave breaches of the Geneva Conventions of 1949, crimes against humanity, and genocide. Specific offenses under these categories include, extermination, murder, willful killing, rape, torture, and forced deportations of civilian populations.

HISTORY

Individuals have committed crimes during armed conflicts throughout history, including in ancient Egypt, China, India, and Israel. In relatively modern times, the World War I (1914–1918) and World War II (1939–1045) played an important part in how war criminals are investigated, brought to justice, and prosecuted. The Leipzig war crimes trials of 12 Germans following World War I were seen largely as a failure. Following World War II, 24 of the major German war criminals were tried by the International Military Tribunal at Nuremberg by the allied victors. Charges included war crimes, crimes against humanity, crimes against peace, and instigating a war of aggression.

The decisions resulting from these and related trials set precedent for the conduct of combatants during armed conflict, the jurisdiction to prosecute, and the defenses available to the accused war criminals. Similarly, Tomoyuki Yamashita, the Imperial Japanese Army general during World War II, was convicted by the International Criminal Tribunal for the Far East of war crimes committed by his subordinates, which cemented the legal notion of command responsibility for war crimes.

MOTIVATION

There are varying reasons that attempt to explain why individuals commit war crimes. The answers are as wide as those that relate to crime causation from criminological perspectives. Some offenders claim to simply follow the orders of their superiors. Others had been ordinary criminals or racketeers before the armed conflict and seized the opportunity to exploit the circumstances of war. Ideology, whether national or religious, often serves as the basis of motivation, and some, such as mercenaries, participate in the war and commit crimes both for the money and the thrill of the kill.

Antisocial personality disorders such as sadism and psychopathy sometimes provide the underlying reasons for the commission of atrocity crimes. For example, Irma Grese, a Nazi concentration camp guard, was a true sadist who enjoyed torturing and murdering civilian victims during World War II. William Laws Calley, who was one of the U.S. army officers responsible for the My Lai massacre in South Vietnam (1968), asserted that he was an automaton who could not refuse superior orders, even those that were manifestly unlawful.

FUGITIVES

Some of the more infamous war crimes fugitives were Nazis that fled Germany after the fall of Berlin in 1945. Many known and indicted war criminals fled to South America, mostly Argentina, where there was a level of protection by the government. Adolf Hitler and his right-hand man, Martin Bormann, never made it out of Berlin, but Adolf Eichmann, one of the major organizers of the Holocaust, was captured by Israeli security service agents on the streets of Buenos Aires, Argentina, in 1960. The Mossad agents smuggled him back to Israel, where he was tried, found guilty, and executed. Dr. Josef Mengele, a high-ranking Nazi medical officer that tortured, maimed, and murdered civilians, fled Argentina for other South American countries after Eichmann's arrest and was never captured.

Following the Yugoslav war of the 1990s, the International Criminal Tribunal for the Former Yugoslavia (ICTY) indicted over 150 war criminals, many of whom went on the run. The ICTY had a fugitive task force that was composed of criminal investigators and intelligence officers recruited from national jurisdictions to coordinate the pursuit and capture of individuals charged with heinous crimes, including genocide, extermination, mass murder, torture, and rape. ICTY war crimes investigators also worked closely with INTERPOL in tracking down and arresting war crimes fugitives. Nevertheless, the ICTY relied heavily on national governments to carry out and effect arrests, many of which were undertaken by tier 1 special operations forces, such as the U.S. Navy SEALs, Delta Force, and the British Special Air Service. In 2008, Radovan Karadžić, the "Butcher of Bosnia" was captured. Three years later, both Ratko Mladić and Goran Hadžić, the last two ICTY-indicted war crimes fugitives were arrested and transferred to The Hague, in the Netherlands, which was the seat of the tribunal.

TRIALS OF WAR CRIMINALS

Once in custody, accused war criminals make an initial appearance before the court with jurisdiction over the offense and the accused. The trial could take place in a national civilian court, a military court, or an international tribunal. Generally speaking, the burden is on the prosecutor to prove the guilt of the accused beyond a reasonable doubt. If an accused is found guilty, he can appeal the decision. If found not guilty, the judgment of the court is final in most national jurisdictions, such as the United States. However, some international venues allow the prosecutor to appeal a finding of not guilty, which in the United States is barred by the Fifth Amendment prohibition against double jeopardy.

Notable war criminals include Saddam Hussein, the deposed president of Iraq, who was found guilty and executed under orders of the Iraqi Special Tribunal. Pol Pot (Cambodia), Charles Taylor (Liberia), Augusto Pinochet (Chile), and Slobodan Milošević (former Yugoslavia) are also known for the horrific war crimes committed under their commands.

John R. Cencich

See also: Genocide; Humanitarian Law; International Criminal Court; International Criminal Tribunal for Rwanda; International Criminal Tribunal for the Former Yugoslavia (ICTY); International Military Tribunal at Nuremberg; International Military Tribunal for the Far East; UN War Crimes Commission; War Crimes

Further Reading

Bryant, Michael. 2015. *A World History of War Crimes: From Antiquity to the Present.* London: Bloomsbury Academic.

Cencich, John. 2013. *The Devil's Garden: A War Crimes Investigator's Story.* Washington, D.C.: Potomac Books.

Gourevitch, Philip, and Morris, Errol. 2009. *The Ballad of Abu Ghraib.* London: Penguin Books.

Marrus, Michael. 1997. *The Nuremberg War Crimes Trial, 1945–46: A Documentary History.* New York: Bedford-St. Martin's.

Tanaka, Yuki. 2017. *Hidden Horrors: Japanese War Crimes in World War II (Asian Voices).* 2nd ed. Lanham, MD: Rowman & Littlefield.

Waste Crime

Waste crime is the term identifying the trade and disposal of waste in contravention of national and international laws (INTERPOL 2018). This definition includes a wide spectrum of illegal activities, ranging from the transnational trafficking of waste by organized crime groups to minor operations such as the improper storage or disposal of waste. The key driver of waste crimes lies in the economic profit they generate. Profit can arise from payments for safe disposal of waste that is either dumped or unsafely disposed at a much lower cost. Economic rewards are also generated through the sale of waste declared as secondhand goods when, in fact, the discarded products are not functioning or did not receive a proper treatment. Waste crime operations have increasingly acquired a global dimension, fueled by the constant growth in the amount of waste produced and due to the globalization of the markets. The improper disposal of waste caused by such illegal activities may have severe implications for the environment and human health, besides imposing an economic disadvantage on law-abiding competitors.

Waste crime has become a global concern after the tightening of environmental regulations in the late 1980s. Such regulations led to an upsurge in the costs of treating and disposing of waste in industrialized countries, where existing waste facilities were failing to absorb the rising demand for waste treatment services. On the other hand, waste facilities in developing countries were often able to offer such services at a much lower price, as they have very low technical and health standards to comply with and low labor costs. The differential in waste treatment costs between industrialized and developing countries has been the main incentive leading to the development of a north-south route of waste exports. However, developing countries often do not have the means to treat imported waste in an environmentally sound manner. Consequently, countries decided to regulate the transboundary movements and disposal of waste through some legal mechanisms, such as the Basel, Rotterdam, and Stockholm Conventions, which formally established the rules for international waste trade, and decided to consider some waste exports as illegal.

ACTORS, ROUTES, AND MODUS OPERANDI

Evidence from waste crime cases showed that such illegal operations are perpetuated both by established organized crime groups, who see the opportunity of making large profits, and small private entities with no criminal background. Often, the main actors engaging in waste crime operations are firms who run legitimate businesses, such as those in the import/export business or in the financial services. However, waste crime constitutes an alarming threat when considering the involvement of organized crime. Due to weak enforcement efforts and the lack of statistics and reporting, the shipment of toxic material provides a significant opportunity for money laundering and diversification of criminal proceeds.

Illegal waste flows typically go from relatively rich to poorer nations. Large-scale shipments of hazardous waste produced in Western Europe are mainly headed to West Africa and Eastern Europe, while shipments of waste produced in the United States, Japan, and Australia often have South and Southeast Asia as their final destination (Rucevska et al. 2015).

Differently from other criminal activities, waste crime can take place in the context of a very broad chain of legal operations. Illegal activities can characterize any of the stages of the waste cycle: the initial transfer from waste producers to firms specialized in waste management, transit and storage operations, and the final treatment or disposal of waste. Common modus operandi employed in this type of crime include the falsification of shipping documents to hide the real nature of waste and the forgery of evidence of a waste treatment that in reality never occurred.

EXTENT OF WASTE CRIME

The true dimension of waste crime is unknown. This is a consequence of the complexity of this crime, the scarce development of appropriate recording systems, and its "victimless" nature, which leads to it often going unreported. The few available estimates refer to illegal shipments and indicate that, at the global level, approximately 1.5 million of waste-loaded containers are shipped illegally every year, which translates into 40,000,000 tons of waste illegally trafficked (IMPEL 2012).

Cecilia Meneghini

See also: Basel Convention on the Control of Transboundary Movements of Hazardous Wastes and Their Disposal; Environmental Crimes

Further Reading

European Union Network for the Implementation and Enforcement of Environmental Law (IMPEL). 2012. *Waste Sites Manual: Identification and Control of 'Upstream' Storage and Treatment Facilities Used for Problematic Waste Export.* Brussels, Belgium: IMPEL.

INTERPOL. 2018. "Environmental Crime." Accessed February 16, 2018. Accessed January 21, 2019. https://www.interpol.int/Crime-areas/Environmental-crime/Environmental-crime.

Liddick, Don. 2010. "The Traffic in Garbage and Hazardous Wastes: An Overview." *Trends in Organized Crime* 13 (2–3): 134–146. https://doi.org/10.1007/s12117-009-9089-6.

Rucevska, Ieva, Christian Nellemann, Nancy Isarin, Wanhua Yang, Ning Liu, Keili Yu, Siv Sandnæs, et al. 2015. *Waste Crime–Waste Risks: Gaps in Meeting the Global Waste Challenge.* A UNEP Rapid Response Assessment. Nairobi, Kenya: United Nations Environment Programme and GRID-Arendal.

Weapons Sales

The sale of weapons, regardless of size or type, can be legal or illegal. And, it is not always easy to determine the difference. Speaking of a particular type of weapon, one researcher notes that all guns start out as legal guns, but a lot of them move into illegal hands (Ingraham 2016). Or, as Marsh (2002) puts it, the legal and illegal trade in small arms are essentially two sides of the same coin. That is, the illegal weapons used by criminals, rebels, and paramilitaries around the world were once manufactured and often sold perfectly legally. For this reason, understanding illegal weapons sales requires that attention also be paid to legal sales.

WEAPONS SALES IN CONTEXT

According to the shared disposition on how to conduct legal arms transfers, all the commercial arms exports have to be licensed by the government of the exporting state that, before issuing the license, has to obtain an end-user certificate signed by a member of the government of the importing state. The aim of this certificate is to verify that the final recipient of the arms is not subject to any restrictions. The certificate has to report the final user of the arms and, in some cases, the use that the user will make of them (Marsh 2002).

The UN Protocol against the Illicit Manufacturing of and Trafficking in Firearms, Their Parts and Components, and Ammunition introduced some additional standards for the legal trade. Among these, the governments have to exchange documents whenever an arms shipment leaves, transits, or arrives in their territory to make diverting arms for illegal purposes more difficult, and firearms have to be indelibly marked at the time of manufacture and import. In addition, the governments have to keep comprehensive records on the trade in firearms.

In 1998, the European Union (EU) adopted a regional Code of Conduct on Arms Exports. It identified common standards to use when making arms export decisions and to increase transparency among EU states on arms exports. In particular, it stressed the importance of consulting and informing each other to avoid having an EU state grant a license previously denied by another EU state. The code also defined cases in which states should not approve arms exports (e.g., when arms could be used in a conflict, for internal repression, or against another state).

Some research institutions collect data on the volume of legal international transfers of weapons. Among these, the Stockholm International Peace Research Institute (SIPRI) has developed the "SIPRI Arms Transfers Database" that contains information on all transfers of major conventional weapons from 1950 to the most recent full calendar year (Stockholm International Peace Research Institute n.d.). According to those data (as of March 2018), after a reduction of the transfers from 1980s to 2000s, the volume has progressively increased, registering a rise of 10 percent in the period 2013–2017 compared to the period 2008–2012.

Focusing on the more recent period, SIPRI identified 67 exporters of major weapons, the five largest are the United States, Russia, France, Germany, and China. Together, these five countries accounted for more than 74 percent of all arms exports (United States 34%, Russia 22%, France 6.7%, Germany 5.8%, and China 5.7%). The five largest importers in the same period are India, Saudi Arabia, Egypt, the United Arab Emirates, and China. Together, they received 35 percent of all arms imports (India 12%, Saudi Arabia 10%, Egypt 4.5%, United Arab Emirates 4.4%, and China 4% percent) (Wezeman et al. 2018).

Despite the existence of instruments to regulate the legal weapons sales among countries, a correspondent illegal firearms market exists. It occurs every time an arms transfer breaches international law or the laws of the exporting, transit, and importing states. The illegal trade can be divided into gray and black markets. The first is generally conducted by or with the complicity of national governments, and the second is conducted by private individuals and criminal organizations acting without any government's control (Marsh 2002).

ILLEGAL WEAPONS SALES

The existence of restrictions in the selling of firearms to some states, as well as the high demand for firearms from people and criminal organizations that cannot purchase them in the legal market, explains the proliferation of illegal firearms sales.

Two main methods are used to circumvent the end-user certificate:

1. Postdelivery onward diversion: This occurs after the delivery of the firearms to the official end user. In this case, the destination state is complicit in the illegal transaction, as no alerting signals were available to refuse the request for export.
2. Point of departure diversion: This occurs when the transactions are carried out using unauthorized or fake end-user certificates. In this case, the arms are directly diverted to an embargoed state or group. This illicit movement is possible in case of negligence of the exporting states in verifying that the country named in the end-user certificate has actually requested the arms or when some representatives of these states are corrupted. (UNODC 2010)

Besides these strategies that request the involvement of the states, other diversion procedures exist.

Almost all firearms in the black market were originally manufactured under government control and diverted to the primary market mainly through

- Leakage from factories or surplus stocks;
- Loss of control over government stockpiles;
- Thefts from dealers or individual owners; or
- Firearm conversion, mainly reactivation of deactivated firearms, modification of semiautomatic firearms into fully automatic ones, conversion of replicas (i.e., devices that are not real firearms but have been designed to look exactly like real firearms), and conversion of blank-firing firearms (i.e., firearms producing noise and flash without expelling projectiles). (Bevan 2008; CSES 2014; Cukier 2008; De Martino and Atwood 2015; EU Commission 2013)

These illegal sales are mainly conducted and facilitated by

- Private individuals (e.g., hobbyists and amateurs) with a wide expertise in altering firearms;
- Criminal organizations that smuggle firearms in addition to other illicit activities taking advantage of their strong expertise in illicit markets, that is, contacts and routes; or
- Corrupted officials and professionals that avoid controls over the goods and the documents. (Savona and Mancuso 2017)

A last emerging illicit channel for selling firearms is the dark web. It allows users to provide hidden content, to connect, and to exchange information and products anonymously, making difficult for law enforcement agencies to identify and tackle online illicit transactions of firearms (Europol 2017; Savona and Mancuso 2017).

RECENT INITIATIVES TO PREVENT ILLEGAL WEAPONS SALES

In the last years, the European Union applied other measures with the aim of preventing the illegal weapons sales while protecting and enhancing the licit market of firearms. Among these, the 2008 amendment of the 1991 Firearms Directive requires of EU member states that any firearm has to be marked with a unique identifying mark and registered in a computerized data filing system. The last amendment to the Firearms Directive occurred in 2017 stresses the need to

- Harmonize the rules on the marking of firearms combined with the establishment of a mutual recognition system of marking among the states;
- Establish common technical guidelines on the convertibility of replica, alarm, and signal weapons;
- Set up a system of information exchange among the states; and
- Adopt strict controls on the online acquisition of firearms, parts, and ammunitions.

Two others EU initiatives are crucial. Regulation No. 258/2012 seeks to harmonize or improve (administrative) procedures or systems in the European Union on the export, import, transit, and transshipment of firearms for civilian purposes. Regulation No. 2403/2015 introduces common and stringent binding deactivation standards to achieve a common and safe level for the deactivation of firearms.

Marina Mancuso

See also: Arms Brokers; Bout, Viktor; Small Arms and Light Weapons, Trafficking in; Small Arms Survey

Further Reading

Bevan, James. 2008. "Arsenal Adrift: Arms and Ammunition Diversion." In *Small Arms Survey 2008: Risk and Resilience*, edited by Small Arms Survey, 43–75. Geneva: Small Arms Survey.

Centre for Strategy & Evaluation Services (CSES). 2014. *Study to Support an Impact Assessment on Options for Combatting Illicit Firearms Trafficking in the European Union.* Brussels: Centre for Strategy & Evaluation Services.

Cukier, Wendy. 2008. *The Illicit Trade in Small Arms: Addressing the Problem of Diversion.* Project Ploughshares. http://ploughshares.ca/pl_publications/the-illicit-trade-in-small-arms-addressing-the-problem-of-diversion/.

De Martino, Luigi, and David Atwood. 2015. *Reducing Illicit Arms Flows and the New Development Agenda.* Research Note 50. Armed Violence. Geneva: Small Arms Survey.

EU Commission. 2013. *Firearms and the Internal Security of the EU: Protecting Citizens and Disrupting Illegal Trafficking.* Brussels: European Commission. https://eur-lex.europa.eu/legal-content/EN/TXT/?uri=CELEX%3A52013DC0716

Europol. 2017. *SOCTA 2017. EU Serious and Organized Crime Threat Assessment. Crime in the Age of Technology.* The Hague: European Police Office.

Ingraham, Christopher. 2016. "New Evidence Confirms What Gun Rights Advocates Have Said for a Long Time about Crime." *Washington Post*, July 27. Accessed January 12, 2019. https://www.washingtonpost.com/news/wonk/wp/2016/07/27/new-evidence-confirms-what-gun-rights-advocates-have-been-saying-for-a-long-time-about-crime/?utm_term=.90ba81b3fc01.

Marsh, Nicholas. 2002. "Two Sides of the Same Coin—The Legal and Illegal Trade in Small Arms." *Brown Journal of World Affairs* 9 (1): 217–228.

Savona, Ernesto U., and Marina Mancuso, eds. 2017. *Fighting Illicit Firearms Trafficking Routes and Actors at European Level.* Final Report of Project FIRE. Milano: Transcrime–Università Cattolica del Sacro Cuore.

Stockholm International Peace Research Institute. n.d. "SIPRI Arms Transfers Database." Accessed September 25, 2018. https://www.sipri.org/databases/armstransfers.

United Nations Office on Drugs and Crime (UNODC). 2010. *The Globalization of Crime: A Transnational Organized Crime Threat Assessment.* Vienna: UNODC.

Wezeman, Pieter D., Aude Fleurant, Alexandra Kuimova, Nan Tian, and Siemon T. Wezeman. 2018. *Trends in International Arms Transfers, 2017.* SIPRI Fact Sheet March 2018. https://www.sipri.org/publications/2018/sipri-fact-sheets/trends-international-arms-transfers-2017

Whaling

Whaling is a specific type of cybercrime that targets persons in high-profile positions, such as bankers, corporate executives, and others in powerful positions. The goal of this type of attack is to trick the target into disclosing personal or corporate information.

Whaling falls within the broader category of phishing attacks (attempts to obtain a person's login information to a specific Web platform) and, as such, follows techniques similar to those used in phishing. In a phishing attack, the victim typically receives an e-mail from what purports to be a trustworthy source—their bank, a utility company, or Facebook—and contains a faulty link infected with malware, which logs the victim's keystrokes as they attempt to log into a site (Chandra, Challa, and Pasupuleti 2016). Once the login information is copied, the phisher then uses the site to obtain banking information or to extort the victim.

Whaling, however, primarily focuses on social engineering. In a whaling attack, the victim—for example, an agency employee with access to financial records or monetary transfer authority—will receive an e-mail from someone masquerading as a senior executive that asks the employee to transfer money or send sensitive documents. This type of attack exploits the professional relationship between employees, often when the high-ranking executive is out of the office or on vacation, so an in-person conversation is not feasible. The masquerading occurs in one of two ways, either the whaler had obtained access to the executive's e-mail—possibly through a phishing scheme—or he or she had spoofed the e-mail address of the executive, creating an e-mail address so close that most people would not notice the change. As the whaler personally constructed the e-mail, spam filters are unable to detect the fake domain or human-written language. Additionally, due to the use of social engineering, the whaling effort is bolstered and legitimized by extensive research into the executive, employees, company protocol, and transfer procedures.

The preparatory work required for a whaling attack results in big rewards for the attackers. From 2013 to 2016, in the United States alone, law enforcement received over 17,000 whaling reports that amounted to over $2.3 billion in losses (McCabe 2016). Additionally, since 2016, the Federal Bureau of Investigation (FBI) has reported a 270 percent increase in identified victims and exposed loses

(McCabe 2016). In 2017, cybercrime was estimated to cost over $500 billion globally, with projected damages of upward of $6 trillion by 2021 (Baker 2018). Unfortunately, due to the global component of the crime and the ability for highly skilled attackers to hide their trails on the Internet, many of the perpetrators are never caught and are suspected to be outside the countries they target with attacks.

What makes whaling so different from other cybercrime is the extensive level of social engineering present in the attack. The high level of research accompanying an attack provides offenders with high rewards if successful and low risk if unsuccessful (Chandra, Challa, and Pasupuleti 2016). The personal details and human-written e-mails inherent in whaling attacks allow offenders to dodge high-tech malware and spam filters. Committing the crime electronically and from a separate cover also provides whalers cover and a high-reward/low-risk environment. Ultimately, experts warn instances of whaling will only increase, with higher frequency of attacks and larger losses for corporations.

As whaling attacks continue to avoid detection from technological programs, law enforcement advises all businesses, large and small, to educate staff on how to recognize whaling attacks and to double and triple check any requests involving transfers of funds or delivery of sensitive documents with in-person or phone conversations.

Jessica C. Smith

See also: Cyberattack; Cybercrime; Identity-Related Crimes; Phishing

Further Reading

Baker, Noel. 2018. "Cybersecurity Experts Warn on 'Whaling Attacks.'" *Irish Examiner*, February 19. Accessed January 21, 2019. https://www.irishexaminer.com/ireland/cybersecurity-experts-warn-on-whaling-attacks-467338.html.

Chandra, J. Vijaya, Narasimham Challa, and Sai Kiran Pasupuleti. 2016. "A Practical Approach to E-Mail Spam Filters to Protect Data from Advanced Persistent Threat." *2016 International Conference on Circuit, Power and Computing Technologies (ICCPCT).* Nagercoil, India, March 18–19. Accessed January 21, 2019. https://ieeexplore.ieee.org/abstract/document/7530239.

McCabe, Andrew. 2016. "FBI Warns of Dramatic Increase in Business E-Mail Scams." Federal Bureau of Investigation press release, April 4. Accessed January 21, 2019. https://www.fbi.gov/contact-us/field-offices/phoenix/news/press-releases/fbi-warns-of-dramatic-increase-in-business-e-mail-scams.

Wildlife and Forest Crime

Wildlife crime encompasses the illegal exploitation and commerce of the world's flora and fauna. It is the illegal taking, trading, trafficking, importing, exporting, possessing, killing, or consumption of animals or plants in contravention of national or international laws. When forest crime is added, the reference expands to include the illicit obtaining of timber and nontimber forest products.

WILDLIFE CRIME

Wildlife crime can take many forms, and it can be difficult to know when the crime has actually occurred. It ranges from the illicit exploitation of natural resources (such as the poaching of elephants and rhinos and uprooting of rare flowers) to subsequent acts that include transporting, selling, possessing, and others. It also includes the concealment and laundering of the financial benefits of these crimes.

There are many examples of wildlife crime, including the poaching of elephants, rhinos, tigers, and parrots. Alares (n.d.) explains that thousands of elephants are killed each year for their ivory tusks, rhinos are killed in the mistaken belief that their horn can cure diseases, and tiger parts are sold for use in folk remedies and to show status.

Products of wildlife crime are common in such industries as food, furniture making, art and décor, jewelry, fashion, cosmetics and perfume, tonics, and medicine. Moreover, the animals trafficked can be sold to zoos, sold as pets, or used for breeding.

The money generated by wildlife crime is used for various purposes. In some cases, money goes to financing terrorism and therefore contributes to political and social instability. These crimes are also closely interlinked to other crimes, such as money laundering, counterfeiting, fraud, corruption, and murder.

FOREST CRIME

Flora is affected to such a degree that the concept of forest crime is often added to wildlife crime. A few examples are the uprooting of rare flowers, unauthorized logging of trees, and illegal trafficking of timber.

Due to wildlife and forest crime, fragile ecosystems are destroyed and biodiversity is reduced or remarkably altered. For instance, the introduction of alien species to new habitats can ruin the natural biodiversity of local areas and the cross border smuggling of plants and animals can spread diseases that are life-threatening, such as Ebola. (Bouley and Thompson 2017).

VALUE AND LOSSES OF WILDLIFE AND FOREST CRIME

Illegal wildlife trafficking is the fourth most lucrative global crime after drugs, humans, and arms. It has an estimated value of between $7 billion and $23 billion each year (World Economic Forum 2016). Nonetheless, the criminal revenue as a whole is extremely difficult to calculate due to the volatility that affects some key wildlife commodities (UNODC 2016) and, of course, due to its illegal essence. According to a report from the United Nations Environment Programme (UNEP) and INTERPOL, for instance, the value of wildlife crime in 2016 ranged from $91 to $258 billion, 26 percent more than in 2014 (WildLeaks 2017). Also consistent with UNEP and INTERPOL's study (2016), the amount of money lost due to environmental crime only is 10,000 times greater than the amount of money spent by international agencies on combating it, which ranges from $20 to $30 million.

Wildlife and forest crime is not only a threat to the ecological stability but also to local and international economies, public health, and even security and criminal justice systems. Particularly for developing countries, wildlife crime generates significant losses in assets and revenues, and, above all, it threatens the livelihood of rural communities, impacting whole ecosystems and affecting human health and food security.

INTERNATIONAL FRAMEWORK AND LAW ENFORCEMENT

Despite the wide security implications of wildlife crime, governments and organizations tend to see the problem as an environmental issue rather than a serious transnational organized crime. Moreover, the fact that it is a "human victim free" type of crime contributes to that. It often remains outside the "mainstream" crime, impairing the collection of data and even the effective law enforcement.

However, over the years, the international community has started to pay more attention to wildlife crime. A diverse range of high-level initiatives and events to tackle wildlife trade and other related illegal activities have taken place at local, national, and global levels. To start, the United Nations Convention against Transnational Organized Crime includes transnational wildlife crime among what it is considered organized crime (any pattern of profit-motivated criminal activity).

Moreover, the Convention on International Trade in Endangered Species of Wild Fauna and Flora (CITES) provides a framework to protect and regulate international trade in certain species to ensure their survival. It was the first international framework and agreement to address wildlife crime and was adopted by more than 80 governments in 1963 at a meeting of members of the International Union for the Conservation of Nature (IUCN).

Nonetheless, regarding this and other regulations, few countries have the capacity to keep track of the complex and changing world of foreign wildlife regulation or to gather evidence on offenses committed on the other side of the world. For most countries, combating wildlife crime is not a priority, and it almost always remains overlooked and poorly understood (WildLeaks 2017). National wildlife law enforcement agencies, especially those in developing states, face many challenges, such as inadequate legislations, lack of resources, limited training, and a limited appreciation among prosecutors, among others.

COMBATING WILDLIFE AND FOREST CRIME

Wildlife crime and forest crimes are global epidemics, and criminal networks are getting more sophisticated than ever; but so are the methods used to identify them, shut them down, and bring perpetrators to justice. New high-tech approaches are being developed, which include the use of DNA technologies, acoustic traps, thermal imaging, advanced analytics and mapping, a spatial monitoring and reporting tool (SMART) and CyberTracker, mobile apps, crowdfunding campaigns, and GPS-enabled cameras and smartphones, among others (Raxter 2015). The aim of these methods is not just to make arrests but also to dissuade potential poachers.

For instance, in March 2017, the International Symposium on Human Identification reported that DNA analysis can show a difference between individual animals by targeting specific genetic markers that are highly variable within species.

By separating out these markers from physical samples (such as a rhino horn or a piece of rosewood), forensic scientists are often able to determine where the animal or plant came from, what its parentage might be, the age of the sample, and how this relates to other seized shipments. Occasionally, it is possible to uncover more information about the criminal networks behind the trade by detailing where the plants or animals were killed and which ports were used to transport them.

Another example is the use of thermal imaging cameras to develop a new anti-poaching system—one that combines thermal imaging cameras and human detection software. This was reported by James Morgan, from the International League of Conservation Photographers, in 2016, and it is one of the first times this technology has been used outside of the military and law enforcement.

While methods like these have greatly improved the odds that wildlife criminals will be caught and brought to justice, there are still some obstacles that remain. Such issues as data sharing, lab and sample collecting standards, and budgets need to be examined (ISHI 2017).

Ana Carolina Paci and Dafne Calderón Burgoa

See also: Convention on International Trade in Endangered Species of Wild Fauna and Flora; UN Global Programme for Combating Wildlife and Forest Crime

Further Reading

Alares, Marcas. n.d. "The Elephants, Rhinos and Tigers Are Still Endangered by Poaching." Maquia for Wildlife. Accessed August 18, 2018. http://www.maquiaambiental.com/en/los-elefantes-los-rinocerontes-y-los-tigres-siguen-en-peligro-por-la-caza-furtiva.

Bouley, Timothy, and Sara Thompson. 2014. "Trafficking Wildlife and Transmitting Disease: Bold Threats in an Era of Ebola." World Bank, *Voices* (blog), October 2. Accessed January 13, 2019. https://blogs.worldbank.org/voices/trafficking-wildlife-and-transmitting-disease-bold-threats-era-ebola.

"Elephants and the Ivory Trade: The Crisis in Africa." 2016. *BBC*, Newsround, October 5. Accessed January 13, 2019. http://www.bbc.co.uk/newsround/37373034.

Fedotov, Yury. 2014. "How Wildlife and Forest Crime Undermines Development and Ravages Global Biodiversity." *UN Chronicle: The Magazine of the United Nations*. Accessed January 13, 2019. https://unchronicle.un.org/article/how-wildlife-and-forest-crime-undermines-development-and-ravages-global-biodiversity.

ISHI. 2017. "How DNA Technologies Are Being Used to Combat Wildlife Crime." *ISHI News* (blog), March 13. Accessed January 13, 2019. https://www.ishinews.com/how-dna-technologies-are-being-used-to-combat-wildlife-crime.

Morgan, James. 2016. "Using Technology to Combat Wildlife Crime." Save the Elephants. Accessed January 20, 2019. http://www.savetheelephants.org/about-elephants-2-3-2/elephant-news-post/?detail=using-technology-to-combat-wildlife-crime.

Raxter, Patricia. 2015. "11 Ways Technology Stops Crime against Endangered Animals." *National Geographic News*, July 6. Accessed January 21, 2019. https://news.nationalgeographic.com/2015/07/150706-wildlife-crime-technology-poaching-endangered-animals.

United Nations Environment Programme (UNEP) and INTERPOL. 2016. "The Rise of Environmental Crime." https://wedocs.unep.org/handle/20.500.11822/7662.

United Nations Office on Drugs and Crime (UNODC). 2016. *World Wildlife Crime Report: Trafficking in Protected Species*. Vienna: UNODC. Accessed January 13,

2019. http://www.unodc.org/documents/data-and-analysis/wildlife/World_Wildlife_Crime_Report_2016_final.pdf.

WildLeaks. 2017. "What Is Wildlife Crime." Accessed January 13, 2019. https://wildleaks.org/what-is-wildlife-crime.

World Economic Forum. 2017. "Wildlife Crime: A $23 Billion Trade That's Destroying Our Planet." Accessed January 21, 2019. https://www.weforum.org/agenda/2016/09/fighting-illegal-wildlife-and-forest-trade.

World Wildlife Fund. 2017. "Stop Wildlife Crime." Accessed January 21, 2019. https://www.worldwildlife.org/pages/stop-wildlife-crime.

Women and Transnational Crime

Women's role in transnational crime has not been extensively examined or studied by criminologists. Indeed, available information regarding women's contribution and engagement in criminal activity is limited and incomplete (Arsovska and Allum 2014). Historically, gender bias was at the forefront of 19th-century criminology. Positivist theory's founding father, Italian physician Cesare Lombroso (1835–1909), posited that women are genetically inferior to men (Lombroso and Ferrero 1895). As such, women have been underestimated in all aspects of society, and this includes their participation in transnational crime.

The imperfection of crime statistics in regard to gendered crimes, such as sexual and labor exploitation and human trafficking, is a problem, especially when attempting to measure crime's prevalence in communities around the world (Arsovska and Allum 2014). While in the last few decades, women's involvement in prominent leadership roles has begun to receive more public attention, because men commit a majority of recorded crimes, these examples continue to be the exception rather than the norm. For this reason, the bulk of academic articles and reports from humanitarian and law enforcement agencies focus on instances and statistics in which women are the victims, rather than the actors and perpetrators, of crime. There is much to indicate that this trend will continue to persist in the near future.

WOMEN AS PERPETRATORS

There are a few prominent examples of women at the helm of organized criminal organizations that have broken with the traditional view of women as passive and submissive victims of crime (Arsovska and Allum 2014). Although Latin American drug cartels, Italian mafia organizations, and human trafficking networks are traditionally male-dominated structures, women have been gaining and yielding power as high-ranking drug lords in Colombia and Mexico, as mafia bosses in the Neapolitan Camorra, and as leaders in Nigerian human trafficking organizations, often after having been human trafficking victims themselves.

Before being killed outside of a butcher shop in Medellín, Colombia, in 2012, Griselda Blanco was considered by many as a pioneer in the drug smuggling trade: for instance, in her use of humans as "mules" to carry cocaine from Latin

America into the United States (Otis 2012). For decades, Blanco worked as a ruthless drug lord and cocaine smuggler in Colombia's Medellín Cartel and stands accused of ordering the murders of hundreds of people throughout the 1970s and 1980s (Otis 2012). In *United States v. Blanco* (1975), the Southern District of New York charged Blanco with conspiring to manufacture, import, and distribute cocaine into the United States. However, Blanco, who was never extradited from Colombia but was able to return to the United States with the assistance of a document forger, was finally arrested in 1985 by the DEA in California, where she was living under a false name. Blanco went on to serve 15 years in prison and was fined $25,000 (*United States v. Blanco* 1988).

In Mexico, Sandra Avila Beltran, known as La Reina del Pacifico, was arrested in Mexico City in 2007 for her role as a top connector to Mexican and Colombian drug cartels. Charged in the shipment of nine tons of Colombian cocaine bound for the United States, Beltran, who had been extradited to the United States in 2012, agreed to a plea deal. She finished her prison sentence in Mexico and was released in 2015 (Flannery 2015).

In the meantime, in Italy, the mafia's presence and monopolization of certain economic sectors—much like the drug cartels in Latin America—has long been a matter of political and public concern. Although the different mafia groups stem from regions in Southern Italy and Sicily, their influence transcends national boundaries. Traditionally, while Sicily's Cosa Nostra operated as a vertical and strictly male hierarchy, the Neapolitan Camorra has functioned more as a horizontal business structure, which Maurizio Catino contends is "characterized by the absence of higher levels of coordination" (Catino 2014, 117). As a result, women, have been able to take advantage of the looser structure to assert themselves into its clans.

Up until her arrest in 2001, Maria Licciardi was a prominent and active leader in the Camorra. A callous strategist, she is credited with allegedly unifying the group's various clans. However, a disagreement with a rival clan over a shipment of heroine that Licciardi deemed unsuitable for use—but which was distributed against her orders—led to the deaths of scores of Italian drug users in the Neapolitan metropolitan area and incited territorial violence, including retaliatory murders (Carroll 2000).

Raffaella D'Alterio, another female leader of the Neapolitan Camorra, took over the criminal activities of her husband, Nicola Pianese, after his arrest in 2002. According to a United Nations Office on Drugs and Crime (UNODC) E4J University Module on Organized Crime (UNODC n.d.-a), she oversaw a criminal group that "made an estimated profit of more than $100 billion" a year. After Pianese was released from prison, D'Alterio, who allegedly did not want to relinquish her hold on power, was believed to have been behind her husband's murder. Upon her arrest in 2012, the carabinieri confiscated property valued at over $10 million.

A UNODC report on trafficking and gender (UNODC 2015) indicates that up to 28 percent of human traffickers are women. As human trafficking investigations are based on victim testimonies, the report posits that a possible explanation for the high number of female human traffickers is tied to the reality that women tend to be low-level traffickers responsible for recruitment, and as such they face a greater risk of both detection and conviction. In turn, because those at the top of the command chain, who tend to be men, orchestrate under the radar of law enforcement, they often evade detection. Increased female involvement in human trafficking might be rooted in the fact that, because a majority of victims of human trafficking are also women, their gender might be perceived as an asset, as the implied trust between women might facilitate the recruitment process.

One of the consequences of the current migrant crisis in Europe is the increase in human trafficking and sexual exploitation. Over the last few years, Nigerians have increasingly been making the perilous journey to Italy. According to the International Organization for Migration (IOM), the number of Nigerian women coming into Italy steadily increased from 1,450 in 2014 to 11,009 in 2016. Specifically, the IOM believes that 80 percent of the 11,009 Nigerian women that came in to Italy in 2016 "were trafficked, and will go on to live a life of forced prostitution in Italy and other countries in Europe" (Kelly 2017). In other words, these women repaid their transportation debt through forced sex work. As the UNODC report on human trafficking in Europe confirms, this cycle of exploitation is further complicated by the fact that "women may 'evolve' over time from victim to exploiter" (UNODC n.d.-b, 6). According to the UNODC report, most Nigerian human trafficking networks are "loose structures" that "operate mainly in and from Nigeria," although they also have "bases in Europe" that are "handled by resident Nigerian women, referred to as 'madams'" (UNODC n.d.-b, 6). Thus, because female perpetrators of crime were often once victims of these very same crimes, the emotional line between victim and abuser becomes blurred, which further complicates prosecution as well.

WOMEN AS VICTIMS

Despite the aforementioned examples, women around the world are more likely to be victims of transnational crime than its perpetrators. Human trafficking and violence against women are prevalent, with a UN Women report (2017) finding that 71 percent of all human trafficking victims are women and girls. Indeed, a majority of the women and girls trafficked in Europe are trafficked into sex work. A 2002 report from the United Nations estimates that 80 percent of trafficked girls and women in Italy belong to Nigeria's Edo ethnic group, and a *Guardian* article asserts, "According to police data, 90% of prostitutes in Palermo come from Nigeria" (Tondo 2016).

Similarly, in Asia, a report on trafficking within the Greater Mekong Delta Sub-Region emphasizes the transnational nature of sexual exploitation in the region, indicating that the Pat Pong district in Bangkok, Thailand, notorious for its sex market, was the creation of foreign investors during the 1950s and 1960s (UNODC n.d.-c, 17). The report also indicates that in most, if not all, global sex markets, the vast majority of sex workers, and thus victims of sexual exploitation, are women.

A report by the International Labour Organization (ILO; 2017) estimates that 40.3 million people were in modern slavery in 2016, which for the ILO includes conditions of forced labor exploitation, debt bondage, forced marriage, human trafficking, and other slavery-like practices. The ILO report also determined that women and girls are disproportionately affected by forced labor, accounting for 99 percent of victims in the commercial sex industry and 58 percent in other sectors. Jini L. Roby (2005) estimates that 1.2 million women and girls become involved each year in the sex trade, generating $1.5 billion in profit. As such, the profit organized criminal groups stand to gain from partaking in organized criminal activities that are so often gendered, such as human trafficking rings and sexual exploitation networks, also points to women's economical exploitation, as they are rarely, if ever, those who reap the benefits from their potentially dangerous labor. Indeed, the profit angle is crucial to understanding the continued existence of female exploitation, and it underscores the intersectionality of transnational crimes and the way in which crimes in one country often involve various international borders and criminal organizations.

CONCLUSION

Due to a dearth of information in the criminology field that grapples with women's role in transnational crime and the extent of their engagement in criminal activity, the general idea we have of the implications and impact of their contributions are far from holistic While high-profile examples of women in drug cartels and mafia organizations yielding great power and influence are crucial, as they provide a more nuanced understanding of the subject, women are still overwhelmingly the targets of transnational crime. Ultimately, by being so disproportionally affected by crime on a global scale, women's human rights are compromised and jeopardized on a daily basis. As such, front and center in the struggle for gender equality is the quest for more thorough research on the topic as well as the need for increased resources to fight the prejudice and discrimination that enables crimes against women to proliferate in the first place.

Julia Pagnamenta

See also: Blanco, Griselda; Cartel Organization; Colombian Drug Cartels; Gender-Based Violence; Human Trafficking; Organized Crime; Sex Exploitation

Further Reading

Arsovska, J., and F. Allum, 2014. "Introduction: Women and Transnational Organized Crime." *Trends in Organized Crime* 17 (1–2): 1–15.

Carroll, R. 2000. "Italy's Most Wanted Mamma." *The Guardian*, June 30. Accessed January 21, 2019. https://www.theguardian.com/g2/story/0,,338148,00.html.

Catino, M. 2014. "How Do Mafias Organize? Conflict and Violence in Three Mafia Organizations." *European Journal of Sociology* 55 (2): 177–220.

Flannery Parish, N. 2015. "Mexico's Organized Crime Queenpin Released from Prison." *Forbes*, February 9. Accessed January 21, 2019. https://www.forbes.com/sites/nathanielparishflannery/2015/02/09/mexicos-organized-crime-queenpin-released-from-prison/#27b17ef04cc0.

Franklin, J. 2016. "Queen of Cartels: Most Famous Female Leader of Mexico's Underworld Speaks Out." *The Guardian*, May 16. Accessed January 21, 2019. https://www.theguardian.com/society/2016/may/16/mexico-drug-cartels-famous-female-leader-sandra-avila.

International Labour Organization (ILO). 2017. "Global Estimates of Modern Slavery: Forced Labour and Forced Marriage." Accessed January 21, 2019. http://www.ilo.org/wcmsp5/groups/public/---dgreports/---dcomm/documents/publication/wcms_575479.pdf.

Kelly, A. 2017. "Number of Nigerian Women Trafficked to Italy for Sex Almost Doubled in 2016." *The Guardian*, January 12. Accessed January 21, 2019. https://www.theguardian.com/global-development/2017/jan/12/nigerian-women-trafficked-to-italy-for-sex-doubled-2016.

Lombroso, C., and W. Ferrero. 1895. *The Female Offender*. New York: D. Appleton and Company. (Original work published in 1893.)

Otis, J. 2012. "'Cocaine Godmother' Griselda Blanco Killed in Colombia." *PRI*, September 4. Accessed January 21, 2019. https://www.pri.org/stories/2012-09-04/cocaine-godmother-griselda-blanco-killed-colombia.

Roby, J. L. 2005 "Women and Children in the Global Sex Trade: Toward More Effective Policy." *International Social Work* 48 (2): 136–147.

Tondo, L. 2016. "Mafia at a Crossroads as Nigerian Gangsters Hit Sicily's Shores." *The Guardian*, June 11. Accessed January 21, 2019. https://www.theguardian.com/global-development/2016/jun/11/mafia-palermo-nigerian-gangsters-hit-sicily-shores.

UN Women. 2017. "Facts and Figures: Ending Violence against Women." August. Accessed January 21, 2019. http://www.unwomen.org/en/what-we-do/ending-violence-against-women/facts-and-figures.

United Nations Office on Drugs and Crime (UNODC). 2015. "Trafficking in Persons and Gender." Accessed January 21, 2019. http://www.heuni.fi/material/attachments/heuni/projects/wmPiHN4hb/Trafficking_in_Persons_and_Gender.pdf.

United Nations Office on Drugs and Crime (UNODC). n.d.-a. "E4J University Module Series: Organized Crime. Module 6: Causes and Facilitating Factors of Organized Crime." Accessed January 21, 2019. https://www.unodc.org/e4j/en/organized-crime/module-6/exercises/case-studies.html.

United Nations Office on Drugs and Crime (UNODC). n.d.-b. "Trafficking in Persons to Europe for Sexual Exploitation." Accessed January 21, 2019. https://www.unodc.org/documents/publications/TiP_Europe_EN_LORES.pdf.

United Nations Office on Drugs and Crime (UNODC). n.d.-c. "Trafficking of Women and Girls for Sexual Exploitation within the Greater Mekong Sub-Region." Accessed January 21, 2019. https://www.unodc.org/documents/toc/Reports/TOCTA-EA-Pacific/TOCTA_EAP_c02.pdf.

United States v. Griselda Blanco. 1975. No. 1187, Docket 85-1423. Accessed January 21, 2019. https://www.unodc.org/cld/case-law-doc/drugcrimetype/usa/1988/united_states_v_blanco.html.

World Bank

The World Bank Group (frequently shortened to "The World Bank") is a financial organization that provides financial loans to nations throughout the world for capital improvement and humanitarian projects. It is headquartered in the Foggy Bottom neighborhood of Washington, D.C., adjacent to the U.S. State Department.

Crime and violence make it difficult, if not impossible, for a country to sustain economic and social gains. The World Bank believes prevention is crucial in combating the toll that crime takes on development and in human lives. To that end, the World Bank includes among its projects and initiatives those that can support crime prevention efforts ranging from reducing violence through increased access to basic urban infrastructure and services to financing of projects designed to better manage forest resources and to fight wildlife crime (World Bank 2017a, 2017b). To better appreciate the World Bank's efforts to combat global crime, it is important to understand its operation.

HISTORY

From July 1 to July 22, 1944, delegates from all 44 Allied nations gathered at the United Nations Monetary and Financial Conference (also known as the Bretton Woods Conference) to discuss the restoration of global financial stability in the aftermath of World War II. Following the conference, member governments signed multilateral agreements creating the United Nations' International Monetary Fund and the International Bank for Reconstruction and Development, which evolved into the World Bank Group.

STRUCTURE

The World Bank Group is composed of five different organizations: the International Bank for Reconstruction and Development (IBRD); the International Finance Corporation (IFC); the International Development Association (IDA); the International Centre for Settlement of Investment Disputes (ICSID); and the Multilateral Investment Guarantee Agency (MIGA). Established in 1944 for the purpose of assisting the reconstruction of Europe following World War II (1939–1945), the IBRD is now responsible for loans to middle-income developing countries. The IFC, established in 1956 as an entity of the World Bank, focuses on private-sector, for-profit investment in economic development projects aimed to reduce poverty.

The IDA was established in 1960 to assist the poorest nations with loans aimed at growing national income, improving credit ratings, and raising the per capita income. The ICSID, founded in 1965, acts as an arbiter responsible for resolving disputes between international investors in an effort to safeguard investment across international borders. The MIGA was established in 1988 as an insurance provider, offering coverage to investors seeking to protect their investments from political risk in developing countries.

MEMBERSHIP

Membership into the World Bank Group is not inclusive to all five organizations of the bank, and membership into some is conditional on membership into others. A requirement of membership is that a member country must first join the International Monetary Fund (IMF), which comes with its own criteria and conditions, as decided by the United Nations. The lowest level of World Bank membership is the IBRD. Once IBRD membership is established, member countries are eligible to join the IDA, IFC, and MIGA. As of August 2018, there are 189 members of the IBRD.

FUNDING

The World Bank primarily funds its programs and operations through three revenue sources. First, member nations purchase a shareholder stake in the bank in exchange for capital payments from that nation. Second, the World Bank sells bonds to global investors. Third, loans to developing countries are repaid according to market value. As of 2010, the WBG voting shares reflected a concentration of 49.7 percent of power being held by 10 member countries: the United States (15.85%), Japan (6.84%), China (4.42%), Germany (4%), the United Kingdom (3.75%), France (3.75%), India (2.91%), Russia (2.77%), Saudi Arabia (2.77%), and Italy (2.64%) ("Developing Nations Get More Say in World Bank Affairs" 2010). Due to the World Bank charter requiring an 85 percent super majority vote for amendment, the United States, by virtue of almost a 20 percent share, can effectively veto changes in the World Bank's charter (Lobe 2003).

ACTIVITIES

The World Bank Group organizes its functions according to two ambitious goals, targeted for the year 2030. The first is to end extreme poverty by decreasing the percentage of people living on less than $1.90 a day to no more than 3 percent, and the second is to promote shared prosperity by fostering the income growth of the bottom 40 percent of every country.

These two goals are pursued in a variety of projects that are divided among 11 different sectors: agriculture, education, energy and extractives, the financial sector, health, industry and trade/services, information and communication, public administration and governance, social protection, transportation, and water/sanitation/waste. The primary services provided by the World Bank are low-interest loans, zero to low-interest lines of credit, and grants. In addition to these financial products, the World Bank supports a global information network intended for member nations to provide accurate monitoring and evaluation data on projects and programs. Through this information, the World Bank is able to identify corrupt uses of the financing packages, ensuring that the program outcomes minimize criminal activity and that the international community is united in pursuing malicious actors who detract from these ambitious organizational goals.

CRITICISM

Despite its original intent on rebuilding areas of the world ruined by war, the World Bank evolved over the latter half of the 20th century to be an instrument of global poverty reduction (Birdsall and Londoño 1997); however, new criticism has developed to question whether it is nothing more than a global agent for global superpowers to exert influence over the developing world (Clemens and Kremer 2016).

Corey B. Miles

See also: Corruption; Failed State; Intergovernmental Organization

Further Reading

Birdsall, Nancy, and Juan Luis Londoño. 1997. "Asset Inequality Matters: An Assessment of the World Bank's Approach to Poverty Reduction." *American Economic Review* 87 (2): 32–37.

Clemens, Michael A., and Michael Kremer. 2016. "The New Role for the World Bank." *Journal of Economic Perspectives* 30 (1): 53–76.

"Developing Nations Get More Say in World Bank Affairs." 2010. *Times of India*, April 26. Accessed January 21, 2019. https://timesofindia.indiatimes.com/india/Developing-nations-get-more-say-in-World-Bank-affairs/articleshow/5858176.cms.

Lobe, Jim. 2003. "US Blocks Stronger African Voice at World Bank—NGO." *Global Policy Forum*. Last updated June 26, 2003. Accessed January 21, 2019. https://www.globalpolicy.org/component/content/article/209/43377.html.

World Bank. 2017a. "Congo: Additional Financing for Forest and Econ. Diversification Proj." Projects & Operations. Last modified May 4, 2017. http://projects.worldbank.org/P158604?lang=en.http://projects.worldbank.org/P124085/forestry-economic-diversification-project?lang=en

World Bank. 2017b. "GT: Urban Infrastructure and Violence Prevention." Projects & Operations. Last modified January 17, 2017.

World Bank. n.d. "What We Do." Accessed August 22, 2018. http://www.worldbank.org/en/what-we-do.

World Intellectual Property Organization

The World Intellectual Property Organization (WIPO) is an international organization designed to promote the worldwide protection of intellectual property, while simultaneously encouraging future intellectual, creative activity. As one of the 15 specialized agencies of the United Nations—which are agencies working with the United Nations through the United Nations Economic and Social Council and the Chief Executives Board—WIPO aims to be the leading global forum for intellectual property services, cooperation, policy, and information (Birkbeck 2016). After its establishment in 1967, WIPO has grown to comprise 191 member states that are responsible for determining the direction, activities, and budget for WIPO. These member states directly uphold the main objective of WIPO, which is to sponsor the protection of intellectual property throughout the world through cooperation among states and international organizations.

HISTORY

In 1883, 11 countries agreed on the Paris Convention for the Protection of Industrial Property, establishing one of the first intellectual property treaties, which helped inventors ensure that their intellectual property was being protected in other countries. In 1886, 10 countries agreed on the Berne Convention for the Protection of Literary and Artistic Works, establishing a system that gave artistic creators the right to control and receive compensation for their creative works on an international level. In 1983, the United International Bureaux for the Protection of Intellectual Property was established to administer both the Berne and Paris conventions, ultimately founding the immediate predecessor to WIPO. In 1967, 42 countries signed the convention establishing the World Intellectual Property Organization in Stockholm, Sweden, and subsequently entered into force in 1970 following the addition of eight further signatories. In 1974, WIPO joined the United Nations family of organizations, acquiring the specialized agency title it holds today.

INTELLECTUAL PROPERTY

Intellectual property protected under WIPO encompasses both industrial property and copyrighted materials. First, industrial property consists of invention designs, scientific discoveries, industrial designs, trademarks, service marks, and commercial names/designations. In addition, WIPO-protected industrial property includes the unequivocal protection against unfair competition, which is a business strategy utilized to cause economic harm to other businesses or consumers (WIPO n.d.-a). Second, WIPO-protected copyrighted materials include any literary, photographic, musical, scientific, and artistic works as well as artistic performances, phonograms, and broadcasts (WIPO n.d.-a).

All WIPO-protected intellectual property is secured by law—for example, through the use of patents, copyrights, and trademarks—thus enabling individuals to receive recognition, and sometimes financial profits, for the intellectual property they invent or create. WIPO strives to strike a balance between innovator interests and societal interests, ultimately seeking to foster an environment in which intellectual property and innovation can flourish. This balance transpires in a highly dynamic, changing environment, thus requiring WIPO to be an extremely efficient and receptive organization. The dynamics surrounding intellectual property protection necessitate WIPO be well-equipped in delivering leadership on intellectual property issues as well as achieving the basic organizational functions steering its existence.

FUNCTIONS

To adhere to their organizational objectives, WIPO functions in a variety of manners. First, WIPO promotes and develops various means to protect intellectual property around the world. This is achieved through the harmonization of regional, national, and international legislation in the field of intellectual property protection. Second, WIPO agrees to undertake and participate in any intellectual property agreements designed to promote the protection of intellectual property. WIPO further enforces this goal by encouraging the conclusion, and championship, of any international agreement designed to promote intellectual property protection.

Third, WIPO routinely offers its cooperation to states requesting assistance with legal-technical issues of intellectual property protection. Fourth, WIPO assembles and disseminates pertinent information surrounding intellectual property protection. This is achieved through WIPO's promotion and publication of various studies and investigations within the field of intellectual property protection. Finally, WIPO maintains a variety of services facilitating the international protection of intellectual property and, where appropriate, provides for registration in this field and the publication of the data concerning the registrations.

Jessie L. Slepicka

See also: Counterfeit Goods and Money; Digital Piracy; Intellectual Property Crime

Further Reading

Birkbeck, Carolyn D. 2016. *The World Intellectual Property Organization (WIPO): A Reference Guide*. Cheltenham, UK: Edward Elgar Publishing.

United Nations. 1998. "WIPO: World Intellectual Property Organization." Accessed May 16, 2018. http://www.un.org/Pubs/ourlives/wipo.htm.

United Nations Systems. n.d. "World Intellectual Property Organization." Accessed May 16, 2018. https://www.unsceb.org/content/wipo.

WIPO. n.d.-a. "Convention Establishing the World Intellectual Property Organization." Accessed May 16, 2018. http://www.wipo.int/treaties/en/text.jsp?file_id=283854.

WIPO. n.d.-b. "Inside WIPO: What Is WIPO?" Accessed May 16, 2018. http://www.wipo.int/about-wipo/en.

WIPO. n.d.-c. "WIPO—A Brief History." Accessed May 16, 2018. http://www.wipo.int/about-wipo/en/history.html.

World Wildlife Crime Report

The World Wildlife Crime Report, published in 2016, reported on the current status of wildlife crime, specifically wildlife trafficking. This multidepartmental and international effort was an informational report based on statistics from 120 countries and data from species experts. Due to the scope of the research analyzed, this report provides both a general and in-depth perspective of wildlife trafficking, both nationally and globally. This report is significant due to its showing the globalization of wildlife trafficking and the limitations of current regulations.

BACKGROUND

Wildlife trafficking has global repercussions by not only having implications on international economic systems but also on the sustainability of thousands of species and ecosystems. The World Wildlife Crime Report was a significant effort to shine a light on illicit trafficking of wildlife, both of flora and fauna species. It was completed by the United Nations Office on Drug and Crime (UNODC), with cooperation by the International Consortium on Combating Wildlife Crime (ICCWC).

The report split wildlife trafficking into common markets: furniture; art, décor, and jewelry; fashion; cosmetics and perfume; food, tonics, and medicines; pets, zoos, and breeding; and seafood. These case studies delved into the specifics of wildlife trafficking, while still emphasizing the general data that was presented in the beginning of the report. This binary nature showed the scope of such criminality and the effects it has on multiple facets of life.

RESEARCH

The report was created as an effort to compile and analyze data on wildlife crime to gain a deeper understanding of wildlife trafficking. The data that was used was predominantly supplied by the World Wildlife Seizure database (World WISE). This database includes information of 164,000 seizures from 120 countries and covers 35,000 protected species. Additional research was collected by species experts to broaden the scope of the report (United Nations 2016).

This research provides a more in-depth understanding of wildlife crime and the connection it has with current and future policies. Illicit wildlife trade was shown to be made up of related but distinct markets, with an influx in legal markets as well. Each path is made up of unique characteristics, making seeing trends all the more difficult on top of changing regulations. The most known trends are seen with documented data, lending to the policy implications suggested in the report. These policy suggestions are the result of the lack of standardization and the surplus of uncertainty that was found in the data.

GLOBAL IMPACT

A significant aspect of this report highlights the fact that wildlife crime spans the globe and is more prominent than previously believed. Based on data from World WISE, approximately 7,000 species have been seized, including mammals, reptiles, corals, birds, and fish. Most notably about such data, no single species accounts for more than 6 percent of the seizures, and a country does not account for more than 15 percent of said shipments (United Nations 2016). This statistic alludes to the vastness and diversity associated with wildlife crime. This variety is seen at all points of criminality, including animals being poached and trafficked, countries of origin, countries of destination, and nationality of traffickers.

By showcasing the global phenomenon associated with wildlife crime, the report uncovered limitations that inevitably enable such trade. This report included potential policy changes that allude to such shortcomings. Said changes include standardization of statutes, expansion of laws to include both international and national markets, increasing research and monitoring, and increasing international support to support local law enforcement (United Nations 2016).

Despite wildlife crime being a global issue, there lacks a global consensus on legislation and law enforcement. The World Wildlife Crime Report is substantive by creating a comprehensive report that showcases the globalization of such criminality and the potential to unify transnational variation.

Christina Lynn Richardson and Shanell Sanchez

See also: Convention on International Trade in Endangered Species of Wild Fauna and Flora; Poaching; Wildlife and Forest Crime

Further Reading

Scanlon, John E. 2016. "CITES Secretary-General's Remarks at the Special High-Level Event and Launch of the First 'World Wildlife Crime' Report—UN Headquarters New York." Convention on International Trade in Endangered Species of Wild Fauna and Flora, June 6. Accessed January 21, 2019. https://www.cites.org/eng/Remarks_CITES_SG_at_Special_High-level_event_and_Launch_first_World_Wildlife_Crime_Report.

United Nations Office on Drugs and Crime (UNODC). 2016 "World Wildlife Crime Report: Trafficking in Protected Species." https://www.unodc.org/unodc/en/data-and-analysis/wildlife.html

United Nations Office on Drugs and Crime (UNODC). 2018. "Wildlife Crime Assessed Globally for the First Time in New UNODC Report." Accessed January 21, 2019. https://www.unodc.org/unodc/en/frontpage/2016/May/wildlife-crime-assessed-globally-for-the-first-time-in-new-unodc-report.html.

Y

Yamaguchi-Gumi (1915–)

Yamaguchi-Gumi is identified as a yakuza, which refers to criminal organizations or transnational organized crime groups from Japan, that operates in 44 of Japan's 47 prefectures (districts). Considered one of the largest criminal organizations in the world, it is internationally active and frequently linked to construction companies tied to criminal organizations. The Yamaguchi-Gumi has an estimated annual revenue of over $6 billion. Having recently experienced internal conflicts and other challenges, the organization's dynamics have altered in response.

HISTORY

The Yamaguchi-Gumi, named after its founder, Harukichi Yamaguchi, was established in 1915 in Kobe, Japan. The Yamaguchi-Gumi has a formal headquarters located in Nada Wada, Kobe, with organization members' names and crests appearing on the buildings it occupies. There are over 23,000 members, which is roughly half of Japan's gangster population, who are often visible and active in their communities. Members typically wear a pin badge linked to the organization. The leader of the organization is referred to as *Kumicho*, a "boss" or "godfather." Published manuals outlining how to commit crimes and avoid punishment for such crimes are part of the gangster tradition in Japan.

Yamaguchi-Gumi has experienced relatively stable leadership since its inception. It has had six leaders in more than 100 years, although in times of conflict or war, an elder would fill the void if necessary. Harukichi Yamaguchi (1915–1925) was followed by his son Noboru Yamaguchi (1925–1942); then Kazuo Taoka (1946–1981), who was followed by Masahisa Takenaka (1984–1985); then Yoshinori Watanabe (1989–2005) and its current and sixth leader, Shinobu Tsukasa, who is also known as Kenich Shinoda (2005–). Yamaguchi-Gumi is officially referred to as the "Sixth Yamaguchi-Gumi" because it has its sixth formal leader.

ACTIVITIES

The Yamaguchi-Gumi, which has been in existence for more than 100 years, controls companies involved in entertainment, construction, and real estate. It is also one of Japan's largest private equity groups because of its involvement in the stock market. The organization has increased and solidified its power through gambling, violence, sex, murder, drugs, extortion, real estate kickbacks, gun smuggling, construction, blackmail, and other fraudulent activities. Although Yamaguchi-Gumi has generally been more active in Kobe, Kansai, Kyoto, and Osaka, it has operations across Japan, the United States, and other parts of Asia. The organization has engaged in both illegal and legal activities. At times, the Yamaguchi-Gumi has also engaged in humanitarian efforts. For example, members provided disaster relief after the 1995 earthquake in Kobe. The organization generally exercises caution to maintain civility with non-gang members and those residing close by.

CHALLENGES AND CONFLICT

In 1984, a split occurred in the Yamaguchi-Gumi after elders in the organization selected Masahisa Takenaka to be its fourth leader, which led to Hiroshi Yamamoto, an elder in the organization, along with several of its members leaving the organization to form Ichiwa-Kai, a rival organization. A rivalry between the two organizations developed, and Takenaka was assassinated along with some other elders in 1985.

In more recent years, the Yamaguchi-Gumi has been struggling with internal rivalry and disloyalty, which have led to some of its members breaking away from the organization and forming a new and alternate organization. As a consequence, there are approximately 72 factions of Yamaguchi-Gumi, and in 2015, during its 100th anniversary, there were concerns about potential violence, which heightened law enforcement concerns. The gang's rift was related to Tsukasa, the sixth leader of Yamaguchi-Gumi, who some members accused of giving preferential treatment to Kodo-Kai, a rival organization, which Tsukasa had established in Nagoya (located on the east coast) in 1984. Tsukasa, who spent years in prison, first for murder and then for weapon possession, also wanted to expand Kodo-Kai in various parts of eastern Japan and move the organization's headquarters to Nagoya, which angered more traditional Yamaguchi-Gumi associates in the western part of the country. Under Tsukasa's leadership, the Yamaguchi-Gumi has been punitive and doled out harsh punishment against those who fail to pay the monthly membership fee or disobey orders.

Although some outlets and publications have attributed more members and affiliates of the organization than others, recent evidence suggests membership in Yamaguchi-Gumi has declined slightly. However, the Yamaguchi-Gumi continues to exert its influence in Japan and other countries, but they are less visible today than in previous years.

Marika Dawkins

See also: Japanese Yakuza; Organized Crime

Further Reading

Adelstein, Jake. 2017a. "Gangsters Prefer to Do Things by the Book." *Japan Times*, September 30. Accessed November 22, 2017. https://www.japantimes.co.jp.

Adelstein, Jake. 2017b. "Japan's Crime Syndicates Are Shooting Themselves in the Foot." *Japan Times*, November 4. Accessed November 22, 2017. https://www.japantimes.co.jp.

Matthews, Chris. 2014. "Fortune 5: The Biggest Organized Crime Groups in the World." *Fortune*, September 14. Accessed November 22, 2017. https://fortune.com.

McCurry, Justin. 2015. "Japanese Gang War Feared as Largest Yakuza Syndicate Splits." *The Guardian*, September 7. Accessed November 22, 2017. https://theguardian.com.

McNeil, David. 2015. "Largest Yakuza Outfit Triggers Fear of Tokyo Turf War." *Irish Times*, September 12. Accessed December 13, 2017. https://irishtimes.com.

Yoshida, Reiji. 2005. "Yamaguchi-Gumi Split, Toughened Laws Will Weaken Gangs: Experts." *Japan Times*, October 20. Accessed January 4, 2017. https://www.japantimes.co.jp.

PRIMARY DOCUMENTS

1 United Nations Convention on the Prevention and Punishment of the Crime of Genocide

United Nations General Assembly

Adopted December 9, 1948; Entered into force January 12, 1951

The United Nations Convention on the Prevention and Punishment of the Crime of Genocide (the Genocide Convention) was adopted by the UN General Assembly in 1948 and entered into force in 1951, becoming the first human rights instrument adopted by the United Nations. As of August 2018, there were 149 parties to the convention. The convention defines genocide as the act of killing, mentally or physically harming, or creating conditions with "the intent to destroy, in whole or in part, a national, ethnic, racial, or religious group." Parties to the convention "confirm that genocide, whether committed in time of peace or in time of war, is a crime under international law which they undertake to prevent and to punish." In addition, the convention criminalizes the conspiracy and attempt to commit genocide, complicity in genocide, and direct and public incitement to commit genocide. The convention states that anyone, even heads of state and public officials, can be punished for the crime of genocide. Although most countries have passed laws making genocide a criminal act, examples of genocide continue to occur, as seen in the cases coming before the International Criminal Court.

Convention on the Prevention and Punishment of the Crime of Genocide
Approved and proposed for signature and ratification or accession by General Assembly resolution 260 A (III) of 9 December 1948
Entry into force: 12 January 1951, in accordance with article XIII

The Contracting Parties,

Having considered the declaration made by the General Assembly of the United Nations in its resolution 96 (I) dated 11 December 1946 that genocide is a crime under international law, contrary to the spirit and aims of the United Nations and condemned by the civilized world,

Recognizing that at all periods of history genocide has inflicted great losses on humanity, and

Being convinced that, in order to liberate mankind from such an odious scourge, international co-operation is required,

Hereby agree as hereinafter provided:

Article I

The Contracting Parties confirm that genocide, whether committed in time of peace or in time of war, is a crime under international law which they undertake to prevent and to punish.

Article II

In the present Convention, genocide means any of the following acts committed with intent to destroy, in whole or in part, a national, ethnical, racial or religious group, as such:

(a) Killing members of the group;
(b) Causing serious bodily or mental harm to members of the group;
(c) Deliberately inflicting on the group conditions of life calculated to bring about its physical destruction in whole or in part;
(d) Imposing measures intended to prevent births within the group;
(e) Forcibly transferring children of the group to another group.

Article III

The following acts shall be punishable:

(a) Genocide;
(b) Conspiracy to commit genocide;
(c) Direct and public incitement to commit genocide;
(d) Attempt to commit genocide;
(e) Complicity in genocide.

Article IV

Persons committing genocide or any of the other acts enumerated in article III shall be punished, whether they are constitutionally responsible rulers, public officials or private individuals.

Article V

The Contracting Parties undertake to enact, in accordance with their respective Constitutions, the necessary legislation to give effect to the provisions of the present Convention, and, in particular, to provide effective penalties for persons guilty of genocide or any of the other acts enumerated in article III.

Article VI

Persons charged with genocide or any of the other acts enumerated in article III shall be tried by a competent tribunal of the State in the territory of which the act was committed, or by such international penal tribunal as may have jurisdiction with respect to those Contracting Parties which shall have accepted its jurisdiction.

Article VII

Genocide and the other acts enumerated in article III shall not be considered as political crimes for the purpose of extradition.

The Contracting Parties pledge themselves in such cases to grant extradition in accordance with their laws and treaties in force.

Article VIII

Any Contracting Party may call upon the competent organs of the United Nations to take such action under the Charter of the United Nations as they consider appropriate for the prevention and suppression of acts of genocide or any of the other acts enumerated in article III.

Article IX

Disputes between the Contracting Parties relating to the interpretation, application or fulfilment of the present Convention, including those relating to the responsibility of a State for genocide or for any of the other acts enumerated in article III, shall be submitted to the International Court of Justice at the request of any of the parties to the dispute.

Article X

The present Convention, of which the Chinese, English, French, Russian and Spanish texts are equally authentic, shall bear the date of 9 December 1948.

Article XI

The present Convention shall be open until 31 December 1949 for signature on behalf of any Member of the United Nations and of any non-member State to which an invitation to sign has been addressed by the General Assembly.

The present Convention shall be ratified, and the instruments of ratification shall be deposited with the Secretary-General of the United Nations.

After 1 January 1950, the present Convention may be acceded to on behalf of any Member of the United Nations and of any non-member State which has received an invitation as aforesaid.

Instruments of accession shall be deposited with the Secretary-General of the United Nations.

Article XII

Any Contracting Party may at any time, by notification addressed to the Secretary-General of the United Nations, extend the application of the present Convention to all or any of the territories for the conduct of whose foreign relations that Contracting Party is responsible.

Article XIII

On the day when the first twenty instruments of ratification or accession have been deposited, the Secretary-General shall draw up a procès-verbal and transmit a copy thereof to each Member of the United Nations and to each of the non-member States contemplated in article XI.

The present Convention shall come into force on the ninetieth day following the date of deposit of the twentieth instrument of ratification or accession.

Any ratification or accession effected subsequent to the latter date shall become effective on the ninetieth day following the deposit of the instrument of ratification or accession.

Article XIV

The present Convention shall remain in effect for a period of ten years as from the date of its coming into force.

It shall thereafter remain in force for successive periods of five years for such Contracting Parties as have not denounced it at least six months before the expiration of the current period.

Denunciation shall be effected by a written notification addressed to the Secretary-General of the United Nations.

Article XV

If, as a result of denunciations, the number of Parties to the present Convention should become less than sixteen, the Convention shall cease to be in force as from the date on which the last of these denunciations shall become effective.

Article XVI

A request for the revision of the present Convention may be made at any time by any Contracting Party by means of a notification in writing addressed to the Secretary-General.

The General Assembly shall decide upon the steps, if any, to be taken in respect of such request.

Article XVII

The Secretary-General of the United Nations shall notify all Members of the United Nations and the non-member States contemplated in article XI of the following:

(a) Signatures, ratifications and accessions received in accordance with article XI;
(b) Notifications received in accordance with article XII;
(c) The date upon which the present Convention comes into force in accordance with article XIII;
(d) Denunciations received in accordance with article XIV;
(e) The abrogation of the Convention in accordance with article XV;
(f) Notifications received in accordance with article XVI.

Article XVIII

The original of the present Convention shall be deposited in the archives of the United Nations.

A certified copy of the Convention shall be transmitted to each Member of the United Nations and to each of the non-member States contemplated in article XI.

Article XIX

The present Convention shall be registered by the Secretary-General of the United Nations on the date of its coming into force.

Source: United Nations General Assembly. 1948. "United Nations Convention on the Prevention and Punishment of the Crime of Genocide." Accessed November 21, 2018. https://treaties.un.org/doc/Publication/UNTS/Volume%2078/v78.pdf.

2 Convention on the Means of Prohibiting and Preventing the Illicit Import, Export and Transfer of Ownership of Cultural Property

United Nations Educational, Scientific and Cultural Organization

Adopted November 14, 1970; Entered into force April 24, 1972

The Convention on the Means of Prohibiting and Preventing the Illicit Import, Export and Transfer of Ownership of Cultural Property was adopted by the United Nations Educational, Scientific and Cultural Organization at its General Conference in 1970 and came into force in 1972. As of August 2018, there are 134 states parties to the convention. In the late 1960s and early 1970s, thefts in museums and archaeological sites were increasing. and objects that had been fraudulently imported or were of unidentified origin were being offered for sale. The convention was created to address such situations. To monitor the legislative and administrative provisions that have been adopted and other actions taken in implementing the convention, states parties must submit reports at four-year intervals. The 2105 reports illustrate the progress made and obstacles encountered. For example, the U.S. report notes that there is a recurring problem of illegal excavations, primarily impacting Native American sites, that has been ongoing for decades. Also noted is the lack of reliable statistics on the size of the cultural goods market in the United States.

Convention on the Means of Prohibiting and Preventing the Illicit Import, Export and Transfer of Ownership of Cultural Property 1970

The General Conference of the United Nations Educational, Scientific and Cultural Organization, meeting in Paris from 12 October to 14 November 1970, at its sixteenth session,

Recalling the importance of the provisions contained in the Declaration of the Principles of International Cultural Co-operation, adopted by the General Conference at its fourteenth session,

Considering that the interchange of cultural property among nations for scientific, cultural and educational purposes increases the knowledge of the civilization of Man, enriches the cultural life of all peoples and inspires mutual respect and appreciation among nations,

Considering that cultural property constitutes one of the basic elements of civilization and national culture, and that its true value can be appreciated only in relation to the fullest possible information regarding is origin, history and traditional setting,

Considering that it is incumbent upon every State to protect the cultural property existing within its territory against the dangers of theft, clandestine excavation, and illicit export,

Considering that, to avert these dangers, it is essential for every State to become increasingly alive to the moral obligations to respect its own cultural heritage and that of all nations,

Considering that, as cultural institutions, museums, libraries and archives should ensure that their collections are built up in accordance with universally recognized moral principles,

Considering that the illicit import, export and transfer of ownership of cultural property is an obstacle to that understanding between nations which it is part of UNESCO's mission to promote by recommending to interested States, international conventions to this end,

Considering that the protection of cultural heritage can be effective only if organized both nationally and internationally among States working in close co-operation . . .

Adopts this Convention on the fourteenth day of November 1970.

Article 1

For the purposes of this Convention, the term 'cultural property' means property which, on religious or secular grounds, is specifically designated by each State as being of importance for archaeology, prehistory, history, literature, art or science and which belongs to the following categories:

(a) Rare collections and specimens of fauna, flora, minerals and anatomy, and objects of palaeontological interest;
(b) property relating to history, including the history of science and technology and military and social history, to the life of national leaders, thinkers, scientists and artist and to events of national importance;
(c) products of archaeological excavations (including regular and clandestine) or of archaeological discoveries;
(d) elements of artistic or historical monuments or archaeological sites which have been dismembered;
(e) antiquities more than one hundred years old, such as inscriptions, coins and engraved seals;
(f) objects of ethnological interest;
(g) property of artistic interest, such as:
    (i) pictures, paintings and drawings produced entirely by hand on any support and in any material (excluding industrial designs and manufactured articles decorated by hand);
    (ii) original works of statuary art and sculpture in any material;
    (iii) original engravings, prints and lithographs;
    (iv) original artistic assemblages and montages in any material;

(h) rare manuscripts and incunabula, old books, documents and publications of special interest (historical, artistic, scientific, literary, etc.) singly or in collections;
(i) postage, revenue and similar stamps, singly or in collections;
(j) archives, including sound, photographic and cinematographic archives;
(k) articles of furniture more than one hundred years old and old musical instruments.

Article 2

1. The States Parties to this Convention recognize that the illicit import, export and transfer of ownership of cultural property is one of the main causes of the impoverishment of the cultural heritage of the countries of origin of such property and that international co-operation constitutes one of the most efficient means of protecting each country's cultural property against all the dangers resulting there from.
2. To this end, the States Parties undertake to oppose such practices with the means at their disposal, and particularly by removing their causes, putting a stop to current practices, and by helping to make the necessary reparations.

Article 3

The import, export or transfer of ownership of cultural property effected contrary to the provisions adopted under this Convention by the States Parties thereto, shall be illicit.

Article 4

The States Parties to this Convention recognize that for the purpose of the Convention property which belongs to the following categories forms part of the cultural heritage of each State:

(a) Cultural property created by the individual or collective genius of nationals of the State concerned, and cultural property of importance to the State concerned created within the territory of that State by foreign nationals or stateless persons resident within such territory;
(b) cultural property found within the national territory;
(c) cultural property acquired by archaeological, ethnological or natural science missions, with the consent of the competent authorities of the country of origin of such property;
(d) cultural property which has been the subject of a freely agreed exchange;
(e) cultural property received as a gift or purchased legally with the consent of the competent authorities of the country of origin of such property . .

Article 6

The States Parties to this Convention undertake:

(a) To introduce an appropriate certificate in which the exporting State would specify that the export of the cultural property in question is authorized. The certificate should accompany all items of cultural property exported in accordance with the regulations;

(b) to prohibit the exportation of cultural property from their territory unless accompanied by the above-mentioned export certificate

(c) to publicize this prohibition by appropriate means, particularly among persons likely to export or import cultural property.

Article 7

The States Parties to this Convention undertake:

(a) To take the necessary measures, consistent with national legislation, to prevent museums and similar institutions within their territories from acquiring cultural property originating in another State Party which has been illegally exported after entry into force of this Convention, in the States concerned . . .

(b) (i) to prohibit the import of cultural property stolen from a museum or a religious or secular public monument or similar institution in another State Party to this Convention after the entry into force of this Convention for the States concerned, provided that such property is documented as appertaining to the inventory of that institution;
(ii) at the request of the State Party of origin, to take appropriate steps to recover and return any such cultural property imported after the entry into force of this Convention in both States concerned, provided, however, that the requesting State shall pay just compensation to an innocent purchaser or to a person who has valid title to that property . . .

Article 9

Any State Party to this Convention whose cultural patrimony is in jeopardy from pillage of archaeological or ethnological materials may call upon other States Parties who are affected . . .

Article 10

The States Parties to this Convention undertake:

(a) To restrict by education, information and vigilance, movement of cultural property illegally removed from any State Party to this Convention and, as appropriate for each country, oblige antique dealers, subject to penal or administrative sanctions, to maintain a register recording the origin of each item of cultural property, names and addresses of the supplier, description and price of each item sold and to inform the purchaser of the cultural property of the export prohibition to which such property may be subject;

(b) to endeavour by educational means to create and develop in the public mind a realization of the value of cultural property and the threat to the cultural heritage created by theft, clandestine excavations and illicit exports.

Article 11

The export and transfer of ownership of cultural property under compulsion arising directly or indirectly from the occupation of a country by a foreign power shall be regarded as illicit.

Source: United Nations Educational, Scientific and Cultural Organization (UNESCO). 1970. "Convention on the Means of Prohibiting and Preventing the Illicit Import, Export and Transfer of Ownership of Cultural Property." Accessed January 9, 2019. http://www.unesco.org/new/en/culture/themes/illicit-trafficking-of-cultural-property/1970-convention/text-of-the-convention.

3 Convention on International Trade in Endangered Species of Wild Fauna and Flora

International Union for Conservation of Nature

Adopted on March 3, 1973; Entered into force on July 1, 1975

The Convention on International Trade in Endangered Species of Wild Fauna and Flora (CITES) resulted from resolutions proposed at meetings as early as 1964 of the International Union for Conservation of Nature (IUCN) and the adoption of a formal text at a 1973 meeting of members of the IUCN in Washington, D.C. CITES entered into force in 1975, and as of August 2018 there are 183 states parties to the agreement. The convention regulates worldwide commercial trade in wild animal and plant species and ensures that international trade in plants and animals does not threaten their survival in the wild. After more than four decades, CITES remains a foundation of international conservation that requires governments to follow rules to monitor, regulate, or ban international trade in species that are under threat. It also brings together law enforcement officers from wildlife authorities, national parks, customs, and police agencies to collaborate on efforts to combat wildlife crime targeted at animals. Each CITES state party must submit reports on how it is implementing the convention, and those reports provide an assessment of successes and areas needing improvement. Representatives of CITES nations meet every two to three years at a Conference of the Parties to review progress and adjust the list of protected species.

Convention on International Trade in Endangered Species of Wild Fauna and Flora

The Contracting States,

Recognizing that wild fauna and flora in their many beautiful and varied forms are an irreplaceable part of the natural systems of the earth which must be protected for this and the generations to come;

Conscious of the ever-growing value of wild fauna and flora from aesthetic, scientific, cultural, recreational and economic points of view;

Recognizing that peoples and States are and should be the best protectors of their own wild fauna and flora;

Recognizing, in addition, that international co-operation is essential for the protection of certain species of wild fauna and flora against over-exploitation through international trade;

Convinced of the urgency of taking appropriate measures to this end;

Have agreed as follows:

Article I Definitions

For the purpose of the present Convention, unless the context otherwise requires:

(a) "Species" means any species, subspecies, or geographically separate population thereof; (b) "Specimen" means:
   (i) any animal or plant, whether alive or dead;
   (ii) in the case of an animal: for species included in Appendices I and II, any readily recognizable part or derivative thereof; and for species included in Appendix III, any readily recognizable part or derivative thereof specified in Appendix III in relation to the species; and
   (iii) in the case of a plant: for species included in Appendix I, any readily recognizable part or derivative thereof; and for species included in Appendices II and III, any readily recognizable part or derivative thereof specified in Appendices II and III in relation to the species;

(c) "Trade" means export, re-export, import and introduction from the sea;
(d) "Re-export" means export of any specimen that has previously been imported;
(e) "Introduction from the sea" means transportation into a State of specimens of any species which were taken in the marine environment not under the jurisdiction of any State;
(f) "Scientific Authority" means a national scientific authority designated in accordance with Article IX;
(g) "Management Authority" means a national management authority designated in accordance with Article IX;
(h) "Party" means a State for which the present Convention has entered into force.

Article II Fundamental principles

1. Appendix I shall include all species threatened with extinction which are or may be affected by trade. Trade in specimens of these species must be subject to particularly strict regulation in order not to endanger further their survival and must only be authorized in exceptional circumstances.
2. Appendix II shall include:
   (a) all species which although not necessarily now threatened with extinction may become so unless trade in specimens of such species is subject to strict regulation in order to avoid utilization incompatible with their survival; and
   (b) other species which must be subject to regulation in order that trade in specimens of certain species referred to in sub-paragraph (a) of this paragraph may be brought under effective control.
3. Appendix III shall include all species which any Party identifies as being subject to regulation within its jurisdiction for the purpose of preventing or restricting exploitation, and as needing the co-operation of other Parties in the control of trade.
4. The Parties shall not allow trade in specimens of species included in Appendices I, II and III except in accordance with the provisions of the present Convention.

Article III Regulation of trade in specimens of species included in Appendix I

1. All trade in specimens of species included in Appendix I shall be in accordance with the provisions of this Article.
2. The export of any specimen of a species included in Appendix I shall require the prior grant and presentation of an export permit. An export permit shall only be granted when the following conditions have been met:
   (a) a Scientific Authority of the State of export has advised that such export will not be detrimental to the survival of that species;
   (b) a Management Authority of the State of export is satisfied that the specimen was not obtained in contravention of the laws of that State for the protection of fauna and flora;
   (c) a Management Authority of the State of export is satisfied that any living specimen will be so prepared and shipped as to minimize the risk of injury, damage to health or cruel treatment; and
   (d) a Management Authority of the State of export is satisfied that an import permit has been granted for the specimen.
3. The import of any specimen of a species included in Appendix I shall require the prior grant and presentation of an import permit and either an export permit or a re-export certificate. An import permit shall only be granted when the following conditions have been met:
   (a) a Scientific Authority of the State of import has advised that the import will be for purposes which are not detrimental to the survival of the species involved;
   (b) a Scientific Authority of the State of import is satisfied that the proposed recipient of a living specimen is suitably equipped to house and care for it; and
   (c) a Management Authority of the State of import is satisfied that the specimen is not to be used for primarily commercial purposes.

Article IV Regulation of trade in specimens of species included in Appendix II

1. All trade in specimens of species included in Appendix II shall be in accordance with the provisions of this Article.
2. The export of any specimen of a species included in Appendix II shall require the prior grant and presentation of an export permit. An export permit shall only be granted when the following conditions have been met:
   (a) a Scientific Authority of the State of export has advised that such export will not be detrimental to the survival of that species;
   (b) a Management Authority of the State of export is satisfied that the specimen was not obtained in contravention of the laws of that State for the protection of fauna and flora; and

(c) a Management Authority of the State of export is satisfied that any living specimen will be so prepared and shipped as to minimize the risk of injury, damage to health or cruel treatment.

3. A Scientific Authority in each Party shall monitor both the export permits granted by that State for specimens of species included in Appendix II and the actual exports of such specimens. Whenever a Scientific Authority determines that the export of specimens of any such species should be limited in order to maintain that species throughout its range at a level consistent with its role in the ecosystems in which it occurs and well above the level at which that species might become eligible for inclusion in Appendix I, the Scientific Authority shall advise the appropriate Management Authority of suitable measures to be taken to limit the grant of export permits for specimens of that species.
4. The import of any specimen of a species included in Appendix II shall require the prior presentation of either an export permit or a re-export certificate.

. . .

Article V Regulation of trade in specimens of species included in Appendix III

1. All trade in specimens of species included in Appendix III shall be in accordance with the provisions of this Article.
2. The export of any specimen of a species included in Appendix III from any State which has included that species in Appendix III shall require the prior grant and presentation of an export permit. An export permit shall only be granted when the following conditions have been met:
   (a) a Management Authority of the State of export is satisfied that the specimen was not obtained in contravention of the laws of that State for the protection of fauna and flora; and
   (b) a Management Authority of the State of export is satisfied that any living specimen will be so prepared and shipped as to minimize the risk of injury, damage to health or cruel treatment.
3. The import of any specimen of a species included in Appendix III shall require, except in circumstances to which paragraph 4 of this Article applies, the prior presentation of a certificate of origin and, where the import is from a State which has included that species in Appendix III, an export permit.

Source: "Convention on International Trade in Endangered Species of Wild Fauna and Flora." 1973. Accessed January 9, 2019. https://www.cites.org/sites/default/files/eng/disc/CITES-Convention-EN.pdf.

4 United Nations Convention on the Law of the Sea

United Nations General Assembly

Adopted December 10, 1982; Entered into force November 16, 1994

The United Nations Convention on the Law of the Sea (UNCLOS) was adopted by the UN General Assembly in 1982 and entered into force in 1994. As of August 2018, there were 168 parties to the convention. The more than 300 articles and annexes comprising UNCLOS establish rules governing all uses of the oceans and their resources. Although the United States was an original architect of the treaty, ratification by the U.S. Senate has remained stalled through three successive presidential administrations, and therefore the United States is not a party to the convention. UNCLOS is criticized for its lack of clear definitions, for its restricted definition of piracy and lack of dealing with other forms of maritime crime, and for having inadequate environmental protections.

United Nations Convention on the Law of the Sea

PREAMBLE

The States Parties to this Convention,

Prompted by the desire to settle, in a spirit of mutual understanding and cooperation, all issues relating to the law of the sea and aware of the historic significance of this Convention as an important contribution to the maintenance of peace, justice and progress for all peoples of the world,

Noting that developments since the United Nations Conferences on the Law of the Sea held at Geneva in 1958 and 1960 have accentuated the need for a new and generally acceptable Convention on the law of the sea,

Conscious that the problems of ocean space are closely interrelated and need to be considered as a whole,

Recognizing the desirability of establishing through this Convention, with due regard for the sovereignty of all States, a legal order for the seas and oceans which will facilitate international communication, and will promote the peaceful uses of the seas and oceans, the equitable and efficient utilization of their resources, the conservation of their living resources, and the study, protection and preservation of the marine environment,

Bearing in mind that the achievement of these goals will contribute to the realization of a just and equitable international economic order which takes into account the interests and needs of mankind as a whole and, in particular, the special interests and needs of developing countries, whether coastal or land-locked,

Believing that the codification and progressive development of the law of the sea achieved in this Convention will contribute to the strengthening of peace, security, cooperation and friendly relations among all nations in conformity with the principles of justice and equal rights and will promote the economic and social advancement of all peoples of the world, in accordance with the Purposes and Principles of the United Nations as set forth in the Charter,

Affirming that matters not regulated by this Convention continue to be governed by the rules and principles of general international law,

Have agreed as follows:

PART I

INTRODUCTION

Article 1
Use of terms and scope

1. For the purposes of this Convention:

(1) "Area" means the seabed and ocean floor and subsoil thereof, beyond the limits of national jurisdiction;

(2) "Authority" means the International Seabed Authority;

(3) "activities in the Area" means all activities of exploration for, and exploitation of, the resources of the Area;

(4) "pollution of the marine environment" means the introduction by man, directly or indirectly, of substances or energy into the marine environment, including estuaries, which results or is likely to result in such deleterious effects as harm to living resources and marine life, hazards to human health, hindrance to marine activities, including fishing and other legitimate uses of the sea, impairment of quality for use of sea water and reduction of amenities . . .

PART II

TERRITORIAL SEA AND CONTIGUOUS ZONE

SECTION 1. GENERAL PROVISIONS

Article 2
Legal status of the territorial sea, of the air space over the territorial sea and of its bed and subsoil

1. The sovereignty of a coastal State extends, beyond its land territory and internal waters and, in the case of an archipelagic State, its archipelagic waters, to an adjacent belt of sea, described as the territorial sea.

2. This sovereignty extends to the air space over the territorial sea as well as to its bed and subsoil.

3. The sovereignty over the territorial sea is exercised subject to this Convention and to other rules of international law . . .

PART III

STRAITS USED FOR INTERNATIONAL NAVIGATION

SECTION 1. GENERAL PROVISIONS

Article 34
Legal status of waters forming straits used for international navigation

1. The regime of passage through straits used for international navigation established in this Part shall not in other respects affect the legal status of the waters forming such straits or the exercise by the States bordering the straits of their sovereignty or jurisdiction over such waters and their air space, bed and subsoil.

2. The sovereignty or jurisdiction of the States bordering the straits is exercised subject to this Part and to other rules of international law . . .

PART VII

HIGH SEAS

SECTION 1. GENERAL PROVISIONS

Article 86
Application of the provisions of this Part

The provisions of this Part apply to all parts of the sea that are not included in the exclusive economic zone, in the territorial sea or in the internal waters of a State, or in the archipelagic waters of an archipelagic State. This article does not entail any abridgement of the freedoms enjoyed by all States in the exclusive economic zone in accordance with article 58.

Article 87
Freedom of the high seas

1. The high seas are open to all States, whether coastal or land-locked. Freedom of the high seas is exercised under the conditions laid down by this Convention and by other rules of international law. It comprises, inter alia, both for coastal and land-locked States:
(a) freedom of navigation; (b) freedom of overflight;
(c) freedom to lay submarine cables and pipelines, subject to Part VI;
(d) freedom to construct artificial islands and other installations permitted under international law, subject to Part VI;
(e) freedom of fishing, subject to the conditions laid down in section 2;
(f) freedom of scientific research, subject to Parts VI and XIII.

2. These freedoms shall be exercised by all States with due regard for the interests of other States in their exercise of the freedom of the high seas, and also with due regard for the rights under this Convention with respect to activities in the Area.

Article 88
Reservation of the high seas for peaceful purposes

The high seas shall be reserved for peaceful purposes.

Article 89
Invalidity of claims of sovereignty over the high seas

No State may validly purport to subject any part of the high seas to its sovereignty.

Article 90
Right of navigation

Every State, whether coastal or land-locked, has the right to sail ships flying its flag on the high seas . . .

Article 91
Nationality of ships

1. Every State shall fix the conditions for the grant of its nationality to ships, for the registration of ships in its territory, and for the right to fly its flag. Ships have the nationality of the State whose flag they are entitled to fly. There must exist a genuine link between the State and the ship.
2. Every State shall issue to ships to which it has granted the right to fly its flag documents to that effect.

PART XII

PROTECTION AND PRESERVATION OF THE MARINE ENVIRONMENT

SECTION 1. GENERAL PROVISIONS

Article 192
General obligation

States have the obligation to protect and preserve the marine environment.

Article 193
Sovereign right of States to exploit their natural resources

States have the sovereign right to exploit their natural resources pursuant to their environmental policies and in accordance with their duty to protect and preserve the marine environment.

Article 194
Measures to prevent, reduce and control pollution of the marine environment

1. States shall take, individually or jointly as appropriate, all measures consistent with this Convention that are necessary to prevent, reduce and control pollution of the marine environment from any source, using for this purpose the best practicable means at their disposal and in accordance with their capabilities, and they shall endeavour to harmonize their policies in this connection.
2. States shall take all measures necessary to ensure that activities under their jurisdiction or control are so conducted as not to cause damage by pollution to other States and their environment, and that pollution arising from incidents or activities under their jurisdiction or control does not spread beyond the areas where they exercise sovereign rights in accordance with this Convention.

PART XIII

MARINE SCIENTIFIC RESEARCH SECTION 1. GENERAL PROVISIONS

Article 238
Right to conduct marine scientific research

All States, irrespective of their geographical location, and competent international organizations have the right to conduct marine scientific research subject to the rights and duties of other States as provided for in this Convention.

Article 239

Promotion of marine scientific research

States and competent international organizations shall promote and facilitate the development and conduct of marine scientific research in accordance with this Convention.

SECTION 2. INTERNATIONAL COOPERATION

Article 242

Promotion of international cooperation

1. States and competent international organizations shall, in accordance with the principle of respect for sovereignty and jurisdiction and on the basis of mutual benefit, promote international cooperation in marine scientific research for peaceful purposes.

2. In this context, without prejudice to the rights and duties of States under this Convention, a State, in the application of this Part, shall provide, as appropriate, other States with a reasonable opportunity to obtain from it, or with its cooperation, information necessary to prevent and control damage to the health and safety of persons and to the marine environment.

Source: UN General Assembly. 1982. "Convention on the Law of the Sea." Accessed January 9, 2019. https://www.un.org/depts/los/convention_agreements/texts/unclos/unclos_e.pdf.

5 Computer Fraud and Abuse Act of 1986

The Computer Fraud and Abuse Act (CFAA) became U.S. law in 1986 (Public Law No. 99-474) and formally exists as 18 USC § 1030. The CFAA criminalizes the intentional accessing of a computer or network without authorization or proceeding beyond authorized access. It is the most important federal statute on computer crime and provides the primary legislation protecting computers and digital information from unauthorized intrusion. When it was passed in 1986, "computer crime" was understood to involve hacking or accessing computer systems or data. Now, more than 30 years later, computer crime looks very different, and, as a result, the CFAA has been expanded and amended several times. For example, a 1994 amendment allows civil actions under the statute, and the 2008 amendment (the most recent) increased penalties and added forfeiture of assets as a possible penalty. Critics argue that the original law was so poorly and broadly written (for example, there is no clear definition of "without authorization") that prosecutors have been able to use the law in situations for which it could not have been originally intended.

COMPUTER FRAUD AND ABUSE ACT OF 1986

SEPTEMBER 3, 1986.-Ordered to be printed
Filed under authority of the order of the Senate of August 16
(legislative day, August 11), 1986
Mr. THURMOND, from the Committee on the Judiciary, submitted the following

REPORT

together with

ADDITIONAL VIEWS
[To accompany S. 2281, as amended]

The Committee on the Judiciary, to which was referred the bill (S. 2281) to amend title 18, United States Code, to provide additional penalties for fraud and related activities in connection with access devices and computers, and for other purposes, having considered the same, reports favorably thereon with amendments and recommends that the bill, as amended, do pass.

I. GENERAL STATEMENT AND HISTORY OF THE LEGISLATION

During the past several years, the Congress has been investigating the problems of computer fraud and abuse to determine whether Federal criminal laws should be revised to cope more effectively with such acts. The Judiciary Committee's concern about these problems has become more pronounced as computers proliferate in businesses and homes across the nation and as evidence mounts that existing criminal laws are insufficient to address the problem of computer crime.

For some time, the United States has been in the midst of a technological explosion. The Federal Government alone operates more than 18,000 medium-scale and large-scale computers at some 4,500 different sites, and the Office of Technology Assessment estimates the Government's investment in computers over the past four years at roughly $60 billion. The General Services Administration estimates that there will be 250,000 to 500,000 computers in use by the Federal Government by 1990.

Computer use has also become much more widespread among the nation's private sector. In 1978, there were an estimated 5,000 desk-top computers in this country; today there are nearly 5 million. Financial institutions, in particular, rely heavily on computer communications; for instance, the Bureau of Justice Statistics reported that in 1983, corporate transfers of funds via computer totaled more than $100 trillion. In addition, more than 100,000 personal computers have been installed in the country's schools, and computers are found in millions of American homes.

This technological explosion has made the computer a mainstay of our communications system, and it has brought a great many benefits to the government, to American businesses, and to all of our lives. But it has also created a new type of criminal-one who uses computers to steal, to defraud, and to abuse the property of others. The proliferation of computers and computer data has spread before the nation's criminals a vast array of property that, in many cases, is wholly unprotected against crime.

In June 1984, the American Bar Association Task Force on Computer Crime, chaired by Joseph Tompkins, Jr., issued its Report on Computer Crime (hereinafter referred to as the "ABA Report"), a study based upon a survey of approximately 1,000 private organizations and public agencies. The ABA Report found that more than 50 percent of the 283 respondents had been victimized by some form of computer crime, and that more than 25 percent of the respondents had sustained financial losses totaling between an estimated $145 million and $730 million during one twelve-month period. The ABA Report also concluded that computer crime is among the worst white-collar offenses. The Committee agrees but notes particularly that computer crimes pose a threat that is not solely financial in nature.

In 1983, for example, a group of adolescents known as the "414 Gang" broke into the computer system at Memorial Sloan-Kettering Cancer Center in New York. In so doing, they gained access to the radiation treatment records of 6,000 past and present cancer patients and had at their fingertips the ability to alter the radiation treatment levels that each patient received. No financial losses were at stake in this case, but the potentially life-threatening nature of such mischief is a source of serious concern to the Committee.

Similarly, so-called "pirate bulletin boards" have sprung up around the country for the sole purpose of exchanging passwords to other people's computer systems. The *Richmond (Va.) Times-Dispatch* recently reported that three such bulletin boards operating in Virginia carry information on how to break into the computers of the U.S. Defense Department and the Republican National Committee. While financial losses resulting from such pirate bulletin boards may not be imminent, the Committee believes that knowingly trafficking in other people's computer passwords should be proscribed.

It is clear that much computer crime can be prevented by those who are potential targets of such conduct. The ABA Report indicated that while the respondents to the survey overwhelmingly supported a Federal computer crime statute, they also believed that the most effective means of preventing and deterring computer crime is "more comprehensive and effective self-protection by private business" and that the primary responsibility for controlling the incidence of computer crime falls upon private industry and individual users, rather than on the Federal, State, or local governments. The Committee strongly agrees with these views.

The Committee also finds that education programs for both computer users and the general public should be undertaken to make young people and others aware of the ethical and legal questions at stake in the use of computers and to deflate the myth that computer crimes are glamorous, harmless pranks. The respondents to the ABA survey indicated strong support for such programs, many of which are underway throughout the nation. The Committee commends those education and security improvement efforts and urges their continuation.

At the same time, the Committee finds that Federal criminal penalties for computer crime are an appropriate punishment for certain acts and can serve to deter would-be computer criminals and to reinforce education and security improvement programs.

To that end, both the Senate and House have devoted considerable attention to determining how the Federal Government can best approach computer-related crimes. The first Federal computer crime statute was enacted in 1984 as part of P.L. 98-473. This is the present 18 U.S.C. 1030, which makes it a felony to access classified information in a computer without authorization and makes it a misdemeanor to access financial records or credit histories in financial institutions or to trespass into a Government computer.

. . .

Throughout its consideration of computer crime, the Committee has been especially concerned about the appropriate scope of Federal jurisdiction in this area. It has been suggested that, because some States lack comprehensive computer crime statutes of their own, the Congress should enact as sweeping a Federal statute as possible so that no computer crime is potentially uncovered. The Committee rejects this approach and prefers instead to limit Federal jurisdiction over computer crime to those cases in which there is a compelling Federal interest, i.e., where computers of the Federal Government or certain financial institutions are involved, or where the crime itself is interstate in nature. The Committee is convinced that this approach strikes the appropriate balance between the Federal Government's interest in computer crime and the interests and abilities of the States to proscribe and punish such offenses. S. 2281, as reported by the Committee, is a consensus bill aimed at deterring and punishing certain "high-tech" crimes in a manner consistent with the States' own criminal laws in this area.

. . .

CHAPTER 47—FRAUD AND FALSE STATEMENTS

§1030. Fraud and related activity in connection with computers

(a) Whoever—

(1) knowingly accesses a computer without authorization [,or having accessed a computer with authorization, uses the opportunity such access

provides for purposes to which such authorization does not extend] or *exceeds authorized access,* and by means of such conduct obtains information that has been determined by the United States Government pursuant to an Executive order or statute to require protection against unauthorized disclosure for reasons of national defense or foreign relations, or any restricted data, as defined in paragraph r. of section 11 of the Atomic Energy Act of 1954, with the intent or reason to believe that such information so obtained is to be used to the injury of the United States, or to the advantage of any foreign nation;

(2) [knowingly] *intentionally* accesses a computer without authorization [, or having accessed a computer with authorization, uses the opportunity such access provides for purposes to which such authorization does not extend] or *exceeds authorized access*, and thereby obtains information contained in a financial record of a financial institution, [as such terms are defined in the Right to Financial Privacy Act of 1978 (12 U.S.C. 3401 et seq.),] or contained in a file of a consumer reporting agency on a consumer, as such terms are defined in the Fair Credit Reporting Act (15 U.S.C. 1681 et seq.); or

(3) [knowingly accesses a computer without authorization, or having accessed a computer with authorization, uses the opportunity such access provides for purposes to which such authorization does not extend, and by means of such conduct knowingly uses, modifies, destroys, or discloses information in, or prevents authorized use of, such computer, if such computer is operated for or on behalf of the Government of the United States and such conduct affects such operation;] *intentionally, without authorization to access any computer of a department or agency of the United States, accesses such a computer of that department or agency that is exclusively for the use of the Government of the United States or, in the case of a computer not exclusively for such use, is used by or for the Government of the United States and such conduct affects the use of the Governments operation of such computer;*

(4) Knowingly and with intent to defraud, accesses a Federal interest computer without authorization, or exceeds authorized access, and by means of such conduct furthers the intended fraud and obtains anything of value, unless the object of the fraud and the thing obtained consists only of the use of the computer;

(5) intentionally accesses a Federal interest computer without authorization, and by means of one or more instances of such conduct alters, damages, or destroys information in any such Federal interest computer, or prevents authorized use of any such computer or information, and thereby—

- *(A) causes loss to one or more others of a value aggregating $1,000 or more during any one year period; or*
- *(B) modifies or impairs, or potentially modifies or impairs, the medical examination, medical diagnosis, medical treatment, or medical care of one or more individuals; or*

(6) knowingly and with intent to defraud traffics (as defined in section 1029) in any password or similar information through which a computer may be accessed without authorization, if—

(A) such trafficking affects interstate or foreign commerce; or

(B) such computer is used by or for the Government of the United States;

(b)

[1] Whoever attempts to commit an offense under subsection (a) of this section shall be punished as provided in subsection (c) of this section.

[(2) Whoever is a party to a conspiracy of two or more persons to commit an offense under subsection (a) of this section, if any of the parties engages in any conduct in furtherance of such offense, shall be fined an amount not great than the amount provided as the maximum fine for such offense under subsection (c) of this section or imprisoned not longer than one-half the period provided as the maximum imprisonment for such offense under subsection (c) of this section, or both.]

(c) The punishment for an offense under subsection (a) or (b)(l) of this section is—

(l)

(A) a fine [of not more than the greater $10,000 or twice the value obtained by the offense] *under this title* or imprisonment for not more than ten years, or both, in the case of an offense under subsection (a)(1) of this section which does not occur after a conviction for another offense under such subsection, or an attempt to commit an offense punishable under this subparagraph; and

(B) a fine [of not more than the greater of $100,000 or twice the value obtained by the offense] *under this title* or imprisonment for not more than twenty years, or both, in the case of an offense under subsection (a)(l) of this section which occurs after a conviction for another offense under such subsection, or an attempt to commit an offense punishable under this sub paragraph; and

(2)

(A) a fine [of not more than the greater of $5,000 or twice the value obtained or loss created by the offense] *under this title* or imprisonment for not more than one year, or both, in the case of an offense under subsection (a)(2) [*or (a)(3)], (a)(3) or (a)(6)* of this section which does not occur after a conviction for another offense under such subsection, or an attempt to commit an offense punishable under this subparagraph; and

(B) a fine [of not more than the greater of $10,000 or twice the value obtained or loss created by the offense] *under this title* or imprisonment for [not than] *not more than* ten years, or both, in the case of an offense under subsection (a)(2) [*or (a)(3)], (a)(3) or (a)(6)* of this section which occurs after a conviction for another offense under such subsection, or an attempt to commit an offense punishable under this subparagraph; and

(3)

(A) a fine under this title or imprisonment for not more than five years, or both, in the case of an offense under subsection (a)(4) or (a)(5) of this section which does not occur after a conviction for another offense under such subsection, or an attempt to commit an offense punishable under this subparagraph; and

(B) a fine under this title or imprisonment for not more than ten years, or both, in the case of an offense under subsection (a)(4) or (a)(5) of this section which occurs after a conviction for another offense under such subsection, or an attempt to commit an offense punishable under this subparagraph.

(e) As used in this *section*—

(1) the term "computer" means an electronic, magnetic, optical, electrochemical, or other high speed data processing device performing logical, arithmetic, or storage functions, and includes any data storage facility or communications facility directly related to or operating in conjunction with such device, but such term does not include an automated typewriter or typesetter, a portable hand held calculator, or other similar device;

(2) the term "Federal interest computer" means a computer—

(A) exclusively for the use of a financial institution or the United States Government, or, in the case of a computer not exclusively for such use, used by or for a financial institution or the United States Government and the conduct constituting the offense affects the use of the financial institution's operation or the Government's operation of such computer; or

(B) which is one of two or more computers used in committing the offense, not all of which are located in the same State;

(3) the term "State" includes the District of Columbia, the Commonwealth of Puerto Rico, and any other possession or territory of the United States;

(4) the term "financial institution" means—

(A) a bank with deposits insured by the Federal Deposit Insurance Corporation;

(B) the Federal Reserve or a member of the Federal Reserve including any Federal Reserve Bank;

(C) an institution with accounts insured by the Federal Savings and Loan Insurance Corporation;

(D) a credit union with accounts insured by the National Credit Union Administration;

(E) a member of the Federal home loan bank system and any home loan bank; and

(F) any institution of the Farm Credit System under the Farm Credit Act of 1971;

(5) the term "financial record" means information derived from any record held by a financial institution pertaining to a customer's relationship with the financial institution;

(6) *the term "exceeds authorized access" means to access a computer with authorization and to use such access to obtain or alter information in the computer that the accesser is not entitled so to obtain or alter; and*

(7) *the term "department of the United States" means the legislative or judicial branch of the Government or one of the executive departments enumerated in section 101 of title 5.*

(8) *This section does not prohibit any lawfully authorized investigative, protective, or intelligence activity of a law enforcement agency of the United States, a State, or a political subdivision of a State, or of an intelligence agency of the United States.*

Source: Senate Report 99-432, September 3, 1986. Accessed January 9, 2019. https://www.cia.gov/library/readingroom/document/cia-rdp87b00858r000400480020-8.

6 The Basel Convention on the Control of Transboundary Movements of Hazardous Wastes and Their Disposal

United Nations Environment Programme

Adopted on March 22, 1989; Entered into force May 5, 1992

The Basel Convention on the Control of Transboundary Movements of Hazardous Wastes and Their Disposal (the Basel Convention) was adopted in 1989 in Basel, Switzerland, in response to a public outcry following the 1980s discovery in Africa and other parts of the developing world of deposits of toxic wastes imported from abroad. It entered into force in 1992 and as of 2018 has 186 states parties. The convention's overarching objective was to protect human health and the environment against the adverse effects of hazardous wastes. The cornerstone of the convention is a regulatory system based on the concept of prior informed consent. The convention also provides for cooperation between parties, ranging from exchange of information on issues relevant to the implementation of the convention to technical assistance, particularly to developing countries. The convention has three principal aims: (1) the reduction of hazardous waste generation and promotion of environmentally sound management; (2) the restriction of transboundary movements of waste, except in cases of environmentally sound management; and (3) establishing a regulatory system applying to all permissible transboundary movements.

BASEL CONVENTION ON THE CONTROL OF TRANSBOUNDARY MOVEMENTS OF HAZARDOUS WASTES AND THEIR DISPOSAL

PREAMBLE

The Parties to this Convention,

Recognizing also that hazardous wastes and other wastes should be transported in accordance with relevant international conventions and recommendations,

Convinced also that the transboundary movement of hazardous wastes and other wastes should be permitted only when the transport and the ultimate disposal of such wastes is environmentally sound, and

Determined to protect, by strict control, human health and the environment against the adverse effects which may result from the generation and management of hazardous wastes and other wastes,

HAVE AGREED AS FOLLOWS:

ARTICLE 1: SCOPE OF THE CONVENTION

1. The following wastes that are subject to transboundary movement shall be "hazardous wastes" for the purposes of this Convention:

(a) Wastes that belong to any category contained in Annex I, unless they do not possess any of the characteristics contained in Annex III; and

(b) Wastes that are not covered under paragraph (a) but are defined as, or are considered to be, hazardous wastes by the domestic legislation of the Party of export, import or transit.

2. Wastes that belong to any category contained in Annex II that are subject to transboundary movement shall be "other wastes" for the purposes of this Convention.

3. Wastes which, as a result of being radioactive, are subject to other international control systems, including international instruments, applying specifically to radioactive materials, are excluded from the scope of this Convention.

4. Wastes which derive from the normal operations of a ship, the discharge of which is covered by another international instrument, are excluded from the scope of this Convention.

ARTICLE 4: GENERAL OBLIGATIONS

1. (a) Parties exercising their right to prohibit the import of hazardous wastes or other wastes for disposal shall inform the other Parties of their decision pursuant to Article 13.
   (b) Parties shall prohibit or shall not permit the export of hazardous wastes and other wastes to the Parties which have prohibited the import of such wastes, when notified pursuant to subparagraph (a) above.
   (c) Parties shall prohibit or shall not permit the export of hazardous wastes and other wastes if the State of import does not consent in writing to the specific import, in the case where that State of import has not prohibited the import of such wastes.
2. Each Party shall take the appropriate measures to:
   (a) Ensure that the generation of hazardous wastes and other wastes within it is reduced to a minimum, taking into account social, technological and economic aspects;
   (b) Ensure the availability of adequate disposal facilities, for the environmentally sound management of hazardous wastes and other wastes, that shall be located, to the extent possible, within it, whatever the place of their disposal;
   (c) Ensure that persons involved in the management of hazardous wastes or other wastes within it take such steps as are necessary to prevent pollution due to hazardous wastes and other wastes arising from such management and, if such pollution occurs, to minimize the consequences thereof for human health and the environment;
   (d) Ensure that the transboundary movement of hazardous wastes and other wastes is reduced to the minimum consistent with the environmentally sound and efficient management of such wastes, and is conducted in a manner which will protect human health and the environment against the adverse effects which may result from such movement;

(e) Not allow the export of hazardous wastes or other wastes to a State or group of States belonging to an economic and/or political integration organization that are Parties, particularly developing countries, which have prohibited by their legislation all imports, or if it has reason to believe that the wastes in question will not be managed in an environmentally sound manner, according to criteria to be decided on by the Parties at their first meeting;
(f) Require that information about a proposed transboundary movement of hazardous wastes and other wastes be provided to the States concerned, according to Annex V A, to state clearly the effects of the proposed movement on human health and the environment;
(g) Prevent the import of hazardous wastes and other wastes if it has reason to believe that the wastes in question will not be managed in an environmentally sound manner;
(h) Co-operate in activities with other Parties and interested organizations, directly and through the Secretariat, including the dissemination of information on the transboundary movement of hazardous wastes and other wastes, in order to improve the environmentally sound management of such wastes and to achieve the prevention of illegal traffic.

3. The Parties consider that illegal traffic in hazardous wastes or other wastes is criminal.
4. Each Party shall take appropriate legal, administrative and other measures to implement and enforce the provisions of this Convention, including measures to prevent and punish conduct in contravention of the Convention.
5. A Party shall not permit hazardous wastes or other wastes to be exported to a non-Party or to be imported from a non-Party.
6. The Parties agree not to allow the export of hazardous wastes or other wastes for disposal within the area south of 60° South latitude, whether or not such wastes are subject to transboundary movement.
7. Furthermore, each Party shall:

(a) Prohibit all persons under its national jurisdiction from transporting or disposing of hazardous wastes or other wastes unless such persons are authorized or allowed to perform such types of operations;
(b) Require that hazardous wastes and other wastes that are to be the subject of a transboundary movement be packaged, labelled, and transported in conformity with generally accepted and recognized international rules and standards in the field of packaging, labelling, and transport, and that due account is taken of relevant internationally recognized practices;
(c) Require that hazardous wastes and other wastes be accompanied by a movement document from the point at which a transboundary movement commences to the point of disposal.

8. Each Party shall require that hazardous wastes or other wastes, to be exported, are managed in an environmentally sound manner in the State of import or elsewhere. Technical guidelines for the environmentally sound management of wastes subject to this Convention shall be decided by the Parties at their first meeting.
9. Parties shall take the appropriate measures to ensure that the transboundary movement of hazardous wastes and other wastes only be allowed if:

   (a) The State of export does not have the technical capacity and the necessary facilities, capacity or suitable disposal sites in order to dispose of the wastes in question in an environmentally sound and efficient manner; or
   (b) The wastes in question are required as a raw material for recycling or recovery industries in the State of import; or
   (c) The transboundary movement in question is in accordance with other criteria to be decided by the Parties, provided those criteria do not differ from the objectives of this Convention.

10. The obligation under this Convention of States in which hazardous wastes and other wastes are generated to require that those wastes are managed in an environmentally sound manner may not under any circumstances be transferred to the States of import or transit.
11. Nothing in this Convention shall prevent a Party from imposing additional requirements that are consistent with the provisions of this Convention, and are in accordance with the rules of international law, in order better to protect human health and the environment.
12. Nothing in this Convention shall affect in any way the sovereignty of States over their territorial sea established in accordance with international law, and the sovereign rights and the jurisdiction which States have in their exclusive economic zones and their continental shelves in accordance with international law, and the exercise by ships and aircraft of all States of navigational rights and freedoms as provided for in international law and as reflected in relevant international instruments.
13. Parties shall undertake to review periodically the possibilities for the reduction of the amount and/or the pollution potential of hazardous wastes and other wastes which are exported to other States, in particular to developing countries.

ARTICLE 10
INTERNATIONAL CO-OPERATION

1. The Parties shall co-operate with each other in order to improve and achieve environmentally sound management of hazardous wastes and other wastes.
2. To this end, the Parties shall:

   (a) Upon request, make available information, whether on a bilateral or multilateral basis, with a view to promoting the environmentally sound management of hazardous wastes and other wastes, including harmonization of technical standards and practices for the adequate management of hazardous wastes and other wastes;

(b) Co-operate in monitoring the effects of the management of hazardous wastes on human health and the environment;

(c) Co-operate, subject to their national laws, regulations and policies, in the development and implementation of new environmentally sound low-waste technologies and the improvement of existing technologies with a view to eliminating, as far as practicable, the generation of hazardous wastes and other wastes and achieving more effective and efficient methods of ensuring their management in an environmentally sound manner, including the study of the economic, social and environmental effects of the adoption of such new or improved technologies;

(d) Co-operate actively, subject to their national laws, regulations and policies, in the transfer of technology and management systems related to the environmentally sound management of hazardous wastes and other wastes. They shall also co-operate in developing the technical capacity among Parties, especially those which may need and request technical assistance in this field;

(e) Co-operate in developing appropriate technical guidelines and/or codes of practice.

3. The Parties shall employ appropriate means to co-operate in order to assist developing countries in the implementation of subparagraphs a, b, c and d of paragraph 2 of Article 4.
4. Taking into account the needs of developing countries, co-operation between Parties and the competent international organizations is encouraged to promote, inter alia, public awareness, the development of sound management of hazardous wastes and other wastes and the adoption of new low-waste technologies.

Source: United Nations Environment Programme. 1989. "Basel Convention on the Control of Transboundary Movements of Hazardous Wastes and Their Disposal." Accessed January 9, 2019. http://www.basel.int/Portals/4/Basel%20Convention/docs/text/BaselConventionText-e.pdf.

7 UN Convention against Illicit Traffic in Narcotic Drugs and Psychotropic Substances

United Nations General Assembly

Adopted on December 20, 1988; Entered into force on November 11, 1990

The UN Convention against Illicit Traffic in Narcotic Drugs and Psychotropic Substances was adopted in 1988 and entered into force in 1990. As of August 2018, there are 190 parties to the convention. In the face of growing dangers stemming from the 1970s and 1980s demand for narcotics and the increased involvement of organized crime groups, the United Nations sought to encourage legal mechanisms for enforcing anti–drug trafficking measures. The convention's goal was to promote cooperation among countries so they could effectively address the various aspects of illicit traffic in narcotic drugs and psychotropic substances. Under provisions of the convention, state parties are obliged to take steps that include legislative and administrative measures, in conformity with their respective domestic legislative systems. The convention is seen by some as a globalization of the war on drugs because the United States provided significant pressure on the United Nations to convene the conference that eventually resulted in the convention and because the convention obliges countries to impose repressive measures and criminal sanctions in a manner similar to those provided by U.S. legislation in its own war on drugs.

UNITED NATIONS CONVENTION AGAINST ILLICIT TRAFFIC IN NARCOTIC DRUGS AND PSYCHOTROPIC SUBSTANCES

UNITED NATIONS

1989

Adopted by the Conference at its 6th plenary meeting on 19 December 1988

The Parties to this Convention,

Deeply concerned by the magnitude of and rising trend in the illicit production of, demand for and traffic in narcotic drugs and psychotropic substances, which pose a serious threat to the health and welfare of human beings and adversely affect the economic, cultural and political foundations of society,

Deeply concerned also by the steadily increasing inroads into various social groups made by illicit traffic in narcotic drugs and psychotropic substances, and particularly by the fact that children are used in many parts of the world as an illicit drug consumers market and for purposes of illicit production, distribution and trade in narcotic drugs and psychotropic substances, which entails a danger of incalculable gravity,

Recognizing the links between illicit traffic and other related organized criminal activities which undermine the legitimate economies and threaten the stability, security and sovereignty of States,

Recognizing also that illicit traffic is an international criminal activity, the suppression of which demands urgent attention and the highest priority,

Aware that illicit traffic generates large financial profits and wealth enabling transnational criminal organizations to penetrate, contaminate and corrupt the structures of government, legitimate commercial and financial business, and society at all levels,

Determined to deprive persons engaged in illicit traffic of the proceeds of their criminal activities and thereby eliminate their main incentive for doing so,

Desiring to eliminate the root causes of the problem of abuse of narcotic drugs and psychotropic substances, including the illicit demand for such drugs and substances and the enormous profits derived from illicit traffic,

Considering that measures are necessary to monitor certain substances, including precursors, chemicals and solvents, which are used in the manufacture of narcotic drugs and psychotropic substances, the ready availability of which has led to an increase in the clandestine manufacture of such drugs and substances,

Determined to improve international co-operation in the suppression of illicit traffic by sea,

Recognizing that eradication of illicit traffic is a collective responsibility of all States and that, to that end, co-ordinated action within the framework of international co-operation is necessary . . .

Desiring to conclude a comprehensive, effective and operative international convention that is directed specifically against illicit traffic and that considers the various aspects of the problem as a whole, in particular those aspects not envisaged in the existing treaties in the field of narcotic drugs and psychotropic substances,

Hereby agree as follows:

Article 1

Definitions

Except where otherwise expressly indicated or where the context otherwise requires, the following definitions shall apply throughout this Convention:

a) "Board" means the International Narcotics Control Board established by the Single Convention on Narcotic Drugs, 1961, and that Convention as amended by the 1972 Protocol Amending the Single Convention on Narcotic Drugs, 1961;
b) "Cannabis plant" means any plant of the genus Cannabis;
c) "Coca bush" means the plant of any species of the genus Erythroxylon;
d) "Commercial carrier" means any person or any public, private or other entity engaged in transporting persons, goods or mails for remuneration, hire or any other benefit . . .

Article 2

SCOPE OF THE CONVENTION

1. The purpose of this Convention is to promote co-operation among the Parties so that they may address more effectively the various aspects of illicit traffic in

narcotic drugs and psychotropic substances having an international dimension. In carrying out their obligations under the Convention, the Parties shall take necessary measures, including legislative and administrative measures, in conformity with the fundamental provisions of their respective domestic legislative systems.

Article 3

OFFENCES AND SANCTIONS

1. Each Party shall adopt such measures as may be necessary to establish as criminal offences under its domestic law, when committed intentionally:
   a. i) The production, manufacture, extraction; preparation, offering, offering for sale, distribution, sale, delivery on any terms whatsoever, brokerage, dispatch, dispatch in transit, transport, importation or exportation of any narcotic drug or any psychotropic substance . . .
      ii) The cultivation of opium poppy, coca bush or cannabis plant for the purpose of the production of narcotic drugs . . .
      iii) The possession or purchase of any narcotic drug or psychotropic substance for the purpose of any of the activities enumerated in i) above;
      iv) The manufacture, transport or distribution of equipment, materials or of substances listed in Table I and Table II, knowing that they are to be used in or for the illicit cultivation, production or manufacture of narcotic drugs or psychotropic substances . . .
2. Subject to its constitutional principles and the basic concepts of its legal system, each Party shall adopt such measures as may be necessary to establish as a criminal offence under its domestic law, when committed intentionally, the possession, purchase or cultivation of narcotic drugs or psychotropic substances for personal consumption . . .

Article 7

MUTUAL LEGAL ASSISTANCE

1. The Parties shall afford one another, pursuant to this article, the widest measure of mutual legal assistance in investigations, prosecutions and judicial proceedings in relation to criminal offences established in accordance with article 3, paragraph 1 . . .

20. The Parties shall consider, as may be necessary, the possibility of concluding bilateral or multilateral agreements or arrangements that would serve the purposes of, give practical effect to, or enhance the provisions of this article . . .

Article 9

OTHER FORMS OF CO-OPERATION AND TRAINING

1. The Parties shall co-operate closely with one another, consistent with their respective domestic legal and administrative systems, with a view to enhancing

the effectiveness of law enforcement action to suppress the commission of offences established in accordance with article 3, paragraph 1 . . .

Article 14

MEASURES TO ERADICATE ILLICIT CULTIVATION OF NARCOTIC PLANTS AND TO ELIMINATE ILLICIT DEMAND FOR NARCOTIC DRUGS AND PSYCHOTROPIC SUBSTANCES

1. Any measures taken pursuant to this Convention by Parties shall not be less stringent than the provisions applicable to the eradication of illicit cultivation of plants containing narcotic and psychotropic substances and to the elimination of illicit demand for narcotic drugs and psychotropic substances under the provisions of the 1961 Convention, the 1961 Convention as amended and the 1971 Convention.
2. Each Party shall take appropriate measures to prevent illicit cultivation of and to eradicate plants containing narcotic or psychotropic substances, such as opium poppy, coca bush and cannabis plants, cultivated illicitly in its territory. The measures adopted shall respect fundamental human rights and shall take due account of traditional licit uses, where there is historic evidence of such use, as well as the protection of the environment.
3. a) The Parties may co-operate to increase the effectiveness of eradication efforts. Such co-operation may, inter alia, include support, when appropriate, for integrated rural development leading to economically viable alternatives to illicit cultivation. Factors such as access to markets, the availability of resources and prevailing socio-economic conditions should be taken into account before such rural development programmes are implemented. The Parties may agree on any other appropriate measures of co-operation.
   b) The Parties shall also facilitate the exchange of scientific and technical information and the conduct of research concerning eradication . . .

Article 15

COMMERCIAL CARRIERS

1. The Parties shall take appropriate measures to ensure that means of transport operated by commercial carriers are not used in the commission of offences established in accordance with article 3, paragraph 1; such measures may include special arrangements with commercial carriers . . .

Article 17

ILLICIT TRAFFIC BY SEA

1. The Parties shall co-operate to the fullest extent possible to suppress illicit traffic by sea, in conformity with the international law of the sea . . .

Article 24

APPLICATION OF STRICTER MEASURES THAN THOSE REQUIRED BY THIS CONVENTION

A Party may adopt more strict or severe measures than those provided by this Convention if, in its opinion, such measures are desirable or necessary for the prevention or suppression of illicit traffic.

Source: UN General Assembly. 1988. "UN Convention against Illicit Traffic in Narcotic Drugs and Psychotropic Substances." Accessed January 9, 2019. https://www.unodc.org/pdf/convention_1988_en.pdf.

8 International Convention for the Suppression of the Financing of Terrorism

United Nations General Assembly

Adopted on December 9, 1999; Entered into force on April 10, 2002

The International Convention for the Suppression of the Financing of Terrorism (known as the Terrorist Financing Convention) was adopted by the UN General Assembly in 1999 and entered into force in 2002. As of August 2018, there are 188 states parties to the convention. The convention's goal is to help countries prevent and counteract the way terrorists and terrorist organizations receive financial support. State parties to the convention are required to have legislation that allows the freezing and seizure of funds that have been deemed intended for terrorist activities. Countries are encouraged to share the forfeited funds or to make them available to victims of the crimes. Although the convention does not define terrorism, it does list specific terrorist crimes and provides a list of activities that should be recognized in domestic law as terrorism financing. In 2017, the convention was used in an interesting way in the International Court of Justice (ICJ) when Ukraine brought action against the Russian Federation, claiming that Russia's annexation of Crimea violated, in part, aspects of the Terrorist Financing Convention. The ICJ concluded that conditions required to show a Russian violation of the convention were not met—although the ICJ did rule that Russia must act in ways to assure compliance with the International Convention on the Elimination of All Forms of Racial Discrimination.

International Convention for the Suppression of the Financing of Terrorism

Preamble

The States Parties to this Convention,

Bearing in mind the purposes and principles of the Charter of the United Nations concerning the maintenance of international peace and security and the promotion of good-neighbourliness and friendly relations and cooperation among States,

Deeply concerned about the worldwide escalation of acts of terrorism in all its forms and manifestations,

Considering that the financing of terrorism is a matter of grave concern to the international community as a whole,

Noting that the number and seriousness of acts of international terrorism depend on the financing that terrorists may obtain,

Noting also that existing multilateral legal instruments do not expressly address such financing,

Being convinced of the urgent need to enhance international cooperation among States in devising and adopting effective measures for the prevention of the financing of terrorism, as well as for its suppression through the prosecution and punishment of its perpetrators,

Have agreed as follows . . .

Article 2

1. Any person commits an offence within the meaning of this Convention if that person by any means, directly or indirectly, unlawfully and wilfully, provides or collects funds with the intention that they should be used or in the knowledge that they are to be used, in full or in part, in order to carry out:

(a) An act which constitutes an offence within the scope of and as defined in one of the treaties listed in the annex; or

(b) Any other act intended to cause death or serious bodily injury to a civilian, or to any other person not taking an active part in the hostilities in a situation of armed conflict, when the purpose of such act, by its nature or context, is to intimidate a population, or to compel a government or an international organization to do or to abstain from doing any act . . .

3. For an act to constitute an offence set forth in paragraph 1, it shall not be necessary that the funds were actually used to carry out an offence referred to in paragraph 1, subparagraphs (a) or (b) . . .

Article 3

This Convention shall not apply where the offence is committed within a single State, the alleged offender is a national of that State and is present in the territory of that State and no other State has a basis under article 7, paragraph 1, or article 7, paragraph 2, to exercise jurisdiction, except that the provisions of articles 12 to 18 shall, as appropriate, apply in those cases.

Article 4

Each State Party shall adopt such measures as may be necessary:

(a) To establish as criminal offences under its domestic law the offences set forth in article 2;

(b) To make those offences punishable by appropriate penalties which take into account the grave nature of the offences . . .

Article 6

Each State Party shall adopt such measures as may be necessary, including, where appropriate, domestic legislation, to ensure that criminal acts within the scope of this Convention are under no circumstances justifiable by considerations of a political, philosophical, ideological, racial, ethnic, religious or other similar nature.

Article 7

1. Each State Party shall take such measures as may be necessary to establish its jurisdiction over the offences set forth in article 2 when:

(a) The offence is committed in the territory of that State;

(b) The offence is committed on board a vessel flying the flag of that State or an aircraft registered under the laws of that State at the time the offence is committed;

(c) The offence is committed by a national of that State.

2. A State Party may also establish its jurisdiction over any such offence when:

(a) The offence was directed towards or resulted in the carrying out of an offence referred to in article 2, paragraph 1, subparagraph (a) or (b), in the territory of or against a national of that State;

(b) The offence was directed towards or resulted in the carrying out of an offence referred to in article 2, paragraph 1, subparagraph (a) or (b), against a State or government facility of that State abroad, including diplomatic or consular premises of that State;

(c) The offence was directed towards or resulted in an offence referred to in article 2, paragraph 1, subparagraph (a) or (b), committed in an attempt to compel that State to do or abstain from doing any act;

(d) The offence is committed by a stateless person who has his or her habitual residence in the territory of that State;

(e) The offence is committed on board an aircraft which is operated by the Government of that State . . .

Article 8

1. Each State Party shall take appropriate measures, in accordance with its domestic legal principles, for the identification, detection and freezing or seizure of any funds used or allocated for the purpose of committing the offences set forth in article 2 as well as the proceeds derived from such offences, for purposes of possible forfeiture.

2. Each State Party shall take appropriate measures, in accordance with its domestic legal principles, for the forfeiture of funds used or allocated for the purpose of committing the offences set forth in article 2 and the proceeds derived from such offences.

3. Each State Party concerned may give consideration to concluding agreements on the sharing with other States Parties, on a regular or case-by-case basis, of the funds derived from the forfeitures referred to in this article.

4. Each State Party shall consider establishing mechanisms whereby the funds derived from the forfeitures referred to in this article are utilized to compensate the victims of offences referred to in article 2, paragraph 1, subparagraph (a) or (b), or their families . . .

Article 9

1. Upon receiving information that a person who has committed or who is alleged to have committed an offence set forth in article 2 may be present in its territory, the State Party concerned shall take such measures as may be necessary under its domestic law to investigate the facts contained in the information.

2. Upon being satisfied that the circumstances so warrant, the State Party in whose territory the offender or alleged offender is present shall take the appropriate measures under its domestic law so as to ensure that person's presence for the purpose of prosecution or extradition.

3. Any person regarding whom the measures referred to in paragraph 2 are being taken shall be entitled to:

(a) Communicate without delay with the nearest appropriate representative of the State of which that person is a national or which is otherwise entitled to protect that person's rights or, if that person is a stateless person, the State in the territory of which that person habitually resides;

(b) Be visited by a representative of that State;

(c) Be informed of that person's rights under subparagraphs (a) and (b).

4. The rights referred to in paragraph 3 shall be exercised in conformity with the laws and regulations of the State in the territory of which the offender or alleged offender is present, subject to the provision that the said laws and regulations must enable full effect to be given to the purposes for which the rights accorded under paragraph 3 are intended . . .

Article 12

1. States Parties shall afford one another the greatest measure of assistance in connection with criminal investigations or criminal or extradition proceedings in respect of the offences set forth in article 2, including assistance in obtaining evidence in their possession necessary for the proceedings.

2. States Parties may not refuse a request for mutual legal assistance on the ground of bank secrecy . . .

Article 16

1. A person who is being detained or is serving a sentence in the territory of one State Party whose presence in another State Party is requested for purposes of identification, testimony or otherwise providing assistance in obtaining evidence for the investigation or prosecution of offences set forth in article 2 may be transferred if the following conditions are met:

(a) The person freely gives his or her informed consent;

(b) The competent authorities of both States agree, subject to such conditions as those States may deem appropriate . . .

Article 17

Any person who is taken into custody or regarding whom any other measures are taken or proceedings are carried out pursuant to this Convention shall be guaranteed fair treatment, including enjoyment of all rights and guarantees in conformity with the law of the State in the territory of which that person is present and applicable provisions of international law, including international human rights law.

Article 18

1. States Parties shall cooperate in the prevention of the offences set forth in article 2 by taking all practicable measures, *inter alia*, by adapting their domestic legislation, if necessary, to prevent and counter preparations in their respective territories for the commission of those offences within or outside their territories, including:

(a) Measures to prohibit in their territories illegal activities of persons and organizations that knowingly encourage, instigate, organize or engage in the commission of offences set forth in article 2;

(b) Measures requiring financial institutions and other professions involved in financial transactions to utilize the most efficient measures available for the identification of their usual or occasional customers, as well as customers in whose interest accounts are opened, and to pay special attention to unusual or suspicious transactions and report transactions suspected of stemming from a criminal activity . . .

3. States Parties shall further cooperate in the prevention of the offences set forth in article 2 by exchanging accurate and verified information in accordance with their domestic law and coordinating administrative and other measures taken, as appropriate, to prevent the commission of offences set forth in article 2 . . .

4. States Parties may exchange information through the International Criminal Police Organization (Interpol).

Source: UN General Assembly. 1999. "International Convention for the Suppression of the Financing of Terrorism." Accessed January 9, 2019. http://www.un.org/law/cod/finterr.htm.

9 Trafficking Victims Protection Act of 2000

Public Law 106-386, 106th Congress; 22 USC § 7102

October 28, 2000

The Trafficking Victims Protection Act (TVPA) became U.S. law in 2000 (Public Law No: 106-386) and formally exists as 22 USC § 7102. The TVPA was the U.S. response to its obligation upon becoming a state party to the UN Protocol to Prevent, Suppress and Punish Trafficking in Persons, Especially Women and Children. With the TVPA, human trafficking is defined as a federal crime and services for victims of human trafficking are identified. The TVPA has been reauthorized in 2003, 2005, 2008, and 2013, but a 2017 reauthorization attempt had not progressed through Congress by August 2018. The TVPA has had considerable influence on human trafficking legislation in individual states and continues to provide a framework for legislative action and victim services nationally and internationally.

VICTIMS OF TRAFFICKING AND VIOLENCE PROTECTION ACT OF 2000

Public Law 106-386
106th Congress

An Act

To combat trafficking in persons, especially into the sex trade, slavery, and involuntary servitude, to reauthorize certain Federal programs to prevent violence against women, and for other purposes.

Be it enacted by the Senate and House of Representatives of the United States of America in Congress assembled,

SECTION 1. SHORT TITLE.

This Act may be cited as the "Victims of Trafficking and Violence Protection Act of 2000".

SEC. 102. PURPOSES AND FINDINGS.

(a) Purposes.—The purposes of this division are to combat trafficking in persons, a contemporary manifestation of slavery whose victims are predominantly women and children, to ensure just and effective punishment of traffickers, and to protect their victims.

(b) Findings.—Congress finds that:

(1) As the 21st century begins, the degrading institution of slavery continues throughout the world. Trafficking in persons is a modern form of slavery, and it is the largest manifestation of slavery today. At least 700,000 persons annually, primarily women and children, are trafficked within or across international borders. Approximately 50,000 women and children are trafficked into the United States each year.

(2) Many of these persons are trafficked into the international sex trade, often by force, fraud, or coercion. The sex industry has rapidly expanded over the

past several decades. It involves sexual exploitation of persons, predominantly women and girls, involving activities related to prostitution, pornography, sex tourism, and other commercial sexual services. The low status of women in many parts of the world has contributed to a burgeoning of the trafficking industry.

(3) Trafficking in persons is not limited to the sex industry. This growing transnational crime also includes forced labor and involves significant violations of labor, public health, and human rights standards worldwide.

(4) Traffickers primarily target women and girls, who are disproportionately affected by poverty, the lack of access to education, chronic unemployment, discrimination, and the lack of economic opportunities in countries of origin. Traffickers lure women and girls into their networks through false promises of decent working conditions at relatively good pay as nannies, maids, dancers, factory workers, restaurant workers, sales clerks, or models. Traffickers also buy children from poor families and sell them into prostitution or into various types of forced or bonded labor.

(5) Traffickers often transport victims from their home communities to unfamiliar destinations, including foreign countries away from family and friends, religious institutions, and other sources of protection and support, leaving the victims defenseless and vulnerable.

(6) Victims are often forced through physical violence to engage in sex acts or perform slavery-like labor. Such force includes rape and other forms of sexual abuse, torture, starvation, imprisonment, threats, psychological abuse, and coercion.

(7) Traffickers often make representations to their victims that physical harm may occur to them or others should the victim escape or attempt to escape. Such representations can have the same coercive effects on victims as direct threats to inflict such harm.

(8) Trafficking in persons is increasingly perpetrated by organized, sophisticated criminal enterprises. Such trafficking is the fastest growing source of profits for organized criminal enterprises worldwide. Profits from the trafficking industry contribute to the expansion of organized crime in the United States and worldwide. Trafficking in persons is often aided by official corruption in countries of origin, transit, and destination, thereby threatening the rule of law.

. . .

(14) Existing legislation and law enforcement in the United States and other countries are inadequate to deter trafficking and bring traffickers to justice, failing to reflect the gravity of the offenses involved. No comprehensive law exists in the United States that penalizes the range of offenses involved in the trafficking scheme. Instead, even the most brutal instances of trafficking in the sex industry are often punished under laws that also apply to lesser offenses, so that traffickers typically escape deserved punishment.

. . .

(21) Trafficking of persons is an evil requiring concerted and vigorous action by countries of origin, transit or destination, and by international organizations.

. . .

(24) Trafficking in persons is a transnational crime with national implications. To deter international trafficking and bring its perpetrators to justice, nations including the United States must recognize that trafficking is a serious offense. This is done by prescribing appropriate punishment, giving priority to the prosecution of trafficking offenses, and protecting rather than punishing the victims of such offenses. The United States must work bilaterally and multilaterally to abolish the trafficking industry by taking steps to promote cooperation among countries linked together by international trafficking routes. The United States must also urge the international community to take strong action in multilateral fora to engage recalcitrant countries in serious and sustained efforts to eliminate trafficking and protect trafficking victims.

SEC. 103. DEFINITIONS.

In this division:

(2) Coercion.—The term "coercion" means—

(A) threats of serious harm to or physical restraint against any person;

(B) any scheme, plan, or pattern intended to cause a person to believe that failure to perform an act would result in serious harm to or physical restraint against any person; or

(C) the abuse or threatened abuse of the legal process.

(3) Commercial sex act.—The term "commercial sex act" means any sex act on account of which anything of value is given to or received by any person.

(4) Debt bondage.—The term "debt bondage" means the status or condition of a debtor arising from a pledge by the debtor of his or her personal services or of those of a person under his or her control as a security for debt, if the value of those services as reasonably assessed is not applied toward the liquidation of the debt or the length and nature of those services are not respectively limited and defined.

(5) Involuntary servitude.—The term "involuntary servitude" includes a condition of servitude induced by means of—

(A) any scheme, plan, or pattern intended to cause a person to believe that, if the person did not enter into or continue in such condition, that person or another person would suffer serious harm or physical restraint; or

(B) the abuse or threatened abuse of the legal process.

(8) Severe forms of trafficking in persons.—The term "severe forms of trafficking in persons" means—

(A) sex trafficking in which a commercial sex act is induced by force, fraud, or coercion, or in which the person induced to perform such act has not attained 18 years of age; or

(B) the recruitment, harboring, transportation, provision, or obtaining of a person for labor or services, through the use of force, fraud, or coercion for the purpose of subjection to involuntary servitude, peonage, debt bondage, or slavery.

(9) Sex trafficking.—The term "sex trafficking" means the recruitment, harboring, transportation, provision, or obtaining of a person for the purpose of a commercial sex act.

. . .

SEC. 107. PROTECTION AND ASSISTANCE FOR VICTIMS OF TRAFFICKING.

(a) Assistance for Victims in Other Countries.—

(1) In general.—The Secretary of State and the Administrator of the United States Agency for International Development, in consultation with appropriate nongovernmental organizations, shall establish and carry out programs and initiatives in foreign countries to assist in the safe integration, reintegration, or resettlement, as appropriate, of victims of trafficking. Such programs and initiatives shall be designed to meet the appropriate assistance needs of such persons and their children, as identified by the Task Force.

(2) Additional requirement.—In establishing and conducting programs and initiatives described in paragraph (1), the Secretary of State and the Administrator of the United States Agency for International Development shall take all appropriate steps to enhance cooperative efforts among foreign countries, including countries of origin of victims of trafficking, to assist in the integration, reintegration, or resettlement, as appropriate, of victims of trafficking, including stateless victims.

(b) Victims in the United States.—

(1) Assistance.—

(A) Eligibility for benefits and services.—Notwithstanding title IV of the Personal Responsibility and Work Opportunity Reconciliation Act of 1996, an alien who is a victim of a severe form of trafficking in persons shall be eligible for benefits and services under any Federal or State program or activity funded or administered by any official or agency described in subparagraph (B) to the same extent as an alien who is admitted to the United States as a refugee under section 207 of the Immigration and Nationality Act.

(B) Requirement to expand benefits and services.—Subject to subparagraph (C) and, in the case of nonentitlement programs, to the availability of appropriations, the Secretary of Health and Human Services, the Secretary of Labor, the Board of Directors of the Legal Services Corporation, and the heads of other Federal agencies shall expand benefits and services to victims of severe forms of trafficking in persons in the United States, without regard to the immigration status of such victims.

(C) Definition of victim of a severe form of trafficking in persons.—For the purposes of this paragraph, the term "victim of a severe form of trafficking in persons" means only a person—

(i) who has been subjected to an act or practice described in section 103(8) as in effect on the date of the enactment of this Act; and

(ii)(I) who has not attained 18 years of age; or

(II) who is the subject of a certification under subparagraph (E).

Source: U.S. Congress. 2000. "Trafficking Victims Protection Act of 2000." Accessed January 9, 2019. https://www.congress.gov/106/plaws/publ386/PLAW-106publ386.pdf.

10 United Nations Convention against Transnational Organized Crime

United Nations General Assembly

Adopted November 15, 2000; Entered into force September 29, 2003

The United Nations Convention against Transnational Organized Crime (UNTOC) was adopted by the UN General Assembly in 2000 and entered into force in 2003. There are 189 states parties as of August 2018. Also called the Palermo Convention for the Italian city where it was signed, UNTOC is the primary international instrument in the fight against transnational organized crime. The convention was a direct result of concerns about the growth of organized cross border criminal activities during the 1990s and the understanding that transnational crime must be responded to with transnational efforts to prevent and combat its occurrence. UNTOC is designed to provide countries with a framework for international cooperation in combating such criminal activities as money laundering, corruption, illicit trafficking in endangered species, offenses against cultural heritage, and the links between terrorism and transnational organized crime. Although UNTOC is criticized for lacking a clear definition of transnational crime and for using broad and ambiguous terms for organized crime groups, it has significantly influenced domestic laws and international crime-fighting efforts.

United Nations Convention against Transnational Organized Crime

The General Assembly,

Deeply concerned by the negative economic and social implications related to organized criminal activities, and convinced of the urgent need to strengthen cooperation to prevent and combat such activities more effectively at the national, regional and international levels,

Noting with deep concern the growing links between transnational organized crime and terrorist crimes, taking into account the Charter of the United Nations and the relevant resolutions of the General Assembly,

Strongly convinced that the United Nations Convention against Transnational Organized Crime will constitute an effective tool and the necessary legal framework for international cooperation in combating, inter alia, such criminal activities as money-laundering, corruption, illicit trafficking in endangered species of wild flora and fauna, offences against cultural heritage and the growing links between transnational organized crime and terrorist crimes . . .

6. *Calls upon* all States to recognize the links between transnational organized criminal activities and acts of terrorism, taking into account the relevant General Assembly resolutions, and to apply the United Nations Convention against Transnational Organized Crime in combating all forms of criminal activity, as provided therein . . .

Annex I
United Nations Convention against Transnational Organized Crime

Article 1
Statement of purpose

The purpose of this Convention is to promote cooperation to prevent and combat transnational organized crime more effectively.

Article 2
Use of terms

For the purposes of this Convention:

(*a*) "Organized criminal group" shall mean a structured group of three or more persons, existing for a period of time and acting in concert with the aim of committing one or more serious crimes or offences established in accordance with this Convention, in order to obtain, directly or indirectly, a financial or other material benefit . . .

Article 3
Scope of application

1. This Convention shall apply, except as otherwise stated herein, to the prevention, investigation and prosecution of:

(*a*) The offences established in accordance with articles 5, 6, 8 and 23 of this Convention; and

(*b*) Serious crime as defined in article 2 of this Convention;

where the offence is transnational in nature and involves an organized criminal group.

2. For the purpose of paragraph 1 of this article, an offence is transnational in nature if:

(*a*) It is committed in more than one State;

(*b*) It is committed in one State but a substantial part of its preparation, planning, direction or control takes place in another State;

(*c*) It is committed in one State but involves an organized criminal group that engages in criminal activities in more than one State; or

(*d*) It is committed in one State but has substantial effects in another State .

Article 5
Criminalization of participation in an organized criminal group

1. Each State Party shall adopt such legislative and other measures as may be necessary to establish as criminal offences, when committed intentionally:

(*a*) Either or both of the following as criminal offences distinct from those involving the attempt or completion of the criminal activity:

(i) Agreeing with one or more other persons to commit a serious crime for a purpose relating directly or indirectly to the obtaining of a financial or other material benefit and, where required by domestic law, involving an act undertaken by one of the participants in furtherance of the agreement or involving an organized criminal group;

(ii) Conduct by a person who, with knowledge of either the aim and general criminal activity of an organized criminal group or its intention to commit the crimes in question, takes an active part in:

a. Criminal activities of the organized criminal group;
b. Other activities of the organized criminal group in the knowledge that his or her participation will contribute to the achievement of the above- described criminal aim;
(*b*) Organizing, directing, aiding, abetting, facilitating or counselling the commission of serious crime involving an organized criminal group . . .

Article 7
Measures to combat money-laundering
1. Each State Party:
(*a*) Shall institute a comprehensive domestic regulatory and supervisory regime for banks and non-bank financial institutions and, where appropriate, other bodies particularly susceptible to money-laundering, within its competence, in order to deter and detect all forms of money-laundering, which regime shall emphasize requirements for customer identification, record-keeping and the reporting of suspicious transactions . . .

Article 8
Criminalization of corruption
1. Each State Party shall adopt such legislative and other measures as may be necessary to establish as criminal offences, when committed intentionally:
(*a*) The promise, offering or giving to a public official, directly or indirectly, of an undue advantage, for the official himself or herself or another person or entity, in order that the official act or refrain from acting in the exercise of his or her official duties;
(*b*) The solicitation or acceptance by a public official, directly or indirectly, of an undue advantage, for the official himself or herself or another person or entity, in order that the official act or refrain from acting in the exercise of his or her official duties . . .

Article 9
Measures against corruption
1. In addition to the measures set forth in article 8 of this Convention, each State Party shall, to the extent appropriate and consistent with its legal system, adopt legislative, administrative or other effective measures to promote integrity and to prevent, detect and punish the corruption of public officials . . .

Article 11
Prosecution, adjudication and sanctions
1. Each State Party shall make the commission of an offence established in accordance with articles 5, 6, 8 and 23 of this Convention liable to sanctions that take into account the gravity of that offence . . .

Article 18
Mutual legal assistance
1. States Parties shall afford one another the widest measure of mutual legal assistance in investigations, prosecutions and judicial proceedings in relation to the

offences covered by this Convention as provided for in article 3 and shall reciprocally extend to one another similar assistance where the requesting State Party has reasonable grounds to suspect that the offence referred to in article 3, paragraph 1 (*a*) or (*b*), is transnational in nature, including that victims, witnesses, proceeds, instrumentalities or evidence of such offences are located in the requested State Party and that the offence involves an organized criminal group . . .

Article 19
Joint investigations

States Parties shall consider concluding bilateral or multilateral agreements or arrangements whereby, in relation to matters that are the subject of investigations, prosecutions or judicial proceedings in one or more States, the competent authorities concerned may establish joint investigative bodies. In the absence of such agreements or arrangements, joint investigations may be undertaken by agreement on a case-by-case basis. The States Parties involved shall ensure that the sovereignty of the State Party in whose territory such investigation is to take place is fully respected . . .

Article 24
Protection of witnesses

1. Each State Party shall take appropriate measures within its means to provide effective protection from potential retaliation or intimidation for witnesses in criminal proceedings who give testimony concerning offences covered by this Convention and, as appropriate, for their relatives and other persons close to them . . .

Article 25
Assistance to and protection of victims

1. Each State Party shall take appropriate measures within its means to provide assistance and protection to victims of offences covered by this Convention, in particular in cases of threat of retaliation or intimidation.

2. Each State Party shall establish appropriate procedures to provide access to compensation and restitution for victims of offences covered by this Convention.

3. Each State Party shall, subject to its domestic law, enable views and concerns of victims to be presented and considered at appropriate stages of criminal proceedings against offenders in a manner not prejudicial to the rights of the defence . . .

Article 27
Law enforcement cooperation

1. States Parties shall cooperate closely with one another, consistent with their respective domestic legal and administrative systems, to enhance the effectiveness of law enforcement action to combat the offences covered by this Convention . . .

2. With a view to giving effect to this Convention, States Parties shall consider entering into bilateral or multilateral agreements or arrangements on direct cooperation between their law enforcement agencies and, where such agreements or arrangements already exist, amending them . . .

Article 29
Training and technical assistance

1. Each State Party shall, to the extent necessary, initiate, develop or improve specific training programmes for its law enforcement personnel, including prosecutors, investigating magistrates and customs personnel, and other personnel charged with the prevention, detection and control of the offences covered by this Convention. Such programmes may include secondments and exchanges of staff . . .

Article 31
Prevention

1. States Parties shall endeavour to develop and evaluate national projects and to establish and promote best practices and policies aimed at the prevention of transnational organized crime.

2. States Parties shall endeavour, in accordance with fundamental principles of their domestic law, to reduce existing or future opportunities for organized criminal groups to participate in lawful markets with proceeds of crime, through appropriate legislative, administrative or other measures.

Source: UN General Assembly. 2000. "Convention against Transnational Organized Crime." Accessed January 9, 2019. https://www.unodc.org/documents/treaties/UNTOC/Publications/TOC%20Convention/TOCebook-e.pdf.

11 United Nations Protocol against the Smuggling of Migrants by Land, Sea, and Air, Supplementing the United Nations Convention against Transnational Organized Crime

United Nations General Assembly

Adopted November 15, 2000; Entered into force January 28, 2004

The Protocol against the Smuggling of Migrants by Land, Sea and Air (Smuggling Protocol) is one of three protocols attached to the UN Convention against Transnational Organized Crime (UNTOC). It was adopted by the UN General Assembly along with UNTOC in 2000. Because it required a signature separate from that required for UNTOC, it did not come into force until January 28, 2004. As of August 2018, there were 146 parties to the protocol. The Smuggling Protocol, which provided the first agreed upon definition of human smuggling in a legally binding convention, aimed to prevent and combat the smuggling of migrants but also to protect the rights of smuggled migrants. The problem of determining what constituted smuggling was approached by focusing on the illegal entry of foreign nationals in exchange for financial and other material benefit. Thus, human smuggling for purposes of the protocol is distinguished from smuggling that occurs, for example, as a favor to one's family members.

Annex III

Protocol against the Smuggling of Migrants by Land, Sea and Air, supplementing the United Nations Convention against Transnational Organized Crime

Preamble

The States Parties to this Protocol,

Declaring that effective action to prevent and combat the smuggling of migrants by land, sea and air requires a comprehensive international approach, including cooperation, the exchange of information and other appropriate measures, including socio-economic measures, at the national, regional and international levels,

Convinced of the need to provide migrants with humane treatment and full protection of their rights,

Taking into account the fact that, despite work undertaken in other international forums, there is no universal instrument that addresses all aspects of smuggling of migrants and other related issues,

Concerned at the significant increase in the activities of organized criminal groups in smuggling of migrants and other related criminal activities set forth in this Protocol, which bring great harm to the States concerned,

Also concerned that the smuggling of migrants can endanger the lives or security of the migrants involved,

Convinced that supplementing the United Nations Convention against Transnational Organized Crime with an international instrument against the smuggling of migrants by land, sea and air will be useful in preventing and combating that crime,

Have agreed as follows:

I. General provisions

Article 1. Relation with the United Nations Convention against Transnational Organized Crime

1. This Protocol supplements the United Nations Convention against Transnational Organized Crime. It shall be interpreted together with the Convention.

2. The provisions of the Convention shall apply, mutatis mutandis, to this Protocol unless otherwise provided herein.

3. The offences established in accordance with article 6 of this Protocol shall be regarded as offences established in accordance with the Convention.

Article 2. Statement of purpose

The purpose of this Protocol is to prevent and combat the smuggling of migrants, as well as to promote cooperation among States Parties to that end, while protecting the rights of smuggled migrants.

Article 3. Use of terms

For the purposes of this Protocol:

(a) "Smuggling of migrants" shall mean the procurement, in order to obtain, directly or indirectly, a financial or other material benefit, of the illegal entry of a person into a State Party of which the person is not a national or a permanent resident;

(b) "Illegal entry" shall mean crossing borders without complying with the necessary requirements for legal entry into the receiving State;

(c) "Fraudulent travel or identity document" shall mean any travel or identity document:

- (i) That has been falsely made or altered in some material way by anyone other than a person or agency lawfully authorized to make or issue the travel or identity document on behalf of a State; or
- (ii) That has been improperly issued or obtained through misrepresentation, corruption or duress or in any other unlawful manner; or
- (iii) That is being used by a person other than the rightful holder;

(d) "Vessel" shall mean any type of water craft, including non-displacement craft and seaplanes, used or capable of being used as a means of transportation on water, except a warship, naval auxiliary or other vessel owned or operated by a Government and used, for the time being, only on government non-commercial service.

Article 5. Criminal liability of migrants

Migrants shall not become liable to criminal prosecution under this Protocol for the fact of having been the object of conduct set forth in article 6 of this Protocol.

Article 6. Criminalization

1. Each State Party shall adopt such legislative and other measures as may be necessary to establish as criminal offences, when committed intentionally and in order to obtain, directly or indirectly, a financial or other material benefit:

(a) The smuggling of migrants;

(b) When committed for the purpose of enabling the smuggling of migrants:

(i) Producing a fraudulent travel or identity document;

(ii) Procuring, providing or possessing such a document;

(c) Enabling a person who is not a national or a permanent resident to remain in the State concerned without complying with the necessary requirements for legally remaining in the State by the means mentioned in sub-paragraph *(b)* of this paragraph or any other illegal means.

II. Smuggling of migrants by sea

Article 7. Cooperation

States Parties shall cooperate to the fullest extent possible to prevent and suppress the smuggling of migrants by sea, in accordance with the international law of the sea.

Article 8. Measures against the smuggling of migrants by sea

1. A State Party that has reasonable grounds to suspect that a vessel that is flying its flag or claiming its registry, that is without nationality or that, though flying a foreign flag or refusing to show a flag, is in reality of the nationality of the State Party concerned is engaged in the smuggling of migrants by sea may request the assistance of other States Parties in suppressing the use of the vessel for that purpose. The States Parties so requested shall render such assistance to the extent possible within their means.

Article 9. Safeguard clauses

1. Where a State Party takes measures against a vessel in accordance with article 8 of this Protocol, it shall:

(a) Ensure the safety and humane treatment of the persons on board;

(b) Take due account of the need not to endanger the security of the vessel or its cargo;

(c) Take due account of the need not to prejudice the commercial or legal interests of the flag State or any other interested State;

(d) Ensure, within available means, that any measure taken with regard to the vessel is environmentally sound.

III. Prevention, cooperation and other measures

Article 10. Information

1. Without prejudice to articles 27 and 28 of the Convention, States Parties, in particular those with common borders or located on routes along which migrants are smuggled, shall, for the purpose of achieving the objectives of this Protocol, exchange among themselves, consistent with their respective domestic legal and administrative systems, relevant information

Article 11. Border measures

1. Without prejudice to international commitments in relation to the free movement of people, States Parties shall strengthen, to the extent possible, such border controls as may be necessary to prevent and detect the smuggling of migrants.

Article 14. Training and technical cooperation

1. States Parties shall provide or strengthen specialized training for immigration and other relevant officials in preventing the conduct set forth in article 6 of this Protocol and in the humane treatment of migrants who have been the object of such conduct, while respecting their rights as set forth in this Protocol.

Article 15. Other prevention measures

1. Each State Party shall take measures to ensure that it provides or strengthens information programmes to increase public awareness of the fact that the conduct set forth in article 6 of this Protocol is a criminal activity frequently perpetrated by organized criminal groups for profit and that it poses serious risks to the migrants concerned.

Article 16. Protection and assistance measures

1. In implementing this Protocol, each State Party shall take, consistent with its obligations under international law, all appropriate measures, including legislation if necessary, to preserve and protect the rights of persons who have been the object of conduct set forth in article 6 of this Protocol as accorded under applicable international law, in particular the right to life and the right not to be subjected to torture or other cruel, inhuman or degrading treatment or punishment.

2. Each State Party shall take appropriate measures to afford migrants appropriate protection against violence that may be inflicted upon them, whether by individuals or groups, by reason of being the object of conduct set forth in article 6 of this Protocol.

. . .

4. In applying the provisions of this article, States Parties shall take into account the special needs of women and children.

Article 18. Return of smuggled migrants

1. Each State Party agrees to facilitate and accept, without undue or unreasonable delay, the return of a person who has been the object of conduct set forth in article 6 of this Protocol and who is its national or who has the right of permanent residence in its territory at the time of return.

Source: UN General Assembly. 2000. "Protocol against the Smuggling of Migrants by Land, Sea and Air," Annex III, page 53. Accessed January 9, 2019. http://www.unodc.org/documents/treaties/UNTOC/Publications/TOC%20Convention/TOCebook-e.pdf.

12 United Nations Protocol to Prevent, Suppress, and Punish Trafficking in Persons, Especially Women and Children, Supplementing the United Nations Convention against Transnational Organized Crime

United Nations General Assembly

Adopted November 15, 2000; Entered into force December 25, 2003

The Protocol to Prevent, Suppress and Punish Trafficking in Persons, Especially Women and Children (the Trafficking Protocol) is one of three protocols attached to the UN Convention against Transnational Organized Crime (UNTOC). It was adopted by the UN General Assembly along with UNTOC in 2000. Because it required a signature separate from that required for UNTOC, it did not come into force until December 25, 2003. As of August 2018, there were 173 parties to the Trafficking Protocol. The Trafficking Protocol is the first global legally binding instrument with an agreed upon definition of trafficking in persons. In addition to providing a definition, it includes provisions for assistance to and protection for victims, preventive measures, actions to discourage the demand, and procedures for the exchange of information and training by the states parties. The Trafficking Protocol has had significant impact on domestic legislation worldwide, especially in how human trafficking is defined. For example, the U.S. Trafficking Victims Protection Act draws heavily from the definitions and provisions of the Trafficking Protocol.

Protocol to Prevent, Suppress and Punish Trafficking in Persons, Especially Women and Children, supplementing the

United Nations Convention against

Transnational Organized Crime

Preamble

The States Parties to this Protocol,

Declaring that effective action to prevent and combat trafficking in persons, especially women and children, requires a comprehensive international approach in the countries of origin, transit and destination that includes measures to prevent such trafficking, to punish the traffickers and to protect the victims of such trafficking, including by protecting their internationally recognized human rights,

Taking into account the fact that, despite the existence of a variety of international instruments containing rules and practical measures to combat the exploitation of persons, especially women and children, there is no universal instrument that addresses all aspects of trafficking in persons,

Concerned that, in the absence of such an instrument, persons who are vulnerable to trafficking will not be sufficiently protected,

Convinced that supplementing the United Nations Convention against Transnational Organized Crime with an international instrument for the prevention, suppression and punishment of trafficking in persons, especially women and children, will be useful in preventing and combating that crime,

Have agreed as follows:

I. General provisions

Article 1. Relation with the United Nations Convention against Transnational Organized Crime

1. This Protocol supplements the United Nations Convention against Transnational Organized Crime. It shall be interpreted together with the Convention.

2. The provisions of the Convention shall apply, mutatis mutandis, to this Protocol unless otherwise provided herein.

3. The offences established in accordance with article 5 of this Protocol shall be regarded as offences established in accordance with the Convention.

Article 2. Statement of purpose

The purposes of this Protocol are:

(a) To prevent and combat trafficking in persons, paying particular attention to women and children;

(b) To protect and assist the victims of such trafficking, with full respect for their human rights; and

(c) To promote cooperation among States Parties in order to meet those objectives.

Article 3. Use of terms

For the purposes of this Protocol:

(a) "Trafficking in persons" shall mean the recruitment, transportation, transfer, harbouring or receipt of persons, by means of the threat or use of force or other forms of coercion, of abduction, of fraud, of deception, of the abuse of power or of a position of vulnerability or of the giving or receiving of payments or benefits to achieve the consent of a person having control over another person, for the purpose of exploitation. Exploitation shall include, at a minimum, the exploitation of the prostitution of others or other forms of sexual exploitation, forced labour or services, slavery or practices similar to slavery, servitude or the removal of organs; exploitation set forth in subparagraph *(a)* of this article shall be irrelevant where any of the means set forth in subparagraph *(a)* have been used;

(c) The recruitment, transportation, transfer, harbouring or receipt of a child for the purpose of exploitation shall be considered "trafficking in persons" even if this does not involve any of the means set forth in subparagraph *(a)* of this article;

(d) "Child" shall mean any person under eighteen years of age.

Article 5. Criminalization

1. Each State Party shall adopt such legislative and other measures as may be necessary to establish as criminal offences the conduct set forth in article 3 of this Protocol, when committed intentionally.

II. Protection of victims of trafficking in persons

Article 6. Assistance to and protection of victims of trafficking in persons

1. In appropriate cases and to the extent possible under its domestic law, each State Party shall protect the privacy and identity of victims of trafficking.

2. Each State Party shall ensure that its domestic legal or administrative system contains measures that provide to victims of trafficking in persons, in appropriate cases:

(a) Information on relevant court and administrative proceedings;

(b) Assistance to enable their views and concerns to be presented and considered at appropriate stages of criminal proceedings against offenders, in a manner not prejudicial to the rights of the defence.

Article 7. Status of victims of trafficking in persons in receiving States

1. In addition to taking measures pursuant to article 6 of this Protocol, each State Party shall consider adopting legislative or other appropriate measures that permit victims of trafficking in persons to remain in its territory, temporarily or permanently, in appropriate cases.

Article 8. Repatriation of victims of trafficking in persons

1. The State Party of which a victim of trafficking in persons is a national or in which the person had the right of permanent residence at the time of entry into the territory of the receiving State Party shall facilitate and accept, with due regard for the safety of that person, the return of that person without undue or unreasonable delay.

III. Prevention, cooperation and other measures

Article 9. Prevention of trafficking in persons

1. States Parties shall establish comprehensive policies, programmes and other measures:

(a) To prevent and combat trafficking in persons; and

(b) To protect victims of trafficking in persons, especially women and children, from revictimization.

2. States Parties shall endeavour to undertake measures such as research, information and mass media campaigns and social and economic initiatives to prevent and combat trafficking in persons.

3. Policies, programmes and other measures established in accordance with this article shall, as appropriate, include cooperation with non-governmental organizations, other relevant organizations and other elements of civil society.

4. States Parties shall take or strengthen measures, including through bilateral or multilateral cooperation, to alleviate the factors that make persons, especially women and children, vulnerable to trafficking, such as poverty, underdevelopment and lack of equal opportunity.

5. States Parties shall adopt or strengthen legislative or other measures, such as educational, social or cultural measures, including through bilateral and multilateral cooperation, to discourage the demand that fosters all forms of exploitation of persons, especially women and children, that leads to trafficking.

Article 11. Border measures

1. Without prejudice to international commitments in relation to the free movement of people, States Parties shall strengthen, to the extent possible, such border controls as may be necessary to prevent and detect trafficking in persons.

Source: UN General Assembly. 2000. "Protocol to Prevent, Suppress and Punish Trafficking in Persons, Especially Women and Children," Annex II, page 41. Accessed January 9, 2019. http://www.unodc.org/documents/treaties/UNTOC/Publications/TOC%20Convention/TOCebook-e.pdf.

13 United Nations Protocol against the Illicit Manufacturing of and Trafficking in Firearms, Their Parts and Components and Ammunition

Adopted May 31, 2001; Entered into force July 3, 2005

The United Nations Protocol Against the Illicit Manufacturing of and Trafficking in Firearms, Their Parts and Components and Ammunition (the Firearms Protocol) was adopted by the UN General Assembly in 2001 and entered into force in 2005. It supplements the United Nations Convention against Transnational Organized Crime. As of October 2018, there were 116 parties to the protocol. The Firearms Protocol was designed to counter the illicit manufacturing of, and trafficking in, firearms—as well as their parts and components and ammunition—at the global level. State parties to the protocol are expected to have domestic laws that make criminal the illicit manufacturing of and trafficking in firearms and to have effective control and security measures that can prevent the theft illicit distribution of firearms. In addition, governments are to have a system of tracking firearms from manufacturer to purchaser to deter their illicit trafficking. The United States is one of 10 countries in the world that has not signed the Firearms Protocol. Many in the United States believe that provisions of the protocol contradict the Second Amendment to the U.S. Constitution, which provides for access to firearms. Specific concerns are with the protocol's requirement for a registry of firearm ownership and also with the prohibition of manufacturing firearms without government authorization—a point that amateur firearm manufacturers find unacceptable.

Preamble

The States Parties to this Protocol,

Aware of the urgent need to prevent, combat and eradicate the illicit manufacturing of and trafficking in firearms, their parts and components and ammunition, owing to the harmful effects of those activities on the security of each State, region and the world as a whole, endangering the well-being of peoples, their social and economic development and their right to live in peace,

Convinced, therefore, of the necessity for all States to take all appropriate measures to this end, including international cooperation and other measures at the regional and global levels,

Recalling General Assembly resolution 53/111 of 9 December 1998, in which the Assembly decided to establish an open-ended intergovernmental ad hoc committee for the purpose of elaborating a comprehensive international convention against transnational organized crime and of discussing the elaboration of, inter alia, an international instrument combating the illicit manufacturing of and trafficking in firearms, their parts and components and ammunition,

Bearing in mind the principle of equal rights and self-determination of peoples, as enshrined in the Charter of the United Nations and the Declaration on Principles of International Law concerning Friendly Relations and Cooperation among States in accordance with the Charter of the United Nations,

Convinced that supplementing the United Nations Convention against Transnational Organized Crime with an international instrument against the illicit manufacturing of and trafficking in firearms, their parts and components and ammunition will be useful in preventing and combating those crimes,
Have agreed as follows:

I. General provisions

Article 1

Relation with the United Nations Convention against Transnational Organized Crime

1. This Protocol supplements the United Nations Convention against Transnational Organized Crime. It shall be interpreted together with the Convention.

2. The provisions of the Convention shall apply, mutatis mutandis, to this Protocol unless otherwise provided herein.

3. The offences established in accordance with article 5 of this Protocol shall be regarded as offences established in accordance with the Convention.

Article 2

Statement of purpose

The purpose of this Protocol is to promote, facilitate and strengthen cooperation among States Parties in order to prevent, combat and eradicate the illicit manufacturing of and trafficking in firearms, their parts and components and ammunition.

Article 3

Use of terms

For the purposes of this Protocol:

(a) "Firearm" shall mean any portable barrelled weapon that expels, is designed to expel or may be readily converted to expel a shot, bullet or projectile by the action of an explosive, excluding antique firearms or their replicas. Antique firearms and their replicas shall be defined in accordance with domestic law. In no case, however, shall antique firearms include firearms manufactured after 1899;

(b) "Parts and components" shall mean any element or replacement element specifically designed for a firearm and essential to its operation, including a barrel, frame or receiver, slide or cylinder, bolt or breech block, and any device designed or adapted to diminish the sound caused by firing a firearm;

(c) "Ammunition" shall mean the complete round or its components, including cartridge cases, primers, propellant powder, bullets or projectiles, that are used in a firearm, provided that those components are themselves subject to authorization in the respective State Party;

(d) "Illicit manufacturing" shall mean the manufacturing or assembly of firearms, their parts and components or ammunition:

- (i) From parts and components illicitly trafficked;
- (ii) Without a licence or authorization from a competent authority of the State Party where the manufacture or assembly takes place; or

(iii) Without marking the firearms at the time of manufacture, in accordance with article 8 of this Protocol; Licensing or authorization of the manufacture of parts and components shall be in accordance with domestic law;

(e) "Illicit trafficking" shall mean the import, export, acquisition, sale, delivery, movement or transfer of firearms, their parts and components and ammunition from or across the territory of one State Party to that of another State Party if any one of the States Parties concerned does not authorize it in accordance with the terms of this Protocol or if the firearms are not marked in accordance with article 8 of this Protocol;

(f) "Tracing" shall mean the systematic tracking of firearms and, where possible, their parts and components and ammunition from manufacturer to purchaser for the purpose of assisting the competent authorities of States Parties in detecting, investigating and analysing illicit manufacturing and illicit trafficking.

Article 4
Scope of application

1. This Protocol shall apply, except as otherwise stated herein, to the prevention of illicit manufacturing of and trafficking in firearms, their parts and components and ammunition and to the investigation and prosecution of offences established in accordance with article 5 of this Protocol where those offences are transnational in nature and involve an organized criminal group.

2. This Protocol shall not apply to state-to-state transactions or to state transfers in cases where the application of the Protocol would prejudice the right of a State Party to take action in the interest of national security consistent with the Charter of the United Nations.

Article 5
Criminalization

1. Each State Party shall adopt such legislative and other measures as may be necessary to establish as criminal offences the following conduct, when committed intentionally:

(a) Illicit manufacturing of firearms, their parts and components and ammunition;

(b) Illicit trafficking in firearms, their parts and components and ammunition;

(c) Falsifying or illicitly obliterating, removing or altering the marking(s) on firearms required by article 8 of this Protocol.

2. Each State Party shall also adopt such legislative and other measures as may be necessary to establish as criminal offences the following conduct:

(a) Subject to the basic concepts of its legal system, attempting to commit or participating as an accomplice in an offence established in accordance with paragraph 1 of this article; and

(b) Organizing, directing, aiding, abetting, facilitating or counselling the commission of an offence established in accordance with paragraph 1 of this article.

Article 6
Confiscation, seizure and disposal

1. Without prejudice to article 12 of the Convention, States Parties shall adopt, to the greatest extent possible within their domestic legal systems,

such measures as may be necessary to enable confiscation of firearms, their parts and components and ammunition that have been illicitly manufactured or trafficked.

2. States Parties shall adopt, within their domestic legal systems, such measures as may be necessary to prevent illicitly manufactured and trafficked firearms, parts and components and ammunition from falling into the hands of unauthorized persons by seizing and destroying such firearms, their parts and components and ammunition unless other disposal has been officially authorized, provided that the firearms have been marked and the methods of disposal of those firearms and ammunition have been recorded.

II. Prevention

Article 7
Record-keeping

Each State Party shall ensure the maintenance, for not less than ten years, of information in relation to firearms and, where appropriate and feasible, their parts and components and ammunition that is necessary to trace and identify those firearms and, where appropriate and feasible, their parts and components and ammunition which are illicitly manufactured or trafficked and to prevent and detect such activities. Such information shall include:

(a) The appropriate markings required by article 8 of this Protocol;

(b) In cases involving international transactions in firearms, their parts and components and ammunition, the issuance and expiration dates of the appropriate licences or authorizations, the country of export, the country of import, the transit countries, where appropriate, and the final recipient and the description and quantity of the articles.

Article 8
Marking of firearms

1. For the purpose of identifying and tracing each firearm, States Parties shall:

(a) At the time of manufacture of each firearm, either require unique marking providing the name of the manufacturer, the country or place of manufacture and the serial number, or maintain any alternative unique user-friendly marking with simple geometric symbols in combination with a numeric and/or alphanumeric code, permitting ready identification by all States of the country of manufacture;

(b) Require appropriate simple marking on each imported firearm, permitting identification of the country of import and, where possible, the year of import and enabling the competent authorities of that country to trace the firearm, and a unique marking, if the firearm does not bear such a marking. The requirements of this subparagraph need not be applied to temporary imports of firearms for verifiable lawful purposes;

(c) Ensure, at the time of transfer of a firearm from government stocks to permanent civilian use, the appropriate unique marking permitting identification by all States Parties of the transferring country.

2. States Parties shall encourage the firearms manufacturing industry to develop measures against the removal or alteration of markings.

Article 9
Deactivation of firearms

A State Party that does not recognize a deactivated firearm as a firearm in accordance with its domestic law shall take the necessary measures, including the establishment of specific offences if appropriate, to prevent the illicit reactivation of deactivated firearms, consistent with the following general principles of deactivation:

(a) All essential parts of a deactivated firearm are to be rendered permanently inoperable and incapable of removal, replacement or modification in a manner that would permit the firearm to be reactivated in any way;

(b) Arrangements are to be made for deactivation measures to be verified, where appropriate, by a competent authority to ensure that the modifications made to a firearm render it permanently inoperable;

(c) Verification by a competent authority is to include a certificate or record attesting to the deactivation of the firearm or a clearly visible mark to that effect stamped on the firearm.

Article 10
General requirements for export, import and transit licensing or authorization systems

1. Each State Party shall establish or maintain an effective system of export and import licensing or authorization, as well as of measures on international transit, for the transfer of firearms, their parts and components and ammunition.

2. Before issuing export licences or authorizations for shipments of firearms, their parts and components and ammunition, each State Party shall verify:

(a) That the importing States have issued import licences or authorizations; and

(b) That, without prejudice to bilateral or multilateral agreements or arrangements favouring landlocked States, the transit States have, at a minimum, given notice in writing, prior to shipment, that they have no objection to the transit.

3. The export and import licence or authorization and accompanying documentation together shall contain information that, at a minimum, shall include the place and the date of issuance, the date of expiration, the country of export, the country of import, the final recipient, a description and the quantity of the firearms, their parts and components and ammunition and, whenever there is transit, the countries of transit. The information contained in the import licence must be provided in advance to the transit States.

4. The importing State Party shall, upon request, inform the exporting State Party of the receipt of the dispatched shipment of firearms, their parts and components or ammunition.

5. Each State Party shall, within available means, take such measures as may be necessary to ensure that licensing or authorization procedures are secure and that the authenticity of licensing or authorization documents can be verified or validated.

6. States Parties may adopt simplified procedures for the temporary import and export and the transit of firearms, their parts and components and ammunition for

verifiable lawful purposes such as hunting, sport shooting, evaluation, exhibitions or repairs.

Article 11

Security and preventive measures

In an effort to detect, prevent and eliminate the theft, loss or diversion of, as well as the illicit manufacturing of and trafficking in, firearms, their parts and components and ammunition, each State Party shall take appropriate measures:

(a) To require the security of firearms, their parts and components and ammunition at the time of manufacture, import, export and transit through its territory; and

(b) To increase the effectiveness of import, export and transit controls, including, where appropriate, border controls, and of police and customs transborder cooperation.

Article 12

Information

1. Without prejudice to articles 27 and 28 of the Convention, States Parties shall exchange among themselves, consistent with their respective domestic legal and administrative systems, relevant case-specific information on matters such as authorized producers, dealers, importers, exporters and, whenever possible, carriers of firearms, their parts and components and ammunition.

2. Without prejudice to articles 27 and 28 of the Convention, States Parties shall exchange among themselves, consistent with their respective domestic legal and administrative systems, relevant information on matters such as:

(a) Organized criminal groups known to take part or suspected of taking part in the illicit manufacturing of or trafficking in firearms, their parts and components and ammunition;

(b) The means of concealment used in the illicit manufacturing of or trafficking in firearms, their parts and components and ammunition and ways of detecting them;

(c) Methods and means, points of dispatch and destination and routes customarily used by organized criminal groups engaged in illicit trafficking in firearms, their parts and components and ammunition; and

(d) Legislative experiences and practices and measures to prevent, combat and eradicate the illicit manufacturing of and trafficking in firearms, their parts and components and ammunition.

3. States Parties shall provide to or share with each other, as appropriate, relevant scientific and technological information useful to law enforcement authorities in order to enhance each other's abilities to prevent, detect and investigate the illicit manufacturing of and trafficking in firearms, their parts and components and ammunition and to prosecute the persons involved in those illicit activities.

4. States Parties shall cooperate in the tracing of firearms, their parts and components and ammunition that may have been illicitly manufactured or trafficked. Such cooperation shall include the provision of prompt responses to requests for assistance in tracing such firearms, their parts and components and ammunition, within available means.

5. Subject to the basic concepts of its legal system or any international agreements, each State Party shall guarantee the confidentiality of and comply with

any restrictions on the use of information that it receives from another State Party pursuant to this article, including proprietary information pertaining to commercial transactions, if requested to do so by the State Party providing the information. If such confidentiality cannot be maintained, the State Party that provided the information shall be notified prior to its disclosure.

Article 13
Cooperation

1. States Parties shall cooperate at the bilateral, regional and international levels to prevent, combat and eradicate the illicit manufacturing of and trafficking in firearms, their parts and components and ammunition.

2. Without prejudice to article 18, paragraph 13, of the Convention, each State Party shall identify a national body or a single point of contact to act as liaison between it and other States Parties on matters relating to this Protocol.

3. States Parties shall seek the support and cooperation of manufacturers, dealers, importers, exporters, brokers and commercial carriers of firearms, their parts and components and ammunition to prevent and detect the illicit activities referred to in paragraph 1 of this article.

Article 14
Training and technical assistance

States Parties shall cooperate with each other and with relevant international organizations, as appropriate, so that States Parties may receive, upon request, the training and technical assistance necessary to enhance their ability to prevent, combat and eradicate the illicit manufacturing of and trafficking in firearms, their parts and components and ammunition, including technical, financial and material assistance in those matters identified in articles 29 and 30 of the Convention.

Article 15
Brokers and brokering

1. With a view to preventing and combating illicit manufacturing of and trafficking in firearms, their parts and components and ammunition, States Parties that have not yet done so shall consider establishing a system for regulating the activities of those who engage in brokering. Such a system could include one or more measures such as:

(a) Requiring registration of brokers operating within their territory;

(b) Requiring licensing or authorization of brokering; or

(c) Requiring disclosure on import and export licences or authorizations, or accompanying documents, of the names and locations of brokers involved in the transaction.

Source: UN General Assembly. 2001. “United Nations Protocol against the Illicit Manufacturing of and Trafficking in Firearms, Their Parts and Components and Ammunition.” Accessed January 9, 2019. https://treaties.un.org/doc/source/recenttexts/18-12_c_e.pdf.

14 Programme of Action to Prevent, Combat and Eradicate the Illicit Trade in Small Arms and Light Weapons in All Its Aspects

Adopted July 20, 2001

New York, NY

The United Nations Conference on the Illicit Trade in Small Arms and Light Weapons in All Its Aspects convened in New York City from July 9–20, 2001. At its meeting, on July 20, 2001, the conference adopted the orally amended draft Programme of Action to Prevent, Combat and Eradicate the Illicit Trade in Small Arms and Light Weapons in All Its Aspects. A Programme of Action (PoA) provides a way to encourage voluntary cooperation among countries, rather than requiring certain actions as is true with treaties, conventions, and protocols. Under this PoA, governments agreed to improve national small-arms laws to better control availability and access to these weapons. In addition, countries would also improve their import/export controls, stockpile management, and engage in cooperation and assistance. The countries agreed to have periodic meetings and to provide reports on progress made in implementing the PoA. In 2005, they also adopted the International Tracing Instrument (ITI), which requires states to ensure that weapons are properly marked and recorded and to provide a framework for cooperation in weapons tracing. Since the PoA was adopted, there have been improvements in the control and tracing of small-arms weapons, but there is general agreement that a gap exists between the commitments made and the actions that have been taken.

I. Introduction

1. In its resolution 54/54 V of 15 December 1999, the General Assembly decided to convene the United Nations Conference on the Illicit Trade in Small Arms and Light Weapons in All Its Aspects in June/July 2001.

2. In the same resolution, the General Assembly decided to establish a preparatory committee open to participation by all States, which would hold no fewer than three sessions, the first to be held in New York from 28 February to 3 March 2000.

3. The Preparatory Committee subsequently held its first session at United Nations Headquarters in New York from 28 February to 3 March 2000; its second session in New York from 8 to 19 January 2001; and its third session in New York from 19 to 30 March 2001. The reports of the Preparatory Committee for the Conference are contained in document A/CONF.192/1.

4. By its decision 55/415 of 20 November 2000, the General Assembly decided to convene the United Nations Conference on the Illicit Trade in Small Arms and Light Weapons in All Its Aspects in New York, from 9 to 20 July 2001.

Programme of Action to Prevent, Combat and Eradicate the Illicit Trade in Small Arms and Light Weapons in All Its Aspects

I. Preamble

1. We, the States participating in the United Nations Conference on the Illicit Trade in Small Arms and Light Weapons in All Its Aspects, having met in New York from 9 to 20 July 2001,

2. Gravely concerned about the illicit manufacture, transfer and circulation of small arms and light weapons and their excessive accumulation and uncontrolled spread in many regions of the world, which have a wide range of humanitarian and socio-economic consequences and pose a serious threat to peace, reconciliation, safety, security, stability and sustainable development at the individual, local, national, regional and international levels,

3. Concerned also by the implications that poverty and underdevelopment may have for the illicit trade in small arms and light weapons in all its aspects,

4. Determined to reduce the human suffering caused by the illicit trade in small arms and light weapons in all its aspects and to enhance the respect for life and the dignity of the human person through the promotion of a culture of peace,

5. Recognizing that the illicit trade in small arms and light weapons in all its aspects sustains conflicts, exacerbates violence, contributes to the displacement of civilians, undermines respect for international humanitarian law, impedes the provision of humanitarian assistance to victims of armed conflict and fuels crime and terrorism,

6. Gravely concerned about its devastating consequences on children, many of whom are victims of armed conflict or are forced to become child soldiers, as well as the negative impact on women and the elderly, and in this context, taking into account the special session of the United Nations General Assembly on children,

7. Concerned also about the close link between terrorism, organized crime, trafficking in drugs and precious minerals and the illicit trade in small arms and light weapons, and stressing the urgency of international efforts and cooperation aimed at combating this trade simultaneously from both a supply and demand perspective,

8. Reaffirming our respect for and commitment to international law and the purposes and principles enshrined in the Charter of the United Nations, including the sovereign equality of States, territorial integrity, the peaceful resolution of international disputes, non-intervention and non-interference in the internal affairs of States,

9. Reaffirming the inherent right to individual or collective self-defence in accordance with Article 51 of the Charter of the United Nations,

10. Reaffirming also the right of each State to manufacture, import and retain small arms and light weapons for its self-defence and security needs, as well as

A/CONF.192/15 8 for its capacity to participate in peacekeeping operations in accordance with the Charter of the United Nations,

11. Reaffirming the right of self-determination of all peoples, taking into account the particular situation of peoples under colonial or other forms of alien domination or foreign occupation, and recognizing the right of peoples to take legitimate action in accordance with the Charter of the United Nations to realize their inalienable right of self-determination. This shall not be construed as authorizing or encouraging any action that would dismember or impair, totally or in part, the territorial integrity or political unity of sovereign and independent States conducting themselves in compliance with the principle of equal rights and self-determination of peoples,

12. Recalling the obligations of States to fully comply with arms embargoes decided by the United Nations Security Council in accordance with the Charter of the United Nations,

13. Believing that Governments bear the primary responsibility for preventing, combating and eradicating the illicit trade in small arms and light weapons in all its aspects and, accordingly, should intensify their efforts to define the problems associated with such trade and find ways of resolving them,

14. Stressing the urgent necessity for international cooperation and assistance, including financial and technical assistance, as appropriate, to support and facilitate efforts at the local, national, regional and global levels to prevent, combat and eradicate the illicit trade in small arms and light weapons in all its aspects,

15. Recognizing that the international community has a duty to deal with this issue, and acknowledging that the challenge posed by the illicit trade in small arms and light weapons in all its aspects is multi-faceted and involves, inter alia, security, conflict prevention and resolution, crime prevention, humanitarian, health and development dimensions,

16. Recognizing also the important contribution of civil society, including non-governmental organizations and industry in, inter alia, assisting Governments to prevent, combat and eradicate the illicit trade in small arms and light weapons in all its aspects, . . .

22. Resolve therefore to prevent, combat and eradicate the illicit trade in small arms and light weapons in all its aspects by:

(a) Strengthening or developing agreed norms and measures at the global, regional and national levels that would reinforce and further coordinate efforts to prevent, combat and eradicate the illicit trade in small arms and light weapons in all its aspects;
(b) Developing and implementing agreed international measures to prevent, combat and eradicate illicit manufacturing of and trafficking in small arms and light weapons;

(c) Placing particular emphasis on the regions of the world where conflicts come to an end and where serious problems with the excessive and destabilizing accumulation of small arms and light weapons have to be dealt with urgently;
(d) Mobilizing the political will throughout the international community to prevent and combat illicit transfers and manufacturing of small arms and light weapons in all their aspects, to cooperate towards these ends and to raise awareness of the character and seriousness of the interrelated problems associated with the illicit manufacturing of and trafficking in these weapons;
(e) Promoting responsible action by States with a view to preventing the illicit export, import, transit and retransfer of small arms and light weapons.

II. Preventing, combating and eradicating the illicit trade in small arms and light weapons in all its aspects

1. We, the States participating in this Conference, bearing in mind the different situations, capacities and priorities of States and regions, undertake the following measures to prevent, combat and eradicate the illicit trade in small arms and light weapons in all its aspects:

At the national level

2. To put in place, where they do not exist, adequate laws, regulations and administrative procedures to exercise effective control over the production of small arms and light weapons within their areas of jurisdiction and over the export, import, transit or retransfer of such weapons, in order to prevent illegal manufacture of and illicit trafficking in small arms and light weapons, or their diversion to unauthorized recipients.

3. To adopt and implement, in the States that have not already done so, the necessary legislative or other measures to establish as criminal offences under their domestic law the illegal manufacture, possession, stockpiling and trade of small arms and light weapons within their areas of jurisdiction, in order to ensure that those engaged in such activities can be prosecuted under appropriate national penal codes.

4. To establish, or designate as appropriate, national coordination agencies or bodies and institutional infrastructure responsible for policy guidance, research and monitoring of efforts to prevent, combat and eradicate the illicit trade in small arms and light weapons in all its aspects. This should include aspects of the illicit manufacture, control, trafficking, circulation, brokering and trade, as well as tracing, finance, collection and destruction of small arms and light weapons.

5. To establish or designate, as appropriate, a national point of contact to act as liaison between States on matters relating to the implementation of the Programme of Action.

6. To identify, where applicable, groups and individuals engaged in the illegal manufacture, trade, stockpiling, transfer, possession, as well as financing for acquisition, of illicit small arms and light weapons, and take action under appropriate national law against such groups and individuals.

7. To ensure that henceforth licensed manufacturers apply an appropriate and reliable marking on each small arm and light weapon as an integral part of the production process. This marking should be unique and should identify the country of manufacture and also provide information that enables the national authorities of that country to identify the manufacturer and serial number so that the authorities concerned can identify and trace each weapon.

8. To adopt where they do not exist and enforce, all the necessary measures to prevent the manufacture, stockpiling, transfer and possession of any unmarked or inadequately marked small arms and light weapons.

9. To ensure that comprehensive and accurate records are kept for as long as possible on the manufacture, holding and transfer of small arms and light A/CONF.192/15 11 weapons under their jurisdiction. These records should be organized and maintained in such a way as to ensure that accurate information can be promptly retrieved and collated by competent national authorities.

10. To ensure responsibility for all small arms and light weapons held and issued by the State and effective measures for tracing such weapons.

11. To assess applications for export authorizations according to strict national regulations and procedures that cover all small arms and light weapons and are consistent with the existing responsibilities of States under relevant international law, taking into account in particular the risk of diversion of these weapons into the illegal trade. Likewise, to establish or maintain an effective national system of export and import licensing or authorization, as well as measures on international transit, for the transfer of all small arms and light weapons, with a view to combating the illicit trade in small arms and light weapons.

12. To put in place and implement adequate laws, regulations and administrative procedures to ensure the effective control over the export and transit of small arms and light weapons, including the use of authenticated end-user certificates and effective legal and enforcement measures.

13. To make every effort, in accordance with national laws and practices, without prejudice to the right of States to re-export small arms and light weapons that they have previously imported, to notify the original exporting State in accordance with their bilateral agreements before the retransfer of those weapons.

14. To develop adequate national legislation or administrative procedures regulating the activities of those who engage in small arms and light weapons brokering. This legislation or procedures should include measures such as registration of brokers, licensing or authorization of brokering transactions as well as the appropriate penalties for all illicit brokering activities performed within the State's jurisdiction and control.

15. To take appropriate measures, including all legal or administrative means, against any activity that violates a United Nations Security Council arms embargo in accordance with the Charter of the United Nations.

16. To ensure that all confiscated, seized or collected small arms and light weapons are destroyed, subject to any legal constraints associated with the preparation of criminal prosecutions, unless another form of disposition or use has been officially authorized and provided that such weapons have been duly marked and registered.

17. To ensure, subject to the respective constitutional and legal systems of States, that the armed forces, police or any other body authorized to hold small arms and light weapons establish adequate and detailed standards and procedures relating to the management and security of their stocks of these weapons. These standards and procedures should, inter alia, relate to: appropriate locations for stockpiles; physical security measures; control of access to stocks; inventory management and accounting control; staff training; security, accounting and control of small arms and light weapons held or A/CONF.192/15 12 transported by operational units or authorized personnel; and procedures and sanctions in the event of thefts or loss.

18. To regularly review, as appropriate, subject to the respective constitutional and legal systems of States, the stocks of small arms and light weapons held by armed forces, police and other authorized bodies and to ensure that such stocks declared by competent national authorities to be surplus to requirements are clearly identified, that programmes for the responsible disposal, preferably through destruction, of such stocks are established and implemented and that such stocks are adequately safeguarded until disposal.

19. To destroy surplus small arms and light weapons designated for destruction, taking into account, inter alia, the report of the Secretary-General of the United Nations on methods of destruction of small arms, light weapons, ammunition and explosives (S/2000/1092) of 15 November 2000.

20. To develop and implement, including in conflict and post-conflict situations, public awareness and confidence-building programmes on the problems and consequences of the illicit trade in small arms and light weapons in all its aspects, including, where appropriate, the public destruction of surplus weapons and the voluntary surrender of small arms and light weapons, if possible, in cooperation with civil society and non-governmental organizations, with a view to eradicating the illicit trade in small arms and light weapons.

21. To develop and implement, where possible, effective disarmament, demobilization and reintegration programmes, including the effective collection, control, storage and destruction of small arms and light weapons, particularly in post-conflict situations, unless another form of disposition or use has been duly authorized and such weapons have been marked and the alternate form of disposition or use has been recorded, and to include, where applicable, specific provisions for these programmes in peace agreements.

22. To address the special needs of children affected by armed conflict, in particular the reunification with their family, their reintegration into civil society, and their appropriate rehabilitation.

23. To make public national laws, regulations and procedures that impact on the prevention, combating and eradicating of the illicit trade in small arms and light weapons in all its aspects and to submit, on a voluntary basis, to relevant regional and international organizations and in accordance with their national practices, information on, inter alia, (a) small arms and light weapons confiscated or destroyed within their jurisdiction; and (b) other relevant information such as illicit trade routes and techniques of acquisition that can contribute to the eradication of the illicit trade in small arms and light weapons in all its aspects . . .

At the global level

32. To cooperate with the United Nations system to ensure the effective implementation of arms embargoes decided by the United Nations Security Council in accordance with the Charter of the United Nations.

33. To request the Secretary-General of the United Nations, within existing resources, through the Department for Disarmament Affairs, to collate and circulate data and information provided by States on a voluntary basis and including national reports, on implementation by those States of the Programme of Action.

34. To encourage, particularly in post-conflict situations, the disarmament and demobilization of ex-combatants and their subsequent reintegration into civilian life, including providing support for the effective disposition, as stipulated in paragraph 17 of this section, of collected small arms and light weapons.

35. To encourage the United Nations Security Council to consider, on a case by-case basis, the inclusion, where applicable, of relevant provisions for disarmament, demobilization and reintegration in the mandates and budgets of peacekeeping operations.

36. To strengthen the ability of States to cooperate in identifying and tracing in a timely and reliable manner illicit small arms and light weapons.

37. To encourage States and the World Customs Organization, as well as other relevant organizations, to enhance cooperation with the International Criminal Police Organization (Interpol) to identify those groups and individuals engaged in the illicit trade in small arms and light weapons in all its aspects in order to allow national authorities to proceed against them in accordance with their national laws.

38. To encourage States to consider ratifying or acceding to international legal instruments against terrorism and transnational organized crime.

39. To develop common understandings of the basic issues and the scope of the problems related to illicit brokering in small arms and light weapons with a view to preventing, combating and eradicating the activities of those engaged in such brokering.

40. To encourage the relevant international and regional organizations and States to facilitate the appropriate cooperation of civil society, including nongovernmental organizations, in activities related to the prevention, combat and eradication of the illicit trade in small arms and light weapons in all its aspects, in view of the important role that civil society plays in this area.

41. To promote dialogue and a culture of peace by encouraging, as appropriate, education and public awareness programmes on the problems of the illicit trade in small arms and light weapons in all its aspects, involving all sectors of society.

Source: United Nations Office for Disarmament Affairs. 2006. "Report of the United Nations Conference on the Illicit Trade in Small Arms and Light Weapons in All Its Aspects." Accessed January 9, 2019. www.un.org/events/smallarms2006/pdf/192.15%20(E).pdf.

15 United Nations Convention against Corruption

United Nations General Assembly

Adopted on October 31, 2003; Entered into Force on December 14, 2005

The Convention against Corruption (UNCAC) was adopted by the UN General Assembly in 2003 and as of 2018 has 186 states parties. It is the first global anti-corruption convention and provides the base for legislation to prevent and combat corruption. The convention covers such corruption acts as domestic and foreign bribery, embezzlement, and money laundering. UNCAC requires states parties to establish as criminal offenses basic forms of public- and private-sector corruption and to take anticorruption action such as enhanced transparency and making public servants subject to codes of conduct. The goal is to promote the prevention, detection, and sanctioning of corruption and to encourage international cooperation among countries on these matters.

United Nations Convention against Corruption

Chapter I General provisions

Article 1. Statement of purpose

The purposes of this Convention are:

(a) To promote and strengthen measures to prevent and combat corruption more efficiently and effectively;
(b) To promote, facilitate and support international cooperation and technical assistance in the prevention of and fight against corruption, including in asset recovery;
(c) To promote integrity, accountability and proper management of public affairs and public property.

Article 2. Use of terms

For the purposes of this Convention:

(a) "Public official" shall mean: (i) any person holding a legislative, executive, administrative or judicial office of a State Party, whether appointed or elected, whether permanent or temporary, whether paid or unpaid, irrespective of that person's seniority; (ii) any other person who performs a public function, including for a public agency or public enterprise, or provides a public service, as defined in the domestic law of the State Party and as applied in the pertinent area of law of that State Party; (iii) any other person defined as a "public official" in the domestic law of a State Party. However, for the purpose of some specific measures contained in chapter II of this Convention, "public official" may mean any person who performs a public function or provides a public service as defined in the domestic law of the State Party and as applied in the pertinent area of law of that State Party;
(b) "Foreign public official" shall mean any person holding a legislative, executive, administrative or judicial office of a foreign country, whether appointed or

elected; and any person exercising a public function for a foreign country, including for a public agency or public enterprise;

(c) "Official of a public international organization" shall mean an inter- national civil servant or any person who is authorized by such an organization to act on behalf of that organization;

(d) "Property" shall mean assets of every kind, whether corporeal or in- corporeal, movable or immovable, tangible or intangible, and legal documents or instruments evidencing title to or interest in such assets;

(e) "Proceeds of crime" shall mean any property derived from or obtained, directly or indirectly, through the commission of an offence;

(f) "Freezing" or "seizure" shall mean temporarily prohibiting the transfer, conversion, disposition or movement of property or temporarily assuming custody or control of property on the basis of an order issued by a court or other competent authority;

(g) "Confiscation", which includes forfeiture where applicable, shall mean the permanent deprivation of property by order of a court or other competent authority;

(h) "Predicate offence" shall mean any offence as a result of which proceeds have been generated that may become the subject of an offence as defined in article 23 of this Convention;

(i) "Controlled delivery" shall mean the technique of allowing illicit or suspect consignments to pass out of, through or into the territory of one or more States, with the knowledge and under the supervision of their competent authorities, with a view to the investigation of an offence and the identification of persons involved in the commission of the offence . . .

Chapter II Preventive measures
Article 5. Preventive anti-corruption policies and practices

1. Each State Party shall, in accordance with the fundamental principles of its legal system, develop and implement or maintain effective, coordinated anti-corruption policies that promote the participation of society and reflect the principles of the rule of law, proper management of public affairs and public property, integrity, transparency and accountability . . .

Article 6. Preventive anti-corruption body or bodies

1. Each State Party shall, in accordance with the fundamental principles of its legal system, ensure the existence of a body or bodies, as appropriate, that prevent corruption by such means as:

(a) Implementing the policies referred to in article 5 of this Convention and, where appropriate, overseeing and coordinating the implementation of those policies;
(b) Increasing and disseminating knowledge about the prevention of corruption . . .

Article 8. Codes of conduct for public officials

1. In order to fight corruption, each State Party shall promote, inter alia, integrity, honesty and responsibility among its public officials, in accordance with the fundamental principles of its legal system.
2. In particular, each State Party shall endeavour to apply, within its own institutional and legal systems, codes or standards of conduct for the correct, honourable and proper performance of public functions . . .

Article 10. Public reporting
Taking into account the need to combat corruption, each State Party shall, in accordance with the fundamental principles of its domestic law, take such measures as may be necessary to enhance transparency in its public administration, including with regard to its organization, functioning and decision- making processes, where appropriate . . .

Article 12. Private sector
1. Each State Party shall take measures, in accordance with the fundamental principles of its domestic law, to prevent corruption involving the private sector, enhance accounting and auditing standards in the private sector and, where appropriate, provide effective, proportionate and dissuasive civil, administrative or criminal penalties for failure to comply with such measures . . .

Article 13. Participation of society
1. Each State Party shall take appropriate measures, within its means and in accordance with fundamental principles of its domestic law, to promote the active participation of individuals and groups outside the public sector, such as civil society, non-governmental organizations and community-based organizations, in the prevention of and the fight against corruption and to raise public awareness regarding the existence, causes and gravity of and the threat posed by corruption . . .

Chapter III Criminalization and law enforcement
Article 15. Bribery of national public officials

Each State Party shall adopt such legislative and other measures as may be necessary to establish as criminal offences, when committed intentionally:
(a) The promise, offering or giving, to a public official, directly or indirectly, of an undue advantage, for the official himself or herself or another person or entity, in order that the official act or refrain from acting in the exercise of his or her official duties;
(b) The solicitation or acceptance by a public official, directly or indirectly, of an undue advantage, for the official himself or herself or another person or entity, in order that the official act or refrain from acting in the exercise of his or her official duties.

Article 16. Bribery of foreign public officials and officials of public international organizations

1. Each State Party shall adopt such legislative and other measures as may be necessary to establish as a criminal offence, when committed intention- ally, the

promise, offering or giving to a foreign public official or an official of a public international organization, directly or indirectly, of an undue advantage, for the official himself or herself or another person or entity, in order that the official act or refrain from acting in the exercise of his or her official duties, in order to obtain or retain business or other undue advantage in relation to the conduct of international business . . .

Article 17. Embezzlement, misappropriation or other diversion of property by a public official

Each State Party shall adopt such legislative and other measures as may be necessary to establish as criminal offences, when committed intentionally, the embezzlement, misappropriation or other diversion by a public official for his or her benefit or for the benefit of another person or entity, of any property, public or private funds or securities or any other thing of value entrusted to the public official by virtue of his or her position.

Article 18. Trading in influence

Each State Party shall consider adopting such legislative and other measures as may be necessary to establish as criminal offences, when committed intentionally:
(a) The promise, offering or giving to a public official or any other per- son, directly or indirectly, of an undue advantage in order that the public official or the person abuse his or her real or supposed influence with a view to obtaining from an administration or public authority of the State Party an undue advantage for the original instigator of the act or for any other person;
(b) The solicitation or acceptance by a public official or any other person, directly or indirectly, of an undue advantage for himself or herself or for another person in order that the public official or the person abuse his or her real or supposed influence with a view to obtaining from an administration or public authority of the State Party an undue advantage.

Article 19. Abuse of functions

Each State Party shall consider adopting such legislative and other measures as may be necessary to establish as a criminal offence, when committed intentionally, the abuse of functions or position, that is, the performance of or failure to perform an act, in violation of laws, by a public official in the discharge of his or her functions, for the purpose of obtaining an undue advantage for himself or herself or for another person or entity.

Article 20. Illicit enrichment

Subject to its constitution and the fundamental principles of its legal sys- tem, each State Party shall consider adopting such legislative and other measures as may be necessary to establish as a criminal offence, when committed intentionally, illicit enrichment, that is, a significant increase in the assets of a public official that he or she cannot reasonably explain in relation to his or her lawful income.

Article 21. Bribery in the private sector

Each State Party shall consider adopting such legislative and other measures as may be necessary to establish as criminal offences, when committed intentionally in the course of economic, financial or commercial activities:
(a) The promise, offering or giving, directly or indirectly, of an undue advantage to any person who directs or works, in any capacity, for a private sector entity, for the person himself or herself or for another person, in order that he or she, in breach of his or her duties, act or refrain from acting;
(b) The solicitation or acceptance, directly or indirectly, of an undue advantage by any person who directs or works, in any capacity, for a private sector entity, for the person himself or herself or for another person, in order that he or she, in breach of his or her duties, act or refrain from acting.

Article 22. Embezzlement of property in the private sector

Each State Party shall consider adopting such legislative and other measures as may be necessary to establish as a criminal offence, when committed intentionally in the course of economic, financial or commercial activities, embezzlement by a person who directs or works, in any capacity, in a private sector entity of any property, private funds or securities or any other thing of value entrusted to him or her by virtue of his or her position . . .

Article 30. Prosecution, adjudication and sanctions

1. Each State Party shall make the commission of an offence established in accordance with this Convention liable to sanctions that take into account the gravity of that offence . . .

Article 32. Protection of witnesses, experts and victims

1 Each State Party shall take appropriate measures in accordance with its domestic legal system and within its means to provide effective protection from potential retaliation or intimidation for witnesses and experts who give testimony concerning offences established in accordance with this Convention and, as appropriate, for their relatives and other persons close to them . . .

Article 33. Protection of reporting persons

Each State Party shall consider incorporating into its domestic legal system appropriate measures to provide protection against any unjustified treatment for any person who reports in good faith and on reasonable grounds to the competent authorities any facts concerning offences established in accordance with this Convention . . .

Article 37. Cooperation with law enforcement authorities

1. Each State Party shall take appropriate measures to encourage persons who participate or who have participated in the commission of an offence established in accordance with this Convention to supply information useful to competent authorities for investigative and evidentiary purposes and to provide factual,

specific help to competent authorities that may contribute to depriving offenders of the proceeds of crime and to recovering such proceeds . . .

Article 38. Cooperation between national authorities

Each State Party shall take such measures as may be necessary to encourage, in accordance with its domestic law, cooperation between, on the one hand, its public authorities, as well as its public officials, and, on the other hand, its authorities responsible for investigating and prosecuting criminal offences. Such cooperation may include:
(a) Informing the latter authorities, on their own initiative, where there are reasonable grounds to believe that any of the offences established in accordance with articles 15, 21 and 23 of this Convention has been committed; or
(b) Providing, upon request, to the latter authorities all necessary information.

Article 39. Cooperation between national authorities and the private sector

1. Each State Party shall take such measures as may be necessary to encourage, in accordance with its domestic law, cooperation between national investigating and prosecuting authorities and entities of the private sector, in particular financial institutions, relating to matters involving the commission of offences established in accordance with this Convention . . .

Chapter IV International Cooperation
Article 43. International cooperation

1. States Parties shall cooperate in criminal matters in accordance with articles 44 to 50 of this Convention. Where appropriate and consistent with their domestic legal system, States Parties shall consider assisting each other in investigations of and proceedings in civil and administrative matters relating to corruption . . .

Article 46. Mutual legal assistance

1. States Parties shall afford one another the widest measure of mutual legal assistance in investigations, prosecutions and judicial proceedings in relation to the offences covered by this Convention . . .

Article 48. Law enforcement cooperation

1. States Parties shall cooperate closely with one another, consistent with their respective domestic legal and administrative systems, to enhance the effectiveness of law enforcement action to combat the offences covered by this Convention . . .

2. With a view to giving effect to this Convention, States Parties shall consider entering into bilateral or multilateral agreements or arrangements on direct cooperation between their law enforcement agencies and, where such agreements or arrangements already exist, amending them . . .

Article 49. Joint investigations

States Parties shall consider concluding bilateral or multilateral agreements or arrangements whereby, in relation to matters that are the subject of investigations, prosecutions or judicial proceedings in one or more States, the competent authorities concerned may establish joint investigative bodies . . .

Chapter VIII Final provisions
Article 65. Implementation of the Convention

1. Each State Party shall take the necessary measures, including legislative and administrative measures, in accordance with fundamental principles of its domestic law, to ensure the implementation of its obligations under this Convention.
2. Each State Party may adopt more strict or severe measures than those provided for by this Convention for preventing and combating corruption . . .

Source: United Nations Office on Drugs and Crime (UNODC). 2003. "United Nations Convention against Corruption." Accessed January 9, 2019. https://www.unodc.org/unodc/en/corruption/tools_and_publications/UN-convention-against-corruption.html.

16 United Kingdom Modern Slavery Act

United Kingdom Parliament

Passed March 26, 2015

In 2015 the United Kingdom Parliament passed legislation making various types of human trafficking illegal and protecting the rights of victims. Although the United Kingdom had ratified the UN Protocol to Prevent, Suppress and Punish Trafficking in Persons, Especially Women and Children in 2006, the British government was criticized for having an inadequate response to the issues of trafficking for sexual exploitation and for labor exploitation. The act also includes a provision on transparency in supply chains that holds companies accountable for abuses that occur along their whole chain of operations. That provision was modeled on the California Transparency in Supply Chains Act. Since its enactment, the Modern Slavery Act improved the United Kingdom's domestic and international response to modern slavery by providing law enforcement with the powers needed to bring offenders to justice and by enhancing the protection given to victims. By 2018, there were more than 600 investigations ongoing, and the British Home Office had announced that an independent review of the act would take place to make sure the legislation is keeping pace with the crime.

MODERN SLAVERY ACT 2015

2015 CHAPTER 30

An Act to make provision about slavery, servitude and forced or compulsory labour and about human trafficking, including provision for the protection of victims; to make provision for an Independent Anti-slavery Commissioner; and for connected purposes. [26th March 2015]

BE IT ENACTED by the Queen's most Excellent Majesty, by and with the advice and consent of the Lords Spiritual and Temporal, and Commons, in this present Parliament assembled, and by the authority of the same, as follow:—

PART 1
OFFENCES

Offences

1 Slavery, servitude and forced or compulsory labour

(1) A person commits an offence if—

(a) the person holds another person in slavery or servitude and the circumstances are such that the person knows or ought to know that the other person is held in slavery or servitude, or

(b) the person requires another person to perform forced or compulsory labour and the circumstances are such that the person knows or ought to know that the other person is being required to perform forced or compulsory labour.

(2) In subsection (1) the references to holding a person in slavery or servitude or requiring a person to perform forced or compulsory labour are to be construed in accordance with Article 4 of the Human Rights Convention.
(3) In determining whether a person is being held in slavery or servitude or required to perform forced or compulsory labour, regard may be had to all the circumstances.
(4) For example, regard may be had—

(a) to any of the person's personal circumstances (such as the person being a child, the person's family relationships, and any mental or physical illness) which may make the person more vulnerable than other persons;
(b) to any work or services provided by the person, including work or services provided in circumstances which constitute exploitation within section 3(3) to (6).

(5) The consent of a person (whether an adult or a child) to any of the acts alleged to constitute holding the person in slavery or servitude, or requiring the person to perform forced or compulsory labour, does not preclude a determination that the person is being held in slavery or servitude, or required to perform forced or compulsory labour.

2 Human trafficking

(1) A person commits an offence if the person arranges or facilitates the travel of another person ("V") with a view to V being exploited.
(2) It is irrelevant whether V consents to the travel (whether V is an adult or a child).
(3) A person may in particular arrange or facilitate V's travel by recruiting V, transporting or transferring V, harbouring or receiving V, or transferring or exchanging control over V.
(4) A person arranges or facilitates V's travel with a view to V being exploited only if—

(a) the person intends to exploit V (in any part of the world) during or after the travel, or
(b) the person knows or ought to know that another person is likely to exploit V (in any part of the world) during or after the travel.

(5) "Travel" means—

(a) arriving in, or entering, any country,
(b) departing from any country,
(c) travelling within any country.

(6) A person who is a UK national commits an offence under this section . . .

3 Meaning of exploitation

(1) For the purposes of section 2 a person is exploited only if one or more of the following subsections apply in relation to the person.

Slavery, servitude and forced or compulsory labour

(2) The person is the victim of behaviour—

(a) which involves the commission of an offence under section 1, or
(b) which would involve the commission of an offence under that section if it took place in England and Wales.

Sexual exploitation

(3) Something is done to or in respect of the person—

(a) which involves the commission of an offence under—

(i) section 1(1)(a) of the Protection of Children Act 1978 (indecent photographs of children), or
(ii) Part 1 of the Sexual Offences Act 2003 (sexual offences), as it has effect in England and Wales, or

(b) which would involve the commission of such an offence if it were done in England and Wales.

Removal of organs etc.

(4) The person is encouraged, required or expected to do anything—

(a) which involves the commission, by him or her or another person, of an offence under section 32 or 33 of the Human Tissue Act 2004 (prohibition of commercial dealings in organs and restrictions on use of live donors) as it has effect in England and Wales, or
(b) which would involve the commission of such an offence, by him or her or another person, if it were done in England and Wales.

Securing services etc by force, threats or deception

(5) The person is subjected to force, threats or deception designed to induce him or her—

(a) to provide services of any kind,
(b) to provide another person with benefits of any kind, or
(c) to enable another person to acquire benefits of any kind.

Securing services etc from children and vulnerable persons

(6) Another person uses or attempts to use the person for a purpose within paragraph (a), (b) or (c) of subsection (5), having chosen him or her for that purpose on the grounds that—

(a) he or she is a child, is mentally or physically ill or disabled, or has a family relationship with a particular person, and
(b) an adult, or a person without the illness, disability, or family relationship, would be likely to refuse to be used for that purpose . . .

PART 5
PROTECTION OF VICTIMS

45 Defence for slavery or trafficking victims who commit an offence

(1) A person is not guilty of an offence if—

(a) the person is aged 18 or over when the person does the act which constitutes the offence,

(b) the person does that act because the person is compelled to do it,
(c) the compulsion is attributable to slavery or to relevant exploitation, and
(d) a reasonable person in the same situation as the person and having the person's relevant characteristics would have no realistic alternative to doing that act.

(2) A person may be compelled to do something by another person or by the person's circumstances.

(3) Compulsion is attributable to slavery or to relevant exploitation only if—

(a) it is, or is part of, conduct which constitutes an offence under section 1 or conduct which constitutes relevant exploitation, or
(b) it is a direct consequence of a person being, or having been, a victim of slavery or a victim of relevant exploitation.

(4) A person is not guilty of an offence if—

(a) the person is under the age of 18 when the person does the act which constitutes the offence,
(b) the person does that act as a direct consequence of the person being, or having been, a victim of slavery or a victim of relevant exploitation, and
(c) a reasonable person in the same situation as the person and having the person's relevant characteristics would do that act . . .

PART 7
MISCELLANEOUS AND GENERAL

General

56 Interpretation

(1) For the purposes of this Act a person is a victim of slavery if he or she is a victim of—

(a) conduct which constitutes an offence under section 1, or
(b) conduct which would have constituted an offence under that section if that section had been in force when the conduct occurred.

(2) For the purposes of this Act a person is a victim of human trafficking if he or she is the victim of—

(a) conduct which constitutes an offence under section 2, or would constitute an offence under that section if the person responsible for the conduct were a UK national, or
(b) conduct which would have been within paragraph (a) if section 2 had been in force when the conduct occurred.

(3) In this Act—

"child" means a person under the age of 18.

Source: United Kingdom Parliament. 2015. "Modern Slavery Act 2015." Accessed January 9, 2019. http://www.legislation.gov.uk/ukpga/2015/30/contents/enacted. Contains public sector information licensed under the Open Government Licence v3.0.

17 Doha Declaration on Integrating Crime Prevention and Criminal Justice into the Wider United Nations Agenda to Address Social and Economic Challenges and to Promote the Rule of Law at the National and International Levels, and Public Participation

Thirteenth United Nations Congress on Crime Prevention and Criminal Justice

Doha, Qatar April 2015

The Doha Declaration is the formal outcome of the Thirteenth United Nations Congress on Crime Prevention and Criminal Justice, organized in April 2015 in Doha, Qatar. In this consolidated declaration, Congress delegates call on states parties to make more effective use of globally agreed upon frameworks for cooperation, such as the UN conventions on transnational organized crime, corruption, drug control, and terrorism, as well as the UN standards and norms on crime prevention and criminal justice. It has specific importance to global crime because it encouraged the inclusion among the United Nations Sustainable Development Goals (adopted by the General Assembly later in 2015) of a goal recognizing the importance of the rule of law and justice in any discussion of sustainable development.

UNITED NATIONS OFFICE ON DRUGS AND CRIME, Vienna

Doha Declaration on Integrating Crime Prevention and Criminal Justice into the Wider United Nations Agenda to Address Social and Economic Challenges and to Promote the Rule of Law at the National and International Levels, and Public Participation

We, Heads of State and Government, Ministers and Representatives of Member States,

Having assembled at the Thirteenth United Nations Congress on Crime Prevention and Criminal Justice in Doha, from 12 to 19 April 2015, to reaffirm our shared commitment to uphold the rule of law and to prevent and counter crime in all its forms and manifestations, at the domestic and international levels, to ensure that our criminal justice systems are effective, fair, humane and accountable, to provide access to justice for all, to build effective, accountable, impartial and inclusive institutions at all levels, and to uphold the principle of human dignity and the universal observance and respect of all human rights and fundamental freedoms,

To that end, declare the following:

1. We acknowledge the 60-year legacy and continuing significant role of the United Nations congresses on crime prevention and criminal justice as one of the largest and most diverse international forums for the exchange of views and experiences in research, law and policy and programme development between States,

intergovernmental organizations and individual experts representing various professions and disciplines in order to identify emerging trends and issues in the field of crime prevention and criminal justice . . .

2. We reaffirm the cross-cutting nature of crime prevention and criminal justice issues and the consequent need to integrate those issues into the wider agenda of the United Nations in order to enhance system-wide coordination . . .

3. We recognize the importance of effective, fair, humane and accountable crime prevention and criminal justice systems and the institutions comprising them as a central component of the rule of law . . .

4. We acknowledge that sustainable development and the rule of law are strongly interrelated and mutually reinforcing . . .

5. We reaffirm our commitment and strong political will in support of effective, fair, humane and accountable criminal justice systems and the institutions comprising them, and encourage the effective participation and inclusion of all sectors of society, thus creating the conditions needed to advance the wider United Nations agenda, while respecting fully the principles of sovereignty and territorial integrity of States and recognizing the responsibility of Member States to uphold human dignity, all human rights and fundamental freedoms for all, in particular for those affected by crime and those who may be in contact with the criminal justice system, including vulnerable members of society, regardless of their status, who may be subject to multiple and aggravated forms of discrimination, and to prevent and counter crime motivated by intolerance or discrimination of any kind . . .

6. We welcome the work of the Expert Group on the Standard Minimum Rules for the Treatment of Prisoners and take note of the draft updated Standard Minimum Rules for the Treatment of Prisoners, as finalized by the Expert Group at its meeting held in Cape Town, South Africa, from 2 to 5 March 2015, and look forward to the consideration of this revised draft, and action thereon, by the Commission on Crime Prevention and Criminal Justice.

7. We emphasize that education for all children and youth, including the eradication of illiteracy, is fundamental to the prevention of crime and corruption and to the promotion of a culture of lawfulness that supports the rule of law and human rights while respecting cultural identities. In this regard, we also stress the fundamental role of youth participation in crime prevention efforts . . .

8. We endeavour to strengthen international cooperation as a cornerstone of our efforts to enhance crime prevention and ensure that our criminal justice systems are effective, fair, humane and accountable, and ultimately to prevent and counter all crimes . . .

9. We endeavour to ensure that the benefits of economic, social and technological advancements become a positive force to enhance our efforts in preventing and countering new and emerging forms of crime. We recognize our responsibility to adequately respond to emerging and evolving threats posed by such crimes . . .

10. We support the development and implementation of consultative and participatory processes in crime prevention and criminal justice in order to engage all members of society, including those at risk of crime and victimization, to make our prevention efforts more effective and to galvanize public trust and confidence in criminal justice systems . . .

11. As we continue our efforts to achieve the objectives set forth in this Declaration, to enhance international cooperation, to uphold the rule of law and to ensure that our crime prevention and criminal justice systems are effective, fair, humane and accountable, we reaffirm the importance of adequate, long-term, sustainable and effective technical assistance and capacity-building policies and programmes . . .

Source: United Nations Office on Drugs and Crime (UNODC). 2015. "Doha Declaration on Integrating Crime Prevention and Criminal Justice into the Wider United Nations Agenda to Address Social and Economic Challenges and to Promote the Rule of Law at the National and International Levels, and Public Participation." Accessed January 9, 2019. http://www.unodc.org/documents/congress/Declaration/V1504151_English.pdf.

Bibliography

Aas, Katja Franko. 2013. *Globalization and Crime*. 2nd ed. *Key Approaches to Criminology*. London: Sage Publications.

Albanese, Jay S. 2003. "Conclusion: Challenges for the Future." In *Organized Crime: World Perspectives*, edited by Jay S. Albanese, Dilip K. Das, and Arvind Verma, 438–459. Upper Saddle River, NJ: Prentice Hall.

Albanese, Jay S. 2008. "White Collar Crimes and Casino Gambling: Looking for Empirical Links to Forgery, Embezzlement, and Fraud." *Crime Law and Social Change* 49 (5): 333–347.

Albanese, Jay S. 2011. *Transnational Crime and the 21st Century: Criminal Enterprise, Corruption, and Opportunity*. New York: Oxford University Press.

Albanese, Jay S. 2012. "Deciphering the Linkages between Organized Crime and Transnational Crime." *Journal of International Affairs* 66 (1): 1–16.

Albanese, Jay S. 2015. *Organized Crime: From the Mob to Transnational Organized Crime*. 7th ed. New York: Routledge

Albanese, Jay S. 2017a. "Crime Control Measures, Individual Liberties, and Crime Rates: An Assessment of 40 Countries." *International Criminal Justice Review* 27 (1): 5–18.

Albanese, Jay S. 2017b. "Global Injustice and Crime Control." *Policing and Society* 27 (6): 688–689.

Alexey, V. P. 2017. "The International Legal Framework of Combating Crimes of Corruption." *Legal Science and Practice-Bulletin of Nizhniy Novgorod Academy of the Ministry If the Interior of Russia* 37 (1): 66–68.

Amrani, Hanafi. 2017. "Understanding the Transnational Character of Money Laundering: The Changing Face of Law Enforcement from Domestic Affairs to the International Cooperation." *Journal of Advanced Research in Law and Economics* 8 (1): 7.

Andreas, Peter, and Kelly M. Greenhill. 2010. *Sex, Drugs, and Body Counts: The Politics of Numbers in Global Crime and Conflict*. Ithaca, NY: Cornell University Press.

Arsovska, Jana. 2015. *Decoding Albanian Organized Crime: Culture, Politics, and Globalization*. Oakland: University of California Press.

Arsovska, Jana, and Felia Allum. 2014. "Introduction: Women and Transnational Organized Crime." *Trends in Organized Crime* 17 (1): 1–15.

Arsovska, Jana, and Popy Begum. 2014. "From West Africa to the Balkans: Exploring Women's Poles in Transnational Organized Crime." *Trends in Organized Crime* 17 (1–2): 89–109.

Arsovska, Jana, and Stef Janssens. 2009. "Human Trafficking and Policing: Good and Bad Practices." In *Strategies against Human Trafficking: The Role of the Security Sector*, edited by Cornelius Friesendorf, 169–211. Vienna: National Defense Academy and Austrian Ministry of Defence and Sports.

Bagheri, Alireza, and Francis L. Delmonico. 2013. "Global Initiatives to Tackle Organ Trafficking and Transplant Tourism." *Medicine, Health Care and Philosophy* 16 (4): 887–895.

Baldwin, Fletcher N., Jr., and Theresa A. DiPerna. 2007. "The Rule of Law: An Essential Component of the Financial War against Organized Crime and Terrorism in the Americas." *Journal of Financial Crime* 14 (4): 405–437.

Ballina, Santiago. 2011. "The Crime–terror Continuum Revisited: A Model for the Study of Hybrid Criminal Organisations." *Journal of Policing, Intelligence and Counter Terrorism* 6 (2): 121–136.

Banks, Cyndi, and James Baker. 2016. *Comparative, International and Global Justice: Perspectives from Criminology and Criminal Justice*. Los Angeles: Sage Publications.

Barberet, Rosemary. 2014a. "Measuring and Researching Transnational Crime." In *Handbook of Transnational Crime and Justice*, edited by Philip L. Reichel and Jay S. Albanese, 47–62. Los Angeles: Sage Publications.

Barberet, Rosemary. 2014b. "Theory and Method." In *Women, Crime and Criminal Justice: A Global Enquiry*, 15–30. London and New York: Routledge, Taylor & Francis Group.

Barberet, Rosemary. 2014c. *Women, Crime and Criminal Justice: A Global Enquiry, Global Issues in Crime and Justice*. London and New York: Routledge, Taylor & Francis Group.

Barclay, Eliza. 2010. "Crime in Latin America." *CQ Global Researcher* 4 (9): 211–234.

Beare, Margaret E. 2013. *Transnational Organized Crime: The Library of Essays on Transnational Crime*. Farnham, Surrey, England; Burlington, VT: Ashgate.

Bennett, Richard R. 2004. "Comparative Criminology and Criminal Justice Research: The State of Our Knowledge." *Justice Quarterly* 21 (1): 1–21.

Biegus, O., and C. Bueger. 2017. "Poachers and Pirates: Improving Coordination of the Global Response to Wildlife Crime." *South African Crime Quarterly-Sacq* 60: 29–36.

Birdsall, A. 2010. "The 'Monster That We Need to Slay'? Global Governance, the United States, and the International Criminal Court." *Global Governance* 16 (4): 451–469.

Blunt, G. D. 2015. "Is Global Poverty a Crime against Humanity?" *International Theory* 7 (3): 539–571.

Bobic, Marinko. 2014. "Transnational Organised Crime and Terrorism: Nexus Needing a Human Security Framework." *Global Crime* 15 (3–4): 241–258.

Bobic, Marinko. 2015. "The Unlawful Society: Global Crime and Security in a Complex World." *Global Crime* 16 (3): 259–261.

Broadhurst, R. 2006. "Developments in the Global Law Enforcement of Cyber-Crime." *Policing—An International Journal of Police Strategies and Management* 29 (3): 408–433.

Bruinsma, Gerben, ed. 2015. *Histories of Transnational Crime*. New York: Springer.

Bussmann, K. D., and M. M. Werle. 2006. "Addressing Crime in Companies—First Findings from a Global Survey of Economic Crime." *British Journal of Criminology* 46 (6): 1128–1144.

Campanaro, J. 2001. "Women, War, and International Law: The Historical Treatment of Gender-based War Crimes." *Georgetown Law Journal* 89 (8): 2557–2592.

Campbell, K. 2013. "The Making of Global Legal Culture and International Criminal Law." *Leiden Journal of International Law* 26 (1): 155–172.

Carrapico, Helena, Daniela Irrera, and Bill Tupman. 2014. "Transnational Organised Crime and Terrorism: Different Peas, Same Pod?" *Global Crime* 15 (3–4): 213–218.

Casey, John. 2010. *Policing the World: The Practice of International and Transnational Policing*. Durham, NC: Carolina Academic Press.

Chesney-Lind, M., and A. V. Merlo. 2015. "Global War on Girls? Policing Girls' Sexuality and Criminalizing Their Victimization." *Women and Criminal Justice* 25 (1–2): 71–82.

Christensen, Mikkel Jarle, and Neil Boister. 2018. *New Perspectives on the Structure of Transnational Criminal Justice, Transnational Crime*. Leiden: Brill.

Clarke, Colin P. 2018. "The Financing of Terrorism and Insurgency through Drug Trafficking." In *Transnational Crime and Global Security*, edited by Philip Reichel and Ryan Randa, 149–166. Santa Barbara, CA: Praeger.

Clifford, W. 1978. "Culture and Crime—Global Perspective." *International Journal of Criminology and Penology* 6 (1): 61–80.

Columb, Seán. 2017. "Excavating the Organ Trade: An Empirical Study of Organ Trading Networks in Cairo, Egypt." *British Journal of Criminology* 57 (6): 1301–1321.

Costa, Jacopo. 2018. "The Globalised Network of a Dirty Game: Match-fixing, Illegal Betting and Transnational Organised Crime in Italian Football." *Global Crime* 19 (2): 125–145.

Cox, P. 2012. "History and Global Criminology." *British Journal of Criminology* 52 (1): 17–31.

Crawford, Mary. 2017. "International Sex Trafficking." *Women and Therapy* 40 (1–2): 101–122.

Crawford, Thomas Adam Michael. 2011. *International and Comparative Criminal Justice and Urban Governance: Convergence and Divergence in Global, National and Local Settings*. Cambridge and New York: Cambridge University Press.

de Haan, W. 2015. "Knowing What We Know Now International Crimes in Historical Perspective." *Journal of International Criminal Justice* 13 (4): 783–799.

Defossez, D. 2017. "The Current Challenges of Money Laundering Law in Russia." *Journal of Money Laundering Control* 20 (4): 367–385.

Densley, James A. 2012. "The Organisation of London's Street Gangs." *Global Crime* 13 (1): 42–64.

Đorđević, Saša. 2009. Understanding Transnational Organized Crime as a Security Threat and Security Theories. *Western Balkans Security Observer* 13 (April–June): 39–52.

Edwards, A., and P. Gill. 2002. "Crime as Enterprise? The Case of 'Transnational Organised Crime.'" *Crime Law and Social Change* 37 (3): 203–223.

Evertsson, Nubia. 2013. "Political Corruption and Electoral Funding: A Cross-national Analysis." *International Criminal Justice Review* 23 (1): 75–94.

Farbiarz, M. 2016. "Extraterritorial Criminal Jurisdiction." *Michigan Law Review* 114 (4): 507–558.

Farrell, Amy, Rebecca Pfeffer, Meredith Dank, and Colleen Owens. 2018. "Human Trafficking for Labor Exploitation." In *Transnational Crime and Global Security*, edited by Philip Reichel and Ryan Randa, 233–250. Santa Barbara, CA: Praeger.

Fedina, Lisa. 2015. "Use and Misuse of Research in Books on Sex Trafficking: Implications for Interdisciplinary Researchers, Practitioners, and Advocates." *Trauma, Violence, and Abuse* 16 (2): 188–198.

Fichtelberg, Aaron. 2014. "Adjudicating International Crimes." In *Handbook of Transnational Crime and Justice*, edited by Philip L. Reichel and Jay S. Albanese, 353–373. Los Angeles: Sage Publications.

Fisher, K. J. 2009. "The Distinct Character of International Crime: Theorizing the Domain." *Contemporary Political Theory* 8 (1): 44–67.

Fraser, A., and J. M. Hagedorn. 2018. "Gangs and a Global Sociological Imagination." *Theoretical Criminology* 22 (1): 42–62.

Galeotti, Mark. 2006. *Global Crime Today: The Changing Face of Organised Crime*. New York: Routledge.

Galeotti, Mark. 2011. "Global Crime: Political Challenges and Responses." *Perspectives on Politics* 9 (3): 597–601.

Gal-Or, N. 2015. "The Formation of a Customary International Crime: Global Terrorism Human (In) Security." *International Criminal Law Review* 15 (4): 665–699.

Garbett, C. 2017. "The International Criminal Court and Restorative Justice: Victims, Participation and the Processes of Justice." *Restorative Justice—An International Journal* 5 (2): 198–220.

Garzón, Juan Carlos, Marianna Olinger, Daniel M. Rico, and Gema Santamaria. 2013. *The Criminal Diaspora: The Spread of Transnational Organized Crime and How to Contain Its Expansion*. Washington, D.C.: The Wilson Center. Accessed January 15, 2019. https://www.wilsoncenter.org/sites/default/files/CRIMINAL_DIASPORA%20%28Eng%20Summary%29_0.pdf.

Gibbs, C., E. F. McGarrell, and M. Axelrod. 2010. "Transnational White-collar Crime and Risk: Lessons from the Global Trade in Electronic Waste." *Criminology and Public Policy* 9 (3): 543–560.

Gilman, Nils, Jesse Goldhammer, and Steven Weber. 2013. "Deviant Globalization." In *Convergence: Illicit Networks and National Security in the Age of Globalization*, edited by Michael Miklaucic and Jacqueline Brewer, 3–13. Washington, D.C.: National Defense University Press.

Glasius, M. 2009. "What Is Global Justice and Who Decides? Civil Society and Victim Responses to the International Criminal Court's First Investigations." *Human Rights Quarterly* 31 (2): 496–520.

Gleditsch, K. S. 2011. "Sex, Drugs, and Body Counts: The Politics of Numbers in Global Crime and Conflict." *Journal of Peace Research* 48 (6): 817–818.

Glenn, H. Patrick. 2014. *Legal Traditions of the World: Sustainable Diversity in Law*. 5th ed. Oxford, UK; New York: Oxford University Press.

Goldson, Barry. 2019. *Juvenile Justice in Europe: Past, Present and Future*. Abingdon, Oxon, UK; New York: Routledge.

Graycar, Adam, and Aiden Sidebottom. 2012. "Corruption and Control: A Corruption Reduction Approach." *Journal of Financial Crime* 19 (4): 384–399.

Greenbaum, B. 2016. "Sex Crimes: Transnational Problems and Global Perspectives." *Journal of Aggression Maltreatment and Trauma* 25 (9): 1019–1020.

Grey, R. 2017. "Interpreting International Crimes from a 'Female Perspective': Opportunities and Challenges for the International Criminal Court." *International Criminal Law Review* 17 (2): 325–350.

Haberfeld, M. R., and Ibrahim Cerrah, eds. 2008. *Comparative Policing: The Struggle for Democratization*. Los Angeles: Sage Publications.

Hall, Tim. 2010. "Where the Money Is: The Geographies of Organised Crime." *Geography* 95 (Spring): 4–13.

Halliday, T. C., and P. Osinsky. 2006. "Globalization of Law." *Annual Review of Sociology* 32: 447–470.

Hanes, Richard C., Sharon M. Hanes, Sarah Hermsen, and Kelly Rudd, eds. 2005. *Organized Crime*. Vol. 1, *Crime and Punishment in America Reference Library*. Detroit: UXL.

Harfield, C. 2008. "The Organization of 'Organized Crime Policing' and Its International Context." *Criminology a Criminal Justice* 8 (4): 483–507.

Harrendorf, S. 2014. "How Can Criminology Contribute to an Explanation of International Crimes?" *Journal of International Criminal Justice* 12 (2): 231–252.

Hartley, Richard D. 2008. *Corporate Crime: A Reference Handbook*. Santa Barbara, CA: ABC-CLIO.

Hauck, P., and S. Peterke. 2010. "Organized Crime and Gang Violence in National and International Law." *International Review of the Red Cross* 92 (878): 407–436.

Heller, K. J. 2017. "What Is an International Crime? (A Revisionist History)." *Harvard International Law Journal* 58 (2): 353–420.

Henry, N. 2009. "Witness to Rape: The Limits and Potential of International War Crimes Trials for Victims of Wartime Sexual Violence." *International Journal of Transitional Justice* 3 (1): 114–134.

Henry, N., and A. Powell. 2016. "Sexual Violence in the Digital Age: The Scope and Limits of Criminal Law." *Social and Legal Studies* 25 (4): 397–418.

Hill, Gary, and Matti Joutsen. 2018. "Combatting Transnational Crime Takes a Public-Private Partnership." In *Transnational Crime and Global Security*, edited by Philip Reichel and Ryan Randa, 275–290. Santa Barbara, CA: Praeger.

Hislope, Robert, and Anthony Mughan. 2012. *Introduction to Comparative Politics: The State and Its Challenges*. Cambridge and New York: Cambridge University Press.

Holmes, L. 2009. "Good Guys, Bad Guys: Transnational Corporations, Rational Choice Theory and Power Crime." *Crime Law and Social Change* 51 (3–4): 383–397.

Howard, Gregory J., and Graeme R. Newman. 2001. *Varieties of Comparative Criminology, International Studies in Sociology and Social Anthropology*. Leiden and Boston: Brill.

Hughes, Christopher W., and Yew Meng Lai. 2011. *Security Studies: A Reader*. London and New York: Routledge.

Huhn, Sebastian, and Hannes Warnecke-Berger. 2017. *Politics and History of Violence and Crime in Central America*. New York: Palgrave Macmillan.

Hume, Deborah L., and Nancy M. Sidun. 2017. "Human Trafficking of Women and Girls: Characteristics, Commonalities, and Complexities." *Women and Therapy* 40 (1–2): 7–11.

Jakobi, A. P. 2017. "Global Norms and US Foreign Policy Change: The Governance of Transnational Crime." *International Politics* 54 (6): 683–697.

Jenks, David A., and John R. Fuller. 2017. *Global Crime and Justice*. New York: Routledge, Taylor & Francis Group.

Joutsen, Matti. 2014a. "A View from the Trenches: The Reality of International Cooperation." In *Handbook of Transnational Crime and Justice*, edited by Philip L. Reichel and Jay S. Albanese, 419–423. Los Angeles: Sage Publications.

Joutsen, Matti. 2014b. "International Instruments on Cooperation in Responding to Transnational Crime." In *Handbook of Transnational Crime and Justice*, edited by Philip L. Reichel and Jay S. Albanese, 303–322. Los Angeles: Sage Publications.

Junger-Tas, J., Ineke Haen Marshall, Dirk Enzmann, Martin Killias, and Majone Steketee. 2012. *The Many Faces of Youth Crime: Contrasting Theoretical Perspectives on Juvenile Delinquency across Countries and Cultures*. New York: Springer.

Kaldor, Mary, and Iavor Rangelov, eds. 2014. *The Handbook of Global Security Policy*. Handbook of Global Policy Series. West Sussex: UK: John Wiley & Sons Inc.

Karstedt, S. 2001. "Comparing Cultures, Comparing Crime: Challenges, Prospects and Problems for a Global Criminology." *Crime Law and Social Change* 36 (3): 285–308.

Katel, Peter. 2014. "Transnational Crime." *CQ Researcher* 24 (30): 697–720.

Katel, Peter. 2015. "Central American Gangs." *CQ Researcher* 25 (5): 97–120.

Kerrey, B. 2002. "International Justice, War Crimes, and Terrorism." *Social Research* 69 (4): 1019–1030.

Kethineni, Sesha. 2014. *Comparative and International Policing, Justice, and Transnational Crime*. 2nd ed. Durham, NC: Carolina Academic Press.

Khamidova, M. F. 2017. "Creation of the International Criminal Court and Legal Issues of Responsibility for International Crimes." *Vestnik of Saint Petersburg University-Law-Vestnik Sankt-Peterburgskogo Universiteta-Pravo* 8 (3): 337–348.

Kiener, Robert. 2012. "Human Trafficking and Slavery." *CQ Global Researcher* 6 (20): 473–496.

King, E. B. L. 2015. "Big Fish, Small Ponds: International Crimes in National Courts." *Indiana Law Journal* 90 (2): 829–849.

Kleemans, Edward R. 2015. "Criminal Organization and Transnational Crime." In *Histories of Transnational Crime*, edited by Gerben Bruinsma, 171–185. New York: Springer.

Kosloski, A. E. 2014. "Trafficking and Global Crime Control." *Security Journal* 27 (3): 341–343.

Kramer, R. C. 2016. "State-Organized Crime, International Law and Structural Contradictions." *Critical Criminology* 24 (2): 231–245.

Lasslett, K. 2017. "Uncovering the Transnational Networks, Organisational Techniques and State-Corporate Ties Behind Grand Corruption: Building an Investigative Methodology." *International Journal for Crime Justice and Social Democracy* 6 (4): 29–54.

Lawless, M. 2007. "Terrorism—An International Crime." *International Journal* 63 (1): 139–159.

Lerner, K. Lee, and Brenda Wilmoth Lerner, eds. 2006. *Introduction to Global Terrorist Movements, Terrorism: Essential Primary Sources*. Detroit: Gale.

Leukfeldt, E. R., E. R. Kleemans, and W. P. Stol. 2017. "Origin, Growth and Criminal Capabilities of Cybercriminal Networks: An International Empirical Analysis." *Crime Law and Social Change* 67 (1): 39–53.

Leuprecht, C., A. Aulthouse, and O. Walther. 2016. "The Puzzling Resilience of Transnational Organized Criminal Networks." *Police Practice and Research* 17 (4): 376–387.

Leuprecht, C., O. Walther, D. B. Skillicorn, and H. Ryde-Collins. 2017. "Hezbollah's Global Tentacles: A Relational Approach to Convergence with Transnational Organized Crime." *Terrorism and Political Violence* 29 (5): 902–921.

Levi, Michael, A. Doig, R. Gundur, D. Wall, and M. Williams. 2017. "Cyberfraud and the Implications for Effective Risk-based Responses: Themes from UK Research." *Crime Law and Social Change* 67 (1): 77–96.

Levi, Michael, and Mike Maguire. 2004. "Reducing and Preventing Organised Crime: An Evidence-based Critique." *Crime, Law and Social Change* 41 (5): 397–469.

Levinger, Matthew. 2010. "Enhancing Security through Peacebuilding." In *Great Decisions 2010*, edited by Foreign Policy Association, 93–102. New York: Foreign Policy Association.

L'Hoiry, X. 2018. Review of *Global Organized Crime: A 21st Century Approach* (2nd ed.), by Mitchel P. Roth. *Policing and Society* 28 (2): 244–246.

Liddick, Donald R., Jr. 2004. *The Global Underworld: Transnational Crime and the United States.* Westport, CT: Praeger.

Ligeti, Katalin, and Stanislaw Tosza. 2018. *White Collar Crime: A Comparative Perspective.* Portland, OR: Hart Publishing.

Liss, C., and J. C. Sharman. 2015. "Global Corporate Crime-Fighters: Private Transnational Responses to Piracy and Money Laundering." *Review of International Political Economy* 22 (4): 693–718.

Lugo, Kristina. 2018. "Transnational Sex Trafficking: An Issue of State and Human Security." In *Transnational Crime and Global Security*, edited by Philip Reichel and Ryan Randa, 207–231. Santa Barbara, CA: Praeger.

Lynch, Michael J., and Paul B. Stretesky. 2010. "Global Warming, Global Crime: A Green Criminological Perspective." In *Global Environmental Harm: Criminological Perspectives*, edited by Rob White, 62–84. Portland, OR: Willan Publishing.

Lynch, Michael J., M. A. Long, K. L. Barrett, and P. B. Stretesky. 2013. "Is It a Crime to Produce Ecological Disorganization? Why Green Criminology and Political Economy Matter in the Analysis of Global Ecological Harms." *British Journal of Criminology* 53 (6): 997–1016.

Madsen, Frank G. 2009. *Transnational Organized Crime, Routledge Global Institutions.* London and New York: Routledge.

Makarenko, Tamara. 2004. "The Crime-Terror Continuum: Tracing the Interplay between Transnational Organised Crime and Terrorism." *Global Crime* 6 (1): 129–145.

Makkai, T. 2006. "Researching Transnational Crime: The Australian Institute of Criminology." *Global Governance* 12 (2): 119–125.

Marhia, Natasha. 2014. "Gender and Security." In *The Handbook of Global Security Policy*, edited by Mary Kaldor and Iavor Rangelov, 51–67. West Sussex: UK: John Wiley & Sons Inc.

Marmo, Marinella. 2016. *Transnational Crime and Criminal Justice.* 1st ed. Thousand Oaks, CA: Sage Publications.

Masters, Adam. 2018. "How the Transnational Crime of Corruption Impacts Global Security." In *Transnational Crime and Global Security*, edited by Philip Reichel and Ryan Randa, 253–280. Santa Barbara, CA: Praeger.

McCusker, R. 2006. "Transnational Organised Cyber Crime: Distinguishing Threat from Reality." *Crime Law and Social Change* 46 (4–5): 257–273.

McGuinness, S., and J. V. McHale. 2014. "Transnational Crimes Related to Health: How Should the Law Respond to the Illicit Organ Tourism?" *Legal Studies* 34 (4): 682–708.

McKinnon, C. 2017. "Endangering Humanity: An International Crime?" *Canadian Journal of Philosophy* 47 (2–3): 395–415.

Megret, F. 2015. "What Sort of Global Justice is 'International Criminal Justice'?" *Journal of International Criminal Justice* 13 (1): 77–96.

Miguel Cruz, José. 2010. "Central American Maras: From Youth Street Gangs to Transnational Protection Rackets." *Global Crime* 11 (4): 379–398.

Mitsilegas, Balsamis, Peter Alldridge, and Leonidas Cheliotis. eds. 2015. *Globalisation Criminal Law and Criminal Justice: Theoretical, Comparative and Transnational Perspectives* Oxford, UK: Hart Publishing.

Natarajan, Mangai. 2011. *International Crime and Justice*. Cambridge and New York: Cambridge University Press.

Negri, S. 2016. "Transplant Ethics and the International Crime of Organ Trafficking." *International Criminal Law Review* 16 (2): 287–303.

Nouwen, S. M. H., and W. G. Werner. 2015. "Monopolizing Global Justice International Criminal Law as Challenge to Human Diversity." *Journal of International Criminal Justice* 13 (1): 157–176.

Obokata, Tom. 2017. "The Value of International Law in Combating Transnational Organized Crime in the Asia-Pacific." *Asian Journal of International Law* 7 (1): 39–60.

Obokata, Tom, and Brian Payne. 2017. *Transnational Organised Crime: A Comparative Analysis, Routledge Research in Transnational Crime and Criminal Law*. Milton Park; New York: Routledge.

O'Brien, M. 2016. "'Don't Kill Them, Let's Choose Them as Wives': The Development of the Crimes of Forced Marriage, Sexual Slavery and Enforced Prostitution in International Criminal Law." *International Journal of Human Rights* 20 (3): 386–406.

Palmiotto, Michael, and N. Prabha Unnithan. 2011. *Policing and Society: A Global Approach*. Clifton Park, NY: Delmar Cengage Learning.

Passas, Nikos. 1999. *Transnational Crime, International Library of Criminology, Criminal Justice, and Penology*. Aldershot, Hants, England; Brookfield, VT: Ashgate.

Perri, Frank S., and Richard G. Brody. 2011. "The Dark Triad: Organized Crime, Terror and Fraud." *Journal of Money Laundering Control* 14 (1): 44–59.

Pinotti, Paolo. 2015. "The Causes and Consequences of Organised Crime: Preliminary Evidence Across Countries." *Economic Journal* 125 (586): F158–F174.

Pol, R. F. 2018. "Anti–money Laundering Effectiveness: Assessing Outcomes or Ticking Boxes?" *Journal of Money Laundering Control* 21 (2): 215–230.

Popovski, V. 2000. "International Criminal Court—A Necessary Step towards Global Justice." *Security Dialogue* 31 (4): 405–419.

Puniskis, M. 2012. "Trafficking and Global Crime Control." *Criminology and Criminal Justice* 12 (2): 222–224.

Rabkin, J. 2005. "Global Criminal Justice: An Idea Whose Time Has Passed." *Cornell International Law Journal* 38 (3): 753–777.

Reichel, Philip L. 2018. *Comparative Criminal Justice Systems: A Topical Approach*. 7th ed. New York: Pearson.

Reichel, Philip L., and Jay S. Albanese. 2014. *Handbook of Transnational Crime and Justice*. 2nd ed. Los Angeles: Sage Publications.

Reichel, Philip L., and Ryan Randa. 2018. *Transnational Crime and Global Security*. Santa Barbara, CA: Praeger Security International.

Renzo, M. 2012. "Crimes against Humanity and the Limits of International Criminal Law." *Law and Philosophy* 31 (4): 443–476.

Reuter, P., and D. O'Regan. 2017. "Smuggling Wildlife in the Americas: Scale, Methods, and Links to Other Organised Crimes." *Global Crime* 18 (2): 77–99.

Reyes, L. E., and S. Dinar. 2015. "The Convergence of Terrorism and Transnational Crime in Central Asia." *Studies in Conflict and Terrorism* 38 (5): 380–393.

Richardson, L. S. 2008. "Due Process for the Global Crime Age: A Proposal." *Cornell International Law Journal* 41 (2): 347–382.

Riggs, Thomas, and Gale (Firm). 2018. *Legal Issues across the Globe*. Farmington Hills, MI: Gale, a Cengage Learning.

Roberts, Anthea, Paul B. Stephan, Pierre-Hugues Verdier, and Mila Versteeg. 2018. *Comparative International Law*. New York: Oxford University Press.

Rollins, John, Liana Sun Wyler, and Seth Rosen. 2010. International Terrorism and Transnational Crime: Security Threats, U.S. Policy, and Considerations for Congress. *CRS Report for Congress* (January 5): 1–31.

Rose-Ackerman, Susan, and Bonnie J. Palifka. 2016. *Corruption and Government: Causes, Consequences, and Reform*. 2nd ed. New York: Cambridge University Press.

Ruggerio, Rosemarie. 2008. *Transnational Crime: Globalizing and Adapting*. New York: Nova Science Publishers.

Runhovde, S. R. 2017. "Taking the Path of Least Resistance? Decision-Making in Police Investigations of Illegal Wildlife Trade." *Policing—A Journal of Policy and Practice* 11 (1): 87–102.

Saha, A. 2009. "Rape as a War Crime: The Position of International Law since World War II." *Journal of East Asia and International Law* 2 (2): 497–516.

Sandu, Adriana Magdalena, and Mirela Loredana Nitu. 2013. "Corruption and Organized Crime." *Contemporary Readings in Law and Social Justice* 5 (2): 454–460.

Saul, B. 2017. "The Legal Relationship between Terrorism and Transnational Crime." *International Criminal Law Review* 17 (3): 417–452.

Schabas, W. A. 2011. "International War Crimes Tribunals and the United States." *Diplomatic History* 35 (5): 769–786.

Schneider, E. M., J. R. Iglesias, K. Hallberg, and M. N. Kuperman. 2014. "Crimes against Humanity: The Role of International Courts." *Plos One* 9 (6). https://doi.org/10.1371/journal.pone.0099064.

Schonhofer, J. 2017. "Political Determinants of Efforts to Protect Victims of Human Trafficking." *Crime Law and Social Change* 67 (2): 153–185.

Sergi, A. 2017. "Countering the Australian 'Ndrangheta: The Criminalisation of Mafia Behaviour in Australia between National and Comparative Criminal Law." *Australian and New Zealand Journal of Criminology* 50 (3): 321–340.

Sharlach, L. 2017. "Sex Crimes: Transnational Problems and Global Perspectives." *International Feminist Journal of Politics* 19 (2): 265–266.

Shelley, Louise. 2004. "The Unholy Trinity: Transnational Crime, Corruption, and Terrorism." *Brown Journal of World Affairs* 11 (2): 101–111.

Shelley, Louise I., and John T. Picarelli. 2005. "Methods and Motives: Exploring Links between Transnational Organized Crime and International Terrorism." *Trends in Organized Crime* 9 (2): 52–67.

Shelley, Louise I., and Sharon A. Melzer. 2008. "The Nexus of Organized Crime and Terrorism: Two Case Studies in Cigarette Smuggling." *International Journal of Comparative and Applied Criminal Justice* 32 (1): 43–63.

Shen, Anqi. 2016. "Female Membership in the Black-Society Style Criminal Organizations: Evidence from a Female Prison in China." *Feminist Criminology* 11 (1): 69–90.

Sheptycki, J. W. E. 2011. *Transnational Crime and Policing: Selected Essays*. Pioneers in Contemporary Criminology Series. Farnham, Surrey, England; Burlington, VT: Ashgate.

Sheptycki, J. W. E. 2015. *Transnational Crime: Critical Concepts in Criminology*. Abingdon, Oxon, UK; New York: Routledge.

Siegel, Dina. 2014. "Women in Transnational Organized Crime." *Trends in Organized Crime* 17 (1–2): 52–65.

Siems, Mathias M. 2018. *Comparative Law*. 2nd ed. The Law in Context Series. Cambridge, UK; New York: Cambridge University Press.

Silverstone, Daniel. 2011. "From Triads to Snakeheads: Organised Crime and Illegal Migration within Britain's Chinese Community." *Global Crime* 12 (2): 93–111.

Simmons, B. A., P. Lloyd, and B. M. Stewart. 2018. "The Global Diffusion of Law: Transnational Crime and the Case of Human Trafficking." *International Organization* 72 (2): 249–281.

Smolka, K., and K. Gronwald. 2017. "Operation Pangea—Standing Together in Combat against International Pharmaceutical Crime." *Bundesgesundheitsblatt-Gesundheitsforschung-Gesundheitsschutz* 60 (11): 1233–1239.

Srikanth, H. 2016. "Combating Transnational Crimes in the Era of Globalization: Strategies for India and the ASEAN." *International Studies* 53 (2): 91–104.

Stamatel, Janet P. 2009. "Overcoming Methodological Challenges in International and Comparative Criminology: Guest Editor's Introduction." *International Journal of Comparative and Applied Criminal Justice* 33 (2): 167–170.

Stephens, G. 2003. "Global Trends in Crime." *Futurist* 37 (3): 40–46.

Stoica, Ionel. 2016. "Transnational Organized Crime: An (Inter)national Security Perspective." *Journal of Defense Resources Management* 7 (2): 13.

Studies and Threat Analysis Section. 2010. "The Threat of Transnational Organized Crime." In *The Globalization of Crime: A Transnational Organized Crime Threat Assessment*, edited by UNODC, 25–36. Vienna: United Nations Office on Drugs and Crime.

Sullivan, John P. 2014. "Transnational Crime." In *The Handbook of Global Security Policy*, edited by Mary Kaldor and Iavor Rangelov, 160–174. West Sussex, UK: John Wiley & Sons Inc.

Tak, M., M. P. Sam, and S. J. Jackson. 2018. "The Problems and Causes of Match-fixing: Are Legal Sports Betting Regimes to Blame?" *Journal of Criminological Research Policy and Practice* 4 (1): 73–87.

Tehrani, P. M., N. A. Manap, and H. Taji. 2013. "Cyber Terrorism Challenges: The Need for a Global Response to a Multi-jurisdictional Crime." *Computer Law and Security Review* 29 (3): 207–215.

Telesetsky, A. 2014. "Laundering Fish in the Global Undercurrents: Illegal, Unreported, and Unregulated Fishing and Transnational Organized Crime." *Ecology Law Quarterly* 41 (4): 939–997.

Thachuk, Kimberley L., ed. 2007. *Transnational Threats: Smuggling and Trafficking in Arms, Drugs, and Human Life*. Westport, CT: Praeger Security International.

Tonry, Michael. 2015. "Is Cross-national and Comparative Research on the Criminal Justice System Useful?" *European Journal of Criminology* 12 (4): 505–516.

Tonry, Michael. 2016. *Sentencing Policies and Practices in Western Countries: Comparative and Cross-national Perspectives, Crime and Justice*. Chicago and London: University of Chicago Press.

United Nations. 2000. "United Nations Convention against Transnational Organized Crime and the Protocols Thereto." Accessed July 16, 2018. https://www.unodc.org/unodc/en/organized-crime/intro/UNTOC.html.

van der Pijl, Y., B. C. O. Breuil, and D. Siegel. 2011. "Is There Such Thing as 'Global Sex Trafficking'? A Patchwork Tale on Useful (Mis)understandings." *Crime Law and Social Change* 56 (5): 567–582.

van der Wilt, H. 2013. "Corporate Criminal Responsibility for International Crimes: Exploring the Possibilities." *Chinese Journal of International Law* 12 (1): 43–77.

van Dijk, Jan. 2008. *The World of Crime: Breaking the Silence on Problems of Security, Justice, and Development across the World*. Los Angeles: Sage Publications.

van Dijk, Jan, and Toine Spapens. 2014. "Transnational Organized Crime Networks." In *Handbook of Transnational Crime and Justice*, edited by Philip L. Reichel and Jay S. Albanese, 213–226. Los Angeles: Sage Publications.

Vines, A. 2012. "Small Arms, Crime and Conflict: Global Governance and the Threat of Armed Violence." *International Affairs* 88 (2): 399–401.

von Lampe, Klaus. 2012. "Transnational Organized Crime Challenges for Future Research." *Crime Law and Social Change* 58 (2): 179–194.

Waldman, R. 2012. "Sex, Drugs, and Body Counts: The Politics of Numbers in Global Crime and Conflict." *Global Public Health* 7 (7): 795–797.

Walklate, S. 2016. "Whither Criminology: Its Global Futures?" *Asian Journal of Criminology* 11 (1): 47–59.

Wang, Peng. 2011. "The Chinese Mafia: Private Protection in a Socialist Market Economy." *Global Crime* 12 (4): 290–311.

White, Rob. 2017. "The Four Ways of Eco-global Criminology." *International Journal for Crime Justice and Social Democracy* 6 (1): 8–22.

Williams, Phil, and Dimitri Vlassis. 2001. *Combating Transnational Crime: Concepts, Activities, and Responses*. London and Portland: Frank Cass .Williams, Phil, and Ernesto U. Savona, eds. 1996. *The United Nations and Transnational Organized Crime*. London: Frank Cass & Co.

Williams, Phil, and R. Godson. 2002. "Anticipating Organized and Transnational Crime." *Crime Law and Social Change* 37 (4): 311–355.

Wilt, Harmen van der, and Christophe Paulussen. 2017. *Legal Responses to Transnational and International Crimes: Towards an Integrative Approach.* Cheltenham, UK: Edward Elgar Publishing.

Winterdyk, John, Philip L. Reichel, and Benjamin Perrin. 2012. *Human Trafficking: Exploring the International Nature, Concerns, and Complexities.* Boca Raton, FL: CRC Press.

Wyatt, T., K. Johnson, L. Hunter, R. George, and R. Gunter. 2018. "Corruption and Wildlife Trafficking: Three Case Studies Involving Asia." *Asian Journal of Criminology* 13 (1): 35–55.

Zamora, C. M. 2016. "Transnational Organized Crime as Policy without Insurgency: The Experience of Central America." *Desafíos* 28 (2): 177–211.

About the Editor and Contributors

EDITOR

PHILIP L. REICHEL, PhD, is emeritus professor at the University of Northern Colorado and associate professor at California University of Pennsylvania. He is author of *Comparative Criminal Justice Systems: A Topical Approach*, coauthor of *Corrections* (Justice Series), and coeditor of the *Handbook of Transnational Crime and Justice* and *Transnational Crime and Global Security*. Reichel has also authored or coauthored more than 40 articles and book chapters. His areas of expertise include corrections, comparative justice systems, and transnational crime. He currently serves as the NGO Representative to the United Nations for the Academy of Criminal Justice Sciences.

CONTRIBUTORS

JAY S. ALBANESE is professor and criminologist in the Wilder School of Government & Public Affairs at Virginia Commonwealth University. He served as chief of the International Center at the National Institute of Justice, the research arm of the U.S. Department of Justice. He is author and editor of 20 books on topics that include organized crime, corruption, ethics, and transnational crime, and he is a past president and fellow of the Academy of Criminal Justice Sciences.

KRISTINE ARTELLO is an associate professor of Criminal Justice at the Virginia Commonwealth University. She holds a PhD in criminology, law and society from the University of California, Irvine. She serves on the Faculty Senate Leadership as the chair of Academic and Professional Status Committee. Her areas of interest include public policy and the intersection of law and social service. She was also a social worker for six years.

ANTHONY AZARI is currently a graduate student at the University of Northern Colorado where he is pursuing his master's in criminology and criminal justice. His research interests include prison reform, corrections, international crime, and evidence-based crime prevention programs and policies.

DANIEL BRASLAVSKY is a graduate of John Jay College of Criminal Justice of the City University of New York. As an international criminal justice major and political science minor, his specialization is in transnational organized crime and rebel groups. He has previously conducted research on rebel groups and militias on behalf of the U.S. Department of State.

KARIN BRUCKMÜLLER is project leader with the Departments of Criminal Law at the Ludwig-Maximilians University Munich (Germany) and the Johannes Kepler University Linz (Austria). She holds a PhD from the University of Vienna. Her research fields are medical criminal law (and bioethics), criminal law and innovative techniques, and prevention of human trafficking.

TAMAR BURRIS is an independent writer and researcher. She is the owner of Tab Writers, Inc. She has worked with the Discovery Channel, PBS, ESPN, and with various educational stations, publications, and websites, as both a writer and educational curriculum expert.

FRANCESCA M. CALAMUNCI is a third-year PhD student in economics, management, and statistics at the University of Messina. During her second year, she spent seven months as a Fulbright Scholar at the John Jay College. She has an MS (2016) in economic and financial science and a BS (2014) in economics and management from the University of Messina. She is researching the infiltration of organized crime into legitimate businesses to study the direct and indirect effects of the presence of criminal organization on the firms' performance.

DAFNE CALDERÓN BURGOA holds a bachelor's degree in marketing from the EBC in México City. She also holds a master's in international peace studies from the UN University for Peace in Costa Rica. Dafne has volunteered with several organizations throughout her career such as the Peace Crane Project, Habesha Project, and a center for education in México for underserved communities. Dafne is the current field operations manager at FIMRC Project Restauracion in the Dominican Republic.

MARIANA CAMMISA studied International Relations in Córdoba, Argentina (2015). After graduating, she pursued the MA in international peace studies at the United Nations–mandated University for Peace (2017). She worked in political affairs in the United Nations Office at Geneva (2017), and she currently works in the Buenos Aires City Government in the localization of the 2030 Agenda for Sustainable Development (2018).

CARLOTTA CARBONE is a PhD candidate in criminology at the Università Cattolica del Sacro Cuore in Milan (Italy) and a researcher at Transcrime. At Transcrime she is involved in projects aimed at assessing corruption and collusion risks in public procurement (e.g., EU DIGIWHIST project). Her research interests include corruption, bid-rigging, and social network analysis. In 2015, she obtained a master's degree in public policies at Università Cattolica.

JOHN R. CENCICH, PhD, is a tenured professor and director of the Pennsylvania Center for Investigative and Forensic Sciences and the director of Criminal Justice Graduate Programs. He has also served as chair of the International Section and vice chair of the Law and Public Policy Section of the Academy of Criminal Sciences. In addition, he has been a consultant to the National Institute of Justice and the United Nations. His expertise is in cold cases, wrongful convictions, and war crimes. He is the author of numerous books and features in a television show called *Hunting Hitler*.

ELLIOT P. CHODOFF is a military and political analyst at the University of Haifa, currently as a doctoral candidate writing a dissertation on international relations. He also serves as a Population Officer for the IDF Northern Command and a lecturer for Hamartzim Educational Services. Chodoff regularly freelances for popular publications on issues of national security and foreign policy and is the editor and founder of the e-journal *MidEast: On Target*. He received his MA in sociology at the University of Chicago and his BA in sociology at University of New York at Stony Brook.

SOMBO MUZATA CHUNDA is a PhD student in the L. Douglas Wilder School of Government and Public Affairs at Virginia Commonwealth University. Previously, she worked as country manager in Zambia for Diakonia, a Swedish international development organization. Sombo is a chartered accountant and a fellow of the ACCA, and she holds an MBA specializing in strategic planning. She believes fighting corruption and promoting social entrepreneurship (her research interests) are game changers for sustainable development in developing countries.

JOHNMICHAEL DA SILVA is a graduate student of organized crime, terrorism, and security at the University of Essex in the United Kingdom. He received his bachelor's degree in international criminal justice from the City University of New York. He was also an intern with the New York Police Department for four months.

MARIKA DAWKINS is an assistant professor in the Department of Criminal Justice at the University of Texas Rio Grande Valley, in Edinburg, Texas. She has published on both criminal and juvenile justice-related issues. Her research interests include issues such as comparative juvenile justice, delinquency prevention, crime and justice in the Caribbean, and policing. Her professional memberships include the American Society of Criminology, the Academy of Criminal Justice Sciences, and the Southwestern Association of Criminal Justice.

MARK W. DENNISTON is an assistant professor in the Criminal Justice Department at Weber State University in Ogden, Utah. After law school, he clerked for Justice Jerry L. Larson of the Iowa Supreme Court and practiced law in suburban Des Moines, Iowa. He then earned his PhD in political science from the University of Colorado at Boulder, where he studied why state supreme courts expand state constitutional rights.

JÓZEF J. DOELLINGER is a doctorate student in law in Department of Criminal Procedure at Białystok University in Poland. He is a former graduate student of the School of Criminology and Criminal Justice at Northeastern University in Boston. He is a junior lawyer and assistant of legal counsel in law office in the city of Bielsko-Biała, Poland. He is a member of the American Society of Criminology. His subjects of interest include disclosure and discovery in criminal cases, penal studies, criminology, psychology of law, and judicial decision-making process.

EMILIA DUNGEL is Communications Coordinator at the Small Arms Survey.

PUCK VAN EIJK earned her master's degree from the University for Peace in Costa Rica. She works in the Department of Multilateral Affairs and Human Rights in the Netherlands at present. She is the cofounder and treasurer of the Sovereignty of Subjectivity (SOS), a nonprofit organization that champions peace and social justice, based in Stockholm, Sweden.

ARIUN ENKHSAIKHAN currently works at the Law Offices of Thais P. Saad, researching country conditions for humanitarian parole applications and asylum seekers. She previously worked for the International Peace Institute and Robert F. Kennedy Human Rights. Ariun holds a bachelor of arts degree in international criminal justice from John Jay College of Criminal Justice (CUNY).

BRIAN FEDOREK is an associate professor in the Criminology and Criminal Justice Department at Southern Oregon University. He earned his doctorate at Indiana University of Pennsylvania. He has taught classes on terrorism, comparative criminal justice, and theories of criminal behavior, to name a few. His research interests include media and crime, criminological theory, and criminal violence. He has served on the board of Western Association of Criminal Justice.

LAURA FINLEY is an assistant professor of sociology and criminology at Barry University. She received a BA in secondary education, an MA in education and professional development, and a PhD in sociology, all from Western Michigan University. Finley is the author of *Juvenile Justice* and *The Torture and Prisoner Abuse Debate*, the coauthor of *Beyond Burning Bras: Feminist Activism for Everyone*, and the editor of *Encyclopedia of Juvenile Violence*. In addition, Finley is actively involved in local and national human rights, social justice, and peace movements.

TAYLOR S. FISHER is an instructor at the University of Alabama in the Department of Criminology and Criminal Justice. She received her BA in criminal justice and psychology and her MS in criminology and criminal justice from UA. Her research interests include the treatment of the mentally ill in the criminal justice system and the social implications of marijuana legalization.

TINA FOWLER entered the PhD program in juvenile justice at Prairie View A&M University in 2017. She earned her master of science in social work from the

University of Tennessee in 2006. Her primary research interests include juvenile justice, mental health, foster care, and educational disparities, but she is broadly interested in research questions related to policy analysis and community policing. Her teaching interests include human behavior, trauma and crisis intervention, diversity, ethics, and policy.

CHRISTINE MARIE GANCAYCO is a Filipina-American who hopes to improve the world through environmental justice and sustainability, youth care, and justice. She will graduate from CUNY John Jay College in May 2019 with a BA in international criminal justice. She hopes to return to John Jay to pursue a MA in forensic mental health counseling to be able to understand the behaviors of children living in troubled environments and to provide them with proper assistance.

ADAM K. GHAZI-TEHRANI is an assistant professor in the Department of Criminology and Criminal Justice at the University of Alabama. His work focuses on white-collar, corporate, state, and cybercrimes; his recent publications are comparative and cover the Asian sphere.

CAMILLE GIBSON, PhD, CRC, a native of Jamaica, is the interim dean of the College of Juvenile Justice and Psychology and executive director of the Texas Juvenile Crime Prevention Center at Prairie View A&M University. She recently served on the board of the Academy of Criminal Justice Sciences, and she is a past president of the Southwestern Association of Criminal Justice. She is a recipient of the Felix Fabian Award and the Niederhoffer Memorial Fellowship.

AMANDA R. GRAVES is a recent graduate of the University of Alabama who earned a bachelor's degree in criminal justice with minors in cyber criminology and French. During her last undergraduate semester, Graves received the Dean's Award of Merit and the Chairperson's Award of Merit. She continued her studies at her alma mater to graduate with a master of science in criminal justice one year later. Graves is now pursuing a career in federal law enforcement.

KENNETH GRAY is a former FBI agent, FBI SWAT member, naval officer in the Surface Warfare community, and crisis coordinator for the New Haven, Connecticut, Division of the FBI. He is a PhD candidate of criminal justice at the University of New Haven, and he teaches classes on criminal justice and investigation. His academic interests include intelligence and terrorism, crisis management, and interrogations.

WESSEL GROOT earned a master of science degree in international relations and transnational governance from the VU University Amsterdam and a master of arts degree in International Peace Studies at the United Nations-mandated University for Peace in Costa Rica. In 2014 he was elected as the youngest municipal councilor of the municipality of Drechterland in the Netherlands. He is currently working as a policy officer at the Dutch city of Zwolle.

HARRY RAYMOND HUESTON joined the Department of Criminal Justice in May 2000. Dr. Hueston retired as the Chief of Police from the University of Arizona in May 2000, after 30 years in law enforcement serving in various positions in Ohio, California, Arizona, and the U.S. Army Military Police. He received his B.S. degree in education from Kent State University in 1971. He received master's degrees in public administration and criminal justice administration from Ohio State University in 1975. He received his PhD from the University of Arizona in education and criminal justice administration in 1997. He is certified as a peace officer in Ohio, Arizona, and with the U.S. Army.

LAUREN M. GUYER is a sociology graduate student at the University of Northern Colorado. Most recently, she has collaborated on research aimed at understanding the needs and experiences of victims and survivors of sex trafficking. Lauren and her research team presented preliminary findings examining commercial sexual exploitation at the 2018 American Men's Studies Association conference. Additionally, Lauren has collaborated on survey design for evaluating first-offender restoration workshops for men arrested or ticketed for buying commercial sex.

DONALD P. HAIDER-MARKEL is professor and chair of political science at the University of Kansas. His specialties include public policy, American politics, public opinion, civil rights, criminal justice, and counterterrorism. He is author and coauthor of numerous articles and books. His articles have appeared in the *Journal of Politics*, *Legislative Studies Quarterly*, *American Politics Quarterly*, and *Politics & Gender*, among other journals.

ABBEY HARBERT earned her master's degree in criminology and criminal justice from the University of Alabama. She is currently a graduate teaching assistant at the same university.

LILLA HEINS is a Macaulay Honors student at John Jay College of Criminal Justice, CUNY. Her research interests include counterterrorism, mobilization of foreign fighters, and organized crime. She has previously worked as a research assistant for the United States Extremist Crime Database and has interned in the Public Affairs Section of the U.S. Department of State in Tashkent, Uzbekistan.

ANGIE HENDERSON is a professor of sociology at the University of Northern Colorado. She has published over 20 peer-reviewed journal articles, 4 book chapters, and one coauthored textbook. Her most recent research focuses on commercial sexual exploitation. Dr. Henderson collaborates with a nationally serving nonprofit organization dedicated to helping women exit sex trafficking, Free Our Girls. In this role, she has advised the organization on data collection and analysis used to inform programming and services.

KAITLYN HOOVER is currently a master's student in criminology and criminal justice at the University of Alabama and will graduate in May of 2019. Her specialties include the effects of mental illness and substance use on criminal behavior and mass homicide. She plans to continue her educational career and receive her doctorate degree in criminology in the future. She has recently coauthored a paper for publication comparing the ages of mass shooters. Kaitlyn currently resides in Tuscaloosa, Alabama.

DANIEL BRENDAN HUGHES recently received his bachelor's degree in political science from the John Jay College of Criminal Justice at the City University of New York. He also received an advanced certificate in counterterrorism from the same university. His interests are in counterterrorism efforts.

MIKAEL JOHANSSON is the coordinator of the United Nations Crime Prevention and Criminal Justice Program Network of Institutes. He has been a member of the board of directors of the International Society for the Reform of Criminal Law since 2011. He earned his master's degree in law from Lund University in Sweden with a focus on international human rights and humanitarian law. He is currently the university's senior policy adviser on anti-corruption and human rights.

JUSTIN JOSEPH has been a pre-doctoral fellow for the Center for Justice Research at Texas Southern University. Mr. Joseph is currently a fourth-year doctoral student in the Juvenile Studies Department in the College of Juvenile Justice and Psychology at Prairie View A&M University. Mr. Joseph has previously worked as a graduate research assistant on Conduct Disorder and Texas Juvenile Mental Health Courts. Mr. Joseph has a BA in psychology and art from Morehead State University and an MA in criminology from the same university.

MATTI JOUTSEN is a Finnish criminologist, lawyer, and civil servant. Especially as the longtime director of the European Institute for Crime Prevention and Control (HEUNI), he has played a key role in negotiations on intergovernmental criminal policy within the framework of the United Nations and also in the European Union and the Council of Europe. Following his retirement from HEUNI in 2017, he is serving as special advisor to the Thailand Institute of Justice.

MARIANA KAKARAKIS is currently an international criminal justice and political science student at John Jay College of Criminal Justice, the City University of New York. Her interests include transnational crime prevention, human rights, and public policy. Mariana aims to build a career where she can fight issues related to drugs, crime, terrorism, organized crime, and corruption.

NICOLE KALCZYNSKI is a secretary for the International Student's Association at John Jay College of Criminal Justice for the City University of New York. She received her bachelor's degree in international criminal justice from the same university. She has previously been a diplomacy lab researcher for the United States Department of State.

BEVERLY MERRILL KELLEY earned her PhD from UCLA in 1977. She founded the Communication Department at California Lutheran University in

1981 and helped start the KCLU FM radio station and the Educational Television for the Conejo TV channel. She is the author of the three-volume *Reelpolitik* series on film and political ideologies and has been a *Ventura County Star* opinion columnist since 1997. She is also the author of numerous scholarly articles and convention papers and provides analysis on politics, pop culture, and the media for radio, television, and newspapers.

JULIA KELLNER is a staff member and tutor at the Ludwig-Maximilians-University, Munich (Germany) in the field of criminal law.

DOROTHY KERSHA-AERGA is an associate professor of criminal justice with the Department of Social and Behavioral Sciences, at Elizabeth City State University, North Carolina. She is a Nigerian trained attorney and holds an MS and PhD in Juvenile Justice from Prairie View A&M University, Texas. Her research interest includes gender issues, gangs, and juvenile delinquency.

SESHA KETHINENI, professor at Prairie View A&M University, received a PhD from Rutgers—The State University of New Jersey and an LL.M. from the University of Illinois. She has over 50 publications, including books, book chapters, and journal articles. Her research interests include comparative juvenile justice, domestic violence, international criminal justice, human rights, and cybercrime. She served as the chair of the International Division of the American Society of Criminology (2013–2015).

STEPHEN KOMISARJEVSKY is a community representative and immigration caseworker for the United States House of Representatives. He received his master's degree in criminology and criminal justice from the University of Alabama, and he has two bachelor's degrees in criminal justice and Spanish from the same university. He was previously a congressional intern for the U.S. House of Representatives in Washington, D.C. His current casework involves immigration, naturalization, Equal Opportunity Commission (EOC) casework, and the Department of State.

KANDYL KOTTA is a Tanzanian student pursuing a master's degree in security and resilience studies from Northeastern University. Additionally, she holds a bachelor's in business administration with concentrations in marketing and supply chain management. Interests lie in immigration policy, especially as it relates to skilled and unskilled workers, and the impact of globalization on developing countries.

LYN LAFAVE is a graduate student in the Department of Criminology and Criminal Justice at the University of Alabama. She holds a bachelor's in psychology and criminology from the University of Alabama. Her research interests include cybercrime and the media's relationship to crime. She is pursuing a law enforcement career upon completion of her MS in criminology.

ZBIGNIEW LASOCIK, PhD, is a professor of law and criminology at University of Warsaw; director of the Human Trafficking Studies Centre; author of numerous publications in criminology, human rights, human trafficking, torture prevention and prison systems; visiting scholar (i.a.) at Columbia University, Harvard University, John Jay College of Criminal Justice and London School of Economics; expert of the UN, EU, OSCE, and Council of Europe; and former member of the UN Subcommittee on Prevention of Torture.

ALEXIS S. LEMANSKI is a student at the University of Alabama.

HOLLIE MACDONALD, M.S., is a lecturer of criminal justice studies at Longwood University in Farmville, Virginia. MacDonald holds a master of science degree in criminal justice studies from Virginia Commonwealth University and a bachelor of science degree in psychology from Longwood University. MacDonald also has experience working with the Virginia Department of Corrections as a court and legal specialist. Her research interests include criminological theory and criminal justice policy.

PHILIP J. MACFARLANE was a writer/editor for ABC-CLIO's award-winning Solutions databases.

MARINA MANCUSO is an assistant professor at Università Cattolica del Sacro Cuore in Milan and a researcher at Transcrime—Joint Research Centre on Transnational Crime, Italy. Her research focuses on organized crime and illicit markets with a particular attention to illicit trafficking in firearms, trafficking in human beings, sexual exploitation, and illicit trade in tobacco products.

MARTINA E. MARCHESI is a PhD candidate in criminology at Università Cattolica del Sacro Cuore in Milan. She holds a master's degree with honors in international cooperation policies for development. Since September 2016, she has been working as a researcher at Transcrime, collaborating on several research projects. Since January 2018, she is managing editor of the *European Journal on Criminal Policy and Research*. Her research interests include transnational organized crime and illicit markets.

VESNA MARKOVIC is an associate professor in justice, law and public safety studies at Lewis University. Her research areas include terrorism (particularly suicide bombings, financing terrorism, and vehicle-ramming attacks), transnational crime, and comparative criminal justice. She has presented at professional conferences and has been invited to give presentations worldwide. She is a senior lecturer for the NATO Center of Excellence Defense against Terrorism courses in Ankara, Turkey, which are offered to ranking military officials.

INEKE HAEN MARSHALL, PhD, is a professor of sociology and anthropology, as well as criminology and criminal justice at Northeastern University in Boston,

Massachusetts. She was previously an American Society of Criminology lead liaison to the Economic and Social Council of the United Nations from 2005 to 2011. She is the chair of the Steering Committee of the International Self-Report Study of Delinquency, which is a global collaboration of scholars who research the subject. She has coauthored numerous books and peer-reviewed articles. Her current areas of interest include crime policy, motivation and crime, and juvenile delinquency.

ADAM B. MASTERS teaches courses about organized crime and corruption at the Centre for Social Research and Methods at the Australian National University. His teaching is based on his research, and he has also published on political rhetoric and the influence of organizational and professional culture on organizations, including Interpol. Before obtaining his PhD, Dr. Masters spent 18 years with the Australian Federal Police.

KLEO MCHUGH is a recent graduate of the Department of Criminology and Criminal Justice at the University of Alabama. She holds a bachelor's in applied neuropsychology and neuroethics from the University of Alabama. Her research interests include terrorism, cybercrime, and forensic science. She plans to pursue a career with the federal government in law enforcement and foreign relations.

RACHEL L. MCNEALEY is a criminology and criminal justice graduate student pursuing a doctoral degree in criminology, specializing in cyber criminology.

CECILIA MENEGHINI is a PhD candidate in criminology at Università Cattolica del Sacro Cuore in Milan, Italy. She holds a master's degree with honors in economic and social sciences from Bocconi University. Since March 2017, she has been working as a researcher and data analyst at Transcrime, collaborating on different projects on illicit trafficking and organized crime. Her research interests include organized crime, illicit markets, and social network analysis.

QINGLI MENG received a PhD in public policy from the University of North Carolina at Charlotte. Meng's research areas include white-collar crime and victimology. A monograph, *Corruption in Transitional China: A 33-Year Study*, was published in 2013. It was also published in China (as a translated version). Meng is currently an assistant professor of criminology in the Department of Sociology, Anthropology, and Criminology at the University of Northern Iowa.

AILI MIAO graduated from the Chinese Academy of Social Sciences and received a doctorate in criminal law. Since 2013, she has been working in the Law Department of Zhejiang Police College in Hangzhou, China. She is primarily engaged in the teaching and researching of criminal law, with particular interest in the punishment system and in property crime.

COREY B. MILES is currently a PhD candidate in public policy and administration at Virginia Commonwealth University. He holds a BA in political science from Hampden-Sydney College, an MPA from Old Dominion University, and a graduate certificate in business communication from Harvard University

Extension School. In addition to his time in Ecuador with the U.S. Peace Corps, he has held a variety of roles in international law firms, political campaigns, private industry, and university development.

TAMBA MONDEH is currently a master's student in public policy at Duke University. He completed a master's degree in criminology and criminal justice at the University of Alabama. His graduate thesis focused on how education outcomes and social bond theory explains the relationship between recreation and juvenile delinquency.

MARIA CRISTINA MONTEFUSCO currently works in the Organized Crime Branch of the United Nations Office on Drugs and Crimes (UNODC) as focal point for UNODC's Knowledge Management Portal SHERLOC, performing substantive legal research and analysis on different forms of organized crime.

HENA MUSTAFA has two bachelor's degrees in psychology and in criminology and criminal justice from Southern Oregon University. She currently resides in Atlanta, Georgia, and is in a doctorate program for clinical forensic psychology. She hopes to work in sex offender rehabilitation and legislation of sex crimes.

MANGAI NATARAJAN earned her PhD in criminal justice from the School of Criminal Justice, Rutgers, at the State University of New Jersey. She received her master's degree in criminology from the University of Madras, India. She is currently the director of the International Criminal Justice BA program at the John Jay College of Criminal Justice at the City University of New York. Her areas of expertise include women in policing, violence against women, drug trafficking, and international crime and justice. She has edited and coedited numerous books on similar subjects.

SABRINA NEIMEISTER is a current master's student in the Department of Criminology and Criminal Justice at the University of Alabama. After graduation in December of 2018, Ms. Neimeister aspires to teach on a collegiate level as an instructor in the field of criminology and sociology.

NATALIA OLLUS is the director of the European Institute for Crime Prevention and Control, based in Finland. She is also a board member of the Scandinavian Research Council for Criminology, as well as a member of the Eurostat Task Force on the Development of a Survey on Gender-based Violence. She has a PhD in law and a master's degree in social anthropology. Her areas of research include violence against women, victimology, the exploitation of migrant workers and trafficking, and more.

DONNA OSSORIO is a doctoral candidate in the Department of Justice Studies in the College of Juvenile Justice and Psychology at Prairie View A&M University. Donna earned her master of science in juvenile justice from Prairie View A&M University in 2015 and her bachelor of science in psychology from the University of Houston in 2012. Her primary research interest includes foster care, juvenile justice, and juvenile corrections. Her primary interest is in policy and program evaluations.

ANA CAROLINA PACI is an assistant for the United Nations Global compact in Brazil. She earned her master's degree in international peace studies with a specialization in media, peace, and conflict studies from the University for Peace in Costa Rica.

JULIA PAGNAMENTA is a master's student in criminal justice, concentrating in criminology and deviance, at CUNY's John Jay College. She received a bachelor's degree in English at the University of Chicago. Over the last several years, Julia has been working as a freelance fact-checker for various publications, including *VICE Magazine*. Prior to returning to school to get her master's, she worked for nearly four years as a cultural administrator at the New York Public Library's Cullman Center for Scholars and Writers.

YALI PANG is a PhD student in public administration and policy at L. Douglas Wilder School of Government and Public Affairs, Virginia Commonwealth University (VCU). She is the diversity fellow at the Partnership for People with Disabilities at VCU, where she is working on research projects on cultural brokering intervention for culturally diverse families of children with disabilities. Yali is also an adjunct instructor at the Department of Political Science at VCU.

JAIRO PATIÑO is a doctoral candidate at the University of New Haven's College of Criminal Justice and Forensic Science. His key areas of research include transnational organized crime, Mexican cartels, terrorism, civil unrest, law enforcement, crime prevention, and open source analytics.

PAUL G. PIERPAOLI JR. is a fellow in Military History at ABC-CLIO and the associate editor of ABC-CLIO's Military History series. A recipient of the Harry S. Truman Dissertation Fellowship, he received his MA and PhD degrees from The Ohio State University. He has also served on the faculties of numerous schools, including Hampden-Sydney College and the University of Arizona. Dr. Pierpaoli has been the assistant editor for *Diplomatic History* as well as the *Journal of Military History.*

AIDA PORTILLO is a lawyer born in El Salvador and currently residing in Asia. She holds a bachelor in law, a master of laws, and a master's in international law and human rights obtained in El Salvador, South Korea, and Costa Rica, respectively. Her international background and professional experience has allowed her to have a deep understanding and a unique perspective on organized crime. Her current research work focuses on sustainable development for developing countries.

PAULA K. PRIEBE is interested in the intersection of urban planning and peace building. After completing her undergraduate education at the University of Michigan, she served as a community development volunteer in South Africa with the United States Peace Corps. She earned a master of urban planning from the

University of Wisconsin–Milwaukee and a master of Arts in international peace studies from the University of Peace.

MELANIE PRUD'HOMME is a second-year doctoral student at Prairie View A&M University in the Juvenile Justice program. She holds a BA and two MAs from the University of Louisiana at Monroe in psychology, criminal justice, and marriage and family therapy, respectively. Her research interest includes race, trauma, mental health treatments, and juvenile delinquency.

RIIKKA PUTTONEN (DJur) is a trained judge in her home country of Finland and currently works in the Organized Crime Branch of the United Nations Office on Drugs and Crimes (UNODC) as the team leader on knowledge management and legislative assistance on the UN Organized Crime Convention.

DAVID A. REMBERT is an assistant professor in the Department of Justice Studies in the College of Juvenile Justice and Psychology at Prairie View A&M University. He is committed to using rigorous quantitative research methods to create an unbiased criminal justice system by promoting reforms in corrections, sentencing, and community supervision. David is interested in research questions related to racial disparities and practices, child welfare, legal aspects, policy, offender risk assessment, and program evaluation.

BRADFORD W. REYNS, PhD, is an associate professor in the Department of Criminal Justice at Weber State University. His research focuses on different dimensions of criminal victimization, particularly victimological theory, victim decision making, and the relationship between technology use and victimization. His recent work on these topics has appeared in *Justice Quarterly*, *Journal of Criminal Justice*, and *Journal of Research in Crime and Delinquency*.

CHRISTINA LYNN RICHARDSON is an Honors College student at Southern Oregon University (SOU). She is earning her bachelor's degrees in psychology and criminology and criminal justice, as well as a certificate in conflict resolution. She is the student trustee on the SOU Foundation's Board of Trustees, and she is the student representative on the SOU University Assessment Committee. She plans on pursuing a career in forensic psychology and research.

MITCHEL P. ROTH is a professor in the College of Criminal Justice at Sam Houston State University, Huntsville, Texas. His research interests include the histories of crime, policing, corrections, terrorism, and organized crime. Among the books he has authored are *Global Organized Crime: A Reference Handbook*, *Crime and Punishment*, and *Houston Blue: The Story of the Houston Police Department* (with Tom Kennedy). He earned a PhD in history from the University of California, Santa Barbara, in 1993.

AMANDA RUDE is a graduate student of criminology and criminal justice at the University of Alabama.

CONNOR RUTHERFORD is a native of upstate New York and works as an investigative auditor for the New York City Department of Investigation. He is also a graduate student at John Jay College for the City University of New York, pursuing his master's degree in international crime and justice. Previously he received his bachelor's degree in accounting from Siena College and his master's degree in forensic accounting from the University at Albany.

ADRIANA SALCEDO holds a PhD in conflict analysis and resolution from George Mason University, Virginia, where she has taught and conducted research on refugees' and migrants' identities and integration processes in host societies. She is currently a visiting faculty at United Nations mandated University for Peace (Costa Rica) and works as an independent consultant for organizations such as UNICEF, the Canadian International Development Agency (CIDA), and the Caribbean Observatory of Migration (OBMICA), among others.

RACHEL SALTER is currently a cyber intelligence analyst for the University of Alabama. She received her master's degree in criminal justice from the same university, and she previously received her bachelor's degree in criminology from Mississippi State University. She has been an active volunteer for at-risk youth. Her areas of interest include recidivism, women and substance abuse, and the darknet.

SHANELL SANCHEZ is an assistant professor of criminology and criminal justice at Southern Oregon University. She earned her doctorate in sociology at the University of Nebraska-Lincoln. Her teaching and research interests focused on social change and justice, inequality, and comparative crime and justice.

ERNESTO UGO SAVONA is the director of Transcrime and a professor of criminology at the University Cattolicà del Sacro Cuore in Milan, Italy. Previously, he has been a consultant to the United Nations Council of Europe and was one of an elite group of seven members of the Scientific and Criminological Council. He was also appointed editor in chief of the *European Journal on Criminal Policy and Research*, and he was chair of the Global Agenda Council on Organized Crime of the World Economic Forum from 2011 to 2012. His research interests include organized economic crime, corruption, laundering, crime statistics, and social change.

ALBERT SCHERR is a professor of law at the University of New Hampshire. He is the chair of the school's International Criminal Law and Justice Programs and is the chair and president of the New Hampshire Civil Liberties Union. In addition, he is a member of the American Civil Liberties Union's National Board of Directors and is the chair of the board's Patents and Civil Liberties Committee. He received his JD from Vermont Law School and teaches courses on investigation, witnesses and evidence, and international criminal law. His areas of expertise include forensic and scientific evidence, criminal procedure, and homicide cases.

CHEYENNE REYES SELBY is a graduate student at the University of Alabama, where she studies criminal justice. She currently researches fatal police encounters and the media. She has been a teacher's assistant at the University of Alabama for two courses: Organization and Management Concept in Criminal Justice, and Juvenile Delinquency. She was previously an intern probation officer for Cook County Juvenile Courts in Chicago, Illinois, where she managed a small caseload.

JESSIE L. SLEPICKA is a master's student in the Department of Criminology and Criminal Justice at the University of Northern Colorado. He graduated summa cum laude from the University of Northern Colorado with a bachelor of arts in criminal justice and a minor in leadership studies. His research interests include criminological theory, texting while driving, and green criminology.

GREYSON SMITH is a student at the University of Alabama.

JESSICA C. SMITH is a doctoral student and graduate teaching assistant at the L. Douglas Wilder School of Government and Public Affairs at Virginia Commonwealth University. She previously worked for the Commonwealth of Virginia, first as the public safety initiatives coordinator at the Attorney General's Office until 2012, and most recently as the school, campus, and public safety resource specialist at the Center for School and Campus Safety until 2017. She is a 2007 graduate of NC State University, where she received a BA in political science, and she's a 2017 graduate of VCU, where she received her MS in criminal justice.

KAREN JUDD SMITH is a best-selling author, resilience trainer, and former deputy secretary general and director of the Office of United Nations Relations. She is the chair of the New York Alliance of NGOs on Crime Prevention and Criminal Justice, and she founded NGO-Academy.com, which is an online training program for international NGO representatives and volunteers to the United Nations. She spent a total of 20 years in the United Nations' crime prevention and criminal justice global policy field. Now, she owns the Global Development Enterprise, where she helps organizations cultivate their leaders and resiliency.

RUSSELL G. SMITH is principal criminologist at the Australian Institute of Criminology, Australia's national research and knowledge center on crime and justice, with qualifications in law, psychology, and criminology from the University of Melbourne. He has a PhD from King's College London. He is also a professor in the College of Business, Government, and Law at Flinders University in South Australia and has published extensively on aspects of computer crime, fraud control, and professional regulation.

A. J. SMUSKIEWICZ is a freelance writer and editor specializing in science, health and medicine, and contemporary issues. He earned a BS in biology at Governors State University in 1988. He has worked as a biologist, a naturalist, and an artist/designer. His writing/editing experience included staff positions with World Book Publishing and the American Osteopathic Association. In recent years, he has focused much of his writing on human sexuality and LGBT issues.

RIANNA P. STARHEIM is a writer who supports the National Institute of Justice. She helped launch the Institute's Notes from the Field publication series, which profiles leading voices on issues such as the opioid crisis and prison reform. Starheim previously directed a communications company in Afghanistan, leading multimedia projects with agencies including USAID, the World Bank, and the European Commission. She frequently publishes on human rights. She is a paramedic and a graduate of Dartmouth College.

NANCY L. STOCKDALE is associate professor of history at the University of North Texas, where she began teaching in 2006. She teaches a variety of courses on topics such as modern Middle Eastern history and gender, race, and class issues in Middle Eastern history. Stockdale received her PhD in history from the University of California, Santa Barbara. She is author of *Colonial Encounters Among English and Palestinian Women, 1800–1948*.

STEVEN STROM was a writer/editor for ABC-CLIO's award-winning Solutions databases.

ANAMIKA A. TWYMAN-GHOSHAL is an associate professor of criminology at Stonehill College in Easton, Massachusetts. She earned her PhD in criminology and justice policy from Northeastern University in Boston. She also has a bachelor's degree in law and a master's degree in international law from the University of Wolverhampton and the University of London, respectively. She previously worked for the International Maritime Bureau in London. Her areas of interest include maritime crime, fraud, international corruption, and corporate crime.

KRISTINA NICOLE VAN WYK received her master's degree in criminal justice from the University of Alabama. She was previously an intern for the Florida Department of Agriculture and Consumer Services Office, where she shadowed officers in the field and assisted with various administrative tasks.

JÉSSICA VIALES LÓPEZ is a project director for Discover Panamá, a youth development program by the nonprofit, U.S.-based Amigos de las Américas. She previously collaborated with the Peace Crane Project as a communications associate and with UNESCO San José, supporting the communication and information sector. Jéssica holds a MA in international peace studies from the United Nations' mandated University for Peace, as well as a BA in international relations and a Lic. in international business.

LORENA VILLAVICENCIO is a graduate student in the Advanced Certificate Program for Crime Prevention and Analysis at John Jay College of Criminal Justice, City University of New York (CUNY). She holds a double undergraduate degree in forensic psychology and international criminal justice from John Jay College. Her research interests include youth gangs, migrant women, and refugee issues.

YULIA VOROBYEVA is a junior fellow at the United Nations Interregional Crime and Justice Research Institute (UNICRI), where she conducts research on illicit financial flows. She holds a PhD in international studies from the University of Miami. Her research interests also include drug trafficking and organized crime, with a focus on Latin America and Russia. In 2016–2017, Yulia was a researcher at Florida International University, where she studied gang violence in Central America.

SERITA WHITING is a doctoral student at Prairie View A&M University Juvenile Justice Department. She currently works as research assistant at Prairie View University. She received her master's in criminal justice from the University of Houston Downtown and her bachelor's in communications from the University of Houston Downtown. Her research interests include racially biased sentencing, policing, and racial issues throughout the criminal justice system.

FAY V. WILLIAMS has a bachelor of science in community health education, a master's degree in public health, and a PhD in juvenile justice. After completing the PhD degree, she worked as the program coordinator of the criminal justice program at Northern Caribbean University. She currently lectures criminology at Lakehead University in Canada and is an external examiner in criminology for the St. Augustus campus of the University of the West Indies.

SERGIO YÉPEZ CORDERO is a Caracas, Venezuela, native who studied international relations and received a master's degree in Latin American studies with a focus in development and culture. He lives in San Jose, Costa Rica, where he works with local law enforcement and the INTERPOL office in San Jose combating international organized criminal groups.

YULIYA ZABYELINA is an assistant professor in the Department of Political Science at John Jay College of Criminal Justice, City University of New York (CUNY). Her research focuses on transnational organized crime and the existing mechanisms for its prevention and control.

Index

Page numbers in **bold** indicate the location of main entries.